S0-BRC-728

THIRTEENTH EDITION

Patterns for College Writing

A RHETORICAL READER AND GUIDE

Laurie G. Kirszner
University of the Sciences, Emeritus

Stephen R. Mandell
Drexel University

BEDFORD/ST. MARTIN'S
Boston • New York

For Peter Phelps (1936–1990), with thanks

For Bedford/St. Martin's
Vice President, Editorial, Macmillan Higher Education Humanities: Edwin Hill
Editorial Director for English and Music: Karen S. Henry
Publisher for Composition and Business and Technical Writing: Leasa Burton
Executive Editor for Readers: John Sullivan
Senior Production Editor: Ryan Sullivan
Senior Production Supervisor: Jennifer Wetzel
Executive Marketing Manager: Jane Helms
Copy Editor: Diana P. George
Indexer: Kirsten Kite
Director of Rights and Permissions: Hilary Newman
Senior Art Director: Anna Palchik
Text Design: Brian Salisbury
Cover Design: Donna Lee Dennison
Cover Art: Janet Fish, *Butterfly Wings.* © www.StewartStewart.com 1991.
Composition: Achorn International, Inc.
Printing and Binding: RR Donnelley and Sons

Copyright © 2015, 2012, 2010, 2007 by Bedford/St. Martin's
All rights reserved. No part of this book may be reproduced, stored in a retrieval system, or transmitted in any form or by any means, electronic, mechanical, photocopying, recording, or otherwise, except as may be expressly permitted by the applicable copyright statutes or in writing by the Publisher.

1   2   3   4   5   6   18   17   16   15   14

For information, write: Bedford/St. Martin's, 75 Arlington Street, Boston, MA 02116
(617-399-4000)

ISBN 978-1-4576-6652-0 (Student Edition)
ISBN 978-1-4576-9941-2 (Instructor's Edition)
ISBN 978-1-4576-7870-7 (High School Edition)

Acknowledgments
Text acknowledgments and copyrights appear at the back of the book on pages 778–82, which constitute an extension of the copyright page. Art acknowledgments and copyrights appear on the same page as the art selections they cover. It is a violation of the law to reproduce these selections by any means whatsoever without the written permission of the copyright holder.

PREFACE

Since it was first published, *Patterns for College Writing* has been used by millions of students at colleges and universities across the United States. We have been delighted by the overwhelmingly positive response to the first twelve editions of *Patterns,* and we continue to be gratified by positive feedback from the many instructors who find *Patterns* to be the most accessible and the most pedagogically sound rhetoric-reader they have ever used. In preparing this thirteenth edition, we have worked hard to fine-tune the features that have made *Patterns* the most popular composition reader available today and to develop new features to enhance the book's usefulness for both instructors and students.

What Instructors and Students Like about *Patterns for College Writing*

An Emphasis on Critical Reading

The Introduction, "How to Use This Book," and Chapter 1, "Reading to Write: Becoming a Critical Reader," prepare students to become analytical readers and writers by showing them how to apply critical reading strategies to a typical selection and by providing sample responses to the various kinds of writing prompts in the book. Not only does this material introduce students to the book's features, but it also prepares them to tackle reading and writing assignments in their other courses.

Extensive Coverage of the Writing Process

The remaining chapters in Part One, "The Writing Process" (Chapters 2 through 5), comprise a "mini-rhetoric," offering advice on drafting, writing, revising, and editing as they introduce students to activities such as freewriting, brainstorming, clustering, and journal writing. These chapters also include numerous writing exercises to give students opportunities for immediate practice.

Detailed Coverage of the Patterns of Development

In Part Two, "Readings for Writers," Chapters 6 through 14 explain and illustrate the patterns of development that students typically use in their college writing assignments: narration, description, exemplification, process, cause and effect, comparison and contrast, classification and division, definition, and argumentation. Each chapter begins with a comprehensive introduction that presents a definition and a paragraph-length example of the pattern to be discussed and then explains the particular writing strategies and applications associated with it. Next, each chapter analyzes one or two annotated student essays to show how the pattern can be used in particular college writing situations. Chapter 15, "Combining the Patterns," illustrates how the various patterns of development discussed in Chapters 6 through 14 can work together in an essay.

A Diverse and Popular Selection of Readings

Varied in subject, style, and cultural perspective, the sixty-eight professional selections engage students while providing them with outstanding models for writing. We have tried to achieve a balance between classic authors (George Orwell, Jessica Mitford, E. B. White, Martin Luther King Jr.) and newer voices (Bich Minh Nguyen, Farhad Manjoo, Max Brooks) so that instructors have a broad range of readings to choose from.

More Student Essays Than Any Comparable Text

To provide students with realistic models for improving their own writing, we include eighteen sample student essays (two new to this edition).

Helpful Coverage of Grammar Issues

Grammar in Context boxes in chapter introductions offer specific advice on how to identify and correct the grammar, mechanics, and punctuation problems that students are likely to encounter when they work with particular patterns of development.

Apparatus Designed to Help Students Learn

Each professional essay in the text is followed by three types of questions. These questions are designed to help students assess their understanding of the essay's content and of the writer's purpose and audience; to recognize the stylistic and structural techniques used to shape the essay; and to become sensitive to the nuances of language. Each essay is also accompanied by a Journal Entry prompt, Writing Workshop topics (suggestions for full-length writing assignments), and Thematic Connections that identify related readings in the text. Also following each essay is a Combining the Patterns feature that focuses on different patterns of development used in the essay and possible alternatives to these patterns. Each chapter ends with a list of Writing Assignments and a Collaborative Activity. Many of these assignments and activities have been updated to reflect the most current topics as well as the most up-to-date trends and sites available on the Web.

Extensive Cultural and Historical Background for All Readings

In addition to a biographical headnote, each reading is preceded by a headnote containing essential background information to help students make connections between the reading and the historical, social, and economic forces that shaped it.

An Introduction to Visual Texts

Every rhetorical chapter includes a visual text — such as a photograph, a piece of fine art, or panels from a graphic novel — that provides an accessible introduction to each rhetorical pattern. Apparatus that helps students discuss the pattern in its visual form follows each image.

Thorough Coverage of Working with Sources

Part Three, "Working with Sources," takes students through the process of writing a research paper and includes a model student paper in MLA style. (The Appendix addresses APA style and includes a model APA paper.)

What's New in This Edition

Engaging New Readings

The twenty-two new professional essays treat topics of current interest. Maggie Koerth-Baker explains "Why Rational People Buy into Conspiracy Theories." Juan Williams compares the "Songs of the Summer of 1963 . . . and 2013." Maia Szalavitz shows "Ten Ways We Get the Odds Wrong." In all cases, readings have been carefully selected for their high-interest subject matter as well as for their effectiveness as teachable models for student writing.

Argumentation Chapter Updated

The argument chapter includes a new debate ("Is the Student Loan Crisis a Myth?") and two new casebooks ("Is Football Too Dangerous?" and "Should Guns Be Allowed on College Campuses?") as well as a new sample student essay, "Just Say No."

Now with LaunchPad Solo

Ten interactive and assignable multimodal readings are now included in LaunchPad Solo for *Patterns for College Writing*. Multimodal selections such as videos and infographics illustrate each of the rhetorical patterns and are accompanied by questions and writing assignments. Selections include an infographic, "What Are the Hardest Languages to Learn?" and

"Dear Motorist: Pledge to Share the Road," a video arguing for drivers to watch out for bicyclists. In addition, tutorials on critical reading and analysis and LearningCurve adaptive quizzing focus students on the writing and common grammar topics they need the most help with. To package LaunchPad Solo free with *Patterns for College Writing,* use ISBN 978-1-319-01312-7.

Get the Most out of Your Course with *Patterns for College Writing*

Bedford/St. Martin's offers resources and format choices that help you and your students get even more out of your book and course. To learn more about or to order any of the following products, contact your Bedford/St. Martin's sales representative, e-mail sales support (**sales_support@bfwpub.com**), or visit the website at **macmillanhighered.com/patterns/catalog**.

LaunchPad Solo for *Patterns for College Writing*: Where Students Learn

LaunchPad Solo provides engaging content and new ways to get the most out of your course. Get **unique, book-specific materials** in a fully customizable course space; then assign and mix our resources with yours.

- **Curated content** — including readings, videos, tutorials, and more — is **easy to adapt and assign** by adding your own materials and mixing them with our high-quality multimedia content and ready-made assessment options, such as **LearningCurve** adaptive quizzing.
- A **streamlined interface** helps students focus on what's due, and social commenting tools let them **engage**, make connections, and learn from each other. Use LaunchPad Solo on its own or integrate it with your school's learning management system so that your class is always on the same page.

To get the most out of your course, order LaunchPad Solo for *Patterns for College Writing* packaged with the print book **at no additional charge**. (LaunchPad Solo for *Patterns for College Writing* can also be purchased on its own.) An activation code is required. To order LaunchPad Solo for *Patterns for College Writing* with the print book, use ISBN 978-1-319-01312-7.

Choose from Alternative Formats of *Patterns for College Writing*

Bedford/St. Martin's offers a range of affordable formats, allowing students to choose the one that works best for them. For more details, visit **macmillanhighered.com/patterns/formats**.

- *Bedford e-Book to Go.* A portable, downloadable e-book is available at about half the price of the print book. To order the Bedford e-Book to Go, use ISBN 978-1-4576-9946-7.
- *Other popular e-book formats.* For details, visit **macmillanhighered .com/ebooks**.

Package with Another Bedford/St. Martin's Title and Save 20%

Get the most value for your students by packaging *Patterns for College Writing* with a Bedford/St. Martin's handbook or any other Bedford/ St. Martin's title for a significant discount. To order, please request a package ISBN from your sales representative or e-mail sales support (**sales _support@bfwpub.com**).

Select Value Packages. Add value to your text by packaging one of the following resources with *Patterns for College Writing.* To learn more about package options for any of these products, contact your Bedford/St. Martin's sales representative or visit **macmillanhighered.com/patterns /catalog**.

LearningCurve for Readers and Writers, Bedford/St. Martin's adaptive quizzing program, quickly learns what students already know and helps them practice what they don't yet understand. Game-like quizzing motivates students to engage with their course, and reporting tools help teachers discern their students' needs. LearningCurve for Readers and Writers can be packaged with *Patterns for College Writing* at a significant discount. An activation code is required. To order LearningCurve packaged with the print book, contact your sales representative for a package ISBN. For details, visit **learningcurveworks.com**.

i-series. This popular series presents multimedia tutorials in a flexible format — because there are things you can't do in a book.

- *ix visualizing composition 2.0* helps students put into practice key rhetorical and visual concepts. To order *ix visualizing composition* packaged with the print book, contact your sales representative for a package ISBN.
- *i·claim: visualizing argument* offers a new way to see argument — with six multimedia tutorials, an illustrated glossary, and a wide array of multimedia arguments. To order *i·claim: visualizing argument* packaged with the print book, contact your sales representative for a package ISBN.

Portfolio Keeping, **Third Edition, by Nedra Reynolds and Elizabeth Davis,** provides all the information students need to use the portfolio method successfully in a writing course. *Portfolio Teaching,* a companion guide for instructors, provides the practical information instructors and writing program administrators need to use the portfolio method successfully in a writing course. To order *Portfolio Keeping* packaged with the print book, contact your sales representative for a package ISBN.

Make Learning Fun with *Re:Writing 3*
bedfordstmartins.com/rewriting

New open online resources with videos and interactive elements engage students in new ways of writing. You'll find tutorials about using common digital writing tools; an interactive peer-review game, Extreme Paragraph Makeover; and more — all for free and for fun. Visit **bedfordstmartins .com/rewriting**.

Instructor Resources
macmillanhighered.com/patterns/catalog

You have a lot to do in your course. Bedford/St. Martin's wants to make it easy for you to find the support you need — and to get it quickly.

Resources for Instructors Using Patterns for College Writing is available as a PDF that can be downloaded from the Bedford/St. Martin's online catalog at the URL above. In addition to chapter overviews, the instructor's manual includes model syllabi, tips for using collaborative activities, overviews of each part, summaries of each selection, and guidance for assignment questions.

Teaching Central (**macmillanhighered.com/teachingcentral**) offers the entire list of Bedford/St. Martin's print and online professional resources in one place. You'll find landmark reference works, sourcebooks on pedagogical issues, award-winning collections, and practical advice for the classroom — all free for instructors.

Bits (**bedfordbits.com**) collects creative ideas for teaching a range of composition topics in an easily searchable blog format. A community of teachers — leading scholars, authors, and editors — discuss revision, research, grammar and style, technology, peer review, and much more. Take, use, adapt, and pass the ideas around. Then, come back to the site to comment or share your own suggestions.

Acknowledgments

As always, friends, colleagues, students, and family all helped this project along. Of particular value were the responses to the questionnaires sent to the following instructors, who provided frank and helpful advice: Heidi Ajrami, Victoria College; Amelia Magallanes Arguijo, Laredo Community College; Debra Benedetti, Pierpont Community and Technical College; Brett Bodily, North Lake College; Mary-Beth Brophy, University of Phoenix; Terri Brown, Arizona Western College; Thomas Chester, Ivy Tech Community College; Joyce Cottonham, Southern University–Shreveport; Edward Coursey, Hillsborough Community College, Dale Mabry Campus; Larnell Dunkley, Harold Washington College; Crystal Edmonds, Robeson Community College; Sallyanne Fitzgerald, Polk State College; Denice Fregozo, Arizona Western College; Holly French-Hart, Bossier Parish Community College; Deborah Goodwyn, Virginia State University; Annette Graham, Motlow State Community College; William Hays, Delta State University; Rebecca Heintz, Polk State College; Joanne Jacobs, Shenandoah University; Melanie Jenkins, Snow College; Amy Lakin, Benedictine University at Springfield; Michael Landers, Mount Pleasant High School; Patricia Leonard, Carl Sandburg High School; Julie Long, College of the Albemarle; John Lusk, St. Clair County Community College; Joyce Mosher, Colorado Mountain College; Maureen Murphy-Smolka, Sussex County Community College; Phaye Poliakoff-Chen, Goucher College; Sharon Prince, Wharton County Junior College; Theresa Scott, Hillsborough Community College–Southshore; Lynette Shaw-Smith, Benedictine University at Springfield; Mary Stahoviak, Victoria College; Bruce Symes, Allen Community College; Charlotte Teague, Alabama A&M University; June Gordon White, Norfolk State University; Hoda Zaki, Camden County College. We are also grateful to Sean C. Smith, Ivy Tech/Community College of Indiana–East Central, for his comments on coverage of APA documentation.

Special thanks go to Jeff Ousborne for his help with some of the apparatus and for revising the headnotes and the *Resources for Instructors*.

Through thirteen editions of *Patterns for College Writing,* we have enjoyed a wonderful working relationship with Bedford/St. Martin's. We have always found the editorial and production staff to be efficient, cooperative, and generous with their time and advice. As always, we appreciate the encouragement and advice of our longtime friend, Nancy Perry. In addition, we thank Joan Feinberg, past president of Bedford/St. Martin's, for her support for this project and for her trust in us. During our work on this edition, we have benefited from our productive relationship with John Sullivan, our editor, who helped us make this edition of *Patterns* the best it could be. We are also grateful to Ryan Sullivan, project editor, and Elise Kaiser, managing editor, for their work overseeing the production of this edition; William Boardman for the attractive new cover; and editorial assistant Jennifer Prince for her invaluable help with tasks large and small.

We are fortunate to have enjoyed our long and fulfilling collaboration; we know how rare a successful partnership like ours is. We also know how lucky we are to have our families help keep us in touch with the things that really matter.

Laurie G. Kirszner
Stephen R. Mandell

CONTENTS

   "The summer I was twelve, my family went away on a 'vacation' — one of my father's half-baked get-to-know-our-country-better-by-sleeping-in-the-van extravaganzas — and when we returned to Jersey, exhausted, battered, we found our front door unlocked. . . . The thieves had kept it simple; they'd snatched a portable radio, some of my Dungeons & Dragons hardcovers, and, of course, Mami's remittances."

   "Confronted by the immediacy of destruction, technology is the first thing that flees. I was reduced to tossing bits of dried weed into the air to check the direction of the wind. You think: water, family, pets. What do I put in the car first? By then the mass of orange-brown smoke had taken over the north sky."

> "For me, a child of Vietnamese immigrants growing up in Michigan in the 1980s, Twinkies were a ticket to assimilation: the golden cake, more golden than the hair I wished I had, filled with sweet white cream. Back then, junk foods seemed to represent an ideal of American indulgence."

> "Like me, perhaps, the people around me had in mind images from television and newspaper pictures: the collapsing buildings, the running office workers, the black plume of smoke against a bright blue sky. Like me, they were probably trying to superimpose those terrible images onto the industrious emptiness right in front of them."

> "There was a horrifying rush of cheddar taste, followed immediately by the dull tang of soybean flour — the main ingredient in Gaines-burgers."

> "There's a reason landfills are tucked away, on the edge of town, in otherwise untraveled terrain, camouflaged by hydroseeded, neatly tiered slopes. If people saw what happened to their waste, lived with the stench, witnessed the scale of destruction, they might start asking difficult questions."

> "Summertime, oh summertime, pattern of life indelible, the fade-proof lake, the woods unshatterable, the pasture with the sweetfern and the juniper forever and ever. . . ."

"My first view in the mirror blotted out the hurting. I'd seen some pretty conks, but when it's the first time, on your *own* head, the transformation, after the lifetime of kinks, is staggering."

"You will face a coordination problem if you are a general deploying troops, tanks, helicopters, food, tents, and medical supplies, or if you are the CEO of a large company juggling the demands of design, personnel, inventory, and production. . . . And these days, you will face a coordination problem if you want to get a cup of coffee."

"Vending machines are extremely heavy and can cause major injury if they tip over. Carefully bang on the side of the machine. Do not hit glass areas."

"People can be executed in places like Shea Stadium before immense paying audiences. . . . As with all sports events, a certain ritual would

10   Cause and Effect   319

Norman Cousins, *Who Killed Benny Paret?*   337

"'They don't come out to see a tea party,' he said evenly. 'They come out to see the knockout. They come out to see a man hurt. If they think anything else, they're kidding themselves.'"

Maggie Koerth-Baker, *Why Rational People Buy into Conspiracy Theories*   342

"Perfectly sane minds possess an incredible capacity for developing narratives, and even some of the wildest conspiracy theories can be grounded in rational thinking, which makes them that much more pernicious."

Lawrence Otis Graham, *The "Black Table" Is Still There*   348

"What did the table say about the integration that was supposedly going on in homerooms and gym classes? What did it say about the black kids? The white kids? What did it say about me when I refused to sit there, day after day, for three years?"

Linda M. Hasselstrom, *A Peaceful Woman Explains Why She Carries a Gun*   353

"People who have not grown up with the idea that they are capable of protecting themselves — in other words, most women — might have to work hard to convince themselves of their ability, and of the necessity. Handgun ownership need not turn us into gunslingers, but it can be part of believing in, and relying on, *ourselves* for protection."

Max Brooks, *The Movies That Rose from the Grave*   359

"Zombie movies present people with an outlet for their apocalyptic anxieties without directly confronting them. The living dead are a fictional threat, as opposed to tsunamis or avian flu. No matter how scary or realistic the particular story might be, their unquestionably fictional nature makes them 'safe.'"

Janice Mirikitani, *Suicide Note* (Poetry)   364

"I apologize.
Tasks do not come easily.
Each failure, a glacier.
Each disapproval, a bootprint.
Each disappointment,
ice above my river."

"When Ulysses S. Grant and Robert E. Lee met in the parlor of a modest house at Appomattox Court House, Virginia, on April 9, 1865, to work out the terms for the surrender of Lee's Army of Northern Virginia, a great chapter in American life came to a close, and a great new chapter began."

"What I wish for all students is some release from the clammy grip of the future. I wish them a chance to savor each segment of their education as an experience in itself and not as a grim preparation for the next step. I wish them the right to experiment, to trip and fall, to learn that defeat is as instructive as victory and is not the end of the world."

"With a show of energy and creativity that would be admirable if applied to the (missing) assignments in question, my students persist, week after week, semester after semester, year after year, in offering excuses about why their work is not ready. Those reasons fall into several broad categories: the family, the best friend, the evils of dorm life, the evils of technology, and the totally bizarre."

"I spend a great deal of my time thinking about the power of language — the way it can evoke an emotion, a visual image, a complex idea, or a

"We hold these truths to be self-evident, that all men are created equal, that they are endowed by their Creator with certain unalienable rights, that among these are life, liberty, and the pursuit of happiness."

"The history of mankind is a history of repeated injuries and usurpations on the part of man toward woman, having in direct object the establishment of an absolute tyranny over her. To prove this, let facts be submitted to a candid world."

"For years now I have heard the word 'Wait!' It rings in the ear of every Negro with piercing familiarity. This 'Wait' has almost always meant 'Never.' We must come to see, with one of our distinguished jurists, that 'justice too long delayed is justice denied.'"

"Horror stories of students drowning in $100,000+ debt might discourage young people from enrolling in college, but they are as rare as they are terrifying."

frenzy — in a football-crazed country, no less. But statistics, experience, and observation strongly suggest that the people playing football are healthier than those watching it — and even those refusing to watch."

THEMATIC GUIDE TO THE CONTENTS

Business and Work

Sports

Race and Culture

Gender

Nature and the Environment

Media and Society

History and Politics

Ethics

Introduction: How to Use This Book

This is a book of readings, but it is also a book about writing. Every reading selection here is followed by questions and exercises designed to help you become a thoughtful and proficient writer. The study questions that accompany the essays in this text encourage you to think critically about writers' ideas. Although some of the questions (particularly those listed under **Comprehension**) call for fairly straightforward, factual responses, other questions (particularly the **Journal Entry** assignments) invite more complex responses that reflect your individual reaction to the selections.

The essay that begins on the following page, "'What's in a Name?'" by Henry Louis Gates Jr., is typical of those that appear in this text. It is preceded by a **headnote** that gives readers information about the author's life and career. This headnote includes a **background** section that provides a social, historical, and cultural context for the essay.

"What's in a Name?"

Henry Louis Gates Jr. was born in 1950 in Keyser, West Virginia, and grew up in the small town of Piedmont. Currently Alphonse Fletcher Jr. University Professor and director of the W. E. B. Du Bois Institute for African and African American Research at Harvard, he has edited many collections of works by African-American writers and published several volumes of literary criticism. However, he is probably best known as a social critic whose books and articles for a general audience explore a wide variety of issues and themes, often focusing on race and culture. In the following essay, which originally appeared in the journal *Dissent*, Gates recalls a childhood experience that occurred during the mid-1950s.

Background on the civil rights movement In the mid-1950s, the first stirrings of the civil rights movement were under way, and in 1954 and 1955 the U.S. Supreme Court handed down decisions declaring racial segregation unconstitutional in public schools. Still, much of the country — particularly the South — remained largely segregated until Congress passed the Civil Rights Act of 1964, which prohibited discrimination based on race, color, religion, or national origin in businesses (including restaurants and theaters) covered by interstate commerce laws, as well as in employment. This was followed by the Voting Rights Act of 1965, which guaranteed equal access to the polls, and the Civil Rights Act of 1968, which prohibited discrimination in housing and real estate. At the time of the experience Gates recalls here — before these laws were enacted — prejudice and discrimination against African Americans were the norm in many communities, including those outside the South.

The question of color takes up much space in these pages, but the question of color, especially in this country, operates to hide the graver questions of the self.

—JAMES BALDWIN, 1961

. . . blood, darky, Tar Baby, Kaffir, shine . . . moor, blackamoor, Jim Crow, spook . . . quadroon, meriney, red bone, high yellow . . . Mammy, porch monkey, home, homeboy, George . . . spearchucker, schwarze, Leroy, Smokey . . . mouli, buck. Ethiopian, brother, sistah.

—TREY ELLIS, 1989

I had forgotten the incident completely, until I read Trey Ellis's essay 1 "Remember My Name" in a recent issue of the *Village Voice* (June 13, 1989). But there, in the middle of an extended italicized list of the bynames of "the race" ("the race" or "our people" being the terms my parents used in polite or reverential discourse, "jigaboo" or "nigger" more commonly used in anger, jest, or pure disgust), it was: "George." Now the events of that very brief exchange return to mind so vividly that I wonder why I had forgotten it.

My father and I were walking home at dusk from his second job. He "moonlighted" as a janitor in the evenings for the telephone company. Every day but Saturday, he would come home at 3:30 from his regular job at the paper mill, wash up, eat supper, then at 4:30 head downtown to his second job. He used to make jokes frequently about a union official who moonlighted. I never got the joke, but he and his friends thought it was hilarious. All I knew was that my family always ate well, that my brother and I had new clothes to wear, and that all of the white people in Piedmont, West Virginia, treated my parents with an odd mixture of resentment and respect that even we understood at the time had something directly to do with a small but certain measure of financial security. 2

He had left a little early that evening because I was with him and I had to be in bed early. I could not have been more than five or six, and we had stopped off at the Cut-Rate Drug Store (where no black person in town but my father could sit down to eat, and eat off real plates with real silverware) so that I could buy some caramel ice cream, two scoops in a wafer cone, please, which I was busy licking when Mr. Wilson walked by. 3

Mr. Wilson was a very quiet man, whose stony, brooding, silent manner seemed designed to scare off any overtures of friendship, even from white people. He was Irish, as was one-third of our village (another third being Italian), the more affluent among whom sent their children to "Catholic School" across the bridge in Maryland. He had white straight hair, like my Uncle Joe, whom he uncannily resembled, and he carried a black worn metal lunch pail, the kind that Riley* carried on the television show. My father always spoke to him, and for reasons that we never did understand, he always spoke to my father. 4

"Hello, Mr. Wilson," I heard my father say. 5
"Hello, George." 6
I stopped licking my ice cream cone, and asked my Dad in a loud voice why Mr. Wilson had called him "George." 7

"Doesn't he know your name, Daddy? Why don't you tell him your name? Your name isn't George. 8

For a moment I tried to think of who Mr. Wilson was mixing Pop up with. But we didn't have any Georges among the colored people in Piedmont; nor were there colored Georges living in the neighboring towns and working at the mill. 9

> " Doesn't he know your name, Daddy? Why don't you tell him your name? Your name isn't George. . . . "

"Tell him your name, Daddy." 10
"He knows my name, boy," my father said after a long pause. "He calls all colored people George." 11

---

* Eds. note — The lead character in the 1950s television program *The Life of Riley*, about a white working-class family and their neighbors.

A long silence ensued. It was "one of those things," as my Mom would   12
put it. Even then, that early, I knew when I was in the presence of "one
of those things," one of those things that provided a glimpse, through a
rent curtain, at another world that we could not affect but that affected
us. There would be a painful moment of silence, and you would wait for it
to give way to a discussion of a black superstar such as Sugar Ray or Jackie
Robinson.

"Nobody hits better in a clutch than Jackie Robinson."   13

"That's right. Nobody."   14

I never again looked Mr. Wilson in the eye.   15

· · ·

Responding to an Essay

The study questions that follow each essay will help you to **think critically**
about what you are reading — that is, to ask questions and draw conclusions. (Critical thinking and reading are discussed in Chapter 1 of this book.)
Four types of questions follow each essay:

- *Comprehension* questions help you to measure your understanding of
  what the writer is saying.
- *Purpose and Audience* questions ask you to consider why, and for
  whom, each selection was written and to examine the implications
  of the writer's choices in view of a particular purpose or intended
  audience.
- *Style and Structure* questions encourage you to examine the decisions
  the writer has made about elements such as arrangement of ideas,
  paragraphing, sentence structure, and imagery. One question in this
  category, designated **Vocabulary Project**, focuses on word choice
  and connotation.
- *Journal Entry* assignments ask you to write a short, informal
  response to what you read and to speculate freely about related
  ideas — perhaps exploring ethical issues raised by the selection or
  offering your opinions about the writer's statements. Briefer, less
  polished, and less structured than full-length essays, journal entries
  may suggest ideas for more formal kinds of writing.

Following these sets of questions are three additional features:

- *Writing Workshop* assignments ask you to write essays structured
  according to the pattern of development explained and illustrated
  in the chapter. Some of these assignments, designated **Working
  with Sources**, will ask you to cite the essay or an outside source. In
  these cases, you will be reminded to include parenthetical documentation and a works-cited page that conform to MLA documentation
  style.

- *Combining the Patterns* questions focus on the various patterns of development — other than the essay's dominant pattern — that the writer uses. These questions ask why a writer uses particular patterns (narration, description, exemplification, process, cause and effect, comparison and contrast, classification and division, definition), what each pattern contributes to the essay, and what other choices the writer might have had.
- *Thematic Connections* identify other readings in this book that explore similar themes. Reading these related works will enhance your understanding and appreciation of the original work and perhaps give you material to write about.

Following are some examples of study questions and possible responses, as well as a **Writing Workshop** assignment and a list of **Thematic Connections**, for " 'What's in a Name?' " (page 2). The numbers in parentheses after quotations refer to the paragraphs in which the quotations appear.

Comprehension

1. *In paragraph 1, Gates wonders why he forgot about the exchange between his father and Mr. Wilson. Why do you think he forgot about it?*

   Gates may have forgotten about the incident simply because it was something that happened a long time ago or because such incidents were commonplace when he was a child. Alternatively, he may *not* have forgotten the exchange between his father and Mr. Wilson but pushed it out of his mind because he found it so painful. (After all, he says he never again looked Mr. Wilson in the eye.)

2. *How is the social status of Gates's family different from that of other African-American families in Piedmont, West Virginia? How does Gates account for this difference?*

   Gates's family is different from other African-American families in town in that they are treated with "an odd mixture of resentment and respect" (2) by whites. Although other blacks are not permitted to eat at the drugstore, Mr. Gates is. Gates attributes this social status to his family's "small but certain measure of financial security" (2). Even so, when Mr. Wilson insults Mr. Gates, the privileged status of the Gates family is revealed as a sham.

3. *What does Gates mean when he says, "It was 'one of those things,' as my Mom would put it" (12)?*

   Gates's comment indicates that the family learned to see such mistreatment as routine. In context, the word *things* in paragraph 12 refers to the kind of incident that gives Gates and his family a glimpse of the way the white world operates.

4. *Why does Gates's family turn to a discussion of a "black superstar" after a "painful moment of silence" (12) such as the one he describes?*

   Although Gates does not explain the family's behavior, we can infer that they speak of African-American heroes like prizefighter Sugar Ray

Robinson and baseball player Jackie Robinson to make themselves feel better. Such discussions are a way of balancing the negative images of African Americans created by incidents such as the one Gates describes and of bolstering the low self-esteem the family felt as a result. These heroes seem to have won the respect denied to the Gates family; to mention them is to participate vicariously in their glory.

5. *Why do you think Gates "never again looked Mr. Wilson in the eye" (15)?*

    Gates may have felt that Mr. Wilson was somehow the enemy, not to be trusted, because he had insulted Gates's father. Or, he may have been ashamed to look him in the eye because he believed his father should have insisted on being addressed properly.

Purpose and Audience

1. *Why do you think Gates introduces his narrative with the two quotations he selects? How do you suppose he expects his audience to react to these quotations? How do you react?*

    Gates begins with two quotations, both by African-American writers, written nearly thirty years apart. Baldwin's words seem to suggest that, in the United States, "the question of color" is a barrier to understanding "the graver questions of the self." That is, the labels *black* and *white* may mask more fundamental characteristics or issues. Ellis's list of names (many pejorative) for African Americans illustrates the fact that epithets can dehumanize people — they can, in effect, rob a person of his or her "self." This issue of the discrepancy between a name and what lies behind it is central to Gates's essay. In one sense, then, Gates begins with these two quotations because they are relevant to the issues he will discuss. More specifically, he is using the two quotations — particularly Ellis's shocking string of unpleasant names — to arouse interest in his topic and provide an intellectual and emotional context for his story. He may also be intending to make his white readers uncomfortable and his black readers angry. How you react depends on your attitudes about race (and perhaps about language).

2. *What is the point of Gates's narrative? That is, why does he recount the incident?*

    Certainly Gates wishes to make readers aware of the awkward, and potentially dangerous, position of his father (and, by extension, of other African Americans) in a small southern town in the 1950s. He also shows us how names help to shape people's perceptions and actions: as long as Mr. Wilson can call all black men "George," he can continue to see them as insignificant and treat them as inferiors. The title of the piece suggests that the way names shape perceptions is the writer's main point.

3. *The title of this selection, which Gates places in quotation marks, is an allusion to act 2, scene 2, of Shakespeare's* Romeo and Juliet, *in which Juliet says, "What's in a name? That which we call a rose / By any other name would smell as sweet." Why do you think Gates chose this title? Does he expect his audience to recognize the quotation?*

Because his work was originally published in a journal read by a well-educated audience, Gates would have expected readers to recognize the **allusion** (and also to know a good deal about 1950s race relations). Although Gates could not have been certain that all members of this audience would recognize the reference to *Romeo and Juliet*, he could have been reasonably sure that if they did, it would enhance their understanding of the selection. In Shakespeare's play, the two lovers are kept apart essentially because of their names: she is a Capulet and he is a Montague, and the two families are involved in a bitter feud. In the speech from which Gates takes the title quotation, Juliet questions the logic of such a situation. In her view, what a person is called should not determine how he or she is regarded — and this, of course, is Gates's point as well. Even if readers do not recognize the allusion, the title still foreshadows the selection's focus on names.

Style and Structure

1. *Does paragraph 1 add something vital to the narrative, or would Gates's story make sense without the introduction? Could another kind of introduction work as well?*

    Gates's first paragraph supplies the context in which the incident is to be read — that is, it makes clear that Mr. Wilson's calling Mr. Gates "George" was not an isolated incident but part of a pattern of behavior that allowed those in positions of power to mistreat those they considered inferior. For this reason, it is an effective introduction. Although the narrative would make sense without paragraph 1, the story's full impact would probably not be as great. Still, Gates could have begun differently. For example, he could have started with the incident itself (paragraph 2) and interjected his comments about the significance of names later in the piece. He also could have begun with the exchange of dialogue in paragraphs 5 through 11 and then introduced the current paragraph 1 to supply the incident's context.

2. *What does the use of dialogue contribute to the narrative? Would the selection have a different impact without dialogue? Explain.*

    Gates was five or six years old when the incident occurred, and the dialogue helps to establish the child's innocence as well as his father's quiet acceptance of the situation. In short, the dialogue is a valuable addition to the piece because it creates two characters, one innocent and one resigned to injustice, both of whom contrast with the voice of the adult narrator: wise, worldly, but also angry and perhaps ashamed, the voice of a man who has benefited from the sacrifices of men like Gates's father.

3. *Why do you think Gates supplies the specific details he chooses in paragraphs 2 and 3? In paragraph 4? Is all this information necessary?*

    The details Gates provides in paragraphs 2 and 3 help to establish the status of his family in Piedmont; because readers have this information, the fact that the family was ultimately disregarded and discounted by some whites emerges as deeply ironic. The information in paragraph 4 also contributes to this **irony**. Here we learn that Mr. Wilson was not liked by many whites, that he looked like Gates's Uncle Joe, and that he carried a lunch box — in other words, that he had no special status in the town apart from that conferred by race.

4. **Vocabulary Project.** *Consider the connotations of the words* colored *and* black, *both used by Gates to refer to African Americans. What different associations does each word have? Why does Gates use both — for example,* colored *in paragraph 9 and* black *in paragraph 12? What is your response to the father's use of the term* boy *in paragraph 11?*

In the 1950s, when the incident Gates describes took place, the term *colored* was still widely used, along with *Negro,* to designate Americans of African descent. In the 1960s, the terms *Afro-American* and *black* replaced the earlier names, with *black* emerging as the preferred term and remaining dominant through the 1980s. Today, although *black* is preferred by some, *African American* is used more and more often. Because the term *colored* is the oldest designation, it may seem old-fashioned and even racist today; *black,* which connoted a certain degree of militancy in the 1960s, is probably now considered a neutral term by most people. Gates uses both words because he is speaking from two time periods. In paragraph 9, re-creating the thoughts and words of a child in a 1950s southern town, he uses the term *colored*; in paragraph 12, the adult Gates, commenting in 1989 on the incident, uses *black.* The substitution of *African American* for the older terms might give the narrative a more contemporary flavor, but it might also seem awkward or forced — and, in paragraph 9, inappropriately formal. As far as the term *boy* is concerned, different readers are apt to have different responses. Although the father's use of the term can be seen as affectionate, it can also be seen as derisive in this context since it echoes the bigot's use of *boy* for all black males, regardless of age or accomplishments.

Journal Entry

Do you think Gates's parents should have used experiences like the one in " 'What's in a Name?' " to educate him about the family's social status in the community? Why do you think they chose instead to dismiss such incidents as "one of those things" (12)?

Your responses to these questions will reflect your own opinions, based on your background and experiences as well as on your interpretation of the reading selection.

Writing Workshop

Write about a time when you, like Gates's father, could have spoken out in protest but chose not to. Would you make the same decision today?

By the time you approach the Writing Workshop assignments, you will have read an essay, responded to study questions about it, discussed it in class, and perhaps considered its relationship to other essays in the text. Often, your next step will be to write an essay in response to one of the Writing Workshop questions. (Chapters 2–4 follow Laura Bobnak, a first-year composition student, through the process of writing an essay in response to this Writing Workshop assignment.)

Combining the Patterns

Although **narration** *is the pattern of development that dominates "'What's in a Name?'" and gives it its structure, Gates also uses* **exemplification**, *presenting an extended example to support his thesis. What is this example? What does it illustrate? Would several brief examples have been more convincing?*

The extended example is the story of the encounter between Gates's father and Mr. Wilson, which compellingly illustrates the kind of behavior African Americans were often forced to adopt in the 1950s. Because Gates's introduction focuses on "the incident" (1), one extended example is enough (although he alludes to other incidents in paragraph 12).

Thematic Connections

- "'Girl'" (page 259)
- "The 'Black Table' Is Still There" (page 348)

As you read and think about the selections in this text, you should begin to see thematic links among them. Such parallels can add to your interest and understanding as well as give you ideas for class discussion and writing.

For example, Jamaica Kincaid's short story "Girl," also by an African-American writer, has some parallels with Gates's autobiographical essay. Like Gates, Kincaid's protagonist seems to occupy a subservient position in a society whose rules she must obey. The lessons in life skills that are enumerated in the story are also similar to the lesson Gates learns from his father.

Another related work is Lawrence Otis Graham's "The 'Black Table' Is Still There." The writer, an African-American man, returns in 1991 to his junior high school, where he sees the lunch tables as segregated as they were when he was a student there. Unlike Gates's essay, which discusses a specific incident that took place in the South in the 1950s, Graham's examines an ongoing situation that may apply to schools all over the United States. Thus, it provides a more contemporary — and, perhaps, wider — context for discussing issues of race and class.

In the process of thinking about Gates's narrative, discussing it in class, or preparing to write an essay on a related topic (such as the one listed under Writing Workshop on page 8), you might find it useful to read Kincaid's story and Graham's essay.

Responding to Other Texts

The first selection in Chapters 6 through 14 of this book is a visual text. It is followed by **Reading Images** questions, a **Journal Entry**, and a short list of **Thematic Connections** that will help you understand the image and shape your response to it.

The final selection in each chapter, a story or poem, is followed by **Reading Literature** questions, a **Journal Entry**, and **Thematic Connections**.

NOTE: At the end of each chapter, **Writing Assignments** offer additional practice in writing essays structured according to a particular pattern of development. Some of these assignments, designated **Working with Sources**, will ask you to refer to one or more of the essays in the chapter (or to an outside source). In these cases, you will be asked to include MLA parenthetical documentation and a works-cited page. Finally, a **Collaborative Activity** suggests an idea for a group project.

PART ONE

The Writing Process

Every reading selection in this book is the result of a struggle between a writer and his or her material. If a writer's struggle is successful, the finished work is welded together without a visible seam, and readers have no sense of the frustration the writer experienced while rearranging ideas or hunting for the right word. Writing is no easy business, even for a professional writer. Still, although there is no simple formula for good writing, some approaches are easier and more productive than others.

At this point you may be asking yourself, "So what? What has this got to do with me? I'm not a professional writer." True enough, but during the next few years you will be doing a good deal of writing. Throughout your college career, you will write midterms, final exams, lab reports, essays, and research papers. In your professional life, you may write progress reports, proposals, business correspondence, and memos. As diverse as these tasks are, they have something in common: they can be made easier if you are familiar with the stages of the **writing process** — a process experienced writers follow when they write.

THE WRITING PROCESS

- **Invention** (also called **prewriting**) During invention, you decide what to write about and gather information to support or explain what you want to say.
- **Arrangement** During arrangement, you decide how you are going to organize your ideas.
- **Drafting and revising** During drafting and revising, you write several drafts as you reconsider your ideas and refine your style and structure.
- **Editing and proofreading** During editing, you focus on grammar and punctuation as well as on sentence style and word choice. During proofreading, you correct spelling, mechanical errors, and typos and check your essay's format.

Although the writing process is usually presented as a series of neatly defined steps, that model does not reflect the way people actually write. Ideas do not always flow easily, and the central point you set out to develop does not always wind up in the essay you ultimately write. In addition, writing often progresses in fits and starts, with ideas occurring sporadically or not at all. Surprisingly, much good writing occurs when a writer gets stuck or confused but continues to work until ideas begin to take shape.

Because the writing process is so erratic, its stages overlap. Most writers engage in invention, arrangement, drafting and revision, and editing simultaneously — finding ideas, considering possible methods of organization, looking for the right words, and correcting grammar and punctuation all at the same time. In fact, writing is such an idiosyncratic process that no two writers approach the writing process in exactly the same way. Some people outline; others do not. Some take elaborate notes during the invention stage; others keep track of everything in their heads.

The writing process discussed throughout this book reflects the many choices writers make at various stages of composition. But regardless of writers' different approaches, one thing is certain: the more you write, the better acquainted you will become with your personal writing process and the better you will learn how to modify it to suit various writing tasks.

Because much of your college writing will be done in response to texts you read, Chapter 1 of this text introduces you to critical reading; then, Chapters 2 through 5 discuss the individual stages of the writing process. These chapters will help you to define your needs as a writer and to understand your options as you approach writing tasks in college and beyond.

1

Reading to Write: Becoming a Critical Reader

On a purely practical level, you will read the selections in this text to answer study questions and prepare for class discussions (and, often, for writing). More significantly, however, you will also read to evaluate the ideas of others, to form judgments, and to develop original viewpoints. In other words, you will engage in **critical reading**.

By introducing you to new ideas and new ways of thinking about familiar concepts, reading prepares you to respond critically to the ideas of others and to develop ideas of your own. When you read critically, you can form opinions, exchange insights with others in conversation, ask and answer questions, and develop ideas that can be further explored in writing. For all of these reasons, critical reading is a vital part of your education.

Understanding Critical Reading

Reading is a two-way street. Readers are presented with a writer's ideas, but they also bring their own ideas to what they read. After all, readers have different national, ethnic, cultural, and geographic backgrounds and different kinds of knowledge and experiences, so they may react differently to a particular essay or story. For example, readers from an economically and ethnically homogeneous suburban neighborhood may have difficulty understanding a story about class conflict, but they may also be more objective than readers who are struggling with such conflict in their own lives.

These differences in readers' responses do not mean that every interpretation is acceptable, that an essay (or story or poem) may mean whatever a reader wants it to mean. Readers must make sure they are not distorting a writer's words, overlooking (or ignoring) significant details, or seeing things in an essay or story that do not exist. It is not important for all readers to agree on a particular interpretation of a work. It *is* important, however, for each reader to develop an interpretation that the work itself supports.

When you read an essay in this book, or any text that you expect to discuss in class, you should read it carefully, ideally more than once. If a text is accompanied by a headnote or other background material, as those in this book are, you should read this material as well because it will help you to understand the text. Keep in mind that some of the texts you read may eventually be used as sources for writing. In these cases, it is especially important that you understand what you are reading and can formulate a thoughtful response to the writer's ideas. (For information on how to evaluate the sources you read, see Chapter 16.)

 TECH TIP: Naming Your Files

If you take notes about your sources on your computer, it's important to give each file an accurate and descriptive title so you can find it when you need it. Your file name should identify the class for which you're writing and the due date.

Comp-Plagiarism essay-9.25

Once you develop a system that works for you, you should use it consistently — for example, always listing elements (class, assignment, date) in the same order for each project. You can also create a separate folder for each class and then use subfolders for each assignment, gathering together all your notes and drafts for an assignment.

To get the most out of your reading, you should use **active reading** strategies. In practical terms, this means actively participating in the reading process: approaching an assigned reading with a clear understanding of your purpose and marking the text to help you understand what you are reading.

Determining Your Purpose

Even before you start reading, you should consider some questions about your **purpose** — why you are reading. The answers to these questions will help you understand what kind of information you hope to get out of your reading and how you will use this information.

✔**CHECKLIST**   **Questions about Your Purpose**

☐ Will you be expected to discuss what you are reading? If so, will you discuss it in class? In a conference with your instructor?
☐ Will you have to write about what you are reading? If so, will you be expected to write an informal response (for example, a journal entry) or a more formal one (for example, an essay)?
☐ Will you be tested on the material?

Previewing

When you **preview**, you try to get a sense of the writer's main idea, key supporting points, and general emphasis. At this stage, you don't read every word; instead, you **skim** the text. You can begin by focusing on the title, the first paragraph (which often contains a purpose statement or overview), and the last paragraph (which may contain a summary of the writer's main idea). You should also look for clues to the writer's message in the passage's other **visual signals**.

Using Visual Signals

- Look at the title.
- Look at the opening and closing paragraphs.
- Look at each paragraph's first sentence.
- Look for headings.
- Look for *italicized* and **boldfaced** words.
- Look for numbered lists.
- Look for bulleted lists (like this one).
- Look at any visuals (graphs, charts, tables, photographs, and so on).
- Look at any information that is boxed.
- Look at any information that is in color.

When you have finished previewing the passage, you should have a general sense of what the writer wants to communicate.

As you read and reread, you will record your reactions in writing. These notations will help you to understand the writer's ideas and your own thoughts about those ideas. Every reader develops a different system of recording responses, but many readers learn to use a combination of *highlighting* and *annotating*.

Highlighting

When you **highlight**, you mark the text. You might, for example, underline (or double underline) important concepts, box key terms, number a series of related points, circle an unfamiliar word (or place a question mark beside it), draw a vertical line in the margin beside a particularly interesting passage, draw arrows to connect related points, or star discussions of the central issues or main idea.

At this stage, you continue to look for visual signals, but now, as you read more closely, you also begin to pay attention to the text's **verbal signals**.

Using Verbal Signals

- Look for phrases that signal emphasis ("The *primary* reason"; "The *most important* idea").
- Look for repeated words and phrases.

- Look for words that signal addition (*also, in addition, furthermore*).
- Look for words that signal time sequence (*first, after, then, next, finally*).
- Look for words that identify causes and effects (*because, as a result, for this reason*).
- Look for words that introduce examples (*for example, for instance*).
- Look for words that signal comparison (*likewise, similarly*).
- Look for words that signal contrast (*unlike, although, in contrast*).
- Look for words that signal contradiction (*however, on the contrary*).
- Look for words that signal a narrowing of the writer's focus (*in fact, specifically, in other words*).
- Look for words that signal summaries or conclusions (*to sum up, in conclusion*).

The following pages reprint a column by journalist Brent Staples that focuses on the issue of plagiarism among college students. The column, "Cutting and Pasting: A Senior Thesis by (Insert Name)," and the accompanying headnote and background material, have been highlighted by a student.

BRENT STAPLES

Cutting and Pasting: A Senior Thesis by (Insert Name)

Born in 1951 in Chester, Pennsylvania, Brent Staples is a writer and member of the editorial board of the *New York Times*. He often writes about culture, politics, race, and education. Staples has a B.A. in behavioral science from Widener University and a Ph.D. in psychology from the University of Chicago. Before joining the *New York Times*, he wrote for the *Chicago Sun-Times*, *Chicago Reader*, *Chicago Magazine*, and the jazz magazine *Down Beat*. His work has also appeared in publications such as *Ms.* and *Harper's*. Staples is the author of a memoir, *Parallel Time: Growing Up in Black and White* (1994).

Background on prevalence of cheating and plagiarism in high school and college Recent studies suggest that high school and college students are increasingly likely to cheat or plagiarize. For example, one Duke University study conducted from 2002 to 2005 showed that 70 percent of the 50,000 undergraduate students surveyed admitted to cheating on occasion. A 2008 survey of high school students by the Center for Youth Ethics at the Josephson Institute showed that 82 percent had copied from another student's work, while 36 percent said that they had used the Internet to plagiarize an assignment. Moreover, students tend to view such academic dishonesty with indifference: according to surveys by the Center for Academic Integrity, only 29 percent of undergraduates believe unattributed copying from the Web rises to the level of "serious cheating."

Observers have proposed various reasons for the prevalence of plagiarism. Some point to new technologies that allow instant access to an apparently "common" store of unlimited information, as sites like Wikipedia challenge traditional notions of singular authorship, originality, and intellectual property. Others see the problem as the result of declining personal morality and of a culture that rewards shady behavior. And many view plagiarism as the unavoidable consequence of the pressures many students feel.

Academic institutions have responded to the problem in a number of ways. Most colleges now use the Internet-based detection service Turnitin .com, which scans students' essays for plagiarism. But a recent study by the National Bureau of Economic Research concluded that simply showing a Web tutorial on the issue could reduce instances of plagiarism by two-thirds. Schools such as Duke University and Bowdoin College now require incoming students to complete this online instruction before they enroll. Additionally, the research of Rutgers professor Ronald McCabe, who founded the Center for Academic Integrity, indicates that honor codes — already in place at many colleges and universities — help create a campus culture of academic integrity.

A friend who teaches at a well-known eastern uni- 1
versity told me recently that plagiarism was turning
him into a cop. He begins the semester collecting evidence, in the form of an in-class essay that gives him a
sense of how well students think and write. He looks
back at the samples later when students turn in papers
that feature their own, less-than-perfect prose alongside expertly written passages lifted verbatim from the
Web.

"I have to assume that in every class, someone will 2
do it," he said. "It doesn't stop them if you say, 'This is
plagiarism. I won't accept it.' I have to tell them that it is
a failing offense and could lead me to file a complaint
with the university, which could lead to them being put
on probation or being asked to leave."

Not everyone who gets caught knows enough about 3
what they did to be remorseful. Recently, for example, a
student who plagiarized a sizable chunk of a paper essentially told my friend to keep his shirt on, that what
he'd done was no big deal. Beyond that, the student
said, he would be ashamed to go home to the family
with an F.

As my friend sees it: "This represents a shift away 4
from the view of education as the process of intellectual
engagement through which we learn to think critically
and toward the view of education as mere training. In
training, you are trying to find the right answer at any
cost, not trying to improve your mind."

Like many other professors, he no longer sees tradi- 5
tional term papers as a valid index of student competence. To get an accurate, Internet-free reading of how
much students have learned, he gives them written
assignments in class — where they can be watched.

These kinds of precautions are no longer unusual in 6
the college world. As Trip Gabriel pointed out in the
Times recently, more than half the colleges in the country have retained services that check student papers for
material lifted from the Internet and elsewhere. Many
schools now require incoming students to take online
tutorials that explain what plagiarism is and how to
avoid it.

Nationally, discussions about plagiarism tend to 7
focus on questions of ethics. But as David Pritchard,
a physics professor at the Massachusetts Institute of
Technology, told me recently: "The big sleeping dog

here is not the moral issue. The problem is that kids don't learn if they don't do the work."

Prof. Pritchard and his colleagues illustrated the point in a study of cheating behavior by M.I.T. students who used an online system to complete homework. The students who were found to have copied the most answers from others started out with the same math and physics skills as their harder-working classmates. But by skipping the actual work in homework, they fell behind in understanding and became significantly more likely to fail. 8

∗ ∗   The Pritchard axiom — that repetitive cheating undermines learning — has ominous implications for a world in which even junior high school students cut and paste from the Internet instead of producing their own writing. 9

If we look closely at plagiarism as practiced by youngsters, we can see that they have a different relationship to the printed word than did the generations before them. When many young people think of writing, they don't think of fashioning original sentences into a sustained thought. They think of making something like a collage of found passages and ideas from the Internet. 10

✓   They become like rap musicians who construct what they describe as new works by "sampling" (which is to say, cutting and pasting) beats and refrains from the works of others. 11

This habit of mind is already pervasive in the culture and will be difficult to roll back. But parents, teachers, and policy makers need to understand that this is not just a matter of personal style or generational expression. It's a question of whether we can preserve the methods through which education at its best teaches people to think critically and originally. 12

• • •

The student who highlighted Staples's column and its headnote was preparing for a class discussion of a group of related articles on the problem of academic cheating. To prepare for class, she began by highlighting the essay to identify the writer's key ideas and mark points she might want to think further about. This highlighting laid the groundwork for the careful annotations she would make when she reread the article.

Exercise 1

Preview the following essay. Then, highlight it to identify the writer's main idea and key supporting points. (Previewing and highlighting the article's headnote, including the background material provided, will help you to understand the article's ideas.) You might circle unfamiliar words, underline key terms or concepts, or draw lines or arrows to connect related ideas.

ZEV CHAFETS

Let Steroids into the Hall of Fame

A versatile journalist and novelist, American-Israeli writer Zev Chafets was born in Pontiac, Michigan, in 1947. After graduating from the University of Michigan, he moved to Israel, where he worked for the Government Press Office and founded the *Jerusalem Report* magazine. He has written for many publications, including the *New York Times Sunday Magazine* and the *Los Angeles Times*. Chafets writes regularly about sports, politics, and the Middle East; he has also written five works of fiction. His most recent books are *Cooperstown Confidential: Heroes, Rogues, and the Inside Story of the Baseball Hall of Fame* (2009) and *Roger Ailes: Off Camera* (2013).

Background on steroids In 1991, then-Commissioner of Baseball Fay Vincent added steroids to the list of banned substances under Major League Baseball's drug policy — although the league instituted no testing program at the time. The 1990s and early 2000s witnessed an explosion of home-run hitting, highlighted in 1998 by the home-run race between Sammy Sosa and Mark McGwire, both of whom used steroids. In the years since, Major League Baseball has cracked down on steroid use under scrutiny and pressure from Congress. Steroids, which increase muscle mass and endurance, can have dangerous side effects, including depression, mood swings, liver damage, and cancer.

1　When the Baseball Hall of Fame commemorates its 70th anniversary with an exhibition game in Cooperstown, N.Y., on Sunday, five of its members will play on the national field of dreams. At least two of them — Paul Molitor and Ferguson Jenkins — were busted in the 1980s for using cocaine. Molitor later said he was sure he wasn't the only player on the team using drugs.

2　Given what we now know about baseball's drug habit, the remark sounds quaint. This week's report that Sammy Sosa tested positive for performance-enhancing drugs in 2003 is only the latest in a long string of revelations. Barry Bonds, Roger Clemens, Alex Rodriguez, Manny Ramirez, Mark McGwire — what great players haven't been linked to drug use?

3　Since the dawn of baseball, players have used whatever substances they believed would help them perform better, heal faster, or relax during a long and stressful season. As far back as 1889, the pitcher Pud Galvin ingested monkey testosterone. During Prohibition, Grover Cleveland Alexander, also a pitcher, calmed his nerves with federally banned alcohol, and no less an expert than Bill Veeck, who owned several major-league teams, said that Alexander was a better pitcher drunk than sober.

4　In 1961, during his home run race with Roger Maris, Mickey Mantle developed a sudden abscess that kept him on the bench. It came from an infected needle used by Max Jacobson, a quack who injected Mantle with a home-brew containing steroids and speed. In his autobiography, Hank Aaron admitted once taking an amphetamine tablet during a game. The Pirates' John Milner testified at a drug dealer's trial that his teammate, Willie Mays, kept "red juice," a liquid form of speed, in his locker. (Mays denied it.) After he retired, Sandy Koufax admitted that he was often "half high" on the mound from the drugs he took for his ailing left arm.

For decades, baseball beat writers — the Hall of Fame's designated elec- 5
toral college — shielded the players from scrutiny. When the Internet (and exposés by two former ballplayers, Jim Bouton and Jose Canseco) allowed fans to see what was really happening, the baseball writers were revealed as dupes or stooges. In a rage, they formed a posse to drive the drug users out of the game.

But today's superstars have lawyers and a union. They know how to use 6
the news media. And they have plenty of money. The only way to punish them is to deny them a place in Cooperstown. The punishment has already been visited on Mark McGwire, and many more are on deck.

This makes no sense. On any given day, 7
the stands are packed with youngsters on Adderall and Ritalin (stimulants used to treat attention deficit hyperactivity disorder) and college students who use Provigil (an anti-narcolepsy drug) as a study aid. The guy who sings the national anthem has probably taken a beta blocker to calm his stage fright. Like it or not, chemical enhancement is here to stay. And it is as much a part of the national game as $5.50 hot dogs, free agency, and Tommy John elbow surgery.

> "Like it or not, chemical enhancement is here to stay."

Purists say that steroids alter the game. But since the Hall opened its 8
doors, baseball has never stopped changing. Batters now wear body padding and helmets. The pitcher's mound has risen and fallen. Bats have more pop. Night games affect visibility. Players stay in shape in the off-season. Expansion has altered the game's geography. And its demography has changed beyond recognition. Babe Ruth never faced a black pitcher. As Chris Rock put it, Ruth's record consisted of "714 affirmative-action home runs." This doesn't diminish Ruth's accomplishment, but it puts it into context.

Statistics change, too. In 1908, Ed Walsh pitched 464 innings; in 2008, 9
C. C. Sabathia led the majors with 253. So what? They were both first under the prevailing conditions of the time.

Despite these changes, or because of them, Americans continue to love 10
baseball. Fans will accept anything except the sense that they are being lied to. Chemical enhancement won't kill the game; it is the cover-up that could be fatal.

Baseball, led by the Hall of Fame, needs to accept this and replace 11
mythology and spin with realism and honesty. If everyone has access to the same drugs and training methods, and the fans are told what these are, then the field is level and fans will be able to interpret what they are seeing on the diamond and in the box scores.

The purists' last argument is that players' use of performance-enhancing 12
drugs sets a bad example for young athletes. But baseball players aren't
children; they are adults in a very stressful and competitive profession. If
they want to use anabolic steroids, or human growth hormone or bull's
testosterone, it should be up to them. As for children, the government can
regulate their use of these substances as they do with tobacco, alcohol, and
prescription medicine.

The Baseball Hall of Fame, which started as a local tourist attraction 13
and a major-league publicity stunt, has since become a national field of
dreams — and now, a battlefield. If it surrenders to the moralists who want
to turn back the clock to some imagined golden era, and excommunicates
the greatest stars anyone has ever seen, it will suffer the fate of all battle-
fields located on the wrong side of history. Obscurity.

• • •

Annotating

When you **annotate**, you carry on a conversation with the text. In marginal notes, you can ask questions, suggest possible parallels with other
reading selections or with your own experiences, argue with the writer's
points, comment on the writer's style or word choice, or define unfamiliar
terms and concepts.

⧉ TECH TIP: Taking Notes

If you use your computer when you take notes instead of writing annotations on the
page, be sure to label each note so you remember where it came from. (You will need
this information for your paper's parenthetical references and works-cited page.)
Include the author's name and the title of the reading selection as well as the page on
which the information you are citing appears. Also note the page and paragraph
number where you found the information so you will be able to find it again.

The questions below can guide you as you read and help you make useful annotations.

✓ CHECKLIST   Questions for Critical Reading

- ☐ What is the writer's general subject?
- ☐ What is the writer's main point?
- ☐ What are the writer's key supporting points?
- ☐ Does the writer seem to have a particular purpose in mind?
- ☐ What kind of audience is the writer addressing?
- ☐ What are the writer's assumptions about audience? About subject?
- ☐ Are the writer's ideas consistent with your own?

(continued)

☐ Does the writer reveal any biases?
☐ Do you have any knowledge that challenges the writer's ideas?
☐ Is any information missing?
☐ Are any sequential or logical links missing?
☐ Can you identify themes or ideas that also appear in other works you have read?
☐ Can you identify parallels with your own experience?

The following pages reproduce the student's highlighting of "Cutting and Pasting: A Senior Thesis by (Insert Name)" from pages 18–19 and also include her annotations. (She annotated the headnote and background material as well, but these annotations are not shown here.)

Teachers as cops

A friend who teaches at a well-known eastern university told me recently that plagiarism was turning him into a cop. He begins the semester collecting evidence, in the form of an in-class essay that gives him a sense of how well students think and write. He looks back at the samples later when students turn in papers that feature their own, less-than-perfect prose alongside expertly written passages lifted verbatim from the Web. 1

Teachers resigned to situation

"I have to assume that in every class, someone will do it," he said. "It doesn't stop them if you say, 'This is plagiarism. I won't accept it.' I have to tell them that it is a failing offense and could lead me to file a complaint with the university, which could lead to them being put on probation or being asked to leave." 2

Not everyone who gets caught knows enough about what they did to be remorseful. Recently, for example, a student who plagiarized a sizable chunk of a paper essentially told my friend to keep his shirt on, that what he'd done was no big deal. Beyond that, the student said, he would be ashamed to go home to the family with an F. 3

Key problem—Move from "intellectual engagement" and critical thinking to "mere training"

＊ As my friend sees it: "This represents a shift away from the view of education as the process of intellectual engagement through which we learn to think critically and toward the view of education as mere training. In training, you are trying to find the right answer at any cost, not trying to improve your mind." 4

Like many other professors, he no longer sees traditional term papers as a valid index of student compe- 5 tence. To get an accurate, Internet-free reading of how much students have learned, he gives them written assignments in class — where they can be watched.

These kinds of precautions are no longer unusual in 6 the college world. As Trip Gabriel pointed out in the *Times* recently, more than half the colleges in the country have retained services that check student papers for material lifted from the Internet and elsewhere. Many schools now require incoming students to take online tutorials that explain what plagiarism is and how to avoid it.

Colleges as police states!

Nationally, discussions about plagiarism tend to 7 focus on questions of ethics. But as David Pritchard, a physics professor at the Massachusetts Institute of Technology, told me recently: "The big sleeping dog here is not the moral issue. The problem is that kids don't learn if they don't do the work."

Problem isn't just ethics

*

Prof. Pritchard and his colleagues illustrated the 8 point in a study of cheating behavior by M.I.T. students who used an online system to complete homework. The students who were found to have copied the most answers from others started out with the same math and physics skills as their harder-working classmates. But by skipping the actual work in homework, they fell behind in understanding and became significantly more likely to fail.

* *

The Pritchard axiom — that repetitive cheating 9 undermines learning — has ominous implications for a world in which even junior high school students cut and paste from the Internet instead of producing their own writing.

If we look closely at plagiarism as practiced by 10 youngsters, we can see that they have a different relationship to the printed word than did the generations before them. When many young people think of writing, they don't think of fashioning original sentences into a sustained thought. They think of making something like a collage of found passages and ideas from the Internet.

True

They become like rap musicians who construct 11 what they describe as new works by "sampling" (which is to say, cutting and pasting) beats and refrains from the works of others.

"Cutting and pasting" = "sampling"

√

This habit of mind is already pervasive in the cul- 12 ture and will be difficult to roll back. But parents, teachers, and policy makers need to understand that this is

What's the answer to this question? (What can schools do? Who is responsible for solving the problem?)

not just a matter of personal style or generational expression. It's a question of whether we can preserve the methods through which education at its best teaches people to think critically and originally.

• • •

As illustrated above, the student who annotated Staples's column on plagiarism supplemented her highlighting with brief marginal summaries to help her understand key points. She also wrote down questions that she thought would help her focus her responses.

SUMMARIZING KEY IDEAS

One strategy that can help you understand what you are reading is **summarizing** a writer's key ideas, as the student writer does in her marginal annotations of the Staples column on pages 24–26. Putting a writer's ideas into your own words can make an unfamiliar or complex concept more accessible and useful to you. For more on summarizing, see page 720.

Exercise 2

Now, add annotations to the Chafets essay and related material that you highlighted for Exercise 1. This time, focus on summarizing the writer's key points and on asking questions that will prepare you for discussing (and perhaps writing about) this essay.

Reading Visual Texts

The process you use when you react to a **visual text** — a photograph; an advertisement; a diagram, graph, or chart; an infographic; or a work of fine art, for example — is much the same as the one you use when you respond to a written text. Here too, your goal is to understand the text, and highlighting and annotating a visual text can help you interpret it.

With visual texts, however, instead of identifying elements such as particular words and ideas, you identify visual elements. These might include the use of color; the arrangement of shapes; the contrast between large and small or light and dark; and, of course, the particular images the visual includes.

As you approach a visual, you might ask questions like those on the following checklist.

✓**CHECKLIST**   **Reading Visual Texts**

☐ Why was the visual created?

☐ What kind of audience is it aimed at?

☐ How would you characterize the visual? For example, is it fine art? An advertisement? A technical diagram? A chart or graph? An infographic?

☐ What is the visual's most important or most striking image? What makes this image dominate the page?

☐ How is blank space used to emphasize (or de-emphasize) individual images?

☐ How does contrast between light and dark (or use of color) work to emphasize (or de-emphasize) individual images?

☐ What objects are depicted in the visual?

☐ Does the visual include any images of people? If so, how do the people depicted interact with one another? What is their relationship to various objects depicted in the visual?

☐ Does the visual include any words? If so, what is their function? What is the relationship between the visual's words and its images?

The following photograph, one of four included in "Four Tattoos" (page 222), illustrates a student's highlighting and annotating of a visual text. (See page 223 for study questions about these images.)

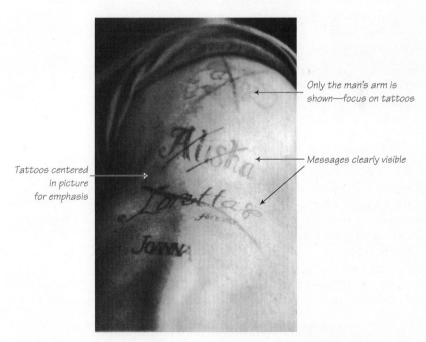

Charles Thatcher, "~~Alisha, Loretta~~" (© Charles Thatcher/The Image Bank/Getty Images)

Exercise 3

In this text, visuals are included in Chapters 6–14, where they are the first reading selection in each chapter. Choose one of these visuals, and highlight and annotate it. When you have finished, write a sentence that sums up what you think the visual is trying to communicate and how successful it is at accomplishing its goals.

2

Invention

Invention, or **prewriting**, is an important (and, frequently, the most neglected) part of the writing process. During invention, you discover what interests you about your subject and consider what ideas to develop in your essay.

When you are given a writing assignment, you may be tempted to start writing a first draft immediately. Before writing, however, you should be sure you understand your assignment and its limits, and you should think about what you want to say. Time spent on these issues now will pay off later when you draft your essay.

Understanding Your Assignment

Almost everything you write in college begins as an **assignment**. Some assignments will be direct and easy to understand:

Write about an experience that changed your life.

Discuss the procedure you used to synthesize ammonia.

Others will be difficult and complex:

Using Jonathan Kozol's essay "The Human Cost of an Illiterate Society" as source material, write an essay using as your thesis the following statement by James Madison: "A people who mean to be their own governors must arm themselves with the power knowledge gives."

Before beginning to write, you need to understand exactly what your assignment is asking you to do. If the assignment is a question, read it carefully several times, and underline its key words. If the assignment is given orally by your instructor, be sure to copy it accurately. (A mistaken word — *analyze* for *compare,* for example — can make quite a difference.) If you are confused about anything, ask your instructor for clarification. Remember that no matter how well written an essay is, it will fall short if it does not address the assignment.

Setting Limits

Once you understand the assignment, you should consider its *length, purpose, audience,* and *occasion* and your own *knowledge* of the subject. Each of these factors helps you determine what you will say about your subject.

Length

Often, your instructor will specify the **length** of a paper, and this word or page limit has a direct bearing on your paper's focus. For example, you would need a narrower topic for a two-page essay than for a ten-page one. Similarly, you could not discuss a question as thoroughly during an hour-long exam as you might in a paper written over several days.

If your instructor sets no page limit, consider how the nature of the assignment suggests a paper's length. A *summary* of a chapter or an article, for instance, should be much shorter than the original, whereas an *analysis* of a poem will most likely be longer than the poem itself. If you are uncertain about the appropriate length for your paper, consult your instructor.

Purpose

Your **purpose** also limits what you say and how you say it. For example, if you were writing a job application letter, you would not emphasize the same elements of college life as you would in an email to a friend. In the first case, you would want to convince the reader to hire you, so you might include your grade-point average, a list of the relevant courses you took, and perhaps the work you did for a service-learning course. In the second case, you would want to inform and perhaps entertain, so you might share anecdotes about dorm life or describe one of your favorite instructors. In each case, your purpose would help you determine what information to include to evoke a particular response in a specific audience.

In general, you can classify your purposes for writing according to your relationship to the audience.

- In **expressive writing**, you convey personal feelings or impressions to readers. Expressive writing is used in diaries, personal emails, and journals, and often in narrative and descriptive essays as well.
- In **informative writing**, you inform readers about something. Informative writing is used in essay exams, lab reports, and expository essays as well as in some research papers and personal Web pages.
- In **persuasive writing**, you try to convince readers to act or think in a certain way. Persuasive writing is used in editorials, argumentative essays, proposals, research papers, and many types of electronic documents.

In addition to these general purposes, you might have a more specific purpose — to analyze, entertain, hypothesize, assess, summarize, question, report, recommend, suggest, evaluate, describe, recount, request, instruct, and so on. For example, suppose you wrote a report on homelessness in your community. Your general purpose might be to *inform* readers of the situation, but you might also want to *assess* the problem and *instruct* readers how to help those in need.

Audience

To be effective, your essay should be written with a particular **audience** in mind. An audience can be an *individual* (your instructor, for example), or it can be a *group* (like your classmates or coworkers). Your essay can address a *specialized* audience (such as a group of medical doctors or economists) or a *general* or *universal* audience whose members have little in common (such as the readers of a newspaper or magazine).

In college, your audience is usually your instructor, and your purpose in most cases is to demonstrate your mastery of the subject matter, your reasoning ability, and your competence as a writer. Other audiences may include classmates, professional colleagues, or members of your community. Considering the age and gender of your audience, its political and religious values, its social and educational level, and its interest in your subject may help you define it.

Often, you will find that your audience is just too diverse to be categorized. In such cases, many writers imagine a general (or universal) audience and make points that they think will appeal to a variety of readers. At other times, writers identify a common denominator, a role that characterizes the entire audience. For instance, when a report on the dangers of smoking asserts, "Now is the time for health-conscious individuals to demand that cigarettes be removed from the market," it automatically casts its audience in the role of health-conscious individuals.

After you define your audience, you have to determine how much (or how little) its members know about your subject. This consideration helps you decide how much information your readers will need in order to understand the discussion. Are they highly informed? If so, you can present your points without much explanation. Are they relatively uninformed? If this is the case, you will have to include definitions of key terms, background information, and summaries of basic research.

Keep in mind that experts in one field will need background information in other fields. If, for example, you were writing an analysis of Joseph Conrad's *Heart of Darkness,* you could assume that the literature instructor who assigned the work would not need a plot summary. However, if you wrote an essay for your history instructor that used *Heart of Darkness* to illustrate the evils of European colonialism in nineteenth-century Africa, you would probably include a short plot summary. (Even though your history instructor would know a lot about colonialism in Africa, she might not be familiar with Conrad's work.)

Occasion

Occasion refers to the situation (or situations) that leads someone to write about a topic. In an academic writing situation, the occasion is almost always a specific assignment. The occasion suggests a specific audience — for example, a history instructor — as well as a specific purpose — for example, to discuss the causes of World War I. In fact, even the format of a paper — whether you use (or do not use) headings or whether you present your response to an assignment as an essay, as a technical report, or as a Power-Point presentation — is determined by the occasion for your writing. For this reason, a paper suitable for a psychology or sociology class might not be suitable for a composition class.

Like college writing assignments, each writing task you do outside of school requires an approach that suits the occasion. An email to coworkers, for instance, may be less formal than a report to a manager. In addition, the occasion suggests how much (or how little) information the piece of writing includes. Finally, your occasion suggests your purpose. For example, a message to members of an online discussion group might be strictly informational, whereas an email to a state senator about preserving a local landmark would be persuasive as well as informative.

Knowledge

What you know (and do not know) about a subject determines what you can say about it. Before writing about any subject, ask yourself what you know about the subject and what you need to find out.

Different writing situations require different kinds of knowledge. A personal essay will draw on your own experiences and observations; an argumentative essay may require you to do research. In many cases, your page limit and the amount of time you have to do the assignment will help you decide how much information you need to gather before you can begin.

✔CHECKLIST   **Setting Limits**

Length

☐ Has your instructor specified a length?
☐ Does the nature of your assignment suggest a length?

Purpose

☐ Is your general purpose to express personal feelings? To inform? To persuade?
☐ In addition to your general purpose, do you have any more specific purposes?
☐ Does your assignment provide any guidelines about purpose?

Audience

☐ Is your audience a group or an individual?
☐ Are you going to address a specialized or a general audience?

☐ Should you take into consideration the audience's age, gender, education, biases, or political or social values?
☐ Should you cast your audience in a particular role?
☐ How much can you assume your audience knows about your subject?

Occasion

☐ Are you writing in class or at home?
☐ Are you addressing a situation outside the academic setting?
☐ What special approaches does your occasion for writing require?

Knowledge

☐ What do you know about your subject?
☐ What do you need to find out?

Exercise 1

Decide whether or not each of the following topics is appropriate for the stated limits, and then write a few sentences to explain why each topic is or is not acceptable.

1. *A two-to-three-page paper*   A history of animal testing in medical research labs
2. *A two-hour final exam*   The effectiveness of bilingual education programs
3. *A one-hour in-class essay*   An interpretation of one of Andy Warhol's paintings of Campbell's soup cans
4. *An email to your college newspaper*   A discussion of your school's policy on plagiarism

Exercise 2

Make a list of the different audiences to whom you speak or write in your daily life. (Consider all the different people you see regularly, such as family members, your roommate, instructors, your boss, your friends, and so on.) Then, record your answers to the following questions:

1. Do you speak or write to each person in your life in the same way and about the same things? If not, how do your approaches to these people differ?
2. List some subjects that would interest some of these people but not others. How do you account for these differences?
3. Choose one of the following subjects, and describe how you would speak or write to different audiences about it.
   - A change that improved your life
   - Censoring Internet content
   - Taking a year off before college
   - Reality TV shows

Moving from Subject to Topic

Although many essays begin as specific assignments, some begin as broad areas of interest or concern. These **general subjects** always need to be narrowed to **specific topics** that can be discussed within the limits of the assignment. For example, a subject like fracking could be interesting, but it is too broad to write about. You need to limit such a subject to a topic that can be covered within the time and space available.

GENERAL SUBJECT	SPECIFIC TOPIC
Tablets	The benefits of using tablets in elementary school classrooms
Herman Melville's *Billy Budd*	Billy Budd as a Christ figure
Constitutional law	One unforeseen result of the *Miranda* ruling
Fracking	Should fracking be banned?

Two strategies can help you narrow a general subject to a specific topic: *questions for probing* and *freewriting*.

Questions for Probing

One way to move from a general subject to a specific topic is to examine your subject by asking a series of questions about it. These **questions for probing** are useful because they reflect how your mind operates — for instance, finding similarities and differences or dividing a whole into its parts. By asking the questions on the following checklist, you can explore your subject systematically. Not all questions will work for every subject, but any single question may elicit many different answers, and each answer is a possible topic for your essay.

✓ CHECKLIST   **Questions for Probing**

What happened?
When did it happen?
Where did it happen?
Who did it?
What does it look like?
What are its characteristics?
What impressions does it make?
What are some typical cases or examples of it?
How did it happen?
What makes it work?
How is it made?
Why did it happen?

What caused it?
What does it cause?
What are its effects?
How is it like other things?
How is it different from other things?
What are its parts or types?
How can its parts or types be separated or grouped?
Do its parts or types fit into a logical order?
Into what categories can its parts or types be arranged?
On what basis can it be categorized?
How can it be defined?
How does it resemble other members of its class?
How does it differ from other members of its class?

When applied to a subject, some of these questions can yield many workable topics, including some you might never have considered had you not asked the questions. For example, by applying this approach to the general subject "the Brooklyn Bridge," you can generate more ideas and topics than you need:

What happened? A short history of the Brooklyn Bridge

What does it look like? A description of the Brooklyn Bridge

How is it made? The construction of the Brooklyn Bridge

What are its effects? The impact of the Brooklyn Bridge on American writers

How does it differ from other members of its class? Innovations in the design of the Brooklyn Bridge

At this point in the writing process, you want to come up with possible topics, and the more ideas you have, the wider your choice. Begin by jotting down all the topics you think of. (You can repeat the process of probing several times to limit topics further.) Once you have a list of topics, eliminate those that do not interest you or are too complex or too simple to fit your assignment. When you have discarded these less promising topics, you should have several left. You can then select the topic that best suits your paper's length, purpose, audience, and occasion, as well as your interests and your knowledge of the subject.

TECH TIP: Questions for Probing

You can store the questions for probing listed on pages 34–35 in a file that you can open whenever you have a new subject. Make sure you keep a record of your answers. If the topic you have chosen is too difficult or too narrow, you can return to the questions-for-probing file and probe your subject again.

Exercise 3

Indicate whether each of the following is a general subject or a specific topic that is narrow enough for a short essay.

1. An argument against fast-food ads that are aimed at young children
2. Home schooling
3. Cell phones and driving
4. Changes in U.S. immigration laws
5. Requiring college students to study a foreign language
6. The advantages of providing free health care for children of undocumented workers
7. A comparison of small-town and big-city living
8. Student loans
9. The advantages of service-learning courses
10. The drawbacks of electric cars

Exercise 4

In preparation for writing a 750-word essay, choose two of the following general subjects, and generate three or four specific topics from each by using as many of the questions for probing as you can.

1. Credit-card fraud
2. Job interviews
3. Identity theft
4. Genetically modified food
5. Substance abuse
6. Climate change
7. The minimum wage
8. Age discrimination
9. Cyberbullying
10. The need for recycling
11. The person you admire most
12. Rising college tuition
13. Online courses
14. Sensational trials
15. The widespread use of surveillance cameras

Freewriting

Another strategy for moving from subject to topic is **freewriting**. You can use freewriting at any stage of the writing process — for example, to generate supporting information or to find a thesis. However, freewriting is a particularly useful way to narrow a general subject or assignment.

When you freewrite, you write for a fixed period, perhaps five or ten minutes, without stopping and without paying attention to spelling, grammar, or punctuation. Your goal is to get your ideas down on paper so that you can react to them and shape them. If you have nothing to say, write down anything until ideas begin to emerge — and in time they will. The secret is to *keep writing*. Try to focus on your subject, but don't worry if you wander off in other directions. The object of freewriting is to let your ideas flow. Often, your best ideas will come from the unexpected connections you make as you write.

After completing your freewriting, read what you have written, and look for ideas you can write about. Some writers underline ideas they think they might explore in their essays. Any of these ideas could become essay topics, or they could become subjects for other freewriting exercises. You might want to freewrite again, using a new idea as your focus. This process of writing more and more specific freewriting exercises — called **focused freewriting** or **looping** — can often yield a great deal of useful information and help you decide on a workable topic.

 TECH TIP: **Freewriting**

If you freewrite on a computer, you may find that staring at your own words causes you to go blank. One possible solution is to turn down the brightness until the screen becomes dark and then to freewrite. This technique allows you to block out distracting elements and concentrate on just your ideas. Once you finish freewriting, turn up the brightness, and see what you have.

A STUDENT WRITER: **Freewriting**

After reading, highlighting, and annotating Henry Louis Gates Jr.'s "'What's in a Name?'" (page 2), Laura Bobnak, a student in a composition class, decided to write an essay in response to this Writing Workshop question.

> Write about a time when you, like Gates's father, could have spoken out in protest but chose not to. Would you make the same decision today?

In an attempt to narrow this assignment to a workable topic, Laura did the following freewriting exercise.

> Write for ten minutes . . . ten minutes . . . at 9 o'clock in the morning — Just what I want to do in the morning — If you can't think of something to say, just write about anything. Right! Time to get this over with — An experience — should have talked — I can think of plenty of times I should have kept quiet! I should have brought a bottle of water to class. I wonder what the people next to me are writing about. That reminds me. Next to me. Jeff Servin in chemistry. The time I saw him cheating. I was mad but I didn't do anything.

> I studied so hard and all he did was cheat. I was so mad. Nobody else seemed
> to care. What's the difference between now and then? It's only a year and a
> half. . . . Honor code? Maturity? A lot of people cheated in high school.
> I bet I could write about this — Before and after, etc. My attitude then and
> now.

After some initial thought, Laura discovered an idea that could be the basis
for her essay. Although her discussion of the incident still had to be developed, Laura's freewriting helped her come up with a possible topic for her
essay: a time she saw someone cheating and did not speak out.

Exercise 5

Do a five-minute freewriting exercise on one of the topics you generated in
Exercise 4 (page 36).

Exercise 6

Read what you have just written, underline the most interesting ideas, and
choose one idea as a topic you could write about in a short essay. Freewrite
about this topic for another five minutes to narrow it further and to generate ideas for your essay. Underline the ideas that seem most useful.

Finding Something to Say

Once you have narrowed your subject to a workable topic, you need to
find something to say about it. *Brainstorming* and *journal writing* are useful
tools for generating ideas, and both can be helpful at this stage of the writing process (and whenever you need to find additional material).

Brainstorming

Brainstorming is a way of discovering ideas about your topic. You
can brainstorm in a group, exchanging ideas with several students in your
composition class and noting the most useful ideas. You can also brainstorm on your own, quickly recording every fact, idea, or detail you can
think of that relates to your topic. Your notes might include words,
phrases, statements, questions, or even drawings or diagrams. Jot them
down in the order in which you think of them. Some of the items may be
inspired by your class notes; others may be ideas you got from reading or
from talking with friends; and still other items may be ideas you have begun to wonder about, points you thought of while moving from subject to
topic, or thoughts that occurred to you as you brainstormed.

A STUDENT WRITER: Brainstorming

To narrow her topic further and find something to say about it, Laura Bobnak made the brainstorming notes shown on page 40. After reading these notes several times, Laura decided to concentrate on the differences between her current and earlier attitudes toward cheating. She knew that she could write a lot about this idea and relate it to the assignment, and she felt confident that her topic would be interesting both to her instructor and to the other students in the class.

 TECH TIP: Brainstorming

Your word-processing program makes it easy to create bulleted or numbered lists and gives you the flexibility to experiment with ways of arranging and grouping items from your brainstorming notes. You can even use the drawing tools to make diagrams.

Journal Writing

Journal writing can be a useful source of ideas at any stage of the writing process. Many writers routinely keep a journal, jotting down experiences and ideas they may want to use when they write. They write journal entries even when they have no particular writing project in mind. Often, these journal entries are the kernels from which longer pieces of writing develop. Your instructor may ask you to keep a writing journal, or you may decide to do so on your own. In either case, you will find your journal entries are likely to be more narrowly focused than freewriting or brainstorming, perhaps examining a small part of a reading selection or even one particular statement. Sometimes you will write in your journal in response to specific questions, such as the Journal Entry assignments that appear throughout this book. Assignments like these can help you start thinking about a reading selection that you may later discuss in class or write about.

A STUDENT WRITER: Journal Writing

In the following journal entry, Laura Bobnak explores one idea from her brainstorming notes — her thoughts about her college's honor code.

> At orientation, the dean of students talked about the college's honor code.
> She talked about how we were a community of scholars who were here for a
> common purpose — to take part in an intellectual conversation. According to
> her, the purpose of the honor code is to make sure this conversation continues
> uninterrupted. This idea sounded dumb at orientation, but now it makes sense.
> If I saw someone cheating, I'd tell the instructor. First, though, I'd ask the
> *student* to go to the instructor. I don't see this as "telling" or "squealing." We're

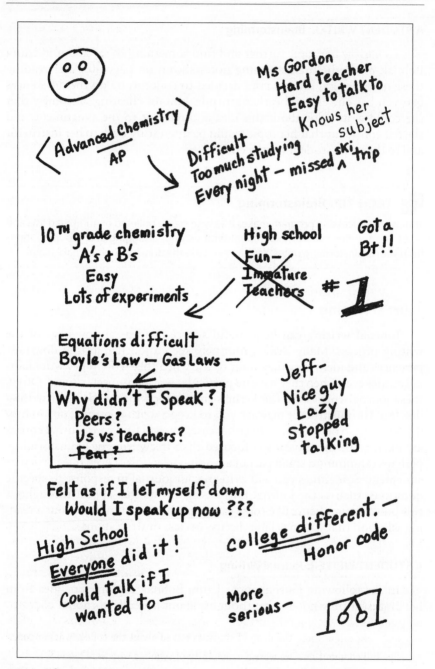

Laura's brainstorming notes

all here to get an education, and we should be able to assume everyone is being honest and fair. Besides, why should I go to all the trouble of studying while someone else does nothing and gets the same grade?

Even though Laura eventually included only a small part of this entry in her paper, writing in her journal helped her focus her ideas about her topic.

 TECH TIP: Keeping a Journal

Keeping your journal in a computer file has some obvious advantages. Not only can you maintain a neat record of your ideas, but you can also easily move entries from your journal into an essay without retyping them. Make sure, however, that you clearly distinguish between your ideas and those of your sources. If you paste material from your sources directly into your journal and then paste that material into your paper without documenting it, you are committing plagiarism. (For information on avoiding plagiarism, see Chapter 17.)

Grouping Ideas

Once you have generated material for your essay, you will want to group ideas that belong together. *Clustering* and *outlining* can help you do this.

Clustering

Clustering is a way of visually arranging ideas so that you can tell at a glance where ideas belong and whether or not you need more information. Although you can use clustering at an earlier stage of the writing process, it is especially useful now for seeing how your ideas fit together. (Clustering can also help you narrow your paper's topic even further. If you find that your cluster diagram is too detailed, you can write about just one branch of the cluster.)

Begin clustering by writing your topic in the center of a sheet of paper. After circling the topic, surround it with the words and phrases that identify the major points you intend to discuss. (You can get ideas from your brainstorming notes, from your journal, and from your freewriting.) Circle these words and phrases, and connect them to the topic in the center. Next, construct other clusters of ideas relating to each major point, and draw lines connecting them to the appropriate point. By dividing and subdividing your points, you get more specific as you move outward from the center. In the process, you identify the facts, details, examples, and opinions that illustrate and expand your main points.

A STUDENT WRITER: Clustering

Because Laura Bobnak was not very visually oriented, she chose not to use this method of grouping her ideas. If she had, however, her cluster diagram would have looked like this.

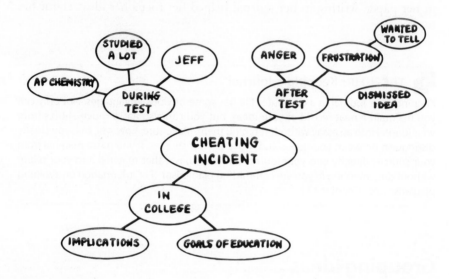

Making an Informal Outline

As an alternative or follow-up to clustering, you can organize your notes from brainstorming or other invention techniques into an **informal outline**. Informal outlines do not include all the major divisions and sub-divisions of your paper the way formal outlines do; they simply suggest the shape of your emerging essay. Quite often an informal outline is just a list of your major points presented in a tentative order. Sometimes, however, an informal outline will include supporting details or suggest a pattern of development.

 TECH TIP: Making an Informal Outline

You can easily arrange the notes you generated in your invention activities into an informal outline. You can construct an informal outline by typing words or phrases from your notes and rearranging them until the order makes sense. Later on, if you need to make a formal outline, you can use the categories from this informal outline to construct it (see page 62).

A STUDENT WRITER: Making an Informal Outline

The following informal outline shows how Laura Bobnak grouped her ideas.

During test
   Found test hard
   Saw Jeff cheating
After test
   Got angry
   Wanted to tell
   Dismissed idea
In college
   Understand implications of cheating
   Understand goals of education

Exercise 7

Continue your work on the topic you selected in Exercise 6 (page 38). Brainstorm about your topic; then, select the ideas you plan to explore in your essay, and use either clustering or an informal outline to help you group related ideas together.

Understanding Thesis and Support

Once you have grouped your ideas, you need to consider your essay's thesis. A **thesis** is the main idea of your essay, its central point. The concept

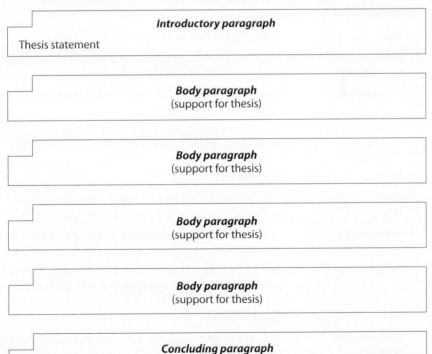

Introductory paragraph
Thesis statement

Body paragraph
(support for thesis)

Body paragraph
(support for thesis)

Body paragraph
(support for thesis)

Body paragraph
(support for thesis)

Concluding paragraph
Restatement of thesis or review of key points

of **thesis and support** — stating your thesis and developing ideas that explain and expand it — is central to college writing.

The essays you write will consist of several paragraphs: an **introduction** that presents your thesis statement, several **body paragraphs** that develop and support your thesis, and a **conclusion** that reinforces your thesis and provides closure. Your thesis holds this structure together; it is the center that the rest of your essay develops around.

Developing a Thesis

Defining the Thesis Statement

A **thesis statement** is more than a *title*, an *announcement of your intent*, or a *statement of fact*. Although a descriptive title orients your readers, it is not detailed enough to reveal your essay's purpose or direction. An announcement of your intent can reveal more, but it is stylistically distracting. Finally, a statement of fact — such as a historical fact or a statistic — is a dead end and therefore cannot be developed into an essay. For example, a statement like "Alaska became a state in 1959" or "Tuberculosis is highly contagious" or "The population of Greece is about ten million" provides your essay with no direction. However, a judgment or opinion *can* be an effective thesis — for instance, "The continuing threat of tuberculosis, particularly in the inner cities, suggests it is necessary to frequently test high-risk populations."

Title	Hybrid Cars: Pro and Con
Announcement of intent	I will examine the pros and cons of hybrid cars that use both gasoline and electricity.
Statement of fact	Hybrid cars are more energy efficient than cars with standard gasoline engines.
Thesis statement	Although hybrid cars could decrease our country's dependence on foreign oil, they have disadvantages.
Title	Orwell's "A Hanging"
Announcement of intent	This paper will discuss George Orwell's attitude toward the death penalty in his essay "A Hanging."
Statement of fact	In his essay, Orwell describes a hanging that he witnessed in Burma.
Thesis statement	In "A Hanging," George Orwell shows that capital punishment is not only brutal but also immoral.
Title	Speaking Out
Announcement of intent	This essay will discuss a time when I could have spoken out but did not.

Statement of fact	Once I saw someone cheating and did not speak out.
Thesis statement	As I look back at the cheating I witnessed, I wonder why I kept silent and what would have happened if I had acted.

WHAT A GOOD THESIS DOES

For writers

It helps writers plan an essay.
It helps writers organize ideas in an essay.
It helps writers unify all the ideas in an essay.

For readers

It identifies the main idea of an essay.
It guides readers through an essay.
It clarifies the subject and the focus of an essay.

Deciding on a Thesis

No rules determine when you draft your thesis; the decision depends on the scope of your assignment, your knowledge of the subject, and your method of writing. When you know a lot about a subject, you may come up with a thesis before doing any invention activities (freewriting or brainstorming, for example). At other times, you may have to review your notes and then think of a single statement that communicates your position on the topic. Occasionally, your assignment may specify a thesis by telling you to take a particular position on a topic. In any case, you should decide on a thesis statement before you begin to write your first draft.

As you write, you will continue to discover new ideas, and you will probably move in directions that you did not anticipate. For this reason, the thesis statement you develop at this stage of the writing process is only **tentative**. Still, because a tentative thesis helps you to focus your ideas, it is essential at the initial stages of writing. As you draft your essay, review your thesis statement in light of the points you make, and revise it accordingly.

Stating Your Thesis

It is a good idea to include a one-sentence statement of your thesis early in your essay. An effective thesis statement has three characteristics:

1. **An effective thesis statement clearly expresses your essay's main idea.**   It does more than state your topic; it indicates what you will say about your topic, and it signals how you will approach your material. The following thesis statement, from the essay "Grant and Lee: A Study in Contrasts" by Bruce Catton (page 393), clearly communicates the writer's main idea.

> They [Grant and Lee] were two strong men, these oddly different generals, and they represented the strengths of two conflicting currents that, through them, had come into final collision.

This statement says that the essay will compare and contrast Grant and Lee. Specifically, it indicates that Catton will present the two Civil War generals as symbols of two opposing historical currents. If the statement had been less fully developed — for example, had Catton written, "Grant and Lee were quite different from each other" — it would have just echoed the essay's title.

2. **An effective thesis statement communicates your essay's purpose.** Whether your purpose is to evaluate or analyze or simply to describe or inform, your thesis statement should communicate that purpose to your readers. In general terms, your thesis can be **expressive**, conveying a mood or impression; it can be **informative**, perhaps listing the major points you will discuss or presenting an objective overview of the essay; or it can be **persuasive**, taking a strong stand or outlining the position you will argue.

Each of the following thesis statements communicates a different purpose.

To express feelings	The city's homeless families live in heartbreaking surroundings.
To inform	The plight of the homeless has become so serious that it is a major priority for many city governments.
To persuade	The best way to address the problems of the homeless is to renovate abandoned city buildings to create suitable housing for homeless families.

3. **An effective thesis statement is clearly worded.**   To communicate your essay's main idea, an effective thesis statement should be clearly worded. (It should also speak for itself. It is not necessary to write, "My thesis is that . . . ." or "The thesis of this paper is. . . .") The thesis statement should give a straightforward and accurate indication of what follows, and it should not mislead readers about the essay's direction, emphasis, scope, content, or viewpoint. Vague language, irrelevant details, and unnecessarily complex terminology have no place in a thesis statement. Keep in mind, too, that your thesis statement should not make promises that your essay is not going to keep. For example, if you are going to discuss just the *effects* of new immigration laws, your thesis statement should not emphasize the *causes* that led to their passage.

Your thesis statement should not include every point you will discuss in your essay. Still, it should be specific enough to indicate your direction and scope. The sentence "Immigration laws have not been effective" is not an effective thesis statement because it does not give your essay much focus. The following sentence, however, *is* an effective thesis statement. It clearly indicates what the writer is going to discuss, and it establishes a specific direction for the essay.

> Because they do not take into account the economic causes of immigration, current immigration laws do little to decrease the number of undocumented workers coming into the United States.

Implying a Thesis

Like an explicitly stated thesis, an **implied thesis** conveys an essay's main focus, but it does not do so explicitly. Instead, the selection and arrangement of the essay's ideas suggest the focus. Professional writers sometimes prefer this option because an implied thesis is subtler than a stated thesis. (An implied thesis is especially useful in narratives, descriptions, and some arguments, where an explicit thesis would seem heavy-handed or arbitrary.) In most college writing, however, you should state your thesis to avoid any risk of being misunderstood or of wandering away from your topic.

A STUDENT WRITER: Developing a Thesis

After experimenting with different ways of arranging her ideas for her essay, Laura Bobnak summed them up in a tentative thesis statement.

> As I look back at the cheating I witnessed, I wonder why I kept silent and what would have happened if I had acted.

✓ **CHECKLIST**   **Stating Your Thesis**

☐ Do you state your thesis in one complete, concise sentence?
☐ Does your thesis indicate your purpose?
☐ Is your thesis suited to the assignment?
☐ Does your thesis clearly convey the main idea you intend to support in your essay?
☐ Does your thesis suggest how you will organize your essay?

Exercise 8

Assess the strengths and weaknesses of the following as thesis statements.

1. My instructor has an attendance policy.
2. My instructor should change her attendance policy because it is bad.

3. My instructor should change her attendance policy because it is unreasonable, inflexible, and unfair.
4. For many students, a community college makes more sense than a four-year college or university.
5. Some children exhibit violent behavior.
6. Violence is a problem in our society.
7. Conflict-resolution courses should be taught to help prevent violence in America's schools.
8. Social networking sites such as Facebook can cause problems.
9. Facebook attracts many college students.
10. College students should be careful of what material they put on their Facebook pages because prospective employers routinely check them.

Exercise 9

Rewrite the following factual statements to make them effective thesis statements. Make sure each thesis statement is a clearly and specifically worded sentence.

1. Henry David Thoreau thought that we should get in touch with nature and lead more meaningful lives.
2. Several Supreme Court decisions have said that art containing explicit sexual images is not necessarily pornographic.
3. Many women earn less money than men do, in part because they drop out of the workforce during their child-rearing years.
4. People who watch more than five hours of television a day tend to think the world is more violent than do people who watch less than two hours of television daily.
5. In recent years, the suicide rate among teenagers — especially middle- and upper-middle-class teenagers — has risen dramatically.

Exercise 10

Read the following sentences from "The Argument Culture" by Deborah Tannen. Then, formulate a one-sentence thesis statement that summarizes the key points Tannen makes about the nature of argument in our culture.

- "More and more, our public interactions have become like arguing with a spouse."
- "Nearly everything is framed as a battle or game in which winning or losing is the main concern."
- "The argument culture pervades every aspect of our lives today."
- "Issues from global warming to abortion are depicted as two-sided arguments, when in fact most Americans' views lie somewhere in the middle."
- "What's wrong with the argument culture is the ubiquity, the knee-jerk nature of approaching any issue, problem, or public person in an adversarial way."

- "If you fight to win, the temptation is great to deny facts that support your opponent's views and say only what supports your side."
- "We must expand the notion of 'debate' to include more dialogue."
- "Perhaps it is time to re-examine the assumption that audiences always prefer a fight."
- "Instead of insisting on hearing 'both sides,' let's insist on hearing 'all sides.'"

Exercise 11

Going through as many steps as you need, draft an effective thesis statement for the essay you have been working on.

3

Arrangement

Each of the tasks discussed in Chapter 2 represents choices you have to make about your topic and your material. Now, before you actually begin to write, you have another choice to make — how to arrange your material into an essay.

Recognizing a Pattern

Deciding how to structure an essay is easy when your assignment specifies a particular pattern of development. This may be the case in a composition class, where the instructor may assign a descriptive or a narrative essay. Also, certain assignments or exam questions suggest how your material should be structured. For example, an instructor might ask you to tell about how something works, or an exam question might ask you to trace the circumstances leading up to an event. If you are perceptive, you will realize that your instructor is asking for a process essay and that the exam question is asking for either a narrative or a cause-and-effect response. The most important thing is to recognize the clues that such assignments give (or those that you find in your topic or thesis statement) and to structure your essay accordingly.

One clue to structuring your essay can be found in the questions that proved most helpful when you probed your subject (see pages 34–35). For example, if questions like "What happened?" and "When did it happen?" yielded the most useful information about your topic, you should consider structuring your paper as a narrative. The chart on page 52 links various questions to the patterns of development that they suggest. Notice how the terms in the right-hand column — narration, description, and so on — identify patterns of development that can help order your ideas. Chapters 6 through 13 explain and illustrate each of these patterns.

☑ CHECKLIST   **Recognizing a Pattern**

What happened?
When did it happen?   ⎫
Where did it happen?   ⎬ Narration
Who did it?   ⎭

What does it look like?   ⎫
What are its characteristics?   ⎬ Description
What impressions does it make?   ⎭

What are some typical cases   ⎫
    or examples of it?   ⎬ Exemplification

How did it happen?   ⎫
What makes it work?   ⎬ Process
How is it made?   ⎭

Why did it happen?   ⎫
What caused it?   ⎬
What does it cause?   ⎬ Cause and effect
What are its effects?   ⎭

How is it like other things?   ⎫
How is it different from other   ⎬ Comparison and contrast
    things?   ⎭

What are its parts or types?   ⎫
How can its parts or types be   ⎪
    separated or grouped?   ⎪
Do its parts or types fit into a   ⎪
    logical order?   ⎬ Classification and division
Into what categories can its   ⎪
    parts or types be arranged?   ⎪
On what basis can it be   ⎪
    categorized?   ⎭

How can it be defined?   ⎫
How does it resemble other   ⎪
    members of its class?   ⎬ Definition
How does it differ from other   ⎪
    members of its class?   ⎭

Understanding the Parts of the Essay

No matter what pattern of development you use, your essay should have a beginning, a middle, and an end — that is, an *introduction,* a *body,* and a *conclusion.*

The Introduction

The **introduction** of your essay, usually one paragraph and rarely more than two, introduces your subject, creates interest, and often states your thesis.

You can use a variety of strategies to introduce an essay and create reader interest. Here are several options for beginning an essay (in each of these introductory paragraphs, the thesis statement is underlined).

1. You can begin with *background information*. This approach works particularly well on exams, where there is no need (or time) for subtlety.

> With inflation low, many companies have understandably lowered prices, and the oil industry should be no exception. Consequently, homeowners have begun wondering whether the high price of home heating oil is justified given the economic climate. It makes sense, therefore, for us to start examining the pricing policies of the major American oil companies.   (economics essay)

2. You can introduce an essay with your own original *definition* of a relevant term or concept. This technique is especially useful for research papers or exams, where the meaning of a specific term is crucial.

> Democracy is a form of government in which power is given to and exercised by the people. This may be true in theory, but some recent elections have raised concerns about the future of democracy. Extensive voting-machine irregularities and "ghost voting" have jeopardized people's faith in the democratic process.   (political science exam)

3. You can begin your essay with an *anecdote* or *story* that leads readers to your thesis.

> Three years ago, I went with my grandparents to my first auction. They live in a small town outside of Lancaster, Pennsylvania, where it is common for people to auction off the contents of a home when someone moves or dies. As I walked through the crowd, I smelled the funnel cakes frying in the food trucks, heard the hypnotic chanting of the auctioneer, and sensed the excitement of the crowd. Two hours later, I walked off with an old trunk that I had bought for thirty dollars and a passion for auctions that I still have today.   (composition essay)

4. You can begin with a *question*.

> What was it like to live through the Holocaust? Elie Wiesel, in *One Generation After*, answers this question by presenting a series of accounts about ordinary people who found themselves imprisoned in Nazi death camps. As he does so, he challenges some of the assumptions we have about the Holocaust and those who survived.   (sociology book report)

5. You can begin with a *quotation*. If it arouses interest, it can encourage your audience to read further.

"The rich are different," F. Scott Fitzgerald said more than eighty years ago. Apparently, they still are. As an examination of the tax code shows, the wealthy receive many more benefits than the middle class or the poor do.   (accounting paper)

6. You can begin with a *surprising statement*. An unexpected statement catches readers' attention and makes them want to read more.

Believe it or not, many people who live in the suburbs are not white and rich. My family, for example, fits into neither of these categories. Ten years ago, my family and I came to the United States from Pakistan. My parents were poor then, and by some standards, they are still poor even though they both work two jobs. Still, they eventually saved enough to buy a small house in the suburbs of Chicago. Throughout the country, there are many suburban families like mine who are working hard to make ends meet so that their children can get a good education and go to college.
                                                                                              (composition essay)

7. You can begin with a *contradiction*. You can open your essay with an idea that most people believe is true and then get readers' attention by showing that it is inaccurate or ill advised.

Many people think that after the Declaration of Independence was signed in 1776, the colonists defeated the British army in battle after battle. This commonly held belief is incorrect. The truth is that the colonial army lost most of its battles. The British were defeated not because the colonial army was stronger, but because George Washington refused to be lured into a costly winner-take-all battle and because the British government lost interest in pursuing an expensive war three thousand miles from home.   (history take-home exam)

8. You can begin with a *fact* or *statistic*.

In 2013, the National Council on Teacher Quality released a report that said that of the 1,400 teacher-preparation programs in the United States, 1,100 are inadequate. According to this report, undergraduate teacher-preparation programs are not rigorous enough and do not include sufficient classroom-teaching experience. In addition, future educators are rarely required to major in the specific subject areas they are going to teach. Although many educators agree with this negative assessment, they do not agree on what should be done to remedy the situation. Instead of trying to modify existing programs, educators should look at new, more cost-effective ways of improving teacher training.   (education essay)

No matter which strategy you select, your introduction should be consistent in tone with the rest of your essay. If it is not, it can misrepresent your intentions and even damage your credibility. (For this reason, it is a good idea not to write your introduction until after you have finished your rough draft.) A technical report, for instance, should have an introduction that reflects the formality and objectivity the occasion requires. The introduction to an autobiographical essay, however, should have a more informal, subjective tone.

☑ CHECKLIST   **What Not to Do in an Introduction**

☐ **Don't apologize.** Never use phrases such as "in my opinion" or "I may not be an expert, but. . . ." By doing so, you suggest that you don't really know your subject.

☐ **Don't begin with a dictionary definition.** Avoid beginning an essay with phrases like "According to Webster's Dictionary. . . ." This type of introduction is overused and trite. If you want to use a definition, develop your own.

☐ **Don't announce what you intend to do.** Don't begin with phrases such as "In this paper I will . . ." or "The purpose of this essay is to. . . ." Use your introduction to create interest in your topic, and let readers discover your intention when they get to your thesis statement.

☐ **Don't wander.** Your introduction should draw readers into your essay as soon as possible. Avoid irrelevant comments or annoying digressions that will distract readers and make them want to stop reading.

Exercise 1

Look through magazine articles or the essays in this book, and find one example of each kind of introduction. Why do you think each introductory strategy was chosen? What other strategies might have worked?

The Body Paragraphs

The middle section, or **body**, of your essay develops your thesis. The body paragraphs present the support that convinces your audience your thesis is reasonable. To do so, each body paragraph should be *unified, coherent,* and *well developed.* It should also follow a particular pattern of development and should clearly support your thesis.

• *Each body paragraph should be unified.* A paragraph is **unified** when each sentence relates directly to the main idea of the paragraph. Frequently, the main idea of a paragraph is stated in a **topic sentence**. Like a thesis statement, a topic sentence acts as a guidepost, making it easy for readers to follow the paragraph's discussion. Although the placement of a topic sentence depends on a writer's purpose and subject, beginning writers often make it the first sentence of a paragraph.

Sometimes the main idea of a paragraph is not stated but **implied** by the sentences in the paragraph. Professional writers often use this technique because they believe that in some situations — especially narratives and descriptions — a topic sentence can seem forced or awkward. As a beginning writer, however, you will find it helpful to use topic sentences to keep your paragraphs focused.

Whether or not you include a topic sentence, remember that each sentence in a paragraph should develop the paragraph's main idea. If the sentences in a paragraph do not support the main idea, the paragraph will lack unity.

In the following excerpt from a student essay, notice how the topic sentence (underlined) unifies the paragraph by summarizing its main idea:

> <u>Another problem with fast food is that it contains additives.</u> Fast-food companies know that to keep their customers happy, they have to give them food that tastes good, and this is where the trouble starts. For example, to give fries flavor, McDonald's used to fry their potatoes in beef fat. Shockingly, their fries actually had more saturated fat than their hamburgers did. When the public found out how unhealthy their fries were, the company switched to vegetable oil. What most people don't know, however, is that McDonald's adds a chemical derived from animals to the vegetable oil to give it the taste of beef tallow.

The topic sentence, placed at the beginning of the paragraph, enables readers to grasp the writer's point immediately. The examples that follow all relate to that point, making the paragraph unified.

• *Each body paragraph should be coherent.*   A paragraph is **coherent** if its sentences are smoothly and logically connected to one another. Coherence can be strengthened in three ways. First, you can repeat **key words** to carry concepts from one sentence to another and to echo important terms. Second, you can use **pronouns** to refer to key nouns in previous sentences. Finally, you can use **transitions**, words or expressions that show chronological sequence, cause and effect, and so on (see the list of transitions on page 57). These three strategies for connecting sentences — which you can also use to connect paragraphs within an essay — indicate for your readers the exact relationships among your ideas.

The following paragraph, from George Orwell's "Shooting an Elephant" (page 133), uses repeated key words, pronouns, and transitions to achieve coherence.

> I got up. The Burmans were already racing past me across the mud. It was obvious that the elephant would never rise again, but he was not dead. He was breathing very rhythmically with long rattling gasps, his great mound of a side painfully rising and falling. His mouth was wide open — I could see far down into caverns of pale pink throat. I waited a long time for him to die, but his breathing did not weaken. Finally I fired my two remaining shots into the spot where I thought his heart must be. The thick blood welled out of him like red velvet, but still he did not die. His body did not even jerk when the shots hit him, the tortured breathing continued without a pause. He was dying, very slowly and in great agony, but in some world remote from me where not even a bullet could damage him further. I felt that I had got to put an end to that dreadful noise. It seemed dreadful to see the great beast lying there, powerless to move and yet powerless to die, and not even to be able to finish him. I sent back for my small rifle and poured shot after shot into his heart and down his throat. They seemed to make no impression. The tortured gasps continued as steadily as the ticking of a clock.

TRANSITIONS

SEQUENCE OR ADDITION

again	first, . . . second, . . . third	next
also	furthermore	one . . . another
and	in addition	still
besides	last	too
finally	moreover	

TIME

afterward	finally	simultaneously
as soon as	immediately	since
at first	in the meantime	soon
at the same time	later	subsequently
before	meanwhile	then
earlier	next	until
eventually	now	

COMPARISON

also	likewise
in comparison	similarly
in the same way	

CONTRAST

although	in contrast	on the one hand . . .
but	instead	on the other hand . . .
conversely	nevertheless	still
despite	nonetheless	whereas
even though	on the contrary	yet
however		

EXAMPLES

for example	specifically
for instance	that is
in fact	thus
namely	

CONCLUSIONS OR SUMMARIES

as a result	in summary
in conclusion	therefore
in short	thus

CAUSES OR EFFECTS

as a result	so
because	then
consequently	therefore
since	

Orwell keeps his narrative coherent by using transitional expressions (*already, finally, when the shots hit him*) to signal the passing of time. He uses pronouns (*he, his*) in nearly every sentence to refer back to the elephant, the topic of his paragraph. Finally, he repeats key words like *shots* and *die* (and its variants *dead* and *dying*) to link the whole paragraph's sentences together.

• *Each body paragraph should be well developed.* A paragraph is **well developed** if it contains the **support** — examples, reasons, facts, and so on — that readers need to understand its main idea. If a paragraph is not adequately developed, readers will feel they have been given only a partial picture of the subject.

If you decide you need more information in a paragraph, you can look back at your brainstorming notes. If this doesn't help, you can freewrite or brainstorm again, talk with friends and instructors, read more about your topic, or (with your instructor's permission) do some research. Your assignment and your topic will determine the kind and amount of information you need.

TYPES OF SUPPORT

- **Examples** Specific illustrations of a general idea or concept
- **Reasons** Underlying causes or explanations
- **Facts** Pieces of information that can be verified or proved
- **Statistics** Numerical data (for example, results of studies by reputable authorities or organizations)
- **Details** Parts or portions of a whole (for example, steps in a process)
- **Expert opinions** Statements by recognized authorities in a particular field
- **Personal experiences** Events that you lived through
- **Visuals** Diagrams, charts, graphs, or photographs

✓ CHECKLIST   Effective Support

☐ **Support should be relevant.** Body paragraphs should clearly relate to your essay's thesis. Irrelevant material — material that does not pertain to the thesis — should be deleted.

☐ **Support should be specific.** Body paragraphs should contain support that is specific, not general or vague. Specific examples, clear reasons, and precise explanations engage readers and communicate your ideas to them.

☐ **Support should be adequate.** Body paragraphs should contain enough facts, reasons, and examples to support your thesis. How much support you need depends on your audience, your purpose, and the scope of your thesis.

☐ **Support should be representative.** Body paragraphs should present support that is typical, not atypical. For example, suppose you write a paper claiming that flu shots do not work. Your support for this claim is that your grandmother got the flu even though she was vaccinated. This example is not representative because studies show that most people who get vaccinated do not get the flu.

☐ **Support should be documented.** Support that comes from research (print sources and the Internet, for example) should be documented. (For more information on proper documentation, see the Appendix.) **Plagiarism** — failure to document the ideas and words of others — is not only unfair but also dishonest. Always use proper documentation to acknowledge your debt to your sources — and keep in mind that words and ideas you borrow from the essays in this book must also be documented. (For more information on avoiding plagiarism, see Chapter 17.)

The following student paragraph uses two examples to support its topic sentence.

Example 1

Just look at how males have been taught that extravagance is a positive characteristic. Scrooge, the main character of Dickens's *A Christmas Carol*, is portrayed as an evil man until he gives up his miserly ways and freely distributes gifts and money on Christmas day. This behavior, of course, is rewarded when people change their opinions about him and decide that he isn't such a bad person after all.

Example 2

Diamond Jim Brady is another interesting example. This individual was a nineteenth-century financier who was known for his extravagant taste in women and food. On any given night, he would eat enough food to feed at least ten of the numerous poor who roamed the streets of New York at that time. Yet, despite his selfishness and infantile self-gratification, Diamond Jim Brady's name has become associated with the good life.

• *Each body paragraph should follow a particular pattern of development.* In addition to making sure your body paragraphs are unified, coherent, and well developed, you need to organize each paragraph according to a specific pattern of development. (Chapters 6 through 13 each begin with a paragraph-length example of the pattern discussed in the chapter.)

• *Each body paragraph should clearly support the thesis statement.* No matter how many body paragraphs your essay has — three, four, five, or even more — each paragraph should introduce and develop an idea that supports the essay's thesis. Each paragraph's topic sentence should express one of these supporting points. The diagram on page 60 illustrates this thesis-and-support structure.

Introductory paragraph

Thesis statement: Despite the emphasis by journalists on objective reporting, there are <u>three reasons</u> why television news is anything but objective.

Body paragraph

Topic sentence: Television news is not objective because the people who gather and report the news are biased.

Body paragraph

Topic sentence: In addition, television news is not objective because networks face pressure from sponsors.

Body paragraph

Topic sentence: Finally, television news is not objective because networks focus on ratings rather than content.

Concluding paragraph

Restatement of thesis: Even though television journalists claim to strive for objectivity, the truth is that this ideal has been impossible to achieve.

Exercise 2

Choose a body paragraph from one of the essays in this book. Using the criteria discussed on pages 55–60, decide whether the paragraph is unified, coherent, and well developed.

Exercise 3

Choose one essay in this book, and underline its thesis statement. Then, determine how its body paragraphs support that thesis statement. (Note that in a long essay, several body paragraphs may develop a single supporting point, and some paragraphs may serve as transitions from one point to another.)

The Conclusion

Since readers remember best what they read last, your **conclusion** is very important. Always end your essay in a way that reinforces your thesis and your purpose.

Like your introduction, your conclusion is rarely longer than a paragraph. Regardless of its length, however, your conclusion should be consistent with the rest of your essay—that is, it should not introduce points you have not discussed earlier. Frequently, a conclusion will restate your essay's main idea or review your key points.

Here are several strategies you can use to conclude an essay:

1. You can conclude your essay by *reviewing your key points* or by *restating your thesis in different words*.

> Rotation of crops provided several benefits. It enriched soil by giving it a rest; it enabled farmers to vary their production; and it ended the cycle of "boom or bust" that had characterized the prewar South's economy when cotton was the primary crop. Of course, this innovation did not solve all the economic problems of the postwar South, but it did lay the groundwork for the healthy economy this region enjoys today.
>
> (history exam)

2. You can end a discussion of a problem with a *recommendation of a course of action*.

> Well-qualified teachers are becoming harder and harder to find. For this reason, school boards should reassess their ideas about what qualifies someone to teach. At the present time, people who have spent their lives working in a particular field are denied certification because they have not taken education courses. This policy deprives school systems of talented teachers. In order to ensure that students have the best possible teachers, school boards should consider applicants' real-world experience when evaluating their qualifications.   (education essay)

3. You can conclude with a *prediction*. Be sure, however, that your prediction follows logically from the points you have made in the essay. Your conclusion is no place to make new points or to change direction.

> Campaign advertisements should help people understand a political candidate's qualifications and where he or she stands on critical issues. They should not appeal to people's fears or greed. Above all, they should not personally attack other candidates or oversimplify complex issues. If campaign advertisements continue to do these things, the American people will disregard them and reject the candidates they promote.
>
> (political science essay)

4. You can end with a relevant *quotation*.

> In *Walden*, Henry David Thoreau says, "The mass of men lead lives of quiet desperation." This sentiment is reinforced by a drive through the Hill District of our city. Perhaps the work of the men and women who run the clinic on Jefferson Street cannot totally change this situation, but it can give us hope to know that some people, at least, are working for the betterment of us all.   (public health essay)

✔CHECKLIST   **What Not to Do in a Conclusion**

☐ **Don't end by repeating the exact words of your thesis and listing your main points.** Avoid boring endings that tell readers what they already know.

☐ **Don't end with an empty phrase.** Avoid ending with a cliché like "This just goes to prove that you can never be too careful."

☐ **Don't introduce new points or go off in new directions.** Your conclusion should not introduce new points for discussion. It should reinforce the points you have already made in your essay.

☐ **Don't end with an unnecessary announcement.** Don't end by saying that you are ending — for example, "In conclusion, let me say...." The tone of your conclusion should signal that the essay is drawing to a close.

Exercise 4

Look through magazine articles or the essays in this book, and find one example of each kind of conclusion. Why do you think each concluding strategy was chosen? What other strategies might have worked?

Constructing a Formal Outline

Before you begin to write, you may decide to construct a **formal outline** to guide you. Whereas informal outlines are preliminary lists that remind you which points to discuss, formal outlines are detailed, multilevel constructions that indicate the exact order in which you will present your key points and supporting details. The complexity of your assignment determines which type of outline you need. For a short paper, an informal outline like the one on page 43 is usually sufficient. For a longer, more complex essay, however, you will need a formal outline.

One way to construct a formal outline is to copy down the main headings from your informal outline. Then, arrange ideas from your brainstorming notes or cluster diagram as subheadings under the appropriate headings. As you work on your outline, make sure each idea you include supports your thesis. Ideas that don't fit should be reworded or discarded. As you revise your essay, continue to refer to your outline to make sure your thesis and support are logically related. The guidelines that follow will help you prepare a formal outline.

✔CHECKLIST   **Constructing a Formal Outline**

☐ Write your thesis statement at the top of the page.

☐ Group main headings under roman numerals (*I, II, III, IV,* and so on), and place them flush with the left-hand margin.

☐ Indent each subheading under the first word of the heading above it. Use capital letters before major points and numbers before supporting details.

☐ Capitalize the first letter of the first word of each heading.

☐ Make your outline as simple as possible, avoiding overly complex divisions of ideas. (Try not to go beyond third-level headings — *1, 2, 3,* and so on.)

☐ Construct either a **topic outline**, with headings expressed as short phrases or single words ("Advantages and disadvantages") or a **sentence outline**, with headings expressed as complete sentences ("The advantages of advanced placement chemistry outweigh the disadvantages"). *Never use both phrases and complete sentences in the same outline.*

☐ Express all headings at the same level in parallel terms. (If roman numeral *I* is a noun, *II, III,* and *IV* should also be nouns.)

☐ Make sure each heading contains at least two subdivisions. You cannot have a *1* without a *2* or an *A* without a *B.*

☐ Make sure your headings do not overlap.

A STUDENT WRITER: Constructing a Formal Outline

The topic outline Laura Bobnak constructed follows the guidelines discussed above. Notice that her outline focuses on the body of her paper and does not include the introduction or conclusion: these are usually developed after the body has been drafted. (Compare this formal outline with the informal outline on page 43 where Laura simply grouped her brainstorming notes under three general headings.)

Thesis statement: As I look back at the cheating I witnessed, I wonder why I kept silent and what would have happened if I had acted.

I. The incident
   A. Test situation
   B. My observation
   C. My reactions
      1. Anger
      2. Silence
II. Reasons for keeping silent
   A. Other students' attitudes
   B. My fears
III. Current attitude toward cheating
   A. Effects of cheating on education
   B. Effects of cheating on students

This outline enabled Laura to arrange her points so that they supported her thesis. As she went on to draft her essay, the outline reminded her to emphasize the contrast between her present and former attitudes toward cheating.

 TECH TIP: **Constructing a Formal Outline**

You can use your word-processing program to arrange and rearrange your headings until your outline is logical and complete. (Your word-processing program will have an outline function that automatically indents and numbers items.) If you saved your pre-writing notes in computer files, you can refer to them while working on your outline and perhaps add or modify headings to reflect what you find.

Exercise 5

Read the thesis statement you developed in Chapter 2, Exercise 11 (on page 49), as well as all the notes you made for the essay you are planning. Then, make a topic outline that lists the points you will discuss in your essay. When you are finished, check to make sure your outline conforms to the guidelines on the checklist on pages 62–63.

Drafting and Revising

After you decide on a thesis and an arrangement for your ideas, you can begin to draft and revise your essay. Keep in mind that even as you carry out these activities, you may have to generate more material or revise your thesis statement.

Writing Your First Draft

The purpose of your **first draft** is to get your ideas down on paper so that you can react to them. Experienced writers know that the first draft is nothing more than a work in progress; it exists to be revised. With this in mind, you should expect to cross out and extensively rearrange material. In addition, don't be surprised if you think of new ideas as you write. If a new idea comes to you, go with it. Some of the best writing comes from unexpected turns or accidents. The following guidelines will help you prepare your first draft.

> ✔ CHECKLIST   **Drafting**
> - ☐ **Begin with the body paragraphs.** Because your essay will probably be revised extensively, don't take the time at this stage to write an introduction or conclusion. Let your thesis statement guide you as you draft the body paragraphs of your essay. Later, when you have finished, you can write an appropriate introduction and conclusion.
> - ☐ **Get your ideas down quickly.** Don't worry about grammar or word choice, and try not to interrupt the flow of your writing with concerns about style.
> - ☐ **Take regular breaks as you write.** Don't write until you are so exhausted you can't think straight. Many writers divide their writing into stages,

(continued)

65

perhaps completing one or two body paragraphs and then taking a short break. This strategy is more efficient than trying to write a complete first draft without stopping.
☐ **Leave yourself time to revise.** Remember, your first draft is a *rough draft*. All writing benefits from revision, so allow enough time to write two or more drafts.

A STUDENT WRITER: Writing a First Draft

Here is the first draft of Laura Bobnak's essay on the following topic: "Write about a time when you, like Henry Louis Gates Jr.'s father, could have spoken out but chose not to. Would you make the same decision today?"

When I was in high school, I had an experience like the one Henry Louis Gates Jr. talks about in his essay. It was then that I saw a close friend cheat in chemistry class. As I look back at the cheating I witnessed, I wonder why I kept silent and what would have happened if I had acted.

1

The incident I am going to describe took place during the final exam for my advanced placement chemistry class. I had studied hard for it, but even so, I found the test difficult. As I struggled to balance a particularly difficult equation, I noticed that my friend Jeff, who was sitting across from me, was acting strangely. I noticed that he was copying material from a paper. After watching him for a while, I dismissed the incident and got back to my test.

2

After the test was over, I began to think about what I had seen. The more I thought about it the angrier I got. It seemed unfair that I had studied for weeks to memorize formulas and equations while all Jeff had done was to copy them onto a cheat sheet. For a moment I considered going to the teacher, but I quickly rejected this idea. After all, cheating was something everybody did. Besides, I was afraid if I told on Jeff, my friends would stop talking to me.

3

Now that I am in college I see the situation differently. I find it hard to believe that I could ever have been so calm about cheating. Cheating is certainly something that students should not take for granted. It undercuts the education process and is unfair to teachers and to the majority of students who spend their time studying.

4

If I could go back to high school and relive the experience, I now know that I would have gone to the teacher. Naturally Jeff would have been angry at me, but at least I would have known I had the courage to do the right thing.

5

Exercise 1

Write a draft of the essay you have been working on in Chapters 2 and 3. Be sure to look back at all your notes as well as your outline.

Revising Your Essay

Revision is not something you do after your paper is finished. It is a continuing process during which you consider the logic and clarity of your ideas as well as how effectively they are presented.

Revision is not simply a matter of proofreading or editing, of crossing out one word and substituting another or correcting errors in spelling and punctuation; revision involves reseeing and rethinking what you have written. When you revise, you may find yourself adding and deleting extensively, reordering whole sentences or paragraphs as you reconsider what you want to communicate to your audience.

Revision can take a lot of time, so don't be discouraged if you have to go through three or four drafts before you think your essay is ready to submit. The following advice can help you when you revise your essay.

- *Give yourself a cooling-off period.*   Put your first draft aside for several hours or even a day or two if you can. This cooling-off period lets you distance yourself from your essay so that you can read it more objectively when you return to it. When you read it again, you will see things you missed the first time.
- *Revise on hard copy.*   Because a printed-out draft shows you all the pages of your paper and enables you to see your handwritten edits, revise on hard copy instead of directly on the computer screen.
- *Read your draft aloud.*   Before you revise, read your draft aloud to help you spot choppy sentences, missing words, or phrases that do not sound right.
- *Take advantage of opportunities to get feedback.*   Your instructor may organize peer-editing groups, distribute a revision checklist, refer students to a writing center, or schedule one-on-one conferences. Make use of as many of these opportunities for feedback as you can; each offers you a different way of gaining information about what you have written.
- *Try not to get overwhelmed.*   It is easy to become overwhelmed by all the feedback you get about your draft. To avoid this, approach revision systematically. Don't automatically make all the changes people suggest; consider the validity of each change. Also ask yourself whether comments suggest larger issues. For example, does a comment about a series of choppy sentences suggest a need for you to add transitions, or does it mean you need to rethink your ideas?
- *Don't let your ego get in the way.*   Everyone likes praise, and receiving negative criticism is never pleasant. Experienced writers know, however, that they must get honest feedback if they are going to improve their work. Learn to see criticism — whether from an instructor or from your peers — as a necessary part of the revision process.
- *Revise in stages.*   Deal with the large elements (essay and paragraph structure) before moving on to the smaller elements (sentence structure and word choice).

How you revise — what specific strategies you decide to use — depends on your own preference, your instructor's instructions, and the time available. Like the rest of the writing process, revision varies from student to student and from assignment to assignment. Four of the most useful revision strategies are *revising with a checklist, revising with an outline, revising with a peer critique,* and *revising with your instructor's comments.*

Revising with a Checklist

If you have time, you can use the following revision checklist, adapting it to your own writing process.

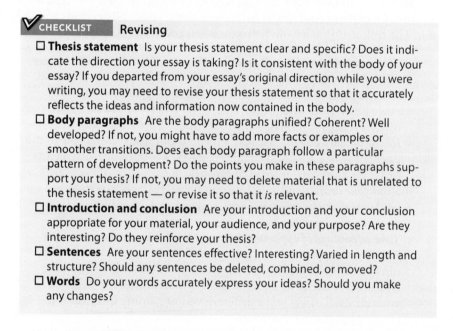

CHECKLIST   Revising

☐ **Thesis statement** Is your thesis statement clear and specific? Does it indicate the direction your essay is taking? Is it consistent with the body of your essay? If you departed from your essay's original direction while you were writing, you may need to revise your thesis statement so that it accurately reflects the ideas and information now contained in the body.

☐ **Body paragraphs** Are the body paragraphs unified? Coherent? Well developed? If not, you might have to add more facts or examples or smoother transitions. Does each body paragraph follow a particular pattern of development? Do the points you make in these paragraphs support your thesis? If not, you may need to delete material that is unrelated to the thesis statement — or revise it so that it *is* relevant.

☐ **Introduction and conclusion** Are your introduction and your conclusion appropriate for your material, your audience, and your purpose? Are they interesting? Do they reinforce your thesis?

☐ **Sentences** Are your sentences effective? Interesting? Varied in length and structure? Should any sentences be deleted, combined, or moved?

☐ **Words** Do your words accurately express your ideas? Should you make any changes?

Revising with an Outline

If you do not have time to consult a detailed checklist, you can check your essay's structure by making a **review outline**. Either an informal outline or a formal one can show you whether you have left out any important points. An outline can also show you whether your essay follows a particular pattern of development. Finally, an outline can clarify the relationship between your thesis statement and your body paragraphs. (See pages 62–64 for guidelines for constructing an outline.)

Revising in a Peer-Editing Group

Another revision strategy involves getting feedback from other students. Sometimes this process is formal: an instructor may require students to exchange papers and evaluate their classmates' work according to certain standards, perhaps by completing a **peer-editing worksheet**. (See pages 71–72 for an example.) Often, however, soliciting feedback from others is an informal process. Even if a friend is unfamiliar with your topic, he or she can still tell you whether you are getting your point across — and maybe even advise you about how to communicate more effectively. (Remember, though, that your critic should be only your reader, not your ghostwriter.)

Getting feedback from others mirrors how people in the real world actually write. For example, businesspeople circulate reports to get feedback from coworkers; academics routinely collaborate when they write. (And, as you may have realized, even this book is the result of a collaboration.)

Your classmates can be helpful as you write the early drafts of your essay, providing suggestions that can guide you through the revision process. In addition, they can respond to questions you may have about your essay — for example, whether your introduction works or whether one of your supporting points needs more explanation. When friends ask *you* to critique their work, the guidelines below should help you.

 TECH TIP: Revising

When you revise, make sure you do not delete text you may need later. Move this information to the end of the draft or to a separate file. That way, if you change your mind about a deletion or if you find you need information you took out of a draft, you can recover it easily.

✔ CHECKLIST   **Guidelines for Peer Critiques**

☐ **Be positive.** Remember that your purpose is to help other students improve their essays.

☐ **Be tactful.** Be sure to emphasize the good points about the essay. Mention one or two things the writer has done particularly well before you offer your suggestions.

☐ **Be specific.** Offer concrete suggestions about what the writer could do better. Vague words like *good* or *bad* provide little help.

☐ **Be involved.** If you are doing a critique orally, make sure you interact with the writer. Ask questions, listen to responses, and explain your comments.

☐ **Look at the big picture.** Don't focus exclusively on issues such as spelling and punctuation. At this stage, the clarity of the thesis statement, the effectiveness of the support, and the organization of the writer's ideas are much more important.

☐ **Be thorough.** When possible, write down and explain your comments, either on a form your instructor provides or in the margins of the draft you are reviewing.

Revising with Your Instructor's Comments

Your instructor's **written comments** on a draft of your essay can also help you revise by suggesting changes in content, arrangement, or style. For example, these comments may question your logic, suggest a clearer thesis statement, ask for more explicit transitions, recommend that a paragraph be relocated, or even propose a new direction for your essay. They may also recommend stylistic changes or ask you to provide more support in one or more of your body paragraphs. You may decide to incorporate these suggestions into the next draft of your essay, or you may decide not to. Whatever the case, you should take your instructor's comments seriously and make reading and responding to them a part of your revision process.

Here is a paragraph from the first draft of Laura Bobnak's essay, which she submitted by email. Her instructor used Microsoft Word's *Comment* tool to insert comments onto her draft.

> Your tentative thesis statement is good — as far as it goes. It doesn't address the second half of the assignment — namely, would you make the same decision today?

When I was in high school, I had an experience like the one Henry Louis Gates Jr. talks about in his essay. It was then that I saw a close friend cheat in chemistry class. As I look back at the cheating I witnessed, I wonder why I kept silent and what would have happened if I had acted.

 TECH TIP: Revising

It is usually not a good idea to revise directly on the computer screen. Since many screens show only a portion of a page, the connections between ideas are hard to see and to keep track of. Even with the split-screen option, you cannot view several pages of a draft at once or easily compare one draft to another. For these reasons, it is a good idea to revise on a hard copy of your essay. Once you have made your handwritten corrections, you can type them into your paper.

Your instructor's **oral comments** at a one-on-one conference can also help you revise. If your instructor encourages (or requires) you to schedule a conference, come to the conference prepared. Read all your drafts carefully and bring a copy of your most recent draft as well as a list of any questions you have. During the conference, ask your instructor to clarify marginal comments or to help you revise a particular section of your essay that is giving you trouble. Make sure you take notes during the conference so that you will have a record of what you and your instructor discussed. Remember that the more prepared for the conference you are, the more you will get out of it. (Some instructors use email, video links, or a chat room to answer questions and to give students feedback.)

A STUDENT WRITER: Revising a First Draft

When she revised the first draft of her essay (page 66), Laura Bobnak followed the revision process discussed above. After writing her rough draft, she put it aside for a few hours and then reread it. Later, her instructor divided the class into pairs and had them read each other's essays and fill out **peer-editing worksheets**. After reading and discussing the following worksheet (filled out by one of her classmates), Laura focused on a number of areas that she thought needed revision.

PEER-EDITING WORKSHEET

1. What is the essay's thesis? Is it clearly worded? Does it provide a focus for the essay?

    "As I look back at the cheating I witnessed, I wonder why I kept silent and what would have happened if I had acted." The thesis is clear and gives a good idea of what the essay is about.

2. Do the body paragraphs clearly support the essay's thesis? Should any of the topic sentences be revised? Which, if any, could be more clearly worded?

    The topic sentences seem fine — each one seems to tell what the paragraph is about.

3. How do the body paragraphs develop the essay's main idea? Where could the writer have used more detail?

    Each of the body paragraphs tells a part of the narrative. You could add more detail about how the exam room was set up — I really can't picture the scene.

4. Can you follow the writer's ideas? Does the essay need transitions?

    I have no problem following your ideas. Maybe you could have added some more transitions, but I think the essay moves OK.

5. Which points are especially clear? What questions do you have that are not answered in the essay?

    I think you clearly explained what you didn't like about Jeff's cheating. I'm not sure what AP chemistry is like, though. Do people cheat because it's so hard?

6. If this were your essay, what would you change before you handed it in?

    I'd add more detail and explain more about AP chemistry. Also, what were the other students doing while the cheating was going on?

(continued)

7. Overall, do you think the paper is effective? Explain.

> Good paper; cheating is a big issue, and I think your essay really gets this across.

A peer-editing worksheet for each pattern of development appears at the end of the introductions for Chapters 6 through 15.

Points for Special Attention: First Draft

The Introduction

When she wrote her first draft, Laura knew she would have to expand her introduction. At this stage, though, she was more concerned with her thesis statement — which, as her instructor's comments pointed out, didn't address the second half of the assignment: to explain whether she would act differently today.

Keeping in mind the feedback she received, Laura rewrote her introduction. First, she created a context for her discussion by specifically linking her story to Gates's essay. Next, she decided to postpone mentioning her subject — cheating — until later in the paper, hoping this strategy would stimulate the curiosity of her readers and make them want to read further. Finally, she revised her thesis statement to reflect the specific wording of the assignment.

The Body Paragraphs

The students in her peer-editing group said Laura needed to expand her body paragraphs. Although she had expected most of her readers to be familiar with courses like advanced placement chemistry, she discovered this was not the case. In addition, some students in her group thought she should expand the paragraph in which she described her reaction to the cheating. They wondered what the other students had thought about the incident. Did they know? Did they care? Laura's classmates were curious, and they thought other readers would be, too.

Before revising the body paragraphs, Laura did some brainstorming for additional ideas. She decided to describe the difficulty of advanced placement chemistry and the pressure the students in the class had felt. She also decided to summarize discussions she had had with several of her classmates after the test. In addition, she wanted to explain in more detail her present views on cheating; she felt that the paragraph presenting these ideas did not contrast enough with the paragraphs dealing with her high school experiences.

To make sure her sentences led smoothly into one another, Laura added transitions and rewrote entire sentences when necessary, signaling the progression of her thoughts by adding words and phrases such as *therefore, for this reason, for example,* and *as a result.* In addition, she repeated key words so that important concepts would be reinforced.

The Conclusion

Laura's biggest concern as she revised was to make sure her readers would see the connection between her essay and the assignment. To make this connection clear, she decided to mention in her conclusion a specific effect the incident had on her: its impact on her friendship with Jeff. She also decided to link her reactions to those of Henry Louis Gates Jr. Like him, she had been upset by the actions of someone she knew. By employing this strategy, she was able to bring her essay full circle and develop an idea she had alluded to in her introduction. Thus, rewriting her conclusion helped Laura to reinforce her thesis statement and provide closure to her essay.

A STUDENT WRITER: Revising a Second Draft

The following draft incorporates Laura's revisions, as well as some preliminary editing of grammar and punctuation.

Speaking Out

In his essay "'What's in a Name?'" Henry Louis Gates Jr. recalls an incident   1
from his past in which his father did not speak up. Perhaps he kept silent
because he was afraid or because he knew that nothing he said or did would
change the situation in Piedmont, West Virginia. Although I have never
encountered the kind of prejudice Gates describes, I did have an experience in
high school where, like Gates's father, I could have spoken up but did not. As I
now look back at the cheating I witnessed, I know I would not make the same
decision today.

The incident I am going to describe took place during the final   2
examination in my advanced placement chemistry class. The course was very
demanding and required hours of studying every night. Every day after school,
I would meet with other students to outline chapters and answer homework
questions. Sometimes we would even work on weekends. We would often ask
ourselves whether we had gotten in over our heads. As the semester dragged on,
it became clear to me, as well as to the other students in the class, that passing
the course was not something we could take for granted. Test after test came
back with grades that were well below the "As" and "Bs" I was used to getting in
the regular chemistry course I took in tenth grade. By the time we were ready to

take the final exam, most of us were worried that we would fail the course —
despite the teacher's assurances that she would mark on a curve.

The final examination for advanced placement chemistry was given on   3
a Friday morning from nine to twelve o'clock. As I struggled to balance a
particularly complex equation, I noticed that the person sitting across from me
was acting strangely. I thought I was imagining things, but as I stared I saw Jeff,
my friend and study partner, fumbling with his test booklet. I realized that he
was copying material from a paper he had taped inside the cuff of his shirt. After
watching him for a while, I dismissed the incident and finished my test.

Surprisingly, when I mentioned the incident to others in the class, they all   4
knew what Jeff had done. The more I thought about Jeff's actions, the angrier
I got. It seemed unfair that I had studied for weeks to memorize formulas and
equations while all Jeff had done was to copy them onto a cheat sheet. For a
moment I considered going to the teacher, but I quickly rejected this idea.
Cheating was nothing new to me or to others in my school. Many of my
classmates cheated at one time or another. Most of us saw school as a war
between us and the teachers, and cheating was just another weapon in our
arsenal. The worst crime I could commit would be to turn Jeff in. As far as I
was concerned, I had no choice. I fell in line with the values of my high school
classmates and dismissed the incident as "no big deal."

I find it hard to believe that I could ever have been so complacent about   5
cheating. The issues that were simple in high school now seem complex. I now
ask questions that never would have occurred to me in high school. Interestingly,
Jeff and I are no longer very close. Whenever I see him, I have the same reaction
Henry Louis Gates Jr. had when he met Mr. Wilson after he had insulted his
father.

Points for Special Attention: Second Draft

Laura could see that her second draft was stronger than her first, but
she decided to schedule a conference with her instructor to help her improve
her draft further.

The Introduction

Although Laura was satisfied with her introduction, her instructor
identified a problem. Laura had assumed that everyone reading her essay
would be familiar with Gates's essay. However, her instructor pointed out
that this might not be the case. So he suggested that she add a brief explanation of the problems Gates's father had faced, in order to accommodate
readers who didn't know about or remember Gates's comments.

The Body Paragraphs

After rereading her first body paragraph, Laura thought she could sharpen its focus. Her instructor agreed, suggesting she delete the first sentence of the paragraph, which seemed too conversational. She also decided she could delete the sentences that explained how difficult advanced placement chemistry was — even though she had added this material at the suggestion of a classmate. After all, cheating, not advanced placement chemistry, was the subject of her paper. She realized that if she included this kind of detail, she might distract readers from the real subject of her discussion.

Her instructor also pointed out that in the second body paragraph, the first and second sentences did not seem to be connected, so Laura decided to connect these ideas by adding a short discussion of her own reaction to the test. Her instructor also suggested that Laura add more transitional words and phrases to this paragraph to clarify the sequence of events she was describing. Phrases such as *at first* and *about a minute passed* would help readers follow her discussion.

Laura thought the third body paragraph was her best, but, even so, she thought she needed to add more material. She and her instructor decided she should expand her discussion of the students' reactions to cheating. More information — perhaps some dialogue — would help Laura make the point that cheating was condoned by the students in her class.

The Conclusion

Laura's conclusion began by mentioning her present attitude toward cheating and then suddenly shifted to the effect cheating had on her relationship with Jeff. Her instructor suggested that she take her discussion about her current view of cheating out of her conclusion and put it in a separate paragraph. By doing this, she could focus her conclusion on the effect cheating had on both Jeff and her. This strategy enabled Laura to present her views about cheating in more detail and also helped her end her essay forcefully.

Working with Sources

Her instructor also suggested that Laura consider adding a quotation from Gates's essay to her conclusion to connect his experience to Laura's. He reminded her not to forget to document the quotation and to use correct MLA documentation format (as explained and illustrated in Chapter 18 of this text).

The Title

Laura's original title was only a working title, and now she wanted one that would create interest and draw readers into her essay. She knew, however, that a humorous, cute, or catchy title would undermine the seriousness of her essay. After she rejected a number of possibilities, she decided on "The Price of Silence." This title was thought provoking and also descriptive, and it prepared readers for what was to follow in the essay.

CHOOSING A TITLE

Because it is the first thing in your essay that readers see, your title should create interest. Usually, single-word titles and cute ones do little to draw readers into your essay. To be effective, a title should reflect your purpose and your tone. The titles of some of the essays in this book illustrate the various kinds of titles you can use:

> *Statement of essay's focus:* "Grant and Lee: A Study in Contrasts"
> *Question:* "Who Killed Benny Paret?"
> *Unusual angle:* "Thirty-Eight Who Saw Murder Didn't Call the Police"
> *Controversy:* "A Peaceful Woman Explains Why She Carries a Gun"
> *Provocative wording:* "No Wonder They Call Me a Bitch"
> *Quotation:* "The 'Black Table' Is Still There"
> *Humor:* "The Dog Ate My Flash Drive, and Other Tales of Woe"

A STUDENT WRITER: Preparing a Final Draft

Based on the decisions she made during and after her conference, Laura revised and edited her draft and handed in this final version of her essay.

The Price of Silence

Introduction (provides background)   In his essay "'What's in a Name?'" Henry Louis Gates Jr. recalls an incident from his past in which his father encountered prejudice and did not speak up. Perhaps he kept silent because he was afraid or because he knew that nothing he said or did would change the racial situation in Piedmont, West Virginia. Although I have never encountered the kind of prejudice Gates describes, I did have an experience in high school where, like Gates's father, I *Thesis statement*   could have spoken out but did not. As I look back at the cheating incident that I witnessed, I realize that I have outgrown the immaturity and lack of confidence that made me keep silent.   1

Narrative begins   In my senior year in high school I, along with fifteen other students, took advanced placement chemistry. The course was very demanding and required hours of studying every night. As the semester dragged on, it became clear to me, as well as to the other   2 students in the class, that passing the course was not something we could take for granted. Test after test came back with grades that were well below the As and Bs I was used to getting in the regular chemistry course I had taken in tenth grade. By the time we were ready to take the final exam, most of us were worried that we would fail the course — despite the teacher's assurances that she would mark on a curve.

Key incident occurs

The final examination for advanced placement chemistry   3
was given on a Friday morning between nine o'clock and noon. I had studied all that week, but, even so, I found the test difficult. I knew the material, but I had a hard time answering the long questions that were asked. As I struggled to balance a particularly complex equation, I noticed that the person sitting across from me was acting strangely. At first I thought I was imagining things, but as I stared I saw Jeff, my friend and study partner, fumbling with his test booklet. About a minute passed before I realized that he was copying material from a paper he had taped to the inside of his shirt cuff. After a short time, I stopped watching him and finished my test.

Narrative continues: reactions to the incident

It was not until after the test that I began thinking   4
about what I had seen. Surprisingly, when I mentioned the incident to others in the class, they all knew what Jeff had done. Some even thought that Jeff's actions were justified. "After all," one student said, "the test was hard." But the more I thought about Jeff's actions, the angrier I got. It seemed unfair that I had studied for weeks to memorize formulas and equations while all Jeff had done was copy them onto a cheat sheet. For a moment I considered going to the teacher, but I quickly rejected this idea. Cheating was nothing new to me or to others in my school. Many of my classmates cheated at one time or another. Most of us saw school as a war between us and the teachers, and cheating was just another weapon in our arsenal. The worst crime I could

Narrative ends

commit would be to turn Jeff in. As far as I was concerned, I had no choice. I fell in line with the values of my high school classmates and dismissed the incident as "no big deal."

Analysis of key incident

Now that I am in college, however, I see the situation   5
differently. I find it hard to believe that I could ever have been so complacent about cheating. The issues that were simple in high school now seem complex — especially in light of the honor code that I follow in college. I now ask questions that never would

have occurred to me in high school. What, for example, are the implications of cheating? What would happen to the educational system if cheating became the norm? What are my obligations to all those who are involved in education? Aren't teachers and students interested in achieving a common goal? The answers to these questions give me a sense of the far-reaching effects of my failure to act. If confronted with the same situation today, I know I would speak out regardless of the consequences.

Jeff is now a first-year student at the state university and, like me, he was given credit for AP chemistry. I feel certain that by not turning him in, I failed not only myself but also Jeff. I gave in to peer pressure instead of doing what I knew to be right. The worst that would have happened to Jeff had I spoken up is that he would have had to repeat chemistry in summer school. By doing so, he would have proven to himself that he could, like the rest of us in the class, pass on his own. In the long run, this knowledge would have served him better than the knowledge that he could cheat whenever he faced a difficult situation.   6

Conclusion (aftermath of incident)   Interestingly, Jeff and I are no longer very close. Whenever I see him, I have the same reaction Henry Louis Gates Jr. had when he met Mr. Wilson after he had insulted his father: "'I never again looked [him] in the eye'" (4).   7

Work Cited

Gates, Henry Louis, Jr. "'What's in a Name?'" *Patterns for College Writing*. 13th ed. Ed. Laurie G. Kirszner and Stephen R. Mandell. Boston: Bedford, 2014. 2–4. Print.

With each draft of her essay, Laura sharpened the focus of her discussion. In the process, she clarified her thoughts about her subject and reached some new and interesting conclusions. Although much of Laura's paper is a narrative, it also includes a contrast between her current ideas about cheating and the ideas she had in high school. Perhaps Laura could have explained the reasons behind her current ideas about cheating more fully. Even so, her paper gives a straightforward account of the incident and analyzes its significance without drifting off into clichés or simplistic moralizing. Especially effective is Laura's conclusion, in which she discusses the long-term effects of her experience and quotes Gates. By concluding in this way, she makes sure her readers will not lose sight of the implications of her experience. Finally, Laura documents the quotation she uses in her conclusion and includes a works-cited page at the end of her essay.

Exercise 2

Use the checklist on page 68 to help you revise your draft. If you prefer, outline your draft and use that outline to help you revise.

Exercise 3

Have another student read your second draft. Then, using the student's peer-critique checklist on page 69 as your guide, revise your draft.

Exercise 4

Using the essay on pages 76–78 as your guide, label the final draft of your own essay. In addition to identifying your introduction, conclusion, and thesis statement, you should also label the main points of your essay.

Editing and Proofreading

When you finish revising your essay, it is tempting to print it out, hand it in, and breathe a sigh of relief. This is one temptation you should resist. You still have to *edit* and *proofread* your paper to correct any problems that may remain after you revise.

When you **edit**, you search for grammatical errors, check punctuation, and look over your sentence style and word choice one last time. When you **proofread**, you look for surface errors, such as spelling errors, typos, incorrect spacing, or problems with your essay's format. The idea is to look carefully for any error, no matter how small, that might weaken your essay's message or undermine your credibility. Remember, this is your last chance to make sure your essay says exactly what you want it to say.

Editing for Grammar

As you edit, keep in mind that certain grammatical errors occur more frequently than others — and even more frequently in particular kinds of writing. By concentrating on these errors, as well as on those errors you yourself are most likely to make, you will learn to edit your essays quickly and efficiently.

Learning the few rules that follow will help you identify the most common errors. Later on, when you practice writing essays in various patterns of development, you can use the **Grammar in Context** section in each chapter to help you correct any errors you find.

Be Sure Subjects and Verbs Agree

Subjects and verbs must agree in number. A singular subject takes a singular verb.

Stephanie Ericsson discusses ten kinds of liars.

A plural subject takes a plural verb.

Chronic liars are different from occasional liars.

Liars and plagiarists have a lot in common.

For information on editing for subject-verb agreement with indefinite pronoun subjects, see the Grammar in Context section of Chapter 15 (page 665).

Be Sure Verb Tenses Are Accurate and Consistent

Unintentional shifts in verb tense can be confusing to readers. Verb tenses in the same passage should be the same unless you are referring to two different time periods.

Single time period:	*past tense* Lee surrendered to Grant on April 9, 1865, and *past tense* then he addressed his men.
Two different time periods:	In "Songs of the Summer of 1963 . . . and 2013," *present tense* Juan Williams compares contemporary music with *past tense* music that was popular fifty years earlier.

For more information on editing for consistent verb tenses, as well as to eliminate unwarranted shifts in voice, person, and mood, see the Grammar in Context section of Chapter 9 (page 270).

Be Sure Pronoun References Are Clear

A pronoun is a word that takes the place of a noun in a sentence. Every pronoun should clearly refer to a specific **antecedent**, the word (a noun or pronoun) it replaces. Pronouns and antecedents must agree in number.

• Singular pronouns refer to singular antecedents.

When she was attacked, Kitty Genovese was on her way home.

• Plural pronouns refer to plural antecedents.

The people who watched the attack gave different reasons for their failure to help.

For information on editing for pronoun-antecedent agreement with indefinite pronouns, see the Grammar in Context section of Chapter 15 (page 665).

Be Sure Sentences Are Complete

A **sentence** is a group of words that includes a subject and a verb and expresses a complete thought. A **fragment** is an incomplete sentence, one that is missing a subject, a verb, or both a subject and a verb — or that has a subject and a verb but does not express a complete thought.

Sentence:	Although it was written in 1963, Martin Luther King's "Letter from Birmingham Jail" remains powerful today.
Fragment (no subject):	Remains powerful today.
Fragment (no verb):	Martin Luther King's "Letter from Birmingham Jail."
Fragment (no subject or verb):	Written in 1963.
Fragment (includes subject and verb but does not express a complete thought):	Although it was written in 1963.

To correct a sentence fragment, you need to supply the missing part of the sentence (a subject, a verb, or both — or an entire independent clause). Often, you will find that the missing words appear in an adjacent sentence in your essay.

Be Careful Not to Run Sentences Together without Proper Punctuation

There are two kinds of **run-ons**: *comma splices* and *fused sentences*.

A **comma splice** is an error that occurs when two independent clauses are connected by just a comma.

Comma splice:	Women who live alone need to learn how to protect themselves‚ sometimes this means carrying a gun.

A **fused sentence** is an error that occurs when two independent clauses are connected without any punctuation.

Fused sentence:	Residents of isolated rural areas may carry guns for protection sometimes these guns may be used against them.

For more information on editing run-ons, including additional ways to correct them, see the Grammar in Context section of Chapter 6 (page 102).

Be Careful to Avoid Misplaced and Dangling Modifiers

Modifiers are words and phrases that describe other words in a sentence. To avoid confusion, place modifiers as close as possible to the words they modify.

Limited by their illiteracy, millions of Americans are ashamed to seek help.

Hoping to draw attention to their plight, Jonathan Kozol wrote *Illiterate America.*

A **misplaced modifier** appears to modify the wrong word because it is placed incorrectly in the sentence.

Misplaced modifier:	Judith Ortiz Cofer wonders why Latin women are so often stereotyped as either "hot tamales" or low-level workers in her essay "The Myth of the Latin Woman: I Just Met a Girl Named Maria." (*Does Cofer's essay stereotype Latin women?*)
Correct:	In her essay "The Myth of the Latin Woman: I Just Met a Girl Named Maria," Judith Ortiz Cofer wonders why Latin women are so often stereotyped as either "hot tamales" or low-level workers.

A **dangling modifier** "dangles" because it cannot logically describe any word in the sentence.

Dangling modifier:	Going back to his old junior high school, the "black table" was still there. (*Who went back to his old school?*)
Correct:	Going back to his old junior high school, Lawrence Otis Graham discovered that the "black table" was still there.

For more information on editing to correct misplaced and dangling modifiers, see the Grammar in Context section of Chapter 7 (page 160).

Be Sure Sentence Elements Are Parallel

Parallelism is the use of matching grammatical elements (words, phrases, clauses) to express similar ideas. Used effectively — for example, with paired items or items in a series — parallelism makes the links between related ideas clear and emphasizes connections.

Paired items:	As Deborah Tannen points out, men speak more than women in public but less than women at home.
Items in a series:	Amy Tan says, "I spend a great deal of my time thinking about the power of language — the way it can evoke an emotion, a visual image, a complex idea, or a simple truth" (463).

Faulty parallelism — using items that are not parallel in a context in which parallelism is expected — makes ideas difficult to follow and will likely confuse your readers.

<table>
<tr><td>Faulty parallelism:</td><td>As Deborah Tannen points out, men speak more than women in public, but at home less talking is done by them.</td></tr>
<tr><td>Correct:</td><td>As Deborah Tannen points out, men tend to speak more than women in public, but they tend to talk less at home.</td></tr>
<tr><td>Faulty parallelism:</td><td>Amy Tan says, "I spend a great deal of my time thinking about the power of language — the way it can evoke an emotion, visual images, or complex ideas can be suggested, or communicate a simple truth" (463).</td></tr>
<tr><td>Correct:</td><td>Amy Tan says, "I spend a great deal of my time thinking about the power of language—the way it can evoke an emotion, a visual image, a complex idea, or a simple truth" (463).</td></tr>
</table>

For more information on using parallelism to strengthen your writing, see the Grammar in Context section of Chapter 11 (page 376).

✓ CHECKLIST   Editing for Grammar

☐ **Subject-verb agreement** Do all your verbs agree with their subjects? Remember that singular subjects take singular verbs, and plural subjects take plural verbs.

☐ **Verb tenses** Are all your verb tenses accurate and consistent? Have you avoided unnecessary shifts in tense?

☐ **Pronoun reference** Do pronouns clearly refer to their antecedents?

☐ **Fragments** Does each group of words punctuated as a sentence have both a subject and a verb and express a complete thought? If not, can you correct the fragment by adding the missing words or by attaching it to an adjacent sentence?

☐ **Run-ons** Have you been careful not to connect two independent clauses without the necessary punctuation? Have you avoided comma splices and fused sentences?

☐ **Modification** Does every modifier point clearly to the word it modifies? Have you avoided misplaced and dangling modifiers?

☐ **Parallelism** Have you used matching words, phrases, or clauses to express equivalent ideas? Have you avoided faulty parallelism?

Editing for Punctuation

Like grammatical errors, certain punctuation errors are more common than others, particularly in certain contexts. By understanding a few punctuation rules, you can learn to identify and correct these errors in your writing.

Learn When to Use Commas — and When Not to Use Them

Commas separate certain elements of a sentence. They are used most often in the following situations:

- To separate an introductory phrase or clause from the rest of the sentence

  In Janice Mirikitani's poem "Suicide Note," the speaker is a college student.

  According to the speaker, her parents have extremely high expectations for her.

  Although she has tried her best, she has disappointed them.

NOTE: Do not use a comma if a dependent clause *follows* an independent clause: She is the only daughter although her father has six sons.

- To separate two independent clauses that are joined by a coordinating conjunction

  The speaker in "Suicide Note" tried to please her parents, but they always expected more of her.

- To separate elements in a series

  Janice Mirikitani has studied creative writing, edited a literary magazine, and published several books of poetry.

For more information on using commas in a series, see the Grammar in Context section of Chapter 8 (page 213).

- To separate a **nonrestrictive clause** (a clause that does not supply information that is essential to the sentence's meaning) from the rest of the sentence

  The poem's speaker, who is female, thinks her parents would like her to be a son.

NOTE: Do not use commas to set off a **restrictive clause** (a clause that supplies information that is vital to the sentence's meaning): The child who is overlooked is often the daughter.

Learn When to Use Semicolons

Semicolons, like commas, separate certain elements of a sentence. However, semicolons separate only grammatically equivalent elements — for example, two closely related independent clauses.

In Burma, George Orwell learned something about the nature of imperialism; it was not an easy lesson.

Shirley Jackson's "The Lottery" is fiction; however, many early readers thought it was a true story.

In most cases, commas separate items in a series. However, when one or more of the items in a series already include commas, separate the items with semicolons. This will make the sentence easier to follow.

Orwell set his works in Paris, France; London, England; and Moulmein, Burma.

Learn When to Use Apostrophes

Apostrophes have two uses: to indicate missing letters in contractions and to show possession or ownership.

- In contractions:

  As Farhad Manjoo observes, it's become more and more common to see dogs where they don't belong.

- To show possession:

  As Manjoo's essay points out, not everyone loves other people's dogs.

NOTE: Be careful not to confuse contractions with similar-sounding possessive pronouns.

CONTRACTION	POSSESSIVE
they're (= they are)	their
it's (= it is, it has)	its
who's (= who is, who has)	whose
you're (= you are)	your

Learn When to Use Quotation Marks

Quotation marks are used to set off quoted speech or writing.

At the end of his essay, E. B. White feels "the chill of death" (196).

Special rules govern the use of other punctuation marks with quotation marks:

- Commas and periods are always placed before quotation marks.
- Colons and semicolons are always placed after quotation marks.
- Question marks and exclamation points can go either before or after quotation marks, depending on whether or not they are part of the quoted material.

Quotation marks are also used to set off the titles of essays ("Once More to the Lake"), stories ("The Lottery"), and poems ("Sadie and Maud").

NOTE: Italics are used to set off titles of books, periodicals, and plays: *Life on the Mississippi, College English, Hamlet.*

For information on formatting quotations in research papers, see Chapter 17.

Learn When to Use Dashes and Colons

Dashes are occasionally used to set off and emphasize information within a sentence.

> Jessica Mitford wrote a scathing critique of the funeral industry — and touched off an uproar. Her book *The American Way of Death* was widely read around the world.

However, because this usage is somewhat informal, dashes should be used in moderation in your college writing.

Colons are used to introduce lists, examples, and clarifications. A colon should always be preceded by a complete sentence.

> As Norman Cousins observes in "Who Killed Benny Paret?" one simple cause was ultimately responsible for Paret's death: the fact that spectators came to the fight expecting to see a knockout.

For more information on using colons, see the **Grammar in Context** section of Chapter 12 (page 439).

✔ CHECKLIST   **Editing for Punctuation**

☐ **Commas** Have you used commas when necessary — and only when necessary?

☐ **Semicolons** Have you used semicolons between only grammatically equivalent elements?

☐ **Apostrophes** Have you used apostrophes in contractions and possessive nouns and (when necessary) in possessive pronoun forms?

☐ **Quotation marks** Have you used quotation marks to set off quoted speech or writing and to set off titles of essays, stories, and poems? Have you used other punctuation correctly with quotation marks?

☐ **Dashes and colons** Have you used dashes in moderation? Is every colon that introduces a list, an example, or a clarification preceded by a complete sentence?

Exercise 1

Reread the essay you wrote in Chapters 2–4, and edit it for grammar and punctuation.

 TECH TIP: Editing

Just as you do when you revise, you should edit on a hard copy of your essay. Seeing your work on the printed page makes it easy for you to spot surface-level errors in grammar and punctuation. You can also run a grammar check to help you find grammar and punctuation errors, but you should keep in mind that grammar checkers are far from perfect. They often miss errors (such as faulty modification), and they frequently highlight areas of text (such as a long sentence) that may not contain an error.

Exercise 2

Run a grammar check, and then make any additional corrections you think are necessary.

Editing for Sentence Style and Word Choice

As you edit your essay for grammar and punctuation, you should also be looking one last time at how you construct sentences and choose words. So that your essay is as clear, readable, and convincing as possible, your sentences should be not only correct but also concise and varied. In addition, every word should mean exactly what you want it to mean, and your language should be free of clichés.

Eliminate Awkward Phrasing

As you review your essay's sentences, check carefully for awkward phrasing, and do your best to smooth it out.

Awkward:	The reason Thomas Jefferson drafted the Declaration of Independence was because he felt the king was a tyrant.
Correct:	The reason Thomas Jefferson drafted the Declaration of Independence was that he felt the king was a tyrant.

For more information about this error, see the Grammar in Context section of Chapter 10 (page 329).

Awkward:	*Work* is where you earn money.
Correct:	*Work* is an activity you do to earn money.

For more information about this error, see the Grammar in Context section of Chapter 13 (page 493).

Be Sure Your Sentences Are Concise

A **concise** sentence is efficient; it is not overloaded with extra words and complicated constructions. To make sentences concise, you need to eliminate repetition and redundancy, delete empty words and expressions, and cut everything that is not absolutely necessary.

Wordy:	Brent Staples's essay "Just Walk On By" explores his feelings, thoughts, and ideas about various events and experiences that were painful to him as a black man living in a large metropolitan city.
Concise:	Brent Staples's essay "Just Walk On By" explores his ideas about his painful experiences as a black man living in a large city.

Be Sure Your Sentences Are Varied

To add interest to your paper, vary the length and structure of your sentences, and vary the way you open them.

- Mix long and short sentences.

  As time went on, and as he saw people's hostile reactions to him, Staples grew more and more uneasy. Then, he had an idea.

- Mix simple, compound, and complex sentences.

  Simple sentence (*one independent clause*): Staples grew more and more uneasy.

  Compound sentence (*two independent clauses*): Staples grew more and more uneasy, but he stood his ground.

  Complex sentence (*dependent clause, independent clause*): Although Staples grew more and more uneasy, he continued to walk in the neighborhood.

For more information on how to form compound and complex sentences, see the Grammar in Context section of Chapter 14 (page 541).

- Vary your sentence openings. Instead of beginning every sentence with the subject (particularly with a pronoun like *he* or *this*), begin some sentences with an introductory word, phrase, or clause that ties it to the preceding sentence.

  The 1964 murder of Kitty Genovese, discussed in Martin Gansberg's "Thirty-Eight Who Saw Murder Didn't Call the Police," remains relevant today for a number of reasons. For one thing, urban crime remains a problem, particularly for women. Moreover, many people are still reluctant to report crimes. Although more than fifty years have gone by, the story of Kitty Genovese and the people who watched her die still stirs strong emotional responses.

Choose Your Words Carefully

- Choose **specific** words that identify particular examples and details.

  Vague: Violence in sports is a bad thing.

  Specific: Violence in boxing is a serious problem that threatens not just the lives of the boxers but also the sport itself.

- Avoid **clichés**, overused expressions that rely on tired figures of speech.

  Clichés: When he was hit, the boxer stood for a moment like a deer caught in the headlights, and then he fell to the mat like a ton of bricks.

  Revised: When he was hit, the boxer stood frozen for a moment, and then he fell to the mat.

✔CHECKLIST   **Editing for Sentence Style and Word Choice**

- ☐ **Awkward phrasing** Have you eliminated awkward constructions?
- ☐ **Concise sentences** Have you eliminated repetition, empty phrases, and excess words? Is every sentence as concise as it can be?
- ☐ **Varied sentences** Have you varied the length and structure of your sentences? Have you varied your sentence openings?
- ☐ **Word choice** Have you selected specific words? Have you eliminated clichés?

Exercise 3

Check your essay's sentence style and word choice.

Proofreading Your Essay

When you proofread, you check your essay for surface errors, such as commonly confused words, misspellings, faulty capitalization, and incorrect italic use; then, you check for typographical errors.

Check for Commonly Confused Words

Even if you have carefully considered your choice of words during the editing stage, you may have missed some errors. As you proofread, look carefully to see if you can spot any **commonly confused words** — *its* for *it's, there* for *their,* or *affect* for *effect,* for example — that a spell check will not catch.

For more information on how to distinguish between *affect* and *effect,* see the Grammar in Context section of Chapter 10 (page 329).

Check for Misspellings and Faulty Capitalization

It makes no sense to work hard on an essay and then undermine your credibility with spelling and mechanical errors. If you have any doubt about how a word is spelled or whether or not to capitalize it, check a dictionary (in print or online).

Check for Typos

The last step in the proofreading process is to read carefully and look for typos. Make sure you have spaced correctly between words and have not accidentally typed an extra letter, omitted a letter, or transposed two letters. Reading your essay *backwards* — one sentence at a time — will help you focus on individual sentences, which in turn will help you see errors more clearly.

 CHECKLIST   Proofreading

☐ **Commonly confused words** Have you proofread for errors involving words that are often confused with each other?
☐ **Misspelled words and faulty capitalization** Have you proofread for errors in spelling and capitalization? Have you run a spell check?
☐ **Typos** Have you checked carefully to eliminate typing errors?

TECH TIP: Spell Checkers

You should certainly run a spell check to help you locate misspelled words and incorrect strings of letters caused by typos, but keep in mind that a spell checker will not discover every error. For example, it will not identify many misspelled proper nouns or foreign words, nor will it highlight words that are spelled correctly but used incorrectly — *work* for *word* or *form* for *from*, for example. For this reason, you must still proofread carefully — even after you run a spell check.

Exercise 4

Proofread your essay.

Checking Your Paper's Format

The final thing to consider is your paper's **format** — how your paragraphs, sentences, and words look on the page. Your instructor will give you some general guidelines about format — telling you, for example, to type your last name and the page number at the top right of each page — and, of course, you should follow these guidelines. Students writing in the humanities usually follow the format illustrated on page 93. (For information on MLA documentation format, see Chapter 18.)

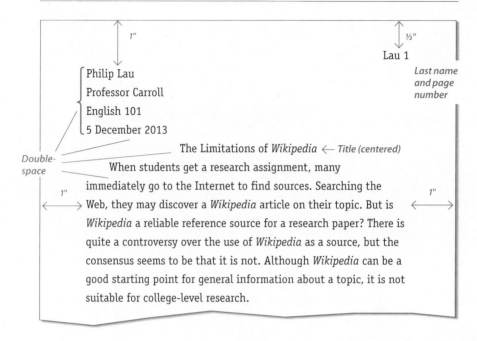

1"

½"

Lau 1

Philip Lau

Professor Carroll

English 101

5 December 2013

Last name and page number

The Limitations of *Wikipedia* ← *Title (centered)*

Double-space

When students get a research assignment, many immediately go to the Internet to find sources. Searching the Web, they may discover a *Wikipedia* article on their topic. But is *Wikipedia* a reliable reference source for a research paper? There is quite a controversy over the use of *Wikipedia* as a source, but the consensus seems to be that it is not. Although *Wikipedia* can be a good starting point for general information about a topic, it is not suitable for college-level research.

1"

1"

✔ CHECKLIST   **Checking Your Paper's Format**

☐ **Format** Have you followed your instructor's format guidelines?
☐ **Spacing** Have you double-spaced throughout?
☐ **Type size** Have you used ten- or twelve-point type?
☐ **Paragraphing** Have you indented the first line of every paragraph?
☐ **Visuals** If you used one or more visuals in your essay, did you insert each visual as close as possible to where it is discussed?
☐ **Documentation** Have you documented each source — and each visual — you used? Have you included a works-cited page?

Exercise 5

Make any necessary corrections to your essay's format, and then print out a final draft.

PART TWO

Readings for Writers

The relationship between reading and writing is a complex one. Sometimes you will write an essay based on your own experience; more often than not, however, you will respond in writing to something you have read. The essays in this book give you a chance to do both.

As you are probably aware, the fact that information appears in print or on the Internet does not mean it should be taken at face value. Of course, many of the books and articles you read will be reliable, but some — especially material found on many websites and blogs — will include contradictions, biased ideas, or even inaccurate or misleading information. For this reason, your goal should not be simply to understand what you read but to assess the credibility of the writers and, eventually, to judge the soundness of their ideas.

When you read the essays and other texts in this book, you should approach them critically. In other words, you should question (and sometimes challenge) the writer's ideas — and, in the process, try to create new interpretations that you can explore in your writing. Approaching a text in this way is not easy, for it requires you to develop your own analytical and critical skills and your own set of standards to help you judge and interpret what you read. Only after you have read and critically evaluated a text can you begin to draw your ideas together and write about them.

Every reading selection in Chapters 6 through 15 is accompanied by a series of questions intended to guide you through the reading process. In many ways, these questions are a warm-up for the intellectual workout of writing an essay. The more time you devote to them, the more you will be practicing your analytical skills. In a real sense, then, these questions will help you develop the critical thinking skills you will need when you write. In becoming a proficient reader, you will also gain confidence in yourself as a writer.

Each of the reading selections in Chapters 6 through 14 is organized around one dominant pattern of development. In your outside reading, however, you will often find more than one pattern used in a single piece of writing (as in Chapter 15, Combining the Patterns, page 663). When you write, then, do not feel you must follow these patterns blindly; instead, think of them as tools for making your writing more effective, and adapt them to your subject, your audience, and your purpose for writing.

In addition to the reading selections, each chapter also includes a visual text — for example, a piece of fine art, an advertisement, or a photograph. By visually reinforcing the chapter's basic rhetorical concept, each visual text serves as a bridge to the chapter's essays. Following each visual is a set of questions designed to help you understand not just the image but also the rhetorical pattern that is the chapter's focus.

6

Narration

What Is Narration?

Narration tells a story by presenting events in an orderly, logical sequence. In the following paragraph from "The Stone Horse," essayist Barry Lopez recounts the history of the exploration of the California desert.

<table>
<tr>
<td>Topic sentence</td>
<td>Western man did not enter the California desert until the end of the eighteenth century, 250 years after Coronado brought his soldiers into the Zuni pueblos in a bewildered search for the cities of Cibola. The earliest appraisals of the land were cursory, hurried. People traveled through it, en route to Santa Fe or the California coastal settlements.</td>
</tr>
<tr>
<td>Narrative traces developments through the nineteenth century</td>
<td>Only miners tarried. In 1823 what had been Spain's became Mexico's, and in 1848 what had been Mexico's became America's; but the bare, jagged mountains and dry lake beds, the vast and uniform plains of creosote bush and yucca plants, remained as obscure as the northern Sudan until the end of the nineteenth century.</td>
</tr>
</table>

Narration can be the dominant pattern in many kinds of writing (as well as in speech). Histories, biographies, and autobiographies follow a narrative form, as do personal letters, diaries, journals, and some of the content on personal Web pages or social networking sites. Narration is the dominant pattern in many works of fiction and poetry, and it is an essential part of casual conversation. Narration also underlies folk and fairy tales and many news reports. In short, anytime you tell what happened, you are using narration.

Using Narration

Narration can provide the structure for an entire essay, but narrative passages may also appear in essays that are not primarily narrative. In an argumentative essay supporting stricter gun-safety legislation, for example, you might devote one or two paragraphs to the story of a child accidentally killed by a handgun. In this chapter, however, we focus on narration as the dominant pattern of a piece of writing.

Throughout your college career, many of your assignments will call for narration. In an English composition class, you may be asked to write about an experience that was important to your development as an adult; on a European history exam, you may need to relate the events that led to Napoleon's defeat at the Battle of Waterloo; and in a technical writing class, you may be asked to write a report tracing a company's negligent actions. In each of these situations (as well as in many additional assignments), your writing has a primarily narrative structure, and the narrative supports a thesis.

The skills you develop in narrative writing will also help you in other kinds of writing. A *process essay,* such as an explanation of a laboratory experiment, is like a narrative because it outlines a series of steps in chronological order; a *cause-and-effect essay,* such as your answer to an exam question that asks you to analyze the events that caused the Great Depression, also resembles a narrative in that it traces a sequence of events. Although a process essay explains how to do something and a cause-and-effect essay explains why events occur, writing both these kinds of essays will be easier after you master narration. (Process essays and cause-and-effect essays are discussed and illustrated in Chapters 9 and 10, respectively.)

Planning a Narrative Essay

Developing a Thesis Statement

Although the purpose of a narrative may be simply to recount events or to create a particular mood or impression, in college writing a narrative essay is more likely to present a sequence of events for the purpose of supporting a thesis. For instance, in a narrative about your problems with credit card debt, your purpose may be to show your readers that college students should not have easy access to credit cards. Accordingly, you do not simply tell the story of your unwise spending. Rather, you select and arrange details to show your readers why having a credit card encouraged you to spend money you didn't have. Although it is usually best to include an explicit **thesis statement** ("My negative experiences with credit have convinced me that college students should not have access to credit cards"), you may also imply your thesis through your selection and arrangement of events.

Including Enough Detail

Narratives, like other types of writing, need to include rich, specific details if they are to be convincing. Each detail should help to create a picture for the reader; even exact times, dates, and geographic locations can be helpful. Look, for example, at the following paragraph from the essay "My

Mother Never Worked" by Bonnie Smith-Yackel, which appears later in this chapter:

> In the winter she sewed night after night, endlessly, begging cast-off clothing from relatives, ripping apart coats, dresses, blouses, and trousers to remake them to fit her four daughters and son. Every morning and every evening she milked cows, fed pigs and calves, cared for chickens, picked eggs, cooked meals, washed dishes, scrubbed floors, and tended and loved her children. In the spring she planted a garden once more, dragging pails of water to nourish and sustain the vegetables for the family. In 1936 she lost a baby in her sixth month.

This list of details adds interest and authenticity to the narrative. The central figure in the narrative is a busy, productive woman, and readers know this because they are given an exhaustive catalog of her activities.

Varying Sentence Structure

When narratives present a long series of events, all the sentences can begin to sound alike: "She sewed dresses. She milked cows. She fed pigs. She fed calves. She cared for chickens." Such a predictable string of sentences may become monotonous for your readers. You can eliminate this monotony by varying your sentence structure — for instance, by using a variety of sentence openings or by combining simple sentences as Smith-Yackel does in "My Mother Never Worked": "In the winter she sewed night after night, endlessly. . . . Every morning and every evening she milked cows, fed pigs and calves, cared for chickens. . . ."

Maintaining Clear Narrative Order

Many narratives present events in the exact order in which they occurred, moving from first event to last. Whether or not you follow a strict **chronological order** depends on the purpose of your narrative. If you are writing a straightforward account of a historical event or summarizing a record of poor management practices, you will probably want to move directly from beginning to end. In a personal-experience essay or a fictional narrative, however, you may want to engage your readers' interest by beginning with an event from the middle of your story, or even from the end, and then presenting the events that led up to it. You may also decide to begin in the present and then use one or more **flashbacks** (shifts into the past) to tell your story. To help readers follow the order of events in your narrative, it is very important to use correct verb tenses and clear transitional words and phrases.

Using Accurate Verb Tenses. Verb tense is extremely important in writing that recounts events in a fixed order because tenses indicate temporal (time) relationships. When you write a narrative, you should be careful to keep verb tenses consistent and accurate so that your readers can follow the sequence of events. Naturally, you need to shift tenses to reflect an actual time shift in your narrative. For instance, convention requires that you use present tense when discussing works of literature ("When Hamlet's mother *marries* his uncle . . ."), but a flashback to an earlier point in the story calls for a shift from present to past tense ("Before his mother's marriage, Hamlet *was* . . ."). Nevertheless, you should avoid unwarranted shifts in verb tense; they will make your narrative confusing.

Using Transitions. Transitions — connecting words or phrases — help link events in time, enabling narratives to flow smoothly. Without them, narratives would lack coherence, and readers would be unsure of the correct sequence of events. Transitions indicate the order of events, and they also signal shifts in time. In narrative writing, the transitions commonly used for these purposes include *first, second, next, then, later, at the same time, meanwhile, immediately, soon, before, earlier, after, afterward, now,* and *finally.* In addition to transitional words and phrases, specific time markers — such as *three years later, in 1927, after two hours,* and *on January 3* — indicate how much time has passed between events. (A more complete list of transitions appears on page 57.)

Structuring a Narrative Essay

Like other essays, a **narrative** essay has an introduction, a body, and a conclusion. If your essay's thesis is explicitly stated, it will, in most cases, appear in the **introduction**. The **body paragraphs** of your essay will recount the events that make up your narrative, following a clear and orderly plan. Finally, the **conclusion** will give your readers the sense that your narrative is complete, perhaps by restating your thesis in different words or by summarizing key points or events.

Suppose you are assigned a short history paper about the Battle of Waterloo. You plan to support the thesis that if Napoleon had kept more troops in reserve, he might have defeated the British troops serving under Wellington. Based on this thesis, you decide that the best way to organize your paper is to present the five major phases of the battle in chronological order. An informal outline of your essay might look like this.

Sample Outline **Narration**	
Introduction:	Thesis statement — If Napoleon had kept more troops in reserve, he might have broken Wellington's line with another infantry attack and thus won the Battle of Waterloo.
Phase 1 of the battle:	Napoleon attacked the Château of Hougoumont.
Phase 2 of the battle:	The French infantry attacked the British lines.

Phase 3 of the battle:	The French cavalry staged a series of charges against the British lines that had not been attacked before; Napoleon committed his reserves.
Phase 4 of the battle:	The French captured La Haye Sainte, their first success of the day but an advantage that Napoleon, having committed troops elsewhere, could not maintain without reserves.
Phase 5 of the battle:	The French infantry was decisively defeated by the combined thrust of the British infantry and the remaining British cavalry.
Conclusion:	Restatement of thesis (in different words) or review of key points or events.

By discussing the five phases of the battle in chronological order, you clearly support your thesis. As you expand your informal outline into a historical narrative, exact details, dates, times, and geographic locations are extremely important. Without them, your statements are open to question. In addition, to keep your readers aware of the order of events, you must select appropriate transitional words and phrases and pay careful attention to verb tenses.

Revising a Narrative Essay

When you revise a narrative essay, consider the items on the revision checklist on page 68. In addition, pay special attention to the items on the following checklist, which apply specifically to narrative essays.

✔️ REVISION CHECKLIST   **Narration**
- ☐ Does your assignment call for narration?
- ☐ Does your essay's thesis communicate the significance of the events you discuss?
- ☐ Have you included enough specific detail?
- ☐ Have you varied your sentence structure?
- ☐ Is the order of events clear to readers?
- ☐ Have you varied sentence openings and combined short sentences to avoid monotony?
- ☐ Do your transitions indicate the order of events and signal shifts in time?

Editing a Narrative Essay

When you edit your narrative essay, follow the guidelines on the editing checklists on pages 85, 88, and 91. In addition, focus on the grammar, mechanics, and punctuation issues that are particularly relevant to narrative essays. One of these issues — avoiding run-on sentences — is discussed below.

GRAMMAR IN CONTEXT **Avoiding Run-Ons**

When writing narrative essays, particularly personal narratives and essays that include dialogue, writers can easily lose sight of sentence boundaries and create **run-ons**. There are two kinds of run-ons: *fused sentences* and *comma splices*.

A **fused sentence** occurs when two sentences are incorrectly joined without punctuation.

CORRECT (TWO SENTENCES): "The sun came out hot and bright, endlessly, day after day. The crops shriveled and died" (Smith-Yackel 124).

FUSED SENTENCE: The sun came out hot and bright, endlessly, day after day the crops shriveled and died.

A **comma splice** occurs when two sentences are incorrectly joined with just a comma.

COMMA SPLICE: The sun came out hot and bright, endlessly, day after day, the crops shriveled and died.

Five Ways to Correct These Errors

1. **Use a period to create two separate sentences.**

   The sun came out hot and bright, endlessly, day after day. The crops shriveled and died.

2. **Join the sentences with a comma and a coordinating conjunction (*and, or, nor, for, so, but, yet*).**

   The sun came out hot and bright, endlessly, day after day, and the crops shriveled and died.

3. **Join the sentences with a semicolon.**

   The sun came out hot and bright, endlessly, day after day; the crops shriveled and died.

4. **Join the sentences with a semicolon and a transitional word or phrase (followed by a comma), such as *however, therefore,* or *for example*. (See page 57 for a list of transitional words and phrases.)**

   The sun came out hot and bright, endlessly, day after day; eventually, the crops shriveled and died.

5. **Create a complex sentence by adding a subordinating conjunction (*although, because, if,* and so on) or a relative pronoun (*who, which, that,* and so on) to one of the sentences.**

   As the sun came out hot and bright, endlessly, day after day, the crops shriveled and died.

☑ **EDITING CHECKLIST**   **Narration**

☐ Have you avoided run-ons?
☐ Do your verb tenses clearly indicate time relationships between events?
☐ Have you avoided unnecessary tense shifts?
☐ If you use dialogue, have you punctuated correctly and capitalized where necessary?

A STUDENT WRITER: Literacy Narrative

In the following essay, student Erica Sarno traces her development as a writer. Her assignment was to write a **literacy narrative**, a personal account focusing on her experiences with reading and writing.

Becoming a Writer

Introduction

I used to think that writing was just about filling pages. 1 Composing an essay for school meant getting the job done and checking it off my to-do list. During my last two years of high school, however, my attitude started to change. Several experiences helped me understand that writing is not a skill that some people are born with and others are not. If I wanted to write, all I needed was a desire to express myself to others and a willing audience.

Thesis statement

Realizing that there was someone on the other side of the page, eager to listen, helped me develop into a more effective writer.

Narrative begins (junior year)

My first real lesson in my development as a writer took place 2 in Mrs. Strickland's junior English class. Mrs. Strickland was hard to approach. She dressed as if she expected to be giving a press conference at the White House. She wore tan suits and silk scarves, and she had a helmet of dyed blonde hair. We seemed to disappoint her just because we were high school students. Maybe I saw her lack of interest in us and our work as a challenge because, one day, I took a risk and wrote a very personal essay about losing my aunt to cancer. When I got the paper back, Mrs. Strickland had written only, "Did you read the instructions?" I could not believe it. For the first time, I had actually written about what was important to me rather than just filling the pages with words, and she had not even read past my introduction! Still, I knew then that I had something to say. I just needed someone to listen.

Narrative continues (senior year)

The next year, I had Dr. Kelleher for senior English. My year 3 with Dr. K profoundly changed the way I see myself as a writer (and as a reader). Finally, a teacher was paying attention to what I had written. His only rule for writing was "Don't be boring!" I rewrote sentences, hoping for an exclamation point or one of Dr. K's other special marks in the margin. Dr. K had a whole list of codes and abbreviations, like "BTH" ("Better than Hemingway") or "the knife" (when the writer slayed the opponent in an argument). I also relied on Dr. K to tell me when I was falling into my old habit of just filling the page. He would write a funny comment like, "Come back! Log out of Facebook!" Then, he would give me a chance to try again. Trusting him to be a generous reader and an honest critic helped me develop my voice and my confidence as a writer.

Narrative shifts to focus on reading

Meanwhile, I started to become a better reader, too. I could   4
tell when a writer was writing to me, wanting me to understand. I could also tell when a writer was writing just to get the job done. Instead of just skimming the assigned reading, I got in the habit of writing in the margins and making notes about what I thought. I underlined ideas that spoke to me, and I wrote "Really??" next to ideas that seemed silly. Instead of assuming a reading would be boring, I gave every assignment a chance. Whether I liked a book or not, I felt that I could explain my reasons. I was finally seeing for myself that writing is just another way for people to talk to each other.

Narrative moves outside the classroom

Eventually, in the spring of my senior year, I experienced   5
what it feels like to connect with a broader audience. I suggested a column about "senioritis" to the school paper, and even though I had never written for the public before, the editor loved my idea. I knew what I wanted to say, and I knew I could collect plenty of stories to help me illustrate my ideas. What I did not predict was how much I would learn from the experience of writing those six columns. Knowing that hundreds of people would be reading my pieces, I revised them over and over again. When Dr. K read one of my last columns aloud to our class, I got to see how my work affected people. Watching the expressions on my classmates' faces and hearing them laugh at the funny parts helped me understand what good writing is. In that moment, I truly connected with my audience.

Conclusion

Although I still have a lot to learn, I now understand how   6
important the relationship between the writer and the reader is. When I write, I am writing to be heard. When I read, I am reading to understand. The communication may not be perfect, but I know

I am not alone in my task. And even though I am not in Dr. K's class anymore, I still sometimes imagine that he will be reading what I have written. Thinking about him reminds me that someone cares about what I have to say.

Points for Special Attention

Assignment. Erica's assignment was to write a literacy narrative. At first, she considered writing about her favorite childhood books or about how she learned to read, but in the end she decided to focus on more recent experiences because she could remember them more clearly (and, therefore, could include more specific detail).

Thesis Statement and Title. Because her focus was on her development as a writer, Erica was careful to include the words *develop* and *writer* in her thesis statement. Her thesis statement also clearly explains the key factor that encouraged her development — the presence of an interested reader.

Structure. In her essay's first two body paragraphs, Erica discusses her junior and senior English classes. However, instead of just contrasting the two teachers, she explains how she herself changed as a result of their different approaches. In paragraph 4, she explains the connection between her reading and her writing, and in paragraph 5, she recounts her development into a reader writing for a wider audience.

Topic Sentences. To move her narrative along, Erica was careful to include transitional words and phrases — *The next year, Meanwhile, Eventually* — in her topic sentences to show the movement from one stage of her development to the next.

Working with Sources. Erica's assignment made it clear that although other assignments in the course would be source-based, this narrative essay should be based solely on her own memories and reflections.

Focus on Revision

When she reread an early draft of her essay, Erica immediately saw a problem: she had written a comparison-and-contrast essay instead of a narrative. Instead of focusing on her development as a writer, she had simply compared her junior- and senior-year English classes. This problem was revealed by her draft's thesis statement — "The difference between junior and senior year of high school was the difference between being ignored and being heard" — as well as by the topic sentences of her first two body paragraphs:

First body paragraph: Mrs. Strickland was an uninspiring teacher.

Second body paragraph: Unlike Mrs. Strickland, Dr. Kelleher encouraged me as a writer.

Erica also noticed that her entire essay dealt with classroom style, further highlighting the contrast between her two teachers. Realizing that her development as a writer had also taken place outside the classroom, she condensed her discussion of the two English classes and added material about reading (paragraph 4) and about writing for her school paper (paragraph 5).

When she wrote her next draft, Erica was careful to include transitions and topic sentences that signaled her focus on her development over time, not on the differences between two classes or two teachers. Finally, as she reviewed her draft, she noticed that her original summary statement — "Knowing that there was someone on the other side of the page made me a better writer" — could be expanded into an appropriate and effective thesis statement.

A STUDENT WRITER: Narration

The following essay is typical of the informal narrative writing many students are asked to do in English composition classes. It was written by Tiffany Forte in response to the assignment "Write an informal essay about a goal or dream you had when you were a child."

My Field of Dreams

Introduction   When I was young, I was told that when I grew up I could   1
be anything I wanted to be, and I always took for granted that
this was true. I knew exactly what I was going to be, and I would
spend hours dreaming about how wonderful my life would be when
Thesis statement   I grew up. One day, though, when I did grow up, I realized that
things had not turned out the way I had always expected they
would.

Narrative begins   When I was little, I never played with baby dolls or Barbies.   2
I wasn't like other little girls; I was a tomboy. I was the only girl
in the neighborhood where I lived, so I always played with boys.
We would play army or football or (my favorite) baseball.

Almost every summer afternoon, all the boys in my   3
neighborhood and I would meet by the big oak tree to get a
baseball game going. Surprisingly, I was always one of the first to
be picked for a team. I was very fast, and (for my size) I could hit
the ball far. I loved baseball more than anything, and I wouldn't
miss a game for the world.

My dad played baseball too, and every Friday night I would   4
go to the field with my mother to watch him play. It was just like
the big leagues, with lots of people, a snack bar, and lights that
shone so high and bright you could see them a mile away. I loved
to go to my dad's games. When all the other kids would wander
off and play, I would sit and cheer on my dad and his team. My
attention was focused on the field, and my heart would jump with
every pitch.

Even more exciting than my dad's games were the major   5
league games. The Phillies were my favorite team, and I always
looked forward to watching them on television. My dad would make
popcorn, and we would sit and watch in anticipation of a Phillies
victory. We would go wild, yelling and screaming at all the big
plays. When the Phillies would win, I would be so excited I couldn't
sleep; when they would lose, I would go to bed angry, just like
my dad.

Key experience introduced (pars. 6–7)

It was when my dad took me to my first Phillies game   6
that I decided I wanted to be a major league baseball player. The
excitement began when we pulled into the parking lot of the old
Veterans Stadium. There were thousands of cars. As we walked
from the car to the stadium, my dad told me to hold on to his
hand and not to let go no matter what. When we gave the man
our tickets and entered the stadium, I understood why. There were
mobs of people everywhere. They were walking around the stadium
and standing in long lines for hot dogs, beer, and souvenirs. It was
the most wonderful thing I had ever seen. When we got to our
seats, I looked down at the tiny baseball diamond below and felt
as if I were on top of the world.

The cheering of the crowd, the singing, and the chants were   7
almost more than I could stand. I was bursting with enthusiasm.
Then, in the bottom of the eighth inning, with the score tied and
two outs, Mike Schmidt came up to bat and hit the game-winning
home run. The crowd went crazy. Everyone in the whole stadium
was standing, and I found myself yelling and screaming along
with everyone else. When Mike Schmidt came out of the dugout
to receive his standing ovation, I felt a lump in my throat and
butterflies in my stomach. He was everyone's hero that night, and
I could only imagine the pride he must have felt. I slept the whole
way home and dreamed of what it would be like to be the hero of
the game.

Narrative continues

The next day, when I met with the boys at the oak tree, I   8
told them that when I grew up, I was going to be a major league
baseball player. They all laughed at me and said I could never be a
baseball player because I was a girl. I told them that they were all
wrong and that I would show them.

Analysis of childhood experiences

In the years to follow, I played girls' softball in a   9
competitive fast-pitch league, and I was very good. I always
wanted to play baseball with the boys, but there were no mixed
leagues. After a few years, I realized that the boys from the oak
tree were right: I was never going to be a major league baseball
player. I realized that what I had been told when I was younger
wasn't the whole truth. What no one had bothered to tell me was
that I could be anything I wanted to be — as long as it was
something that was appropriate for a girl to do.

Conclusion

In time, I would get over the loss of my dream. I found new   10
dreams, acceptable for a young woman, and I moved on to other
things. Still, every time I watch a baseball game and someone hits
a home run, I get those same butterflies in my stomach and think,
for just a minute, about what might have been.

Points for Special Attention

Assignment. Tiffany's assignment was to write about a goal or dream
she had when she was a child. As a nontraditional student, a good deal older
than most of her classmates, Tiffany found this assignment challenging at
first. She wondered if her childhood dreams would be different from those
of her classmates, and she was somewhat hesitant to share her drafts with
her peer-editing group. As it turned out, though, her childhood dreams
were not very different from those of the other students in her class.

Introduction. Tiffany's introduction is straightforward, yet it arouses
reader interest by setting up a contrast between what she expected and
what actually happened. Her optimistic expectation — that she could be
anything she wanted to be — is contradicted by her thesis statement, encouraging readers to read on to learn how things turned out and why.

Thesis Statement. Although the assignment called for a personal narrative, the instructor made it clear that the essay should have an explicitly
stated thesis that made a point about a childhood goal or dream. Tiffany
knew she wanted to write about her passion for baseball, but she also knew
that just listing a series of events would not fulfill the assignment. Her thesis statement — "One day, though, when I did grow up, I realized that

things had not turned out the way I had always expected they would" — puts her memories in context, suggesting that she will use them to support a general conclusion about the gap between dreams and reality.

Structure. The body of Tiffany's essay traces the chronology of her involvement with baseball — playing with the neighborhood boys, watching her father's games, watching baseball on television, and, finally, attending her first major league game. Each body paragraph introduces a different aspect of her experience with baseball, culminating in the vividly described Phillies game. The balance of the essay (paragraphs 8–10) summarizes the aftermath of that game, gives a brief overview of Tiffany's later years in baseball, and presents her conclusion.

Detail. Personal narratives like Tiffany's need a lot of detail because the writers want readers to see and hear and feel what they did. To present an accurate picture, Tiffany includes all the significant sights and sounds she can remember: the big oak tree, the lights on the field, the popcorn, the excited cheers, the food and souvenir stands, the crowds, and so on. She also names Mike Schmidt ("everyone's hero"), his team, and the stadium where she saw him play. Despite all these details, though, she omits some important information — for example, how old she was at each stage of her essay.

Working with Sources. Tiffany's essay is very personal, and she supports her thesis with experiences and observations from her own childhood. Although she could have consulted sources to find specific information about team standings or players' stats — or even quoted her hero, Mike Schmidt — she decided that her own memories would provide convincing support for her thesis.

Verb Tense. Maintaining clear chronological order is very important in narrative writing, where unwarranted shifts in verb tenses can confuse readers. Knowing this, Tiffany was careful to avoid unnecessary tense shifts. In her conclusion, she shifts from past to present tense, but this shift is both necessary and clear. Elsewhere she uses *would* to identify events that recurred regularly. For example, in paragraph 5 she says, "My dad *would* make popcorn" rather than "My dad *made* popcorn," which would have suggested that he did so only once.

Transitions. Tiffany's skillful use of transitional words and expressions links her sentences and moves her readers smoothly through her essay. In addition to transitional words such as *when* and *then,* she uses specific time markers — "When I was little," "Almost every summer afternoon," "every Friday night," "As we walked," "The next day," "In the years to follow," and "After a few years" — to advance the narrative and carry her readers along.

Focus on Revision

In their responses to an earlier draft of Tiffany's essay, several students in her peer-editing group recommended that she revise one particularly monotonous paragraph. (As one student pointed out, all its sentences began with the subject, making the paragraph seem choppy and its ideas disconnected.) Here is the paragraph from her draft:

> My dad played baseball too. I went to the field with my mother every Friday night to watch him play. It was just like the big leagues. There were lots of people and a snack bar. The lights shone so high and bright you could see them a mile away. I loved to go to my dad's games. All the other kids would wander off and play. I would sit and cheer on my dad and his team. My attention was focused on the field. My heart would jump with every pitch.

In the revised version of the paragraph (now paragraph 4 of her essay), Tiffany varies sentence length and opening strategies:

> My dad played baseball too, and every Friday night I would go to the field with my mother to watch him play. It was just like the big leagues, with lots of people, a snack bar, and lights that shone so high and bright you could see them a mile away. I loved to go to my dad's games. When all the other kids would wander off and play, I would sit and cheer on my dad and his team. My attention was focused on the field, and my heart would jump with every pitch.

After reading Tiffany's revised draft, another student suggested that she might still polish her essay a bit. For instance, she could add some dialogue, quoting the boys' taunts and her own reply in paragraph 8. She could also revise to eliminate **clichés** (overused expressions), substituting fresher, more original language for phrases such as "I felt a lump in my throat and butterflies in my stomach" and "felt as if I were on top of the world." In the next draft of her essay, Tiffany followed up on these suggestions.

PEER-EDITING WORKSHEET: Narration

1. What point is the writer making about the essay's subject? Is this point explicitly stated in a thesis statement? If so, where? If not, can you state the essay's thesis in one sentence?

2. List some details that enrich the narrative. Where could more detail be added? What kind of detail? Be specific.

3. Does the writer vary sentence structure and avoid monotonous strings of similar sentences? Should any sentences be combined? If so, which ones? Can you suggest different openings for any sentences?

4. Should any transitions be added to clarify the order in which events occurred? If so, where?

5. Do verb tenses establish a clear chronological order? Identify any verb tenses that you believe need to be changed.

6. Does the writer avoid run-on sentences? Point out any fused sentences or comma splices.

7. What could the writer *add* to this essay?

8. What could the writer take out of this essay?

9. What is the essay's greatest strength? Why?

10. What is the essay's greatest weakness? What steps should the writer take to correct this problem?

The selections that follow illustrate some of the many possibilities open to writers of narratives. The first selection, a visual text, is followed by questions designed to illustrate how narration can operate in visual form. (A multimodal text for narration is located online at **macmillanhighered .com/patterns**.)

MARJANE SATRAPI

from *Persepolis II* (Graphic Fiction)*

TO KEEP US FROM STRAYING OFF THE STRAIGHT PATH, OUR STUDIOS WERE SEPARATED FROM THOSE OF THE BOYS.

I'M YOUR ANATOMY PROFESSOR. IN THE PAST, WE DREW NUDES, BUT THINGS HAVE CHANGED. YOUR MODEL WILL BE COVERED. TRY TO MAKE THE BEST OF IT.

WE TRIED,

WE LOOKED...

...FROM EVERY DIRECTION...

...AND FROM EVERY ANGLE...

BUT NOT A SINGLE PART OF HER BODY WAS VISIBLE.

WE NEVERTHELESS LEARNED TO DRAW DRAPES.

• • •

From *Persepolis II: The Story of a Return*, by Marjane Satrapi, translation © 2004 by Anjali Singh. Used by permission of Pantheon Books, an imprint of the Knopf Doubleday Publishing Group, a division of Random House, LLC. All rights reserved.

* These panels, from the graphic novel *Persepolis II*, tell part of a story about the changes in the life of a young girl during Iran's Islamic revolution. In 1979, the secular monarch was overthrown, and a government run by Islamic religious leaders instituted new rules, including extreme regulations on how women could dress.

Reading Images

1. Look carefully at the panels on page 112, and read the footnote that appears below them. Then, list the events depicted in the panels in the order in which they are shown.

2. What visual elements link each panel to the one that follows? Can you identify any words that serve as transitions? What additional transitional words and phrases might help to move readers from one panel to the next?

3. What do you think happened right before (and right after) the events depicted here?

Journal Entry

Write a narrative paragraph summarizing the story told in these panels. Begin with a sentence that identifies the characters and the setting. Next, write a sentence that summarizes the events that might have preceded the first panel. Then, tell the story the pictures tell. In your last sentence, bring the sequence of events to a logical close. Be sure to use present tense and to include all necessary transitions.

Thematic Connections

- "The Myth of the Latin Woman: I Just Met a Girl Named Maria" (page 230)
- "The Ways We Lie" (page 471)
- "The Wife-Beater" (page 514)
- "Your Flip-Flops Are Grossing Me Out" (page 687)

JUNOT DÍAZ

The Money

Born in the Dominican Republic in 1968 and raised in New Jersey, Junot Díaz earned his bachelor's degree from Rutgers University and an M.F.A. in creative writing from Cornell University. He is the author of several works of fiction, including *Drown* (1996), *The Brief Wondrous Life of Oscar Wao* (2007), and *This Is How You Lose Her* (2012). The winner of many awards, including a Pulitzer Prize and MacArthur and Guggenheim Fellowships, Díaz is the fiction editor at *Boston Review* and the Rudge and Nancy Allen Professor of Writing at the Massachusetts Institute of Technology.

Background on Dominicans in the United States Dominicans living in the United States account for 3 percent of the U.S. Hispanic population; they numbered about 1.5 million when the Census Bureau made its American Community Survey in 2011. For many years, the northeast has been home to the majority of Dominicans in the United States. Although historically almost half settled in New York City, in recent years they have established sizable populations in several other northeastern states, such as New Jersey, Massachusetts, and Pennsylvania. Dominicans living in the United States are significantly more likely to have been born outside the U.S., as Díaz was, than the general Hispanic population (56 percent versus 36 percent). The Dominican population also has a slightly higher poverty rate compared to all Hispanics; however, it can also claim a higher level of education. Dominicans have had an impact on American food, music, and culture, and they are an integral part of social and commercial life in the United States, where they are teachers, bankers, lawyers, small business owners, entrepreneurs, and workers. With a long history of activism, Dominicans have also begun to wield political influence as elected officials in U.S. state, city, and local governments.

All the Dominicans I knew in those days sent money home. My mother 1 didn't have a regular job besides caring for us five kids, so she scrimped the loot together from whatever came her way. My father was always losing his forklift jobs, so it wasn't like she ever had a steady flow. But my grandparents were alone in Santo Domingo, and those remittances, beyond material support, were a way, I suspect, for Mami to negotiate the absence, the distance, caused by our diaspora. She chipped dollars off the cash Papi gave her for our daily expenses, forced our already broke family to live even broker. That was how she built the nut — two, maybe three hundred dollars — that she sent home every six months or so.

We kids knew where the money was hidden, but we also knew that to 2 touch it would have meant a violent punishment approaching death. I, who could take the change out of my mother's purse without thinking, couldn't have brought myself even to look at that forbidden stash.

So what happened? Exactly what you'd think. The summer I was   3
twelve, my family went away on a "vacation" — one of my father's half-
baked get-to-know-our-country-better-by-sleeping-in-the-van extravaganzas — and when we returned to Jersey, exhausted, battered, we found our
front door unlocked. My parents' room, which was where the thieves had
concentrated their search, looked as if it had been tornado-tossed. The
thieves had kept it simple; they'd snatched a portable radio, some of my
Dungeons & Dragons hardcovers, and, of course, Mami's remittances.

It's not as if the robbery came as a huge   4
surprise. In our neighborhood, cars and
apartments were always getting jacked, and
the kid stupid enough to leave a bike unat-
tended for more than a tenth of a second was
the kid who was never going to see that bike
again. Everybody got hit; no matter who you
were, eventually it would be your turn.

> " Everybody got hit;
> no matter who you
> were, eventually it
> would be your turn. "

And that summer it was ours.   5

Still, we took the burglary pretty hard. When you're a recent immigrant,   6
it's easy to feel targeted. Like it wasn't just a couple of assholes that had it
in for you but the whole neighborhood — hell, maybe the whole country.

No one took the robbery as hard as my mom, though. She cursed the   7
neighborhood, she cursed the country, she cursed my father, and of course
she cursed us kids, swore that we had run our gums to our idiot friends and
they had done it.

And this is where the tale should end, right? Wasn't as if there was   8
going to be any "C.S.I."-style investigation or anything. Except that a
couple of days later I was moaning about the robbery to these guys I was
hanging with at that time and they were cursing sympathetically, and out
of nowhere it struck me. You know when you get one of those moments of
mental clarity? When the nictitating membrane obscuring the world suddenly lifts? That's what happened. I realized that these two dopes I called
my friends had done it. They were shaking their heads, mouthing all the
right words, but I could see the way they looked at each other, the Raskolnikov glances. I *knew*.

Now, it wasn't like I could publicly denounce these dolts or go to the   9
police. That would have been about as useless as crying. Here's what I did: I
asked the main dope to let me use his bathroom (we were in front of his
apartment) and while I pretended to piss I unlatched the window. Then we
all headed to the park as usual, but I pretended that I'd forgotten something back home. Ran to the dope's apartment, slid open the bathroom
window, and in broad daylight wriggled my skinny ass in.

Where the hell did I get these ideas? I have not a clue. I guess I was read-   10
ing way too much Encyclopedia Brown and the Three Investigators in those
days. And if mine had been a normal neighborhood this is when the cops
would have been called and my ass would have been caught *burglarizing*.

The dolt and his family had been in the U.S. all their lives and they had   11
a ton of stuff, a TV in every room, but I didn't have to do much searching. I

popped up the dolt's mattress and underneath I found my D.&D. books and most of my mother's money. He had thoughtfully kept it in the same envelope.

And that was how I solved the Case of the Stupid Morons. My one and   12
only case.

The next day at the park, the dolt announced that someone had bro-   13
ken into *his* apartment and stolen all his savings. This place is full of thieves, he complained bitterly, and I was, like, No kidding.

It took me two days to return the money to my mother. The truth was I   14
was seriously considering keeping it. But in the end the guilt got to me. I guess I was expecting my mother to run around with joy, to crown me her favorite son, to cook me my favorite meal. Nada. I'd wanted a party or at least to see her happy, but there was nothing. Just two hundred and some dollars and fifteen hundred or so miles — that's all there was.

·   ·   ·

Comprehension

1. Díaz grew up poor. How does he communicate this fact to readers?

2. According to Díaz, why is the money in his mother's "forbidden stash" (2) different from the money in her purse? Do you think this distinction makes sense?

3. How did Díaz solve "the Case of the Stupid Morons" (12)?

4. What does Díaz mean when he says, "Just two hundred and some dollars and fifteen hundred or so miles — that's all there was" (14)?

Purpose and Audience

1. Even though Díaz uses a very informal style, full of slang expressions, he also uses words like *diaspora* (1) and expressions like "Raskolnikov glances" (8). What does this tell you about him — and about how he sees his audience?

2. This essay does not have a stated thesis. What is Díaz's main idea? Write a sentence that could serve as a thesis statement. Where in the essay could this sentence be added? *Should* such a sentence be added? Why or why not?

3. Does this essay have an informative or a persuasive purpose, or is Díaz just trying to share his memories with readers? Explain.

Style and Structure

1. Identify the one- and two-sentence paragraphs in this essay. Are these very brief paragraphs effective as they are, or should they be expanded or combined with other paragraphs? Explain.

2. This is a personal, informal essay, and it uses first person and contractions. It also includes a number of sentence fragments. Identify a few fragments,

and try to turn each one into a complete sentence. Then, explain why you think Díaz used each fragment.

3. In paragraphs 3, 8, and 10, Díaz asks **rhetorical questions**. How would you answer these questions?

4. **Vocabulary Project.** What words, besides *morons,* does Díaz use to describe the thieves? Which word seems most appropriate to you? Why?

5. Like a crime story, Díaz's narrative moves readers through events from the crime itself to its impact to its final outcome. Identify each of these sections of the narrative.

Journal Entry

Do you think Díaz feels more angry at the "morons" or at himself? Does he also feel frustration? Disappointment? If so, with whom (or what)?

Writing Workshop

1. Díaz mentions Encyclopedia Brown and the Three Investigators, fictional young detectives whose adventures he followed. When you were young, what was as important to you as these fictional characters were to Díaz? In a narrative essay, trace the development of your fascination with a particular fictional character, pastime, or hobby.

2. When he returns the money to his mother, Díaz expects "a party or at least to see her happy" (14), but that isn't the reaction he gets. Write a narrative essay about a time when you expected a particular reaction or outcome but were disappointed or surprised.

3. **Working with Sources.** Consult several dictionaries to find out what the term *diaspora* has meant throughout history. Then, write a narrative essay tracing your own family's diaspora, focusing on their movement from one country, region, or neighborhood to another. Include a definition from one of the dictionaries you consult, and be sure to include parenthetical documentation and a works-cited page. (See Chapter 18 for information on MLA documentation.)

Combining the Patterns

Díaz discusses both his family's life in a Dominican neighborhood in New York City and his relatives' lives back in Santo Domingo. If he wanted to write a **comparison-and-contrast** paragraph comparing his life to his relatives', what details might he include? Do you think he should add such a paragraph? If so, why — and where?

Thematic Connections

- "Indian Education" (page 142)
- "The Ways We Lie" (page 471)
- "Tortillas" (page 506)

ALAN DEAN FOSTER

Living with Fire

Fantasy and science-fiction writer Alan Dean Foster earned a B.A. and an M.F.A. from the University of California, Los Angeles. He has published dozens of novels and short stories, including books set in the Humanx Commonwealth Universe; the Spellsinger series; and novelizations of *Star Trek, Alien,* and *Transformers* films. He is also the author of many standalone novels, including *Kingdoms of Light* (2001) and *Sagramanda* (2006).

Background on wilderness fires In this essay, Foster writes about the Yarnell Hill wildfire, near his home in Prescott, Arizona, which burned from June 28 to July 10 in 2013. Before it was over, the fire had burned 8,500 acres (over 13 square miles), killed 19 people, and destroyed many buildings and homes. Such fires have always been part of America's landscape: the Peshtigo wildfire of 1871 in Peshtigo, Wisconsin, burned 1.2 million acres and killed more than 1,500 people; in 1910, a fire in Montana killed 80. High-profile disasters aside, fires are a natural part of the life cycle of wilderness areas, and they are often beneficial, clearing dead brush, wood, and undergrowth. But over the last several decades, the number — and the destructive power — of such fires has increased significantly. According to U.S. Forest Service Chief Thomas Tidwell, more than 9.3 million acres in the United States burned in 2012, and 51 wildfires exceeded 40,000 acres. Moreover, over the last forty years, the length of the fire season has increased by two months. Researchers cite several variables that may be contributing to this phenomenon, from irresponsible campers and changes in weather patterns to logging practices and the composition of insect populations, but two possible factors stand out. First, climate change may be leading to hotter, drier summers, as well as to shifts in regional weather in Western states such as Arizona and California. Second, as the population grows in the American South and West, homes are increasingly being built in areas prone to fires. Ironically, attempts to control and prevent forest and wilderness fires may actually be contributing to the problem as well because smaller, naturally occurring burns can often remove the deadwood and brush that could lead to much more devastating fires.

When you build a fire in a fireplace, you start with paper, add kindling, 1 and finally arrange the larger logs on top. That perfectly describes the summertime environment in the southwestern mountains of the United States.

Yet many thousands of us choose to live here. 2

I live in Prescott, Arizona, where a wildfire called the Doce fire is now 3 almost completely contained, after burning 6,767 tinder-dry acres. It started two weeks ago, six miles or so from the house where my wife and I have lived for more than thirty years.

We live in the bottom of a small canyon, and it took a moment for me 4 to realize that the smoke I was seeing from the study window was all wrong. Distant fires, which we are used to, score the blue sky with a thin haze, like a watercolorist's brown wash. But this cloud was massive, a darker brown, moving too fast, and flush with orange .

I drove to the top of the highest hill behind our house and as I swung 5 around the crest, between homes with neat desert landscaping, a view opened before me that bordered on the apocalyptic. Someone had switched the channel of my life.

The mountains were on fire. At that moment the wind was so strong 6 that much of the smoke was lying down, the flames blown almost parallel to the ground. It didn't look like a movie. I could smell it.

Confronted by the immediacy of destruction, technology is the first 7 thing that flees. I was reduced to tossing bits of dried weed into the air to check the direction of the wind. You think: water, family, pets. What do I put in the car first? By then the mass of orange-brown smoke had taken over the north sky.

Move, your mind tells you. Yet you can't stop staring. If you stare at it 8 long enough, perhaps it will go away.

But the monster doesn't go away. It burns north-northeast, luckily 9 almost directly away from our house. It burns right into the backyards of some homes, but no structures are lost, no lives are lost, thanks to the coordination of multiple fire units.

Among the best of these, the front-line fighters, are the Hotshots. 10 They're the best trained, the best conditioned, the hardest working of all. They go right up to the fire line, and sometimes into it.

On Sunday they showed up to fight another fire, near the small, pic- 11 turesque town of Yarnell, some thirty miles southwest of here. At first it wasn't a big fire, nor was it considered a dangerous one.

But a monsoon blew up. The southwest monsoon is not technically 12 a monsoon, but that's what we call it. Rain poured down in Prescott — welcome, drenching rain. Out in front of the storm, however, winds rose, turned erratic.

The fire essentially flipped over a team of Hotshots, the Granite Moun- 13 tain Hotshots, from Prescott. Nineteen of them died, the worst loss of firefighter life in a wildland fire in Arizona's history, the worst in the country in eighty years. The greatest tragedy to strike the firefighting profession since 9/11.

I did not know any of them personally, 14 but based on the group photo that has been widely distributed, I think some of them went to my gym. It's strange to think I won't see them again. Small blank spaces in one's existence that used to be occupied by actual people.

> " No place is safe. Not on this planet. "

Terrible calamity, the television anchors keep repeating. Horrible trag- 15 edy. If you live here, you don't need those words. You call those you know to make sure they're O.K. You meet people in the drugstore, on the street. A knowing look, a regretful nod convey all that needs to be said. People living in proximity to disaster don't shout; they just prepare in case it turns and comes for them.

Two major fires in two weeks. Why stay there, people who live else- 16 where must wonder as they watch such tragedies unfold. Why not move someplace where you don't spend every summer wondering if your house is going to burn down.

Why do humans live on the slopes of active volcanoes? Why do they 17 live atop major earthquake faults? Why on earth do people continue to dwell, year after year, in a part of the country called Tornado Alley?

Because such places are beautiful, are peaceful, and, for better or worse, 18 are home. No place is safe. Not on this planet. So you choose your home for what you love about it, and not what you fear. If we let fear dictate where we should live, we would all end up huddled together in one great shivering ball of humanity, and that wouldn't be safe, either.

The Doce fire could have been infinitely worse. All it would have taken 19 was a shift in the wind. Yarnell is still burning. But I have to go feed the towhees and the hummingbirds, maybe shoo away a too-curious coyote. This is my home, and I'll deal with Mother Nature's dark side when and if it comes my way. As must we all.

• • •

Comprehension

1. Why was Foster confused when he first saw the fire from his study window?

2. In paragraph 7, Foster says, "Confronted by the immediacy of destruction, technology is the first thing that flees." What does he mean?

3. What immediate response did Foster have as he looked at the fire from the hill behind his house? In what sense is his reaction a **paradox**?

4. Who are the Granite Mountain Hotshots?

5. Foster observes that people who live "in proximity to disaster don't shout" (15). What do they do instead? Why?

6. According to Foster, why do people choose to live in areas that are prone to natural disasters?

Purpose and Audience

1. What is Foster's thesis? How would you restate it in your own words? What do you think he wants his essay to accomplish?

2. At several points in the essay, Foster asks rhetorical questions. What do these questions suggest about Foster's view of his audience?

3. Why do you think Foster includes the story of the Granite Mountain Hotshots? How does it support his overall purpose?

4. What do you think Foster hopes to accomplish in his essay's last two sentences? Do you think he is successful?

Style and Structure

1. Foster begins his essay with an **analogy**. Is this an appropriate opening strategy? Why or why not?

2. In paragraph 15, Foster writes, "If you live here, you don't need those words." To which words is he referring?

3. **Vocabulary Project.** When Foster sees the fire from a hill near his house, the view "bordered on the apocalyptic" (5). What does *apocalyptic* mean? Do you think the choice of this word is appropriate, or does the word seem overdramatic? Explain.

4. How would you describe Foster's attitude toward the fire and its consequences? Fearful? Angry? Exhilarated? How does he convey this attitude to the reader?

Journal Entry

In this essay, Foster writes about the experience of confronting the "immediacy of destruction" (7). Have you ever had an experience of this kind? Even if you have not witnessed disaster or tragedy on a grand scale, have you ever confronted a scene or situation that "switched the channel" (5) in your life? If so, how did you respond? Did you learn anything from the experience?

Writing Workshop

1. In paragraphs 16 and 17, Foster asks several rhetorical questions about people (like himself) who choose to live in areas prone to natural disasters. Consider the dangers — from nature or from other factors — that have threatened you (or that you think might threaten you in the future) in the place where you live. Then, write a narrative essay about a danger that you have faced (or might face) in your home or neighborhood.

2. **Working with Sources.** As the headnote explains, Foster is a fantasy and science-fiction writer. In what sense does this essay incorporate elements of fantasy or science fiction? How could the landscape it describes, and the central "apocalyptic" event, serve as background for a fantasy or science-fiction story? Write a fictional narrative that traces the events Foster describes. If you quote Foster's essay, be sure to cite your source and to include a works-cited page. (See Chapter 18 for information on MLA documentation.)

3. Think about the factors that Foster identifies as important: beauty, peacefulness, and the sense that some places are just "home" (18). Then, consider the power of a natural or man-made disaster to destroy that sense of home. In a narrative essay, write about a disaster that you witnessed or read about. How did this disaster shape (or change) what *home* means to you?

Combining the Patterns

How does Foster incorporate **description** into his narrative? Point to specific examples. Given the overall purpose of his essay, do you think Foster might want to limit his use of description and focus more on narrative action? Or should he do just the reverse?

Thematic Connections

- "Ground Zero" (page 175)
- "The Storm" (page 198)
- "A Peaceful Woman Explains Why She Carries a Gun" (page 353)
- "Homeless" (page 510)

BONNIE SMITH-YACKEL

My Mother Never Worked

Bonnie Smith-Yackel was born into a farm family in Willmar, Minnesota, in 1937. She began writing as a young homemaker in the early 1960s and for the next fourteen years published short stories, essays, and book reviews in such publications as *Catholic Digest, Minnesota Monthly,* and *Ms.* magazine, as well as in several local newspapers. As Smith-Yackel explains it, "The catalyst for writing the [following] essay shortly after my mother's death was recounting my telephone conversation with Social Security to the lawyer who was helping me settle my mother's estate. When I told him what the SS woman had said, he responded: 'Well, that's right. Your mother didn't work, you know.' At which point I stood and said, 'She worked harder throughout her life than you or a hundred men like you!' and stomped out of his office, drove home, sat down and wrote the essay in one sitting." Although this narrative essay, first published in *Women: A Journal of Liberation* in 1975, is based on personal experience, it also makes a broader statement about how society values "women's work."

Background on Social Security benefits Social Security is a federal insurance program that requires workers to contribute a percentage of their wages to a fund that they may draw benefits from if they become unemployed due to disability. After retirement, workers can receive a monthly income from this fund, which also provides a modest death benefit to survivors. The contribution is generally deducted directly from a worker's paycheck, and employers must contribute a matching amount. According to federal law, a woman who is a homemaker, who has never been a wage earner, is eligible for Social Security benefits only through the earnings of her deceased husband. (The same would be true for a man if the roles were reversed.) Therefore, a homemaker's survivors would not be eligible for the death benefit. Although the law has been challenged in the courts, the survivors of a homemaker who has never been a wage earner are still not entitled to a Social Security death benefit.

"Social Security Office." (The voice answering the telephone sounds very self-assured.) 1

"I'm calling about . . . my mother just died . . . I was told to call you and see about a . . . death-benefit check, I think they call it. . . ." 2

"I see. Was your mother on Social Security? How old was she?" 3

"Yes . . . she was seventy-eight. . . ." 4

"Do you know her number?" 5

"No . . . I, ah . . . don't you have a record?" 6

"Certainly. I'll look it up. Her name?" 7

"Smith. Martha Smith. Or maybe she used Martha Ruth Smith? . . . Sometimes she used her maiden name . . . Martha Jerabek Smith?" 8

"If you'd care to hold on, I'll check our records — it'll be a few minutes." 9

"Yes. . . ." 10

Her love letters — to and from Daddy — were in an old box, tied with 11
ribbons and stiff, rigid-with-age leather thongs: 1918 through 1920; hers
written on stationery from the general store she had worked in full-time
and managed, single-handed, after her graduation from high school in
1913; and his, at first, on YMCA or Soldiers and Sailors Club stationery
dispensed to the fighting men of World War I. He wooed her thoroughly
and persistently by mail, and though she reciprocated all his feelings for
her, she dreaded marriage. . . .

"It's so hard for me to decide when to have my wedding day — that's all 12
I've thought about these last two days. I have told you dozens of times that
I won't be afraid of married life, but when it comes down to setting the date
and then picturing myself a married woman with half a dozen or more kids
to look after, it just makes me sick. . . . I am weeping right now — I hope
that some day I can look back and say how foolish I was to dread it all."

They married in February, 1921, and began farming. Their first baby, a 13
daughter, was born in January, 1922, when my mother was twenty-six years
old. The second baby, a son, was born in March, 1923. They were renting
farms; my father, besides working his own fields, also was a hired man for
two other farmers. They had no capital initially, and had to gain it slowly,
working from dawn until midnight every day. My town-bred mother
learned to set hens and raise chickens, feed pigs, milk cows, plant and harvest a garden, and can every fruit and vegetable she could scrounge. She
carried water nearly a quarter of a mile from the well to fill her wash boilers
in order to do her laundry on a scrub board. She learned to shuck grain,
feed threshers, shock and husk corn, feed corn pickers. In September, 1925,
the third baby came, and in June, 1927, the fourth child — both daughters.
In 1930, my parents had enough money to buy their own farm, and that
March they moved all their livestock and belongings themselves, fifty-five
miles over rutted, muddy roads.

In the summer of 1930 my mother and her two eldest children re- 14
claimed a forty-acre field from Canadian thistles, by chopping them all out
with a hoe. In the other fields, when the oats and flax began to head out,
the green and blue of the crops were hidden by the bright yellow of wild
mustard. My mother walked the fields day after day, pulling each mustard
plant. She raised a new flock of baby chicks — five hundred — and she
spaded up, planted, hoed, and harvested a half-acre garden.

During the next spring their hogs caught cholera and died. No cash 15
that fall.

And in the next year the drought hit. My mother and father trudged 16
from the well to the chickens, the well to the calf pasture, the well to the
barn, and from the well to the garden. The sun came out hot and bright,
endlessly, day after day. The crops shriveled and died. They harvested half
the corn, and ground the other half, stalks and all, and fed it to the cattle as
fodder. With the price at four cents a bushel for the harvested crop, they
couldn't afford to haul it into town. They burned it in the furnace for fuel
that winter.

In 1934, in February, when the dust was still so thick in the Minnesota   17
air that my parents couldn't always see from the house to the barn, their
fifth child — a fourth daughter — was born. My father hunted rabbits daily,
and my mother stewed them, fried them, canned them, and wished out
loud that she could taste hamburger once more. In the fall the shotgun
brought prairie chickens, ducks, pheasant, and grouse. My mother plucked
each bird, carefully reserving the breast feathers for pillows.

In the winter she sewed night after night, endlessly, begging cast-off   18
clothing from relatives, ripping apart coats, dresses, blouses, and trousers
to remake them to fit her four daughters and son. Every morning and every
evening she milked cows, fed pigs and calves, cared for chickens, picked
eggs, cooked meals, washed dishes, scrubbed floors, and tended and loved
her children. In the spring she planted a garden once more, dragging pails
of water to nourish and sustain the vegetables for the family. In 1936 she
lost a baby in her sixth month.

In 1937 her fifth daughter was born. She was forty-two years old. In   19
1939 a second son, and in 1941 her eighth child — and third son.

But the war had come, and prosperity of a sort. The herd of cattle had   20
grown to thirty head; she still milked morning and evening. Her garden
was more than a half acre — the rains had come, and by now the Rural Electricity Administration and indoor plumbing. Still she sewed — dresses and
jackets for the children, housedresses and aprons for herself, weekly patching of jeans, overalls, and denim shirts. She still made pillows, using feathers she had plucked, and quilts every year — intricate patterns as well as
patchwork, stitched as well as tied — all necessary bedding for her family.
Every scrap of cloth too small to be used in quilts was carefully saved and
painstakingly sewed together in strips to make rugs. She still went out in
the fields to help with the haying whenever there was a threat of rain.

In 1959 my mother's last child graduated from high school. A year   21
later the cows were sold. She still raised chickens and ducks, plucked feathers, made pillows, baked her own bread, and every year made a new quilt —
now for a married child or for a grandchild. And her garden, that huge,
undying symbol of sustenance, was as large and cared for as in all the years
before. The canning, and now freezing, continued.

In 1969, on a June afternoon, mother and father started out for town   22
so that she could buy sugar to make rhubarb jam for a daughter who lived
in Texas. The car crashed into a ditch. She was paralyzed from the waist
down.

In 1970 her husband, my father, died. My mother struggled to regain   23
some competence and dignity and order
in her life. At the rehabilitation institute,
where they gave her physical therapy and
trained her to live usefully in a wheelchair,
the therapist told me: "She did fifteen push-
ups today — fifteen! She's almost seventy-
five years old! I've never known a woman so
strong!"

> "Well, you see —
> your mother never
> worked."

From her wheelchair she canned pickles, baked bread, ironed clothes, 24
wrote dozens of letters weekly to her friends and her "half dozen or more
kids," and made three patchwork housecoats and one quilt. She made balls
and balls of carpet rags — enough for five rugs. And kept all her love letters.

"I think I've found your mother's records — Martha Ruth Smith; mar- 25
ried to Ben F. Smith?"

"Yes, that's right." 26

"Well, I see that she was getting a widow's pension. . . ." 27

"Yes, that's right." 28

"Well, your mother isn't entitled to our $255 death benefit." 29

"Not entitled! But why?" 30

The voice on the telephone explains patiently: 31

"Well, you see — your mother never worked." 32

· · ·

Comprehension

1. What kind of work did Martha Smith do while her children were growing up? List some of the chores she performed.

2. Why aren't Martha Smith's survivors entitled to a death benefit when their mother dies?

3. How does the government define *work*?

Purpose and Audience

1. What point is the writer trying to make? Why do you suppose her thesis is never explicitly stated?

2. This essay appeared in *Ms.* magazine and other publications whose audiences are sympathetic to feminist goals. Could it have appeared in a magazine whose audience had a more traditional view of gender roles? Explain.

3. Smith-Yackel mentions relatively little about her father in this essay. How can you account for this?

4. This essay was first published in 1975. Do you think it is dated, or do you think the issues it raises are still relevant today?

Style and Structure

1. Is the essay's title effective? If so, why? If not, what alternate title can you suggest?

2. Smith-Yackel could have outlined her mother's life without framing it with the telephone conversation. Why do you think she includes this frame?

3. What strategies does Smith-Yackel use to indicate the passing of time in her narrative?

4. This narrative piles details one on top of another almost like a list. Why does the writer include so many details?

5. In paragraphs 20 and 21, what is accomplished by the repetition of the word *still*?

6. **Vocabulary Project.** Try substituting equivalent words for those italicized in this sentence:

> He *wooed* her *thoroughly* and *persistently* by mail, and though she *reciprocated* all his feelings for her, she *dreaded* marriage . . . (11).

How do your substitutions change the sentence's meaning?

Journal Entry

Do you believe that a homemaker who has never been a wage earner should be entitled to a Social Security death benefit for her survivors? Explain your reasoning.

Writing Workshop

1. **Working with Sources.** Interview one of your parents or grandparents (or another person you know who reminds you of Smith-Yackel's mother) about his or her work history, and write a chronological narrative based on what you learn. Include a thesis statement that your narrative can support, and quote your family member's responses when possible. Be sure to include parenthetical documentation for these quotations, and also include a works-cited page. (See Chapter 18 for information on MLA documentation.)

2. Write Martha Smith's obituary as it might have appeared in her hometown newspaper. (If you are not familiar with the form of an obituary, read a few in your local paper or online at Legacy.com or Obituaries.com.)

3. Write a narrative account of a typical day at the worst job you ever had. Include a thesis statement that expresses your negative feelings.

Combining the Patterns

Because of the repetitive nature of the farm chores Smith-Yackel describes in her narrative, some passages come very close to explaining a **process**, a series of repeated steps that always occur in a predictable order. Identify several such passages. If Smith-Yackel's essay were written entirely as a process explanation, what material would have to be left out? How would these omissions change the essay?

Thematic Connections

- "Midnight" (page 217)
- " 'Girl' " (page 259)
- "Aristotle" (page 481)
- "I Want a Wife" (page 502)

MARTIN GANSBERG

Thirty-Eight Who Saw Murder Didn't Call the Police

Martin Gansberg (1920–1995), a native of Brooklyn, New York, was a reporter and editor for the *New York Times* for forty-three years. The following article, written for the *Times* two weeks after the 1964 murder it recounts, earned Gansberg an award for excellence from the Newspaper Reporters Association of New York. Gansberg's thesis, though not explicitly stated, still retains its power.

Background on the Kitty Genovese murder case The events reported here took place on March 14, 1964, as contemporary American culture was undergoing a complex transition. The relatively placid years of the 1950s were giving way to more troubling times: the civil rights movement was leading to social unrest in the South and in northern inner cities; the escalating war in Vietnam was creating angry political divisions; President John F. Kennedy had been assassinated just four months earlier; violent imagery was increasing in television and film; crime rates were rising; and a growing drug culture was becoming apparent. The brutal, senseless murder of Kitty Genovese — and, more important, her neighbors' failure to respond immediately to her cries for help — became a nationwide, and even worldwide, symbol for what was perceived as an evolving culture of violence and indifference.

In recent years, some of the details Gansberg mentions have been challenged. For example, as the *New York Times* now acknowledges, there were only two attacks on Ms. Genovese, not three; the first attack may have been shorter than first reported; the second attack may have occurred in the apartment house foyer, where neighbors would not have been able to see Genovese; and some witnesses may, in fact, actually *have* called the police. At the time, however, the world was shocked by the incident, and even today social scientists around the world debate the causes of "the Genovese syndrome."

For more than half an hour thirty-eight respectable, law-abiding citizens in Queens watched a killer stalk and stab a woman in three separate attacks in Kew Gardens. 1

Twice their chatter and the sudden glow of their bedroom lights interrupted him and frightened him off. Each time he returned, sought her out, and stabbed her again. Not one person telephoned the police during the assault; one witness called after the woman was dead. 2

That was two weeks ago today. 3

Still shocked is Assistant Chief Inspector Frederick M. Lussen, in charge of the borough's detectives and a veteran of twenty-five years of homicide investigations. He can give a matter-of-fact recitation on many murders. 4

But the Kew Gardens slaying baffles him — not because it is a murder, but because the "good people" failed to call the police.

"As we have reconstructed the crime," he said, "the assailant had three chances to kill this woman during a thirty-five-minute period. He returned twice to complete the job. If we had been called when he first attacked, the woman might not be dead now."

> " Not one person telephoned the police during the assault; one witness called after the woman was dead. " 5

This is what the police say happened beginning at 3:20 A.M. in the staid, middle-class, tree-lined Austin Street area:

3:20 AM 6

Twenty-eight-year-old Catherine Genovese, who was called Kitty by 7 almost everyone in the neighborhood, was returning home from her job as manager of a bar in Hollis. She parked her red Fiat in a lot adjacent to the Kew Gardens Long Island Rail Road Station, facing Mowbray Place. Like many residents of the neighborhood, she had parked there day after day since her arrival from Connecticut a year ago, although the railroad frowns on the practice.

She turned off the lights of her car, locked the door, and started to 8 walk the one hundred feet to the entrance of her apartment at 82-70 Austin Street, which is in a Tudor building, with stores in the first floor and apartments on the second.

The entrance to the apartment is in the rear of the building because the 9 front is rented to retail stores. At night the quiet neighborhood is shrouded in the slumbering darkness that marks most residential areas.

Miss Genovese noticed a man at the far end of the lot, near a seven- 10 story apartment house at 82-40 Austin Street. She halted. Then, nervously, she headed up Austin Street toward Lefferts Boulevard, where there is a call box to the 102nd Police Precinct in nearby Richmond Hill.

She got as far as a street light in front of a bookstore before the man 11 grabbed her. She screamed. Lights went on in the ten-story apartment house at 82-67 Austin Street, which faces the bookstore. Windows slid open and voices punctuated the early-morning stillness.

Miss Genovese screamed: "Oh, my God, he stabbed me! Please help 12 me! Please help me!"

From one of the upper windows in the apartment house, a man called 13 down: "Let that girl alone!"

The assailant looked up at him, shrugged, and walked down Austin 14 Street toward a white sedan parked a short distance away. Miss Genovese struggled to her feet.

Lights went out. The killer returned to Miss Genovese, now trying to 15 make her way around the side of the building by the parking lot to get to her apartment. The assailant stabbed her again.

"I'm dying!" she shrieked. "I'm dying!" 16

Windows were opened again, and lights went on in many apartments. 17 The assailant got into his car and drove away. Miss Genovese staggered to

assailant drove away

her feet. A city bus, 0–10, the Lefferts Boulevard line to Kennedy International Airport, passed. It was 3:35 A.M.

The assailant returned. By then, Miss Genovese had crawled to the back of the building, where the freshly painted brown doors to the apartment house held out hope for safety. The killer tried the first door; she wasn't there. At the second door, 82-62 Austin Street, he saw her slumped on the floor at the foot of the stairs. He stabbed her a third time — fatally.   18

It was 3:50 by the time the police received their first call, from a man who was a neighbor of Miss Genovese. In two minutes they were at the scene. The neighbor, a seventy-year-old woman, and another woman were the only persons on the street. Nobody else came forward.   19

The man explained that he had called the police after much deliberation. He had phoned a friend in Nassau County for advice, and then he had crossed the roof of the building to the apartment of the elderly woman to get her to make the call.   20

"I didn't want to get involved," he sheepishly told police.   21

Six days later, the police arrested Winston Moseley, a twenty-nine-year-old business machine operator, and charged him with homicide. Moseley had no previous record. He is married, has two children, and owns a home at 133-19 Sutter Avenue, South Ozone Park, Queens. On Wednesday, a court committed him to Kings County Hospital for psychiatric observation.   22

When questioned by the police, Moseley also said that he had slain Mrs. Annie May Johnson, twenty-four, of 146-12 133d Avenue, Jamaica, on Feb. 29 and Barbara Kralik, fifteen, of 174-17 140th Avenue, Springfield Gardens, last July. In the Kralik case, the police are holding Alvin L. Mitchell, who is said to have confessed to that slaying.   23

The police stressed how simple it would have been to have gotten in touch with them. "A phone call," said one of the detectives, "would have done it." The police may be reached by dialing "0" for operator or SPring 7-3100.   24

Today witnesses from the neighborhood, which is made up of one-family homes in the $35,000 to $60,000 range with the exception of the two apartment houses near the railroad station, find it difficult to explain why they didn't call the police.   25

A housewife, knowingly if quite casually, said, "We thought it was a lovers' quarrel." A husband and wife both said, "Frankly, we were afraid." They seemed aware of the fact that events might have been different. A distraught woman, wiping her hands in her apron, said, "I didn't want my husband to get involved."   26

One couple, now willing to talk about that night, said they heard the first screams. The husband looked thoughtfully at the bookstore where the killer first grabbed Miss Genovese.   27

"We went to the window to see what was happening," he said, "but the light from our bedroom made it difficult to see the street." The wife, still apprehensive, added: "I put out the light and we were able to see better."   28

Asked why they hadn't called the police, she shrugged and replied: "I 29
don't know."

A man peeked out from a slight opening in the doorway to his apart- 30
ment and rattled off an account of the killer's second attack. Why hadn't
he called the police at the time? "I was tired," he said without emotion. "I
went back to bed."

It was 4:25 A.M. when the ambulance arrived to take the body of Miss 31
Genovese. It drove off. "Then," a solemn police detective said, "the people
came out."

Comprehension

1. According to Gansberg, how much time elapsed between the first stabbing of Kitty Genovese and the time when the people finally came out?

2. What excuses do the neighbors make for not coming to Kitty Genovese's
   aid?

Purpose and Audience

1. This article appeared in 1964. What effect was it intended to have on its
   audience? Do you think it has the same impact today, or has its impact
   changed or diminished?

2. What is the article's main point? Why does Gansberg imply his thesis
   rather than state it explicitly?

3. What is Gansberg's purpose in describing the Austin Street area as "staid,
   middle-class, tree-lined" (6)?

4. Why do you suppose Gansberg provides the police department's phone
   number in his article? (Note that New York City did not have 911 emergency service in 1964.)

Style and Structure

1. Gansberg is very precise in this article, especially in his references to time,
   addresses, and ages. Why?

2. The objective newspaper style is dominant in this article, but the writer's
   anger shows through. Point to words and phrases that reveal his attitude
   toward his material.

3. Because this article was originally set in the narrow columns of a newspaper, it has many short paragraphs. Would the narrative be more effective if some of these brief paragraphs were combined? If so, why? If not,
   why not? Give examples to support your answer.

4. **Vocabulary Project.** The word *assailant* appears frequently in this article.
   Why is it used so often? What impact is this repetition likely to have on
   readers? What other words could have been used?

5. Review the dialogue quoted in this article. Does it strengthen Gansberg's narrative? Would the article be more compelling with additional dialogue? Without dialogue? Explain.

6. This article does not have a formal conclusion; nevertheless, the last paragraph sums up the writer's attitude. How?

Journal Entry

In a similar situation, would you have called the police? Would you have gone outside to help? What factors might have influenced your decision?

Writing Workshop

1. In your own words, write a ten-sentence **summary** (see page 720) of this newspaper article. Try to reflect Gansberg's order and emphasis as well as his ideas, and be sure to include all necessary transitions.

2. Rewrite the article as if it were a blog post by one of the thirty-eight people who watched the murder. Summarize what you saw, and explain why you decided not to call for help. (You may invent details that Gansberg does not include.) If you like, you can first visit the website oldkewgardens.com, which includes a detailed critique of Gansberg's article as well as photos of the area in which the crime took place.

3. **Working with Sources.** If you have ever been involved in or witnessed a situation in which someone was in trouble, write a narrative essay about the incident. If people failed to help the person in trouble, explain why you think no one acted. If people did act, tell how. Be sure to account for your own actions. In your essay's introduction, refer to Gansberg's account of Kitty Genovese's murder. If you quote Gansberg, be sure to include documentation and a works-cited page. (See Chapter 18 for information on MLA documentation.)

Combining the Patterns

Because the purpose of this newspaper article is to give basic factual information, it has no extended descriptions of the victim, the witnesses, or the crime scene. It also does not explain *why* those who watched did not act. Where might passages of **description** or **cause and effect** be added? How might such additions change the article's impact on readers? Do you think they would strengthen the article?

Thematic Connections

- "Shooting an Elephant" (page 133)
- "The Lottery" (page 308)
- "Who Killed Benny Paret?" (page 337)
- "A Peaceful Woman Explains Why She Carries a Gun" (page 353)

GEORGE ORWELL

Shooting an Elephant

George Orwell (1903–1950) was born Eric Blair in Bengal, India, where his father was a British civil servant. Rather than attend university, Orwell joined the Imperial Police in neighboring Burma (now renamed Myanmar), where he served from 1922 to 1927. Finding himself increasingly opposed to British colonial rule, Orwell left Burma to live and write in Paris and London. A political liberal and a fierce moralist, Orwell is best known today for his novels *Animal Farm* (1945) and *1984* (1949), which portray the dangers of totalitarianism. In "Shooting an Elephant," written in 1936, he recalls an incident from his days in Burma that clarified his thinking about British colonial rule.

Background on British imperialism The British had gradually taken over Burma through a succession of wars beginning in 1824; by 1885, the domination was complete. Like a number of other European countries, Britain had forcibly established colonial rule in countries throughout the world during the eighteenth and nineteenth centuries, primarily to exploit their natural resources. This empire building, known as *imperialism,* was justified by the belief that European culture was superior to the cultures of the indigenous peoples, particularly in Asia and Africa. Therefore, imperialist nations claimed, it was "the white man's burden" to bring civilization to these "heathen" lands. In most cases, such control could be achieved only through force. Anti-imperialist sentiment began to grow in the early twentieth century, but colonial rule continued until the mid-twentieth century in much of the less-developed world. Not until the late 1940s did many European colonies begin to gain independence. The British ceded home rule to Burma in 1947.

In Moulmein, in Lower Burma, I was hated by large numbers of 1 people — the only time in my life that I have been important enough for this to happen to me. I was sub-divisional police officer of the town, and in an aimless, petty kind of way anti-European feeling was very bitter. No one had the guts to raise a riot, but if a European woman went through the bazaars alone somebody would probably spit betel juice over her dress. As a police officer I was an obvious target and was baited whenever it seemed safe to do so. When a nimble Burman tripped me up on the football field and the referee (another Burman) looked the other way, the crowd yelled with hideous laughter. This happened more than once. In the end the sneering yellow faces of young men that met me everywhere, the insults hooted after me when I was at a safe distance, got badly on my nerves. The young Buddhist priests were the worst of all. There were several thousands of them in the town and none of them seemed to have anything to do except stand on street corners and jeer at Europeans.

Secretly all
for the
Burmese

All this was perplexing and upsetting. For at that time I had already 2 made up my mind that imperialism was an evil thing and the sooner I chucked up my job and got out of it the better. Theoretically — and secretly, of course — I was all for the Burmese and all against their oppressors, the British. As for the job I was doing, I hated it more bitterly than I can per- haps make clear. In a job like that you see the dirty work of Empire at close quarters. The wretched prisoners huddling in the stinking cages of the lockups, the grey, cowed faces of the long-term convicts, the scarred but- tocks of the men who had been flogged with bamboos — all these oppressed me with an intolerable sense of guilt. But I could get nothing into perspec- tive. I was young and ill-educated and I had had to think out my problems in the utter silence that is imposed on every Englishman in the East. I did not even know that the British Empire is dying, still less did I know that it is a great deal better than the younger empires that are going to supplant it.* All I knew was that I was stuck between my hatred of the empire I served and my rage against the evil-spirited little beasts who tried to make my job impossible. With one part of my mind I thought of the British Raj** as an unbreakable tyranny, as something clamped down, in *saecula saeculorum*,*** upon the will of prostrate peoples; with another part I thought that the greatest joy in the world would be to drive a bayonet into a Buddhist priest's guts. Feelings like these are the normal by-products of imperialism; ask any Anglo-Indian official, if you can catch him off duty.

stuck
between
hatred &
rage

One day something happened which in a roundabout way was enlight- 3 ening. It was a tiny incident in itself, but it gave me a better glimpse than I had had before of the real nature of imperi- alism — the real motives for which despotic governments act. Early one morning the sub- inspector at a police station the other end of the town rang me up on the phone and said that an elephant was ravaging the bazaar. Would I please come and do something about it? I did not know what I could do, but I wanted to see what was happening and I got on to a pony and started out. I took my rifle, an old .44 Winchester and much too small to kill an elephant, but I thought the

> " It was a tiny incident in itself, but it gave me a better glimpse than I had had before of the real nature of imperialism. . . . "

noise might be useful *in terrorem.*† Various Burmans stopped me on the way and told me about the elephant's doings. It was not, of course, a wild ele- phant, but a tame one which had gone "must."‡ It had been chained up, as

in heat

---

* Eds. note — Orwell was writing in 1936, when Hitler and Stalin were in power and World War II was only three years away.

** Eds. note — The former British rule of the Indian subcontinent.

*** Eds. note — From time immemorial.

† Eds. note — For the purpose of frightening.

‡ Eds. note — Was in heat, a condition likely to wear off.

tame elephants always are when their attack of "must" is due, but on the previous night it had broken its chain and escaped. Its mahout,* the only person who could manage it when it was in that state, had set out in pursuit, but had taken the wrong direction and was now twelve hours' journey away, and in the morning the elephant had suddenly reappeared in the town. The Burmese population had no weapons and were quite helpless against it. It had already destroyed somebody's bamboo hut, killed a cow, and raided some fruit-stalls and devoured the stock; also it had met the municipal rubbish van and, when the driver jumped out and took to his heels, had turned the van over and inflicted violences upon it.

The Burmese sub-inspector and some Indian constables were waiting 4 for me in the quarter where the elephant had been seen. It was a very poor quarter, a labyrinth of squalid bamboo huts, thatched with palm-leaf, winding all over a steep hillside. I remember that it was a cloudy, stuffy morning at the beginning of the rains. We began questioning people as to where the elephant had gone, and, as usual, failed to get any definite information. That is invariably the case in the East; a story always sounds clear enough at a distance, but the nearer you get to the scene of events the vaguer it becomes. Some of the people said that the elephant had gone in one direction, some said that he had gone in another, some professed not even to have heard of an elephant. I had almost made up my mind that the whole story was a pack of lies, when we heard yells a little distance away. There was a loud, scandalized cry of "Go away, child! Go away this instant!" and an old woman with a switch in her hand came round the corner of a hut, violently shooing away a crowd of naked children. Some more women followed, clicking their tongues and exclaiming; evidently there was something that the children ought not to have seen. I rounded the hut and saw a man's dead body sprawling in the mud. He was an Indian, a black Dravidian coolie,** almost naked, and he could not have been dead many minutes. The people said that the elephant had come suddenly upon him round the corner of the hut, caught him with its trunk, put its foot on his back, and ground him into the earth. This was the rainy season and the ground was soft, and his face had scored a trench a foot deep and a couple of yards long. He was lying on his belly with arms crucified and head sharply twisted to one side. His face was coated with mud, the eyes wide open, the teeth bared and grinning with an expression of unendurable agony. (Never tell me, by the way, that the dead look peaceful. Most of the corpses I have seen looked devilish.) The friction of the great beast's foot had stripped the skin from his back as neatly as one skins a rabbit. As soon as I saw the dead man I sent an orderly to a friend's house nearby to borrow an elephant rifle. I had already sent back the pony, not wanting it to go mad with fright and throw me if it smelled the elephant.

The orderly came back in a few minutes with a rifle and five cartridges, 5 and meanwhile some Burmans had arrived and told us that the elephant

---

* Eds. note — A keeper and driver of an elephant.

** Eds. note — An unskilled laborer.

was in the paddy* fields below, only a few hundred yards away. As I started forward practically the whole population of the quarter flocked out of the houses and followed me. They had seen the rifle and were all shouting excitedly that I was going to shoot the elephant. They had not shown much interest in the elephant when he was merely ravaging their homes, but it was different now that he was going to be shot. It was a bit of fun to them, as it would be to an English crowd; besides they wanted the meat. It made me vaguely uneasy. I had no intention of shooting the elephant — I had merely sent for the rifle to defend myself if necessary — and it is always unnerving to have a crowd following you. I marched down the hill, looking and feeling a fool, with the rifle over my shoulder and an ever-growing army of people jostling at my heels. At the bottom, when you got away from the huts, there was a metalled road and beyond that a miry waste of paddy fields a thousand yards across, not yet ploughed but soggy from the first rains and dotted with coarse grass. The elephant was standing eight yards from the road, his left side towards us. He took not the slightest notice of the crowd's approach. He was tearing up bunches of grass, beating them against his knees to clean them and stuffing them into his mouth.

I had halted on the road. As soon as I saw the elephant I knew with per- 6 fect certainty that I ought not to shoot him. It is a serious matter to shoot a working elephant — it is comparable to destroying a huge and costly piece of machinery — and obviously one ought not to do it if it can possibly be avoided. And at that distance, peacefully eating, the elephant looked no more dangerous than a cow. I thought then and I think now that his attack of "must" was already passing off; in which case he would merely wander harmlessly about until the mahout came back and caught him. Moreover, I did not in the least want to shoot him. I decided that I would watch him for a little while to make sure that he did not turn savage again, and then go home.

But at that moment I glanced round at the crowd that had followed 7 me. It was an immense crowd, two thousand at the least and growing every minute. It blocked the road for a long distance on either side. I looked at the sea of yellow faces above the garish clothes — faces all happy and excited over this bit of fun, all certain that the elephant was going to be shot. They were watching me as they would watch a conjurer about to perform a trick. They did not like me, but with the magical rifle in my hands I was momentarily worth watching. And suddenly I realized that I should have to shoot the elephant after all. The people expected it of me and I had got to do it; I could feel their two thousand wills pressing me forward, irresistibly. And it was at this moment, as I stood there with the rifle in my hands, that I first grasped the hollowness, the futility of the white man's dominion in the East. Here was I, the white man with his gun, standing in front of the unarmed native crowd — seemingly the leading actor of the piece; but in reality I was only an absurd puppet pushed to and fro by the will of those

---

* Eds. note — Wet land for growing rice.

yellow faces behind. I perceived in this moment that when the white man turns tyrant it is his own freedom that he destroys. He becomes a sort of hollow, posing dummy, the conventionalized figure of a sahib.* For it is the condition of his rule that he shall spend his life in trying to impress the "natives," and so in every crisis he has got to do what the "natives" expect of him. He wears a mask, and his face grows to fit it. I had got to shoot the elephant. I had committed myself to doing it when I sent for the rifle. A sahib has got to act like a sahib; he has got to appear resolute, to know his own mind and do definite things. To come all that way, rifle in hand, with two thousand people marching at my heels, and then to trail feebly away, having done nothing — no, that was impossible. The crowd would laugh at me. And my whole life, every white man's life in the East, was one long struggle not to be laughed at.

But I did not want to shoot the elephant. I watched him beating his 8 bunch of grass against his knees, with the preoccupied grandmotherly air that elephants have. It seemed to me that it would be murder to shoot him. At that age I was not squeamish about killing animals, but I had never shot an elephant and never wanted to. (Somehow it always seems worse to kill a *large* animal.) Besides, there was the beast's owner to be considered. Alive, the elephant was worth at least a hundred pounds; dead, he would only be worth the value of his tusks, five pounds, possibly. But I had got to act quickly. I turned to some experienced-looking Burmans who had been there when we arrived, and asked them how the elephant had been behaving. They all said the same thing: he took no notice of you if you left him alone, but he might charge if you went too close to him.

It was perfectly clear to me what I ought to do. I ought to walk up to 9 within, say, twenty-five yards of the elephant and test his behavior. If he charged I could shoot, if he took no notice of me it would be safe to leave him until the mahout came back. But also I knew that I was going to do no such thing. I was a poor shot with a rifle and the ground was soft mud into which one would sink at every step. If the elephant charged and I missed him, I should have about as much chance as a toad under a steamroller. But even then I was not thinking particularly of my own skin, only of the watchful yellow faces behind. For at that moment, with the crowd watching me, I was not afraid in the ordinary sense, as I would have been if I had been alone. A white man mustn't be frightened in front of "natives"; and so, in general, he isn't frightened. The sole thought in my mind was that if anything went wrong those two thousand Burmans would see me pursued, caught, trampled on, and reduced to a grinning corpse like that Indian up the hill. And if that happened it was quite probable that some of them would laugh. That would never do. There was only one alternative. I shoved the cartridges into the magazine and lay down on the road to get a better aim.

---

* Eds. note — An official. The term was used among Hindus and Muslims in colonial India.

The crowd grew very still, and a deep, low, happy sigh, as of people who   10
see the theatre curtain go up at last, breathed from innumerable throats.
They were going to have their bit of fun after all. The rifle was a beautiful
German thing with cross-hair sights. I did not then know that in shooting
an elephant one would shoot to cut an imaginary bar running from ear-
hole to ear-hole. I ought, therefore, as the elephant was sideways on, to have
aimed straight at his ear-hole; actually I aimed several inches in front of
this, thinking the brain would be further forward.

When I pulled the trigger I did not hear the bang or feel the kick — one   11
never does when a shot goes home — but I heard the devilish roar of glee
that went up from the crowd. In that instant, in too short a time, one would
have thought, even for the bullet to get there, a mysterious, terrible change
had come over the elephant. He neither stirred nor fell, but every line on his
body had altered. He looked suddenly stricken, shrunken, immensely old,
as though the frightful impact of the bullet had paralyzed him without
knocking him down. At last, after what seemed a long time — it might have
been five seconds, I dare say — he sagged flabbily to his knees. His mouth
slobbered. An enormous senility seemed to have settled upon him. One
could have imagined him thousands of years old. I fired again into the
same spot. At the second shot he did not collapse but climbed with desperate slowness to his feet and stood weakly upright, with legs sagging and
head drooping. I fired a third time. That was the shot that did for him. You
could see the agony of it jolt his whole body and knock the last remnant of
strength from his legs. But in falling he seemed for a moment to rise, for as
his hind legs collapsed beneath him he seemed to tower upwards like a
huge rock toppling, his trunk reaching skywards like a tree. He trumpeted,
for the first and only time. And then down he came, his belly towards me,
with a crash that seemed to shake the ground even where I lay.

I got up. The Burmans were already racing past me across the mud. It   12
was obvious that the elephant would never rise again, but he was not dead.
He was breathing very rhythmically with long rattling gasps, his great
mound of a side painfully rising and falling. His mouth was wide open — I
could see far down into caverns of pale pink throat. I waited a long time for
him to die, but his breathing did not weaken. Finally I fired my two remaining shots into the spot where I thought his heart must be. The thick blood
welled out of him like red velvet, but still he did not die. His body did not
even jerk when the shots hit him, the tortured breathing continued without a pause. He was dying, very slowly and in great agony, but in some
world remote from me where not even a bullet could damage him further. I
felt that I had got to put an end to that dreadful noise. It seemed dreadful
to see the great beast lying there, powerless to move and yet powerless to
die, and not even to be able to finish him. I sent back for my small rifle and
poured shot after shot into his heart and down his throat. They seemed to
make no impression. The tortured gasps continued as steadily as the tick-
ing of a clock.

In the end I could not stand it any longer and went away. I heard later 13
that it took him half an hour to die. Burmans were bringing dahs* and baskets even before I left, and I was told they had stripped his body almost to
the bones by the afternoon.

Afterwards, of course, there were endless discussions about the shoot- 14
ing of the elephant. The owner was furious, but he was only an Indian and
could do nothing. Besides, legally I had done the right thing, for a mad elephant has to be killed, like a mad dog, if its owner fails to control it. Among
the Europeans opinion was divided. The older men said I was right, the
younger men said it was a damn shame to shoot an elephant for killing a
coolie, because an elephant was worth more than any damn Coringhee
coolie. And afterwards I was very glad that the coolie had been killed; it put
me legally in the right and it gave me a sufficient pretext for shooting the
elephant. I often wondered whether any of the others grasped that I had
done it solely to avoid looking a fool.

. . .

Comprehension

1. Why is Orwell "hated by large numbers of people" (1) in Burma? Why
   does he have mixed feelings toward the Burmese people?

2. Why do the local officials want something done about the elephant? Why
   does the crowd want Orwell to shoot the elephant?

3. Why does Orwell finally decide to kill the elephant? What makes him hes-
   itate at first?

4. Why does Orwell say at the end he was glad the coolie had been killed?

Purpose and Audience

1. One of Orwell's purposes in telling his story is to show how it gave him a
   glimpse of "the real nature of imperialism" (3). What does he mean? How
   does his essay illustrate this purpose?

2. Do you think Orwell wrote this essay to inform or to persuade his audience? How did Orwell expect his audience to react to his ideas? How can
   you tell?

3. What is the essay's thesis?

Style and Structure

1. What does Orwell's first paragraph accomplish? Where does the introduction end and the narrative itself begin?

---

* Eds. note — Heavy knives.

2. The essay includes almost no dialogue. Why do you think Orwell's voice as narrator is the only one readers hear? Is the absence of dialogue a strength or a weakness? Explain.

3. Why do you think Orwell devotes so much attention to the elephant's misery (11–12)?

4. Orwell's essay includes a number of editorial comments, which appear within parentheses or dashes. How would you characterize these comments? Why are they set off from the text?

5. **Vocabulary Project.** Because Orwell is British, he frequently uses words or expressions that an American writer would not likely use. Substitute a contemporary American word or phrase for each of the following, making sure it is appropriate in Orwell's context.

raise a riot (1)	rubbish van (3)	a bit of fun (5)
rang me up (3)	inflicted violences (3)	I dare say (11)

What other expressions in Orwell's essay might need to be "translated" for a contemporary American audience?

6. Consider the following statements: "Some of the people said that the elephant had gone in one direction, some said that he had gone in another" (4); "Among the Europeans opinion was divided. The older men said I was right, the younger men said it was a damn shame to shoot an elephant" (14). How do these comments reinforce the idea expressed in paragraph 2 ("All I knew was that I was stuck between my hatred of the empire I served and my rage against the evil-spirited little beasts")? What other comments reinforce this idea?

Journal Entry

Do you think Orwell is a coward? Do you think he is a racist? Explain your feelings.

Writing Workshop

1. **Working with Sources.** Orwell says that even though he hated British imperialism and sympathized with the Burmese people, he found himself a puppet of the system. Write a narrative essay about a time when you had to do something that went against your beliefs or convictions. Begin by summarizing Orwell's situation in Burma, and go on to show how your situation was similar to his. If you quote Orwell, be sure to include documentation and a works-cited page. (See Chapter 18 for information on MLA documentation.)

2. Orwell's experience taught him something not only about himself but also about something beyond himself — the way British imperialism worked. Write a narrative essay that reveals how an incident in your life taught you something about some larger social or political force as well as about yourself.

3. Write an objective, factual newspaper article recounting the events Orwell describes.

Combining the Patterns

Implicit in this narrative essay is an extended **comparison and contrast** that highlights the differences between Orwell and the Burmese people. Review the essay, and list the most obvious differences Orwell perceives between himself and them. Do you think his perceptions are accurate? If all of the differences were set forth in a single paragraph, how might such a paragraph change your perception of Orwell's dilemma? Of his character?

Thematic Connections

- "Thirty-Eight Who Saw Murder Didn't Call the Police" (page 128)
- "Just Walk On By: A Black Man Ponders His Power to Alter Public Space" (page 238)
- "The Untouchable" (page 494)

Indian Education (Fiction)

Sherman Alexie, the son of a Coeur d'Alene Indian father and a Spokane Indian mother, was born in 1966 and grew up on the Spokane Reservation in Wellpinit, Washington, home to some eleven hundred Spokane tribal members. Realizing as a teenager that his educational opportunities there were extremely limited, Alexie made the unusual decision to attend high school off the reservation in nearby Reardon. Later a scholarship student at Gonzaga University, he received a bachelor's degree in American studies from Washington State University at Pullman. While in college, he began publishing poetry; within a year of graduation, his first collection, *The Business of Fancydancing* (1992), appeared. This was followed by *The Lone Ranger and Tonto Fistfight in Heaven* (1993), a short-story collection, and the novels *Reservation Blues* (1995) and *Indian Killer* (1996), all of which garnered numerous awards and honors. Alexie also wrote the screenplay for the film *Smoke Signals* (1998) and wrote and directed *The Business of Fancydancing* (2002). His most recent novel, *The Absolutely True Diary of a Part-Time Indian,* won the 2007 National Book Award for Young People's Literature. *War Dances,* a collection of his stories and poems, was published in 2009 and received the PEN/Faulkner Award for Fiction in 2010.

Background on the U.S. government's "Indian schools" By the mid-1800s, most Native American tribes had been overwhelmed by the superior weapons of the U.S. military and confined to reservations. Beginning in the late 1800s and continuing into the 1950s, government policymakers established boarding schools for Native American youth to help them assimilate into the dominant culture and thus become "civilized." To this end, children were forcibly removed from their homes for long periods to separate them from native traditions. At the boarding schools, they were given a cursory academic education and spent most of their time studying Christian teachings and working to offset the cost of their schooling. Students were punished for speaking their own language or practicing their own religion. Responding to protests from the American Indian movement in the 1970s, the U.S. government began to send fewer Native Americans to boarding schools and retreated from its goal of assimilation at boarding schools and at newly established reservation schools. However, such schools still exist. Today, government funding for Native American schools remains considerably lower than for other public schools, and students often make do with inadequate and antiquated facilities, equipment, and textbooks. In part because of such educational failures, few Native American students go on to college, and the incidence of alcohol and drug abuse among Native Americans is higher than in any other U.S. population.

First Grade

My hair was too short and my U.S. Government glasses were horn- 1
rimmed, ugly, and all that first winter in school, the other Indian boys
chased me from one corner of the playground to the other. They pushed
me down, buried me in the snow until I couldn't breathe, thought I'd never
breathe again.

They stole my glasses and threw them over my head, around my out- 2
stretched hands, just beyond my reach, until someone tripped me and sent
me falling again, facedown in the snow.

I was always falling down; my Indian name was Junior Falls Down. 3
Sometimes it was Bloody Nose or Steal-His-Lunch. Once, it was Cries-Like-
a-White-Boy, even though none of us had seen a white boy cry.

Then it was a Friday morning recess and Frenchy SiJohn threw snow- 4
balls at me while the rest of the Indian boys tortured some other *top-yogh-
yaught* kid, another weakling. But Frenchy was confident enough to tor-
ment me all by himself, and most days I would have let him.

But the little warrior in me roared to life that day and knocked Frenchy 5
to the ground, held his head against the snow, and punched him so hard
that my knuckles and the snow made symmetrical bruises on his face. He
almost looked like he was wearing war paint.

But he wasn't the warrior. I was. And I chanted *It's a good day to die, it's a* 6
good day to die, all the way down to the principal's office.

Second Grade

Betty Towle, missionary teacher, redheaded and so ugly that no one 7
ever had a puppy crush on her, made me stay in for recess fourteen days
straight.

"Tell me you're sorry," she said.   8

"Sorry for what?" I asked.   9

"Everything," she said and made me stand straight for fifteen minutes, 10
eagle-armed with books in each hand. One was a math book; the other was
English. But all I learned was that gravity can be painful.

For Halloween I drew a picture of her riding a broom with a scrawny 11
cat on the back. She said that her God would never forgive me for that.

Once, she gave the class a spelling test but set me aside and gave me a 12
test designed for junior high students. When I spelled all the words right,
she crumpled up the paper and made me eat it.

"You'll learn respect," she said.   13

She sent a letter home with me that told my parents to either cut my 14
braids or keep me home from class. My parents came in the next day and
dragged their braids across Betty Towle's desk.

"Indians, indians, indians." She said it without capitalization. She 15
called me "indian, indian, indian."

And I said, *Yes, I am. I am Indian. Indian, I am.*   16

Third Grade

My traditional Native American art career began and ended with my 17
very first portrait: *Stick Indian Taking a Piss in My Backyard.*

As I circulated the original print around the classroom, Mrs. Schluter 18
intercepted and confiscated my art.

Censorship, I might cry now. *Freedom of expression,* I would write in edito- 19
rials to the tribal newspaper.

In third grade, though, I stood alone in the corner, faced the wall, and 20
waited for the punishment to end.

I'm still waiting. 21

Fourth Grade

"You should be a doctor when you grow up," Mr. Schluter told me, 22
even though his wife, the third grade teacher, thought I was crazy beyond
my years. My eyes always looked like I had just hit-and-run someone.

"Guilty," she said. "You always look guilty." 23

"Why should I be a doctor?" I asked Mr. Schluter. 24

"So you can come back and help the tribe. So you can heal people." 25

That was the year my father drank a gallon of vodka a day and the same 26
year that my mother started two hundred different quilts but never finished
any. They sat in separate, dark places in our HUD house and wept savagely.

I ran home after school, heard their Indian tears, and looked in the 27
mirror. *Doctor Victor,* I called myself, invented an education, talked to my
reflection. *Doctor Victor to the emergency room.*

Fifth Grade

I picked up a basketball for the first time and made my first shot. No. I 28
missed my first shot, missed the basket completely, and the ball landed in
the dirt and sawdust, sat there just like I had sat there only minutes before.

But it felt good, that ball in my hands, all those possibilities and angles. 29
It was mathematics, geometry. It was beautiful.

At that same moment, my cousin Steven Ford sniffed rubber cement 30
from a paper bag and leaned back on the merry-go-round. His ears rang, his
mouth was dry, and everyone seemed so far away.

But it felt good, that buzz in his head, all those colors and noises. It was 31
chemistry, biology. It was beautiful.

Oh, do you remember those sweet, almost innocent choices that the Indian 32
boys were forced to make?

Sixth Grade

Randy, the new Indian kid from the white town of Springdale, got into 33
a fight an hour after he first walked into the reservation school.

Stevie Flett called him out, called him a squawman, called him a pussy, 34
and called him a punk.

Randy and Stevie, and the rest of the Indian boys, walked out into the 35
playground.

"Throw the first punch," Stevie said as they squared off.   36

"No," Randy said.   37

"Throw the first punch," Stevie said again.   38

"No," Randy said again.   39

"Throw the first punch!" Stevie said for the third time, and Randy 40
reared back and pitched a knuckle fastball that broke Stevie's nose.

We all stood there in silence, in awe.   41

That was Randy, my soon-to-be first and best friend, who taught me 42
the most valuable lesson about living in the white world: *Always throw the
first punch.*

Seventh Grade

I leaned through the basement window of the HUD house and kissed 43
the white girl who would later be raped by her foster-parent father, who
was also white. They both lived on the reservation, though, and when the
headlines and stories filled the papers later, not one word was made of their
color.

Just Indians being Indians, someone must have said somewhere and they 44
were wrong.

But on the day I leaned through the basement window of the HUD 45
house and kissed the white girl, I felt the good-byes I was saying to my
entire tribe. I held my lips tight against her lips, a dry, clumsy, and ultimately stupid kiss.

But I was saying good-bye to my tribe, to all the Indian girls and women 46
I might have loved, to all the Indian men who might have called me cousin,
even brother.

I kissed that white girl and when I opened my eyes, she was gone from 47
the reservation, and when I opened my eyes, I was gone from the reservation, living in a farm town where a beautiful white girl asked my name.

"Junior Polatkin," I said, and she laughed.   48

After that, no one spoke to me for another five hundred years.   49

Eighth Grade

At the farm town junior high, in the boys' bathroom, I could hear 50
voices from the girls' bathroom, nervous whispers of anorexia and bulimia.
I could hear the white girls' forced vomiting, a sound so familiar and natural to me after years of listening to my father's hangovers.

"Give me your lunch if you're just going to throw it up," I said to one of 51
those girls once.

I sat back and watched them grow skinny from self-pity.   52

•   •   •

Back on the reservation, my mother stood in line to get us commodities. 53
We carried them home, happy to have food, and opened the canned beef
that even the dogs wouldn't eat.

But we ate it day after day and grew skinny from self-pity.   54

There is more than one way to starve.   55

Ninth Grade

At the farm town high school dance, after a basketball game in an over-   56
heated gym where I had scored twenty-seven points and pulled down thirteen rebounds, I passed out during a slow song.

As my white friends revived me and prepared to take me to the emer-   57
gency room where doctors would later diagnose my diabetes, the Chicano
teacher ran up to us.

"Hey," he said. "What's that boy been drinking? I know all about these   58
Indian kids. They start drinking real young."

Sharing dark skin doesn't necessarily make two men brothers.   59

Tenth Grade

I passed the written test easily and nearly flunked the driving, but still 60
received my Washington State driver's license on the same day that Wally
Jim killed himself by driving his car into a pine tree.

No traces of alcohol in his blood, good job, wife and two kids.   61

"Why'd he do it?" asked a white Washington State trooper.   62

All the Indians shrugged their shoulders, looked down at the ground.   63

"Don't know," we all said, but when we look in the mirror, see the his- 64
tory of our tribe in our eyes, taste failure in the tap water, and shake with
old tears, we understand completely.

Believe me, everything looks like a noose if you stare at it long enough. 65

Eleventh Grade

Last night I missed two free throws
which would have won the game against the
best team in the state. The farm town high
school I play for is nicknamed the "Indians,"
and I'm probably the only actual Indian ever
to play for a team with such a mascot.

> "This morning I   66
> pick up the sports
> page and read the
> headline: INDIANS
> LOSE AGAIN."

This morning I pick up the sports page   67
and read the headline: INDIANS LOSE AGAIN.

Go ahead and tell me none of this is supposed to hurt me very much.   68

Twelfth Grade

I walk down the aisle, valedictorian of this farm town high school, and 69 my cap doesn't fit because I've grown my hair longer than it's ever been. Later, I stand as the school-board chairman recites my awards, accomplishments, and scholarships.

I try to remain stoic for the photographers as I look toward the future.   70

Back home on the reservation, my former classmates graduate: a few can't 71 read, one or two are just given attendance diplomas, most look forward to the parties. The bright students are shaken, frightened, because they don't know what comes next.

They smile for the photographer as they look back toward tradition.   72

The tribal newspaper runs my photograph and the photograph of my for- 73 mer classmates side by side.

Postscript: Class Reunion

Victor said, "Why should we organize a reservation high school reunion? 74 My graduating class has a reunion every weekend at the Powwow Tavern."

• • •

Reading Literature

1. Instead of linking events with transitional phrases that establish chronology, Alexie uses headings to move readers through his story. How do these headings indicate the passage of time? Are these headings enough, or do you think Alexie should have opened each section of the story with a transitional phrase? (Try to suggest some possibilities.)

2. The narrator's experiences in each grade in school are illustrated by specific incidents. What do these incidents have in common? What do they reveal about the narrator? About his schools?

3. Explain the meaning of each of these statements in the context of the story:
   • "There is more than one way to starve" (55).
   • "Sharing dark skin doesn't necessarily make two men brothers" (59).
   • "Believe me, everything looks like a noose if you stare at it long enough" (65).

Journal Entry

What does the "Postscript: Class Reunion" section (74) tell readers about Indian education? Is this information consistent with what we have learned in the rest of the story, or does it come as a surprise? Explain.

Thematic Connections

Writing Assignments for Narration

1. Trace the path you expect to follow to establish yourself in your chosen profession, considering possible obstacles you may face and how you expect to deal with them. Include a thesis statement that conveys the importance of your goals. If you like, you may refer to an essay in this book that focuses on work — for example, "My Mother Never Worked" (page 123).

2. Write a personal narrative looking back from some point in the far future on your own life as you hope others will see it. Use third person if you like, and write your own obituary; or, use first person, assessing your life in a letter to your great-grandchildren.

3. Write a news article recounting in objective terms the events described in an essay that appears anywhere in this text — for example, "Who Killed Benny Paret?" (page 337) or "Grant and Lee: A Study in Contrasts" (page 393). Include a descriptive headline.

4. Write the introductory narrative for the home page of your family's (or community's) website. In this historical narrative, trace the roots of your family or your hometown or community. Be sure to include specific detail, dialogue, and descriptions of people and places. (You may also include visuals if you like.)

5. Write an account of one of these "firsts": your first serious argument with your parents; your first experience with physical violence or danger; your first extended stay away from home; your first encounter with someone whose culture was very different from your own; or your first experience with the serious illness or death of a close friend or relative. Make sure your essay includes a thesis statement your narrative can support.

6. **Working with Sources.** Both George Orwell and Martin Gansberg deal with the consequences of failing to act. Write an essay or story recounting what would have happened if Orwell had *not* shot the elephant or if one of the eyewitnesses *had* called the police right away. Be sure to document references to Orwell or Gansberg and to include a works-cited page. (See Chapter 18 for information on MLA documentation.)

7. **Working with Sources.** Write a narrative about a time when you were an outsider, isolated because of social, intellectual, or ethnic differences between you and others. Did you resolve the problems your isolation created? Explain. If you like, you may refer to the Orwell essay in this chapter or to "Just Walk On By" (page 238), taking care to include parenthetical documentation and a works-cited page. (See Chapter 18 for information on MLA documentation.)

8. Imagine a meeting between any two people who appear in this chapter's reading selections. Using dialogue and narrative, write an account of this meeting.

9. Using Sherman Alexie's story as a model, write the story of your own education.

10. List the five books you have read that most influenced you at important stages of your life. Then, write your literary autobiography, tracing your personal development through these books. (Or, write your wardrobe autobiography — discussing what you wore at different times of your life — or your music autobiography.)

Collaborative Activity for Narration

Working with a group of students of about your own age, write a history of your television-viewing habits. Start by working individually to list all your most-watched television shows in chronological order, beginning as far back as you can remember. Then, compile a single list that reflects a consensus of the group's preferences, perhaps choosing one or two representative programs for each stage of your life (preschool, elementary school, and so on). Have a different student write a paragraph on each stage, describing the chosen programs in as much detail as possible and using "we" as the subject. Finally, combine the individual paragraphs to create a narrative essay that traces the group's changing tastes in television shows. The essay's thesis statement should express what your group's television preferences reveal about your generation's development.

7

Description

What Is Description?

You use **description** to tell readers about the physical characteristics of a person, place, or thing. Description relies on the five senses — sight, hearing, taste, touch, and smell. In the following paragraph from "Knoxville: Summer 1915," James Agee uses sight, touch, and sound to re-create a summer's evening for his audience.

Topic sentence

Description using sight

Description using touch

Description using sound

It is not of games children play in the evening that I want to speak now, it is of a contemporaneous atmosphere that has little to do with them; that of fathers and families, each in his space of lawn, his shirt fishlike pale in the unnatural light and his face nearly anonymous, hosing their lawns. The hoses were attached to spigots that stood out of the brick foundations of the houses. The nozzles were variously set but usually so there was a long sweet stream of spray, the nozzle wet in the hand, the water trickling the right forearm and the peeled-back cuff, and the water whishing out a long loose and low-curved cone, and so gentle a sound. First an insane noise of violence in the nozzle, then the still irregular sound of adjustment, then the smoothing into steadiness and a pitch as accurately tuned to the size and style of stream as any violin. So many qualities of sound out of one hose: so many choral differences out of those several hoses that were in earshot. Out of any one hose, the almost dead silence of the release, and the short still arch of the separate big drops, silent as a held breath, and the only noise the flattering noise on leaves and the slapped grass at the fall of each big drop. That, and the intense hiss with the intense stream; that, and the same intensity not growing less but growing more quiet and delicate with the turn of the nozzle, up to that extreme tender whisper when the water was just a wide bell of film.

A descriptive essay tells what something looks like or what it feels like, sounds like, smells like, or tastes like. However, description often goes beyond personal sense impressions: novelists can create imaginary landscapes, historians can paint word pictures of historical figures, and scientists can describe physical phenomena they have never actually seen. When you write description, you use language to create a vivid impression for your readers.

Using Description

In your college writing, you use description in many different kinds of assignments. In a comparison-and-contrast essay, for example, you may describe the designs of two proposed buildings to show that one is more energy efficient than the other. In an argumentative essay, you may describe a fish kill in a local river to make the point that industrial waste dumping is a problem. Through description, you communicate your view of the world to your readers. If your readers come to understand or share your view, they are likely to accept your observations, your judgments, and, eventually, your conclusions. Therefore, in almost every essay you write, knowing how to write effective description is important.

Understanding Objective Description

Description can be objective or subjective. In an **objective description**, you focus on the object itself rather than on your personal reactions to it. Your purpose is to present a precise, literal picture of your subject. Many writing situations require exact descriptions of apparatus or conditions, and in these cases your goal is to construct an accurate picture for your audience. A biologist describing what he sees through an electron microscope and a historian describing a Civil War battlefield would both write objectively. The biologist would not, for instance, say how exciting his observations were, nor would the historian say how disappointed she was at the outcome of the battle. Many newspaper reporters also try to achieve this objectivity, as do writers of technical reports, scientific papers, and certain types of business correspondence. Still, objectivity is an ideal that writers strive for but never fully achieve. In fact, by selecting some details and leaving out others, writers are making subjective decisions.

In the following descriptive passage, Shakespearean scholar Thomas Marc Parrott aims for objectivity by giving his readers the factual information they need to visualize Shakespeare's theater:

The main or outer stage [of Shakespeare's theater] was a large platform, which projected out into the audience. Sections of the floor could be removed to make such things as the grave in the grave digger's scene in *Hamlet,* or they could be transformed into trapdoors through which characters could disappear, as in *The Tempest.* The players referred to the space beneath the platform as the Hell. At the rear of the platform and at the same level was the smaller, inner stage, or alcove. . . . Above the alcove at the level of the second story, there was another curtained stage, the chamber. . . . The action of the play would move from one scene to another, using one, two, or all of them. Above the chamber was the music gallery; . . . and above this were the windows, "The Huts," where characters and lookouts could appear.

Artist's rendering of the Globe Theatre, London.

From Shakespeare: Six Plays and the Sonnets by Thomas Marc Parrott and Edward Hubler, Charles Scribner's Sons, 1956.

Note that Parrott is not interested in responding to or evaluating the theater he describes. Instead, he chooses words that convey sizes and directions, such as *large* and *above*.

Objective descriptions are sometimes accompanied by **visuals**, such as diagrams, drawings, or photographs. A well-chosen visual can enhance a description by enabling writers to avoid tedious passages of description that might confuse readers. For example, the illustration on page 153, which accompanies Parrott's description of Shakespeare's theater, makes the passage much easier to understand, helping readers to visualize the multiple stages where Shakespeare's plays were performed.

✔**CHECKLIST** **Using Visuals Effectively**

If your instructor permits you to use visuals, ask the following questions to make sure that you have used them responsibly and effectively.

☐ **Is your visual directly related to your discussion?** To be effective, a visual should clearly illustrate what is being discussed and not introduce new material.

☐ **Does your visual add something to your paper?** For example, you could use a diagram to help explain a process, a chart or graph to clarify statistics, or a photograph to show an unusual structure.

☐ **Is your visual located as close as possible to where it is discussed in the paper?** This placement will establish the context for the visual and ensure that readers understand the reason why you have included it.

☐ **Have you documented your visual?** Like all material you borrow from a source, visuals must be documented. (For more on documentation, see Chapter 18.)

🖳 **TECH TIP: Finding Visuals**

You can find visuals on the Internet, on DVDs, or in clip-art compilations. You can also scan pictures you find in print sources or download pictures you take with your phone or with a digital camera. Once the visual is downloaded onto your computer as a file, you can cut and paste it into your essay. Remember, however, that all visual material you get from a source — whether print or Internet — must be documented.

Understanding Subjective Description

In contrast to objective description, **subjective description** conveys your personal response to your subject. Here your perspective is not necessarily stated explicitly; often it is revealed indirectly, through your choice of words and phrasing. If an English composition assignment asks you to describe a place that has special meaning to you, you could give a subjective reaction to your topic by selecting and emphasizing details that show your feelings about the place. For example, you could write a subjective description of your room by focusing on particular objects — your desk, your window, and your bookshelves — and explaining the meanings these things have for you. Thus, your desk could be a "warm brown rectangle of wood whose surface reveals the scratched impressions of a thousand school assignments."

A subjective description should convey not just a literal record of sights and sounds but also their significance. For example, if you objectively described a fire that destroyed a house in your neighborhood, you might include its temperature, duration, and scope. In addition, you might describe, as accurately as possible, the fire's movement and intensity. If you subjectively described the fire, however, you would try to re-create for your audience a sense of how the fire made you feel — your reactions to the noise, to the dense smoke, to the destruction.

In the following passage, notice how Mark Twain subjectively describes a sunset on the Mississippi River:

> I still kept in mind a certain wonderful sunset which I witnessed when steamboating was new to me. A broad expanse of the river was turned to blood; in the middle distance the red hue brightened into gold, through which a solitary log came floating, black and conspicuous; in one place a long, slanting mark lay sparkling upon the water; in another the surface was broken by boiling, tumbling rings, that were as many-tinted as an opal.

In this passage, Twain conveys his strong emotional reaction to the sunset by using vivid, powerful images, such as the river "turned to blood," the "solitary log . . . black and conspicuous," and the "boiling, tumbling rings." He also chooses words that suggest great value, such as *gold* and *opal.*

Neither objective nor subjective description exists independently. Objective descriptions usually include some subjective elements, and subjective descriptions need some objective elements to convey a sense of reality. The skillful writer adjusts the balance between objectivity and subjectivity to suit the topic, thesis, audience, and purpose as well as occasion for writing.

Using Objective and Subjective Language

As the passages by Parrott and Twain illustrate, both objective and subjective descriptions rely on language that appeals to readers' senses. But these two types of description use language differently. Objective descriptions rely on precise, factual language that presents a writer's observations without conveying his or her attitude toward the subject. Subjective descriptions, however, often use richer and more suggestive language than objective descriptions do. They are more likely to rely on the **connotations** of words, their emotional associations, than on their **denotations**, or more literal meanings (such as those found in a dictionary). In addition, they may deliberately provoke the reader's imagination with striking phrases or vivid language, including **figures of speech** such as *simile, metaphor, personification,* and *allusion.*

- A **simile** uses *like* or *as* to compare two dissimilar things. These comparisons occur frequently in everyday speech — for example, when someone claims to be "happy as a clam," "free as a bird," or "hungry as a bear." As a rule, however, you should avoid overused expressions like these in your writing. Effective writers constantly strive to create original similes. In his essay "Once More to the Lake" (page 191), for instance, E. B. White uses a striking simile to describe the annoying sound of boats on a lake when he says that in the evening "they whined about one's ears *like mosquitoes.*" Later in the same essay, he describes a thunderstorm as being *"like the revival of an old melodrama* that I had seen long ago with childish awe."

- A **metaphor** compares two dissimilar things without using *like* or *as.* Instead of saying that something is *like* something else, a metaphor says it *is* something else. Mark Twain uses a metaphor when he says, "A broad expanse of the river was turned to blood."

- **Personification** speaks of concepts or objects as if they had life or human characteristics. If you say that the wind whispered or that an engine died, you are using personification.

- An **allusion** is a reference to a person, place, event, or quotation that the writer assumes readers will recognize. In "Letter from Birmingham Jail" (page 563), for example, Martin Luther King Jr. enriches his argument by alluding to biblical passages and proverbs that he expects his audience of clergy to be familiar with.

Your purpose and audience determine whether you should use objective or subjective description. An assignment that specifically asks for reactions calls for a subjective description. Legal, medical, technical, business, and scientific writing assignments, however, require objective descriptions because their primary purpose is to give the audience factual information. Even in these areas, though, figures of speech are often used to describe an unfamiliar object or concept. For example, in their pioneering article on the structure of DNA, scientists James Watson and Francis Crick use a simile when they describe a molecule of DNA as looking like two spiral staircases winding around each other.

Selecting Details

Sometimes inexperienced writers pack their descriptions with general words such as *nice, great, terrific,* or *awful,* substituting their own reactions to an object for the qualities of the object itself. To produce an effective description, however, you must do more than just *say* something is wonderful — you must use details that evoke this response in your readers, as Twain does with the sunset. (Twain does use the word *wonderful* at the beginning of his description, but he then goes on to supply many specific details that make the scene he describes vivid and specific.)

All good descriptive writing, whether objective or subjective, relies on **specific details**. Your aim is not simply to *tell* readers what something looks like but to *show* them. Every person, place, or thing has its special characteristics, and you should use your powers of observation to detect them. Then, you need to select the specific words that will enable your readers to imagine what you describe. Don't be satisfied with "He looked angry" when you can say, "His face flushed, and one corner of his mouth twitched as he tried to control his anger." What's the difference? In the first case, you simply identify the man's emotional state. In the second, you provide enough detail so that readers can tell not only that he was angry but also how he revealed the intensity of his anger.

Of course, you could have provided even more detail by describing the man's beard, his wrinkles, or any number of other features. Keep in mind, however, that not all details are equally useful or desirable. You should include only those that contribute to the dominant impression you wish to create. Thus, in describing a man's face to show how angry he was, you would probably not include the shape of his nose or the color of his hair. (After all, a person's hair color does not change when he or she gets angry.) In fact, the number of particulars you use is less important than their quality and appropriateness. You should select and use only those details relevant to your purpose.

Factors such as the level, background, and knowledge of your audience also influence the kinds of details you include. For example, a description of a DNA molecule written for high school students would contain more basic descriptive details than a description written for college biology majors. In addition, the more advanced description would contain details — the sequence of amino acid groups, for instance — that might be inappropriate for high school students.

Planning a Descriptive Essay

Developing a Thesis Statement

Writers of descriptive essays often use an **implied thesis** when they describe a person, place, or thing. This technique allows them to convey an essay's main idea subtly, through the selection and arrangement of details. When they use description to support a particular point, however, many writers prefer to use an **explicitly stated thesis**. This strategy lets readers see immediately what point the writer is making — for example, "The sculptures that adorn Philadelphia's City Hall are a catalog of nineteenth-century artistic styles."

Whether you state or imply your thesis, the details of your descriptive essay must work together to create a single **dominant impression** — the mood or quality emphasized in the piece of writing. In many cases, your thesis may be just a statement of the dominant impression; sometimes, however, your thesis may go further and make a point about that dominant impression.

Organizing Details

When you plan a descriptive essay, you usually begin by writing down descriptive details in no particular order. You then arrange these details in a way that supports your thesis and communicates your dominant impression. As you consider how to arrange your details, keep in mind that you have a number of options. For example, you can move from a specific description of an object to a general description of other things around it. Or you can reverse this order, beginning with the general and proceeding to the specific. You can also progress from the least important feature to the most important one, from the smallest to the largest item, from the least unusual to the most unusual detail, or from left to right, right to left, top to bottom, or bottom to top. Another option is to combine approaches, using different organizing schemes in different parts of the essay. The strategy you choose depends on the dominant impression you want to convey, your thesis, and your purpose and audience.

Using Transitions

Be sure to include all the transitional words and phrases readers need to follow your description. Without them, readers will have difficulty understanding the relationship between one detail and another. Throughout your description, especially in the topic sentences of your body paragraphs, use words or phrases indicating the spatial arrangement of details. In descriptive essays, the transitions commonly used include *above, adjacent to, at the bottom, at the top, behind, below, beyond, in front of, in the middle, next to, over, under, through,* and *within.* (A more complete list of transitions appears on page 57.)

Structuring a Descriptive Essay

Descriptive essays begin with an **introduction** that presents the **thesis** or establishes the dominant impression that the rest of the essay will develop. Each **body paragraph** includes details that support the thesis or convey the dominant impression. The **conclusion** reinforces the thesis or dominant impression, perhaps echoing an idea stated in the introduction or using a particularly effective simile or metaphor.

Suppose your English composition instructor has asked you to write a short essay describing a person, place, or thing. After thinking about the assignment for a day or two, you decide to write an objective description of the National Air and Space Museum in Washington, DC, because you have visited it recently and many details are fresh in your mind. The museum is large and has many different exhibits, so you know you cannot describe them all. Therefore, you decide to concentrate on one, the heavier-than-air flight exhibit, and you choose as your topic the display you remember most vividly — Charles Lindbergh's airplane, *The Spirit of St. Louis*. You begin by brainstorming to recall all the details you can. When you read over your notes, you realize that you could present the details of the airplane in the order in which your eye took them in, from front to rear. The dominant impression you wish to create is how small and fragile *The Spirit of St. Louis* appears, and your thesis statement communicates this impression. An informal outline for your essay might look like this.

Sample Outline	**Description**
Introduction:	Thesis statement — It is startling that a plane as small as *The Spirit of St. Louis* could fly across the Atlantic.
Front of plane:	Single engine, tiny cockpit
Middle of plane:	Short wingspan, extra gas tanks
Rear of plane:	Limited cargo space filled with more gas tanks
Conclusion:	Restatement of thesis (in different words) or review of key points or details

Revising a Descriptive Essay

When you revise a descriptive essay, consider the items on the revision checklist on page 68. In addition, pay special attention to the items on the following checklist, which apply specifically to descriptive essays.

✔ REVISION CHECKLIST   Description

☐ Does your assignment call for description?
☐ Does your descriptive essay clearly communicate its thesis or dominant impression?
☐ Is your description primarily objective or subjective?
☐ If your description is primarily objective, have you used precise, factual language? Would your essay be enriched by a visual?
☐ If your description is primarily subjective, have you used figures of speech as well as words that convey your feelings and emotions?
☐ Have you included enough specific details?
☐ Have you arranged your details in a way that supports your thesis and communicates your dominant impression?
☐ Have you used the transitional words and phrases that readers need to follow your description?

Editing a Descriptive Essay

When you edit your descriptive essay, follow the guidelines in the editing checklists on pages 85, 88, and 91. In addition, focus on the grammar, mechanics, and punctuation issues that are particularly relevant to descriptive essays. One of these issues — avoiding misplaced and dangling modifiers — is discussed below.

GRAMMAR IN CONTEXT   Avoiding Misplaced
and Dangling Modifiers

When writing descriptive essays, you use **modifying words** and **phrases** to describe people, places, and objects. Because these modifiers are important in descriptive essays, you need to place them correctly to ensure they clearly refer to the words they describe.

Avoiding Misplaced Modifiers A **misplaced modifier** appears to modify the wrong word because it is placed incorrectly in the sentence. Sentences that contain misplaced modifiers are always illogical and frequently humorous.

MISPLACED: E. B. White's son swam in the lake wearing an old bathing suit. (*Was the lake wearing a bathing suit?*)

MISPLACED: From the cabin, the sounds of the woods were heard by E. B. White and his son. (*Were the sounds of the woods inside the cabin?*)

In these sentences, the phrases *wearing an old bathing suit* and *from the cabin* appear to modify words that they cannot logically modify. You can correct these errors and avoid confusion by moving each modifier as close as possible to the word it is supposed to modify.

CORRECT: Wearing an old bathing suit, E. B. White's son swam in the lake.

CORRECT: From the cabin, E. B. White and his son heard the sounds of the woods.

Avoiding Dangling Modifiers A modifier "dangles" when it cannot logically modify any word that appears in the sentence. Often, these **dangling modifiers** come at the beginning of sentences (as present or past participle phrases), where they illogically seem to modify the words that come immediately after them.

DANGLING: Determined to get a better look, the viewing platform next to St. Paul's Chapel was crowded. (*Who was determined to get a better look?*)

DANGLING: Standing on the corner, the cranes, jackhammers, and bulldozers worked feverishly at ground zero. (*Who was standing on the corner?*)

In the preceding sentences, the phrases *determined to get a better look* and *standing on the corner* seem to modify *the viewing platform* and *cranes, jackhammers, and bulldozers*, respectively. However, these sentences make no sense. How can a viewing platform get a better look? How can cranes, jackhammers, and bulldozers stand on a corner? In addition, the two sentences do not contain the words that the modifying phrases are supposed to describe. In each case, you can correct the problem by supplying the missing word and rewriting the sentence accordingly.

CORRECT: Determined to get a better look, people crowded the viewing platform next to St. Paul's Chapel.

CORRECT: Standing on the corner, people watched the cranes, jackhammers, and bulldozers work feverishly at ground zero.

✔ **EDITING CHECKLIST**   **Description**
- ☐ Have you avoided misplaced modifiers?
- ☐ Have you avoided dangling modifiers?
- ☐ Have you used figures of speech effectively?
- ☐ Have you avoided general words such as *nice, great,* and *terrific*?

A STUDENT WRITER: Objective Description

The following essay, an objective description of a globe from 1939, was written by Mallory Cogan for a composition class. The assignment was to write a description of an object that has special meaning for her.

My Grandfather's Globe

Introduction

Each afternoon, sunlight slants through the windows of my grandfather's bedroom. Slowly, slowly, it sweeps over the bookshelves. Late in the day, just before the light disappears altogether, it rests sleepily on a globe in the corner. My grandfather bought this globe in 1939, just before World War II.

Thesis statement

The world has changed since then, and the globe is a record of what it looked like at that time.

Description of Western Hemisphere

Turning the globe left, I begin my world tour. The blue of the Pacific Ocean gives way to the faded pinks, browns, and oranges of North and South America. In the north is a large area

1

2

dotted with lakes and bays. This is the Dominion of Canada, now simply Canada. In the far north, the Canadian mainland breaks into islands that extend into the Arctic Ocean. Below it is the multicolored United States. To the north, Canada sprawls and breaks apart; to the south, Mexico narrows, then curves east, extended by the uneven strip of land that is Central America. This strip of land is connected to the northernmost part of South America. South America, in the same colors as the United States, looks like a face in profile looking east, with a nose extending into the Atlantic Ocean and a long neck that narrows as it reaches toward Antarctica at the South Pole.

Description of Africa

As I trace the equator east across the Atlantic Ocean, I   3
come to French Equatorial Africa. The huge African continent, like a fat boomerang, is labeled with names of European countries. A large, kidney-shaped purple area to the northwest is called French West Africa. To the east, about halfway down the continent, is the Belgian Congo, a substantial orange splotch that straddles the equator. On the eastern coast just above the equator is a somewhat smaller, almost heart-shaped yellow area called Italian East Africa. These regions, once European colonies, are now divided into dozens of independent countries.

Description of Europe

Moving north, I follow the thick blue ribbon of the   4
Mediterranean Sea until I reach Western Europe. I pause on yellow, boot-shaped Italy and glance to the west and southwest at purple France and orange Spain. The northwestern coasts of both countries extend slightly into the Atlantic. To the northwest of France, the pink clusters of the British Isles droop like bunches of grapes.

Description of Europe and changes since 1939

Looking eastward, I see a water stain on Germany. It   5
extends down through Italy and across the Mediterranean, ending in the Sahara Desert on the African continent. Following the stain back into Europe, I look north, where Norway, Sweden, and Finland reach toward the rest of Europe. Returning to Germany, I move east, through Poland. On a modern globe, I would find Belarus and Ukraine on Poland's eastern border. On this globe, however, my finger passes directly into a vast area called the Union of Soviet Socialist Republics. The U.S.S.R. (today called the Russian Federation) cuts a wide swath across the northern part of the Asian continent; there is plenty of room for its long name to be displayed horizontally across the country's light-brown surface. Still in the southern half of the country, I travel east, crossing

the landlocked Caspian Sea into a region of the U.S.S.R. called Turkistan, now the country of Turkmenistan. To the southeast, green Afghanistan sits between light-purple Iran to the west and pink India to the east. India is cone shaped, but with a pointed top, and green rectangular Nepal sits atop its western border.

Description of China and additional changes

Looking north again, I continue moving east. In Tibet, there   6 is a small tear in the globe. I continue into China's vast interior. Just as the U.S.S.R. blankets the northern part of the Asian continent, China spreads over much of the southeast. I notice that China's borders on this globe are different from what they are today. On my grandfather's globe, China includes Mongolia but not a purple region to the northwest labeled Manchoukuo, also known as Manchuria. Following Manchoukuo to its southern border, I see a strip of land that extends into the sea, surrounded by water on three sides. The area is small, so its name — Chosen — has been printed in the Sea of Japan to the east. Today, it is called Korea.

Description of Southeast Asia

Backtracking west and dropping south, past China's   7 southern border, I see Siam, now called Thailand. Siam is a three-leaf clover with a stem that hangs down. Wrapped along its eastern border, bordering two of its "leaves," is a purple country called French Indo-China. Today, this region is divided into the countries of Cambodia, Laos, and Vietnam. Bordering Siam on the west is the larger country of Burma, in pink. Like Siam, Burma is top-heavy, like a flower or a clover with a thin stem.

Description of Indonesia and Australia

Tracing that stem south, I come to the numerous islands of   8 Indonesia, splashes of yellow spreading east-west along, above, and below the equator. I do not need to travel much farther before I arrive at a large landmass: Australia. This country is pink and shaped like half of a very thick doughnut. On Australia's eastern coast is the Pacific; on its western coast is the Indian Ocean.

Conclusion

Of course, it is not surprising that I would end where I   9 started, with the ocean, since water covers seventy percent of the Earth. Still, countries — not oceans — are what interest me most about this globe. The shifting names and borders of countries that no longer exist remind me that although the world seems fixed, just as it did to the people of 1939, it is always changing. The change happens slowly, like the sun crossing my grandfather's room. Caught at any single moment, the world, like the afternoon light, appears still and mysterious.

Points for Special Attention

Objective Description. Because her essay is primarily an objective description, Mallory uses concrete language and concentrates on the shapes, colors, and surroundings of the countries she describes.

This objective description does include a few subjective elements. For example, in her introduction, Mallory says that the sunlight rests "sleepily" on her grandfather's globe. In her conclusion, she observes that the world represented by her grandfather's globe is "still and mysterious." (Her instructor had told the class that they could include a few subjective comments to convey the special meaning that the items they describe have for them.)

Figurative Language. In order to give readers a clear sense of what the countries on the globe look like, Mallory uses figurative language. For example, she uses similes when she describes South America as "like a face in profile" and Africa as looking "like a fat boomerang." She also uses metaphor when she says that the Mediterranean Sea is a "thick blue ribbon" and Siam is "a three-leaf clover with a stem that hangs down." Finally, Mallory uses personification when she says that the Belgian Congo "straddles the equator." By using these figures of speech, Mallory creates a vivid and striking picture of her grandfather's globe.

Structure. Mallory structures her description by moving from north to south as she moves east around the globe. She begins by describing the colors of North America, and then she describes South America. She directs her readers' attention to specific areas — for example, Central America. She then moves east, to Africa, and repeats the process of describing the regions in the north (Western Europe) and then in the south (Africa). As she does so, she notes that some countries, such as the U.S.S.R., have changed names since the globe was made in 1939. She repeats the pattern of moving east, north, and south and ends by describing Australia. Mallory frames her description of the globe with a description of her grandfather's bedroom. In her conclusion, she connects the sunlight in her grandfather's room to the world pictured on the globe by observing that both seem "still and mysterious."

Selection of Detail. Mallory's instructor defined her audience as people who know about the world today but have never seen her grandfather's globe and do not know much about the world in 1939. For this reason, Mallory includes details such as the tear in Tibet and the water stain that runs through Germany and Italy. In addition, she explains how some countries' names and borders differ from those that exist today.

Working with Sources. Before she wrote her essay, Mallory thought about looking at old atlases or history books. She decided that because her assignment called for a description of an object — not an analysis of how the world changed due to war or to the decline of colonialism — she did not have to consult these sources. She did, however, look up a few facts, such as the current name of Manchoukuo, but since facts are considered common knowledge, she did not have to document her sources for this information.

Focus on Revision

During a conference, Mallory's instructor suggested three possible changes. First, he thought that Mallory should consider including descriptions of additional countries, such as Japan in Asia and Chile, Argentina, and Brazil in South America. He thought that without these descriptions, readers might not fully appreciate how much information the globe contained. Next, he suggested that Mallory add more detail about the globe itself, such as its size, whether it was on a table or on a floor stand, and the materials from which it was constructed. Finally, he suggested that Mallory include a picture of the globe in her essay. He thought that this picture would give students a clearer idea of what the globe looked like and would eliminate the need to add more description.

Mallory decided to write a short paragraph (to be inserted between paragraphs 1 and 2) that provided a general description of the globe. She also decided to add a picture because even with all the vivid description she included, she thought that the globe might be hard to picture. However, she decided that she had mentioned enough countries in her essay and that adding more would be repetitious and might cause readers to lose interest.

A STUDENT WRITER: Subjective Description

The essay that follows, a subjective description of an area in Burma (renamed Myanmar after a military coup in 1989), was written by Mary Lim for her composition class. Her assignment was to write an essay about a place that had a profound effect on her. Mary's essay uses **subjective description** so that readers can share, as well as understand, her experience.

The Valley of Windmills

Introduction	In my native country of Burma, strange happenings and exotic scenery are not unusual, for Burma is a mysterious land that in some areas seems to have been ignored by time. Mountains stand jutting their rocky peaks into the clouds as they have for thousands of years. Jungles are so dense with exotic vegetation that human beings or large animals cannot even enter. But
Description (identifying the scene)	one of the most fascinating areas in Burma is the Valley of Windmills, nestled between the tall mountains near the fertile and beautiful city of Taungaleik. In this valley there is beautiful and breathtaking scenery, but there are also old, massive, and gloomy structures that can disturb a person deeply.

1

Description (moving toward the valley)

The road to Taungaleik twists out of the coastal flatlands into those heaps of slag, shale, and limestone that are the Tennesserim Mountains in the southern part of Burma. The air grows rarer and cooler, and stones become grayer, the highway a little more precarious at its edges, until, ahead, standing in ghostly sentinel across the lip of a pass, is a line of squat forms.

Description (immediate view)

They straddle the road and stand at intervals up hillsides on either side. Are they boulders? Are they fortifications? Are they broken wooden crosses on graves in an abandoned cemetery?

These dark figures are windmills standing in the misty atmosphere. They are immensely old and distinctly evil, some merely turrets, some with remnants of arms hanging derelict from their snouts, and most of them covered with dark green moss. Their decayed but still massive forms seem to turn and sneer at visitors.

Description (more distant view)

Down the pass on the other side is a circular green plateau that lies like an arena below, where there are still more windmills. Massed in the plain behind them, as far as the eye can see, in every field, above every hut, stand ten thousand iron windmills, silent and sailless. They seem to await only a call from a watchman to clank, whirr, flap, and groan into action. Visitors suddenly feel cold. Perhaps it is a sense of loneliness, the cool air, the desolation, or the weirdness of the arcane windmills — but something chills them.

Conclusion

As you stand at the lip of the valley, contrasts rush in to overwhelm you. Beyond, glittering on the mountainside like a solitary jewel, is Taungaleik in the territory once occupied by the Portuguese. Below, on rolling hillsides, are the dark windmills, still enveloped in morning mist.

Description (windmills contrasted with city)

Thesis statement

These ancient windmills can remind a person of the impermanence of life and the mystery that still surrounds these hills. In a strange way, the scene in the valley can be disturbing, but it also can offer insight into the contradictions that define life here in Burma.

Points for Special Attention

Subjective Description. One of the first things her classmates noticed when they read Mary's essay was her use of vivid details. The road to Taungaleik is described in specific terms: it twists "out of the coastal flatlands" into the mountains, which are "heaps of slag, shale, and limestone." The iron windmills are decayed and stand "silent and sailless" on a green plateau that "lies like an arena." Through her use of detail, Mary creates her dominant impression of the Valley of Windmills as dark, mysterious, and disquieting. The point of her essay — the thesis — is stated in the last paragraph: the Valley of Windmills embodies the contrasts that characterize life in Burma.

Subjective Language. By describing the windmills, Mary conveys her sense of foreboding. When she first introduces them, she questions whether these "squat forms" are "boulders," "fortifications," or "broken wooden crosses," each of which has a menacing connotation. After telling readers what they are, she uses personification, describing the windmills as dark, evil, sneering figures with "arms hanging derelict." She sees them as ghostly sentinels awaiting "a call from a watchman" to spring into action. With this figure of speech, Mary skillfully re-creates the unearthly quality of the scene.

Structure. Mary's purpose in this paper was to give her readers the experience of being in the Valley of Windmills. She uses an organizing scheme that takes readers along the road to Taungaleik, up into the Tennesserim Mountains, and finally to the pass where the windmills wait. From her perspective on the lip of the valley, she describes the details closest to her and then those farther away, as if following the movement of her eyes. She ends by bringing her readers back to the lip of the valley, contrasting Taungaleik "glittering on the mountainside" with the windmills "enveloped in morning mist." With her description, Mary builds up to her thesis about the nature of life in her country. She withholds the explicit statement of her main point until her last paragraph, when readers are fully prepared for it.

Focus on Revision

Mary's peer-editing group suggested that she make two changes. One student thought that Mary's thesis about life in Burma needed additional support. The student pointed out that although Mary's description is quite powerful, it does not fully convey the contrasts she alludes to in her conclusion.

Mary decided that adding another paragraph discussing something about her life (perhaps her reasons for visiting the windmills) could help supply this missing information. She could, for example, tell her readers that right after her return from the valley, she found out that a friend had been accidentally shot by border guards and that it was this event that had caused her to characterize the windmills as she did. Such information would help explain the passage's somber mood and underscore the ideas presented in the conclusion.

Working with Sources. Another student suggested that Mary add some information about the political situation in Burma. He pointed out that few, if any, students in the class knew much about Burma — for example, that after a coup in 1989, the military threw out the civilian government and changed the name of Burma to Myanmar. In addition, he said that he had no idea how repressive the current government of Burma was. For this reason, the student thought that readers would benefit from a paragraph that gave a short history of Burma. Mary considered this option but decided that such information would distract readers from the main point of her description. (A sample peer-editing worksheet for description appears below.)

PEER-EDITING WORKSHEET: Description

1. What is the essay's dominant impression or thesis?

2. What points does the writer emphasize in the introduction? Should any other points be included? If so, which ones?

3. Would you characterize the essay as primarily an objective or subjective description? What leads you to your conclusion?

4. Point out some examples of figures of speech. Could the writer use figures of speech in other places? If so, where?

5. What specific details does the writer use to help readers visualize what is being described? Where could the writer have used more details? Would a visual have helped readers understand what is being described?

6. Are all the details necessary? Can you identify any that seem excessive or redundant? Where could the writer have provided more details to support the thesis or convey the dominant impression?

7. How are the details in the essay arranged? What other arrangement could the writer have used?

8. List some transitional words and phrases the writer uses to help readers follow the discussion. Which sentences need transitional words or phrases to link them to other sentences?

9. Do any sentences contain misplaced or dangling modifiers? If so, which ones?

10. How effective is the essay's conclusion? Does the conclusion reinforce the dominant impression?

The following selections illustrate various ways description can shape an essay. As you read them, pay particular attention to the differences between objective and subjective description. The first selection, a visual text, is followed by questions designed to illustrate how description can operate in visual form. (A multimodal text for description is located online at **macmillanhighered.com/patterns**.)

ANSEL ADAMS

Jeffrey Pine—Sentinel Dome (Photo)

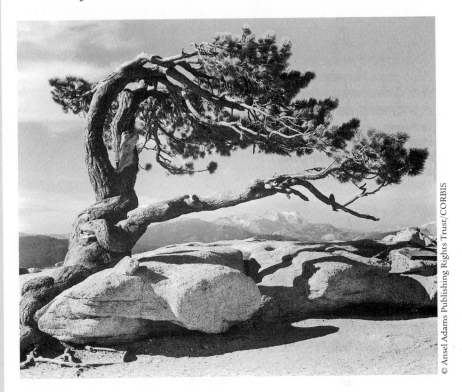

© Ansel Adams Publishing Rights Trust/CORBIS

• • •

Reading Images

1. This photograph, "Jeffrey Pine — Sentinel Dome," was taken by the well-known photographer and environmentalist Ansel Adams. Describe what you see in the picture starting with the image of the tree and then moving left to right (or right to left).

2. Think of a few similes or metaphors that might be used to describe the tree. How would these figures of speech help someone who has not seen the picture to visualize the tree and its surroundings?

3. What dominant impression do you think the photographer wanted to create? How do the details in the picture communicate this dominant impression?

Journal Entry

Go to Google Images and find other photographs by Ansel Adams. Choose one and decide what dominant impression you think Adams was trying to create. Is it different from or similar to the dominant impression created by Adams in the photograph reproduced here?

Thematic Connections

- "Once More to the Lake" (page 191)
- *The Kiss* (page 390)
- "The Untouchable" (page 494)
- "Tortillas" (page 506)

BICH MINH NGUYEN

Goodbye to My Twinkie Days

Writer Bich Minh Nguyen was born in 1974 in the Vietnamese city of Saigon, now known as Ho Chi Minh City. In 1975, her family fled to the United States, where they settled in Grand Rapids, Michigan. Nguyen holds an M.F.A. in creative writing from the University of Michigan and teaches writing and literature at Purdue University. Her books include a memoir, *Stealing Buddha's Dinner* (2007), which won a PEN/Jerard Award from the PEN American Center, and the novel *Short Girls* (2009).

Background on the snack cake Individually wrapped, inexpensive, accessible, and unpretentious — the American snack cake is a democratic and egalitarian representation of mass-produced efficiency. Moreover, these processed products are also a guilty pleasure, even in today's health-conscious era. Although the Twinkie perhaps is the most iconic American snack cake, it is part of a larger history of mass-produced baked goods stretching back to the late nineteenth and early twentieth centuries. Although the Twinkie remains one of the best-selling snack cakes in history, it was not the first one produced. In 1888, Norman Drake established Drake Brothers, a commercial bakery in Brooklyn, New York, which sold individual slices of "Drake's Cakes" pound cake. Eventually, the company became better known for treats such as Yodels and Ring Dings. In the South, the first Moon Pie was sold by the Chattanooga Baking Company in 1917. However, exactly who sold the first mass-produced snack cake remains a subject of dispute. For example, the Philadelphia company Tastykake claims that its individually packaged Junior layer cakes and chocolate cupcakes appeared in 1914 and 1915, predating Hostess products and the Moon Pie by several years. Regardless, no one disagrees that the first Twinkie appeared in 1930, created by baker James Dewar. The Hostess brand filed for bankruptcy in 2011, fueling fears that the Twinkie would disappear forever, yet the snack cake returned to store shelves — with the help of a new parent corporation — in 2013.

1   When I heard this week that the Hostess cake company was going out of business, I decided to pay my respects: I went out and bought a ten-pack box of Twinkies.

2   Though the more immediate cause of the company's trouble is a labor dispute with members of the Bakery, Confectionery, Tobacco Workers and Grain Millers International Union, its demise has been a long time coming. After all, we're not supposed to eat like this anymore. The partially hydrogenated oils, artificial flavors, high fructose corn syrup — Michael Pollan would not approve. Mr. Pollan, I swear that I have not tasted a Twinkie in years. I would not feed them to my kids.

But I can't stop the nostalgia, rising even now in the recitation of   3
names: Ho Hos, Ding Dongs, Sno Balls, Zingers, Donettes, Suzy Q's. Generations of us carried these Hostess treats in our lunchboxes, traded them,
saved bites of frosting and cream for last. Soon, unless another company
buys the brands, they'll be nothing but liquidated assets.

"Junk food" is a phrase at once grotesque   4
and appealing. We know it's bad, and that's
why we want it. The Twinkie, introduced in
1930, was a best-selling treat of the Depression and is still one of the company's top
items. The inventor got the idea after seeing
baking equipment for strawberry cakes go
unused when the fruit was out of season. (It
seems incredible now that mass-production

> "'Junk food' is a phrase at once grotesque and appealing."

of food once shifted with the seasons.) We have Hostess largely to thank for
the very concept of the "snack cake," lifting sweets from dessert time to anytime. Of the company's many products — the chocolate CupCakes with the
white squiggle across the top, Fruit Pies, Dolly Madison cakes, even Wonder
Bread — the Twinkie, fresh from the package or deep-fried at a county fair,
has been its most enduring icon.

For me, a child of Vietnamese immigrants growing up in Michigan in   5
the 1980s, Twinkies were a ticket to assimilation: the golden cake, more
golden than the hair I wished I had, filled with sweet white cream. Back
then, junk foods seemed to represent an ideal of American indulgence.

They've since become a joke, a stereotype of shallow suburbia. For   6
Asian-Americans, to be a twinkie is to be a sellout: yellow on the outside,
white on the inside. Even the name "Hostess" seems quaintly outdated, like
"stewardess" or "butler." On the box of Twinkies I bought there's a cartoon
of a Twinkie as a cowboy; his sidekick is a short, swarthy chocolate cupcake. Whether Hostess meant to evoke the Lone Ranger and Tonto or was
simply trying to recapture a glory-days notion of sweet-toothed kids playing dress-up, the company seems determined to be retro.

Yet maybe that's exactly why the Twinkie has continued to fascinate: it   7
is already a relic. When I opened one, the smell of sugary, fake, buttery-ish
vanilla took me back to my elementary school and the basketball lines on
the floor of the gym that doubled as our lunchroom. The underside of the
cake had the same three white dots where the cream filling had been
punched in, and it tasted like what it was, a blend of shortening and corn
syrup, coating the tongue. I didn't think the Twinkie would thrill the way it
used to, and it didn't. But it tasted like memory.

We might bake our own cakes now, eat whole grain bread, and try to   8
follow those grocery store Food Rules, but who among us can forget being
sugar-shocked by processed goods? What will it mean if Twinkies and
Zingers become footnotes, gone the way of Uneeda Biscuit and Magic
Middles? There's nothing like junk foods, emblems of our shared pop culture, to create a conversation and establish common ground. Losing the
Twinkie will mean losing a connection to our shared past; it will be another

part of the long goodbye to our youth. As Hostess goes under, we become older.

According to popular myth, Twinkies are so stuffed with chemicals 9 and preservatives that they will last for decades. Hostess insists that the shelf life is more like twenty-five days. I decided to store the rest of mine in the cupboard above my refrigerator, out of reach but available, just in case. I may never eat them, but I like knowing that they exist, that I can still taste my way back to the childhood living room where I watched episodes of *Silver Spoons* and dreamed of all the possibilities yet to be consumed.

• • •

Comprehension

1. In spite of saying that she has not eaten a Twinkie in years and that she would not give one to her children, Nguyen buys a ten-pack. Why?
2. According to Nguyen, what is the significance of a "snack cake"?
3. In paragraph 5, Nguyen says, "Twinkies were a ticket to assimilation." What does she mean? In what sense is junk food particularly American?
4. What special meaning do Hostess Twinkies have for Asian Americans?
5. What significance would losing Twinkies have for Nguyen? For all Americans?

Purpose and Audience

1. How much does Nguyen assume her readers know about Twinkies? How can you tell?
2. What is Nguyen's purpose? Is she writing about how much she will miss Twinkies, or is she writing about something else? Explain.
3. Does this essay have an explicitly stated thesis, or is the thesis implied? What dominant impression does Nguyen want to convey?

Style and Structure

1. Nguyen begins her essay with a one-sentence paragraph. How effective is this opening strategy? How else could she have begun her essay?
2. In paragraph 2, Nguyen refers to Michael Pollan, who writes about culture and food—especially about how industrial food production has lost touch with nature. Why does Nguyen mention Pollan? What point is she trying to make?
3. In paragraph 6, Nguyen includes one sentence that contains a colon and another that contains a semicolon. Instead of the colon, why doesn't Nguyen use a comma? Instead of the semicolon, why doesn't she use a period?
4. **Vocabulary Project.** In paragraph 4, Nguyen discusses junk food. What do you think she means by this term? Is your definition of junk food different from Nguyen's? If so, how?

5. In paragraph 6, Nguyen describes the box that contains the Twinkies. In paragraph 7, she describes a Twinkie itself. Are these descriptions primarily objective or subjective? What specific words lead you to your conclusion?

Journal Entry

What snack food do you most associate with your childhood? Is this association positive or negative? Why?

Writing Workshop

1. **Working with Sources.** Write an essay in which you describe a food that is as meaningful to you as Twinkies are to Nguyen. Make sure that your essay has a clear thesis and that it includes at least one reference to Nguyen's essay. Be sure to document all material that you borrow from Nguyen's essay and to include a works-cited page. (See Chapter 18 for information on MLA documentation.)

2. Write an email to someone in another country in which you describe the foods that you traditionally eat on a particular holiday. Assume that the person is not familiar with the foods you describe. Be sure your description conveys a clear dominant impression.

3. Write an essay in which you describe a parent or grandparent (or any other older person) who has had a great influence on you. Make sure you include basic biographical information as a well as a detailed physical description.

Combining the Patterns

In addition to describing Nguyen's fascination for Twinkies, this essay examines **causes and effects** (in paragraph 2). What purpose does this cause-and-effect paragraph serve?

Thematic Connections

- "My Field of Dreams" (page 106)
- "Songs of the Summer of 1963 . . . and 2013" (page 403)
- "Tortillas" (page 506)

SUZANNE BERNE

Ground Zero

Suzanne Berne has worked as a journalist and has also published book reviews and personal essays as well as four well-received novels, including *The Ghost at the Table* (2006) and *Lucille* (2010). She currently teaches English at Boston College. In the following essay, which appeared on the *New York Times* op-ed page in April 2002, Berne describes a personal pilgrimage to the former site of the World Trade Center in New York City.

Background on the terrorist attacks of 9/11 The September 11, 2001, terrorist attacks that destroyed the twin towers of New York's World Trade Center and severely damaged the Pentagon stunned the nation and the world. People watched in horror as camera crews recorded the collapse of the towers while victims jumped to their deaths. The three hijacked aircraft that crashed into these targets, and a fourth that crashed into a field in rural Pennsylvania, caused the deaths of nearly three thousand people. An outpouring of grief, outrage, fear, and patriotism consumed the nation in the ensuing months. While many, like Berne, have felt drawn to visit "ground zero," some family members of the victims — particularly of those whose unidentified remains are still at the site — have expressed concern that it not become a tourist attraction. A memorial at the site, which opened in May 2014, includes two huge reflecting pools where the original twin towers stood. The names of the nearly three thousand people who were killed in the September 11 attacks in New York City, Pennsylvania, and Washington, DC (as well as those killed in the 1993 World Trade Center bombings) are inscribed around the edges of the pools. An underground museum houses exhibits that convey the experiences of responders, victims, and witnesses.

On a cold, damp March morning, I visited Manhattan's financial district, a place I'd never been, to pay my respects at what used to be the World Trade Center. Many other people had chosen to do the same that day, despite the raw wind and spits of rain, and so the first thing I noticed when I arrived on the corner of Vesey and Church Streets was a crowd.

Standing on the sidewalk, pressed against aluminum police barricades, wearing scarves that flapped into their faces and woolen hats pulled over their ears, were people apparently from everywhere. Germans, Italians, Japanese. An elegant-looking Norwegian family in matching shearling coats. People from Ohio and California and Maine. Children, middle-aged couples, older people. Many of them were clutching cameras and video recorders, and they were all craning to see across the street, where there was nothing to see.

At least, nothing is what it first looked like, the space that is now ground zero. But once your eyes adjust to what you are looking at, "nothing" becomes something much more potent, which is absence.

But to the out-of-towner, ground zero looks at first simply like a con- 4
struction site. All the familiar details are there: the wooden scaffolding; the
cranes, the bulldozers, and forklifts; the trailers and construction workers
in hard hats; even the dust. There is the pound of jackhammers, the steady
beep-beep-beep of trucks backing up, the roar of heavy machinery.

So much busyness is reassuring, and it is possible to stand looking at 5
the cranes and trucks and feel that mild curiosity and hopefulness so often
inspired by construction sites.

Then gradually your eyes do adjust, exactly as if you have stepped from 6
a dark theater into a bright afternoon, because what becomes most striking
about this scene is the light itself.

Ground zero is a great bowl of light, an 7
emptiness that seems weirdly spacious and
grand, like a vast plaza amid the dense
tangle of streets in lower Manhattan. Light
reflecting off the Hudson River vaults into
the site, soaking everything — especially on
an overcast morning — with a watery glow.
This is the moment when absence begins to
assume a material form, when what is not
there becomes visible.

> " Ground zero is a
> great bowl of light, an
> emptiness that seems
> weirdly spacious and
> grand. . . . "

Suddenly you notice the periphery, the skyscraper shrouded in black 8
plastic, the boarded windows, the steel skeleton of the shattered Winter
Garden. Suddenly there are the broken steps and cracked masonry in front
of Brooks Brothers. Suddenly there are the firefighters, the waiting ambulance on the other side of the pit, the police on every corner. Suddenly there
is the enormous cross made of two rusted girders.

And suddenly, very suddenly, there is the little cemetery attached to 9
St. Paul's Chapel, with tulips coming up, the chapel and grounds miraculously undamaged except for a few plastic-sheathed gravestones. The iron
fence is almost invisible beneath a welter of dried pine wreaths, banners,
ribbons, laminated poems and prayers and photographs, swags of paper
cranes, withered flowers, baseball hats, rosary beads, teddy bears. And flags,
flags everywhere, little American flags fluttering in the breeze, flags on
posters drawn by Brownie troops, flags on T-shirts, flags on hats, flags
streaming by, tied to the handles of baby strollers.

It takes quite a while to see all of this; it takes even longer to come up 10
with something to say about it.

An elderly man standing next to me had been staring fixedly across the 11
street for some time. Finally he touched his son's elbow and said: "I watched
those towers being built. I saw this place when they weren't there." Then
he stopped, clearly struggling with, what for him, was a double negative,
recalling an absence before there was an absence. His son, waiting patiently,
took a few photographs. "Let's get out of here," the man said at last.

Again and again I heard people say, "It's unbelievable." And then they 12
would turn to each other, dissatisfied. They wanted to say something more
expressive, more meaningful. But it *is* unbelievable, to stare at so much

devastation, and know it for devastation, and yet recognize that it does not look like the devastation one has imagined.

Like me, perhaps, the people around me had in mind images from tele- 13 vision and newspaper pictures: the collapsing buildings, the running office workers, the black plume of smoke against a bright blue sky. Like me, they were probably trying to superimpose those terrible images onto the indus-trious emptiness right in front of them. The difficulty of this kind of men-tal revision is measured, I believe, by the brisk trade in World Trade Center photograph booklets at tables set up on street corners.

Determined to understand better what I was looking at, I decided to 14 get a ticket for the viewing platform beside St. Paul's. This proved no easy task, as no one seemed to be able to direct me to South Street Seaport, where the tickets are distributed. Various police officers whom I asked for directions waved me vaguely toward the East River, differing degrees of boredom and resignation on their faces. Or perhaps it was a kind of incred-ulousness. Somewhere around the American Stock Exchange, I asked a security guard for help and he frowned at me, saying, "You want tickets to the disaster?"

Finally I found myself in line at a cheerfully painted kiosk, watching a 15 young juggler try to entertain the crowd. He kept dropping the four red balls he was attempting to juggle, and having to chase after them. It was noon; the next available viewing was at 4 P.M.

Back I walked, up Fulton Street, the smell of fish in the air, to wander 16 again around St. Paul's. A deli on Vesey Street advertised a view of the World Trade Center from its second-floor dining area. I went in and ordered a pastrami sandwich, uncomfortably aware that many people be-fore me had come to that same deli for pastrami sandwiches who would never come there again. But I was here to see what I could, so I carried my sandwich upstairs and sat down beside one of the big plate-glass windows.

And there, at last, I got my ticket to the disaster.   17

I could see not just into the pit now, but also its access ramp, which 18 trucks had been traveling up and down since I had arrived that morning. Gathered along the ramp were firefighters in their black helmets and black coats. Slowly they lined up, and it became clear that this was an honor guard, and that someone's remains were being carried up the ramp toward the open door of an ambulance.

Everyone in the dining room stopped eating. Several people stood up, 19 whether out of respect or to see better, I don't know. For a moment, every-thing paused.

Then the day flowed back into itself. Soon I was outside once more, 20 joining the tide of people washing around the site. Later, as I huddled with a little crowd on the viewing platform, watching people scrawl their names or write "God Bless America" on the plywood walls, it occurred to me that a form of repopulation was taking effect, with so many visitors to this place, thousands of visitors, all of us coming to see the wide emptiness where so many were lost. And by the act of our visiting — whether we are motivated by curiosity or horror or reverence or grief, or by something confusing that combines them all — that space fills up again.

• • •

Comprehension

1. What does Berne mean when she says that as her eyes adjust to what she is seeing, " 'nothing' becomes something much more potent, which is absence" (3)?
2. Why does it take "quite a while" (10) to see all the details at ground zero? Why does it take "even longer" (10) to think of something to say about it?
3. According to Berne, how were the television pictures of ground zero different from the actual experience of seeing it?
4. How does the area around ground zero contrast with the site itself? How does Berne react to this contrast?
5. What does Berne mean in her conclusion when she says that with so many visitors coming to see ground zero, a form of "repopulation" (20) is taking place? Do you think she is being **sarcastic**?

Purpose and Audience

1. Does Berne state or imply her thesis? Why do you think she makes the decision she does? State Berne's thesis in your own words.
2. What is Berne's purpose in writing her essay?
3. What assumptions does Berne make about her readers' ideas about ground zero? How can you tell?

Style and Structure

1. Why does Berne begin her essay by saying she had never before visited Manhattan's financial district?
2. What organizational scheme does Berne use? What are the advantages and disadvantages of this scheme?
3. In paragraph 3, Berne says that ground zero at first looks like "nothing"; in paragraph 4, she says that it looks like a construction site. Then, in paragraph 7, she describes ground zero as "a great bowl of light." And finally, in her conclusion, she refers to it as a "pit" (18). Why do you think Berne describes ground zero in so many different ways?
4. Berne leaves a space between paragraphs 17 and 18. In what way does the space (as well as paragraph 17) reinforce a shift in her essay's focus?
5. Why does Berne end her essay with a description of the crowd standing on the viewing platform? Why do you suppose she feels the need to include these observations?

6. In paragraphs 8 and 9, Berne repeats the word *suddenly*. What is the effect of this repetition? Could she have achieved this effect some other way?

7. **Vocabulary Project.** Go to dictionary.com and look up the meaning of the term *ground zero*. What connotations does this term have? Do you think this is an appropriate title for Berne's essay?

Journal Entry

Go to the website wtc.vjs.org and look at film clips of ground zero just after the twin towers collapsed. Are your reactions to these images similar to or different from Berne's?

Writing Workshop

1. **Working with Sources.** Write an essay describing what you saw in the film clips you watched for your journal entry. Be sure to include an explicitly stated thesis and to use descriptive details to convey your reactions to the event. Try to include a quotation from Berne's essay in your paper. Be sure to document the quotation and to include a works-cited page. (See Chapter 18 for information on MLA documentation.)

2. Write a description of a place from several different vantage points, as Berne does. Make sure each of your perspectives provides different information about the place you are describing.

3. Write a subjective description of a scene you remember from your childhood. In your thesis statement and in your conclusion, explain how your adult impressions of the scene differ from those of your childhood.

Combining the Patterns

In addition to containing a great deal of description, this essay also uses **comparison and contrast**. In paragraphs 1 through 10, what two ways of seeing ground zero does Berne compare? What points about each view of ground zero does she contrast?

Thematic Connections

- From *Persepolis II* (page 112)
- "Living with Fire" (page 118)
- "Shooting an Elephant" (page 133)
- "Once More to the Lake" (page 191)

ANN HODGMAN

No Wonder They Call Me a Bitch

Ann Hodgman, who was born in 1956, is a humorist, food writer, and children's author. She has published many books, including *You Know You're 40 When . . .* (2005), *The House of a Million Pets* (2007), and *How to Die of Embarrassment Every Day* (2011). A former contributing editor at *Spy*, an influential humor magazine in the 1980s, Hodgman has also written for *Good Housekeeping* and the *New York Times*.

Background on pet food Ohioan James Spratt created Spratt's Meat Fibrine Dog Cakes, the first commercially prepared dog food, in 1860. However, the industry truly boomed during the first half of the twentieth century, with products like Milk-Bones and Ken-L Ration, the first canned dog food. Ken-L Ration was also a pioneer in advertising dog food, first as a sponsor for the radio show *The Adventures of Rin Tin Tin* and then on television, advertising on programs like *The Adventures of Ozzie and Harriet*. The food's commercial tagline at the time is instructive: "This dog food uses only USDA, government-inspected horse meat." Indeed, while dog-food advertising has long relied on images of satisfied and healthy dogs with shiny coats, as well as on claims of appetizing ingredients ("Real beef!"), the product's contents have long been the subject of curiosity and even satire. Now, the dog-food business is largely an extension of the industrial food system of humans, as it makes use of offal, waste, and animal by-products deemed unfit for human consumption. Still, through a "miracle of beauty and packaging" (in Hodgman's words), it is also a $10 billion industry.

I've always wondered about dog food. Is a Gaines-burger really like a 1 hamburger? Can you fry it? Does dog food "cheese" taste like real cheese? Does Gravy Train actually make gravy in a dog's bowl, or is that brown liquid just dissolved crumbs? And what exactly *are* by-products?

Having spent the better part of a week eating dog food, I'm sorry to say 2 that I now know the answers to these questions. While my dachshund, Shortie, watched in agonies of yearning, I gagged my way through can after can of stinky, white-flecked mush and bag after bag of stinky, fat-drenched nuggets. And now I understand exactly why Shortie's breath is so bad.

Of course, Gaines-burgers are neither mush nor nuggets. They are, 3 rather, a miracle of beauty and packaging — or at least that's what I thought when I was little. I used to beg my mother to get them for our dogs, but she always said they were too expensive. When I finally bought a box of cheese-flavored Gaines-burgers — after twenty years of longing — I felt deliciously wicked.

"Dogs love real beef," the back of the box proclaimed proudly. "That's 4 why Gaines-burgers is the only beef burger for dogs with real beef and no meat by-products!" The copy was accurate: meat by-products did not appear in the list of ingredients. Poultry by-products did, though — right there next to preserved animal fat.

One Purina spokesman told me that poultry by-products consist of necks, intestines, undeveloped eggs, and other "carcass remnants," but not feathers, heads, or feet. When I told him I'd been eating dog food, he said, "Oh, you're kidding! Oh, *no!*" (I came to share his alarm when, weeks later, a second Purina spokesman said that Gaines-burgers *do* contain poultry heads and feet — but *not* undeveloped eggs.)

Up close my Gaines-burger didn't much resemble chopped beef. Rather, it looked — and felt — like a single long, extruded piece of redness that had been chopped into segments and formed into a patty. You could make one at home if you had a Play-Doh Fun Factory.

I turned on the skillet. While I waited for it to heat up I pulled out a shred of cheese-colored material and palpated it. Again, like Play-Doh, it was quite malleable. I made a little cheese bird out of it; then I counted to three and ate the bird.

There was a horrifying rush of cheddar taste, followed immediately by the dull tang of soybean flour — the main ingredient in Gaines-burgers. Next I tried a piece of red extrusion. The main difference between the meat-flavored and cheese-flavored extrusions is one of texture. The "cheese" chews like fresh Play-Doh, whereas the "meat" chews like Play-Doh that's been sitting out on the rug for a couple of hours.

> " There was a horrifying rush of cheddar taste, followed immediately by the dull tang of soybean flour — the main ingredient in Gaines-burgers. "

Frying only turned the Gaines-burger black. There was no melting, no sizzling, no warm meat smells. A cherished childhood illusion was gone. I flipped the patty into the sink, where it immediately began leaking rivulets of red dye.

As alarming as the Gaines-burgers were, their soy meal began to seem like an old friend when the time came to try some *canned* dog foods. I decided to try the Cycle foods first. When I opened them, I thought about how rarely I use can openers these days, and I was suddenly visited by a long-forgotten sensation of can-opener distaste. *This* is the kind of unsavory place can openers spend their time when you're not watching! Every time you open a can of, say, Italian plum tomatoes, you infect them with invisible particles of by-product.

I had been expecting to see the usual homogeneous scrapple inside, but each can of Cycle was packed with smooth, round, oily nuggets. As if someone at Gaines had been tipped off that a human would be tasting the stuff, the four Cycles really were different from one another. Cycle-1, for puppies, is wet and soyish. Cycle-2, for adults, glistens nastily with fat, but it's passably edible — a lot like some canned Swedish meatballs I once got in a Care package at college. Cycle-3, the "lite" one, for fatties, had no specific flavor; it just tasted like dog food. But at least it didn't make me fat.

Cycle-4, for senior dogs, had the smallest nuggets. Maybe old dogs can't   12
open their mouths as wide. This kind was far sweeter than the other three
Cycles — almost like baked beans. It was also the only one to contain "dried
beef digest," a mysterious substance that the Purina spokesman defined as
"enzymes" and my dictionary defined as "the products of digestion."

Next on the menu was a can of Kal Kan Pedigree with Chunky Chicken.   13
Chunky *chicken*? There were chunks in the can, certainly — big, purplish-
brown chunks. I forked one chunk out (by now I was becoming callous)
and found that while it had no discernible chicken flavor, it wasn't bad
except for its texture — like meat loaf with ground-up chicken bones.

In the world of canned dog food, a smooth consistency is a sign of low   14
quality — lots of cereal. A lumpy, frightening, bloody, stringy horror is a
sign of high quality — lots of meat. Nowhere in the world of wet dog foods
was this demonstrated better than in the fanciest I tried — Kal Kan's Pedigree Select Dinners. These came not in a can but in a tiny foil packet with a
picture of an imperious Yorkie. When I pulled open the container, juice
spurted all over my hand, and the first chunk I speared was trailing a long
gray vein. I shrieked and went instead for a plain chunk, which I was able to
swallow only after taking a break to read some suddenly fascinating office
equipment catalogues. Once again, though, it tasted no more alarming
than, say, canned hash.

Still, how pleasant it was to turn to *dry* dog food! Gravy Train was the   15
first I tried, and I'm happy to report that it really does make a "thick, rich,
real beef gravy" when you mix it with water. Thick and rich, anyway. Except
for a lingering rancid-fat flavor, the gravy wasn't beefy, but since it tasted
primarily like tap water, it wasn't nauseating either.

My poor dachshund just gets plain old Purina Dog Chow, but Purina   16
also makes a dry food called Butcher's Blend that comes in Beef, Bacon &
Chicken flavor. Here we see dog food's arcane semiotics at its best: a red
triangle with a *T* stamped into it is supposed to suggest beef; a tan curl,
chicken; and a brown *S*, a piece of bacon. Only dogs understand these messages. But Butcher's Blend does have an endearing slogan: "Great Meaty
Tastes — without bothering the Butcher!" *You know, I wanted to buy some
meat, but I just couldn't bring myself to bother the butcher.*

Purina O.N.E. ("Optimum Nutritional Effectiveness") is targeted at   17
people who are unlikely ever to worry about bothering a tradesperson. "We
chose chicken as a primary ingredient in Purina O.N.E. for several reasonings [sic]," the long, long essay on the back of the bag announces. Chief
among these reasonings, I'd guess, is the fact that chicken appeals to people
who are — you know — *like us*. Although our dogs do nothing but spend
eighteen-hour days alone in the apartment, we still want them to be *premium* dogs. We want them to cut down on red meat, too. We also want dog
food that comes in a bag with an attractive design, a subtle typeface, and no
kitschy pictures of slobbering golden retrievers.

Besides that, we want a list of the Nutritional Benefits of our dog   18
food — and we get it on O.N.E. One thing I especially like about this list is

its constant references to a dog's "hair coat," as in "Beef tallow is good for the dog's skin and hair coat." (On the other hand, beef tallow merely provides palatability, while the dried beef digest in Cycle provides palatability *enhancement.*)

I hate to say it, but O.N.E. was pretty palatable. Maybe that's because it 19 has about 100 percent more fat than, say, Butcher's Blend. Or maybe I'd been duped by the packaging; that's been known to happen before.

As with people food, dog snacks taste much better than dog meals. 20 They're better looking, too. Take Milk-Bone Flavor Snacks. The loving-hands-at-home prose describing each flavor is colorful; the writers practically choke on their own exuberance. Of bacon they say, "It's so good, your dog will think it's hot off the frying pan." Of liver: "The only taste your dog wants more than liver — is even more liver!" Of poultry: "All those farm fresh flavors deliciously mixed in one biscuit. Your dog will bark with delight!" And of vegetable: "Gardens of taste! Specially blended to give your dog that vegetable flavor he wants — but can rarely get!"

Well, I may be a sucker, but advertising *this* emphatic just doesn't convince me. I lined up all seven flavors of Milk-Bone Flavor Snacks on the floor. Unless my dog's palate is a lot more sensitive than mine — and considering that she steals dirty diapers out of the trash and eats them, I'm loath to think it is — she doesn't detect any more difference in the seven flavors than I did when I tried them.

I much preferred Bonz, the hard-baked, bone-shaped snack stuffed 22 with simulated marrow. I liked the bone part, that is; it tasted almost exactly like the cornmeal it was made of. The mock marrow inside was a bit more problematic: in addition to looking like the sludge that collects in the treads of my running shoes, it was bursting with tiny hairs.

I'm sure you have a few dog food questions of your own. To save us 23 time, I've answered them in advance.

Q. *Are those little cans of Mighty Dog actually branded with the sizzling word* 24 BEEF, *the way they show in the commercials?*

A. You should know by now that that kind of thing never happens. 25

Q. *Does chicken-flavored dog food taste like chicken-flavored cat food?* 26

A. To my surprise, chicken cat food was actually a little better — 27 more chickeny. It tasted like inferior canned pâté.

Q. *Was there any dog food that you just couldn't bring yourself to try?* 28

A. Alas, it was a can of Mighty Dog called Prime Entree with Bone Mar- 29 row. The meat was dark, dark brown, and it was surrounded by gelatin that was almost black. I knew I would die if I tasted it, so I put it outside for the raccoons.

. . .

Comprehension

1. Why did Hodgman decide to try eating dog food? Do you find her reasons convincing?

2. According to Hodgman, how does the packaging of dog food contrast with its taste?

3. Which brand of dog food does Hodgman like best? Which does she like least?

4. How does Hodgman describe the advertising copy that appears on the packages of dog food? What message does this advertising try to convey to purchasers?

Purpose and Audience

1. Does "No Wonder They Call Me a Bitch" have an explicitly stated thesis? If so, where? If not, why not?

2. What dominant impression is Hodgman trying to create in her essay? How successful is she?

3. How do you think Hodgman expects readers to react to her essay? How can you tell? How do these expectations affect Hodgman's treatment of her subject?

Style and Structure

1. What is your reaction to the title of this essay? What are the advantages and disadvantages of using a word like *bitch* in this title?

2. What determines how the details in this description are arranged? Would another organizing principle have been more effective?

3. Does Hodgman develop her description of the various dog foods fully enough? Where could she have provided more detail? Where, if anywhere, do you think she gives too much detail?

4. What figures of speech does Hodgman use to help readers understand her description? How do these figures of speech help Hodgman make her points?

5. Why does Hodgman end her essay by answering questions that readers may have? Do you think this is an effective strategy? Explain.

6. **Vocabulary Project.** Make a list of the adjectives Hodgman uses to describe the dog foods she tasted. How effectively do these adjectives convey the look, feel, taste, and smell of the various foods?

Journal Entry

Why do you think Hodgman uses humor so extensively in this essay? Include some specific examples to support your answer.

Writing Workshop

1. **Working with Sources.** Hodgman uses original research to find out about her subject and then writes an essay that describes the results of

her research. Conduct your own food-tasting on a type of food product — for example, kinds of energy drinks, snack foods, or fast-food burgers. Then, write an essay that describes the results of your research. Be sure to document all references to Hodgman's essay and to include a works-cited page. (See Chapter 18 for information on MLA documentation.)

2. Make a list of products that make claims that could be considered exaggerated or false — in TV infomercials or on natural food labels, for example. Then, write an essay in which you describe several of these products. Like Hodgman, use concrete sensory details to convey your dominant impression.

3. In addition to writing essays, Hodgman writes a food column. Read a few food columns online, and then write one that describes the food served in your school cafeteria. Make sure your description supports your thesis statement (or the dominant impression you wish to convey).

Combining the Patterns

At various points in her essay — for example, in paragraphs 7 and 13 — Hodgman uses **narration**. What do these narrative paragraphs add to her essay?

Thematic Connections

- "The Embalming of Mr. Jones" (page 301)
- "Tortillas" (page 506)
- "On Dumpster Diving" (page 672)

HEATHER ROGERS

The Hidden Life of Garbage

Journalist Heather Rogers has written articles on the environmental effects of mass production and consumption for the *New York Times Magazine,* the *Utne Reader, Architecture,* and a variety of other publications. Her 2002 documentary film *Gone Tomorrow: The Hidden Life of Garbage* has been screened at festivals around the world and served as the basis for a book of the same title. Named an Editor's Choice by the *New York Times* and the *Guardian,* the book, published in 2005, traces the history and politics of household garbage in the United States, drawing connections between modern industrial production, consumer culture, and our contemporary throwaway lifestyle. In the following excerpt from the book, Rogers provides a detailed description of a giant landfill in central Pennsylvania and asks readers to think about the ramifications of accumulating so much trash. Her most recent book is *Green Gone Wrong: How Our Economy Is Undermining the Environmental Revolution* (2010).

Background on waste disposal Human beings have always faced the question of how to dispose of garbage. The first city dump was established in ancient Athens, and the government of Rome had begun the collection of municipal trash by 200 C.E. Even as late as the 1800s, garbage was, at worst, simply thrown out into the streets of U.S. cities or dumped into rivers and ditches; in more enlightened communities, it might have been carted to foul-smelling open dumps or burned in incinerators, creating clouds of dense smoke. Experiments with systematically covering the garbage in dumps began as early as the 1920s, and the first true "sanitary landfill," as it was called, was created in Fresno, California, in 1937. Today, more than 60 percent of the solid waste in the United States ends up in landfills, and the amount of waste seems to keep growing. According to the Energy Information Administration, the amount of waste produced in the United States has more than doubled in the past thirty years, and it is estimated that the average American generates an astounding 4.5 pounds of trash every day.

In the dark chill of early morning, heavy steel garbage trucks chug and creep along neighborhood collection routes. A worker empties the contents of each household's waste bin into the truck's rear compaction unit. Hydraulic compressors scoop up and crush the dross, cramming it into the enclosed hull. When the rig is full, the collector heads to a garbage depot called a "transfer station" to unload. From there the rejectamenta is taken to a recycling center, an incinerator, or, most often, to what's called a "sanitary landfill."

Land dumping has long been the favored disposal method in the U.S. thanks to the relative low cost of burial and North America's abundant supply of unused acreage. Although the great majority of our castoffs go to landfills, they are places the public is not meant to see. Today's garbage graveyards are sequestered, guarded, veiled. They are also high-tech, and, increasingly, located in rural areas that receive much of their rubbish from urban centers that no longer bury their own wastes.

There's a reason landfills are tucked away, on the edge of town, in 3 otherwise untraveled terrain, camouflaged by hydroseeded, neatly tiered slopes. If people saw what happened to their waste, lived with the stench, witnessed the scale of destruction, they might start asking difficult questions. Waste Management Inc., the largest rubbish handling corporation in the world, operates its Geological Reclamation Operations and Waste Systems (GROWS) landfill just outside Morrisville, Pennsylvania — in the docile river valley near where Washington momentously crossed the Delaware leading his troops into Trenton in 1776. Sitting atop the landfill's 300-foot-high butte composed entirely of garbage, the logic of our society's unrestrained consuming and wasting quickly unravels.

Up here is where the dumping takes place; it is referred to as the fill's 4 "working face." Clusters of trailer trucks, yellow earthmovers, compacting machines, steamrollers, and water tankers populate this bizarre, thirty-acre nightmare. Churning in slow motion through the surreal landscape, these machines are remaking the earth in the image of garbage. Scores of seagulls hover overhead then suddenly drop into the rotting piles. The ground underfoot is torn from the metal treads of the equipment. Potato chip wrappers, tattered plastic bags, and old shoes poke through the dirt as if floating to the surface. The smell is sickly and sour.

The aptly named GROWS landfill is part of Waste Management Inc.'s 5 (WMI) 6,000-acre garbage treatment complex, which includes a second landfill, an incinerator, and a state-mandated leaf composting lot. GROWS is one of a new breed of waste burial sites referred to as "mega-fills." These high-tech, high-capacity dumps are comprised of a series of earth-covered "cells" that can be ten to one hundred acres across and up to hundreds of feet deep — or tall, as is the case at GROWS. (One Virginia whopper has disposal capacity equivalent to the length of one thousand football fields and the height of the Washington Monument.) As of 2002, GROWS was the single largest recipient of New York City's garbage in Pennsylvania, a state that is the country's biggest depository for exported waste.

WMI's Delaware-side operation sits on land that has long served the 6 interests of industry. Overlooking a rambling, mostly decommissioned US Steel factory, WMI now occupies the former grounds of the Warner Company. In the previous century, Warner surface mined the area for gravel and sand, much of which was shipped to its cement factory in Philadelphia. The area has since been converted into a reverse mine of sorts; instead of extraction, workers dump, pack, and fill the earth with almost forty million pounds of municipal wastes daily.

Back on top of the GROWS landfill, twenty-ton dump trucks gather at 7 the low end of the working face, where they discharge their fetid cargo. Several feet up a dirt bank, a string of large trailers are being detached from semi trucks. In rapid succession each container is tipped almost vertical by a giant hydraulic lift and, within seconds, twenty-four tons of putrescence cascades down into the day's menacing valley of trash. In the middle of the dumping is a "landfill compactor" — which looks like a bulldozer on ste-roids with mammoth metal spiked wheels — that pitches back and forth, its fifty tons crushing the detritus into the earth. A smaller vehicle called a "track loader" maneuvers on tank treads, channeling the castoffs from kitchens and offices into the compactor's path. The place runs like a well-oiled machine, with only a handful of workers orchestrating the burial.

Get a few hundred yards from the landfill's working face and it's hard 8 to smell the rot or see the debris. The place is kept tidy with the help of thirty-five-foot-tall fencing made of "litter netting" that surrounds the perimeter of the site's two landfills. As a backup measure, teams of "paper pickers" constantly patrol the area retrieving discards carried off by the wind. Small misting machines dot fence tops, roads, and hillsides, spraying a fine, invisible chemical-water mixture into the air, which binds with odor molecules and pulls them to the ground.

In new state-of-the-art landfills, the cells that contain the trash are 9 built on top of what is called a "liner." The liner is a giant underground bladder intended to prevent contamination of groundwater by collecting leachate — liquid wastes and the rainwater that seeps through buried trash — and channeling it to nearby water treatment facilities. WMI's two Morrisville landfills leach on average 100,000 gallons daily. If this toxic stew contaminated the site's groundwater it would be devastating.

Once a cell is filled, which might take years, it is closed off or "capped." 10 The capping process entails covering the garbage with several feet of dirt, which gets graded, then packed by steamrollers. After that, layers of clay-embedded fabric, synthetic mesh, and plastic sheeting are draped across the top of the cell and joined with the bottom liner (which is made of the same materials) to encapsulate all those outmoded appliances, dirty dia-pers, and discarded wrappers.

Today's landfill regulations, ranging from liner construction to post- 11 capping oversight, mean that disposal areas like WMI's GROWS are poten-tially less dangerous than the dumps of previous generations. But the fact remains that these systems are short-term solutions to the garbage prob-lem. While they may not seem toxic now, all those underground cells packed with plastics, solvents, paints, batteries, and other hazardous materials will someday have to be treated since the liners won't last forever. Most liners are expected to last somewhere between thirty and fifty years. That time frame just happens to coincide with the post-closure liability private landfill operators are subject to: thirty years after a site is shut-tered, its owner is no longer responsible for contamination, the public is.

> " But what's most striking at these places isn't what they might be hiding; it's what's in plain view. " 12

There is a palpable tension at waste treatment facilities, as though at any minute the visitor will uncover some illegal activity. But what's most striking at these places isn't what they might be hiding; it's what's in plain view. The lavish resources dedicated to destroying used commodities and making that obliteration acceptable, even "green," is what's so astounding. Each landfill (not to mention garbage collection systems, transfer stations, recycling centers, and incinerators) is an expensive, complex operation that uses the latest methods developed and perfected at laboratories, universities, and corporate campuses across the globe.

The more state-of-the-art, the more "environmentally responsible" the operation, the more the repressed question pushes to the surface: what if we didn't have so much trash to get rid of?   13

•   •   •

Comprehension

1. According to Rogers, why are landfills "tucked away, on the edge of town, in otherwise untraveled terrain" (3)?

2. What is the landfill's "working face" (4)? How does it compare with other parts of the landfill?

3. Why does Rogers think that the GROWS landfill is "aptly named" (5)? What **connotations** do you think Waste Management Inc. intended the name GROWS to have? What connotations does Rogers think the name has?

4. What are the dangers of the "new state-of-the-art landfills" (9)? What point does Rogers make about liners being "expected to last somewhere between thirty and fifty years" (11)?

5. According to Rogers, what is the "repressed question" (13) that is not being asked?

Purpose and Audience

1. At what point in the essay does Rogers state her thesis? Why do you think she places the thesis where she does?

2. What dominant impression does Rogers try to create in her description? Is she successful?

3. What is Rogers's attitude toward waste disposal in general — and toward disposal companies like Waste Management Inc. in particular? Do you share her feelings?

Style and Structure

1. Rogers begins her essay with a description of garbage trucks collecting trash. What specific things does she describe? How does this description establish the context for the rest of the essay?

2. What determines the order in which details are arranged in Rogers's essay?

3. Is this essay a subjective or objective description of the landfill? Explain.

4. In paragraph 13, why does Rogers put the phrase *environmentally responsible* in quotation marks? What impression is she trying to convey?

5. Rogers never offers a solution to the problems she writes about. Should she have done so? Is her failure to offer a solution a shortcoming of the essay?

6. **Vocabulary Project.** Some critics of waste disposal methods accuse both municipalities and waste disposal companies of "environmental racism." Research this term on the Web. Do you think the methods described by Rogers are examples of environmental racism? Explain.

Journal Entry

What do you think you and your family could do to reduce the amount of garbage you produce? How realistic are your suggestions?

Writing Workshop

1. Write an essay in which you describe the waste that you see generated at your school, home, or job. Like Rogers, write your description in a way that will motivate people to do something about the problem.

2. **Working with Sources.** In 1986, the city of Philadelphia hired a company to dispose of waste from a city incinerator. Over thirteen thousand tons of waste — some of which was hazardous — was loaded onto a ship called the *Khian Sea,* which unsuccessfully tried to dispose of it. After two years, the cargo mysteriously disappeared. Go to Google Images and find several pictures of the *Khian Sea.* Then, write a description of the ship and its cargo. Make sure the thesis statement of your description clearly conveys your dominant impression. If you wish, you may insert one of the images you found into your essay. Be sure to document the image and to include a works-cited page. (See Chapter 18 for information on MLA documentation.)

3. Describe a place that has played an important role in your life. Include a narrative passage that conveys the place's significance to you.

Combining the Patterns

In paragraphs 9 and 10, Rogers includes a **definition** as well as a **process** description. Explain how these paragraphs help Rogers develop her description.

Thematic Connections

- "What Happens to Plastic That Is Recycled by Us?" (page 281)
- "The Irish Famine, 1845–1849" (page 330)
- "Homeless" (page 510)
- "On Dumpster Diving" (page 672)

E. B. WHITE

Once More to the Lake

Elwyn Brooks White was born in 1899 in Mount Vernon, New York. He joined the newly founded *New Yorker* in 1925 and was associated with the magazine until his death in 1985. In 1937, White moved his family to a farm in Maine and began writing a monthly column for *Harper's* magazine titled "One Man's Meat." A collection of some of these essays appeared under the same title in 1942. In addition to this and other essay collections, White published two popular children's books, *Stuart Little* (1945) and *Charlotte's Web* (1952). He also wrote a classic writer's handbook, *The Elements of Style* (1959), a revision of a text by one of his Cornell professors, William Strunk.

Background on continuity and change In a sense, White's essay is a reflection on continuity and change. While much had remained the same at the Maine lake since 1904, the year White first began coming with his parents, the world outside had undergone a significant transformation by the time he returned years later with his son. Auto and air travel had become commonplace; the invention of innumerable electrical appliances and machines had revolutionized the home and the workplace; movies had gone from primitive, silent, black-and-white shorts to sophisticated productions with sound and sometimes color; and the rise of national advertising had spurred a new and greatly expanded generation of consumer products. Moreover, the country had suffered through World War I, enjoyed a great economic expansion, experienced a period of social revolution, and been devastated by a great economic depression. Within this context, White relives his childhood through his son's eyes.

One summer, along about 1904, my father rented a camp on a lake in 1 Maine and took us all there for the month of August. We all got ringworm from some kittens and had to rub Pond's Extract on our arms and legs night and morning, and my father rolled over in a canoe with all his clothes on; but outside of that the vacation was a success and from then on none of us ever thought there was any place in the world like that lake in Maine. We returned summer after summer — always on August 1st for one month. I have since become a salt-water man, but sometimes in summer there are days when the restlessness of the tides and the fearful cold of the sea water and the incessant wind which blows across the afternoon and into the evening make me wish for the placidity of a lake in the woods. A few weeks ago this feeling got so strong I bought myself a couple of bass hooks and a spinner and returned to the lake where we used to go, for a week's fishing and to revisit old haunts.

I took along my son, who had never had any fresh water up his nose 2 and who had seen lily pads only from train windows. On the journey over to the lake I began to wonder what it would be like. I wondered how time would have marred this unique, this holy spot — the coves and streams, the hills that the sun set behind, the camps and the paths behind the camps. I was sure that the tarred road would have found it out and I wondered in what other ways it would be desolated. It is strange how much you can remember about places like that once you allow your mind to return into the grooves which lead back. You remember one thing, and that suddenly reminds you of another thing. I guess I remembered clearest of all the early mornings, when the lake was cool and motionless, remembered how the bedroom smelled of the lumber it was made of and the wet woods whose scent entered through the screen. The partitions in the camp were thin and did not extend clear to the top of the rooms, and as I was always the first up I would dress softly so as not to wake the others, and sneak out into the sweet outdoors and start out in the canoe, keeping close along the shore in the long shadows of the pines. I remembered being very careful never to rub my paddle against the gunwale for fear of disturbing the stillness of the cathedral.

> " You remember one thing, and that suddenly reminds you of another thing. "

The lake had never been what you would call a wild lake. There were 3 cottages sprinkled around the shores, and it was in farming country although the shores of the lake were quite heavily wooded. Some of the cottages were owned by nearby farmers, and you would live at the shore and eat your meals at the farmhouse. That's what our family did. But although it wasn't wild, it was a fairly large and undisturbed lake and there were places in it which, to a child at least, seemed infinitely remote and primeval.

I was right about the tar: it led to within half a mile of the shore. But 4 when I got back there, with my boy, and we settled into a camp near a farmhouse and into the kind of summertime I had known, I could tell that it was going to be pretty much the same as it had been before — I knew it, lying in bed the first morning, smelling the bedroom, and hearing the boy sneak quietly out and go off along the shore in a boat. I began to sustain the illusion that he was I, and therefore, by simple transposition, that I was my father. This sensation persisted, kept cropping up all the time we were there. It was not an entirely new feeling, but in this setting it grew much stronger. I seemed to be living a dual existence. I would be in the middle of some simple act, I would be picking up a bait box or laying down a table fork, or I would be saying something, and suddenly it would be not I but my father who was saying the words or making the gesture. It gave me a creepy sensation.

We went fishing the first morning. I felt the same damp moss covering 5 the worms in the bait can, and saw the dragonfly alight on the tip of my rod as it hovered a few inches from the surface of the water. It was the arrival of this fly that convinced me beyond any doubt that everything was as it always had been, that the years were a mirage and there had been no years. The small waves were the same, chucking the rowboat under the chin as we fished at anchor, and the boat was the same boat, the same color green and the ribs broken in the same places, and under the floor-boards the same freshwater leavings and débris — the dead helgramite,* the wisps of moss, the rusty discarded fishhook, the dried blood from yesterday's catch. We stared silently at the tips of our rods, at the dragonflies that came and went. I lowered the tip of mine into the water, tentatively, pensively dislodging the fly, which darted two feet away, poised, darted two feet back, and came to rest again a little farther up the rod. There had been no years between the ducking of this dragonfly and the other one — the one that was part of memory. I looked at the boy, who was silently watching his fly, and it was my hands that held his rod, my eyes watching. I felt dizzy and didn't know which rod I was at the end of.

We caught two bass, hauling them in briskly as though they were 6 mackerel, pulling them over the side of the boat in a businesslike manner without any landing net, and stunning them with a blow on the back of the head. When we got back for a swim before lunch, the lake was exactly where we had left it, the same number of inches from the dock, and there was only the merest suggestion of a breeze. This seemed an utterly enchanted sea, this lake you could leave to its own devices for a few hours and come back to, and find that it had not stirred, this constant and trustworthy body of water. In the shallows, the dark, water-soaked sticks and twigs, smooth and old, were undulating in clusters on the bottom against the clean ribbed sand, and the track of the mussel was plain. A school of minnows swam by, each minnow with its small individual shadow, doubling the attendance, so clear and sharp in the sunlight. Some of the other campers were in swim-ming, along the shore, one of them with a cake of soap, and the water felt thin and clear and unsubstantial. Over the years there had been this person with the cake of soap, this cultist, and here he was. There had been no years.

Up to the farmhouse to dinner through the teeming, dusty field, the 7 road under our sneakers was only a two-track road. The middle track was missing, the one with the marks of the hooves and the splotches of dried, flaky manure. There had always been three tracks to choose from in choos-ing which track to walk in; now the choice was narrowed down to two. For a moment I missed terribly the middle alternative. But the way led past the tennis court, and something about the way it lay there in the sun reassured me; the tape had loosened along the backline, the alleys were green with plantains and other weeds, and the net (installed in June and removed in September) sagged in the dry noon, and the whole place steamed with mid-day heat and hunger and emptiness. There was a choice of pie for dessert, and one was blueberry and one was apple, and the waitresses were the same country girls, there having been no passage of time, only the illusion of it as in a dropped curtain — the waitresses were still fifteen; their hair had been

---

* Eds. note — An insect larva often used as bait.

washed, that was the only difference — they had been to the movies and seen the pretty girls with the clean hair.

Summertime, oh summertime, pattern of life indelible, the fade-proof 8 lake, the woods unshatterable, the pasture with the sweetfern and the juniper forever and ever, summer without end; this was the background, and the life along the shore was the design, the cottages with their innocent and tranquil design, their tiny docks with the flagpole and the American flag floating against the white clouds in the blue sky, the little paths over the roots of the trees leading from camp to camp and the paths leading back to the outhouses and the can of lime for sprinkling, and at the souvenir counters at the store the miniature birch-bark canoes and the post cards that showed things looking a little better than they looked. This was the American family at play, escaping the city heat, wondering whether the newcomers in the camp at the head of the cove were "common" or "nice," wondering whether it was true that the people who drove up for Sunday dinner at the farmhouse were turned away because there wasn't enough chicken.

It seemed to me, as I kept remembering all this, that those times and 9 those summers had been infinitely precious and worth saving. There had been jollity and peace and goodness. The arriving (at the beginning of August) had been so big a business in itself, at the railway station the farm wagon drawn up, the first smell of the pine-laden air, the first glimpse of the smiling farmer, and the great importance of the trunks and your father's enormous authority in such matters, and the feel of the wagon under you for the long ten-mile haul, and at the top of the last long hill catching the first view of the lake after eleven months of not seeing this cherished body of water. The shouts and cries of the other campers when they saw you, and the trunks to be unpacked, to give up their rich burden. (Arriving was less exciting nowadays, when you sneaked up in your car and parked it under a tree near the camp and took out the bags and in five minutes it was all over, no fuss, no loud wonderful fuss about trunks.)

Peace and goodness and jollity. The only thing that was wrong now, 10 really, was the sound of the place, an unfamiliar nervous sound of the outboard motors. This was the note that jarred, the one thing that would sometimes break the illusion and set the years moving. In those other summertimes all motors were inboard; and when they were at a little distance, the noise they made was a sedative, an ingredient of summer sleep. They were one-cylinder and two-cylinder engines, and some were make-and-break and some were jump-spark, but they all made a sleepy sound across the lake. The one-lungers throbbed and fluttered, and the twin-cylinder ones purred and purred, and that was a quiet sound too. But now the campers all had outboards. In the daytime, in the hot mornings, these motors made a petulant, irritable sound; at night, in the still evening when the afterglow lit the water, they whined about one's ears like mosquitoes. My boy loved our rented outboard, and his great desire was to achieve singlehanded mastery over it, and authority, and he soon learned the trick of choking it a little (but not too much), and the adjustment of the needle valve. Watching him I would remember the things you could do with the old one-cylinder engine with the heavy flywheel, how you could have it eating out of your hand if you got really close to it spiritually. Motor boats in those days didn't have clutches, and you would make a landing by shutting off the motor at the proper time and coasting in with a dead rudder. But there was a way of reversing them, if you learned the trick, by cutting the switch and putting it on again exactly on the final dying revolution of the flywheel, so that it would kick back against compression and begin reversing. Approaching a dock in a strong following breeze, it was difficult to slow up sufficiently by the ordinary coasting method, and if a boy felt he had complete mastery over his motor, he was tempted to keep it running beyond its time and then reverse it a few feet from the dock. It took a cool nerve, because if you threw the switch a twentieth of a second too soon you could catch the flywheel when it still had speed enough to go up past center, and the boat would leap ahead, charging bull-fashion at the dock.

We had a good week at the camp. The bass were biting well and the sun 11 shone endlessly, day after day. We would be tired at night and lie down in the accumulated heat of the little bedrooms after the long hot day and the breeze would stir almost imperceptibly outside and the smell of the swamp drift in through the rusty screens. Sleep would come easily and in the morning the red squirrel would be on the roof, tapping out his gay routine. I kept remembering everything, lying in bed in the mornings — the small steamboat that had a long rounded stern like the lip of a Ubangi,* how quietly she ran on the moonlight sails, when the older boys played their mandolins and the girls sang and we ate doughnuts dipped in sugar, and how sweet the music was on the water in the shining night, and what it had felt like to think about girls then. After breakfast we would go up to the store and the things were in the same place — the minnows in a bottle, the plugs and spinners disarranged and pawed over by the youngsters from the boys' camp, the fig newtons and the Beeman's gum. Outside, the road was tarred and cars stood in front of the store. Inside, all was just as it had always been, except there was more Coca-Cola and not so much Moxie** and root beer and birch beer and sarsaparilla.*** We would walk out with a bottle of pop apiece and sometimes the pop would backfire up our noses and hurt. We explored the streams, quietly, where the turtles slid off the sunny logs and dug their way into the soft bottom; and we lay on the town wharf and fed worms to the tame bass. Everywhere we went I had trouble making out which was I, the one walking at my side, the one walking in my pants.

One afternoon while we were there at that lake a thunderstorm came 12 up. It was like the revival of an old melodrama that I had seen long ago with

---

* Eds. note — A member of an African tribe known for wearing mouth ornaments that stretch the lips into a saucerlike shape.
** Eds. note — A soft drink that was popular in the early twentieth century.
*** Eds. note — A sweetened carbonated beverage flavored with birch oil and sassafras.

childish awe. The second-act climax of the drama of the electrical distur-
bance over a lake in America had not changed in any important respect.
This was the big scene, still the big scene. The whole thing was so familiar,
the first feeling of oppression and heat and a general air around camp of
not wanting to go very far away. In midafternoon (it was all the same) a
curious darkening of the sky, and a lull in everything that had made life
tick; and then the way the boats suddenly swung the other way at their
moorings with the coming of a breeze out of the new quarter, and the
premonitory rumble. Then the kettle drum, then the snare, then the bass
drum and cymbals, then crackling light against the dark, and the gods
grinning and licking their chops in the hills. Afterward the calm, the rain
steadily rustling in the calm lake, the return of light and hope and spirits,
and the campers running out in joy and relief to go swimming in the rain,
their bright cries perpetuating the deathless joke about how they were getting simply drenched, and the children screaming with delight at the new
sensation of bathing in the rain, and the joke about getting drenched linking the generations in a strong indestructible chain. And the comedian
who waded in carrying an umbrella.

When the others went swimming my son said he was going in too. He   13
pulled his dripping trunks from the line where they had hung all through
the shower, and wrung them out. Languidly, and with no thought of going
in, I watched him, his hard little body, skinny and bare, saw him wince
slightly as he pulled up around his vitals the small, soggy, icy garment. As
he buckled the swollen belt suddenly my groin felt the chill of death.

. . .

Comprehension

1. How are the writer and his son alike? How are they different? What does
   White mean when he says, "I seemed to be living a dual existence" (4)?

2. In paragraph 5, White says that "no years" seemed to have gone by
   between past and present; elsewhere, he senses that things are different.
   How do you account for these conflicting feelings?

3. Why does White feel disconcerted when he discovers that the road to the
   farmhouse has two tracks, not three? What do you make of his comment
   that "now the choice was narrowed down to two" (7)?

4. How does sound "break the illusion and set the years moving" (10)?

5. What is White referring to in the essay's last sentence?

Purpose and Audience

1. What is the thesis of this essay? Is it stated or implied?

2. Do you think White expects the ending of his essay to surprise his audience? Explain.

3. What age group do you think this essay would appeal to most? Why?

Style and Structure

1. List the specific changes that have taken place on the lake. Does White emphasize these changes or play them down? Explain.

2. What ideas and images does White repeat throughout his essay? What is the purpose of this repetition?

3. White goes to great lengths to describe how things look, feel, smell, taste, and sound. How does this help him achieve his purpose in this essay?

4. How does White's conclusion echo the first paragraph of the essay?

5. **Vocabulary Project.** Underline ten words in the essay that refer to one of the five senses, and make a list of synonyms you could use for these words. How close do your substitutions come to capturing White's meaning?

Journal Entry

Do you identify more with the father or with the son in this essay? Why?

Writing Workshop

1. Write a description of a scene you remember from your childhood. In your essay, discuss how your current view of the scene differs from the view you had when you were a child.

2. **Working with Sources.** Assume you are a travel agent. Stressing the benefits White describes, write a descriptive brochure designed to bring tourists to the lake. Remember to include parenthetical documentation for references to White's essay and to include a works-cited page. (See Chapter 18 for information on MLA documentation.)

3. Write an essay describing yourself from the perspective of one of your parents. Make sure your description conveys both the qualities your parent likes and the qualities he or she would want to change.

Combining the Patterns

White opens his essay with a short narrative about his first trip to the lake in 1904. How does this use of **narration** provide a context for the entire essay?

Thematic Connections

- "My Field of Dreams" (page 106)
- "Goodbye to My Twinkie Days" (page 171)
- "The 'Black Table' Is Still There" (page 348)
- "The Park" (page 667)

KATE CHOPIN

The Storm (Fiction)

Kate Chopin (1851–1904) was born Catherine O'Flaherty. In 1870, she married Oscar Chopin and moved with him to New Orleans. After suffering business reversals, Chopin relocated to Cloutierville, Louisiana, to be closer to his extended Creole family. Oscar Chopin died suddenly in 1882, and Kate Chopin, left with six children to raise, returned to St. Louis. There she began writing short stories, many set in the colorful Creole country of central Louisiana. Her first collection, *Bayou Folk,* was published in 1894, followed by *A Night in Arcadie* in 1897. Her literary success was cut short, however, with the publication of her first novel, *The Awakening* (1899), a story of adultery that outraged many of her critics and readers because it was told sympathetically from a woman's perspective. Her work languished until the middle of the twentieth century, when it was rediscovered, largely by feminist literary scholars.

Background on Creole culture The following story was probably written about the same time as *The Awakening,* but Chopin never attempted to publish it. Its frank sexuality — franker than that depicted in her controversial novel — and its focus on an adulterous liaison between two lovers (Calixta and Alcée) would have been too scandalous for middle-class readers of the day. Even within the more liberal Creole culture in which the story is set, Calixta's actions would have been outrageous. While Creole men were expected to have mistresses, Creole wives were expected to remain true to their wedding vows. The Creoles themselves were descendants of the early Spanish and French settlers in Louisiana, and they lived lives quite separate from — and, they believed, superior to — those whose ancestors were British. Their language became a mix of French and English, as did their mode of dress and cuisine. A strong Creole influence can still be found in New Orleans and the surrounding Louisiana countryside; Mardi Gras, for example, is a Creole tradition.

I

The leaves were so still that even Bibi thought it was going to rain. 1
Bobinôt, who was accustomed to converse on terms of perfect equality with his little son, called the child's attention to certain sombre clouds that were rolling with sinister intention from the west, accompanied by a sullen, threatening roar. They were at Friedheimer's store and decided to remain there till the storm had passed. They sat within the door on two empty kegs. Bibi was four years old and looked very wise.

"Mama'll be 'fraid, yes," he suggested with blinking eyes. 2

"She'll shut the house. Maybe she got Sylvie helpin' her this evenin'," 3
Bobinôt responded reassuringly.

"No; she ent got Sylvie. Sylvie was helpin' her yistiday," piped Bibi. 4

Bobinôt arose and going across to the counter purchased a can of 5
shrimps, of which Calixta was very fond. Then he returned to his perch on
the keg and sat stolidly holding the can of shrimps while the storm burst. It
shook the wooden store and seemed to be ripping great furrows in the distant field. Bibi laid his little hand on his father's knee and was not afraid.

II

Calixta, at home, felt no uneasiness for their safety. She sat at a side 6
window sewing furiously on a sewing machine. She was greatly occupied
and did not notice the approaching storm. But she felt very warm and
often stopped to mop her face on which the perspiration gathered in beads.
She unfastened her white sacque at the throat. It began to grow dark, and
suddenly realizing the situation she got up hurriedly and went about closing windows and doors.

Out on the small front gallery she had hung Bobinôt's Sunday clothes 7
to air and she hastened out to gather them before the rain fell. As she
stepped outside, Alcée Laballière rode in at the gate. She had not seen
him very often since her marriage, and never alone. She stood there with
Bobinôt's coat in her hands, and the big rain drops began to fall. Alcée rode
his horse under the shelter of a side projection where the chickens had
huddled and there were plows and a harrow piled up in the corner.

"May I come and wait on your gallery till the storm is over, Calixta?" he 8
asked.

"Come 'long in, M'sieur Alcée."   9

His voice and her own startled her as if from a trance, and she seized 10
Bobinôt's vest. Alcée, mounting to the porch, grabbed the trousers and
snatched Bibi's braided jacket that was about to be carried away by a sudden gust of wind. He expressed an intention to remain outside, but it was
soon apparent that he might as well have been out in the open: the water
beat in upon the boards in driving sheets, and he went inside, closing the
door after him. It was even necessary to put something beneath the door to
keep the water out.

"My! what a rain! It's good two years sence it rain' like that," exclaimed 11
Calixta as she rolled up a piece of bagging and Alcée helped her to thrust it
beneath the crack.

She was a little fuller of figure than five years before when she mar- 12
ried; but she had lost nothing of her vivacity. Her blue eyes still retained
their melting quality; and her yellow hair, dishevelled by the wind and rain,
kinked more stubbornly than ever about her ears and temples.

The rain beat upon the low, shingled roof with a force and clatter that 13
threatened to break an entrance and deluge them there. They were in the
dining room — the sitting room — the general utility room. Adjoining was
her bed room, with Bibi's couch along side her own. The door stood open,
and the room with its white, monumental bed, its closed shutters, looked
dim and mysterious.

Alcée flung himself into a rocker and Calixta nervously began to gather 14 up from the floor the lengths of a cotton sheet which she had been sewing.

"If this keeps up, *Dieu sait** if the levees goin' to stan' it!" she exclaimed. 15

"What have you got to do with the levees?" 16

"I got enough to do! An' there's Bobinôt with Bibi out in that storm — if 17 he only didn't left Friedheimer's!"

"Let us hope, Calixta, that Bobinôt's got sense enough to come in out 18 of a cyclone."

She went and stood at the window with a greatly disturbed look on her 19 face. She wiped the frame that was clouded with moisture. It was stiflingly hot. Alcée got up and joined her at the window, looking over her shoulder. The rain was coming down in sheets obscuring the view of far-off cabins and enveloping the distant wood in a gray mist. The playing of the lightning was incessant. A bolt struck a tall chinaberry tree at the edge of the field. It filled all visible space with a blinding glare and the crash seemed to invade the very boards they stood upon.

Calixta put her hands to her eyes, and with a cry, staggered backward. Alcée's arm encircled her, and for an instant he drew her close and spasmodically to him. 20

> "Calixta put her hands to her eyes, and with a cry, staggered backward." 21

"*Bonté!*"** she cried, releasing herself from his encircling arm and retreating from the window, "the house'll go next! If I only knew w'ere Bibi was!" She would not compose herself; she would not be seated. Alcée clasped her shoulders and looked into her face. The contact of her warm, palpitating body when he had unthinkingly drawn her into his arms, had aroused all the old-time infatuation and desire for her flesh.

"Calixta," he said, "don't be frightened. Nothing can happen. The 22 house is too low to be struck, with so many tall trees standing about. There! aren't you going to be quiet? say, aren't you?" He pushed her hair back from her face that was warm and steaming. Her lips were as red and moist as pomegranate seed. Her white neck and a glimpse of her full, firm bosom disturbed him powerfully. As she glanced up at him the fear in her liquid blue eyes had given place to a drowsy gleam that unconsciously betrayed a sensuous desire. He looked down into her eyes and there was nothing for him to do but to gather her lips in a kiss. It reminded him of Assumption.***

"Do you remember — in Assumption, Calixta?" he asked in a low voice 23 broken by passion. Oh! she remembered; for in Assumption he had kissed her and kissed and kissed her; until his senses would well nigh fail, and to save her he would resort to a desperate flight. If she was not an immaculate dove in those days, she was still inviolate; a passionate creature whose very

---

* Eds. note — God knows.
** Eds. note — Goodness!
*** Eds. note — A parish near New Orleans.

defenselessness had made her defense, against which his honor forbade him to prevail. Now — well, now — her lips seemed in a manner free to be tasted, as well as her round, white throat and her whiter breasts.

They did not heed the crashing torrents, and the roar of the elements 24 made her laugh as she lay in his arms. She was a revelation in that dim, mysterious chamber; as white as the couch she lay upon. Her firm, elastic flesh that was knowing for the first time its birthright, was like a creamy lily that the sun invites to contribute its breath and perfume to the undying life of the world.

The generous abundance of her passion, without guile or trickery, was 25 like a white flame which penetrated and found response in depths of his own sensuous nature that had never yet been reached.

When he touched her breasts they gave themselves up in quivering 26 ecstasy, inviting his lips. Her mouth was a fountain of delight. And when he possessed her, they seemed to swoon together at the very borderland of life's mystery.

He stayed cushioned upon her, breathless, dazed, enervated, with his 27 heart beating like a hammer upon her. With one hand she clasped his head, her lips lightly touching his forehead. The other hand stroked with a soothing rhythm his muscular shoulders.

The growl of the thunder was distant and passing away. The rain beat 28 softly upon the shingles, inviting them to drowsiness and sleep. But they dared not yield.

The rain was over; and the sun was turning the glistening green world 29 into a palace of gems. Calixta, on the gallery, watched Alcée ride away. He turned and smiled at her with a beaming face; and she lifted her pretty chin in the air and laughed aloud.

III

Bobinôt and Bibi, trudging home, stopped without at the cistern to 30 make themselves presentable.

"My! Bibi, w'at will yo' mama say! You ought to be asham'. You oughtn' 31 put on those good pants. Look at 'em! An' that mud on yo' collar! How you got that mud on yo' collar, Bibi? I never saw such a boy!" Bibi was the picture of pathetic resignation. Bobinôt was the embodiment of serious solicitude as he strove to remove from his own person and his son's the signs of their tramp over heavy roads and through wet fields. He scraped the mud off Bibi's bare legs and feet with a stick and carefully removed all traces from his heavy brogans. Then, prepared for the worst — the meeting with an over-scrupulous housewife, they entered cautiously at the back door.

Calixta was preparing supper. She had set the table and was dripping 32 coffee at the hearth. She sprang up as they came in.

"Oh, Bobinôt! You back! My! but I was uneasy. W'ere you been during 33 the rain? An' Bibi? he ain't wet? he ain't hurt?" She had clasped Bibi and was kissing him effusively. Bobinôt's explanations and apologies which he had been composing all along the way, died on his lips as Calixta felt him to see if he were dry, and seemed to express nothing but satisfaction at their safe return.

"I brought you some shrimps, Calixta," offered Bobinôt, hauling the 34
can from his ample side pocket and laying it on the table.

"Shrimps! Oh, Bobinôt! you too good fo' anything!" and she gave him 35
a smacking kiss on the cheek that resounded. "*J'vous réponds*,* we'll have a
feas' tonight! umph-umph!"

Bobinôt and Bibi began to relax and enjoy themselves, and when the 36
three sated themselves at table they laughed much and so loud that anyone
might have heard them as far away as Laballière's.

IV

Alcée Laballière wrote to his wife, Clarisse, that night. It was a loving 37
letter, full of tender solicitude. He told her not to hurry back, but if she and
the babies liked it at Biloxi, to stay a month longer. He was getting on
nicely; and though he missed them, he was willing to bear the separation a
while longer — realizing that their health and pleasure were the first things
to be considered.

V

As for Clarisse, she was charmed upon receiving her husband's letter. 38
She and the babies were doing well. The society was agreeable; many of her
old friends and acquaintances were at the bay. And the first free breath
since her marriage seemed to restore the pleasant liberty of her maiden
days. Devoted as she was to her husband, their intimate conjugal life was
something which she was more than willing to forego for a while.

So the storm passed and everyone was happy. 39

• • •

Reading Literature

1. How does the storm help set in motion the action of the story? List the
   events caused by the storm.
2. Is the last line of the story to be taken literally, or is it meant to be **ironic**
   (that is, does it actually suggest the opposite meaning)? Explain.
3. What do the story's specific descriptive details tell us about Calixta?

Journal Entry

On one level, the story's title refers to the storm that takes place through
much of the story. To what else could the story's title refer?

---

* Eds. note — I tell you.

Thematic Connections

Writing Assignments for Description

1. Choose a character from a book, movie, or video game who you think is interesting. Write a descriptive essay conveying what makes this character so special.

2. Several of the essays in this chapter deal with the way journeys change how the writers see themselves. For example, in "Once More to the Lake," a visit to a campground forces E. B. White to confront his own mortality, and in "The Hidden Life of Garbage," a visit to a landfill outside Morrisville, Pennsylvania, enables Heather Rogers to grasp the enormity of the task of disposing of garbage in the United States. Write an essay describing a place that you traveled to. Make sure that, in addition to describing the place, you explain how it has taught you something about yourself.

3. Locate some photographs of your relatives. Describe three of these pictures, including details that provide insight into the lives of the people you discuss. Use your descriptive passages to support a thesis about your family.

4. **Working with Sources.** Visit an art museum (or go to a museum site on the web), and select a painting that interests you. Study it carefully, and then write an essay-length description of it. Before you write, decide how you will organize your details and whether you will write a subjective or an objective description. If possible, include a photograph of the painting in your essay. Be sure to document the photograph and to include a works-cited page. (See Chapter 18 for information on MLA documentation.)

5. Select an object you are familiar with, and write an objective description of it. Include a diagram.

6. Assume you are writing an email to someone in another country who knows little about life in the United States. Describe to this person something you consider typically American — for example, a state fair or a food court in a shopping mall.

7. Visit your college library, and write a brochure in which you describe the reference area. Be specific, and select an organizing scheme before you begin your description. Your purpose is to acquaint students with some of the reference materials they will use. If possible, include a diagram that will help orient students to this section of the library.

8. Describe your neighborhood to a visitor who knows nothing about it. Include as much specific detail as you can.

9. After reading "Ground Zero," write a description of a sight or scene that fascinated, surprised, or shocked you. Your description should explain why you were so deeply affected by what you saw.

10. Write an essay describing an especially frightening horror film. What specific sights and sounds make this film so horrifying? Include a thesis statement assessing the film's success as a horror film. (Be careful not to simply summarize the plot of the film.)

Collaborative Activity for Description

Working in groups of three or four students, go to Google Maps, Street View, and select a city that you would like to visit. Then, as a group, write a description of a street, a building, or even a block in that city, making sure to include as much physical detail as possible.

8

Exemplification

What Is Exemplification?

Exemplification uses one or more particular cases, or **examples**, to illustrate or explain a general point or an abstract concept. In the following paragraph from *Sexism and Language,* Alleen Pace Nilsen uses a number of well-chosen examples to illustrate her statement that the armed forces use words that have positive masculine connotations to encourage recruitment.

Topic sentence

The armed forces, particularly the Marines, use the positive masculine connotation as part of their recruitment psychology. They promote the idea that to join the Marines (or the Army, Navy, or Air Force) guarantees that you will become a man. But this brings up a problem, because much of the work that is necessary to keep a large organization running is what is traditionally thought of as *woman's work.* Now, how can the Marines ask someone who has signed up for a *man-sized job* to do *woman's work*? Since they can't, they euphemize and give the jobs titles that are more prestigious or, at least, don't make people think of females. Waitresses are called *orderlies,* secretaries are called *clerk-typists,* nurses are called *medics,* assistants are called *adjutants,* and cleaning up an area is called *policing* the area. The same kind of word glorification is used in civilian life to bolster a man's ego when he is doing such tasks as cooking and sewing. For example, a *chef* has higher prestige than a *cook* and a *tailor* has higher prestige than a *seamstress.*

Series of related examples

Using Exemplification

You have probably noticed, when watching interviews on television (or on YouTube or other online sites) or listening to classroom discussions, that the most effective exchanges occur when participants support their points with specific examples. Sweeping generalizations and vague statements are not nearly as effective as specific observations, anecdotes, details, and opinions. It is one thing to say, "The mayor is corrupt and should not be reelected" and another to illustrate your point by saying, "The mayor should not be reelected because he has fired two city workers who refused to contribute to his campaign fund, has put his family and friends on the city payroll, and has used public employees to make improvements to his home." The same principle applies to writing: many of the most effective essays use examples extensively. Exemplification is used in every kind of writing situation to explain and clarify, to add interest, and to persuade.

Using Examples to Explain and Clarify

On a midterm exam in a film course, you might write, "Even though horror movies seem modern, they really aren't." You may think your statement is perfectly clear, but if this is all you say about horror movies, you should not be surprised if your exam comes back with a question mark in the margin next to this sentence. After all, you have only made a general statement about your subject. It is not specific, nor does it anticipate readers' questions about how horror movies are not modern. To be certain that your audience knows exactly what you mean, state your point precisely: "Despite the fact that horror movies seem modern, two of the most memorable ones are adaptations of nineteenth-century Gothic novels." Then, use examples to ensure clarity and avoid ambiguity. For example, you could illustrate your point by discussing two films — *Frankenstein,* directed by James Whale, and *Dracula,* directed by Todd Browning — and linking them to the nineteenth-century novels on which they are based. With the benefit of these specific examples, readers would know what you mean — that the literary roots of such movies are in the past, not that their cinematic techniques or production methods are dated. Moreover, readers would know exactly which horror movies you are discussing.

Using Examples to Add Interest

Writers use well-chosen examples to add interest as well as to clarify their points. Brent Staples does this in his essay "Just Walk On By," which appears later in this chapter. In itself, the claim that during his time away from home, Staples became "thoroughly familiar with the language of fear" is not very interesting. This statement becomes compelling, however, when Staples illustrates it with specific examples — experiences he had while walking the streets at night. For example, his presence apparently inspired so much fear in people that they locked their car doors as he walked past or crossed to the other side of the street when they saw him approaching.

When you use exemplification, choose examples that are interesting as well as pertinent. Test the effectiveness of your examples by putting yourself in your readers' place. If you don't find your essay lively and absorbing, chances are your readers won't either. If this is the case, try to add more thought-provoking and spirited examples. After all, your goal is to communicate ideas to your readers, and imaginative examples can make the difference between an engrossing essay and one that is a chore to read.

Using Examples to Persuade

Although you can use examples to explain or to add interest, examples are also an effective way of persuading people that what you are saying is reasonable and worth considering. A few well-chosen examples can provide effective support for otherwise unconvincing general statements. For instance, a broad statement that school districts across the country cannot cope with the numerous students with limited English skills is one that needs support. If you make such a statement on an exam, you need to back it up with appropriate examples — such as that in Massachusetts alone, the number of students who speak English as a second language has increased by more than 20 percent over the past ten years. In other words, in 2010, 57,000 students lacked proficiency in English. Similarly, a statement in a biology paper that DDT should continue to be banned is unconvincing without persuasive examples such as these to support it:

- Although DDT has been banned since December 31, 1972, scientists are finding traces in the eggs of various fish and waterfowl.
- Certain lakes and streams cannot be used for sport and recreation because DDT levels are dangerously high, presumably because of farmland runoff.
- Because of its stability as a compound, DDT does not degrade quickly; therefore, existing residues will threaten the environment well into the twenty-first century.

Planning an Exemplification Essay

Developing a Thesis Statement

The **thesis statement** of an exemplification essay makes a point that the rest of the essay will support with examples. This statement usually identifies your topic as well as the main point you want to make about it.

The examples you gather during the invention stage of the writing process can help you develop your thesis. By doing so, they can help you test your ideas as well as the ideas of others. For instance, suppose you plan to write an essay for a composition class about students' writing skills. Your tentative thesis is that writing well is an inborn talent and that teachers can do little to help people write better. But is this really true? Has it been true in your own life? To test your point, you brainstorm about the various teachers you have had who tried to help you improve your writing.

As you assemble your list, you remember a teacher you had in high school. She was strict, required lots of writing, and seemed to accept nothing less than perfection. At the time, neither you nor your classmates liked her. But looking back, you recall her one-on-one conferences, her organized lessons, her helpful comments on your essays, and her timely replies to your emails. You realize that after completing her class, you felt much more comfortable writing. When examining some papers you saved, you are surprised to see how much your writing actually improved during that year. These examples lead you to reevaluate your ideas and to revise your thesis:

> Even though some people seem to have a natural flair for writing, a good teacher can make a difference.

Providing Enough Examples

Unfortunately, no general rule exists to tell you when you have enough examples to support your ideas. The number you need depends on your thesis statement. If, for instance, your thesis is that an educational institution, like a business, needs careful financial management, a single detailed examination of one college or university could provide all the examples you need to make your point.

If, however, your thesis is that conflict between sons and fathers is a major theme in Franz Kafka's writing, more than one example would be necessary. A single example would show only that the theme is present in *one* of Kafka's works. In this case, the more examples you include, the more effectively you support your point.

For some thesis statements, however, even several examples would not be enough. Examples alone, for instance, could not demonstrate convincingly that children from small families have more successful careers than children from large families. This thesis would have to be supported with a **statistical study** — that is, by collecting and interpreting numerical data representing a great many examples.

Choosing a Fair Range of Examples

Selecting a sufficient **range of examples** is just as important as choosing an appropriate number. If you want to persuade readers that Colin Powell was an able general, you should choose examples from several stages of his military career. Likewise, if you want to convince readers that outdoor advertising ruins the scenic views from major highways, you should discuss an area larger than your immediate neighborhood. Your objective in each case is to choose a cross section of examples to represent the full range of your topic.

Similarly, if you want to argue for a ban on smoking in all public spaces, you should not limit your examples to restaurants. To be convincing, you should include examples involving many public places, such as office buildings, hotel lobbies, and sports stadiums. For the same reason, one person's experience is not enough to support a general conclusion involving many people unless you can clearly establish that the experience is typical.

If you decide you cannot cite a fair range of examples that support your thesis, reexamine it. Rather than switching to a new topic, try to narrow your thesis. After all, the only way your paper will be convincing is if your readers believe that your thesis is supported by your examples and that your examples fairly represent the scope of your topic.

Of course, to be convincing you must not only *choose* examples effectively but also *use* them effectively. You should keep your thesis statement in mind as you write, taking care not to get so involved with one example that you digress from your main point. No matter how carefully developed, no matter how specific, lively, and appropriate, your examples accomplish nothing if they do not support your essay's main idea.

Using Transitions

Be sure to use transitional words and phrases to introduce your examples. Without them, readers will have difficulty seeing the connection between an example and the general statement it is illustrating. In some cases, transitions will help you connect examples to your thesis statement ("*Another* successful program for the homeless provides telephone answering services for job seekers"). In other cases, transitions will link examples to topic sentences ("*For instance,* I have written articles for my college newspaper"). In exemplification essays, the most frequently used transitions include *for example, for instance, in fact, namely, specifically, that is,* and *thus.* (A more complete list of transitions appears on page 57.)

Structuring an Exemplification Essay

Exemplification essays usually begin with an **introduction** that includes the *thesis statement,* which is supported by examples in the body of the essay. Each **body paragraph** may develop a separate example, present a point illustrated by several brief examples, or explore one part of a single extended example that is developed throughout the essay. The **conclusion** reinforces the essay's main idea, perhaps restating the thesis. At times, however, variations of this basic pattern are advisable and even necessary. For instance, beginning your paper with a striking example might stimulate your reader's interest and curiosity; ending with one might vividly reinforce your thesis.

Exemplification presents one special organizational problem. If you do not select your examples carefully and arrange them effectively, your paper can become a thesis statement followed by a list or by ten or fifteen brief, choppy paragraphs. One way to avoid this problem is to develop your best examples fully in separate paragraphs and then discard the others.

Another effective strategy is to group related examples together in one paragraph.

Within each paragraph, you can arrange examples **chronologically**, beginning with those that occurred first and moving to those that occurred later. You can also arrange examples **in order of increasing complexity**, beginning with the simplest and moving to the most difficult or complex. Finally, you can arrange examples **in order of importance**, beginning with those that are less significant and moving to those that are most significant or persuasive.

The following informal outline for an essay evaluating the nursing care at a hospital illustrates one way to arrange examples. Notice how the writer presents his examples in order of increasing importance under three general headings — *patient rooms, emergency room,* and *clinics.*

Sample Outline	**Exemplification**

Introduction:	Thesis statement — Because of its focus on the patient, the nursing care at Montgomery Hospital can serve as a model for other medical facilities.
In Patient Rooms	
Example 1:	Being responsive
Example 2:	Establishing rapport
Example 3:	Delivering bedside care
In Emergency Room	
Example 4:	Staffing treatment rooms
Example 5:	Circulating among patients in the waiting room
Example 6:	Maintaining good working relationships with physicians
In Clinics	
Example 7:	Preparing patients
Example 8:	Assisting during treatment
Example 9:	Instructing patients after treatment
Conclusion:	Restatement of thesis (in different words) or review of key points or examples

---

Revising an Exemplification Essay

When you revise an exemplification essay, consider the items on the revision checklist on page 68. In addition, pay special attention to the items on the following checklist, which apply specifically to exemplification essays.

✓ REVISION CHECKLIST   **Exemplification**

☐ Does your assignment call for exemplification?
☐ Does your essay have a clear thesis statement that identifies the point you will illustrate?
☐ Do your examples explain and clarify your thesis statement?
☐ Have you provided enough examples?
☐ Have you used a range of examples?
☐ Are your examples persuasive?
☐ Do your examples add interest?
☐ Have you used transitional words and phrases that reinforce the connection between your examples and your thesis statement?

Editing an Exemplification Essay

When you edit your exemplification essay, follow the guidelines on the editing checklists on pages 85, 88, and 91. In addition, focus on the grammar, mechanics, and punctuation issues that are most relevant to exemplification essays. One of these issues — using commas in a series — is discussed here.

GRAMMAR IN CONTEXT   **Using Commas in a Series**

When you write an exemplification essay, you often use a **series of examples** to support a statement or to illustrate a point. When you use a series of three or more examples in a sentence, you must remember to separate them with commas.

- Always use commas to separate three or more items — words, phrases, or clauses — in a series.

  In "Just Walk On By," Brent Staples says, "I was <u>surprised</u>, <u>embarrassed</u>, and <u>dismayed</u> all at once" (239).

  In "Just Walk On By," Staples observes that the woman thought she was being stalked <u>by a mugger</u>, <u>by a rapist</u>, or <u>by something worse</u> (239).

  "Waitresses are called <u>*orderlies*</u>, secretaries are called <u>*clerk-typists*</u>, nurses are called <u>*medics*</u>, assistants are called <u>*adjutants*</u>, and <u>cleaning up an area is called *policing* the area</u>" (Nilsen 207).

NOTE: Although newspaper and magazine writers routinely leave out the comma before the last item in a series of three or more items, you should always include this comma in your college writing.

- Do not use a comma after the final element in a series of three or more items.

INCORRECT: Staples was shocked, horrified, and disillusioned, to be taken for a mugger.

CORRECT: Staples was shocked, horrified, and disillusioned to be taken for a mugger.

• Do not use commas if all the elements in a series of three or more items are separated by coordinating conjunctions (*and, or, but,* and so on).

According to Deborah L. Rhode, society discriminates against unattractive people in three ways: they are less likely to be hired and less likely to get raises and less likely to get promoted. (*no commas*)

✔ **EDITING CHECKLIST**   **Exemplification**

☐ Have you used commas to separate three or more items in a series?
☐ Have you made sure not to use a comma after the last element in a series?
☐ Have you made sure not to use a comma in a series with items separated by coordinating conjunctions?
☐ Are all the elements in a series stated in **parallel** terms (see page 376)?

A STUDENT WRITER: Exemplification

Exemplification is frequently used in nonacademic writing situations, such as business reports, memos, and proposals. One of the most important situations for using exemplification is in a letter you write to apply for a job.* Kristy Bredin's letter of application to a prospective employer follows.

---

* Eds. note — In business letters, paragraphs are not indented and extra space is added between paragraphs.

1028 Geissinger Street
Bethlehem, PA 18018
September 7, 2014

Kim Goldstein
Rolling Stone
1290 Avenue of the Americas
New York, NY 10104-0298

Dear Ms. Goldstein:

Introduction

I am writing to apply for the paid online internship that you   1
posted on RollingStone.com. I believe that both my education and

Thesis statement   my experience in publishing qualify me for the position you
advertised.

Examples

I am currently a senior at Moravian College, where I am majoring   2
in English (with a concentration in creative writing) and music.
Throughout my college career, I have maintained a 3.4 average.
After I graduate in May, I would like to find a full-time job
in publishing. For this reason, I am very interested in your
internship. It would not only give me additional editorial and
administrative experience, but it would also give me insight into
a large-scale publishing operation. An internship at RollingStone
.com would also enable to me to read, edit, and possibly write
articles about popular music — a subject I know a lot about.

Examples

Throughout college, I have been involved in writing and editing. I   3
have served as both secretary and president of the Literary Society
and have written, edited, and published its annual newsletter.
I have also worked as a tutor in Moravian's Writing Center; as a
literature editor for the *Manuscript*, Moravian's literary magazine;
and as a features editor for the *Comeneian*, the student newspaper.
In these jobs I have gained a good deal of practical experience in
publishing as well as insight into dealing with people. In addition,
I acquired professional editing experience as well as experience
posting across platforms this past semester, when I worked as an
intern for Taylor and Francis (Routledge) Publishing in New York.

Conclusion   I believe that my education and my publishing experience make   4
me a good candidate for your position. As your ad requested, I
have enclosed my résumé, information on Moravian's internship
program, and several writing samples for your consideration.
You can contact me by phone at (484) 625-6731 or by email at
stkab@moravian.edu. I will be available for an interview anytime
after September 23. I look forward to meeting with you to discuss
my qualifications.

Sincerely,

Kristy Bredin

Kristy Bredin

Points for Special Attention

Organization. Exemplification is ideally suited for letters of application. The best way Kristy Bredin can support her claims about her qualifications for the internship at RollingStone.com is to give examples of her
educational and professional qualifications. For this reason, the body of
her letter is divided into two categories — her educational record and her
editorial experience.

Each of the body paragraphs has a clear purpose and function. The second paragraph contains two examples pertaining to Kristy's educational
record. The third paragraph contains examples of her editorial experience.
These examples tell the prospective employer what qualifies Kristy for the
internship. Within these two body paragraphs, she arranges her examples
in order of increasing importance. Because her practical experience as an
editor relates directly to the position she is applying for, Kristy considers
this her strongest point and presents it last.

Kristy ends her letter on a strong note, expressing her willingness to be
interviewed and giving the first date she will be available for an interview.
Because people remember best what they read last, a strong conclusion is
essential here, just as it is in other writing situations.

Persuasive Examples. To support a thesis convincingly, examples
should convey specific information, not generalizations. Saying "I am a
good student who is not afraid of responsibility" means very little. It is far
better to say, as Kristy does, "Throughout my college career, I have maintained a 3.4 average" and "I have served as both secretary and president of
the Literary Society." A letter of application should specifically show a prospective employer how your strengths and background correspond to the
employer's needs; well-chosen examples can help you accomplish this goal.

Focus on Revision

After reading her letter, the students in Kristy's peer-editing group identified several areas that they thought needed work.

One student thought Kristy should have mentioned that she had taken a desktop publishing course as an elective and worked with publishing and graphics software when she was the features editor of the student newspaper. Kristy agreed that this expertise would make her a more attractive candidate for the job and thought she could work these examples into her third paragraph.

Another student asked Kristy to explain how her experience as secretary and president of the Literary Society relates to the job she is applying for. If her purpose is to show that she can assume responsibility, she should say so; if it is to illustrate that she can supervise others, she should make this clear.

A third student suggested that she expand the discussion of her internship with Taylor and Francis Publishing in New York. Specific examples of her duties there would be persuasive because they would give her prospective employer a clear idea of her experience. (A peer-editing worksheet for exemplification can be found on pages 220–21.)

Working with Sources. Kristy's instructor recommended that she refer to the ad to which she was responding. He said that this strategy would help her readers — potential employers — to see that she was tailoring her letter to the specific job at RollingStone.com. Kristy considered this suggestion and decided to quote the language of the ad in her letter.

A STUDENT WRITER: Exemplification

The following essay, by Grace Ku, was written for a composition class in response to the following assignment: "Write an essay about the worst job you (or someone you know) ever had. If you can, include a quotation from one of the essays in your textbook. Make sure you include documentation as well as a works-cited page."

Midnight

Introduction   It was eight o'clock, and I was staring at the television   1
set wondering what kind of lesson Dr. Huxtable would teach his
children on a rerun of *The Cosby Show*. I was glued to the set
like an average eleven-year-old while leisurely eating cold Chef
Boyardee spaghetti out of the can. As I watched the show, I fell
asleep on the floor fully clothed in a pair of jeans and a T-shirt,
wondering when my parents would come home. Around midnight
I woke up to a rustling noise: my parents had finally arrived from
Thesis statement   a long day at work. I could see in their tired faces the grief and
hardship of working at a dry-cleaning plant.

Transitional paragraph provides background

Although my parents lived in the most technologically 2
advanced country in the world, their working conditions were
like those of nineteenth-century factory workers. Because they
were immigrants with little formal education and spoke broken
English, they could get jobs only as laborers. Therefore, they
worked at a dry-cleaning plant that was as big as a factory, a
place where hundreds of small neighborhood cleaners sent their
clothes to be processed. Like Bonnie Smith-Yackel's mother in
the essay "My Mother Never Worked," my parents constantly

Quotation from essay in textbook

"struggled to regain some competence and dignity and order" in
their lives (125).

Series of brief examples: physical demands

At work, my parents had to meet certain quotas. Each day 3
they had to clean and press several hundred garments — shirts,
pants, and other clothing. By themselves, every day, they did the
work of four laborers. The muscles of my mother's shoulders and
arms grew hard as iron from working with the press, a difficult
job even for a man. In addition to pressing, my father serviced
the washing machines. As a result, his work clothes always
smelled of oil.

Example: long hours

Not only were my parents' jobs physically demanding, but 4
they also required long hours. My parents went to work at five
o'clock in the morning and came home between nine o'clock at
night and midnight. Each day they worked over twelve hours
at the dry-cleaning plant, where eight-hour workdays and labor
unions did not exist. They were allowed to take only two ten- to
twenty-minute breaks — one for lunch and one for dinner. They

Example: frequent burns

did not stop even when they were burned by a hot iron or by
steam from a press. The scars on their arms made it obvious
that they worked at a dry-cleaning plant. My parents' burned
skin would blister and later peel off, exposing raw flesh. In
time, these injuries would heal, but other burns would soon
follow.

Example: low pay

In addition to having to work long hours and suffering 5
painful injuries, my parents were paid below minimum wage.
Together their paychecks were equal to that of a single unionized
worker (even though they did the work of four). They used this
money to feed and care for a household of five people.

Conclusion

As my parents silently entered our home around midnight, 6
they did not have to complain about their jobs. I could see their
anguish in their faces and their fatigue in the slow movements of

Restatement of thesis their bodies. Even though they did not speak, their eyes said, "We hate our jobs, but we work so that our children will have better lives than we do."

Work Cited

Works-cited list (begins new page) Smith-Yackel, Bonnie. "My Mother Never Worked." *Patterns for College Writing*. 13th ed. Ed. Laurie G. Kirszner and Stephen R. Mandell. Boston: Bedford, 2015. 123–25. Print.

Points for Special Attention

Organization. Grace Ku begins her introduction by describing herself as an eleven-year-old sitting on the floor watching television. At first, her behavior seems typical of many American children, but two things suggest problems: first, she is eating her cold dinner out of a can, and second, even though it is late in the evening, she is still waiting for her parents to return from work. This opening prepares readers for her thesis that her parents' jobs produce only grief and hardship.

In the body of her essay, Grace presents the examples that support her thesis statement. In paragraph 2, she sets the stage for the discussion to follow, explaining that her parents' working conditions were similar to those of nineteenth-century factory workers. In paragraph 3, she presents a series of examples that illustrate how physically demanding her parents' jobs were. In the remaining body paragraphs, she gives three other examples to show how unpleasant the jobs were — how long her parents worked, how often they were injured, and how little they were paid.

Grace concludes her essay by returning to the scene in her introduction, using a quotation that she wants to stay with her readers after they have finished the essay.

Working with Sources. Because her assignment asked students to include a quotation from an essay in their textbook, Grace looked for essays that had to do with work. After reading three of them, she decided that the sentiments expressed by Bonnie Smith-Yackel in "My Mother Never Worked" most closely mirrored her own. For this reason, at the end of paragraph 2, she included a quotation from Smith-Yackel's essay that helped her put her parents' struggles into perspective. Grace was careful to include quotation marks as well as MLA documentation. She also included bibliographic information for the essay in a works-cited page at the end of her essay. (See Chapter 18 for information on MLA documentation.)

Enough Examples. Certainly no single example, no matter how graphic, could adequately support the thesis of this essay. To establish the pain and difficulty of her parents' jobs, Grace uses several examples. Although additional examples would have added even more depth to the essay, the ones she uses are vivid and compelling enough to support her thesis that her parents had to endure great hardship to make a living.

Range of Examples. Grace selects examples that illustrate the full range of her subject. She draws from her parents' daily experience and does not include atypical examples. She also includes enough detail so that her readers, who she assumes do not know much about working in a dry-cleaning plant, will understand her points. She does not, however, provide so much detail that her readers get bogged down and lose interest.

Effective Examples. All of Grace's examples support her thesis statement. While developing these examples, she never loses sight of her main idea; consequently, she does not get sidetracked in irrelevant discussions. She also avoids the temptation to preach to her readers about the injustice of her parents' situation. By allowing her examples to speak for themselves, Grace paints a powerful portrait of her parents and their hardships.

Focus on Revision

After reading this draft, a classmate thought Grace could go into more detail about her parents' situation and could explain her examples in more depth — possibly writing about the quotas her parents had to meet or the other physical dangers of their jobs.

Grace herself thought that she should expand the discussion in paragraph 5 about her parents' low wages, perhaps anticipating questions some of her readers might have about working conditions. For example, was it legal for her parents' employer to require them to work overtime without compensation or to pay them less than the minimum wage? If not, how was the employer able to get away with such practices?

Grace also thought she should move the information about her parents' work-related injuries from paragraph 4 to paragraph 3, where she discusses the physical demands of their jobs.

Finally, she decided to follow the advice of another student and include comments by her parents to make their experiences more immediate to readers.

 PEER-EDITING WORKSHEET: Exemplification

1. What strategy does the writer use in the essay's introduction? Would another strategy be more effective?

2. What is the essay's thesis? Does it make a point that the rest of the essay will support with examples?

3. What specific points do the body paragraphs make?

4. Does the writer use one example or several to illustrate each point? Should the writer use more examples? Fewer? Explain.

5. Does the writer use a sufficient range of examples? Are they explained in enough depth?

6. Do the examples add interest? How persuasive are they? List a few other examples that might be more persuasive.

7. What transitional words and phrases does the writer use to introduce examples? What other transitional words and phrases should be added? Where?

8. In what order are the examples presented? Would another order be more effective? Explain.

9. Has the writer used a series of three or more examples in a single sentence? If so, are these examples separated by commas?

10. What strategy does the writer use in the conclusion? What other strategy could be used?

The selections in this chapter all depend on exemplification to explain and clarify, to add interest, or to persuade. The first selection, a visual text, is followed by questions designed to illustrate how exemplification can operate in visual form. (A multimodal text for exemplification is located online at **macmillanhighered.com/patterns**.)

CHARLES THATCHER, CARRIE VILLINES, OSCAR SÁNCHEZ, AND ANTHONY BRADSHAW*

Four Tattoos (Photos)

Charles Thatcher, "~~Alisha, Loretta~~"

Carrie Villines, "Positive Outlook"

Anthony Bradshaw, "Bar Code"

Oscar Sánchez, "Dragon"

* Photos shown clockwise from top left.

(© Charles Thatcher/The Image Bank/Getty Images; © Carrie Villines/age fotostock/Getty Images; © 2012 OsanchezPhoto/Getty Images; © Anthony Bradshaw/Getty Images)

Reading Images

1. How would you describe each of the four tattoos pictured on the previous page? List the prominent features of each, and then write two or three sentences that describe each of them.

2. After studying the four pictures (and reviewing your answer to question 1), write a one-sentence general statement that sums up your ideas about tattoos. For example, why do you think people get tattoos? Do you see them as a way for people to express themselves? As a way of demonstrating individuality? As a form of rebellion? As an impulsive act? As something else?

3. List several examples that support the general statement you made in question 2. What examples could you use to support this general statement?

Journal Entry

Would you ever get a tattoo? Write a paragraph answering this question. Use your answers to the questions above to support the main idea in your topic sentence. (If you have a tattoo, give several reasons why you decided to get it.)

Thematic Connections

- "Medium Ash Brown" (page 277)
- "My First Conk" (page 283)
- "The Wife-Beater" (page 514)
- "Inked Well" (page 692)

FARHAD MANJOO

No, I Do Not Want to Pet Your Dog

Farhad Manjoo (b. 1978) is a technology columnist for the *New York Times*. Previously, he was a staff writer for *Salon* and *Slate*. He is also a regular contributor for National Public Radio, as well as the author of the book *True Enough: Learning to Live in a Post-Fact Society* (2008). Manjoo attended Cornell University, where he served as editor in chief of the *Cornell Daily Sun*.

Background on domesticated dogs in America The Humane Society of the United States estimates that there are over 83 million pet dogs in North America. Nearly half of all households include at least one canine. The origins of the domestic dog (*Canis lupus familiaris*) are disputed. Some scientists say that dogs are domesticated wolves that joined human communities between 10,000 and 20,000 years ago. Other researchers speculate that canine domestication may go back even further — perhaps 130,000 years. Before the arrival of European colonists in the Americas, Native Americans already had domesticated dogs. When large groups of Europeans arrived in the seventeenth and eighteenth centuries, they brought dogs that had been bred to guard and work, and wealthy people bred dogs as a hobby and for sport. In the nineteenth century, Americans increasingly viewed dogs as loyal companions rather than as guards, workers, and hunters. Their eventual designation as a "best friend" is attributed to Missouri lawyer and politician George Vest. In 1870, he represented a client whose dog had been killed by a sheep farmer. He delivered a sentimental "eulogy" on the loyalty and love of dogs and won the case. Over the last century and a half, dogs such as Toto from *The Wizard of Oz* and animated characters such as Snoopy from *Peanuts* cartoons and Brian from the television show *Family Guy* have become cultural icons. Dogs also work as guides for the disabled, assist in law enforcement, and even serve in the military.

1   The other day I walked into my gym and saw a dog. A half-dozen people were crowding around him, cooing and petting. He was a big dog, a lean and muscular Doberman with, I later learned, the sort of hair-trigger bark you'd prize if you wanted to protect a big stash of gold bullion.

2   "This is Y.," the dog's owner said. No explanation was offered for the pooch's presence, as if it were the most natural thing in the world to have a dog in a place usually reserved for human beings. *Huh*, I thought.

3   The dog came up to me, because in my experience that's what dogs do when you don't want them to come up to you. They get up real close, touching you, licking you, theatrically begging you to respond. The dog pushed his long face toward my hand, the canine equivalent of a high five. And so — in the same way it's rude to leave a high-fiver hanging, especially if the high-fiver has big teeth and a strong jaw — I was expected to pet him. I

224

was expected to pet him

ran my hand across his head half-heartedly. I guess I was fairly sure he wouldn't snap and bite me, but stranger things have happened—for instance, dogs snapping and biting people all the time.

Anyway, happily, I survived.   4

But wait a second. Come on! Why was this dog here? And why was   5
no one perturbed that this dog was here? When this beast was barking at passersby through the window as we were all working out, why did no one go, *Hey, just throwing this out there, should we maybe not have this distracting, possibly dangerous animal by the free weights?*

No one was asking because no one   6
could ask. Sometime in the last decade, dogs
achieved dominion over urban America.
They are everywhere now, allowed in places
that used to belong exclusively to humans,
and sometimes only to human adults: the
office, restaurants, museums, buses, trains,
malls, supermarkets, barber shops, banks,
post offices. Even at the park and other
places where dogs belong, they've been given free rein. Dogs are frequently allowed to wander off leash, to run toward you and around you, to run across the baseball field or basketball court, to get up in your grill. Even worse than the dogs are the owners, who seem never to consider whether there may be people in the gym/office/restaurant/museum who do not care to be in close proximity to their dogs. After all, what kind of monster would have a problem with a poor innocent widdle doggie? It's a dog's world. We just live in it. And it's awful. Bad dogs!

> " Sometime in the last decade, dogs achieved dominion over urban America. "

Not everyone agrees with me on this issue. Some people—or maybe   7
even most people, since dogs, like zombies, have an insidious way of turning opponents into allies—love that dogs abound. If you adore dogs but aren't able to keep one, the world is now your dog park, with pooches everywhere to pet and nuzzle and otherwise brighten your day.

I am not a dog person. (Could you tell?) It's not that I actively despise   8
mutts; I just don't have much time for them, in the same way I don't have time for crossword puzzles or Maroon 5. Now imagine if, everywhere you went, whatever you did, Maroon 5 was always playing and everyone pretended it was totally normal—that this permanent new situation was not in any way offensive, distracting, dirty, and potentially dangerous.

OK, bad example.   9

But here's my problem: There's now a cultural assumption that every-   10
one must love dogs. Dog owners are rarely forced to reckon with the idea that there are people who aren't enthralled by their furry friends, and that taking their dogs everywhere might not be completely pleasant for these folks.

Example: If you're in the office and someone has brought her dog   11
in for the day—because, *fun!*—the dog is sure to come around you, get between your legs, rub against your thigh, take a nap on your feet, or do some other annoying thing.

If the dog's owner notices these antics, I can promise you she won't 12
apologize for the imposition. Nor will she ask you if you mind her dog
doing what he's doing. Nor will she pull on its leash, because there won't be
a leash, this being an office, where dogs are as welcome as Wi-Fi and free
coffee.

Instead, if the owner says anything, it will be on the order of, "Don't 13
worry, he loves people!" Oh, OK then! I guess I'll just take your word for it,
and forget for the moment that 1,000 Americans a day go to emergency
rooms because of dog bites. More Americans seek medical attention for
dog bites than for choking or falls. You're more likely to have to go to a
doctor for a bite than to call the fire department for a home fire. Like it or
not, American dog owner, your pet is a hazard.

But let's leave aside the possibility that I'm scared (maybe legitimately!) 14
of your dog, since you've assured me your dog loves people, and there's no
chance you could be wrong. What if I'm allergic? Or what if I just plain
hate your dog? What if I think he's dirty, since after all he did just put his
nose in another dog's butt? And what if I just want to go through my work-
day without being slobbered on by an animal?

I know this sounds curmudgeonly. You want to shake me and tell me 15
to snap out of it, to get over myself and just love dogs already. But that's
because you like dogs and don't see anything but good in them. For you, a
dog is like ice cream. What churl doesn't like ice cream? Well, I'm that
churl — I'm canine intolerant.

To give you a sense of how I feel when I'm accosted by your dog, let's 16
replace that animal with my two-and-a-half-year-old son. Now, I love my
son, but on any objective scale of socially acceptable behavior, he is the
worst. He's loud. He's inconsiderate of people's personal space — if he's left
free he won't watch where he's walking and will run into you, either on purpose or accidentally. He's jumpy and fidgety in confined spaces; in an airplane it is physically impossible to restrain him from kicking the seat in
front of him. He scratches himself often, sometimes picks his nose, sometimes offers to pick yours. He will constantly say inappropriate things. The
other day at Target, he noticed a little person and commented, for pretty
much everyone to hear, "That lady is short!" On top of all this, he may be
packing a diaper full of urine and feces.

Weirdly, irrationally, despite all this, I feel the same way about my 17
son as you do about your dog: I love him unconditionally and just don't
understand why even strangers wouldn't want him around all the time.
Indeed, I think almost everything he does, even the inappropriate things, is
the cutest behavior ever exhibited in human history.

And yet, still, I rein him in. I realize that, although he's impossibly cute, 18
it's possible he might aggravate some people. For this reason, whenever I
go into public spaces with my toddler, I treat him as if I were handling nuclear waste or a dangerous animal. I keep him confined. I shush him. If he
does anything out of turn — screams, touches people — I make a show of
telling him to quit it and I apologize profusely. And, finally, there are some
places that are completely off-limits to my son: nice restaurants, contem-

plative adult spaces like grown-up museums and coffee shops, the gym, and the office. Especially the office.

Yes, there are parents who don't act this way, awful parents who let   19 their terrible kids run free. The rest of us hate those people because they give all parents a bad name. But I'll submit there are many more such dog owners than there are overindulgent parents. Most parents I know are mortified by the thought that their children might be causing anguish for others. This is evident in the world around you: It's why your co-workers rarely bring their toddlers to work. It's why two-year-olds don't approach you in the park and lick your leg or ask you whether you need to visit the potty. It's why, when a child is being unruly in a supermarket or restaurant, you'll usually see his parents strive to get him to knock it off.

But dog owners? They seem to suffer few qualms about their animals'   20 behavior. That's why there are so many dogs running around at the park, jumping up on the bench beside you while you're trying to read a book, the owner never asking if it's OK with you. That's why, when you're at a café, the dog at the neighboring table feels free to curl up under your seat. That's why there's a dog at your office right at this moment and you're having to pretend that he's just the cutest.

Well, no more, my fellow doggie skeptics. Let's take back the peace   21 we're owed. The next time your young, happy co-worker brings in his dog for the day, tell him the office is not a canine playpen. It's time to take that dog home.

Comprehension

1. In paragraph 6, Manjoo says, "Sometime in the last decade, dogs achieved dominion over urban America." Is Manjoo being serious, or is he being sarcastic? Explain.

2. What, specifically, does Manjoo object to about dogs? Could his objections apply to other types of pets as well — for example, cats?

3. Manjoo says that there is "a cultural assumption that everyone must love dogs" (10). Do you agree? Why or why not?

4. In paragraph 13, Manjoo points out that over one thousand Americans a day are treated for dog bites. Why does he include this statistic?

5. According to Manjoo, how are dogs like his two-and-a-half-year-old child? How are they different? What point is he making with this comparison?

Purpose and Audience

1. Is Manjoo's essay aimed at dog lovers or at people, like him, who don't like dogs? How can you tell?

2. At what point in the essay does Manjoo state his thesis? Why does he wait so long to do so?

3. What does Manjoo hope to accomplish with this essay? Does he want to change people's minds? Inform them? Move them to action? Something else?

Style and Structure

1. Manjoo introduces his essay with an **anecdote** about encountering a dog in a gym. Is this an effective way to begin? Explain.

2. At several points in the essay, Manjoo talks directly to readers — for example, in paragraph 5. Why do you think he uses this strategy?

3. In paragraph 7, Manjoo compares dogs to zombies. What point is he trying to make? Is this a logical comparison? Why or why not?

4. In paragraph 8, Manjoo compares dogs to the rock band Maroon 5. In paragraph 9, he acknowledges that this is a bad example. Why then does he make this comparison?

5. In paragraph 14, Manjoo asks a series of **rhetorical questions**. Why? Is this strategy successful?

6. **Vocabulary Project.** What specific words and phrases convey Manjoo's attitude toward dog lovers? How would you describe the tone these words create? Respectful? Insulting? Sarcastic? Something else?

Journal Entry

Does your own experience support Manjoo's conclusions? Do you think that Manjoo accurately characterizes dog owners, or do you think that he is exaggerating?

Writing Workshop

1. Assume that you are working in an office that is considering instituting a Bring Your Dog to Work Day. Write an email to your supervisor in which you argue for or against this policy. Make sure that you use examples from your own experience to support your position.

2. **Working with Sources.** Manjoo's essay originally appeared as a blog post on Slate.com. Write a response to Manjoo's essay, referring to the specific points that he makes. Be sure to include parenthetical documentation for references to Manjoo's essay, and include a works-cited page. (See Chapter 18 for information on MLA documentation.)

3. Recent studies have shown that when a therapy dog is brought into a retirement home, a veterans hospital, or even a prison, people report being less stressed. Write an essay in which you discuss the possible benefits of having a dog with you in stressful settings or situations — for example, when you are studying for a test or working under a deadline.

Combining the Patterns

Manjoo includes two long **narratives** in his essay — one about a dog in a gym and another about his son. What purposes do these narratives serve?

Thematic Connections

- "Shooting an Elephant" (page 133)
- "No Wonder They Call Me a Bitch" (page 180)
- "Your Flip-Flops Are Grossing Me Out" (page 687)

JUDITH ORTIZ COFER

The Myth of the Latin Woman: I Just Met a Girl Named Maria

Born in Puerto Rico in 1952, Judith Ortiz Cofer moved to New Jersey with her family when she was four. She is now Regents' and Franklin Professor of English and Creative Writing at the University of Georgia. Widely anthologized, Cofer has published three collections of poetry, including *A Love Story Beginning in Spanish* (2005); four essay collections, including *Silent Dancing* (1990) and *The Latin Deli* (1993); four novels, including the young adult novel *Call Me Maria* (2006); and the short-story collection *An Island Like You: Stories of the Barrio* (1995). In a recent interview, she commented on her early writing: "Poetry allowed me to become intimate with English. And it allowed me to master the one skill that I try to teach my students — and if that's the only thing I accomplish, I consider it a success — and that is succinctness: economy and concentration of language. Why use fifteen words when one clear, elegant sentence will do it?"

Background on images of Hispanic women in film During the era of silent film, Hispanic performers found a niche with the popularity of the stereotypical "Latin lover." Although Hispanic actors enjoyed success, only a handful of Hispanic actresses, such as Myrtle Gonzalez and Beatriz Michelena, played in leading roles that did not always cast them as Latina. For example, Mexican-born Dolores del Rio, the only Hispanic actress to achieve international stardom during the period, played characters named Evelyn Iffield and Jeanne Lamont as well as Carlotta de Silva and Carmelita de Granados. However, in the late 1920s, the advent of sound brought many fewer movie roles for Hispanic actresses. Some who found success during the thirties and forties conformed to broad stereotypes — for example, "Mexican Spitfire" Lupe Vélez, Carmen "the Lady in the Tutti-Frutti Hat" Miranda, and Maria Montez's hot-blooded seductresses. Others concealed their Hispanic identities on-screen (as was the case for Margarita Carmen Cansino, whose hair was dyed, eyebrows heavily plucked, and skin lightened to make her into the movie star Rita Hayworth). In the fifties and sixties, actresses such as Katy Jurado and Rita Moreno (who won a supporting actress Academy Award for her performance in *West Side Story*) rarely played leads. The sixties saw the stardom of Raquel Welch (born Jo Raquel Tejada), who, like Hayworth, played down her Hispanic roots; but it was not until the nineties that young performers such as Jessica Alba, Jennifer Lopez, Penelope Cruz, and Salma Hayek came into their own, playing Latinas who are more than stereotypes or characters whose ethnicity is not important.

On a bus trip to London from Oxford University where I was earning 1
some graduate credits one summer, a young man, obviously fresh from a

pub, spotted me and as if struck by inspiration went down on his knees in the aisle. With both hands over his heart he broke into an Irish tenor's rendition of "Maria" from *West Side Story*.* My politely amused fellow passengers gave his lovely voice the round of gentle applause it deserved. Though I was not quite as amused, I managed my version of an English smile: no show of teeth, no extreme contortions of the facial muscles — I was at this time of my life practicing reserve and cool. Oh, that British control, how I coveted it. But "Maria" had followed me to London, reminding me of a prime fact of my life: you can leave the island, master the English language, and travel as far as you can, but if you are a Latina, especially one like me who so obviously belongs to Rita Moreno's** gene pool, the island travels with you.

This is sometimes a very good thing — it may win you that extra minute of someone's attention. But with some people, the same things can make *you* an island — not a tropical paradise but an Alcatraz, a place nobody wants to visit. As a Puerto Rican girl living in the United States*** and wanting like most children to "belong," I resented the stereotype that my Hispanic appearance called forth from many people I met.

Growing up in a large urban center in New Jersey during the 1960s, I suffered from what I think of as "cultural schizophrenia." Our life was designed by my parents as a microcosm of their *casas*† on the island. We spoke in Spanish, ate Puerto Rican food bought at the *bodega*,‡ and practiced strict Catholicism at a church that allotted us a one-hour slot each week for mass, performed in Spanish by a Chinese priest trained as a missionary for Latin America.

As a girl I was kept under strict surveillance by my parents, since my virtue and modesty were, by their cultural equation, the same as their honor. As a teenager I was lectured constantly on how to behave as a proper *senorita*. But it was a conflicting message I received, since the Puerto Rican mothers also encouraged their daughters to look and act like women and to dress in clothes our Anglo friends and their mothers found too "mature" and flashy. The difference was, and is, cultural; yet I often felt humiliated when I appeared at an American friend's party wearing a dress more suitable to a semi-formal than to a playroom birthday celebration. At Puerto Rican festivities, neither the music nor the colors we wore could be too loud.

I remember Career Day in our high school, when teachers told us to come dressed as if for a job interview. It quickly became obvious that to the Puerto Rican girls "dressing up" meant wearing their mother's ornate

---

* Eds. note — A Broadway musical, based on *Romeo and Juliet,* about two rival New York street gangs, one Anglo and one Puerto Rican.

** Eds. note — Puerto Rico–born actress who won an Oscar for her role in the 1960 movie version of *West Side Story*.

*** Eds. note — Although it is an island, Puerto Rico is part of the United States.

† Eds. note — Homes.

‡ Eds. note — Small grocery store.

jewelry and clothing, more appropriate (by mainstream standards) for the company Christmas party than as daily office attire. That morning I had agonized in front of my closet, trying to figure out what a "career girl" would wear. I knew how to dress for school (at the Catholic school I attended, we all wore uniforms), I knew how to dress for Sunday mass, and I knew what dresses to wear for parties at my relatives' homes. Though I do not recall the precise details of my Career Day outfit, it must have been a composite of these choices. But I remember a comment my friend (an Italian American) made in later years that coalesced my impressions of that day. She said that at the business school she was attending, the Puerto Rican girls always stood out for wearing "everything at once." She meant, of course, too much jewelry, too many accessories. On that day at school we were simply made the negative models by the nuns, who were themselves not credible fashion experts to any of us. But it was painfully obvious to me that to the others, in their tailored skirts and silk blouses, we must have seemed "hopeless" and "vulgar." Though I now know that most adolescents feel out of step much of the time, I also know that for the Puerto Rican girls of my generation that sense was intensified. The way our teachers and classmates looked at us that day in school was just a taste of the cultural clash that awaited us in the real world, where prospective employers and men on the street would often misinterpret our tight skirts and jingling bracelets as a "come-on."

Mixed cultural signals have perpetuated certain stereotypes — for example, that of the Hispanic woman as the "hot tamale" or sexual firebrand. It is a one-dimensional view that the media have found easy to promote. In their special vocabulary, advertisers have designated "sizzling" and "smoldering" as the adjectives of choice for describing not only the foods but also the women of Latin America. From conversations in my house I recall hearing about the harassment that Puerto Rican women endured in factories where the "boss-men" talked to them as if sexual innuendo was all they understood, and worse, often gave them the choice of submitting to their advances or being fired.

> " Mixed cultural signals have perpetuated certain stereotypes — for example, that of the Hispanic woman as the 'hot tamale' or sexual firebrand. "

6

It is custom, however, not chromosomes, that leads us to choose scarlet over pale pink. As young girls, it was our mothers who influenced our decisions about clothes and colors — mothers who had grown up on a tropical island where the natural environment was a riot of primary colors, where showing your skin was one way to keep cool as well as to look sexy. Most important of all, on the island, women perhaps felt freer to dress and move more provocatively since, in most cases, they were protected by the traditions, mores, and laws of a Spanish/Catholic system of morality and machismo whose main rule was: *You may look at my sister, but if you touch her I*

7

will kill you. The extended family and church structure could provide a young woman with a circle of safety in her small pueblo on the island; if a man "wronged" a girl, everyone would close in to save her family honor.

My mother has told me about dressing in her best party clothes on   8 Saturday nights and going to the town's plaza to promenade with her girl-friends in front of the boys they liked. The males were thus given an opportunity to admire the women and to express their admiration in the form of *piropos*: erotically charged street poems they composed on the spot. (I have myself been subjected to a few *piropos* while visiting the island, and they can be outrageous, although custom dictates that they must never cross into obscenity.) This ritual, as I understand it, also entails a show of studied indifference on the woman's part; if she is "decent," she must not acknowledge the man's impassioned words. So I do understand how things can be lost in translation. When a Puerto Rican girl dressed in her idea of what is attractive meets a man from the mainstream culture who has been trained to react to certain types of clothing as a sexual signal, a clash is likely to take place. I remember the boy who took me to my first formal dance leaning over to plant a sloppy, over-eager kiss painfully on my mouth; when I didn't respond with sufficient passion, he remarked resent-fully: "I thought you Latin girls were supposed to mature early," as if I were expected to *ripen* like a fruit or vegetable, not just grow into womanhood like other girls.

It is surprising to my professional friends that even today some people,   9 including those who should know better, still put others "in their place." It happened to me most recently during a stay at a classy metropolitan ho-tel favored by young professional couples for weddings. Late one evening after the theater, as I walked toward my room with a colleague (a woman with whom I was coordinating an arts program), a middle-aged man in a tuxedo, with a young girl in satin and lace on his arm, stepped directly into our path. With his champagne glass extended toward me, he exclaimed "Evita!"*

Our way blocked, my companion and I listened as the man half-   10 recited, half-bellowed "Don't Cry for Me, Argentina." When he finished, the young girl said: "How about a round of applause for my daddy?" We complied, hoping this would bring the silly spectacle to a close. I was becoming aware that our little group was attracting the attention of the other guests. "Daddy" must have perceived this too, and he once more barred the way as we tried to walk past him. He began to shout-sing a ditty to the tune of "La Bamba" — except the lyrics were about a girl named Maria whose exploits rhymed with her name and gonorrhea. The girl kept saying "Oh, Daddy" and looking at me with pleading eyes. She wanted me to laugh along with the others. My companion and I stood silently waiting

---

* Eds. note — A Broadway musical about Eva Duarte de Perón, the former first lady of Argentina.

for the man to end his offensive song. When he finished, I looked not at him but at his daughter. I advised her calmly never to ask her father what he had done in the army. Then I walked between them and to my room. My friend complimented me on my cool handling of the situation, but I confessed that I had really wanted to push the jerk into the swimming pool. This same man — probably a corporate executive, well-educated, even worldly by most standards — would not have been likely to regale an Anglo woman with a dirty song in public. He might have checked his impulse by assuming that she could be somebody's wife or mother, or at least *somebody* who might take offense. But, to him, I was just an Evita or a Maria: merely a character in his cartoon-populated universe.

Another facet of the myth of the Latin woman in the United States is 11 the menial, the domestic — Maria the housemaid or countergirl. It's true that work as domestics, as waitresses, and in factories is all that's available to women with little English and few skills. But the myth of the Hispanic menial — the funny maid, mispronouncing words and cooking up a spicy storm in a shiny California kitchen — has been perpetuated by the media in the same way that "Mammy" from *Gone with the Wind* became America's idea of the black woman for generations. Since I do not wear my diplomas around my neck for all to see, I have on occasion been sent to that "kitchen" where some think I obviously belong.

One incident has stayed with me, though I recognize it as a minor 12 offense. My first public poetry reading took place in Miami, at a restaurant where a luncheon was being held before the event. I was nervous and excited as I walked in with notebook in hand. An older woman motioned me to her table, and thinking (foolish me) that she wanted me to autograph a copy of my newly published slender volume of verse, I went over. She ordered a cup of coffee from me, assuming that I was the waitress. (Easy enough to mistake my poems for menus, I suppose.) I know it wasn't an intentional act of cruelty. Yet of all the good things that happened later, I remember that scene most clearly, because it reminded me of what I had to overcome before anyone would take me seriously. In retrospect I understand that my anger gave my reading fire. In fact, I have almost always taken any doubt in my abilities as a challenge, the result most often being the satisfaction of winning a convert, of seeing the cold, appraising eyes warm to my words, the body language change, the smile that indicates I have opened some avenue for communication. So that day as I read, I looked directly at that woman. Her lowered eyes told me she was embarrassed at her faux pas, and when I willed her to look up at me, she graciously allowed me to punish her with my full attention. We shook hands at the end of the reading and I never saw her again. She has probably forgotten the entire incident, but maybe not.

Yet I am one of the lucky ones. There are thousands of Latinas without 13 the privilege of an education or the entrees into society that I have. For them life is a constant struggle against the misconceptions perpetuated by the myth of the Latina. My goal is to try to replace the old stereotypes with a much more interesting set of realities. Every time I give a reading, I hope the stories I tell, the dreams and fears I examine in my work, can achieve some universal truth that will get my audience past the particulars of my skin color, my accent, or my clothes.

I once wrote a poem in which I called all Latinas "God's brown daugh- 14 ters." This poem is really a prayer of sorts, offered upward, but also, through the human-to-human channel of art, outward. It is a prayer for communication and for respect. In it, Latin women pray "in Spanish to an Anglo God/with a Jewish heritage," and they are "fervently hoping/that if not omnipotent,/at least He be bilingual."

· · ·

Comprehension

1. What does Cofer mean by "cultural schizophrenia" (3)?

2. What "conflicting message" (4) did Cofer receive from her family?

3. What points does Cofer make by including each of the following in her essay?
   - The story about the young man in Oxford (1)
   - The story about Career Day (5)
   - The story about the poetry reading (12)

4. According to Cofer, what stereotypes are commonly applied to Latinas?

5. How does Cofer explain why she and other Puerto Rican women like to dress as they do? Why do outsiders think they dress this way?

6. What exactly is "the myth of the Latin woman" (11)?

7. How does Cofer hope to help people see beyond the stereotypes she describes? Is she successful?

Purpose and Audience

1. Which of the following do you think is Cofer's thesis? Why?
   - "[I]f you are a Latina, especially one like me who so obviously belongs to Rita Moreno's gene pool, the island travels with you" (1).
   - "As a Puerto Rican girl living in the United States . . . I resented the stereotype that my Hispanic appearance called forth from many people I met" (2).
   - "My goal is to try to replace the old stereotypes with a much more interesting set of realities" (13).

2. Why does Cofer begin paragraph 13 with "Yet I am one of the lucky ones"? How do you think she expects her audience to react to this statement?

3. Despite its use of Spanish words, this essay is directed at an Anglo audience. How can you tell?

Style and Structure

1. Cofer opens her essay with a story about an incident in her life. Considering her subject matter and her audience, is this an effective opening strategy? Why or why not?

2. What do you think Cofer means to suggest with these expressions in paragraph 8?
   - "erotically charged"
   - "studied indifference"
   - "lost in translation"
   - "mainstream culture"

3. Cofer does not introduce the stereotype of the Latina as "the menial, the domestic" until paragraph 11, when she devotes two paragraphs to this part of the stereotype. Why does she wait so long? Should this discussion have appeared earlier? Should it have been deleted altogether? Explain your reasoning.

4. Cofer uses exemplification to support her thesis. Does she provide enough examples? Are they the right kinds of examples?

5. How do you interpret the lines of poetry that Cofer quotes in her conclusion? Is this an effective concluding strategy? Why or why not?

6. **Vocabulary Project.** Cofer uses Spanish words throughout this essay, and she does not define them. Find definitions of these words in a Spanish/English dictionary, such as SpanishDict.com, or at Google Translate. Would the English equivalents be just as effective as — or even more effective than — the Spanish words?

Journal Entry

On the basis of what she writes here, it seems as if Cofer does not confront the people who stereotype her and does not show anger, even in the incident described in paragraphs 9–10. Do you think she should have acted differently, or do you admire her restraint?

Writing Workshop

1. What stereotypes are applied by outsiders to your racial or ethnic group (or to people of your gender, intended profession, or geographic region)? Write an exemplification essay in which you argue that these stereotypes are untrue and potentially harmful. Support your thesis with passages of narration, comparison and contrast, and cause and effect.

2. Think of some books, films, advertisements, or TV shows that feature characters of your own racial or ethnic group. Write a classification essay in which you discuss the different ways in which these characters are portrayed. Use exemplification and description to explain your categories. In your thesis, evaluate the accuracy of these characterizations.

3. **Working with Sources.** In paragraph 1 of her essay, Cofer says that "you can leave the island, master the English language, and travel as far as you can, but if you are a Latina, especially one like me who so obviously belongs to Rita Moreno's gene pool, the island travels with you." Editing this statement to suit your own "gene pool," use it as the thesis of an essay about the problems you have fitting in to some larger segment of society. Be sure to acknowledge Cofer as your source, including parenthetical documentation for references to her essay, and include a works-cited page. (See Chapter 18 for information on MLA documentation.)

Combining the Patterns

The examples Cofer uses are personal narratives — stories of her own experience. What are the advantages and disadvantages of using **narration** here? Would other kinds of examples be more effective? Explain.

Thematic Connections

- " 'What's in a Name?' " (page 2)
- "Indian Education" (page 142)
- "Just Walk On By: A Black Man Ponders His Power to Alter Public Space" (page 238)

BRENT STAPLES

Just Walk On By: A Black Man Ponders His Power to Alter Public Space

Born in Chester, Pennsylvania, in 1951, Brent Staples joined the staff of the *New York Times* in 1985, writing on culture and politics, and he became a member of its editorial board in 1990. His columns appear regularly on the paper's op-ed pages. Staples has also written a memoir, *Parallel Time: Growing Up in Black and White* (1994), about his escape from the poverty and violence of his childhood.

Background on racial profiling "Just Walk On By" can be read in the light of current controversies surrounding racial profiling of criminal suspects, which occurs, according to the American Civil Liberties Union, "when the police target someone for investigation on the basis of that person's race, national origin, or ethnicity. Examples of profiling are the use of race to determine which drivers to stop for minor traffic violations ('driving while black') and the use of race to determine which motorists or pedestrians to search for contraband." Although law enforcement officials have often denied that they profile criminals solely on the basis of race, studies have shown a high prevalence of police profiling directed primarily at African and Hispanic Americans. A number of states have enacted laws barring racial profiling, and some people have won court settlements when they objected to being interrogated by police solely because of their race. Since the terrorist attacks of September 11, 2001, however, people of Arab descent have been targets of heightened interest at airports and elsewhere. In addition, the passage of a strict anti-illegal immigration law in Arizona in 2010 caused many Hispanics to fear that they would be singled out for scrutiny solely on the basis of race. (Just before the bill was scheduled to take effect, a federal judge blocked sections that required police to check immigration status during traffic violations, detentions, and arrests. The United States Supreme Court subsequently upheld that portion of the law.) Clearly, these events have added to the continuing controversy surrounding the association of criminal behavior with particular ethnic groups.

My first victim was a woman — white, well dressed, probably in her 1 early twenties. I came upon her late one evening on a deserted street in Hyde Park, a relatively affluent neighborhood in an otherwise mean, impoverished section of Chicago. As I swung onto the avenue behind her, there seemed to be a discreet, uninflammatory distance between us. Not so. She cast back a worried glance. To her, the youngish black man — a broad six feet two inches with a beard and billowing hair, both hands shoved into the pockets of a bulky military jacket — seemed menacingly close. After a few more quick glimpses, she picked up her pace and was soon running in earnest. Within seconds she disappeared into a cross street.

That was more than a decade ago. I was twenty-two years old, a graduate student newly arrived at the University of Chicago. It was in the echo of that terrified woman's footfalls that I first began to know the unwieldy inheritance I'd come into — the ability to alter public space in ugly ways. It was clear that she thought herself the quarry of a mugger, rapist, or worse. Suffering a bout of insomnia, however, I was stalking sleep, not defenseless wayfarers. As a softy who is scarcely able to take a knife to a raw chicken — let alone hold it to a person's throat — I was surprised, embarrassed, and dismayed all at once. Her flight made me feel like an accomplice in tyranny. It also made it clear that I was indistinguishable from the muggers who occasionally seeped into the area from the surrounding ghetto. That first encounter, and those that followed, signified that a vast, unnerving gulf lay between nighttime pedestrians — particularly women — and me. And I soon gathered that being perceived as dangerous is a hazard in itself. I only needed to turn a corner into a dicey situation, or crowd some frightened, armed person in a foyer somewhere, or make an errant move after being pulled over by a policeman. Where fear and weapons meet — and they often do in urban America — there is always the possibility of death.

> " It was in the echo of that terrified woman's footfalls that I first began to know the unwieldy inheritance I'd come into — the ability to alter public space in ugly ways. "

In that first year, my first away from my hometown, I was to become thoroughly familiar with the language of fear. At dark, shadowy intersections in Chicago, I could cross in front of a car stopped at a traffic light and elicit the *thunk, thunk, thunk, thunk* of the driver — black, white, male, or female — hammering down the door locks. On less traveled streets after dark, I grew accustomed to but never comfortable with people who crossed to the other side of the street rather than pass me. Then there were the standard unpleasantries with police, doormen, bouncers, cab drivers, and others whose business it is to screen out troublesome individuals *before* there is any nastiness.

I moved to New York nearly two years ago and I have remained an avid night walker. In central Manhattan, the near-constant crowd cover minimizes tense one-on-one street encounters. Elsewhere — visiting friends in SoHo, where sidewalks are narrow and tightly spaced buildings shut out the sky — things can get very taut indeed.

Black men have a firm place in New York mugging literature. Norman Podhoretz in his famed (or infamous) 1963 essay, "My Negro Problem — and Ours," recalls growing up in terror of black males; they "were tougher than we were, more ruthless," he writes — and as an adult on the Upper West Side of Manhattan, he continues, he cannot constrain his nervousness when he meets black men on certain streets. Similarly, a decade later, the essayist and novelist Edward Hoagland extols a New York where once "Negro bitterness bore down mainly on other Negroes." Where some see mere panhandlers, Hoagland sees "a mugger who is clearly screwing up his nerve to do more than just *ask* for money." But Hoagland has "the New Yorker's quick-hunch posture for broken-field maneuvering," and the bad guy swerves away.

I often witness that "hunch posture," from women after dark on the warrenlike streets of Brooklyn where I live. They seem to set their faces on neutral and, with their purse straps strung across their chests bandolier style, they forge ahead as though bracing themselves against being tackled. I understand, of course, that the danger they perceive is not a hallucination. Women are particularly vulnerable to street violence, and young black males are drastically overrepresented among the perpetrators of that violence. Yet these truths are no solace against the kind of alienation that comes of being ever the suspect, against being set apart, a fearsome entity with whom pedestrians avoid making eye contact. 6

It is not altogether clear to me how I reached the ripe old age of twenty-two without being conscious of the lethality nighttime pedestrians attributed to me. Perhaps it was because in Chester, Pennsylvania, the small, angry industrial town where I came of age in the 1960s, I was scarcely noticeable against a backdrop of gang warfare, street knifings, and murders. I grew up one of the good boys, had perhaps a half-dozen fist fights. In retrospect, my shyness of combat has clear sources. 7

Many things go into the making of a young thug. One of those things is the consummation of the male romance with the power to intimidate. An infant discovers that random flailings send the baby bottle flying out of the crib and crashing to the floor. Delighted, the joyful babe repeats those motions again and again, seeking to duplicate the feat. Just so, I recall the points at which some of my boyhood friends were finally seduced by the perception of themselves as tough guys. When a mark cowered and surrendered his money without resistance, myth and reality merged — and paid off. It is, after all, only manly to embrace the power to frighten and intimidate. We, as men, are not supposed to give an inch of our lane on the highway; we are to seize the fighter's edge in work and in play and even in love; we are to be valiant in the face of hostile forces. 8

Unfortunately, poor and powerless young men seem to take all this nonsense literally. As a boy, I saw countless tough guys locked away; I have since buried several, too. They were babies, really — a teenage cousin, a brother of twenty-two, a childhood friend in his mid-twenties — all gone down in episodes of bravado played out in the streets. I came to doubt the virtues of intimidation early on. I chose, perhaps even unconsciously, to remain a shadow — timid, but a survivor. 9

The fearsomeness mistakenly attributed to me in public places often has a perilous flavor. The most frightening of these confusions occurred in the late 1970s and early 1980s when I worked as a journalist in Chicago. One day, rushing into the office of a magazine I was writing for with a deadline story in hand, I was mistaken for a burglar. The office manager called security and, with an ad hoc posse, pursued me through the labyrinthine 10 halls, nearly to my editor's door. I had no way of proving who I was. I could only move briskly toward the company of someone who knew me.

Another time I was on assignment for a local paper and killing time 11 before an interview. I entered a jewelry store on the city's affluent Near North Side. The proprietor excused herself and returned with an enormous red Doberman pinscher straining at the end of a leash. She stood, the dog extended toward me, silent to my questions, her eyes bulging nearly out of her head. I took a cursory look around, nodded, and bade her good night. Relatively speaking, however, I never fared as badly as another black male journalist. He went to nearby Waukegan, Illinois, a couple of summers ago to work on a story about a murderer who was born there. Mistaking the reporter for the killer, police hauled him from his car at gunpoint and but for his press credentials would probably have tried to book him. Such episodes are not uncommon. Black men trade tales like this all the time.

In "My Negro Problem — and Ours," Podhoretz writes that the ha- 12 tred he feels for blacks makes itself known to him through a variety of avenues — one being his discomfort with that "special brand of paranoid touchiness" to which he says blacks are prone. No doubt he is speaking here of black men. In time, I learned to smother the rage I felt at so often being taken for a criminal. Not to do so would surely have led to madness — via that special "paranoid touchiness" that so annoyed Podhoretz at the time he wrote the essay.

I began to take precautions to make myself less threatening. I move 13 about with care, particularly late in the evening. I give a wide berth to nervous people on subway platforms during the wee hours, particularly when I have exchanged business clothes for jeans. If I happen to be entering a building behind some people who appear skittish, I may walk by, letting them clear the lobby before I return, so as not to seem to be following them. I have been calm and extremely congenial on those rare occasions when I've been pulled over by the police.

And on late-evening constitutionals along streets less traveled by, I 14 employ what has proved to be an excellent tension-reducing measure: I whistle melodies from Beethoven and Vivaldi and the more popular classical composers. Even steely New Yorkers hunching toward nighttime destinations seem to relax, and occasionally they even join in the tune. Virtually everybody seems to sense that a mugger wouldn't be warbling bright, sunny selections from Vivaldi's *Four Seasons*. It is my equivalent of the cowbell that hikers wear when they know they are in bear country.

• • •

Comprehension

1. Why does Staples characterize the woman he encounters in paragraph 1 as a "victim"?

2. What does Staples mean when he says he has the power to "alter public space" (2)?

3. Why does Staples walk the streets at night?

4. What things, in Staples's opinion, contribute to "the making of a young thug" (8)? According to Staples, why are young, poor, and powerless men especially likely to become thugs?

5. How does Staples attempt to make himself less threatening?

Purpose and Audience

1. What is Staples's thesis? Does he state it or imply it?

2. Does Staples use logic, emotion, or a combination of the two to appeal to his readers? How appropriate is his strategy?

3. What preconceptions does Staples assume his audience has? How does he challenge these preconceptions?

4. What is Staples trying to accomplish with his first sentence? Do you think he succeeds? Why or why not?

Style and Structure

1. Why does Staples mention Norman Podhoretz? Could he make the same points without referring to Podhoretz's essay?

2. Staples begins his essay with an anecdote. How effective is this strategy? Do you think another opening strategy would be more effective? Explain.

3. Does Staples present enough examples to support his thesis? Are they representative? Would other types of examples be more convincing? Explain.

4. In what order does Staples present his examples? Would another order be more effective? Explain.

5. **Vocabulary Project.** In paragraph 8, Staples uses the word *thug*. List as many synonyms as you can for this word. Do all these words convey the same idea, or do they differ in their connotations? Explain. (If you like, consult an online thesaurus at thesaurus.com.)

Journal Entry

Have you ever been in a situation such as the ones Staples describes, where you perceived someone (or someone perceived you) as threatening? How did you react? After reading Staples's essay, do you think you would react the same way now?

Writing Workshop

1. Use your journal entry to help you write an essay using a single long example to support this statement: "When walking alone at night, you can (or cannot) be too careful."

2. **Working with Sources.** Relying on examples from your own experience and from Staples's essay, write an essay discussing what part you think race plays in people's reactions to Staples. Do you think his perceptions are accurate? Be sure to include parenthetical documentation for Staples's words and ideas, and include a works-cited page. (See Chapter 18 for information on MLA documentation.)

3. How accurate is Staples's observation concerning the "male romance with the power to intimidate" (8)? What does he mean by this statement? What examples from your own experience support (or do not support) the idea that this "romance" is an element of male upbringing in our society?

Combining the Patterns

In paragraph 8, Staples uses **cause and effect** to demonstrate what goes "into the making of a young thug." Would several **examples** have better explained how a youth becomes a thug?

Thematic Connections

- "The 'Black Table' Is Still There" (page 348)
- "A Peaceful Woman Explains Why She Carries a Gun" (page 353)
- "The Ways We Lie" (page 471)
- "The Wife-Beater" (page 514)

DEBORAH L. RHODE

Why Looks Are the Last Bastion of Discrimination

Deborah L. Rhode (b. 1952) is the Ernest McFarland Professor of Law and the Director of the Center on the Legal Profession at Stanford University. She earned her undergraduate and law degrees at Yale University; she also served as a law clerk for former Supreme Court Justice Thurgood Marshall. She has published many books on gender, legal ethics, and professional responsibility, including *The Difference "Difference" Makes: Women and Leadership* (2002) and *The Beauty Bias: The Injustice of Appearance in Life and Law* (2010). A columnist for the *National Law Journal,* Rhode has also written for the *New York Times, Slate,* the *Boston Globe,* and other publications. The following essay originally appeared in the *Washington Post.*

Background on appearance-based discrimination The Constitution bars discrimination on the basis of race, sex, religion, national origin, and ethnicity. Although some see "lookism" as a civil rights issue similar to racism and sexism, others worry that addressing the issue with legislation encroaches on individual freedom and unnecessarily creates another legally protected group. As Rhode notes, however, the state of Michigan and six local jurisdictions throughout the United States have already enacted legal prohibitions on appearance discrimination. In Michigan, for example, a Hooters waitress sued the chain after she was told to lose weight and improve her looks. Lawyers for Hooters argued that employees at the restaurant — who wear tank tops and tight shorts — are entertainers as much as servers. In 2011, the suit was settled out of court.

In the nineteenth century, many American cities banned public appearances by "unsightly" individuals. A Chicago ordinance was typical: "Any person who is diseased, maimed, mutilated, or in any way deformed, so as to be an unsightly or disgusting subject . . . shall not . . . expose himself to public view, under the penalty of a fine of $1 for each offense." 1

Although the government is no longer in the business of enforcing such discrimination, it still allows businesses, schools, and other organizations to indulge their own prejudices. Over the past half-century, the United States has expanded protections against discrimination to include race, religion, sex, age, disability, and, in a growing number of jurisdictions, sexual orientation. Yet bias based on appearance remains perfectly permissible in all but one state and six cities and counties. Across the rest of the country, looks are the last bastion of acceptable bigotry. 2

We all know that appearance matters, but the price of prejudice can be steeper than we often assume. In Texas in 1994, an obese woman was 3

bigotry

rejected for a job as a bus driver when a company doctor assumed she was not up to the task after watching her, in his words, "waddling down the hall." He did not perform any agility tests to determine whether she was, as the company would later claim, unfit to evacuate the bus in the event of an accident.

In New Jersey in 2005, one of the Borgata Hotel Casino's "Borgata babe" cocktail waitresses went from a Size 4 to a Size 6 because of a thyroid condition. When the waitress, whose contract required her to keep "an hourglass figure" that was "height and weight appropriate," requested a larger uniform, she was turned down. "Borgata babes don't go up in size," she was told. (Unless, the waitress noted, they have breast implants, which the casino happily accommodated with paid medical leave and a bigger bustier.)   4

And in California in 2001, Jennifer Portnick, a 240-pound aerobics instructor, was denied a franchise by Jazzercise, a national fitness chain. Jazzercise explained that its image demanded instructors who are "fit" and "toned." But Portnick was both: She worked out six days a week, taught back-to-back classes, and had no shortage of willing students.   5

Such cases are common. In a survey by the National Association to Advance Fat Acceptance, 62 percent of its overweight female members and 42 percent of its overweight male members said they had been turned down for a job because of their weight.   6

And it isn't just weight that's at issue; it's appearance overall. According to a national poll by the Employment Law Alliance in 2005, 16 percent of workers reported being victims of appearance discrimination more generally — a figure comparable to the percentage who in other surveys say they have experienced sex or race discrimination.   7

Conventional wisdom holds that beauty is in the eye of the beholder, but most beholders tend to agree on what is beautiful. A number of researchers have independently found that, when people are asked to rate an individual's attractiveness, their responses are quite consistent, even across race, sex, age, class, and cultural background. Facial symmetry and unblemished skin are universally admired. Men get a bump for height, women are favored if they have hourglass figures, and racial minorities get points for light skin color, European facial characteristics, and conventionally "white" hairstyles.   8

> "Conventional wisdom holds that beauty is in the eye of the beholder, but most beholders tend to agree on what is beautiful."

Yale's Kelly Brownell and Rebecca Puhl and Harvard's Nancy Etcoff have each reviewed hundreds of studies on the impact of appearance. Etcoff finds that unattractive people are less likely than their attractive peers to be viewed as intelligent, likable, and good. Brownell and Puhl have documented that overweight individuals consistently suffer disadvantages at school, at work, and beyond.   9

Among the key findings of a quarter-century's worth of research: Unat- 10
tractive people are less likely to be hired and promoted, and they earn lower
salaries, even in fields in which looks have no obvious relationship to professional duties. (In one study, economists Jeff Biddle and Daniel Hamer-
mesh estimated that for lawyers, such prejudice can translate to a pay cut of
as much as 12 percent.) When researchers ask people to evaluate written essays, the same material receives lower ratings for ideas, style, and creativity
when an accompanying photograph shows a less attractive author. Good-
looking professors get better course evaluations from students; teachers in
turn rate good-looking students as more intelligent.

Not even justice is blind. In studies that simulate legal proceedings, 11
unattractive plaintiffs receive lower damage awards. And in a study released
this month, Stephen Ceci and Justin Gunnell, two researchers at Cornell
University, gave students case studies involving real criminal defendants
and asked them to come to a verdict and a punishment for each. The students gave unattractive defendants prison sentences that were, on average,
twenty-two months longer than those they gave to attractive defendants.

Just like racial or gender discrimination, discrimination based on irrel- 12
evant physical characteristics reinforces invidious stereotypes and undermines equal-opportunity principles based on merit and performance. And
when grooming choices come into play, such bias can also restrict personal
freedom.

Consider Nikki Youngblood, a lesbian who in 2001 was denied a photo 13
in her Tampa high school yearbook because she would not pose in a scoop-
necked dress. Youngblood was "not a rebellious kid," her lawyer explained.
"She simply wanted to appear in her yearbook as herself, not as a fluffed-
up stereotype of what school administrators thought she should look like."
Furthermore, many grooming codes sexualize the workplace and jeopardize employees' health. The weight restrictions at the Borgata, for example,
reportedly contributed to eating disorders among its waitresses.

Appearance-related bias also exacerbates disadvantages based on gen- 14
der, race, ethnicity, age, sexual orientation, and class. Prevailing beauty
standards penalize people who lack the time and money to invest in their
appearance. And weight discrimination, in particular, imposes special costs
on people who live in communities with shortages of healthy food options
and exercise facilities.

So why not simply ban discrimination based on appearance? 15

Employers often argue that attractiveness is job-related; their workers' 16
appearance, they say, can affect the company's image and its profitability.
In this way, the Borgata blamed its weight limits on market demands. Customers, according to a spokesperson, like being served by an attractive
waitress. The same assumption presumably motivated the L'Oreal executive who was sued for sex discrimination in 2003 after allegedly ordering a
store manager to fire a salesperson who was not "hot" enough.

Such practices can violate the law if they disproportionately exclude 17
groups protected by civil rights statutes — hence the sex discrimination
suit. Abercrombie & Fitch's notorious efforts to project what it called a

"classic American" look led to a race discrimination settlement on behalf of minority job-seekers who said they were turned down for positions on the sales floor. But unless the victims of appearance bias belong to groups already protected by civil rights laws, they have no legal remedy.

As the history of civil rights legislation suggests, customer preferences should not be a defense for prejudice. During the early civil rights era, employers in the South often argued that hiring African Americans would be financially ruinous; white customers, they said, would take their business elsewhere. In rejecting this logic, Congress and the courts recognized that customer preferences often reflect and reinforce precisely the attitudes that society is seeking to eliminate. Over the decades, we've seen that the most effective way of combating prejudice is to deprive people of the option to indulge it.

Similarly, during the 1960s and 1970s, major airlines argued that the male business travelers who dominated their customer ranks preferred attractive female flight attendants. According to the airlines, that made sex a bona fide occupational qualification and exempted them from anti-discrimination requirements. But the courts reasoned that only if sexual allure were the "essence" of a job should employers be allowed to select workers on that basis. Since airplanes were not flying bordellos, it was time to start hiring men.

Opponents of a ban on appearance-based discrimination also warn that it would trivialize other, more serious forms of bias. After all, if the goal is a level playing field, why draw the line at looks? "By the time you've finished preventing discrimination against the ugly, the short, the skinny, the bald, the knobbly-kneed, the flat-chested, and the stupid," Andrew Sullivan wrote in the London *Sunday Times* in 1999, "you're living in a totalitarian state." Yet intelligence and civility are generally related to job performance in a way that appearance isn't.

We also have enough experience with prohibitions on appearance discrimination to challenge opponents' arguments. Already, one state (Michigan) and six local jurisdictions (the District of Columbia; Howard County, Md.; San Francisco; Santa Cruz, Calif.; Madison, Wis.; and Urbana, Ill.) have banned such discrimination. Some of these laws date back to the 1970s and 1980s, while some are more recent; some cover height and weight only, while others cover looks broadly; but all make exceptions for reasonable business needs.

Such bans have not produced a barrage of loony litigation or an erosion of support for civil rights remedies generally. These cities and counties each receive between zero and nine complaints a year, while the entire state of Michigan totals about 30, with fewer than one a year ending up in court.

Although the laws are unevenly enforced, they have had a positive effect by publicizing and remedying the worst abuses. Because Portnick, the aerobics instructor turned away by Jazzercise, lived in San Francisco, she was able to bring a claim against the company. After a wave of sympathetic media coverage, Jazzercise changed its policy.

This is not to overstate the power of legal remedies. Given the stigma 24 attached to unattractiveness, few will want to claim that status in public litigation. And in the vast majority of cases, the cost of filing suit and the difficulty of proving discrimination are likely to be prohibitive. But stricter anti-discrimination laws could play a modest role in advancing healthier and more inclusive ideals of attractiveness. At the very least, such laws could reflect our principles of equal opportunity and raise our collective consciousness when we fall short.

. . .

Comprehension

1. Why, according to Rhode, are looks "the last bastion of acceptable bigotry" (2)?
2. Why does the government allow organizations to engage in appearance discrimination?
3. What forms of discrimination do unattractive people face?
4. Why do some people object to banning discrimination based on appearance? How does Rhode address these objections?
5. According to Rhode, how effective are laws that prohibit appearance discrimination? What positive effects might they have?

Purpose and Audience

1. Does Rhode assume that her readers are aware of the problem she discusses? How can you tell?
2. What preconceived attitudes about appearance does Rhode assume her readers have?
3. Where does Rhode state her thesis? Why does she state it where she does instead of earlier in her essay?
4. Is Rhode's purpose simply to inform her readers or to persuade them? Explain.

Style and Structure

1. The first half of Rhode's essay contains a series of short examples. What do these examples illustrate? Do you think Rhode should have made her point with fewer examples developed in more depth?
2. Paragraph 15 is a **rhetorical question**. What is the purpose of this rhetorical question? How effective is it?
3. The second half of Rhode's essay addresses objections to laws banning appearance discrimination. How effectively does Rhode respond to these objections?

4. At several points in her essay, Rhode cites statistics. Is this kind of evidence convincing? Is it more convincing than additional examples would be?

5. **Vocabulary Project.** What words or phrases convey Rhode's feelings toward her subject? Do you think these emotional words and phrases undercut her essay in any way? What other language could she have used instead of these words and phrases?

Journal Entry

Do you believe, as Rhode does, that "stricter anti-discrimination laws could play a modest role in advancing healthier and more inclusive ideals of attractiveness" (24)?

Writing Workshop

1. Do you think Rhode makes a convincing case? Write an email to her in which you agree or disagree with her position.

2. Write an essay that shows how Rhode's ideas apply (or do not apply) to a school, a business, or an organization that you know well.

3. **Working with Sources.** According to an article on the HRM Guide website, unattractive people are not the only ones who face discrimination. "Regardless of who the real person may be," says the article, "stereotypes associated with piercings and tattoos can and do affect others. In general, individuals with tattoos and body piercings are often viewed as 'rougher' or 'less educated.'" Write an essay in which you use examples from your own experience to support or challenge this statement. Be sure that your essay includes at least one reference to Rhode's essay. Document all references to Rhode, and include a works-cited page. (See Chapter 18 for information on MLA documentation.)

Combining the Patterns

In paragraphs 1 and 2, Rhode uses **comparison and contrast**. In these paragraphs, she compares nineteenth-century laws that penalized "'unsightly' individuals" to the actions of government today. How does this comparison help Rhode prepare her readers for her thesis?

Thematic Connections

- "Indian Education" (page 142)
- "Four Tattoos" (page 222)
- "The Myth of the Latin Woman: I Just Met a Girl Named Maria" (page 230)
- "My First Conk" (page 283)
- "Your Flip-Flops Are Grossing Me Out" (page 687)
- "Inked Well" (page 692)

MAIA SZALAVITZ

Ten Ways We Get the Odds Wrong

Maia Szalavitz, a journalist who writes about science, health, addiction, and public policy, has published articles in the *New York Times,* the *Washington Post, New Scientist, Time* magazine, and many other publications. She is the author of *Help at Any Cost: How the Troubled-Teen Industry Cons Parents and Hurts Kids* (2006) as well as the co-author of *The Boy Who Was Raised as a Dog* (2006) and *Born for Love: Why Empathy Is Essential — and Endangered* (2010), with Bruce D. Perry.

Background on odds and risks Odds making is most often associated with sports and casino gambling, although people can place bets on nearly everything from presidential races to celebrity deaths and the weather. For sporting events (such as NFL games), professional oddsmakers are generally less interested in predicting the winner than in setting an appropriate line for "spreadbetting," creating a situation that will attract an equal number of bettors on both sides. The result is that the oddsmakers reduce their risks and make money regardless of the outcome. Odds making and risk assessment are not just confined to sports betting, however. The first stirrings of the modern insurance industry in the seventeenth and eighteenth centuries coincided with advancements in mathematics and probability theory. As a result of advances in both statistics and technology, the actuarial sciences — the use of mathematics and statistics to assess risk — now flourish not only in the insurance sector, but also in finance, global economics, medicine, and public policy. The management of risk has become so central to our social and economic lives that the German sociologist Ulrich Beck famously coined the term "risk society" to define the modern world.

Is your gym locker room crawling with drug-resistant bacteria? Is the guy with the bulging backpack a suicide bomber? And what about that innocent-looking arugula: Will pesticide residue cause cancer, or do the leaves themselves harbor *E. coli*? But wait! Not eating enough vegetables is also potentially deadly.

These days, it seems like everything is risky, and worry itself is bad for your health. The more we learn, the less we seem to know — and if anything makes us anxious, it's uncertainty. At the same time, we're living longer, healthier lives. So why does it feel like even the lettuce is out to get us?

The human brain is exquisitely adapted to respond to risk — uncertainty about the outcome of actions. Faced with a precipice or a predator, the brain is biased to make certain decisions. Our biases reflect the choices that kept our ancestors alive. But we have yet to evolve similarly effective responses to statistics, media coverage, and fear-mongering politicians. For most of human existence twenty-four-hour news channels didn't exist, so we don't have cognitive shortcuts to deal with novel uncertainties.

Still, uncertainty unbalances us, pitching us into anxiety and produc-   4
ing an array of cognitive distortions. Even minor dilemmas like deciding whether to get a cell phone (brain cancer vs. dying on the road because you can't call for help?) can be intolerable for some people. And though emotions are themselves critical to making rational decisions, they were de-signed for a world in which dangers took the form of predators, not pollutants. Our emotions push us to make snap judgments that once were sensible — but may not be anymore.

> " Our emotions push us to make snap judgments that once were sensible — but may not be anymore. "

I. We Fear Snakes, Not Cars

Risk and emotion are inseparable.

Fear feels like anything but a cool and detached computation of the   5
odds. But that's precisely what it is, a lightning-fast risk assessment per-formed by your reptilian brain, which is ever on the lookout for danger. The amygdala flags perceptions, sends out an alarm message, and — before you have a chance to think — your system gets flooded with adrenaline. "This is the way our ancestors evaluated risk before we had statistics," says Paul Slovic, president of Decision Research. Emotions are decision-making shortcuts.

As a result of these evolved emotional algorithms, ancient threats like   6
spiders and snakes cause fear out of proportion to the real danger they pose, while experiences that should frighten us — like fast driving — don't. Dangers like speedy motorized vehicles are newcomers on the landscape of life. The instinctive response to being approached rapidly is to freeze. In the ancestral environment, this reduced a predator's ability to see you — but that doesn't help when what's speeding toward you is a car.

II. We Fear Spectacular, Unlikely Events

Fear skews risk analysis in predictable ways.

Fear hits primitive brain areas to produce reflexive reactions before the   7
situation is even consciously perceived. Because fear strengthens memory, catastrophes such as earthquakes, plane crashes, and terrorist incidents completely capture our attention. As a result, we overestimate the odds of dreadful but infrequent events and underestimate how risky ordinary events are. The drama and excitement of improbable events make them appear to be more common. The effect is amplified by the fact that media tend to cover what's dramatic and exciting, Slovic notes. The more we see something, the more common we think it is, even if we are watching the same footage over and over.

After 9/11, 1.4 million people changed their holiday travel plans to   8
avoid flying. The vast majority chose to drive instead. But driving is far
more dangerous than flying, and the decision to switch caused roughly
1,000 additional auto fatalities, according to two separate analyses comparing traffic patterns in late 2001 to those the year before. In other words,
1,000 people who chose to drive wouldn't have died had they flown instead.

III. We Fear Cancer but Not Heart Disease
We underestimate threats that creep up on us.

Humans are ill-prepared to deal with risks that don't produce immedi-   9
ate negative consequences, like eating a cupcake or smoking cigarettes. As a
result, we are less frightened of heart disease than we should be. Heart disease is the end result of actions that one at a time (one cigarette or one
french fry) aren't especially dangerous. But repeated over the years, those
actions have deadly consequences. "Things that build up slowly are very
hard for us to see," says Kimberly Thompson, a professor of risk analysis at
the Harvard School of Public Health. Obesity and global warming are in
that category. "We focus on the short-term even if we know the long-term
risk."

Our difficulty in understanding how small risks add up accounts for   10
many unplanned pregnancies. At most points during the menstrual cycle,
the odds of pregnancy are low, but after a year of unprotected sex, 85 percent of couples experience it.

IV. No Pesticide in My Backyard — Unless I Put It There
We prefer that which (we think) we can control.

If we feel we can control an outcome, or if we choose to take a risk   11
voluntarily, it seems less dangerous, says David Ropeik, a risk consultant.
"Many people report that when they move from the driver's seat to the passenger's seat, the car in front of them looks closer and their foot goes to the
imaginary brake. You're likely to be less scared with the steering wheel in
your hand, because you can do something about your circumstances, and
that's reassuring." Could explain why your mother always criticizes your
driving.

The false calm a sense of control confers, and the tendency to worry   12
about dangers we can't control, explains why when we see other drivers
talking on cell phones we get nervous but we feel perfectly fine chatting
away ourselves. Similarly, because homeowners themselves benefit if they
kill off bugs that are destroying their lawns, people fear insecticide less if
they are using it in their own backyard than if a neighbor uses the same
chemical in the same concentration, equally close to them. The benefits to
us reduce the level of fear. "Equity is very important," says Slovic, and
research shows that if people who bear the risk also get the benefit, they
tend to be less concerned about it.

V. We Speed Up When We Put Our Seat Belts On

We substitute one risk for another.

Insurers in the United Kingdom used to offer discounts to drivers who 13
purchased cars with safer brakes. "They don't anymore," says John Adams,
a risk analyst and emeritus professor of geography at University College.
"There weren't fewer accidents, just different accidents."

Why? For the same reason that the vehicles most likely to go out of 14
control in snowy conditions are those with four-wheel drive. Buoyed by a
false sense of safety that comes with the increased control, drivers of four-
wheel-drive vehicles take more risks. "These vehicles are bigger and heavier,
which should keep them on the road," says Ropeik. "But police report that
these drivers go faster, even when roads are slippery."

Both are cases of risk compensation: People have a preferred level of 15
risk, and they modulate their behavior to keep risk at that constant level.
Features designed to increase safety — four-wheel drive, seat belts, or air
bags — wind up making people drive faster. The safety features may reduce
risks associated with weather, but they don't cut overall risk. "If I drink a
diet soda with dinner," quips Slovic, "I have ice cream for dessert."

VI. Teens May Think Too Much about Risk — and Not Feel Enough

Why using your cortex isn't always smart.

Parents worry endlessly that their teens will drive, get pregnant, or 16
overdose on drugs; they think youth feel immortal and don't consider negative consequences. Curiously, however, teens are actually less likely than
adults to fall into the trap of thinking, "It won't happen to me." In fact,
teens massively overestimate the odds of things like contracting HIV or
syphilis if they have sex. One study found that teens thought a sexually
active girl had a 60 percent chance of getting AIDS. So why do they do it
anyway?

Teens may not be irrational about risk but too rational, argues Valerie 17
Reyna, a psychologist at Cornell University. Adults asked to consider absurd propositions like "Is it a good idea to drink Drano?" immediately and
intuitively say no. Adolescents, however, take more than twice as long to
think about it. Brain-scan research shows that when teens contemplate
things like playing Russian roulette or drinking and driving, they primarily
use rational regions of the brain — certain regions of cortex — while adults
use emotional regions like the insula.

When risky decisions are weighed in a rational calculus, benefits like 18
fitting in and feeling good now can outweigh real risks. As a result, teaching reasoned decision-making to teens backfires, argues Reyna. Instead,
she says, we should teach kids to rule out risks based on emotional responses — for example, by considering the worst-case scenario, as adults do.
But research suggests there may be no way to speed up the development of
mature decision-making. Repetition and practice are critical to emotional
judgment — which means that it takes time to learn this skill.

VII. Why Young Men Will Never Get Good Rates on Car Insurance

The "risk thermostat" varies widely.

People tend to maintain a steady level of risk, sensing what range of 19 odds is comfortable for them and staying within it. "We all have some propensity to take risk," says Adams. "That's the setting on the 'risk thermostat.'" Some people have a very high tolerance for risk, while others are more cautious.

Forget the idea of a risk-taking personality. If there's a daredevil gene 20 that globally affects risk-taking, researchers haven't found it. Genes do influence impulsivity, which certainly affects the risks people take. And testosterone inclines males to take more risks than females. But age and situation matter as much as gender. Men fifteen to twenty-five are very risk-prone compared to same-age women and older people.

More importantly, one person's risk thermostat may have different set- 21 tings for different types of risk. "Somebody who has their whole portfolio in junk bonds is not necessarily also a mountain climber," explains Baruch Fischhoff, a professor of psychology at Carnegie Mellon University.

VIII. We Worry about Teen Marijuana Use, but Not about Teen Sports

Risk arguments cannot be divorced from values.

If the risks of smoking marijuana are coldly compared to those of 22 playing high-school football, parents should be less concerned about pot smoking. Death by marijuana overdose has never been reported, while thirteen teen players died of football-related injuries in 2006 alone. And marijuana impairs driving far less than the number one drug used by teens: alcohol. Alcohol and tobacco are also more likely to beget addiction, give rise to cancer, and lead to harder drug use.

If the comparison feels absurd, it's because judgments of risk are insep- 23 arable from value judgments. We value physical fitness and the lessons teens learn from sports, but disapprove of unearned pleasure from recreational drugs. So we're willing to accept the higher level of risk of socially preferred activities — and we mentally magnify risks associated with activities society rejects, which leads us to do things like arresting marijuana smokers.

"Risk decisions are not about risks alone," says Slovic. "People usu- 24 ally take risks to get a benefit." The value placed on that benefit is inherently subjective, so decisions about them cannot be made purely "on the science."

IX. We Love Sunlight but Fear Nuclear Power

Why "natural" risks are easier to accept.

The word radiation stirs thoughts of nuclear power, X-rays, and dan- 25 ger, so we shudder at the thought of erecting nuclear power plants in our neighborhoods. But every day we're bathed in radiation that has killed many more people than nuclear reactors: sunlight. It's hard for us to grasp the danger because sunlight feels so familiar and natural.

Our built-in bias for the natural led a California town to choose a toxic 26 poison made from chrysanthemums over a milder artificial chemical to fight mosquitoes: People felt more comfortable with a plant-based product. We see what's "natural" as safe — and regard the new and "unnatural" as frightening.

Any sort of novelty — including new and unpronounceable chemicals — 27 evokes a low-level stress response, says Bruce Perry, a child psychiatrist at Child Trauma Academy. When a case report suggested that lavender and tea-tree oil products caused abnormal breast development in boys, the media shrugged and activists were silent. If these had been artificial chemicals, there likely would have been calls for a ban, but because they are natural plant products, no outrage resulted. "Nature has a good reputation," says Slovic. "We think of natural as benign and safe. But malaria's natural and so are deadly mushrooms."

X. We Should Fear Fear Itself
Why worrying about risk is itself risky.

Though the odds of dying in a terror attack like 9/11 or contracting 28 Ebola are infinitesimal, the effects of chronic stress caused by constant fear are significant. Studies have found that the more people were exposed to media portrayals of the 2001 attacks, the more anxious and depressed they were. Chronically elevated stress harms our physiology, says Ropeik. "It interferes with the formation of bone, lowers immune response, increases the likelihood of clinical depression and diabetes, impairs our memory and our fertility, and contributes to long-term cardiovascular damage and high blood pressure."

The physiological consequences of overestimating the dangers in the 29 world — and revving our anxiety into overdrive — are another reason risk perception matters. It's impossible to live a risk-free life: Everything we do increases some risks while lowering others. But if we understand our innate biases in the way we manage risks, we can adjust for them and genuinely stay safer — without freaking out over every leaf of lettuce.

• • •

Comprehension

1. What does Szalavitz mean in paragraph 3 when she says, "The human brain is exquisitely adapted to respond to risk . . ."?

2. Why, according to Szalavitz, have human beings been unable to develop effective responses to risks posed by "statistics, media coverage, and fear-mongering politicians" (3)?

3. How does Szalavitz explain the following in her essay?
   - We fear snakes but not cars
   - We fear spectacular, unlikely events
   - We fear cancer but not heart disease
   - We fear pesticides in our neighbor's yard but not in our own yard
   - We speed up when we put on seat belts
   - We fear nuclear power but not sunlight

4. What is a "risk thermostat"? What does Szalavitz mean when she says that "one person's risk thermostat may have different settings for different types of risk" (21)?

5. According to Szalavitz, what are the consequences of overestimating the dangers of the world? How does understanding our "innate biases" (29) help us to manage the way we respond to risk?

Purpose and Audience

1. Szalavitz states her thesis at the end of paragraph 4. What information does she present in her first four paragraphs? Would readers be able to understand her thesis without this information? Explain.

2. What preconceived ideas does Szalavitz assume her readers have about risk? How can you tell?

3. What is Szalavitz's purpose in writing this essay? To inform readers? To persuade them? Or does she have some other purpose in mind?

4. Szalavitz's essay appeared in *Psychology Today,* a publication aimed at readers who are interested in psychology. How would Szalavitz have to revise this essay to make it appeal to readers with more general interests?

Style and Structure

1. Szalavitz uses headings and subheadings to introduce the sections of her essay. Why? Would her essay be as effective without these headings and subheadings?

2. Szalavitz presents ten examples to support her thesis. Does she present enough examples? Does she include a fair range of examples? Are all her examples necessary? Are they equally appropriate and convincing?

3. Szalavitz draws some of her examples from research sources. Would the essay have been more or less convincing if all Szalavitz's examples were drawn from her own experience? Explain.

4. Does Szalavitz arrange her examples in any particular order — for example, from least important to most important? Explain.

5. **Vocabulary Project.** At several points in her essay, Szalavitz defines some basic terms — for example, *risk* (3), *fear* (5), and *emotions* (5). Why does she think that she has to define these terms for readers?

Journal Entry

Do you agree with Szalavitz when she says that our emotions cause us to make snap decisions? Could she be accused of overstating her case?

Writing Workshop

1. Choose one of the ten types of risks that Szalavitz discusses. Then, write an essay in which you use several examples from your own experience to illustrate Szalavitz's point about this risk.

2. Do you consider yourself to be risk averse or risk inclined? Write an essay in which you use at least four examples to support your thesis.

3. **Working with Sources.** The following quiz appeared along with Szalavitz's essay. Take the quiz, and then, on the basis of your score, write an essay in which you agree or disagree with Szalavitz's thesis. In your essay, use examples from the quiz as well as from Szalavitz's essay. Be sure to include parenthetical documentation and a works-cited page. (See Chapter 18 for information on MLA documentation.)

How good is your grasp of risk?

1. What's more common in the United States, (a) suicide or (b) homicide?
2. What's the more frequent cause of death in the United States, (a) pool drowning or (b) falling out of bed?
3. What are the top five causes of accidental death in America, following motor-vehicle accidents, and which is the biggest one?
4. Of the top two causes of nonaccidental death in America, (a) cancer and (b) heart disease, which kills more women?
5. What are the next three causes of nonaccidental death in the United States?
6. Which has killed more Americans, (a) bird flu or (b) mad cow disease?
7. How many Americans die from AIDS every year, (a) 12,995, (b) 129,950, or (c) 1,299,500?
8. How many Americans die from diabetes every year, (a) 72,820, (b) 728,200, or (c) 7,282,000?
9. Which kills more Americans, (a) appendicitis or (b) salmonella?
10. Which kills more Americans, (a) pregnancy and childbirth or (b) malnutrition?

ANSWERS (all refer to number of Americans per year, on average):

1. a
2. a
3. In order: drug overdose, fire, choking, falling down stairs, bicycle accidents
4. b
5. In order: stroke, respiratory disease, diabetes

6. No American has died from either one
7. a
8. a
9. a
10. b

Sources:

- Centers for Disease Control and Prevention (Division of Vital Statistics)
- National Transportation Safety Board

Combining the Patterns

Although this essay is primarily an exemplification, it contains several **cause-and-effect** paragraphs — for example, paragraphs 6 and 10. Read these two paragraphs, and determine what they contribute to the essay.

Thematic Connections

- "Ground Zero" (page 175)
- "The Ways We Lie" (page 471)
- "Why Parents Should Let Their Kids Play Dangerous Sports" (page 616)

JAMAICA KINCAID

"Girl" (Fiction)

Jamaica Kincaid's novels, short stories, and nonfiction frequently reflect on race, colonialism, adolescence, gender, and the weight of family relationships and personal history. Born Elaine Potter Richardson in St. John's, Antigua, in 1949, she changed her name to Jamaica Kincaid in 1973 partly to avoid a negative response from her family, who disapproved of her writing. She moved to New York City at 17 and worked as a nanny. She began college but dropped out to write for *Ingenue,* a teen magazine, as well as the *Village Voice.* In 1985, she became a staff writer for the *New Yorker,* where she worked until 1996. Her first published work of fiction, "Girl," appeared in the magazine in 1978. Kincaid credits *New Yorker* editor William Shawn for "show[ing] me what my voice was. . . . He made me feel that what I thought, my inner life, my thoughts as I organized them, were important." The author of *Annie John* (1985), *My Brother* (1997), *Among the Flowers: A Walk in the Himalayas* (2005), and several other books, Kincaid is a professor at Claremont McKenna College.

Background on slavery and colonialism in the West Indies Europeans brought Africans to the Caribbean islands in the sixteenth and seventeenth centuries to work as slaves, primarily on sugar plantations. In her nonfiction book *A Small Place,* Kincaid writes searingly of her native island's dark colonial history, the "large ships filled up with human cargo." The human beings, she says, were "forced to work under conditions that were cruel and inhuman, they were beaten, they were murdered, they were sold, their children were taken from them and these separations lasted forever. . . ." Although the British outlawed slavery in the 1830s, blacks remained the largest percentage of the population in the British Caribbean colonies. Antigua remained a British colony until 1981.

Wash the white clothes on Monday and put them on the stone heap; 1 wash the color clothes on Tuesday and put them on the clothesline to dry; don't walk barehead in the hot sun; cook pumpkin fritters in very hot sweet oil; soak your little cloths right after you take them off; when buying cotton to make yourself a nice blouse, be sure that it doesn't have gum on it, because that way it won't hold up well after a wash; soak salt fish overnight before you cook it; is it true that you sing benna* in Sunday school?; always eat your food in such a way that it won't turn someone else's stomach; on Sundays try to walk like a lady and not like the slut you are so bent on becoming; don't sing benna in Sunday school; you mustn't speak to wharf-rat boys, not even to give directions; don't eat fruits on the street — flies will follow you; *but I don't sing benna on Sundays at all and never in Sunday school;*

* Eds. note — Form of popular music.

this is how to sew on a button; this is how to make a button-hole for the button you have just sewed on; this is how to hem a dress when you see the hem coming down and so to prevent yourself from looking like the slut I know you are so bent on becoming; this is how you iron your father's khaki shirt so that it doesn't have a crease; this is how you iron your father's khaki pants so that they don't have a crease; this is how you grow okra — far from the house, because okra tree harbors red ants; when you are growing da-sheen, make sure it gets plenty of water or else it makes your throat itch when you are eating it; this is how you sweep a corner; this is how you sweep a whole house; this is how you sweep a yard; this is how you smile to some-one you don't like too much; this is how you smile to someone you don't like at all; this is how you smile to someone you like completely; this is how you set a table for tea; this is how you set a table for dinner; this is how you set a table for dinner with an important guest; this is how you set a table for lunch; this is how you set a table for breakfast; this is how to behave in the presence of men who don't know you very well, and this way they won't recognize immediately the slut I have warned you against becoming; be sure to wash every day, even if it is with your own spit; don't squat down to play marbles — you are not a boy, you know; don't pick people's flowers — you might catch some-thing; don't throw stones at blackbirds, because it might not be a blackbird at all; this is how to make a bread pudding; this is how to make doukona;* this is how to make pepper pot; this is how to make a good medicine for a cold; this is how to make a good medicine to throw away a child before it even becomes a child; this is how to catch a fish; this is how to throw back a fish you don't like, and that way something bad won't fall on you; this is how to bully a man; this is how a man bullies you; this is how to love a man, and if this doesn't work there are other ways, and if they don't work don't feel too bad about giving up; this is how to spit up in the air if you feel like it, and this is how to move quick so that it doesn't fall on you; this is how to make ends meet; always squeeze bread to make sure it's fresh; *but what if the baker won't let me feel the bread?*; you mean to say that after all you are really going to be the kind of woman who the baker won't let near the bread?

> " [T]his is how you set a table for lunch; this is how you set a table for breakfast. . . . "

• • •

Reading Literature

1. Who is the speaker in the story? To whom is she speaking?

2. What do the speaker's remarks suggest about being female? Do the speaker's ideas correspond to your own ideas about being female? Explain.

---

* Eds. note — A spiced pudding.

3. Do you think this story has political or social implications? For example, what does the speaker's list suggest about the status of working-class women in the West Indies?

Journal Entry

Write a journal entry in which you record the duties of a woman (or a man) in your family.

Thematic Connections

- "'What's in a Name?'" (page 2)
- "My Mother Never Worked" (page 123)
- "I Want a Wife" (page 502)

Writing Assignments for Exemplification

1. Write a humorous essay about a ritual, ceremony, or celebration you experienced and the types of people who participated in it. Make a point about the event, and use the participants as examples to support your point.

2. Write an essay establishing that you are an optimistic (or pessimistic) person. Use examples to support your case.

3. If you could change three or four things at your school, what would they be? Use examples from your own experience to support your recommendations, and tie your recommendations together in your thesis statement.

4. **Working with Sources.** Write an essay discussing two or three of the greatest challenges facing the United States today. Refer to essays in this chapter, such as "Just Walk On By" (page 238), or to essays elsewhere in this book, such as "The Hidden Life of Garbage" (page 186), "Homeless" (page 510), or "On Dumpster Diving" (page 672). Make sure that you document any references to your sources and that you include a works-cited page. (See Chapter 18 for information on MLA documentation.)

5. Using your family and friends as examples, write an essay suggesting some of the positive or negative characteristics of Americans.

6. Write an essay presenting your formula for achieving success in college. You may, if you wish, talk about things such as scheduling time, maintaining a high energy level, and learning how to relax. Use examples from your own experience to make your point. You may wish to refer to "College Pressures" (page 448).

7. Write an exemplification essay discussing how cooperation has helped you achieve some important goal. Support your thesis with a single well-developed example.

8. Choose an event that you believe illustrates a less-than-admirable moment in your life. Then, write an essay explaining your feelings about it.

9. The popularity of the TV shows *American Idol* and *The Voice* has revealed once again Americans' long-standing infatuation with music icons. Choose several pop groups or stars, old and new — such as Elvis Presley, the Beatles, Michael Jackson, Alicia Keys, 50 Cent, Beyoncé Knowles, Lady Gaga, and Taylor Swift, to name only a few — and use them to illustrate the characteristics that you think make pop stars so appealing.

Collaborative Activity for Exemplification

The following passage appeared in a handbook given to parents of entering students at a midwestern university:

The freshman experience is like no other — at once challenging, exhilarating, and fun. Students face academic challenges as they are exposed to many new ideas. They also face personal challenges as they meet many new people from diverse backgrounds. It is a time to mature and grow. It is an opportunity to explore new subjects and familiar ones. There may be no more challenging and exciting time of personal growth than the first year of university study.

Working in groups of four, brainstorm to identify examples that support or refute the idea that there "may be no more challenging and exciting time of personal growth" than the first year of college. Then, choose one person from each group to tell the class the position the group took and explain the examples you collected. Finally, work together to write an essay that presents your group's position. Have one student write the first draft, two others revise this draft, and the last student edit and proofread the revised draft.

9

Process

What Is Process?

A **process** essay explains how to do something or how something occurs. It presents a sequence of steps and shows how those steps lead to a particular result. In the following paragraph from the college biology textbook *What Is Life? A Guide to Biology*, writer Jay Phelan explains a scientific process.

Process presents series of steps in chronological order

Topic sentence

Researchers have developed a way to make the bacteria of interest identify themselves. First, a chemical is added to the entire population of bacterial cells, separating the double-stranded DNA into single strands. Next, a short sequence of single-stranded DNA is washed over the bacteria. Called a DNA probe, this DNA contains part of the sequence of the gene of interest and has also been modified so that it is radioactive. Bacteria with the gene of interest bind to this probe and glow with radioactivity. These cells can then be separated out and grown in large numbers — for example, vats of *E. coli* that produce human growth hormone.

Process, like narration, presents events in chronological order. Unlike a narrative, however, a process essay explains a particular series of events that produces the same outcome whenever it is duplicated. Because these events form a sequence with a fixed order, clarity is extremely important. Whether your readers will actually perform the process or are simply trying to understand how it occurs, your essay must make clear the exact order of the individual steps, as well as their relationships to one another and to the process as a whole. This means that you need to provide clear, logical transitions between the steps in a process and that you need to present the steps in *strict* chronological order — that is, in the exact order in which they occur or are to be performed.

Depending on its purpose, a process essay can be either a set of *instructions* or a *process explanation*.

Understanding Instructions

The purpose of **instructions** is to enable readers to perform a process. Recipes, information about how to use your library's online databases, and steps for completing online registration for classes are all written as instructions. So are directions for locating an office building in Washington, DC, or for driving from Houston to Pensacola. Instructions use the present tense and, like commands, they use the imperative mood, speaking directly to readers: "*Disconnect* the system, and *check* the electrical source."

Understanding Process Explanations

The purpose of a **process explanation** is not to enable readers to perform a process but rather to help them understand how it is carried out. Such essays may examine anything from how silkworms spin their cocoons to how Michelangelo and Leonardo da Vinci painted their masterpieces on plaster walls and ceilings.

A process explanation may use the first person (*I, we*) or the third (*he, she, it, they*), the past tense or the present. Because its readers need to understand the process, not perform it, a process explanation does not use the second person (*you*) or the imperative mood (commands). The style of a process explanation varies, depending on whether a writer is explaining a process that takes place regularly or one that occurred in the past and also depending on whether the writer or someone else carries out the steps. The following chart suggests the stylistic options available to writers of process explanations.

	First Person	*Third Person*
Present tense	"Before I begin writing my draft, I take some time to plan." *(habitual process performed by the writer)*	"Before he begins writing his draft, he takes some time to plan." *(habitual process performed by someone other than the writer)*
Past tense	"Before I began writing my draft, I took some time to plan." *(process performed in the past by the writer)*	"Before he began writing his draft, he took some time to plan." *(process performed in the past by someone other than the writer)*

Using Process

College writing frequently calls for instructions or process explanations. In a biology paper on genetic testing, you might devote a paragraph to an explanation of the process of amniocentesis; in an editorial about the negative side of fraternity life, you might include a brief account of the process of pledging. You can also organize an entire paper around a process pattern: in a literature essay, you might trace a fictional character's progress toward some new insight; on a finance midterm, you might explain the procedure for approving a commercial loan.

Planning a Process Essay

As you plan a process essay, remember that your primary goal is to explain the process accurately. This means you need to distinguish between what usually or always happens and what occasionally or rarely happens, between necessary steps and optional ones. You should also mentally test all the steps in sequence to be sure the process really works as you say it does, checking carefully for omitted steps or incorrect information. If you are writing about a process you observed, try to test the accuracy of your explanation by observing the process again.

Accommodating Your Audience

As you write, remember to keep your readers' needs in mind. When necessary, explain the reasons for performing the steps, describe unfamiliar materials or equipment, define terms, and warn readers about possible problems that may occur during the process. (Sometimes you may want to include illustrations.) Besides complete information, your readers need a clear and consistent discussion, without ambiguities or digressions. For this reason, you should avoid unnecessary shifts in tense, person, voice, and mood. You should also be careful not to omit articles (*a*, *an*, and *the*); you want your discussion to move smoothly, like an essay — not abruptly, like a cookbook.

Developing a Thesis Statement

Both instructions and process explanations can be written either to persuade or simply to present information. If its purpose is persuasive, a process essay may take a strong stand in a **thesis statement**, such as "Applying for food stamps is a needlessly complex process that discourages many qualified recipients" or "The process of slaughtering baby seals is inhumane and sadistic." Many process essays, however, communicate nothing more debatable than the procedure for blood typing. Even in such a case, though, a process should have a clear thesis statement that identifies the process and perhaps tells why it is performed: "Typing their own blood can familiarize students with some basic laboratory procedures."

Using Transitions

Throughout your essay, be sure to use transitional words and phrases to ensure that each step, each stage, and each paragraph leads logically to the next. Transitions such as *first, second, meanwhile, after this, next, then, at the same time, when you have finished,* and *finally* help to establish sequential and chronological relationships so that readers can follow the process. (A more complete list of transitions appears on page 57.)

Structuring a Process Essay

Like other essays, a process essay generally consists of three sections. The **introduction** identifies the process and indicates why and under what circumstances it is performed. This section may include information about materials or preliminary preparations, or it may present an overview of the process, perhaps even listing its major stages. The paper's thesis is also usually stated in the introduction.

Each paragraph in the **body** of the essay typically treats one major stage of the process. Each stage may group several steps, depending on the nature and complexity of the process. These steps are presented in chronological order, interrupted only for essential definitions, explanations, or cautions. Every step must be included and must appear in its proper place.

A short process essay may not need a formal **conclusion**. If an essay does have a conclusion, however, it will often briefly review the procedure's major stages. Such an ending is especially useful if the paper has outlined a technical procedure that may seem complicated to general readers. The conclusion may also reinforce the thesis by summarizing the results of the process or explaining its significance.

Suppose you are taking a midterm exam in a course in childhood and adolescent behavior. One essay question calls for a process explanation: "Trace the stages that children go through in acquiring language." After thinking about the question, you draft the following thesis statement: "Although individual cases may differ, most children acquire language in a predictable series of stages." You then plan your essay and develop an informal outline, which might look like this.

Sample Outline Process	
Introduction:	Thesis statement — Although individual cases may differ, most children acquire language in a predictable series of stages.
First stage (two to twelve months):	Prelinguistic behavior, including "babbling" and appropriate responses to nonverbal cues.

Second stage (end of first year):	Single words as commands or requests; infant catalogs his or her environment.
Third stage (beginning of second year):	Expressive jargon (flow of sounds that imitates adult speech); real words along with jargon.
Fourth and final stage (middle of second year to beginning of third year):	Two-word phrases; longer strings; missing parts of speech.
Conclusion:	Restatement of thesis (in different words) or review of major stages of process.

This essay, when completed, will show not only what the stages of the process are but also how they relate to one another. In addition, it will support the thesis that children learn language through a well-defined process.

Revising a Process Essay

When you revise a set of instructions or a process explanation, consider the items on the revision checklist on page 68. In addition, pay special attention to the items on the following checklist, which apply specifically to revising process essays.

✔ **REVISION CHECKLIST**   **Process**

☐ Does your assignment call for a set of instructions or a process explanation?
☐ Is your essay's style appropriate for the kind of process essay (instructions or process explanation) you are writing?
☐ Does your essay have a clearly stated thesis that identifies the process and perhaps tells why it is (or was) performed?
☐ Have you included all necessary steps?
☐ Are the steps presented in strict chronological order?
☐ Do transitions clearly indicate where one step ends and the next begins?
☐ Have you included all necessary reminders and cautions?

Editing a Process Essay

When you edit your process essay, follow the guidelines on the editing checklists on pages 85, 88, and 91. In addition, focus on the grammar, mechanics, and punctuation issues that are particularly relevant to process essays. One of these issues — avoiding unnecessary shifts in tense, person, voice, and mood — is discussed on pages 270–71.

Avoiding Unnecessary Shifts

To explain a process to readers, you need to use consistent verb **tense** (past or present), **person** (first, second, or third), **voice** (active or passive), and **mood** (statements or commands). Unnecessary shifts in tense, person, voice, or mood can confuse readers and make it difficult for them to follow your process.

Avoiding Shifts in Tense Use present tense for a process that is performed regularly.

"The body is first laid out in the undertaker's morgue — or rather, Mr. Jones is reposing in the preparation room — to be readied to bid the world farewell" (Mitford 302).

Use past tense for a process that was performed in the past.

"He peeled the potatoes and thin-sliced them into a quart-sized Mason fruit jar" (Malcolm X 283).

Shift from present to past tense only when you need to indicate a change in time: *Usually, I study several days before a test, but this time I studied the night before.*

Avoiding Shifts in Person In process explanations, use first or third person.

FIRST PERSON (*I*):	"I reached for the box of Medium Ash Brown hair color just as my friend Veronica grabbed the box labeled Sparkling Sherry" (Hunt 277).
FIRST PERSON (*WE*):	"We decided to use my bathroom to color our hair" (Hunt 277).
THIRD PERSON (*HE*):	"The embalmer, having allowed an appropriate interval to elapse, returns to the attack, but now he brings into play the skill and equipment of sculptor and cosmetician" (Mitford 304).

In instructions, use second person.

SECOND PERSON (*YOU*):	"If you sometimes forget to pay bills, or if you have large student loans, you may have a problem" (McGlade 272).

When you give instructions, be careful not to shift from third to second person.

INCORRECT:	If a person sometimes forgets to pay bills, or if someone has large student loans, you may have a problem. (shift from third to second person)

CORRECT: If you sometimes forget to pay bills, or if you have large student loans, you may have a problem. (second person used consistently)

Avoiding Shifts in Voice   Use active voice when you want to emphasize the person performing the action.

"In the last four years, I have moved eight times, living in three dorm rooms, two summer sublets, and three apartments in three different cities" (McGlade 272).

Use passive voice to emphasize the action itself, not the person performing it.

"The patching and filling completed, Mr. Jones is now shaved, washed, and dressed" (Mitford 305).

Do not shift between the active and the passive voice, especially within a sentence, unless your intent is to change your emphasis.

INCORRECT: The first draft of my essay was completed, and then I started the second draft. (shift from passive to active voice)

CORRECT: I completed the first draft of my essay, and then I started the second draft. (active voice used consistently)

Avoiding Shifts in Mood   Use the indicative mood (statements) for process explanations.

"He draped the towel around my shoulders, over my rubber apron, and began again vaselining my hair" (Malcolm X 284).

Use the imperative mood (commands) only in instructions.

"Carefully bang on the side of the machine" (Piven and Borgenicht 293).

Be careful not to shift from the imperative mood to the indicative mood.

INCORRECT: First, check your credit report for errors, and you should report any errors you find. (shift from imperative to indicative mood)

CORRECT: First, check your credit report for errors, and report any errors you find. (imperative mood used consistently)

CORRECT: First, you should check your credit report for errors, and you should report any errors you find. (indicative mood used consistently)

> ☑️ **EDITING CHECKLIST**   **Process**
>
> ☐ Have you used commas correctly in a series of three or more steps, including a comma before the *and?*
> ☐ Have you used parallel structure for items in a series?
> ☐ Have you avoided unnecessary shifts in tense?
> ☐ Have you avoided unnecessary shifts in person?
> ☐ Have you avoided unnecessary shifts in voice?
> ☐ Have you avoided unnecessary shifts in mood?

A STUDENT WRITER: Instructions

The following student essay, "The Search," by Eric McGlade, gives readers instructions on how to find an apartment. It was written for a composition class in response to the assignment "Write an essay giving practical instructions for doing something most people you know will need to do at one time or another."

The Search

Introduction

In the last four years, I have moved eight times, living in three dorm rooms, two summer sublets, and three apartments in three different cities. I would not recommend this experience to anyone. Finding an apartment is time consuming, stressful, and expensive, so the best advice is to stay where you are. However, if you must move, here are a few tips to help you survive the search.   1

Thesis statement

First major stage of process: before the search

Before you begin your search, take some time to plan. First, figure out what you can afford. (Here's a hint — you can afford less than you think.) Most experts say you should spend no more than one-third of your net income on rent. Find a budgeting worksheet online, and see for yourself how car insurance, electricity, and cable can add up. Remember, your new landlord may charge a security deposit and the first month's rent, and there may be pet, parking, cleaning, or moving-in fees.   2

First step: review your finances

Second step: check your credit history

Next, consider your credit history. If you sometimes forget to pay bills, or if you have large student loans, you may have a problem. Landlords usually run a credit check on potential renters. If you are particularly concerned about your credit rating, order a credit report from one of the three main credit bureaus: TransUnion, Equifax, or Experian. If you find that your credit isn't perfect, don't panic. First, check your credit report for errors, and report any errors you find to the credit bureau. Second, adopt good financial habits immediately. Start paying bills on time, and   3 try to consolidate any debts at a lower interest rate. If a landlord does question your credit, be prepared to explain any extenuating circumstances in the past and to point out your current good behavior.

Third step: consider where to live

After you know what you can afford, you need to figure   4
out where you want to (and can afford to) live. Keep in mind important factors such as how close the apartment is to your school or workplace and how convenient the neighborhood is. Is public transportation located nearby? Is on-street parking available? Can you easily get to a supermarket, coffee shop, convenience store, and Laundromat? If possible, visit each potential neighborhood both during the day and at night. A business district may be bustling during the day but deserted (and even dangerous) at night. If you visit both early and late, you will get a more accurate impression of how safe the neighborhood feels.

Fourth step: consider a roommate

During this stage, consider whether or not you are willing   5
to live with a roommate. You will sacrifice privacy, but you will be able to afford a better apartment. If you do decide to live with a roommate, the easiest way to proceed is to find a friend who also needs an apartment. If this isn't possible, try to find an apartment that comes with a roommate — one with one roommate moving out but the other roommate remaining in the apartment. The third option is to find another apartment seeker and go apartment hunting together. Some websites, such as www.roommates.com, cater to this type of search, but, unfortunately, most require a fee. However, your school housing office might have a list of students looking for roommates.

Transitional paragraph

Now, you are ready to start looking. You can find the perfect   6
apartment through a real estate agent, by checking your local newspaper or school's housing listings, by asking your friends and family, or by visiting websites such as Craigslist.

Second major stage of process: during the search

Each of these methods has pros and cons. A real estate   7
agent might help you find your dream apartment quickly, but you will usually have to pay for this speedy service. As for newspaper listings, stick to your local paper; unless you are looking for a

First step: do research

second vacation home in Maui, national newspapers are not your best bet. An even better idea is to check your school's housing listings, where you are likely to find fellow students in search of apartments in your price range.

Second step: spread the word

Meanwhile, spread the word. Tell everyone you know that   8
you are apartment hunting. After all, your stepsister's uncle's
mother-in-law may live in a building with a newly vacant
apartment. This method isn't the most efficient, but the results
can be amazing. As a bonus, you will receive practical advice
about your neighborhood, such as what to watch out for and what
problems other renters have had.

Third step: try Craigslist

Finally, if you are hunting in a major city, I have but one   9
word: Craigslist. Craigslist.org has free apartment listings arranged
by city and neighborhood. You can hunt for an apartment by
price, by number of bedrooms, or by length of lease. If you are
on a tight moving schedule and need a place immediately, this
website is especially helpful because of the sheer volume of its
listings. Craigslist also has the added benefit of providing a general
price range for your ideal neighborhood.

Fourth step: visit apartments

Once you have identified some possibilities, it's time to visit   10
the apartments. Get a good look at each one, and ask yourself some
questions. Is it furnished or unfurnished? Are all the appliances in
good working order? Will your bed fit in the bedroom? How much
closet space will you have? Are there phone, cable, and Internet
hookups? Is it a sunny apartment (south facing), or is it dark (north
facing)? In the bathroom, turn on the faucets in the sink and shower;
check for rust and poor water pressure. As you walk through the
apartment, check the cell-phone reception (leaning out the window
of your bathroom to talk on the phone is not fun). Most important,
do not forget to take notes. After seeing fourteen apartments, you
may confuse Apartment A, with the six pets and funny smell, with
Apartment G, with the balcony and renovated kitchen.

Third major stage of process: after the search

First step: check your lease

And now, at last, the search is over: you have found your   11
apartment. Congratulations! Unfortunately, your work is not yet
over. Now, it is time to read your lease. It will be long and boring,
but it is a very important document. Among other things, your
lease should specify the length of the lease, a rent due date, fees
for late rent payments, the amount of the security deposit, and
the conditions required for the return of the security deposit.
If you have decided to live with a roommate, you might ask
the landlord to divide the rent on your lease. This way, if your
roommate moves to Brazil, you will not have to pay his or her
share of the rent. Be sure to read your lease thoroughly and bring
up any concerns with your landlord.

Second step: get insurance and activate utilities

Before you move in, you have a few more things to do: get   12
renter's insurance to protect you from theft or damage to your
possessions; arrange to get your utilities hooked up; submit a
change-of-address form at the post office; and inform your bank
or credit-card company about your future move. Finally, start
packing!

Conclusion

If you plan ahead and shop smart, you can find your   13
perfect apartment. Remember to figure out what you can afford,
check out the neighborhoods, consider a roommate, use multiple
search methods, and take careful notes when you visit potential
apartments. Yes, happy endings do occur. I am now in the third
month of a two-year lease, and I have no plans to move anytime
soon.

Points for Special Attention

Introduction. Eric McGlade's essay begins by giving readers some background on his own experience as an apartment hunter. This strategy gives him some credibility, establishing him as an "expert" who can explain the process. Eric then narrows his focus to the difficulties of apartment hunting and ends his introduction with a thesis statement telling readers that the process can be made easier.

Structure. Eric divides his essay into the three major stages of apartment hunting: what to do before, during, and after the search. After his introduction, Eric includes four paragraphs that explain what to do before the search gets under way. In paragraphs 6 through 10, he explains how to go about the actual hunt for an apartment. Then, in paragraphs 11 and 12, he tells readers what they should do after they locate an apartment (but before they move in). In his conclusion, he restates his thesis, summarizes the steps in the process, and returns to his own experience to reassure readers that a positive outcome is possible.

Purpose and Style. Because Eric's assignment asked him to give practical advice for a process readers could expect to perform, he decided that he should write the essay as a set of instructions. Therefore, he uses the second person ("If *you* find that *your* credit isn't perfect, don't panic") and the present tense, with many of his verbs in the form of commands ("First, *figure out what you can afford*").

Transitions. To make his essay clear and easy to follow, Eric includes transitions that indicate the order in which each step is to be performed ("First," "Next," "Now," "Meanwhile," "Finally," and so on), as well as expressions such as "During this stage." He also includes transitional sentences to move his essay from one stage of the process to the next:

- "Before you begin your search, take some time to plan" (2).
- "Now, you are ready to start looking" (6).
- "Once you have identified some possibilities, it's time to visit the apartments" (10).
- "And now, at last, the search is over: you have found your apartment" (11).

Finally, paragraph 6 serves as a transitional paragraph, moving readers from the preliminary steps to the start of the actual search for an apartment.

Focus on Revision

When he met with his peer-editing group, Eric found that they had all gone through the apartment-hunting process and therefore had some practical suggestions to make. In the draft they reviewed, Eric included a good deal of information about his own experiences, but his readers felt those narratives, although amusing, were distracting and got in the way of the process. Eric agreed, and he deleted these anecdotes. His classmates thought that mentioning his experiences briefly in his introduction would be sufficient, but Eric decided to also return briefly to his own story in his conclusion, adding the two "happy ending" sentences that now conclude his essay. In addition, he followed his classmates' suggestion to expand his conclusion by adding a review of the steps of the process to help readers remember what they had read. These additions gave him a fully developed conclusion.

In terms of his essay's content, his fellow students were most concerned with paragraph 10, which they felt seemed to rush through a very important part of the process: visiting the apartments. They also observed that the information in this paragraph was not arranged in any logical order and that Eric had failed to mention other considerations (for example, whether the apartment needed repairs or painting, whether it was noisy, whether it included air conditioning). One student suggested that Eric expand his discussion and divide the information into two separate paragraphs, one on the apartment's mechanical systems (plumbing, electricity, and so on) and another on its physical appearance (size of rooms, light, and so on). In the final draft of his essay, Eric did just that. (A sample peer-editing worksheet for process appears on page 280.)

Working with Sources. Although the students in Eric's peer-editing group did not suggest any specific revisions to his introductory paragraph, he thought his essay needed a more interesting opening. So, in his final draft, he planned to quote key phrases from some of the Craigslist ads he rejected. He thought this might add some humor to an otherwise straightforward essay.

A STUDENT WRITER: Process Explanation

The essay that follows, "Medium Ash Brown," by Melany Hunt, is a **process explanation**. It was written for a composition class in response to the assignment "Write an essay explaining a process that changed your appearance in some way."

Medium Ash Brown

Introduction

The beautiful chestnut-haired woman pictured on the box   1
seemed to beckon to me. I reached for the box of Medium Ash
Brown hair color just as my friend Veronica grabbed the box
labeled Sparkling Sherry. I can't remember our reasons for wanting
to change our hair color, but they seemed to make sense at the
time. Maybe we were just bored. I do remember that the idea of
transforming our appearance came up unexpectedly. Impulsively,
we decided to change our hair color — and, we hoped, ourselves —

Thesis statement

that very evening. The process that followed taught me that some
impulses should definitely be resisted.

Materials assembled

We decided to use my bathroom to color our hair. Inside   2
each box of hair color, we found two little bottles and a small tube
wrapped in a page of instructions. Attached to the instruction
page itself were two very large, one-size-fits-all plastic gloves,
which looked and felt like plastic sandwich bags. The directions
recommended having some old towels around to soak up any spills
or drips that might occur. Under the sink we found some old,
frayed towels that I figured my mom had forgotten about, and we

First stage of process: preparing the color

spread them around the bathtub. After we put our gloves on, we
began the actual coloring process. First we poured the first bottle
into the second, which was half-full of some odd-smelling liquid.
The smell was not much better after we combined the two bottles.
The directions advised us to cut off a small section of hair to use
as a sample. For some reason, we decided to skip this step.

Second stage of process: applying the color

At this point, Veronica and I took turns leaning over the tub   3
to wet our hair for the color. The directions said to leave the color
on the hair for fifteen to twenty minutes, so we found a little
timer and set it for fifteen minutes. Next, we applied the color to
our hair. Again, we took turns, squeezing the bottle in order to
cover all our hair. We then wrapped the old towels around our
sour-smelling hair and went outside to get some fresh air.

Third stage of process: rinsing

After the fifteen minutes were up, we rinsed our hair.   4
According to the directions, we were to add a little water and

scrub as if we were shampooing our hair. The color lathered up, and we rinsed our hair until the water ran clear. So far, so good.

Last stage of process: applying conditioner

The last part of the process involved applying the small   5
tube of conditioner to our hair (because colored hair becomes brittle and easily damaged). We used the conditioner as directed, and then we dried our hair so that we could see the actual color. Even before I looked in the mirror, I heard Veronica's gasp.

Outcome of process

"Nice try," I said, assuming she was just trying to make me   6
nervous, "but you're not funny."

"Mel," she said, "look in the mirror." Slowly, I turned   7
around. My stomach turned into a lead ball when I saw my reflection. My hair was the putrid greenish-brown color of a winter lawn, dying in patches yet still a nice green in the shade.

The next day in school, I wore my hair tied back under a   8
baseball cap. I told only my close friends what I had done. After they were finished laughing, they offered their deepest, most heartfelt condolences. They also offered many suggestions — none very helpful — on what to do to get my old hair color back.

Conclusion

It is now three months later, and I still have no idea what   9
prompted me to color my hair. My only consolation is that I resisted my first impulse: to use a wild color, like blue or fuchsia. Still, as I wait for my hair to grow out, and as I assemble a larger and larger collection of baseball caps, it is small consolation indeed.

Points for Special Attention

Structure. In Melany's opening paragraph, her thesis statement makes it very clear that the experience she describes is not one she would recommend to others. The temptation she describes in her introduction's first few sentences lures readers into her essay, just as the picture on the box lured her. Her second paragraph lists the contents of the box and explains how she and her friend assembled the other necessary materials. Then, she explains the first stage in the process: preparing the color. Paragraphs 3–5 describe the other stages in the process in chronological order, and paragraphs 6–8 record Melany's and her friend Veronica's reactions to their experiment. In paragraph 9, Melany sums up the impact of her experience and once again expresses her annoyance with herself for her impulsive act.

Purpose and Style. Melany's purpose is not to enable others to duplicate the process she explains; on the contrary, she wants to discourage readers from doing what she did. Consequently, she presents her process not as a set of instructions but as a process explanation, using first person and past tense to explain her and her friend's actions. She also largely eliminates cautions and reminders that her readers, who are not likely to undertake the process, will not need to know.

Detail. Melany's essay includes vivid descriptive detail that gives readers a clear sense of the process and its outcome. Throughout, her emphasis is on the negative aspects of the process — the "odd-smelling liquid" and the "putrid greenish-brown color" of her hair, for instance — and this emphasis is consistent with her essay's purpose.

Transitions. To move readers smoothly through the process, Melany includes clear transitions ("First," "At this point," "Next," "then") and clearly identifies the beginning of the process ("After we put our gloves on, we began the actual coloring process") as well as the end ("The last part of the process").

Focus on Revision

The writing center tutor who read Melany's draft thought it was clearly written and structured and that its ironic, self-mocking tone was well suited to her audience and purpose. He felt, however, that some minor revisions would make her essay even more effective. Specifically, he thought that paragraph 2 began too abruptly: paragraph 1 recorded the purchase of the hair color, and paragraph 2 opened with the sentence "We decided to use my bathroom to color our hair," leaving readers wondering how much time had passed between purchase and application. Because the thesis rests on the idea of the foolishness of an impulsive gesture, it is important for readers to understand that the girls presumably went immediately from the store to Melany's house.

After thinking about this criticism, Melany decided to write a clearer opening for paragraph 2: "As soon as we paid for the color, we returned to my house, where, eager to begin our transformation, we locked ourselves in my bathroom. Inside each box . . ." She also decided to divide paragraph 2 into two paragraphs, one describing the materials and another beginning with "After we put our gloves on," which introduces the first step in the process.

Another possible revision Melany considered was developing Veronica's character further. Although both girls purchase and apply hair color, readers never learn what happens to Veronica. Melany knew she could easily add a brief paragraph after paragraph 7, describing Veronica's "Sparkling Sherry" hair in humorous terms. Her writing center tutor thought this would be a good addition, and Melany planned to add this material in her paper's final draft.

Working with Sources. Melany's tutor suggested that she might refer in her essay to Malcolm X's "My First Conk" (page 283). After all, Malcolm X had also tried to change his appearance and had also been sorry afterward. (In fact, the class's assignment — "Write an essay explaining a process that changed your appearance in some way" — was inspired by their reading of "My First Conk.") Melany considered this suggestion but ultimately decided not to follow her tutor's suggestion. For one thing, she realized that Malcolm X's initial response to his transformation (unlike hers) was positive; only later did he realize that his desire to transform his looks to conform to a white ideal was "ridiculous" and ultimately a "step toward self-degradation" (page 285). More important, Melany thought Malcolm X's serious analysis would not be a good fit for her lighthearted essay. So, even though the topic of Malcolm X's essay was similar to hers, Melany decided that referring to his experience would trivialize his ideas and be out of place in her essay.

PEER-EDITING WORKSHEET: Process

1. What process does this essay describe?

2. Does the writer include all the information the audience needs? Is any vital step or piece of information missing? Is any step or piece of information irrelevant? Is any necessary definition, explanation, or caution missing or incomplete?

3. Is the essay a set of instructions or a process explanation? How can you tell? Why do you think the writer chose this strategy rather than the alternative? Do you think this was the right choice?

4. Does the writer consistently follow the stylistic conventions for the strategy — instructions or process explanation — he or she has chosen?

5. Are the steps presented in a clear, logical order? Are they grouped logically into paragraphs? Should any steps be combined or relocated? If so, which ones?

6. Does the writer use enough transitions to move readers through the process? Should any transitions be added? If so, where?

7. Does the writer need to revise to correct confusing shifts in tense, person, voice, or mood? If so, where?

8. Is the essay interesting? What descriptive details would add interest to the essay? Would a visual be helpful?

9. How would you characterize the writer's opening strategy? Is it appropriate for the essay's purpose and audience? What alternative strategy might be more effective?

10. How would you characterize the writer's closing strategy? Would a different conclusion be more effective? Explain.

The reading selections that follow illustrate how varied the uses of process writing can be. The first selection, a visual text, is followed by questions designed to illustrate how process can operate in visual form. (A multimodal text for process is located online at **macmillanhighered.com /patterns**.)

What Happens to Plastic That Is Recycled by Us? (Infographic)

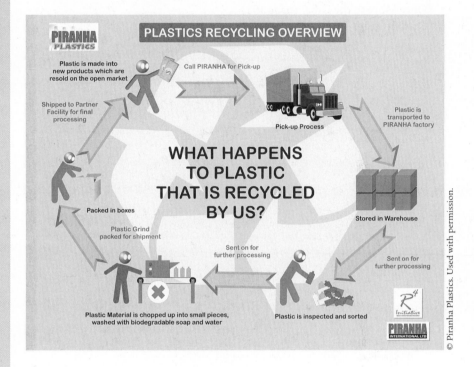

Reading Images

1. How easy (or difficult) is it to understand the information presented in this diagram? Would the information have been more (or less) accessible if it were summarized in paragraph form? Why or why not?

2. Evaluate the icons used in this diagram. Would you suggest including any additional (or different) icons? Do you find the two Piranha company logos distracting?

3. For what purpose do you think this process diagram was created? What makes you think so?

continued

Journal Entry

In one paragraph, answer the question the graphic poses: What happens to plastic that is recycled by Piranha Plastics?

Thematic Connections

- "The Hidden Life of Garbage" (page 186)
- "Once More to the Lake" (page 191)
- "On Dumpster Diving" (page 672)

MALCOLM X

My First Conk

Malcolm X was born Malcolm Little in Omaha, Nebraska, in 1925. As a young man, he had a number of run-ins with the law, and he wound up in prison on burglary charges before he was twenty-one. There he pursued his education and was influenced by the writings of Elijah Muhammad, the founder of the Black Muslims (now known as the Nation of Islam), a black separatist organization. On his release from prison, Malcolm X became a highly visible member of this group and a disciple of its leader. He left the movement in 1963, later converting to orthodox Islam and founding a rival African-American political organization. He was assassinated in 1965.

Background on conks and other African-American hair styles *The Autobiography of Malcolm X* (written with Alex Haley) was published in 1964. The following excerpt from that book describes the painful and painstaking process many African-American men once endured to achieve a style of straight hair called a "conk." (The term probably comes from Congolene, the brand name of one commercial hair straightener.) First popularized in the 1920s by black entertainers such as Cab Calloway, the style continued to be fashionable until the 1960s, when more natural styles, including the Afro, became a symbol of black pride and conked hair came to be seen as a self-loathing attempt to imitate whites. Ironically, perhaps, some African Americans still distinguish between "good" (that is, naturally straight) and "bad" (that is, naturally curly) hair. Today, cosmetically straightened hair (a process that is no longer so arduous) is considered one fashion option among many, including shaved heads, closely cropped hair, braids, cornrows, and dreadlocks.

Shorty soon decided that my hair was finally long enough to be conked. 1 He had promised to school me in how to beat the barbershops' three- and four-dollar price by making up congolene, and then conking ourselves.

I took the little list of ingredients he had printed out for me, and went 2 to a grocery store, where I got a can of Red Devil lye, two eggs, and two medium-sized white potatoes. Then at a drugstore near the poolroom, I asked for a large jar of vaseline, a large bar of soap, a large-toothed comb and a fine-toothed comb, one of those rubber hoses with a metal spray-head, a rubber apron, and a pair of gloves.

"Going to lay on that first conk?" the drugstore man asked me. I 3 proudly told him, grinning, "Right!"

Shorty paid six dollars a week for a room in his cousin's shabby apart- 4 ment. His cousin wasn't at home. "It's like the pad's mine, he spends so much time with his woman," Shorty said. "Now, you watch me —"

He peeled the potatoes and thin-sliced them into a quart-sized Mason 5 fruit jar, then started stirring them with a wooden spoon as he gradually poured in a little over half the can of lye. "Never use a metal spoon; the lye will turn it black," he told me.

A jelly-like, starchy-looking glop resulted from the lye and potatoes, and Shorty broke in the two eggs, stirring real fast — his own conk and dark face bent down close. The congolene turned pale-yellowish. "Feel the jar," Shorty said. I cupped my hand against the outside, and snatched it away. "Damn right, it's hot, that's the lye," he said. "So you know it's going to burn when I comb it in — it burns bad. But the longer you can stand it, the straighter the hair."

> " So you know it's going to burn when I comb it in — it burns bad. But the longer you can stand it, the straighter the hair. "

6

He made me sit down, and he tied the string of the new rubber apron   7
tightly around my neck, and combed up my bush of hair. Then, from the big vaseline jar, he took a handful and massaged it hard all through my hair and into the scalp. He also thickly vaselined my neck, ears, and forehead. "When I get to washing out your head, be sure to tell me anywhere you feel any little stinging," Shorty warned me, washing his hands, then pulling on the rubber gloves, and tying on his own rubber apron. "You always got to remember that any congolene left in burns a sore into your head."

The congolene just felt warm when Shorty started combing it in. But   8
then my head caught fire.

I gritted my teeth and tried to pull the sides of the kitchen table to-   9
gether. The comb felt as if it was raking my skin off.

My eyes watered, my nose was running. I couldn't stand it any lon-   10
ger; I bolted to the washbasin. I was cursing Shorty with every name I could think of when he got the spray going and started soap lathering my head.

He lathered and spray-rinsed, lathered and spray-rinsed, maybe ten or   11
twelve times, each time gradually closing the hot-water faucet, until the rinse was cold, and that helped some.

"You feel any stinging spots?"   12

"No," I managed to say. My knees were trembling.   13

"Sit back down, then. I think we got it all out okay."   14

The flame came back as Shorty, with a thick towel, started drying my   15
head, rubbing hard. *"Easy, man, easy!"* I kept shouting.

"The first time's always worst. You get used to it better before long. You   16
took it real good, homeboy. You got a good conk."

When Shorty let me stand up and see in the mirror, my hair hung down   17
in limp, damp strings. My scalp still flamed, but not as badly; I could bear it. He draped the towel around my shoulders, over my rubber apron, and began again vaselining my hair.

I could feel him combing, straight back, first the big comb, then the   18
fine-tooth one.

Then, he was using a razor, very delicately, on the back of my neck.   19
Then, finally, shaping the sideburns.

My first view in the mirror blotted out the hurting. I'd seen some pretty 20 conks, but when it's the first time, on your *own* head, the transformation, after the lifetime of kinks, is staggering.

The mirror reflected Shorty behind me. We both were grinning and 21 sweating. And on top of my head was this thick, smooth sheen of shining red hair — real red — as straight as any white man's.

How ridiculous I was! Stupid enough to stand there simply lost in ad- 22 miration of my hair now looking "white," reflected in the mirror in Shorty's room. I vowed that I'd never again be without a conk, and I never was for many years.

This was my first really big step toward self-degradation: when I en- 23 dured all of that pain, literally burning my flesh to have it look like a white man's hair. I had joined that multitude of Negro men and women in America who are brainwashed into believing that the black people are "inferior" — and white people "superior" — that they will even violate and mutilate their God-created bodies to try to look "pretty" by white standards.

Look around today, in every small town and big city, from two-bit cat- 24 fish and soda-pop joints into the "integrated" lobby of the Waldorf-Astoria, and you'll see conks on black men. And you'll see black women wearing these green and pink and purple and red and platinum-blonde wigs. They're all more ridiculous than a slapstick comedy. It makes you wonder if the Negro has completely lost his sense of identity, lost touch with himself.

You'll see the conk worn by many, many so-called "upper class" Ne- 25 groes, and, as much as I hate to say it about them, on all too many Negro entertainers. One of the reasons that I've especially admired some of them, like Lionel Hampton and Sidney Poitier, among others, is that they have kept their natural hair and fought to the top. I admire any Negro man who has never had himself conked, or who has had the sense to get rid of it — as I finally did.

I don't know which kind of self-defacing conk is the greater shame — 26 the one you'll see on the heads of the black so-called "middle class" and "upper class," who ought to know better, or the one you'll see on the heads of the poorest, most downtrodden, ignorant black men. I mean the legal-minimum-wage ghetto-dwelling kind of Negro, as I was when I got my first one. It's generally among these poor fools that you'll see a black kerchief over the man's head, like Aunt Jemima; he's trying to make his conk last longer, between trips to the barbershop. Only for special occasions is this kerchief-protected conk exposed — to show off how "sharp" and "hip" its owner is. The ironic thing is that I have never heard any woman, white or black, express any admiration for a conk. Of course, any white woman with a black man isn't thinking about his hair. But I don't see how on earth a black woman with any race pride could walk down the street with any black man wearing a conk — the emblem of his shame that he is black.

To my own shame, when I say all of this, I'm talking first of all about 27 myself — because you can't show me any Negro who ever conked more faithfully than I did. I'm speaking from personal experience when I say of any black man who conks today, or any white-wigged black woman, that if they gave the brains in their heads just half as much attention as they do their hair, they would be a thousand times better off.

. . .

Comprehension

1. What exactly is a conk? Why does Malcolm X want to get his hair conked? What does the conk symbolize to him at the time he gets it? What does it symbolize at the time he writes about it?

2. List the materials Shorty asks Malcolm X to buy. Is the purpose of each explained? If so, where?

3. Outline the major stages in the procedure Malcolm X describes. Are they presented in chronological order? Which, if any, of the major stages are out of place?

Purpose and Audience

1. Why was this selection written as a process explanation instead of as a set of instructions?

2. This selection has an explicitly stated thesis that makes its purpose clear. What is this thesis?

3. *The Autobiography of Malcolm X* was published in 1964, when many African Americans regularly straightened their hair. Is the thesis of this excerpt from the book still relevant today?

4. Why do you think Malcolm X includes so many references to the pain and discomfort he endured as part of the process?

5. What is the relationship between Malcolm X's personal experience and his universal statement about the process he discusses?

Style and Structure

1. Identify some of the transitional words Malcolm X uses to move from step to step.

2. Only about half of this selection is devoted to the process explanation. Where does the process begin? Where does it end?

3. In paragraphs 22–26, Malcolm X encloses several words in quotation marks, occasionally prefacing them with the phrase *so-called*. What is the effect of these quotation marks?

4. **Vocabulary Project.** Because this is an informal piece of writing, Malcolm X uses many **colloquialisms** and **slang** terms. Substitute a more formal word for each of the following.

beat (1)	glop (6)	"sharp" (26)
pad (4)	real (6)	"hip" (26)

Evaluate the possible impact of your substitutions. Do they improve the essay or weaken it?

Journal Entry

Did you ever engage in behavior that you later came to view as unacceptable as your beliefs changed or as your social consciousness developed? What made you change your attitude toward this behavior?

Writing Workshop

1. Write a process explanation of an unpleasant experience you or someone you know has gone through to conform to someone else's standard of physical beauty (for instance, dieting or getting a tattoo). Include a thesis statement that conveys your disapproval of the process.

2. **Working with Sources.** Rewrite Malcolm X's process explanation as he might have written it when he still considered conking a desirable process, worth all the trouble. Include all his steps, but change his thesis and choose words that make the process sound painless and worthwhile. If you quote Malcolm X's words, be sure to include parenthetical documentation and a works-cited page. (See Chapter 18 for information on MLA documentation.)

3. Rewrite this essay as a set of instructions that Shorty might have written for a friend about to help someone conk his hair. Begin by telling the friend what materials to purchase. Be sure to include all necessary cautions and reminders.

Combining the Patterns

Although "My First Conk" is very detailed, it does not include an extended **definition** of a conk. Do you think a definition paragraph should be added? If so, where could it be inserted? What patterns could be used to develop such a definition?

Thematic Connections

- "Four Tattoos" (page 222)
- "Just Walk On By: A Black Man Ponders His Power to Alter Public Space" (page 238)
- "Why Looks Are the Last Bastion of Discrimination" (page 244)
- "Medium Ash Brown" (page 277)
- "Inked Well" (page 692)

STANLEY FISH

Getting Coffee Is Hard to Do

Literary critic and legal scholar Stanley Fish (b. 1938) has had a long and distinguished academic career. An authority on the seventeenth-century poet John Milton, Fish is widely recognized for his revolutionary approach to literary criticism, as summarized in his groundbreaking book *Is There a Text in This Class?: The Authority of Interpretive Communities* (1980). A regular contributor to popular journals and op-ed pages in newspapers nationwide, Fish has also been a guest columnist for the *New York Times*, where the following essay originally appeared. His most recent book is *How to Write a Sentence: And How to Read One* (2011).

Background on U.S. coffee-drinking trends Coffee consumption in the United States goes back to the earliest English settlers. In fact, the British tax imposed on tea that led to the rebellious Boston Tea Party resulted in coffee's becoming the most popular American drink. However, the popularity of gourmet coffees can be traced back to 1966, when Dutch immigrant Alfred Peet, a coffee importer who was unhappy with the general quality of coffee in the United States, opened a shop in Berkeley, California, where he sold his own special roast. Trained in coffee roasting by Peet, the founders of Starbucks opened their first outlet in Seattle in 1971, selling quality coffee beans and coffeemaking equipment. Returning from a buying trip to Italy in 1985, then-marketing director Howard Schultz suggested that Starbucks become a true coffeehouse in the Italian tradition, a gathering spot where people could enjoy freshly roasted and brewed coffee. Despite being met with skepticism, Schultz would eventually take over the business and turn it into a worldwide phenomenon.

A coordination problem (a term of art in economics and management) 1 occurs when you have a task to perform, the task has multiple and shifting components, the time for completion is limited, and your performance is affected by the order and sequence of the actions you take. The trick is to manage it so that the components don't bump into each other in ways that produce confusion, frustration, and inefficiency.

You will face a coordination problem if you are a general deploying 2 troops, tanks, helicopters, food, tents, and medical supplies, or if you are the CEO of a large company juggling the demands of design, personnel, inventory, and production.

And these days, you will face a coordination problem if you want to get 3 a cup of coffee.

It used to be that when you wanted a cup of coffee you went into a 4 nondescript place fitted out largely in linoleum, Formica, and neon, sat down at a counter, and, in response to a brisk "What'll you have, dear?"

said, "Coffee and a cheese Danish." Twenty seconds later, tops, they arrived, just as you were settling into the sports page.

Now it's all wood or concrete floors, lots of earth tones, soft, high-style lighting, open barrels of coffee beans, folk-rock and indie music, photographs of urban landscapes, and copies of *The Onion*. As you walk in, everything is saying, "This is very sophisticated, and you'd better be up to it." 5

> " As you walk in, everything is saying, 'This is very sophisticated, and you'd better be up to it.' "

It turns out to be hard. First you have to 6 get in line, and you may have one or two people in front of you who are ordering a drink with more parts than an internal combustion engine, something about "double shot," "skinny," "breve," "grande," "au lait," and a lot of other words that never pass my lips. If you are patient and stay in line (no bathroom breaks), you get to put in your order, but then you have to find a place to stand while you wait for it. There is no such place. So you shift your body, first here and then there, trying not to get in the way of those you can't help get in the way of.

Finally, the coffee arrives. 7

But then your real problems begin when you turn, holding your prize, 8 and make your way to where the accessories — things you put in, on, and around your coffee — are to be found. There is a staggering array of them, and the order of their placement seems random in relation to the order of your needs. There is no "right" place to start, so you lunge after one thing and then after another with awkward reaches.

Unfortunately, two or three other people are doing the same thing, and 9 each is doing it in a different sequence. So there is an endless round of "excuse me," "no, excuse me," as if you were in an old Steve Martin routine.

But no amount of politeness and care is enough. After all, there are so 10 many items to reach for — lids, cup jackets, straws, napkins, stirrers, milk, half and half, water, sugar, Splenda, the wastepaper basket, spoons. You and your companions may strive for a ballet of courtesy, but what you end up performing is more like bumper cars. It's just a question of what will happen first — getting what you want or spilling the coffee you are trying to balance in one hand on the guy reaching over you.

I won't even talk about the problem of finding a seat. 11

And two things add to your pain and trouble. First, it costs a lot, $3 12 and up. And worst of all, what you're paying for is the privilege of doing the work that should be done by those who take your money. The coffee shop experience is just one instance of the growing practice of shifting the burden of labor to the consumer — gas stations, grocery and drug stores, bagel shops (why should I put on my own cream cheese?), airline check-ins, parking lots. It's insert this, swipe that, choose credit or debit, enter your PIN, push the red button, error, start again. At least when you go on a "vacation" that involves working on a ranch, the work is something you've chosen. But none of us has chosen to take over the jobs of those we pay to serve us.

Well, it's Sunday morning, and you're probably reading this with a cup 13 of coffee. I hope it was easy to get.

. . .

Comprehension

1. How does Fish describe the traditional process of getting a cup of coffee (4)? What does he see as the main difference between getting a cup of coffee in a diner or coffee shop and getting coffee in today's coffee bars?

2. According to Fish, how do the two kinds of coffee shops differ in terms of their physical setting?

3. List some of the obstacles Fish says customers face in a modern-day coffee bar.

4. Whom, or what, does Fish blame for the situation he describes?

5. Note that Fish does not mention paying for the coffee. Do you think the fact that this step is missing is significant in any way?

Purpose and Audience

1. What purpose do the first two paragraphs of this essay serve? Are they necessary, or could the essay begin with paragraph 3?

2. What is the point of this essay? Is Fish simply trying to explain how difficult it has become to get a cup of coffee (as his title suggests), or does he have a more specific — and perhaps more serious — purpose in mind? (Read paragraph 12 carefully before you answer this question.)

3. In one sentence, state this essay's thesis. Does this thesis statement appear in the essay? If so, where?

4. Do you think Fish is exaggerating the difficulty of getting a cup of coffee? If so, what might be his purpose for doing so?

5. Who is the "you" Fish addresses in this essay? What does this use of *you* tell you about how he sees his audience?

Style and Structure

1. This essay includes several one-sentence paragraphs. Locate each one, and explain why you think it is so short. Should any of these one-sentence paragraphs be developed further? If so, how? Should any be combined with an adjacent paragraph?

2. List the steps in the process Fish describes. Then, group the steps into stages in the process.

3. Where does Fish include cautions and reminders? Give some examples. Given his audience's likely familiarity with the process he describes, are these tips necessary? If not, why do you think he includes them?

4. This essay is a process explanation. Do you think it would have been more effective if Fish had written it in the form of instructions? Explain.

5. **Vocabulary Project.** As Fish illustrates, the world of the coffee bar has its own vocabulary. List and define five words that are part of this specialized vocabulary. (You can define words Fish includes here, or you can create your own list.)

6. Would you characterize Fish's tone as amused? Annoyed? Puzzled? What is his attitude toward the process he describes?

Journal Entry

Do you agree with Fish that the process he describes is a problem? Why or why not?

Writing Workshop

1. **Working with Sources.** Write an essay describing another process that is "hard to do" — specifically, something that is more complicated today than it used to be. For possible topics, see paragraph 12 of Fish's essay. Begin by summarizing Fish's position, and be sure to include parenthetical documentation and a works-cited page. (See Chapter 18 for information on MLA documentation.)

2. Write a set of instructions for ordering, eating, and cleaning up after a meal in a fast-food restaurant. Assume your audience has never eaten in a fast-food restaurant before. Use "Getting Fast Food Is Easy to Do" as your essay's title.

Combining the Patterns

Fish includes several other patterns of development in his process essay. Locate examples of **definition, comparison and contrast, description, exemplification,** and **narration**. How do these passages support the process explanation?

Thematic Connections

- "How to Retrieve a Candy Bar Stuck in the Lunchroom Vending Machine" (page 292)
- "Tortillas" (page 506)
- The Declaration of Independence (page 550)

JOSHUA PIVEN AND DAVID BORGENICHT

How to Retrieve a Candy Bar Stuck in the Lunchroom Vending Machine

Joshua Piven and David Borgenicht are the authors of the best-seller *The Worst-Case Scenario Survival Handbook* (1999), which provides expert advice on such dilemmas as "How to Break into a Parked Car" and "How to Escape from a Mountain Lion." The book's success sparked a series that now includes titles such as *The Worst-Case Scenario: Weddings* (2004) and *The Complete Worst-Case Scenario Survival Handbook: Man Skills* (2010).

Background on the history of vending machines The origins of the vending machine have been traced all the way back to the first century AD, when the mathematician and inventor Hero of Alexandria designed a coin-operated water dispenser. Some accounts suggest that the Chinese designed a machine in 1076 that dispensed writing implements. In England in the seventeenth century, early coin-operated vending machines sold snuff and smoking tobacco at taverns. A century later in England, more sophisticated devices were selling books, postcards, handkerchiefs, and candy. In the United States, vending machines arrived in 1888, when the Adams Gum Company began selling Tutti Fruitti gum on the platforms of New York City train stations, charging a nickel for a package of five pieces. The novelty caught on at the end of the nineteenth century, when machines were produced to dispense cigars, newspapers, photographs, and perfume. During the twentieth century in the United States, coin-operated cigarette and soda machines became common in public spaces, and there are now an estimated five million of them in the United States. Worldwide, both the technology and the products continue to develop and change. For example, in Germany and the United Arab Emirates, people can buy gold from machines; in England, people can buy shoes; and in some towns in the United States, people can buy live fishing bait. However, the days of the coin-operated vending machine may be at an end, as more machines rely instead on card-swiping and wireless technology.

1. Wait several seconds.

Newer vending machines may be equipped with special technology 1 that senses when an item has not dropped; the machine may return your money or give you another selection.

2. Purchase the item again.

Depending on how severely the snack is stuck and how much money 2 you have, you may be able to jar it loose and get a second one by selecting the same item again.

3. Choose an item from the row above.

If your snack is stuck at an angle toward the glass at the end of the row, an item dropping from above may knock it free.

4. Jostle the machine.

Vending machines are extremely heavy and can cause major injury if they tip over. Carefully bang on the side of the machine. Do not hit glass areas.

> " Vending machines are extremely heavy and can cause major injury if they tip over."

5. Rock the machine.

Tip the machine backward very slightly (not side-to-side) and let it drop back in place to jar the item loose. Do not press on the glass.

Rock the machine forward and back slightly.

From *Worst-Case Scenario Survival Handbook: Work* © 2003 by Joshua Piven and David Borgenicht. Used with permission from Chronicle Books LLC, San Francisco. Visit ChronicleBooks.com.

6. Push in the vending door and remove the candy.

Once the item — or items — have dropped, reach in and slowly extricate it.

BE AWARE

Anti-theft devices make it virtually impossible to reach in and up past   7
the vending door. Do not risk getting your arm stuck in the machine.

• • •

Comprehension

1. This set of instructions begins very abruptly. What happens before the first step ("Wait several seconds") listed here?
2. Why might someone choose to perform Step 3 instead of Step 2?
3. How much time do you think this process takes?

Purpose and Audience

1. What main idea is implied in this set of instructions? Write a sentence that could serve as the essay's thesis statement.
2. What kinds of readers might find this essay useful? What kinds of readers might react negatively to these instructions?
3. Does the illustration help to explain the process? If so, how? What other purpose might it serve?

Style and Structure

1. This selection is neither structured nor formatted like most of the other essays in this text. What does it include that most other essays do not? What elements are missing that most other essays include? Should any of those missing elements be added? Why or why not?
2. What stylistic features tell you that this is a set of instructions rather than a process explanation?
3. Instructions are usually directed at people who may actually perform a process. Is that the case here? Explain.
4. Where do the writers include the cautions and reminders that are usually present in instructions? Do you think readers need any additional warnings or reminders?
5. How do the writers move readers from one step to the next? Would transitional words and expressions be helpful additions? Suggest some transitions that could be added.
6. **Vocabulary Project.** What words do the writers use in this essay in place of the words "candy bar" in the title? Can you suggest other words they could use?

Journal Entry

What is your reaction to the instructions presented here? If you found yourself unable to retrieve an item from a vending machine, would you follow these instructions or do something different? Why or why not?

Writing Workshop

1. **Working with Sources.** This essay is from one of a series of books by Piven et al. that provides instructions for coping with "worst-case scenarios," such as escaping from a stadium riot or putting out a microwave fire. Find the tables of contents for several of these books on Amazon.com, and choose a scenario to use as the topic for a set of instructions of your own. In your introduction, use some of the listed chapter titles to illustrate the concept of a "worst-case scenario" and to give your essay some context. Be sure to cite Amazon.com as your source, and include a work-cited page. (See Chapter 18 for information on documenting sources.)

2. This selection is more a list of steps than a fully developed essay. Expand these instructions, including an introduction and concluding paragraphs and any additional steps or advice (including warnings) you think are necessary. Be sure to add transitions between sentences and paragraphs to make the process flow smoothly. If you like, you can include illustrations.

Combining the Patterns

In presenting instructions for retrieving a stuck candy bar, the writers could have used **exemplification** to illustrate the different snack items that might become stuck. How would such examples strengthen the essay?

Thematic Connections

- "Goodbye to My Twinkie Days" (page 171)
- "Getting Coffee Is Hard to Do" (page 288)
- *Rube Goldberg Machine* (page 335)
- "Tortillas" (page 506)

ARTHUR MILLER

Get It Right: Privatize Executions

One of the leading playwrights of the twentieth century, Arthur Miller (1915–2005) had his first play produced on Broadway in 1944. Though it was not a success, his next Broadway production, *All My Sons* (1947), received positive reviews and the New York Drama Critics' Circle Award. However, it was his 1949 play *Death of a Salesman* that established Miller as a major voice in the American theater: opening to ecstatic reviews, it went on to win the Pulitzer Prize. Another important play, *The Crucible* (1953), was set during the Salem witch trials of the late seventeenth century but was written as an allegory for the persecution of suspected Communists in the 1950s. (Miller himself was called before the House Un-American Activities Committee and convicted of contempt of Congress because he refused to testify.) While his plays from the 1960s on did not achieve the success of his earlier works, Miller's artistic legacy is assured; his moral vision, as evidenced in the following 1992 essay, continues to move readers and playgoers around the world.

Background on public executions Public executions of convicted felons can be traced back at least as far as the ancient civilizations of Greece and Rome and were common in European countries until well into the nineteenth century (public executions were conducted in England, for example, until 1868). Over time, they have been carried out by crucifixion, stoning, burning at the stake, and beheading, among other methods. However, by the 1600s in England and in the American colonies, public executions were most often accomplished by hanging, usually in a public square. These hangings, which were meant to teach spectators a moral lesson, ironically took on a festive, carnival-like air and were considered a form of free entertainment. By the early 1800s, authorities in a number of states began to require that hangings be performed in the privacy of prisons — in part because the crowds witnessing them had become so rowdy and in part because it was felt that public executions could stir sentiments against capital punishment. Still, public executions persisted in some areas of the United States until the twentieth century; the last was performed in 1936 in Owensboro, Kentucky. Today, public executions continue in countries operating under Muslim law and under repressive regimes, such as that of North Korea. In this essay, Miller makes the somewhat radical suggestion that execution be both "privatized" — that is, run not by the government but by private companies — and public.

The time has come to consider the privatization of executions. 1

There can no longer be any doubt that government — society itself — is 2 incapable of doing anything right, and this certainly applies to the executions of convicted criminals.

At present, the thing is a total loss, to the convicted person, to his family, and to society. It need not be so. 3

People can be executed in places like Shea Stadium* before immense 4 paying audiences. The income from the spectacle could be distributed to the prison that fed and housed him or to a trust fund for prisoner rehabilitation and his own family and/or girlfriend, as he himself chose.

The condemned would of course get a percentage of the gate, to be 5 negotiated by his agent or a promoter, if he so desired.

The take would, without question, be sizable, considering the immense 6 number of Americans in favor of capital punishment. A $200 to $300 ringside seat would not be excessive, with bleachers going for, say, $25.

As with all sports events, a certain ritual would seem inevitable and 7 would quickly become an expected part of the occasion. The electric chair would be set on a platform, like a boxing ring without the rope, around second base.

Once the audience was seated, a soprano would come forward and sing 8 "The Star-Spangled Banner." When she stepped down, the governor, holding a microphone, would appear and describe the condemned man's crimes in detail, plus his many failed appeals.

Then the governor would step aside and a phalanx of police officers or possibly National Guard or Army troops would mount the platform and surround the condemned. This climactic entrance might be accompanied by a trumpet fanfare or other musical number by the police or Army band, unless it was thought to offend good taste. 9

> " Next, a minister or priest would appear and offer a benediction, asking God's blessing on the execution. "

Next, a minister or priest would appear and offer a benediction, asking God's blessing on the execution. 10

The condemned, should he desire, could make a short statement and 11 even a plea of innocence. This would only add to the pathos of the occasion and would of course not be legally binding. He would then be strapped into the chair.

Finally, the executioner, hooded to protect himself from retaliation, 12 would proceed to the platform. He would walk to a console where, on a solemn signal from the governor, he would pull the switch.

The condemned man would instantly surge upward against his bindings, with smoke emitting from his flesh. This by itself would provide a most powerful lesson for anyone contemplating murder. For those not contemplating murder, it would be a reminder of how lucky they are to have been straight and honest in America. 13

---

* Eds. note — Demolished in 2009 and replaced by Citi Field, where the New York Mets now play.

For the state, this would mean additional income; for the audience, an 14 intense and educational experience — people might, for example, wish to bring their children.

And for the condemned, it would have its achievement aspect, because 15 he would know that he had not lived his life for nothing.

Some might object that such proceedings are so fundamentally attrac- 16 tive that it is not too much to imagine certain individuals contemplating murder in order to star in the program. But no solution to any profound social problem is perfect.

Finally, and perhaps most important, it is entirely possible that after 17 witnessing a few dozen privatized executions, the public might grow tired of the spectacle — just as it seizes on all kinds of entertainment only to lose interest once their repetitiousness becomes too tiresomely apparent.

Then perhaps we might be willing to consider the fact that in execut- 18 ing prisoners we merely add to the number of untimely dead without diminishing the number of murders committed.

At that point, the point of boredom, we might begin asking why it is 19 that Americans commit murder more often than any other people. At the moment, we are not bored enough with executions to ask this question; instead, we are apparently going to demand more and more of them, most probably because we never get to witness any in person.

My proposal would lead us more quickly to boredom and away from 20 our current gratifying excitement — and ultimately perhaps to a wiser use of alternating current.

• • •

Comprehension

1. What process does Miller describe? List the individual steps in this process.

2. Which of Miller's recommendations are most outrageous? Is any part of his scheme actually plausible?

3. In paragraph 6, Miller notes that many Americans support capital punishment. Do you think Miller was one of these people? Why or why not?

4. Why, according to Miller, do executions need to be privatized rather than performed by the government?

5. What specific benefits does Miller say will result from his scheme?

6. In paragraph 20, Miller suggests that his proposal might ultimately lead to "a wiser use of alternating current." What does he mean by "alternating current"?

Purpose and Audience

1. This essay begins with an abrupt statement of a very controversial thesis. Why does Miller choose this approach? How successful is it?

2. What kind of reaction do you think Miller hoped to get from his audience? For instance, does he want them to be amused? Shocked? Guilty? Angry? Explain.

3. How would you characterize Miller's primary purpose in writing this essay? What do you think he hoped to accomplish?

Style and Structure

1. Because this essay was first published in a newspaper and set in columns, it has relatively short paragraphs. Which paragraphs, if any, could be combined? Which would you leave as they are? Are there any advantages to using one- or two-sentence paragraphs in this essay?

2. Where does the actual process begin? Where does it end?

3. What words and phrases link the steps in the process? Do you think any additional transitions are needed? If so, where?

4. **Vocabulary Project.** Miller repeats the word *execution* many times. What alternatives does he have? What different connotations does each of these possible alternatives suggest?

5. Much of this essay's tone is ironic, and Miller clearly intended that many of his statements not be taken literally. How do you suppose he expected readers to react to each of the following?

    -   "unless it was thought to offend good taste" (9)
    -   "he would know that he had not lived his life for nothing" (15)
    -   "no solution to any profound social problem is perfect" (16)

6. Miller seems to suggest that executions are not unlike sporting events. How, according to Miller, are they alike? Is this a valid **analogy**?

Journal Entry

Many people who support capital punishment see it as a deterrent to crime. Do you think Miller's scheme, if enacted, would be a deterrent? Why or why not?

Writing Workshop

1. Using past tense, rewrite the process section of Miller's essay from the point of view of someone who has just witnessed a public execution. Give the condemned person an identity, a history, and a family, and explain the crime for which he or she is being punished. In your thesis, take a stand on whether or not this person deserves to be executed.

2. **Working with Sources.** Write a process essay expressing your strong disapproval of the idea of public executions. Quoting Miller where necessary, use the steps in the process he describes to support your position. To convince readers this practice is inhumane, add descriptive details — for

example, information about the observers' reactions and the sensational-ist news coverage. Be sure to include parenthetical documentation that cites Miller as the source of your quoted material and to include a works-cited page. (See Chapter 18 for information on MLA documentation.)

Combining the Patterns

Although the body of this essay is structured as a process, the essay as a whole makes a powerful **argument**. Does Miller have a debatable thesis? Do you think he needs more evidence to support his thesis, or is the process itself enough? Does he consider the possible objections of his audience? Does he refute these objections?

Thematic Connections

- "Shooting an Elephant" (page 133)
- "The Lottery" (page 308)
- "Who Killed Benny Paret?" (page 337)
- "A Modest Proposal" (page 699)

JESSICA MITFORD

The Embalming of Mr. Jones

Jessica Mitford (1917–1996) was born in Batsford Mansion, England, to a wealthy, aristocratic family. Rebelling against her sheltered upbringing, she became involved in left-wing politics and eventually immigrated to the United States. Mitford wrote two volumes of autobiography — *Daughters and Rebels* (1960), about her eccentric family, and *A Fine Old Conflict* (1976). In the 1950s, she began a career in investigative journalism, which produced the books *The American Way of Death* (1963), about abuses in the funeral business; *Kind and Usual Punishment* (1973), about the U.S. prison system; and *The American Way of Birth* (1992), about the crisis in American obstetrical care.

Background on the funeral industry "The Embalming of Mr. Jones" is excerpted from *The American Way of Death*, a scathing critique of the funeral industry in the United States. The book prompted angry responses from morticians but also led to increased governmental regulation, culminating in a 1984 Federal Trade Commission ruling requiring funeral homes to disclose in writing the prices for all goods and services, as well as certain consumer rights; barring funeral homes from forcing consumers to purchase more than they really want; and forbidding funeral directors from misleading consumers regarding state laws governing the disposal of bodies. Still, industry critics charge that many abuses continue. While funeral services can be purchased for less than a thousand dollars, the standard rate is between two and four thousand dollars — and it can go much higher. The difference in cost is based largely on the price of a casket, and grieving family members are often strongly pressured into buying the most expensive caskets, which may be marked up as much as 500 percent. Advocates for reform suggest that consumers choose cremation over burial (of the approximately 2.5 million people who died in the United States in 2006, only some 800,000 were cremated) and that they hold memorial services in churches or other settings, where costs are much lower than in funeral homes.

Embalming is indeed a most extraordinary procedure, and one must 1 wonder at the docility of Americans who each year pay hundreds of millions of dollars for its perpetuation, blissfully ignorant of what it is all about, what is done, how it is done. Not one in ten thousand has any idea of what actually takes place. Books on the subject are extremely hard to come by. They are not to be found in most libraries or bookshops.

In an era when huge television audiences watch surgical operations 2 in the comfort of their living rooms, when, thanks to the animated cartoon, the geography of the digestive system has become familiar territory even to the nursery school set, in a land where the satisfaction of curiosity about almost all matters is a national pastime, the secrecy surrounding embalming can, surely, hardly be attributed to the inherent gruesomeness of the subject. Custom in this regard has within this century suffered a complete reversal. In the early days of American embalming, when it was performed in the home of the deceased, it was almost mandatory for some relative to stay by the embalmer's side and witness the procedure. Today, family members who might wish to be in attendance would certainly be dissuaded by the funeral director. All others, except apprentices, are excluded by law from the preparation room.

A close look at what does actually take place may explain in large measure the undertaker's intractable reticence concerning a procedure that has become his major *raison d'être*.* Is it possible he fears that public information about embalming might lead patrons to wonder if they really want this service? If the funeral men are loath to discuss the subject outside the trade, the reader may, understandably, be equally loath to go on reading at this point. For those who have the stomach for it, let us part the formaldehyde curtain. . . .

> "For those who have the stomach for it, let us part the formaldehyde curtain."

The body is first laid out in the undertaker's morgue — or rather, Mr. Jones is reposing in the preparation room — to be readied to bid the world farewell.

The preparation room in any of the better funeral establishments has the tiled and sterile look of a surgery, and indeed the embalmer-restorative artist who does his chores there is beginning to adopt the term "dermasurgeon" (appropriately corrupted by some mortician-writers as "demi-surgeon") to describe his calling. His equipment, consisting of scalpels, scissors, augers, forceps, clamps, needles, pumps, tubes, bowls, and basin, is crudely imitative of the surgeon's, as is his technique, acquired in a nine- or twelve-month post-high-school course in an embalming school. He is supplied by an advanced chemical industry with a bewildering array of fluids, sprays, pastes, oils, powders, creams, to fix or soften tissue, shrink or distend it as needed, dry it here, restore the moisture there. There are cosmetics, waxes, and paints to fill and cover features, even plaster of Paris to replace entire limbs. There are ingenious aids to prop and stabilize the cadaver: a Vari-Pose Head Rest, the Edwards Arm and Hand Positioner, the Repose Block (to support the shoulders during the embalming), and the Throop Foot Positioner, which resembles an old-fashioned stocks.

Mr. John H. Eckels, president of the Eckels College of Mortuary Science, thus describes the first part of the embalming procedure: "In the hands of a skilled practitioner, this work may be done in a comparatively short time and without mutilating the body other than by slight incision — so slight that it scarcely would cause serious inconvenience if made upon a living person. It is necessary to remove all the blood, and doing this not only

---

* Eds. note — Reason for being (French).

helps in the disinfecting, but removes the principal cause of disfigurements due to discoloration."

Another textbook discusses the all-important time element: "The earlier this is done, the better, for every hour that elapses between death and embalming will add to the problems and complications encountered. . . ." Just how soon should one get going on the embalming? The author tells us, "On the basis of such scanty information made available to this profession through its rudimentary and haphazard system of technical research, we must conclude that the best results are to be obtained if the subject is embalmed before life is completely extinct — that is, before cellular death has occurred. In the average case, this would mean within an hour after somatic death." For those who feel that there is something a little rudimentary, not to say haphazard, about this advice, a comforting thought is offered by another writer. Speaking of fears entertained in early days of premature burial, he points out, "One of the effects of embalming by chemical injection, however, has been to dispel fears of live burial." How true; once the blood is removed, chances of live burial are indeed remote.

To return to Mr. Jones, the blood is drained out through the veins and replaced by embalming fluid pumped in through the arteries. As noted in *The Principles and Practices of Embalming,* "every operator has a favorite injection and drainage point — a fact which becomes a handicap only if he fails or refuses to forsake his favorites when conditions demand it." Typical favorites are the carotid artery, femoral artery, jugular vein, subclavian vein. There are various choices of embalming fluid. If Flextone is used, it will produce a "mild, flexible rigidity. The skin retains a velvety softness, the tissues are rubbery and pliable. Ideal for women and children." It may be blended with B. and G. Products Company's Lyf-Lyk tint, which is guaranteed to reproduce "nature's own skin texture . . . the velvety appearance of living tissue." Suntone comes in three separate tints: Suntan; Special Cosmetic Tint, a pink shade "especially indicated for young female subjects"; and Regular Cosmetic Tint, moderately pink.

About three to six gallons of a dyed and perfumed solution of formaldehyde, glycerin, borax, phenol, alcohol, and water is soon circulating through Mr. Jones, whose mouth has been sewn together with a "needle directed upward between the upper lip and gum and brought out through the left nostril," with the corners raised slightly "for a more pleasant expression." If he should be buck-toothed, his teeth are cleaned with Bon Ami and coated with colorless nail polish. His eyes, meanwhile, are closed with flesh-tinted eye caps and eye cement.

The next step is to have at Mr. Jones with a thing called a trocar. This is a long, hollow needle attached to a tube. It is jabbed into the abdomen, poked around the entrails and chest cavity, the contents of which are pumped out and replaced with "cavity fluid." This done, and the hole in the abdomen sewed up, Mr. Jones's face is heavily creamed (to protect the skin from burns which may be caused by leakage of the chemicals), and he is covered with a sheet and left unmolested for a while. But not

for long — there is more, much more, in store for him. He has been embalmed, but not yet restored, and the best time to start restorative work
is eight to ten hours after embalming, when the tissues have become firm
and dry.

The object of all this attention to the corpse, it must be remembered,   11
is to make it presentable for viewing in an attitude of healthy repose. "Our
customs require the presentation of our dead in the semblance of nor-
mality . . . unmarred by the ravages of illness, disease, or mutilation,"
says Mr. J. Sheridan Mayer in his *Restorative Art.* This is rather a large order since few people die in the full bloom of health, unravaged by illness
and unmarked by some disfigurement. The funeral industry is equal to
the challenge: "In some cases the gruesome appearance of a mutilated or
disease-ridden subject may be quite discouraging. The task of restoration
may seem impossible and shake the confidence of the embalmer. This is
the time for intestinal fortitude and determination. Once the formative
work is begun and affected tissues are cleaned or removed, all doubts of
success vanish. It is surprising and gratifying to discover the results which
may be obtained."

The embalmer, having allowed an appropriate interval to elapse, re-   12
turns to the attack, but now he brings into play the skill and equipment
of sculptor and cosmetician. Is a hand missing? Casting one in plaster of
Paris is a simple matter. "For replacement purposes, only a cast of the back
of the hand is necessary; this is within the ability of the average operator
and is quite adequate." If a lip or two, a nose, or an ear should be missing, the embalmer has at hand a variety of restorative waxes with which
to model replacements. Pores and skin texture are simulated by stippling
with a little brush, and over this cosmetics are laid on. Head off? Decapi-
tation cases are rather routinely handled. Ragged edges are trimmed, and
head joined to torso with a series of splints, wires, and sutures. It is a good
idea to have a little something at the neck — a scarf or high collar — when
time for viewing comes. Swollen mouth? Cut out tissue as needed from
inside the lips. If too much is removed, the surface contour can easily be
restored by padding with cotton. Swollen necks and cheeks are reduced
by removing tissue through vertical incisions made down each side of
the neck. "When the deceased is casketed, the pillow will hide the suture
incisions. . . . as an extra precaution against leakage, the suture may be
painted with liquid sealer."

The opposite condition is more likely to present itself — that of ema-   13
ciation. His hypodermic syringe now loaded with massage cream, the embalmer seeks out and fills the hollowed and sunken areas by injection. In
this procedure the backs of the hands and fingers and the underchin area
should not be neglected.

Positioning the lips is a problem that recurrently challenges the in-   14
genuity of the embalmer. Closed too tightly, they tend to give a stern,
even disapproving expression. Ideally, embalmers feel, the lips should give
the impression of being ever so slightly parted, the upper lip protruding
slightly for a more youthful appearance. This takes some engineering,

however, as the lips tend to drift apart. Lip drift can sometimes be remedied by pushing one or two straight pins through the inner margin of the lower lip and then inserting them between the two front upper teeth. If Mr. Jones happens to have no teeth, the pins can just as easily be anchored in his Armstrong Face Former and Denture Replacer. Another method to maintain lip closure is to dislocate the lower jaw, which is then held in its new position by a wire run through holes which have been drilled through the upper jaws at the midline. As the French are fond of saying, *il faut souffrir pour être belle.**

If Mr. Jones has died of jaundice, the embalming fluid will very likely 15
turn him green. Does this deter the embalmer? Not if he has intestinal fortitude. Masking pastes and cosmetics are heavily laid on, burial garments and casket interiors are color-correlated with particular care, and Jones is displayed beneath rose-colored lights. Friends will say, "How *well* he looks." Death by carbon monoxide, on the other hand, can be rather a good thing from an embalmer's viewpoint: "One advantage is the fact that this type of discoloration is an exaggerated form of a natural pink coloration." This is nice because the healthy glow is already present and needs but little attention.

The patching and filling completed, Mr. Jones is now shaved, washed, 16
and dressed. Cream-based cosmetic, available in pink, flesh, suntan, brunette, and blonde, is applied to his hands and face, his hair is shampooed and combed (and, in the case of Mrs. Jones, set), his hands manicured. For the horny-handed son of toil special care must be taken; cream should be applied to remove ingrained grime, and the nails cleaned. "If he were not in the habit of having them manicured in life, trimming and shaping is advised for better appearance — never questioned by kin."

Jones is now ready for casketing (this is the present participle of the 17
verb "to casket"). In this operation his right shoulder should be depressed slightly "to turn the body a bit to the right and soften the appearance of lying flat on the back." Positioning the hands is a matter of importance, and special rubber positioning blocks may be used. The hands should be cupped slightly for a more lifelike, relaxed appearance. Proper placement of the body requires a delicate sense of balance. It should lie as high as possible in the casket, yet not so high that the lid, when lowered, will hit the nose. On the other hand, we are cautioned, placing the body too low "creates the impression that the body is in a box."

Jones is next wheeled into the appointed slumber room where a few 18
last touches may be added — his favorite pipe placed in his hand or, if he was a great reader, a book propped into position. (In the case of little Master Jones a Teddy bear may be clutched.) Here he will hold open house for a few days, visiting hours 10 A.M. to 9 P.M.

· · ·

* Eds. note — It is necessary to suffer in order to be beautiful.

Comprehension

1. How, according to Mitford, has the public's knowledge of embalming changed? How does she explain this change?

2. To what other professionals does Mitford compare the embalmer? Are these analogies flattering or critical? Explain.

3. What are the major stages in the process of embalming and restoration?

Purpose and Audience

1. Mitford's purpose in this essay is to convince her audience of something. What is her thesis?

2. Do you think Mitford expects her audience to agree with her thesis? How can you tell?

3. In one of her books, Mitford refers to herself as a *muckraker,* one who informs the public of misconduct. Does she achieve this status here? Cite specific examples.

4. Mitford's tone in this essay is subjective, even judgmental. What effect does her tone have on you? Does it encourage you to trust her? Should she have presented her facts in a more objective way? Explain.

Style and Structure

1. Identify the stylistic features that distinguish this process explanation from a set of instructions.

2. In this selection, as in many process essays, a list of necessary materials comes before the procedure. What additional details does Mitford include in her list in paragraph 5? How do these additions affect you?

3. Locate Mitford's remarks about the language of embalming. How do her comments about euphemisms, newly coined words, and other aspects of language help to support her thesis?

4. **Vocabulary Project.** Reread paragraphs 5–9 carefully. Then, list all the words in this section of the essay that suggest surgical techniques and all the words that suggest cosmetic artistry. What do your lists tell you about Mitford's intent in these paragraphs?

5. Throughout the essay, Mitford quotes various experts. How does she use their remarks to support her thesis?

6. Give examples of phrases that serve as transitions that link the various stages of Mitford's process.

7. Mitford uses a good deal of sarcasm and biased language in this essay. Identify some examples. Do you think her use of this kind of language strengthens or weakens her essay? Why?

Journal Entry

What are your thoughts about how your religion or culture deals with death and dying? What practices, if any, make you uncomfortable? Why?

Writing Workshop

1. Use the information in this process explanation to help you prepare a two-page set of instructions for undertakers. Unlike Mitford, keep your essay objective.

2. **Working with Sources.** In the role of a funeral director, write a blog post taking issue with Mitford's essay. As you explain the process of embalming, paraphrase or quote two or three of Mitford's statements and argue against them, making sure to identify the source of these quotations. Your objective is to defend the practice of embalming as necessary and practical. Be sure to include parenthetical documentation citing Mitford as your source, and include a works-cited page. (See Chapter 18 for information on MLA documentation.)

3. Write an explanation of a process you personally find disgusting — or delightful. Make your attitude clear in your thesis statement and in your choice of words.

Combining the Patterns

Although Mitford structures this essay as a process, many passages rely heavily on subjective **description**. Where is her focus on descriptive details most obvious? What is her purpose in describing particular individuals and objects as she does? How do these descriptive passages help to support her essay's thesis?

Thematic Connections

- "My First Conk" (page 283)
- "The Movies That Rose from the Grave" (page 359)
- "The Ways We Lie" (page 471)

SHIRLEY JACKSON

The Lottery (Fiction)

Shirley Jackson (1919–1965) is best known for her subtly macabre stories of horror and suspense, most notably her best-selling novel *The Haunting of Hill House* (1959), which Stephen King has called "one of the greatest horror stories of all time." She also published wryly humorous reflections on her experiences as a wife and mother of four children. Many of her finest stories and novels were not anthologized until after her death.

Background on the initial reaction to "The Lottery" "The Lottery" first appeared in the *New Yorker* in 1948, three years after the end of World War II. Jackson was living somewhat uneasily in the New England college town of Bennington, Vermont, a village very similar to the setting of "The Lottery." She felt herself an outsider there, a sophisticated intellectual in an isolated, closely knit community that was suspicious of strangers. Here, Jackson (whose husband was Jewish) experienced frequent encounters with anti-Semitism. At the time, the full atrocity of Germany's wartime program to exterminate Jews, now called the Holocaust, had led many social critics to contemplate humanity's terrible capacity for evil. Most Americans, however, wished to put the horrors of the war behind them, and many readers reacted with outrage to Jackson's tale of an annual small-town ritual, calling it "nasty," "nauseating," and even "perverted." Others, however, immediately recognized its genius, its power, and its many layers of meaning. This classic tale is now one of the most widely anthologized of all twentieth-century short stories.

The morning of June 27th was clear and sunny, with the fresh warmth 1 of a full-summer day; the flowers were blossoming profusely and the grass was richly green. The people of the village began to gather in the square, between the post office and the bank, around ten o'clock; in some towns there were so many people that the lottery took two days and had to be started on June 26th, but in this village, where there were only about three hundred people, the whole lottery took less than two hours, so it could begin at ten o'clock in the morning and still be through in time to allow the villagers to get home for noon dinner.

The children assembled first, of course. School was recently over for 2 the summer, and the feeling of liberty sat uneasily on most of them; they tended to gather together quietly for a while before they broke into boisterous play, and their talk was still of the classroom and the teacher, of books and reprimands. Bobby Martin had already stuffed his pockets full of stones, and the other boys soon followed his example, selecting the smoothest and roundest stones; Bobby and Harry Jones and Dickie Delacroix — the villagers pronounced his name "Dellacroy" — eventually made a great pile of stones in one corner of the square and guarded it against the raids of the other boys. The girls stood aside, talking among themselves, looking over their shoulders at the boys, and the very small children rolled in the dust or clung to the hands of their older brothers or sisters.

Soon the men began to gather, surveying their own children, speaking of planting and rain, tractors and taxes. They stood together, away from the pile of stones in the corner, and their jokes were quiet and they smiled rather than laughed. The women, wearing faded house dresses and sweaters, came shortly after their menfolk. They greeted one another and exchanged bits of gossip as they went to join their husbands. Soon the women, standing by their husbands, began to call to their children, and the children came reluctantly, having to be called four or five times. Bobby Martin ducked under his mother's grasping hand and ran, laughing, back to the pile of stones. His father spoke up sharply, and Bobby came quickly and took his place between his father and his oldest brother. 3

The lottery was conducted — as were the square dances, the teenage club, the Halloween program — by Mr. Summers, who had time and energy to devote to civic activities. He was a round-faced, jovial man and he ran the coal business, and people were sorry for him, because he had no children and his wife was a scold. When he arrived in the square, carrying the black wooden box, there was a murmur of conversation among the villagers, and he waved and called "Little late today, folks." The postmaster, Mr. Graves, followed him, carrying a three-legged stool, and the stool was put in the center of the square and Mr. Summers set the black box down on it. The villagers kept their distance, leaving a space between themselves and the stool, and when Mr. Summers said, "Some of you fellows want to give me a hand?" there was a hesitation before two men, Mr. Martin and his oldest son, Baxter, came forward to hold the box steady on the stool while Mr. Summers stirred up the papers inside it. 4

The original paraphernalia for the lottery had been lost long ago, and the black box now resting on the stool had been put into use even before Old Man Warner, the oldest man in town, was born. Mr. Summers spoke frequently to the villagers about making a new box, but no one liked to upset even as much tradition as was represented by the black box. There was a story that the present box had been made with some pieces of the box that had preceded it, the one that had been constructed when the first people settled down to make a village here. Every year, after the lottery, Mr. Summers began talking about a new box, but every year the subject was allowed to fade off without anything's being done. The black box grew shabbier each year; by now it was no longer completely black but splintered badly along one side to show the original wood color, and in some places faded and stained. 5

Mr. Martin and his oldest son, Baxter, held the black box securely on the stool until Mr. Summers had stirred the papers thoroughly with his hand. Because so much of the ritual had been forgotten or discarded, Mr. Summers had been successful in having slips of paper substituted for the chips of wood that had been used for generations. Chips of wood, Mr. Summers had argued, had been all very well when the village was tiny, but now that the population was more than three hundred and likely 6 to keep on growing, it was necessary to use something that would fit more easily into the black box. The night before the lottery, Mr. Summers and Mr. Graves made up the slips of paper and put them in the box, and it was then taken to the safe of Mr. Summers' coal company and locked up until Mr. Summers was ready to take it to the square the next morning. The rest of the year, the box was put away, sometimes one place, sometimes another; it had spent one year in Mr. Graves' barn and another year underfoot in the post office, and sometimes it was set on a shelf in the Martin grocery and left there.

There was a great deal of fussing to be done before Mr. Summers declared the lottery open. There were the lists to make up — of heads of families, heads of households in each family, members of each household in each family. There was the proper swearing-in of Mr. Summers by the postmaster, as the official of the lottery; at one time, some people remembered, there had been a recital of some sort, performed by the official of the lottery, a perfunctory, tuneless chant that had been rattled off duly each year; some people believed that the official of the lottery used to stand just so when he said or sang it, others believed that he was supposed to walk among the people, but years and years ago this part of the ritual had been allowed to lapse. There had been, also, a ritual salute, which the official of the lottery had had to use in addressing each person who came up to draw from the box, but this also had changed with time, until now it was felt necessary only for the official to speak to each person approaching. Mr. Summers was very good at all this; in his clean white shirt and blue jeans, with one hand resting carelessly on the black box, he seemed very proper and important as he talked interminably to Mr. Graves and the Martins.   7

Just as Mr. Summers finally left off talking and turned to the assembled villagers, Mrs. Hutchinson came hurriedly along the path to the square, her sweater thrown over her shoulders, and slid into place in the back of the crowd. "Clean forgot what day it was," she said to Mrs. Delacroix, who stood next to her, and they both laughed softly. "Thought my old man was out back stacking wood," Mrs. Hutchinson went on, "and then I looked out the window and the kids were gone, and then I remembered it was the twenty-seventh and came a-running." She dried her hands on her apron, and Mrs. Delacroix said, "You're in time, though. They're still talking away up there."   8

Mrs. Hutchinson craned her neck to see through the crowd and found her husband and children standing near the front. She tapped Mrs. Delacroix on the arm as a farewell and began to make her way through the crowd. The people separated good-humoredly to let her through; two or three people said, in voices just loud enough to be heard across the crowd, "Here comes your Missus, Hutchinson," and "Bill, she made it after all." Mrs. Hutchinson reached her husband, and Mr. Summers, who had been waiting, said cheerfully, "Thought we were going to have to get on without you, Tessie." Mrs. Hutchinson said, grinning, "Wouldn't have me leave m'dishes in the sink, now, would you, Joe?" and soft laughter ran through   9 the crowd as the people stirred back into position after Mrs. Hutchinson's arrival.

"Well, now," Mr. Summers said soberly, "guess we better get started, 10 get this over with, so's we can go back to work. Anybody ain't here?"

"Dunbar," several people said. "Dunbar, Dunbar." 11

Mr. Summers consulted his list. "Clyde Dunbar," he said. "That's right. 12 He's broke his leg, hasn't he? Who's drawing for him?"

"Me, I guess," a woman said, and Mr. Summers turned to look at her. 13 "Wife draws for her husband," Mr. Summers said. "Don't you have a grown boy to do it for you, Janey?" Although Mr. Summers and everyone else in the village knew the answer perfectly well, it was the business of the official of the lottery to ask such questions formally. Mr. Summers waited with an expression of polite interest while Mrs. Dunbar answered.

"Horace's not but sixteen yet," Mrs. Dunbar said regretfully. "Guess I 14 gotta fill in for the old man this year."

"Right," Mr. Summers said. He made a note on the list he was holding. 15 Then he asked, "Watson boy drawing this year?"

A tall boy in the crowd raised his hand. "Here," he said. "I'm draw- 16 ing for m'mother and me." He blinked his eyes nervously and ducked his head as several voices in the crowd said things like "Good fellow, Jack," and "Glad to see your mother's got a man to do it."

"Well," Mr. Summers said, "guess that's everyone. Old Man Warner 17 make it?"

"Here," a voice said, and Mr. Summers nodded. 18

A sudden hush fell on the crowd as Mr. Summers cleared his throat and 19 looked at the list. "All ready?" he called. "Now, I'll read the names — heads of families first — and the men come up and take a paper out of the box. Keep the paper folded in your hand without looking at it until everyone has had a turn. Everything clear?"

The people had done it so many times that they only half listened to 20 the directions; most of them were quiet, wetting their lips, not looking around. Then Mr. Summers raised one hand high and said, "Adams." A man disengaged himself from the crowd and came forward. "Hi, Steve," Mr. Summers said, and Mr. Adams said, "Hi, Joe." They grinned at one another humorlessly and nervously. Then Mr. Adams reached into the black box and took out a folded paper. He held it firmly by one corner as he turned and went hastily back to his place in the crowd, where he stood a little apart from his family, not looking down at his hand.

"Allen," Mr. Summers said. "Anderson. . . . Betham." 21

"Seems like there's no time at all between lotteries any more," Mrs. 22 Delacroix said to Mrs. Graves in the back row. "Seems like we got through the last one only last week."

"Time sure goes fast," Mrs. Graves said. 23

"Clark. . . . Delacroix." 24

"There goes my old man," Mrs. Delacroix said. She held her breath 25 while her husband went forward.

"Dunbar," Mr. Summers said, and Mrs. Dunbar went steadily to the 26
box while one of the women said, "Go on, Janey," and another said, "There
she goes."

"We're next," Mrs. Graves said. She watched while Mr. Graves came 27
around from the side of the box, greeted Mr. Summers gravely, and selected
a slip of paper from the box. By now, all through the crowd there were
men holding the small folded papers in their large hands, turning them
over and over nervously. Mrs. Dunbar and her two sons stood together,
Mrs. Dunbar holding the slip of paper.

"Harburt. . . . Hutchinson."   28

"Get up there, Bill," Mrs. Hutchinson said, and the people near her 29
laughed.

"Jones."   30

"They do say," Mr. Adams said to Old Man Warner, who stood next to 31
him, "that over in the north village they're talking of giving up the lottery."

Old Man Warner snorted. "Pack of crazy fools," he said. "Listening to 32
the young folks, nothing's good enough for *them*. Next thing you know,
they'll be wanting to go back to living in caves, nobody work any more,
live *that* way for a while. Used to be a saying about 'Lottery in June, corn be
heavy soon.' First thing you know, we'd all be eating stewed chickweed and
acorns. There's *always* been a lottery," he added petulantly. "Bad enough to
see young Joe Summers up there joking with everybody."

"Some places have already quit lotteries," Mrs. Adams said.   33

"Nothing but trouble in *that*," Old Man Warner said stoutly. "Pack of 34
young fools."

"Martin." And Bobby Martin watched his father go forward. "Over- 35
dyke. . . . Percy."

"I wish they'd hurry," Mrs. Dunbar said to her older son. "I wish they'd 36
hurry."

"They're almost through," her son said.   37

"You get ready to run tell Dad," Mrs. Dunbar said.   38

Mr. Summers called his own name and then stepped forward precisely 39
and selected a slip from the box. Then he called, "Warner."

"Seventy-seventh year I been in the lottery," Old Man Warner said as he 40
went through the crowd. "Seventy-seventh time."

"Watson." The tall boy came awkwardly through the crowd. Someone 41
said, "Don't be nervous, Jack," and Mr. Summers said, "Take your time, son."

"Zanini."   42

After that, there was a long pause, a breathless pause, until Mr. Sum- 43
mers, holding his slip of paper in the air, said, "All right fellows." For a minute, no one moved, and then all the slips of paper were opened. Suddenly,
all the women began to speak at once, saying, "Who is it?," "Who's got it?,"
"Is it the Dunbars?," "Is it the Watsons?" Then the voices began to say, "It's
Hutchinson. It's Bill," "Bill Hutchinson's got it."

"Go tell your father," Mrs. Dunbar said to her older son.   44

People began to look around to see the Hutchinsons. Bill Hutchinson 45
was standing quiet, staring down at the paper in his hand. Suddenly, Tessie

Hutchinson shouted to Mr. Summers, "You didn't give him time enough to take any paper he wanted. I saw you. It wasn't fair!"

"Be a good sport, Tessie," Mrs. Delacroix called, and Mrs. Graves said, "All of us took the same chance."

"Shut up, Tessie," Bill Hutchinson said.

"Well, everyone," Mr. Summers said, "That was done pretty fast, and now we've got to be hurrying a little more to get it done in time." He consulted his next list. "Bill," he said, "you draw for the Hutchinson family. You got any other households in the Hutchinsons?"

"There's Don and Eva," Mrs. Hutchinson yelled. "Make *them* take their chance!" 49

"Daughters draw with their husbands' families, Tessie," Mr. Summers 50 said gently. "You know that as well as anyone else."

"It wasn't *fair*," Tessie said. 51

"I guess not, Joe," Bill Hutchinson said regretfully. "My daughter draws 52 with her husband's family, that's only fair. And I've got no other family except the kids."

"Then, as far as drawing for families is concerned, it's you," Mr. Sum- 53 mers said in explanation, "and as far as drawing for households is concerned, that's you, too. Right?"

"Right," Bill Hutchinson said. 54

"How many kids, Bill?" Mr. Summers asked formally. 55

"Three," Bill Hutchinson said. "There's Bill, Jr., and Nancy, and little 56 Dave. And Tessie and me."

"All right, then," Mr. Summers said. "Harry, you got their tickets back?" 57

Mr. Graves nodded and held up the slips of paper. "Put them in the 58 box, then," Mr. Summers directed. "Take Bill's and put it in."

"I think we ought to start over," Mrs. Hutchinson said, as quietly as she 59 could. "I tell you it wasn't *fair*. You didn't give him time enough to choose. *Every*body saw that."

Mr. Graves had selected the five slips and put them in the box, and he 60 dropped all the papers but those onto the ground, where the breeze caught them and lifted them off.

"Listen, everybody," Mrs. Hutchinson was saying to the people around 61 her.

"Ready, Bill?" Mr. Summers asked, and Bill Hutchinson, with one 62 quick glance around at his wife and children, nodded.

"Remember," Mr. Summers said, "take the slips and keep them folded 63 until each person has taken one. Harry, you help little Dave." Mr. Graves took the hand of the little boy, who came willingly with him up to the box. "Take a paper out of the box, Davy," Mr. Summers said. Davy put his hand into the box and laughed. "Take just *one* paper," Mr. Summers said. "Harry, you hold it for him." Mr. Graves took the child's hand and removed the

> **46** "'Be a good sport, Tessie,' Mrs. Delacroix called, and Mrs. **47** Graves said, 'All of us took the same **48** chance.'"

folded paper from the tight fist and held it while little Dave stood next to him and looked up at him wonderingly.

"Nancy next," Mr. Summers said. Nancy was twelve, and her school 64 friends breathed heavily as she went forward, switching her skirt, and took a slip daintily from the box. "Bill, Jr.," Mr. Summers said, and Billy, his face red and his feet over-large, nearly knocked the box over as he got a paper out. "Tessie," Mr. Summers said. She hesitated for a minute, looking around defiantly, and then set her lips and went up to the box. She snatched a paper out and held it behind her.

"Bill," Mr. Summers said, and Bill Hutchinson reached into the box 65 and felt around, bringing his hand out at last with the slip of paper in it.

The crowd was quiet. A girl whispered, "I hope it's not Nancy," and the 66 sound of the whisper reached the edges of the crowd.

"It's not the way it used to be," Old Man Warner said clearly. "People 67 ain't the way they used to be."

"All right," Mr. Summers said. "Open the papers. Harry, you open little 68 Dave's."

Mr. Graves opened the slip of paper and there was a general sigh 69 through the crowd as he held it up and everyone could see that it was blank. Nancy and Bill, Jr., opened theirs at the same time, and both beamed and laughed, turning around to the crowd and holding their slips of paper above their heads.

"Tessie," Mr. Summers said. There was a pause, and then Mr. Summers 70 looked at Bill Hutchinson, and Bill unfolded his paper and showed it. It was blank.

"It's Tessie," Mr. Summers said, and his voice was hushed. "Show us 71 her paper, Bill."

Bill Hutchinson went over to his wife and forced the slip of paper out 72 of her hand. It had a black spot on it, the black spot Mr. Summers had made the night before with the heavy pencil in the coal-company office. Bill Hutchinson held it up, and there was a stir in the crowd.

"All right, folks," Mr. Summers said. "Let's finish quickly."   73

Although the villagers had forgotten the ritual and lost the original 74 black box, they still remembered to use stones. The pile of stones the boys had made earlier was ready; there were stones on the ground with the blowing scraps of paper that had come out of the box. Mrs. Delacroix selected a stone so large she had to pick it up with both hands and turned to Mrs. Dunbar. "Come on," she said. "Hurry up."

Mrs. Dunbar had small stones in both hands, and she said, gasping for 75 breath, "I can't run at all. You'll have to go ahead and I'll catch up with you."

The children had stones already, and someone gave little Davy Hutch- 76 inson a few pebbles.

Tessie Hutchinson was in the center of a cleared space by now, and she 77 held her hands out desperately as the villagers moved in on her. "It isn't fair," she said. A stone hit her on the side of the head.

Old Man Warner was saying, "Come on, come on, everyone." Steve 78 Adams was in the front of the crowd of villagers, with Mrs. Graves beside him.

"It isn't fair, it isn't right," Mrs. Hutchinson screamed, and then they 79
were upon her.

. . .

Reading Literature

1. List the stages in the process of the lottery. Then, identify passages explaining the reasons behind each step. How logical are these explanations?
2. What is the significance of the fact that the process has continued essentially unchanged for so many years? What does this fact suggest about the people in the town?
3. Do you see this story as an explanation of a brutal process carried out in one town, or do you see it as a universal statement about dangerous tendencies in modern society — or in human nature? Explain your reasoning.

Journal Entry

What do you think it would take to stop a process like this lottery? What would have to be done — and who would have to do it?

Thematic Connections

- "Thirty-Eight Who Saw Murder Didn't Call the Police" (page 128)
- "Shooting an Elephant" (page 133)
- "Get It Right: Privatize Executions" (page 296)

Writing Assignments for Process

1. Jessica Mitford describes the process of doing a job. Write an essay summarizing the steps you took in applying for, performing, or quitting a job.

2. Write a set of instructions explaining in objective terms how the lottery Shirley Jackson describes should be conducted. Imagine you are setting these steps down in writing for generations of your fellow townspeople to follow.

3. Write a consumer-oriented article for your school newspaper explaining how to apply for financial aid, a work-study job, or an internship.

4. List the steps in the process you follow when you study for an important exam. Then, interview two friends about how they study, and take notes about their usual routine. Finally, combine the most helpful strategies into a set of instructions aimed at students entering your school.

5. **Working with Sources.** Think of a series of steps in a bureaucratic process that you had to go through to accomplish something — getting a driver's license or becoming a U.S. citizen, for instance. Write an essay explaining that process, and include a thesis statement that evaluates the process's efficiency. Before you begin writing, consult a website that explains the process, and refer to this explanation when necessary in your essay. Be sure to document any references to the site, and include a works-cited page. (See Chapter 18 for information on MLA documentation.)

6. Imagine you have encountered a visitor from another country (or another planet) who is not familiar with a social ritual you take for granted. Try to outline the steps involved in the ritual you are familiar with — for instance, choosing sides for a game or pledging a fraternity or sorority.

7. Write a process essay explaining how you went about putting together a collection, a scrapbook, a writing portfolio, or an album of some kind. Be sure your essay makes clear why you collected or compiled your materials.

8. Explain how a certain ritual or ceremony is conducted in your religion. Make sure someone of another faith could understand the process, and include a thesis statement that explains why the ritual is important.

9. Think of a process you believe should be modified or discontinued. Formulate a thesis that presents your negative feelings, and then explain the process so that you make your objections clear to your readers.

10. Write an essay explaining a process you experienced but would not recommend to others — for example, getting a tattoo or a body piercing.

11. Give readers instructions for the process of participating in a potentially dangerous but worthwhile physical activity — for example, skydiving, rock climbing, or white-water rafting. Be sure to include all necessary cautions.

Collaborative Activity for Process

Working with three other students, create an illustrated instructional pamphlet to help new students survive four of your college's first "ordeals" — for example, registering for classes, purchasing textbooks, eating in the cafeteria, and moving into a dorm. Before beginning, decide as a group which processes to write about, whether you want your pamphlet to be practical and serious or humorous and irreverent, and what kinds of illustrations it should include. Then, decide who will write about which process — each student should do one — and who will provide the illustrations. When all of you are ready, assemble your individual efforts into a single unified piece of writing.

Cause and Effect

What Is Cause and Effect?

Process describes *how* something happens; **cause and effect** analyzes *why* something happens. Cause-and-effect essays examine causes, describe effects, or do both. In the following paragraph, journalist Tom Wicker considers the effects of a technological advance on a village in India.

Cause

Effects

Topic sentence

When a solar-powered water pump was provided for a well in India, the village headman took it over and sold the water, until stopped. The new liquid abundance attracted hordes of unwanted nomads. Village boys who had drawn water in buckets had nothing to do, and some became criminals. The gap between rich and poor widened, since the poor had no land to benefit from irrigation. Finally, village women broke the pump, so they could gather again around the well that had been the center of their social lives. Moral: technological advances have social, cultural, and economic consequences, often unanticipated.

Cause and effect, like narration, links situations and events together in time, with causes preceding effects. But causality involves more than sequence: cause-and-effect analysis explains why something happened — or is happening — and predicts what probably will happen.

Sometimes many different causes can be responsible for one effect. For example, as the following diagram illustrates, many elements may contribute to an individual's decision to leave his or her country of origin for the United States.

Causes

Political repression
Desire to further education
Desire to join family members
Desire for economic opportunity
Desire for religious freedom

Effect

Immigrants come to the United States

319

Similarly, a single cause can produce many different effects. Immigration, for instance, has had a variety of effects on the United States.

Cause	*Effects*
Immigrants come to the United States	Diverse culture Demand for new goods and services Competition for jobs Challenges to educational system New political agendas

Using Cause and Effect

Of course, causal relationships are rarely as neat as the preceding boxes suggest; in fact, such relationships are often subtle and complex. As you examine situations that seem suited to cause-and-effect analysis, you will discover that most complex situations involve numerous causes and many different effects.

Consider the two examples that follow.

The Case of the Losing Team. A professional basketball team, recently stocked with the best players money can buy, has had a mediocre season. Because the individual players are talented and were successful under other coaches, fans blame the current coach for the team's losing streak and want him fired. But is the coach alone responsible? Maybe the inability of the players to function well as a team contributed to their poor performance. Perhaps some of the players are suffering from injuries, personal problems, or drug dependency. Or maybe the lack of support from fans has affected the team's morale. Clearly, other elements besides the new coach could have caused the losing streak. (And, of course, the team's losing streak might have any number of consequences, from declining attendance at games to the city's refusal to build a new arena.)

The Case of the Declining SAT Scores. For more than twenty years, from the 1960s to the 1980s, the college-board scores of high school seniors steadily declined, and educators began to look for causes. The decline began soon after television became popular, and therefore many people concluded that the two events were connected. This idea is plausible because children did seem to be reading less to watch television more, and reading comprehension is one of the chief skills the tests evaluate.

But many other elements might have contributed to the decline of test scores during those years. During the same period, for example, many schools reduced the number of required courses and deemphasized traditional subjects and skills, such as reading. Adults were reading less than they used to, and perhaps they were not encouraging their children to read. Furthermore, during the 1960s and 1970s, many colleges changed their policies and admitted students who previously would not have qualified.

These new admission standards encouraged students who would not have taken college boards in earlier years to take the tests. Therefore, the scores may have been lower because they measured the top third of high school seniors rather than the top fifth. In any case, the reason for the lower scores during that twenty-year period remains unclear. Perhaps television was the main cause after all, but nobody knows for sure. In such a case, it is easy — too easy — to claim a cause-and-effect relationship without the evidence to support it.*

And just as the drop in scores may have had many causes, television watching may have had many effects. For instance, it may have made those same students better observers and listeners even if they did less well on standardized written tests. It may have encouraged them to have a national or even international outlook instead of a narrower local perspective. In other words, even if watching television did limit young people in some ways, it might also have expanded their horizons in other ways.

Remember, when you write about situations such as those described above, you need to give a balanced analysis. This means that you should try to consider all possible causes and effects, not just the most obvious ones or the first ones you think of.

Understanding Main and Contributory Causes

Even when you have identified several causes of a particular effect, one — the *main cause* — is always more important than the others, the *contributory causes*. Understanding the distinction between the **main** (most important) **cause** and the **contributory** (less important) **causes** is vital for planning a cause-and-effect paper because once you identify the main cause, you can emphasize it in your paper and downplay the other causes. How, then, can you tell which cause is most important? Sometimes the main cause is obvious, but often it is not, as the following example shows.

The Case of the Hartford Roof Collapse. During one winter a number of years ago, an unusually large amount of snow accumulated on the roof of the Civic Center Auditorium in Hartford, Connecticut, and the roof fell in. Newspapers reported that the weight of the snow had caused the collapse, and they were partly right. Other buildings, however, had not been flattened by the snow, so the main cause seemed to lie elsewhere. Insurance investigators eventually determined that the roof design, not the weight of the snow (which was a contributory cause), was the main cause of the collapse.

---

* With 2006 SAT scores showing their biggest decline since 1975 and 2013 scores averaging twenty points lower than 2006 scores, educators have continued to consider possible reasons for the drop, including changes made to the test in 2006 and the fact that fewer students are taking the test more than once.

These cause-and-effect relationships are shown in this diagram:

Because the main cause is not always the most obvious one, you should be sure to consider the significance of each cause very carefully as you plan your essay — and to continue to evaluate the importance of each cause as you write and revise.

Understanding Immediate and Remote Causes

Another important distinction is the difference between an immediate cause and a remote cause. An **immediate cause** closely precedes an effect and is therefore relatively easy to recognize. A **remote cause** is less obvious, perhaps because it involves something in the past or far away. Assuming that the most obvious cause is always the most important can be dangerous as well as shortsighted.

Reconsidering the Hartford Roof Collapse. Most people agreed that the snow was the immediate cause of the roof collapse. But further study by insurance investigators suggested remote causes that were not so apparent. The design of the roof was the most important remote cause of the collapse, but other remote causes were also examined. Perhaps the materials used in the roof's construction were partly to blame. Maybe maintenance crews had not done their jobs properly, or necessary repairs had not been made. If you were the insurance investigator analyzing the causes of this event, you would want to assess all possible contributing factors. If you did not consider the remote as well as the immediate causes, you would reach an oversimplified and perhaps incorrect conclusion.

This diagram shows the cause-and-effect relationships just summarized.

Remember, remote causes can be extremely important. In the roof-collapse situation, as we have seen, a remote cause — the roof design — was actually the main cause of the accident.

Understanding Causal Chains

Sometimes an effect can also be a cause. This is true in a **causal chain**, where A causes B, B causes C, C causes D, and so on, as shown here.

A
Cause ──────→ B
             Effect
             (Cause) ──────→ C
                          Effect
                          (Cause) ──────→ D
                                       Effect
                                       (Cause) ──────→ E
                                                Effect

In causal chains, the result of one action is the cause of another. Leaving out any link in the chain, or failing to put any link in its proper order, destroys the logic and continuity of the chain.

A simple example of a causal chain is the recent suggestion by a group of retired generals that global warming might be a threat to U.S. national security. According to these generals, global warming could cause worldwide climate changes, such as droughts, which in turn might create a refugee crisis as people leave their homelands in search of clean water. The resulting refugee camps, the generals claim, become a breeding ground for terrorists, and it is these terrorists who threaten our nation's security.

Here is another example of a causal chain.

The Case of the Disappearing Bicycle. In the past forty years, the bicycle as a form of transportation for children has become increasingly rare, with fewer than one percent of children now riding bicycles to school. In addition, fewer children ride bicycles for recreation. Causes cited for this decline include the absence of sidewalks in many newer suburban communities, parents' rising fears about crime and traffic accidents, the rise in the number of students who schedule back-to-back after-school activities (perhaps due in part to the increased number of households with two working parents), the growing popularity of social media and video games, and the increased reliance on after-school jobs by teenagers (who often need cars, not bikes, to get to work). The decreasing number of children who ride bikes has contributed to a corresponding steady decline, since the 1970s, in the sale of bicycles.

As a result of the decline in bicycle sales, bicycle thefts have decreased sharply, and bicycle deaths involving children under sixteen have also dropped dramatically (although this is due in part to the increased use of helmets). However, the number of American children who are obese has doubled since the mid-1980s — in part because children get less and less exercise. So, factors such as fewer sidewalks and more working teenagers may have led to a decline in bicycle sales, which in turn could have had a far-reaching impact on children's health.

If your analysis of a situation reveals a causal chain, this discovery can be useful as you plan your essay. The identification of a causal chain suggests an organizational pattern for a paper, and following the chain helps you to discuss items in their logical order. Be careful, however, to keep your emphasis on the causal connections and not to lapse into narration.

Avoiding *Post Hoc* Reasoning

When developing a cause-and-effect essay, you should not assume that just because event A *precedes* event B, event A has *caused* event B. This illogical assumption, called ***post hoc* reasoning**, equates a chronological sequence with causality. When you fall into this trap — assuming, for instance, that you failed an exam because a black cat crossed your path the day before — you are mistaking coincidence for causality.

Consider a classic example of *post hoc* reasoning.

The Case of the Magical Maggots. Until the late nineteenth century, many scientists accepted the notion of spontaneous generation — that is, they believed living things could arise directly from nonliving matter. To support their beliefs, they pointed to specific situations. For instance, they observed that maggots, the larvae of the housefly, seemed to arise directly from the decaying flesh of dead animals.

These scientists were confusing sequence with causality, assuming that because the presence of decaying meat preceded the appearance of maggots, the two were connected in a causal relationship. In fact, because the dead animals were exposed to the air, flies were free to lay eggs in the animals' bodies, and these eggs hatched into maggots. Therefore, the living maggots were not a direct result of the presence of nonliving matter. Although these scientists were applying the best technology and scientific theory of their time, hindsight reveals that their conclusions were not valid.

Here is a more recent example of *post hoc* reasoning.

The Case of the Female Centenarians. Several years ago, medical researchers published findings reporting that female centenarians — women who reached the age of one hundred — were four times as likely to have given birth when they were past forty as were women in a control group who died at the age of seventy-three. Researchers saw no causal connection between childbirth after forty and long life, suggesting only that the centenarians might have been predisposed to live longer because they reached menopause later than the other women. Local television newscasts and tabloid newspapers, however, misinterpreted the study's implications, presenting the relationship between late childbearing and long life as a causal one. In a vivid example of *post hoc* reasoning, one promotional spot for a local television newscast proclaimed, "Having kids late in life can help you live longer."

In your writing, as well as in your observations, it is neither logical nor fair to assume that a causal relationship exists unless clear, strong evidence supports the connection. When you revise a cause-and-effect paper, make sure you have not confused words such as *because, therefore,* and *consequently* (words that indicate a causal relationship) with words such as *then, next, subsequently, later,* and *afterward* (words that indicate a chronological relationship). When you use a word like *because,* you are signaling to readers that you are telling *why* something happened; when you use a word like *later,* you are only showing *when* it happened.

The ability to identify and analyze cause-and-effect relationships; to distinguish causes from effects and recognize causal chains; and to distinguish immediate from remote, main from contributory, and logical from illogical causes are all skills that will improve your writing.

Planning a Cause-and-Effect Essay

After you have sorted out the cause-and-effect relationships you will write about, you are ready to plan your essay. You have three basic options — to discuss causes, to discuss effects, or to discuss both causes and effects. Often your assignment will suggest which of these options to use. Here are a few likely topics for cause-and-effect essays.

Focus on finding causes	Discuss the factors that contributed to the declining population of state mental hospitals in the 1960s. (social work paper)
	Identify some possible causes of collective obsessional behavior. (psychology exam)
Focus on describing or predicting effects	Evaluate the probable effects of moving elementary school children from a highly structured classroom to a relatively open classroom. (education paper)
	Discuss the impact of World War I on two of Ernest Hemingway's characters. (literature exam)
Focus on both causes and effects	The 1840s were volatile years in Europe. Choose one social, political, or economic event that occurred during those years, analyze its causes, and briefly note how the event influenced later developments in European history. (history exam)

Developing a Thesis Statement

Of course, a cause-and-effect essay usually does more than just enumerate causes or effects; more often, it presents and supports a particular thesis. For example, an economics essay treating the major effects of the Vietnam War on the U.S. economy could be just a straightforward presentation of factual information — an attempt to inform readers of the war's economic impact. It is more likely, however, that the essay would not just list the war's effects but also indicate their significance. In fact, cause-and-effect analysis often requires you to judge various factors so that you can assess their relative significance.

When you draft your **thesis statement**, be sure it identifies the relationships among the specific causes or effects you will discuss. This thesis statement should tell your readers three things: the issues you plan to consider, the position you will take, and whether your emphasis will be on causes, effects, or both. Your thesis statement may also indicate explicitly or implicitly the cause or effect you consider most important and the order in which you will present your points.

Arranging Causes and Effects

When deciding on the sequence in which you will present causes or effects, you have several options. One option, of course, is chronological order: you can present causes or effects in the order in which they occurred. Another option is to introduce the main cause first and then the contributory causes — or you can do just the opposite. If you want to stress positive consequences, begin by briefly discussing the negative ones; if you plan to emphasize negative results, summarize the less important positive effects first. Still another possibility is to begin by dismissing any events that were *not* causes and then explain what the real causes were. (This method is especially effective if you think your readers are likely to jump to *post hoc* conclusions.) Finally, you can begin with the most obvious causes or effects and move on to more subtle factors — and then to your analysis and conclusion.

Using Transitions

Cause-and-effect essays rely on clear transitions — *the first cause, the second cause; one result, another result* — to distinguish causes from effects and to help move readers through the discussion. In essays that analyze complex causal relationships, transitions are even more important because they can help readers distinguish main from contributory causes (*the most important cause, another cause*) and immediate from remote causes (*the most obvious cause, a less apparent cause*). Transitions are also essential in a causal chain, where they can help readers sort out the sequence (*then, next*) as well as the causal relationships (*because, as a result, for this reason*). A more complete list of transitions appears on page 57.

Structuring a Cause-and-Effect Essay

Finding Causes

Suppose you are planning the social work essay mentioned earlier: "Discuss the factors that contributed to the declining population of state mental hospitals in the 1960s." Your assignment specifies an effect — the declining population of state mental hospitals — and asks you to discuss possible causes, which might include the following:

- An increasing acceptance of mental illness in our society
- Prohibitive costs of in-patient care
- Increasing numbers of mental health professionals, which made it possible to treat patients outside of hospitals

Many health professionals, however, believe that the most important cause was the development and use of psychotropic drugs, such as chlorpromazine (Thorazine), which can alter behavior. To emphasize this cause in your paper, you could draft the following thesis statement.

Less important causes	Although society's increasing acceptance of the mentally ill, the high cost of in-patient care, and the rise in the number of mental health profession-
Effect	als were all influential in reducing the population of state mental hospitals in the 1960s, the most
Most important cause	important cause of this decline was the development and use of psychotropic drugs.

This thesis statement fully prepares your readers for your essay. It identifies the points you will consider, and it reveals your position — your assessment of the relative significance of the causes you identify. It states the less important causes first and indicates their secondary importance with *although*. In the body of your essay, the less important causes would come first so that the essay could gradually build up to the most convincing material. An informal outline for your essay might look like the one that follows.

Sample Outline **Finding Causes**

Introduction:	Thesis statement — Although society's increasing acceptance of the mentally ill, the high cost of in-patient care, and the rise in the number of mental health professionals were all influential in reducing the population of state mental hospitals in the 1960s, the most important cause of this decline was the development and use of psychotropic drugs.
First cause:	Increasing acceptance of the mentally ill
Second cause:	High cost of in-patient care

Third cause:	Rise in the number of mental health professionals
Fourth (and most important) cause:	Development and use of psychotropic drugs
Conclusion:	Restatement of thesis (in different words) or summary of key points

Describing or Predicting Effects

Suppose you were planning an education essay on the topic mentioned earlier: "Evaluate the probable effects of moving elementary school children from a highly structured classroom to a relatively open classroom." Here you would focus on effects rather than on causes. After brainstorming and deciding which specific points to discuss, you might draft this thesis statement.

Cause

Effects

Moving children from a highly structured classroom to a relatively open one is desirable because it is likely to encourage more independent play, more flexibility in forming friendship groups, and, ultimately, more creativity.

This thesis statement clearly tells readers the stand you will take and the main points you will consider in your essay. The thesis also clearly indicates that these points are *effects* of the open classroom. After introducing the cause, your essay would treat these three effects in the order in which they are presented in the thesis statement, building up to the most important point. An informal outline of your paper might look like the one below.

Sample Outline	**Describing or Predicting Effects**
Introduction:	Thesis statement — Moving children from a highly structured classroom to a relatively open one is desirable because it is likely to encourage more independent play, more flexibility in forming friendship groups, and, ultimately, more creativity.
First effect:	More independent play
Second effect:	More flexibility in forming friendship groups
Third (and most important) effect:	More creativity
Conclusion:	Restatement of thesis (in different words) or summary of key points

Revising a Cause-and-Effect Essay

When you revise a cause-and-effect essay, consider the items on the revision checklist on page 68. In addition, pay special attention to the items on the following checklist, which apply specifically to cause-and-effect essays.

✔ REVISION CHECKLIST   **Cause and Effect**

☐ Does your assignment call for a discussion of causes, of effects, or of both causes and effects?

☐ Does your essay have a clearly stated thesis that indicates whether you will focus on causes, effects, or both?

☐ Have you considered all possible causes and all possible effects?

☐ Have you distinguished between the main (most important) cause and the contributory (less important) causes?

☐ Have you distinguished between immediate and remote causes?

☐ Have you identified a causal chain in your reasoning?

☐ Have you avoided *post hoc* reasoning?

☐ Have you used transitional words and phrases to show how the causes and effects you discuss are related?

Editing a Cause-and-Effect Essay

When you edit your cause-and-effect essay, follow the guidelines on the editing checklists on pages 85, 88, and 91. In addition, focus on the grammar, mechanics, and punctuation issues that are particularly relevant to cause-and-effect essays. Two of these issues — avoiding faulty "the reason is because" constructions and using *affect* and *effect* correctly — are discussed here.

GRAMMAR IN CONTEXT   Avoiding "The reason is because";
Using *Affect* and *Effect* Correctly

Avoiding "the reason is because" When you discuss causes and effects, you may find yourself using the phrase "the reason is." If you follow this phrase with *because* ("the reason is *because*"), you will create an error.

The word *because* means "for the reason that." Therefore, it is redundant to say "the reason is because" (which literally means "the reason is for the reason that"). You can correct this error by substituting *that* for *because* ("the reason is *that*").

INCORRECT: Lawrence Otis Graham believes that one <u>reason</u> he did not sit with other African-American students in the cafeteria <u>was because</u> he was afraid of losing his white friends.

CORRECT: Lawrence Otis Graham believes that one reason he did not sit with other African-American students in the cafeteria was that he was afraid of losing his white friends.

Using *Affect* and *Effect* Correctly When you write a cause-and-effect essay, you will probably use the words *affect* and *effect* quite often. For this reason, it is important that you know the difference between *affect* and *effect*.

- *Affect,* usually a verb, means "to influence."

  Linda M. Hasselstrom believes that carrying a gun has affected her life in a positive way.

- *Effect,* usually a noun, means "a result."

  Linda M. Hasselstrom believes that carrying a gun has had a positive effect on her life.

NOTE: *Effect* can also be a verb meaning "to bring about" ("She worked hard to effect change in the community").

✔ **EDITING CHECKLIST**   **Cause and Effect**

☐ Have you used verb tenses correctly to distinguish among events that happened earlier, at the same time, and later?
☐ Have you placed a comma after every dependent clause introduced by *because* ("Because the rally was so crowded, we left early") but not used a comma before a dependent clause introduced by *because* ("We left early because the rally was so crowded")?
☐ Have you used "the reason is that" (not "the reason is because")?
☐ Have you used *affect* and *effect* correctly?

A STUDENT WRITER: Cause and Effect

The following midterm exam, written for a history class, analyzes both the causes and the effects of the famine that occurred in Ireland during the 1840s. Notice how the writer, Evelyn Pellicane, concentrates on causes but also discusses briefly the effects of this tragedy, just as the exam question directs.

Question: The 1840s were volatile years in Europe. Choose one social, political, or economic event that occurred during those years, analyze its causes, and briefly note how the event influenced later developments in European history.

The Irish Famine, 1845–1849

Thesis statement   The Irish famine, which brought hardship and tragedy to   1
Ireland during the 1840s, was caused and prolonged by four basic

factors: the failure of the potato crop, the landlord-tenant system, errors in government policy, and the long-standing prejudice of the British toward Ireland.

First cause

The immediate cause of the famine was the failure of the   2
potato crop. In 1845, potato disease struck the crop, and potatoes rotted in the ground. The 1846 crop also failed, and before long people were eating weeds. The 1847 crop was healthy, but there were not enough potatoes to go around, and in 1848 the blight struck again, leading to more and more evictions of tenants by landlords.

Second cause

The tenants' position on the land had never been very secure.   3
Most had no leases and could be turned out by their landlords at any time. If a tenant owed rent, he was evicted—or, worse, put in prison, leaving his family to starve. The threat of prison caused many tenants to leave their land; those who could leave Ireland did so, sometimes with money provided by their landlords. Some landlords did try to take care of their tenants, but most did not. Many were absentee landlords who spent their rent money abroad.

Third cause

Government policy errors, although not an immediate cause   4
of the famine, played an important role in creating an unstable economy and perpetuating starvation. In 1846, the government decided not to continue selling corn, as it had during the first year of the famine, claiming that low-cost purchases of corn by Ireland had paralyzed British trade by interfering with free enterprise. Therefore, 1846 saw a starving population, angry demonstrations, and panic; even those with money were unable to buy food. Still, the government insisted that if it sent food to Ireland, prices would rise in the rest of the United Kingdom and that this would be unfair to hardworking English and Scots. As a result, no food was sent. Throughout the years of the famine, the British government aggravated an already grave situation: they did nothing to improve agricultural operations, to help people adjust to another crop, to distribute seeds, or to reform the landlord-tenant system that made the tenants' position so insecure.

Fourth cause

At the root of this poor government policy was the long-   5
standing British prejudice against the Irish. Hostility between the two countries went back some six hundred years, and the British were simply not about to inconvenience themselves to save the Irish. When the Irish so desperately needed grain to replace the damaged potatoes, it was clear that grain had to be imported from England. This meant, however, that the Corn Laws, which

had been enacted to keep the price of British corn high by taxing imported grain, had to be repealed. The British were unwilling to repeal the Corn Laws. Even when they did supply cornmeal, they made no attempt to explain to the Irish how to cook this unfamiliar food. Moreover, the British government was determined to make Ireland pay for its own poor, so it forced the collection of taxes. Since many landlords could not collect the tax money, they were forced to evict their tenants. The British government's callous and indifferent treatment of the Irish has been called genocide.

Effects As a result of this devastating famine, the population of 6
Ireland was reduced from about nine million to about six and one-half million. During the famine years, men roamed the streets looking for work, begging when they found none. Epidemics of "famine fever" and dysentery reduced the population drastically. The most important historical result of the famine, however, was the massive immigration to the United States, Canada, and Great Britain of poor, unskilled people who had to struggle to fit into a skilled economy and who brought with them a deep-seated hatred of the British. (This same hatred remained strong in Ireland itself—so strong that during World War II, Ireland, then independent, remained neutral rather than coming to England's aid.) Irish immigrants faced slums, fever epidemics, joblessness, and hostility—even anti-Catholic and anti-Irish riots—in Boston, New York, London, Glasgow, and Quebec. In Ireland itself, poverty and discontent continued, and by 1848 those emigrating from Ireland included a more highly skilled class of farmers, the ones Ireland needed to recover and to survive.

Conclusion The Irish famine, one of the great tragedies of the 7
(includes nineteenth century, was a natural disaster compounded by the
restatement insensitivity of the British government and the archaic agricultural
of thesis) system of Ireland. Although the deaths that resulted depleted
Ireland's resources even more, the men and women who immigrated to other countries permanently enriched those nations.

Points for Special Attention

Structure. This is a relatively long essay; if it were not so clearly organized, it would be difficult to follow. Because the essay was to focus primarily on causes, Evelyn first introduces the effect — the famine itself — and then considers its causes. After she examines the causes, she moves on to the results of the famine, treating the most important result last. In this essay, then, the famine is first treated as an effect and then, toward the end, as a cause. In fact, it is the central link in a causal chain.

Evelyn devotes one paragraph to her introduction and one to each cause; she sums up the famine's results in a separate paragraph and devotes the final paragraph to her conclusion. (Depending on a particular essay's length and complexity, more — or less — than one paragraph may be devoted to each cause or effect.) An informal outline for her essay might look like this.

> The Irish Famine
>
> Introduction (including thesis statement)
> First cause: Failure of the potato crop
> Second cause: The landlord-tenant system
> Third cause: Errors in government policy
> Fourth cause: British prejudice
> Results of the famine
> Conclusion

Because Evelyn saw all the causes as important and interrelated, she decided not to present them in order of increasing importance. Instead, she begins with the immediate cause of the famine — the failure of the potato crop — and then digs more deeply until she arrives at the most remote cause, British prejudice. The immediate cause is also the main (most important) cause; the other situations had existed before the famine began.

Transitions. Because Evelyn considers a series of relationships as well as an intricate causal chain, the cause-and-effect relationships in this essay are both subtle and complex. Throughout the essay, many words suggest cause-and-effect connections: *brought, caused, leading to, therefore, as a result, so, since,* and the like. These words help readers identify and understand the causal connections.

Answering an Exam Question. Before planning her answer, Evelyn read the exam question carefully. She saw that it asked for both causes and effects but that its wording directed her to spend more time on causes ("analyze") than on effects ("briefly note"), and this wording helped her to organize her discussion. In addition, she saw that she would need to indicate *explicitly* which were the causes ("government policy . . . played an important role") and which were the effects ("The most important historical result").

Evelyn's purpose was to convey factual information and, in doing so, to demonstrate her understanding of the course material. Rather than waste her limited time choosing a clever opening strategy or making elaborate attempts to engage her audience, she began her essay with a direct statement of her thesis.

Working with Sources. Evelyn was obviously influenced by outside sources; the ideas in the essay are not completely her own. Because this was an exam, however, and because the instructor expected that students would base their essays on class notes and assigned readings, Evelyn was not required to document her sources.

Focus on Revision

Because this essay was written for an exam, Evelyn had no time — and no need — to revise it further. If she had been preparing this assignment outside of class, however, she might have done more. For example, she could have added a more arresting opening, such as a brief eyewitness account of the famine's effects. Her conclusion — appropriately brief and straightforward for an exam answer — could also have been developed further, perhaps with the addition of information about the nation's eventual recovery. Finally, adding statistics, quotations by historians, or a brief summary of life in Ireland before the famine could have further enriched the essay.

PEER-EDITING WORKSHEET: Cause and Effect

1. Paraphrase the essay's thesis. Is it explicitly stated? Should it be?
2. Does the essay focus on causes, effects, or both? Does the thesis statement clearly identify this focus? If not, how should the thesis statement be revised?
3. Does the writer consider *all* relevant causes or effects? Are any key causes or effects omitted? Are any irrelevant causes or effects included?
4. Make an informal outline of the essay. What determines the order of the causes or effects? Is this the most effective order? If not, what revisions do you suggest?
5. List the transitional words and phrases used to indicate causal connections. Are any additional transitions needed? If so, where?
6. Does the writer use *post hoc* reasoning? Point out any examples of illogical reasoning.
7. Are more examples or details needed to help readers understand causal connections? If so, where?
8. Do you agree with the writer's conclusions? Why or why not?
9. Has the writer used any "the reason is because" constructions? If so, suggest revisions.
10. Are *affect* and *effect* used correctly? Point out any errors.

All the selections that follow focus on cause-and-effect relationships. Some readings focus on causes, others on effects. The first selection, a visual text, is followed by questions designed to illustrate how cause and effect can operate in visual form. (A multimodal text for cause and effect is located online at **macmillanhighered.com/patterns**.)

JEFFREY COOLIDGE

Rube Goldberg Machine

© Jeffrey Coolidge/Getty Images

• • •

Reading Images

1. This image shows a device inspired by Rube Goldberg, a cartoonist and inventor known for his complex machines that carry out simple tasks in roundabout, overly complex ways. What task is depicted here? In what straightforward way could it be completed?

2. Study the image carefully. Does every event have a cause? Does every cause have a result? Does this diagram illustrate a causal chain? Why or why not?

3. What is the end result depicted here? Which event do you see as the main cause? Which events are remote causes?

continued

Journal Entry

Write a paragraph summarizing the cause-and-effect relationships depicted in this image.

Thematic Connections

- "Getting Coffee Is Hard to Do" (page 288)
- "How to Retrieve a Candy Bar Stuck in the Lunchroom Vending Machine" (page 292)
- "Aristotle" (page 481)
- "Love and Other Catastrophes: A Mix Tape" (page 518)

NORMAN COUSINS

Who Killed Benny Paret?

Norman Cousins (1915–1990) began his career in journalism writing for the *New York Evening Post* and *Current History* magazine. In 1940, Cousins joined the *Saturday Review*, where he served as editor from 1942 to 1978. A noted social critic, Cousins lectured widely on world affairs. An adjunct professor in the department of psychiatry at the UCLA School of Medicine from 1978 until his death, he is particularly remembered for his many books urging a positive outlook to combat illness, including *Anatomy of an Illness* (1979).

Background on the hazards of boxing Cousins's classic 1962 essay "Who Killed Benny Paret?" focuses on a brutal boxing match at Madison Square Garden between Emile Griffith and Benny (Kid) Paret — a fight that led to Paret's death after nine days in a coma. The event, witnessed by millions of shocked television viewers, is the subject of a 2004 documentary, *Ring of Fire*. The fight went twelve rounds and ended with Griffith driving Paret onto the ropes and relentlessly beating him. Some newspapers reported that Griffith was angry because Paret had questioned his manhood, calling him, in Spanish (Paret was Cuban), a *maricón* (a derogatory name for a gay man). In the aftermath of the fight, many demanded that boxing be banned altogether. As a result of Paret's death, a number of rules for professional boxing were changed, but boxing remains an inherently dangerous sport. More than five hundred ring deaths have occurred in the past century; as recently as 2005, a professional boxer died following a knockout in the ring. In addition, many boxers suffer from chronic latent brain damage, known medically as *dementia pugilistica*. In answering the question posed by his essay's title, Cousins takes a strong stand against violence in boxing.

Sometime about 1935 or 1936 I had an interview with Mike Jacobs, the 1 prize-fight promoter. I was a fledgling reporter at that time; my beat was education but during the vacation season I found myself on varied assignments, all the way from ship news to sports reporting. In this way I found myself sitting opposite the most powerful figure in the boxing world.

There was nothing spectacular in Mr. Jacobs' manner or appearance; 2 but when he spoke about prize fights, he was no longer a bland little man but a colossus who sounded the way Napoleon must have sounded when he reviewed a battle. You knew you were listening to Number One. His saying something made it true.

We discussed what to him was the only important element in suc- 3 cessful promoting — how to please the crowd. So far as he was concerned, there was no mystery to it. You put killers in the ring and the people filled your arena. You hire boxing artists — men who are adroit at feinting, parrying, weaving, jabbing, and dancing, but who don't pack dynamite in their fists — and you wind up counting your empty seats. So you searched for the killers and sluggers and maulers — fellows who could hit with the force of a baseball bat.

I asked Mr. Jacobs if he was speaking literally when he said people came 4 out to see the killer.

"They don't come out to see a tea party," he said evenly. "They come 5 out to see the knockout. They come out to see a man hurt. If they think anything else, they're kidding themselves."

Recently, a young man by the name of 6 Benny Paret was killed in the ring. The killing was seen by millions; it was on television. In the twelfth round, he was hit hard in the head several times, went down, was counted out, and never came out of the coma.

> " The killing was seen by millions; it was on television. "

The Paret fight produced a flurry of in- 7 vestigations. Governor Rockefeller was shocked by what happened and appointed a committee to assess the responsibility. The New York State Boxing Commission decided to find out what was wrong. The District Attorney's office expressed its concern. One question that was solemnly studied in all three probes concerned the action of the referee. Did he act in time to stop the fight? Another question had to do with the role of the examining doctors who certified the physical fitness of the fighters before the bout. Still another question involved Mr. Paret's manager; did he rush his boy into the fight without adequate time to recuperate from the previous one?

In short, the investigators looked into every possible cause except the 8 real one. Benny Paret was killed because the human fist delivers enough impact, when directed against the head, to produce a massive hemorrhage in the brain. The human brain is the most delicate and complex mechanism in all creation. It has a lacework of millions of highly fragile nerve connections. Nature attempts to protect this exquisitely intricate machinery by encasing it in a hard shell. Fortunately, the shell is thick enough to withstand a great deal of pounding. Nature, however, can protect a man against everything except man himself. Not every blow to the head will kill a man — but there is always the risk of concussion and damage to the brain. A prize fighter may be able to survive even repeated brain concussions and go on fighting, but the damage to his brain may be permanent.

In any event, it is futile to investigate the referee's role and seek to 9 determine whether he should have intervened to stop the fight earlier. That is not where the primary responsibility lies. The primary responsibility lies with the people who pay to see a man hurt. The referee who stops a fight too soon from the crowd's viewpoint can expect to be booed. The crowd wants the knockout; it wants to see a man stretched out on the canvas. This is the supreme moment in boxing. It is nonsense to talk about prize fighting as a test of boxing skills. No crowd was ever brought to its feet screaming and cheering at the sight of two men beautifully dodging and weaving out of each other's jabs. The time the crowd comes alive is when a man is hit hard over the heart or the head, when his mouthpiece flies out, when the blood squirts out of his nose or eyes, when he wobbles under the attack and his pursuer continues to smash at him with pole-axe impact.

Don't blame it on the referee. Don't even blame it on the fight manag- 10 ers. Put the blame where it belongs — on the prevailing mores that regard prize fighting as a perfectly proper enterprise and vehicle of entertainment. No one doubts that many people enjoy prize fighting and will miss it if it should be thrown out. And that is precisely the point.

•   •   •

Comprehension

1. Why, according to Mike Jacobs, do people come to see a prize fight? Does Cousins agree with him?
2. What was the immediate cause of Paret's death? What remote causes did the investigators consider? What, according to Cousins, was the main cause — that is, where does the "primary responsibility" (9) lie?
3. Why does Cousins believe "it is futile to investigate the referee's role" (9)?
4. Cousins ends his essay with "And that is precisely the point." What is the "point" he refers to?

Purpose and Audience

1. This persuasive essay has a strong thesis. What is it?
2. This essay appeared on May 5, 1962, a month after Paret died. What do you suppose its impact was on its audience? Do you think the impact on readers is the same today?
3. At whom is this essay aimed — boxing enthusiasts, sportswriters, or a general audience? On what do you base your conclusion?
4. Does Cousins expect his audience to agree with his thesis? How does he try to win sympathy for his position?

Style and Structure

1. Do you think Cousins includes enough detail to convince readers? Where, if anywhere, might more detail be helpful?
2. Explain the complex cause-and-effect relationships discussed in paragraph 9.
3. What strategy does Cousins use in his conclusion? Is it effective? Explain your reasoning.

4. **Vocabulary Project.** The specialized vocabulary of boxing is prominent in this essay, but the facts Cousins presents would apply equally well to any sport in which violence is a potential problem.

   a. Imagine you are writing a similar essay about football, hockey, rugby, or another sport. Think about your audience, and substitute an appropriate equivalent word or phrase for each of the following.

promoter (1)	feinting, parrying, weaving,	knockout (5)
prize fights (2)	jabbing, and dancing (3)	referee (7)
in the ring (3)	killers and sluggers	fighters/fight (7)
boxing artists (3)	and maulers (3)	

   b. Rewrite these sentences so that they suit the sport you have chosen: "The crowd wants the knockout; it wants to see a man stretched out on the canvas. . . . It is nonsense to talk about prize fighting as a test of boxing skills. No crowd was ever brought to its feet screaming and cheering at the sight of two men beautifully dodging and weaving out of each other's jabs" (9).

Journal Entry

Do Cousins's graphic descriptions convince you that boxing should be outlawed? Explain.

Writing Workshop

1. **Working with Sources.** Write a cause-and-effect essay examining how you believe the pressure to excel affects professional or amateur athletes. For example, you might examine steroid use in baseball or head injuries in soccer or football. In your first paragraph, quote Cousins on this issue, citing him as your source; be sure to include a works-cited page. (See Chapter 18 for information on MLA documentation.)

2. Write a cause-and-effect essay about a time when, in response to peer pressure, you encouraged someone to do something you felt was dishonest or unwise. Be sure to identify what caused your actions.

3. Why do you think a young person might turn to a career in boxing? Write a cause-and-effect essay examining the possible motives.

Combining the Patterns

This essay begins with five paragraphs of **narration** that summarize a meeting between Cousins and Mike Jacobs. What function does this narrative introduction serve in the essay? Once Paret's death is mentioned and the persuasive portion of the essay begins, Cousins never resumes the narrative. Do you think he should have returned to this narrative? If so, where might he have continued the story?

Thematic Connections

MAGGIE KOERTH-BAKER

Why Rational People Buy into Conspiracy Theories

Maggie Koerth-Baker (b. 1981) is a science writer and science editor at *Boing Boing*, a blog devoted to technology and culture. She writes regularly for the *New York Times Magazine*, and her work has appeared in *Discover*, *Popular Science*, and other publications. Koerth-Baker is also the author of *Before the Lights Go Out: Conquering the Energy Crisis Before It Conquers Us* (2012).

Background on famous conspiracy theories In her essay, Koerth-Baker refers to historian Richard Hofstadter's famous 1965 work, *The Paranoid Style in American Politics*. For Hofstadter, American politics — and implicitly, American life — was often marked by a sense of "heated exaggeration, suspiciousness, and conspiratorial fantasy." However, the belief in such fantasies knows no geographical or temporal boundaries. For example, anti-Semitic conspiracy theories stretch back to at least the Middle Ages and, later, were infamously promoted in *The Protocols of the Elders of Zion* (1903), a fraudulent text that claimed to reveal a scheme for Jewish world domination. Despite being a hoax, *The Protocols* appealed to prominent figures like Adolf Hitler and Henry Ford. As Hofstadter suggested, however, the United States has long been fertile ground for conspiracy theories, as in the case of nineteenth-century American fears of Catholics and Freemasons. In the twentieth century, many such theories flourished — often related to communism and the dangerous presence of internal enemies. A case in point: Some Americans viewed the widespread fluoridation of the United States water supply in the 1950s and early 1960s as a subversive plot. Other conspiracies have focused on extraterrestrials and the government cover-up of alien activity, as in the case of Area 51, a military installation in Nevada that has long been a topic of conspiracy theorists. As Hofstadter noted, American politics (and political figures) has often attracted conspiratorial thinking. This is evident in such recent theories as "The Clinton Body Count" (a list of people supposedly killed directly or indirectly by President Bill Clinton); the belief that President George W. Bush was actively complicit in the September 11, 2001, terrorist attacks; and the claim that President Barack Obama is not a U.S. citizen.

In the days following the bombings at the Boston Marathon, specula- 1
tion online regarding the identity and motive of the unknown perpetrator or perpetrators was rampant. And once the Tsarnaev brothers were identified and the manhunt came to a close, the speculation didn't cease. It took a new form. A sampling: Maybe the brothers Tsarnaev were just patsies, fall guys set up to take the heat for a mysterious Saudi with high-level connections; or maybe they were innocent, but instead of the Saudis, the actual

bomber had acted on behalf of a rogue branch of our own government; or what if the Tsarnaevs were behind the attacks, but were secretly working for a larger organization?

Crazy as these theories are, those propagating them are not—they're quite normal, in fact. But recent scientific research tells us this much: if you think one of the theories above is plausible, you probably feel the same way about the others, even though they contradict one another. And it's very likely that this isn't the only news story that makes you feel as if shadowy forces are behind major world events.

"The best predictor of belief in a conspiracy theory is belief in other conspiracy theories," says Viren Swami, a psychology professor who studies conspiracy belief at the University of Westminster in England. Psychologists say that's because a conspiracy theory isn't so much a response to a single event as it is an expression of an overarching worldview.

As Richard Hofstadter wrote in his seminal 1965 book, *The Paranoid Style in American Politics*, conspiracy theories, especially those involving meddlesome foreigners, are a favorite pastime in this nation. Americans have always had the sneaking suspicion that somebody was out to get us—be it Freemasons, Catholics, or communists. But in recent years, it seems as if every tragedy comes with a round of yarn-spinning, as the Web fills with stories about "false flag" attacks and "crisis actors"—not mere theorizing but arguments for the existence of a completely alternate version of reality.

Since Hofstadter's book was published, our access to information has vastly improved, which you would think would have helped minimize such wild speculation. But according to recent scientific research on the matter, it most likely only serves to make theories more convincing to the public. What's even more surprising is that this sort of theorizing isn't limited to those on the margins. Perfectly sane minds possess an incredible capacity for developing narratives, and even some of the wildest conspiracy theories can be grounded in rational thinking, which makes them that much more pernicious. Consider this: 63 percent of registered American voters believe in at least one political conspiracy theory, according to a recent poll conducted by Fairleigh Dickinson University.

While psychologists can't know exactly what goes on inside our heads, they have, through surveys and laboratory studies, come up with a set of traits that correlate well with conspiracy belief. In 2010, Swami and a co-author summarized this research in *The Psychologist*, a scientific journal. They found, perhaps surprisingly, that believers are more likely to be cynical about the world in general and politics in particular. Conspiracy theories also seem to be more compelling to those with low self-worth, especially with regard to their sense of agency in the world at large. Conspiracy theories appear to be a way of reacting to uncertainty and powerlessness.

> " Conspiracy theories appear to be a way of reacting to uncertainty and powerlessness. "

Economic recessions, terrorist attacks, and natural disasters are mas- 7
sive, looming threats, but we have little power over when they occur or how
or what happens afterward. In these moments of powerlessness and uncertainty, a part of the brain called the amygdala kicks into action. Paul
Whalen, a scientist at Dartmouth College who studies the amygdala, says it
doesn't exactly do anything on its own. Instead, the amygdala jump-starts
the rest of the brain into analytical overdrive — prompting repeated reas-
sessments of information in an attempt to create a coherent and understandable narrative, to understand what just happened, what threats still
exist, and what should be done now. This may be a useful way to understand how, writ large, the brain's capacity for generating new narratives
after shocking events can contribute to so much paranoia in this country.

"If you know the truth and others don't, that's one way you can reas- 8
sert feelings of having agency," Swami says. It can be comforting to do your
own research even if that research is flawed. It feels good to be the wise old
goat in a flock of sheep.

Surprisingly, Swami's work has also turned up a correlation between 9
conspiracy theorizing and strong support of democratic principles. But
this isn't quite so strange if you consider the context. Kathryn Olmsted, a
historian at the University of California, Davis, says that conspiracy theories wouldn't exist in a world in which real conspiracies don't exist. And
those conspiracies — Watergate or the Iran-Contra Affair — often involve manipulating and circumventing the democratic process. Even people who
believe that the Sandy Hook shooting was actually a drama staged by actors couch their arguments in concern for the preservation of the Second
Amendment.

Our access to high-quality information has not, unfortunately, ush- 10
ered in an age in which disagreements of this sort can easily be solved with
a quick Google search. In fact, the Internet has made things worse. Confirmation bias — the tendency to pay more attention to evidence that supports what you already believe — is a well-documented and common human
failing. People have been writing about it for centuries. In recent years,
though, researchers have found that confirmation bias is not easy to overcome. You can't just drown it in facts.

In 2006, the political scientists Brendan Nyhan and Jason Reifler iden- 11
tified a phenomenon called the "backfire effect." They showed that efforts
to debunk inaccurate political information can leave people more convinced that false information is true than they would have been otherwise.
Nyhan isn't sure why this happens, but it appears to be more prevalent
when the bad information helps bolster a favored worldview or ideology.

In that way, Swami says, the Internet and other media have helped per- 12
petuate paranoia. Not only does more exposure to these alternative narratives help engender belief in conspiracies, he says, but the Internet's tendency toward tribalism helps reinforce misguided beliefs.

And that's a problem. Because while believing George W. Bush helped 13
plan the September 11 attacks might make you *feel* in control, it doesn't

actually make you so. Earlier this year, Karen Douglas, a University of Kent psychologist, along with a student, published research in which they exposed people to conspiracy theories about climate change and the death of Princess Diana. Those who got information supporting the theories but not information debunking them were more likely to withdraw from participation in politics and were less likely to take action to reduce their carbon footprints.

Alex Jones, a syndicated radio host, can build fame as a conspiracy peddler; politicians can hint at conspiracies for votes and leverage; but if conspiracy theories are a tool the average person uses to reclaim his sense of agency and access to democracy, it's an ineffective tool. It can even have dangerous health implications. For example, research has shown that African Americans who believe AIDS is a weapon loosed on them by the government (remembering the abuses of the Tuskegee experiment) are less likely to practice protected sex. And if you believe that governments or corporations are hiding evidence that vaccines harm children, you're less likely to have your children vaccinated. The result: pockets of measles and whooping-cough infections and a few deaths in places with low child-vaccination rates.   14

Psychologists aren't sure whether powerlessness causes conspiracy theories or vice versa. Either way, the current scientific thinking suggests these beliefs are nothing more than an extreme form of cynicism, a turning away from politics and traditional media — which only perpetuates the problem.   15

•   •   •

Comprehension

1. What is a conspiracy theory? List some examples Koerth-Baker gives to illustrate this concept.
2. In paragraph 3, Koerth-Baker cites psychologists who say that "a conspiracy theory isn't so much a response to a single event as it is an expression of an overarching worldview." What do these psychologists mean?
3. What is "confirmation bias" (10)? What is the "backfire effect" (11)?
4. What traits "correlate well with conspiracy belief" (6)? How is belief in conspiracy theories related to "strong support of democratic principles" (9)?
5. How do the Internet and other media help to "perpetuate paranoia" (12)?
6. According to Koerth-Baker, exactly why do "rational people buy into conspiracy theories"?
7. What *effects* of belief in conspiracy theories does Koerth-Baker identify? Does she see these effects as generally positive or negative?

Purpose and Audience

1. This essay addresses a serious issue and relies for support on expert testimony, yet its style and tone are quite informal. What does this tell you about the writer's purpose and intended audience?

2. Koerth-Baker quotes psychology professor Viren Swami and political scientist Richard Hofstadter and also cites historians and scientists. How do these experts support the point she is making?

3. Why do you think Koerth-Baker uses the phrase "rational people" (instead of just "people") in her title? How is her audience likely to respond to this phrase? How does she appeal to her audience in a similar way elsewhere in the essay—for example, with the statistic in paragraph 5?

4. Could any of the following serve as the thesis of this essay?

   - "Crazy as these theories are, those propagating them are not—they're quite normal, in fact." (2)
   - " 'The best predictor of belief in a conspiracy theory is belief in other conspiracy theories.' " (3)
   - "Psychologists aren't sure whether powerlessness causes conspiracy theories or vice versa." (15)

   Why or why not? Can you suggest a more appropriate thesis statement for this essay?

Style and Structure

1. As the title suggests, this essay's primary focus is on the causes of conspiracy theories. Where does Koerth-Baker discuss the effects?

2. Could this essay be diagrammed as a causal chain? Try to create a diagram to show how each effect causes another.

3. **Vocabulary Project.** What is paranoia? Look up this word in a few different dictionaries—including a medical or psychological dictionary—and explain how it might be related to belief in conspiracy theories.

Journal Entry

Reread this essay's first paragraph. Do any of the rumors Koerth-Baker cites seem plausible to you? Why or why not?

Writing Workshop

1. Visit one of the many conspiracy theory sites on the Web, and skim some of the theories described there. Identify one theory that you think makes sense. Then, write a cause-and-effect essay in which you explain what led you to accept this theory.

2. **Working with Sources.** Conspiracy theories have been popular throughout history. Consult a few websites to get an overview of some popular conspiracy theories—for example, those surrounding the moon landing, 9/11, the assassination of JFK, or another historical event—and ask some of your friends which of these theories they find believable. Then, write an essay in which you try to account for what might have caused these theories—and some possible effects of such beliefs. Be sure to provide parenthetical documentation for any references to Koerth-Baker's

essay, and include a works-cited page. (See Chapter 18 for information on MLA documentation.)

Combining the Patterns

Koerth-Baker's essay uses **exemplification** to illustrate the causes and effects of conspiracy theories. Does she include enough examples? Could she have included more, or better, examples?

Thematic Connections

- "Ground Zero" (page 175)
- "Just Walk On By: A Black Man Ponders His Power to Alter Public Space" (page 238)
- "The Lottery" (page 308)
- "The Ways We Lie" (page 471)

LAWRENCE OTIS GRAHAM

The "Black Table" Is Still There

Lawrence Otis Graham was born in 1962 into one of the few African-American families living in an upper-middle-class community in Westchester County, near New York City. A graduate of Princeton University and Harvard Law School, Graham works as a corporate attorney in Manhattan. He is the author of some dozen books, most recently *Our Kind of People: Inside America's Black Upper Class* (1999) and *The Senator and the Socialite: The True Story of America's First Black Dynasty* (2007). The following essay, originally published in the *New York Times* in 1991, is included in Graham's 1995 essay collection, *Member of the Club: Reflections on Life in a Racially Polarized World.*

Background on school segregation In "The 'Black Table' Is Still There," Graham returns to his largely white junior high school and discovers to his dismay how little has changed since the 1970s. Since the 1950s, the United States government has strongly supported integration of public schools. For example, the Supreme Court in 1954 found segregation of public schools unconstitutional; the Civil Rights Act of 1964 required public school systems to implement integration programs; and in 1971, the Supreme Court upheld court-ordered busing as a means of achieving integration. The results of these policies were dramatic. From the mid-1960s to 1972, the number of African-American students attending desegregated schools jumped from 12 percent to 44 percent. By the 1990s, however, this had begun to change as the Supreme Court began to lift desegregation orders in response to local school boards' promises to desegregate voluntarily through magnet schools and the like. A study published in 2003 showed that two-thirds of African-American students attend schools that are predominantly minority and more than 15 percent attend schools that are 99 to 100 percent minority, a significant rise since 1989. Ironically, as Graham observes, when students are given the choice, self-segregation seems to be the norm.

During a recent visit to my old junior high school in Westchester County, I came upon something that I never expected to see again, something that was a source of fear and dread for three hours each school morning of my early adolescence: the all-black lunch table in the cafeteria of my predominantly white suburban junior high school. 1

As I look back on twenty-seven years of often being the first and only black person integrating such activities and institutions as the college newspaper, the high school tennis team, summer music camps, our all-white suburban neighborhood, my eating club at Princeton, or my private social club at Harvard Law School, the one scenario that puzzled me the most then and now is the all-black lunch table. 2

Why was it there? Why did the black kids separate themselves? What 3 did the table say about the integration that was supposedly going on in homerooms and gym classes? What did it say about the black kids? The white kids? What did it say about me when I refused to sit there, day after day, for three years?

Each afternoon, at 12:03 P.M., after the fourth period ended, I found 4 myself among six hundred 12-, 13-, and 14-year-olds who marched into the brightly-lit cafeteria and dashed for a seat at one of the twenty-seven blue formica lunch tables.

No matter who I walked in with — usually a white friend — no matter 5 what mood I was in, there was one thing that was certain: I would not sit at the black table.

I would never consider sitting at the 6 black table.

What was wrong with me? What was I 7 afraid of?

I would like to think that my decision 8 was a heroic one, made in order to express my solidarity with the theories of integration that my community was espousing. But I was just twelve at the time, and there was nothing heroic in my actions.

> " I would never consider sitting at the black table.
> What was wrong with me? What was I afraid of? "

I avoided the black table for a very simple 9 reason: I was afraid that by sitting at the black table I'd lose all my white friends. I thought that by sitting there I'd be making a racist, anti-white statement.

Is that what the all-black table means? Is it a rejection of white people? 10 I no longer think so.

At the time, I was angry that there was a black lunch table. I believed 11 that the black kids were the reason why other kids didn't mix more. I was ready to believe that their self-segregation was the cause of white bigotry.

Ironically, I even believed this after my best friend (who was white) told 12 me I probably shouldn't come to his bar mitzvah because I'd be the only black and people would feel uncomfortable. I even believed this after my Saturday afternoon visit, at age ten, to a private country club pool prompted incensed white parents to pull their kids from the pool in terror.

In the face of this blatantly racist (anti-black) behavior I still somehow 13 managed to blame only the black kids for being the barrier to integration in my school and my little world. What was I thinking?

I realize now how wrong I was. During that same time, there were at 14 least two tables of athletes, an Italian table, a Jewish girls' table, a Jewish boys' table (where I usually sat), a table of kids who were into heavy metal music and smoking pot, a table of middle-class Irish kids. Weren't these tables just as segregationist as the black table? At the time, no one thought so. At the time, no one even acknowledged the segregated nature of these other tables.

Maybe it's the color difference that makes all-black tables or all-black 15
groups attract the scrutiny and wrath of so many people. It scares and angers people; it exasperates. It did those things to me, and I'm black.

As an integrating black person, I know that my decision *not* to join the 16
black lunch table attracted its own kinds of scrutiny and wrath from my
classmates. At the same time that I heard angry words like "Oreo" and
"white boy" being hurled at me from the black table, I was also dodging
impatient questions from white classmates: "Why do all those black kids
sit together?" or "Why don't you ever sit with the other blacks?"

The black lunch table, like those other segregated tables, is a comment 17
on the superficial inroads that integration has made in society. Perhaps I
should be happy that even this is a long way from where we started. Yet,
I can't get over the fact that the twenty-seventh table in my junior high
school cafeteria is still known as the "black table" — fourteen years after my
adolescence.

· · ·

Comprehension

1. What exactly is the "black table"?
2. In paragraph 1, Graham says that on a recent visit to his old school he
   "came upon something that [he] never expected to see again." Why do you
   think the sight of the all-black lunch table was such a surprise to him?
3. In Graham's school, what factors determined where students sat?
4. Why didn't Graham sit at the "black table"?
5. When he was a student, whom did Graham blame for the existence of the
   exclusively black lunch table? Whom or what does he now see as the cause
   of the table's existence?

Purpose and Audience

1. What is Graham's thesis?
2. Rather than introducing outside supporting information — such as statistics, interviews with educators, or sociological studies — Graham relies
   on his own opinions and on anecdotal evidence to support his thesis. Do
   you think this is enough? Explain your reasoning.
3. Why does Graham give background information about himself in this
   essay — for example, in paragraphs 2 and 12? How does this information
   affect your reaction to him as a person? Your reaction to his essay? Do
   you think he needs to supply additional information about himself or
   about his school? If so, what kind of information would be helpful?
4. Do you think Graham's primary purpose here is to criticize a system he
   despises, to change his audience's views about segregated lunch tables, or
   to justify his own behavior? Explain your conclusion.

5. In paragraph 5, Graham tells readers that he usually entered the cafeteria with a white friend; in paragraph 12, he reveals that his best friend was white. Why do you suppose he wants his audience to know these facts?

Style and Structure

1. **Vocabulary Project.** Does the phrase *black table* have a negative connotation for you? Do you think Graham intends it to? What other names could he give to the table that might present it in a more neutral, even positive, light? What names could he give to the other tables he lists in paragraph 14?

2. Throughout his essay, Graham asks **rhetorical questions**. Identify as many of these questions as you can. Are they necessary? Provocative? Distracting? Explain.

3. In paragraph 16, Graham quotes his long-ago classmates. What do these quotations reveal? Should he have included more of them?

4. Is Graham's focus on finding causes, describing effects, or both? Explain.

5. This essay uses first-person pronouns and contractions. Do you think Graham would have more credibility if he used a less personal and more formal style?

Journal Entry

Graham sees the continued presence of the "black table" as a serious problem. Do you agree?

Writing Workshop

1. **Working with Sources.** In paragraph 14, Graham mentions other lunch tables that were limited to certain groups and asks, "Weren't these tables just as segregationist as the black table?" Answer his question in a cause-and-effect essay explaining why you believe "black tables" still exist today. In your introduction, quote Graham's question, and be sure to include parenthetical documentation for any references to Graham's essay; also include a works-cited page. (See Chapter 18 for information on MLA documentation.)

2. In addition to self-segregated lunch tables, many colleges also have single-race social clubs, dormitories, fraternities, and even graduation ceremonies. Do you see such self-segregation as something that divides our society (that is, as a cause) or as something that reflects divisions that already exist (that is, as an effect)? Write an essay discussing this issue, supporting your thesis with examples from your own experience.

3. Do the people at your school or workplace tend to segregate themselves according to race, gender, or some other principle? Do you see a problem

in such behavior? Write an email to your school's dean of students or to your employer explaining what you believe causes this pattern and what effects, positive or negative, you have observed.

Combining the Patterns

In paragraph 14, Graham uses **classification and division**. What is he categorizing? What categories does he identify? What other categories might he include? Why is this pattern of development particularly appropriate for this essay?

Thematic Connections

- "Indian Education" (page 142)
- "The Myth of the Latin Woman: I Just Met a Girl Named Maria" (page 230)
- "Just Walk On By: A Black Man Ponders His Power to Alter Public Space" (page 238)
- "College Pressures" (page 448)

LINDA M. HASSELSTROM

A Peaceful Woman Explains Why She Carries a Gun

Linda M. Hasselstrom (b. 1943) grew up in rural South Dakota in a cattle ranching family. After receiving a master's degree in journalism from the University of Missouri, she returned to South Dakota to run her own ranch and now divides her time between South Dakota and Cheyenne, Wyoming. A highly respected poet, essayist, and writing teacher, she often focuses on everyday life in the American West in her work. Her publications include the poetry collections *Caught by One Wing* (1984), *Roadkill* (1987), and *Dakota Bones* (1991); the essay collection *Land Circle* (1991); and several books about ranching, including *Feels Like Far: A Rancher's Life on the Great Plains* (1999) and *Between Grass and Sky: Where I Live and Work* (2002). Her most recent book is *Dirt Songs: A Plains Duet* (2011). In this essay from *Land Circle*, Hasselstrom explains her reluctant decision to become licensed to carry a concealed handgun.

Background on incidences of sexual assault Hasselstrom's gun ownership can certainly be considered in the context of the ongoing debate over how (and even whether) stricter gun safety measures should be enacted in the United States. In 2008, the Supreme Court overturned a thirty-two-year ban on handguns in Washington, DC, concluding that the ban violated individuals' right to keep and bear arms. In a ruling in 2010, it extended Second Amendment protection to every jurisdiction in the nation. Equally important, however, is the fact that Hasselstrom's reason for carrying a gun is to protect herself from sexual assault. According to the 2008 National Crime Victimization survey, more than 200,000 women reported being sexually assaulted in this country in that year. It is estimated that only one in six instances of sexual assault is actually reported to the police, so the number of such attacks is, in reality, much higher. A 2009 study conducted by the National Shooting Sports Foundation found that gun purchases by women were increasing and that 80 percent of the female gun buyers who responded to the survey had purchased a gun for self-defense.

I am a peace-loving woman. But several events in the past ten years 1 have convinced me I'm safer when I carry a pistol. This was a personal decision, but because handgun possession is a controversial subject, perhaps my reasoning will interest others.

I live in western South Dakota on a ranch twenty-five miles from the 2 nearest town: for several years I spent winters alone here. As a freelance writer, I travel alone a lot — more than 100,000 miles by car in the last four years. With women freer than ever before to travel alone, the odds of our encountering trouble seem to have risen. Distances are great, roads are deserted, and the terrain is often too exposed to offer hiding places.

A woman who travels alone is advised, usually by men, to protect her- 3 self by avoiding bars and other "dangerous situations," by approaching her car like an Indian scout, by locking doors and windows. But these precautions aren't always enough. I spent years following them and still found myself in dangerous situations. I began to resent the idea that just because I am female, I have to be extra careful.

A few years ago, with another woman, I camped for several weeks in the 4 West. We discussed self-defense, but neither of us had taken a course in it. She was against firearms, and local police told us Mace was illegal. So we armed ourselves with spray cans of deodorant tucked into our sleeping bags. We never used our improvised Mace because we were lucky enough to camp beside people who came to our aid when men harassed us. But on one occasion we visited a national park where our assigned space was less than fifteen feet from other campers. When we returned from a walk, we found our closest neighbors were two young men. As we gathered our cooking gear, they drank beer and loudly discussed what they would do to us after dark. Nearby campers, even families, ignored them: rangers strolled past, unconcerned. When we asked the rangers point-blank if they would protect us, one of them patted my shoulder and said, "Don't worry, girls. They're just kidding." At dusk we drove out of the park and hid our camp in the woods a few miles away. The illegal spot was lovely, but our enjoyment of that park was ruined. I returned from the trip determined to reconsider the options available for protecting myself.

At that time, I lived alone on the ranch and taught night classes in 5 town. Along a city street I often traveled, a woman had a flat tire, called for help on her CB radio, and got a rapist who left her beaten. She was afraid to call for help again and stayed in her car until morning. For that reason, as well as because CBs work best along line-of-sight, which wouldn't help much in the rolling hills where I live, I ruled out a CB.

As I drove home one night, a car followed me. It passed me on a narrow 6 bridge while a passenger flashed a blinding spotlight in my face. I braked sharply. The car stopped, angled across the bridge, and four men jumped out. I realized the locked doors were useless if they broke the windows of my pickup. I started forward, hoping to knock their car aside so I could pass. Just then another car appeared, and the men hastily got back in their car. They continued to follow me, passing and repassing. I dared not go home because no one else was there. I passed no lighted houses. Finally they pulled over to the roadside, and I decided to use their tactic: fear. Speeding, the pickup horn blaring, I swerved as close to them as I dared as I roared past. It worked: they turned off the highway. But I was frightened and angry. Even in my vehicle I was too vulnerable.

Other incidents occurred over the years. One day I glanced out at a 7 field below my house and saw a man with a shotgun walking toward a pond full of ducks. I drove down and explained that the land was posted. I politely asked him to leave. He stared at me, and the muzzle of the shotgun began to rise. In a moment of utter clarity I realized that I was alone on the ranch, and that he could shoot me and simply drive away. The moment passed: the man left.

One night, I returned home from teaching a class to find deep tire ruts 8 in the wet ground of my yard, garbage in the driveway, and a large gas tank empty. A light shone in the house: I couldn't remember leaving it on. I was too embarrassed to drive to a neighboring ranch and wake someone up. An hour of cautious exploration convinced me the house was safe, but once inside, with the doors locked, I was still afraid. I kept thinking of how vulnerable I felt, prowling around my own house in the dark.

My first positive step was to take a kung fu class, which teaches eva- 9 sive or protective action when someone enters your space without permission. I learned to move confidently, scanning for possible attackers. I learned how to assess danger and techniques for avoiding it without combat.

I also learned that one must practice several hours every day to be good 10 at kung fu. By that time I had married George: when I practiced with him, I learned how *close* you must be to your attacker to use martial arts, and decided a 120-pound woman dare not let a six-foot, 220-pound attacker get that close unless she is very, very good at self-defense. I have since read articles by several women who were extremely well trained in the martial arts, but were raped and beaten anyway.

I thought back over the times in my life when I had been attacked or 11 threatened and tried to be realistic about my own behavior, searching for anything that had allowed me to become a victim. Overall, I was convinced that I had not been at fault. I don't believe myself to be either paranoid or a risk-taker, but I wanted more protection.

With some reluctance I decided to try carrying a pistol. George had 12 always carried one, despite his size and his training in martial arts. I practiced shooting until I was sure I could hit an attacker who moved close enough to endanger me. Then I bought a license from the county sheriff, making it legal for me to carry the gun concealed.

But I was not yet ready to defend myself. George taught me that the 13 most important preparation was mental: convincing myself I could actually *shoot a person*. Few of us wish to hurt or kill another human being. But there is no point in having a gun — in fact, gun possession might increase your danger — unless you know you can use it. I got in the habit of rehearsing, as I drove or walked, the precise conditions that would be required before I would shoot someone.

People who have not grown up with the idea that they are capable of 14 protecting themselves — in other words, most women — might have to work hard to convince themselves of their ability, and of the necessity. Handgun ownership need not turn us into gunslingers, but it can be part of believing in, and relying on, *ourselves* for protection.

To be useful, a pistol has to be available. In my car, it's within instant 15 reach. When I enter a deserted rest stop at night, it's in my purse, with my hand on the grip. When I walk from a dark parking lot into a motel, it's in my hand, under a coat. At home, it's on the headboard. In short, I take it with me almost everywhere I go alone.

Just carrying a pistol is not protection; avoidance is still the best   16
approach to trouble. Subconsciously watching for signs of danger, I believe I've become more alert. Handgun use, not unlike driving, becomes instinctive. Each time I've drawn my gun — I have never fired it at another human being — I've simply found it in my hand.

I was driving the half-mile to the highway mailbox one day when I saw   17
a vehicle parked about midway down the road. Several men were standing in the ditch, relieving themselves. I have no objection to emergency urination, but I noticed they'd dumped several dozen beer cans in the road. Besides being ugly, cans can slash a cow's feet or stomach.

The men noticed me before they finished and made quite a perfor-   18
mance out of zipping their trousers while walking toward me. All four of them gathered around my small foreign car, and one of them demanded what the hell I wanted.

"This is private land. I'd appreciate it if you'd pick up the beer cans."   19

"What beer cans?" said the belligerent one, putting both hands on the   20
car door and leaning in my window. His face was inches from mine, and the beer fumes were strong. The others laughed. One tried the passenger door, locked; another put his foot on the hood and rocked the car. They circled, lightly thumping the roof, discussing my good fortune in meeting them and the benefits they were likely to bestow upon me. I felt very small and very trapped and they knew it.

"The ones you just threw out," I said politely.   21

"I don't see no beer cans. Why don't you get out here and show them to   22
me, honey?" said the belligerent one, reaching for the handle inside my door.

"Right over there," I said, still being polite. " — there, and over there." I   23
pointed with the pistol, which I'd slipped under my thigh. Within one minute the cans and the men were back in the car and headed down the road.

I believe this incident illustrates several important principles. The men   24
were trespassing and knew it: their judgment may have been impaired by alcohol. Their response to the polite request of a woman alone was to use their size, numbers, and sex to inspire fear. The pistol was a response in the same language. Politeness didn't work: I couldn't match them in size or number. Out of the car, I'd have been more vulnerable. The pistol just changed the balance of power. It worked again recently when I was driving in a desolate part of Wyoming. A man played cat-and-mouse with me for thirty miles, ultimately trying to run me off the road. When his car passed mine with only two inches to spare, I showed him my pistol, and he disappeared.

> "The pistol just changed the balance of power."

When I got my pistol, I told my husband, revising the old Colt slogan,   25
"God made men *and women,* but Sam Colt made them equal." Recently I

have seen a gunmaker's ad with a similar sentiment. Perhaps this is an idea whose time has come, though the pacifist inside me will be saddened if the only way women can achieve equality is by carrying weapons.

We must treat a firearm's power with caution. "Power tends to corrupt, 26 and absolute power corrupts absolutely," as a man (Lord Acton) once said. A pistol is not the only way to avoid being raped or murdered in today's world, but, intelligently wielded, it can shift the balance of power and provide a measure of safety.

. . .

Comprehension

1. According to Hasselstrom, why does she carry a gun? In one sentence, summarize her rationale.

2. List the specific events that led Hasselstrom to her decision to carry a gun.

3. Other than carrying a gun, what means of protecting herself did Hasselstrom try? Why did she find these strategies unsatisfactory? Can you think of other strategies she could have adopted instead of carrying a gun?

4. Where in the essay does Hasselstrom express her reluctance to carry a gun?

5. In paragraph 13, Hasselstrom says that possessing a gun "might increase your danger — unless you know you can use it." Where else does she touch on the possible pitfalls of carrying a gun?

6. What does Hasselstrom mean when she says, "The pistol just changed the balance of power" (24)?

Purpose and Audience

1. How does paragraph 1 establish Hasselstrom's purpose for writing this essay? What other purpose might she have?

2. What purpose does paragraph 5 serve? Is it necessary?

3. Do you think that this essay is aimed primarily at men or at women? Explain.

4. Do you think Hasselstrom expects her readers to agree with her position? Where does she indicate that she expects them to challenge her? How does she address this challenge?

Style and Structure

1. This essay is written in the first person, and it relies heavily on personal experience. Do you see this as a strength or a weakness? Explain.

2. What is the main cause in this cause-and-effect essay — that is, what is the most important reason Hasselstrom gives for carrying a gun? Can you identify any contributory causes?

3. Could you argue that simply being a woman is justification enough for carrying a gun? Do you think this is Hasselstrom's position? Explain.

4. Think of Hasselstrom's essay as the first step in a possible causal chain. What situations might result from her decision to carry a gun?

5. In paragraph 25, Hasselstrom says that "the pacifist inside me will be saddened if the only way women can achieve equality is by carrying weapons." In her title and elsewhere in the essay, Hasselstrom characterizes herself as a "peaceful woman." Do you think she is successful in portraying herself as a peace-loving woman who only reluctantly carries a gun?

6. **Vocabulary Project.** Some of the words and phrases Hasselstrom uses in this essay suggest that she sees her pistol as an equalizer, something that helps to compensate for her vulnerability. Identify the words and phrases she uses to characterize her gun in this way.

Journal Entry

Do you agree that carrying a gun is Hasselstrom's only choice, or do you think she could take other steps to ensure her safety? Explain.

Writing Workshop

1. Hasselstrom lives in a rural area, and the scenarios she describes apply to rural life. Rewrite this essay as "A Peaceful Urban (or Suburban) Woman Explains Why She Carries a Gun."

2. **Working with Sources.** What reasons might a "peace-loving" *man* have for carrying a gun? Write a cause-and-effect essay outlining such a man's motives, using any of Hasselstrom's reasons that might apply to him as well. Be sure to include parenthetical documentation for any references to Hasselstrom's essay and to include a works-cited page. (See Chapter 18 for information on MLA documentation.)

3. Write a cause-and-effect essay presenting reasons to support a position that opposes Hasselstrom's: "A Peaceful Woman (or Man) Explains Why She (or He) Refuses to Carry a Gun."

Combining the Patterns

Several times in her essay, Hasselstrom uses **narration** to support her position. Identify these narrative passages. Are they absolutely essential to the essay? Could they be briefer? Could some be deleted? Explain.

Thematic Connections

MAX BROOKS

The Movies That Rose from the Grave

Born in 1972, Max Brooks is a writer, graphic novelist, actor, and voice-over actor. He is the author of several books on zombies, including *The Zombie Survival Guide: Complete Protection from the Living Dead* (2003) and *World War Z: An Oral History of the Zombie War* (2013). He has also written the graphic novels *G.I. Joe: Hearts and Minds* (2010) and *The Harlem Hellfighters* (2014).

Background on zombies Originating in Haitian folklore and brought into the foreground of American pop culture with the 1968 hit horror film *Night of the Living Dead*, zombies have been a popular fixation ever since. The undead are a pop cultural phenomenon that extends into recent movies such as *The Dead* (2010) and Brooks's *World War Z* (2013); television shows such as *The Walking Dead*; books such as *Pride, Prejudice, and Zombies* (2009); video games such as *All Zombies Must Die!*; and countless websites and graphic novels. Even the U.S. government has taken part in the zombie craze: in 2011, the Centers for Disease Control and Prevention website published a humorous preparedness guide for responding to a zombie apocalypse. As zombies have proliferated in popular culture, so have theories to explain their current — and enduring — popularity. For example, cultural critic Chuck Klosterman has suggested that zombies resonate with us because they are unavoidable and unstoppable, "like the Internet and the media and every conversation we don't want to have." But the twenty-first-century preoccupation with zombies perhaps also speaks to our anxieties about life, disease, and death — as well as to our uneasiness about the rise of consumerism, the loss of community, and the speed of scientific progress.

It will never die! It may disappear for a while, stay out of sight, out of mind, but sooner or later it will rise again, and no matter what we do, or how hard we try, it will never, ever die. A zombie? Hardly, rather our own fascination with what popular culture now refers to as "the living dead." 1

Zombies have dominated mainstream horror for more than half a decade. They're everywhere: movies, books, videogames, comics, even a new Broadway musical adaptation of Sam Raimi's *The Evil Dead*. Not only have they replaced previous alpha-monsters such as vampires and werewolves, but they are continuing to generate more interest (and revenue) than almost all other creatures put together. Given that several years ago the living dead were considered an obscure and largely underground sub-genre, it would not be an exaggeration to state that they have enjoyed a spectacular rebirth unlike anything in the history of modern horror. 2

Where did these creatures come from? Why are they so popular now? And when, if ever, will their reign of terror cease? 3

Although many cultures have their own myths concerning the raising of the dead (one going as far back as the epic of Gilgamesh), the word 4 "zombie" can trace its origins back to west Africa. The legend involves a "houngan" (wizard) using a magical elixir to transform a living human into a mobile, docile, and obedient corpse. The fact that this legend is deeply rooted in reality (Haitian zombie powder was discovered to contain a powerful neurotoxin that caused a live victim to behave like a resurrected corpse) may explain why, when African slaves were brought to the Americas, European colonists also embraced the notion of the living dead.

For several centuries the voodoo zombie remained the staple of tall 5 tales, stage productions, and even early Hollywood movies such as *White Zombie* (1932) and *I Walked with a Zombie* (1943). It wasn't until 1968 that up-and-coming filmmaker George A. Romero gave us a whole new reason to be afraid. *Night of the Living Dead* replaced the image of a harmless voodoo-created zombie with a hostile, flesh-eating ghoul that swelled its numbers to pandemic proportions. This new ghoul was the result of science, not magic, specifically radiation from a returning space probe. This new ghoul could, likewise, only be dispatched by a scientific solution: destroying the brain or severing it from the rest of the body. This new ghoul obeyed no one, other than its own insatiable craving for living, human flesh. In fact, this new ghoul was only referred to throughout the movie as a ghoul. The word "zombie" was never mentioned.

Romero's revolutionary creation set the stage for an entirely new genre, 6 the horror-apocalypse or "horocalypse" movie. Zombies would henceforth be associated with the collapse of modern society, a new form of walking plague that threatened to stamp out humanity. Gone were the days of suspense and darkness, of castles and swamps and remote, isolated violence. Zombies would now be waging all-out war across the silver screen, a tradition that has endured for almost forty years.

Since the premiere of *Night of the Living Dead,* many have sought to capi- 7 talize on Romero's initial success. The Italian movie *Night of the Zombie* (1980) mixed a fictional storyline with real-life footage of cannibalism in New Guinea. A similar movie, *Zombi 2,* witnessed a battle between a corpse-like stuntman and an actual man-eating shark. One Japanese film, *Wild Zero,* attempted to combine the living dead with aliens, transsexuals, and the Japanese garage band Guitar Wolf. Michael Jackson immortalized dancing zombies with his 1983 music video "Thriller." And in 1984, Romero's former writing partner, John Russo, released the zombie comedy *The Return of the Living Dead.*

While all of these works enjoyed a loyal fan base, they remained largely 8 a cult sensation until the turn of this century. The rise began slowly at first. Computer games such as *Resident Evil* and *House of the Dead* were becoming successful enough to warrant their development into movies. On the heels of those came Danny Boyle's *28 Days Later* and the remake of Romero's *Dawn of the Dead,* which knocked Mel Gibson's *The Passion of the Christ* off the top spot in the U.S. Most industry experts predicted this was just a fad. Conventional wisdom predicted a short life for the living dead. Only that didn't happen. More zombie movies were produced, including Romero's own *Land of the Dead. Resident Evil* spawned a sequel, as did *House of the Dead,* and *The Return of the Living Dead.*

The literary world was similarly inundated with zombie fiction, as was 9 the world of comics. New videogames such as *Stubbs the Zombie* and the mega-hit *Dead Rising* took their place alongside *Resident Evil* and *House of the Dead.* Even U.S. television could not escape the walking corpses. Last year, Showtime's *Masters of Horror* series broadcast one episode with dead Iraq War veterans rising from their body bags to vote against the politicians that put them there.

Why now? Why such a sudden and rav- 10 enous obsession with ghouls? Could it be the zombie authors themselves and the new levels of sophistication they are bringing to the genre? Perhaps. This new generation of writers, directors, illustrators, and programmers are the first to have grown up studying the works of Romero and his contemporaries. For them, simply re-creating the monsters of their childhood was not enough. Their zombie projects had to be faster, wilder, and, in some cases, even smarter. In some cases, they have surpassed their predecessors in all aspects. But this rise in product quality does nothing to explain society's phenomenal demand for the living dead.

> "Why now? Why such a sudden and ravenous obsession with ghouls?"

The answer to that question lies not in fiction, but current events. The 11 last six years have witnessed a bombardment of tragic events. Terrorism, war, viral outbreaks, and natural disasters have created a global undercurrent of anxiety not seen since the darkest days of the Cold War. It seems that just turning on the nightly news either shows some present calamity or one that might potentially befall us any day now.

Zombie movies present people with an outlet for their apocalyptic anx- 12 ieties without directly confronting them. The living dead are a fictional threat, as opposed to tsunamis or avian flu. No matter how scary or realistic the particular story might be, their unquestionably fictional nature makes them "safe." Someone can watch, say *Dawn of the Dead,* and witness an orgy of graphic violence and destruction, but still know in the back of their minds that, once they switch off the TV, this particular threat will simply cease to exist, something that cannot be said for terrorist docudrama *Dirty War,* or the classic nuclear nightmare *Threads.* Knowing that zombies can never really rise allows for a feeling of control, a rare and valuable thing these days.

No one can say how long this present undead explosion will be with us. 13 Perhaps they will ebb with the current trend of global chaos. Perhaps, as the dust of this decade settles, and society returns to a semblance of stability, our macabre fascinations will return to more conventional monsters, forsaking flesh-eating ghouls for good old-fashioned werewolves or vampires. No one can say. What is certain is that nothing lasts forever. What else is certain is that the living dead might go away, but they won't be gone forever. They will simply retreat underground again, waiting patiently for the day when they rise again.

•   •   •

Comprehension

1. What is a zombie? Does Brooks provide a formal definition of the word *zombie* anywhere in his essay? If so, where? If not, why not?

2. Brooks poses three questions in paragraph 3. Where does he answer each of these questions? Does he answer them all to your satisfaction?

3. Where did the myth of the zombie originate?

4. How did filmmaker George A. Romero reinvent the zombie?

5. What is a "horocalypse" movie? What two words are combined to form this new word?

6. According to Brooks, why did the zombie craze develop rapidly after the turn of the twenty-first century?

7. In general, how does Brooks account for the initial — and continuing — popularity of zombies? Does he expect this popularity to continue? Why or why not?

Purpose and Audience

1. At what kind of audience does this essay seem to be aimed? What does Brooks expect them to know about his subject? What does he expect them *not* to know? How can you tell?

2. What is this essay's thesis? Does Brooks state it directly? If so, where? If not, suggest a sentence that could serve as the thesis statement.

Style and Structure

1. Do you think Brooks's opening paragraph, with its exclamation and question, is effective? Does it succeed in drawing readers into the essay? Why or why not?

2. In paragraph 10, Brooks asks, "Why now?" and in paragraph 11 he says, "The answer to that question lies not in fiction, but current events." What does he mean? What other answers to the question does he suggest?

3. This essay examines the causes behind the popularity of zombies. Does it also consider the *effects* of this popularity? If so, where?

4. **Vocabulary Project.** What is the origin of the word *zombie*? How are the connotations of this word different from the connotations of the word *ghoul* (5)? Can you think of other synonyms for *zombie*?

Journal Entry

Why do you think zombies are so popular today in films, video games, and literature (including young-adult fiction)?

Writing Workshop

1. **Working with Sources.** How do you account for the current popularity of books, films, and video games about zombies? Write a cause-and-effect essay explaining why zombies continue to live on in the popular imagination. Be sure to include parenthetical documentation for any references to Brooks and to include a works-cited page. (See Chapter 18 for information on MLA documentation.)

2. Write an essay explaining the popularity of another icon or character—for example, the vampire, the avatar, or the transformer—in films, television, graphic fiction, or video games.

3. What effects do you think the proliferation of zombies in popular culture is having on young teenagers? Write a cause-and-effect essay discussing ways in which tales of zombies are a negative (or positive) influence on young people.

Combining the Patterns

In this essay, Brooks uses **exemplification** to illustrate how horror films featuring zombies have changed. In paragraph 5, he gives an extended example, but paragraphs 7 and 8 just offer an overview of various films and computer games. Do you think the examples in paragraphs 7 and 8 should be developed further? Why or why not?

Thematic Connections

- "Ground Zero" (page 175)
- "The Embalming of Mr. Jones" (page 301)
- "Aristotle" (page 481)

JANICE MIRIKITANI

Suicide Note (Poetry)

Janice Mirikitani, a third-generation Japanese American, was born in San Francisco in 1941 and graduated from the University of California at Los Angeles in 1962. In her poetry, Mirikitani often considers how racism in the United States affects Asian Americans, particularly the thousands of Japanese Americans held in internment camps during World War II. Her collections include *Awake in the River* (1978), *Shedding Silence* (1987), and *We, the Dangerous: New and Selected Poems* (1995). She has also edited anthologies of Japanese-American and developing-nation literature, as well as several volumes giving voice to children living in poverty. For many years, she has been president of the Glide Foundation, which sponsors outreach programs for the poor and homeless of San Francisco.

Background on teenage suicide   The following poem, which appears in *Shedding Silence,* takes the form of a suicide note written by a young Asian-American college student to her family and reveals the extreme pressure to excel placed on her by her parents and her culture. The theme, however, has considerable relevance beyond the Asian-American community. Tragically, some five thousand teenagers and young adults commit suicide annually in the United States (there are ten times as many attempts), and suicide is the third leading cause of death among fifteen- to twenty-four-year-olds. Among college students, suicide is the second leading cause of death; approximately one thousand college students take their own lives every year. The number of suicides by college students has tripled since the 1950s. Nationally there are 7.29 suicides per year for every 100,000 students. Recent extensive media coverage of a number of youth suicides caused by bullying has increased awareness of this problem and has led to proposals for stronger anti-harassment legislation.

> How many notes written . . .
> ink smeared like birdprints in snow.
>
> not good enough   not pretty enough   not smart enough
>
> dear mother and father.
> I apologize   5
> for disappointing you.
> I've worked very hard,
>
> not good enough
>
> harder, perhaps to please you.
> If only I were a son, shoulders broad   10
> as the sunset threading through pine,
> I would see the light in my mother's
> eyes, or the golden pride reflected

in my father's dream
of my wide, male hands worthy of work   15
and comfort.
I would swagger through life
muscled and bold and assured,
drawing praises to me
like currents in the bed of wind, virile   20
with confidence.

    not good enough   not pretty enough   not smart enough

I apologize.
Tasks do not come easily.
Each failure, a glacier.   25
Each disapproval, a bootprint.
Each disappointment,
ice above my river.
So I have worked hard.

        not good enough   30

My sacrifice I will drop
bone by bone, perched
on the ledge of my womanhood,
fragile as wings.

        not strong enough   35

It is snowing steadily
surely not good weather
for flying — this sparrow
sillied and dizzied by the wind
on the edge.   40

        not smart enough

I make this ledge my altar
to offer penance.
This air will not hold me,
the snow burdens my crippled wings,   45
my tears drop like bitter cloth
softly into the gutter below.

    not good enough   not pretty enough   not smart enough

        Choices thin as shaved
        ice. Notes shredded   50
        drift like snow

on my broken body,
cover me like whispers
of sorries

sorries.   55
Perhaps when they find me
they will bury
my bird bones beneath
a sturdy pine
and scatter my feathers like   60
unspoken song
over this white and cold and silent
breast of earth.

• • •

Reading Literature

1. An author's note that originally introduced this poem explained the main cause of the student's death.

   An Asian-American college student was reported to have jumped to her death from her dormitory window. Her body was found two days later under a deep cover of snow. Her suicide note contained an apology to her parents for having received less than a perfect four-point grade average.

   What other causes might have contributed to her suicide?

2. Why does the speaker believe her life would be happier if she were male? Do you think she is correct?

3. What words, phrases, and images are repeated in this poem? What effect do these repetitions have on you?

Journal Entry

Whom (or what) do you blame for teenage suicides such as the one the poem describes? How might such deaths be eliminated?

Thematic Connections

- "Midnight" (page 217)
- "Why Chinese Mothers Are Superior" (page 408)
- "College Pressures" (page 448)
- "Aristotle" (page 481)

Writing Assignments for Cause and Effect

1. **Working with Sources.** "Thirty-Eight Who Saw Murder Didn't Call the Police" (page 128), "Who Killed Benny Paret?" (page 337), and "On Dumpster Diving" (page 672) all encourage readers, either directly or indirectly, to take action rather than remain uninvolved. Using information gleaned from these essays (or from others in the text) as support for your thesis, write an essay exploring either the possible consequences of apathy, the possible causes of apathy, or both. Be sure to provide parenthetical documentation for any words or ideas that are not your own, and include a works-cited page. (See Chapter 18 for more information on MLA documentation.)

2. Write an updated version of one of this chapter's essays. For example, you might explore the kinds of pressure Lawrence Otis Graham ("The 'Black Table' Is Still There," page 348) might face as a student today.

3. A recent study concluded that the number of young adults getting driver's licenses has declined over the past few decades. Why do you think this is so? What effects might this decline have on these nondrivers—and on society as a whole? Write an essay exploring the possible causes and effects of this trend.

4. How do you account for the popularity of one of the following: Twitter, Facebook, hip-hop, video games, home schooling, reality TV, fast food, flash mobs, or sensationalist tabloids such as the *Star*? Write an essay considering remote as well as immediate causes for the success of the phenomenon you choose.

5. Between 1946 and 1964, the U.S. birthrate increased considerably. Some of the effects attributed to this "baby boom" include the 1960s antiwar movement, an increase in the crime rate, and the development of the women's movement. Write an essay exploring some possible effects on the nation's economy and politics of the baby-boom generation's growing older. What trends would you expect to find now that the first baby boomers have passed sixty-five?

6. Write an essay tracing a series of events in your life that constitutes a causal chain. Indicate clearly both the sequence of events and the causal connections among them, and be careful not to confuse coincidence with causality.

7. In recent years, almost half of American marriages ended in divorce. However, among married couples of "Generation X," born between 1965 and 1980, the divorce rate is considerably lower. To what do you attribute this decline in divorce rate? Be as specific as possible, citing "case studies" of families you are familiar with.

8. What do you see as the major cause of any one of these problems: binge drinking among college students, voter apathy, school shootings, childhood obesity, or academic cheating? Based on your identification of its cause, formulate some specific solutions for the problem you select.

9. Write an essay considering the likely effects of a severe, protracted shortage of one of the following commodities: clean water, rental

housing, cell phones, flu vaccine, books, or gasoline. You may consider a community-, city-, or statewide shortage or a nation- or worldwide crisis.

10. Write an essay exploring the causes, effects, or both of increased violence among children in the United States.

Collaborative Activity for Cause and Effect

Working in groups of four, discuss your thoughts about the homeless population, and then list four effects the presence of homeless people is having on you, your community, and our nation. Assign each member of your group to write a paragraph explaining one of the effects the group identifies. Then, arrange the paragraphs by increasing importance, moving from the least to the most significant consequence. Finally, work together to turn your individual paragraphs into an essay: write an introduction, a conclusion, and transitions between paragraphs, and include a thesis statement in paragraph 1.

Comparison and Contrast

What Is Comparison and Contrast?

In the narrowest sense, *comparison* shows how two or more things are similar, and *contrast* shows how they are different. In most writing situations, however, the two related processes of **comparison and contrast** are used together. In the following paragraph from *Disturbing the Universe,* scientist Freeman Dyson compares and contrasts two different styles of human endeavor, which he calls "the gray and the green."

Topic sentence (outlines elements of comparison)	In everything we undertake, either on earth or in the sky, we have a choice of two styles, which I call the gray and the green. The distinction between the gray and green is not sharp. Only at the extremes of the spectrum can we say without qualification, this is green and that is gray. The difference between green and gray is better explained by examples than by definitions. Factories are gray, gardens are green. Physics is gray, biology is green. Plutonium is gray, horse manure is green. Bureaucracy is gray, pioneer communities are green. Self-reproducing machines are gray, trees and children are green. Human technology is gray, God's technology is green. Clones are gray, clades* are green. Army field manuals are gray, poems are green.
Point-by-point comparison	

A special form of comparison, called **analogy**, explains one thing by comparing it to a second, more familiar thing. In the following paragraph from *The Shopping Mall High School,* Arthur G. Powell, Eleanor Farrar, and David K. Cohen use analogy to shed light on the nature of contemporary American high schools.

---

* Eds. note — A group of organisms that evolved from a common ancestor.

Topic sentence (identifies elements of analogy)	If Americans want to understand their high schools at work, they should imagine them as shopping malls. Secondary education is another consumption experience in an abundant society. Shopping malls attract a broad range of customers with different tastes and purposes. Some shop at Target, others at Bloomingdale's. In high schools a broad range of students also shop. They too can select from an astonishing variety of products and services conveniently assembled in one place with
Points of similarity	ample parking. Furthermore, in malls and schools many different kinds of transactions are possible. Both institutions bring hopeful purveyors and potential purchasers together. The former hope to maximize sales but can take nothing for granted. Shoppers have a wide discretion not only about what to buy but also about whether to buy.

Using Comparison and Contrast

Throughout our lives, we are bombarded with information from newspapers, television, radio, the Internet, and personal experience: the police strike in Memphis; city workers walk out in Philadelphia; the Senate debates government spending; taxes are raised in New Jersey. Somehow we must make sense of the jumbled facts and figures that surround us. One way we have of understanding information like this is to put it side by side with other data and then to compare and contrast. Do the police in Memphis have the same complaints as the city workers in Philadelphia? What are the differences between the two situations? Is the national debate on spending analogous to the New Jersey debate on taxes? How do they differ?

We apply comparison and contrast every day to matters that directly affect us. When we make personal decisions, we consider alternatives, asking ourselves whether one option seems better than another. Should I major in history or business? What job opportunities will each major offer me? Should I register as a Democrat, a Republican, or an Independent? What are the positions of each political party on government spending, health care, and taxes? To answer questions like these, we use comparison and contrast.

Planning a Comparison-and-Contrast Essay

Because comparison and contrast is central to our understanding of the world, this way of thinking is often called for in essays and on essay exams.

Compare and contrast the attitudes toward science and technology expressed in Fritz Lang's *Metropolis* and George Lucas's *Star Wars*. (film)

What are the similarities and differences between mitosis and meiosis? (biology)

Discuss the relative merits of establishing a partnership or setting up a corporation. (business law)

Discuss both the advantages and disadvantages of bilingual education. (education)

Recognizing Comparison-and-Contrast Assignments

You are not likely to sit down and say to yourself, "I think I'll write a comparison-and-contrast essay today. Now what can I write about?" Instead, your assignment will suggest comparison and contrast, or you will decide comparison and contrast suits your purpose. In the preceding examples, for instance, the instructors phrased their questions to tell students how to treat the material. When you read these questions, certain key words and phrases — *compare and contrast, similarities and differences, relative merits, advantages and disadvantages* — indicate you should use a comparison-and-contrast pattern to organize your essay. Sometimes you may not even need a key phrase. Consider the question "Which of the two Adamses, John or Samuel, had the greater influence on the timing and course of the American Revolution?" Here the word *greater* is enough to suggest a contrast.

Even when your assignment is not worded to suggest comparison and contrast, your purpose may indicate this pattern of development. For instance, when you **evaluate**, you frequently use comparison and contrast. If, as a student in a management course, you are asked to evaluate two health-care systems, you can begin by researching the standards experts use in their evaluations. You can then compare each system's performance with those standards and contrast the systems with each other, concluding perhaps that both systems meet minimum standards but that one is more cost-efficient than the other. Or, if you are evaluating two of this year's new cars for a consumer newsletter, you can establish some criteria — fuel economy, safety features, reliability, handling, style — and compare and contrast the cars on each criterion. If each of the cars is better in different categories, your readers will have to decide which features matter most to them.

Establishing a Basis for Comparison

Before you can compare and contrast two things, you must be sure a **basis for comparison** exists — that the two things have enough in common to justify the comparison. For example, although cats and dogs are very different, they share several significant elements: they are mammals, they make good pets, and they are intelligent. Without these shared elements, there would be no basis for comparison and nothing of importance to discuss.

A comparison should lead you beyond the obvious. For instance, at first the idea of a comparison-and-contrast essay based on an analogy between bees and people might seem absurd: after all, these two creatures differ in species, physical structure, and intelligence. In fact, their differences are so obvious that an essay based on them might seem pointless. But after further analysis, you might decide that bees and people have quite a few similarities. Both are social animals that live in complex social structures, and both have tasks to perform and roles to fulfill in their respective societies. Therefore, you *could* write about them, but you would focus on the common elements that seem most provocative — social structures and roles — rather than on dissimilar elements. If you tried to draw an analogy between bees and SUVs or humans and golf tees, however, you would run into trouble. Although some points of comparison could be found, they would be trivial. Why bother to point out that both bees and SUVs can travel great distances or that both people and tees are needed to play golf? Neither statement establishes a significant basis for comparison.

When two subjects are very similar, the differences may be worth writing about. And when two subjects are not very much alike, you may find that the similarities are worth considering.

Selecting Points for Discussion

After you decide which subjects to compare and contrast, you need to select the points you want to discuss. You do this by determining your emphasis — on similarities, differences, or both — and the major focus of your paper. If your purpose in comparing two types of houseplants is to explain that one is easier to grow than the other, you would select points having to do with plant care, not those having to do with plant biology.

When you compare and contrast, make sure you treat the same (or at least similar) points for each subject you discuss. For instance, if you were going to compare and contrast two novels, you might consider the following points in both works.

NOVEL A	NOVEL B
Minor characters	Minor characters
Major characters	Major characters
Themes	Themes

Try to avoid the common error of discussing entirely different points for each subject. Such an approach obscures any basis for comparison that might exist. The two novels, for example, could not be meaningfully compared or contrasted if you discussed dissimilar points.

NOVEL A	NOVEL B
Minor characters	Author's life
Major characters	Plot
Themes	Symbolism

Developing a Thesis Statement

After selecting the points you want to discuss, you are ready to develop your thesis statement. This **thesis statement** should tell readers what to expect in your essay, identifying not only the subjects to be compared and contrasted but also the point you will make about them. Your thesis statement should also indicate whether you will concentrate on similarities or differences or both. In addition, it may list the points of comparison and contrast in the order in which they will be discussed in the essay.

The structure of your thesis statement can indicate the emphasis of your essay. As the following sentences illustrate, a thesis statement should highlight the essay's central concern by presenting it in the independent, rather than the dependent, clause of the sentence. Notice that the structure of the first thesis statement emphasizes similarities, while the structure of the second highlights differences.

> Despite the fact that television and radio are distinctly different media, they use similar strategies to appeal to their audiences.

> Although Melville's *Moby-Dick* and London's *The Sea Wolf* are both about the sea, the minor characters, major characters, and themes of *Moby-Dick* establish its greater complexity.

Structuring a Comparison-and-Contrast Essay

Like every other type of essay in this book, a comparison-and-contrast essay has an **introduction**, several **body paragraphs**, and a **conclusion**. Within the body of your paper, you can use either of two basic comparison-and-contrast strategies — **subject by subject** or **point by point**.

As you might expect, each organizational strategy has advantages and disadvantages. In general, you should use subject-by-subject comparison when your purpose is to emphasize overall similarities or differences, and you should use point-by-point comparison when your purpose is to emphasize individual points of similarity or difference.

Using Subject-by-Subject Comparison

In a **subject-by-subject comparison**, you essentially write a separate section about each subject, and you discuss the same points for both subjects. Use your basis for comparison to guide your selection of points, and arrange these points in some logical order, usually in order of their increasing significance. The following informal outline illustrates a subject-by-subject comparison.

Introduction:	Thesis statement — Despite the fact that television and radio are distinctly different media, they use similar strategies to appeal to their audiences.
Television audiences	
Point 1:	Men
Point 2:	Women
Point 3:	Children

Radio audiences

Point 1:	Men
Point 2:	Women
Point 3:	Children
Conclusion:	Restatement of thesis (in different words) or review of key points

Subject-by-subject comparisons are most appropriate for short, uncomplicated papers. In longer papers, where you might make many points about each subject, this organizational strategy demands too much of your readers, requiring them to keep track of all your points throughout your paper. In addition, because of the length of each section, your paper may seem like two completely separate essays. For longer or more complex papers, then, it is often best to use point-by-point comparison.

Using Point-by-Point Comparison

In a **point-by-point comparison**, you make a point about one subject and then follow it with a comparable point about the other. This alternating pattern continues throughout the body of your essay until all your points have been made. The following informal outline illustrates a point-by-point comparison.

Introduction:	Thesis statement — Although Melville's *Moby-Dick* and London's *The Sea Wolf* are both about the sea, the minor characters, major characters, and themes of *Moby-Dick* establish its greater complexity.
Minor characters	
Book 1:	*The Sea Wolf*
Book 2:	*Moby-Dick*
Major characters	
Book 1:	*The Sea Wolf*
Book 2:	*Moby-Dick*
Themes	
Book 1:	*The Sea Wolf*
Book 2:	*Moby-Dick*
Conclusion:	Restatement of thesis (in different words) or review of key points

Point-by-point comparisons are useful for longer, more complicated essays in which you discuss many different points. (If you treat only one or two points of comparison, you should consider a subject-by-subject organization.) In a point-by-point essay, readers can follow comparisons or contrasts more easily and do not have to wait several paragraphs to find out, for example, the differences between minor characters in *Moby-Dick* and *The*

Sea Wolf or to remember on page five what was said on page three. Nevertheless, it is easy to fall into a monotonous, back-and-forth movement between points when you write a point-by-point comparison. To avoid this problem, vary your sentence structure as you move from point to point—and be sure to use clear transitions.

Using Transitions

Transitions are especially important in comparison-and-contrast essays because readers need clear signals that identify individual similarities and differences. Without these cues, readers will have trouble following your discussion and may lose track of the significance of the points you are making. Some transitions indicating comparison and contrast are listed in the following box. (A more complete list of transitions appears on page 57.)

USEFUL TRANSITIONS FOR COMPARISON AND CONTRAST

COMPARISON

in comparison	like
in the same way	likewise
just as . . . so	similarly

CONTRAST

although	nevertheless
but	nonetheless
conversely	on the contrary
despite	on the one hand . . . on the other hand
even though	still
however	unlike
in contrast	whereas
instead	yet

Longer essays frequently include **transitional paragraphs** that connect one part of an essay to another. A transitional paragraph can be a single sentence that signals a shift in focus or a longer paragraph that provides a summary of what was said before. In either case, transitional paragraphs enable readers to pause and consider what has already been said before moving on to a new subject.

Revising a Comparison-and-Contrast Essay

When you revise your comparison-and-contrast essay, consider the items on the revision checklist on page 68. In addition, pay special attention to the items on the checklist below, which apply specifically to comparison-and-contrast essays.

✓ **REVISION CHECKLIST**   **Comparison and Contrast**

☐ Does your assignment call for comparison and contrast?
☐ What basis for comparison exists between the two subjects you are comparing?
☐ Does your essay have a clear thesis statement that identifies both the subjects you are comparing and the points you are making about them?
☐ Do you discuss the same or similar points for both subjects?
☐ If you have written a subject-by-subject comparison, have you included a transition paragraph that connects the two sections of the essay?
☐ If you have written a point-by-point comparison, have you included appropriate transitions and varied your sentence structure to indicate your shift from one point to another?
☐ Have you included transitional words and phrases that indicate whether you are discussing similarities or differences?

Editing a Comparison-and-Contrast Essay

When you edit your comparison-and-contrast essay, follow the guidelines on the editing checklists on pages 85, 88, and 91. In addition, focus on the grammar, mechanics, and punctuation issues that are particularly relevant to comparison-and-contrast essays. One of these issues — using parallel structure — is discussed below.

GRAMMAR IN CONTEXT   **Using Parallelism**

Parallelism — the use of matching nouns, verbs, phrases, or clauses to express the same or similar ideas — is frequently used in comparison-and-contrast essays to emphasize the similarities or differences between one point or subject and another.

• Use parallel structure with paired items or with items in a series.

"For women, as for girls, intimacy is the fabric of relationships, and talk is the thread from which it is woven" (Tannen 422).

"Lee was tidewater Virginia, and in his background were family, culture, and tradition . . . the age of chivalry transplanted to a New World which was making its own legends and its own myths" (Catton 393–94).

According to Bruce Catton, Lee was strong, aristocratic, and dedicated to the Confederacy.

- Use parallel structure with paired items linked by correlative conjunctions (*not only/but also, both/and, neither/nor, either/or,* and so on).

"In everything we undertake, **either** on earth **or** in the sky, we have a choice of two styles, which I call the gray and the green" (Dyson 369).

Catton **not only** admires Grant **but also** respects him.

- Use parallel structure to emphasize the contrast between paired items linked by *as* or *than.*

According to Deborah Tannen, conversation between men and women is **as** much a problem for men **as** a problem for women.

As Deborah Tannen observes, most men are socialized to communicate through actions **rather than** to communicate through conversation.

✔ EDITING CHECKLIST   **Comparison and Contrast**

☐ Have you used parallel structure with parallel elements in a series?
☐ Have you used commas to separate three or more parallel elements in a series?
☐ Have you used parallel structure with paired items linked by correlative conjunctions?
☐ Have you used parallel structure with paired items linked by *as* or *than*?

A STUDENT WRITER: Subject-by-Subject Comparison

The following essay, by Mark Cotharn, is a subject-by-subject comparison. It was written for a composition class whose instructor asked students to write an essay comparing two educational experiences.

Brains versus Brawn

Introduction   When people think about discrimination, they usually   1
associate it with race or gender. But discrimination can take other
forms. For example, a person can gain an unfair advantage at a
job interview by being attractive, by knowing someone who works
at the company, or by being able to talk about something (like
sports) that has nothing to do with the job. Certainly, the people
who do not get the job would claim that they were discriminated
against, and to some extent they would be right. As a high school
athlete, I experienced both sides of discrimination. When I was a
sophomore, I benefited from discrimination. When I was a junior,

Thesis statement (emphasizing differences)

however, I was penalized by it, treated as if there were no place for me in a classroom. As a result, I learned that discrimination, whether it helps you or hurts you, is wrong.

First subject: Mark helped by discrimination

Status of football

At my high school, football was everything, and the entire town supported the local team. In the summer, merchants would run special football promotions. Adults would wear shirts with the team's logo, students would collect money to buy equipment, and everyone would go to the games and cheer the team on. Coming out of junior high school, I was considered an exceptional athlete who was eventually going to start as varsity quarterback. Because of my status, I was enthusiastically welcomed by the high school. Before I entered the school, the varsity coach visited my home, and the principal called my parents and told them how well I was going to do.

2

Treatment by teachers

I knew that high school would be different from junior high, but I wasn't prepared for the treatment I received from my teachers. Many of them talked to me as if I were their friend, not their student. My math teacher used to keep me after class just to talk football; he would give me a note so I could be late for my next class. My biology teacher told me I could skip the afternoon labs so that I would have some time for myself before practice. Several of my teachers told me that during football season, I didn't have to hand in homework because it might distract me during practice. My Spanish teacher even told me that if I didn't do well on a test, I could take it over after the season. Everything I did seemed to be perfect.

3

Mark's reaction to treatment

Despite this favorable treatment, I continued to study hard. I knew that if I wanted to go to a good college, I would have to get good grades, and I resented the implication that the only way I could get good grades was by getting special treatment. I had always been a good student, and I had no intention of changing my study habits now that I was in high school. Each night after practice, I stayed up late outlining my notes and completing my class assignments. Any studying I couldn't do during the week, I would complete on the weekends. Of course my social life suffered, but I didn't care. I was proud that I never took advantage of the special treatment my teachers were offering me.

4

Transitional paragraph: signals shift from one subject to another

Then, one day, the unthinkable happened. The township redrew the school-district lines, and I suddenly found myself assigned to a new high school — one that was academically more demanding than the one I attended and, worse, one that had

5

a weak football team. When my parents appealed to the school board to let me stay at my current school, they were told that ~no exception~ if the board made an exception for me, it would have to make exceptions for others, and that would lead to chaos. My principal and my coach also tried to get the board to change its decision, but they got the same response. So, in my junior year, at the height of my career, I changed schools.

Second subject: Mark hurt by discrimination

Status of football

Unlike the people at my old school, no one at my new school seemed to care much about high school football. Many of the students attended the games, but their primary focus was on getting into college. If they talked about football at all, they usually discussed the regional college teams. As a result, I didn't have the status I had when I attended my former school. When I met with the coach before school started, he told me the football team was weak. He also told me that his main goal was to make ~Wow!~ sure everyone on the team had a chance to play. So, even though ☺ I would start, I would have to share the quarterback position with two seniors. Later that day, I saw the principal, who told me that although sports were an important part of school, academic achievement was more important. He made it clear that I would play football only as long as my grades did not suffer.

6

Treatment by teachers

Unlike the teachers at my old school, the teachers at my new school did not give any special treatment to athletes. When I entered my new school, I was ready for the challenge. What I was not ready for was the hostility of most of my new teachers. From the first day, in just about every class, my teachers made it obvious that they had already made up their minds about ~teachers were hostile~ what kind of student I was going to be. Some teachers told me I shouldn't expect any special consideration just because I was the team's quarterback. One even said in front of the class that I would have to study as hard as the other students if I expected

7

Mark's reaction to treatment

to pass. I was hurt and embarrassed by these comments. I didn't expect anyone to give me anything, and I was ready to get the grades I deserved. After all, I had gotten good grades up to this point, and I had no reason to think that the situation would change. Even so, my teachers' preconceived ideas upset me.

Just as I had in my old school, I studied hard, but I didn't know how to deal with the prejudice I faced. At first, it really bothered me and even affected my performance on the football field. However, after a while, I decided that the best way to show my teachers that I was not the stereotypical jock was to prove to

8

them what kind of student I really was. In the long run, far from discouraging me, their treatment motivated me, and I decided to work as hard in the classroom as I did on the football field. By the end of high school, not only had the team won half of its games (a record season), but I had also proved to my teachers that I was a good student. (I still remember the surprised look on the face of my chemistry teacher when she handed my first exam back to me and told me that I had received the second-highest grade in the class.)

Conclusion   Before I graduated, I talked to the teachers about how they had treated me during my junior year. Some admitted they had been harder on me than on the rest of the students, but others denied they had ever discriminated against me. Eventually, I realized that some of them would never understand what they had done. Even so, my experience did have some positive effects. I learned that you should judge people on their merits, not by your own set of assumptions. In addition, I learned that although some people are talented intellectually, others have special skills *Restatement of thesis*   that should also be valued. And, as I found out, discriminatory treatment, whether it helps you or hurts you, is no substitute for fairness.

Points for Special Attention

Basis for Comparison. Mark knew he could easily compare his two experiences. Both involved high school, and both focused on the treatment he had received as an athlete. In one case, Mark was treated better than other students because he was the team's quarterback; in the other, he was stereotyped as a "dumb jock" because he was a football player. Mark also knew that his comparison would make an interesting (and perhaps unexpected) point — that discrimination is unfair even when it gives a person an advantage.

Selecting Points for Comparison. Mark wanted to make certain that he would discuss the same (or at least similar) points for the two experiences he was going to compare. As he planned his essay, he consulted his brainstorming notes and made the following informal outline.

EXPERIENCE 1	EXPERIENCE 2
(gained an advantage)	(was put at a disadvantage)
Status of football	Status of football
Treatment by teachers	Treatment by teachers
My reaction	My reaction

Structure. Mark's essay makes three points about each of the two experiences he compares. Because his purpose was to convey the differences between the two experiences, he decided to use a subject-by-subject strategy. In addition, Mark thought he could make his case more convincingly if he discussed the first experience fully before moving on to the next one, and he believed readers would have no trouble keeping his individual points in mind as they read. Of course, Mark could have decided to do a point-by-point comparison. He rejected this strategy, though, because he thought that shifting back and forth between subjects would distract readers from his main point.

Transitions. Without adequate transitions, a subject-by-subject comparison can read like two separate essays. Notice that in Mark's essay, paragraph 5 is a **transitional paragraph** that connects the two sections of the essay. In it, Mark sets up the comparison by telling how he suddenly found himself assigned to another high school.

In addition to connecting the sections of an essay, transitional words and phrases can identify individual similarities or differences. Notice, for example, how the transitional word *however* emphasizes the contrast between the following sentences from paragraph 1.

WITHOUT TRANSITION

When I was a sophomore, I benefited from discrimination. When I was a junior, I was penalized by it.

WITH TRANSITION

When I was a sophomore, I benefited from discrimination. When I was a junior, *however,* I was penalized by it.

Topic Sentences. Like transitional phrases, topic sentences help to guide readers through an essay. When reading a comparison-and-contrast essay, readers can easily forget the points being compared, especially if the essay is long. Direct, clearly stated topic sentences act as guideposts, alerting readers to the comparisons and contrasts you are making. For example, Mark's straightforward topic sentence at the beginning of paragraph 5 dramatically signals the movement from one experience to the other ("Then, one day, the unthinkable happened"). In addition, as in any effective comparison-and-contrast essay, each point discussed in connection with one subject is also discussed in connection with the other. Mark's topic sentences reinforce this balance.

FIRST SUBJECT

At my high school, football was everything, and the entire town supported the local team.

SECOND SUBJECT

Unlike the people at my old school, no one at my new school seemed to care much about high school football.

Focus on Revision

In general, Mark's classmates thought he could have spent more time talking about what he did to counter the preconceptions about athletes that teachers in *both* his schools had.

One student in his peer-editing group pointed out that the teachers at both schools seemed to think athletes were weak students. The only difference was that the teachers at Mark's first school were willing to make allowances for athletes, while the teachers at his second school were not. The student thought that although Mark alluded to this fact, he should have made his point more explicitly.

Another classmate thought Mark should acknowledge that some student athletes *do* fit the teachers' stereotypes (although many do not). This information would reinforce his thesis and help him demonstrate how unfair his treatment was.

After rereading his essay, along with his classmates' comments, Mark decided to add information about how demanding football practice was. Without this information, readers would have a hard time understanding how difficult it was for him to keep up with his studies. He also decided to briefly acknowledge the fact that though he did not fit the negative stereotype of student athletes, some other student athletes do. This fact, however, did not justify the treatment he received at the two high schools he attended. (A sample peer-editing worksheet for comparison and contrast appears on pages 388–89.)

Working with Sources. One of Mark's classmates suggested that he add a quotation from Judith Ortiz Cofer's essay "The Myth of the Latin Woman: I Just Met a Girl Named Maria" (page 230) to his essay. The student pointed out that Cofer, like Mark, was a victim of discrimination on the basis of stereotyping. By referring to Cofer's essay, Mark could widen the scope of his remarks and show how his experience was similar to that of someone who was stereotyped on the basis of ethnicity. Mark thought this was a good idea, and he decided to refer to Cofer's essay in the next draft of his paper. (Adding this reference would require him to include MLA parenthetical documentation as well as a works-cited page.)

A STUDENT WRITER: Point-by-Point Comparison

The following essay, by Maria Tecson, is a point-by-point comparison. It was written for a composition class whose instructor asked students to compare two websites about a health issue and to determine which is the more reliable information source.

A Comparison of Two Websites on Attention Deficit Disorder

Introduction   At first glance, the National Institute of Mental Health   1
(NIMH) website and ADD.About.com — two sites on Attention
Deficit Disorder — look a lot alike. Both have attractive designs,

headings, and links to other websites. Because anyone can publish on the Internet, however, websites cannot be judged just on how they look. Colorful graphics and an appealing layout can often hide shortcomings that make sites unsuitable research sources. As a comparison of the NIMH and ADD.About.com websites shows, the first site is definitely a more useful source of information than the second.

Thesis statement (emphasizing differences)

The first difference between the two websites is the design   2 of their home pages. The NIMH page looks clear and professional. For example, the logos, tabs, links, search boxes, and text columns are placed carefully on the page (see fig. 1). Words are spelled correctly; tabs help users to navigate; and content is arranged topically, with headings such as "What Is Attention Deficit Hyperactivity Disorder?" and "How Is ADHD Treated?" The page includes links to detailed reference lists and footnotes as well as to resources for further study. Finally, this page and many of the other pages associated with the NIMH site offer accessibility options, such as text in Spanish.

First point: comparing home pages

NIMH home page

The ADD.About.com home page is more crowded than NIMH's   3 ADHD/ADD home page; although it has less text, it contains more design elements, including a number of images and sidebars (see fig. 2). The arrangement of these elements on the page, the focus of the information presented, and the lack of misspellings indicate that it has been carefully designed. This page is engaging and visually stimulating, and it contains many of the same headings as the NIMH page, including sections on defining ADHD and explaining treatments. However, it is not always clear how the photos and videos are related to the information on the page. The home page also lacks any clear accessibility options, which limits the site's use by a wide audience.

ADD home page

Another difference between the two websites is their   4 purposes. The URL for the NIMH website indicates that it is a *.gov* — a website created by a branch of the United States government. The logo at the top left of the home page identifies the National Institute of Mental Health (NIMH) as the sponsor of the site. The "About Us" tab on the upper right-hand side of the page links to a description of NIMH as well as to contact information for this organization. A notice at the bottom of the page informs visitors that NIMH is part of the National Institutes of Health, which is, in turn, a part of the U.S. Department of Health

Second point: comparing sponsors

NIMH site sponsor

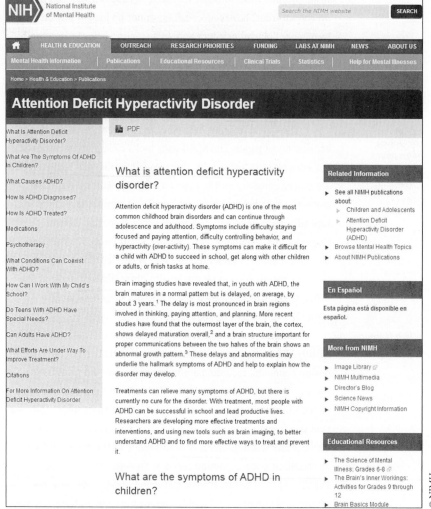

Fig. 1. National Institute of Mental Health. *Attention Deficit Hyperactivity Disorder.* NIMH, n.d. Web. 28 Oct. 2013.

and Human Services. Furthermore, the "About Us" tab includes the NIMH Strategic Plan, which informs readers that NIMH is the "lead federal agency for research on mental and behavioral disorders." This description clearly indicates that the site's purpose is to give the American public the latest information about ADHD. For this reason, the website lists all the medications used to treat ADHD and objectively evaluates the various treatment options available to patients.

Screenshot reprinted by permission of About.com and Keath Low. Photos © Andresr/Shutterstock; Robert Kneschke/Shutterstock; Rocketclips, Inc./Shutterstock; Sergey Nivens/Shutterstock; Giovanni Cancemi/Shutterstock; Olesia Bilkei/Shutterstock.

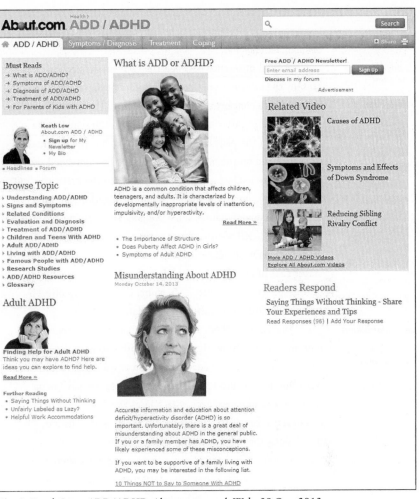

Fig. 2. Keath Low. *ADD/ADHD*. About.com, n.d. Web. 28 Oct. 2013.

ADD site sponsor

The URL for ADD.About.com ends with *.com*, indicating that   5
it is a commercial site. The sponsor of this website is About.com.
At the very bottom of the page, a link called "Our Story" explains
that the goal of About.com is to make "finding accessible, quality
information — on almost every topic — as easy as a simple search."
A careful examination of the site, however, indicates that About
.com's purpose is not just to deliver information about mental
health and behavioral disorders. Although ADD.About.com treats
some of the same topics as the NIMH site, it also includes paid
advertisements. These ads present a limited number of the

treatments and products available for ADHD, which means that the About.com site highlights certain options over others for commercial reasons.

Third point: how sites present information

A final difference between the two websites is how they present the information. The ADHD information on the NIMH site is largely concentrated on a single page. The page is long, listing one topic after another. The links on the sidebar take

6

NIMH information

readers down the page to different sections, but the information is all included on the main page. Links on the right-hand side of the page take readers to other pages, both on the NIMH site and from outside sources, including other organizations working on ADHD, both governmental and academic. There are no ads of any kind on the NIMH website. Most of the sites linked to from the main page have an educational focus. In addition, the site clearly states that links to other sites "do not constitute an endorsement of their policies or products." In short, the NIMH site offers a straightforward presentation of material.

ADD information

On the ADD.About.com website, however, information is presented very differently. All of the information on the ADD.About.com home page is displayed as excerpts, requiring a click-through to "Read More." This means readers have to go through several pages, each with a large number of links, ads, and options, to get to the information they want. Ads are listed along the sides, top, and bottom of the page. This arrangement seems to imply that the paid advertisements are equivalent to the other information on the site. Although the words "Ads" and "Advertisement" appear on the page, these labels are difficult to see. In addition, the ads include everything from brain-training games to college-scholarship information to guides for treating drug addiction. As a result, they disrupt the clarity, focus, and usefulness of the About.com site.

7

Conclusion

A comparison of the NIMH website and ADD.About.com website shows some clear differences between the two. The biggest difference is found in the reliability of information they present. The NIMH website makes it easy for users to understand where the information on the site comes from and why it is included. The About.com site, however, downplays its commercial associations and this possibly misleads readers about the reliability of the information they access. For this reason, the

8

Restatement of thesis   NIMH website is a much more useful source of information than the ADD.About.com website.

Points for Special Attention

Structure. Maria's purpose in writing this essay was to compare two websites that deal with Attention Deficit Hyperactivity Disorder and to determine which is the more useful, more reliable source of information. She structured her essay as a point-by-point comparison, carefully discussing the same point for each subject. With this method of organization, she can be sure her readers will understand the specific differences between the NIMH website and the ADD.About.com website. Had Maria used a subject-by-subject comparison, her readers would have had to keep turning back to compare the points she made about one website with those she made about the other.

Topic Sentences. Without clear topic sentences, Maria's readers would have had difficulty determining where each discussion of the NIMH website ended and each discussion about the ADD.About.com website began. Maria uses topic sentences to distinguish the two subjects of her comparison and to make the contrast between them clear.

Point 1

The NIMH page looks clear and professional.

The ADD.About.com home page is more crowded than NIMH's ADHD/ADD home page; although it has less text, it contains more design elements, including a number of images and sidebars.

Point 2

The URL for the NIMH website indicates that it is a *.gov* — a website created by a branch of the United States government.

The URL for ADD.About.com ends with *.com,* indicating that it is a commercial site.

Point 3

The ADHD information on the NIMH site is largely concentrated on a single page.

On the ADD.About.com website, however, information is presented very differently.

Transitions. In addition to clear and straightforward topic sentences, Maria included **transitional sentences** to help readers move through the essay. These sentences identify the three points of contrast in the essay, and by establishing a parallel structure, they form a pattern that reinforces the essay's thesis.

The first difference between the two websites is the design of their home pages.

Another difference between the two websites is their purposes.

A final difference between the two websites is how they present the information.

Working with Sources. Maria knew that it would be easier for her to compare the NIMH and ADD.About.com websites if she included visuals in her paper. Because readers would be able to see the pages of the sites she was comparing, she would not have to include long passages of description. She could then concentrate on making specific points and not get sidetracked describing physical features. Her instructor pointed out that if she added these two visuals, she would have to include a label (*Fig. 1, Fig. 2,* and so on) along with a caption under each one. He also told her that if the caption included complete source information, there was no need to list the source on her works-cited page. (See Chapter 18 for a discussion of MLA documentation.)

Focus on Revision

Maria's classmates thought the greatest strength of her essay was its use of supporting examples, which made the contrast between the two websites clear, but they thought that more detail would improve her essay. For example, in paragraph 6, Maria could include a list of the other kinds of sites linked to on the NIMH website. In paragraph 7, she could also list some of the specific information presented on the ADD.About.com website and explain why it is problematic.

Maria thought these suggestions made sense. She also thought that she could improve her conclusion: although it summed up the main points of her essay, it included little that would stay with readers after they finished. A sentence or two to caution readers about the need to carefully evaluate the information they find on websites would be a good addition.

PEER-EDITING WORKSHEET: Comparison and Contrast

1. Does the essay have a clearly stated thesis? What is it?

2. What two things are being compared? What basis for comparison exists between the two?

3. Does the essay treat the same or similar points for each of its two subjects? List the points discussed.

FIRST SUBJECT	SECOND SUBJECT
a.	a.
b.	b.
c.	c.
d.	d.

    Are these points discussed in the same order for both subjects? Are the points presented in parallel terms?

4. Does the essay use a point-by-point or subject-by-subject strategy? Is this the best choice? Why?

5. Are transitional words and phrases used appropriately to identify points of comparison and contrast? List some of the transitions used.

6. Are additional transitions needed? If so, where?

7. How could the introductory paragraph be improved?

8. How could the concluding paragraph be improved?

The selections that follow illustrate both subject-by-subject and point-by-point comparisons. The first selection, a pair of visual texts, is followed by questions designed to illustrate how comparison and contrast can operate in visual form. (A multimodal text for comparison and contrast is located online at **macmillanhighered.com/patterns**.)

AUGUSTE RODIN

The Kiss (Sculpture)

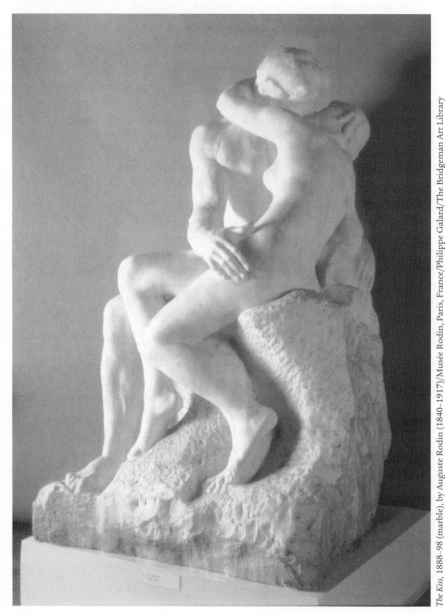

The Kiss, 1888–98 (marble), by Auguste Rodin (1840–1917)/Musée Rodin, Paris, France/Philippe Galard/The Bridgeman Art Library

ROBERT INDIANA

LOVE (Sculpture)

© Amanda Hall/Getty Images

• • •

continued

Reading Images

1. What characteristics do the two sculptures pictured on the preceding pages share? Do they share enough characteristics to establish a basis for comparison? Explain.

2. Make a list of points you could discuss if you were comparing the two sculptures.

3. What general statement could you make about these two sculptures? Do the points you listed in response to question 2 provide enough support for this general statement?

Journal Entry

How does each sculpture convey the idea of love? Which one do you believe conveys this idea more effectively? Why?

Thematic Connections

- "The Storm" (page 198)
- "Sex, Lies, and Conversation" (page 421)
- "Love and Other Catastrophes: A Mix Tape" (page 518)

BRUCE CATTON

Grant and Lee: A Study in Contrasts

Bruce Catton (1899–1978) was a respected journalist and an authority on the American Civil War. His studies were interrupted by his service during World War I, after which he worked as a journalist and then for various government agencies. Catton edited *American Heritage* magazine from 1954 until his death. Among his many books are *Mr. Lincoln's Army* (1951); *A Stillness at Appomattox* (1953), which won both a Pulitzer Prize and a National Book Award; and *Gettysburg: The Final Fury* (1974). Catton also wrote a memoir, *Waiting for the Morning Train* (1972), in which he recalls listening as a young boy to the reminiscences of Union Army veterans.

Background on Grant and Lee "Grant and Lee: A Study in Contrasts," which first appeared in a collection of historical essays titled *The American Story*, focuses on the two generals who headed the opposing armies during the Civil War (1861–1865). Robert E. Lee led the Army of Northern Virginia, the backbone of the Confederate forces, throughout much of the war. Ulysses S. Grant was named commander in chief of the Union troops in March 1864. By the spring of 1865, although it seemed almost inevitable that the Southern forces would be defeated, Lee made an attempt to lead his troops to join another Confederate army in North Carolina. Finding himself virtually surrounded by Grant's forces near the small town of Appomattox, Virginia, Lee chose to surrender to Grant. The following essay considers these two great generals in terms of both their differences and their important similarities.

1   When Ulysses S. Grant and Robert E. Lee met in the parlor of a modest house at Appomattox Court House, Virginia, on April 9, 1865, to work out the terms for the surrender of Lee's Army of Northern Virginia, a great chapter in American life came to a close, and a great new chapter began.

2   These men were bringing the Civil War to its virtual finish. To be sure, other armies had yet to surrender, and for a few days the fugitive Confederate government would struggle desperately and vainly, trying to find some way to go on living now that its chief support was gone. But in effect it was all over when Grant and Lee signed the papers. And the little room where they wrote out the terms was the scene of one of the poignant, dramatic contrasts in American history.

3   They were two strong men, these oddly different generals, and they represented the strengths of two conflicting currents that, through them, had come into final collision.

4   Back of Robert E. Lee was the notion that the old aristocratic concept might somehow survive and be dominant in American life.

5   Lee was tidewater Virginia, and in his background were family, culture, and tradition . . . the age of chivalry transplanted to a New World which

was making its own legends and its own myths. He embodied a way of life that had come down through the age of knighthood and the English country squire. America was a land that was beginning all over again, dedicated to nothing much more complicated than the rather hazy belief that all men had equal rights and should have an equal chance in the world. In such a land Lee stood for the feeling that it was somehow of advantage to human society to have pronounced inequality in the social structure. There should be a leisure class, backed by ownership of land; in turn, society itself should be keyed to the land as the chief source of wealth and influence. It would bring forth (according to this ideal) a class of men with a strong sense of obligation to the community; men who lived not to gain advantage for themselves, but to meet the solemn obligations which had been laid on them by the very fact that they were privileged. From them the country would get its leadership; to them it could look for the higher values — of thought, of conduct, of personal deportment — to give it strength and virtue.

Lee embodied the noblest elements of this aristocratic ideal. Through   6 him, the landed nobility justified itself. For four years, the Southern states had fought a desperate war to uphold the ideals for which Lee stood. In the end, it almost seemed as if the Confederacy fought for Lee; as if he himself was the Confederacy . . . the best thing that the way of life for which the Confederacy stood could ever have to offer. He had passed into legend before Appomattox. Thousands of tired, underfed, poorly clothed Confederate soldiers, long since past the simple enthusiasm of the early days of the struggle, somehow considered Lee the symbol of everything for which they had been willing to die. But they could not quite put this feeling into words. If the Lost Cause, sanctified by so much heroism and so many deaths, had a living justification, its justification was General Lee.

Grant, the son of a tanner on the Western frontier, was everything Lee   7 was not. He had come up the hard way and embodied nothing in particular except the eternal toughness and sinewy fiber of the men who grew up beyond the mountains. He was one of a body of men who owed reverence and obeisance to no one, who were self-reliant to a fault, who cared hardly anything for the past but who had a sharp eye for the future.

These frontier men were the precise opposites of the tidewater aristo-   8 crats. Back of them, in the great surge that had taken people over the Alleghenies and into the opening Western country, there was a deep, implicit dissatisfaction with a past that had settled into grooves. They stood for democracy, not from any reasoned conclusion about the proper ordering of human society, but simply because they had grown up in the middle of democracy and knew how it worked. Their society might have privileges, but they would be privileges each man had won for himself. Forms and patterns meant nothing. No man was born to anything, except perhaps to a chance to show how far he could rise. Life was competition.

Yet along with this feeling had come a deep sense of belonging to a   9 national community. The Westerner who developed a farm, opened a shop, or set up in business as a trader could hope to prosper only as his own community prospered — and his community ran from the Atlantic to the

Pacific and from Canada down to Mexico. If the land was settled, with towns and highways and accessible markets, he could better himself. He saw his fate in terms of the nation's own destiny. As its horizons expanded, so did his. He had, in other words, an acute dollars-and-cents stake in the continued growth and development of his country.

And that, perhaps, is where the contrast between Grant and Lee be- 10 comes most striking. The Virginia aristocrat, inevitably, saw himself in relation to his own region. He lived in a static society which could endure almost anything except change. Instinctively, his first loyalty would go to the locality in which that society existed. He would fight to the limit of endurance to defend it, because in defending it he was defending every- thing that gave his own life its deepest meaning.

The Westerner, on the other hand, would fight with an equal tenacity 11 for the broader concept of society. He fought so because everything he lived by was tied to growth, expansion, and a constantly widening horizon. What he lived by would survive or fall with the nation itself. He could not pos- sibly stand by unmoved in the face of an attempt to destroy the Union. He would combat it with everything he had, because he could only see it as an effort to cut the ground out from under his feet.

So Grant and Lee were in complete   12 contrast, representing two diametrically op- posed elements in American life. Grant was the modern man emerging; beyond him, ready to come on the stage, was the great age of steel and machinery, of crowded cities and a restless burgeoning vitality. Lee might have ridden down from the old age of chiv- alry, lance in hand, silken banner fluttering over his head. Each man was the perfect champion of his cause, drawing both his strengths and his weaknesses from the people he led.

> " So Grant and Lee were in complete contrast, representing two diametrically opposed elements in American life. "

Yet it was not all contrast, after all. Different as they were — in back- 13 ground, in personality, in underlying aspiration — these two great soldiers had much in common. Under everything else, they were marvelous fight- ers. Furthermore, their fighting qualities were really very much alike.

Each man had, to begin with, the great virtue of utter tenacity and 14 fidelity. Grant fought his way down the Mississippi Valley in spite of acute personal discouragement and profound military handicaps. Lee hung on in the trenches at Petersburg after hope itself had died. In each man there was an indomitable quality . . . the born fighter's refusal to give up as long as he can still remain on his feet and lift his two fists.

Daring and resourcefulness they had, too; the ability to think faster 15 and move faster than the enemy. These were the qualities which gave Lee the dazzling campaigns of Second Manassas and Chancellorsville and won Vicksburg for Grant.

Lastly, and perhaps greatest of all, there was the ability, at the end, to 16 turn quickly from war to peace once the fighting was over. Out of the way these two men behaved at Appomattox came the possibility of a peace of reconciliation. It was a possibility not wholly realized, in the years to come, but which did, in the end, help the two sections to become one nation again . . . after a war whose bitterness might have seemed to make such a reunion wholly impossible. No part of either man's life became him more than the part he played in this brief meeting in the McLean house at Appomattox. Their behavior there put all succeeding generations of Americans in their debt. Two great Americans, Grant and Lee — very different, yet under everything very much alike. Their encounter at Appomattox was one of the great moments of American history.

$$\bullet \quad \bullet \quad \bullet$$

Comprehension

1. What took place at Appomattox Court House on April 9, 1865? Why did the meeting at Appomattox signal the closing of "a great chapter in American life" (1)?

2. How does Robert E. Lee represent aristocracy? How does Ulysses S. Grant represent Lee's opposite?

3. According to Catton, where is it that "the contrast between Grant and Lee becomes most striking" (10)?

4. What similarities does Catton see between the two men?

5. Why, according to Catton, are "succeeding generations of Americans" (16) in debt to Grant and Lee?

Purpose and Audience

1. Catton's purpose in contrasting Grant and Lee is to make a statement about the differences between two currents in American history. Summarize these differences. Do you think the differences still exist today? Explain.

2. Is Catton's purpose in comparing Grant and Lee the same as his purpose in contrasting them? That is, do their similarities also make a statement about U.S. history? Explain.

3. State the essay's thesis in your own words.

Style and Structure

1. Does Catton use subject-by-subject or point-by-point comparison? Why do you think he chooses the strategy he does?

2. In this essay, topic sentences are extremely helpful to the reader. Explain the functions of the following sentences: "Grant . . . was everything Lee was not" (7); "So Grant and Lee were in complete contrast" (12); "Yet it was not all contrast, after all" (13); and "Lastly, and perhaps greatest of all . . ." (16).

3. Catton uses transitions skillfully in his essay. Identify the transitional words or expressions that link each paragraph to the preceding one.

4. Why do you suppose Catton provides the background for the meeting at Appomattox but presents no information about the dramatic meeting itself?

5. **Vocabulary Project.** Go to an online thesaurus, and look up **synonyms** for each of the following words. Then, determine whether each synonym would be as effective as the word used in this essay.

   deportment (5)   obeisance (7)   indomitable (14)
   sanctified (6)   diametrically (12)

Journal Entry

Compare your attitudes about the United States with those held by Grant and by Lee. With which man do you agree?

Writing Workshop

1. Write a "study in contrasts" about two people you know well — two teachers, your parents, two relatives, two friends — or about two fictional characters you are very familiar with. Be sure to include a thesis statement.

2. Write a dialogue between two people you know that reveals their contrasting attitudes toward school, work, or any other subject.

3. **Working with Sources.** Using language and syntax appropriate for middle-school students, rewrite this essay for that audience, making the same points Catton makes about the differences between Grant and Lee. Be sure to include parenthetical documentation for any references to Catton's essay, and also include a works-cited page. (See Chapter 18 for information on MLA documentation.)

Combining the Patterns

In several places, Catton uses **exemplification** to structure a paragraph. For instance, in paragraph 7, he uses examples to support the topic sentence "Grant, the son of a tanner on the Western frontier, was everything Lee was not." Identify three paragraphs that use examples to support the topic sentence, and bracket the examples. How do these examples in these paragraphs reinforce the similarities and differences between Grant and Lee?

Thematic Connections

- "Ground Zero" (page 175)
- The Declaration of Independence (page 550)
- "Letter from Birmingham Jail" (page 563)
- "Should American Citizenship Be a Birthright?" (Debate; page 591)

PAMELA HAAG

Your Social Life: Are You a Fox or a Hedgehog?

A writer with a wide range of interests, Pamela Haag graduated from Swarthmore College and earned a Ph.D. in history from Yale University and an M.F.A. from Goucher College. She has written about feminism, American culture, relationships, and transportation issues, as well as autobiographical subjects. She has also been the Director of Research at the American Association of University Women and has held fellowships from the National Endowment for the Humanities and other institutions. In addition to the books *Consent: Sexual Rights and the Transformation of American Liberalism* (1999) and *Marriage Confidential: Love in the Post-Romantic Age* (2011), Haag has written articles for many publications, including the *Chronicle of Higher Education*, the *Washington Post*, and the *American Scholar*.

Background on the fox and the hedgehog parable As Pamela Haag writes, the Greek poet Archilochus is credited with creating the parable of the fox and the hedgehog. In the twentieth century, however, it became associated with the philosopher Isaiah Berlin, who began his 1953 analysis of the Russian novelist Leo Tolstoy with the following line from Archilochus: "The fox knows many things, but the hedgehog knows one big thing." Berlin then went on to explain this distinction: "For there exists a great chasm between those, on one side, who relate everything to a single central vision, one system less or more coherent or articulate . . . a single, universal, organizing principle . . . and, on the other side, those who pursue many ends, often unrelated and even contradictory, connected, if at all, only in some de facto way. . . ." In other words, some writers and thinkers understand the world — and pursue the truth — by means of a single central insight or coherent idea. In contrast, others see the world in complex terms and do not seek a universal organizing principle. Berlin viewed his classification in the context of intellectual playfulness: "I never meant it very seriously," he later said in an interview. "I meant it as a kind of enjoyable intellectual game. . . ." Nevertheless, the distinction endures, probably because the parable of the fox and the hedgehog can be applied to so many different kinds of people and practices — for example, entrepreneurial technology moguls (Steve Jobs as the fox vs. Bill Gates as the hedgehog) and baseball players (versatile, light-hitting foxes vs. home-run-hitting hedgehogs).

The ancient Greek poet Archilochus said that the fox knows many 1 things about a little, but the hedgehog knows one big thing. Philosopher Isaiah Berlin used the fox and hedgehog distinction in his brilliant essay about Leo Tolstoy's view of history and his longing for a unifying insight and understanding.

The hedgehog and the fox is also a good parable for social life today. 2
The hedgehog social life, which is what I think I grew up with, is one where
you know a lot, and deeply, and intimately, about a few friends. You might
count four people as close friends, if that many, but you know the nooks
and crannies of each other's lives, and you'd be comfortable sharing anything with them. If they call you at 3:30 A.M. and need help, you feel obli-
gated to help them.   *hedgehog = few very good friends*

The fox social life, which is what I think social media is selecting for, is 3
one where you know a million little things about a lot of people. The fox
might have an active social life and many acquaintances, but doesn't know
much about them.   *fox = not me*

The hedgehog probes deeply and nar- 4
rowly; the fox skims lightly and broadly.

Obviously, both the hedgehog and the 5
fox social lives have their virtues, and they're
not mutually exclusive. Most of us probably
have both, and are fox-ish or hedgehog-ish,
but not exclusively one or the other.

> The hedgehog
> probes deeply and
> narrowly; the fox
> skims lightly and
> broadly."

Just as Nicholas Carr questions how 6
Google is affecting our brains and cognition, in one of two new book projects I have
underway, I'm questioning (among many other things) how Facebook and
social media are affecting our hearts.

On the surface, although I'm not wedded to this hypothesis, it seems 7
to be inclining us toward the fox social life.   *Social media = fox*

Our attention is dispersed quickly and pithily across hundreds if not 8
thousands of people; we know a little about an awful lot of people. Emotions are more shallow than deeply plumbed. Sadness and grief are certainly expressed, but in delimited ways that are intuitively suitable to the
medium.

Facebook can satiate my social appetite in ways that somewhat trouble 9
me. It can feel like the equivalent of filling up on bread before dinner.   *yup*

I've gotten some social calories in me — some kind of social interac- 10
tion — and it has the benefit of being unencumbered, the ultimate in no
strings attached, and usually affirmative, even effusive, and light. But it is
pure fox.

This happened to me just the other day. I had a social "things to do" 11
list on my desk — people whom I wanted to contact for dinner dates. But I
spent two hours Facebook-mesmerized, scrolling up and down my wall,
liking random comments, reading others, writing some, and then seeing
who might have liked mine and all the rest. I actually participated in an
intellectually substantive conversation, too. I only knew the original poster,
none of the others, but it felt like a first day in a good college seminar.

The "things to do" social list didn't get done. I didn't feel the need. I'd 12
filled up on bread.

My point is that the fox social life might corrode the imperative of hav- 13
ing the hedgehog social life, assuming a zero sum game of social energy.

What constitutes a "friend" relationship in social media spaces also   14
may (or may not) influence fashion standards for friendships that aren't
predominately online. Emphasis is on the curation and presentation of the
self. It's not just that we're updating or communicating with friends about
random goings-on in our lives; we're managing a presence in a media space.
The two processes are inextricable. I wonder if in that old warning from
mom, the online friends might be a "bad influence" on the non-online
ones. It's hard to say right now, but hedgehogs, beware.

The allegation, or observation, that mainstream culture is now a celeb-   15
rity culture rings true for me in some important ways. We collect fans, both
literally and informally; our social life unfolds through a medium of display—like graffiti on a wall or, to be highbrow, a piece of art hanging on a
wall; our self and self-image are ever more conflated, much as they are with
Hollywood celebrities.

My intention isn't to sound like a Luddite crank, although I'm always   16
susceptible to technology nostalgia. In many respects Facebook is a life
saver for me. I work alone, and it's a way to make a fast but positive connection to people during the day, and to find out about stories that are trend-
ing. I can connect with readers on Facebook, which I always enjoy, and get
compliments that they wouldn't bother to send in a letter.

But current research on loneliness finds that a not insignificant per-   17
centage of Americans (although not a majority) do not have a single
friend—not one—in whom they would confide honestly and fully about
meaningful things going on in their lives. They might have a work colleague with whom they share mutual office frustrations. Or they might
have acquaintances with whom they share undemanding news of work, or
their lives. Some might see their spouses as friends, but others lie, deceive,
and/or withhold from their spouses, too, so they can't count them as true
or full confidants, either.

Some might be hedgehogs, and have a life with lots of acquaintances.   18
They might hang out with the other parents in their children's school, or
on teams. But others in the group don't even have that.

I wonder how Facebook will affect this sort of social isolation gener-   19
ally. Ironically, could it make it even worse, while appearing to expand the
lonely, disconnected person's friends by the scores, or even hundreds?

Meanwhile here's my quiz to see if you're more fox-ish or hedgehog-ish: 20

YOU'RE A HEDGEHOG IF ...	YOU'RE A FOX IF ...
you gave your friend a hug	you gave your friend a like
you have actually visited the home of your friend	you don't actually know who all your friends *are*
it would be impossible for one of your friends to be impersonating a man, or a much younger person	some of your friends might really be inmates or precocious ten-year-olds, and you wouldn't know
you talk to a friend and feel filled up for days afterward	you talk to a friend and feel hungry for updates a minute later

· · ·

Comprehension

1. Generally speaking, how are hedgehogs different from foxes?

2. Why does Haag think that the hedgehog and the fox is "a good parable for social life today" (2)?

3. According to Haag, does Facebook incline people toward a fox or a hedgehog social life? Explain.

4. What does current research into loneliness suggest about Americans? Does Haag think that Facebook makes this situation better or worse? Do you agree with her?

5. What does Haag mean in paragraph 9 when she says, "Facebook can satiate my social appetite in ways that somewhat trouble me. It can feel like the equivalent of filling up on bread before dinner"?

Purpose and Audience

1. Do you think Haag expects readers to be receptive or hostile to her ideas? How can you tell?

2. Where does Haag state her thesis? In your own words, summarize this thesis.

3. Why do you think Haag wrote her essay? To persuade? To inform? To enlighten? For some other reason? Explain.

Style and Structure

1. This essay's title is a question. Why do you think Haag chose this title? What other titles can you suggest?

2. Haag's introduction consists of two paragraphs. What do each of these paragraphs accomplish?

3. In comparing her two subjects, Haag relies mainly on a point-by-point comparison. What are the advantages and disadvantages of this kind of organization?

4. Underline the transitional words and phrases in this essay. Should Haag have used more transitions to emphasize the contrast between her two subjects, or does she have enough? Explain.

5. Haag ends her essay with a quiz. Is this an effective conclusion? Should she have ended differently? Explain.

6. **Vocabulary Project.** Haag uses several words that might be unfamiliar to many readers — for example, *parable* (2), *cognition* (6), and *Luddite* (16). Go through the essay, and underline any unfamiliar words. Look them up in a dictionary, and then think of some synonyms for each word. Would any of your substitutions improve the essay? Why or why not?

Journal Entry

Haag uses the parable of the fox and the hedgehog to contrast two different kinds of social lives. Use this parable to contrast two other things — for example, types of teachers, students, or parents.

Writing Workshop

1. Expand your journal entry into a comparison-and-contrast essay. Make sure that you explain the difference between the fox and the hedgehog in your introduction and that your thesis statement identifies the two things you are going to contrast.

2. **Working with Sources.** Write a comparison-and-contrast essay in which you answer the question posed by Haag's title. Be sure to refer specifically to some of the points that Haag makes and to document references to her essay. Don't forget to include a works-cited page. (See Chapter 18 for information on MLA documentation.)

3. Decide which of your friends is like the fox in the parable and which is like the hedgehog. Then, write an essay in which you compare your two friends, making sure that you explain the parable in your introduction and identify the major differences you are going to discuss in your thesis statement.

Combining the Patterns

Paragraph 11 of this essay is a **narrative** that tells what happened to Haag "the other day." What point does this paragraph make? What does this paragraph add to the essay?

Thematic Connections

- "No, I Do Not Want to Pet Your Dog" (page 224)
- "I'm Your Teacher, Not Your Internet-Service Provider" (page 415)
- "Sadie and Maud" (page 428)
- "I Want a Wife" (page 502)

JUAN WILLIAMS

Songs of the Summer of 1963 . . . and 2013

Born in Panama in 1954, Juan Williams grew up in Brooklyn, New York, after his family came to the United States. He earned a B.A. from Haverford College. Williams has had a long and varied career in journalism, including a two-decade association with the *Washington Post*, where he not only wrote editorials and opinion columns but also covered the White House as a reporter. His books include *Eyes on the Prize: America's Civil Rights Years, 1954–1965* (1987) and *Muzzled: The Assault on Honest Debate* (2011). He has written for the *New York Times Sunday Magazine,* the *Atlantic Monthly*, *Ebony*, and other publications. For many years, he was a reporter and host for National Public Radio. Currently, he is a political analyst for Fox News.

Background on the 1963 March on Washington Although the August 28, 1963, March on Washington is primarily associated with the civil rights movement — and, in particular, with Martin Luther King's famous "I Have a Dream" speech — the event was originally planned as a response to the high rate of unemployment among African Americans. In 1961, A. Philip Randolph, an African-American labor activist and civil rights pioneer, proposed a "Jobs Rights March and Mobilization." Over the course of the next two years, several organizations, including the National Association for the Advancement of Colored People (NAACP), the Congress for Racial Equality (CORE), the Negro American Labor Council (NALC), and Martin Luther King Jr.'s Southern Christian Leadership Conference (SCLC), organized the event, which was ultimately called "The March on Washington for Jobs and Freedom." The platform of the march included calls for civil rights legislation; a national two-dollar-per-hour minimum wage; school desegregation; job training programs; and other political, social, and economic measures. Over 200,000 people took part in the march, a crowd that stretched from the Washington Monument to the Lincoln Memorial. Following the march, King and other civil rights leaders attended a meeting in the White House with President John Kennedy and Vice President Lyndon Johnson. Among the political legacies of the march are the Civil Rights Act of 1964 and the Voting Rights Act of 1965.

Fifty years after the March on Washington, mystical memories of that 1 seminal moment in the civil-rights era are less likely to focus on movement politics than on the great poetry and great music.

The emotional uplift of the monumental march is a universe of time 2 away from today's degrading rap music — filled with the n-word, bitches, and "hoes" — that confuses and depresses race relations in America now.

The poetry of August 28, 1963, is best on view when Martin Luther 3
King Jr. went off his speech script and started using a musical, chanting
reprise — "I have a dream." The transforming insight born of the power of
the interracial gathering at that time of turmoil, combined with the power
of the spoken word, created an emotional message that still grips the American mind.

"I have a dream that one day on the red hills of Georgia, sons of former 4
slaves and the sons of former slave owners will be able to sit down together
at the table of brotherhood," King said, in verse that somehow spanned a
history of slavery and the Founding Fathers' uniquely American promise
of equality.

"I have a dream that one day even the state of Mississippi, a state swel- 5
tering with the heat of injustice, sweltering with the heat of oppression,
will be transformed into an oasis of freedom and justice. I have a dream
that my four little children will one day live in a nation where they will not
be judged by the color of their skin, but the content of their character. I
have a dream today!"

That poetry rose above the reality that as King spoke the civil-rights 6
movement was stalled. Few schools had integrated after the Supreme
Court's *Brown v. Board of Education* decision nine years earlier. One hundred
years after the Emancipation Proclamation, the Civil Rights Act was stuck
in Congress. NAACP leader Medgar Evers had been killed in June. After a
violent April in Alabama, in which protest marchers were beaten and set
upon by police dogs, an estimated fifteen thousand more civil-rights activists had been arrested at protests across the country that summer.

King sailed past all those sad realities to invoke his soaring vision of 7
the nation at racial peace. When he finished speaking, the crowd spontaneously broke into singing "We Shall Overcome," holding hands and swaying
as if in communal prayer.

That sense of unity, promise, and pur- 8
pose was also evident in the music of the
march. It's music that still stirs emotions to
this day.

> "That sense of unity, promise, and purpose was also evident in the music of the 9
> march. It's music that still stirs emotions to this day."

Bob Dylan's "Blowin' in the Wind," written in 1962, hit number two on the Bill-
board charts just before the crowd gathered
in Washington. When the folk-music trio
Peter, Paul and Mary sang the song for the
250,000 people in front of the Lincoln Memorial that day, it became an interracial
anthem for change. The song itself drew in-
spiration from two others: The lyrics brought to mind Woody Guthrie's
"Bound for Glory," which included an allegory about newspapers blowing
down city streets, and its melody came from a slave protest song called "No
More Auction Block."

And so they sang in Washington: "Yes, how many years can some 10
people exist before they're allowed to be free? Yes, how many times can a

man turn his head, pretending that he just doesn't see? The answer, my friend, is blowin' in the wind, the answer is blowin' in the wind."

Sam Cooke, the black gospel and rhythm-and-blues singer, began per- 11
forming the Dylan song immediately after the march. He had been work-ing on a song about the hurt he felt as a black man living with racism yet also with hope for better times. In December 1963, Cooke recorded "A Change Is Gonna Come." The song became a hit on black radio, another anthem of yearning for a nation without racial rancor.

"I go to the movie and I go downtown, somebody keep telling me don't 12
hang around," Cooke wrote. "It's been a long time coming, but I know a change is gonna come, oh yes it will."

The next year, in 1964, Curtis Mayfield — also openly inspired by the 13
music of the march — wrote an even more hopeful song: "People Get Ready." It, too, picked up on a frequent image of American folklore, the train of salvation.

Just as Woody Guthrie and Johnny Cash had sung "This Train's Bound 14
for Glory," Mayfield, a black Chicago singer steeped in church gospel music and the blues, sang about faith in the American struggle for racial justice.

"People get ready, there's a train a-comin'; you don't need no baggage, 15
you just get on board . . . there ain't no room for the hopeless sinner who would hurt all mankind just to save his own. Have pity on those whose chances grow thinner, for there's no hiding place against the Kingdom's throne."

The uplifting lyrics made "People Get Ready" one of the earliest hits on 16
both black and white radio. Bob Marley later used some of the words in his poignant song "One Love." Bruce Springsteen used the song as a healing anthem at concerts after the 9/11 terror attacks.

The songs by Dylan, Cooke, and Mayfield have been ranked four- 17
teenth, twelfth, and twenty-fourth on *Rolling Stone* magazine's list of great-est songs of all time. All three have roots in the March on Washington.

Now, half a century after the lyrical promise of that inspiring music 18
and poetry, there is the inescapable and heartbreaking contrast with the malignant, self-aggrandizing rap songs that define today's most popular music.

In Jay-Z's current hit, "Holy Grail," he sings about "psycho bitches" 19
and uses the n-word seven times while bragging that he is "Living the life . . . Illest [n-word] alive." Another top rapper, Lil Wayne, released a song in the spring with an obscenity *in the title,* using the n-word repeatedly and depicting himself as abusing "hoes" and "bitches."

Similar examples abound in the rap-music world and have persisted 20
for years with scarcely any complaint from today's civil-rights leaders. Their failure to denounce these lyrics for the damage they do to poor and minor-ity families — words celebrating tattooed thugs and sexually indiscriminate women as icons of "keeping it real" — is a sad reminder of how long it has been since the world heard the sweet music of the March on Washington.

• • •

Comprehension

1. What is the "great poetry" to which Williams alludes in paragraph 1?
2. Williams says that when King delivered his "I Have a Dream" speech, "the civil-rights movement was stalled" (6). What does he mean?
3. How do the songs of 1962 and 1963 reflect the different moods of those two years? How would you define each of these two moods?
4. In his essay, Williams refers to songs by Bob Dylan, Sam Cooke, and Curtis Mayfield. According to Williams, what do these songs have in common?
5. How is today's mood different from that of the civil-rights era? How does contemporary popular music reflect this difference?

Purpose and Audience

1. Does Williams assume that his readers will be familiar with the events he discusses? How can you tell?
2. Do you think Williams expects readers to know the songs he refers to? Why or why not?
3. What is Williams's purpose in writing this essay? What effect does he want his essay to have on his readers?

Style and Structure

1. How do the first two paragraphs set up the discussion for the rest of the essay?
2. Write a one-sentence summary of Williams's thesis.
3. Throughout most of his essay, Williams discusses the music from the early 1960s. Only in paragraph 19 does he survey contemporary rap music. Should he have spent more time discussing the music from 2013? Why or why not?
4. This essay is organized as a subject-by-subject comparison. Where does Williams move from one subject to the other? What transition does he use to signal this shift?
5. What point does Williams emphasize in his conclusion? Does his conclusion reinforce his thesis statement? Explain.
6. **Vocabulary Project.** In paragraph 18, Williams talks about both the music of the early sixties and the music of 2013. What adjectives does he use to describe each type of music? How do these adjectives convey Williams's attitude toward the two types of music?

Journal Entry

Do you think that Williams's assessment of contemporary rap music is accurate, or do you think that he exaggerates the harm it does (or misrepresents its effects)?

Writing Workshop

1. Compare the music you listened to when you were younger to the music you listen to now. What do the two types of music tell about you and how you have changed? Write a comparison-and-contrast essay in which you discuss your conclusions.

2. **Working with Sources.** Write an essay in which you compare and contrast two different popular songs, focusing on lyrics, music, or political or social messages. Be sure to quote lyrics from the songs, and include parenthetical documentation and a works-cited page. (See Chapter 18 for information on MLA documentation.)

3. **Working with Sources.** Find several of the songs that Williams mentions on YouTube, and listen to them. Then, write an email to Williams in which you agree or disagree with his assessments. Make sure that you structure your email as a comparison-and-contrast essay and that you refer specifically to Williams's essay as well as to the lyrics of the songs. Include parenthetical documentation where necessary, as well as a works-cited page, and also include YouTube links to the performances you watched. (See Chapter 18 for information on MLA documentation.)

Combining the Patterns

Williams uses a number of **exemplification** paragraphs in his essay. Identify two or three of these exemplification paragraphs, and determine what they add to the essay.

Thematic Connections

- "Goodbye to My Twinkie Days" (page 171)
- "Once More to the Lake" (page 191)
- "The 'Black Table' Is Still There" (page 348)
- "Letter from Birmingham Jail" (page 563)

AMY CHUA

Why Chinese Mothers Are Superior

Amy Chua was born in Champaign, Illinois, in 1962. She graduated from Harvard College and earned her J.D. at Harvard Law School, where she was an executive editor of the *Harvard Law Review*. Chua is now the John M. Duff Professor of Law at Yale Law School, where she focuses on international law and business, ethnic conflict, and globalization and the law. She has written two scholarly books, *World on Fire: How Exporting Free Market Democracy Breeds Ethnic Hatred and Global Instability* (2003) and *Days of Empire: How Hyperpowers Rise to Global Dominance — and Why They Fall* (2007). Today, however, Chua is best known for her parenting memoir, *Battle Hymn of the Tiger Mother* (2011).

Background on parenting styles Chua writes disapprovingly about contemporary "Western" parents who, she claims, are "extremely anxious about their children's self-esteem." Such anxieties are relatively new, especially when one surveys the history of parenting — from the ancient Greeks, who commonly left unwanted children in the woods to die of exposure, to seventeenth-century American Puritans, who practiced a philosophy of visual "Better whipt than damned." French Enlightenment figure Jean-Jacques Rousseau (1712–1778) proposed a more sympathetic view of the child, writing that when "children's wills are not spoiled by our fault, children want nothing uselessly." But in the nineteenth and early twentieth centuries, American parenting philosophies usually focused on discipline, emotional detachment, and the wisdom of experts. As Dr. Luther Emmett Holt wrote in *The Care and Feeding of Children* (1894), "instinct and maternal love are too often assumed to be a sufficient guide for a mother." Pediatrician Benjamin Spock, who published his enormously influential *Baby and Child Care* in 1946, is often credited with — or blamed for — a social shift toward more permissive child-rearing, especially in the context of the baby-boom generation. Spock urged parents to trust their own judgment and to meet their children's needs rather than worrying about "spoiling" the child. In the decades that followed, this parenting approach accompanied an increasing emphasis on children's self-esteem, both at home and in school.

A lot of people wonder how Chinese parents raise such stereotypically 1 successful kids. They wonder what these parents do to produce so many math whizzes and music prodigies, what it's like inside the family, and whether they could do it too. Well, I can tell them, because I've done it. Here are some things my daughters, Sophia and Louisa, were never allowed to do:

- attend a sleepover
- have a playdate
- be in a school play

- complain about not being in a school play
- watch TV or play computer games
- choose their own extracurricular activities
- get any grade less than an A
- not be the No. 1 student in every subject except gym and drama
- play any instrument other than the piano or violin
- not play the piano or violin.

I'm using the term "Chinese mother" loosely. I know some Korean, 2
Indian, Jamaican, Irish, and Ghanaian parents who qualify too. Conversely,
I know some mothers of Chinese heritage, almost always born in the West,
who are not Chinese mothers, by choice or otherwise. I'm also using the
term "Western parents" loosely. Western parents come in all varieties.

When it comes to parenting, the Chinese seem to produce children 3
who display academic excellence, musical mastery, and professional success — or so the stereotype goes. *WSJ*'s* Christina Tsuei speaks to two
moms raised by Chinese immigrants who share what it was like growing up
and how they hope to raise their children.

All the same, even when Western parents think they're being strict, 4
they usually don't come close to being Chinese mothers. For example, my
Western friends who consider themselves strict make their children practice their instruments 30 minutes every day. An hour at most. For a Chinese mother, the first hour is the easy part. It's hours two and three that get
tough.

Despite our squeamishness about cultural stereotypes, there are tons 5
of studies out there showing marked and quantifiable differences between
Chinese and Westerners when it comes to parenting. In one study of fifty
Western American mothers and forty-eight Chinese immigrant mothers,
almost 70 percent of the Western mothers said either that "stressing academic success is not good for children" or that "parents need to foster the
idea that learning is fun." By contrast, roughly 0 percent of the Chinese
mothers felt the same way. Instead, the vast majority of the Chinese mothers said that they believe their children can be "the best" students, that
"academic achievement reflects successful parenting," and that if children
did not excel at school then there was "a problem" and parents "were not
doing their job." Other studies indicate that
compared to Western parents, Chinese parents spend approximately ten times as long
every day drilling academic activities with
their children. By contrast, Western kids are
more likely to participate in sports teams.

> " What Chinese parents understand is that nothing is fun until you're good at it. "

What Chinese parents understand is 6
that nothing is fun until you're good at it.
To get good at anything you have to work,
and children on their own never want to

---

* Eds. note — *Wall Street Journal*.

work, which is why it is crucial to override their preferences. This often requires fortitude on the part of the parents because the child will resist; things are always hardest at the beginning, which is where Western parents tend to give up. But if done properly, the Chinese strategy produces a virtuous circle. Tenacious practice, practice, practice is crucial for excellence; rote repetition is underrated in America. Once a child starts to excel at something — whether it's math, piano, pitching, or ballet — he or she gets praise, admiration, and satisfaction. This builds confidence and makes the once not-fun activity fun. This in turn makes it easier for the parent to get the child to work even more.

Chinese parents can get away with things that Western parents can't. 7 Once when I was young — maybe more than once — when I was extremely disrespectful to my mother, my father angrily called me "garbage" in our native Hokkien dialect. It worked really well. I felt terrible and deeply ashamed of what I had done. But it didn't damage my self-esteem or anything like that. I knew exactly how highly he thought of me. I didn't actually think I was worthless or feel like a piece of garbage.

As an adult, I once did the same thing to Sophia, calling her "garbage" 8 in English when she acted extremely disrespectfully toward me. When I mentioned that I had done this at a dinner party, I was immediately ostracized. One guest named Marcy got so upset she broke down in tears and had to leave early. My friend Susan, the host, tried to rehabilitate me with the remaining guests.

The fact is that Chinese parents can do things that would seem un- 9 imaginable — even legally actionable — to Westerners. Chinese mothers can say to their daughters, "Hey fatty — lose some weight." By contrast, Western parents have to tiptoe around the issue, talking in terms of "health" and never ever mentioning the f-word, and their kids still end up in therapy for eating disorders and negative self-image. (I also once heard a Western father toast his adult daughter by calling her "beautiful and incredibly competent." She later told me that made her feel like garbage.)

Chinese parents can order their kids to get straight As. Western parents 10 can only ask their kids to try their best. Chinese parents can say, "You're lazy. All your classmates are getting ahead of you." By contrast, Western parents have to struggle with their own conflicted feelings about achievement, and try to persuade themselves that they're not disappointed about how their kids turned out.

I've thought long and hard about how Chinese parents can get away 11 with what they do. I think there are three big differences between the Chinese and Western parental mind-sets.

First, I've noticed that Western parents are extremely anxious about 12 their children's self-esteem. They worry about how their children will feel if they fail at something, and they constantly try to reassure their children about how good they are notwithstanding a mediocre performance on a test or at a recital. In other words, Western parents are concerned about their children's psyches. Chinese parents aren't. They assume strength, not fragility, and as a result they behave very differently.

For example, if a child comes home with an A-minus on a test, a Western parent will most likely praise the child. The Chinese mother will gasp in horror and ask what went wrong. If the child comes home with a B on the test, some Western parents will still praise the child. Other Western parents will sit their child down and express disapproval, but they will be careful not to make their child feel inadequate or insecure, and they will not call their child "stupid," "worthless," or "a disgrace." Privately, the Western parents may worry that their child does not test well or have aptitude in the subject or that there is something wrong with the curriculum and possibly the whole school. If the child's grades do not improve, they may eventually schedule a meeting with the school principal to challenge the way the subject is being taught or to call into question the teacher's credentials. 13

If a Chinese child gets a B — which would never happen — there would first be a screaming, hair-tearing explosion. The devastated Chinese mother would then get dozens, maybe hundreds of practice tests and work through them with her child for as long as it takes to get the grade up to an A. 14

Chinese parents demand perfect grades because they believe that their child can get them. If their child doesn't get them, the Chinese parent assumes it's because the child didn't work hard enough. That's why the solution to substandard performance is always to excoriate, punish, and shame the child. The Chinese parent believes that their child will be strong enough to take the shaming and to improve from it. (And when Chinese kids do excel, there is plenty of ego-inflating parental praise lavished in the privacy of the home.) 15

Second, Chinese parents believe that their kids owe them everything. The reason for this is a little unclear, but it's probably a combination of Confucian filial piety and the fact that the parents have sacrificed and done so much for their children. (And it's true that Chinese mothers get in the trenches, putting in long grueling hours personally tutoring, training, interrogating, and spying on their kids.) Anyway, the understanding is that Chinese children must spend their lives repaying their parents by obeying them and making them proud. 16

By contrast, I don't think most Westerners have the same view of children being permanently indebted to their parents. My husband, Jed, actually has the opposite view. "Children don't choose their parents," he once said to me. "They don't even choose to be born. It's parents who foist life on their kids, so it's the parents' responsibility to provide for them. Kids don't owe their parents anything. Their duty will be to their own kids." This strikes me as a terrible deal for the Western parent. 17

Third, Chinese parents believe that they know what is best for their children and therefore override all of their children's own desires and preferences. That's why Chinese daughters can't have boyfriends in high school and why Chinese kids can't go to sleepaway camp. It's also why no Chinese kid would ever dare say to their mother, "I got a part in the school play! I'm Villager Number Six. I'll have to stay after school for rehearsal every day from 3:00 to 7:00, and I'll also need a ride on weekends." God help any Chinese kid who tried that one. 18

Don't get me wrong: It's not that Chinese parents don't care about their children. Just the opposite. They would give up anything for their children. It's just an entirely different parenting model.   19

. . . Western parents worry a lot about their children's self-esteem. But as a parent, one of the worst things you can do for your child's self-esteem is to let them give up. On the flip side, there's nothing better for building confidence than learning you can do something you thought you couldn't.   20

There are all these new books out there portraying Asian mothers as scheming, callous, overdriven people indifferent to their kids' true interests. For their part, many Chinese secretly believe that they care more about their children and are willing to sacrifice much more for them than Westerners, who seem perfectly content to let their children turn out badly. I think it's a misunderstanding on both sides. All decent parents want to do what's best for their children. The Chinese just have a totally different idea of how to do that.   21

Western parents try to respect their children's individuality, encouraging them to pursue their true passions, supporting their choices, and providing positive reinforcement and a nurturing environment. By contrast, the Chinese believe that the best way to protect their children is by preparing them for the future, letting them see what they're capable of, and arming them with skills, work habits, and inner confidence that no one can ever take away.   22

• • •

Comprehension

1. What does Chua mean when she says, "What Chinese parents understand is that nothing is fun until you're good at it" (6)? Do you agree with her?

2. Does Chua's husband agree or disagree with her child-rearing methods? Why does he react the way he does?

3. According to Chua, why are Chinese parents able to do things that Western parents cannot?

4. How does Chua respond to the charge that Chinese parents don't care about their children?

5. According to Chua, how do Chinese child-rearing practices prepare children for life?

Purpose and Audience

1. What preconceptions about Chinese mothers does Chua think Westerners have? Do you think she is right?

2. Does Chua seem to expect her readers to be receptive, hostile, or neutral to her ideas? What evidence can you find to support your impression? How do you know?

3. What is Chua's thesis? Where does she state it?

4. In an interview, Chua said that the editors of the *Wall Street Journal,* not she, chose the title of her essay. Why do you think the editors chose the title they did? What title do you think Chua would have chosen? What title would you give the essay?

Style and Structure

1. Why does Chua begin her essay with a list of things her two daughters were not allowed to do as they were growing up? How do you think she expects readers to react to this list? How do you react?

2. Is this essay a point-by-point comparison, a subject-by-subject comparison, or a combination of the two organizational strategies? Why does Chua arrange her comparison the way she does?

3. What evidence does Chua present to support her view that there are marked differences between the parenting styles of Chinese and Western parents?

4. Chua was born in the United States. Does this fact undercut her conclusions about the differences between Western and Chinese child-rearing? Explain.

5. What points does Chua emphasize in her conclusion? How else could she have ended her essay?

6. **Vocabulary Project.** In paragraph 2, Chua says she is using the terms "Chinese mother" and "Western parents" loosely. What does she mean? How does she define these two terms? How would you define them?

Journal Entry

Do you think Chua's essay perpetuates a cultural stereotype? Why or why not?

Writing Workshop

1. Write an essay in which you compare your upbringing to that of Chua's daughters. Were your parents "Western" or "Chinese" parents (or, were they a combination of the two)? In your thesis, take a stand on the question of which kind of parent is "superior." Use examples from your childhood to support your thesis.

2. **Working with Sources.** Read the poem "Suicide Note" by Janice Mirikitani (page 364). Then, write an essay in which you compare Chua's positive view of Asian child-rearing practices with the feelings expressed by the speaker in Mirikitani's poem. Be sure to include parenthetical documentation for any references to the two sources and to include a works-cited page. (See Chapter 18 for information on MLA documentation.)

3. When Chua's essay was published, it elicited thousands of responses, many of which were negative. For example, some readers thought that her parenting methods were tantamount to child abuse, while some readers admired Chua for her resolve and her emphasis on hard work, and others

said that her methods reminded them of their own upbringings. Chua herself responded to readers' comments by saying that her "tough love" approach was grounded in her desire to make sure her children were the best that they could be. Write an email to Chua in which you respond to her essay. Be sure to address each of her major points and to compare your opinions to hers.

Combining the Patterns

Throughout her essay, Chua includes **exemplification** paragraphs. Identify two exemplification paragraphs, and explain how they help Chua make her point about the superiority of Chinese mothers.

Thematic Connections

- "Indian Education" (page 142)
- "Suicide Note" (page 364)
- "College Pressures" (page 448)
- "Mother Tongue" (page 463)

ELLEN LAIRD

I'm Your Teacher, Not Your Internet-Service Provider

An educator and essayist for over thirty years, Ellen Laird believes that technology has forever changed both teaching and learning, as the following essay, originally published in the *Chronicle of Higher Education,* suggests. Laird teaches at Hudson Valley Community College in New York.

Background on "distance learning" Correspondence schools began to appear in the United States in the late nineteenth century, facilitated to a large degree by an extensive and efficient national postal service. These schools allowed students to receive study materials by mail and to complete examinations and other written work that they then submitted, again by mail, to a central departmental office for response and grading by instructors. For the most part, correspondence schools tended to focus on technical curricula, although some programs were geared toward a more traditional liberal arts curriculum. By the 1930s, correspondence schools had entered a period of decline as an increase in the number of high school graduates and the rise of junior colleges meant that students were more likely to have hands-on educational opportunities close to home. Then, beginning in the 1960s, the concept was revived through the broadcast of publicly funded televised courses, again with a mail-based system for transmitting written materials. Today, many universities have Internet-based distance-learning programs. They find that the Internet is a cost-effective, flexible, and efficient way to deliver courses to a large number of students — many of whom cannot commute to campus.

The honeymoon is over. My romance with distance teaching is losing 1 its spark. Gone are the days when I looked forward to each new online encounter with students, when preparing and posting a basic assignment was a thrilling adventure, when my colleagues and friends were well-wishers, cautiously hopeful about my new entanglement. What remains is this instructor, alone, often in the dark of night, facing the reality of my online class and struggling to make it work.

After four years of Internet teaching, I must pause. When pressed to 2 demonstrate that my online composition class is the equivalent of my classroom-based composition sections, I can do so professionally and persuasively. On the surface, course goals, objectives, standards, outlines, texts, Web materials, and so forth, are identical. But my fingers are crossed.

The two experiences are as different as a wedding reception and a rave. 3 The nonlinear nature of online activity and the well-ingrained habits of Web use involve behavior vastly different from that which fosters success in the traditional college classroom. Last fall, my online students ranged from ages fifteen to fifty, from the home-schooled teen to the local union president. Yet all brought to class assumptions and habits that sometimes interfered with learning and often diminished the quality of the experience for all of us. As a seasoned online instructor, I knew what to expect and how to help students through the inevitable. But for the uninitiated, the reality of online teaching can be confounding and upsetting. It can make a talented teacher feel like an unmitigated failure.

> " The honeymoon is over. My romance with distance teaching is losing its spark. "

If faculty members, whether well established or new, are to succeed 4 in online teaching, they must be prepared for attitudes and behaviors that permeate Web use but undermine teaching and learning in the Web classroom. Potential online instructors are generally offered technical training in file organization, course-management software use, and the like. But they would be best served by an unfiltered look at what really happens when the student logs into class, however elegantly designed the course may be. A few declarative sentences drafted for my next online syllabus may suffice:

The syllabus is not a restaurant menu.

In sections offered in campus classrooms, my students regard the syl- 5 labus as a fixed set of requirements, not as a menu of choices. They accept the sequence and format in which course material is provided for them. They do not make selections among course requirements according to preference.

Online? Not so. Each semester, online students howl electronically 6 about having to complete the same assignments in the same sequence required of my face-to-face students. Typical Internet users, these students are accustomed to choices online. They enjoy the nonlinear nature of Web surfing; they would be hard pressed to replicate the sequence of their activity without the down arrow beside the URL box on their browsers.

To their detriment, many of these students fail to consider that Web 7 learning is different from Web use, particularly in a skills-based course like composition. They find it hard to accept, for example, that they must focus on writing a solid thesis before tackling a research paper. Most would prefer to surf from one module of material to the next and complete what appeals to them rather than what is required of them.

The difference between students' expectations and reality frustrates us 8 all. In traditional classrooms, students do not pick up or download only the handouts that appeal to them; most do not try to begin the semester's final project without instruction in the material on which it is based. Yet, online students expect such options.

Even Cinderella had a deadline.

Students in my traditional classes certainly miss deadlines. But they 9 generally regard deadlines as real, if not observable; they recognize an instructor's right to set due dates; and they accept the consequences of missing them to be those stated on the syllabus.

Not so with my online students. Neither fancy font nor flashing bullet 10 can stir the majority to submit work by the published deadline. Students seem to extend the freedom to choose the time and place of their course work to every aspect of the class. Few request extensions in the usual manner. Instead, they announce them. One student, for example, emailed me days after a paper was due, indicating that he had traveled to New York for a Yankees' game and would submit the essay in a couple of weeks.

All course components do not function at the speed of the Internet.

As relaxed as my online students are about meeting deadlines, they 11 begin the course expecting instantaneous service. The speed of Internet transmission seduces them into seeking and expecting speed as an element of the course. Naturally, students' emphasis on rapidity works against them. The long, hard, eventually satisfying work of thinking, doing research, reading, and writing has no relationship to bandwidth, processor speed, or cable modems.

At the same time, it takes me a long time to respond thoughtfully to 12 students' work, particularly their writing. Each semester, online students require help in understanding that waiting continues to be part of teaching and learning, that the instructor is not another version of an Internet-service provider, to be judged satisfactory or not by processing speed and 24/7 availability.

There are no sick or personal days in cyberspace.

In my traditional classes, I refrain from informing students that I will 13 be out of town for a weekend, that I need a root canal, or that my water heater failed before work. My face-to-face students can read my expression and bearing when they see me; thus, I can usually keep personal explanations to a professional minimum.

In my online class, however, students cannot see the bags under my 14 eyes or the look of exuberance on my face. They cannot hear the calm or the shake in my voice. Thus, for the smooth functioning of the course, I willingly provide details about where I am and what I am doing, so students can know what to expect.

However, I am still troubled by the email message from an online stu- 15 dent that began, "I know you are at your father's funeral right now, but I just wondered if you got my paper." Surely, he hesitated before pushing "send," but his need for reassurance prevailed. And so it goes, all semester long. There simply isn't room in an online class for the messiness of ordinary life, the students' or mine. Nor is there room for the extraordinary — the events of September 11, for example. As long as the server functions, the course is always on, bearing down hard on both students and instructor.

Still, students will register for online classes under circumstances that 16 would prohibit them from enrolling in a course on the campus. The welder compelled to work mandatory overtime, the pregnant woman due before midsemester, and the newly separated security guard whose wife will not surrender the laptop all arrive online with the hope and the illusion that, in cyberspace, they can accomplish what is temporarily impossible for them on campus.

I am not on your buddy list.

The egalitarian atmosphere of the Internet chat room transfers rap- 17 idly and inappropriately to the online classroom. Faceless and ageless on-line, I am, at first, addressed as a peer. If students knew that I dress like many of their mothers, or that my hair will soon be more gray than brown, would their exchanges with me be different? I reveal what I want them to know — the date of my marathon, my now-deceased dog's consumption of a roll of aluminum foil, my one gig as a cocktail-lounge pianist — but little of what one good look at me, in my jumper and jewelry, would tell them.

They, on the other hand, hold back nothing. Confessional writing, 18 always a challenge in composition, can easily become the norm online. So can racist, sexist, and otherwise offensive remarks — even admissions of crimes. The lack of a face to match with a rhetorical voice provides the illusion of anonymity, and thus the potential for a no-holds-barred qual-ity to every discussion thread. The usual restraint characterizing conversa-tion among classroom acquaintances evaporates online within about two weeks. Private conversations fuse with academic discussion before an in-structor can log in.

Are there strategies to manage these and similar difficulties? Of course 19 there are. Thus, I continue with online teaching and welcome both its chal-lenges and its rewards. But educators considering online teaching need to know that instruction in person and online are day and night. They must brace themselves for a marriage of opposites, and build large reserves of commitment, patience, and wherewithal if the relationship is to succeed.

Comprehension

1. Why does Laird say that her "honeymoon" with online teaching is over (1)?

2. According to Laird, why are online teaching and classroom-based teach-ing different? How does she explain the differences?

3. What does Laird mean when she says that potential online instructors "would be best served by an unfiltered look at what really happens when the student logs into class" (4)?

4. In what way does classroom-based teaching limit students' choices? How is online teaching different?

5. In paragraph 11, Laird says, "The long, hard, eventually satisfying work of thinking, doing research, reading, and writing has no relationship to bandwidth, processor speed, or cable modems." What does she mean?

Purpose and Audience

1. What is the thesis of this essay?

2. To whom do you think Laird is addressing her essay? Instructors? Students? Both?

3. What do you think Laird is trying to accomplish in her essay? Is she successful?

4. Does Laird assume that her readers are familiar with online teaching, or does she assume they are relatively unfamiliar with it? How can you tell?

Style and Structure

1. Is this essay a point-by-point or subject-by-subject comparison? Why do you think Laird chose this strategy?

2. Laird highlights a "few declarative sentences" (4) as boldfaced headings throughout her essay. What is the function of these headings?

3. Does Laird seem to favor one type of teaching over another? Is she optimistic or pessimistic about the future of online education? Explain.

4. Does Laird indicate how students feel about online teaching? Should she have spent more time exploring this issue?

5. In her conclusion, Laird asks, "Are there strategies to manage these and similar difficulties?" Her answer: "Of course there are." Should she have listed some of these strategies in her conclusion? Why do you think she does not?

6. **Vocabulary Project.** In paragraph 3, Laird says, "The two experiences are as different as a wedding reception and a rave." What are the denotations and connotations of *wedding reception* and *rave*? What point is Laird trying to make with this comparison?

Journal Entry

Do you agree or disagree with Laird's assessment of distance learning and classroom-based learning? (If you have never taken an online course, discuss only her analysis of classroom-based learning.)

Writing Workshop

1. Write an essay in which you discuss whether you would like to take an online writing course. How do you think such a course would compare with a traditional classroom-based course? (If you are already taking such a course, compare it with a traditional writing course.)

2. **Working with Sources.** Write an email to Laird in which you explain that like her, students also have difficulty adapting to online instruction. Address the specific difficulties that students encounter in such courses, and compare these difficulties with those they experience when they take a classroom-based course. Include at least one quotation from Laird's essay, and be sure to include parenthetical documentation for the quotation and to include a works-cited page. (See Chapter 18 for information on MLA documentation.)

3. Read the following list of advantages of taking online courses:

   - A student who is ill will not miss classes.
   - Students who are employed and cannot come to campus can take courses.
   - Nontraditional students — the elderly and disabled, for example — can take courses.
   - Courses are taken at any time, day or night.
   - Guest speakers who cannot travel to campus can be integrated into the course.

   Then, make a list of disadvantages (for example, students never have face-to-face contact with an instructor). Finally, write an essay in which you discuss whether the advantages of online instruction outweigh the disadvantages.

Combining the Patterns

Laird begins her essay with two **narrative** paragraphs. What is the purpose of these paragraphs? What other strategy could Laird have used to introduce her essay?

Thematic Connections

- "Indian Education" (page 142)
- "What I Learned (and Didn't Learn) in College" (page 440)
- "College Pressures" (page 448)
- "The Dog Ate My Flash Drive, and Other Tales of Woe" (page 457)

DEBORAH TANNEN

Sex, Lies, and Conversation

Deborah Tannen was born in Brooklyn, New York, in 1945 and currently teaches at Georgetown University. Tannen has written and edited several scholarly books on the problems of communicating across cultural, class, ethnic, and sexual divides. She has also presented her research to the general public in newspapers and magazines and in her best-selling books *That's Not What I Meant!* (1986), *You Just Don't Understand: Women and Men in Conversation* (1990), and *Talking from 9 to 5* (1994). Her most recent book is *You Were Always Mom's Favorite: Sisters in Conversation throughout Their Lives* (2010).

Background on men's and women's communication styles Tannen wrote "Sex, Lies, and Conversation" because the chapter in *That's Not What I Meant!* on the difficulties men and women have communicating with one another got such a strong response. She realized the chapter might raise some controversy — that discussing their different communication styles might be used to malign men or to put women at a disadvantage — and indeed, some critics have seen her work as reinforcing stereotypes. Still, her work on the subject, along with that of other writers (most notably John Gray in his *Men Are from Mars, Women Are from Venus* series), has proved enormously popular. Much of the research about male and female differences in terms of brain function, relational styles and expectations, and evolutionary roles is controversial and continues to stir debate.

I was addressing a small gathering in a suburban Virginia living 1 room — a women's group that had invited men to join them. Throughout the evening, one man had been particularly talkative, frequently offering ideas and anecdotes, while his wife sat silently beside him on the couch. Toward the end of the evening, I commented that women frequently complain that their husbands don't talk to them. This man quickly concurred. He gestured toward his wife and said, "She's the talker in our family." The room burst into laughter; the man looked puzzled and hurt. "It's true," he explained. "When I come home from work I have nothing to say. If she didn't keep the conversation going, we'd spend the whole evening in silence."

This episode crystallizes the irony that although American men tend 2 to talk more than women in public situations, they often talk less at home. And this pattern is wreaking havoc with marriage.

The pattern was observed by political scientist Andrew Hacker in 3 the late '70s. Sociologist Catherine Kohler Riessman reports in her new book *Divorce Talk* that most of the women she interviewed — but only a few of the men — gave lack of communication as the reason for their divorces. Given the current divorce rate of nearly 50 percent, that amounts to millions of cases in the United States every year — a virtual epidemic of failed conversation.

In my own research, complaints from women about their husbands 4 most often focused not on tangible inequities such as having given up the chance for a career to accompany a husband to his, or doing far more than their share of daily life-support work like cleaning, cooking, social arrangements, and errands. Instead, they focused on communication: "He doesn't listen to me," "He doesn't talk to me." I found, as Hacker observed years before, that most wives want their husbands to be, first and foremost, conversational partners, but few husbands share this expectation of their wives.

In short, the image that best represents the current crisis is the stereo- 5 typical cartoon scene of a man sitting at the breakfast table with a newspaper held up in front of his face, while a woman glares at the back of it, wanting to talk.

Linguistic Battle of the Sexes

How can women and men have such different impressions of communication in marriage? Why the widespread imbalance in their interests and expectations? 6

In the April issue of *American Psychologist,* Stanford University's Eleanor Maccoby reports the results of her own and others' research showing that children's development is most influenced by the social structure of peer interactions. Boys and girls tend to play with children of their own gender, and their sex-separate groups have different organizational structures and interactive norms. 7

> " How can women and men have such different impressions of communication in marriage? Why the widespread imbalance in their interests and expectations? "

I believe these systematic differences in childhood socialization make 8 talk between women and men like cross-cultural communication, heir to all the attraction and pitfalls of that enticing but difficult enterprise. My research on men's and women's conversations uncovered patterns similar to those described for children's groups.

For women, as for girls, intimacy is the fabric of relationships, and talk 9 is the thread from which it is woven. Little girls create and maintain friendships by exchanging secrets; similarly, women regard conversation as the cornerstone of friendship. So a woman expects her husband to be a new and improved version of a best friend. What is important is not the individual subjects that are discussed but the sense of closeness, of a life shared, that emerges when people tell their thoughts, feelings, and impressions.

Bonds between boys can be as intense as girls', but they are based less 10 on talking, more on doing things together. Since they don't assume talk is the cement that binds a relationship, men don't know what kind of talk women want, and they don't miss it when it isn't there.

Boys' groups are larger, more inclusive, and more hierarchical, so boys   11
must struggle to avoid the subordinate position in the group. This may
play a role in women's complaints that men don't listen to them. Some
men really don't like to listen, because being the listener makes them feel
one-down, like a child listening to adults or an employee to a boss.

But often when women tell men, "You aren't listening," and the men   12
protest, "I am," the men are right. The impression of not listening results
from misalignments in the mechanics of conversation. The misalignment
begins as soon as a man and a woman take physical positions. This became
clear when I studied videotapes made by psychologist Bruce Dorval of children and adults talking to their same-sex best friends. I found that at every
age, the girls and women faced each other directly, their eyes anchored on
each other's faces. At every age, the boys and men sat at angles to each other
and looked elsewhere in the room, periodically glancing at each other. They
were obviously attuned to each other, often mirroring each other's movements. But the tendency of men to face away can give women the impression they aren't listening even when they are. A young woman in college
was frustrated: Whenever she told her boyfriend she wanted to talk to him,
he would lie down on the floor, close his eyes, and put his arm over his face.
This signaled to her, "He's taking a nap." But he insisted he was listening
extra hard. Normally, he looks around the room, so he is easily distracted.
Lying down and covering his eyes helped him concentrate on what she was
saying.

Analogous to the physical alignment that women and men take in con-   13
versation is their topical alignment. The girls in my study tended to talk at
length about one topic, but the boys tended to jump from topic to topic.
The second-grade girls exchanged stories about people they knew. The
second-grade boys teased, told jokes, noticed things in the room, and
talked about finding games to play. The sixth-grade girls talked about
problems with a mutual friend. The sixth-grade boys talked about fifty-five
different topics, none of which extended over more than a few turns.

Listening to Body Language

Switching topics is another habit that gives women the impression   14
men aren't listening, especially if they switch to a topic about themselves.
But the evidence of the tenth-grade boys in my study indicates otherwise.
The tenth-grade boys sprawled across their chairs with bodies parallel and
eyes straight ahead, rarely looking at each other. They looked as if they
were riding in a car, staring out the windshield. But they were talking
about their feelings. One boy was upset because a girl had told him he
had a drinking problem, and the other was feeling alienated from all his
friends.

Now, when a girl told a friend about a problem, the friend responded   15
by asking probing questions and expressing agreement and understanding. But the boys dismissed each other's problems. Todd assured Richard
that his drinking was "no big problem" because "sometimes you're funny

when you're off your butt." And when Todd said he felt left out, Richard responded, "Why should you? You know more people than me."

Women perceive such responses as belittling and unsupportive. But 16 the boys seemed satisfied with them. Whereas women reassure each other by implying, "You shouldn't feel bad because I've had similar experiences," men do so by implying, "You shouldn't feel bad because your problems aren't so bad."

There are even simpler reasons for women's impression that men don't 17 listen. Linguist Lynette Hirschman found that women make more listener-noise, such as "mhm," "uhuh," and "yeah," to show "I'm with you." Men, she found, more often give silent attention. Women who expect a stream of listener-noise interpret silent attention as no attention at all.

Women's conversational habits are as frustrating to men as men's are 18 to women. Men who expect silent attention interpret a stream of listener-noise as overreaction or impatience. Also, when women talk to each other in a close, comfortable setting, they often overlap, finish each other's sentences, and anticipate what the other is about to say. This practice, which I call "participatory listenership," is often perceived by men as interruption, intrusion, and lack of attention.

A parallel difference caused a man to complain about his wife, "She 19 just wants to talk about her own point of view. If I show her another view, she gets mad at me." When most women talk to each other, they assume a conversationalist's job is to express agreement and support. But many men see their conversational duty as pointing out the other side of an argument. This is heard as disloyalty by women, and refusal to offer the requisite support. It is not that women don't want to see other points of view, but that they prefer them phrased as suggestions and inquiries rather than as direct challenges.

In his book *Fighting for Life*, Walter Ong points out that men use "ago- 20 nistic," or warlike, oppositional formats to do almost anything; thus discussion becomes debate, and conversation a competitive sport. In contrast, women see conversation as a ritual means of establishing rapport. If Jane tells a problem and June says she has a similar one, they walk away feeling closer to each other. But this attempt at establishing rapport can backfire when used with men. Men take too literally women's ritual "troubles talk," just as women mistake men's ritual challenges for real attack.

The Sounds of Silence

These differences begin to clarify why women and men have such dif- 21 ferent expectations about communication in marriage. For women, talk creates intimacy. Marriage is an orgy of closeness: you can tell your feelings and thoughts, and still be loved. Their greatest fear is being pushed away. But men live in a hierarchical world, where talk maintains independence and status. They are on guard to protect themselves from being put down and pushed around.

This explains the paradox of the talkative man who said of his silent 22 wife, "She's the talker." In the public setting of a guest lecture, he felt challenged to show his intelligence and display his understanding of the lecture. But at home, where he has nothing to prove and no one to defend against, he is free to remain silent. For his wife, being home means she is free from the worry that something she says might offend someone, or spark disagreement, or appear to be showing off; at home she is free to talk.

The communication problems that endanger marriage can't be fixed 23 by mechanical engineering. They require a new conceptual framework about the role of talk in human relationships. Many of the psychological explanations that have become second nature may not be helpful, because they tend to blame either women (for not being assertive enough) or men (for not being in touch with their feelings). A sociolinguistic approach by which male-female conversation is seen as cross-cultural communication allows us to understand the problem and forge solutions without blaming either party.

Once the problem is understood, improvement comes naturally, as it 24 did to the young woman and her boyfriend who seemed to go to sleep when she wanted to talk. Previously, she had accused him of not listening, and he had refused to change his behavior, since that would be admitting fault. But then she learned about and explained to him the differences in women's and men's habitual ways of aligning themselves in conversation. The next time she told him she wanted to talk, he began, as usual, by lying down and covering his eyes. When the familiar negative reaction bubbled up, she reassured herself that he really was listening. But then he sat up and looked at her. Thrilled, she asked why. He said, "You like me to look at you when we talk, so I'll try to do it." Once he saw their differences as cross-cultural rather than right and wrong, he independently altered his behavior.

Women who feel abandoned and deprived when their husbands won't 25 listen to or report daily news may be happy to discover their husbands trying to adapt once they understand the place of small talk in women's relationships. But if their husbands don't adapt, the women may still be comforted that for men, this is not a failure of intimacy. Accepting the difference, the wives may look to their friends or family for that kind of talk. And husbands who can't provide it shouldn't feel their wives have made unreasonable demands. Some couples will still decide to divorce, but at least their decisions will be based on realistic expectations.

In these times of resurgent ethnic conflicts, the world desperately 26 needs cross-cultural understanding. Like charity, successful cross-cultural communication should begin at home.

• • •

Comprehension

1. What pattern of communication does Tannen identify at the beginning of her essay?

2. According to Tannen, what do women complain about most in their marriages?

3. What gives women the impression that men do not listen?

4. What characteristics of women's speech do men find frustrating?

5. According to Tannen, what can men and women do to remedy the communication problems that exist in most marriages?

Purpose and Audience

1. What is Tannen's thesis?

2. What is Tannen's purpose in writing this essay? Do you think she wants to inform or to persuade? On what do you base your conclusion?

3. Is Tannen writing for an expert audience or for an audience of general readers? To men, women, or both? How can you tell?

Style and Structure

1. What does Tannen gain by stating her thesis in paragraph 2 of the essay? Would there be any advantage in postponing the thesis statement until the end? Explain.

2. Is this essay a subject-by-subject or a point-by-point comparison? What does Tannen gain by organizing her essay the way she does?

3. Throughout her essay, Tannen cites scholarly studies and quotes statistics. How effectively does this information support her points? Could she have made a strong case without this material? Why or why not?

4. Would you say Tannen's tone is hopeful, despairing, sarcastic, angry, or something else? Explain.

5. Tannen concludes her essay with a far-reaching statement. What do you think she hopes to accomplish with this conclusion? Is she successful? Explain your reasoning.

6. **Vocabulary Project.** Where does Tannen use professional **jargon** in this essay? Would the essay be more or less effective without these words? Explain.

Journal Entry

Based on your own observations of male-female communication, how accurate is Tannen's analysis? Can you relate an anecdote from your own life that illustrates (or contradicts) her thesis?

Writing Workshop

1. **Working with Sources.** In another essay, Tannen contrasts the communication patterns of male and female students in classroom settings. After observing students in a few of your own classes, write an essay of your

own that draws a comparison between the communication patterns of your male and female classmates. Include quotations from both male and female students. Be sure to include parenthetical documentation for these quotations as well as for any references to Tannen's essay; also include a works-cited page. (See Chapter 18 for information on MLA documentation.)

2. Write an essay comparing the way male and female characters speak (or behave) in films or on television. Use examples to support your points.

3. Write an essay comparing the vocabulary used in two different sports. Does one sport use more violent language than the other? For example, baseball uses the terms *bunt* and *sacrifice,* and football uses the terms *blitz* and *bomb.* Use as many examples as you can to support your thesis.

Combining the Patterns

Tannen begins her essay with an anecdote. Why does she begin with this paragraph of **narration**? How does this story set the tone for the rest of the essay?

Thematic Connections

- "I Want a Wife" (page 502)
- "The Wife-Beater" (page 514)
- "Love and Other Catastrophes: A Mix Tape" (page 518)
- Declaration of Sentiments and Resolutions, Seneca Falls Convention, 1848 (page 556)

GWENDOLYN BROOKS

Sadie and Maud (Poetry)

Poet Gwendolyn Brooks (1917–2000) was born in Topeka, Kansas, and graduated from Wilson Junior College in Chicago, where she lived most of her life. She was on the faculty of Columbia College and Northeastern Illinois State College, and she was named the poet laureate of Illinois. Her first volume of poetry was *A Street in Bronzeville* (1945), named for the African-American neighborhood on the South Side of Chicago where she grew up. Among her many later collections are *Annie Allen* (1949), for which she was the first African American to win a Pulitzer Prize; *Riot* (1969), based on the violent unrest that gripped many inner-city neighborhoods following the assassination of Martin Luther King Jr.; and *Blacks* (1987). She also published books for children, a novel, and two volumes of her memoirs. The following poem is from *A Street in Bronzeville*.

Background on African Americans in the 1940s Because deed restrictions in Chicago in the 1940s prevented blacks from buying property outside of Bronzeville, the area was home to African Americans from all income levels as well as to many thriving black-owned businesses. Still, the opportunities available to women like Sadie and Maud in the 1940s were limited. Nationally, only about 12 percent of African Americans completed four years of high school (although numbers were higher in the North than in the South), and many fewer went on to college. Six out of ten African-American women were employed in low-paying domestic service positions, while fewer than one percent held professional positions, primarily as teachers in segregated schools.

Maud went to college.
Sadie stayed at home.
Sadie scraped life
With a fine-tooth comb.

She didn't leave a tangle in.   5
Her comb found every strand.
Sadie was one of the livingest chits
In all the land.

Sadie bore two babies
Under her maiden name.   10
Maud and Ma and Papa
Nearly died of shame.

When Sadie said her last so-long
Her girls struck out from home.
(Sadie had left as heritage   15
Her fine-tooth comb.)

Maud, who went to college,
Is a thin brown mouse.
She is living all alone
In this old house.   20

. . .

Reading Literature

1. What two ideas is Brooks comparing in the poem? How does the speaker
   let readers know when she is shifting from one subject to another?

2. How accurate do you think the speaker's portrayals are? Is the speaker
   stereotyping the two women?

3. What comment do you think the poem is making about education?
   About society? About women? About African-American women?

Journal Entry

Brooks wrote "Sadie and Maud" in 1945. What changes do you think she
would make if she wrote her poem today?

Thematic Connections

- "My Mother Never Worked" (page 123)
- "The Myth of the Latin Woman: I Just Met a Girl Named Maria" (page 230)
- " 'Girl' " (page 259)
- Declaration of Sentiments and Resolutions, Seneca Falls Convention, 1848
  (page 556)

Writing Assignments for Comparison and Contrast

1. Find a description of the same news event in two different magazines or newspapers. Write a comparison-and-contrast essay discussing the similarities and differences between the two stories.

2. **Working with Sources.** In your local public library, locate two children's books on the same subject — one written in the 1950s and one written within the past ten years. Write an essay discussing which elements are the same and which are different. Include a thesis statement about the significance of the differences between the two books. Make sure that you document all material you take from the two books and that you include a works-cited page. (See Chapter 18 for information on MLA documentation.)

3. Write an essay about a relative or friend you have known since you were a child. Consider how your opinion of this person is different now from what it was then.

4. Write an essay comparing and contrasting the expectations that college professors and high school teachers have for their students. Cite your own experiences as examples.

5. Since you started college, how have you changed? Write a comparison-and-contrast essay that answers this question.

6. Taking careful notes, watch a local television news program and then a national news broadcast. Write an essay comparing the two programs, paying particular attention to the news content and to the journalists' broadcasting styles.

7. Write an essay comparing your own early memories of school with those of a parent or an older relative.

8. How are the attitudes toward education different among students who work to finance their own education and students who do not? Your thesis statement should indicate what differences exist and why.

9. Compare and contrast the college experiences of commuters and students who live in dorms on campus. Interview people in your classes to use as examples.

10. Write an essay comparing any two groups that have divergent values — vegetarians and meat eaters or smokers and nonsmokers, for example.

11. How is being a participant — playing a sport or acting in a play, for instance — different from being a spectator? Write a comparison-and-contrast essay in which you answer this question.

Collaborative Activity for Comparison and Contrast

Form groups of four students each. Assume your college has hired these groups as consultants to suggest solutions for several problems students have been complaining about. Select the four areas — food, campus safety, parking, and class scheduling, for example — you think need improvement. Then, as a group, write a short report to your college describing the present conditions in these areas, and compare them to the improvements you envision. (Be sure to organize your report as a comparison-and-contrast essay.) Finally, have one person from each group read the group's report to the class. Decide as a class which group has the best suggestion.

12

Classification and Division

What Is Classification and Division?

Division is the process of breaking a whole into parts; **classification** is the process of sorting individual items into categories. In the following paragraph from "Pregnant with Possibility," Gregory J. E. Rawlins divides Americans into categories based on their access to computer technology.

Topic sentence
identifies categories

> Today's computer technology is rapidly turning us into three completely new races: the superpoor, the rich, and the superrich. The superpoor are perhaps eight thousand in every ten thousand of us. The rich — me and you — make up most of the remaining two thousand, while the superrich are perhaps the last two of every ten thousand. Roughly speaking, the decisions of two superrich people control what almost two thousand of us do, and our decisions, in turn, control what the remaining eight thousand do. These groups are really like races since the group you're born into often determines which group your children will be born into.

Through **classification and division**, we can make sense of seemingly random ideas by putting scattered bits of information into useful, coherent order. By breaking a large group into smaller categories and assigning individual items to larger categories, we can identify relationships between a whole and its parts and relationships among the parts themselves. Keep in mind, though, that classification involves more than simply comparing two items or listing examples; when you classify, you sort individual examples into different categories.

In countless practical situations, classification and division bring order to chaos. For example, your iPod will *classify* your music, sorting individual songs into distinct genres — alternative rock, hip-hop, country,

Ranchera, and so on. Similarly, phone numbers listed in your cell phone's address book are *divided* into three clearly defined categories: home, work, and mobile. Thus, order can be brought to your music and your phone numbers — just as it is brought to newspapers, department stores, supermarkets, biological hierarchies, and libraries — when a whole is divided into categories or sections and individual items are assigned to one or another of these subgroups.

Understanding Classification

Even though the interrelated processes of classification and division invariably occur together, they are two separate operations. When you **classify**, you begin with individual items and sort them into categories. Since a given item invariably has several different attributes, it can be classified in various ways. For example, the most obvious way to classify the students who attend your school might be according to their year in college. But you could also classify students according to their major, home state, grade-point average, or any number of other principles. The **principle of classification** that you choose — the quality your items have in common — would depend on how you wish to approach the members of this large and diverse group.

Understanding Division

Division is the opposite of classification. When you **divide**, you start with a whole (an entire class) and break it into its individual parts. For example, you might start with the large general class *television shows* and divide it into categories: *sitcoms, action/adventure, reality shows,* and so forth. You could then divide each of these still further. *Action/adventure programs,* for example, might include *Westerns, crime dramas, spy dramas,* and so on — and each of these categories could be further divided as well. Eventually, you would need to identify a particular principle of classification to help you assign specific programs to one category or another — that is, to classify them.

Using Classification and Division

Whenever you write an essay, you use classification and division to bring order to the invention stage of the writing process. For example, when you brainstorm, as Chapter 2 explains, you begin with your topic and list all the ideas you can think of. Next, you *divide* your topic into logical categories and *classify* the items in your brainstorming notes into one category or another, perhaps narrowing, expanding, or eliminating some categories — or some ideas — as you go along. This sorting and grouping enables you to condense and shape your material until it eventually suggests a thesis and the main points your essay will develop.

More specifically, certain topics and questions, because of the way they are worded, immediately suggest a classification-and-division pattern. Suppose, for example, you are asked, "What kinds of policies can government implement to reduce the nation's budget deficit?" Here the word *kinds* suggests classification and division. Other words — such as *types, varieties, aspects,* and *categories* — can also indicate that this pattern of development is called for.

Planning a Classification-and-Division Essay

Once you decide to use a classification-and-division pattern, you need to identify a **principle of classification**. Every group of people, things, or ideas can be categorized in many different ways. When you are at your college bookstore with limited funds, the cost of different books may be the only principle of classification you use when deciding which ones to buy. As you consider which books to carry across campus, however, weight may matter more. Finally, as you study and read, the usefulness of the books will determine which ones you concentrate on. Similarly, when you organize an essay, the principle of classification you choose is determined by your writing situation — your assignment, your purpose, your audience, and your special knowledge and interests.

Selecting and Arranging Categories

After you define your principle of classification and apply it to your topic, you should select your categories by dividing a whole class into parts and grouping a number of different items together within each part. Next, you should decide how you will treat the categories in your essay. Just as a comparison-and-contrast essay makes comparable points about its subjects, so your classification-and-division essay should treat all categories similarly. When you discuss comparable points for each category, your readers are able to understand your distinctions among categories as well as your definition of each category.

Finally, you should arrange your categories in some logical order so that readers can see how the categories are related and what their relative importance is. Whatever order you choose, it should be consistent with your purpose and with your essay's thesis.

Developing a Thesis Statement

Like other kinds of essays, a classification-and-division essay should have a thesis. Your **thesis statement** should identify your subject, introduce the categories you will discuss, and perhaps show readers the relationships of your categories to one another and to the subject as a whole. In

✓CHECKLIST   Establishing Categories

☐ **All the categories should derive from the same principle.** If you decide to divide *television shows* into *sitcoms, reality shows,* and the like, it is not logical to include *children's programs,* for this category results from one principle (target audience) while the others result from another principle (genre). Similarly, if you were classifying undergraduates at your school according to their year, you would not include the category *students receiving financial aid.*

☐ **All the categories should be at the same level.** In the series *sitcoms, action/adventure,* and *Westerns,* the last item, *Westerns,* does not belong because it is at a lower level — that is, it is a subcategory of *action/adventure.* Likewise, *sophomores* (a subcategory of *undergraduates*) does not belong in the series *undergraduates, graduate students, continuing education students.*

☐ **You should treat all categories that are significant and relevant to your discussion.** Include enough categories to make your point, with no important omissions and no overlapping categories. In a review of a network's fall television lineup, the series *sitcoms, reality shows, crime shows,* and *detective shows* is incomplete because it omits important categories such as *news programs, game shows,* and *documentaries;* moreover, *detective shows* may overlap with *crime shows.* In the same way, the series *freshmen, sophomores, juniors,* and *transfers* is illogical: the important group *seniors* has been omitted, and *transfers* may include *freshmen, sophomores,* and *juniors.*

addition, your thesis statement should tell your readers why your categories are significant or establish their relative value. For example, if you were writing an essay about investment strategies, a thesis statement that simply listed different kinds of investments would be pointless. Instead, your thesis statement might note their relative strengths and weaknesses and perhaps make recommendations based on this assessment. Similarly, a research paper about a writer's major works would accomplish little if it merely categorized his or her writings. Instead, your thesis statement should communicate your evaluation of these works, perhaps demonstrating that some deserve higher public regard than others.

Using Transitions

When you write a classification-and-division essay, you use transitional words and phrases both to introduce your categories (*the first category, one category,* and so on) and to move readers from one category to the next (*the second category, another category,* and so on). In addition, transitional words and expressions can show readers the relationships between categories — for example, whether one category is more important than another (*a more important category, the most important category,* and so on). A more complete list of transitions appears on page 57.

Structuring a Classification-and-Division Essay

Once you have drafted your essay's thesis statement and established your categories, you should plan your classification-and-division essay around the same three major sections that other essays have: *introduction, body,* and *conclusion.* Your **introduction** should orient your readers by identifying your topic, the principle for classifying your material, and the individual categories you plan to discuss; your thesis is also usually stated in the introduction. In the **body paragraphs**, you should discuss your categories one by one, in the same order in which you mentioned them in your introduction. Finally, your **conclusion** should restate your thesis in different words, summing up the points you have made and perhaps considering their implications.

Suppose you are preparing a research paper on Mark Twain's nonfiction works for an American literature course. You have read selections from *Roughing It, Life on the Mississippi,* and *The Innocents Abroad.* Besides these travel narratives, you have read parts of Twain's autobiography and some of his correspondence and essays. When you realize that the works you have studied can easily be classified as four different types of Twain's nonfiction — travel narratives, essays, letters, and autobiography — you decide to use classification and division to structure your essay. So, you first divide the large class *Twain's nonfiction prose* into major categories — his travel narratives, essays, autobiography, and letters. Then, you classify the individual works, assigning each work to one of these categories, which you will discuss one at a time. Your purpose is to persuade readers to reconsider the reputations of some of these works, and you word your thesis statement accordingly. You might then prepare a formal outline like the one that follows for the body of your paper.

Sample Outline   **Classification and Division**

Thesis statement: Most readers know Mark Twain as a novelist, but his nonfiction works — his travel narratives, essays, letters, and especially his autobiography — deserve more attention.

I. Travel narratives
   A. *Roughing It*
   B. *The Innocents Abroad*
   C. *Life on the Mississippi*

II. Essays
   A. "Fenimore Cooper's Literary Offenses"
   B. "How to Tell a Story"
   C. "The Awful German Language"
III. Letters
   A. To W. D. Howells
   B. To his family
IV. Autobiography

Because this will be a long essay, each of the outline's divisions will have several subdivisions, and each subdivision might require several paragraphs.

This outline illustrates the characteristics of an effective classification-and-division essay. First, Twain's nonfiction works are classified according to a single principle of classification — literary genre. (Depending on your purpose, another principle — such as theme or subject matter — could work just as well.) The outline also reveals that the paper's four categories are on the same level (each is a different literary genre) and that all relevant categories are included. Had you left out *essays,* for example, you would have been unable to classify several significant works of nonfiction.

This outline also arranges the four categories so that they will support your thesis most effectively. Because you believe Twain's travel narratives are somewhat overrated, you plan to discuss them early in your paper. Similarly, because you think the autobiography would make your best case for the merit of the nonfiction works as a whole, you decide it should be placed last. (Of course, you could arrange your categories in several other orders, such as from shorter to longer works or from least to most popular, depending on the thesis your paper will support.)

Finally, this outline reminds you to treat all categories comparably in your paper. Your case would be weakened if, for example, you inadvertently skipped style in your discussion of Twain's letters while discussing style for every other category. This omission might lead your readers to suspect that you had not done enough research on the letters or that the style of Twain's letters did not measure up to the style of his other works.

Revising a Classification-and-Division Essay

When you revise a classification-and-division essay, consider the items on the revision checklist on page 68. In addition, pay special attention to the items on the following checklist, which apply specifically to revising classification-and-division essays.

✓ **REVISION CHECKLIST**   **Classification and Division**

☐ Does your assignment call for classification and division?
☐ Have you identified a principle of classification for your material?
☐ Have you identified the categories you plan to discuss and decided how you will treat them?
☐ Have you arranged your categories in a logical order?
☐ Have you treated all categories similarly?
☐ Does your essay have a clearly stated thesis that identifies your subject and the categories you will discuss and indicates the significance of your classification?
☐ Have you used transitional words and phrases to show the relationships among categories?

Editing a Classification-and-Division Essay

When you edit your classification-and-division essay, you should follow the guidelines on the editing checklists on pages 85, 88, and 91. In addition, you should focus on the grammar, mechanics, and punctuation issues that are particularly relevant to classification-and-division essays. One of these issues — using a colon to introduce your categories — is discussed below.

GRAMMAR IN CONTEXT   **Using a Colon to Introduce Your Categories**

When you state the thesis of a classification-and-division essay, you often give readers an overview by listing the categories you will discuss. You introduce this list of categories with a **colon**, a punctuation mark whose purpose is to direct readers to look ahead for a series, list, clarification, or explanation.

When you use a colon to introduce your categories, the colon must be preceded by a complete sentence.

CORRECT: Carolyn Foster Segal's essay identifies kinds of student excuses with five headings: The Family, The Best Friend, The Evils of Dorm Life, The Evils of Technology, and The Totally Bizarre.

INCORRECT: The headings that Carolyn Foster Segal uses to identify kinds of student excuses are: The Family, The Best Friend, The Evils of Dorm Life, The Evils of Technology, and The Totally Bizarre.

In any list or series of three or more categories, the categories should be separated by commas, with a comma preceding the *and* that separates the last two items. This last comma prevents confusion by ensuring that readers will be able to see at a glance exactly how many categories you are discussing.

CORRECT: The Family, The Best Friend, The Evils of Dorm Life, The Evils of Technology, and The Totally Bizarre (five categories)

INCORRECT: The Family, The Best Friend, The Evils of Dorm Life, The Evils of Technology and The Totally Bizarre (without the final comma, it might appear you are only discussing four categories)

NOTE: Items on a list or in a series are always expressed in **parallel** terms.

☑ EDITING CHECKLIST   **Classification and Division**

☐ Do you introduce your list of categories with a colon preceded by a complete sentence?
☐ Are the items on your list of categories separated by commas?
☐ Do you include a comma before the *and* that connects the last two items on your list?
☐ Do you express the items on your list in parallel terms?

A STUDENT WRITER: Classification and Division

The following classification-and-division essay was written by Josie Martinez for an education course. Her assignment was to look back at her own education and to consider what she had learned so far, referring in her essay to William Zinsser's "College Pressures" (page 448). Josie's essay divides a whole — college classes — into four categories.

What I Learned (and Didn't Learn) in College

Introduction

In "College Pressures," William Zinsser notes the   1
disappearance of a time when college students "journeyed through college with a certain relaxation, sampling a wide variety of courses — music, art, philosophy, classics, anthropology, poetry, religion — that would send them out as liberally educated men and women" (450). The change in college students' focus is even more noticeable today than when Zinsser wrote his essay, and it represents a real loss for students. Taking a variety of different kinds of courses can educate students about a wide range of subjects, and it can also teach them about themselves.

Categories listed and explained

Despite the variety of experiences that different students   2
have with different courses, most college classes can be classified
into one of four categories: ideal classes, worthless classes,
disappointing classes, and unexpectedly valuable classes. First are
courses that students love — ideal learning environments in which
they enjoy both the subject matter and the professor-student
interaction. Far from these ideal courses are those that students
find completely worthless in terms of subject matter, atmosphere,
and teaching style. Somewhere between these two extremes are
two kinds of courses that can be classified into another pair of
opposites: courses that students expect to enjoy and to learn
much from but are disappointing and courses that students are
initially not interested in but that exceed their expectations.

Thesis statement

Understanding these four categories can help students accept *thesis*
the fact that one disappointing class is not a disaster and can
encourage them to try classes with different kinds of subjects,
class sizes, and instructors.

First category: ideal class

One of the best courses I have taken so far as a college   3
student was my Shakespeare class. The professor who taught it
had a great sense of humor and was liberal in terms of what she
allowed in her classroom — for example, controversial Shakespeare *discussion*
adaptations and virtually any discussion, relevant or irrelevant.
The students in the class — English majors and non-English majors,
those who were interested in the plays as theater and those who
preferred to study them as literature — shared an enthusiasm for
Shakespeare, and they were eager to engage in lively discussions.
This class gave us a thorough knowledge of Shakespeare's plays
(tragedies, histories, comedies) as well as an understanding
of his life. We also developed our analytical skills through our
discussions of the plays and films as well as through special
projects — for example, a character profile presentation and an
abstract art presentation relating a work of art to one of the plays.
This class was an ideal learning environment not only because
of the wealth of material we were exposed to but also because *respect*
of the respect with which our professor treated us: we were her
colleagues, and she was as willing to learn from us as we were to
learn from her.

Second category: worthless class

In contrast to this ideal class, one of the most worthless   4
courses I have taken in college was Movement Education. As an
education major, I expected to like this class, and several other

students who had taken it told me it was both easy and enjoyable. The class consisted of playing children's games and learning what made certain activities appropriate and inappropriate for children of various ages. The only requirement for this class was that we had to write note cards explaining how to play each game so that we could use them for reference in our future teaching experiences. Unfortunately, I never really enjoyed the games we played, and I have long since discarded my note cards and forgotten how to play the games — or even what they were.

Third category: disappointing class

Although I looked forward to taking Introduction to Astronomy, I was very disappointed in this class. I had hoped to satisfy my curiosity about the universe outside our solar system, but the instructor devoted most of the semester to a detailed study of the Earth and the other bodies in our own solar system. In addition, a large part of our work included charting orbits and processing distance equations — work that I found both difficult and boring. Furthermore, we spent hardly any class time learning how to use a telescope and how to locate objects in the sky. In short, I gained little information from the class, learning only how to solve equations I would never confront again and how to chart orbits that had already been charted.

Fourth category: unexpectedly valuable class

In direct contrast to my astronomy class, a religion class called Paul and the Early Church was much more rewarding than I had anticipated. Having attended Catholic school for thirteen years, I assumed this course would offer me little that was new to me. However, because the class took a historical approach to studying Paul's biblical texts, I found that I learned more about Christianity than I had in all my previous religion classes. We learned about the historical validity of Paul and other texts in the Bible and how they were derived from various sources and passed orally through several generations before being written down and translated into different languages. We approached the texts from a linguistic perspective, determining the significance of certain words and learning how various meanings can be derived from different translations of the same passage. This class was unlike any of my other religion classes in that it encouraged me to study the texts objectively, leaving me with a new and valuable understanding of material I had been exposed to for most of my life.

5

6

Conclusion   Although each student's learning experience in college   7
will be different — because every student has a different learning
style, is interested in different subjects, and takes courses at
different schools taught by different professors — all college
students' experiences are similar in one respect. All students

Summary of will encounter the same kinds of courses: those that are ideal,
four categories those that are worthless, those that they learn little from despite
their interest in the subject, and those that they learn from and

Restatement become engaged in despite their low expectations. Understanding
of thesis that these categories exist is important because it gives students
the freedom and courage to try new things, as college students
did years ago. After all, even if one course is a disappointment,
another may be more interesting — or even exciting. For this
reason, college students should not be discouraged by a course
they do not like; the best classes are almost certainly still in their
future.

Work Cited

Works-cited list Zinsser, William. "College Pressures." *Patterns for College Writing: A*
(begins new page) *Rhetorical Reader and Guide.* 13th ed. Ed. Laurie G. Kirszner
and Stephen R. Mandell. Boston: Bedford, 2015. 448–54. Print.

Points for Special Attention

Working with Sources. Josie's teacher asked students to cite William
Zinsser's "College Pressures," which they had just discussed, somewhere in
their own essays. Josie knew that the passage she chose to quote or paraphrase would have to be directly relevant to her own paper's subject, so
she knew it would have to focus on academic (rather than economic or
social) pressures. When she discovered Zinsser's comments on students'
tendency not to experiment with a wide variety of courses, she knew she
had found material that could give her essay a more global, less personal
focus. For this reason, she decided to refer to Zinsser in her essay's first
paragraph. (Note that she includes parenthetical documentation and a
separate works-cited page.)

Thesis and Support. Josie's purpose in writing this essay was to
communicate to her professor and the other students in her education
class what she had learned from the classes she had taken so far in college,
and both the thesis she states in paragraph 2 and the restatement of this
thesis in her conclusion make this clear: what she has learned is to take a
wide variety of courses. Knowing that few, if any, students in her class
would have taken any of the courses she took, Josie realized she had to
provide a lot of detail to show what these classes taught her.

Organization. As she reviewed the various courses she had taken and assessed their strengths and weaknesses, Josie saw a classification scheme emerging. As soon as she noticed this, she organized her material into four categories. Rather than discuss the four kinds of classes from best to worst or from worst to best, Josie decided to present them as two opposing pairs: ideal class and worthless class, surprisingly disappointing class and unexpectedly worthwhile class. In paragraph 2, Josie lists the four categories she plans to discuss in her essay and gives readers an overview of these categories to help prepare them for her thesis.

Transitions between Categories. Josie uses clear topic sentences to move readers from one category to the next and to indicate the relationship of each category to another.

One of the best courses I have taken so far as a college student was my Shakespeare class. (3)

In contrast to this ideal class, one of the most worthless courses I have taken in college was Movement Education. (4)

Although I looked forward to taking Introduction to Astronomy, I was very disappointed in this class. (5)

In direct contrast to my astronomy class, a religion class called Paul and the Early Church was much more rewarding than I had anticipated. (6)

These four sentences distinguish the four categories from one another and also help to communicate Josie's direction and emphasis.

Focus on Revision

An earlier draft of Josie's essay, which she discussed with her instructor in a conference, did not include very specific topic sentences. Instead, the sentences were vague and unfocused:

One class I took in college was a Shakespeare course.

Another class I took was Movement Education.

I looked forward to taking Introduction to Astronomy.

My experience with a religion class was very different.

Although her essay's second paragraph listed the categories and explained how they differed, Josie's instructor advised her to revise her topic sentences so that it would be clear which category she was discussing in each body paragraph. Josie took his advice and revised these topic sentences. After reading her next draft, she felt confident that her categories — listed in paragraph 2 and repeated in her topic sentences and in her conclusion — were clear and distinct.

Even after making these revisions, however, Josie felt her paper needed some additional fine-tuning. For example, in her final draft, she planned to add some material to paragraphs 4 and 5. At first, because she had dismissed Movement Education as completely worthless and Introduction to Astronomy as disappointing, Josie felt she did not have to say much about them. When she reread her paper, however, she realized she needed to explain the shortcomings of the two classes more fully so that her readers would understand why these classes had little value for her.

PEER-EDITING WORKSHEET: Classification and Division

1. Paraphrase the essay's thesis.

2. What whole is being divided into parts in this essay? Into what general categories is the whole divided?

3. Is each category clearly identified and explained? If not, what revisions can you suggest? (For example, can you suggest a different title for a particular category? A different topic sentence to introduce it?)

4. Where does the writer list the categories to be discussed? Is the list introduced by a colon (preceded by a complete sentence)? If not, suggest revisions.

5. Are the categories arranged in a logical order, one that indicates their relationships to one another and their relative importance? If not, how could they be rearranged?

6. Does the writer treat all relevant categories and no irrelevant ones? Which categories, if any, should be added, deleted, or combined?

7. Does the writer include all necessary items, and no unnecessary ones, within each category? What additional items could be added? Should any items be located elsewhere?

8. Does the writer treat all categories similarly, discussing comparable points for each? Should any additional points be discussed? If so, where?

9. Do topic sentences clearly signal the movement from one category to the next? Should any topic sentences be strengthened to mark the boundaries between categories more clearly? If so, which ones?

10. Could the writer use another pattern of development to structure this essay, or is classification and division the best choice? Explain.

Each of the following selections is developed by means of classification and division. In some cases, the pattern is used to explain ideas; in others, it is used to persuade the reader. The first selection, a visual text, is followed by questions designed to illustrate how classification and division can operate in visual form. (Two multimodal texts for classification and division are located online at **macmillanhighered.com/patterns**.)

Key to Chalk Marks Designating Medical Conditions of Immigrants, Ellis Island (Chart)

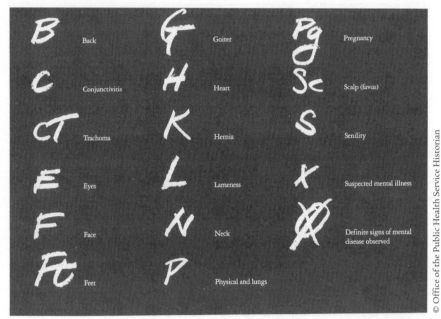

© Office of the Public Health Service Historian

• • •

Reading Images

1. The photo above shows symbols, written in chalk on early-twentieth-century immigrants' clothing, representing medical conditions that could disqualify them from entry into the United States. What different principles of classification might be used to sort these symbols into categories? Which principle of classification seems to make the most sense? Why?

2. Guided by the principle of classification you selected in question 1, arrange the various symbols into three or four distinct categories. Are there any that do not fit into your classification scheme?

3. The chalk mark system illustrated here is no longer in use, but visitors' health is still a consideration. What medical conditions do you think should disqualify a visitor for entry into the United States today? List

some possible criteria for exclusion, and arrange these criteria into categories.

Journal Entry

Do you think the United States should exclude any potential immigrants solely for medical reasons? Why or why not?

Thematic Connections

- "Why Looks Are the Last Bastion of Discrimination" (page 244)
- "The Untouchable" (page 494)
- "Should American Citizenship Be a Birthright?" (Debate; page 591)

WILLIAM ZINSSER

College Pressures

William Zinsser has worked as a newspaper and magazine writer and has taught English at Yale University. He is also the author of numerous books on writing, including *On Writing Well: The Classic Guide to Writing Nonfiction* (twenty-fifth anniversary edition, 2001) and *Writing about Your Life: A Journey into the Past* (2004). His works on American culture include *Spring Training* (1989), about the culture of baseball, and *Easy to Remember: Great American Songwriters and Their Songs* (2001). In 2010–11, Zinsser wrote a weekly online column, Zinsser on Friday, for the *American Scholar*.

Background on college pressures today Although the following essay focuses on the kinds of pressures facing Yale students in 1979, many of these remain relevant (and, in some cases, even more relevant) for college students today. These pressures include the need to develop time management and study skills appropriate for college work, the desire for good grades, the desire to meet parents' expectations, and the need to find employment in a competitive job market after graduation. In addition, many college students today face pressures unknown to most students in the late 1970s. According to the U.S. Department of Education's National Center for Education Statistics, only about 25 percent of current undergraduates fit the "traditional" model of eighteen- to twenty-two-year-old full-time students still supported primarily by their parents. Increasingly, college undergraduates are adults, supporting themselves — and sometimes families — and funding their own education through full- or part-time employment in addition to loans. In 2014, the average student debt was $30,000 and growing. Unemployment for recent college graduates varies by undergraduate major. (The highest unemployment rate — 7 to 8 percent — is among liberal arts and social science majors.)

Dear Carlos: I desperately need a dean's excuse for my chem midterm which will begin in about one hour. All I can say is that I totally blew it this week. I've fallen incredibly, inconceivably behind. 1

Carlos: Help! I'm anxious to hear from you. I'll be in my room and won't leave it until I hear from you. Tomorrow is the last day for . . . 2

Carlos: I left town because I started bugging out again. I stayed up all night to finish a take home make-up exam and am typing it to hand in on the 10th. It was due on the 5th. P.S. I'm going to the dentist. Pain is pretty bad. 3

Carlos: Probably by Friday I'll be able to get back to my studies. Right now I'm going to take a long walk. This whole thing has taken a lot out of me. 4

Carlos: I'm really up the proverbial creek. The problem is I really *bombed* the history final. Since I need that course for my major . . . 5

Carlos: Here follows a tale of woe. I went home this weekend, had to help my   6
Mom, & caught a fever so didn't have much time to study. My professor . . .

Carlos: Aargh! Nothing original but everything's piling up at once. To be brief,   7
my job interview . . .

Hey Carlos, good news! I've got mononucleosis.   8

Who are these wretched supplicants, scribbling notes so laden with   9
anxiety, seeking such miracles of postponement and balm? They are men
and women who belong to Branford College, one of the twelve residential
colleges at Yale University, and the messages are just a few of the hundreds
that they left for their dean, Carlos Hortas — often slipped under his door
at 4 A.M. — last year.

But students like the ones who wrote those notes can also be found on   10
campuses from coast to coast — especially in New England and at many
other private colleges across the country that have high academic standards and highly motivated students. Nobody could doubt that the notes
are real. In their urgency and their gallows humor they are authentic voices
of a generation that is panicky to succeed.

My own connection with the message writers is that I am master of   11
Bradford College. I live in its Gothic quadrangle and know the students
well. (We have 485 of them.) I am privy to their hopes and fears — and also
to their stereo music and their piercing cries in the dead of night ("Does
anybody *ca-a-are?*"). If they went to Carlos to ask how to get through tomorrow, they come to me to ask how to get through the rest of their lives.

Mainly I try to remind them that the road ahead is a long one and that   12
it will have more unexpected turns than they think. There will be plenty of
time to change jobs, change careers, change whole attitudes and approaches.
They don't want to hear such liberating news. They want a map — right
now — that they can follow unswervingly to career security, financial security, Social Security, and, presumably, a prepaid grave.

What I wish for all students is some release from the clammy grip of   13
the future. I wish them a chance to savor each segment of their education
as an experience in itself and not as a grim
preparation for the next step. I wish them
the right to experiment, to trip and fall, to
learn that defeat is as instructive as victory
and is not the end of the world.

 his wishes – unrealistic

> One of the few
> rights that America
> does not proclaim is
> the right to fail.

My wish, of course, is naive. One of the   14
few rights that America does not proclaim is
the right to fail. Achievement is the national
god, venerated in our media — the million-   *right to fail.*
dollar athlete, the wealthy executive — and glorified in our praise of possessions. In the presence of such a potent state religion, the young are growing
up old.

I see four kinds of pressure working on college students today: eco-   15
nomic pressure, parental pressure, peer pressure, and self-induced pressure.

[margin note: No Villains]

It is easy to look around for villains — to blame the colleges for charging too much money, the professors for assigning too much work, the parents for pushing their children too far, the students for driving themselves too hard. But there are no villains, only victims.

[margin note: only victims]

"In the late 1960s," one dean told me, "the typical question that I got from students was 'Why is there so much suffering in the world?' or 'How can I make a contribution?' Today it's 'Do you think it would look better for getting into law school if I did a double major in history and political science, or just majored in one of them?'" Many other deans confirmed this pattern. One said: "They're trying to find an edge — the intangible something that will look better on paper if two students are about equal." 16

[margin note: find an edge]

Note the emphasis on looking better. The transcript has become a sacred document, the passport to security. How one appears on paper is more important than how one appears in person. *A* is for Admirable and *B* is for Borderline, even though, in Yale's official system of grading, *A* means "excellent" and *B* means "very good." Today, looking very good is no longer good enough, especially for students who hope to go on to law school or medical school. They know that entrance into the better schools will be an entrance into the better law firms and better medical practices where they will make a lot of money. They also know that the odds are harsh. Yale Law School, for instance, matriculates 170 students from an applicant pool of 3,700; Harvard enrolls 550 from a pool of 7,000. 17

It's all very well for those of us who write letters of recommendation for our students to stress the qualities of humanity that will make them good lawyers or doctors. And it's nice to think that admission officers are really reading our letters and looking for the extra dimension of commitment or concern. Still, it would be hard for a student not to visualize these officers shuffling so many transcripts studded with *A*s that they regard a *B* as positively shameful. 18

The pressure is almost as heavy on students who just want to graduate and get a job. Long gone are the days of the "gentleman's C," when students journeyed through college with a certain relaxation, sampling a wide variety of courses — music, art, philosophy, classics, anthropology, poetry, religion — that would send them out as liberally educated men and women. If I were an employer I would rather employ graduates who have this range and curiosity than those who narrowly pursued safe subjects and high grades. I know countless students whose inquiring minds exhilarate me. I like to hear the play of their ideas. I don't know if they're getting *A*s or *C*s, and I don't care. I also like them as people. The country needs them, and they will find satisfying jobs. I tell them to relax. They can't. 19

[margin note: yes!]

Nor can I blame them. They live in a brutal economy. Tuition, room, and board at most private colleges now comes to at least $7,000, not counting books and fees.* This might seem to suggest that the colleges are getting rich. But they are equally battered by inflation. Tuition covers only 20

[margin note: in 1979]

---

* Eds. note — Zinsser's essay was published in 1979; the figures quoted for tuition and other expenses would be a great deal higher today.

60 percent of what it costs to educate a student, and ordinarily the remainder comes from what colleges receive in endowments, grants, and gifts. Now the remainder keeps being swallowed by cruel costs — higher every year — of just opening the doors. Heating oil is up. Insurance is up. Postage is up. Health-premium costs are up. Everything is up. Deficits are up. We are witnessing in America the creation of a brotherhood of paupers — colleges, parents, and students, joined by the common bond of debt. *loans*

Today it is not unusual for a student, even if he works part-time at 21 college and full-time during the summer, to accrue $5,000 in loans after four years — loans that he must start to repay within one year after graduation. Exhorted at commencement to go forth into the world, he is already behind as he goes forth. How could he not feel under pressure throughout college to prepare for this day of reckoning? I have used "he" incidentally, only for brevity. Women at Yale are under no less pressure to justify their expensive education to themselves, their parents, and society. In fact, they *women* are probably under more pressure. For although they leave college superbly equipped to bring fresh leadership to traditionally male jobs, society hasn't yet caught up with this fact.

Along with economic pressure goes parental pressure. Inevitably, the 22 two are deeply intertwined.

I see many students taking pre-medical courses with joyless tenacity. 23 They go off to their labs as if they were going to the dentist. It saddens me because I know them in other corners of their life as cheerful people.

"Do you want to go to medical school?" I ask them. 24

"I guess so," they say, without conviction, or "Not really." 25

"Then why are you going?" 26

"Well, my parents want me to be a doctor. They're paying all this 27 money and . . ."

Poor students, poor parents. They are caught in one of the oldest webs 28 of love and duty and guilt. The parents mean well; they are trying to steer their sons and daughters toward a secure future. But the sons and daughters want to major in history or classics or philosophy — subjects with no "practical" value. Where's the payoff on the humanities? It's not easy to *liberal* persuade such loving parents that the humanities do indeed pay off. The *arts* intellectual faculties developed by studying subjects like history and classics — an ability to synthesize and relate, to weigh cause and effect, to see *✳* events in perspective — are just the faculties that make creative leaders in business or almost any general field. Still, many fathers would rather put their money on courses that point toward a specific profession — courses that are pre-law, pre-medical, pre-business, or, as I sometimes heard it put, "pre-rich."

But the pressure on students is severe. They are truly torn. One part 29 of them feels obliged to fulfill their parents' expectations; after all, their parents are older and presumably wiser. Another part tells them that the expectations that are right for their parents are not right for them.

I know a student who wants to be an artist. She is very obviously an 30 artist and will be a good one — she has already had several modest exhibits.

UNCW   12+ credit hours   — in state =
                                    $3345.33

Meanwhile she is growing as a well-rounded person and taking humanistic subjects that will enrich the inner resources out of which her art will grow. But her father is strongly opposed. He thinks that an artist is a "dumb" thing to be. The student vacillates and tries to please everybody. She keeps up with her art somewhat furtively and takes some of the "dumb" courses her father wants her to take — at least they are dumb courses for her. She is a free spirit on a campus of tense students — no small achievement in itself — and she deserves to follow her muse.

Peer pressure and self-induced pressure are also intertwined, and they 31 begin almost at the beginning of freshman year.

"I had a freshman student I'll call Linda," one dean told me, "who came 32 in and said she was under terrible pressure because her roommate, Barbara, was much brighter and studied all the time. I couldn't tell her that Barbara had come in two hours earlier to say the same thing about Linda."

The story is almost funny — except that it's not. It's symptomatic of all 33 the pressures put together. When every student thinks every other student is working harder and doing better, the only solution is to study harder still. I see students going off to the library every night after dinner and coming back when it closes at midnight. I wish they could sometimes forget about their peers and go to a movie. I hear the clacking of typewriters in the hours before dawn. I see the tension in their eyes when exams are approaching and papers are due: *"Will I get everything done?"*

Probably they won't. They will get sick. They will get "blocked." They 34 will sleep. They will oversleep. They will bug out. *Hey Carlos, help!*

Part of the problem is that they do more than they are expected to do. 35 A professor will assign five-page papers. Several students will start writing ten-page papers to impress him. Then more students will write ten-page papers, and a few will raise the ante to fifteen. Pity the poor student who is still just doing the assignment.

"Once you have twenty or thirty percent of the student population 36 deliberately overexerting," one dean points out, "it's bad for everybody. When a teacher gets more and more effort from his class, the student who is doing normal work can be perceived as not doing well. The tactic works, psychologically."

Why can't the professor just cut back and not accept longer papers? 37 He can, and he probably will. But by then the term will be half over and the damage done. Grade fever is highly contagious and not easily reversed. Besides, the professor's main concern is with his course. He knows his students only in relation to the course and doesn't know that they are also overexerting in their other courses. Nor is it really his business. He didn't sign up for dealing with the student as a whole person and with all the emotional baggage the student brought along from home. That's what deans, masters, chaplains, and psychiatrists are for.

To some extent this is nothing new: a certain number of professors 38 have always been self-contained islands of scholarship and shyness, more comfortable with books than with people. But the new pauperism has widened the gap still further, for professors who actually like to spend time with students don't have as much time to spend. They also are overexerting. If they are young, they are busy trying to publish in order not to perish, hanging by their fingernails onto a shrinking profession. If they are old and tenured, they are buried under the duties of administering departments — as departmental chairmen or members of committees — that have been thinned out by the budgetary axe.

Ultimately it will be the students' own business to break the circles in 39 which they are trapped. They are too young to be prisoners of their parents' dreams and their classmates' fears. They must be jolted into believing in themselves as unique men and women who have the power to shape their own future.

"Violence is being done to the undergraduate experience," says Carlos 40 Hortas. "College should be open-ended: at the end it should open many, many roads. Instead, students are choosing their goal in advance, and their choices narrow as they go along. It's almost as if they think that the country has been codified in the type of jobs that exist — that they've got to fit into certain slots. Therefore, fit into the best-paying slot.

"They ought to take chances. Not taking chances will lead to a life of 41 colorless mediocrity. They'll be comfortable. But something in the spirit will be missing."

I have painted too drab a portrait of today's students, making them 42 seem a solemn lot. That is only half of their story; if they were so dreary I wouldn't so thoroughly enjoy their company. The other half is that they are easy to like. They are quick to laugh and to offer friendship. They are not introverts. They are usually kind and are more considerate of one another than any student generation I have known.

Nor are they so obsessed with their studies that they avoid sports and 43 extracurricular activities. On the contrary, they juggle their crowded hours to play on a variety of teams, perform with musical and dramatic groups, and write for campus publications. But this in turn is one more cause of anxiety. There are too many choices. Academically, they have 1,300 courses to select from; outside class they have to decide how much spare time they can spare and how to spend it.

This means that they engage in fewer extracurricular pursuits than 44 their predecessors did. If they want to row on the crew and play in the symphony they will eliminate one; in the '60s they would have done both. They also tend to choose activities that are self-limiting. Drama, for instance, is flourishing in all twelve of Yale's residential colleges as it never has before. Students hurl themselves into these productions — as actors, directors, carpenters, and technicians — with a dedication to create the best possible play, knowing that the day will come when the run will end and they can get back to their studies.

They also can't afford to be the willing slave of organizations like the 45 *Yale Daily News*. Last spring at the one-hundredth anniversary banquet of that paper — whose past chairmen include such once and future kings as

Potter Stewart, Kingman Brewster, and William F. Buckley Jr.* — much was made of the fact that the editorial staff used to be small and totally committed and that "newsies" routinely worked fifty hours a week. In effect they belonged to a club; Newsies is how they defined themselves at Yale. Today's student will write one or two articles a week, when he can, and he defines himself as a student. I've never heard the word Newsie except at the banquet.

46   If I have described the modern undergraduate primarily as a driven creature who is largely ignoring the blithe spirit inside who keeps trying to come out and play, it's because that's where the crunch is, not only at Yale but throughout American education. It's why I think we should all be worried about the values that are nurturing a generation so fearful of risk and so goal-obsessed at such an early age.

47   I tell students that there is no one "right" way to get ahead — that each of them is a different person, starting from a different point and bound for a different destination. I tell them that change is a tonic and that all the slots are not codified nor the frontiers closed. One of my ways of telling them is to invite men and women who have achieved success outside the academic world to come and talk informally with my students during the year. They are heads of companies or ad agencies, editors of magazines, politicians, public officials, television magnates, labor leaders, business executives, Broadway producers, artists, writers, economists, photographers, scientists, historians — a mixed bag of achievers.

48   I ask them to say a few words about how they got started. The students assume that they started in their present profession and knew all along that it was what they wanted to do. Luckily for me, most of them got into their field by a circuitous route, to their surprise, after many detours. The students are startled. They can hardly conceive of a career that was not preplanned. They can hardly imagine allowing the hand of God or chance to nudge them down some unforeseen trail.

· · ·

Comprehension

1. What advice does Zinsser give students when they bring their problems to him?

2. What does Zinsser wish for his students? Why does he believe his wish is naive?

3. What four kinds of pressure does Zinsser identify?

4. Whom does Zinsser blame for the existence of these pressures? Explain.

---

* Eds. note — Stewart was a U.S. Supreme Court justice, Brewster was a president of Yale, and Buckley was a conservative editor and columnist.

5. How, according to Zinsser, is his evaluation of students different from their own and from their potential employers' assessments?

6. Why does Zinsser believe that women are probably under even more pressure than men? Do you think this is true today?

7. How does what Zinsser calls the "new pauperism" (38) affect professors?

8. Who, according to Zinsser, is ultimately responsible for eliminating college pressures? Explain.

9. In what sense are sports and other extracurricular activities another source of anxiety for students? How do students adapt to this pressure?

Purpose and Audience

1. Is Zinsser's intent in this essay simply to expose a difficult situation or does he want to effect change? What makes you think so?

2. On what kind of audience do you think this essay would have the most significant impact: students, teachers, parents, potential employers, graduate school admissions committees, or college administrators? Why?

3. What do you think Zinsser hopes to accomplish in paragraphs 42–46? How would the essay be different without this section?

4. What assumptions does Zinsser make about his audience? Do you think these assumptions are valid? Explain.

Style and Structure

1. Evaluate the essay's introductory strategy. What impact do you think including the notes to Carlos is likely to have on readers?

2. Identify the boundaries of Zinsser's actual classification. How does he introduce the first category? How does he indicate that his treatment of the final category is complete?

3. What function do paragraphs 22 and 31 serve in the essay?

4. Zinsser is careful to explain that when he refers to students as *he,* he includes female students as well. However, he also refers to professors as *he* (for example, in paragraphs 35–37). Assuming that not all professors at Yale are male, what other stylistic options does Zinsser have?

5. At various points in the essay, Zinsser quotes deans and students at Yale. What is the effect of these quotations?

6. Zinsser notes that his categories are "intertwined" (22, 31). In what ways do the categories overlap? Does this overlap weaken the essay? Explain.

7. What, if anything, seems to determine the order in which Zinsser presents categories? Is this order effective? Why or why not?

8. **Vocabulary Project.** At times Zinsser uses religious language — *national god, sacred document* — to describe the students' quest for success. Identify other examples of such language, and explain why it is used.

Journal Entry

Which of the pressures Zinsser identifies has the greatest impact on you? Why? Do you have any pressures Zinsser does not mention?

Writing Workshop

1. Zinsser describes problems faced by students at an elite private college in the late 1970s. Are the pressures you experience as a college student similar to or different from the ones Zinsser identifies? Classify your own college pressures, and write an email to your academic adviser or dean. Include a thesis statement that takes a strong stand against the forces responsible for these pressures. *point to a specific issue*

2. **Working with Sources.** Write a classification essay supporting a thesis about college students' drive for success. Categorize students you know either by the degree of their need to succeed or by the different ways in which they wish to succeed. Include a reference to Zinsser's essay — or to Carolyn Foster Segal's essay on page 457 — to support your thesis. Be sure to include parenthetical documentation and a works-cited page. (See Chapter 18 for information on MLA documentation.)

3. Zinsser takes a negative view of the college pressures he identifies. Using his four categories, write an essay arguing that, in the long run, these pressures are not only necessary but also valuable.

Combining the Patterns

Exemplification is an important secondary pattern in this classification-and-division essay. Identify as many passages of exemplification as you can. What do these examples add to Zinsser's essay? What other kinds of examples might be helpful to readers?

Thematic Connections

- "Suicide Note" (page 364)
- "Why Chinese Mothers Are Superior" (page 408)
- "I'm Your Teacher, Not Your Internet-Service Provider" (page 415)
- "The Dog Ate My Flash Drive, and Other Tales of Woe" (page 457)
- "Is the Student Loan Crisis a Myth?" (Debate; page 578)

CAROLYN FOSTER SEGAL

The Dog Ate My Flash Drive, and Other Tales of Woe

Carolyn Foster Segal (b. 1950) teaches English at Cedar Crest College in Allentown, Pennsylvania. Segal has published poetry, fiction, and essays in a number of publications, including the *Chronicle of Higher Education,* where the following essay originally appeared. She sums up her ideas about writing as follows: "Writing — and it does not matter if it is writing about a feature of the landscape, an aspect of human nature, or a work of literature — begins with observation. The other parts are curiosity, imagination, and patience." She has received hundreds of responses from other instructors corroborating the experiences she describes here.

Background on academic integrity and honor codes While making up an excuse for being unprepared for class may seem like a minor infraction, it may still be considered a breach of academic integrity. At many colleges, honor codes define academic integrity and set penalties for those who violate its rules. The concept of college honor codes in the United States goes back to one developed by students at the University of Virginia in 1840, but reports of widespread cheating on college campuses in the early 1990s brought renewed interest in such codes. (Surveys show that more than three-quarters of college students have cheated at least once during their schooling, and an even greater number see cheating as the norm among successful students.) In 1992, the Center for Academic Integrity was established to help colleges and universities find ways to promote "honesty, trust, fairness, respect, and responsibility" among students and faculty members. Its original twenty-five-member group has grown to include more than two hundred institutions, and many other colleges have adopted its goals as well. The main focus of most honor codes is on discouraging plagiarism — copying the work of others and presenting the work of others as one's own — and various forms of cheating on tests. The Center for Academic Integrity sees promoting individual honesty as the fundamental issue underlying all of these concerns.

Taped to the door of my office is a cartoon that features a cat explain- 1
ing to his feline teacher, "The dog ate my homework." It is intended as a gently humorous reminder to my students that I will not accept excuses for late work, and it, like the lengthy warning on my syllabus, has had absolutely no effect. With a show of energy and creativity that would be admirable if applied to the (missing) assignments in question, my students persist, week after week, semester after semester, year after year, in offering excuses about why their work is not ready. Those reasons fall into several

broad categories: the family, the best friend, the evils of dorm life, the evils of technology, and the totally bizarre.

The Family

The death of the grandfather/grandmother is, of course, the grandmother of all excuses. What heartless teacher would dare to question a student's grief or veracity? What heartless student would lie, wishing death on a revered family member, just to avoid a deadline? Creative students may win extra extensions (and days off) with a little

> " Those reasons fall into several broad categories: the family, the best friend, the evils of dorm life, the evils of technology, and the totally bizarre. "

2

careful planning and fuller plot development, as in the sequence of "My grandfather/grandmother is sick"; "Now my grandfather/grandmother is in the hospital"; and finally, "We could all see it coming — my grandfather/grandmother is dead."

Another favorite excuse is "the family emergency," which (always) goes 3 like this: "There was an emergency at home, and I had to help my family." It's a lovely sentiment, one that conjures up images of Louisa May Alcott's* little women rushing off with baskets of food and copies of *Pilgrim's Progress*,** but I do not understand why anyone would turn to my most irresponsible students in times of trouble.

The Best Friend

This heartwarming concern for others extends beyond the family to 4 friends, as in, "My best friend was up all night and I had to (a) stay up with her in the dorm, (b) drive her to the hospital, or (c) drive to her college because (1) her boyfriend broke up with her, (2) she was throwing up blood [no one catches a cold anymore; everyone throws up blood], or (3) her grandfather/grandmother died."

At one private university where I worked as an adjunct, I heard an inter- 5 esting spin that incorporated the motifs of both best friend and dead relative: "My best friend's mother killed herself." One has to admire the cleverness here: A mysterious woman in the prime of her life has allegedly committed suicide, and no professor can prove otherwise! And I admit I was moved, until finally I had to point out to my students that it was amazing how the simple act of my assigning a topic for a paper seemed to drive

---

* Eds. note — Nineteenth-century sentimental novelist, author of *Little Women*.
** Eds. note — Eighteenth-century allegory by John Bunyan describing a Christian's journey from the City of Destruction to the Celestial City.

large numbers of otherwise happy and healthy middle-aged women to their deaths. I was careful to make that point during an off week, during which no deaths were reported.

The Evils of Dorm Life

These stories are usually fairly predictable; almost always feature the evil roommate or hallmate, with my student in the role of the innocent victim; and can be summed up as follows: My roommate, who is a horrible person, likes to party, and I, who am a good person, cannot concentrate on my work when he or she is partying. Variations include stories about the two people next door who were running around and crying loudly last night because (a) one of them had boyfriend/girlfriend problems; (b) one of them was throwing up blood; or (c) someone, somewhere, died. A friend of mine in graduate school had a student who claimed that his roommate attacked him with a hammer. That, in fact, was a true story; it came out in court when the bad roommate was tried for killing his grandfather. 6

yes!

The Evils of Technology

The computer age has revolutionized the student story, inspiring almost as many new excuses as it has Internet businesses. Here are just a few electronically enhanced explanations: 7

- The computer wouldn't let me save my work.
- The printer wouldn't print.
- The printer wouldn't print this file.
- The printer wouldn't give me time to proofread.
- The printer made a black line run through all my words, and I know you can't read this, but do you still want it, or wait, here, take my flash drive. File name? I don't know what you mean.
- I swear I attached it.
- It's my roommate's computer, and she usually helps me, but she had to go to the hospital because she was throwing up blood.
- I did write to the listserv, but all my messages came back to me.
- I just found out that all my other listserv messages came up under a diferent name. I just want you to know that its really me who wrote all those messages, you can tel which ones our mine because I didnt use the spelcheck! But it was yours truely :) Anyway, just in case you missed those messages or dont belief its my writting. I'll repeat what I sad: I thought the last movie we watched in clas was borring.

The Totally Bizarre

I call the first story "The Pennsylvania Chain Saw Episode." A commuter student called to explain why she had missed my morning class. She 8 had gotten up early so that she would be wide awake for class. Having a bit of extra time, she walked outside to see her neighbor, who was cutting some wood. She called out to him, and he waved back to her with the saw. Wouldn't you know it, the safety catch wasn't on or was broken, and the blade flew right out of the saw and across his lawn and over her fence and across her yard and severed a tendon in her right hand. So she was calling me from the hospital, where she was waiting for surgery. Luckily, she reassured me, she had remembered to bring her paper and a stamped envelope (in a plastic bag, to avoid bloodstains) along with her in the ambulance, and a nurse was mailing everything to me even as we spoke.

That wasn't her first absence. In fact, this student had missed most of 9 the class meetings, and I had already recommended that she withdraw from the course. Now I suggested again that it might be best if she dropped the class. I didn't harp on the absences (what if even some of this story were true?). I did mention that she would need time to recuperate and that making up so much missed work might be difficult. "Oh, no," she said, "I can't drop this course. I had been planning to go on to medical school and become a surgeon, but since I won't be able to operate because of my accident, I'll have to major in English, and this course is more important than ever to me." She did come to the next class, wearing — as evidence of her recent trauma — a bedraggled Ace bandage on her left hand.

You may be thinking that nothing could top that excuse, but in fact I 10 have one more story, provided by the same student, who sent me a letter to explain why her final assignment would be late. While recuperating from her surgery, she had begun corresponding on the Internet with a man who lived in Germany. After a one-week, whirlwind Web romance, they had agreed to meet in Rome, to rendezvous (her phrase) at the papal Easter Mass. Regrettably, the time of her flight made it impossible for her to attend class, but she trusted that I — just this once — would accept late work if the pope wrote a note.

• • •

Comprehension

1. What exactly is Segal classifying in this essay?

2. In paragraph 3, Segal says, "I do not understand why anyone would turn to my most irresponsible students in times of trouble." Do you see this comment as fair?

3. Which of the excuses Segal discusses do you see as valid? Which do you see as just excuses? Why?

4. Do you see Segal as rigid and unsympathetic, or do you think her frustration is justified? Do you think her students are irresponsible procrastinators or simply overworked?

5. What lessons do you think Segal would like her students to learn from her? Would reading this essay teach them what she wants them to learn?

Purpose and Audience

1. This essay was originally published in the *Chronicle of Higher Education,* a periodical for college teachers and administrators. How do you think these readers responded to the essay? How do you respond?

2. Do you see Segal's purpose here as being to entertain, to let off steam, to warn, to criticize, or to change students' habits? Explain.

3. In paragraph 7, Segal lists some specific excuses in the "evils of technology" category, paraphrasing students' remarks and even imitating their grammar and style. Why does she do this? Considering her likely audience, is this an effective strategy?

Style and Structure

1. In paragraph 1, Segal lists the five categories she plans to discuss. Is this list necessary? Why or why not?

2. Are Segal's categories mutually exclusive, or do they overlap? Could she combine any categories? Can you think of any categories she does not include?

3. What determines the order in which Segal introduces her categories? Is this order logical, or should she present her categories in a different order?

4. Does Segal discuss comparable points for each category? What points, if any, need to be added?

5. Segal frequently uses **sarcasm** in this essay. Give some examples. Given her intended audience, do you think this tone is appropriate? How do you react to her sarcasm?

6. **Vocabulary Project.** Every profession has its own unique **jargon**. What words and expressions in this essay characterize the writer as a college professor?

7. Throughout her essay, Segal returns again and again to two excuses: "my grandfather/grandmother died" and "throwing up blood." Locate different versions of these excuses in the essay. Why do you think she singles out these two excuses?

8. Although Segal deals with a serious academic problem, she includes many expressions — such as "Wouldn't you know it" (8) — that give her essay an informal tone. Identify some other examples. What is your reaction to the essay's casual, offhand tone?

9. Review the category Segal calls "The Evils of Technology." Can you add to (and update) her list? Can you create subcategories?

Journal Entry

Do you think this essay is funny? Explain your reaction.

Writing Workshop

1. **Working with Sources.** Write an email to Segal explaining why your English paper will be late, presenting several different kinds of original excuses for your paper's lateness. Before you present your own superior excuses, be sure to acknowledge the inadequacies of the excuses Segal lists, quoting a few and including parenthetical documentation and a works-cited page. (See Chapter 18 for information about MLA documentation.)

2. Write an essay identifying four or five categories of legitimate excuses for handing in work late. If you like, you can use narrative examples from your own life as a student to explain each category.

3. Using a humorous (or even sarcastic) tone, write an essay identifying several different categories of teachers in terms of their shortcomings — for instance, teachers who do not cover the assigned work or teachers who do not grade papers in a timely fashion. Be sure to give specific examples of teachers in each category.

Combining the Patterns

In paragraphs 8–10, Segal uses **narration** to tell two stories. What do these stories add to her essay? Do you think she should have added more stories like these to her essay? If so, where?

Thematic Connections

- "Cutting and Pasting: A Senior Thesis by (Insert Name)" (page 24)
- "I'm Your Teacher, Not Your Internet-Service Provider" (page 415)
- "College Pressures" (page 448)
- "The Ways We Lie" (page 471)

AMY TAN

Mother Tongue

Amy Tan was born in 1952 in Oakland, California, the daughter of recent Chinese immigrants. In 1984, when she began to write fiction, she started to explore the contradictions she faced as a Chinese American who was also the daughter of immigrant parents. Three years later, she published *The Joy Luck Club* (1987), a best-selling novel about four immigrant Chinese women and their American-born daughters. Her most recent books are the novels *Rules for Virgins* (2011) and *The Valley of Amazement* (2013). In the following 1990 essay, Tan considers her mother's heavily Chinese-influenced English, as well as the different "Englishes" she herself uses, especially in communicating with her mother. She then discusses the potential limitations of growing up with immigrant parents who do not speak fluent English.

Background on Asian Americans and standardized tests The children of Asian immigrants tend to be highly assimilated and are often outstanding students, in part because their parents expect them to work hard and do well. Most who were born in the United States speak and read English fluently. Yet on standardized tests, they have generally scored much higher in math than in English. For example, the average SAT scores nationally in 2009 were 515 in math, 501 in critical reading, and 493 in writing. Asian-American students had average scores of 587 in math, 516 in critical reading, and 520 in writing. The verbal scores represent a recent improvement over previous years, in which Asian-American students generally scored lower than average in the verbal sections of the SAT. In some cases, as Tan suggests, the perception that Asian-American students have greater skill in math than in reading and writing, based on average standardized test scores, may lead teachers to discourage these students from pursuing degrees in fields outside of math and science.

1 I am not a scholar of English or literature. I cannot give you much more than personal opinions on the English language and its variations in this country or others.

2 I am a writer. And by that definition, I am someone who has always loved language. I am fascinated by language in daily life. I spend a great deal of my time thinking about the power of language — the way it can evoke an emotion, a visual image, a complex idea, or a simple truth. Language is the tool of my trade. And I use them all — all the Englishes I grew up with.

3 Recently, I was made keenly aware of the different Englishes I do use. I was giving a talk to a large group of people, the same talk I had already given to half a dozen other groups. The nature of the talk was about my writing, my life, and my book, *The Joy Luck Club*. The talk was going along well enough, until I remembered one major difference that made the whole

talk sound wrong. My mother was in the room. And it was perhaps the first time she had heard me give a lengthy speech, using the kind of English I have never used with her. I was saying things like, "The intersection of memory upon imagination" and "There is an aspect of my fiction that relates to thus-and-thus" — a speech filled with carefully wrought grammatical phrases, burdened, it suddenly seemed to me, with nominalized forms, past perfect tenses, conditional phrases, all the forms of standard English that I had learned in school and through books, the forms of English I did not use at home with my mother.

Just last week, I was walking down the street with my mother, and I again found myself conscious of the English I was using, and the English I do use with her. We were talking about the price of new and used furniture and I heard myself saying this: "Not waste money that way." My husband was with us as well, and he didn't notice any switch in my English. And then I realized why. It's because over the twenty years we've been together I've often used that same kind of English with him, and sometimes he even uses it with me. It has become our language of intimacy, a different sort of English that relates to family talk, the language I grew up with.

So you'll have some idea of what this family talk I heard sounds like, I'll quote what my mother said during a recent conversation which I videotaped and then transcribed. During this conversation my mother was talking about a political gangster in Shanghai who had the same last name as her family's, Du, and how the gangster in his early years wanted to be adopted by her family, which was rich by comparison. Later, the gangster became more powerful, far richer than my mother's family, and one day showed up at my mother's wedding to pay his respects. Here's what she said in part:

"Du Yusong having business like fruit stand. Like off the street kind. He is Du like Du Zong — but not Tsung-ming Island people. The local people call putong, the river east side, he belong to that side local people. The man want to ask Du Zong father take him in like become own family. Du Zong father wasn't looking down on him, but didn't take seriously, until that man big like become a mafia. Now important person very hard to inviting him. Chinese way, come only to show respect, don't stay for dinner. Respect for making big celebration, he shows up. Mean gives lots of respect. Chinese custom. Chinese social life that way. If too important won't have to stay too long. He come to my wedding. I didn't see. I heard it. I gone to boy's side, they have YMCA dinner. Chinese age I was nineteen."

You should know that my mother's expressive command of English belies how much she actually understands. She reads the *Forbes* report, listens to *Wall Street Week,* converses daily with her stockbroker, reads all of Shirley MacLaine's books with ease — all kinds of things I can't begin to understand. Yet some of my friends tell me they understand 50 percent of what my mother says. Some say they understand 80 to 90 percent. Some say they understand none of it, as if she were speaking pure Chinese. But to me, my mother's English is perfectly clear, perfectly natural. It's my mother's tongue. Her language, as I hear it, is vivid, direct, full of observation and imagery. This was the language that helped shape the way I saw things, expressed things, made sense of the world.

Lately, I've been giving more thought to the kind of English my mother 8 speaks. Like others, I have described it to people as "broken" or "fractured" English. But I wince when I say that. It has always bothered me that I can think of no way to describe it other than "broken," as if it were damaged and needed to be fixed, as if it lacked a certain wholeness and soundness. I've heard other terms used, "limited English," for example. But they seem just as bad, as if everything is limited, including people's perceptions of the limited English speaker.

I know this for a fact, because when I was growing up, my mother's 9 "limited" English limited *my* perception of her. I was ashamed of her English. I believed that her English reflected the quality of what she had to say. That is, because she expressed them imperfectly her thoughts were imperfect. And I had plenty of empirical evidence to support me: the fact that people in department stores, at banks, and at restaurants did not take her seriously, did not give her good service, pretended not to understand her, or even acted as if they did not hear her.

My mother has long realized the limitations of her English as well. 10 When I was fifteen, she used to have me call people on the phone to pretend I was she. In this guise, I was forced to ask for information or even complain and yell at people who had been rude to her. One time it was a call to her stockbroker in New York. She had cashed out her small portfolio and it just so happened we were going to go to New York the next week, our very first trip outside California. I had to get on the phone and say in an adolescent voice that was not very convincing, "This is Mrs. Tan."

And my mother was standing in the back whispering loudly, "Why he 11 don't send me check, already two weeks late. So mad he lie to me, losing me money."

And then I said in perfect English, "Yes, I'm getting rather concerned. 12 You had agreed to send the check two weeks ago, but it hasn't arrived."

Then she began to talk more loudly. "What he want, I come to New 13 York tell him front of his boss, you cheating me?" And I was trying to calm her down, make her be quiet, while telling the stockbroker, "I can't tolerate any more excuses. If I don't receive the check immediately I am going to have to speak to your manager when I'm in New York next week." And sure enough, the following week there we were in front of this astonished stockbroker, and I was sitting there red-faced and quiet, and my mother, the real Mrs. Tan, was shouting at his boss in her impeccable broken English.

We used a similar routine just five days ago, for a situation that was far 14 less humorous. My mother had gone to the hospital for an appointment, to find out about a benign brain tumor a CAT scan had revealed a month ago. She said she had spoken very good English, her best English, no mistakes. Still, she said, the hospital did not apologize when they said they had

What?!?

lost the CAT scan and she had come for nothing. She said they did not seem to have any sympathy when she told them she was anxious to know the exact diagnosis, since her husband and son had both died of brain tumors. She said they would not give her any more information until the next time and she would have to make another appointment for that. So she said she would not leave until the doctor called her daughter. She wouldn't budge. And when the doctor finally called her daughter, me, who spoke in perfect English — lo and behold — we had assurances the CAT scan would be found, promises that a conference call on Monday would be held, and apologies for any suffering my mother had gone through for a most regrettable mistake.

Wow

I think my mother's English almost had an effect on limiting my pos- 15 sibilities in life as well. Sociologists and linguists probably will tell you that a person's developing language skills are more influenced by peers. But I do think that the language spoken in the family, especially in immigrant families which are more insular, plays a large role in shaping the language of the child. And I believe that it affected my results on achievement tests, IQ tests, and the SAT. While my English skills were never judged as poor, compared to math, English could not be considered my strong suit. In grade school I did moderately well, getting perhaps B's, sometimes B-pluses, in English and scoring perhaps in the sixtieth or seventieth percentile on achievement tests. But those scores were not good enough to override the opinion that my true abilities lay in math and science, because in those areas I achieved A's and scored in the ninetieth percentile or higher.

This was understandable. Math is precise; there is only one correct 16 answer. Whereas, for me at least, the answers on English tests were always a judgment call, a matter of opinion and personal experience. Those tests were constructed around items like fill-in-the-blank sentence completion, such as "Even though Tom was _____, Mary thought he was _____." And the correct answer always seemed to be the most bland combinations of thoughts, for example, "Even though Tom was shy, Mary thought he was charming," with the grammatical structure "even though" limiting the correct answer to some sort of semantic opposites, so you wouldn't get answers like, "Even though Tom was foolish, Mary thought he was ridiculous." Well, according to my mother, there were very few limitations as to what Tom could have been and what Mary might have thought of him. So I never did well on tests like that.

The same was true with word analogies, pairs of words in which you 17 were supposed to find some sort of logical, semantic relationship — for example, "*Sunset* is to *nightfall* as _____ is to _____." And here you would be presented with a list of four possible pairs, one of which showed the same kind of relationship: *red* is to *stoplight*, *bus* is to *arrival*, *chills* is to *fever*, *yawn* is to *boring*. Well, I could never think that way. I knew what the tests were asking, but I could not block out of my mind the images already created by the first pair, "*sunset* is to *nightfall*" — and I would see a burst of colors against a darkening sky, the moon rising, the lowering of a curtain of stars. And all the other pairs of words — red, bus, stoplight, boring — just threw up a mass of confusing images, making it impossible for me to sort out something as logical as saying: "A sunset precedes nightfall" is the same as "a chill precedes a fever." The only way I would have gotten that answer right would have been to imagine an associative situation, for example, my being disobedient and staying out past sunset, catching a chill at night, which turns into feverish pneumonia as punishment, which indeed did happen to me.

I have been thinking about all this lately, about my mother's English, about achievement tests. Because lately I've been asked, as a writer, why there are not more Asian Americans represented in American literature. Why are there few Asian Americans enrolled in creative writing programs? Why do so many Chinese students go into engineering? Well, these are broad sociological questions I can't begin to answer. But I have noticed in surveys — in fact, just last week — that Asian students, as a whole, always do significantly better on math achievement tests than in English. And this makes me think that there are other Asian-American students whose English spoken in the home might also be described as "broken" or "limited." And perhaps they also have teachers who are steering them away from writing and into math and science, which is what happened to me.

> " Why are there few Asian Americans enrolled in creative writing programs? Why do so many Chinese students go into engineering? "

18

Fortunately, I happen to be rebellious in nature and enjoy the challenge of disproving assumptions made about me. I became an English major my first year in college, after being enrolled as pre-med. I started writing nonfiction as a freelancer the week after I was told by my former boss that writing was my worst skill and I should hone my talents toward account management. 19

But it wasn't until 1985 that I finally began to write fiction. And at first I wrote using what I thought to be wittily crafted sentences, sentences that would finally prove I had mastery over the English language. Here's an example from the first draft of a story that later made its way into *The Joy Luck Club,* but without this line: "That was my mental quandary in its nascent state." A terrible line, which I can barely pronounce. — **HA** 20

Fortunately, for reasons I won't get into today, I later decided I should envision a reader for the stories I would write. And the reader I decided upon was my mother because these were stories about mothers. So with this reader in mind — and in fact she did read my early drafts — I began to write stories using all the Englishes I grew up with: the English I spoke to my mother, which for lack of a better term might be described as "simple"; the English she used with me, which for lack of a better term might be described as "broken"; my translation of her Chinese, which could certainly be described as "watered down"; and what I imagined to be her translation of her Chinese if she could speak in perfect English, her internal language, 21 and for that I sought to preserve the essence, but neither an English nor a Chinese structure. I wanted to capture what language ability tests can never reveal: her intent, her passion, her imagery, the rhythms of her speech, and the nature of her thoughts.

Apart from what any critic had to say about my writing, I knew I had 22 succeeded where it counted when my mother finished reading my book and gave me her verdict: "So easy to read."

· · ·

Comprehension

1. What is Tan classifying in this essay? What individual categories does she identify?

2. Where does Tan identify the different categories she discusses in "Mother Tongue"? Should she have identified these categories earlier? Explain your reasoning.

3. Does Tan illustrate each category she identifies? Does she treat all categories equally? If she does not, do you see this as a problem? Explain.

4. In what specific situations does Tan say her mother's "limited English" was a handicap? In what other situations might Mrs. Tan face difficulties?

5. What effects has her mother's limited English had on Tan's life?

6. How does Tan account for the difficulty she had in answering questions on achievement tests, particularly word analogies? Do you think her problems in this area can be explained by the level of her family's language skills, or might other factors also be to blame? Explain.

7. In paragraph 18, Tan considers the possible reasons for the relatively few Asian Americans in the fields of language and literature. What explanations does she offer? What other explanations can you think of?

Purpose and Audience

1. Why do you suppose Tan begins her essay by explaining her qualifications? Why, for example, does she tell her readers she is "not a scholar of English or literature" (1) but rather a writer who is "fascinated by language in daily life" (2)?

2. Do you think Tan expects most of her readers to be Asian American? To be familiar with Asian-American languages and culture? How can you tell?

3. Is Tan's primary focus in this essay on language or on her mother? Explain your conclusion.

Style and Structure

1. This essay's style is relatively informal. For example, Tan uses *I* to refer to herself and addresses her readers as *you*. Identify other features that char-

acterize her style as informal. Do you think a more formal style would strengthen her credibility? Explain your reasoning.

2. In paragraph 6, Tan quotes a passage of her mother's speech. What purpose does Tan say she wants this quotation to serve? What impression does it give of her mother? Do you think this effect is what Tan intended? Explain.

3. **Vocabulary Project.** In paragraph 8, Tan discusses the different words and phrases that might be used to describe her mother's spoken English. Which of these terms seems most accurate? Do you agree with Tan that these words are unsatisfactory? What other term for her mother's English would be both neutral and accurate?

4. In paragraphs 10 through 13, Tan juxtaposes her mother's English with her own. What point do these quoted passages make?

5. Consider the expression *Mother Tongue* in Tan's title. What does this expression usually mean? What does it seem to mean here?

6. In paragraph 20, Tan quotes a "terrible line" from an early draft of part of her novel *The Joy Luck Club*. Why do you suppose she quotes this line? How is it different from the writing style she uses in "Mother Tongue"?

Journal Entry

In paragraph 9, Tan says that when she was growing up she was sometimes ashamed of her mother because of her limited English proficiency. Have you ever felt ashamed of a parent (or a friend) because of his or her inability to "fit in" in some way? How do you feel now about your earlier reaction?

Writing Workshop

1. What different "Englishes" (or other languages) do you use in your day-to-day life as a student, employee, friend, and family member? Write a classification-and-division essay identifying, describing, and illustrating each kind of language and explaining the purpose it serves.

2. **Working with Sources.** What kinds of problems does a person whose English is as limited as Mrs. Tan's face in the age of social media and instant communication? Write a classification-and-division essay that identifies and explains the kinds of problems you might encounter today if the level of your spoken English were comparable to Mrs. Tan's. Try to update some of the specific situations Tan describes, quoting Tan where necessary, and be sure to document any borrowed words or ideas and to include a works-cited page. (See Chapter 18 for information on MLA documentation.)

3. Tan's essay focuses on spoken language, but people also use different kinds of *written* language in different situations. Write a classification-and-division essay that identifies and analyzes three different kinds of written English: one appropriate for your parents, one for a teacher or

employer, and one for a friend. Illustrate each kind of language with a few sentences directed at each audience about your plans for your future. In your thesis statement, explain why all three kinds of language are necessary.

Combining the Patterns

Tan develops her essay with a series of anecdotes about her mother and about herself. How does this use of **narration** strengthen her essay? Could she have made her point about the use of different "Englishes" without these anecdotes? What other strategy could she have used?

Thematic Connections

- "Midnight" (page 217)
- "Why Chinese Mothers Are Superior" (page 408)
- "The Park" (page 667)

STEPHANIE ERICSSON

The Ways We Lie

Stephanie Ericsson (b. 1953) grew up in San Francisco and began writing as a teenager. She has been a screenwriter and an advertising copywriter and has published several books based on her own life. *Shamefaced: The Road to Recovery* and *Women of AA: Recovering Together* (both 1985) focus on her experiences with addiction; *Companion through the Darkness: Inner Dialogues on Grief* (1993) deals with the sudden death of her husband; and *Companion into the Dawn: Inner Dialogues on Loving* (1994) is a collection of essays.

Background on lies in politics and business The following piece originally appeared in the *Utne Reader* as the cover article of the January 1993 issue, which was devoted to the theme of lies and lying. The subject had particular relevance after a year when the honesty of Bill Clinton — the newly elected U.S. president — had been questioned. (It also followed the furor surrounding the confirmation hearings of U.S. Supreme Court nominee Clarence Thomas, who denied allegations by attorney Anita Hill of workplace sexual harassment; here the question was who was telling the truth and who was not.) Six years later, President Clinton was accused of perjury and faced a Senate impeachment trial. In subsequent years, lying was featured prominently in the news as executives at a number of major corporations were charged with falsifying records at the expense of employees and shareholders, and George W. Bush's administration was accused of lying about the presence of weapons of mass destruction in Iraq to justify going to war.

More recently, major mortgage lenders were found to have lied about their reviews of documents justifying many thousands of foreclosures. In 2010, lying was again featured prominently in the news as investigations of the oil company BP found that the company was aware of problems with a safety device on the Deepwater Horizon oil rig prior to an explosion that killed eleven workers and spilled millions of gallons of oil, but covered up those concerns in an attempt to increase its profits. BP has also been accused of lying to Congress about its estimate of the extent of the spill.

The bank called today and I told them my deposit was in the mail, even 1
though I hadn't written a check yet. It'd been a rough day. The baby I'm pregnant with decided to do aerobics on my lungs for two hours, our three-year-old daughter painted the living-room couch with lipstick, the IRS put me on hold for an hour, and I was late to a business meeting because I was tired.

I told my client the traffic had been bad. When my partner came home, 2
his haggard face told me his day hadn't gone any better than mine, so when he asked, "How was your day?" I said, "Oh, fine," knowing that one more straw might break his back. A friend called and wanted to take me to lunch.

We all lie!

I said I was busy. Four lies in the course of a day, none of which I felt the least bit guilty about.

We lie. We all do. We exaggerate, we minimize, we avoid confrontation, 3 we spare people's feelings, we conveniently forget, we keep secrets, we justify lying to the big-guy institutions. Like most people, I indulge in small falsehoods and still think of myself as an honest person. Sure I lie, but it doesn't hurt anything. Or does it?

I once tried going a whole week without telling a lie, and it was paralyzing. I discovered that telling the truth all the time is nearly impossible. It means living with some serious consequences: The bank charges me $60 in overdraft fees, my partner keels over when I tell him about my travails, my client fires me for telling her I didn't feel like being on time, and my friend takes it personally when I say I'm not hungry. There must be some merit to lying.

> *not lying = serious consequences*

> " I once tried going a whole week without telling a lie, and it was paralyzing. "

4

But if I justify lying, what makes me any different from slick politicians 5 or the corporate robbers who raided the S&L industry? Saying it's okay to lie one way and not another is hedging. I cannot seem to escape the voice deep inside me that tells me: When someone lies, someone loses. !!

What far-reaching consequences will I, or others, pay as a result of my 6 lie? Will someone's trust be destroyed? Will someone else pay *my* penance because I ducked out? We must consider the *meaning of our actions.* Deception, lies, capital crimes, and misdemeanors all carry meanings. *Webster's* definition of *lie* is specific:

1: a false statement or action especially made with the intent to deceive;

2: anything that gives or is meant to give a false impression.

A definition like this implies that there are many, many ways to tell a 7 lie. Here are just a few.

The White Lie

A man who won't lie to a woman has very little consideration for her feelings.

—BERGEN EVANS

The white lie assumes that the truth will cause more damage than a 8 simple, harmless untruth. Telling a friend he looks great when he looks like hell can be based on a decision that the friend needs a compliment more than a frank opinion. But, in effect, it is the liar deciding what is best for the lied to. Ultimately, it is a vote of no confidence. It is an act of subtle arrogance for anyone to decide what is best for someone else.

Yet not all circumstances are quite so cut-and-dried. Take, for instance, 9 the sergeant in Vietnam who knew one of his men was killed in action but listed him as missing so that the man's family would receive indefinite compensation instead of the lump-sum pittance the military gives widows and children. His intent was honorable. Yet for twenty years this family kept their hopes alive, unable to move on to a new life.   *terrible*

Facades

> Et tu, Brute?
>
> *Create an illusion*
>
> —CAESAR*

We all put up facades to one degree or another. When I put on a suit to go to see a client, I feel as though I am putting on another face, obeying the expectation that serious businesspeople wear suits rather than sweatpants. But I'm a writer. Normally, I get up, get the kid off to school, and sit at my computer in my pajamas until four in the afternoon. When I answer the phone, the caller thinks I'm wearing a suit (though the UPS man knows better).   10

But facades can be destructive because they are used to seduce others into an illusion. For instance, I recently realized that a former friend was a liar. He presented himself with all the right looks and the right words and offered lots of new consciousness theories, fabulous books to read, and fascinating insights. Then I did some business with him, and the time came for him to pay me. He turned out to be all talk and no walk. I heard a plethora of reasonable excuses, including in-depth descriptions of the big break around the corner. In six months of work, I saw less than a hundred bucks. When I confronted him, he raised both eyebrows and tried to convince me that I'd heard him wrong, that he'd made no commitment to me. A simple investigation into his past revealed a crowded graveyard of disenchanted former friends.   11

Ignoring the Plain Facts

> Well, you must understand that Father Porter is only human. . . .
>
> —A MASSACHUSETTS PRIEST

In the '60s, the Catholic Church in Massachusetts began hearing complaints that Father James Porter was sexually molesting children. Rather than relieving him of his duties, the ecclesiastical authorities simply moved him from one parish to another between 1960 and 1967, actually providing him with a fresh supply of unsuspecting families and innocent children to abuse. After treatment in 1967 for pedophilia, he went back to   12

---

* Eds. note — "And you, Brutus?" (Latin). In Shakespeare's play *Julius Caesar,* Caesar asks this question when he sees Brutus, whom he has believed to be his friend, among the conspirators who are stabbing him.

work, this time in Minnesota. The new diocese was aware of Father Porter's obsession with children, but they needed priests and recklessly believed treatment had cured him. More children were abused until he was relieved of his duties a year later. By his own admission, Porter may have abused as many as a hundred children.

Ignoring the facts may not in and of itself be a form of lying, but consider the context of this situation. If a lie is *a false action done with the intent to deceive,* then the Catholic Church's conscious covering for Porter created irreparable consequences. The church became a co-perpetrator with Porter. 13

Deflecting

> When you have no basis for an argument, abuse the plaintiff.
>
> —CICERO

I've discovered that I can keep anyone from seeing the true me by being selectively blatant. I set a precedent of being up-front about intimate issues, but I never bring up the things I truly want to hide; I just let people assume I'm revealing everything. It's an effective way of hiding. 14

Any good liar knows that the way to perpetuate an untruth is to deflect attention from it. When Clarence Thomas exploded with accusations that the Senate hearings were a "high-tech lynching," he simply switched the focus from a highly charged subject to a radioactive subject. Rather than defending himself, he took the offensive and accused the country of racism. It was a brilliant maneuver. Racism is now politically incorrect in official circles — unlike sexual harassment, which still rewards those who can get away with it. 15

Some of the most skillful deflectors are passive-aggressive people who, when accused of inappropriate behavior, refuse to respond to the accusations. This you-don't-exist stance infuriates the accuser, who, understandably, screams something obscene out of frustration. The trap is sprung and the act of deflection successful, because now the passive-aggressive person can indignantly say, "Who can talk to someone as unreasonable as you?" The real issue is forgotten and the sins of the original victim become the focus. Feeling guilty of name-calling, the victim is fully tamed and crawls into a hole, ashamed. I have watched this fighting technique work thousands of times in disputes between men and women, and what I've learned is that the real culprit is not necessarily the one who swears the loudest. 16

Omission

> The cruelest lies are often told in silence.
>
> —R. L. STEVENSON

Omission involves telling most of the truth minus one or two key facts whose absence changes the story completely. You break a pair of glasses 17 that are guaranteed under normal use and get a new pair, without mentioning that the first pair broke during a rowdy game of basketball. Who hasn't tried something like that? But what about omission of information that could make a difference in how a person lives his or her life?

For instance, one day I found out that rabbinical legends tell of another 18 woman in the Garden of Eden before Eve. I was stunned. The omission of the Sumerian goddess Lilith from Genesis — as well as her demonization by ancient misogynists as an embodiment of female evil — felt like spiritual robbery. I felt like I'd just found out my mother was really my stepmother. To take seriously the tradition that Adam was created out of the same mud as his equal counterpart, Lilith, redefines all of Judeo-Christian history.

Some renegade Catholic feminists introduced me to a view of Lilith 19 that had been suppressed during the many centuries when this strong goddess was seen only as a spirit of evil. Lilith was a proud goddess who defied Adam's need to control her, attempted negotiations, and when this failed, said adios and left the Garden of Eden.

This omission of Lilith from the Bible was a patriarchal strategy to 20 keep women weak. Omitting the strong-woman archetype of Lilith from Western religions and starting the story with Eve the Rib has helped keep Christian and Jewish women believing they were the lesser sex for thousands of years.

Stereotypes and Clichés

> Where opinion does not exist, the status quo becomes stereotyped and all
> originality is discouraged.   *form of shorthand*
>   —BERTRAND RUSSELL

Stereotype and cliché serve a purpose as a form of shorthand. Our need 21 for vast amounts of information in nanoseconds has made the stereotype vital to modern communication. Unfortunately, it often shuts down original thinking, giving those hungry for the truth a candy bar of misinformation instead of a balanced meal. The stereotype explains a situation with just enough truth to seem unquestionable.

All the "isms" — racism, sexism, ageism, et al. — are founded on and 22 fueled by the stereotype and the cliché, which are lies of exaggeration, omission, and ignorance. They are always dangerous. They take a single tree and make it a landscape. They destroy curiosity. They close ⸻inds and separate people. The single mother on welfare is assumed to be ⸻ black male could tell you how much of his identity is oblite⸻ types. Fat people, ugly people, beautiful people, old ⸻ women, short men, the mentally ill, and the home⸻ how much more they are like us than we want to th⸻ a group of people that I had a mouth like a truck ⸻ prise, a man stood up and said, "I'm a truck driver⸻ less to say, I was humbled.

Groupthink

> Who is more foolish, the child afraid of the dark, or the man afraid of the light?
>
> *loyalty to group*
>
> —MAURICE FREEHILL

Irving Janis, in *Victims of GroupThink,* defines this sort of lie as a psycho- 23 logical phenomenon within decision-making groups in which loyalty to the group has become more important than any other value, with the result that dissent and the appraisal of alternatives are suppressed. If you've ever worked on a committee or in a corporation, you've encountered group-think. It requires a combination of other forms of lying — ignoring facts, selective memory, omission, and denial, to name a few.

The textbook example of groupthink came on December 7, 1941. From 24 as early as the fall of 1941, the warnings came in, one after another, that Japan was preparing for a massive military operation. The Navy command in Hawaii assumed Pearl Harbor was invulnerable — the Japanese weren't stupid enough to attack the United States' most important base. On the other hand, racist stereotypes said the Japanese weren't smart enough to invent a torpedo effective in less than 60 feet of water (the fleet was docked in 30 feet); after all, U.S. technology hadn't been able to do it.

On Friday, December 5, normal weekend leave was granted to all the 25 commanders at Pearl Harbor, even though the Japanese consulate in Hawaii was busy burning papers. Within the tight, good-ole-boy cohesive-ness of the U.S. command in Hawaii, the myth of invulnerability stayed well entrenched. No one in the group considered the alternatives. The rest is history.

Out-and-Out Lies

> The only form of lying that is beyond reproach is lying for its own sake.
>
> —OSCAR WILDE

Of all the ways to lie, I like this one the best, probably because I get 26 tired of trying to figure out the real meanings behind things. At least I can trust the bald-faced lie. I once asked my five-year-old nephew, "Who broke the fence?" (I had seen him do it.) He answered, "The murderers." Who could argue?

At least when this sort of lie is told it can be easily confronted. As the 27 person who is lied to, I know where I stand. The bald-faced lie doesn't toy with my perceptions — it argues with them. It doesn't try to refashion real-ity, it tries to refute it. *Read my lips.* . . . No sleight of hand. No guessing. If this were the only form of lying, there would be no such thing as floating anxiety or the adult-children of alcoholics movement.

issal

tention to that man behind the curtain! I am the Great Oz!

—THE WIZARD OF OZ

Dismissal is perhaps the slipperiest of all lies. Dismissing feelings, per- 28
ceptions, or even the raw facts of a situation ranks as a kind of lie that can
do as much damage to a person as any other kind of lie.

The roots of many mental disorders can be traced back to the dismissal 29
of reality. Imagine that a person is told from the time she is a tot that her
perceptions are inaccurate. *"Mommy, I'm scared."* "No, you're not, darling."
"I don't like that man next door, he makes me feel icky." "Johnny, that's a terrible
thing to say, of course you like him. You go over there right now and be nice
to him."

I've often mused over the idea that madness is actually a sane reaction 30
to an insane world. Psychologist R. D. Laing supports this hypothesis in
Sanity, Madness & the Family, an account of his investigations into families
of schizophrenics. The common thread that ran through all of the families   *Wow!*
he studied was a deliberate, staunch dismissal of the patient's perceptions
from a very early age. Each of the patients started out with an accurate
grasp of reality, which, through meticulous and methodical dismissal, was
demolished until the only reality the patient could trust was catatonia.

Dismissal runs the gamut. Mild dismissal can be quite handy for for- 31
giving the foibles of others in our day-to-day lives. Toddlers who have just
learned to manipulate their parents' attention sometimes are dismissed
out of necessity. Absolute attention from the parents would require so
much energy that no one would get to eat dinner. But we must be careful
and attentive about how far we take our "necessary" dismissals. Dismissal
is a dangerous tool, because it's nothing less than a lie.

Delusion

> We lie loudest when we lie to ourselves.
>
> —ERIC HOFFER

I could write the book on this one. Delusion, a cousin of dismissal, is 32
the tendency to see excuses as facts. It's a powerful lying tool because it filters out information that contradicts what we want to believe. Alcoholics
who believe that the problems in their lives are legitimate reasons for drinking rather than results of the drinking offer the classic example of deluded
thinking. Delusion uses the mind's ability to see things in myriad ways to
support what it wants to be the truth.

But delusion is also a survival mechanism we all use. If we were to fully 33
contemplate the consequences of our stockpiles of nuclear weapons or
global warming, we could hardly function on a day-to-day level. We don't
want to incorporate that much reality into our lives because to do so would
be paralyzing.

Delusion acts as an adhesive to keep the status quo intact. It shame- 34
lessly employs dismissal, omission, and amnesia, among other sorts of lies.
Its most cunning defense is that it cannot see itself.   *cannot see itself*

> The liar's punishment . . . is that he cannot believe anyone else.
>
> —GEORGE BERNARD SHAW

These are only a few of the ways we lie. Or are lied to. As I said earlier,   35
it's not easy to entirely eliminate lies from our lives. No matter how pious
we may try to be, we will still embellish, hedge, and omit to lubricate the
daily machinery of living. But there is a world of difference between telling
functional lies and living a lie. Martin Buber* once said, "The lie is the
spirit committing treason against itself." Our acceptance of lies becomes a
cultural cancer that eventually shrouds and reorders reality until moral
garbage becomes as invisible to us as water is to a fish.

How much do we tolerate before we become sick and tired of being sick   36
and tired? When will we stand up and declare our *right* to trust? When do
we stop accepting that the real truth is in the fine print? Whose lips do we
read this year when we vote for president? When will we stop being so reti-
cent about making judgments? When do we stop turning over our personal
power and responsibility to liars?

Maybe if I don't tell the bank the check's in the mail I'll be less tolerant   37
of the lies told me every day. A country song I once heard said it all for me:
"You've got to stand for something or you'll fall for anything."

· · ·

Comprehension

1. List and briefly define each of the ten kinds of lies Ericsson identifies.

2. Why, in Ericsson's view, is each kind of lie necessary?

3. According to Ericsson, what is the danger of each kind of lie?

4. Why does Ericsson like "out-and-out lies" (26–27) best?

5. Why is "dismissal" the "slipperiest of all lies" (28)?

Purpose and Audience

1. Is Ericsson's thesis simply that "there are many, many ways to tell a
   lie" (7)? Or is she defending — or attacking — the practice of lying? Try
   to state her thesis in a single sentence.

2. Do you think Ericsson's choice of examples reveals a political bias? If so,
   do you think she expects her intended audience to share her political
   views? Explain your conclusion.

Style and Structure

1. Despite the seriousness of her subject matter, Ericsson's essay is informal;
   her opening paragraphs are especially personal and breezy. Why do you
   think she chose to use this kind of opening? Do you think her decision
   makes sense?

---

* Eds. note — Austrian-born Judaic philosopher (1878–1965).

2. Ericsson introduces each category of lie with a quotation. What function do these quotations serve? Do you think her essay would be less (or more) effective without them? Why or why not?

3. In addition to a heading and a quotation, what other elements does Ericsson include in her treatment of each kind of lie? Are all the discussions parallel — that is, does her discussion of each category include the same elements? If not, do you think this lack of balance is a problem? Explain.

4. What, if anything, determines the order in which Ericsson arranges her categories in this essay? Do you think any category should be relocated? If so, why?

5. Throughout her essay, Ericsson uses **rhetorical questions**. Why do you suppose she uses this stylistic device?

6. **Vocabulary Project.** Ericsson uses many **colloquialisms** in this essay — for example, "I could write the book on this one" (32). Identify as many of these informal expressions as you can. Why do you think she uses colloquialisms instead of more formal expressions? Do they have a positive or negative effect on your reaction to her ideas? Explain.

7. Ericsson occasionally cites the views of experts. Why does she include these references? If she wanted to cite additional experts, what professional backgrounds or fields of study do you think they should represent? Why?

8. In paragraph 29, Ericsson says, "Imagine that a person is told from the time she is a tot. . . ." Does she use *she* in similar contexts elsewhere in the essay? Do you find the feminine form of the personal pronoun appropriate or distracting? Explain.

9. Paragraphs 35–37 constitute Ericsson's conclusion. How does this conclusion parallel the essay's introduction in terms of style, structure, and content?

Journal Entry

In paragraph 3, Ericsson says, "We lie. We all do." Later in the paragraph, she comments, "Sure I lie, but it doesn't hurt anything. Or does it?" Answer her question.

Writing Workshop

1. **Working with Sources.** Choose three or four of Ericsson's categories, and write a classification-and-division essay called "The Ways I Lie." Base your essay on personal experience, and include an explicit thesis statement that defends your own lies — or is sharply critical of their use. Be sure to document Ericsson's essay when you cite her categories and to include a works-cited page. (See Chapter 18 for information on MLA documentation.)

2. In paragraph 22, Ericsson condemns stereotypes. Write a classification-and-division essay with the following thesis statement: "Stereotypes are usually inaccurate, often negative, and always dangerous." In your essay, consider the stereotypes applied to three or four of the following groups: people who are disabled, overweight, or elderly; urban teenagers; politicians; housewives; and immigrants.

3. Using the thesis provided in question 2, write a classification-and-division essay that considers the stereotypes applied to three or four of the following occupations: police officers, librarians, used-car dealers, flight attendants, lawyers, construction workers, rock musicians, accountants, and telemarketers.

Combining the Patterns

A dictionary **definition** is a familiar — even tired — strategy for an essay's introduction. Do you think Ericsson should delete the definition in paragraph 6 for this reason, or do you believe it is necessary? Explain.

Thematic Connections

- " 'What's in a Name?' " (page 2)
- "The Money" (page 114)
- "Thirty-Eight Who Saw Murder Didn't Call the Police" (page 128)
- "The Hidden Life of Garbage" (page 186)
- "The Lottery" (page 308)

BILLY COLLINS

Aristotle (Poetry)

Former United States Poet Laureate Billy Collins was born in New York City in 1941 and received an undergraduate degree from the College of the Holy Cross and a Ph.D. in English from the University of California, Riverside. Collins's poetry is artful, accessible, and self-effacing in its style and in its focus on ordinary experiences. Collins writes with his reader in mind: "I always tend to begin a poem with something fairly clear or a piece of common knowledge . . . something we all know, some little common ground that becomes the grounding wire." Collins's recent work includes the haiku collection *She Was Just Seventeen* (2006) and *Ballistics* (2008) as well as *Bright Wings: An Illustrated Anthology of Poems about Birds* (2009), which he edited.

Background on Aristotle and the Dramatic Unities The Greek philosopher Aristotle (384–322 BCE) is a foundational figure in Western rhetoric, physics, logic, and politics. He also wrote the earliest known work of literary theory, *Poetics* (c. 335 BCE), which examines the principles behind effective poetry and drama. According to Aristotle, the plot of a play requires three elements to be a complete, unified whole.

> A whole is that which has a beginning, a middle, and an end. A beginning is that which does not itself follow anything by causal necessity, but after which something naturally is or comes to be. An end, on the contrary, is that which itself naturally follows some other thing, either by necessity, or as a rule, but has nothing following it. A middle is that which follows something as some other thing follows it. A well constructed plot, therefore, must neither begin nor end at haphazard, but conform to these principles.

Collins has acknowledged that the same principle guides his own work: "My poems tend to have rhetorical structures; what I mean by that is they tend to have a beginning, a middle, and an end."

This is the beginning. 1
Almost anything can happen.
This is where you find
the creation of light, a fish wriggling onto land,
the first word of *Paradise Lost** on an empty page. 5
Think of an egg, the letter *A*,
a woman ironing on a bare stage
as the heavy curtain rises.
This is the very beginning.

---

* Eds. note — Epic poem written by English poet John Milton and published in 1667.

The first-person narrator introduces himself,   10
tells us about his lineage.
The mezzo-soprano stands in the wings.
Here the climbers are studying a map
or pulling on their long woolen socks.
This is early on, years before the Ark, dawn.   15
The profile of an animal is being smeared
on the wall of a cave,
and you have not yet learned to crawl.
This is the opening, the gambit,
a pawn moving forward an inch.   20
This is your first night with her,
your first night without her.
This is the first part
where the wheels begin to turn,
where the elevator begins its ascent,   25
before the doors lurch apart.

This is the middle.
Things have had time to get complicated,
messy, really. Nothing is simple anymore.
Cities have sprouted up along the rivers   30
teeming with people at cross-purposes —
a million schemes, a million wild looks.
Disappointment unshoulders his knapsack
here and pitches his ragged tent.
This is the sticky part where the plot congeals,   35
where the action suddenly reverses
or swerves off in an outrageous direction.
Here the narrator devotes a long paragraph
to why Miriam does not want Edward's child.
Someone hides a letter under a pillow.   40
Here the aria rises to a pitch,
a song of betrayal, salted with revenge.
And the climbing party is stuck on a ledge
halfway up the mountain.
This is the bridge, the painful modulation.   45
This is the thick of things.
So much is crowded into the middle —
the guitars of Spain, piles of ripe avocados,
Russian uniforms, noisy parties,
lakeside kisses, arguments heard through a wall —   50
too much to name, too much to think about.

And this is the end,
the car running out of road,

the river losing its name in an ocean,
the long nose of the photographed horse   55
touching the white electronic line.
This is the colophon, the last elephant in the parade,
the empty wheelchair,
and pigeons floating down in the evening.
Here the stage is littered with bodies,   60
the narrator leads the characters to their cells,
and the climbers are in their graves.
It is me hitting the period
and you closing the book.
It is Sylvia Plath in the kitchen   65
and St. Clement with an anchor around his neck.
This is the final bit
thinning away to nothing.
This is the end, according to Aristotle,
what we have all been waiting for,   70
what everything comes down to,
the destination we cannot help imagining,
a streak of light in the sky,
a hat on a peg, and outside the cabin, falling leaves.

• • •

Reading Literature

1. What three categories does this poem explore? Are the categories mutually exclusive, or do they overlap?

2. Are the three categories treated in similar terms? That is, do they include
   the same kind of examples? Do they all seem to be of equal importance?

3. What additional examples could you include in each category?

Journal Entry

Why is this poem called "Aristotle"? (Read this selection's headnote before
you answer this question.) Do you see this poem as a commentary on poetry
or on life?

Thematic Connections

- "Ground Zero" (page 175)
- "Once More to the Lake" (page 191)
- "'Girl'" (page 259)
- "Suicide Note" (page 364)
- "Love and Other Catastrophes: A Mix Tape" (page 518)

Writing Assignments for Classification and Division

1. Choose a film you have seen recently, and list all the elements you consider significant — plot, direction, acting, special effects, and so on. Then, further subdivide each category (for instance, listing each of the major special effects). Using this list as an outline, write a review of the film.

2. Write an essay classifying the teachers or bosses you have had into several distinct categories, and form a judgment about the relative effectiveness of the individuals in each group. Give each category a name, and be sure your essay has a thesis statement.

3. What fashion styles do you observe on your college campus? Establish four or five distinct categories, and write an essay classifying students on the basis of how they dress. Give each group of students a descriptive title.

4. **Working with Sources.** Look through this book's thematic table of contents (page xxxiii), and choose three essays on the same general subject. Then, write a classification-and-division essay discussing the different ways writers can explore the same theme. Be sure your topic sentences clearly define your three categories. Include parenthetical documentation for all references to the essays you choose, and also include a works-cited page. (See Chapter 18 for information on MLA documentation.)

5. Many consider violence in sports to be a serious problem. Write an essay expressing your views on this problem. Using a classification-and-division structure, categorize information according to sources of violence (such as the players, the nature of the game, and the fans).

6. Classify television shows according to type (reality show, crime drama, and so forth), audience (preschoolers, school-age children, adults, and so on), or any other logical principle. Write an essay based on your system of classification, making sure to include a thesis statement. For instance, you might assert that the relative popularity of one kind of program over others reveals something about television watchers or that one kind of program shows signs of becoming obsolete.

7. Write a lighthearted classification-and-division essay discussing kinds of snack foods, cartoons, pets, status symbols, shoppers, vacations, weight-loss diets, hairstyles, or drivers.

8. Write a classification-and-division essay assessing the relative merits of several different politicians, websites, blogs, or academic majors.

9. What kinds of survival skills does a student need to get through college successfully? Write a classification-and-division essay identifying and discussing several kinds of skills and indicating why each category is important. If you like, you may write your essay in the form of an email to a beginning college student.

10. Divide your Facebook friends into categories according to some logical principle. Then, write a classification-and-division essay that includes a thesis statement indicating how different the various groups are.

Collaborative Activity for Classification and Division

Working in a group of four students, devise a classification system encompassing all the different kinds of popular music the members of your group favor. You may begin with general categories, such as country, pop, and rhythm and blues, but you should also include more specific categories, such as rap and heavy metal, in your classification system. After you decide on categories and subcategories that represent the tastes of all group members, fill in examples for each category. Then, devise several different options for arranging your categories into an essay.

Definition

What Is Definition?

A **definition** tells what a term means and how it differs from other terms in its class. In the following paragraph from "Altruistic Behavior," anthropologist Desmond Morris defines *altruism,* the key term of his essay.

Topic sentence	Altruism is the performance of an unselfish act. As a pattern of behavior, this act must have two
Extended definition defines term by *enumeration* and *negation*	properties: it must benefit someone else, and it must do so to the disadvantage of the benefactor. It is not merely a matter of being helpful; it is helpfulness at a cost to yourself.

Most people think of definition in terms of print or online dictionaries, which give brief, succinct explanations – called **formal definitions** – of what words mean. But definition also includes explaining what something, or even someone, *is* – that is, its essential nature. Sometimes a definition requires a paragraph, an essay, or even a whole book. These longer, more complex definitions are called **extended definitions**.

Understanding Formal Definitions

Look at any dictionary, and you will notice that many definitions have a standard three-part structure. First, they present the *term* to be defined, then the general *class* it is a part of, and finally the *qualities that differentiate it* from the other terms in the same class.

TERM	CLASS	DIFFERENTIATION
behaviorism	a theory	that regards the objective facts of a subject's actions as the only valid basis for psychological study
cell	a unit of protoplasm	with a nucleus, cytoplasm, and an enclosing membrane

naturalism	a literary movement	whose original adherents believed writers should treat life with scientific objectivity
mitosis	a process	of nuclear division of cells, consisting of prophase, metaphase, anaphase, and telophase
authority	a power	to command and require obedience

Understanding Extended Definitions

Many extended-definition essays include short formal definitions like those in dictionaries. In such an essay, a brief formal definition can introduce readers to the extended definition, or it can help to support the essay's thesis. However, an extended definition does not follow a set **pattern of development**. Instead, it uses whatever strategies best suit the writer's purpose, the term being defined, and the writing situation. In fact, any one (or more than one) of the essay patterns illustrated in this book can be used to structure a definition essay.

Using Definition

Providing a formal definition of each term you use is usually not necessary or desirable. Readers will either know what a word means or be able to look it up. Still, it is often helpful to provide a brief definition of any term that is key to your readers' understanding of your essay — especially if a key term has more than one meaning, if you are using it in an unusual way, or if you are fairly certain that the term will be unfamiliar to your readers.

Many situations call for extended definitions. On an exam, for example, you might be asked to define *behaviorism*; tell what a *cell* is; explain the meaning of the literary term *naturalism*; include a comprehensive definition of *mitosis* in your answer; or define *authority*. Such exam questions cannot always be answered in a sentence or two. In fact, the definitions they call for often require a full paragraph — or even several paragraphs.

Extended definitions are useful in many academic assignments besides exams. For example, definitions can explain abstractions such as *freedom*, controversial terms such as *right to life*, or **slang** terms (informal expressions whose meanings may vary from locale to locale or change as time passes).

Planning a Definition Essay

Developing a Thesis Statement

The thesis of a definition essay should do more than simply identify the term to be defined — and more than just define it. The thesis statement needs to make clear to readers the larger purpose for which you are defining the term. For example, assume you set out to write an extended definition of *behaviorism*. If your goal is to show its usefulness for treating patients with certain psychological disorders, a statement like "This essay will define behaviorism" will not be very helpful. Even a formal definition — "Behaviorism is a theory that regards the objective facts of a subject's actions as the only valid basis for psychological study" — is not enough. Your thesis statement needs to suggest the *value* of this kind of therapy, not just tell what it is — for example, "Contrary to some critics' objections, behaviorism is a valid approach for treating a wide variety of psychological dysfunctions."

Deciding on a Pattern of Development

You can organize a definition essay according to one or more of the patterns of development described in this book. As you plan your essay and jot down your ideas about the term or subject you will define, you will see which of the patterns are most useful. For example, the formal definitions of the five terms discussed on pages 487–88 could be expanded with five different patterns of development:

• **Exemplification** To explain *behaviorism,* you could give **examples**. Carefully chosen cases could show how this theory of psychology applies to different situations. These examples could help readers see exactly how behaviorism works and what it can and cannot account for. Often, examples are the clearest way to explain something. Defining dreams as "the symbolic representation of mental states" might convey little to readers who do not know much about psychology, but a few examples would help you make your meaning clear. Many students have dreams about taking exams — perhaps dreaming that they are late for the test, that they remember nothing about the course, or that they are writing their answers in disappearing ink. You might explain the nature of dreams by interpreting these particular dreams, which may reflect anxiety about a course or about school in general.

• **Description** You can explain the nature of something by **describing** it. For example, the concept of a *cell* is difficult to grasp from just a formal definition, but your readers would understand the concept more clearly if you were to describe what a cell looks like, possibly with the aid of a diagram or two. Concentrating on the cell membrane, cytoplasm, and nucleus, you could detail each structure's appearance and function. These descriptions would enable readers to visualize the whole cell and understand its workings. Of course, description involves more than the visual: a definition of a tsunami might describe the sounds and the appearance of this enormous ocean wave, and a definition of Parkinson's disease might include a description of how its symptoms affect a patient.

• **Comparison and contrast** An extended definition of *naturalism* could use a **comparison-and-contrast** structure. Naturalism is one of several major movements in American literature, so its literary aims could be contrasted with those of other literary movements, such as romanticism or realism. Or, you might compare and contrast the plots and characters of several naturalistic works with those of romantic or realistic works. Anytime you need to define something unfamiliar, you can compare it to something familiar to your readers. For example, your readers may never have heard of the Chinese dish sweet-and-sour cabbage, but you can help them imagine it by saying it tastes something like coleslaw. You can also define a thing by contrasting it with something unlike it, especially if the two have some qualities in common. For instance, one way to explain the British sport of rugby might be to contrast it with American football, which is not as violent.

- **Process** Because mitosis is a process, an extended definition of *mitosis* should be organized as a **process explanation**. By tracing the process from stage to stage, you would clearly define this type of cell division for your readers. Process is also a suitable pattern for defining objects in terms of what they do. For example, because a computer carries out certain processes, an extended definition of a computer would probably include a process explanation.

- **Classification and division** You could define *authority* by using **classification and division**. Basing your extended definition on the model developed by the German sociologist Max Weber, you could divide the class *authority* into the subclasses *traditional authority, charismatic authority,* and *legal-bureaucratic authority*. By explaining each type of authority, you could clarify this very broad term for your readers. In both extended and formal definitions, classification and division can be very useful. By identifying the class something belongs to, you are explaining what kind of thing it is. For instance, *monetarism* is an economic theory; *The Adventures of Huckleberry Finn* is a novel; and *emphysema* is a disease. Likewise, by dividing a class into subclasses, you are defining something more specifically. Emphysema, for instance, is a disease of the lungs and can therefore be classified with tuberculosis but not with appendicitis.

Phrasing Your Definition

Whatever form your definitions take, make certain that they clearly define your terms. Be sure to provide a true definition, not just a descriptive statement such as "Happiness is a four-day weekend." Also, remember that repetition is not definition, so don't include the term you are defining in your definition. For instance, the statement "Abstract art is a school of artists whose works are abstract" clarifies nothing for your readers. Finally, define as precisely as possible. Name the class of the term you are defining — "mitosis is *a process* of cell division" — and define this class as narrowly and as accurately as you can, clearly differentiating your term from other members of its class. Careful attention to the language and structure of your definition will help readers understand your meaning.

Structuring a Definition Essay

Like other essays, a definition essay should have an introduction, a body, and a conclusion. Although a formal definition strives for objectivity, an extended definition usually does not. Instead, it is likely to define a term in a way that reflects your attitude toward the subject or your reason for defining it. For example, your extended-definition paper about literary *naturalism* might argue that the significance of this movement's major works has been underestimated by literary scholars. Similarly, your definition of *authority* might criticize its abuses. In such cases, the **thesis statement** provides a focus for your definition essay, showing readers your approach to the definition.

The **introduction** identifies the term to be defined, perhaps presents a brief formal definition, and goes on to state the essay's thesis. The body of the essay expands the definition, using any one (or several) of the patterns of development explained and illustrated in this text.

In addition to using various patterns of development, you can expand the **body** of your definition by using any of the following strategies:

- You can define a term by using **synonyms** (words with similar meanings).
- You can define a term by using **negation** (telling what it is *not*).
- You can define a term by using **enumeration** (listing its characteristics).
- You can define a term by using an **analogy** (identifying similarities between an unfamiliar term and something likely to be more familiar to readers).
- You can define a term by discussing its **origin and development** (the word's derivation, original meaning, and usages).

NOTE: If you are describing something that is unfamiliar to your readers, you can also include a **visual** — a drawing, painting, diagram, or photograph — to supplement your definition.

Your essay's **conclusion** reminds readers why you have chosen to define the term, perhaps restating your thesis in different words.

Suppose your assignment is to write a short paper for your introductory psychology course. You decide to examine *behaviorism*. Of course, you can define the word in one sentence, or possibly two. But to explain the *concept* of behaviorism and its status in the field of psychology, you must go beyond the dictionary.

Now, you have to decide what kinds of explanations are most suitable for your topic and for your intended audience. If you are trying to define *behaviorism* for readers who know very little about psychology, you might use analogies that relate behaviorism to your readers' experiences, such as how they were raised or how they train their pets. You might also use examples, but the examples would relate not to psychological experiments or clinical treatment but to experiences in everyday life. If, however, you are directing your paper to your psychology instructor, who obviously already knows what behaviorism is, your purpose is to show that you know, too. One way to do this is to compare behaviorism with other psychological theories; another way is to give examples of how behaviorism works in practice; still another is to briefly summarize the background and history of the theory. (In a long paper, you might use all of these strategies.)

After considering your paper's scope and audience, you might decide that because behaviorism is somewhat controversial, your best strategy is to supplement a formal definition with examples showing how behaviorist assumptions and methods are applied in specific situations. These examples, drawn from your class notes and textbook, would support your thesis that behaviorism is a valid approach for treating certain psychological dysfunctions. Together, your examples would define *behaviorism* as it is understood today.

An informal outline for your essay might look like this.

Sample Outline	Definition
Introduction:	Thesis statement — Contrary to its critics' objections, behaviorism is a valid approach for treating a wide variety of psychological dysfunctions.
Background:	Definition of behaviorism, including its origins and evolution
First example:	The use of behaviorism to help psychotic patients function in an institutional setting
Second example:	The use of behaviorism to treat neurotic behavior, such as chronic anxiety, a phobia, or a pattern of destructive acts
Third example:	The use of behaviorism to treat normal but antisocial or undesirable behavior, such as heavy smoking or overeating
Conclusion:	Restatement of thesis (in different words) or review of key points

Notice how the three examples in this essay define behaviorism with the kind of complexity, detail, and breadth that a formal definition could not duplicate. This definition is more like a textbook explanation — and, in fact, textbook explanations are often written as extended definitions.

Revising a Definition Essay

When you revise a definition essay, consider the items on the revision checklist on page 68. In addition, pay special attention to the items on the following checklist, which apply specifically to revising definition essays.

☑ **REVISION CHECKLIST**   **Definition**

☐ Does your assignment call for definition?
☐ Does your essay include a clearly worded thesis statement — one that identifies the term you will be defining and tells readers why you are defining it?
☐ Have you included a formal definition of your subject? Have you defined other key terms that may not be familiar to your readers?
☐ Have you used appropriate patterns of development to expand your definition?
☐ Do you need to use other strategies — such as synonyms, negation, enumeration, or analogies — to expand your definition?
☐ Do you need to discuss the origin and development of the term you are defining?
☐ Do you need to include a visual?

Editing a Definition Essay

When you edit your definition essay, follow the guidelines on the editing checklists on pages 85, 88, and 91. In addition, focus on the grammar, mechanics, and punctuation issues that are particularly relevant to definition essays. One of these issues — avoiding the phrases *is when* and *is where* in formal definitions — is discussed below.

GRAMMAR IN CONTEXT   *Avoiding is when and is where*

Many extended definitions include a one-sentence formal definition. As you have learned, such definitions must include the term you are defining, the class to which the term belongs, and the characteristics that distinguish the term from other terms in the same class.

Sometimes, however, when you are defining a term or concept, you may find yourself departing from this structure and using the phrase *is when* or *is where*. If so, your definition is not complete because it omits the term's class. (In fact, the use of *is when* or *is where* indicates that you are actually presenting an example of the term and not a definition.)

You can avoid this error by making certain that the form of the verb *be* in your definition is always followed by a noun.

INCORRECT: As described by Ajoy Mahtab in his essay "The Untouchable," *prejudice* is when someone forms an irrational bias or negative opinion of a person or group.

CORRECT: As described by Ajoy Mahtab in his essay "The Untouchable," *prejudice* is an irrational bias or negative opinion of a person or group.

INCORRECT:	*Homelessness* is where a person has no permanent place to live.
CORRECT:	*Homelessness* is the state of being without a permanent place to live.

✔ **EDITING CHECKLIST**   **Definition**

☐ Have you avoided using *is when* and *is where* in your formal definitions?
☐ Have you used the present tense for your formal definition — even if you have used the past tense elsewhere in your essay?
☐ In your formal definition, have you italicized the term you are defining and placed the definition itself in quotation marks?

A STUDENT WRITER: Definition

The following student essay, written by Ajoy Mahtab for a composition course, defines the untouchables, members of a caste that is shunned in India. In his essay, Ajoy, who grew up in Calcutta, presents a thesis that is sharply critical of the practice of ostracizing untouchables. Note that he includes a photograph to help readers understand the unfamiliar term he is defining.

The Untouchable

Introduction: background

A word that is extremely common in India yet uncommon   1
to the point of incomprehension in the West is the word *untouchable*. It is a word that has had very sinister connotations throughout India's history. A rigorously worked-out caste system has traditionally existed in Indian society. At the top of the social ladder sat the Brahmins, the clan of the priesthood. These people had renounced the material world for a spiritual one. Below them came the Kshatriyas, or the warrior caste. This caste included the kings and all their nobles along with their armies. Third on the social ladder were the Vaishyas, who were the merchants of the land. Trade was their only form of livelihood. Last came the Shudras — the menials. Shudras were employed by the prosperous as sweepers and laborers. Originally a person's caste was determined only by his profession. Thus, if the son of a merchant joined the army, he automatically converted from a Vaishya to a Kshatriya. However, the system soon became hereditary and rigid. Whatever one's occupation, one's caste was determined from birth according to the caste of one's father.

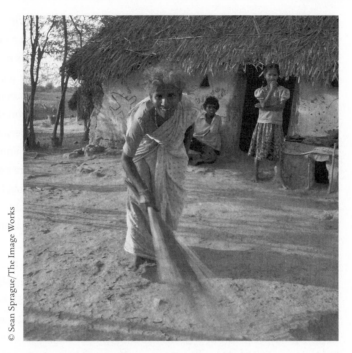

© Sean Sprague/The Image Works

Fig. 1. Sean Sprague. *Untouchable Woman Sweeping in Front of Her House in a Village in Tamil Nadu, India.* 2003. The Image Works. Web. 4 Nov. 2011.

Outside of this structure were a group of people, human   2
beings treated worse than dogs and shunned far more than lepers,
people who were not considered even human, people who defiled
with their very touch. These were the Achhoots: the untouchables,
Formal definition   one of whom is shown in fig. 1. The word *untouchable* is commonly
Historical   defined as "that which cannot or should not be touched." In India,
background   however, it was taken to a far greater extreme. The untouchables
of a village lived in a separate community downwind of the
borders of the village. They had a separate water supply, for they
would make the village water impure if they were to drink from
it. When they walked, they were made to bang two sticks together
continuously so that passersby could hear them coming and
thus avoid an untouchable's shadow. Tied to their waists, trailing
behind them, was a broom that would clean the ground they had
walked on. The penalty for not following these or any other rules
was death for the untouchable and, in many instances, for the
entire untouchable community.

Present situation   One of the pioneers of the fight against untouchability was   3
Mahatma Gandhi. Thanks to his efforts and those of many others,

untouchability no longer presents anything like the horrific picture described above. In India today, in fact, recognition of untouchability is punishable by law. Theoretically, there is no such thing as untouchability anymore. But old traditions linger on, and a deep-rooted fear passed down from generation to generation does not disappear overnight. Even today, caste is an important factor in most marriages. Most Indian surnames reveal a person's caste immediately, so it is a difficult thing to hide. The shunning of the untouchable is more prevalent in South India, where people are much more devout, than in the North. Some people would rather starve than share food and water with an untouchable. This concept is very difficult to accept in the West, but it is true all the same.

Example   I remember an incident from my childhood. I could not   4
have been more than eight or nine at the time. I was on a holiday staying at my family's house on the river Ganges. A festival was going on, and, as is customary, we were giving the servants small presents. I was handing them out when an old lady, bent with age, slowly hobbled into the room. She stood in the far corner of the room all alone, and no one so much as looked at her. When the entire line ended, she stepped hesitantly forward and stood in front of me, looking down at the ground. She then held a cloth stretched out in front of her. I was a little confused about how I was supposed to hand her her present, since both her hands were holding the cloth. Then, with the help of prompting from someone behind me, I learned that I was supposed to drop the gift into the cloth without touching the cloth itself. It was only later that I found out that she was an untouchable. This was the first time I had actually come face to face with such prejudice, and it felt like a slap in the face. That incident was burned into my memory, and I do not think I will ever forget it.

Conclusion   The word *untouchable* is not often used in the West, and   5
begins
when it is, it is generally used as a complimentary term. For example, an avid fan might say of an athlete, "He was absolutely untouchable. Nobody could even begin to compare with him." It seems rather ironic that a word could be so favorable in one culture and so negative in another. Why does a word that gives happiness in one part of the world cause pain in another? Why does the same word have different meanings to different people around the globe? Why do certain words cause rifts and others

forge bonds? I do not think anyone can tell me the answers to these questions.

Conclusion continues   No actual parallel can be found today that compares to the   6
horrors of untouchability. For an untouchable, life itself was a

Thesis statement   crime. The day was spent just trying to stay alive. From the misery of the untouchables, the world should learn a lesson: isolating and punishing any group of people is dehumanizing and immoral.

Points for Special Attention

Thesis Statement. Ajoy Mahtab's assignment was to write an extended definition of a term he assumed would be unfamiliar to his audience. Because he had definite ideas about the unjust treatment of the untouchables, Ajoy wanted his essay to have a strong thesis that communicated his disapproval. Still, because he knew his American classmates would need a good deal of background information before they would understand the context for such a thesis, he decided not to present it in his introduction. Instead, he decided to lead up to his thesis gradually and state it at the end of his essay. When other students in the class reviewed his draft, this subtlety was one of the points they reacted to most favorably.

Structure. Ajoy's introduction establishes the direction of his essay by introducing the word he will define; he then places this word in context by explaining India's rigid caste system. In paragraph 2, he gives the formal definition of the word *untouchable* and goes on to sketch the term's historical background. Paragraph 3 explains the status of the untouchables in present-day India, and paragraph 4 gives a vivid example of Ajoy's first encounter with an untouchable. As he begins his conclusion in paragraph 5, Ajoy brings his readers back to the word his essay defines. Here he uses two strategies to add interest: he contrasts a contemporary American usage of *untouchable* with its pejorative meaning in India, and he asks a series of **rhetorical questions** (questions asked for effect and not meant to be answered). In paragraph 6, Ajoy presents a summary of his position to lead into his thesis statement.

Patterns of Development. This essay uses a number of strategies commonly incorporated into extended definitions: it includes a formal definition, explains the term's origin, and explores some of the term's connotations. The essay also uses several familiar patterns of development. For instance, paragraph 1 uses classification and division to explain India's caste system; paragraphs 2 and 3 use brief examples to illustrate the plight of the untouchable; and paragraph 4 presents a narrative. Each of these patterns enriches the definition.

Working with Sources. Ajoy includes a visual — a photograph of an untouchable — to supplement his passages of description and to help his readers understand this very unfamiliar concept. He places the photograph early in his essay, where it will be most helpful, and he refers to it in paragraph 2 with the phrase "one of whom is shown in fig. 1." In addition, he includes a caption below the photo with full source information.

Focus on Revision

Because the term Ajoy defined was so unfamiliar to his classmates, many of the peer-editing worksheets students filled in asked for more information. One suggestion in particular — that he draw an analogy between the unfamiliar term *untouchable* and a concept more familiar to American students — appealed to Ajoy as he planned his revision. Another student suggested that Ajoy could compare untouchables to other groups who have been shunned — for example, people with AIDS. Although Ajoy states in his conclusion that no parallel exists, an attempt to find common ground between untouchables and other groups could make his essay more meaningful to his readers — and bring home to them a distinctly alien idea. Such a connection could also make his conclusion especially powerful.

PEER-EDITING WORKSHEET: Definition

1. What term is the writer defining? Does the essay include a formal definition? If so, where? If no formal definition is included, should one be added?

2. Why is the writer defining the term? Does the essay include a thesis statement that makes this purpose clear? If not, suggest revisions.

3. What patterns does the writer use to develop the definition? What other patterns could be used? Would a visual be helpful?

4. Does the essay define the term appropriately for its audience? Does the definition help you understand the meaning of the term?

5. Does the writer use synonyms to develop the definition? If so, where? If not, where could synonyms be used to help communicate the term's meaning?

6. Does the writer use negation to develop the definition? If so, where? If not, could the writer strengthen the definition by explaining what the term is not?

7. Does the writer use enumeration to develop the definition? If so, where? If not, where in the essay might the writer list the term's special characteristics?

8. Does the writer use analogies to develop the definition? If so, where? Do you find these analogies helpful? What additional analogies might help readers understand the term more fully?

9. Does the writer explain the term's origin and development? If so, where? If not, do you believe this information should be added?

10. Reread the essay's introduction. If the writer uses a formal definition as an opening strategy, try to suggest an alternative opening.

The selections that follow use exemplification, description, narration, and other methods of developing extended definitions. The first selection, a visual text, is followed by questions designed to illustrate how definition can operate in visual form. (A multimodal text for definition is located online at **macmillanhighered.com/patterns**.)

U.S. CENSUS BUREAU

U.S. Census 2010 Form (Questionnaire)

→ **NOTE: Please answer BOTH Question 8 about Hispanic origin and Question 9 about race. For this census, Hispanic origins are not races.**

8. Is Person 1 of Hispanic, Latino, or Spanish origin?

☐ **No**, not of Hispanic, Latino, or Spanish origin
☐ Yes, Mexican, Mexican Am., Chicano
☐ Yes, Puerto Rican
☐ Yes, Cuban
☐ Yes, another Hispanic, Latino, or Spanish origin — *Print origin, for example, Argentinean, Colombian, Dominican, Nicaraguan, Salvadoran, Spaniard, and so on.* ↘

9. What is Person 1's race? *Mark* ☒ *one or more boxes.*

☐ White
☐ Black, African Am., or Negro
☐ American Indian or Alaska Native — *Print name of enrolled or principal tribe.* ↘

☐ Asian Indian   ☐ Japanese   ☐ Native Hawaiian
☐ Chinese   ☐ Korean   ☐ Guamanian or Chamorro
☐ Filipino   ☐ Vietnamese   ☐ Samoan
☐ Other Asian — *Print race, for example, Hmong, Laotian, Thai, Pakistani, Cambodian, and so on.* ↘   ☐ Other Pacific Islander — *Print race, for example, Fijian, Tongan, and so on.* ↘

☐ Some other race — *Print race.* ↘

Courtesy of the U.S. Dept. of Commerce/Bureau of the Census

• • •

Reading Images

1. In a single complete sentence, define yourself in terms of your race, religion, or ethnicity (whatever is most important to you).

2. Look at the U.S. Census questions on the form. Which boxes would you mark? Do you see this choice as an accurate expression of what you consider yourself to be? Explain.

3. Only recently has the Census Bureau permitted respondents to mark "one or more boxes" to indicate their ethnic identity. Do you think this option is a good idea?

Journal Entry

Why do you think the U.S. government needs to know what a person considers himself/herself to be? Do you think it is important for the government to know how people define themselves, or do you consider this information an unwarranted violation of a person's privacy? Explain.

Thematic Connections

- "'What's in a Name?'" (page 2)
- "Indian Education" (page 142)
- "The Myth of the Latin Woman: I Just Met a Girl Named Maria" (page 230)
- "Mother Tongue" (page 463)
- "On Dumpster Diving" (page 672)

JUDY BRADY

I Want a Wife

Judy Brady has published articles on many social issues. Diagnosed with breast cancer in 1980, she became active in the politics of cancer and has edited *Women and Cancer* (1990) and *One in Three: Women with Cancer Confront an Epidemic* (1991). She also helped found the Toxic Links Coalition, an organization devoted to lobbying for cancer and environmental issues.

Background on the status of women Brady has been active in the women's movement since 1969, and "I Want a Wife" first appeared in the premiere issue of the feminist *Ms.* magazine in 1972. That year represented perhaps the height of the feminist movement in the United States. The National Organization for Women, established in 1966, had hundreds of chapters around the country. The Equal Rights Amendment, barring discrimination against women, passed in Congress (although it was ratified by only thirty-five of the necessary thirty-eight states), and Congress also passed Title IX of the Education Amendments Act, which required equal opportunity (in sports as well as academics) for all students in any school that receives federal funding. At that time, women accounted for just under 40 percent of the labor force (up from 23 percent in 1950), a number that has grown to almost 50 percent today, in part because of the severe recession that started in 2008, which has caused more job losses for men than for women. Of mothers with children under age eighteen, fewer than 40 percent were employed in 1970; today, three-quarters work, 38 percent of them full-time and year-round. As for stay-at-home fathers, their numbers have increased from virtually zero to nearly 160,000.

I belong to that classification of people known as wives. I am A Wife. And, not altogether incidentally, I am a mother.

Not too long ago a male friend of mine appeared on the scene fresh from a recent divorce. He had one child, who is, of course, with his ex-wife. He is looking for another wife. As I thought about him while I was ironing one evening, it suddenly occurred to me that I, too, would like to have a wife. Why do I want a wife?

I would like to go back to school so that I can become economically independent, support myself, and, if need be, support those dependent upon me. I want a wife who will work and send me to school. And while I am going to school I want a wife to take care of my children. I want a wife to keep track of the children's doctor and dentist appointments. And to keep track of mine, too. I want a wife to make sure my children eat properly and are kept clean. I want a wife who will wash the children's clothes and keep them mended. I want a wife who is a good nurturant attendant to my children, who arranges for their schooling, makes sure that they have an adequate social life with their peers, takes them to the park, the zoo, etc. I want a wife who takes care of the children when they are sick, a wife who arranges to be around when the children need special care, because, of course, I cannot miss classes at school. My wife must arrange to lose time at work and not lose the job. It may mean a small cut in my wife's income from time to time, but I guess I can tolerate that. Needless to say, my wife will arrange and pay for the care of the children while my wife is working.

I want a wife who will take care of *my* physical needs. I want a wife who 4 will keep my house clean. A wife who will pick up after my children, a wife who will pick up after me. I want a wife who will keep my clothes clean, ironed, mended, replaced when need be, and who will see to it that my personal things are kept in their proper place so that I can find what I need the minute I need it. I want a wife who cooks the meals, a wife who is a *good* cook. I want a wife who will plan the menus, do the necessary grocery shopping, prepare the meals, serve them pleasantly, and then do the cleaning up while I do my studying. I want a wife who will care for me when I am sick and sympathize with my pain and loss of time from school. I want a wife to go along when our family takes a vacation so that someone can continue to care for me and my children when I need a rest and change of scene.

I want a wife who will not bother me with rambling complaints about 5 a wife's duties. But I want a wife who will listen to me when I feel the need to explain a rather difficult point I have come across in my course of studies. And I want a wife who will type my papers for me when I have written them.

I want a wife who will take care of the details of my social life. When my 6 wife and I are invited out by my friends, I want a wife who will take care of the babysitting arrangements. When I meet people at school that I like and want to entertain, I want a wife who will have the house clean, will prepare a special meal, serve it to me and my friends, and not interrupt when I talk about things that interest me and my friends. I want a wife who will have arranged that the children are fed and ready for bed before my guests arrive so that the children do not bother us. I want a wife who takes care of the needs of my guests so that they feel comfortable, who makes sure that they have an ashtray, that they are passed the hors d'oeuvres, that they are offered a second helping of the food, that their wine glasses are replenished when necessary, that their coffee is served to them as they like it. And I want a wife who knows that sometimes I need a night out by myself.

I want a wife who is sensitive to my sexual needs, a wife who makes love passionately and eagerly when I feel like it, a wife who makes sure that I am satisfied. And, of course, I want a wife who will not demand sexual attention when I am not in the mood for it. I want a wife who assumes the complete responsibility for birth control, because I do not want more children. I want a wife who will remain sexually faithful to me so that I do not have to clutter up my intellectual life with jealousies. And I want a wife who understands that *my* sexual needs may

> " My God, who *wouldn't* want a wife? "

7

entail more than strict adherence to monogamy. I must, after all, be able to relate to people as fully as possible.

If, by chance, I find another person more suitable as a wife than the 8 wife I already have, I want the liberty to replace my present wife with another one. Naturally, I will expect a fresh new life; my wife will take the children and be solely responsible for them so that I am left free.

When I am through with school and have a job, I want my wife to quit 9 working and remain at home so that my wife can more fully and completely take care of a wife's duties.

My God, who *wouldn't* want a wife? 10

. . .

Comprehension

1. In one sentence, define what Brady means by *wife*. Does this ideal wife actually exist? Explain.

2. List some of the specific duties of the wife Brady describes. Into what five general categories does Brady arrange these duties?

3. What complaints does Brady apparently have about the life she actually leads? To what does she seem to attribute her problems?

4. Under what circumstances does Brady say she would consider leaving her wife? What would happen to the children if she left?

Purpose and Audience

1. This essay was first published in *Ms.* magazine. In what sense is it appropriate for the audience of this feminist publication? Where else can you imagine it appearing?

2. Does this essay have an explicitly stated thesis? If so, where is it? If the thesis is implied, paraphrase it.

3. Do you think Brady *really* wants the kind of wife she describes? Explain your response.

Style and Structure

1. Throughout the essay, Brady repeats the words "I want a wife." What is the effect of this repetition?

2. The first and last paragraphs of this essay are quite brief. Does this weaken the essay? Why or why not?

3. In enumerating a wife's duties, Brady frequently uses the verb *arrange*. What other verbs does she use repeatedly? How do these verbs help her make her point?

4. Brady never uses the personal pronouns *he* or *she* to refer to the wife she defines. Why not?

5. **Vocabulary Project.** Going beyond the dictionary definitions, decide what Brady means to suggest by each of the following words. Is she using any of these terms sarcastically? Explain.

proper (4)   necessary (6)   suitable (8)
pleasantly (4)   demand (7)   free (8)
bother (6)   clutter up (7)

Journal Entry

Is Brady's 1972 characterization of a wife still accurate today? Which of the characteristics she describes have remained the same? Which have changed? Why?

Writing Workshop

1. Write an essay defining your ideal boss, parent, teacher, or pet.
2. Write an essay titled "I Want a Husband." Taking an **ironic** stance, use society's notions of the ideal husband to help you shape your definition.
3. Write a definition essay called "The Ideal Couple," in which you try to divide household chores and other responsibilities equitably between the two partners. (Your essay can be serious or humorous.) Develop your definition with examples.

Combining the Patterns

Like most definition essays, "I Want a Wife" uses several patterns of development. Which ones does it use? Which of these do you consider most important for supporting Brady's thesis? Why?

Thematic Connections

- "My Mother Never Worked" (page 123)
- "Sex, Lies, and Conversation" (page 421)
- Declaration of Sentiments and Resolutions, Seneca Falls Convention, 1848 (page 556)

JOSÉ ANTONIO BURCIAGA

Tortillas

José Antonio Burciaga (1940–1996) was the founder of *Diseños Literarios,* a publishing company in California, as well as the comedy troupe Culture Clash. He contributed fiction, poetry, and articles to many anthologies, as well as to journals and newspapers. He also published several books of poems, drawings, and essays, including the poetry collection *Undocumented Love* (1992) and the essay collection *Drink Cultura* (1993). "Tortillas," originally titled "I Remember Masa," was first published in *Weedee Peepo* (1988), a collection of essays in Spanish and English.

Background on tortillas Tortillas have been a staple of Mexican cooking for thousands of years. These thin, round griddlecakes made of cornmeal *(masa)* are often eaten with every meal, and the art of making them is still passed from generation to generation (although they now are widely available commercially as well). The earliest Mexican immigrants introduced them to the United States, and in the past twenty-five years tortillas, along with many other popular items of Mexican cuisine, have entered the country's culinary landscape (as, over the decades, has a wide variety of other "ethnic" foods, such as pizza, egg rolls, bagels, sushi, and gyros). Still, tortillas have special meaning for Mexican Americans, and in this essay Burciaga discusses the role of the tortilla within his family's culture.

My earliest memory of *tortillas* is my *Mamá* telling me not to play with 1
them. I had bitten eyeholes in one and was wearing it as a mask at the dinner table.

As a child, I also used *tortillas* as hand warmers on cold days, and my 2
family claims that I owe my career as an artist to my early experiments with *tortillas.* According to them, my clowning around helped me develop a strong artistic foundation. I'm not so sure, though. Sometimes I wore a *tortilla* on my head, like a *yarmulke,* and yet I never had any great urge to convert from Catholicism to Judaism. But who knows? They may be right.

For Mexicans over the centuries, the *tortilla* has served as the spoon and 3
the fork, the plate and the napkin. *Tortillas* originated before the Mayan civilizations, perhaps predating Europe's wheat bread. According to Mayan mythology, the great god Quetzalcoatl, realizing that the red ants knew the secret of using maize as food, transformed himself into a black ant, infiltrated the colony of red ants, and absconded with a grain of corn. (Is it any wonder that to this day, black ants and red ants do not get along?) Quetzalcoatl then put maize on the lips of the first man and woman, Oxomoco and Cipactonal, so that they would become strong. Maize festivals are still celebrated by many Indian cultures of the Americas.

When I was growing up in El Paso, *tortillas* were part of my daily life. 4
I used to visit a *tortilla* factory in an ancient adobe building near the

open *mercado* in Ciudad Juárez. As I approached, I could hear the rhythmic slapping of the *masa* as the skilled vendors outside the factory formed it into balls and patted them into perfectly round corn cakes between the palms of their hands. The wonderful aroma and the speed with which the women counted so many dozens of *tortillas* out of warm wicker baskets still linger in my mind. Watching them at work convinced me that the most handsome and *deliciosas tortillas* are handmade. Although machines are faster, they can never adequately replace generation-to-generation experience. There's no place in the factory assembly line for the tender slaps that give each *tortilla* character. The best thing that can be said about mass-producing *tortillas* is that it makes it possible for many people to enjoy them.

> " For Mexicans over the centuries, the *tortilla* has served as the spoon and the fork, the plate and the napkin. "

In the *mercado* where my mother shopped, we frequently bought *taquitos de nopalitos,* small tacos filled with diced cactus, onions, tomatoes, and *jalapeños.* Our friend Don Toribio showed us how to make delicious, crunchy *taquitos* with dried, salted pumpkin seeds. When you had no money for the filling, a poor man's *taco* could be made by placing a warm *tortilla* on the left palm, applying a sprinkle of salt, then rolling the *tortilla* up quickly with the fingertips of the right hand. My own kids put peanut butter and jelly on *tortillas,* which I think is truly bicultural. And speaking of fast foods for kids, nothing beats a *quesadilla,* a *tortilla* grilled-cheese sandwich. 5

Depending on what you intend to use them for, *tortillas* may be made in various ways. Even a run-of-the-mill *tortilla* is more than a flat corn cake. A skillfully cooked homemade *tortilla* has a bottom and a top; the top skin forms a pocket in which you put the filling that folds your *tortilla* into a taco. Paper-thin *tortillas* are used specifically for *flautas,* a type of taco that is filled, rolled, and then fried until crisp. The name *flauta* means *flute,* which probably refers to the Mayan bamboo flute; however, the only sound that comes from an edible *flauta* is a delicious crunch that is music to the palate. In México *flautas* are sometimes made as long as two feet and then cut into manageable segments. The opposite of *flautas* is *gorditas,* meaning *little fat ones.* These are very thick small *tortillas.* 6

The versatility of *tortillas* and corn does not end here. Besides being tasty and nourishing, they have spiritual and artistic qualities as well. The Tarahumara Indians of Chihuahua, for example, concocted a corn-based beer called *tesgüino,* which their descendants still make today. And everyone has read about the woman in New Mexico who was cooking her husband a *tortilla* one morning when the image of Jesus Christ miraculously appeared on it. Before they knew what was happening, the man's breakfast had become a local shrine. 7

Then there is *tortilla* art. Various Chicano artists throughout the Southwest have, when short of materials or just in a whimsical mood, used a dry *tortilla* as a small, round canvas. And a few years back, at the height of the 8

Chicano movement, a priest in Arizona got into trouble with the Church after he was discovered celebrating mass using a *tortilla* as the host. All of which only goes to show that while the *tortilla* may be a lowly corn cake, when the necessity arises, it can reach unexpected distinction.

· · ·

Comprehension

1. What exactly is a tortilla?
2. List the functions — both practical and whimsical — that tortillas serve.
3. In paragraph 7, Burciaga cites the "spiritual and artistic qualities" of tortillas. Do you think he is being serious? Explain your reasoning.

Purpose and Audience

1. Burciaga states his thesis explicitly in his essay's final sentence. Paraphrase this thesis. Why do you think he does not state it sooner? Do you think this was the right decision?
2. Do you think Burciaga expects most of his readers to be of Hispanic descent? To be familiar with tortillas? How can you tell?
3. Why do you think Burciaga uses humor in this essay? Is it consistent with his essay's purpose? Could the humor have a negative effect on his audience? Explain.
4. Why are tortillas so important to Burciaga? Is it just their versatility he admires, or do they represent something more to him?

Style and Structure

1. Where does Burciaga provide a formal definition of *tortilla*? Why does he locate this formal definition where he does?
2. Burciaga uses many Spanish words, but he defines only some of them — for example, *taquitos de nopalitos* and *quesadilla* in paragraph 5 and *flautas* and *gorditas* in paragraph 6. Why do you think he defines some Spanish terms but not others? Should he have defined them all?
3. Does Burciaga use synonyms or negation to define *tortilla*? Does he discuss the word's origin and development? If so, where? If not, do you think any of these strategies would improve his essay? Explain.
4. **Vocabulary Project.** Look up each of the following words in a Spanish-English dictionary, and try to supply its English equivalent.

mercado (4)   deliciosas (4)
masa (4)   jalapeños (5)

Journal Entry

Explore some additional uses — practical or frivolous — for tortillas that Burciaga does not discuss.

Writing Workshop

1. **Working with Sources.** Write an essay defining a food that is important to your family, ethnic group, or circle of friends. Begin with your own "earliest memory" of the food, comparing it with Burciaga's, and use several patterns of development, as Burciaga does. Assume your audience is not familiar with the food you define. Your thesis should indicate why the food is so important to you. Be sure to document references to Burciaga's essay and to include a works-cited page. (See Chapter 18 for information on MLA documentation.)

2. Relying primarily on description and exemplification, define a food that is sure to be familiar to all your readers. Do not name the food until your essay's last sentence.

3. Write an essay defining a food — but include a thesis statement that paints a very favorable portrait of a much-maligned food (for example, Spam or brussels sprouts) or a very negative picture of a popular food (for example, chocolate or ice cream).

Combining the Patterns

Burciaga uses several patterns of development in his extended definition. Where, for example, does he use **description**, **narration**, **process**, and **exemplification**? Does he use any other patterns?

Thematic Connections

- "Goodbye to My Twinkie Days" (page 171)
- "Once More to the Lake" (page 191)
- "The Case for Birthright Citizenship" (page 593)
- "The Park" (page 667)

ANNA QUINDLEN

Homeless

A prolific journalist, columnist, children's author, and novelist, Anna Quindlen was born in 1952 and graduated from Barnard College. She is probably best known for her Pulitzer Prize–winning opinion columns for the *New York Times* in the 1980s and 1990s. From 2000 to 2009, Quindlen wrote the Last Word column for *Newsweek* magazine. She is the author of many books of fiction and nonfiction, including *One True Thing* (1994), *Good Dog. Stay.* (2007), and *Every Last One: A Novel* (2010). Her latest novel is *Still Life with Bread Crumbs* (2013).

Background on homelessness in the United States Given the economic conditions of the last several years — a deep recession, the 2008 global financial collapse, a housing crisis, and chronically high unemployment — some people may be surprised to discover that America's homeless population has actually declined during the last decade. Recent figures from the National Alliance to End Homelessness estimate the homeless population at around 633,000, a 17 percent decline since 2005; a 2013 report from the U.S. Department of Housing and Urban Development (HUD) gives a slightly lower estimate: 610,042 homeless people. According to HUD, 65 percent of this population was living in emergency shelters or transitional housing. A more recent decline in homelessness was evident across a range of demographics, including homeless veterans and the chronically homeless. The numbers vary by region. For example, in some states, such as New York, the homeless population has increased even as the national number decreased. (Of course, measuring this population, which is often marginal or even invisible, can be difficult.) The causes of homelessness are complex; poverty, unemployment, domestic violence, mental illness, and substance abuse often play a role. The Institute for Children, Poverty, and Homelessness also points to a lack of affordable housing, particularly as the production of federal subsidized housing units has decreased. Anna Quindlen wrote the following essay in 1987, when homelessness was a more prominent social issue. Although homelessness receives less attention today than it did in the past, it remains a serious problem in the United States.

Her name was Ann, and we met in the Port Authority Bus Terminal 1
several Januarys ago. I was doing a story on homeless people. She said I was
wasting my time talking to her; she was just passing through, although
she'd been passing through for more than two weeks. To prove to me that
this was true, she rummaged through a tote bag and a manila envelope and
finally unfolded a sheet of typing paper and brought out her photographs.

They were not pictures of family, or friends, or even a dog or cat, its 2
eyes brown-red in the flashbulb's light. They were pictures of a house. It
was like a thousand houses in a hundred towns, not suburb, not city, but
somewhere in between, with aluminum siding and a chain-link fence, a

narrow driveway running up to a one-car garage, and a patch of backyard. The house was yellow. I looked on the back for a date or a name, but neither was there. There was no need for discussion. I knew what she was trying to tell me, for it was something I had often felt. She was not adrift, alone, anonymous, although her bags and her raincoat with the grime shadowing its creases had made me believe she was. She had a house, or at least once upon a time had had one. Inside were curtains, a couch, a stove, potholders. You are where you live. She was somebody.

I've never been very good at looking at the big picture, taking the global 3 view, and I've always been a person with an overactive sense of place, the legacy of an Irish grandfather. So it is natural that the thing that seems most wrong with the world to me right now is that there are so many people with no homes. I'm not simply talking about shelter from the elements, or three square meals a day, or a mailing address to which the welfare people can send the check — although I know that all these are important for survival. I'm talking about a home, about precisely those kinds of feelings that have wound up in cross-stitch and French knots on samplers over the years.

Home is where the heart is. There's no place like it. I love my home with a ferocity totally out of proportion to its appearance or location. I love dumb things about it: the hot-water heater, the plastic rack you drain dishes in, the roof over my head, which occasionally leaks. And yet it is precisely those dumb things that make it what it is — a place of certainty, stability, predictability, privacy, for me and for my family. It is where I live. What more can you say about a place than that? That is everything.

> " It is where I live. What more can you say about a place than that? That is everything. "

[handwritten margin note: Mothin]

Yet it is something that we have been edging away from gradually dur- 5 ing my lifetime and the lifetimes of my parents and grandparents. There was a time when where you lived often was where you worked and where you grew the food you ate and even where you were buried. When that era passed, where you lived at least was where your parents had lived and where you would live with your children when you became enfeebled. Then, suddenly, where you lived was where you lived for three years, until you could move on to something else and something else again.

And so we have come to something else again, to children who do not 6 understand what it means to go to their rooms because they have never had a room, to men and women whose fantasy is a wall they can paint a color of their own choosing, to old people reduced to sitting on molded plastic chairs, their skin blue-white in the lights of a bus station, who pull pictures of houses out of their bags. Homes have stopped being homes. Now they are real estate.

People find it curious that those without homes would rather sleep sit- 7 ting up on benches or huddled in doorways than go to shelters. Certainly some prefer to do so because they are emotionally ill, because they have

[handwritten margin note at bottom: Now real estate]

been locked in before and they are determined not to be locked in again. Others are afraid of the violence and trouble they may find there. But some seem to want something that is not available in shelters, and they will not compromise, not for a cot, or oatmeal, or a shower with special soap that kills the bugs. "One room," a woman with a baby who was sleeping on her sister's floor once told me, "painted blue." That was the crux of it; not the size or location, but pride of ownership. Painted blue.

This is a difficult problem, and some wise and compassionate people 8 are working hard at it. But in the main I think we work around it, just as we walk around it when it is lying on the sidewalk or sitting in the bus terminal—the problem, that is. It has been customary to take people's pain and lessen our own participation in it by turning it into an issue, not a collection of human beings. We turn an adjective into a noun: the poor, not poor people; the homeless, not Ann or the man who lives in the box or the woman who sleeps on the subway grate.

Sometimes I think we would be better off if we forgot about the broad 9 strokes and concentrated on the details. Here is a woman without a bureau. There is a man with no mirror, no wall to hang it on. They are not the homeless. They are people who have no homes. No drawer that holds the spoons. No window to look out upon the world. My God. That is everything.

. . .

Comprehension

1. Where does Quindlen define *homeless, homelessness, homeless people,* and *home*? Which of these terms is the primary focus of her essay?

2. In paragraph 3, Quindlen says that "the thing that seems most wrong with the world to me right now is that there are so many people with no homes." What does she mean by *homes* in this context?

3. How does Quindlen define *home* in paragraph 4? Is her meaning here the same as her meaning in paragraph 3?

4. What does Quindlen mean when she says in paragraph 9, "They are not the homeless. They are people who have no homes." What distinction is she making here? Is this a meaningful distinction? Why or why not?

Purpose and Audience

1. Quindlen begins her essay with two paragraphs discussing her encounter with a woman named Ann. Is this an effective opening strategy? Is it likely to engage her audience? Why or why not?

2. In one sentence, state this essay's thesis. Does this thesis appear in the essay? If so, where? If not, do you think an implied thesis is a good strategy here? Explain.

3. What do you think Quindlen hoped to accomplish by writing this essay? Do you think her points are as relevant today as they were in 1987, when she wrote her essay? Are they perhaps *more* relevant?

Style and Structure

1. Identify sentences that reveal Quindlen's emotional response to the problem she is examining. Do you think she is too emotionally involved with her topic?

2. What purpose does paragraph 5 serve in this essay? How does this paragraph use comparison and contrast to develop a definition of *home*?

3. Do you think Quindlen should have included statistics or expert testimony, or is her essay convincing without this type of supporting evidence?

4. Where does Quindlen define by negation—by telling what a term is *not*?

5. Where does Quindlen use exemplification to develop her definition? Where does she use description?

6. **Vocabulary Project.** In paragraph 6, Quindlen says, "Homes have stopped being homes. Now they are real estate." Use a dictionary or thesaurus to help you identify the different connotations of the word *home*. Then, find a definition of the term *real estate*. How are these terms alike in meaning? How are they different?

Journal Entry

Do you agree with Quindlen when she says that "we would be better off if we forgot about the broad strokes and concentrated on the details" (9)? Briefly outline your own views on how to address the problem of homelessness.

Writing Workshop

1. **Working with Sources.** Who are the homeless? Visit the website of the National Coalition for the Homeless (or a similar site) to find out what kinds of people are homeless in the United States today. Then, write an essay defining the term *homeless,* using classification and division to structure your essay. Be sure to include parenthetical documentation for references to Quindlen and to include a works-cited page. (See Chapter 18 for information on MLA documentation.)

2. Write an extended definition of *home,* developing your definition with narration, description, and exemplification. (You can also use negation, explaining what a home is *not*.)

Combining the Patterns

In her definition essay, Quindlen also presents an **argument**. What is her position on the issue she is examining? How could she make a stronger argument?

Thematic Connections

- " 'What's in a Name?' " (page 2)
- "Midnight" (page 217)
- "On Dumpster Diving" (page 672)

GAYLE ROSENWALD SMITH

The Wife-Beater

Gayle Rosenwald Smith, an attorney, currently practices family law. She has published articles in a variety of journals and periodicals and is coauthor of *What Every Woman Should Know about Divorce and Custody* (1998) and *Divorce and Money: Everything You Need to Know* (2004). The following essay appeared in the *Philadelphia Inquirer* in 2001.

Background on the "wife-beater" shirt As Smith notes here, *wife-beater* is a slang term for a type of sleeveless undershirt that has in recent years become fashionable. An Internet search of the term found a number of businesses that actually market such shirts as "wife-beaters." The corresponding shirts for women are often called "boy-beaters." A Texas-based firm offers adult-sized shirts emblazoned with the slogan, as well as "Lil' Wife Beater" shirts for babies. The firm's website — which plays the song "Smack My Bitch Up" — includes a background screen showing a woman being spanked and provides a link to a "Wife Beater Hall of Fame." It also offers to send a second shirt at half price to any customer convicted of domestic violence (proof of conviction required, photos not acceptable). In another twist, a feminist retail site offered a "Wife Beater Beater" shirt with a cartoon image of a woman kicking a man in the groin. Ironically, this retail site was shut down when a *man* complained that it was offensive.

Everybody wears them. The Gap sells them. Fashion designers Dolce 1
and Gabbana have lavished them with jewels. Their previous greatest resurgence occurred in the 1950s, when Marlon Brando's Stanley Kowalski wore one in Tennessee Williams' *A Streetcar Named Desire.* They are all the rage.

What are they called? 2

The name is the issue. For they are known as "wife-beaters." 3

A Web search shows that kids nationwide are wearing the skinny- 4
ribbed white T-shirts that can be worn alone or under another shirt. Women have adopted them with the same gusto as men. A search of boutiques shows that these wearers include professionals who wear them, adorned with designer accessories, under their pricey suits. They are available in all colors, sizes, and price ranges.

Wearers under twenty-five do not seem to be disturbed by the name. 5
But I sure am.

It's an odd name for an undershirt. And even though the ugly stereo- 6
types behind the name are both obvious and toxic, it appears to be cool to say the name without fear of (or without caring about) hurting anyone.

That the name is fueled by stereotype is now an academically estab- 7
lished fact, although various sources disagree on exactly when shirt and name came together. The *Oxford Dictionary* defines the term *wife-beater* as:

1. A man who physically abuses his wife and

2. Tank-style underwear shirts. Origin: based on the stereotype that physically abusive husbands wear that particular type of shirt.

The *World Book Dictionary* locates the origin of the term *wife-beater* in 8 the 1970s, from the stereotype of the Midwestern male wearing an undershirt while beating his wife. The shirts are said to have been popular in the 1980s at all types of sporting events, especially ones at which one sits in the sun and develops "wife-beater marks." The undershirts also attained popularity at wet T-shirt contests, in which the wet, ribbed tees accentuated contestants' breasts.

In an article in the style section of the *New York Times,* Jesse Scheidlower, 9 principal editor of the *Oxford English Dictionary*'s American office, says the association of the undershirt and the term *wife-beater* arose in 1997 from varied sources, including gay and gang subcultures and rap music.

> " So *manly* equals *violent*? Not by me, and I hope not by anyone on any side of age twenty-five. "

In the article, some sources argued that 10 the reference in the term was not to spousal abuse per se but to popular-culture figures such as Ralph Cramden and Tony Soprano. And what about Archie Bunker?

It's not just the name that worries me. 11 Fashion headlines reveal that we want to overthrow '90s grunge and return to shoulder pads and hardware-studded suits. Am I reading too much into a fashion statement that the return is also to male dominance where physical abuse is acceptable as a means of control?

There has to be a better term. After all, it's a pretty rare piece of cloth- 12 ing that can make both men and women look sexier. You'd expect a term connoting flattery — not violence.

Wearers under twenty-five may not want to hear this, but here it is. 13 More than four million women are victims of severe assaults by boyfriends and husbands each year. By conservative estimate, family violence occurs in two million families each year in the United States. Average age of the batterer: thirty-one.

Possibly the last statistic is telling. Maybe youth today would rather 14 ignore the overtones of the term *wife-beater.* It is also true, however, that the children of abusers often learn the behavior from their elders.

Therein lies perhaps the worst difficulty: that this name for this shirt 15 teaches the wrong thing about men. Some articles quote women who felt the shirts looked great, especially on guys with great bodies. One woman stated that it even made guys look "manly."

So *manly* equals *violent*? Not by me, and I hope not by anyone on any 16 side of age twenty-five.

•   •   •

Comprehension

1. Why is Smith "disturbed" (5) by the name "wife-beater"? Do you think her concern is justified?

2. In paragraph 3, Smith says, "The name is the issue"; in paragraph 11, she says, "It's not just the name that worries me." What does she mean by each statement? Do these two statements contradict each other?

3. What relationship does Smith see between the name of a sleeveless undershirt and the prevalence of family violence? Does she believe a causal connection does — or could — exist? If so, which is the cause, and which is the effect?

4. In paragraph 12, Smith acknowledges that the shirt "can make both men and women look sexier." Does this remark in any way undercut her credibility? Explain.

5. How, according to Smith, does calling a shirt a wife-beater teach women "the wrong thing about men" (15)?

Purpose and Audience

1. How do you think Smith expects her audience to react to her opening statement ("Everybody wears them")?

2. Why do you think Smith wrote this essay? Does she hope to change the name of the T-shirt, or does she seem to have a more ambitious purpose? Explain.

3. Twice in her essay, Smith mentions a group she calls "wearers under 25" (5, 13). Does she seem to direct her remarks at these young adults or at older readers? At wearers of the shirts or at a more general audience?

4. Restate Smith's thesis in your own words.

Style and Structure

1. Why do you think Smith begins her essay by explaining the popularity of sleeveless undershirts? Is this an effective opening strategy?

2. In paragraph 7, Smith reproduces a formal definition from the *Oxford Dictionary*. Why does she include this definition when she has already defined her term? What, if anything, does the formal definition add?

3. In paragraph 12, Smith says, "There has to be a better term." Can you think of a "better term" — one that does not suggest violence — for the shirt Smith describes?

4. Where does Smith present information on the history of the wife-beater? Why does she include this kind of information?

5. Where does Smith quote statistics? Do you see this information as relevant or incidental to her argument?

6. **Vocabulary Project.** Visit several different online dictionary sites — for example, dictionary.com and Merriam-Webster Online at m-w.com — and compare their definitions of the term *wife-beater*. How are these definitions alike? How are they different?

Journal Entry

Do you agree with Smith that the casual use of terms like *wife-beater* is dangerous, or do you think she is exaggerating the problem?

Writing Workshop

1. **Working with Sources.** Relying primarily on description and exemplification, define an article of clothing that is essential to your wardrobe. Begin by checking Internet sites on fashion history, such as fashion-era .com, to learn the item's history and the origin of its name. If you use information from a site in your essay, be sure to cite your source and to include a works-cited page. (See Chapter 18 for information on MLA documentation.)

2. Using comparison and contrast to structure your essay, define what a particular item of clothing means to you — and what it means to one of your parents.

3. Do members of your religious or ethnic group wear an item of clothing that is not well known to others — or not well understood by them? Define the article of clothing, and explain its significance and its history in terms that outsiders can understand.

Combining the Patterns

Do you think Smith should have spent more time in this essay on developing the **cause-and-effect** relationship, if any, between the "wife-beater" shirt and family violence? What additional information would she have to provide?

Thematic Connections

- "Four Tattoos" (page 222)
- "My First Conk" (page 283)
- "A Peaceful Woman Explains Why She Carries a Gun" (page 353)
- "Your Flip-Flops Are Grossing Me Out" (page 687)

AMANDA BROWN

Love and Other Catastrophes: A Mix Tape (Fiction)

Amanda Brown graduated with a B.F.A. in literature, writing, and publishing from Emerson College in 2002. As an undergraduate, she wrote "Love and Other Catastrophes: A Mix Tape" for a class assignment that required students to write a "list story." With her husband, Brown runs the Los Angeles–based record label Not Not Fun. Her first novel, *Drain You*, was published under the pseudonym M. Beth Bloom in 2012.

Background on music as the "soundtrack of our lives" For most of human history, the only way for people to hear music was to listen to it performed live — or to sing and play an instrument themselves. Since Thomas Edison invented the phonograph in 1877, however, music has become increasingly portable, accessible, and ubiquitous. Coin-operated jukeboxes appeared at the end of the nineteenth century; the first portable radio was introduced by Zenith in 1924; and vinyl 33 and 45 rpm records became dominant in the 1950s, later competing with eight-track tapes and then with compact cassettes. In the 1980s, home tape decks and devices like the Walkman led to the popularity of the hand-made "mix tape": a personal compilation of songs both reflecting the idiosyncratic taste of its creator and communicating a specific message to its recipient. As the poet and essayist Geoffrey O'Brien notes, mix tapes are an art form in themselves, a "self-portrait, a gesture of friendship, prescription for an ideal party . . . an environment consisting solely of what is most ardently loved." While some lament the decline of cassette culture, other mix-tape enthusiasts argue that compact discs and MP3 files have made the creation of personal mixes more convenient and accessible.

"All by Myself" (Eric Carmen). "Looking for Love" (Lou Reed). "I Wanna 1
Dance with Somebody" (Whitney Houston). "Let's Dance" (David Bowie).
"Let's Kiss" (Beat Happening). "Let's Talk about Sex" (Salt N' Pepa). "Like a
Virgin" (Madonna). "We've Only Just Begun" (The Carpenters). "I Wanna
Be Your Boyfriend" (The Ramones). "I'll Tumble 4 Ya" (Culture Club).
"Head over Heels" (The Go-Go's). "Nothing Compares to You" (Sinead
O'Connor). "My Girl" (The Temptations). "Could This Be Love?" (Bob Mar-
ley). "Love and Marriage" (Frank Sinatra). "White Wedding" (Billy Idol).
"Stuck in the Middle with You" (Stealers Wheel). "Tempted" (Squeeze).
"There Goes My Baby" (The Drifters). "What's Going On?" (Marvin Gaye).
"Where Did You Sleep Last Night?" (Leadbelly). "Whose Bed Have Your
Boots Been Under?" (Shania Twain). "Jealous Guy" (John Lennon). "Your
Cheatin' Heart" (Tammy Wynette). "Shot through the Heart" (Bon Jovi).
"Don't Go Breaking My Heart" (Elton John and Kiki Dee). "My Achy Breaky

Heart" (Billy Ray Cyrus). "Heartbreak Hotel" (Elvis Presley). "Stop, in the Name of Love" (The Supremes). "Try a Little Tenderness" (Otis Redding). "Try (Just a Little Bit Harder)" (Janis Joplin). "All Apologies" (Nirvana). "Hanging on the Telephone" (Blondie). "I Just Called to Say I Love You" (Stevie Wonder). "Love Will Keep Us Together" (Captain and Tennille). "Let's Stay Together" (Al Green). "It Ain't Over 'til It's Over" (Lenny Kravitz). "What's Love Got to Do with It?" (Tina Turner). "You Don't Bring Me Flowers Anymore" (Barbra Streisand and Neil Diamond). "I Wish You Wouldn't Say That" (Talking Heads). "You're So Vain" (Carly Simon). "Love Is a Battlefield" (Pat Benatar). "Heaven Knows I'm Miserable Now" (The Smiths). "(Can't Get No) Satisfaction" (Rolling Stones). "Must Have Been Love (But It's Over Now)" (Roxette). "Breaking Up Is Hard to Do" (Neil Sedaka). "I Will Survive" (Gloria Gaynor). "Hit the Road, Jack" (Mary McCaslin and Jim Ringer). "These Boots Were Made for Walking" (Nancy Sinatra). "All Out of Love" (Air Supply). "All by Myself" (Eric Carmen).

• • •

Reading Literature

1. What is defined in this "list story"?
2. What patterns are used to develop this definition?
3. In what sense is love a "catastrophe"? What are the "other catastrophes" to which the title refers?

Journal Entry

Write a ten-item "list story," using a series of song titles to define *childhood, adolescence, college,* or *work.* Give your story a descriptive title.

Thematic Connections

- "The Storm" (page 198)
- *The Kiss/LOVE* (page 390)
- "The Ways We Lie" (page 471)
- "I Want a Wife" (page 502)
- "The Wife-Beater" (page 514)

Writing Assignments for Definition

1. Choose a document or ritual that is a significant part of your religious or cultural heritage. Define it, using any pattern or combination of patterns you choose, but be sure to include a formal definition somewhere in your essay. Assume your readers are not familiar with the term you are defining.

2. Define an abstract term — for example, *stubbornness, security, courage,* or *fear* — by making it concrete. You can develop your definition with a series of brief examples or with an extended narrative that illustrates the characteristic you are defining.

3. The readings in this chapter define (among other things) a food, a family role, and an item of clothing. Write an essay using examples and description to define one of these topics — for instance, ramen noodles (food), a stepmother (family role), or a chador (item of clothing).

4. **Working with Sources.** Visit webmd.com (for adult health issues) or kidshealth.org (for children's health issues) to learn about one of these medical conditions: angina, migraine, Down syndrome, attention deficit disorder, schizophrenia, autism, or Alzheimer's disease. Then, write an extended definition essay explaining the condition to an audience of high school students. Be sure to include parenthetical documentation for references to your source, and include a works-cited page. (See Chapter 18 for information on MLA documentation.)

5. Use a series of examples to support a thesis in an essay that defines *racism, sexism, ageism, homophobia,* or another type of bigotry.

6. Choose a term that is central to one of your courses — for instance, *naturalism, behaviorism,* or *authority* — and write an essay defining the term. Assume your audience is made up of students who have not yet taken the course. You may begin with an overview of the term's origin if you believe this is appropriate. Then, develop your essay with examples and analogies that will facilitate your audience's understanding of the term. Your purpose is to convince readers that understanding the term you are defining is important.

7. Assume your audience is from a culture unfamiliar with present-day American children's pastimes. Write a definition essay for this audience describing the form and function of a Frisbee, a Barbie doll, an action figure, a skateboard, or a video game.

8. Review any one of the following narrative essays in Chapter 6, and use it to help you develop an extended definition of one of the following terms.

    -   "The Money" — revenge
    -   "Living with Fire" — responsibility
    -   "My Mother Never Worked" — work
    -   "Thirty-Eight Who Saw Murder Didn't Call the Police" — apathy
    -   "Shooting an Elephant" — power

Be sure to document any words or ideas you borrow from a source, and include a works-cited page. (See Chapter 18 for information on MLA documentation.)

9. What constitutes an education? Define the term *education* by identifying several different sources of knowledge, formal or informal, and explaining what each contributes. To get ideas for your essay, look at the excerpt from *Persepolis II* (page 112), "Indian Education" (page 142), or "My First Conk" (page 283).

10. What qualifies someone as a hero? Developing your essay with a series of examples, define the word *hero*. Include a formal definition, and try to incorporate at least one paragraph defining the term by explaining and illustrating what a hero is *not*.

Collaborative Activity for Definition

Working as a group, choose one of the following words to define: *pride, hope, sacrifice,* or *justice*. Then, define the term with a series of extended examples drawn from films your group members have seen, with each of you developing an illustrative paragraph based on a different film. (Before beginning, your group may decide to focus on one particular genre of film.) When everyone in the group has read each paragraph, work together to formulate a thesis that asserts the vital importance of the quality your examples have defined. Finally, write suitable opening and closing paragraphs for the essay, and arrange the body paragraphs in a logical order, adding transitions where necessary.

14

Argumentation

What Is Argumentation?

Argumentation is a process of reasoning that asserts the soundness of a debatable position, belief, or conclusion. Argumentation takes a stand — supported by evidence — and urges people to share the writer's perspective and insights. In the following paragraph from *To Sell Is Human: The Surprising Truth about Moving Others*, Daniel Pink argues that the impact of the smartphone has been much greater than most people realize.

<table>
<tr>
<td valign="top" width="30%">

Topic sentence (takes a stand)

</td>
<td valign="top" rowspan="4">

While the Web has enabled more microentrepreneurs to flourish, its overall impact might seem quaint compared with the smartphone. As Marc Andreessen, the venture capitalist who in the early 1990s created the first Web browser, has said, "The smartphone revolution is *under*hyped." These handheld mini-computers certainly can destroy certain aspects of sales. Consumers can use them to conduct research, comparison-shop, and bypass salespeople altogether. But once again, the net effect is more creative than destructive. The same technology that renders certain types of salespeople obsolete has turned even more people into potential sellers. For instance, the existence of smartphones has birthed an entire app economy that didn't exist before 2007, when Apple shipped its first iPhone. Now the production of apps itself is responsible for nearly half a million jobs in the United States alone, most of them created by bantamweight entrepreneurs. Likewise, an array of new technologies, such as Square from one of the founders of Twitter, PayHere from eBay, and GoPayment from Intuit, make it easier for individuals to accept credit card payments directly on their mobile devices — allowing anyone with a phone to become a shopkeeper.

</td>
</tr>
<tr>
<td valign="top">

Background presents both sides of issue

</td>
</tr>
<tr>
<td valign="top">

Evidence (examples)

</td>
</tr>
<tr>
<td></td>
</tr>
</table>

Argumentation can be used to convince other people to accept (or at least acknowledge the validity of) your position; to defend your position, even if you cannot convince others to agree; or to question or refute a position you believe to be misguided, untrue, dangerous, or evil (without necessarily offering an alternative).

Understanding Argumentation and Persuasion

Although the terms *persuasion* and *argumentation* are frequently used interchangeably, they do not mean the same thing. **Persuasion** is a general term that refers to how a writer influences an audience to adopt a belief or follow a course of action. To persuade an audience, a writer relies on various kinds of appeals — appeals based on emotion (*pathos*), appeals based on logic (*logos*), and appeals based on the character reputation of the writer (*ethos*).

Argumentation is the appeal to reason (*logos*). In an argument, a writer connects a series of statements so that they lead logically to a conclusion. Argumentation is different from persuasion in that it does not try to move an audience to action; its primary purpose is to demonstrate that certain ideas are valid and others are not. Moreover, unlike persuasion, argumentation has a formal structure: an argument makes points, supplies evidence, establishes a logical chain of reasoning, refutes opposing arguments, and accommodates the audience's views.

As the selections in this chapter demonstrate, however, most effective arguments combine two or more appeals: even though their primary appeal is to reason, they may also appeal to emotions. For example, you could use a combination of logical and emotional appeals to argue against lowering the drinking age in your state from twenty-one to eighteen. You could appeal to *reason* by constructing an argument leading to the conclusion that the state should not condone policies that have a high probability of injuring or killing citizens.

You could support your conclusion by presenting statistics showing that alcohol-related traffic accidents kill more teenagers than disease does. You could also cite a study showing that when the drinking age was raised from eighteen to twenty-one, fatal accidents declined. In addition, you could include an appeal to the *emotions* by telling a particularly poignant story about an eighteen-year-old alcoholic or by pointing out how an increased number of accidents involving drunk drivers would cost some innocent people their lives. Keep in mind, however, that although appeals to your audience's emotions may reinforce the central point of your argument, they do not take the place of sound logic and compelling evidence. The appeals you choose and how you balance them depend on your purpose and your sense of your audience.

As you consider what strategies to use, remember that some extremely effective appeals are unfair. Although most people would agree that lies, threats, misleading statements, and appeals to greed and prejudice are unacceptable ways of reaching an audience, such appeals are used in daily conversation, in political campaigns, and even in international diplomacy. Nevertheless, in your college writing you should use only those appeals that most people would consider fair. To do otherwise will undercut your audience's belief in your trustworthiness and weaken your argument.

Planning an Argumentative Essay

Choosing a Topic

In an argumentative essay, as in all writing, choosing the right topic is important. Ideally, you should have an intellectual or emotional stake in your topic. Still, you should be open-minded and willing to consider all sides of a question. If the evidence goes against your position, you should be willing to change your position. You should also be able, from the outset, to consider your topic from other people's viewpoints; this will help you determine what their beliefs are and how they are likely to react to your argument. You can then use this knowledge to build your case and to refute opposing viewpoints. If you cannot be open-minded, you should choose another topic you can deal with more objectively.

Other factors should also influence your selection of a topic. First, you should be well informed about your topic. In addition, you should choose an issue narrow enough to be treated in the space available to you or be willing to confine your discussion to one aspect of a broad issue. It is also important to consider what you expect your argument to achieve. If your topic is so far-reaching that you cannot identify what point you want to make, or if your position is overly idealistic or unreasonable, your essay will suffer.

Developing a Thesis

After you have chosen your topic, you are ready to state the position you will argue in the form of a **thesis**. Keep in mind that in an argumentative essay, your thesis must take a stand — in other words, it must be **debatable**. A good argumentative thesis states a proposition that at least some people will object to. Arguing a statement of fact or an idea that most people accept as self-evident is pointless. Consider the following thesis statement.

> Education is the best way to address the problem of increased drug use among teenagers.

This thesis statement presents ideas that some people might take issue with: it says that increased drug use is a problem among teenagers, that more than one possible solution to this problem exists, and that education is a better solution than any other. Your argumentative essay will go on to support each of these three points logically and persuasively.

A good way to test the suitability of your thesis for an argumentative essay is to formulate an **antithesis**, a statement that asserts the opposite position. If you think that some people would support the antithesis, you can be certain your thesis is indeed debatable.

Thesis: Education is the best way to address the problem of increased drug use among teenagers.

Antithesis: Education is not the best way to address the problem of increased drug use among teenagers.

Analyzing Your Audience

Before writing any essay, you should analyze the characteristics, values, and interests of your audience. In argumentation, it is especially important to consider what beliefs or opinions your readers are likely to have and whether your audience is likely to be friendly, neutral, or hostile to your thesis.

In an argumentative essay, you face a dual challenge. You must appeal to readers who are neutral or even hostile to your position, and you must influence those readers so that they are more receptive to your viewpoint. For example, it would be relatively easy to convince college students that tuition should be lowered or to convince instructors that faculty salaries should be raised. You could be reasonably sure, in advance, that each group would agree with your position. But argument requires more than just telling people what they already believe. It would be much harder to convince college students that tuition should be raised to pay for an increase in instructors' salaries or to persuade instructors to forgo raises so that tuition can remain the same. Remember, your audience will not just take your word for the claims you make. You must provide evidence that will support your thesis and establish a line of reasoning that will lead logically to your conclusion.

It is probably best to assume that some, if not most, of your readers are **skeptical** — that they are open to your ideas but need to be convinced. This assumption will keep you from making claims you cannot support. If your position is controversial, you should assume that an informed (and possibly determined) opposition is looking for holes in your argument.

Gathering and Documenting Evidence

All the points you make in your essay must be supported. If they are not, your audience will dismiss them as unfounded, irrelevant, or unclear. Sometimes you can support a statement with appeals to emotion, but most of the time you support your argument's points by appealing to reason — by providing **evidence**: facts and opinions in support of your position.

As you gather evidence and assess its effectiveness, keep in mind that evidence in an argumentative essay never proves anything conclusively. If it did, there would be no debate — and hence no point in arguing. The best that evidence can do is convince your audience that an assertion is reasonable and worth considering.

Kinds of Evidence. Evidence can be *fact* or *opinion*. **Facts** are statements that people generally agree are true and that can be verified independently. For example, it is a fact that fewer people were killed in U.S. automobile accidents in 2014 than in 1975. It is also a fact that this decrease came about, in part, because of better-engineered cars.

Facts are often accompanied by **opinions** — judgments or beliefs that are not substantiated by proof. Opinions do not carry the same weight as facts, but they can be quite persuasive, particularly when they are the opinions of experts in a relevant field. For example, you could offer the opinion that automobile deaths could be reduced if vehicles were equipped with automatic crash-avoidance systems. You could then make this statement more persuasive by supporting it with **expert opinion** — for example, by saying that David Zuby, the chief researcher at the Insurance Institute for Highway Safety, believes that automatic crash-avoidance systems should be standard equipment for all automobiles.

Keep in mind that not all opinions are equally convincing. The opinions of experts are more convincing than are those of individuals who have limited knowledge of an issue. Your personal opinions can be excellent evidence (provided you are knowledgeable about your subject), but they are usually less convincing to your audience than an expert's opinion. In the final analysis, what is important is not just the quality of the evidence but also the **credibility** (or believability) of the person offering it.

What kind of evidence might change readers' minds? That depends on the readers, the issue, and the facts at hand. Put yourself in the place of your readers, and ask what would make them receptive to your thesis. Why, for example, should a student agree to pay higher tuition? You might concede that tuition is high but point out that it has not been raised for three years while the college's costs have kept going up. The cost of heating and maintaining the buildings has increased, and professors' salaries have not, with the result that several excellent teachers have recently left the college for higher-paying jobs. Furthermore, cuts in federal and state funding have already caused a reduction in the number of courses offered. Similarly, how could you convince a professor to agree to accept no raise at all, especially in light of the fact that faculty salaries have not kept up with inflation? You could say that because cuts in government funding have already reduced course offerings and because the government has also reduced funds for student loans, any further rise in tuition to pay faculty salaries would cause some students to drop out — and that in turn would eventually cost some instructors their jobs. As you can see, the evidence you use in an argument depends to a great extent on whom you want to persuade and what you know about them.

Criteria for Evidence. As you select and review material, choose your evidence with the following three criteria in mind:

1. Your evidence should be **relevant**. It should support your thesis and be pertinent to your argument. As you present evidence, be careful not to concentrate so much on a single example that you lose sight of the broader position you are supporting. Such digressions may confuse your readers. For example, in arguing for more medical aid to Africa, one student made the point that AIDS in Africa remains at epidemic proportions. To illustrate this point, he discussed the bubonic plague in fourteenth-century Europe. Although interesting, this example is not relevant. To show its relevance, the student would have to link his discussion to his assertions about AIDS, possibly by comparing the spread of the bubonic plague in the fourteenth century to the spread of AIDS in Africa today.

2. Your evidence should be **representative**. It should represent the full range of opinions about your subject, not just one side. For example, in an essay arguing against the use of animals in medical experimentation, you would not just use information provided by animal rights activists. You would also use information supplied by medical researchers, pharmaceutical companies, and medical ethicists.

The examples and expert opinions you include should also be **typical**, not aberrant. Suppose you are writing an essay in support of creating bike lanes on your city's streets. To support your thesis, you present the example of Philadelphia, which has a successful bike-lane program. As you consider your evidence, ask yourself if Philadelphia's experience with bike lanes is typical. Did other cities have less success? Take a close look at the opinions that disagree with the position you plan to take. If you understand your opposition, you can refute it effectively when you write your paper.

3. Your evidence should be **sufficient**. It should include enough facts, opinions, and examples to support your claims. The amount of evidence you need depends on the length of your essay, your audience, and your thesis. It stands to reason that you would use fewer examples in a two-page essay than in a ten-page research project. Similarly, an audience that is favorably disposed to your thesis might need only one or two examples to be convinced, whereas a skeptical or hostile audience would need many more. As you develop your thesis, think about the amount of support you will need to write your essay. You may decide that a narrower, more limited thesis will be easier to support than a more inclusive one.

Documentation of Evidence. After you decide on a topic, you should begin to gather evidence. Sometimes you can use your own ideas and observations to support your claims. Most of the time, however, you will have to use the print and electronic resources of the library or search the Internet to locate the information you need.

Whenever you use such evidence in your essay, you have to **document** it by providing the source of the information. (When documenting sources, follow the documentation format recommended by the Modern Language Association, which is explained in Chapter 18 of this book.) If you don't document your sources, your readers are likely to dismiss your evidence, thinking that it may be inaccurate, unreliable, or simply false. **Documentation** gives readers the ability to evaluate the sources you cite and to consult them if they wish. When you document sources, you establish credibility by showing readers that you are honest and have nothing to hide.

Documentation also helps you avoid **plagiarism** — presenting the ideas or words of others as if they were your own. Certainly you don't have to document every idea you use in your paper. For example, **common knowledge** — information you could easily find in several reference sources — can be presented without documentation, and so can your own ideas. You must, however, document any use of a direct quotation and any ideas, statistics, charts, diagrams, or pictures that you obtain from your source. (See Chapter 17 for information on plagiarism.)

Dealing with the Opposition

When gathering evidence, you should not ignore arguments against your position. In fact, you should always try to identify the most obvious — and even the not-so-obvious — objections to your position. By directly addressing these objections in your essay, you will help convince readers that your own position is valid. This part of an argument, called **refutation**, is essential to making the strongest case possible.

You can **refute** opposing arguments by showing that they are unsound, unfair, or weak. Frequently, you will present evidence to show the weakness of your opponent's points and to reinforce your own case. Careful use of definition and cause-and-effect analysis may also prove effective. In the following passage from the classic essay "Politics and the English Language," George Orwell refutes an opponent's argument:

> I said earlier that the decadence of our language is probably curable. Those who deny this would argue, if they produced an argument at all, that language merely reflects existing social conditions, and that we cannot influence its development by any direct tinkering with words and constructions. So far as the general tone or spirit of a language goes, this may be true, but it is not true in detail. Silly words and expressions have often disappeared, though not through any evolutionary process but owing to the conscious actions of a minority.

In the excerpt above, Orwell begins by stating the point he wants to make, goes on to define the argument against his position, and then identifies the weakness of this opposing argument. Later in the essay, Orwell strengthens his argument by presenting examples that support his point.

When an opponent's argument is so compelling that it cannot be easily dismissed, you should **concede** its strength (admit that it is valid). By acknowledging that a point is well taken, you reinforce the impression that you are a fair-minded person. After conceding the strength of the opposing argument, try to identify its limitations and then move your argument to more solid ground. (Often an opponent's strong point addresses only *one* facet of a multifaceted problem.) Notice in the example above that Orwell concedes an opposing argument when he says, "So far as the general tone or spirit of a language goes, this may be true." Later in his discussion, he refutes this argument by pointing out its shortcomings.

When planning an argumentative essay, write down all the arguments against your thesis that you can think of. Then, as you gather your evidence, decide which points you will refute, keeping in mind that careful readers will expect you to refute the most compelling of your opponent's arguments. Be careful, however, not to distort an opponent's argument by making it seem weaker than it actually is. This technique, called creating a **straw man**, can backfire and actually turn fair-minded readers against you.

Understanding Rogerian Argument

Not all arguments are (or should be) confrontational. Psychologist Carl Rogers has written about how to argue without assuming an adversarial relationship. According to Rogers, traditional strategies of argument rely on confrontation — trying to prove that an opponent's position is wrong. With this method of arguing, one person is "wrong" and one is "right." By attacking an opponent and repeatedly hammering home the message that his or her arguments are incorrect or misguided, a writer forces the opponent into a defensive position. The result is conflict, disagreement, and frequently ill will and hostility.

Rogers recommends that you think of those who disagree with you as colleagues, not adversaries. With this approach, now known as **Rogerian argument**, you enter into a cooperative relationship with opponents. Instead of aggressively refuting opposing arguments, you emphasize points of agreement and try to find common ground. You thus collaborate to find mutually satisfying solutions. By adopting a conciliatory attitude, you demonstrate your respect for opposing viewpoints and your willingness to compromise and work toward a position that both you and those who disagree with you will find acceptable. To use a Rogerian strategy in your writing, follow the guidelines below.

✔ **CHECKLIST**   **Guidelines for Using Rogerian Argument**

☐ Begin by summarizing opposing viewpoints.
☐ Carefully consider the position of those who disagree with you. What are their legitimate concerns? If you were in their place, how would you react?
☐ Present opposing viewpoints accurately and fairly. Demonstrate your respect for the ideas of those who disagree with you.
☐ Concede the strength of a compelling opposing argument.
☐ Acknowledge the concerns you and your opposition share.
☐ Point out to readers how they will benefit from the position you are defining.
☐ Present the evidence that supports your viewpoint.

Using Deductive and Inductive Arguments

In an argument, you move from evidence to a conclusion in two ways. One method, called **deductive reasoning**, proceeds from a general premise or assumption to a specific conclusion. Deduction is what most people mean when they speak of logic. Using strict logical form, deduction holds that if all the statements in the argument are true, the conclusion must also be true.

The other method of moving from evidence to conclusion is called **inductive reasoning**. Induction proceeds from individual observations to a more general conclusion and uses no strict form. It requires only that all the relevant evidence be stated and that the conclusion fit the evidence better than any other conclusion would.

Most written arguments use a combination of deductive and inductive reasoning, but it is simpler to discuss and illustrate them separately.

Using Deductive Arguments

The basic form of a deductive argument is a **syllogism**. A syllogism consists of a **major premise**, which is a general statement; a **minor premise**, which is a related but more specific statement; and a **conclusion**, which is drawn from those premises. Consider the following example.

Major premise:	All Olympic runners are fast.
Minor premise:	Jesse Owens was an Olympic runner.
Conclusion:	Therefore, Jesse Owens was fast.

As you can see, if you grant both the major and minor premises, then you must also grant the conclusion. In fact, it is the only conclusion you can properly draw. You cannot reasonably conclude that Jesse Owens was slow because that conclusion contradicts the premises. Nor can you conclude (even if it is true) that Jesse Owens was tall because that conclusion goes beyond the premises.

Of course, this argument seems obvious, and it is much simpler than an argumentative essay would be. In fact, a deductive argument's premises can be fairly elaborate. The Declaration of Independence, which appears later in this chapter, has at its core a deductive argument that could be summarized in this way:

Major premise:	Tyrannical rulers deserve no loyalty.
Minor premise:	King George III is a tyrannical ruler.
Conclusion:	Therefore, King George III deserves no loyalty.

The major premise is a statement that the Declaration claims is **self-evident** — so obvious that it needs no proof. Much of the Declaration consists of evidence to support the minor premise that King George is a tyrannical ruler. The conclusion, because it is drawn from those premises, has the force of irrefutable logic: the king deserves no loyalty from his American subjects, who are therefore entitled to revolt against him.

When a conclusion follows logically from the major and minor premises, then the argument is said to be **valid**. But if the syllogism is not logical, the argument is not valid, and the conclusion is not sound. For example, the following syllogism is not logical:

Major premise:	All dogs are animals.
Minor premise:	All cats are animals.
Conclusion:	Therefore, all dogs are cats.

Of course, the conclusion is absurd. But how did we wind up with such a ridiculous conclusion when both premises are obviously true? The answer is that the syllogism actually contains two major premises. (Both the major and minor premises begin with *all*.) Therefore, the syllogism is defective, and the argument is invalid. Consider the following example of an invalid argument:

Major premise:	All dogs are animals.
Minor premise:	Ralph is an animal.
Conclusion:	Therefore, Ralph is a dog.

Here, an error in logic occurs because the minor premise refers to a term in the major premise that is **undistributed** — it covers only some of the items in the class it denotes. (To be valid, the minor premise must refer to the term in the major premise that is **distributed** — it covers *all* the items in the class it denotes.) In the major premise, *dogs* is the distributed term; it designates *all dogs*. The minor premise, however, refers to *animals*, which is undistributed because it refers only to animals that are dogs. As the minor premise establishes, Ralph is an animal, but it does not logically follow that he is a dog. He could be a cat, a horse, or even a human being.

Even if a syllogism is valid — that is, correct in its form — its conclusion will not necessarily be **true**. The following syllogism draws a false conclusion:

Major premise:	All dogs are brown.
Minor premise:	My poodle Toby is a dog.
Conclusion:	Therefore, Toby is brown.

As it happens, Toby is black. The conclusion is false because the major premise is false: many dogs are *not* brown. If Toby were actually brown, the conclusion would be correct, but only by chance, not by logic. To be **sound**, a syllogism must be both logical and true.

The advantage of a deductive argument is that if your audience accepts your major and minor premises, they must grant your conclusion. Therefore, you should try to select premises that you know your audience accepts or that are self-evident — that is, premises that most people believe to be true. Do not assume, however, that "most people" refers only to your friends and acquaintances. Consider, too, those who may hold different views. If you think your premises are too controversial or difficult to establish firmly, you should use inductive reasoning.

Using Inductive Arguments

Unlike deduction, induction has no distinctive form, and its conclusions are less definitive than those of syllogisms. Still, much inductive thinking (and writing based on that thinking) tends to follow a particular process.

- First, you decide on a question to be answered — or, especially in the sciences, a tentative answer to such a question, called a **hypothesis**.
- Then, you gather the evidence that is relevant to the question and that may be important to finding the answer.
- Finally, you move from your evidence to your conclusion by making an **inference** — a statement about the unknown based on the known — that answers the question and takes the evidence into account.

Here is a very simple example of the inductive process:

Question:	How did that living-room window get broken?
Evidence:	There is a baseball on the living-room floor.
	The baseball was not there this morning.
	Some children were playing baseball this afternoon.
	They were playing in the vacant lot across from the window.
	They stopped playing a little while ago.
	They aren't in the vacant lot now.
Conclusion:	One of the children hit or threw the ball through the window; then, they all ran away.

The conclusion, because it takes all of the evidence into account, seems obvious. But if it turned out that the children had been playing volleyball, not baseball, this additional piece of evidence would make the conclusion doubtful. Even if the conclusion is believable, you cannot necessarily assume it is true: after all, the window could have been broken in some other way. For example, perhaps a bird flew against it, and perhaps the baseball in the living room had gone unnoticed all day, making the second piece of "evidence" on the list not true.

Considering several possible conclusions is a good way to avoid reaching an unjustified or false conclusion. In the preceding example, a hypothesis like this one might follow the question:

Hypothesis:	One of those children playing baseball broke the living-room window.

Many people stop reasoning at this point, without considering the evidence. But when the gap between your evidence and your conclusion is too great, you may reach a conclusion that is not supported by the facts. This well-named error is called **jumping to a conclusion** because it amounts to a premature inductive leap. In induction, the hypothesis is merely the starting point. The rest of the inductive process continues as if the question were still to be answered — as in fact it is until all the evidence has been taken into account.

Because inductive arguments tend to be more complicated than the example on page 533, it is not always easy to move from the evidence you have collected to a sound conclusion. Of course, the more pertinent information you gather, the smaller the gap between your evidence and your conclusion. Still, whether large or small, the crucial step from evidence to conclusion always involves what is called an **inductive leap**. For this reason, it is important to remember that inductive conclusions are just inferences and opinions (not facts). Therefore, inductive conclusions are never certain, only highly probable.

Using Toulmin Logic

Another approach for structuring arguments has been advanced by philosopher Stephen Toulmin. Known as **Toulmin logic**, this method tries to describe how the argumentative strategies a writer uses lead readers to respond the way they do. Toulmin puts forth a model that divides arguments into three parts: the *claim,* the *grounds,* and the *warrant.*

- The **claim** is the main point of the essay. Usually the claim is stated directly as the thesis, but in some arguments it may be implied.
- The **grounds** — the material a writer uses to support the claim — can be evidence (facts or expert opinion) or appeals to the emotions or values of the audience.
- The **warrant** is the inference that connects the claim to the grounds. It can be a belief that is taken for granted or an assumption that underlies the argument.

In its simplest form, an argument following Toulmin logic would look like this example.

Claim:	Carol should be elected class president.
Grounds:	Carol is an honor student.
Warrant:	A person who is an honor student would make a good class president.

When you formulate an argument using Toulmin logic, you can still use inductive and deductive reasoning. You derive your claim inductively from facts and examples, and you connect the grounds and warrant to your claim deductively. For example, the deductive argument in the Declaration of Independence that was summarized on page 531 can be represented as shown here.

Claim:	King George III deserves no loyalty.
Grounds:	King George III is a tyrannical ruler.
Warrant:	Tyrannical rulers deserve no loyalty.

As Toulmin points out, the clearer your warrant, the more likely readers will be to agree with it. Notice that in the two preceding examples, the warrants are very explicit.

Recognizing Fallacies

Fallacies are illogical statements that may sound reasonable or true but are actually deceptive and dishonest. When readers detect them, such statements can turn even a sympathetic audience against your position. Here are some of the more common fallacies that you should avoid.

Begging the Question. This fallacy assumes that a statement is true when it actually requires proof. It requires readers to agree that certain points are self-evident when in fact they are not.

> Unfair and shortsighted policies that limit free trade are a threat to the American economy.

Restrictions against free trade may or may not be unfair and shortsighted, but emotionally loaded language does not constitute proof. The statement begs the question because it assumes what it should be proving — that policies that limit free trade are unfair and shortsighted.

Argument from Analogy. An **analogy** explains something unfamiliar by comparing it to something familiar. Although analogies can help explain abstract or unclear ideas, they do not constitute proof. An argument based on an analogy frequently ignores important dissimilarities between the two things being compared. When this occurs, the argument is fallacious.

> Overcrowded conditions in some parts of our city have forced people together like rats in a cage. Like rats, they will eventually turn on one another, fighting and killing until a balance is restored. It is therefore necessary that we vote to appropriate funds to build low-cost housing.

No evidence is offered to establish that people behave like rats under these or any other conditions. Just because two things have some characteristics in common, you should not assume they are alike in other respects.

Personal Attack (Argument *Ad Hominem*). This fallacy tries to divert attention from the facts of an argument by attacking the motives or character of the person making the argument.

> The public should not take seriously Dr. Mason's plan for improving county health services. He is overweight and a smoker.

This attack on Dr. Mason's character says nothing about the quality of his plan. Sometimes a connection exists between a person's private and public lives — for example, in a case of conflict of interest. However, no evidence of such a connection is presented here.

Jumping to a Conclusion. Sometimes called a *hasty* or *sweeping generalization,* this fallacy occurs when a conclusion is reached on the basis of too little evidence.

> Because our son benefited from home schooling, every child should be educated in this way.

Perhaps other children would benefit from home schooling, and perhaps not, but no conclusion about children in general can be reached on the basis of just one child's experience.

False Dilemma (Either/Or Fallacy). This fallacy occurs when a writer suggests that only two alternatives exist even though there may be others.

> We must choose between life and death, between intervention and genocide. No one can be neutral on this issue.

An argument like this oversimplifies an issue and forces people to choose between extremes instead of exploring more moderate positions.

Equivocation. This fallacy occurs when the meaning of a key term changes at some point in an argument. Equivocation makes it seem as if a conclusion follows from premises when it actually does not.

> As a human endeavor, computers are a praiseworthy and even remarkable accomplishment. But how human can we hope to be if we rely on computers to make our decisions?

The use of *human* in the first sentence refers to the entire human race. In the second sentence, *human* means "merciful" or "civilized." By subtly shifting this term to refer to qualities characteristic of people as opposed to machines, the writer makes the argument seem more sound than it is.

Red Herring. This fallacy occurs when the focus of an argument is shifted to divert the audience from the actual issue.

> The mayor has proposed building a new sports stadium. How can he even consider allocating millions of dollars to this scheme when so many professional athletes are being paid such high salaries?

The focus of this argument should be the merits of the sports stadium. Instead, the writer shifts to the irrelevant issue of athletes' high salaries.

You Also (*Tu Quoque*). This fallacy asserts that an opponent's argument has no value because the opponent does not follow his or her own advice.

> How can that judge favor stronger penalties for convicted drug dealers? During his confirmation hearings, he admitted smoking marijuana when he was in college.

Appeal to Doubtful Authority. Often people will attempt to strengthen an argument with references to experts or famous people. These appeals have merit when the person referred to is an expert in the area being discussed. They do not have merit, however, when the individuals cited have no expertise on the issue.

> According to Diane Sawyer, interest rates will remain low during the next fiscal year.

Although Diane Sawyer is a respected journalist, she is not an expert in business or finance. Therefore, her pronouncements about interest rates are no more than a personal opinion or, at best, an educated guess.

Misleading Statistics. Although statistics are a powerful form of factual evidence, they can be misrepresented or distorted in an attempt to influence an audience.

> Women will never be competent firefighters; after all, 50 percent of the women in the city's training program failed the exam.

Here, the writer has neglected to mention that there were only two women in the program. Because this statistic is not based on a large enough sample, it cannot be used as evidence to support the argument.

Post Hoc, Ergo Propter Hoc **(After This, Therefore Because of This).** This fallacy, known as *post hoc* **reasoning**, assumes that because two events occur close together in time, the first must be the cause of the second.

> Every time a Republican is elected president, a recession follows. If we want to avoid another recession, we should elect a Democrat.

Even if it were true that recessions always occur during the tenure of Republican presidents, no causal connection has been established. (See pages 324–25.)

Non Sequitur **(It Does Not Follow).** This fallacy occurs when a statement does not logically follow from a previous statement.

> Disarmament weakened the United States after World War I. Disarmament also weakened the United States after the Vietnam War. For this reason, the city's efforts to limit gun sales will weaken the United States.

The historical effects of disarmament have nothing to do with current efforts to control the sale of guns. Therefore, the conclusion is a *non sequitur.*

Using Transitions

Transitional words and **phrases** are extremely important in argumentative essays. Without these words and phrases, readers could easily lose track of your argument.

Argumentative essays use transitions to signal a shift in focus. For example, paragraphs that present the specific points in support of your argument can signal this purpose with transitions such as *first, second, third, in addition,* and *finally.* In the same way, paragraphs that refute opposing arguments can signal this purpose with transitions such as *still, nevertheless, however,* and *yet.* Transitional words and phrases — such as *therefore* and *for these reasons* — are also useful when you are presenting your argument's conclusions.

USEFUL TRANSITIONS FOR ARGUMENTATION

all in all	in conclusion
as a result	in other words
finally	in short
first, second, third	in summary
for example	nevertheless
for instance	on the one hand . . . on the other hand
for these reasons	still
however	therefore
in addition	thus
in brief	yet

A more complete list of transitions appears on page 57.

Structuring an Argumentative Essay

An argumentative essay, like other kinds of essays, has an **introduction**, a **body**, and a **conclusion**. However, an argumentative essay has its own special structure, one that ensures that ideas are presented logically and convincingly. The Declaration of Independence follows the typical structure of many classic arguments.

Sample Outline	**Argumentation**
Introduction:	Introduces the issue
	States the thesis
Body:	Induction — offers evidence to support the thesis
	Deduction — uses syllogisms to support the thesis
	States the arguments against the thesis and refutes them
Conclusion:	Restates the thesis in different words
	Makes a forceful closing statement

Jefferson begins the Declaration by presenting the issue that the document addresses: the obligation of the people of the American colonies to tell the world why they must separate from Great Britain. Next, Jefferson states his thesis that because of the tyranny of the British king, the colonies must replace his rule with another form of government. In the body of the Declaration, he offers as evidence twenty-eight examples of injustice endured by the colonies. Following the evidence, Jefferson refutes counterarguments by explaining how again and again the colonists have appealed to the British for redress, but without result. In his concluding paragraph, he restates the thesis and reinforces it one final time. He ends with a flourish: speaking for the representatives of the United States, he explicitly dissolves all political connections between England and America.

Not all arguments, however, follow this pattern. Your material, your thesis, your purpose, your audience, the type of argument you are writing, and the limitations of your assignment all help you determine the strategies you use. If your thesis is especially novel or controversial, for example, the refutation of opposing arguments may come first. In this instance, opposing positions might even be mentioned in the introduction — provided they are discussed more fully later in the argument.

Suppose your journalism instructor gives you the following assignment:

> Select a controversial topic that interests you, and write a brief editorial about it. Direct your editorial to readers who do not share your views, and try to convince them that your position is reasonable. Be sure to acknowledge the view your audience holds and to refute possible criticisms of your argument.

You are well informed about one local issue because you have just read a series of articles on it. A citizens' group is lobbying for a local ordinance that would authorize government funding for religious schools. Since you have also recently studied the doctrine of separation of church and state in your American government class, you know you could argue fairly and strongly against the position taken by this group.

An informal outline of your essay might look like this:

Sample Outline	**Argumentation**
Issue introduced:	Should public tax revenues be spent on aid to religious schools?
Thesis statement:	Despite the pleas of citizen groups like Religious School Parents United, using tax dollars to support church-affiliated schools violates the U.S. Constitution.
Evidence (deduction):	Explain general principle of separation of church and state.

Evidence (induction):	Present recent examples of court cases interpreting and applying this principle.
Evidence (deduction):	Explain how the court cases apply to your community's situation.
Opposing arguments refuted:	Identify and refute arguments used by Religious School Parents United. Concede the point that religious schools educate many children who would otherwise have to be educated in public schools at taxpayers' expense. Then, explain the limitations of this argument.
Conclusion:	Restate the thesis (in different words); end with a strong closing statement.

Revising an Argumentative Essay

When you revise an argumentative essay, consider the items on the revision checklist on page 68. In addition, pay special attention to the items on the following checklist, which apply specifically to argumentative essays.

✔ REVISION CHECKLIST   **Argumentation**

☐ Does your assignment call for argumentation?
☐ Have you chosen a topic you can argue about effectively?
☐ Do you have a debatable thesis?
☐ Have you considered the beliefs and opinions of your audience?
☐ Is your evidence relevant, representative, and sufficient?
☐ Have you documented evidence you have gathered from sources? Have you included a works-cited page?
☐ Have you made an effort to address your audience's possible objections to your position?
☐ Have you refuted opposing arguments?
☐ Have you used inductive or deductive reasoning (or a combination of the two) to move from your evidence to your conclusion?
☐ Have you avoided logical fallacies?
☐ Have you used appropriate transitional words and phrases?

Editing an Argumentative Essay

When you edit your argumentative essay, follow the guidelines on the editing checklists on pages 85, 88, and 91. In addition, focus on the grammar, mechanics, and punctuation issues that are particularly relevant to argumentative essays. One of these issues — using coordinating and subordinating conjunctions to link ideas — is discussed in the pages that follow.

When you write an argumentative essay, you often have to use **conjunctions** — words that join other words or groups of words — to express the logical and sequential relationships between ideas in your sentences. Conjunctions are especially important because they help readers follow the logic of your argument. For this reason, you should be certain that the conjunctions you select clearly and accurately communicate the connections between the ideas you are discussing.

Using Coordinating Conjunctions A **compound sentence** is made up of two or more independent clauses (simple sentences) connected by a coordinating conjunction. **Coordinating conjunctions** join two independent clauses that express ideas of equal importance, and they also indicate how those ideas are related.

independent clause   *independent clause*
[People can disobey unjust laws], or [they can be oppressed by them].

COORDINATING CONJUNCTIONS

and (*indicates addition*)
but, yet (*indicate contrast or contradiction*)
or (*indicates alternatives*)
nor (*indicates an elimination of alternatives*)
so, for (*indicate a cause-and-effect connection*)

According to Thomas Jefferson, the king has refused to let governors pass important laws, and he has imposed taxes without the consent of the people.

Elizabeth Cady Stanton says that women are equal to men, but men think that they are superior to women.

Martin Luther King Jr. does not believe that all laws are just, nor does he believe that it is wrong to protest unjust laws.

When you use a coordinating conjunction to join together two independent clauses, you should always place a comma before the coordinating conjunction.

Using Subordinating Conjunctions A **complex sentence** is made up of one independent clause (simple sentence) and one or more dependent clauses. (A dependent clause cannot stand alone as a sentence.) Subordinating conjunctions link dependent and independent clauses that express ideas of unequal importance, and they also indicate how those ideas are related.

independent clause

[According to Martin Luther King Jr., he led protests]

dependent clause

[so that he could fight racial injustice].

SUBORDINATING CONJUNCTIONS

SUBORDINATING CONJUNCTION	RELATIONSHIP BETWEEN CLAUSES
after, before, since, until, when, whenever, while	Time
as, because, since, so that	Cause or effect
even if, if, unless	Condition
although, even though, though	Contrast

"All segregation statutes are unjust because segregation distorts the soul and damages the personality" (King 568).

"If this philosophy had not emerged, by now many streets of the South would, I am convinced, be flowing with blood" (King 571).

"Before the pen of Jefferson etched the majestic words of the Declaration of Independence across the pages of history, we were here" (King 574).

When you use a subordinating conjunction to join two clauses, place a comma after the dependent clause when it comes *before* the independent clause. Do not use a comma when the dependent clause comes *after* the independent clause.

When they signed the Declaration of Independence, Thomas Jefferson and the others knew they were committing treason. (*comma*)

Thomas Jefferson and the others knew they were committing treason when they signed the Declaration of Independence. (*no comma*)

✔ EDITING CHECKLIST   Argumentation

☐ Have you used coordinating conjunctions correctly to connect two or more independent clauses?

☐ Do the coordinating conjunctions accurately express the relationship between the ideas in the independent clauses?

☐ Have you placed a comma before the coordinating conjunction?

☐ Have you used subordinating conjunctions correctly to connect an independent clause and one or more dependent clauses?

☐ Do the subordinating conjunctions accurately express the relationship between the ideas in the dependent and independent clauses?

☐ Have you placed a comma after the dependent clause when it comes before the independent clause?

☐ Have you remembered not to use a comma when the dependent clause comes after the independent clause?

A STUDENT WRITER: Argumentation

The following essay, written by Marta Ramos for her composition course, illustrates the techniques discussed earlier in this chapter.

Just Say No

Introduction

Summary of controversy

Thesis statement

Recently, the increase in the use of so-called study drugs has   1
become a hotly debated subject. Many students now routinely take prescription medications such as Ritalin or Adderall to improve their academic performance. On the one hand, students who take these medications say that they help them concentrate and improve their ability to study and to get high grades. On the other hand, medical professionals warn that the effects of prolonged exposure to these drugs can be harmful and in some cases even fatal. Unfortunately, these warnings have not stopped an ever-increasing number of students — both in high school and in college — from taking such drugs. They argue that parental pressure and the need to succeed have forced them to take extreme measures. In the final analysis, however, the risks that these drugs present far outweigh their supposed advantages.

Argument (inductive)

Evidence

Despite the claims of users, there is little empirical evidence   2
to show that study drugs actually improve attention or enhance memory. A recent article in the *Huffington Post* examined a range of research on the effectiveness of Ritalin and Adderall. It concluded, "In study after study examining the effect of the drugs on so-called healthy subjects, the findings have been underwhelming. At best, the drugs show a small effect; more often, researchers come up with negative findings. . . ." Moreover, researchers have concluded that Adderall, in particular, "makes you think you're doing better than you actually are" (Schwartz). This probably accounts for the anecdotal evidence of the drug's effectiveness. In short, even though students who take study drugs think they work, there is little hard evidence to suggest they actually do.

Argument (inductive)

Adding to the problem, study drugs are often obtained illegally 3
or under false pretenses. Students either buy them from friends or fake conditions such as Attention Deficit Disorder (ADD) to get doctors to prescribe them. Because Adderall is an amphetamine, its side effects are unpredictable — especially when it is abused or mixed with alcohol. For this reason, taking drugs like Adderall without proper medical supervision can — and often does — have

Evidence

severe physical and mental consequences. For example, a student named Steven Roderick, cited in a *New York Times* article about study drugs, began taking Adderall during his first year in college. In the beginning, a small amount of the drug seemed to improve his academic performance, but as time went on, he needed to increase the dosage to experience the same effect. By his senior year, Roderick was taking large amounts of Adderall in the morning before classes and taking other drugs at night to get to sleep. Eventually, the Adderall stopped working, and because he could not concentrate without it, he was forced to drop out of school (Cohen).

Argument (inductive)

Even though the physical effects of study drugs are   4
obvious, other negative effects can be subtle and quite insidious. Current research suggests that study drugs can "alter personality and constrain the very self that should be supported to live authentically" (Graf et al. 1257). In other words, study drugs provide a false sense of self to students at a time when they should be testing their abilities and pursuing authenticity. It goes without saying that college is a time of self-discovery and that any substance that interferes with this process is, therefore, harmful and should be avoided. Unfortunately, the temptation to take study drugs is encouraged by a society that values superficiality over depth, instant gratification over determination, and winning at all costs over fairness and personal development.

Refutation of opposing argument

Of course, not everyone agrees with this assessment of   5
study drugs. Some argue that concerns about these medications are overblown and that they are more like caffeinated drinks than steroids or amphetamines. In an article on *Slate.com,* Will Oremus asks, "What if Adderall turns out to be the new coffee — a ubiquitous, mostly harmless little helper that enables us to spend more time poring over spreadsheets and less time daydreaming or lolling about in bed?" The answer to this question is simple. Unlike drinking coffee, the abuse of illicitly obtained prescription drugs is not "mostly harmless." On the contrary, it can undermine the academic mission of colleges; it can damage the physical and mental well-being of students; and it can hurt society as a whole by compromising its core values.

Conclusion

Because of the dangers of study drugs, educators, medical   6
professionals, and parents should inform students of the risks and discourage their use. Medical professionals should be on the lookout for students who are trying to fool them into prescribing Adderall.

Parents should be educated to recognize the behavior associated with the excessive use of study drugs. Finally, colleges should make it clear to students that the use of study drugs is unacceptable and will not be tolerated. Only by adopting these measures can the use of study drugs be curtailed — and, eventually, eliminated.

Works Cited

Works-cited list (begins new page)

Cohen, Roger. "The Competition Drug." *New York Times*. New York Times, 4 Mar. 2013. Web. 14 Mar. 2014.

Graf, William D., et al. "Pediatric Neuroenhancement: Ethical, Legal, Social, and Neurodevelopmental Implications." *Neurology* 80.13 (203): 1251-60. Print.

Oremus, Will. "The New Stimulus Package." *Slate.com*. Washington Post Newsweek Interactive, 27 Mar. 2013. Web. 14 Mar. 2014.

Schwartz, Casey. "Busting the Adderall Myth." *Huffington Post*. Huffington Post, 20 Dec. 2010. Web. 14 Mar. 2014.

Points for Special Attention

Choosing a Topic. For her composition course, Marta Ramos was asked to write an argumentative essay on a topic of her choice. Because her college newspaper had recently run an editorial on the use of study drugs, she decided to explore this topic. Although Marta had no direct experience with study drugs, such as Adderall and Ritalin, she knew people who used them. Given the timeliness and seriousness of the issue, Marta thought that it would be a good topic for her to write about. Because she had read the article in her school newspaper, as well as the many responses (both pro and con) that it elicited, she thought that she understood both sides of the controversy. She knew that she was against the use of study drugs, but even so, she believed that she could approach the topic with an open mind and that she would be able to reconsider her opinion if the evidence led her in a different direction.

Gathering Evidence. Marta realized that she could not rely on personal experience to support her position. For this reason, she used information from several outside sources to develop her argument. For example, she found an article in the academic journal *Neurology*, which increased her understanding of her subject. She also found a newspaper article about a student whose story illustrated the practical dangers of study drugs. In addition, she decided to address Will Oremus's 2013 defense of study drugs, which she found both interesting and troubling. She took notes on her sources and recorded their bibliographic information for her works-cited page.

Organization. Marta begins her essay by supplying the context for her argument and then stating her thesis:

> In the final analysis, however, the risks that these drugs present far outweigh their supposed advantages.

In her first body paragraph, Marta addresses the misconception that study drugs are effective. She includes material from an article by Casey Schwartz that summarizes several studies on the use of Ritalin and Adderall by college students, and she combines this information with her own ideas to make the point that study drugs give users a false sense of confidence.

Marta goes on to discuss the harmful physical and psychological effects of study drugs. She begins by saying that because study drugs are often obtained illegally or under false pretenses, their use is extremely risky. She illustrates this point with an anecdote about a student who began taking Adderall to improve his academic performance but eventually had to drop out of college because he could no longer concentrate.

Finally, Marta explains how study drugs have insidious effects on users. In this paragraph, she presents a deductive argument:

Major premise:	Students should discover their authentic selves in college.
Minor premise:	Any substance that interferes with this discovery process is harmful to students.
Conclusion:	Therefore, study drugs are harmful and should be avoided.

Refuting Opposing Arguments. Marta spends one paragraph addressing Will Oremus's point that taking study drugs may be no more harmful than drinking coffee. She refutes this claim by pointing out that unlike coffee, study drugs can do real harm to students as well as to colleges and to society. Here, as in the rest of her essay, Marta is careful to appear both reasonable and respectful. She makes her points clearly and concisely, taking care to avoid name-calling, personal attacks, and jumping to conclusions.

Focus on Revision

When Marta's instructor returned her essay along with his comments, he told her that she had made a very strong argument but that the argument would have been even stronger had she refuted more than one opposing argument. For example, she could have addressed the argument that taking study drugs is not unethical because these medications only help you if you have studied in the first place. Marta could also have considered other issues related to this controversy. For instance, is it unfair for some students to use study drugs while others do not? Does the increasing use of study drugs indicate a problem with the educational system? Does pressure to excel put students under too much pressure? Should the colleges be doing more to limit the number of courses that students can carry? Would more student aid enable students to concentrate more on studying and less on earning money to pay tuition?

PEER-EDITING WORKSHEET: Argumentation

1. Does the essay take a stand on an issue? What is it? At what point does the writer state his or her thesis? Is the thesis debatable?

2. What evidence does the writer include to support his or her position? What additional evidence could the writer supply?

3. Has the writer used information from outside sources? If so, is documentation included? Identify any information that the writer should have documented but did not.

4. Does the essay summarize and refute the opposing arguments? List these arguments.

5. How effective are the writer's refutations? Should the writer address any other arguments?

6. Does the essay use inductive reasoning? Deductive reasoning? Both? Provide an example of each type of reasoning used in the essay.

7. Does the essay include any logical fallacies? How would you correct these fallacies?

8. Do coordinating and subordinating conjunctions convey the logical and sequential connections between ideas?

9. How could the introduction be improved?

10. How could the conclusion be improved?

The essays that follow represent a wide variety of topics, and the purpose of each essay is to support a debatable thesis. In addition to three classic arguments, this chapter also includes two debates and two casebooks that focus on current issues. Each of the debates pairs two essays that take opposing stands on the same issue. In the casebooks, four essays on a single topic offer a greater variety of viewpoints. The first selection, a visual text, is followed by questions designed to illustrate how argumentation can operate in visual form. (A multimodal text for argumentation is located online at **macmillanhighered.com/patterns**.)

You Don't Want Them Responding to Your Text (Ad)

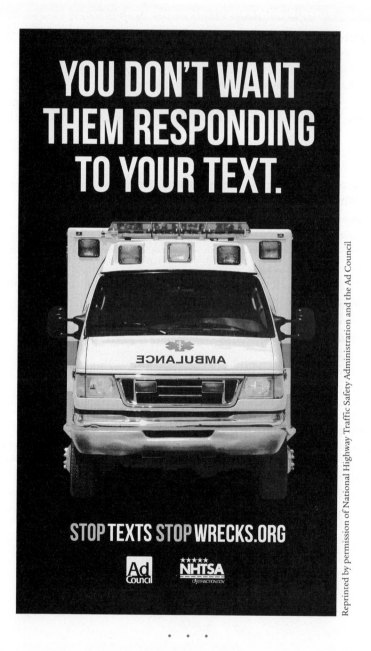

Reprinted by permission of National Highway Traffic Safety Administration and the Ad Council

Reading Images

1. At whom is this ad directed?
2. What point does the headline make? How does the image support this point?
3. Does this ad appeal primarily to logic, to emotion, or to both? Explain.
4. Visit the website StopTextsStopWrecks.org. What additional information does the site include that supports the message of the advertisement?

Journal Entry

Do you have additional suggestions about how to combat this problem? Post your comments in the "Have More Solutions?" box on StopTextsStopWrecks .org.

Thematic Connections

- "Ten Ways We Get the Odds Wrong" (page 250)
- "The Embalming of Mr. Jones" (page 301)
- "The Lottery" (page 308)
- "Who Killed Benny Paret?" (page 337)

THOMAS JEFFERSON

The Declaration of Independence

Thomas Jefferson was born in 1743 in what is now Albemarle County, Virginia. A lawyer, he was elected to Virginia's colonial legislature in 1769 and began a distinguished political career that strongly influenced the early development of the United States. In addition to his participation in the Second Continental Congress of 1775–1776, which ratified the Declaration of Independence, he served as governor of Virginia; as minister to France; as secretary of state under President George Washington; as vice president under John Adams; and, finally, as president from 1801 to 1809. After his retirement, he founded the University of Virginia. He died on July 4, 1826.

Background on the struggle for American independence By the early 1770s, many residents of the original thirteen American colonies were convinced that King George III and his ministers wielded too much power over the colonists. In particular, they objected to a series of taxes imposed on them by the British Parliament, and, being without political representation, they asserted that "taxation without representation" amounted to tyranny. In response to a series of laws Parliament passed in 1774 to limit the political and geographic freedom of the colonists, representatives of each colony met at the Continental Congress of 1774 to draft a plan of reconciliation, but it was rejected.

As cries for independence increased, British soldiers and state militias began to engage in armed conflict, which by 1776 had become a full-fledged war. On June 11, 1776, the Second Continental Congress chose Jefferson, Benjamin Franklin, and several other delegates to draft a declaration of independence. The draft was written by Jefferson, with suggestions and revisions contributed by other commission members. Jefferson's Declaration of Independence challenges a basic assumption of its time — that the royal monarch ruled by divine right — and, in so doing, it became one of the most important political documents in world history.

As you read, keep in mind that to the British, the Declaration of Independence was a call for open rebellion. For this reason, the Declaration's final sentence, in which the signatories pledge their lives, fortunes, and honor, is no mere rhetorical flourish. Had England defeated the colonists, everyone who signed the Declaration of Independence would have been arrested, charged with treason or sedition, stripped of his property, and probably hanged.

When in the course of human events, it becomes necessary for one 1
people to dissolve the political bonds which have connected them with another, and to assume among the powers of the earth, the separate and equal station to which the Laws of Nature and of Nature's God entitle them, a decent respect to the opinions of mankind requires that they should declare the causes which impel them to the separation.

We hold these truths to be self-evident, that all men are created equal, that they are endowed by their Creator with certain unalienable rights, that among these are life, liberty, and the pursuit of happiness. That to secure these rights, governments are instituted among men, deriving their just powers from the consent of the governed.

> " We hold these truths to be self-evident, that all men are created equal. . . . "

2

That whenever any form of government becomes destructive to these ends, it is the right of the people to alter or to abolish it, and to institute new government, laying its foundation on such principles and organizing its powers in such form, as to them shall seem most likely to effect their safety and happiness. Prudence, indeed, will dictate that governments long established should not be changed for light and transient causes; and accordingly all experience hath shown, that mankind are more disposed to suffer, while evils are sufferable, than to right themselves by abolishing the forms to which they are accustomed. But when a long train of abuses and usurpations, pursuing invariably the same object, evinces a design to reduce them under absolute despotism, it is their right, it is their duty, to throw off such government, and to provide new guards for their future security. Such has been the patient sufferance of these Colonies; and such is now the necessity which constrains them to alter their former systems of government. The history of the present king of Great Britain is a history of repeated injuries and usurpations, all having in direct object the establishment of an absolute tyranny over these States. To prove this, let facts be submitted to a candid world.

He has refused his assent to laws, the most wholesome and necessary 3
for the public good.

He has forbidden his Governors to pass laws of immediate and pressing importance, unless suspended in their operation till his assent should be obtained; and when so suspended, he has utterly neglected to attend to them. 4

He has refused to pass other laws for the accommodation of large districts of people, unless those people would relinquish the right of representation in the legislature, a right inestimable to them and formidable to tyrants only. 5

He has called together legislative bodies at places unusual, uncomfortable, and distant from the depository of their public records, for the sole purpose of fatiguing them into compliance with his measure. 6

He has dissolved representative houses repeatedly, for opposing with manly firmness his invasions on the rights of people. 7

He has refused for a long time, after such dissolutions, to cause others to be elected; whereby the legislative powers, incapable of annihilation, have returned to the people at large for their exercise; the State remaining in the meantime exposed to all the dangers of invasion from without, and convulsions within. 8

He has endeavoured to prevent the population of these states; for that purpose obstructing the laws for naturalization of foreigners; refusing to 9 pass others to encourage their migration hither, and raising the conditions of new appropriations of lands.

He has obstructed the administration of justice, by refusing his assent 10 to laws for establishing judiciary powers.

He has made judges dependent on his will alone, for the tenure of their 11 offices, and the amount and payment of their salaries.

He has erected a multitude of new offices, and sent hither swarms of 12 officers to harass our people, and eat out their substance.

He has kept among us, in times of peace, standing armies without the 13 consent of our legislatures.

He has affected to render the military independent of and superior to 14 the civil power.

He has combined with others to subject us to a jurisdiction foreign to 15 our constitution, and unacknowledged by our laws; giving his assent to their acts of pretended legislation:

For quartering large bodies of troops among us: 16

For protecting them, by a mock trial, from punishment for any mur- 17 ders which they should commit on the inhabitants of these States:

For cutting off our trade with all parts of the world: 18

For imposing taxes on us without our consent: 19

For depriving us in many cases, of the benefits of trial by jury: 20

For transporting us beyond seas to be tried for pretended offences: 21

For abolishing the free system of English laws in a neighbouring 22 Province, establishing therein an arbitrary government, and enlarging its boundaries so as to render it at once an example and fit instrument for introducing the same absolute rule into these Colonies:

For taking away our Charters, abolishing our most valuable laws, and 23 altering fundamentally the forms of our governments:

For suspending our own legislatures, and declaring themselves invested 24 with power to legislate for us in all cases whatsoever.

He has abdicated government here, by declaring us out of his protec- 25 tion and waging war against us.

He has plundered our seas, ravaged our coasts, burnt our towns, and 26 destroyed the lives of our people.

He is at this time transporting large armies of foreign mercenaries to 27 complete the works of death, desolation and tyranny, already begun with circumstances of cruelty and perfidy scarcely paralleled in the most barbarous ages, and totally unworthy the head of a civilized nation.

He has constrained our fellow citizens taken captive on the high seas to 28 bear arms against their country, to become the executioners of their friends and brethren, or to fall themselves by their hands.

He has excited domestic insurrections amongst us, and has endeav- 29 oured to bring on the inhabitants of our frontiers, the merciless Indian savages, whose known rule of warfare, is an undistinguished destruction of all ages, sexes, and conditions.

In every stage of these oppressions we have petitioned for redress in the 30 most humble terms: our repeated petitions have been answered only by repeated injury. A prince whose character is thus marked by every act which may define a tyrant, is unfit to be the ruler of a free people.

Nor have we been wanting in attentions to our British brethren. We 31 have warned them from time to time of attempts by their legislature to extend an unwarrantable jurisdiction over us. We have reminded them of the circumstances of our emigration and settlement here. We have appealed to their native justice and magnanimity, and we have conjured them by the ties of our common kindred to disavow these usurpations, which would inevitably interrupt our connections and correspondence. They too have been deaf to the voice of justice and of consanguinity. We must, therefore, acquiesce in the necessity, which denounces our separation, and hold them, as we hold the rest of mankind, enemies in war, in peace friends.

We, therefore, the Representatives of the United States of America, in 32 General Congress, assembled, appealing to the Supreme Judge of the world for the rectitude of our intentions, do, in the name, and by authority of the good people of these Colonies, solemnly publish and declare, That these United Colonies are, and of right ought to be Free and Independent States; that they are absolved from all allegiance to the British Crown, and that all political connection between them and the state of Great Britain, is and ought to be totally dissolved; and that as Free and Independent States, they have full power to levy war, conclude peace, contract alliances, establish commerce, and to do all other acts and things which Independent States may of right do. And for the support of this declaration, with a firm reliance on the protection of divine Providence, we mutually pledge to each other our lives, our fortunes, and our sacred honor.

. . .

Comprehension

1. What "truths" does Jefferson say are "self-evident" (2)?
2. What does Jefferson say is the source from which governments derive their powers?
3. What reasons does Jefferson give to support his premise that the United States should break away from Great Britain?
4. What conclusions about British rule does Jefferson draw from the evidence he presents?

Purpose and Audience

1. What is the major premise of Jefferson's argument? Should Jefferson have done more to establish the truth of this premise?
2. The Declaration of Independence was written during a period now referred to as the Age of Reason. In what ways has Jefferson tried to make his document appear reasonable?
3. For what audience (or audiences) was the document intended? Which groups of readers would have been most likely to accept it? Explain.

4. How effectively does Jefferson anticipate and refute the opposition?

5. In paragraph 31, following the list of grievances, why does Jefferson address his "British brethren"?

6. At what point does Jefferson state his thesis? Why does he state it where he does?

Style and Structure

1. Does the Declaration of Independence rely primarily on inductive or deductive reasoning? Identify examples of each.

2. What techniques does Jefferson use to create smooth and logical transitions from one paragraph to another?

3. Why does Jefferson list all of his twenty-eight grievances? Why doesn't he just summarize them or mention a few representative grievances?

4. Jefferson begins the last paragraph of the Declaration of Independence with "We, therefore." How effective is this conclusion? Explain.

5. **Vocabulary Project.** Underline ten words that have negative connotations. How does Jefferson use these words to help him make his point? Do you think words with more neutral connotations would strengthen or weaken his case? Why?

6. **Vocabulary Project.** What words does Jefferson use that are rarely used today? Would the Declaration of Independence be more meaningful to today's readers if it were updated, with more familiar words substituted? To help you formulate your response, try rewriting a paragraph or two, and assess your updated version. Look up any unfamiliar words in an online dictionary such as dictionary.com.

Journal Entry

Do you think Jefferson is being fair to the king? Do you think he should be?

Writing Workshop

1. Following Jefferson's example, write a declaration of independence from your school, job, family, or any other institution with which you are associated.

2. **Working with Sources.** Go to the website ushistory.org/declaration /document/congress.htm, and look at the revisions that Congress made to Jefferson's original draft of the Declaration of Independence. Decide which version you think is better. Then, write an essay in which you present your case. Make sure you document references to both versions of the Declaration, and include a works-cited page. (See Chapter 18 for information on MLA documentation.)

3. **Working with Sources.** In an argumentative essay written from the viewpoint of King George III, answer Jefferson. Try to convince the colonists

that they should not break away from Great Britain. If you can, refute some of the points Jefferson makes. Make sure that you include parenthetical documentation for all references to the Declaration and that you include a works-cited page. (See Chapter 18 for information on MLA documentation.)

Combining the Patterns

The middle section of the Declaration of Independence is developed by means of **exemplification**: it presents a series of examples to support Jefferson's assertion that the colonists have experienced "repeated injuries and usurpations" (2). Are these examples relevant? Representative? Sufficient? What other pattern of development could Jefferson have used to support his assertion?

Thematic Connections

- "The 'Black Table' Is Still There" (page 348)
- "Grant and Lee: A Study in Contrasts" (page 393)
- "Aristotle" (page 481)
- "Letter from Birmingham Jail" (page 563)

ELIZABETH CADY STANTON

Declaration of Sentiments and Resolutions, Seneca Falls Convention, 1848

Elizabeth Cady was born in Johnstown, New York, in 1815 and attended the Troy Female Seminary. At the age of twenty-five, she married the writer and abolitionist Henry Brewster Stanton, joining him in the struggle to end slavery. She also became active in the women's suffrage movement, lobbying for the right of women to vote. This movement had its beginnings in the United States at the first Woman's Rights Convention, which was organized by Stanton and other early petitioners for women's rights and held in Seneca Falls, New York, in July 1848. There, the following declaration was first presented, amended, and then unanimously adopted by the three hundred delegates. (All the resolutions were passed unanimously except for the one calling for women's right to vote, which was thought by some to be extreme enough to discredit the feminist movement.) Stanton went on to lead the National Woman Suffrage Movement from 1869 to 1890 and to coedit *Revolution,* a feminist periodical. A popular lecturer and a skilled writer, she continued to work toward the goal of equality for women until her death in 1902.

Background on the women's suffrage movement In 1848, women were considered inferior to men in terms of intelligence and the ability to reason, so the Founding Fathers' statement "all men are created equal" did not apply to them. In fact, the idea for the Seneca Falls Convention was spurred by Stanton's experiences at the 1840 World Anti-Slavery Convention in London, which she attended with her husband and which refused to admit women delegates to the floor. When made public, the Declaration of Sentiments was universally derided by the press and by contemporary religious leaders — even Henry Stanton thought his wife had gone too far. The Civil War interrupted the budding women's rights movement, but at its close, when emancipated African-American men were granted the right to vote, the movement picked up steam again. Its leaders lobbied for an amendment to the U.S. Constitution allowing women to vote and pressed state legislatures for voting rights as well. It was a long road, however. By 1913, only twelve states had extended voting rights to women, and not until the Nineteenth Amendment to the Constitution was ratified in 1920 did American women gain this right.

Declaration of Sentiments

When, in the course of human events, it becomes necessary for one portion of the family of man to assume among the people of the earth a position different from that which they have hitherto occupied, but one to which the laws of nature and of nature's God entitle them, a decent respect to the opinions of mankind requires that they should declare the causes that impel them to such a course.

We hold these truths to be self-evident: that all men and women are 2 created equal; that they are endowed by their Creator with certain inalienable rights; that among these are life, liberty, and the pursuit of happiness; that to secure these rights governments are instituted, deriving their just powers from the consent of the governed. Whenever any form of government becomes destructive of these ends, it is the right of those who suffer from it to refuse allegiance to it, and to insist upon the institution of a new government, laying its foundation on such principles, and organizing its powers in such form, as to them shall seem most likely to effect their safety and happiness. Prudence, indeed, will dictate that governments long established should not be changed for light and transient causes; and accordingly all experience hath shown that mankind are more disposed to suffer, while evils are sufferable, than to right themselves by abolishing the forms to which they were accustomed. But when a long train of abuses and usurpations, pursuing invariably the same object, evinces a design to reduce them under absolute despotism, it is their duty to throw off such government, and to provide new guards for their future security. Such has been the patient sufferance of the women under this government, and such is now the necessity which constrains them to demand the equal station to which they are entitled.

The history of mankind is a history of repeated injuries and usurpa- 3 tions on the part of man toward woman, having in direct object the establishment of an absolute tyranny over her. To prove this, let facts be submitted to a candid world.

> " The history of mankind is a history of repeated injuries and usurpations on the part of man toward woman. . . . "

He has never permitted her to exer- 4 cise her inalienable right to the elective franchise.

He has compelled her to submit to 5 laws, in the formation of which she had no voice.

He has withheld from her rights which 6 are given to the most ignorant and degraded men — both natives and foreigners.

Having deprived her of this first right of a citizen, the elective franchise, 7 thereby leaving her without representation in the halls of legislation, he has oppressed her on all sides.

He has made her, if married, in the eye of the law, civilly dead. 8

He has taken from her all right in property, even to the wages she 9 earns.

He has made her, morally, an irresponsible being, as she can commit 10 many crimes with impunity, provided they be done in the presence of her husband. In the covenant of marriage, she is compelled to promise obedience to her husband, he becoming, to all intents and purposes, her master — the law giving him power to deprive her of her liberty, and to administer chastisement.

He has so framed the laws of divorce, as to what shall be the proper 11 causes, and in case of separation, to whom the guardianship of the children shall be given, as to be wholly regardless of the happiness of women — the law, in all cases, going upon the false supposition of the supremacy of man, and giving all power into his hands.

After depriving her of all rights as a married woman, if single, and the 12 owner of property, he has taxed her to support a government which recognizes her only when her property can be made profitable to it.

He has monopolized nearly all the profitable employments, and from 13 those she is permitted to follow, she receives but a scanty remuneration. He closes against her all the avenues to wealth and distinction which he considers most honorable to himself. As a teacher of theology, medicine, or law, she is not known.

He has denied her the facilities for obtaining a thorough education, all 14 colleges being closed against her.

He allows her in Church, as well as State, but a subordinate position, 15 claiming Apostolic authority for her exclusion from the ministry, and, with some exceptions, from any public participation in the affairs of the Church.

He has created a false public sentiment by giving to the world a differ- 16 ent code of morals for men and women, by which moral delinquencies which exclude women from society, are not only tolerated, but deemed of little account in man.

He has usurped the prerogative of Jehovah himself, claiming it as his 17 right to assign for her a sphere of action, when that belongs to her conscience and to her God.

He has endeavored, in every way that he could, to destroy her confi- 18 dence in her own powers, to lessen her self-respect, and to make her willing to lead a dependent and abject life.

Now, in view of this entire disenfranchisement of one-half the people 19 of this country, their social and religious degradation — in view of the unjust laws above mentioned, and because women do feel themselves aggrieved, oppressed, and fraudulently deprived of their most sacred rights, we insist that they have immediate admission to all the rights and privileges which belong to them as citizens of the United States.

In entering upon the great work before us, we anticipate no small 20 amount of misconception, misrepresentation, and ridicule; but we shall use every instrumentality within our power to effect our object. We shall employ agents, circulate tracts, petition the State and National legislatures, and endeavor to enlist the pulpit and the press in our behalf. We hope this Convention will be followed by a series of Conventions embracing every part of the country.

Resolutions

Whereas, The great precept of nature is conceded to be, that "man 21 shall pursue his own true and substantial happiness." Blackstone* in his Commentaries remarks, that this law of Nature being coeval with mankind, and dictated by God himself, is of course superior in obligation to any other. It is binding over all the globe, in all countries and at all times; no human laws are of any validity if contrary to this, and such of them as are valid, derive all their force, and all their validity, and all their authority, mediately and immediately, from this original; therefore,

Resolved, That such laws as conflict, in any way, with the true and sub- 22 stantial happiness of woman, are contrary to the great precept of nature and of no validity, for this is "superior in obligation to any other."

Resolved, That all laws which prevent woman from occupying such a sta- 23 tion in society as her conscience shall dictate, or which place her in a position inferior to that of man, are contrary to the great precept of nature, and therefore of no force or authority.

Resolved, That woman is man's equal — was intended to be so by the Cre- 24 ator, and the highest good of the race demands that she should be recognized as such.

Resolved, That the women of this country ought to be enlightened in 25 regard to the laws under which they live, that they may no longer publish their degradation by declaring themselves satisfied with their present position, nor their ignorance, by asserting that they have all the rights they want.

Resolved, That inasmuch as man, while claiming for himself intellectual 26 superiority, does accord to woman moral superiority, it is preeminently his duty to encourage her to speak and teach, as she has an opportunity, in all religious assemblies.

Resolved, That the same amount of virtue, delicacy, and refinement of 27 behavior that is required of woman in the social state, should also be required of man, and the same transgressions should be visited with equal severity on both man and woman.

Resolved, That the objection of indelicacy and impropriety, which is 28 so often brought against woman when she addresses a public audience, comes with a very ill-grace from those who encourage, by their attendance, her appearance on the stage, in the concert, or in feats of the circus.

Resolved, That woman has too long rested satisfied in the circumscribed 29 limits which corrupt customs and a perverted application of the Scriptures have marked out for her, and that it is time she should move in the enlarged sphere which her great Creator has assigned her.

Resolved, That it is the duty of the women of this country to secure to 30 themselves their sacred right to the elective franchise.

---

* Eds. note — Sir William Blackstone (1723–1780), English jurist. Many regard his *Commentaries* (1765–1769) as the most thorough treatment of English law ever produced.

Resolved, That the equality of human rights results necessarily from the   31
fact of the identity of the race in capabilities and responsibilities.

Resolved, therefore, That, being invested by the Creator with the same   32
capabilities, and the same consciousness of responsibility for their exercise,
it is demonstrably the right and duty of woman, equally with man, to promote every righteous cause by every righteous means; and especially in
regard to the great subjects of morals and religion, it is self-evidently her
right to participate with her brother in teaching them, both in private and
in public, by writing and by speaking, by any instrumentalities proper to be
used, and in any assemblies proper to be held; and this being a self-evident
truth growing out of the divinely implanted principles of human nature,
any custom or authority adverse to it, whether modern or wearing the hoary
sanction of antiquity, is to be regarded as a self-evident falsehood, and at
war with mankind.

Resolved, That the speedy success of our cause depends upon the zealous   33
and untiring efforts of both men and women, for the overthrow of the
monopoly of the pulpit, and for the securing to woman an equal participation with men in the various trades, professions, and commerce.*

•   •   •

Comprehension

1. According to Stanton, why is it necessary for women to declare their
   sentiments?

2. What truths does Stanton say are "self-evident" (2)?

3. What injuries does Stanton list? Which injuries seem most important?

4. What type of reception does Stanton expect the Declaration of Sentiments and Resolutions to receive? What does she propose to do about
   this reception?

5. What conclusion does Stanton draw? According to her, what self-evident
   right do women have? What does she believe should be regarded as "a self-
   evident falsehood" (32)?

Purpose and Audience

1. Is Stanton addressing men, women, or both? How can you tell? Does she
   consider one segment of her audience more receptive to her ideas than
   another? Explain.

2. What strategies does Stanton use to present herself as reasonable? Do you
   think she is successful? Explain.

3. What is Stanton's thesis? At what point does she state it? Why do you
   think she states it when she does?

---

* Eds. note — This last resolution was given by Lucretia Mott at the actual convention. All the previous resolutions were drafted earlier by Elizabeth Cady Stanton.

4. What is Stanton's purpose? Do you think she actually expects to change people's ideas and behavior, or does she have some other purpose in mind?

Style and Structure

1. The Declaration of Sentiments and Resolutions imitates the tone, style, and, in some places, even the wording of the Declaration of Independence. What are the advantages of this strategy? What are the disadvantages?

2. In paragraphs 2 and 32, Stanton mentions "self-evident" truths. Are these truths really self-evident? Should she have done more to establish the validity of these statements?

3. What are the major and minor premises of Stanton's argument? Do these premises lead logically to her conclusion?

4. How do transitional words and phrases help Stanton move readers from one section of her argument to another? Are the transitions effective?

5. Should Stanton have specifically refuted arguments against her position? Could she be accused of ignoring her opposition?

6. **Vocabulary Project.** Today, many people would consider the language of some of the passages in the Declaration of Sentiments and Resolutions stiff and overly formal. Find a paragraph that fits this description, and rewrite it using less formal diction. What is lost in your revision, and what is gained?

Journal Entry

Review Stanton's list of injuries to women. How many of these wrongs have been corrected? How many have yet to be addressed?

Writing Workshop

1. Choose an issue you care about, and write your own Declaration of Sentiments and Resolutions. Like Stanton, echo the phrasing of the Declaration of Independence in your essay.

2. **Working with Sources.** Reread your journal entry, and select one of the injuries to women that has not yet been corrected. Research this issue, and then write an essay arguing that this issue needs to be resolved. In your essay, refer specifically to the Declaration of Sentiments and Resolutions, as well as your other sources. Make sure you document all references to your sources, and include a works-cited page. (See Chapter 18 for information on MLA documentation.)

3. When the Declaration of Sentiments and Resolutions was voted on at the Seneca Falls Convention in 1848, the only resolution not passed unanimously was the one that called for women to win the right to vote (see paragraph 30). Write a letter to the convention calling on the delegates to

vote for this resolution. Make sure you refute the main argument against this resolution — that it would alienate so many people that it would discredit the feminist movement.

Combining the Patterns

Like the Declaration of Independence, the Declaration of Sentiments and Resolutions is partly developed by **exemplification**. A series of examples supports Stanton's assertion that women now "demand the equal station to which they are entitled" (2). How effective are these examples? Are they relevant? Representative? Sufficient?

Thematic Connections

- "My Mother Never Worked" (page 123)
- "A Peaceful Woman Explains Why She Carries a Gun" (page 353)
- "I Want a Wife" (page 502)
- The Declaration of Independence (page 550)

MARTIN LUTHER KING JR.

Letter from Birmingham Jail

Martin Luther King Jr. was born in Atlanta, Georgia, in 1929. After receiving his doctorate in theology from Boston University in 1955, he became pastor of the Dexter Avenue Baptist Church in Montgomery, Alabama. There, he organized a 382-day bus boycott that led to the 1956 Supreme Court decision outlawing segregation on Alabama's buses. As leader of the Southern Christian Leadership Conference, he was instrumental in securing the civil rights of black Americans, using methods based on a philosophy of nonviolent protest. His books include *Stride towards Freedom* (1958) and *Why We Can't Wait* (1964). In 1964, King was awarded the Nobel Peace Prize. He was assassinated in 1968 in Memphis, Tennessee.

Background on racial segregation In 1896, the Supreme Court ruled in *Plessy v. Ferguson* that "separate but equal" accommodations on railroad cars gave African Americans the equal protection guaranteed by the Fourteenth Amendment of the Constitution. This decision was used to justify separate public facilities — including schools — for blacks and whites well into the twentieth century.

In the mid-1950s, state support for segregation and discrimination against blacks had begun to be challenged. Supreme Court decisions in 1954 and 1955 declared segregation in public schools and other publicly financed venues unconstitutional, while blacks and whites alike were calling for an end to discrimination. Their actions took the form of marches, boycotts, and sit-ins (organized protests whose participants refuse to move from a public area). Many whites, however, particularly in the South, vehemently resisted any change in race relations.

By 1963, when Martin Luther King Jr. organized a campaign against segregation in Birmingham, Alabama, tensions ran deep. He and his followers met fierce opposition from the police, as well as from white moderates, who considered him an "outside agitator." During the demonstrations, King was arrested and jailed for eight days. While imprisoned, he wrote his "Letter from Birmingham Jail" to white clergymen to explain his actions and answer those who urged him to call off the demonstrations.

April 16, 1963

My Dear Fellow Clergymen:

While confined here in the Birmingham city jail, I came across your 1
recent statement calling my present activities "unwise and untimely." Seldom do I pause to answer criticism of my work and ideas. If I sought to answer all the criticisms that cross my desk, my secretaries would have little time for anything other than such correspondence in the course of the day, and I would have no time for constructive work. But since I feel that you are

men of genuine good will and that your criticisms are sincerely set forth, I want to try to answer your statement in what I hope will be patient and reasonable terms.

I think I should indicate why I am here in Birmingham, since you have 2 been influenced by the view which argues against "outsiders coming in." I have the honor of serving as president of the Southern Christian Leadership Conference, an organization operating in every southern state, with headquarters in Atlanta, Georgia. We have some eighty-five affiliated organizations across the South, and one of them is the Alabama Christian Movement for Human Rights. Frequently we share staff, educational, and financial resources with our affiliates. Several months ago the affiliate here in Birmingham asked us to be on call to engage in a nonviolent direct-action program if such were deemed necessary. We readily consented, and when the hour came we lived up to our promise. So I, along with several members of my staff, am here because I was invited here. I am here because I have organizational ties here.

But more basically, I am in Birmingham because injustice is here. Just 3 as the prophets of the eighth century B.C. left their villages and carried their "thus saith the Lord" far beyond the boundaries of their home towns, and just as the Apostle Paul left his village of Tarsus and carried the gospel of Jesus Christ to the far corners of the Greco-Roman world, so am I compelled to carry the gospel of freedom beyond my own home town. Like Paul, I must constantly respond to the Macedonian call for aid.

Moreover, I am cognizant of the interrelatedness of all communities 4 and states. I cannot sit idly by in Atlanta and not be concerned about what happens in Birmingham. Injustice anywhere is a threat to justice everywhere. We are caught in an inescapable network of mutuality, tied in a single garment of destiny. Whatever affects one directly, affects all indirectly. Never again can we afford to live with the narrow, provincial, "outside agitator" idea. Anyone who lives inside the United States can never be considered an outsider anywhere within its bounds.

You deplore the demonstrations taking place in Birmingham. But your 5 statement, I am sorry to say, fails to express a similar concern for the conditions that brought about the demonstrations. I am sure that none of you would want to rest content with the superficial kind of social analysis that deals merely with effects and does not grapple with underlying causes. It is unfortunate that demonstrations are taking place in Birmingham, but it is even more unfortunate that the city's white power structure left the Negro community with no alternative.

In any nonviolent campaign there are four basic steps: collection of the 6 facts to determine whether injustices exist; negotiation; self-purification; and direct action. We have gone through all these steps in Birmingham. There can be no gainsaying the fact that racial injustice engulfs this community. Birmingham is probably the most thoroughly segregated city in the United States. Its ugly record of brutality is widely known. Negroes have experienced grossly unjust treatment in courts. There have been more unsolved bombings of Negro homes and churches in Birmingham than in any other city in the nation. These are the hard, brutal facts of the case. On the basis of these conditions, Negro leaders sought to negotiate with the city fathers. But the latter consistently refused to engage in good-faith negotiation.

Then, last September, came the opportunity to talk with leaders of Birmingham's economic community. In the course of the negotiations, certain promises were made by the merchants — for example, to remove the stores' humiliating racial signs. On the basis of these promises, the Reverend Fred Shuttlesworth and the leaders of the Alabama Christian Movement for Human Rights agreed to a moratorium on all demonstrations. As the weeks and months went by, we realized that we were the victims of a broken promise. A few signs, briefly removed, returned; the others remained. 7

As in so many past experiences, our hopes had been blasted, and the shadow of deep disappointment settled upon us. We had no alternative except to prepare for direct action, whereby we would present our very bodies as means of laying our case before the conscience of the local and the national community. Mindful of the difficulties involved, we decided to undertake a process of self-purification. We began a series of workshops on nonviolence, and we repeatedly asked ourselves: "Are you able to accept blows without retaliating?" "Are you able to endure the ordeal of jail?" We decided to schedule our direct-action program for the Easter season, realizing that except for Christmas, this is the main shopping period of the year. Knowing that a strong economic-withdrawal program would be the by-product of direct action, we felt that this would be the best time to bring pressure to bear on the merchants for the needed change. 8

Then it occurred to us that Birmingham's mayoral election was coming up in March, and we speedily decided to postpone action until after election day. When we discovered that the Commissioner of Public Safety, Eugene "Bull" Connor, had piled up enough votes to be in the run-off, we decided again to postpone action until the day after the run-off so that the demonstrations could not be used to cloud the issues. Like many others, we waited to see Mr. Connor defeated, and to this end we endured postponement after postponement. Having aided in this community need, we felt that our direct-action program could be delayed no longer. 9

You may well ask, "Why direct action? Why sit-ins, marches, and so forth? Isn't negotiation a better path?" You are quite right in calling for negotiation. Indeed, this is the very purpose of direct action. Nonviolent direct action seeks to create such a crisis and foster such a tension that a community which has constantly refused to negotiate is forced to confront the issue. It seeks so to dramatize the issue that it can no longer be ignored. My citing the creation of tension as part of the work of the nonviolent-resister may sound rather shocking. But I must confess that I am not afraid of the word "tension." I have earnestly opposed violent tension, but there is a type of constructive, nonviolent tension which is necessary for growth. Just as Socrates felt that it was necessary to create a tension in the mind so that individuals could rise from the bondage of myths and half-truths to 10 the unfettered realm of creative analysis and objective appraisal, so must we see the need for nonviolent gadflies to create the kind of tension in society that will help men rise from the dark depths of prejudice and racism to the majestic heights of understanding and brotherhood.

The purpose of our direct-action program is to create a situation so 11 crisis-packed that it will inevitably open the door to negotiation. I therefore concur with you in your call for negotiation. Too long has our beloved Southland been bogged down in a tragic effort to live in monologue rather than dialogue.

One of the basic points in your statement is that the action that I and 12 my associates have taken in Birmingham is untimely. Some have asked: "Why didn't you give the new city administration time to act?" The only answer that I can give to this query is that the new Birmingham administration must be prodded about as much as the outgoing one, before it will act. We are sadly mistaken if we feel that the election of Albert Boutwell as mayor will bring the millennium to Birmingham. While Mr. Boutwell is a much more gentle person than Mr. Connor, they are both segregationists, dedicated to maintenance of the status quo. I have hoped that Mr. Boutwell will be reasonable enough to see the futility of massive resistance to desegregation. But he will not see this without pressure from devotees of civil rights. My friends, I must say to you that we have not made a single gain in civil rights without determined legal and nonviolent pressure. Lamentably, it is an historical fact that privileged groups seldom give up their privileges voluntarily. Individuals may see the moral light and voluntarily give up their unjust posture; but, as Reinhold Niebuhr* has reminded us, groups tend to be more immoral than individuals.

We know through painful experience that freedom is never voluntarily 13 given by the oppressor; it must be demanded by the oppressed. Frankly, I have yet to engage in a direct-action campaign that was "well timed" in the view of those who have not suffered unduly from the disease of segregation. For years now I have heard the word "Wait!" It rings in the ear of every Negro with piercing familiarity. This "Wait" has almost always meant "Never." We must come to see, with one of our distinguished jurists, that "justice too long delayed is justice denied."

We have waited for more than 340 years 14 for our constitutional and God-given rights. The nations of Asia and Africa are moving with jetlike speed toward gaining political independence, but we still creep at horse-and-buggy pace toward gaining a cup of coffee at a lunch counter. Perhaps it is easy for those who have never felt the stinging darts of segregation to say, "Wait." But when you have seen vicious mobs lynch your mothers

> We must come to see, with one of our distinguished jurists, that 'justice too long delayed is justice denied.'

---

* Eds. note — American religious and social thinker (1892–1971).

and fathers at will and drown your sisters and brothers at whim; when you have seen hate-filled policemen curse, kick, and even kill your black brothers and sisters; when you see the vast majority of your twenty million Negro brothers smothering in an airtight cage of poverty in the midst of an affluent society; when you suddenly find your tongue twisted and your speech stammering as you seek to explain to your six-year-old daughter why she can't go to the public amusement park that has just been advertised on television, and see tears welling up in her eyes when she is told that Funtown is closed to colored children, and see ominous clouds of inferiority beginning to form in her little mental sky, and see her beginning to distort her personality by developing an unconscious bitterness toward white people; when you have to concoct an answer for a five-year-old son who is asking, "Daddy, why do white people treat colored people so mean?"; when you take a cross-country drive and find it necessary to sleep night after night in the uncomfortable corners of your automobile because no motel will accept you; when you are humiliated day in and day out by nagging signs reading "white" and "colored"; when your first name becomes "nigger," your middle name becomes "boy" (however old you are), and your last name becomes "John," and your wife and mother are never given the respected title "Mrs."; when you are harried by day and haunted at night by the fact that you are a Negro, living constantly at tiptoe stance, never quite knowing what to expect next, and are plagued with inner fears and outer resentments; when you are forever fighting a degenerating sense of "nobodiness" — then you will understand why we find it difficult to wait. There comes a time when the cup of endurance runs over, and men are no longer willing to be plunged into the abyss of despair. I hope, sirs, you can understand our legitimate and unavoidable impatience.

You express a great deal of anxiety over our willingness to break laws. 15 This is certainly a legitimate concern. Since we so diligently urge people to obey the Supreme Court's decision of 1954 outlawing segregation in the public schools, at first glance it may seem rather paradoxical for us consciously to break laws. One may well ask: "How can you advocate breaking some laws and obeying others?" The answer lies in the fact that there are two types of laws: just and unjust. I would be the first to advocate obeying just laws. One has not only a legal but a moral responsibility to obey just laws. Conversely, one has a moral responsibility to disobey unjust laws. I would agree with St. Augustine* that "an unjust law is no law at all."

Now, what is the difference between the two? How does one determine 16 whether a law is just or unjust? A just law is a man-made code that squares with the moral law or the law of God. An unjust law is a code that is out of harmony with the moral law. To put it in the terms of St. Thomas Aquinas:** An unjust law is a human law that is not rooted in eternal law and natural law. Any law that uplifts human personality is just. Any law that degrades

---

* Eds. note — Early church father and philosopher (354–430).
** Eds. note — Italian philosopher and theologian (1225–1274).

human personality is unjust. All segregation statutes are unjust because segregation distorts the soul and damages the personality. It gives the segregator a false sense of superiority and the segregated a false sense of inferiority. Segregation, to use the terminology of the Jewish philosopher Martin Buber, substitutes an "I-it" relationship for an "I-thou" relationship and ends up relegating persons to the status of things. Hence segregation is not only politically, economically, and sociologically unsound, it is morally wrong and sinful. Paul Tillich* has said that sin is separation. Is not segregation an existential expression of man's tragic separation, his awful estrangement, his terrible sinfulness? Thus it is that I can urge men to obey the 1954 decision of the Supreme Court, for it is morally right; and I can urge them to disobey segregation ordinances, for they are morally wrong.

Let us consider a more concrete example of just and unjust laws. An 17 unjust law is a code that a numerical or power majority group compels a minority group to obey but does not make binding on itself. This is *difference* made legal. By the same token, a just law is a code that a majority compels a minority to follow and that it is willing to follow itself. This is *sameness* made legal.

Let me give another explanation. A law is unjust if it is inflicted on a 18 minority that, as a result of being denied the right to vote, had no part in enacting or devising the law. Who can say that the legislature of Alabama which set up that state's segregation laws was democratically elected? Throughout Alabama all sorts of devious methods are used to prevent Negroes from becoming registered voters, and there are some counties in which, even though Negroes constitute a majority of the population, not a single Negro is registered. Can any law enacted under such circumstances be considered democratically structured?

Sometimes a law is just on its face and unjust in its application. For 19 instance, I have been arrested on a charge of parading without a permit. Now, there is nothing wrong in having an ordinance which requires a permit for a parade. But such an ordinance becomes unjust when it is used to maintain segregation and to deny citizens the First-Amendment privilege of peaceful assembly and protest.

I hope you are able to see the distinction I am trying to point out. In no 20 sense do I advocate evading or defying the law, as would the rabid segregationist. That would lead to anarchy. One who breaks an unjust law must do so openly, lovingly, and with a willingness to accept the penalty. I submit that an individual who breaks a law that conscience tells him is unjust, and who willingly accepts the penalty of imprisonment in order to arouse the conscience of the community over its injustice, is in reality expressing the highest respect for law.

Of course, there is nothing new about this kind of civil disobedi- 21 ence. It was evidenced sublimely in the refusal of Shadrach, Meshach, and

---

* Eds. note — American philosopher and theologian (1886–1965).

Abednego* to obey the laws of Nebuchadnezzar, on the ground that a higher moral law was at stake. It was practiced superbly by the early Christians, who were willing to face hungry lions and the excruciating pain of chopping blocks rather than submit to certain unjust laws of the Roman Empire. To a degree, academic freedom is a reality today because Socrates practiced civil disobedience. In our own nation, the Boston Tea Party represented a massive act of civil disobedience.

We should never forget that everything Adolph Hitler did in Germany 22 was "legal" and everything the Hungarian freedom fighters did in Hungary was "illegal." It was "illegal" to aid and comfort a Jew in Hitler's Germany. Even so, I am sure that, had I lived in Germany at the time, I would have aided and comforted my Jewish brothers. If today I lived in a Communist country where certain principles dear to the Christian faith are suppressed, I would openly advocate disobeying that country's antireligious laws.

I must make two honest confessions to you, my Christian and Jewish 23 brothers. First, I must confess that over the past few years I have been gravely disappointed with the white moderate. I have almost reached the regrettable conclusion that the Negro's great stumbling block in his stride toward freedom is not the White Citizens Counciler or the Ku Klux Klanner, but the white moderate, who is more devoted to "order" than to justice; who prefers a negative peace which is the absence of tension to a positive peace which is the presence of justice; who constantly says, "I agree with you in the goal you seek, but I cannot agree with your methods of direct action"; who paternalistically believes he can set the timetable for another man's freedom; who lives by a mythical concept of time and who constantly advises the Negro to wait for a "more convenient season." Shallow understanding from people of good will is more frustrating than absolute misunderstanding from people of ill will. Lukewarm acceptance is much more bewildering than outright rejection.

I had hoped that the white moderate would understand that law and 24 order exist for the purpose of establishing justice and that when they fail in this purpose they become the dangerously structured dams that block the flow of social progress. I had hoped that the white moderate would understand that the present tension in the South is a necessary phase of the transition from an obnoxious negative peace, in which the Negro passively accepted his unjust plight, to a substantive and positive peace, in which all men will respect the dignity and worth of human personality. Actually, we who engage in nonviolent direct action are not the creators of tension. We merely bring to the surface the hidden tension that is already alive. We bring it out in the open, where it can be seen and dealt with. Like a boil that can never be cured so long as it is covered up but must be opened with all its ugliness to the natural medicines of air and light, injustice must be

---

* Eds. note — In the Book of Daniel, three men who were thrown into a blazing fire for refusing to worship a golden statue.

exposed, with all the tension its exposure creates, to the light of human conscience and the air of national opinion, before it can be cured.

In your statement you assert that our actions, even though peaceful, 25 must be condemned because they precipitate violence. But is this a logical assertion? Isn't this like condemning a robbed man because his possession of money precipitated the evil act of robbery? Isn't this like condemning Socrates because his unswerving commitment to truth and his philosophical inquiries precipitated the act by the misguided populace in which they made him drink hemlock? Isn't this like condemning Jesus because his unique God-consciousness and never-ceasing devotion to God's will precipitated the evil act of crucifixion? We must come to see that, as the federal courts have consistently affirmed, it is wrong to urge an individual to cease his efforts to gain his basic constitutional rights because the quest may precipitate violence. Society must protect the robbed and punish the robber.

I had also hoped that the white moderate would reject the myth con- 26 cerning time in relation to the struggle for freedom. I have just received a letter from a white brother in Texas. He writes: "All Christians know that the colored people will receive equal rights eventually, but it is possible that you are in too great a religious hurry. It has taken Christianity almost two thousand years to accomplish what it has. The teachings of Christ take time to come to earth." Such an attitude stems from a tragic misconception of time, from the strangely irrational notion that there is something in the very flow of time that will inevitably cure all ills. Actually, time itself is neutral; it can be used either destructively or constructively. More and more I feel that the people of ill will have used time much more effectively than have the people of good will. We will have to repent in this generation not merely for the hateful words and actions of the bad people, but for the appalling silence of the good people. Human progress never rolls in on wheels of inevitability; it comes through the tireless efforts of men willing to be coworkers with God, and without this hard work, time itself becomes an ally of the forces of social stagnation. We must use time creatively, in the knowledge that the time is always ripe to do right. Now is the time to make real the promise of democracy and transform our pending national elegy into a creative psalm of brotherhood. Now is the time to lift our national policy from the quicksand of racial injustice to the solid rock of human dignity.

You speak of our activity in Birmingham as extreme. At first I was 27 rather disappointed that fellow clergymen would see my nonviolent efforts as those of an extremist. I began thinking about the fact that I stand in the middle of two opposing forces in the Negro community. One is a force of complacency, made up in part of Negroes who, as a result of long years of oppression, are so drained of self-respect and a sense of "somebodiness" that they have adjusted to segregation; and in part of a few middle-class Negroes who, because of a degree of academic and economic security and because in some ways they profit by segregation, have become insensitive to the problems of the masses. The other force is one of bitterness and hatred, and it comes perilously close to advocating violence. It is expressed in the various black nationalist groups that are springing up across the nation, the largest and best-known being Elijah Muhammad's Muslim movement. Nourished by the Negro's frustration over the continued existence of racial discrimination, this movement is made up of people who have lost faith in America, who have absolutely repudiated Christianity, and who have concluded that the white man is an incorrigible "devil."

I have tried to stand between these two forces, saying that we need 28 emulate neither the "do-nothingism" of the complacent nor the hatred and despair of the black nationalist. For there is the more excellent way of love and nonviolent protest. I am grateful to God that, through the influence of the Negro church, the way of nonviolence became an integral part of our struggle.

If this philosophy had not emerged, by now many streets of the South 29 would, I am convinced, be flowing with blood. And I am further convinced that if our white brothers dismiss as "rabble-rousers" and "outside agitators" those of us who employ nonviolent direct action, and if they refuse to support our nonviolent efforts, millions of Negroes will, out of frustration and despair, seek solace and security in black-nationalist ideologies — a development that would inevitably lead to a frightening racial nightmare.

Oppressed people cannot remain oppressed forever. The yearning for 30 freedom eventually manifests itself, and that is what has happened to the American Negro. Something within has reminded him of his birthright of freedom, and something without has reminded him that it can be gained. Consciously or unconsciously, he has been caught up by the *Zeitgeist*, and with his black brothers of Africa and his brown and yellow brothers of Asia, South America, and the Caribbean, the United States Negro is moving with a sense of great urgency toward the promised land of racial justice. If one recognizes this vital urge that has engulfed the Negro community, one should readily understand why public demonstrations are taking place. The Negro has many pent-up resentments and latent frustrations, and he must release them. So let him march; let him make prayer pilgrimages to the city hall; let him go on freedom rides — and try to understand why he must do so. If his repressed emotions are not released in nonviolent ways, they will seek expression through violence; this is not a threat but a fact of history. So I have not said to my people, "Get rid of your discontent." Rather, I have tried to say that this normal and healthy discontent can be channeled into the creative outlet of nonviolent direct action. And now this approach is being termed extremist.

But though I was initially disappointed at being categorized as an 31 extremist, as I continued to think about the matter I gradually gained a measure of satisfaction from the label. Was not Jesus an extremist for love: "Love your enemies, bless them that curse you, do good to them that hate you, and pray for them which despitefully use you, and persecute you." Was not Amos an extremist for justice: "Let justice roll down like waters and righteousness like an everflowing stream." Was not Paul an extremist for the Christian gospel: "I bear in my body the marks of the Lord Jesus." Was not Martin Luther an extremist: "Here I stand; I cannot do otherwise, so help me God." And John Bunyan: "I will stay in jail to the end of my days before I make a butchery of my conscience." And Abraham Lincoln: "This nation cannot survive half slave and half free." And Thomas Jefferson: "We hold these truths to be self-evident, that all men are created equal. . . ." So the question is not whether we will be extremists, but what kind of extremists we will be. Will we be extremists for hate or for love? Will we be extremists for the preservation of injustice or for the extension of justice? In that dramatic scene of Calvary's hill three men were crucified. We must never forget that all three were crucified for the same crime — the crime of extremism. Two were extremists for immorality, and thus fell below their environment. The other, Jesus Christ, was an extremist for love, truth, and goodness, and thereby rose above his environment. Perhaps the South, the nation, and the world are in dire need of creative extremists.

I hoped that the white moderate would see this need. Perhaps I was too 32 optimistic; perhaps I expected too much. I suppose I should have realized that few members of the oppressor race can understand the deep groans and passionate yearnings of the oppressed race, and still fewer have the vision to see that injustice must be rooted out by strong, persistent, and determined action. I am thankful, however, that some of our white brothers in the South have grasped the meaning of this social revolution and committed themselves to it. They are still all too few in quantity, but they are big in quality. Some — such as Ralph McGill, Lillian Smith, Harry Golden, James McBride Dabbs, Ann Braden, and Sarah Patton Boyle — have written about our struggle in eloquent and prophetic terms. Others have marched with us down nameless streets of the South. They have languished in filthy, roach-infested jails, suffering the abuse and brutality of policemen who view them as "dirty nigger-lovers." Unlike so many of their moderate brothers and sisters, they have recognized the urgency of the movement and sensed the need for powerful "action" antidotes to combat the disease of segregation.

Let me take note of my other major disappointment. I have been so 33 greatly disappointed with the white church and its leadership. Of course, there are some notable exceptions. I am not unmindful of the fact that each of you has taken some significant stands on this issue. I commend you, Reverend Stallings, for your Christian stand on this past Sunday, in welcoming Negroes to your worship service on a nonsegregated basis. I commend the Catholic leaders of this state for integrating Spring Hill College several years ago.

But despite these notable exceptions, I must honestly reiterate that I 34 have been disappointed with the church. I do not say this as one of those negative critics who can always find something wrong with the church. I say this as a minister of the gospel, who loves the church; who was nurtured in its bosom; who has been sustained by its spiritual blessings and who will remain true to it as long as the cord of life shall lengthen.

When I was suddenly catapulted into the leadership of the bus protest 35 in Montgomery, Alabama, a few years ago, I felt we would be supported by the white church. I felt that the white ministers, priests, and rabbis of the South would be among our strongest allies. Instead, some have been outright opponents, refusing to understand the freedom movement and misrepresenting its leaders; all too many others have been more cautious than courageous and have remained silent behind the anesthetizing security of stained-glass windows.

In spite of my shattered dreams, I came to Birmingham with the hope 36 that the white religious leadership of this community would see the justice of our cause and, with deep moral concern, would serve as the channel through which our just grievances could reach the power structure. I had hoped that each of you would understand. But again I have been disappointed.

There was a time when the church was very powerful — in the time 37 when the early Christians rejoiced at being deemed worthy to suffer for what they believed. In those days the church was not merely a thermometer that recorded the ideas and principles of popular opinion; it was a thermostat that transformed the mores of society. Whenever the early Christians entered a town, the people in power became disturbed and immediately sought to convict the Christians for being "disturbers of the peace" and "outside agitators." But the Christians pressed on, in the conviction that they were "a colony of heaven," called to obey God rather than man. Small in number, they were big in commitment. They were too God-intoxicated to be "astronomically intimidated." By their effort and example they brought an end to such ancient evils as infanticide and gladiatorial contests.

Things are different now. So often the contemporary church is a weak, 38 ineffectual voice with an uncertain sound. So often it is an archdefender of the status quo. Far from being disturbed by the presence of the church, the power structure of the average community is consoled by the church's silent — and often even vocal — sanction of things as they are.

But the judgment of God is upon the church as never before. If today's 39 church does not recapture the sacrificial spirit of the early church, it will lose its authenticity, forfeit the loyalty of millions, and be dismissed as an irrelevant social club with no meaning for the twentieth century. Every day I meet young people whose disappointment with the church has turned into outright disgust.

Perhaps I have once again been too optimistic. Is organized religion 40 too inextricably bound to the status quo to save our nation and the world? Perhaps I must turn my faith to the inner spiritual church, the church within the church, as the true *ekklesia** and the hope of the world. But again I am thankful to God that some noble souls from the ranks of organized religion have broken loose from the paralyzing chains of conformity and joined us as active partners in the struggle for freedom. They have left their secure congregations and walked the streets of Albany, Georgia, with us.

* Eds. note — Greek word for the early Christian church.

They have gone down the highways of the South on tortuous rides for freedom. Yes, they have gone to jail with us. Some have been dismissed from their churches, have lost the support of their bishops and fellow ministers. But they have acted in the faith that right defeated is stronger than evil triumphant. Their witness has been the spiritual salt that has preserved the true meaning of the gospel in these troubled times. They have carved a tunnel of hope through the dark mountain of disappointment.

41   I hope the church as a whole will meet the challenge of this decisive hour. But even if the church does not come to the aid of justice, I have no despair about the future. I have no fear about the outcome of our struggle in Birmingham, even if our motives are at present misunderstood. We will reach the goal of freedom in Birmingham and all over the nation, because the goal of America is freedom. Abused and scorned though we may be, our destiny is tied up with America's destiny. Before the pilgrims landed at Plymouth, we were here. Before the pen of Jefferson etched the majestic words of the Declaration of Independence across the pages of history, we were here. For more than two centuries our forebears labored in this country without wages; they made cotton king; they built the homes of their masters while suffering gross injustice and shameful humiliation — and yet out of a bottomless vitality they continued to thrive and develop. If the inexpressible cruelties of slavery could not stop us, the opposition we now face will surely fail. We will win our freedom because the sacred heritage of our nation and the eternal will of God are embodied in our echoing demands.

42   Before closing I feel impelled to mention one other point in your statement that has troubled me profoundly. You warmly commended the Birmingham police for keeping "order" and "preventing violence." I doubt that you would have so warmly commended the police force if you had seen its dogs sinking their teeth into unarmed, nonviolent Negroes. I doubt that you would so quickly commend the policemen if you were to observe their ugly and inhumane treatment of Negroes here in the city jail; if you were to watch them push and curse old Negro women and young Negro girls; if you were to see them slap and kick old Negro men and young boys; if you were to observe them, as they did on two occasions, refuse to give us food because we wanted to sing our grace together. I cannot join you in your praise of the Birmingham police department.

43   It is true that the police have exercised a degree of discipline in handling the demonstrators. In this sense they have conducted themselves rather "nonviolently" in public. But for what purpose? To preserve the vile system of segregation. Over the past few years I have consistently preached that nonviolence demands that the means we use must be as pure as the ends we seek. I have tried to make clear that it is wrong to use immoral means to attain moral ends. But now I must affirm that it is just as wrong, or perhaps even more so, to use moral means to preserve immoral ends. Perhaps Mr. Connor and his policemen have been rather nonviolent in public, as was Chief Pritchett in Albany, Georgia, but they have used the moral means of nonviolence to maintain the immoral end of racial injus-

tice. As T. S. Eliot has said, "The last temptation is the greatest treason: To do the right deed for the wrong reason."

I wish you had commended the Negro sit-inners and demonstrators of 44 Birmingham for their sublime courage, their willingness to suffer, and their amazing discipline in the midst of great provocation. One day the South will recognize its real heroes. They will be the James Merediths,* with the noble sense of purpose that enables them to face jeering and hostile mobs, and with the agonizing loneliness that characterizes the life of the pioneer. They will be old, oppressed, battered Negro women, symbolized in a seventy-two-year-old woman in Montgomery, Alabama, who rose up with a sense of dignity and with her people decided not to ride segregated buses, and who responded with ungrammatical profundity to one who inquired about her weariness: "My feets is tired, but my soul is at rest." They will be the young high school and college students, the young ministers of the gospel and a host of their elders, courageously and nonviolently sitting in at lunch counters and willingly going to jail for conscience's sake. One day the South will know that when these disinherited children of God sat down at lunch counters, they were in reality standing up for what is best in the American dream and for the most sacred values in our Judaeo-Christian heritage, thereby bringing our nation back to those great wells of democracy which were dug deeply by the founding fathers in their formulation of the Constitution and the Declaration of Independence.

Never before have I written so long a letter. I'm afraid it is much too 45 long to take your precious time. I can assure you that it would have been much shorter if I had been writing from a comfortable desk, but what else can one do when he is alone in a narrow jail cell, other than write long letters, think long thoughts, and pray long prayers?

If I have said anything in this letter that overstates the truth and indi- 46 cates an unreasonable impatience, I beg you to forgive me. If I have said anything that understates the truth and indicates my having a patience that allows me to settle for anything less than brotherhood, I beg God to forgive me.

I hope this letter finds you strong in the faith. I also hope that cir- 47 cumstances will soon make it possible for me to meet each of you, not as an integrationist or a civil-rights leader but as a fellow clergyman and a Christian brother. Let us all hope that the dark clouds of racial prejudice will soon pass away and the deep fog of misunderstanding will be lifted from our fear-drenched communities, and in some not too distant tomorrow the radiant stars of love and brotherhood will shine over our great nation with all their scintillating beauty.

Yours for the cause of Peace and Brotherhood,
Martin Luther King Jr.

• • •

---

* Eds. note — James Meredith was the first African American to enroll at the University of Mississippi.

Comprehension

1. King says he seldom answers criticism. Why not? Why, then, does he decide to do so in this instance?

2. Why do the other clergymen consider King's activities to be " 'unwise and untimely' " (1)?

3. What reasons does King give for the demonstrations? Why does he think it is too late for negotiations?

4. What does King say *wait* means to black people?

5. What are the two types of laws King defines? What is the difference between the two?

6. What does King find illogical about the claim that the actions of his followers precipitate violence?

7. Why is King disappointed in the white church?

Purpose and Audience

1. Why, in the first paragraph, does King establish his setting (the Birmingham city jail) and define his intended audience?

2. Why does King begin his letter with a reference to his audience as "men of genuine good will" (1)? Is this phrase **ironic** in light of his later criticism of them? Explain.

3. What indicates that King is writing his letter to an audience other than his fellow clergymen?

4. What is the thesis of this letter? Is it stated or implied?

Style and Structure

1. Where does King seek to establish that he is a reasonable person?

2. Where does King address the objections of his audience?

3. As in the Declaration of Independence, transitions are important in King's letter. Identify the transitional words and phrases that connect the different parts of his argument.

4. Why does King cite Jewish, Catholic, and Protestant philosophers to support his position?

5. Throughout his letter, King cites theologians and philosophers (Augustine, Aquinas, Buber, Tillich, and others). Why do you think he does this?

6. King uses both induction and deduction in his letter. Find an example of each, and explain how they function in his argument.

7. Throughout the body of his letter, King criticizes his audience of white moderates. In his conclusion, however, he seeks to reestablish a harmonious relationship with them. How does he do this? Is he successful?

8. **Vocabulary Project.** Locate five **allusions** to the Bible in this essay. Look up these allusions online. Then, determine how these allusions help King express his ideas.

9. In paragraph 14, King refers to his "cup of endurance." What is this a reference to? How is the original phrase worded?

Journal Entry

Do you believe King's remarks go too far? Do you believe they do not go far enough? Explain.

Writing Workshop

1. Write an argumentative essay supporting a deeply held belief of your own. Assume that your audience, like King's, is not openly hostile to your position.

2. **Working with Sources.** Assume you are a militant political leader responding to Martin Luther King Jr. Argue that King's methods do not go far enough. Be sure to address potential objections to your position. You might want to consult a website such as http://mlk-kpp01.stanford .edu or read some newspapers and magazines from the 1960s to help you prepare your argument. Make sure you document all references to your sources, and include a works-cited page. (See Chapter 18 for information on MLA documentation.)

3. **Working with Sources.** Read your local newspaper for several days, collecting articles about a controversial subject that interests you. Using information from the articles, take a position on the issue, and write an essay supporting it. Make sure you document all references to your sources, and include a works-cited page. (See Chapter 18 for information on MLA documentation.)

Combining the Patterns

In "Letter from Birmingham Jail," King includes several passages of **narration**. Find two of these passages, and discuss what use King makes of narration. Why do you think narration plays such an important part in King's argument?

Thematic Connections

- "Indian Education" (page 142)
- "Just Walk On By: A Black Man Ponders His Power to Alter Public Space" (page 238)
- "The 'Black Table' Is Still There" (page 348)
- "Should American Citizenship Be a Birthright?" (Debate; page 591)

Is the Student Loan Crisis a Myth?

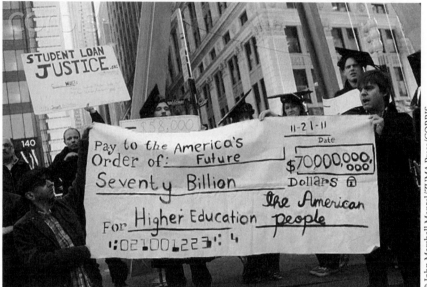

"Occupy Student Debt" protesters march against burdensome student loans in New York City on November 21, 2011.

·   ·   ·

Overall student debt now tops $1 trillion, making it the single largest source of consumer debt. The average college senior now graduates with over $30,000 in loans, and the number of parents who go into debt to finance their children's higher education is increasing. According to the Department of Education, the student loan default rate is now 10 percent, which is the highest it has been in sixteen years.

Many interrelated factors have contributed to this situation. For example, college tuition rates have tripled over the last thirty years, and the rising costs of higher education increasingly make financial assistance a necessity for those seeking degrees. At the same time, in the wake of a weak economy, states have cut higher education funding, which has made even less-expensive public institutions more difficult to afford. With a persistently high unemployment rate, recent graduates have a hard time finding work or must settle for low-paying jobs. This situation makes paying back loans difficult. Moreover, student loan debt can be a drag on the national economy as a whole because people who must make loan payments delay other purchases, such as houses and cars.

Not surprisingly, discussions of the student loan crisis also spill over into other areas. The evolution of American higher education is a story of widening accessibility and democratization, from the establishment of land-grant universities and "free" colleges like the College of the City of New York (CCNY), to the post–World War II GI Bill, the community college system, and widely available Stafford Loans. This evolution reflects a long-standing American belief that education is the key to socioeconomic mobility as well as a necessity for an informed citizenry and a competitive workforce in the global marketplace. However, anxieties about student debt have led many people to ask questions: Is a college education still worth the cost? Are American universities performing as well as they should? What role should the federal government play in helping Americans gain access to higher education? These questions stem, in no small part, from heightened scrutiny of college debt. But is there really a student-loan debt crisis?

The following two selections take opposing points of view. In "The Myth of the Student Loan Crisis," Nicole Allan and Derek Thompson argue that the crisis is overblown. Moreover, they make the case that a college degree remains an excellent financial investment. Chris Lewis and Layla Zaidane respond to Allan and Thompson with "Here's Your Crisis: Student Loan Debt Isn't a Myth," highlighting several factors that suggest the student loan crisis is, in fact, a real crisis.

NICOLE ALLAN AND DEREK THOMPSON

The Myth of the Student Loan Crisis

Nicole Allan is a senior editor at the *Atlantic Monthly*. A graduate of Yale University, she has written for *Slate* and the *New Republic*. Derek Thompson directs the *Atlantic*'s Business Channel. His work has appeared in *Slate*, *Business Week*, and the *Daily Beast*.

Background on Sallie Mae Any discussion of student loan debt over the past several decades must include the role of Sallie Mae. Although other forms of federal financial aid preceded it, the Student Loan Marketing Association (Sallie Mae) was created in 1972 as a GSE, or government-sponsored enterprise: a public-private partnership that helped provide private lenders with a large market of borrowers: students seeking financial assistance for their education. As a GSE, Sallie Mae could borrow at low interest rates because the company was backed by the full faith and credit of the U.S. government. Over the past four decades, Sallie Mae has become the single largest source of private student loans. Beginning in the 1990s, however, the company moved toward full privatization; Congress terminated its federal charter in 2004. The continued evolution of Sallie Mae has been rocky. In 2007, for example, the company was at the center of a scandal involving unethical financial relationships with several colleges, which resulted in inflated loan prices. A number of schools, including the University of Pennsylvania and New York University, reimbursed students for several million dollars. More recently, President Barack Obama initiated reforms that allow students to take out low-interest loans directly from the government and bypass private lenders such as Sallie Mae.

This month, college-admission letters are being accompanied by national anxiety over the growing "student debt crisis." The cost of college has spiked 150 percent since 1995, compared with a 50 percent increase in the cost of other goods and services. Last year, outstanding student loans soared to nearly $1 trillion — a 300 percent jump since 2003. College is an undeniably risky investment, seemingly more so than ever. But are rising debt levels a national crisis? [1]

> " College is such a good investment, in fact, that it might even justify *more* student debt. "

1. One year at Harvard costs **$57,950**. But most students don't go to Harvard. The average yearly tab for a first-time, full-time student living on campus, it turns out, is **$27,453** at four-year schools and **$15,267** at two-year schools.

2. Even most of the students who do go to Harvard don't end up paying full price. Taking grants and scholarships into account, these students owed **$16,459** for the 2009–10 school year; nationwide, the average four-year student who received aid owed **$17,360**.

3. Horror stories of students drowning in $100,000+ debt might discourage young people from enrolling in college, but they are as rare as they are terrifying.

INDEBTED STUDENTS, BY AMOUNT OWED

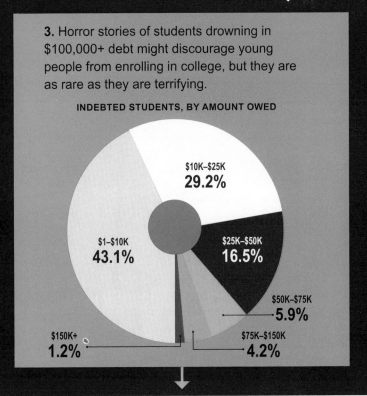

$10K–$25K
29.2%

$1–$10K
43.1%

$25K–$50K
16.5%

$50K–$75K
5.9%

$150K+
1.2%

$75K–$150K
4.2%

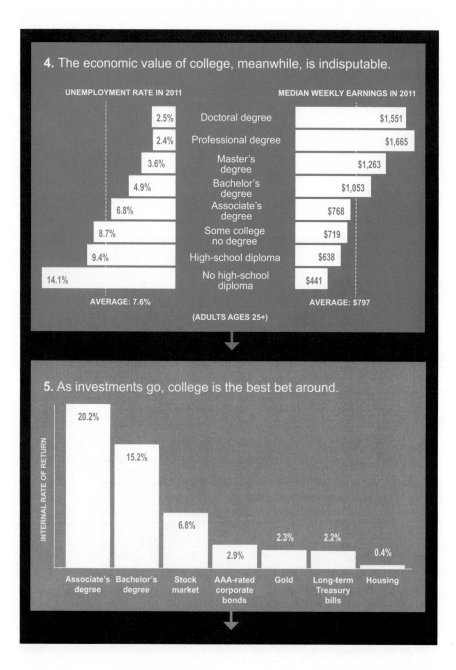

4. The economic value of college, meanwhile, is indisputable.

UNEMPLOYMENT RATE IN 2011 — MEDIAN WEEKLY EARNINGS IN 2011

Degree	Unemployment Rate	Median Weekly Earnings
Doctoral degree	2.5%	$1,551
Professional degree	2.4%	$1,665
Master's degree	3.6%	$1,263
Bachelor's degree	4.9%	$1,053
Associate's degree	6.8%	$768
Some college no degree	8.7%	$719
High-school diploma	9.4%	$638
No high-school diploma	14.1%	$441

AVERAGE: 7.6%   AVERAGE: $797

(ADULTS AGES 25+)

5. As investments go, college is the best bet around.

INTERNAL RATE OF RETURN

Category	Rate
Associate's degree	20.2%
Bachelor's degree	15.2%
Stock market	6.8%
AAA-rated corporate bonds	2.9%
Gold	2.3%
Long-term Treasury bills	2.2%
Housing	0.4%

6. College is such a good investment, in fact, that it might even justify *more* student debt. A 2012 study found that **1 in 6** full-time students at four-year schools who were eligible for government loans weren't taking advantage of them. Another found that low-income families are likely to overestimate the cost of college, and suggested that they may be scared off by the complexity of financial-aid forms. But for students from these families, not going to college can be more expensive than going to college.

7. Each of the 6.7 million Americans ages 16 to 24 who are neither employed nor in school costs the country **$37,450** a year in low wages, lost tax revenue, and higher public spending. Compared with this figure, the cost of college is a bargain—for students and taxpayers.

1. Harvard University; National Center for Education Statistics. 2. National Center for Education Statistics. 3. Federal Reserve Bank of New York. 4. Bureau of Labor Statistics. 5. Brookings Institution. 6. Brian C. Cadena, University of Colorado at Boulder, and Benjamin J. Keys, University of Chicago; Eric Bettinger et al., National Bureau of Economic Research. 7. Clive R. Belfield et al., Civic Enterprises.

•   •   •

Comprehension

1. For the 2009–2010 school year, what did the average four-year college student who received financial aid owe? Why is this figure important?

2. The writers refer to the "horror stories of students drowning in $100,000+ debt." What specific effect do Allan and Thompson think such "horror stories" might have on young people?

3. According to a study cited in the infographic, how do many low-income families view the prospect of college costs and financial aid?

4. Allan and Thompson assert that for some students, "not going to college can be more expensive than going to college." What do they mean? Given the costs of higher education, how is that possible?

Purpose and Audience

1. For what purpose was this infographic created? Do you think the writers are trying to inform? Persuade? Encourage readers to take a specific point of view?

2. Who is the audience for this infographic? How can you tell?

3. What preconceptions do Allan and Thompson think their readers might have? How do they address these preconceptions?

4. What is the thesis of this infographic? Restate it in your own words.

Style and Structure

1. Instead of presenting their argument in words alone, the writers created an infographic, combining charts and graphs with text. What are the advantages of this approach? What are the disadvantages?

2. Allan and Thompson assert that the economic value of a college degree is "indisputable" (panel 4). Are they **begging the question**? Explain.

3. **Vocabulary Project.** Allan and Thompson present college as an "investment," claiming, "As investments go, college is the best bet around" (panel 5). What is an "investment"? In what context do we usually use this term? Do you consider a college education primarily an investment? Does it make sense to compare it to bonds or stocks? Explain.

Journal Entry

How did the costs of higher education factor into your decision to attend college or to choose a specific school? Have these costs in any way determined the field you chose to study?

Writing Workshop

1. **Working with Sources.** What is your view of the student loan crisis? Create your own infographic composed of five to seven numbered panels using charts, figures, and brief explanations to present the information to make your argument. Use the sources cited by Allan and Thompson, taking care to document all material that you refer to and to include a works-cited page. (See Chapter 18 for information on MLA documentation.)

2. **Working with Sources.** If you agree with the writers' main argument, how would you make a case that the student debt crisis is overblown and

that college remains a good investment? Using the sources that Allan and Thompson cite in their infographic, write an essay that further develops their argument that the student loan crisis is a "myth." In particular, you might focus on addressing the "horror stories" about student debt and highlight valuable aspects of higher education that Allan and Thompson do not take into account. Be sure to document all references to your sources, and include a works-cited page. (See Chapter 18 for information on MLA documentation.)

3. The writers present the value of a college education primarily in financial terms. Is that how you view higher education? What other factors might come into play in this discussion? Write an essay that takes a position on whether a college degree is valuable financially or otherwise.

Combining the Patterns

Where in this infographic do the writers use **classification and division**? Where do they use **cause and effect**? Why are these patterns important for their argument?

Thematic Connections

- "The Money" (page 114)
- "Ten Ways We Get the Odds Wrong" (page 250)
- "College Pressures" (page 448)

CHRIS LEWIS AND LAYLA ZAIDANE

Here's Your Crisis: Student Loan Debt Isn't a Myth

Chris Lewis is a reporter for Generation Progress (formerly Campus Progress), a nonprofit organization whose work focuses on U.S. college campuses and younger Americans. He graduated from American University, and his work has appeared in the *Washington City Paper,* the *Miami Herald,* and other publications. Layla Zaidane is the online communications associate for Generation Progress. She graduated from Georgetown University's School of Foreign Service.

Background on proposals to alleviate student debt According to the Consumer Finance Protection Bureau, total student debt is over $1 trillion. That includes all student loans taken out from private entities such as Sallie Mae as well as federal loans originating directly from the Department of Education. The average debt burden of a college graduate with loans is now over $30,000. Struggling through a sluggish economy and rising tuitions, students have been defaulting on their college loans at record rates, and this situation has led to various proposals for alleviating student debt. Some officials have suggested bankruptcy reform: many kinds of debt can be discharged and mitigated through the legal process of bankruptcy, but most student debt cannot. Others have proposed overall loan forgiveness. For example, Strike Debt, part of the Occupy Wall Street movement, has created what it calls the Rolling Jubilee: essentially, it buys up discounted student debt that would otherwise be sold to debt collectors and then "liberates" the debtors. For its part, the federal government has tried to move toward various income-contingent repayment plans for those who have taken out federal student loans. Some observers have expressed a more general concern that federal involvement in financial aid only fuels a higher-education bubble; some also worry that allowing graduates to avoid paying back their loans in full — or granting them loan forgiveness — encourages an abdication of personal responsibility.

The student loan crisis is a myth.   1

So say Nicole Allan and Derek Thompson, who argue in this month's   2
issue of the *Atlantic* that the economic returns of college far outweigh the
burden of student loan debt.

"Horror stories of students drowning in $100,000+ debt might dis-   3
courage young people from enrolling in college, but they are as rare as they
are terrifying," Allan and Thompson wrote in the article. "The economic
value of college, meanwhile, is indisputable."

Allan and Thompson looked for crisis in the wrong places. Six-figure   4
calamities are indeed rare, but millions of Americans are caught between
stubbornly weak labor markets and increasingly costly higher education.

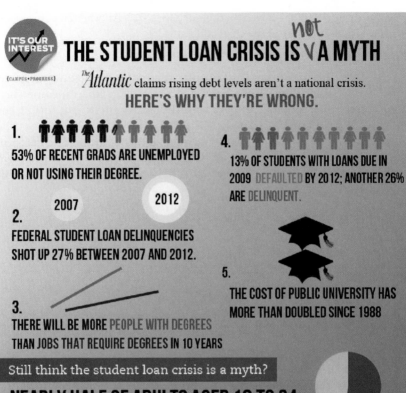

THE STUDENT LOAN CRISIS IS ~~not~~ A MYTH

IT'S OUR INTEREST
{CAMPUS•PROGRESS}

*The*Atlantic claims rising debt levels aren't a national crisis.
HERE'S WHY THEY'RE WRONG.

1. 53% OF RECENT GRADS ARE UNEMPLOYED OR NOT USING THEIR DEGREE.

2007   2012

2. FEDERAL STUDENT LOAN DELINQUENCIES SHOT UP 27% BETWEEN 2007 AND 2012.

3. THERE WILL BE MORE PEOPLE WITH DEGREES THAN JOBS THAT REQUIRE DEGREES IN 10 YEARS

4. 13% OF STUDENTS WITH LOANS DUE IN 2009 DEFAULTED BY 2012; ANOTHER 26% ARE DELINQUENT.

5. THE COST OF PUBLIC UNIVERSITY HAS MORE THAN DOUBLED SINCE 1988

Still think the student loan crisis is a myth?

NEARLY HALF OF ADULTS AGED 18 TO 34
WITHOUT DEGREES (48%) CAN'T AFFORD TO GO TO COLLEGE

SOURCES: The Wall Street Journal, CNN Money, Associated Press, The Atlantic

itsourinterest.org

1. The employment prospects for young grads are pretty gloomy. According to an Associated Press analysis, 53 percent of recent college graduates are either unemployed or not putting their degree to use.

2. Because of the weak job market, borrowers are struggling more and more to keep up with payments. According to TransUnion, federal student loan delinquencies shot up 27 percent between 2007 and 2012. (Private loan delinquencies dropped 2 percent.)

3. Don't expect the problem to go away once the economy picks up. As Campus Progress recently reported, the growth in Americans with degrees is far outpacing the growth in jobs that require them, meaning jobs that offer a secure path to debt repayment will become ever more competitive.

4. But repayment is already causing hardship: 13 percent of students whose loans

> "It's not just a debt crisis — it's an affordability crisis."

came due in 2009 defaulted on their debt by 2012. Another 26 percent are delinquent, on the cusp of default.

5. It's not just a debt crisis — it's an affordability crisis.

CNN Money found that the cost of attending a public university has   5
more than doubled since 1988, even as Americans' median income stag-
nated. If our incomes had kept pace with the cost of higher education, the
average American would now make $77,000 yearly.

Finally, the cost of college prevents many low-income Americans from   6
even seeking a higher education. Forty-eight percent of adults aged eighteen to thirty-four without degrees told the *Wall Street Journal* that they
can't afford to go to college.

Among high schoolers who score highly on the SAT and ACT, 80 per-   7
cent of kids from wealthy families go on to get college degrees, compared
with just 44 percent of those from low-income families. Student loan
debt not only makes life miserable for many graduates, it prevents some
Americans from even setting foot on a college campus. That's what we call
a crisis.

•   •   •

Comprehension

1. According to the writers, what specific factors indicate that student debt
    is a national crisis?

2. The writers point out that a large number of recent graduates with jobs
    are "not putting their degree to use" (4). What do they mean by this? If
    these graduates are employed, what does the fact that they are not using
    the degrees they earned have to do with the student loan crisis?

3. What do the terms "delinquent" and "default" (4) mean in the context of
    the infographic?

4. How much has the cost of a public university increased since 1988? Why
    do you think the writers emphasize public universities rather than private
    ones?

Purpose and Audience

1. How would you restate the thesis of this selection's infographic in your
    own words?

2. Who is the intended audience for the infographic? How can you tell?

3. How would you describe the purpose of the infographic? To present
    information? To persuade?

4. "Here's Your Crisis: Student Loan Debt Isn't a Myth" was created as a
    response to the infographic "The Myth of the Student Loan Crisis"
    (page 580). Do the authors of "Here's Your Crisis: Student Loan Debt

Isn't a Myth" assume that their readers have seen the earlier infographic? Do they represent that infographic fairly and accurately? Does this infographic present a convincing response to "The Myth of the Student Loan Crisis"? Explain.

Style and Structure

1. Which information seems the most effective in supporting the main point of the infographic? Which is the least effective or convincing? Explain.

2. Is the infographic's use of icons effective? Why or why not? What other icons would you suggest they use?

3. How would you describe the tone of the language used in the infographic? Does it seem objective? Biased? Serious? Sarcastic?

4. **Vocabulary Project.** The title of this essay is "Here's Your Crisis: Student Loan Debt Isn't a Myth." What does the word *myth* mean in this context? What other meanings and connotations does the word have?

Journal Entry

Do you have student loans? Have you received financial aid of any kind? Do you find your own college financing to be stressful? Does it seem like a "crisis"?

Writing Workshop

1. **Working with Sources.** The authors of "The Myth of the Student Loan Crisis" (page 580) believe that there is no student loan crisis. The authors of "Here's Your Crisis: Student Loan Debt Isn't a Myth" disagree. Consider both arguments, and then investigate and research the subject on your own. Write an essay that answers the question, "Is the student loan crisis a myth?" Be sure to document any sources you use and to include a works-cited page. (See Chapter 18 for information on MLA documentation.)

2. Based on the two examples in this debate, how effective are infographics at presenting credible and persuasive arguments? Write a critique that examines the strengths and weaknesses of the two infographics. For instance, do any facts or statistics seem to be presented out of context? Do these infographics seem more objective than an argument written in essay form? Do they present enough support for their arguments?

3. **Working with Sources.** According to "Here's Your Crisis: Student Loan Debt Isn't a Myth," student loan delinquencies and defaults have risen over the last several years. What can be done to ease the burden of student loans? Investigate some recent proposals, ideas, and strategies that have been put forth for helping students deal with debt, and then write an

essay suggesting some solutions to the problem. Be sure to document the sources you use and to include a works-cited page. (See Chapter 18 for information on MLA documentation.)

Combining the Patterns

How do the writers use **definition** to make their main point?

Thematic Connections

- "I'm Your Teacher, Not Your Internet-Service Provider" (page 415)
- "The Dog Ate My Flash Drive, and Other Tales of Woe" (page 457)

Should American Citizenship Be a Birthright?

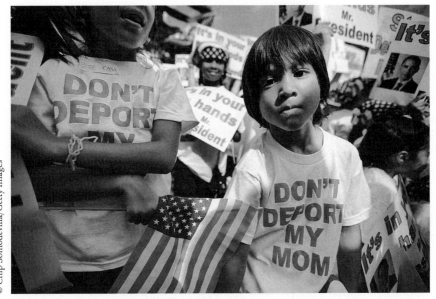

U.S.-born children with their undocumented parents demonstrating in Washington against deportations.

•   •   •

The United States is a nation of immigrants. In ways both large and small, immigrants have contributed to American culture, to its economic and physical growth, to its political power, and to its reputation as a beacon of freedom and opportunity to the world. However, immigration has also been a source of controversy in the United States — a controversy that existed even before the nation's founding. In 1753, for example, Benjamin Franklin worried about the influx of Germans to Pennsylvania: "They will soon outnumber us . . . and even our government will be precarious."

Still, from the earliest years of the republic, America has had mechanisms for assimilating people from other countries. In 1790, the United States passed the first naturalization law, which established the process for foreign nationals to become American citizens. In addition, in 1868, the Fourteenth Amendment made birthright citizenship a part of the United States Constitution. The amendment begins, "All persons born or naturalized in the United States, and subject to the jurisdiction thereof, are citizens of the United States and of the State wherein they reside." In the last several years, however, some Americans have questioned the merits of birthright citizenship — especially as debates about illegal immigration have become more heated and contentious.

Currently, approximately 11 million undocumented immigrants live in the United States. Opponents of birthright citizenship argue that this policy increases the country's immigration problem by encouraging foreign nationals to have so-called "anchor babies," who they hope will give them access to social services — and, eventually, to citizenship. A 2010 study by the Pew Hispanic Center estimated that the number of children of undocumented immigrants who have received birthright citizenship grew from 2.7 million in 2003 to 4.5 million in 2010. As Speaker of the U.S. House of Representatives John Boehner says, "In certain parts of our country, clearly, our schools, our hospitals are being overrun by illegal immigrants, a lot of whom came here just so their children could become U.S. citizens." Some officials have proposed a constitutional amendment to end birthright citizenship. Other lawmakers opposed to birthright citizenship are considering legal measures at the state level.

For most legal scholars and historians, however, the long-standing interpretation of the Fourteenth Amendment is settled law. Supporters of birthright citizenship argue that the practice reflects the country's democratic character, its constitutional values, and its tradition of widening the community of people regarded as "Americans." Moreover, some political officials argue that targeting the Fourteenth Amendment is merely a distraction from enacting real immigration reform. In "The Case for Birthright Citizenship," Linda Chavez argues that abandoning this principle is a "terrible idea" that would "fundamentally change what it means to be an American." She also warns that doing so will "jeopardize the electoral future of the GOP by alienating Hispanics." George F. Will makes the case against birthright citizenship in "An Argument to Be Made about Immigrant Babies and Citizenship." To "drain some scalding steam from immigration arguments," Will proposes a reading of the Fourteenth Amendment that brings it "into conformity with what the authors of its text intended, and with common sense."

LINDA CHAVEZ

The Case for Birthright Citizenship

Linda Chavez is chair of the Center for Equal Opportunity, a Virginia-based public policy research organization. In 1983, President Ronald Reagan named her staff director for the U.S. Commission on Civil Rights. She subsequently held a number of other government posts, including chair of the National Commission on Migrant Education. Chavez is the author of *Out of the Barrio: Toward a New Politics of Hispanic Assimilation* (1991), *An Unlikely Conservative: The Transformation of an Ex-Liberal, or How I Became the Most Hated Hispanic in America* (2002), and *Betrayal: How Union Bosses Shake Down Their Members and Corrupt American Politics* (2004). She is also a columnist whose work has appeared in the *Washington Post,* the *Wall Street Journal,* and many other publications. In 2000, Chavez was named a Library of Congress "Living Legend" for her contributions to America's cultural and social heritage.

Background on birthright citizenship in other countries Originally enacted to guarantee citizenship to freed slaves, the Fourteenth Amendment to the United States Constitution grants automatic citizenship to anyone born on American soil—including the children of undocumented immigrants. This principle is known as *jus soli,* or "right of the soil." Many countries practice *jus soli* citizenship, including Argentina, Mexico, Canada, and Pakistan. France, the United Kingdom, and other states use a modified version of *jus soli,* imposing an additional requirement for citizenship, such as having a parent who is a permanent resident. Most countries, however, still use the principle of *jus sanguina,* or "right of blood." Under this rule, an individual gains citizenship by having an ancestor who is a national or citizen of the state. For example, Israel's *jus sanguina* system automatically grants citizenship to Jews and the descendants of Israeli Arabs all over the world but not to the offspring of foreign workers within the country. Likewise, Ireland allows any person with an Irish grandparent to become a citizen—and to pass that right to Irish nationality on to his or her own children. Germany, which traditionally had a strong *jus sanguina* system, has recently loosened its citizenship laws. As of 2002, children born on German soil can claim citizenship if one of their parents has lived in the country legally for eight years. Debates about birthright citizenship lead to larger questions about the meaning of the word "citizen." For example, is citizenship a function of both blood and heritage? What standards must an individual meet to be a citizen?

Republican leaders in Congress are now flirting with changing portions of the Fourteenth Amendment — which grants citizenship to "all persons born or naturalized in the United States and subject to the jurisdiction thereof" — to deny citizenship to children born here to illegal immigrants.

The idea of modifying birthright citizenship has been around for de-   2
cades but was previously relegated to the fringes of the immigration restriction movement. Yet in recent days, Sens. John McCain, Lindsey Graham, and Jon Kyl have embraced the idea; Senate and House GOP leaders
Mitch McConnell and John Boehner have proposed hearings.

Repealing birthright citizenship is a ter-   3
rible idea. It will unquestionably jeopardize
the electoral future of the GOP by alienating
Hispanics — the largest minority and fastest-
growing segment of the U.S. population.
More importantly, ending birthright citizenship would fundamentally change what
it means to be an American.

> "Since the abolition of slavery, we have never denied citizenship to any group of children born in the U.S. . . ."

Proponents of repeal argue that the   4
Fourteenth Amendment was passed after
the Civil War to guarantee citizenship to
freed slaves, and that it was never intended to grant rights to the offspring
of illegal aliens. But this argument is a non sequitur. At the time of the
adoption of the amendment, there was no category of "illegal alien" because immigration was unrestricted and unregulated. If you secured passage to the United States, or simply walked across the open border with
Mexico or Canada, you could stay permanently as a resident alien or apply
to be naturalized after a certain number of years. And if you happened to
give birth while still an alien, your child was automatically a citizen — a right
dating back to English common law.

The most serious challenge to birthright citizenship for the children of   5
aliens came in 1898, and it involved a class of aliens who were every bit as
unpopular as present-day illegal immigrants: the Chinese. Like most illegal
immigrants today, the Chinese came here to work as common laborers,
eagerly recruited by employers but often deeply resented by the workers
with whom they competed. This popular resentment, coupled with racial
prejudice, led to America's first immigration restriction law, the Chinese
Exclusion Act of 1882. It was followed by successively more restrictive federal and state laws that denied Chinese aliens — and, later, other Asians —
the right to own property, to marry, to return to the U.S. if they left, or to
become American citizens.

With anti-Chinese alien sentiment still high, the Supreme Court took   6
up the case *U.S. v. Wong Kim Ark* in 1898. Born in San Francisco to alien parents who later returned to China, Wong traveled to his parents' homeland
for a visit and was denied re-entry on his return in 1895. The government
argued that Wong had no right to birthright citizenship under the Fourteenth Amendment because his parents remained "subjects of the emperor
of China" not subject to U.S. jurisdiction, even while residing in California
at the time of his birth. In a 7–2 vote, the Supreme Court ruled otherwise.

The court found that the only persons Congress intended to exclude   7
from birthright citizenship under the Fourteenth Amendment were chil-

dren born to diplomats — an ancient, universally recognized exception even under common law; Indians, who by treaty were considered members of sovereign nations; and children of an occupying enemy. "The amendment, in clear words and in manifest intent, includes the children born within the territory of the United States of all other persons, of whatever race or color, domiciled within the United States," wrote Justice Horace Gray for the majority. To hold otherwise, he noted, would be to deny citizenship to the descendants of English, Irish, German, and other aliens who had always been considered citizens even if their parents were citizens of other countries. For more than 100 years, the court has consistently upheld this analysis.

Our history has been largely one of continuously expanding the com-   8 munity of people regarded as Americans, from native-born whites to freed slaves to Indians to naturalized citizens of all races and ethnicities. Since the abolition of slavery, we have never denied citizenship to any group of children born in the U.S. — even when we denied citizenship to their parents, as we did Asian immigrants from 1882 to 1943. This expansive view of who is an American has been critical to our successful assimilation of millions of newcomers.

Conservatives should not betray these values based on a misreading of   9 American history and legal precedent. Instead of amending the Constitution to eliminate "anchor babies" — the ugly term opponents of birthright citizenship use to describe these U.S. citizens — Republicans should be helping them become good Americans.

•   •   •

Comprehension

1. What specific events motivated Chavez to write this column?
2. Chavez claims that repealing birthright citizenship is a "terrible idea" (3). What consequences does she see for the Republican Party if Republicans repeal birthright citizenship?
3. According to Chavez, what "class of aliens" once occupied a place similar to "present-day illegal immigrants" (5)?
4. At the time of the adoption of the Fourteenth Amendment, why was there no category of "illegal alien"?

Purpose and Audience

1. Where does Chavez state her thesis? Restate it in your own words.
2. Chavez's column was published in the politically conservative, pro-business *Wall Street Journal*. Do you think she expects her audience to agree with her position? How can you tell?
3. Chavez implies that illegal immigrants are unpopular. How might politicians use this sentiment to their own advantage?

4. Chavez makes a number of broad statements about American history. Give some examples. How do these statements support her argument? How convincing are they?

Style and Structure

1. Where does Chavez address opposing arguments? Does she refute them effectively?

2. Chavez claims that her opponents commit a logical fallacy. Which fallacy is it? Do you agree with her?

3. Paragraph 3 opens with the direct statement, "Repealing birthright citizenship is a terrible idea." Given Chavez's audience, do you think this is an effective opening strategy, or do you think she should have stated her position with more subtlety?

4. What point does Chavez make in paragraph 7? Do you find it persuasive? Why or why not?

5. Where does Chavez use **analogy**? Do you find the comparisons she makes effective? Explain.

6. **Vocabulary Project.** According to the writer, *anchor babies* is an "ugly term" (9). Do you agree? Why or why not?

Journal Entry

Chavez refers to America's "successful assimilation of millions" of immigrants (8). What qualities indicate to you that an immigrant has "successfully assimilated"?

Writing Workshop

1. **Working with Sources.** George F. Will (page 598) considers birthright citizenship to be at odds both with common sense and with a correct interpretation of the Fourteenth Amendment. In contrast, Chavez claims that arguments such as Will's are based on a *non sequitur*. Which writer do you find more persuasive? Write an essay that evaluates their respective positions and explains your own position on this issue. Make sure that you document references to the essays and that you include a works-cited page. (See Chapter 18 for information on MLA documentation.)

2. **Working with Sources.** Chavez implies that illegal aliens are unpopular with most Americans. Do you think she is correct? Using information from newspapers, magazines, popular media, the Internet, and other sources, write an essay in which you take a stand on this issue. Make sure that you document references to your sources and that you include a works-cited page. (See Chapter 18 for information on MLA documentation.)

3. In paragraph 3, Chavez writes that "ending birthright citizenship would fundamentally change what it means to be an American." Do you agree? Why or why not? Write an essay justifying your position.

Combining the Patterns

What pattern of development does Chavez use to support her claim that American history "has been largely one of continuously expanding the community of people regarded as Americans" (8)?

Thematic Connections

- "Goodbye to My Twinkie Days" (page 171)
- "Midnight" (page 217)
- "Mother Tongue" (page 463)
- "U.S. Census 2010 Form" (page 500)

GEORGE F. WILL

An Argument to Be Made about Immigrant Babies and Citizenship

Pulitzer Prize–winning political columnist George F. Will was born in 1941 in Champaign, Illinois. After receiving an undergraduate degree at Trinity College and a master's degree from Oxford, Will earned an M.A. and a Ph.D. in political science at Princeton University. He taught at the University of Toronto and the University of Michigan and then served on the staff of Colorado senator Gordon Allot from 1970 to 1972. Will began his journalism career as a writer and editor at the *National Review,* a conservative magazine, in the early 1970s. Since 1974, Will has written a nationally syndicated political column for the *Washington Post.* He is also the author of several books, including *Men at Work: The Craft of Baseball* (1988), *Restoration: Congress, Term Limits, and the Recovery of Deliberative Democracy* (1992), and *One Man's America: The Pleasures and Provocations of Our Singular Nation* (2008), a collection of his columns.

Background on children born to non-U.S. citizens George Will cites congressional testimony estimating that nearly 10 percent of all recent U.S. births "have been to mothers who are here illegally." According to a 2010 report by the nonpartisan Pew Hispanic Center, that figure is largely correct. The study found that while undocumented immigrants make up just under 4 percent of the population (3.7 percent), they are producing 8 percent of the nation's babies: 350,000 of the children born in the United States between March 2009 and March 2010. Estimates of the total undocumented immigrant population generally vary between 11 and 12 million; according to the Pew Center, 11.7 million were living in the United States in 2012, down slightly from a peak of 12 million in 2007. Researchers attribute the decline both to a weak economy and to stricter border enforcement. Most undocumented immigrants come from Mexico (6 million), followed by other countries in Latin America (2.6 million) and Asia (1.3 million). California has the largest population of undocumented immigrants in the United States, with 2.45 million. California's Department of Health Services birth statistics do not include the legal status of new parents, but the department's records indicate that nearly half the state's babies are born to immigrant mothers.

A simple reform would drain some scalding steam from immigration 1 arguments that may soon again be at a roiling boil. It would bring the interpretation of the Fourteenth Amendment into conformity with what the authors of its text intended, and with common sense, thereby removing an incentive for illegal immigration.

To end the practice of "birthright citizenship," all that is required is to 2 correct the misinterpretation of that amendment's first sentence: "All persons born or naturalized in the United States, and subject to the jurisdiction thereof, are citizens of the United States and of the State wherein they reside." From these words has flowed the practice of conferring citizenship on children born here to illegal immigrants.

A parent from a poor country, writes professor Lino Graglia of the University of Texas law school, "can hardly do more for a child than make him or her an American citizen, entitled to all the advantages of the American welfare state." Therefore, "It is difficult to imagine a more irrational and self-defeating legal system than one which makes unauthorized entry into this country a criminal offense and simultaneously provides perhaps the greatest possible inducement to illegal entry."

> " There cannot be a more total or forceful denial of consent to a person's citizenship than to make the source of that person's presence in the nation illegal. "

3

Writing in the *Texas Review of Law and Politics*, Graglia says this irrationality is rooted in a misunderstanding of the phrase "subject to the jurisdiction thereof." What was this intended or understood to mean by those who wrote it in 1866 and ratified it in 1868? The authors and ratifiers could not have intended birthright citizenship for illegal immigrants because in 1868 *there were and never had been any illegal immigrants* because *no law ever had restricted immigration.*

4

If those who wrote and ratified the Fourteenth Amendment *had* imagined laws restricting immigration — and had anticipated huge waves of illegal immigration — is it reasonable to presume they would have wanted to provide the reward of citizenship to the children of the violators of those laws? Surely not.

5

The Civil Rights Act of 1866 begins with language from which the Fourteenth Amendment's citizenship clause is derived: "All persons born in the United States, *and not subject to any foreign power,* excluding Indians not taxed, are hereby declared to be citizens of the United States." (Emphasis added.) The explicit exclusion of Indians from birthright citizenship was not repeated in the Fourteenth Amendment because it was considered unnecessary. Although Indians were at least partially subject to U.S. jurisdiction, they owed allegiance to their tribes, not the United States. This reasoning — divided allegiance — applies equally to exclude the children of resident aliens, legal as well as illegal, from birthright citizenship. Indeed, today's regulations issued by the departments of Homeland Security and Justice stipulate:

6

"A person born in the United States to a foreign diplomatic officer accredited to the United States, as a matter of international law, is not subject to the jurisdiction of the United States. That person is not a United States citizen under the 14th Amendment."

7

Senator Lyman Trumbull of Illinois was, Graglia writes, one of two "principal authors of the citizenship clauses in [the] 1866 act and the Fourteenth Amendment." He said that "subject to the jurisdiction of the United

8

States" meant subject to its "complete" jurisdiction, meaning "not owing allegiance to anybody else." Hence children whose Indian parents had tribal allegiances were excluded from birthright citizenship.

Appropriately, in 1884 the Supreme Court held that children born to   9
Indian parents were not born "subject to" U.S. jurisdiction because, among other reasons, the person so born could not change his status by his "own will without the action or assent of the United States." And "no one can become a citizen of a nation without its consent." Graglia says this decision "seemed to establish" that U.S. citizenship is "a consensual relation, requiring the consent of the United States." So: "This would clearly settle the question of birthright citizenship for children of illegal aliens. There cannot be a more total or forceful denial of consent to a person's citizenship than to make the source of that person's presence in the nation illegal."

Congress has heard testimony estimating that more than two-thirds of   10
all births in Los Angeles public hospitals, and more than half of all births in that city, and nearly 10 percent of all births in the nation in recent years, have been to mothers who are here illegally. Graglia seems to establish that there is no constitutional impediment to Congress ending the granting of birthright citizenship to those whose presence here is "not only without the government's consent but in violation of its law."

· · ·

Comprehension

1. Will notes that debates about immigration are contentious. What reform, according to Will, could quiet down the controversy? Do you agree with his suggestion?

2. In Will's view, where does the concept of birthright citizenship come from?

3. Throughout his essay, Will cites legal scholar Lino Graglia. Why does Graglia think parents from poor countries give birth to children in the United States? What does he see as the primary "inducement" (3)?

4. According to Will, how do we know that the "authors and ratifiers" of the Fourteenth Amendment "could not have intended birthright citizenship for illegal immigrants" (4)?

5. According to Will, what groups — historically and presently — are already excluded from birthright citizenship? How do these exceptions strengthen his argument?

Purpose and Audience

1. What is Will's thesis? How would you restate it in your own words?

2. What is the purpose of this essay? That is, what does Will hope to achieve?

3. Will quotes extensively from Lino Graglia's scholarly article published in the *Texas Review of Law and Politics*. Who is Will's audience? How is it similar to or different from Graglia's?

Style and Structure

1. Will believes that a particular interpretation of the Fourteenth Amendment will change the terms of the immigration debate, particularly regarding birthright citizenship. In what sense is his essay a deductive argument?

2. Do you think Will should have included evidence from a wider range of sources? Does the Graglia article provide enough support?

3. Will does not specifically address any opposing arguments. Do you think this weakens his argument? Why or why not?

4. Will closes his essay by citing statistics on birthrates among undocumented immigrants. Why does he end this way? Do you think this concluding strategy is effective? Can you suggest an additional closing sentence that would end his argument more forcefully?

5. In what respects is this a definition essay? What is being defined? How is the definition developed?

6. **Vocabulary Project.** How is the word *Indian* (9) different from terms such as *Native American, Amerindian,* or even *indigenous people*? Is the word *Indian* appropriate in this context, or should Will have used another term in his essay?

Journal Entry

Will's essay addresses the legal meaning of citizenship in the context of debates about immigration. What does *citizenship* mean to you? What privileges and obligations go along with it? How is its meaning for you shaped by your own ethnic or cultural background?

Writing Workshop

1. Do you support birthright citizenship? Why or why not? Write an argumentative essay that takes a position on the issue.

2. **Working with Sources.** George Will cites law professor Lino Graglia, who (in Will's view) interprets the Fourteenth Amendment in "conformity with what the authors of its text intended, and with common sense" (1). Read the amendment yourself, and then do some research to find a legal expert with an opinion that is different from Graglia's. Write an essay explaining which interpretation of the amendment you find most convincing, and why. Be sure to document all references to your sources, and include a works-cited page. (See Chapter 18 for information on MLA documentation.)

3. According to Will, almost 10 percent of recent U.S. births have been to mothers who are in the United States illegally. What is your reaction to this statistic? Do you think illegal immigration is a major problem in America? Write an essay that explains your view of the immigration debate.

Combining the Patterns

Find an example of **classification and division** in Will's essay. How does this pattern strengthen his argument?

Thematic Connections

- "The Money" (page 114)
- "Indian Education" (page 142)
- "U.S. Census 2010 Form" (page 500)

Is Football Too Dangerous?

© AP Photo/Chris O'Meara

Miami running back Duke Johnson is injured during the second quarter of an NCAA college football game on Saturday, September 28, 2013, in Tampa, Florida. Wide receiver Herb Waters looks on.

·   ·   ·

The first intercollegiate football game took place on November 6, 1869, when Princeton played Rutgers University. In the early years of the twentieth century, Yale football coach Walter Camp — the "father of football" — implemented rules that shaped football into the game we recognize now: legalizing the forward pass; designing a system of "downs" to determine

603

possession; and establishing the "line of scrimmage" as well as point values for touchdowns and field goals. In 1920, the American Professional Football Association was created. It became the National Football League (NFL) in 1922. In the years since, college and professional football have become tremendously popular — and lucrative.

Youth football is also very popular. Currently, an estimated 2.8 million children play in youth leagues. Likewise, over 1 million high school students play football. And, like its professional and college counterparts, high school football is more than just a sport; in certain areas of the country, it has achieved mythic status, as exemplified by the popular television show *Friday Night Lights*.

Recently, however, public attention has focused on football's physical risks and long-term health effects. Several retired NFL players have committed suicide over the last few years, and medical evidence suggests that brain damage — the consequence of years of violent on-field collisions and concussions — may have played a role in these deaths. Other players — for example, Pittsburgh Steelers Hall of Fame center Mike Webster and Chicago Bears quarterback Jim MacMahon — have suffered dementia and physical deterioration.

Many have wondered if increased fears about the game's risks will cause parents to be less likely to allow their children to play football. Each year about a dozen high school and college players die. Some of these deaths are due to underlying conditions such as heart disease and asthma, but others are the result of head trauma, broken necks, and abdominal injuries. Even President Barack Obama has said, "I'm a big football fan, but I have to tell you, if I had a son, I'd have to think long and hard before I let him play football."

All the essays in this casebook address the dangers of football. In "What Price Football?" Don Banks makes the case that if football is going to have a future, it has to change to make the game safer for players. In "Would Football without Concussions Still Be Football?" Nina Burleigh acknowledges her love of the sport but argues that real changes and increased safety measures must start at the local and youth-league level. In "Why Parents Should Let Their Kids Play Dangerous Sports," Jeb Golinkin argues that risky activities and team sports are essential for children's spiritual and emotional development. Finally, in "Football Does a Body Good (Nannyism Doesn't)," Daniel J. Flynn sees the recent "anti-football frenzy" as unfounded, overhyped "hysteria" based on speculation, not on empirical evidence.

DON BANKS

What Price Football?

Don Banks is a senior writer for *Sports Illustrated,* where he covers the National Football League. He worked previously as a sports reporter at the *St. Paul Pioneer Press,* the *Minneapolis Star Tribune,* and the *St. Petersburg Times.* He has received several newspaper honors, including two Society of Professional Journalists Minnesota Page One Awards (1998 and 2000), two Associated Press Sports Editors awards for news and investigative reporting (1994 and 1997), and a feature-writing award from the Florida Sports Writers Association.

Background on traumatic brain injuries in the NFL Football is a contact sport, and concussions have been common in the National Football League over the last several decades. Until recently, players who suffered concussions would often return to the game shortly after their injuries. In fact, there has always been a strong incentive for coaches, fans, the league, and the players themselves to keep stars on the field even if that meant playing through pain. But recently, the long-term effects of these injuries — particularly chronic traumatic encephalopathy (CTE) or brain trauma — have become more apparent. High-profile retired players, including Chicago Bears safety Dave Duerson and All-Pro linebacker Junior Seau, have committed suicide, possibly because of CTE, while others have suffered from early forms of dementia attributable to concussions caused by collisions on the field. The focus on football's dark side has led some observers to suggest that the long-term health costs of professional football may be too high for the sport to continue in its present form.

They trumpeted it as a "settlement," but of course the $765 million in 1 restitution that the NFL has agreed to pay to former players to make those concussion-related lawsuits go away didn't really settle everything. Certainly not the biggest question of all: will America's love affair with football continue unchanged and unabated, now that we're finally coming to grips with how much the game can ultimately cost some of its players?

In other words, what price football? 2

It's not an easy question to grapple with, but given the stakes, it has 3 to be done, and it has be done by everyone from couch potatoes to commissioners.

Now that we all know enough to know there's hard evidence connect- 4 ing football to traumatic brain injuries, and realize it's a game that has been played far too dangerously for too long, there are new realities.

We have to let the game change, and we have to embrace that change. 5 For the safety of the men who play the sport for our weekly entertainment, and for the preservation of the game itself.

The NFL is quick to point out it didn't have to accept liability as part of its concussion litigation settlement with former players. But culpability is no longer the point, responsibility is, and the responsibility to make things right and to let football evolve into a safer game is something that every fan, media member, coach, player, and team or league executive has a part in.

> "We have to let the game change, and we have to embrace that change."

6

Where football goes from here depends on it.

7

Ignore the voices that resist change and cling to the way the game was played when they first learned it. The game has already changed in significant ways on the safety front in recent years, and it will continue to do so. Football isn't being ruined by these changes, it's being saved. At least hopefully, if they go far enough and work effectively.

8

Decide to see the wisdom of those changes, not just the flaws. Banning crown-of-the-helmet blows in the open field is not a loss to the game, it's a common-sense move to protect the head and lower the amount of punishment it absorbs. Helmet-to-helmet hits aren't to be argued and complained about by players, coaches, and anyone who wants to paint them as unavoidable. Some perhaps are, but they're dangerous and need to be eliminated as much as possible, like driving without a seat belt or running around in a lightning storm.

9

If the decision to remove the hazardous kickoff from the game comes along in the near future, let's not whine about a cherished part of the game lost. If it makes the game safer, it makes sense. Case closed. Players will always say it's too hard to change the way they play, but they can and will change the way they play, because it's too important not to.

10

Worry less about new rules "ruining" the game and more about the lives that have been ruined by the game, thanks to the effects of dementia, depression, and suicides related to brain trauma. What we know about those issues today might wind up being just the tip of that scary iceberg.

11

The game of football should resist the notion that everything's going to be fine. Record ratings, record profits, and wall-to-wall coverage are here today, but they're not guaranteed indefinitely if the sport doesn't keep taking steps to become less violent and less risky when it comes to long-term brain damage. It's not a given that youth leaguers will continue to play in high school, taking their game to college and then the best of those into the professional ranks. Football needs a feeder system, but it needs one that doesn't start to dry up due to fears of the game's unintended consequences.

12

Change, even if it's uncomfortable at first, must keep coming to the game of football. Nothing will ever make football 100 percent safe, but that doesn't mean you don't set the goal high and keep striving. It's going to take more rule changes, better science and equipment, and increased emphasis and education when it comes to safety. And it's going to take accepting that the change is for the better, and for the good of the game.

13

What price football? It's a question that needs to be asked by everyone   14
who has a sporting interest in the game America loves, and for all those
who understand the need to protect the players of today better than the
players of the past. If we learn to live with a game that features fewer devastating hits but helps secure football's long-term future, it won't be just the
players who will feel the lasting impact.

. . .

Comprehension

1. In paragraphs 1 and 2, the writer discusses a $765 million restitution paid
   by the NFL. Who is this money being paid to? Why is it being paid?

2. In paragraph 4, Banks says that "we all know enough to know there's hard
   evidence connecting football to traumatic brain injuries." Do you think
   he is **begging the question**? Does he supply the evidence to support this
   statement? Explain.

3. In paragraph 12, Banks says, "Football needs a feeder system, but it needs
   one that doesn't start to dry up due to fears of the game's unintended
   consequences." What does he mean by "feeder system," and what are the
   "unintended consequences" he refers to?

4. Banks says that if new rules are put in place to make football safer, "it
   won't be just the players who will feel the lasting impact" (14). Who else
   will feel the impact? What will that impact be?

Purpose and Audience

1. The title of this essay is in the form of a question, and the writer repeats
   the same question several times throughout his essay. To whom is the
   question being asked? Who do you think is supposed to answer it?

2. What is Banks's thesis? Restate it in your own words.

3. How would you characterize Banks's attitude toward football and football fans? Do you think NFL fans are the intended audience for this essay?
   Why or why not?

4. What is Banks's purpose in writing this essay? Is he trying to change the
   way people feel about football? Would he like to see football abolished?
   Explain.

Style and Structure

1. Banks says that several cause-and-effect relationships have shaped the
   sport of football. Identify two examples of these relationships. How convincing are they? How do they help support his overall argument?

2. In paragraph 1, Banks puts quotation marks around the word *settlement*.
   He does the same in paragraph 11 with the word *ruining*. Why does he use
   these quotation marks?

3. In paragraph 9, Banks compares helmet-to-helmet hits to "driving without a seat belt or running around in a lightning storm." How effective are these **analogies**.

4. **Vocabulary Project.** In paragraph 6, Banks contrasts the words *liability* and *culpability* with *responsibility*. How are these terms different? How does Banks's emphasis on *responsibility* instead of *liability* or *culpability* reflect his position on the dangers of football?

5. Banks begins paragraphs 8, 9, and 11 with commands. How do these commands affect the tone of his essay?

Journal Entry

Banks's essay asks, "What price football?" What are some of the "costs" Banks alludes to? Would you call football an "expensive" pastime? Who "pays the price" for football? What other pastimes or activities can you think of that have a similarly high "price"?

Writing Workshop

1. **Working with Sources.** In paragraph 10, Banks mentions the possibility of eliminating the kickoff from football. Research this issue. Then, write an essay that either supports or refutes Banks's statement that this change "makes sense." Be sure to document any references to sources, and include a works-cited page. (See Chapter 18 for information on ML A documentation.)

2. **Working with Sources.** According to Banks, "It's not a given that youth leaguers will continue to play in high school, taking their game to college and then the best of those into the professional ranks" (12). Has there been a drop in youth football? If so, what are the possible causes of this drop? After researching this issue, write an essay that either agrees or disagrees with Banks's comment. Include parenthetical documentation for references to source material, and include a works-cited page. (See Chapter 18 for information on MLA documentation.)

3. Although Banks does not argue for an outright ban of professional football, he does support some major changes. Do you agree with him? What do you think should be done about football injuries? Should the fate of football be left to the fans, the players, and the league, or is legislation needed? Write an essay that takes a position on these questions.

Combining the Patterns

How does Banks use **exemplification** in this essay? Does he give examples to clarify, explain, add interest, or persuade? How do his examples support his overall argument?

Thematic Connections

- "Thirty-Eight Who Saw Murder Didn't Call the Police" (page 128)
- "Ten Ways We Get the Odds Wrong" (page 250)
- "Who Killed Benny Paret?" (page 337)

NINA BURLEIGH

Would Football without Concussions Still Be Football?

Writer and journalist Nina Burleigh earned a B.A. in English at MacMurray College, an M.A. in English from the University of Chicago, and an M.A. in public affairs reporting from the University of Illinois. Her work has appeared in *Time*, *New York Magazine*, the *Washington Post*, and other publications. She is also the author of several books, including *Mirage: Napoleon's Scientist and the Unveiling of Egypt* (2007) and *The Fatal Gift of Beauty* (2011).

Background on football as America's most popular sport Professional football is currently the most popular spectator sport in the United States. It is also enormously lucrative, generating almost $10 billion per year — not including the highly popular and profitable business of college football. (By way of comparison, Major League Baseball brings in $7 billion, and NBA basketball earns $4 billion.) The NFL originated in the 1920s as the American Professional Football Conference and became the National Football League in 1922. The league expanded in both size and popularity over the next two decades, but its dominance grew enormously with the advent of television. Many consider the televised 1958 championship game between the Baltimore Colts and the New York Giants to be the key moment in football's ascension: the live national coverage on NBC brought about unprecedented publicity and enthusiasm for the sport. Currently, the Super Bowl is the most watched sporting event in the United States, and it is also seen by millions of people around the world.

Earlier this fall, two squads of pint-size players clashed in the crisp air 1 at a peewee football field in Southbridge, Massachusetts. The boys on one team were much larger than the others, and within six plays, three of the smaller boys had been carried off with head injuries, one with his eyes rolling back in their sockets.

By the end of the game, a 52–0 rout, five boys on the losing team were 2 receiving emergency medical care for concussions.

Even as the smaller boys on the field were hit hard and carted off one 3 by one, their own parents did not try to stop the game. Moms and dads stood on the sidelines, cheering. Though later suspended after a hearing, the refs and coaches continued playing, concerned about notching up another game for the 2012 Pop Warner football schedule.

This was not a Monty Python* bit or a *South Park* episode. This really 4 happened in Southbridge a few weeks ago.

---

* Eds. note — A British comedy troupe known for its zany, surreal humor.

Such is the glory and delirium of American football — invigorating 5
autumn air, the crack of a beer at the tailgate, the snuggly team-logo sweat-
shirt, boys with men in showers.

It's been a bad year for America's favorite fall sport, what with lawsuits 6
by former NFL players, the Penn State scandal, pro player suicides, college
and high school deaths, and brain injuries at all levels. The NFL just threw
$30 million at the National Institutes of Health in a Hail Mary philan-
thropic pass to avert the PR and legal mess over a link between football's
repeated concussions and early-onset Alzheimer's. The commissioner is
using words like "evolve" to describe football's future.

It's been building for years, but the sport 7
seems to have reached a crisis point. The
National Center for Catastrophic Sport Injury Research says all football games (from
sandlot to NFL) cause an average of nine
deaths a year. Just last week, a nineteen-year-
old kid named William Wayne Jones III collapsed and died during a practice on the field
at Tennessee State University. The cause of
death is yet to be determined.

> "It's been building
> for years, but the
> sport seems to have
> reached a crisis
> point."

Then there are the deaths off the field: in August, Tennessee Titans 8
wide receiver O. J. Murdock shot himself in a car and died at age twenty-
five, becoming the sixth NFL player to commit suicide in two years, a phenomenon that may be related to brain injury.

The dead are far outnumbered by the walking wounded. A study re- 9
leased in September found that NFL players faced a higher-than-average
risk of Alzheimer's. The study followed 3,400 long-term NFL players between 1959 and 1988 and found that their risk of developing the disease
was four times that of the general population.

Thousands of former players have sued the league claiming the NFL 10
failed to inform them of the long-term danger of brain damage from repeated concussions. Plaintiffs are seeking to hold the league responsible
for the care of players suffering from these problems.

But is there any way to reconcile player safety and the sport's inherent 11
crowd-pleasing brutality?

Baseball is often called America's pastime, but the tapestry of physical 12
grace and brute strength at the heart of football is the more perfect distillation of our national essence. We are the only nation that plays real football,
not the delicate "futbol" of the rest of the world. Perhaps only British and
Australian rugby teams or Spanish bullfighters match us in terms of public
blood sport.

The NFL retirees deserve to win their lawsuits, although knocking 13
brains out of their own and other men's heads is what they signed up for.
Unlike the gladiators of ancient Rome, who were literal slaves forced onto
the stadium grounds to fight for their lives, pro football players choose the
sport, and get paid quite a lot. The median NFL player's salary is $770,000.
Of course the money's not quite so staggering when you consider that the

average career lasts just three and a half years, unless you include an announcer gig or a Ford dealership.

Is $2 million just compensation for relinquishing one's *compos mentis* 14 years long before one's peers? It's too late to ask Michael "Iron Mike" Webster, the famed Pittsburgh Steelers center who, like so many other players, was diagnosed with chronic traumatic encephalopathy — a degenerative disease — only after his death, following years of depression, pain, and dementia.

Trouble is, college ball is dangled as one way out of poverty for big, ath- 15 letic kids. The pot of gold is alluring, and it's hard to blame kids for choosing the sport. But the de facto commodification of poor strong kids means that players are all still property of the team "owners."

And what owners they are. The average team is worth more than a bil- 16 lion dollars, and rakes in an average of $261 million a season. Ads for the Super Bowl sold for $116,667 per second last year, according to Bloomberg.

Advertisers and billionaires are not the only ones invested: average 17 Americans finance the great stadiums where the clashes play out, as the public till is poured into construction projects instead of childhood education. The Lucas Oil Stadium in Indianapolis, where the Super Bowl was played last year, cost $720 million — much of it taxpayer-financed.

Despite all the money invested in the sport, the bloom is coming off 18 the Rose Bowl. Publicity about the long-term symptoms suffered by brain-injured football players has lowered participation in the sport at the youth level, according to reports from around the country this fall.

The NFL is scrambling to deal with the fallout. Commissioner Roger 19 Goodell, speaking at the Harvard School of Public Health recently, insisted the game can "evolve" and be made safer. He said the league has changed rules, including outlawing the flying wedge tackle to make the game safer, and introducing enhanced helmet technology.

"Not long ago, the game allowed the head-slap, tackling by the face 20 mask, horse-collar tackles, dangerous blocks, and hits to the head of defenseless receivers and quarterbacks. All of that has changed," he said.

Mr. Goodell claimed the new attention to long-term effects of brain 21 injuries means the game is potentially safer. The league has taken strides to move up the kickoff line, penalize hits to the head, and more quickly diagnose concussions on the sideline.

On one recent Sunday, three NFL quarterbacks — Alex Smith, Jay Cut- 22 ler, and Michael Vick — were taken out of games with concussions, with Mr. Vick's injury described as "pretty significant." Quarterbacks have probably been spending Sunday nights with concussions ever since pro football hit the airwaves. But three taken off the field on one afternoon is unusual, and likely related to the NFL's newfound consideration for players' brains.

About now, I sound like I'd rather be watching *Masterpiece Theatre** on 23 Thanksgiving, but *au contraire,* I love these brutes. I can't get enough of the

---

* Eds. note — Long-running public television drama series associated with an educated audience.

prancing beauty of the running back or the quarterback's soaring arc of a pass, the human perfection of Tom Brady and his throwing arm in the second before being crushed by the troglodytes of the defensive line. Who can resist the clash of helmets, the crunch of flesh and bone slamming to earth? Primal savagery delivered to our living rooms is sort of the whole point. Without it, it's "futbol."

But the price paid by brain-injured boys and teens, and by potentially 24 thousands of grown men reduced to shuffling around with early-onset Alzheimer's, is a pretty bill to pay for couch-potato thrills.

More publicity about football and brain injuries is anecdotally causing 25 more parents to keep their kids off the field. Some changes underway include handing out penalties for tackling with the head, and emphasizing safer defensive techniques. But high school players still suffer 67,000 concussions a year in football, fueling a multibillion-dollar obsession that thrives on their new blood. Every Friday night this time of year, college scouts haunt the high school stands with binoculars and charts, scoping out boys like race horses.

Pop Warner, the sport's equivalent of Little League, has made some 26 changes, including limiting contact drills to one-third practice and prohibiting full-speed, head-on drills. One brain injury expert has advised "no tackle" football until age fourteen, yet Pop Warner phased out safer flag football in 2005 because parents insisted on the full-contact version. The league even added tackle for five- and six-year-olds.

The NFL can throw millions at brain injury and helmet research, but 27 the real changes have to start at the local level, on fields like the one in Southbridge, Massachusetts. Parents should demand that leagues and schools install stiffer rules to protect their kids and that coaches actually enforce them. If that means a kinder, gentler game, so be it.

·   ·   ·

Comprehension

1. According to Burleigh, it has been a "bad year for America's favorite fall sport" (6). What does she mean?

2. In paragraph 9, Burleigh refers to the results of a study released in September of 2012. What did the study find? Why does she include this information?

3. Although Burleigh says that brain-damaged NFL retirees deserve to win their lawsuits against the league, she qualifies this statement. How? Do you agree with this qualification?

4. What is the median salary of an NFL player? How long does the average NFL player's career last?

5. Why, according to Burleigh, did the Pop Warner youth football organization phase out "safer flag football" (26) for young children in 2005?

Purpose and Audience

1. After Burleigh describes a Pop Warner football league game, she says, "This was not a Monty Python bit or a *South Park* episode" (4). What does she mean? What does this comment indicate about how she sees her readers?

2. In paragraph 23, Burleigh describes her own attitude toward football. What is this attitude?

3. Does Burleigh see her readers as friendly, hostile, neutral, or something else? How do you know?

4. What do you think Burleigh hopes to accomplish with this essay? Explain.

Style and Structure

1. Burleigh begins her essay with an **anecdote** about a youth-league football game. Why does she begin this way? How does this anecdote relate to her main point?

2. Paragraph 5 is a single sentence. How does this paragraph connect Burleigh's introduction to the rest of the essay?

3. **Vocabulary Project.** In paragraph 14, Burleigh asks, "Is $2 million just compensation for relinquishing one's *compos mentis* years long before one's peers?" What is the meaning of *compos mentis*? Why do you think she uses this Latin term instead of its English equivalent?

4. Burleigh compares and contrasts modern football players to Roman gladiators, who were slaves (13–15). Near the end of the essay, she writes about the college scouts who "haunt the high school stands with binoculars and charts, scoping out boys like race horses" (25). How do these comparisons support the overall point she makes in this essay? Are they persuasive? Are they fair? Explain.

5. In paragraphs 20 and 21, Burleigh refers to the "strides" that the NFL has taken to make the game safer; then, in paragraph 22, she describes games from a "recent Sunday." What point is she making here? Is she being serious or sarcastic? How can you tell?

Journal Entry

Burleigh places much of the responsibility for making football safer on parents. If you had (or have) children, would (or do) you allow them to play football? Why or why not?

Writing Workshop

1. **Working with Sources.** In paragraph 18, Burleigh claims that publicity about football-related brain injuries has "lowered participation in the sport at the youth level." Later, she claims this same publicity is "anecdot-

ally causing more parents to keep their kids off the field" (25). Do some research to determine if Burleigh's claim is justified. Then, write an argumentative essay that presents your conclusions. Be sure to include parenthetical documentation and a works-cited page. (See Chapter 18 for information on MLA documentation.)

2. **Working with Sources.** In paragraph 11, Burleigh asks, "[I]s there any way to reconcile player safety and the sport's inherent crowd-pleasing brutality?" Write an essay that answers her question, referring to any of the essays in this casebook (as well as any outside sources you may find). Be sure to document references to your sources, and include a works-cited page. (See Chapter 18 for information on MLA documentation.)

3. According to Burleigh, "Baseball is often called America's pastime, but the tapestry of physical grace and brute strength at the heart of football is the more perfect distillation of our national essence" (12). Do you agree? Write an essay in which you support or challenge Burleigh's assessment. (You may instead write about another sport that you think is a "distillation of our national essence.")

Combining the Patterns

Where does Burleigh use **description**? Point to specific examples. How do her descriptions contribute to the overall effect of the essay?

Thematic Connections

- "Indian Education" (page 142)
- "Ten Ways We Get the Odds Wrong" (page 250)
- "Who Killed Benny Paret?" (page 337)
- "Brains versus Brawn" (page 377)

JEB GOLINKIN

Why Parents Should Let Their Kids Play Dangerous Sports

Jeb Golinkin, a graduate of the University of Texas School of Law, writes about U.S. politics and policy for *TheWeek.com*. From 2008 to 2011, he served as an editor and reporter for *Frum Forum/New Majority*, a political website that is now part of the *Daily Beast*.

Background on the X Games The X Games are annual, seasonal competitions sponsored and broadcast by ESPN. Events focus on "extreme" or "action sports," such as "vert skateboarding," in which skateboarders do tricks on ramps; "freestyle motocross," in which motorcyclists try to impress judges with aerial stunts; or "crashed ice," which involves downhill speed skating in an urban environment. Not surprisingly, these activities involve considerable risk, as the recent death of Caleb Moore, snowmobile freestyle competitor, illustrates. Although Moore is the first person to die at the Winter X Games, others have been seriously injured or died in extreme events. For example, daredevil motocross star Jeremy Lusk, a well-known participant in the X Games, died trying to complete a motorcycle backflip during a one-hundred-foot jump at an action sports competition in Costa Rica. Indeed, injuries are so common that the X Games now have competitions for disabled athletes called "Adaptive" events. Although action sports were originally curiosities on the fringes of athletic competition, they have become mainstream despite the dangers. In fact, some formerly "extreme" events, like snowboarding and ski slopestyle, are now official events in Olympic competition.

1 "Are you not entertained? Are you *not* entertained? Is this not why you are here?"

2 So shouts Russell Crowe's character Maximus in the most powerful scene of Ridley Scott's award-winning film *Gladiator*, after Maximus vanquishes his opponent with such aggressiveness that it leaves the crowd in stunned silence. Maximus's point — that the crowd was there for the violence and the danger — remains as true as ever. But today, our collective fascination with bigger, faster, stronger, higher, more aggressive, more dangerous, and more powerful athletic enterprises has very real costs for the participants who deliver the thrills.

3 The most recent and extreme example of the dangers of our sporting culture comes from the world of extreme snowmobiling. On Thursday, a twenty-five-year-old Texan called Caleb Moore died from injuries sustained when his snowmobile came crashing down on his head after one of his tricks went horribly wrong during his run in the Snowmobile FreeStyle

competition in the Winter X Games in Aspen, Colorado. Moore suffered his injuries after he attempted to do a backflip on his snowmobile. He came up short and the skis on the front of his snowmobile caught the lip of the landing area, sending Moore flying over the handlebars. When Moore hit the snow, his 450-pound snowmobile came crashing down on his head, causing injuries that ultimately led to his death. The death was the first to occur in the X Games' eighteen-year history, which is something of a miracle given the activities involved. The injury that led to Moore's death was broadcast live on ESPN.

This is only the latest in a long list of recent episodes illustrating the 4 undeniable fact that the sports we love are killing the athletes we worship for playing them. For example, San Diego Chargers legend Junior Seau shot himself in the chest — allowing his brain to be preserved and studied. Researchers concluded that Seau suffered from chronic traumatic encephalopathy (CTE), a type of chronic brain damage that is increasingly becoming a side effect of being an NFL football player.

The list of dangerous sports goes on and on — hockey, soccer, rugby, 5 skiing, snowboarding, baseball. And these realizations have given rise to a debate at dinner tables and in living rooms across the United States: Should children play sports, like football, that are demonstrably dangerous, and that have long-lasting health consequences?

Indeed, no less a figure than Barack Obama recently told the *New* 6 *Republic,* "If I had a son, I'd have to think long and hard before I let him play football."

But children should absolutely be allowed to play such sports. Parental fear threatens to deprive many young people of the lessons of organized athletics — lessons they cannot learn anywhere else.

> "Sports, even violent and dangerous sports, continue to represent something noble about the human spirit."

7

8

I respect the president's comments, and I think they reflect the views of many parents in the United States. But I also think it is a shame that people would not allow their children to play football or ski or play hockey because of the risk of concussions. Sports, even violent and dangerous sports, continue to represent something noble about the human spirit.

Many people watch the trick that Caleb Moore died trying and think, 9 "what kind of lunatic would even think to do such a thing?" or "what kind of parent would allow their child to do such an obviously stupid thing?" But we nevertheless watch because the tricks are so audacious, so dangerous, so . . . crazy. Caleb Moore's death is a tragedy, but it should also be recognized that Moore died doing what all great humans do in one way or another: Pushing the limits of the possible. He literally died trying to fly.

Physical safety matters. But our collective obsession with protecting 10 our children from harm threatens to turn out a generation of children ill-equipped spiritually or emotionally to deal with the brave new world order in which only the tough and the persistent will thrive. Children in modern America are growing up in a country paralyzed by complacency and fear. Our political leaders are hardly great, and our economic power is sputtering. Life is not going to be easy, or safe, even for the competent. We would do well to remember that spiritual development is every bit as important as physical safety.

Between the lines, our children learn the importance of teamwork, 11 sportsmanship, toughness, and competitiveness. Between the lines, our children learn to strive, to succeed, and, most importantly, how to fail. When the time comes, let your kid play football, or hockey . . . or whatever, and let him decide for himself. He may break his leg or suffer a concussion, but he will be far better off for it over the course of his life than if he stays inside and plays video games.

• • •

Comprehension

1. What does Golinkin say is an "undeniable fact" (4)? What evidence does he use to support this statement?

2. According to Golinkin, what is a "dangerous sport"? What do all these sports have in common?

3. Why does Golinkin believe that parents should let children play "even violent and dangerous sports" (8)? What does he see as the advantages of these sports?

4. Although Golinkin concedes that Caleb Moore's death was a "tragedy" (9), he says that we should understand its significance. What does he mean? Do you agree?

5. What qualities does Golinkin think will be essential for children in the "brave new world order" (10)? What is the "new world order"? Why, according to Golinkin, will protected children be "ill-equipped" to survive?

Purpose and Audience

1. Where does Golinkin state his thesis? Why does he wait so long to state it?

2. Evaluate Golinkin's title. Does he expect it to arouse interest, to surprise, or to do something else? Explain.

3. Does Golinkin expect his readers to be receptive to his ideas? How do you know?

Style and Structure

1. Golinkin opens the essay by describing a scene from *Gladiator,* an explicitly violent film set in ancient Rome. Why does he begin his essay in this way?

What point is he making by comparing contemporary sports figures to gladiators?

2. At the end of paragraph 5, Golinkin asks a **rhetorical question**. What is the purpose of this question? How does it signal a shift in the essay?

3. Throughout the essay, Golinkin uses the first person plural, which is signaled by pronouns like *we* and *our*. Why do you think he chose to use these pronouns?

4. Golinkin devotes the first six paragraphs of the essay to establishing that sports can have a dangerous and deadly human cost. Does this opening strategy undermine his argument? Is the second part of his essay as strong as the first part? Explain.

5. Do you think Golinkin should have provided more evidence to support his thesis? If so, what kind? Explain.

6. **Vocabulary Project.** Golinkin claims, "Life is not going to be easy, or safe, even for the competent" (10). What does the word *competent* mean in this context?

Journal Entry

Do you like to take physical risks? Why or why not? What is your impression of those who engage in extreme sports?

Writing Workshop

1. Golinkin claims that children learn lessons from organized athletics that "they cannot learn anywhere else" (7). Write an essay in which you agree or disagree with this claim. Use your own experience to support your thesis.

2. In paragraph 10, Golinkin says that overprotectiveness threatens children's spiritual and emotional growth and makes them ill prepared to cope with the future. Do you think that today's parents are too protective of their children? Write an essay in which you agree or disagree with Golinkin's position.

3. **Working with Sources.** According to Golinkin, parents should let their children play "dangerous" sports, even if it results in a broken leg or a concussion. Do you agree? To prepare for this assignment, review the other essays in this casebook, and try to answer the following questions. (If you need more information, research these questions online.)

   • How dangerous are youth sports?
   • How many children are seriously injured each year?
   • How many children die?
   • What are the long-term effects of these sports injuries?

   Be sure to include parenthetical documentation for references to your sources as well as to Golinkin's essay, and include a works-cited page. (See Chapter 18 for information on MLA documentation.)

Combining the Patterns

Where in the essay does Golinkin use **cause and effect**? How does it support his overall point and purpose?

Thematic Connections

- "Let Steroids into the Hall of Fame" (page 21)
- "Ten Ways We Get the Odds Wrong" (page 250)
- "Brains versus Brawn" (page 377)
- "Why Chinese Mothers Are Superior" (page 408)

DANIEL J. FLYNN

Football Does a Body Good (Nannyism Doesn't)

Daniel J. Flynn writes a regular column for *Spectator.org*. His writing has also appeared in the *Boston Globe,* the *American Conservative,* the *National Review,* and other publications. He has written several books, including *A Conservative History of the American Left* (2008) and *Blue Collar Intellectuals: When the Enlightened and the Everyman Elevated America* (2011). Flynn also blogs about politics, movies, and sports.

Background on youth football and head injuries Over a million teenagers play high school football; an estimated 2.8 million more children play the sport below the high school level. Not surprisingly, recent studies of brain injuries, traumas that can happen to even the youngest players, have attracted the attention of youth football leagues. For example, a 2011 study from Virginia Tech University examined seven- and eight-year-olds who played youth-league football; the results showed that children experienced hits to the head that were similar to the collisions of adult players. As a result, some sports leagues have taken steps to try to make the game safer. For example, Pop Warner, America's largest youth football organization, changed its rules to limit collisions and other potentially dangerous forms of contact, and many football associations at the college and high school levels have also implemented safety measures. Perhaps the larger question, however, is whether parents should continue to encourage their children to participate in a sport that could cause physical injury, including brain damage.

Should consenting adults be allowed to play football? 1

Prior to a debate on the subject at New York University earlier this 2 month, 53 percent of the audience opposed a ban on college football (and just 16 percent supported). Following the debate, 53 percent of the audience supported a ban.

That dramatic opinion shift comes in the wake of several decleaters to 3 the game's reputation.

In March, the NFL came down hard on the New Orleans Saints, whose 4 bounty program offered financial incentives to defenders for injuring opposing players. More than 1,500 players have joined lawsuits against the league for not informing them of the dangers of the game. The suicide of Junior Seau, whose extremely long and violent NFL career unleashed not unreasonable speculation that so many jarring hits may have unmoored the beloved linebacker's mental circuits, has hurt the league worse in every way imaginable than the Saints or the suits.

"American football is dying," John Kass writes in the *Chicago Tribune*. 5 "It's about time." He thinks parents will forbid their children from playing, thus starving the NFL of fans and participants. For parents who shuttle their kids to Pop Warner practices, he advises: "So why not make it simple and just give the kids packs of cigarettes instead?"

There's strong evidence, not speculation, that cigarettes cause cancer. 6 There's no evidence, just speculation, that football caused Junior Seau to kill himself. Writers making connections between the self-administered demises of two retired stars (Seau and Dave Duerson) and the gridiron might as well ponder the pitfalls of their own profession. Do the unhappy endings of Ernest Hemingway, Hunter Thompson, and Arthur Koestler demonstrate a link between scribbling and suicide?

Journalists have parlayed a few tragic anecdotes among tens of thou- 7 sands of retired professional athletes into a national anti-football frenzy— in a football-crazed country, no less. But statistics, experience, and observation strongly suggest that the people playing football are healthier than those watching it—and even those refusing to watch.

A government study commissioned by the NFL Players Association 8 found that athletes in the league lived longer than their male counterparts in American society. The study looked at 3,439 men who played for five years or longer in the league between 1959 and 1993 and discovered 334 deaths. Had the results mirrored statistical norms among American men, the researchers would have found 625 deaths. It turns out that professional football players have lower rates of cancer and heart disease.

Who would have guessed that there are health benefits to all that run- 9 ning, jumping, pushing, and pulling?

The number of football deaths at all levels has fallen dramatically over 10 the last half century. Present hysteria aside, rule changes and advances in equipment have made it a safer game. During the second half of the 1960s, brain-injury deaths averaged more than twenty per year for football players. That figure is now less than five per year in a sport played by millions.

Perhaps four deaths annually, and an uncountable number of concus- 11 sions, is an unacceptable price for what amounts to an amusement. Former *American Spectator* writer Malcolm Gladwell said as much in that NYU debate by wondering aloud about the ethics of *watching* a game in which contestants risk life and limb. But every year about 40 Americans die skiing, about 800 die bicycling, and about 3,500 die swimming.

Are those dangerous activities permissi- 12 ble because they haven't captured voyeurs the way the NFL has?

Like football, there are benefits to ski- 13 ing, cycling, and swimming. There aren't figures on how many lives those activities extend and enhance. But sensible people know that skiing, cycling, and swimming are on the whole good for you.

> " It's a shame that the smart-set isn't smart enough to grasp the benefits of contact sports. "

So is football.   14

When I played in high school, I spent five to six days a week working 15
out in the weight room and sprinting on the track in anticipation of the
season. I strangely ran with weighed-down tires roped to my waist, broad-
jumped my way up stadium bleachers, and imbibed powder-based con-
coctions that the vitamin store insisted were healthy but that my palate
insisted were not. All that trouble resulted in a touchdown reception, a
fumble recovery, and a few special teams tackles. I spent most of my senior
year on the sidelines rather than on the field.

Football never bruised my brain. It bruised my ego.   16

One senses an ego bruise may be responsible for the football-phobic 17
jumping on the pile. Eggheads resenting all the attention jocks received
way back when now relish bestowing the wrong kind of attention upon
them. Thus, a cultural tic masquerades as a public-health crusade.

It's a shame that the smart-set isn't smart enough to grasp the benefits 18
of contact sports.

One rarely sees neighborhood kids in pickup football games anymore. 19
They're too busy playing video games, text messaging, and friending strangers on Facebook. The unhealthy aversion to football (and other sports not
named "soccer") has little to do with head injuries and much to do with an
indoor society that's lost its head. Surely strenuous outdoor activity is a
fine remedy for what ails climate-controlled, obese, antiseptic adolescence.

Playing football is good for you. Being a wuss isn't.   20

•   •   •

Comprehension

1. According to Flynn, what recent events have changed some people's opinions of football?

2. Flynn quotes newspaper columnist John Kass, who compares playing
   youth football to smoking cigarettes. How does Flynn respond to Kass's
   comment? Do you agree?

3. Who does Flynn blame for the current "national anti-football frenzy" (7)?

4. In paragraph 8, Flynn refers to a study sponsored by the NFL Players
   Association, which looked at 3,439 men who played for five years or longer in the NFL. What were the results of this study?

5. According to Flynn, what are the benefits of football and other contact
   sports? Do you think that these benefits outweigh the potential risks?
   Why or why not?

Purpose and Audience

1. This essay originally appeared in the *American Spectator,* a review of conservative political opinion. Does the writer's argument have any social or
   political implications? If so, what are they?

2. What do you think Flynn hopes to accomplish with his essay? Does he want to change people's minds? Move people to action? Something else? Explain.

3. Does Flynn expect his readers to be sympathetic to his argument? How do you know?

Style and Structure

1. Where does Flynn address opposing points of view? Why do you think he chose to address these opposing points of view where he does?

2. In paragraph 7, Flynn implies that journalists writing about the dangers of football are committing a logical **fallacy**. What is this logical fallacy? (See "Recognizing Fallacies," page 535.) Do you agree with his assessment?

3. Flynn's essay includes several one-sentence paragraphs. What is the function of these paragraphs? How do they affect the tone of the essay?

4. **Vocabulary Project.** In paragraph 10, Flynn refers to the "present hysteria" about the dangers of football. What does the word *hysteria* mean? Investigate the word's origins and connotations. How does this word choice reinforce Flynn's argument?

5. What does Flynn emphasize in his two-sentence conclusion? Should he have emphasized a different point (or points)? Explain.

Journal Entry

When discussing the suicides of two retired football players in paragraph 6, Flynn dismisses the connection between the sport and their deaths. Do you find this dismissal convincing? Why or why not?

Writing Workshop

1. **Working with Sources.** In paragraph 8, Flynn cites a study commissioned by the NFL that indicated that former NFL players were healthier than men in the general population. Investigate this study further on your own. Then, write an essay that takes a position on the health effects of football. Make sure that you include parenthetical documentation for information you find as well as for specific references to Flynn's essay and that you include a works-cited page. (See Chapter 18 for information on MLA documentation.)

2. Flynn suggests that contact sports like football are beneficial. What did he gain from his own experiences playing football in high school? Reflect on your own participation in a sport. What did you learn? Was the experience valuable? Write an essay that uses your own background and observations to support or challenge Flynn's position.

3. Flynn says that young people are often overprotected by an "indoor society that's lost its head" and trapped in a "climate-controlled, obese, anti-

septic adolescence" (19). Do you agree with him? Write an essay that responds to Flynn's claims.

Combining the Patterns

Where does Flynn use **cause and effect** in this essay? Why? Explain your answer.

Thematic Connections

- "Let Steroids into the Hall of Fame" (page 21)
- "Who Killed Benny Paret?" (page 337)
- "A Peaceful Woman Explains Why She Carries a Gun" (page 353)

Should Guns Be Allowed on College Campuses?

In this photo taken on March 1, 2011, Adrienne O'Reilly, Oklahoma director for Students for Concealed Carry on Campus, carries an empty gun holster on the Oklahoma State University campus in Stillwater, Oklahoma, to show support for proposed legislation that would allow concealed weapons to be carried on school grounds.

© James Gibbard/Associated Press

•　•　•

Statistically, colleges and universities are relatively safe environments for students, faculty, and administrators. Indeed, they are probably among the safest public spaces in the United States. According to some studies, the homicide rate on campuses is one in one million students, as compared to fifty-seven deaths per million people in the general population. On average, there are fewer than twenty homicides a year on the grounds of American colleges and universities. This general pattern holds true across a range of crimes even when researchers take into account the lengthy semester breaks that leave campuses sparsely populated. The pattern also remains consistent regardless of a college's location. "Contrary to the concerns of many parents . . . about sending their children to college in some 'dangerous big city,' campuses in urban centers do not tend to have higher rates of victimization than do those in remote, rural locations," writes Northeastern University criminology professor James Alan Fox.

Of course, colleges and universities are not crime- or violence-free, although suicides are one hundred times more likely on campus than homicides. And despite their relative rarity, recent high-profile mass shootings on campuses have captured — and horrified — the public imagination. The 2007 massacre at Virginia Tech was the deadliest shooting by a single shooter in U.S. history; in that incident, a student killed thirty-two people and injured seventeen others. In 2008, an undergraduate at Louisiana Technical College killed two people and herself in a classroom. Also in 2008, a former graduate student at Northern Illinois University killed five people and injured twenty-one. Since 1990, there have been more than twenty multiple-victim shooting incidents on college campuses.

These and similar incidents have led to a nationwide conversation among public officials, college administrators, students, and others about how to make colleges safer. The discussion often boils down to two issues: how to prevent such events and how to respond to such events. Solutions include a range of measures, from profiling troubled individuals and focusing on the general psychological health of students to improving communications during emergencies and setting up procedures for locking down campuses. Perhaps the most controversial response to these events, however, involves the status of firearms and policies banning — or allowing — students and others to carry guns on campuses. As always, the discussion of gun rights touches on fundamental issues of personal freedom and public safety. These issues come into even sharper focus in the context of college and university campuses, which tend to be seen as orderly, peaceful places.

The four essays in this casebook illuminate the complex — and often polarizing — aspects of this discussion. In "Do We Really Need More Guns on Campus?" David Skorton and Glenn Altschuler argue that allowing more guns on campus will make colleges and universities less safe. For example, they note that a proliferation of armed students would make it far more difficult for campus police and law enforcement officials to respond to an emergency with multiple shooters. The essay by Students for Gun-Free Schools, an advocacy organization that emerged in the wake of the Virginia Tech shootings, makes a comprehensive case against allowing guns on campus ("Why Our Campuses Are Safer without Concealed Handguns"); among other points, the writers suggest that the presence of concealed firearms will detract from a free and open learning environment. In "Why Our Campuses Are *Not* Safer without Concealed Handguns," Students for Concealed Carry, another advocacy organization, offers point-by-point counterarguments to the claims made by Students for Gun-Free Schools. Finally, Timothy Wheeler, a retired physician and gun rights activist, criticizes public policy experts, medical professionals, and "timid" college bureaucrats for restricting the rights of those who wish to carry guns on campus and elsewhere ("There's a Reason They Choose Schools").

DAVID SKORTON AND GLENN ALTSCHULER

Do We Really Need More Guns on Campus?

David Skorton (b. 1949), President of Cornell University, is a professor of medicine who previously served as president of the University of Iowa, among other posts. Glenn Altschuler (b. 1950) is Cornell's Vice President for University Relations, Dean of the School of Continuing Education, and the Thomas and Dorothy Litwin Professor of American Studies.

Background on the 2007 Virginia Tech shootings and gun policies On April 16, 2007, a Virginia Tech senior shot and killed thirty-two people and wounded seventeen others on the university's campus. In the wake of this horrific event — the most deadly mass killing by a single shooter in United States history — Americans reflected on the causes of the massacre as well as on possible preventative measures. The student shooter had a history of psychological and behavioral problems. He had been declared a danger to himself by a Virginia court in 2005; his professors had reported strange behavior, and the university had previously investigated him for stalking female students. Still, he had been able to purchase weapons because of a gap in the federal and state laws that forbid individuals legally declared mentally unsound from buying guns. The Virginia Tech shooting led to the first federal gun legislation in thirteen years: the new law strengthened procedures for identifying and tracking mentally ill people and stopping them from buying guns. However, some — for example, Students for Concealed Carry, an organization that advocates for those who wish to carry legally concealed weapons on campuses — disagree with this emphasis on restricting firearms, especially on campuses. (Some colleges do allow concealed weapons on their campuses.)

Given a sense of urgency by the murders at Sandy Hook Elementary 1 School, the gun control debate rages on across the nation. Less well known is that this year many state legislatures will consider whether to require public colleges and universities to allow guns on campus. We oppose legislation that will prevent colleges from setting their own gun policies — and will make students, staff, and faculty less safe.

Today the vast majority of U.S. colleges and universities, public and 2 private, prohibit guns. Federal law is silent on the issue, and the states are somewhat divided. Five states — Colorado, Mississippi, Oregon, Utah, and Wisconsin — have laws allowing "concealed carry" at public colleges and universities.

Details of the laws vary. In Wisconsin administrators can prohibit 3 weapons from campus facilities if they post no-weapons signs on each building. Mississippi allows concealed carry on campus only for those who complete a firearm safety course. Utah is the only state that specifically forbids public colleges and universities from banning the carrying of concealed weapons.

The rest of the states divide into those that do not allow concealed 4 weapons on campuses (twenty-one) and those that permit colleges to set their own gun policies (twenty-four).

After the shootings at Virginia Tech in 2007, in which thirty-three 5 people died, and at Northern Illinois University, where six were killed in 2008, debates on campus gun policies in state legislatures soared. Two years ago only one state permitted concealed carry at public institutions, compared with five today. In 2011 and 2012 state legislators introduced at least thirty-four bills to allow concealed firearms on campuses. Although most of those measures failed to pass, many of them are back on the docket this year.

Proponents of concealed carry laws usually argue that the constitu- 6 tional right to bear arms should apply everywhere, on campuses as well as off; that people are safer when they have guns to protect themselves; and that an armed bystander could put a stop to a mass shooting in progress. "The current rules guarantee criminals a free shot," says David Burnett of Students for Concealed Carry, which the *Wall Street Journal* calls a "major force" for guns on campus. "Allowing licensed concealed carry would give potential attackers pause and ultimately give innocent victims a fighting chance."

With that view in mind, let's look at what actually happens on college 7 campuses.

Colleges and universities are far safer than most public spaces in the United States. The campus homicide rate is about one death per one million people, compared to fifty-seven deaths per million in the general population. In the college-age population in general, moreover, homicide is the second leading cause of death, while on college campuses it remains a rare event.

> " Colleges and universities are far safer than most public spaces in the United States. "

Still, no campus is crime-free. Would 9 more guns on campus prevent crimes?

In the *Chronicle of Higher Education* last June, Gary Olson, former pro- 10 vost of Idaho State University, stated categorically that "there is no recorded incident in which a victim — or spectator — of a violent crime on a campus has prevented that crime by brandishing a weapon." As for the extremely rare case of an active shooter, we shudder at the prospect of campus police, who often do bear arms, rushing into a scene where more than one person is firing a gun. As Regina G. Lawson, chief of police at Wake Forest University, said at a 2008 conference on higher-education law, "When you're responding to a situation like that, and someone's in plain clothes with a gun, who's the bad guy? Who are you going to take out to save the lives of the ten thousand other students you're trying to protect?"

Like all police officers, campus police would likely have a low rate of 11 accuracy in such chaotic situations, given the likelihood that the officer is moving, the target is moving, and victims are fleeing in every direction. (*Time* magazine reported in January that New York City police in gunfights hit their target 18 percent of the time.) The average student, professor, or staff member carrying a weapon is likely to be far less accurate, substantially raising the odds of more innocent victims.

Campuses are a risky environment for guns in other ways as well. We 12 don't need to put more firearms in the hands of college students, a cohort that includes emotionally volatile young men and women and abusers of alcohol and drugs. How many accidental shootings will happen under the influence? How many disputes will turn deadly if a gun is nearby?

Consider also an even more compelling fact: suicide is the second lead- 13 ing cause of death for college students (after accidents). According to the Harvard Injury Control Research Center, 85 percent of attempted suicides using guns are fatal, compared to only 2 percent of attempts by a far more common method, drug overdose. If guns are more readily available, many more suicide attempts will likely succeed.

By all means, let's get on with the national and state-level debate about 14 how best to balance second-amendment rights with public safety. We applaud President Obama's directive to scale up federally funded research on gun violence — research that for decades has been squelched by the political muscle of gun rights advocates. More research means better-informed choices.

But meanwhile, let our colleges and universities set their own policies. 15 We believe that the great majority will continue to prohibit guns, and our campus communities will be all the safer.

•   •   •

Comprehension

1. According to the writers, what is the firearms policy of a "vast majority" (2) of American colleges and universities? Why is it important for the writers to point out the prevalence of this policy?

2. What has caused an increase in debates about gun policies in state legislatures over the last several years?

3. According to the writers, how would armed students cause problems for campus police?

4. Why are campuses "a risky environment for guns" (12)? How do the writers characterize college students? Do you think this characterization is accurate?

Purpose and Audience

1. What is the writers' purpose? Are they writing to change their readers' minds? Propose a course of action? Attract national attention or support for a cause? Inform their readers? Something else? Explain.

2. In paragraphs 2–4, the writers provide a brief overview of various state laws and campus policies. Do you think the essay would benefit from more information about these laws? Would more specific explanation better serve the writers' purpose? Why or why not?

3. What is the function of paragraph 8? Why is it important to the writers' overall argument and purpose?

Style and Structure

1. Where do the writers state their thesis? How would you restate it in your own words?

2. Where do the writers address opposing arguments? Do you think they represent these opposing views fairly and accurately?

3. Paragraph 7 consists of a single sentence. How would you describe the writers' tone in this sentence, particularly given the paragraph that precedes it? What does this sentence accomplish?

4. In paragraph 10, the writers quote two authorities and use these quotations to support the essay's thesis. Do you find these appeals to authority effective and persuasive? Why or why not?

5. **Vocabulary Project.** Skorton and Altschuler write: "In the *Chronicle of Higher Education* last June, Gary Olson, former provost of Idaho State University, stated categorically that 'there is no recorded incident in which a victim — or spectator — of a violent crime on a campus has prevented that crime by brandishing a weapon'" (10). What does the word *categorically* mean in this context? Why do you think the writers use this word to modify *stated*? Is it necessary?

Journal Entry

The writers worry about putting more guns in the hands of college students: "How many accidental shootings will happen under the influence [of alcohol and drugs]? How many disputes will turn deadly if a gun is nearby?" (12). Do you agree that college is "a risky environment for guns" (12)? Is this assessment consistent with your own experiences and your observations of the college students you know?

Writing Workshop

1. **Working with Sources.** What is the firearms policy on your college campus? Find out the rules, and learn whether they are determined by the state or by the school. Then, talk to campus security personnel, college officials, students, and other people on campus to gather a range of views on this topic, and write an essay that takes a position on the appropriateness of your school's firearms policy. Be sure to document your sources and to include a works-cited page. (See Chapter 18 for information on MLA documentation.)

2. Skorton and Altschuler argue that colleges and universities should be able to set policies regarding the possession of firearms on campus. Do you agree that they should be the final authority, or do you think such decisions should be better left to individual states or to the federal government — or to individual gun owners? Write an essay that takes a position on this issue.

3. The writers quote gun rights proponent David Burnett, who argues, "The current rules [prohibiting firearms on campus] guarantee criminals a free shot. . . . Allowing licensed concealed carry would give potential attackers pause and ultimately give innocent victims a fighting chance" (6). How do you respond to this argument? Do you agree with Burnett's logic? Write an essay that responds to Burnett.

Combining the Patterns

Where in the essay do the authors use **classification and division**? Why is this pattern necessary for their overall purpose?

Thematic Connections

- "Thirty-Eight Who Saw Murder Didn't Call the Police" (page 128)
- "College Pressures" (page 448)

Why Our Campuses Are Safer without Concealed Handguns

Students for Gun-Free Schools is a public advocacy organization founded by a number of people, including Omar Samaha and Randa Samaha, whose sister Reema was killed in the 2007 Virginia Tech massacre. The organization, which now has dozens of chapters at universities across the country, opposes laws that allow students to carry concealed firearms on college campuses. In 2009, a chapter at the University of Texas in Austin organized a large rally and walk-out protesting state legislation allowing guns on campuses. SGFS's motto is "Armed with knowledge, not guns."

Background on campus crime and safety Generally, colleges are relatively safe places. For example, a student is much less likely to die in a homicide on his or her campus than away from it. Recent work by researchers such as professor James Alan Fox at Northeastern University indicates that college campuses have low rates of violence and violent crimes overall — a reality that holds true at both urban and rural institutions. Horrific events like the Virginia Tech massacre understandably capture the public imagination and lead to concerns about the safety of students. However, the more common dangers of campus life are tied to binge drinking and to suicide (almost 1,200 college students commit suicide every year).

In the wake of tragic shootings at Virginia Tech and Northern Illi- 1 nois University, a group called Students for Concealed Carry on Campus formed to advocate for the "right" of students and faculty to carry concealed handguns at colleges and universities in the United States. This group was quickly joined by the National Rifle Association and other pro-gun organizations that had been lobbying for years to liberalize America's concealed carry laws.

Frequently lost in the national debate that ensued was the fact that our 2 nation's colleges and universities are some of the safest places in our country in large part because their campuses, in almost all cases, have remained gun-free.

The overwhelming majority of the 4,314 colleges and universities in 3 the United States prohibit students and faculty from carrying concealed handguns on campus (the exceptions include public colleges and universities in Utah; Blue Ridge Community College in Weyers Cave, Virginia; and Colorado State University in Fort Collins, Colorado). Despite high-profile shootings like the ones mentioned above, homicides at American colleges and universities remain rare events.

A 2001 study by the U.S. Department of Education found that the 4 overall homicide rate at postsecondary education institutions was 0.07 per 100,000 of enrollment in 1999. By comparison, the criminal homicide rate in the United States was 5.7 per 100,000 persons overall in 1999, and 14.1 per 100,000 for persons ages seventeen to twenty-nine. Another study, conducted by the Department of Justice, found that 93 percent of violent crimes that victimize college students occur off campus. This research demonstrates conclusively that students on the campuses of postsecondary institutions are significantly safer than both their off-campus counterparts and the nation as a whole.

Students for Gun-Free Schools (SGFS) believes these results can be 5 attributed largely to strict policies that have kept firearms off our nation's campuses. Our colleges and universities are safe sanctuaries for learning, and we believe they would be endangered by the presence of concealed handguns for the following reasons:

1. Concealed handguns would detract from a healthy learning environment;

2. More guns on campus would create additional risk for students;

3. Shooters would not be deterred by concealed carry permit holders;

4. Concealed carry permit holders are not always "law-abiding" citizens; and

5. Concealed carry permit holders are not required to have law enforcement training.

1. Concealed Handguns Would Detract from a Healthy Learning Environment

In order to foster a healthy learning environment at America's colleges 6 and universities, it is critical that students and faculty feel safe on campus. If concealed carry were allowed on America's campuses, there is no doubt that many students would feel uncomfortable about not knowing whether their professors and/or fellow students were carrying handguns. Students and teachers must be able to express themselves freely in classroom environments, where discussions frequently touch on controversial topics that arouse passion. The introduction of handguns on our campuses would inhibit this dialogue by creating fear of possible retaliation. Whether it's a classroom debate, a student-teacher conversation about a grade, or an informal interaction in a dormitory, the presence of hidden handguns would restrain the open exchange of ideas that is so critical to the college experience.

Americans, in overwhelming numbers, believe that guns have no place 7 at our colleges and universities. In one national survey, 94 percent of Americans answered "No" when asked, "Do you think regular citizens should be allowed to bring their guns [onto] college campuses?"

2. More Guns on Campus Would Create Additional Risk for Students

Allowing concealed carry permit holders to bring handguns onto col-   8
lege campuses would raise a host of public safety concerns for institutions
that have a legal duty to provide secure environments for their students,
faculty, and visitors. As noted in a 2007 report by the Brady Campaign to
Prevent Gun Violence, there are four reasons why gun violence would be
likely to increase if more guns were present on college campuses: (1) The
prevalence of drugs and alcohol; (2) The risk of suicide and mental health
issues; (3) The likelihood of gun thefts; and (4) An increased risk of accidental shootings .

A 2007 study by the National Center on Addiction and Substance   9
Abuse at Columbia University found that "[N]early half of America's
5.4 million full-time college students abuse drugs or drink alcohol on
binges at least once a month." Another study found that alcohol is involved
in 95 percent of the violent crime on campus. The combination of alcohol,
drugs, and guns is a dangerous mix that could lead to additional, and more
lethal, violence on campus. A 2002 study by the Harvard School of Public
Health compared students who have a firearm at college with those who do
not have a firearm. They found that students who have a firearm at college
are more likely to binge drink, drive a motor vehicle after binge drinking,
use illegal drugs, vandalize property, and get into trouble with the police.

Suicide and mental health are also substantial issues on college cam-   10
puses. One study found that 24 percent of college students had thought
about attempting suicide and 5 percent had actually attempted to kill themselves. Firearms, of course, make many types of violence more lethal. Suicide
attempts are successful more than 90 percent of the time when a firearm is
used. By comparison, such attempts are fatal only 3 percent of the time
when a drug overdose is the method used. One study that examined college
student suicide from 1920–2004 found that, "It is the reduced use of firearms as a method of suicide that is responsible for virtually all of the benefit
associated with being a student . . . and that the relationship between student status and firearms may be the key to understanding why students
commit suicide at a lower rate than does the general U.S. population."

Allowing concealed handguns on campus would also increase the risk   11
of gun theft and accidental shootings. College dorm rooms are typically
small, with few places available to lock up or secure a handgun. They also
experience considerable numbers of visitors who could gain unauthorized
access to these firearms.

3. Shooters Would Not Be Deterred by Concealed Carry Permit Holders

The gun lobby frequently advances the argument that shooters target   12
gun-free zones such as college campuses for their attacks because they are
unlikely to receive initial resistance.

This ignores the fact that homicides and shootings at American col- 13
leges and universities are rare events in large part because of these institutions' current policies regarding firearms on campus. In 2003, for example,
there were 11,920 total gun homicides in the United States, but only ten
total murders on the nation's college campuses.

Campus shooters are also frequently suicidal. Most of the campus 14
shootings in America in recent years (i.e., Virginia Tech, Northern Illinois
University, Louisiana Technical College, etc.) were murder-suicides. These
shooters left home on the morning of their attacks knowing they were
going to die by gunfire before the day was over — their goal was simply to
take as many people with them as they could. It is unlikely these shooters
would have been deterred by the knowledge that their fellow students (or
campus faculty) might be armed. In fact, it is possible that a college campus that allows staff and faculty to carry concealed handguns might provide a more attractive target to such shooters. Lacking any fear of death,
they might welcome the opportunity to provoke shootouts and crossfire
among relatively untrained concealed carry permit holders in order to increase casualties.

There have also been numerous incidents in recent years where shoot- 15
ers have targeted what might be deemed "gun-full zones" for their attacks,
including:

> May 8, 2006 — Michael Kennedy, eighteen, attacks Fairfax County Police
> Sully District Station in Virginia, firing more than seventy rounds and
> killing two officers before police are able to take him down. Kennedy is
> armed with five handguns and two rifles, including a semiautomatic
> AK-47 assault rifle, and carries more than three hundred rounds of am-
> munition.

> May 19, 2007 — Jason Hamilton shoots and kills his wife at home and then
> attacks a sheriff's department at Latah County Courthouse and a church
> in Moscow, Idaho. Hamilton kills a total of three people, including a police
> officer, before taking his own life. He is armed with an AK-47 assault rifle
> and an M1 carbine despite a long history of domestic violence, mental ill-
> ness, and run-ins with the police. Local resident and University of Idaho
> student Pete Hussmann, twenty, races to the courthouse on his bike armed
> with a .45 caliber handgun and is shot
> four times by Hamilton. "It was like a war
> zone," says Hussmann. Two other law en-
> forcement officers are wounded.

" There is no evidence
that suicidal shooters
would be deterred   16
from attacks on
college campuses
by concealed carry
permit holders. "

There is no evidence that suicidal shooters would be deterred from attacks on college campuses by concealed carry permit
holders. To the extent that they could provoke firefights with such individuals in
crowded college classrooms and create additional mayhem, they might even seek out
such confrontations.

4. Concealed Carry Permit Holders Are Not Always "Law-Abiding" Citizens

The gun lobby frequently claims that those with permits to carry concealed handguns are "law-abiding citizens," or even the most law-abiding citizens in their communities. This is not always true. Two states, Alaska and Vermont, do not even require residents to obtain a permit to carry a concealed weapon. Individuals in these states can buy a handgun through an unregulated private sale (no background check required) and then carry it in public. [17]

Thirty-eight states have a "shall-issue" policy for concealed carry permits, meaning that officials may not arbitrarily deny an application to those who meet a basic set of requirements. The primary requirement for obtaining a permit in these states is to pass a background check through the National Instant Criminal Background Check System (NICS). The purpose of the background check is to ascertain whether the applicant is prohibited under federal law from owning and purchasing firearms. Those with felony convictions are automatically prohibited. The only misdemeanor convictions that would prohibit someone from owning and purchasing firearms, however, are those related to incidents of domestic violence. Someone who obtains a concealed carry permit in a shall-issue state could have a rap sheet with other types of misdemeanor convictions, including violent offenses. [18]

The National Instant Criminal Background Check System is also not foolproof. A recent study found that the NICS database is "deeply flawed" and missing millions of disqualifying records. Most troubling, nine out of ten mental health records that would disqualify individuals from purchasing firearms are not currently in the database. One-fourth of felony conviction records have also not been submitted to NICS by the states. [19]

The bottom line is that even if someone passes a background check and qualifies for a concealed carry permit (if their state requires one), that person is not necessarily a law-abiding citizen. They could have a substantial criminal record involving misdemeanor offenses, or a history of mental illness. It is notable that campus shooters including Gang Lu, Wayne Lo, Robert Flores, Biswanath Halder, Seung-Hui Cho, Latina Williams, and Steven Kazmierczak passed background checks in acquiring the firearms used in their attacks. Some possessed a concealed carry permit in their home states; others would have qualified had they applied. Finally, individuals who are prohibited under federal law from owning or purchasing firearms can still pass a background check (and potentially qualify for a concealed carry permit) if their disqualifying records have not been transferred to NICS. [20]

Research has demonstrated that those who obtain concealed carry permits can pose a threat to public safety. [21]

A Violence Policy Center study found that Texas concealed handgun license holders were arrested for weapon-related offenses at a rate 81 percent higher than the general population of Texas aged twenty-one and [22] older (offenses included 279 assaults, 671 unlawfully carrying a weapon, and 172 deadly conduct/discharge of a firearm). Between January 1, 1996, and August 31, 2001, Texas concealed handgun license holders were arrested for 5,314 crimes — including murder, rape, kidnapping, and theft.

A 2007 investigation by the Florida *Sun-Sentinel* found that the state's 23 permit system had granted concealed carry permits to more than 1,400 individuals who pled guilty or no contest to a felony, 216 individuals with outstanding warrants, 128 individuals with active domestic violence restraining orders, and 6 registered sex offenders.

5. Concealed Carry Permit Holders Are Not Required to Have Law Enforcement Training

The forty-eight states in the U.S. that allow residents to carry concealed 24 handguns do not require them to have any formal law enforcement training. The training requirement to obtain a concealed carry permit in a "shall-issue" state is typically a day class. Many shall-issue states do not even require the applicant to fire his/her handgun at a range to demonstrate proficiency or even basic competency with the weapon. An example would be Virginia, where a four-hour sit-down session in a classroom is sufficient to meet the state's training requirement.

This is in direct contrast to the intensive training required of law en- 25 forcement officers who are currently called on to safeguard our nation's colleges and universities. These officers start receiving training in how to safely handle a sidearm — and in demonstrating discretion in using lethal force — long before they ever see actual duty in their communities. This training then continues throughout their career in law enforcement. Police departments typically require their officers to qualify one to four times a year with their duty weapon.

Nonetheless, even trained law enforcement officers rarely hit their tar- 26 gets when firing at other human beings. One 2006 study examined three decades of bullet hit rates among larger U.S. police departments and found that officers hit their targets approximately 20 percent of the time. The New York City Police Department's Firearms Discharge report for 2006 showed similar results. That year, their officers intentionally fired a gun at a person 364 times, hitting their target only 103 times — a success rate of 28.3 percent. Commenting on that success rate, New York City Police Commissioner Ray Kelly said, "When you factor in all of the other elements that are involved in shooting at an adversary, that's a high hit rate. The adrenaline flow, the movement of the target, the movement of the shooter, the officer, the lighting conditions, the weather . . . I think it is a high rate when you consider all of the variables."

Given the record of trained law enforcement officers, how often would 27 relatively untrained concealed carry permit holders hit their targets when opening fire on college campuses? Recent shootings on America's campuses have occurred in crowded classrooms and involved a great deal of chaos, with students panicked and running for their lives. Concealed carry permit holders discharging their weapons in such situations would be unlikely to have clear lines of fire. If multiple students drew handguns, just identifying the actual "shooter" or target would be challenging. The potential for collateral damage is enormous, even assuming that concealed carry permit holders would make sound decisions about when to discharge their handguns.

Law enforcement officers responding to such emergencies would also 28 face enormous difficulties. If police arrived on the scene of a campus shooting and found multiple students with handguns drawn, how would they know who their target is? This scenario was contemplated by the Virginia Tech Review Panel, which commented: "If numerous people had been rushing around with handguns outside Norris Hall on the morning of April 16, [2007,] the possibility of accidental or mistaken shootings would have increased significantly. The campus police said that the probability would have been high that anyone emerging from a classroom at Norris Hall holding a gun would have been shot."

Despite the fact that there are more than 200 million firearms in pri- 29 vate hands in the United States and forty-eight states now allow some form of concealed carry, instances in which law-abiding citizens successfully shoot and kill criminals are exceedingly rare. In 2005, there were a total of 12,352 gun-related homicides in the United States. Yet, during the same year, the FBI reported only 143 justifiable homicides involving a firearm. A 2000 study by the Harvard School of Public Health concluded that, "Guns are used to threaten and intimidate far more often than they are used in self-defense. Most self-reported self-defense gun uses may well be illegal and against the interests of society." This is no doubt partially due to the lack of formal training among those purchasing firearms and receiving permits to carry concealed handguns in the United States.

The notion that individuals with concealed carry permits are going to 30 make prudent decisions about when to discharge their firearms on school campuses is dubious at best, as is the notion that these individuals would successfully take down active shooters while avoiding collateral damage in chaotic situations. The safest policy to limit potential violence is to prohibit students and faculty from keeping handguns on campus and allow trained law enforcement officers to provide for campus security.

•   •   •

Comprehension

1. According to the writers, what often gets "lost in the national debate" (2) about gun laws after high-profile school shootings? Why is this important to the writers' main point?

2. According to the 2007 Brady Campaign report cited by the writers, why will gun violence likely increase if guns are allowed on campuses? What four reasons does the report give?

3. The writers discuss "shall-issue" policies (18) for concealed carry permits. What is a "shall-issue" policy?

4. According to the writers, what is the "bottom line" with regard to "law-abiding" (20) concealed carry permit holders? Why are the writers skeptical of the "gun lobby" on this issue?

Purpose and Audience

1. Students for Gun-Free Schools is a national organization devoted to keeping guns off campuses. For example, it works to influence legislation and policy directly. How do you think this mission affects the writers' purpose in this essay?

2. Before the writers list their reasons for keeping guns off campus, they establish that campuses are relatively safe places. Why do you think they do so?

3. How would you restate the essay's thesis in your own words?

4. The writers often refer to claims made by the "gun lobby," but they do not define this term. Should they have done so? Why or why not?

5. Why do the writers bring up the "bullet hit rate" (26) of the New York City Police Department? How is it related to their main argument?

Style and Structure

1. In their opening paragraph, why do the writers put the word *right* in quotation marks?

2. In paragraph 7, the writers cite an unnamed "national survey" indicating that 94 percent of Americans think that citizens should not be allowed to bring guns on campuses. Is this information convincing? Is it relevant to the main issue?

3. What is the purpose of the two examples used in paragraph 15?

4. **Vocabulary Project.** In paragraph 27, the writers discuss the "potential for collateral damage" if more students are armed on campus. What connotations does the expression *collateral damage* have? What connotations do you think the writers want it to have in this essay?

Journal Entry

The writers argue that guns on campus would encourage an unhealthy learning environment, restraining exchanges of ideas, inhibiting discussions, making students uncomfortable, and discouraging passionate debate by "creating fear of possible retaliation" (6). Does this seem like a reasonable concern? Why or why not?

Writing Workshop

1. The writers argue that college campuses are relatively safe places. Do you agree? Do you feel safe at your school? Do you think allowing students to carry guns on campus would make colleges less safe? Would you feel more

secure knowing your fellow students and professors might be armed? Write an essay that presents your position on these questions.

2. **Working with Sources.** In the first paragraph, the writers refer to the National Rifle Association and "other pro-gun organizations" that lobby to "liberalize America's concealed carry laws." Do you think gun laws should be "liberalized" or made more restrictive? Write an essay that takes a position on this issue. Before you begin, consult the NRA's website at nra.org and the website of the Brady Campaign Against Gun Violence at bradycampaign.org to get an overview of the opposing positions on this issue. Be sure to document any sources you use and to include a works-cited page. (See Chapter 18 for information on MLA documentation.)

3. Students for Gun-Free Schools was founded in the wake of the Virginia Tech shootings in 2007, and much of the discussion and activism in the aftermath of Virginia Tech and other shootings has focused on guns. Do you believe that guns are the central problem in these events, or even a main cause? Or, do you think the emphasis on firearms and gun laws is misplaced in the context of other issues, such as mental health? Write an essay that answers these questions.

Combining the Patterns

Where in the essay do the writers use **comparison and contrast**? How does this pattern help the writers to develop their main argument?

Thematic Connections

- "Shooting an Elephant" (page 133)
- "Just Walk On By: A Black Man Ponders His Power to Alter Public Space" (page 238)

Why Our Campuses Are *Not* Safer without Concealed Handguns

Founded in 2007, Students for Concealed Carry is a national organization of U.S. college students, faculty, staff, and others who support allowing those with concealed handgun licenses to carry their guns on campuses. The group seeks to raise public awareness about the issue of campus safety and to persuade legislators and college administrators to (in the words of the organization's website) "grant concealed handgun license holders the same rights on college campuses that those licensees currently enjoy in most other unsecured locations." Students for Concealed Carry is known for its national campus "empty holster" protests, in which members visibly wear empty holsters and distribute literature in support of their cause.

Background on concealed carry The phrase *concealed carry* refers to the practice of carrying a concealed gun or other weapon. Concealed carry laws are determined by individual states, not federal law; however, in 2012 a federal court overturned a long-standing Illinois ban on concealed weapons as unconstitutional. Generally, concealed carry laws fall into several categories, including "shall-issue" and "may-issue." In "shall-issue" states, such as Idaho and Pennsylvania, permits are granted to those who meet specific requirements. In "may-issue" states, such as Massachusetts and Maryland, the issuing of permits remains at the discretion of local or state authorities even if the applicant meets basic requirements. In some cases, those applying for concealed carry licenses must demonstrate "good cause" for desiring a permit. States generally require applicants to meet basic criteria. For example, those who have been judged mentally incompetent in court or who have been committed to a mental institution are ineligible. Over the last two decades, more states have become "shall-issue" jurisdictions, which suggests an easing of gun restrictions.

In response to the unprecedented media attention and public support 1 generated by Students for Concealed Carry (SCC), the organization leading the charge to extend concealed carry (of handgun) rights to college campuses, a counter-movement has emerged, operating under the banner Students for Gun-Free Schools (SGFS). SGFS recently released an essay titled "Why Our Campuses Are Safer without Concealed Handguns." This attack on the positions of SCC brings few, if any, new arguments to the table and relies instead on the well-worn arguments put forth by groups like the Brady Campaign to Prevent Gun Violence.

The crux of the SGFS essay is the undeniable fact that college cam- 2 puses typically have lower crime rates than the cities in which they reside.

Tossing academic standards of research and citation to the wind, the essay's introduction simply points out this fact and concludes, "Students for Gun-Free Schools (SGFS) believes these results can be attributed largely to strict policies that have kept firearms off our nation's campuses." Without citing corroborating facts or research, the same gun control advocates who want us to believe that lax gun control laws in nearby states negate the effectiveness of strict gun control laws in the District of Columbia and other tightly regulated cities/states now want us to believe that strict gun control regulations on college campuses are able to stand up against the lax gun control laws in the very cities in which those campuses reside.

To assume a cause-and-effect relationship between the unenforceable 3 gun control regulations on college campuses and the relative safety of college campuses constitutes an astoundingly naïve leap in logic. A similar disparity can be found between the relatively low crime rates in affluent neighborhoods and the higher crime rates in the cities in which those neighborhoods exist. After all, what are college campuses but, essentially, large, affluent neighborhoods?

After making the unsubstantiated claim that strict gun control regula- 4 tions make college campuses safer, the essay moves on to present five reasons why SGFS believes that allowing concealed carry on college campuses would make colleges less safe:

1. Concealed handguns would detract from a healthy learning environment;
2. More guns on campus would create additional risk for students;
3. Shooters would not be deterred by concealed carry permit holders;
4. Concealed carry permit holders are not always "law-abiding" citizens; and
5. Concealed carry permit holders are not required to have law enforcement training.

1. Concealed Handguns Would *Not* Detract from a Healthy Learning Environment

An opponent of concealed carry on campus isn't doing his or her job 5 unless he or she argues, "Concealed handguns would detract from a healthy learning environment." The SGFS essay contends, "If concealed carry were allowed on America's campuses, there is no doubt that many students would feel uncomfortable about not knowing whether their professors and/or fellow students were carrying handguns." This argument not only ignores the fact that, in the absence of metal detectors and X-ray machines at every campus entrance, students already have no way of knowing who, if anyone, is carrying a gun; it also assumes that students would be made more uncomfortable by the presence of guns on campus than they are by the presence of guns off campus.

In most U.S. states approximately 1 percent of the population (one 6
person out of a hundred) is licensed to carry a concealed handgun. Are
students afraid to sit in three-hundred-seat movie theaters knowing that,
statistically speaking, as many as three of their fellow moviegoers may
be legally carrying concealed handguns? Are they afraid to walk through
crowded shopping malls knowing that one out of every hundred shoppers
they pass is potentially carrying a legally concealed handgun? Or do they
go through their daily routines, both on and off campus, never giving
much thought to what is concealed beneath the clothing and within
the handbags of the people they pass? Does SGFS honestly contend that
students on the one hundred U.S. college campuses where concealed carry
is currently allowed, including all public colleges in the states of Utah,
Colorado, Mississippi, and recently Idaho, are afraid to engage in intelligent debate for fear that somebody nearby might have a gun? Does concealed carry discourage debate on the floor of the state legislatures in
Texas and Virginia and the other states where it is allowed in the state
capitol?

The SGFS essay points to a 1999 survey that asked 1,500 respondents, 7
"Do you think regular citizens should be allowed to bring their guns [onto]
college campuses?" This survey, which asked only about "regular citizens"
and made no distinction for concealed handgun license holders, took place
ten years ago, when America's right-to-carry laws were still in their infancy
and before many current right-to-carry states adopted "shall-issue" licensing laws. At that time very few Americans were familiar with the process or
even the notion of obtaining a concealed handgun license, and it is absurd
to suggest that this outdated poll reflects current national opinion on the
rights of trained, licensed adults. However, accepting for the sake of argument that a majority of the general public does oppose allowing concealed
carry on college campuses, what does that prove? Beyond the 1 percent
who possess concealed handgun licenses, what percentage of Americans
can tell you the requirements to obtain a concealed handgun license in
their state, much less accurately comment on whether or not concealed
carry leads to more or less crime? Public opinion does not always dictate
public policy on complicated issues of public safety. The FDA does not poll
the public on acceptable procedures for sanitizing meatpacking plants.

2. More Guns on Campus Would Create Little If Any
   Additional Risk for Students

The SGFS essay goes on to assert, "More guns on campus would create 8
additional risk for students." Citing a study by the Brady Campaign, the
essay points to "(1) The prevalence of drugs and alcohol; (2) The risk of suicide and mental health issues; (3) The likelihood of gun thefts; and (4) An
increased risk of accidental shootings." The essay doesn't mention that
after allowing concealed carry on campus for a combined total of one hundred semesters, none of the aforementioned twelve U.S. colleges have seen

a single resulting incident of a student under the influence of drugs or alcohol using or brandishing a weapon on campus, a single resulting suicide, a single resulting gun theft, or a single resulting gun accident.

The essay points to a 2007 Columbia University study that concluded, 9 "[N]early half of America's 5.4 million full-time college students abuse drugs or drink alcohol on binges at least once a month"; however, the essay fails to differentiate between underclassmen and upperclassmen. Since the age limit to obtain a concealed handgun license in most states is twenty-one, it seems only fair to note that a three-year study by the Task Force on College Drinking, commissioned by the National Institute on Alcohol Abuse and Alcoholism (NIAAA), found that ages eighteen through twenty-one is the period of heaviest alcohol consumption for most drinkers in the United States, that college students under the age of twenty-one are more likely than older students to binge drink and have alcohol-related problems, and that the average levels of drinking drop off significantly by the age of twenty-three. In July of 2008 more than one hundred university chancellors and college presidents, recognizing that binge drinking is primarily a problem among students under the age of twenty-one and convinced that college binge drinking occurs because students under the age of twenty-one are not allowed to drink in the same safe, controlled environments as students over the age of twenty-one, signed on to the Amethyst Initiative, a movement aimed at creating a dialogue over the wisdom of the national drinking age.

According to Dr. Robert D. Foss, manager of alcohol studies at the 10 University of North Carolina Highway Safety Research Center (HSRC), "Almost everybody misperceives how much college students actually drink. When people are asked to estimate it, they almost always way overshoot the reality." Between 1999 and 2003, HSRC conducted a study that used breathalyzers (as opposed to the anonymous surveys used in the studies cited by SGFS) to gauge the drinking habits of students at the University of North Carolina. According to Dr. Foss, "Our findings ran counter to reports in the national media that portrayed excessive college student drinking as a rampant epidemic." The study found that two out of three students returning to their residences on Friday and Saturday nights had not had anything to drink and that many of the remaining one-third had only had a few drinks. The rate of alcohol consumption during the rest of the week was found to be much lower.

The SGFS essay also points to a 2002 Harvard University study that 11 found that students who have firearms at college are more likely to binge drink, drive while under the influence, use illegal drugs, vandalize property, and get into trouble with the police. What the essay doesn't point out is that a comparison of the Harvard study's data to concealed handgun licensing data from that same period of time suggests that fewer (most likely far fewer) than 5 percent of the gun owners surveyed were concealed handgun license holders. Studies[1] show that concealed handgun license holders, unlike unlicensed gun owners, are significantly less likely than the general population to engage in criminal behavior.

Despite all of these statistics, the issue of alcohol consumption and 12
reckless behavior by college students is a moot point — this is not a debate
about keeping guns out of the hands of college students. Allowing concealed carry on college campuses would not change the rules about who
can purchase a firearm or who can obtain a concealed handgun license. It
also wouldn't change the rules at off-campus parties and bars, the places
where individuals over the age of twenty-one are most likely to consume
alcohol. And it would not make it legal to carry a handgun while under the
influence of drugs or alcohol. Changing the rules would simply allow the
same trained, licensed adults who carry concealed handguns, without incident when not on campus, to do so on campus. There is no reason to
assume that the same individuals who aren't getting drunk and shooting
people outside of college campuses would suddenly get drunk and start
shooting people on college campuses.

SGFS's arguments about suicide and the vulnerability of dorm rooms 13
to theft carry very little weight when viewed in light of the fact that this is
not a debate about who can own or carry a gun. The overwhelming majority of suicides are committed in the victim's home. Under current regulations, the only students prohibited from keeping firearms in their homes
are students living in on-campus housing. At most colleges, on-campus
housing is occupied primarily by freshmen and sophomores, students typically too young to obtain a concealed handgun license. A comparison of
housing statistics at the University of Texas (a major university with over
fifty thousand students) to Texas concealed handgun licensing statistics
shows a probability of only ten to twenty concealed handgun license holders living in on-campus housing. Statistically speaking, how many of those
ten to twenty individuals are likely to commit suicide in a given year? As for
theft, the vulnerability of dorms to theft does not necessitate a campus-
wide ban on concealed carry. There are a multitude of security options, from
floor safes to safes that bolt to bed frames to community gun lockups.

Concerns about accidental discharges are overblown, to say the least. 14
Accidental discharges of concealed firearms are very rare — particularly because modern firearms are designed with safety in mind and because a
handgun's trigger is typically not exposed when it is concealed — and only
a small fraction of accidental discharges result in injury. It is silly to suggest that citizens should be denied a right simply because that right is
accompanied by a negligible risk.

3. Shooters May or May Not Be Deterred by Concealed Carry Permit Holders, but Deterring Shooting Sprees Is Only One of Several Potential Benefits

SGFS goes on to argue, "Shooters would not be deterred by concealed 15
carry permit holders." To quote Louisiana State Representative Ernest D.
Wooton, speaking at the 2008 SCC (then Students for Concealed Carry
on Campus) National Conference in Washington, D.C., "If we don't try it,
are we going to know?"

Though campus shooters are frequently suicidal, they are not simply 16
suicidal — if they were, they would simply shoot themselves at home and
leave everyone else alone. Campus shooters go on armed rampages because
they misguidedly seek to make a point or attain infamy. It's hard to attain
infamy if a concealed handgun license holder ends your shooting spree
before it begins. Even if the knowledge that concealed handgun license
holders might be present isn't enough to deter all would-be gunmen, an
attempted shooting spree thwarted by a licensee might be enough to deter
a few.

The SGFS essay points to two attacks on facilities where the shooters 17
knew that law enforcement officers would be present, as evidence that suicidal gunmen are not deterred by armed resistance. Those particular shooters may not have been deterred, but they also didn't cause nearly as great a
loss of life as is often caused by shooters in "gun-free zones." In those two
incidents, the shooters killed a combined total of five people, less than one-
sixth the total body count from the Virginia Tech massacre.

The issue of concealed carry on college campuses is not just about pre- 18
venting campus shooting sprees. Though it's the mass shootings that get
the headlines, college campuses play host to assaults, rapes, and every type
of criminal activity found in the rest of society. The question of whether or
not concealed carry would deter would-be mass-shooters should not be
the determining factor in whether or not it is allowed on college campuses.
Why should a 105-pound woman who is allowed the means to defend herself against a 250-pound would-be rapist outside of campus not be afforded
that same right on campus? Why should a professor who is allowed the
means to defend himself at the local bank and at his neighborhood church
be forced to hide under his desk listening to gunshots getting closer, with
no recourse but to hope and pray the gunman doesn't find him?

4. Concealed Carry Permit Holders Are Not Always "Law-Abiding" Citizens, but They're Statistically More Law-Abiding Than Most

Students for Gun-Free Schools unnecessarily points out, "Concealed 19
carry permit holders are not always 'law-abiding' citizens." This is true.
Likewise, law enforcement officers, elected officials, and clergy members
are not always "law-abiding" citizens. Every segment of society has its bad
apples, but statistically speaking, concealed carry has fewer than most.
Numerous studies[1] by independent researchers and state agencies suggest
that concealed handgun license holders are five times less likely than non-
license holders to commit violent crimes. A comparison of statistics[2] in the
mid-nineties, when Florida was still one of the few shall-issue states, found
that Florida concealed handgun license holders were three times less likely
to be arrested than were New York City police officers.

Despite the fact that Students for Concealed Carry on Campus does 20
not advocate concealed carry by unlicensed individuals, SGFS finds it necessary to point out that Alaska and Vermont do not require (though Alaska
offers) a license to carry a concealed handgun. The essay then goes on to

erroneously suggest, "The primary requirement for obtaining a permit in [the thirty-eight shall-issue] states is to pass a background check through the National Instant Criminal Background Check System." In reality, many states, such as Texas, require applicants to submit to extensive state and federal fingerprint and background checks that often take one to three months (far from instant) to complete.

The essay further blurs the line between the requirements to purchase 21 a firearm and the requirements to obtain a concealed handgun license by stating, "The only misdemeanor convictions that would prohibit someone from owning and purchasing firearms, however, are those related to incidents of domestic violence. Someone who obtains a concealed carry permit in a shall-issue state could have a rap sheet with other types of misdemeanor convictions, including violent offenses." The factors that can disqualify an individual from obtaining a concealed handgun license vary from state to state, but most states place certain restrictions and time limits on misdemeanor offenders. For instance, in the state of Texas you cannot obtain a concealed handgun license if you have had any misdemeanor convictions greater than a traffic citation in the past five years. A current license holder who commits a misdemeanor greater than a traffic violation would immediately have his or her license revoked.

The SGFS essay refers to several mass-shooters and erroneously suggests that several of them either possessed or would have qualified for concealed handgun licenses. For example, the essay mentions Seung-Hui Cho, the Virginia Tech shooter, even though his adjudication as a danger to himself and others would have disqualified him from obtaining a concealed handgun license in most shall-issue states. Contrary to the claims of SGFS, mental health rulings are commonly considered by states when deciding whether or not to issue a concealed handgun license.

> " Contrary to the claims of SGFS, mental health rulings are commonly considered by states when deciding whether or not to issue a concealed handgun license. "

22

Perhaps most discrediting of SGFS's 23 many claims is its citation of a widely discredited 2001 study by the Violence Policy Center, a highly biased gun control advocacy group. The study claims that Texas concealed handgun license holders were arrested for weapon-related offenses at a rate 81 percent higher than the general population of Texas age twenty-one and older, between January 1, 1996, and December 31, 2000 (SGFS mistakenly lists the end date as August 31, 2001). This study, which took place during the first five years of Texas's concealed handgun licensing program, when police officers were not always clear on the new weapons laws and often took a "better safe than sorry" approach to making arrests, focused solely on arrests, not convictions. According to Texas Department of Corrections statistics from that same period of time, Texas concealed handgun license holders were 7.6 times *less* likely than non-license holders to be arrested for *violent* crimes (as opposed to the weapons crimes — which can include non-violent offenses such as attempting to carry a concealed handgun into a federal building — researched by the Violence Policy Center). A four-year study by engineering statistician William E. Sturdevant found that Texas concealed handgun license holders were 5.5 times less likely than non-license holders to be *convicted* of violent crimes. According to statistics from the Texas Department of Public Safety and the U.S. Census Bureau, reported by the *San Antonio Express-News* in September 2000, Texas concealed handgun license holders were 14 times less likely than the non-license holders to commit a crime of any kind and 5 times less likely to commit a violent crime. The SGFS essay mentions murder as one of the crimes for which Texas concealed handgun license holders were arrested during the course of the VPC study, but the essay fails to mention that in the first ten years of Texas's concealed handgun licensing program (during which time over a quarter of a million concealed handgun licenses were issued), only eight Texas concealed handgun license holders were convicted of murder. As of January 1, 2007, no Texas concealed handgun license holder had ever been convicted of capital murder. The discrepancy between arrests and convictions is caused, in large part, by the way law enforcement officers respond to a self-defense shooting. If the facts of a self-defense shooting are not immediately evident, a shooter who acted within the letter of the law may still be arrested for murder and held until investigators are able to sort out the sequence of events.

The SGFS essay concludes its attack on the integrity of concealed   24
handgun license holders by pointing to a 2007 investigation by the Florida *Sun-Sentinel* that purportedly found more than 1,400 convicted felons in possession of Florida concealed handgun licenses. Though the Florida licensing system may have a few cracks in its screening process, the cracks appear to be relatively minor. Those 1,400 convicted felons constitute only about 0.1 percent of all Florida concealed handgun license holders. And the cracks apparently aren't causing problems. Statistics show that Florida concealed handgun license holders are still significantly less likely than non-license holders to commit violent crimes. In fact, according to Florida state agencies, you are more than twice as likely to be attacked by an alligator than by a concealed handgun license holder in the state of Florida.

The truth is that possessing a concealed handgun license and/or hav-   25
ing the right to legally carry a firearm does not enable a person to carry a gun or commit a crime. There are no checkpoints where officials screen for guns and check licenses. A person intent on carrying a gun can easily do so throughout modern American society, including on college campuses, regardless of whether or not he or she is licensed to do so. An individual engaged in criminal activity is typically not concerned with the prospect of committing a misdemeanor (carrying a concealed handgun without a license) on his or her way to commit a felony (armed robbery, assault, rape, murder, etc.).

5. Concealed Carry Permit Holders Are Not Required to Have Law Enforcement Training Because They're Not Law Enforcement Officers

For its final argument, the essay points out, "Concealed carry permit 26 holders are not required to have law enforcement training." This is true. Concealed carry permit holders are not required to have law enforcement training because they are not law enforcement officers. Law enforcement officers do not go through academy training to learn to carry concealed handguns for self-defense; they go through academy training to learn to be law enforcement officers. Concealed handgun license holders have no need of most of the training received by law enforcement officers. Concealed handgun license holders don't need to know how to drive police cars at high speeds or how to kick down doors or how to conduct traffic stops or how to make arrests or how to use handcuffs. And concealed handgun license holders definitely don't need to spend weeks memorizing radio codes and traffic laws.

Contrary to what SGFS and other opponents of concealed carry might 27 claim, concealed handgun license holders don't need extensive tactical training because they are not charged with protecting the public. Concealed handgun license holders don't go looking for bad guys — it's not their job to act like amateur, one-man SWAT teams. All a concealed handgun license holder needs to know is how to use his or her concealed handgun to stop an immediate threat of death or serious bodily harm. That type of training *can* be accomplished in the one-day training courses required to obtain a concealed handgun license in most states.

The SGFS essay accurately points out that police officers in the field 28 typically hit their intended targets approximately 25 percent of the time. What it fails to point out is that police officers frequently encounter scenarios that a concealed handgun license holder would never encounter. License holders do not chase bad guys down dark alleys or raid drug labs or engage in standoffs with criminals barricaded inside buildings. According to experts on the issue, most self-defense shootings occur at close range and are over in a matter of seconds.

Interestingly enough, law enforcement officers in most states are only 29 required to requalify with their weapons once a year, and in some states, such as Texas, the requalification test for law enforcement officers varies very little from the shooting test that must be passed by concealed handgun license applicants.

Not surprisingly, the SGFS essay presents the typical far-fetched sce- 30 narios of self-defense shootings resulting in "collateral damage" and of multiple students drawing weapons and finding themselves unable to identify the actual "shooter" in prolonged shootouts. This ignores both the findings of a 1997 FBI study[3] that concluded that most shootouts last less than ten seconds and the fact that the rate of concealed carry among individuals in their twenties is typically about one half of one percent. How nine seconds of exchanged gunfire between two armed individuals could possibly lead to greater loss of life than a nine-minute, uncontested execution-style massacre, such as the one that occurred at Virginia Tech, is something Students for Gun-Free Schools, like most opponents of concealed carry on campus, doesn't attempt to explain. Likewise, they make no attempt to explain how one of these brief shootouts could lead to multiple students drawing their weapons and losing track of the shooter, when statistically speaking, only about one out of every two hundred students would be armed. Given the fact that even a huge four-hundred-seat lecture hall would statistically contain only two students with concealed handgun licenses, the chance of one of those armed students losing track of the actual shooter during a few seconds of exchanged gunfire is highly unlikely.

Students for Gun-Free Schools concludes its essay by suggesting that 31 the relatively small number of justified shooting deaths each year somehow proves that concealed carry is ineffective. Like many opponents of concealed carry, they fail to realize that the key factor is not the number of bad guys killed but, rather, the number of good guys saved. According to a 1991 FBI study,[4] less than one out of a thousand lawful defensive uses of a firearm results in the death of the attacker. By that estimate, firearms are used almost five times more frequently to save lives than to take lives in the U.S.

In the end, Students for Gun-Free Schools' arguments against con- 32 cealed carry on campus, like all arguments against concealed carry on campus, rely entirely on speculation, false assumptions, and emotion. Most college campuses in America are surrounded by neighborhoods where concealed handgun license holders, including college students, lawfully carry concealed handguns at movie theaters, grocery stores, shopping malls, office buildings, restaurants, churches, banks, etc. Yet, we don't hear of spates of accidental discharges or alcohol-fueled shootings by licensees in those places. If the majority of college campuses are safer than their surrounding areas because they don't allow concealed carry on campus, why don't we see higher crime rates at the twelve U.S. colleges that do allow concealed carry on campus? After a combined total of one hundred semesters, why haven't we seen *any* negative results on those twelve campuses? There is absolutely no verifiable evidence to suggest that allowing concealed carry on college campuses makes campuses any less safe; therefore, reason dictates that current school policies and state laws against concealed carry on campus serve only to stack the odds in favor of dangerous criminals who have no regard for school policy or state law. SCC simply seeks to take the advantage away from those who seek to harm the innocent.

SCC
Better armed because we're armed with knowledge and *guns!*

Endnotes

1. "Crime, Deterrence, and Right-to-Carry Concealed Handguns,"
   John Lott and David Mustard, *Journal of Legal Studies* (v. 26, no. 1,

pages 1–68, January 1997); "An Analysis of the Arrest Rate of Texas Concealed Handgun License Holders as Compared to the Arrest Rate of the Entire Texas Population," William E. Sturdevant, September 1, 2000; Florida Department of Justice statistics, 1998; Florida Department of State, "Concealed Weapons/Firearms License Statistical Report," 1998; Texas Department of Public Safety and the U.S. Census Bureau, reported in *San Antonio Express-News,* September 2000; Texas Department of Corrections data, 1996–2000, compiled by the Texas State Rifle Association.

2. A comparison of statistics on arrests of police officers, published by the *Washington Post* on 08/28/94, to Florida Department of Law Enforcement statistics submitted to the governor on 03/15/95.

3. "In the Line of Fire: Violence against Law Enforcement," U.S. Department of Justice, Federal Bureau of Investigation, National Institute of Justice, 1997.

4. "Critical Incidents in Policing," Federal Bureau of Investigation, 1991.

• • •

Comprehension

1. Why do the writers discuss the Texas and Virginia state legislatures? What is significant about them?

2. According to the writers, what misperception do people generally have about the drinking habits of college students?

3. What kind of training do the writers say can be "accomplished in the one-day training courses required to obtain a concealed handgun license in most states" (27)?

4. The writers claim that arguments against concealed carry on campus rely entirely on three premises. What are these three premises?

Purpose and Audience

1. How would you state the thesis of this essay in your own words?

2. In paragraphs 2 and 3, the writers accuse their opponents of committing a logical **fallacy**. What is this fallacy? Why do you think the writers choose to make this claim near the beginning of their essay? How does it serve their overall purpose?

3. Do you think the writers are primarily trying to persuade those who disagree with them or addressing those who already agree with their position? How can you tell?

4. How do the writers characterize the views of the American public on the issues of guns and gun control? What is their opinion of the general population? Do you think this opinion influences their argument?

5. The writers accuse opponents of concealed carry on campus of relying on emotion to make their arguments. Do the writers of this essay use any

emotional arguments to build their own case? If so, point to an example, and explain how this kind of emotional appeal supports (or does not support) their overall purpose.

Style and Structure

1. This essay is structured as a point-by-point rebuttal of arguments made by Students for Gun-Free Schools (page 633). Do you find this approach effective? Would the strategy work for those who have not read the original SGFS article that prompted this response? Why or why not?

2. Where in the essay do the writers use **analogies**? Do you find the comparisons logical? Persuasive? Why or why not?

3. **Vocabulary Project.** The writers claim that the "issue of alcohol consumption and reckless behavior by college students is a moot point" (12). What is a "moot point"? Do you agree that this issue is a "moot point"?

4. In paragraph 23, the writers address a study by the Violence Policy Center, referring to the organization as a "highly biased gun control advocacy group." Is this characterization fair? What are they trying to accomplish by labeling the Violence Policy Center in this way? Do they achieve their goal?

5. Where in this essay do the writers use expert opinion? Where do they use statistics? Do you find these kinds of support persuasive? Why or why not?

Journal Entry

In paragraph 13, the writers discuss the security options of those who wish to keep their guns while living on campus, including "safes that bolt to bed frames" and "community gun lockups." Would you feel less safe (or safer) living in a college dorm or residence with guns on the premises? Explain your answer.

Writing Workshop

1. **Working with Sources.** Referring to accidental gun discharges, the writers claim, "It is silly to suggest that citizens should be denied a right simply because that right is accompanied by a negligible risk" (14). Indeed, arguments about gun laws and policies invariably lead to debates about the meaning of the noun *right*. How do you view the right of an individual to possess firearms? What are its limits? In what ways, if any, should public safety be balanced against the individual's right to own a gun? Write an essay that explores and tries to answer these questions. Be sure to document any sources you use and to include a works-cited page. (See Chapter 18 for information on MLA documentation.)

2. The writers discuss the general public's opinion of concealed carry laws, but they suggest that the public is uninformed. Moreover, they argue that

public opinion may be irrelevant in this context, saying, "Public opinion does not always dictate public policy on complicated issues of public safety. The FDA does not poll the public on acceptable procedures for sanitizing meatpacking plants" (7). Do you think these are valid arguments? Do you share the writers' overall view of the public and the public's ability to understand complex policies or issues? Write an essay that addresses these questions.

3. In their last paragraph, the writers say that all arguments against concealed carry on campus "rely entirely on speculation, false assumptions, and emotion." Do you agree? After reading both this essay and the essay by Students for Gun-Free Schools (page 633), consider where you stand on the issue of guns on campus. Write an essay that presents and supports your position.

Combining the Patterns

The writers examine — and propose — several **cause-and-effect** relationships in this essay. Point to a specific example, and explain how it supports their overall argument or purpose.

Thematic Connections

- "A Peaceful Woman Explains Why She Carries a Gun" (page 353)
- The Declaration of Independence (page 550)

TIMOTHY WHEELER

There's a Reason They Choose Schools

A retired surgeon, Timothy Wheeler is the director of Doctors for Responsible Gun Ownership, a national group of physicians, medical students, scientists, and others who support — and advocate for — gun rights as well as the safe and lawful use of firearms. DRGO is associated with the Claremont Institute, a conservative think tank. Wheeler's writing has appeared in the *Washington Times,* the *National Review Online,* and other publications.

Background on gun violence as a public health issue More than thirty thousand people are killed every year by gun violence. As Wheeler's essay suggests, many physicians and health-care experts view this problem as a public health issue — and even a public health crisis. Wheeler cites the 2007 issue of the American Medical Association's *Disaster Medicine and Public Health Preparedness,* which focused on the Virginia Tech massacre. The AMA, the largest association of physicians in the United States, has long viewed the problem in a public health context. After the 2013 shootings at Sandy Hook Elementary School in Connecticut, the AMA and fifty-two other medical organizations sent a letter to President Barack Obama. The signatories advocated several proposals, including an assault weapons ban, increased mental health services, and more research on violence prevention. In the past, the government funded extensive research for studying (and reducing) gun violence at the Centers for Disease Control, but gun rights advocates, including the NRA, lobbied for legal restrictions on the CDC, requiring that "[n]one of the funds made available . . . may be used to advocate or promote gun control." Such public health research is not limited to the public sector, of course. For example, the University of Chicago Crime Lab, founded in 2008, explores the causes and effects of gun violence in the United States. For gun rights activists such as Wheeler, these physicians, researchers, and health-care experts too often put the "emphasis on guns and not on the humans who misuse them."

Wednesday's shooting at yet another school has a better outcome than 1 most in recent memory. No one died at Cleveland's Success Tech Academy except the perpetrator. The two students and two teachers he shot are in stable condition at Cleveland hospitals.

What is depressingly similar to the mass murders at Virginia Tech and 2 Nickel Mines, Pennsylvania,* and too many others was the killer's choice of venue — that steadfastly gun-free zone, the school campus. Although murderer Seung-Hui Cho at Virginia Tech and Asa Coon, the Cleveland

---

* Eds. note — On October 2, 2006, Charles Carl Roberts shot five students and injured five others in an Amish one-room schoolhouse.

shooter, were both students reported to have school-related grudges, other school killers have proved to be simply taking advantage of the lack of effective security at schools. The Bailey, Colorado, multiple rapes and murder of September 2006, the Nickel Mines massacre of October 2006, and Buford Furrow's murderous August 1999 invasion of a Los Angeles Jewish day-care center were all committed by adults. They had no connection to the schools other than being drawn to the soft target a school offers such psychopaths.

This latest shooting comes only a few weeks after the American Medi-   3
cal Association released a theme issue of its journal *Disaster Medicine and Public Health Preparedness*. This issue is dedicated to analyzing the April 2007 Virginia Tech shootings, in which thirty-two people were murdered. The authors are university officials, trauma surgeons, and legal analysts who pore over the details of the incident, looking for "warning signs" and "risk factors" for violence. They rehash all the tired rhetoric of bureaucrats and public-health wonks, including the public-health mantra of the 1990s that guns are the root cause of violence.

Sheldon Greenberg, a dean at Johns Hopkins, offers this gem: "Rein-   4
force a 'no weapons' policy and, when violated, enforce it quickly, to include expulsion. Parents should be made aware of the policy. *Officials should dispel the politically driven notion that armed students could eliminate an active shooter*" (emphasis added). Greenberg apparently isn't aware that at the Appalachian School of Law in 2002 another homicidal Virginia student was stopped from shooting more of his classmates when another student held him at gunpoint. The Pearl High School murderer Luke Woodham was stopped cold when vice principal Joel Myrick got his Colt .45 handgun out of his truck and pointed it at the young killer.

Virginia Tech's 2005 no-guns-on-campus policy was an abject failure at   5
deterring Seung-Hui Cho. Greenberg's audacity in ignoring the obvious is typical of arrogant school officials. What the AMA journal authors studiously avoid are on one hand the repeated failures of such feel-good steps as no-gun policies, and on the other hand the demonstrated success of armed first responders. These responders would be the students themselves, such as the trained and licensed law student, or their similarly qualified teachers.

> " It is encouraging that college students themselves have a   6
> much better grasp on reality than their politically correct elders. "

In Cleveland this week and at Virginia Tech the shooters took time to walk the halls, searching out victims in several rooms, and then shooting them. Virginia Chief Medical Examiner Marcella Fierro describes the locations of the dead in Virginia Tech's Norris Hall. Dead victims were found in groups ranging from one to thirteen, scattered throughout four rooms and a stairwell. If any one of the victims had, like the Appalachian School of Law student, used armed force to stop Cho, lives could have been saved.

The people of Virginia actually had a chance to implement such a plan 7 last year. House Bill 1572 was introduced in the legislature to extend the state's concealed-carry provisions to college campuses. But the bill died in committee, opposed by the usual naysayers, including the Virginia Association of Chiefs of Police and the university itself. Virginia Tech spokesman Larry Hincker was quoted in the *Roanoke Times* as saying, "I'm sure the university community is appreciative of the General Assembly's actions because this will help parents, students, faculty, and visitors feel safe on our campus."

It is encouraging that college students themselves have a much better 8 grasp on reality than their politically correct elders. During the week of October 22–26, Students for Concealed Carry on Campus will stage a nationwide "empty holster" demonstration (peaceful, of course) in support of their cause.

School officials typically base violence-prevention policies on irratio- 9 nal fears more than real-world analysis of what works. But which is more horrible, the massacre that timid bureaucrats fear might happen when a few good guys (and gals) carry guns on campus, or the one that actually did happen despite Virginia Tech's progressive violence-prevention policy? Can there really be any more debate?

AMA journal editor James J. James, M.D, offers up this nostrum: 10

> We must meaningfully embrace all of the varied disciplines contributing to preparedness and response and be more willing to be guided and informed by the full spectrum of research methodologies, including not only the rigid application of the traditional scientific method and epidemiological and social science applications but also the incorporation of observational/empirical findings, as necessary, in the absence of more objective data.

Got that?   11

I prefer the remedy prescribed by self-defense guru Massad Ayoob. 12 When good people find themselves in what he calls "the dark place," confronted by the imminent terror of a gun-wielding homicidal maniac, the picture becomes clear. Policies won't help. Another federal gun law won't help. The only solution is a prepared and brave defender with the proper lifesaving tool — a gun.

· · ·

Comprehension

1. What does Wheeler see as "depressingly similar" (2) about the sites of recent mass shootings?

2. The American Medical Association devoted an entire issue of one of its journals to dealing with tragedies such as school shootings. How does Wheeler view the AMA's reaction and policy proposals?

3. According to Wheeler, what do the AMA journal authors "studiously avoid" (5)?

4. In Wheeler's view, what is the basis of most anti-violence policies on school campuses?

5. According to Wheeler, what is the only effective way to deal with the "imminent terror of a gun-wielding homicidal maniac" (12)?

Purpose and Audience

1. The writer, a doctor, is the director of Doctors for Responsible Gun Ownership. How does your knowledge of his professional background affect your view of his argument? Do you think he should have mentioned his background in the essay? Why or why not?

2. This article originally appeared in the *National Review Online,* a conservative publication. Given his likely audience, what do you think the writer's purpose is? For example, do you think he wants to change readers' minds? To reinforce what they already believe? Explain.

3. How would you restate Wheeler's thesis in your own words?

4. Wheeler writes about the positions and policies of school officials and public health experts. If they read this article, how do you think they would react?

5. In paragraph 8, Wheeler refers to an "encouraging" sign. What is this sign? How does it support his overall purpose?

6. In paragraph 10, Wheeler includes a passage by AMA journal editor James J. James, M.D. Why does he include this long quotation?

Style and Structure

1. Where does Wheeler address opposing points of view? How does he respond to these arguments against his position? Are his responses effective? Explain.

2. How does Wheeler characterize those with opposing viewpoints? What specific words does he use? How do you respond to this characterization?

3. In paragraph 3, why does Wheeler place quotation marks around the terms "warning signs" and "risk factors"? How does this use of quotation marks affect the meaning and connotation of those phrases?

4. **Vocabulary Project.** In paragraph 3, Wheeler refers to a "public health mantra." What is a mantra? What connotations does this word have? Why do you think Wheeler chose to use *mantra* in this context?

5. What purpose does paragraph 4 serve? How does it help to support Wheeler's thesis?

Journal Entry

In his conclusion, Wheeler discusses the "imminent terror" of a "gun-wielding homicidal maniac." Mass shootings have captured the public imagination; they understandably evoke fear and horror. Do you think the public tends to overreact to mass shootings, or do you think their reactions are appropriate? Explain.

Writing Workshop

1. Wheeler writes: "Policies won't help. Another federal law won't help. The only solution is a prepared and brave defender with the proper lifesaving tool — a gun" (12). Do you agree that policies and laws "won't help"? Is the solution to the problem as clear-cut as the one Wheeler presents in his conclusion? Write an essay that addresses these questions.

2. The writer seems to have little use for school officials. For example, in paragraph 8, he suggests that college students "have a much better grasp on reality than their politically correct elders"; and in paragraph 9, he refers to college administrators as "timid bureaucrats." Consider your own college or university. What are your school's policies with regard to firearms on campus and emergency procedures? Do you think administrators and officials are making policies based on "irrational fears" instead of "real-world analysis" (9)? Write an essay that examines and evaluates your school's policies.

3. **Working with Sources.** The title of this essay is "There's a Reason They Choose Schools." The writer refers to colleges as "soft targets" for shooters because campuses are usually gun-free zones. How safe are the elementary schools, high schools, and colleges in your community? Do you see these schools as "soft targets"? Why or why not? Write an argumentative essay that answers these questions and makes recommendations that address the problems you identify. Be sure to document any sources you cite and to include a works-cited page. (See Chapter 18 for information on MLA documentation.)

Combining the Patterns

Where does the writer use **comparison and contrast** in this essay? How does the pattern work to support his main point?

Thematic Connections

- "Thirty-Eight Who Saw Murder Didn't Call the Police" (page 128)
- "Ground Zero" (page 175)

Writing Assignments for Argumentation

1. Write an argumentative essay discussing whether parents have a right to spank their children. If your position is that they do, under what circumstances? What limitations should exist? If your position is that they do not, how should parents discipline children? How should they deal with inappropriate behavior?

2. Visit the American Library Association's website at www.ala.org, and read the list of banned and challenged books of the twenty-first century. Choose a book from the list that you have read. Assume that a library in your town has decided that the book you have chosen is objectionable and has removed it from the shelves. Write an email to your local newspaper arguing for or against the library's actions. Make a list of the major arguments that might be advanced against your position, and try to refute some of them in your email.

3. In Great Britain, cities began installing video surveillance systems in public areas in the 1970s. Police departments claim that these cameras help them do their jobs more efficiently. For example, such cameras enabled police to identify and capture terrorists who bombed the London subway in 2005. Opponents of the cameras say that the police are creating a society that severely compromises the right of personal privacy. How do you feel about this issue? Assume that the police department in your city is proposing to install cameras in the downtown and other pedestrian areas. Write an editorial for your local paper presenting your views on the topic.

4. Write an essay discussing under what circumstances, if any, animals should be used for scientific experimentation.

5. **Working with Sources.** Each year, a growing number of high school graduates are choosing to take a year off before going to college. The idea of this kind of "gap year" has been the source of some debate. Proponents say that a gap year gives students time to mature, time to decide what they want to get out of their education. It also gives them the opportunity to travel or to save some money for college. Detractors of a gap year point out that some students have trouble getting back into the academic routine when the year is over. In addition, students who take a year off are a year behind their classmates when they return. Research the pros and cons of the gap year. Then, write an essay in which you argue for or against taking a year off before college. Be sure to document your sources and to include a works-cited page. (See Chapter 18 for information on MLA documentation.)

6. **Working with Sources.** Visit the website deathpenalty.org, and research some criminal cases that resulted in the death penalty. Write an essay using these accounts to support your arguments either for or against the death penalty. Be sure to document your sources and to include a works-cited page. (See Chapter 18 for information about MLA documentation.)

7. Write an argumentative essay discussing under what circumstances a nation has an obligation to go (or not to go) to war.

8. Since the events of September 11, 2001, the idea of arming pilots of commercial passenger planes has been debated. Those opposed to arming pilots claim that the risks — that a gun will fall into the hands of hijackers or that a passenger will be accidentally shot — outweigh any benefits. Those who support the idea say that the pilot is the last line of defense and must be able to defend the cockpit from terrorists. Due to public pressure in favor of arming pilots, a small trial program has been instituted. Do you think all pilots of commercial airplanes should be armed? Write an argumentative essay presenting your views on this subject.

9. In the Declaration of Independence, Jefferson says that all individuals are entitled to "life, liberty and the pursuit of happiness." Write an essay arguing that these rights are not absolute.

10. Write an argumentative essay on one of these topics:

    - Should high school students be required to recite the Pledge of Allegiance at the start of each school day?
    - Should college students be required to do community service?
    - Should public school teachers be required to pass periodic competency tests?
    - Should the legal drinking age be raised (or lowered)?
    - Should the children of undocumented immigrants qualify for in-state tuition rates at public colleges?
    - Should sugary drinks be banned in all public schools and government workplaces?
    - Do Facebook and other social networking sites do more harm than good?

Collaborative Activity for Argumentation

Working with three other students, select a controversial topic — one not covered in any of the debates in this chapter — that interests all of you. (You can review the Writing Assignments for Argumentation to get ideas.) State your topic the way a topic is stated in a formal debate:

Resolved: The federal government should censor Internet content.

Then, divide into two-member teams, and decide which team will take the pro position and which will take the con. Each team should list the arguments on its side of the issue and then write two or three paragraphs summarizing its position. Finally, the teams should stage a ten-minute debate — five minutes for each side — in front of the class. (The pro side presents its argument first.) At the end of each debate, the class should decide which team has presented the stronger arguments.

15

Combining the Patterns

Many paragraphs combine several patterns of development. In the following paragraph, for example, Paul Hoffman uses narration, exemplification, and cause and effect to explain why we tend to see numbers as more than "instruments of enumeration."

Topic sentence

Narration

Exemplification

Cause and effect

The idea that numbers are not mere instruments of enumeration but are sacred, perfect, friendly, lucky, or evil goes back to antiquity. In the sixth century B.C. Pythagoras, whom schoolchildren associate with the famous theorem that in a right triangle the square of the hypotenuse always equals the sum of the squares of its sides, not only performed brilliant mathematics but made a religion out of numbers. In numerology, the number 12 has always represented completeness, as in the 12 months of the year, the 12 signs of the zodiac, the 12 hours of the day, the 12 gods of Olympus, the 12 labors of Hercules, the 12 tribes of Israel, the 12 apostles of Jesus, the 12 days of Christmas, and, more recently perhaps, the 12 eggs in an egg carton. Since 13 exceeds 12 by only one, the number lies just beyond completeness and, hence, is restless to the point of being evil.

Like paragraphs, essays do not usually follow a single pattern of development; in fact, nearly every essay, including those in this text, combines a variety of patterns. Even though an essay may be organized according to one dominant pattern, it is still likely to include paragraphs, and even groups of paragraphs, shaped by other patterns of development. For example, a process essay can use **cause and effect** to show the results of the process, and a cause-and-effect essay can use **exemplification** to illustrate possible causes or effects. In many cases, a dominant pattern is supported by other patterns; in fact, combining various patterns in a single essay gives writers the flexibility to express their ideas most effectively. For this reason, each essay in Chapters 6 through 14 of this text is followed by a Combining the Patterns question that focuses on how the essay uses (or might use) other patterns of development along with its dominant pattern.

Structuring an Essay by Combining the Patterns

Essays that combine various patterns of development, like essays structured primarily by a single pattern, include an **introduction**, several **body paragraphs**, and a **conclusion**. The introduction typically ends with the thesis statement that gives the essay its focus, and the conclusion often restates that thesis in different words or summarizes the essay's main points. Each body paragraph (or group of paragraphs) is structured according to the pattern of development that best suits the material it develops.

Suppose you are planning your answer to the following question on a take-home essay exam for a sociology of religion course.

> For what reasons are people attracted to cults? Why do they join? Support your answer with specific examples that illustrate how cults recruit and retain members.

The wording of this exam question ("for what reasons") suggests that the essay's dominant pattern of development will be **cause and effect**; the wording also suggests that this cause-and-effect structure will include **exemplification** ("specific examples"). In addition, you may decide to develop your essay with **definition** and **process**.

An informal outline for your essay might look like this.

Sample Outline	Combining the Patterns
Introduction:	Definition of *cult* (defined by negation — telling what it is *not* — and by comparison and contrast with *religion*). Thesis statement (suggests cause and effect): Using aggressive recruitment tactics and isolating potential members from their families and past lives, cults appeal to new recruits by offering them a highly structured environment.
Cause and effect:	Why people join cults
Process:	How cults recruit new members
Exemplification:	Tactics various cults use to retain members (series of brief examples)
Conclusion:	Restatement of thesis or review of key points

Combining the Patterns: Revising and Editing

When you revise an essay that combines several patterns of development, consider the items on the revision checklist on page 68, as well as any of the more specific revision checklists in Chapters 6 through 14 that apply to the patterns in your essay. As you edit your essay, refer to the editing checklists on pages 85, 88, and 91, and to the individual editing checklists in Chapters 6 through 14. You may also wish to consult the Grammar in Context sections that appear throughout the book, as well as the one that follows.

GRAMMAR IN CONTEXT   Agreement with Indefinite Pronouns

A **pronoun** is a word that takes the place of a noun or another pronoun in a sentence. Unlike most pronouns, an **indefinite pronoun** (*anyone, either, each,* and so on) does not refer to a specific person or thing.

Subject-Verb Agreement Pronoun subjects must agree in number with their verbs: singular pronouns (*I, he, she, it,* and so on) take singular verbs, and plural pronouns (*we, they,* and so on) take plural verbs.

"I have learned much as a scavenger" (Eighner 673).

"We were free like comets in the heavens" (Truong 667).

Indefinite pronoun subjects must also agree in number with their verbs: singular indefinite pronouns take singular verbs, and plural indefinite pronouns take plural verbs. Most indefinite pronouns are singular, but some are plural.

SUBJECT–VERB AGREEMENT WITH INDEFINITE PRONOUN SUBJECTS

SINGULAR INDEFINITE PRONOUNS

another	anyone	everyone	one	each
either	neither	anything	everything	

"Everyone was darker or lighter than we were" (Truong 669).

"Everything seems to stink" (Eighner 678).

PLURAL INDEFINITE PRONOUNS

both	many	few	several	others

"Many are discarded for minor imperfections that can be pared away" (Eighner 675).

NOTE: A few indefinite pronouns — *some, all, any, more, most,* and *none* — may be either singular or plural, depending on their meaning in the sentence.

SINGULAR: According to David Kirby, some of the history of tattoos is surprising. (*Some* refers to *history*, so the verb is singular.)

PLURAL: Some of the tattoos David Kirby discusses serve as a kind of "record book," while others create a "canvas" (695). (*Some* refers to *tattoos*, so the verb is plural.)

Pronoun-Antecedent Agreement An **antecedent** is the noun or pronoun that a pronoun refers to in a sentence. Pronouns must agree in number with their antecedents.

Use a singular pronoun to refer to a singular indefinite pronoun antecedent.

Each day has its surprises for Lars Eighner and his dog, Lizbeth.

Use a plural pronoun to refer to a plural indefinite pronoun antecedent.

Many of the people who pass Eighner and Lizbeth avert their eyes.

NOTE: Although the indefinite pronoun *everyone* is singular, it is often used with a plural pronoun in everyday speech and informal writing.

INFORMAL: Everyone turns their heads when Eighner and Lizbeth walk by.

This usage is generally acceptable in informal situations, but college writing requires correct pronoun-antecedent agreement.

CORRECT: People turn their heads when Eighner and Lizbeth walk by.

The essays in this chapter illustrate how different patterns of development work together in a single piece of writing. The first two essays — "The Park" by Michael Huu Truong, a student, and "On Dumpster Diving" by Lars Eighner — include marginal annotations that identify the various patterns these writers use. Truong's essay relies primarily on narration, but he also uses description and exemplification to convey his memories of childhood. Eighner's combines sections of definition, exemplification, classification and division, cause and effect, comparison and contrast, and process; at the same time, he tells the story (narration) and provides vivid details (description) of his life as a homeless person.

Following these annotated essays are three additional selections that combine patterns: Dana Stevens's "Your Flip-Flops Are Grossing Me Out," David Kirby's "Inked Well," and Jonathan Swift's classic satire "A Modest Proposal." Each of the essays in this chapter is followed by the same types of questions that accompany the reading selections that appear elsewhere in the text.

A STUDENT WRITER: Combining the Patterns

This essay was written by Michael Huu Truong for a first-year composition course in response to the assignment "Write an essay about the person and/or place that defined your childhood."

The Park

Background

My childhood did not really begin until I came to this country from the jungle of Vietnam. I can't really remember much from this period, and the things I do remember are vague images that I have no desire or intention to discuss. However, my childhood in the States was a lot different, especially after I met

Thesis statement

my friend James. While it lasted, it was paradise.

Narrative begins

It was a cold wintry day in February after a big snowstorm —

Description: effects of cold

the first I'd ever seen. My lips were chapped, my hands were frozen stiff, and my cheeks were burning from the biting wind, and yet I loved it. I especially loved the snow. I had come from

Comparison and contrast: U.S. vs. Vietnam

a country where the closest things to snow were white paint and cotton balls. But now I was in America. On that frosty afternoon, I was determined to build a snowman. I had seen them in books, and I had heard they could talk. I knew they could come alive, and I couldn't wait.

"Eyryui roeow ierog," said a voice that came out of nowhere.

Description: James

I turned around, and right in my face was a short, red-faced (probably from the cold wind) Korean kid with a dirty, runny nose. I responded, "Wtefkjkr ruyjft gsdfr" in my own tongue. We understood each other perfectly, and we expressed our

Narration: the first day

understanding with a smile. Together, we built our first snowman. We were disappointed that evening when the snowman just stood there; however, I was happy because I had made my first friend.

Analogies

Ever since then we've been a team like Abbott and Costello (or, when my cousin joined us, the Three Stooges). The two of us were inseparable. We could've made the greatest Krazy Glue commercial ever.

Narration: what they did that summer

The summer that followed the big snowstorm, from what I can recall, was awesome. We were free like comets in the heavens, and we did whatever our hearts wanted. For the most part, our desires were fulfilled in a little park across the street. This park was ours; it was like our own planet guarded by our own robot army (disguised as trees). Together we fought against the bigger people who always tried to invade and take over our world. The

1

2

3

4

5

enemy could never conquer our fortress because they would have to destroy our robots, penetrate our force field, and then defeat us; this last feat would be impossible.

Narrative continues

Examples: what they banished

This park was our fantasy land where everything we wished   6
for came true and everything we hated was banished forever. We banished vegetables, cheese, bigger people, and — of course — girls. The land was enchanted, and we could be whatever we felt like. We were super ninjas one day and millionaires the next; we became the heroes we idolized and lived the lives we dreamed

Examples: superhero fantasies

about. I had the strength of Bruce Lee and Superman; James possessed the power of Clint Eastwood and the Bionic Man. My weapons were the skills of Bruce and a cape. James, however, needed a real weapon for Clint, and the weapon he made was awesome. The Death Ray could destroy a building with one blast, and it even had a shield so that James was always protected. Even with all his mighty weapons and gadgets, though, he was still no match for Superman and Bruce Lee. Every day, we fought until death (or until our parents called us for dinner).

Narrative continues

When we became bored with our super powers, the park   7
became a giant spaceship. We traveled all over the Universe, conquering and exploring strange new worlds and mysterious planets. Our ship was a top-secret indestructible space warship

Examples: new worlds and planets

called the X–007. We went to Mars, Venus, Pluto, and other alien planets, destroying all the monsters we could find. When necessary, our spacecraft was transformed into a submarine for deep-sea adventures. We found lost cities, unearthed treasures, and saved Earth by destroying all the sea monsters that were plotting against us. We became heroes — just like Superman, Bruce Lee, the Bionic Man, and Clint Eastwood.

Cause and effect: prospect of school leads to problems

James and I had the time of our lives in the park that   8
summer. It was great — until we heard about the horror of starting school. Shocked and terrified, we ran to our fortress to escape. For some reason, though, our magic kingdom had lost its powers. We fought hard that evening, trying to keep the bigger people out of our planet, but the battle was soon lost. Bruce Lee, Superman, the Bionic Man, and Clint Eastwood had all lost their special powers.

Narrative continues

School wasn't as bad as we'd thought it would be. The first   9
day, James and I sat there with our hands folded. We didn't talk or move, and we didn't dare look at each other (we would've cracked

up because we always made these goofy faces). Even though we had pens that could be transformed into weapons, we were still scared.

Description: school

Everyone was darker or lighter than we were, and the   10
teacher was speaking a strange language (English). James and I giggled as she talked. We giggled softly when everyone else talked, and they laughed out loud when it was our turn to speak.

Narrative continues

The day dragged on, and all we wanted to do was go home   11
and rebuild our fortress. Finally, after an eternity, it was almost three o'clock. James and I sat at the edge of our seats as we counted under our breath: "10, 9, 8, 7, 6, 5, 4, 3, 2, 1." At last, the bell sounded. We dashed for the door and raced home and across the street — and then we stopped. We stood still in the middle of the street with our hearts pounding like the beats of a drum. The cool September wind began to pick up, and everything

Description: the fence

became silent. We stood there and watched the metal of the fence reflect the beautiful colors of the sun. It was beautiful, and yet we hated everything about it. The new metal fence separated us from our fortress, our planet, our spaceship, our submarine — and, most important of all, from our heroes and our dreams.

We stood there for a long time. As the sun slowly turned   12
red and sank beneath the ground, so did our dreams, heroes, and hearts. Darkness soon devoured the park, and after a while we walked home with only the memories of the summer that came after the big snowstorm.

Points for Special Attention

Writing a Personal Experience Essay. Michael's instructor specified that he was to write an essay about a person or place to help his readers — other students — understand what his childhood was like. Because the assignment called for a personal experience essay, Michael was free to use the first-person pronouns *I* and *we*, as well as contractions, although neither would be acceptable in a more formal essay.

Thesis Statement. Because Michael's primary purpose in this essay was to communicate personal feelings and impressions, an argumentative thesis statement (such as "If every television in the United States disappeared, more people would have childhoods like mine") would have been inappropriate. Still, Michael states his thesis explicitly in order to unify his essay around the dominant impression he wants to convey: "While it lasted, it was paradise."

Working with Sources. Michael's assignment did not require him to consult any outside sources. If it had, he could have included background information about immigration from Vietnam to the United States — particularly data about when Vietnamese people came to the United States, where immigrants settled, how children adjusted to school and learned English, and how quickly they assimilated. Such information could have provided some context for his childhood memories.

Combining the Patterns. Michael also had more specific purposes, and these determined the patterns that shape his essay. His essay's dominant pattern is *narration,* but to help students visualize the person (James) and the place (the park) he discusses, he includes sections that *describe* and give concrete, specific *examples* as well as summarize his daily routine. These patterns work together to create an essay that conveys the nature of his childhood to readers.

Transitions. The transitions between the individual sentences and paragraphs of Michael's essay — "But now," "Ever since," "The summer that followed the big snowstorm" — serve primarily to move readers through time. This is appropriate because narration is the dominant pattern that determines the essay's overall structure.

Detail. "The Park" is full of specific detail — for example, quoted bits of dialogue in paragraph 3 and names of Michael's heroes and of particular games (and related equipment and weapons) elsewhere. The descriptive details that re-create the physical scenes — in particular, the snow, cold, frost, and wind of winter and the sun reflected on the fence — are vivid enough to help readers visualize the places Michael writes about.

Figures of Speech. Michael's essay describes a time when his imagination wandered without the restraints of adulthood. Appropriately, he uses **simile**, **metaphor**, and **personification** — "We were free like comets in the heavens"; "the park became a giant spaceship"; "We found lost cities, unearthed treasures, and saved Earth"; "Darkness soon devoured the park" — to evoke the time and place he describes.

Focus on Revision

Michael's assignment asked him to write about his childhood, and he chose to focus on his early years in the United States. When his peer-editing group discussed his essay, however, a number of students were curious about his life in Vietnam. Some of them thought he should add a paragraph summarizing the "vague images" he remembered of his earlier childhood, perhaps contrasting it with his life in the United States, as he does in passing in paragraph 2. When Michael asked his instructor about this idea, she suggested instead that he consider deleting the sentence in paragraph 1 that states he has "no desire or intention to discuss" this part of his life because it raises issues his essay does not address. After thinking about these suggestions, Michael decided to delete this sentence in his next draft and to add a brief paragraph about his life in Vietnam, contrasting the park and his friendship with James with some of his earlier, less idyllic memories.

PEER-EDITING WORKSHEET: Combining the Patterns

1. Using the annotations for "The Park" (page 667) or "On Dumpster Diving" (page 672) as a guide, annotate the essay to identify the patterns of development it uses.

2. What is the essay's thesis? If it is not explicitly stated, state it in your own words. What pattern or patterns of development are suggested by the wording of the thesis statement?

3. What dominant pattern of development determines the essay's overall structure?

4. What patterns does the writer use to develop the body paragraphs of the essay? Explain why each pattern is used in a particular paragraph or group of paragraphs.

5. What patterns are not used? Where, if anywhere, might one of these patterns serve the writer's purpose?

6. Review the essay's topic sentences. Is the wording of each topic sentence consistent with the particular pattern that structures the paragraph? If not, suggest possible ways some of the topic sentences might be reworded.

Each of the following essays combines several patterns, blending strategies to achieve the writer's purpose.

LARS EIGHNER

On Dumpster Diving

Lars Eighner (b. 1948) dropped out of the University of Texas at Austin after his third year and took a job at a state mental hospital. After leaving his job over a policy dispute in 1988 and falling behind in his rent payments, Eighner became homeless. For three years, he traveled between Austin and Los Angeles with his dog, Lizbeth, earning what money he could from writing stories for magazines. Eighner's memories of his experiences living on the street, *Travels with Lizbeth* (1993), was written on a computer he found in a Dumpster. The following chapter from that book details the practical dangers as well as the many possibilities he discovered in his "Dumpster diving." Eighner now lives in Austin and works as a freelance writer and writing coach.

Background on the homeless Although the number of homeless people in the United States is difficult to measure accurately, homelessness has become a highly visible issue in the past two decades. It is estimated, for example, that as many as ten million people experienced homelessness in this country in the late 1980s alone. This surge in homelessness has a number of causes. Perhaps most important, a booming real estate market led to a significant drop in affordable housing in many areas of the country. In several cities, single-room-occupancy hotels, which had long provided cheap lodging, were demolished or converted into luxury apartments. At the same time, new technologies left many unskilled workers jobless. Government policies against detaining the nondangerous mentally ill against their will also played a significant role. (About a quarter of all homeless people are thought to be mentally ill.) More recently, a real estate bubble and the subsequent foreclosure crisis have forced hundreds of thousands out of their houses, leading many cities to report increased demand for emergency shelter. Currently, the U.S. Department of Health and Human Services estimates that homelessness affects two to three million Americans each year, of which approximately 40 percent are children.

This chapter was composed while the author was homeless. The present tense has been preserved.

Definition: Dumpster

Long before I began Dumpster diving I was im- 1
pressed with Dumpsters, enough so that I wrote the
Merriam-Webster research service to discover what I
could about the word *Dumpster*. I learned from them
that it is a proprietary word belonging to the Dempsey
Dumpster company. Since then I have dutifully capitalized the word, although it was lowercased in almost
all the citations Merriam-Webster photocopied for me.
Dempsey's word is too apt. I have never heard these

things called anything but Dumpsters. I do not know anyone who knows the generic name for these objects. From time to time I have heard a wino or hobo give some corrupted credit to the original and call them Dipsy Dumpsters.

Narration: Eighner's story begins

I began Dumpster diving about a year before I became homeless. 2

Definition: Dumpster diving

I prefer the word *scavenging* and use the word *scrounging* when I mean to be obscure. I have heard people, evidently meaning to be polite, use the word *foraging,* but I prefer to reserve that word for gathering nuts and berries and such, which I do also according to the season and the opportunity. *Dumpster diving* seems to me to be a little too cute and, in my case, inaccurate because I lack the athletic ability to lower myself into the Dumpsters as the true divers do, much to their increased profit. 3

I like the frankness of the word *scavenging,* which I can hardly think of without picturing a big black snail on an aquarium wall. I live from the refuse of others. I am a scavenger. I think it a sound and honorable niche, although if I could I would naturally prefer to live the comfortable consumer life, perhaps — and only perhaps — as a slightly less wasteful consumer, owing to what I have learned as a scavenger. 4

Narration: story continues

While Lizbeth and I were still living in the shack on Avenue B as my savings ran out, I put almost all my sporadic income into rent. The necessities of daily life I began to extract from Dumpsters. Yes, we ate from them. Except for jeans, all my clothes came from Dumpsters. Boom boxes, candles, bedding, toilet paper, a virgin male love doll, medicine, books, a typewriter, dishes, furnishings, and change, sometimes amounting to many dollars — I acquired many things from Dumpsters. 5

Exemplification: things found in Dumpsters

Thesis statement

I have learned much as a scavenger. I mean to put some of what I have learned down here, beginning with the practical art of Dumpster diving and proceeding to the abstract. 6

What is safe to eat? 7

After all, the finding of objects is becoming something of an urban art. Even respectable employed people will sometimes find something tempting sticking out of a Dumpster or standing beside one. Quite a number of people, not all of them of the bohemian type, are willing to brag that they found this or that piece of trash. But eating from Dumpsters is what separates the dilettanti 8 from the professionals. Eating safely from the Dumpsters involves three principles: using the senses and common sense to evaluate the condition of the found materials, knowing the Dumpsters of a given area and checking them regularly, and seeking always to answer the question "Why was this discarded?"

Comparison and contrast: Dumpster divers vs. others

Perhaps everyone who has a kitchen and a regular 9 supply of groceries has, at one time or another, made a sandwich and eaten half of it before discovering mold on the bread or got a mouthful of milk before realizing the milk had turned. Nothing of the sort is likely to happen to a Dumpster diver because he is constantly reminded that most food is discarded for a reason. Yet a lot of perfectly good food can be found in Dumpsters.

Classification and division: different kinds of food found in Dumpsters and their relative safety

Canned goods, for example, turn up fairly often 10 in the Dumpsters I frequent. All except the most phobic people will be willing to eat from a can, even if it came from a Dumpster. Canned goods are among the safest foods to be found in Dumpsters but are not utterly foolproof.

Although very rare with modern canning methods, 11 botulism is a possibility. Most other forms of food poisoning seldom do lasting harm to a healthy person, but botulism is almost certainly fatal and often the first symptom is death. Except for carbonated beverages, all canned goods should contain a slight vacuum and suck air when first punctured. Bulging, rusty, and dented cans and cans that spew when punctured should be avoided, especially when the contents are not very acidic or syrupy.

Heat can break down the botulin, but this requires 12 much more cooking than most people do to canned goods. To the extent that botulism occurs at all, of course, it can occur in cans on pantry shelves as well as in cans from Dumpsters. Need I say that home-canned goods are simply too risky to be recommended.

From time to time one of my companions, aware of 13 the source of my provisions, will ask, "Do you think these crackers are really safe to eat?" For some reason it is most often the crackers they ask about.

This question has always made me angry. Of course 14 I would not offer my companion anything I had doubts about. But more than that, I wonder why he cannot evaluate the condition of the crackers for himself. I have no special knowledge and I have been wrong before. Since he knows where the food comes from, it seems to me he ought to assume some of the responsibility for deciding what he will put in his mouth. For myself I have few qualms about dry foods such as crackers, cookies, cereal, chips, and pasta if they are free of visible contaminates and still dry and crisp. Most often such things are found in the original packaging, which is not so much a positive sign as it is the absence of a negative one.

Raw fruits and vegetables with intact skins seem 15 perfectly safe to me, excluding of course the obviously rotten. Many are discarded for minor imperfections that can be pared away. Leafy vegetables, grapes, cauliflower, broccoli, and similar things may be contaminated by liquids and may be impractical to wash.

Candy, especially hard candy, is usually safe if it has 16 not drawn ants. Chocolate is often discarded only because it has become discolored as the cocoa butter de-emulsified. Candying, after all, is one method of food preservation because pathogens do not like very sugary substances.

All of these foods might be found in any Dump- 17 ster and can be evaluated with some confidence largely on the basis of appearance. Beyond these are foods that cannot be correctly evaluated without additional information.

I began scavenging by pulling pizzas out of the 18 Dumpster behind a pizza delivery shop. In general, prepared food requires caution, but in this case I knew when the shop closed and went to the Dumpster as soon as the last of the help left.

Such shops often get prank orders; both the orders 19 and the products made to fill them are called *bogus*. Because help seldom stays long at these places, pizzas are often made with the wrong topping, refused on delivery for being cold, or baked incorrectly. The products to be discarded are boxed up because inventory is kept by counting boxes: A boxed pizza can be written off; an unboxed pizza does not exist.

I never placed a bogus order to increase the supply 20 of pizzas and I believe no one else was scavenging in this Dumpster. But the people in the shop became suspicious and began to retain their garbage in the shop overnight. While it lasted I had a steady supply of fresh, sometimes warm pizza. Because I knew the Dumpster I knew the source of the pizza, and because I visited the Dumpster regularly I knew what was fresh and what was yesterday's.

*Cause and effect:
why Eighner visits
certain Dumpsters;
why students throw
out food*

The area I frequent is inhabited by many affluent   21
college students. I am not here by chance; the Dumpsters in this area are very rich. Students throw out many
good things, including food. In particular they tend to
throw everything out when they move at the end of a
semester, before and after breaks, and around midterm,
when many of them despair of college. So I find it advan-
tageous to keep an eye on the academic calendar.

Students throw food away around breaks because   22
they do not know whether it has spoiled or will spoil
before they return. A typical discard is a half jar of
peanut butter. In fact, nonorganic peanut butter does
not require refrigeration and is unlikely to spoil in any
reasonable time. The student does not know that, and
since it is Daddy's money, the student decides not to
take a chance. Opened containers require caution and
some attention to the question "Why was this discarded?" But in the case of discards from student apartments, the answer may be that the item was thrown out
through carelessness, ignorance, or wastefulness. This
can sometimes be deduced when the item is found with
many others, including some that are obviously perfectly good.

Some students, and others, approach defrosting a   23
freezer by chucking out the whole lot. Not only do the
circumstances of such a find tell the story, but also the
mass of frozen goods stays cold for a long time and
items may be found still frozen or freshly thawed.

Yogurt, cheese, and sour cream are items that are   24
often thrown out while they are still good. Occasionally
I find cheese with a spot of mold, which of course I just
pare off, and because it is obvious why such a cheese was
discarded, I treat it with less suspicion than an apparently perfect cheese found in similar circumstances. Yogurt is often discarded, still sealed, only because the
expiration date on the carton had passed. This is one of
my favorite finds because yogurt will keep for several
days, even in warm weather.

Students throw out canned goods and staples at the   25
end of semesters and when they give up college at midterm. Drugs, pornography, spirits, and the like are often
discarded when parents are expected — Dad's Day, for
example. And spirits also turn up after big party weekends, presumably discarded by the newly reformed.
Wine and spirits, of course, keep perfectly well even once
opened, but the same cannot be said of beer.

My test for carbonated soft drinks is whether they 26
still fizz vigorously. Many juices or other beverages are
too acidic or too syrupy to cause much concern, provided they are not visibly contaminated. I have discovered nasty molds in the vegetable juices, even when the
product was found under its original seal; I recommend
that such products be decanted slowly into a clear glass.
Liquids always require some care. One hot day I found a
large jug of Pat O'Brien's Hurricane mix. The jug had
been opened but was still ice cold. I drank three large
glasses before it became apparent to me that someone
had added rum to the mix, and not a little rum. I never
tasted the rum, and by the time I began to feel the effects I had already ingested a very large quantity of the
beverage. Some divers would have considered this a
boon, but being suddenly intoxicated in a public place
in the early afternoon is not my idea of a good time.

Examples: liquids that require care

I have heard of people maliciously contaminating 27
discarded food and even handouts, but mostly I have
heard of this from people with vivid imaginations who
have had no experience with Dumpsters themselves.
Just before the pizza shop stopped discarding its garbage at night, jalapeños began showing up on most of
the thrown-out pizzas. If indeed this was meant to discourage me, it was a wasted effort because I am a native
Texan.

For myself, I avoid game, poultry, pork, and egg- 28
based foods, whether I find them raw or cooked. I seldom have the means to cook what I find, but when I do I
avail myself of plentiful supplies of beef, which is often
in very good condition. I suppose fish becomes disagreeable before it becomes dangerous. Lizbeth is happy to
have any such thing that is past its prime and, in fact,
does not recognize fish as food until it is quite strong.

Home leftovers, as opposed to surpluses from res- 29
taurants, are very often bad. Evidently, especially among
students, there is a common type of personality that
carefully wraps up even the smallest leftover and shoves
it into the back of the refrigerator for six months or so
before discarding it. Characteristic of this type are the
reused jars and margarine tubs to which the remains are
committed. I avoid ethnic foods I am unfamiliar with. If
I do not know what it is supposed to look like when it is
good, I cannot be certain I will be able to tell if it is bad.

No matter how careful I am I still get dysentery at 30
least once a month, oftener in warmer weather. I do not

want to paint too romantic a picture. Dumpster diving has serious drawbacks as a way of life.

Process: how to scavenge

I learned to scavenge gradually, on my own. Since 31 then I have initiated several companions into the trade. I have learned that there is a predictable series of stages a person goes through in learning to scavenge.

At first the new scavenger is filled with disgust and 32 self-loathing. He is ashamed of being seen and may lurk around, trying to duck behind things, or he may try to dive at night. (In fact, most people instinctively look away from a scavenger. By skulking around, the novice calls attention to himself and arouses suspicion. Diving at night is ineffective and needlessly messy.)

Every grain of rice seems to be a maggot. Everything 33 seems to stink. He can wipe the egg yolk off the found can, but he cannot erase from his mind the stigma of eating garbage.

That stage passes with experience. The scavenger 34 finds a pair of running shoes that fit and look and smell brand-new. He finds a pocket calculator in perfect working order. He finds pristine ice cream, still frozen, more than he can eat or keep. He begins to understand: People throw away perfectly good stuff, a lot of perfectly good stuff.

At this stage, Dumpster shyness begins to dissipate. 35 The diver, after all, has the last laugh. He is finding all manner of good things that are his for the taking. Those who disparage his profession are the fools, not he.

He may begin to hang on to some perfectly good 36 things for which he has neither a use nor a market. Then he begins to take note of the things that are not perfectly good but are nearly so. He mates a Walkman with broken earphones and one that is missing a battery cover. He picks up things that he can repair.

At this stage he may become lost and never recover. 37 Dumpsters are full of things of some potential value to someone and also of things that never have much intrinsic value but are interesting. All the Dumpster divers I have known come to the point of trying to acquire everything they touch. Why not take it, they reason, since it is all free? This is, of course, hopeless. Most divers come to realize that they must restrict themselves to items of relatively immediate utility. But in some cases the diver simply cannot control himself. I have met several of these pack-rat types. Their ideas of the values of various pieces of junk verge on the psychotic. Every bit of glass may be a diamond, they think, and all that glisters,* gold.

I tend to gain weight when I am scavenging. Partly 38 this is because I always find far more pizza and dough-nuts than water-packed tuna, nonfat yogurt, and fresh vegetables. Also I have not developed much faith in the reliability of Dumpsters as a food source, although it has been proven to me many times. I tend to eat as if I have no idea where my next meal is coming from. But mostly I just hate to see food go to waste and so I eat much more than I should. Something like this drives the obsession to collect junk.

As for collecting objects, I usually restrict myself to 39 collecting one kind of small object at a time, such as pocket calculators, sunglasses, or campaign buttons. To live on the street I must anticipate my needs to a certain extent: I must pick up and save warm bedding I find in August because it will not be found in Dumpsters in November. As I have no access to health care, I often hoard essential drugs, such as antibiotics and antihista-mines. (This course can be recommended only to those with some grounding in pharmacology. Antibiotics, for example, even when indicated are worse than useless if taken in insufficient amounts.) But even if I had a home with extensive storage space, I could not save everything that might be valuable in some contingency.

I have proprietary feelings about my Dumpsters. As 40 I have mentioned, it is no accident that I scavenge from ones where good finds are common. But my limited experience with Dumpsters in other areas suggests to me that even in poorer areas, Dumpsters, if attended with sufficient diligence, can be made to yield a live-lihood. The rich students discard perfectly good kiwi fruit; poorer people discard perfectly good apples. Slacks and Polo shirts are found in one place; jeans and T-shirts in the other. The population of competitors rather than the affluence of the dumpers most affects the feasibility of survival by scavenging. The large num-ber of competitors is what puts me off the idea of trying to scavenge in places like Los Angeles.

Curiously, I do not mind my direct competition, 41 other scavengers, so much as I hate the can scroungers.

People scrounge cans because they have to have 42 a little cash. I have tried scrounging cans with an able-bodied companion. Afoot a can scrounger simply

Marginal notes:

Cause and effect: why Eighner gains weight when he scavenges

Cause and effect: why Eighner saves items

Comparison and contrast: Dumpsters in rich and poorer areas

Cause and effect: why people scrounge cans

---

* Eds. note — Glitters.

cannot make more than a few dollars in a day. One can extract the necessities of life from the Dumpsters directly with far less effort than would be required to accumulate the equivalent value in cans. (These observations may not hold in places with container redemption laws.)

Can scroungers, then, are people who must have 43 small amounts of cash. These are drug addicts and winos, mostly the latter because the amounts of cash are so small. Spirits and drugs do, like all other commodities, turn up in Dumpsters and the scavenger will from time to time have a half bottle of a rather good wine with his dinner. But the wino cannot survive on these occasional finds; he must have his daily dose to stave off the DTs. All the cans he can carry will buy about three bottles of Wild Irish Rose.

Comparison and contrast: can scroungers vs. true scavengers

I do not begrudge them the cans, but can scroungers 44 tend to tear up the Dumpsters, mixing the contents and littering the area. They become so specialized that they can see only cans. They earn my contempt by passing up change, canned goods, and readily hockable items.

There are precious few courtesies among scaven- 45 gers. But it is common practice to set aside surplus items: pairs of shoes, clothing, canned goods, and such. A true scavenger hates to see good stuff go to waste, and what he cannot use he leaves in good condition in plain sight.

Can scroungers lay waste to everything in their path 46 and will stir one of a pair of good shoes to the bottom of a Dumpster, to be lost or ruined in the muck. Can scroungers will even go through individual garbage cans, something I have never seen a scavenger do.

Cause and effect: why scavengers do not go through individual garbage cans

Individual garbage cans are set out on the public 47 easement only on garbage days. On the other days going through them requires trespassing close to a dwelling. Going through individual garbage cans without scattering litter is almost impossible. Litter is likely to reduce the public's tolerance of scavenging. Individual cans are simply not as productive as Dumpsters; people in houses and duplexes do not move so often and for some reason do not tend to discard as much useful material. Moreover, the time required to go through one garbage can that serves one household is not much less than the time required to go through a Dumpster that contains the refuse of twenty apartments.

But my strongest reservation about going through 48 individual garbage cans is that this seems to me a very personal kind of invasion to which I would object if I were a householder. Although many things in Dumpsters are obviously meant never to come to light, a Dumpster is somehow less personal.

I avoid trying to draw conclusions about the people   49
who dump in the Dumpsters I frequent. I think it would be unethical to do so, although I know many people will find the idea of scavenger ethics too funny for words.

*Examples: things
found in Dumpsters*
Dumpsters contain bank statements, correspon-   50
dence, and other documents, just as anyone might expect. But there are also less obvious sources of information. Pill bottles, for example. The labels bear the name of the patient, the name of the doctor, and the name of the drug. AIDS drugs and antipsychotic medicines, to name but two groups, are specific and are seldom prescribed for any other disorders. The plastic compacts for birth-control pills usually have complete label information.

Despite all of this sensitive information, I have had   51
only one apartment resident object to my going through the Dumpster. In that case it turned out the resident was a university athlete who was taking bets and who was afraid I would turn up his wager slips.

Occasionally a find tells a story. I once found a small   52
paper bag containing some unused condoms, several partial tubes of flavored sexual lubricants, a partially used compact of birth-control pills, and the torn pieces of a picture of a young man. Clearly she was through with him and planning to give up sex altogether.

Dumpster things are often sad — abandoned teddy   53
bears, shredded wedding books, despaired-of sales kits. I find many pets lying in state in Dumpsters. Although I hope to get off the streets so that Lizbeth can have a long and comfortable old age, I know this hope is not very realistic. So I suppose when her time comes she too will go into a Dumpster. I will have no better place for her. And after all, it is fitting, since for most of her life her livelihood has come from the Dumpster. When she finds something I think is safe that has been spilled from a Dumpster, I let her have it. She already knows the route around the best ones. I like to think that if she survives me she will have a chance of evading the dog catcher and of finding her sustenance on the route.

Silly vanities also come to rest in the Dumpsters. I   54
am a rather accomplished needleworker. I get a lot of material from the Dumpsters. Evidently sorority girls,

hoping to impress someone, perhaps themselves, with their mastery of a womanly art, buy a lot of embroider-by-number kits, work a few stitches horribly, and eventually discard the whole mess. I pull out their stitches, turn the canvas over, and work an original design. Do not think I refrain from chuckling as I make gifts from these kits.

I find diaries and journals. I have often thought of 55 compiling a book of literary found objects. And perhaps I will one day. But what I find is hopelessly commonplace and bad without being, even unconsciously, camp. College students also discard their papers. I am horrified to discover the kind of paper that now merits an A in an undergraduate course. I am grateful, however, for the number of good books and magazines the students throw out.

In the area I know best I have never discovered ver- 56 min in the Dumpster, but there are two kinds of kitty surprise. One is alley cats whom I meet as they leap, claws first, out of Dumpsters. This is especially thrilling when I have Lizbeth in tow. The other kind of kitty surprise is a plastic garbage bag filled with some ponderous, amorphous mass. This always proves to be used cat litter.

City bees harvest doughnut glaze and this makes 57 the Dumpster at the doughnut shop more interesting. My faith in the instinctive wisdom of animals is always shaken whenever I see Lizbeth attempt to catch a bee in her mouth, which she does whenever bees are present. Evidently some birds find Dumpsters profitable, for birdie surprise is almost as common as kitty surprise of the first kind. In hunting season all kinds of small game turn up in Dumpsters, some of it, sadly, not entirely dead. Curiously, summer and winter, maggots are uncommon.

The worst of the living and near-living hazards of 58 the Dumpsters are the fire ants. The food they claim is not much of a loss, but they are vicious and aggressive. It is very easy to brush against some surface of the Dumpster and pick up half a dozen or more fire ants, usually in some sensitive area such as the underarm. One advantage of bringing Lizbeth along as I make Dumpster rounds is that, for obvious reasons, she is very alert to ground-based fire ants. When Lizbeth recognizes a fire-ant infestation around our feet, she does the Dance of the Zillion Fire Ants. I have learned not to ignore this warning from Lizbeth, whether I perceive the tiny ants or not, but to remove ourselves at Lizbeth's first *pas de bourée.** All the more so because the ants are the worst in the summer months when I wear flip-flops if I have them. (Perhaps someone will misunderstand this. Lizbeth does the Dance of the Zillion Fire Ants when she recognizes more fire ants than she cares to eat, not when she is being bitten. Since I have learned to react promptly, she does not get bitten at all. It is the isolated patrol of fire ants that falls in Lizbeth's range that deserves pity. She finds them quite tasty.)

Process: how to go through a Dumpster

By far the best way to go through a Dumpster is to lower yourself into it. Most of the good stuff tends to settle at the bottom because it is usually weightier than the rubbish. My more athletic companions have often demonstrated to me that they can extract much good material from a Dumpster I have already been over. 59

To those psychologically or physically unprepared to enter a Dumpster, I recommend a stout stick, preferably with some barb or hook at one end. The hook can be used to grab plastic garbage bags. When I find canned goods or other objects loose at the bottom of a Dumpster, I lower a bag into it, roll the desired object into the bag, and then hoist the bag out — a procedure more easily described than executed. Much Dumpster diving is a matter of experience for which nothing will do except practice. 60

Dumpster diving is outdoor work, often surprisingly pleasant. It is not entirely predictable; things of interest turn up every day and some days there are finds of great value. I am always very pleased when I can turn up exactly the thing I most wanted to find. Yet in spite of the element of chance, scavenging more than most other pursuits tends to yield returns in some proportion to the effort and intelligence brought to bear. It is very sweet to turn up a few dollars in change from a Dumpster that has just been gone over by a wino. 61

The land is now covered with cities. The cities are full of Dumpsters. If a member of the canine race is ever able to know what it is doing, then Lizbeth knows that when we go around to the Dumpsters, we are hunting. I think of scavenging as a modern form of self-reliance. In any event, after having survived nearly ten years of government service, where everything is geared to the lowest common denominator, I find it refreshing to have work that rewards initiative and effort. Certainly I 62

* Eds. note — A ballet step.

Cause and effect: results of Eighner's experiences as a scavenger

would be happy to have a sinecure again, but I am no longer heartbroken that I left one.

I find from the experience of scavenging two rather 63 deep lessons. The first is to take what you can use and let the rest go by. I have come to think that there is no value in the abstract. A thing I cannot use or make useful, perhaps by trading, has no value however rare or fine it may be. I mean useful in some broad sense — some art I would find useful and some otherwise.

I was shocked to realize that some things are not 64 worth acquiring, but now I think it is so. Some material things are white elephants that eat up the possessor's substance. The second lesson is the transience of material being. This has not quite converted me to a dualist,* but it has made some headway in that direction. I do not suppose that ideas are immortal, but certainly mental things are longer lived than other material things.

Once I was the sort of person who invests objects 65 with sentimental value. Now I no longer have those objects, but I have the sentiments yet.

Many times in our travels I have lost everything but 66 the clothes I was wearing and Lizbeth. The things I find in Dumpsters, the love letters and rag dolls of so many lives, remind me of this lesson. Now I hardly pick up a thing without envisioning the time I will cast it aside. This I think is a healthy state of mind. Almost everything I have now has already been cast out at least once, proving that what I own is valueless to someone.

Anyway, I find my desire to grab for the gaudy 67 bauble has been largely sated. I think this is an attitude I share with the very wealthy — we both know there is plenty more where what we have came from. Between us are the rat-race millions who nightly scavenge the cable channels looking for they know not what.

I am sorry for them.   68

• • •

Comprehension

1. In your own words, give a one-sentence definition of *Dumpster diving*.
2. List some of Eighner's answers to the question "Why was this discarded?" (8). What additional reasons can you think of?
3. What foods does Eighner take particular care to avoid? Why?

---

* Eds. note — Someone who believes that the world consists of two opposing forces, such as mind and matter.

4. In paragraph 30, Eighner comments, "Dumpster diving has serious drawbacks as a way of life." What drawbacks does he cite in his essay? What additional drawbacks are implied? Can you think of others?

5. Summarize the stages in the process of learning to scavenge.

6. In addition to food, what else does Eighner scavenge for? Into what general categories do these items fall?

7. Why does Eighner hate can scroungers?

8. What lessons has Eighner learned as a Dumpster diver?

Purpose and Audience

1. In paragraph 6, Eighner states his purpose: to record what he has learned as a Dumpster diver. What additional purposes do you think he had in setting his ideas down on paper?

2. Do you think most readers are apt to respond to Eighner's essay with sympathy? Pity? Impatience? Contempt? Disgust? How do you react? Why?

3. Why do you think Eighner chose not to provide much background about his life — his upbringing, education, or work history — before he became homeless? Do you think this decision was a wise one? How might such information (for example, any of the details in the headnote that precedes the essay) have changed readers' reactions to his discussion?

4. In paragraph 8, Eighner presents three principles one must follow to eat safely from a Dumpster; in paragraphs 59–60 he explains how to go through a Dumpster; and throughout the essay he includes many cautions and warnings. Clearly, he does not expect his audience to take up Dumpster diving. What, then, is his purpose in including such detailed explanations?

5. When Eighner begins paragraph 9 with "Perhaps everyone who has a kitchen," he encourages readers to identify with him. Where else does he make efforts to help readers imagine themselves in his place? Are these efforts successful? Explain your response.

6. What effect do you think the essay's last sentence is calculated to have on readers? What effect does it have on you?

Style and Structure

1. Eighner opens his essay with a fairly conventional strategy: extended definitions of *Dumpster* and *Dumpster diving*. What techniques does he use in paragraphs 1 through 3 to develop these definitions? Is beginning with definitions the best strategy for this essay? Explain your answer.

2. **Vocabulary Project.** In paragraph 3, Eighner suggests several alternative words for *diving* as he uses it in his essay. Consult an unabridged dictionary to determine the connotations of each of his alternatives. What are the pros and cons of substituting one of these words for *diving* in Eighner's title and throughout the essay?

3. This long essay contains three one-sentence paragraphs. Why do you think Eighner isolates these sentences? Do you think any of them should be combined with an adjacent paragraph? Explain your reasoning.

4. As the introductory note explains, Eighner chose to retain the present tense even though he was no longer homeless when the essay was published. Why do you think he decided to preserve the present tense?

5. Eighner's essay includes a number of lists that catalog items he came across (for example, in paragraphs 5 and 50). Identify as many of these lists as you can. Why do you think Eighner includes such extensive lists?

Journal Entry

In paragraphs 21–25, Eighner discusses the discarding of food by college students. Does your own experience support his observations? Do you think he is being too hard on students, or does his characterization seem accurate?

Writing Workshop

1. Write an essay about a homeless person you have seen in your community. Use any patterns you like to structure your paper. When you have finished, annotate your essay to identify the patterns you have used.

2. Write an email to your school's dean of students recommending steps that can be taken on your campus to redirect discarded (but edible) food to the homeless. Use process and exemplification to structure your message, and use information from Eighner's essay to support your points. (Be sure to acknowledge your source.)

3. **Working with Sources.** Taking Eighner's point of view and using information from his essay, write an argumentative essay with a thesis statement that takes a strong stand against homelessness and recommends government or private measures to end it. If you like, you may write your essay in the form of a statement by Eighner to a congressional committee. Be sure to document any words or ideas you borrow from Eighner, and include a works-cited page. (See Chapter 18 for information on MLA documentation.)

Combining the Patterns

Review the annotations that identify each pattern of development used in this essay. Which patterns seem to be most effective in helping you understand and empathize with the life of a homeless person? Why?

Thematic Connections

- "The Untouchable" (page 494)
- "Homeless" (page 510)
- The Declaration of Independence (page 550)

DANA STEVENS

* "Composing tirades" (handwritten annotation)

Your Flip-Flops Are Grossing Me Out

Dana Stevens (b. 1966), a film critic at *Slate* magazine, grew up in New York and Texas and earned a Ph.D. in comparative literature at the University of California, Berkeley. She has written for the *New York Times,* the *Atlantic Monthly,* and the *Washington Post,* among other publications.

Background on the social contract In the following essay, Dana Stevens suggests that flip-flops separate "the wearer's behavior from the social contract." Although her tone here may be tongue-in-cheek, the idea of a "social contract" has its origins in philosophy and political theory. Briefly, the social contract is an agreement among members of a society, or between a government and its citizens, that defines, codifies, and limits the rights and obligations of each. Such a contract might include a shared code of morality or rules of behavior that people accept on the condition that other members of the society also accept them. Philosophers such as Thomas Hobbes, Jean-Jacques Rousseau, John Locke, and John Rawls, among others, have sought to define and explain the origins of social contracts.

1   "Some slow week in summer, I should write a tirade against flip-flops," I unwisely remarked to my editor one disgusting August afternoon a few years back, as we walked back from lunch behind a woman whose street-blackened soles could be glimpsed anew with each *schlapp!*-ing step. Now, during an early-July lull between big summer movie releases, he's gone and called my bluff. And the truth is, I'm not really one for composing tirades. I'm a live-and-let-live sort when it comes to personal grooming and style, and whatever qualities I'm remembered for at my funeral, I'm fairly certain neither hygiene nor chic will top the list. But the increasing prevalence of all-day urban flip-flop wear during the summer months is something we need to talk about as a culture.

2   I won't deny that this ancient shoe design, which can be seen in Egyptian murals dating back to 4000 B.C. (the British Museum owns a 1,500-year-old pair made of papyrus) has its situational utility. On the beach, by the pool, showering at the gym, taking out the garbage, making a quick run to the Laundromat — all these are moments in which the advantages of lightweight, easy-to-don-and-doff footwear are self-evident (even if personally, as a non-fan of the feeling of rigid objects wedged between my toes, I'd prefer an across-the-foot "slide" in those moments). I understand, too, that there are parts of the world where the inexpensive, mass-produced flip-flop is widely worn for reasons other than aesthetic choice; in many circumstances, it may be the only shoe that's both available and affordable. But we are not here to discuss the footwear choices of impoverished

yup! (handwritten annotation)

villagers, just-showered athletes, or Jimmy Buffett strumming his six-string on his front porch in Margaritaville.* We're talking about grown adults in affluent societies — people presumably in possession of at least one pair of actual shoes — who see fit to navigate the grimy sidewalks of large cities shod only in a loosely flapping, half-inch-thick slip of rubber. Those people — you, if you're among them — need to face the reality that you are, in essence, going barefoot, and it's grossing the rest of us out.

From what angle to approach the wrongness first? The crux of the flip- 3 flop problem, for me, lies in the decoupling of footwear from foot with each step — and the attendant decoupling of the wearer's behavior from the social contract. Extended flip-flop use seems to transport people across some sort of etiquette Rubicon where the distinction between public and private, inside and outside, shod and barefoot, breaks down entirely. I've witnessed flip-flop wearers on the New York City subway slip their "shoes" off altogether and cross their feet on the train-car floor with a contented sigh, as though they were already home and kicking back in front of a DVR'd *Cheers*** marathon. We would all look askance at a person who removed his socks and sneakers on the train before ostentatiously propping his naked dogs in plain sight. Why do people get a break just because they happen to be wearing footgear that takes them 90 percent of the way there?

> " The crux of the flip-flop problem, for me, lies in the . . . decoupling of the wearer's behavior from the social contract. "

Then there's the lack of support and protection the flip-flop offers its 4 wearer's foot. Of course, the same might be said of any flat, thin-soled shoe — but as soon as you slap a heel strap and a buckle onto that sad, flapping sole, my objections disappear. Individual sandals and clogs are subject to scrutiny as to their wearability and visual appeal: Tevas and Crocs may be aesthetic abominations unto the Lord, but at least they perform most of the basic functions of shoes. They permit the wearer to break into a run or take a step backward when needed (who can predict when you'll need to sprint to catch a bus or help a friend move his couch on short notice?). And with their thicker soles and foot-harnessing straps, they at least go some way toward protecting the feet from the most egregious aggressors in the outside environment: broken glass, loose nails at construction sites, wads of gum, pools of motor oil, piles of dog poop, puddles of human effluvia. (If this unappetizing imagery is skeeving out you flip-flop loyalists, welcome to the mental world of *everyone who looks at your feet*.)

It's tough to find hard numbers for the growing pervasiveness of 5 flip-flops as city footwear, though the explosive growth of the popular,

---

* Eds. note — American singer-songwriter associated with music about escapism, relaxation, and drinking.

** Eds. note — Popular television sitcom that ran from 1982 to 1993.

Brazilian-owned Havaianas brand over the past two decades suggests that wherever we're choosing to wear them, we're certainly buying more of the things than ever. But anecdotally, it's evident that flip-flop culture is steadily gaining ground. In 2005, several members of the Northwestern women's lacrosse team wore them on a visit to the Bush White House, sparking a national conversation about whether shoes originally worn to ward off fungus at the gym were also appropriate for trekking through the Oval Office. By 2011, the stigma had diminished to the extent that Obama became the first-ever president to be photographed wearing a pair of flip-flops (though to the president's credit, the context — an ice-cream shop in his native Hawaii, where he was vacationing with his family — was entirely flip-flop appropriate. It's not like he was meeting with foreign dignitaries).

I contacted some professionals to confirm my suspicion that flip-flops 6 are not only unappealing and unsanitary, but actively bad for the health of the human foot. Dr. Richard Kushner, a podiatrist in New York City, stopped just short of committing to the condemnation of flip-flops per se — though he allowed that they left the foot more vulnerable to injury, and that any thin-soled, unsupportive shoe would encourage the eventual degradation of the structures that maintain the joints of the foot: "If the foot is too flat on the ground, there's a clawing effect that happens with the toes." Asked about the hygienic properties of the flip-flop as city street-wear, he replied, "That's another matter. That's something that I myself certainly wouldn't . . ." He trailed off, joining me in a moment of anguished silence.

Jeff Gray, C. Ped., a pedorthist and director of education at the or- 7 thotics company Superfeet Worldwide in Ferndale, Washington, was more voluble in his condemnation of the rubber-soled scourge. "I see young people going through airports wearing flip-flops and I want to run after them and say 'I can help you.' And half their foot isn't even on the shoe; it's collapsed off the shoe. . . . I believe twenty years from now we're going to see a whole generation who will have foot problems when they're in their thirties and forties — soft tissue problems, joint problems, arthritis." I asked him to lay out the precise anatomical problem with locomotion via flip-flop: "Mother Nature knew that when your foot hit the ground it needed to be a loose bag of bones; then when you push off it converts to a rigid lever. Shoes are really a timing device that manages the transition between those two states."

With the ordinary flip-flop, he continued, the "bag of bones" stage of 8 the step lasts too long, leaving the foot in the pronated (inwardly rolled) position. (This would explain why flip-flop soles tend to wear out from the inside edge first, and why people walking in them often seem to have inwardly collapsing ankles.) Gray also believes that backless shoes in general are a major cause of injuries and falls, especially among older people, thanks to their lack of maneuverability: "Go and take the lug nuts off your car and see how well you corner."

My final line of argument against flip-flops is a more nebulous one, 9 having to do with their laziness and lack of character as footwear. Because of the ease with which they're put on and removed — along, perhaps, with their generic ubiquity — flip-flops connote a sort of half-dressed slatternliness, a sense that the wearer has forgotten to do anything at all with his or her body from the ankles down. I was going to call them "foot underwear" (nomenclature that would be consistent with their older U.S. designation as "thongs," a term still used in Australia), but that's not quite right — after all, it's not like you're going to put a pair of real shoes on top. More precisely, flip-flops are foot *robes,* and seeing hundreds of strangers walk by in dirty, sidewalk-sweeping bathrobes barely held on with loosely tied belts (the analogy holds up all the way through) is no one's idea of summer fun. Unless your daily commute is a stroll from your hammock across white sands to the piña colada stand you manage in Waikiki, please consider leaving the foot robes at home.

· · ·

Comprehension

1. According to Stevens, what prompted her to write this essay?

2. In paragraph 2, Stevens provides some background about flip-flops. What else does she accomplish in this paragraph?

3. According to Stevens, how are flip-flops different from other kinds of casual footwear?

4. Under what circumstances does Stevens find flip-flops appropriate?

5. What, according to Stevens, is the "crux of the flip-flop problem" (3)?

6. In paragraph 5, Stevens notes that "anecdotally, it's evident that flip-flop culture is steadily gaining ground." How does she support this statement?

7. What is Stevens's greatest objection to flip-flops?

Purpose and Audience

1. Do you think this essay's primary purpose is to amuse, to inform, or to persuade? Explain.

2. How does Stevens characterize herself in this essay — for example, in paragraph 1? Is this characterization likely to establish common ground with her readers or to alienate them?

3. This article originally appeared in *Slate,* an online magazine that covers culture and politics. Whom do you think Stevens considers her primary audience — those who wear flip-flops or those (like herself) who object to them? How can you tell?

4. At the end of paragraph 1, Stevens says, "But the increasing prevalence of all-day urban flip-flop wear during the summer months is something we need to talk about as a culture." Is this her essay's thesis? If not, is there another sentence in the essay that could serve as a thesis statement?

Style and Structure

1. Where does Stevens cite expert opinion to support her position on flip-flops? Where does she use personal opinion? Where does she use anecdotal evidence? Which kind of support for her position do you find most convincing? Why?

2. Do you think the essay's title is effective, or would you prefer a more objective, less informal title?

3. **Vocabulary Project.** What other meanings does the word *flip-flop* have? Given these other meanings, is *flip-flop* the best term for this kind of footwear? What other name might be more appropriate?

4. In paragraph 9, Stevens refers to flip-flops as "foot underwear" and "foot *robes*." What other terms can you coin to describe them?

Journal Entry

What is your position on flip-flops? Do you share Stevens's views, or do you disagree with her? Why?

Writing Workshop

1. Write an essay taking a position on the appropriateness or attractiveness of another common item of casual apparel — for example, T-shirts, sweatshirts, baseball caps, tank tops, or cutoffs.

2. **Working with Sources.** Find some information on the origin of one of the items listed in question 1 above (or another kind of casual apparel). Then, write an essay in which you trace this item's development, describing it and comparing and contrasting it with similar items. In your thesis statement, take a position on the item's attractiveness, functionality, and appropriateness for a twenty-first-century lifestyle. Be sure to document all material from your sources and to include a works-cited page. (See Chapter 18 for information on MLA documentation.)

Combining the Patterns

What patterns of development does Stevens use in this essay? Annotate the essay to identify each pattern. Use the annotations accompanying "On Dumpster Diving" (page 672) as a guide.

Thematic Connections

- From *Persepolis II* (page 112)
- "My First Conk" (page 283)
- "The Wife-Beater" (page 514)
- "Inked Well" (page 692)

DAVID KIRBY

Inked Well

Poet David Kirby is a longtime professor of English at Florida State University, where he teaches nineteenth-century American literature and creative writing. He has authored or coauthored twenty-nine books, including the poetry collections *The Ha-Ha* (2003) and *The House on Boulevard Street* (2007), literary studies such as *Mark Strand and the Poet's Place in Contemporary Culture* (1990) and *Herman Melville* (1993), and the essay collection *Ultra-Talk: Johnny Cash, the Mafia, Shakespeare, Drum Music, St. Teresa of Avila, and 17 Other Colossal Topics of Conversation* (2007).

Background on tattoos People have sported tattoos for more than five thousand years. In some cultures, tattoos have marked a rite of passage into adulthood. They have also symbolized spiritual protection, status within a clan, fertility, and social ostracism, among other things. (Interestingly, the teachings of both Judaism and Islam specifically prohibit tattooing.) In modern Western culture, tattoos primarily serve as body adornment, although there are some exceptions — for example, the Nazis forcibly tattooed identifying numbers on many Jews, and members of some street gangs wear tattoos that signify membership. In the United States today, the most popular tattoos include skulls, hearts, eagles, and crosses as well as abstract tribal designs based on motifs that originated among Polynesian Islanders (historically, some of the most heavily tattooed people in the world). Celtic designs, flowers and butterflies, angels, stars, dragons, Chinese characters, and swallows are also popular, and anchors, once staples among sailors, are now making a comeback. Increasingly, tattoo artists are being taken seriously, and an original design may be worth thousands of dollars, or even more. Today, conventions of tattoo enthusiasts, such as the traveling Bodyart Expo, draw millions of participants each year. The cost of getting a tattoo can be as much as a hundred dollars an hour. (Getting rid of a tattoo can cost considerably more.)

Some tattooed people are easier to read than others.   1

When Richard Costello tried to sell stolen motorcycle parts on eBay   2 earlier this year, he put the items on the floor and photographed them, though the photos also included his bare feet, with the word *White* tattooed on one and *Trash* on the other. The bike's lawful owner did a Web search, found what appeared to be the stolen parts, and notified the Clearwater, Florida, police department. Since jail records typically include identifying marks, it didn't take long for local detectives to identify Mr. Costello and set up a sting. He was arrested after showing up with a van full of stolen parts and is now facing trial. According to Sgt. Greg Stewart, Mr. Costello "just tiptoed his way back to jail."

L'Affaire White Trash confirmed just about everything that I thought 3
about tattoos until recently; namely, that in addition to being nasty and
unsanitary, tattoos only grace the skins of either bottom feeders or those
who want to pretend they are. Richard Costello's phenomenal act of self-
betrayal wouldn't have been a surprise at all to modernist architect Adolph
Loos, whose influential 1908 essay "Ornament and Crime" is still cited
today as a potent argument against frills and fancy stuff. Mr. Loos wrote in
effect a manifesto opposing decoration, which he saw as a mark of primitive cultures, and in favor of simplicity, which is a sign of, well, modernism.
Thus, Mr. Loos reasoned, it's OK for a Pacific Islander to cover himself and
all his possessions with ink and carvings, whereas "a modern person [i.e., a
European] who tattoos himself is either a criminal or a degenerate. . . .
People with tattoos not in prison are either latent criminals or degenerate
aristocrats."

So, presuming the kid with a Tweety Bird tattoo on his forearm who 4
delivered your pizza last night isn't a down-on-his-luck baronet who's trying to earn enough money to return to his ancestral estate in Northumber-
land and claim his seat on the Queen's Privy Council, does the fact that
he's slinging pies mean that he simply hasn't lived long enough to commit
his first murder? Not necessarily: tattoos have a richer social history than
one might think.

Tattoos were brought to Europe from Polynesia by eighteenth-century 5
British explorers, as Margo DeMello writes in *Bodies of Inscription: A Cultural
History of the Modern Tattoo Community* (2000). Europeans who had tattoos
in those days were not social bottom dwellers. And as Charles C. Mann
points out in *1491* (2005), Americans first saw tattoos in the New World on
their conflicted Indian hosts as early as 1580. To Protestants of ascetic tem-
peraments, these exotic displays were of a piece with the colonists' propensity to see Indians as primeval savages.

Perhaps predictably, however, tattoos came ultimately to signify patri- 6
otism rather than exoticism in the United States. The first known professional tattoo artist in the United States was one Martin Hildebrandt, who
set up shop in New York City in 1846. Mr. Hildebrandt became instrumental in establishing the tradition of the tattooed serviceman by practicing
his craft on soldiers and sailors on both sides in the Civil War as he mi-
grated from one camp to another.

And then occurred one of those curious little shifts that make history 7
so delicious. Tattoos became fashionable among members of the European
aristocracy, who encountered the practice during nineteenth-century trips
to the Far East.

By the beginning of World War I, though, the lords and ladies had all 8
but abandoned bodily decoration. Why? Because by then, anybody could
get a tattoo. The laborious process involving hand-tapping ink into the
skin with a single needle was made obsolete with the invention of the electric tattoo machine in 1891. Tattooing suddenly became easier, less painful, and, mainly, cheaper. This led to the speedy spread of the practice
throughout the working class and its abandonment by the rich.

By the middle of the twentieth century, tattooing seemed largely the 9
province of bikers, convicts, and other groups on the margins of society,
much as Mr. Loos had predicted. Except for all those patriotic servicemen,
a century ago tattoos were the tribal marks that you paid somebody to cut
into your skin so that everyone would know you belonged to a world populated by crooks and creeps, along with a few bored aristocrats who would
probably have been attracted to living a life of crime had their trust funds
not rendered it redundant. And if things had stayed that way, I wouldn't be
writing this essay: tattoos would be simply one more way of differentiating
"Them" from "Us."

But "We" are the ones who are tattooed now: in the late twentieth cen- 10
tury, the middle class began showing up in droves at tattoo parlors. A study
in the June 2006 issue of the *Journal of the American Academy of Dermatology*
reveals that as many as 24 percent of men and women between the ages of
eighteen and fifty have one or more tattoos — up from just 15 to 16 percent
in 2003. Men and women are equally likely to be tattooed, though the
women surveyed are more likely to have body piercings, as well.

How did this change come to pass? Those of us who are certain we'll 11
never get a tattoo will always shudder with joy when we read about knuckle-
heads like Richard Costello. But more and more people who wouldn't have
dreamed of being tattooed a few years back are paying good money to have
sketches of boom boxes, court jesters, and spider webs incised into their
hides. Why, and what does it say about the world we live in?

To answer these questions, I walked the streets of Tallahassee, Florida, 12
accosting total and sometimes menacing-looking strangers with the intent of asking them questions about the most intimate parts of their bodies. Any stereotypes of tattooed "victims" I had fell by the wayside rather
quickly.

One of my first lessons was that people can get the biggest, most color- 13
ful tattoos either for exceedingly complex reasons or none at all. Jen (I'll use
first names only), a pretty, slender brunette in her late twenties, said getting a tattoo was simply on a list of things she wanted to do. Melissa, a grad
student in modern languages whom I spied in a bookstore wearing a pair
of low-slung jeans, got a black and blue love knot high on one hip because
she and her friend wanted identical tattoos, "even though she's not my
friend anymore." Becky wanted a tattoo that would be a means of "making
a promise to myself that I would become the person I wanted to be, that I
would improve my life through hard work."

Of the dozen or so subjects I interviewed, Jodie was the sweetest, the 14
most articulate, and the most heavily inked — her arms were fully sleeved in
tattoos, and she was making plans to get started on her hands and neck.
Jodie explained that she had been a "cutter" who "was having a lot of
trouble with hurting myself physically for various reasons, so I began to get
tattooed. It didn't take me long to realize that getting tattooed was quite
comparable to cutting myself; it was a way for me to 'bleed out' the emotional pains which I was unable to deal with otherwise."

Jodie is smart as well as troubled. She knew she was hurting herself and 15
would continue to do so, so she sublimated her self-destruction and made
art of it, as surely as, say, poet Sylvia Plath* did — temporarily, anyway.

It seems that more and more people from every walk of life in these 16
United States are getting tattooed. These pioneers are "deterritorializing"
tattoos, in Ms. DeMello's words, liberating them from patriotic sailors and
dim-bulb motorcycle thieves and making them available to soccer moms
and dads.

Tattoos have always been a means of identifying oneself, notes Ms. 17
DeMello, and are always meant to be read — even a tattoo that's hidden
becomes a secret book of sorts. When you get a tattoo, you write yourself,
in a manner of speaking, and make it possible for others to read you, which
means that every tattoo has a story.

There are primarily two types of tattoo narratives, the Record Book 18
and the Canvas. Melissa, the young woman who got her tattoo to signify
bonding with a friend, was capturing a relationship as one might with a
photograph. In the pop music world, rap artists and other musicians sometimes get tattoos of friends or relatives who have died violently or merely
passed away. The Dixie Chicks agreed to get a little chick footprint on the
insteps of their feet for every No. 1 album they had.

If your body is a Record Book, then you and everyone who sees you is 19
looking back at the events depicted there. But if you see your body as a Canvas, then the story you tell is, at least in its conception and execution, as
inner-driven as any by Faulkner or Hemingway. Jodie, for example, is going
over every inch of her body, using it as a way to tell herself a story she's
beginning to understand only gradually. The more she understands, the
more she "revises," just as any other artist might: her first tattoo was "a
horrible butterfly thing," she told me, "which has since been covered up
with a lovely raven."

Every person with a tattoo is a link in a chain of body modification 20
that goes back to the dawn of human history. Researchers have found
sharpened pieces of manganese dioxide —
black crayons, really — that Neanderthals
may have used to color animal skins as well
as their own. The ancient Egyptians practiced simple tattooing. Today, radically different cultures share an obsession with body
remodeling that goes far beyond mere tattooing. African tribes pierce and scar the
body routinely; weightlifters pump their pecs until they bulge like grape-
fruit; women pay for cosmetic breast enlargement or reduction. And if
that's not enough evidence that body modification is endemic, I have one
word for you: *Botox.*

> In a word, tattoos
> are now officially OK
> by me.

---

* Eds. note — American confessional poet who committed suicide in 1963 at the
age of thirty-one.

The point of all this is self-expression — and we seem to be living in a   21
time where that's what nearly everybody (word carefully chosen) wants to
do, in one way or another. As with all lifestyle changes, the tricky part is
knowing when to stop.

As I said, I used to think tattoos were for either lowlifes or those who   22
wanted to pretend they were, but my mind now stands changed by the
thoughtful, articulate people I talked to and the spectacular designs that
had been inked into their bodies. In a word, tattoos are now officially OK
by me.

Does that mean I'd get one? Not on your life.   23

Comprehension   — Self -expression

1. Explain the possible meanings of "Inked Well," the essay's title.

2. Kirby opens his essay with a narrative that recounts "L'Affaire White
   Trash" (3). Why does he begin with this narrative? What does it illustrate
   about tattoos?

3. Where does Kirby present information on the history of tattoos? Why
   does he include this background? Is it necessary? Why does he return to
   this historical background in paragraph 20?

4. According to Kirby, how has the tattooed population changed over the
   years? What factors explain these changes?

5. What does Kirby mean when he says, " 'We' are the ones who are tattooed
   now" (10)?

6. What two kinds of "tattoo narratives" does Kirby identify? How are they
   different?

7. According to Kirby, for what reasons do people get tattoos? Can you
   think of additional reasons?

8. How have Kirby's ideas about tattoos changed over the years? *Why* have
   they changed?

Purpose and Audience

1. Is Kirby's primary purpose to provide information about tattoos, to
   entertain readers, to explore his own feelings about tattoos, or to persuade readers to consider getting (or not getting) tattoos? Explain.

2. In paragraph 4, Kirby says that "tattoos have a richer social history than
   one might think." Is this his essay's thesis? If not, what is the thesis of
   "Inked Well"?

3. Why do you think Kirby mentions the universal "obsession with body
   remodeling" in paragraph 20? How do you think he expects this reference
   to affect his audience's reactions to his thesis? How do you react?

Style and Structure

1. **Vocabulary Project.** What is the origin of the word *tattoo*? Check an online dictionary to find out. Then, visit a tattoo website such as tattoos .com, and list some words and phrases that are part of the vocabulary of the tattoo industry. Define several of these words and expressions in lay-person's terms.

2. What do you see as this essay's dominant pattern of development? Why?

3. Kirby's first and last paragraphs are each just one line long. Are his short introduction and conclusion effective? If you were to expand them, what would you add? Why?

4. Where does Kirby cite experts? Where does he include statistics? What do these kinds of information add to his essay?

Journal Entry

Do you see tattoos as art or as a kind of defacement or self-mutilation? Explain your feelings.

Writing Workshop

1. **Working with Sources.** Find some pictures of tattoos online. Then, write a classification-and-division essay that discusses the kinds of tattoos you find there. (You might want to begin by looking at "Four Tattoos," page 222.) Be sure your essay has a thesis statement that makes a point about tattoos, and use exemplification, description, and comparison and contrast to support your thesis. If you like, you may illustrate your essay with photos or drawings you find on the Web, but if you do, remember to document your sources and to include a works-cited page. (See Chapter 18 for information on MLA documentation.)

2. In paragraph 11, Kirby asks what the prevalence of tattoos says about the world we live in. Using cause and effect as your dominant pattern of development, write an essay that tries to explain what accounts for this phenomenon. Use description and exemplification to support your points.

3. In paragraph 17, Kirby says, "When you get a tattoo, you write yourself, in a manner of speaking, and make it possible for others to read you, which means that every tattoo has a story." What story would you like your own tattoo (or tattoos) to tell?

Combining the Patterns

What patterns of development does Kirby use in his essay? Annotate the essay to identify each pattern. Use the annotations accompanying "On Dumpster Diving" (page 672) as a guide.

Thematic Connections

- "Four Tattoos" (page 222)
- "Why Looks Are the Last Bastion of Discrimination" (page 244)
- "Medium Ash Brown" (page 277)
- "My First Conk" (page 283)
- "The Wife-Beater" (page 514)

JONATHAN SWIFT

A Modest Proposal

Jonathan Swift (1667–1745) was born in Dublin, Ireland, and spent much of his life journeying between his homeland, where he had a modest income as an Anglican priest, and England, where he wished to be part of the literary establishment. The author of many satires and political pamphlets, he is best known today for *Gulliver's Travels* (1726), a sharp satire that, except among academics, is now read primarily as a fantasy for children.

Background on the English-Irish conflict At the time Swift wrote "A Modest Proposal," Ireland had been essentially under British rule since 1171, with the British often brutally suppressing rebellions by the Irish people. When Henry VIII of England declared a Protestant Church of Ireland, many of the Irish remained fiercely Roman Catholic, and this led to even greater contention. By the early 1700s, the English-controlled Irish Parliament had passed laws that severely limited the rights of Irish Catholics, and British trade policies had begun to seriously depress the Irish economy. A fierce advocate for the Irish people in their struggle under British rule, Swift published several works supporting the Irish cause. The following sharply ironic essay was written during the height of a terrible famine in Ireland, when the British were proposing a devastating tax on the impoverished Irish citizenry. Note that Swift does not write in his own voice here but adopts the persona of one who does not recognize the barbarity of his "solution."

It is a melancholy object to those who walk through this great town* or travel in the country, when they see the streets, the roads, and cabin doors, crowded with beggars of the female sex, followed by three, four, or six children, all in rags and importuning every passenger for an alms. These mothers, instead of being able to work for their honest livelihood, are forced to employ all their time in strolling to beg sustenance for their helpless infants, who, as they grow up, either turn thieves for want of work, or leave their dear native country to fight for the Pretender in Spain, or sell themselves to the Barbadoes.**

I think it is agreed by all parties that this prodigious number of children in the arms, or on the backs, or at the heels of their mothers, and frequently of their fathers, is in the present deplorable state of the kingdom a very great additional grievance; and therefore whoever could find out a fair, cheap, and easy method of making these children sound, useful members

---

* Eds. note — Dublin.
** Eds. note — Many young Irishmen left their country to fight as mercenaries in Spain's civil war or to work as indentured servants in the West Indies.

of the commonwealth would deserve so well of the public as to have his statue set up for a preserver of the nation.

But my intention is very far from being confined to provide only for 3 the children of professed beggars; it is of a much greater extent, and shall take in the whole number of infants at a certain age who are born of parents in effect as little able to support them as those who demand our charity in the streets.

As to my own part, having turned my thoughts for many years upon 4 this important subject, and maturely weighed the several schemes of the other projectors, I have always found them grossly mistaken in their computation. It is true, a child just dropped from its dam may be supported by her milk for a solar year, with little other nourishment; at most not above the value of two shillings, which the mother may certainly get, or the value in scraps, by her lawful occupation of begging; and it is exactly at one year old that I propose to provide for them in such a manner as instead of being a charge upon their parents or the parish, or wanting food and raiment for the rest of their lives, they shall on the contrary contribute to the feeding, and partly to the clothing, of many thousands.

There is likewise another great advantage in my scheme, that it will 5 prevent those involuntary abortions, and that horrid practice of women murdering their bastard children, alas, too frequent among us, sacrificing the poor innocent babies, I doubt, more to avoid the expense than the shame, which would move tears and pity in the most savage and inhuman breast.

The number of souls in this kingdom being usually reckoned one mil- 6 lion and a half, of these I calculate there may be about two hundred thousand couples whose wives are breeders, from which number I subtract thirty thousand couples who are able to maintain their own children, although I apprehend there cannot be so many under the present distress of the kingdom; but this being granted, there will remain an hundred and seventy thousand breeders. I again subtract fifty thousand for those women who miscarry, or whose children die by accident or disease within the year. There only remain an hundred and twenty thousand children of poor parents annually born. The question therefore is, how this number shall be reared and provided for, which, as I have already said, under the present situation of affairs, is utterly impossible by all the methods hitherto proposed. For we can neither employ them in handicraft nor agriculture; we neither build houses (I mean in the country) nor cultivate land. They can very seldom pick up livelihood by stealing till they arrive at six years old, except where they are of towardly parts,* although I confess they learn the rudiments much earlier, during which time they can however be looked upon only as probationers, as I have been informed by a principal gentleman in the country of Cavan, who protested to me that he never knew above one or two instances under the age of six, even in a part of the kingdom so renowned for the quickest proficiency in that art.

---

* Eds. note — Precocious.

I am assured by our merchants that a boy or a girl before twelve years 7
old is no salable commodity; and even when they come to this age, they will
not yield above three pounds, or three pounds and half a crown at most on
the Exchange; which cannot turn to account either to the parents or the
kingdom, the charge of nutriment and rags having been at least four times
that value.

I shall now therefore humbly propose my own thoughts, which I hope 8
will not be liable to the least objection.

I have been assured by a very knowing American of my acquaintance in 9
London, that a young healthy child well nursed is at a year old a most delicious, nourishing, and wholesome food, whether stewed, roasted, baked,
or boiled; and I make no doubt that it will equally serve in fricassee or a
ragout.

I do therefore humbly offer it to public consideration that of the hun- 10
dred and twenty thousand children, already computed, twenty thousand
may be reserved for breed, whereof only one fourth part to be males, which
is more than we allow to sheep, black cattle, or swine; and my reason is that
these children are seldom the fruits of marriage, a circumstance not much
regarded by our savages, therefore one male will be sufficient to serve
four females. That the remaining hundred thousand may at a year old be
offered in sale to the persons of quality and fortune through the kingdom,
always advising the mother to let them suck plentifully in the last month,
so as to render them plump and fat for a good table. A child will make two
dishes at an entertainment for friends; and when the family dines alone,
the fore or hind quarter will make a reason-
able dish, and seasoned with a little pepper
or salt, will be very good boiled on the fourth
day, especially in winter.

I have reckoned upon a medium that a
child just born will weigh twelve pounds,
and in a solar year if tolerably nursed in-
creaseth to twenty-eight pounds.

I grant this food will be somewhat dear,
and therefore very proper for landlords, who,
as they have already devoured most of the
parents, seem to have the best title to the
children.

Infant's flesh will be in season throughout the year, but more plentiful in March,
and a little before and after. For we are told
by a grave author, an eminent French phy-
sician,* that fish being a prolific diet, there are more children born in
Roman Catholic countries about nine months after Lent, than at any other
season; therefore, reckoning a year after Lent, the markets will be more
glutted than usual, because the number of popish infants is at least three

> " I grant this food
> will be somewhat
> dear, and therefore   11
> very proper for
> landlords, who, as
> they have already   12
> devoured most of the
> parents, seem to have
> the best title to the
> children. "   13

---

* Eds. note — François Rabelais, a sixteenth-century satirical writer.

to one in this kingdom; and therefore it will have one other collateral advantage, by lessening the number of Papists* among us.

I have already computed the charge of nursing a beggar's child (in which list I reckon all cottagers, laborers, and four fifths of the farmers) to be about two shillings per annum, rags included; and I believe no gentleman would repine to give ten shillings for the carcass of a good fat child, which, as I have said, will make four dishes of excellent nutritive meat, when he hath only some particular friend or his own family to dine with him. Thus the squire will learn to be a good landlord, and grow popular among the tenants; the mother will have eight shillings net profit, and be fit for work till she produces another child. 14

Those who are more thrifty (as I must confess the times require) may flay the carcass; the skin of which artificially** dressed will make admirable gloves for ladies, and summer boots for fine gentlemen. 15

As to our city of Dublin, shambles*** may be appointed for this purpose in the most convenient parts of it, and butchers we may be assured will not be wanting; although I rather recommend buying the children alive, and dressing them hot from the knife as we do roasting pigs. 16

A very worthy person, a true lover of his country, and whose virtues I highly esteem, was lately pleased in discoursing on this matter to offer a refinement upon my scheme. He said that many gentlemen of his kingdom, having of late destroyed their deer, he conceived that the want of venison might be well supplied by the bodies of young lads and maidens, not exceeding fourteen years of age nor under twelve, so great a number of both sexes in every county being now ready to starve for want of work and service; and these to be disposed of by their parents, if alive, or otherwise by their nearest relations. But with due deference to so excellent a friend and so deserving a patriot I cannot be altogether in his sentiments; for as to the males, my American acquaintance assured me from frequent experience that their flesh was generally tough and lean, like that of our schoolboys, by continual exercise, and their taste disagreeable; and to fatten them would not answer the charge. Then as to the females, it would, I think with humble submission, be a loss to the public, because they soon would become breeders themselves; and besides, it is not improbable that some scrupulous people might be apt to censure such a practice (although indeed very unjustly) as a little bordering upon cruelty; which, I confess, hath always been with me the strongest objection against any project, how well soever intended. 17

But in order to justify my friend, he confessed that this expedient was put into his head by the famous Psalmanazar,† a native of the island Formosa, who came from thence to London above twenty years ago, and in 18

---

* Eds. note — Roman Catholics.

** Eds. note — Skillfully.

*** Eds. note — A slaughterhouse or meat market.

† Eds. note — Frenchman who passed himself off as a native of Formosa (present-day Taiwan).

conversation told my friend that in his country when any young person happened to be put to death, the executioner sold the carcass to the persons of quality as a prime dainty; and that in his time the body of a plump girl of fifteen, who was crucified for an attempt to poison the emperor, was sold to the Imperial Majesty's prime minister of state, and other great mandarins of the court, in joints from the gibbet, at four hundred crowns. Neither indeed can I deny that if the same use were made of several plump young girls in this town, who without one single groat to their fortunes cannot stir abroad without a chair,* and appear at the playhouse and assemblies in foreign fineries which they never will pay for, the kingdom would not be the worse.

Some persons of a desponding spirit are in great concern about the 19 vast number of poor people who are aged, diseased, or maimed, and I have been desired to employ my thoughts what course may be taken to ease the nation of so grievous an encumbrance. But I am not in the least pain upon that matter, because it is very well known that they are every day dying and rotting by cold and famine, and filth and vermin, as fast as can be reasonably expected. And as to the younger laborers, they are now in almost as hopeful a condition. They cannot get work, and consequently pine away for want of nourishment to a degree that if any time they are accidentally hired to common labor, they have not strength to perform it; and thus the country and themselves are happily delivered from the evils to come.

I have too long digressed, and therefore shall return to my subject. I 20 think the advantages by the proposal which I have made are obvious and many, as well as of the highest importance.

For first, as I have already observed, it would greatly lessen the number 21 of Papists, with whom we are yearly overrun, being the principal breeders of the nation as well as our most dangerous enemies; and who stay at home on purpose to deliver the kingdom to the Pretender, hoping to take their advantage by the absence of so many good Protestants, who have chosen rather to leave their country than to stay at home and pay tithes against their conscience to an Episcopal curate.

Secondly, the poorer tenants will have something valuable of their 22 own, which by law may be made liable to distress,** and help to pay their landlord's rent, their corn and cattle being already seized and money a thing unknown.

Thirdly, whereas the maintenance of an hundred thousand children, 23 from two years old and upwards, cannot be computed at less than ten shillings a piece per annum, the nation's stock will be thereby increased fifty thousand pounds per annum, besides the profit of a new dish introduced to the tables of all gentlemen of fortune in the kingdom who have any refinement in taste. And the money will circulate among ourselves, the goods being entirely of our own growth and manufacture.

---

* Eds. note — A sedan chair; that is, a portable covered chair designed to seat one person and then to be carried by two men.

** Eds. note — Property could be seized by creditors.

Fourthly, the constant breeders, besides the gain of eight shillings ster- 24
ling per annum by the sale of their children, will be rid of the charge for
maintaining them after the first year.

Fifthly, this food would likewise bring great custom to taverns, where 25
the vintners will certainly be so prudent as to procure the best receipts* for
dressing it to perfection, and consequently have their houses frequented by
all the fine gentlemen, who justly value themselves upon their knowledge
in good eating; and a skillful cook, who understands how to oblige his
guests, will contrive to make it as expensive as they please.

Sixthly, this would be a great inducement to marriage, after which all 26
wise nations have either encouraged by rewards or enforced by laws and
penalties. It would increase the care and tenderness of mothers toward
their children, when they were sure of a settlement for life to the poor
babes, provided in some sort by the public, to their annual profit instead of
expense. We should see an honest emulation among the married women,
which of them could bring the fattest child to the market. Men would
become as fond of their wives during the time of pregnancy as they are
now of their mares in foal, their cows in calf, or sows when they are ready
to farrow; nor offer to beat or kick them (as is too frequent a practice) for
fear of miscarriage.

Many other advantages might be enumerated. For instance, the addi- 27
tion of some thousand carcasses in our exportation of barreled beef, the
propagation of swine's flesh, and improvements in the art of making good
bacon, so much wanted among us by the great destruction of pigs, too frequent at our tables, which are no way comparable in taste or magnificence
to a well-grown, fat, yearling child, which roasted whole will make a considerable figure at a lord mayor's feast or other public entertainment. But this
and many others I omit, being studious of brevity.

Supposing that one thousand families in this city would be constant 28
customers for infants' flesh, besides others who might have it at merry
meetings, particularly weddings and christenings, I compute that Dublin
would take off annually about twenty thousand carcasses, and the rest of
the kingdom (where probably they will be sold somewhat cheaper) the
remaining eighty thousand.

I can think of no one objection that will possibly be raised against this 29
proposal, unless it should be urged that the number of people will be
thereby much lessened in the kingdom. This I freely own, and it was indeed
one principal design in offering it to the world. I desire the reader will
observe; that I calculate my remedy for this one individual kingdom of Ireland and for no other that ever was, is, or I think ever can be upon earth.
Therefore, let no man talk to me of other expedients: of taxing our absen-
tees at five shillings a pound: of using neither clothes nor household furniture except what is of our own growth and manufacture: of utterly rejecting
the materials and instruments that promote foreign luxury: of curing the
expensiveness of pride, vanity, idleness, and gaming in our women: of in-

---

* Eds. note — Recipes.

troducing a vein of parsimony, prudence, and temperance: of learning to love our country, in the want of which we differ even from Lowlanders and the inhabitants of Topinamboo:* of quitting our animosities and factions, nor acting any longer like the Jews,** who were murdering one another at the very moment their city was taken: of being a little cautious not to sell our country and conscience for nothing: of teaching landlords to have at least one degree of mercy toward their tenants: lastly, of putting a spirit of honesty, industry, and skill into our shopkeepers; who, if a resolution could now be taken to buy only our native goods, would immediately unite to cheat and exact upon us in the price, the measure, and the goodness, nor could ever yet be brought to make one fair proposal of just dealing, though often and earnestly invited to it.

Therefore, I repeat, let no man talk to me of these and the like expedients, till he hath at least some glimpse of hope that there will ever be some hearty and sincere attempt to put them in practice.*** 30

But as to myself, having been wearied out for many years with offering 31 vain, idle, visionary thoughts, and at length utterly despairing of success, I fortunately fell upon this proposal, which, as it is wholly new, so it hath something solid and real, of no expense and little trouble, full in our own power, and whereby we can incur no danger in disobliging England. For this kind of commodity will not bear exploration, the flesh being of too tender a consistence to admit a long continuance in salt, although perhaps I could name a country which would be glad to eat up our whole nation without it.

After all, I am not so violently bent upon my own opinion as to reject 32 any offer proposed by wise men, which shall be found equally innocent, cheap, easy, and effectual. But before something of that kind shall be advanced in contradiction to my scheme, and offering a better, I desire the author or authors will be pleased maturely to consider two points. First, as things now stand, how they will be able to find food and raiment for an hundred thousand useless mouths and backs. And secondly, there being a round million of creatures in human figure throughout this kingdom, whose sole subsistence put into a common stock would leave them in debt two million of pounds sterling, adding those who are beggars by profession to the bulk of farmers, cottagers, and laborers, with their wives and children who are beggars in effect; I desire those politicians who dislike my overture, and may perhaps be so bold to attempt an answer, that they will first ask the parents of these mortals whether they would not at this day think it a great happiness to have been sold for food at a year old in this manner I prescribe, and thereby have avoided such a perpetual scene of misfortunes as they have since gone through by the oppression of landlords, the impossibility of paying rent without money or trade, the want of

---

* Eds. note — A place in the Brazilian jungle.

** Eds. note — In the first century B.C., the Roman general Pompey could conquer Jerusalem in part because the citizenry was divided among rival factions.

*** Eds. note — Note that these measures represent Swift's true proposal.

common sustenance, with neither house nor clothes to cover them from the inclemencies of the weather, and the most inevitable prospect of entailing the like or greater miseries upon their breed forever.

I profess, in the sincerity of my heart, that I have not the least personal   33 interest in endeavoring to promote this necessary work, having no other motive than the public good of my country, by advancing our trade, providing for infants, relieving the poor, and giving some pleasure to the rich. I have no children by which I can propose to get a single penny; the youngest being nine years old, and my wife past childbearing.

· · ·

Comprehension

1. What problem does Swift identify? What general solution does he recommend?

2. What advantages does Swift see in his plan?

3. What does he see as the alternative to his plan?

4. What clues indicate that Swift is not serious about his proposal?

5. In paragraph 29, Swift lists and rejects a number of "other expedients." What are they? Why do you think he presents and rejects these ideas?

Purpose and Audience

1. Swift's target here is the British government, in particular its poor treatment of the Irish. How would you expect British government officials to respond to his proposal? How would you expect Irish readers to react?

2. What do you think Swift hoped to accomplish in this essay? Do you think his purpose was simply to amuse and shock, or do you think he wanted to change people's minds — or even inspire them to take some kind of action? Explain.

3. In paragraphs 6, 14, 23, and elsewhere, Swift presents a series of mathematical calculations. What effect do you think he expected these computations to have on his readers?

4. Explain why each of the following groups might have been offended by this essay: women, Catholics, butchers, the poor.

5. How do you think Swift expected the appeal in his conclusion to affect his audience?

Style and Structure

1. **Vocabulary Project.** In paragraph 6, Swift uses the word *breeders* to refer to fertile women. What connotations does this word have? Why does he use this word rather than a more neutral alternative?

2. What purpose does paragraph 8 serve in the essay? Do the other short paragraphs have the same function? Explain.

3. Swift's remarks are presented as an argument. Where, if anywhere, does Swift anticipate and refute his readers' objections?

4. **Vocabulary Project.** Swift applies to infants many words usually applied to animals who are slaughtered to be eaten — for example, *fore or hind quarter* (10) and *carcass* (15). Identify as many examples of this kind of usage as you can. Why do you think Swift uses such words?

5. Throughout his essay, Swift cites the comments of others — "our merchants" (7), "a very knowing American of my acquaintance" (9), and "an eminent French physician" (13), for example. Find some additional examples. What, if anything, does he accomplish by referring to these people?

6. A **satire** is a piece of writing that uses wit, **irony**, and ridicule to attack foolishness, incompetence, or evil. How does "A Modest Proposal" fit this definition of satire?

7. Evaluate the strategy Swift uses to introduce each advantage he cites in paragraphs 21 through 26.

8. Swift uses a number of parenthetical comments in his essay — for example, in paragraphs 14, 17, and 26. Identify as many of these parenthetical comments as you can, and consider what they contribute to the essay.

9. Swift begins paragraph 20 with "I have too long digressed, and therefore shall return to my subject." Has he in fact been digressing? Explain.

10. The title of this essay states that Swift's proposal is a "modest" one; elsewhere he says he proposes his ideas "humbly" (8). Why do you think he chooses these words? Does he really mean to present himself as modest and humble?

Journal Entry

What is your emotional reaction to this essay? Do you find it amusing or offensive? Why?

Writing Workshop

1. Write a "modest proposal," either straightforward or satirical, for solving a problem in your school or community.

2. Write a "modest proposal" for achieving one of these national goals:
   - Banning assault weapons
   - Eliminating binge drinking on college campuses
   - Promoting sexual abstinence among teenagers

3. Write a letter to an executive of the tobacco industry, a television network, or an industry that threatens the environment. In your letter, set forth a "modest proposal" for making the industry more responsible.

Combining the Patterns

What patterns of development does Swift use in his argument? Annotate the essay to identify each pattern. Use the annotations accompanying "On Dumpster Diving" (page 672) as a guide.

Thematic Connections

- "The Embalming of Mr. Jones" (page 301)
- "The Irish Famine, 1845–1849" (page 330)
- "I Want a Wife" (page 502)

Writing Assignments for Combining the Patterns

1. Reread Michael Huu Truong's essay at the beginning of this chapter. Responding to the same assignment he was given ("Write an essay about the person and/or place that defined your childhood"), use several different patterns of development to communicate to readers what your own childhood was like.

2. Write an essay about the political, social, or economic events (local, national, or international) that you believe have dominated and defined your life (or a stage of your life). Use cause and effect and any other patterns you think are appropriate to explain and illustrate why these events were important to you and how they affected you.

3. Develop a thesis statement that draws a general conclusion about the nature, quality, or effectiveness of advertising in online media or in print media (in newspapers or magazines or on billboards). Write an essay that supports this thesis statement with a series of very specific paragraphs. Use the patterns of development that best help you to characterize particular advertisements. Include visuals if you like.

4. Exactly what do you think it means to be an American? Write a definition essay that answers this question, developing your definition with whatever patterns best serve your purpose.

5. Many of the essays in this text recount the writers' personal experiences. Identify one essay that describes experiences that are either similar to your own or in sharp contrast to your own. Then, write a comparison-and-contrast essay *either* comparing *or* contrasting your experiences with those of the writer. Use several different patterns to develop your essay.

Collaborative Activity for Combining the Patterns

Working in pairs, choose an essay from Chapters 6 through 14 of this text. Then, working individually, identify the various patterns of development used in the essay. When you have finished, compare notes with your classmate. Have both of you identified the same patterns in the essay? If not, try to reach a consensus. Working together, write a paragraph summarizing why each pattern is used and explaining how the various patterns combine to support the essay's thesis.

PART THREE

Working with Sources

Some students see research as a complicated, time-consuming process that seems to have no obvious benefit. They can't understand why instructors assign topics that involve research or why they have to spend so much time considering other people's ideas. These are fair questions that deserve straightforward answers.

For one thing, doing research enables you to become part of an academic community — one that attempts to answer some of the most interesting and profound questions being asked today. For example, what steps should be taken to ensure privacy on the Internet? What is the value of a college education? What is the role of print journalism in the electronic age? How much should the government be involved in people's lives? These and other questions need to be addressed not just because they are interesting but also because the future of our society depends on the answers.

In addition, research teaches sound methods of inquiry. By doing research, you learn to ask questions, to design a research plan, to meet deadlines, to collect and analyze information, and to present your ideas in a well-organized essay. Above all, research encourages you to **think critically** — to consider different sources of information, to evaluate conflicting points of view, to understand how the information you discover fits in with your own ideas about your subject, and to reach logical conclusions. Thus, doing research helps you become a more thoughtful writer as well as a more responsible, more informed citizen — one who is capable of sorting through the vast amount of information you encounter each day and of making informed decisions about the important issues that confront us all.

When you use sources in an essay, you follow the same process that guides you when you write any essay. However, in addition to using your own ideas to support your points, you use information that you find in the library and on the Internet. Because working with sources presents special challenges, there are certain issues that you should be aware of before you engage in research. The chapters in Part Three identify these issues and give you practical suggestions for dealing with them. Chapter 16 discusses how to find sources and how to determine if those sources are authoritative, accurate, objective, current, and comprehensive. Chapter 17 discusses how to paraphrase, summarize, and quote sources and how to avoid committing plagiarism. Finally, Chapter 18 explains how to use the documentation style recommended by the Modern Language Association (MLA) to acknowledge the source information you use in your papers. (The documentation style recommended by the American Psychological Association [APA] is illustrated in the Appendix.)

Finding and Evaluating Sources

In some essays you write — personal narratives or descriptions, for example — you can use your own ideas and observations to support the points you make. In other essays, however, you will have to supplement your own ideas with **research**, looking for information in magazines, newspapers, journals, and books as well as in the library's electronic databases or on the Internet.

Finding Information in the Library

Although many students turn first to the Internet, the best place to begin your research is in your college library, which contains electronic and print resources that you cannot find anywhere else. Of course, your college library houses books, magazines, and journals, but it also gives you access to the various **databases** to which it subscribes as well as to reference works that contain facts and statistics.

THE RESOURCES OF THE LIBRARY

The Online Catalog

An **online catalog** enables you to search all the resources of the library. You can access the online catalog in the library or remotely though an Internet portal. By typing in keywords related to your topic, you can find articles, books, or other sources of information to use in your research.

Electronic Databases

Libraries subscribe to **electronic databases** — for example, *Expanded Academic ASAP* or *LexisNexis Academic Universe*. These electronic databases enable you to access information from hundreds of newspapers, magazines, and journals. Some contain lists of bibliographic citations as well as **abstracts** (summaries of articles); many others enable you to retrieve entire articles or books.

Reference Works

Libraries also contain **reference works** — in print and in electronic form — that can give you an overview of your topic as well as key facts, dates, and names. **General encyclopedias** — such as the *New Encyclopaedia Britannica* — include articles on a wide variety of topics. **Specialized encyclopedias** — such as the *Encyclopedia of Law Enforcement* — contain articles that give you detailed information about a specific field (sociology or law enforcement, for example).

Sources for Facts and Statistics

Reference works such as *Facts on File*, the *Information Please Almanac*, and the *Statistical Abstract of the United States* can help you locate reliable facts or statistics that you may need to support your points. (These resources are available online as well as in the reference section of your college library.)

Much of the information in library databases — for example, the full text of many scholarly articles — cannot be found on the Internet. In addition, because your college librarians oversee all material coming into the library, the sources you find there are generally more reliable, more focused, and more useful than many you will find on the Internet.

INTERNET	LIBRARY DATABASES
Coverage is general, haphazard	Coverage is focused and often discipline-specific
Sources may not contain bibliographic information	Sources will contain bibliographic information
Web postings are not filtered	Databases are created by librarians and scholars
Material is posted by anyone, regardless of qualifications	Material is checked for accuracy and quality

Exercise 1

Assume that you are writing a three- to five-page paper on one of the general topics listed below.

Eating disorders	Women in combat
Alternative medicine	Green construction projects
Government health care	Legalizing marijuana
Offshore drilling	Electric cars

Using your college library's online catalog, see how much information you can find. How easy was this system to use? Where did you have difficulty?

Finding Information on the Internet

When most people refer to the **Internet**, they are actually referring to the **Web**, which is part of the Internet. Once you connect to the Web with your browser, you use a search engine such as Google or Yahoo! to sort through the millions of documents that are available there. There are three ways to access information on the Web: *entering a website's URL, doing a keyword search*, and *doing a subject search*.

Entering a website's URL. All browsers have a box in which you can enter a website's **uniform resource locator (URL)**. When you hit the computer's Enter or Return key, the browser will connect you to the website.

Doing a keyword search. All search engines enable you to do a **keyword search**. You type a search term into a box, and the search engine looks for documents that contain the term. If you type in a broad term like *civil war,* you will get millions of hits — many more than you could possibly consider. If you narrow your search by using a more specific search term — *Battle of Gettysburg,* for example — you will get fewer hits. You can focus your search even further by connecting search terms with *and* (in capital letters) — for example, *Battle of Gettysburg* AND *military strategy*. The documents you retrieve will contain both these search terms, not just one or the other. You can also put quotation marks around a search term — for example, "Lee's surrender at Appomattox." If you do this, the search engine will retrieve only documents that contain this specific phrase.

Doing a subject search. Some search engines, such as Ask.com and Yahoo!, enable you to do a **subject search** (also called a *directory search*). First, you choose a subject from a list of general subjects: *The Arts, Business, Computers, Science,* and so on. Each of these general subjects leads you to more specific subjects and, eventually, to the subtopic that you want. For example, you could start your search by selecting the general topic *Science*. Clicking on this topic would lead you to *Environment* and then to *Forests and Rainforests*. Finally, you would get a list of websites that could be useful to you.

Exercise 2

Carry out an Internet search of the topic you chose for Exercise 1. How much useful information were you able to find? How does this information compare to the information you found when you used the library's online catalog?

ACCESSING WEBSITES: TROUBLESHOOTING

Sometimes you will be unable to connect to the site you want. Before giving up, try these strategies:

- **Check to make sure that the URL is correct.** Any error in typing the URL — an extra space or an added letter — will send you to the wrong site or to no site at all.
- **Try using part of the URL.** If the URL is long, try deleting everything after the last slash. If this doesn't work, use just the part of the URL that ends in .com or .gov. If this part of the URL doesn't work, you have an incorrect (or inoperable) URL.
- **Try revisiting the site later.** Sometimes websites experience technical problems that prevent you from accessing them. Wait a while, and then try accessing your site again.

Evaluating Sources

Not every source contains trustworthy information. For this reason, even after you find information (either in print or online), you still have to **evaluate** it — that is, determine its suitability. When you use print information from your college library, you can be reasonably certain that it has been evaluated in some way. Material from the Web presents special problems, however, because so much of it is either anonymous or written by people who have little or no knowledge of their subject.

To evaluate a source, ask the following questions.

Is the source authoritative? A source is **authoritative** when it is written by an expert. Given the volume and variety of information on the Web, it is important to determine if it is written by a well-respected scholar or expert in the field. (This is especially true for Wiki sites where information is constantly being rewritten or revised — often by people with little or no expertise in a field.) To determine if the author has the expertise to write about a subject, find out what else he or she has written on the same subject, and then do a Web search to see if other authorities recognize the author as an expert.

Trying to determine the legitimacy of information on websites, online publications, and blogs can often be difficult or even impossible. Some sites do not list authors, and if they do, they do not always include their credentials. In addition, you may not be able to determine how a website decides what to publish. (Does one person decide, or does an editorial board make decisions?) Finally, you might have difficulty evaluating (or even identifying) the sponsoring organization of a site. If you cannot determine if a website is authoritative, do not use the site as a source.

Is the source accurate? A source is **accurate** if its information is factual, correct, detailed, and up-to-date. If a university press or scholarly journal published a book or article, you can be reasonably certain that experts in the field reviewed it to confirm its accuracy. Books published by commercial presses or articles in high-level magazines, such as the *Atlantic* and the *Economist*, may also be suitable for your research — provided experts wrote them. The same is true for newspaper articles. Articles in respected newspapers, such as the *New York Times* or the *Wall Street Journal*, have much more credibility than articles in tabloids, such as the *National Enquirer* or the *Globe*.

You can judge the accuracy of a source by comparing specific information it contains to the same information in several other sources. If you find discrepancies, you should assume that the source contains other errors as well. You should also check to see if an author includes citations for the information he or she uses. Such documentation can help readers determine the accuracy (and the quality) of the information in the source. Perhaps the best (and safest) course to follow is that if you can't verify the information you find on a website, don't use it.

Is the source objective? A source is **objective** when it is not unduly influenced by personal opinions or feelings. Of course, all sources reflect the **biases** of their authors, regardless of how impartial they may try to be. Some sources — such as those that support one political position over another — make no secret of their biases. In fact, bias does not automatically disqualify a source. At the very least, it should alert you to the fact that you are seeing just one side of an issue and that you have to look elsewhere to get a fuller picture. Bias becomes a problem, however, when it is so extreme that a source distorts an issue or misrepresents opposing points of view.

As a researcher, you should ask yourself if a writer's conclusions are supported by evidence or if they are the result of emotional reactions or preconceived ideas. You can make this determination by looking at the writer's choice of words and seeing if the language is slanted and also by seeing if the writer ignores (or attacks) opposing points of view.

With websites, you should try to determine if advertising that appears on the site affects its objectivity. Also try to determine if the site has a commercial purpose. If it does, the writer may have a conflict of interest. (Sometimes, commercially motivated content is not easy to recognize. Critics have recently charged that individuals were paid to write favorable Wikipedia articles to promote companies or products.) The same need to assess objectivity exists when a political group or special-interest group sponsors a site. These organizations have agendas, and you should make sure that they are not manipulating facts to promote their own goals.

Is the source current? A source is **current** if the information it contains is up-to-date. It is relatively easy to find out how current a print source is. You can find the publication date of a book on the page that lists its publication information, and you can find the publication date of a periodical on its front cover.

Websites and blogs, however, may present problems. First, check to see when a website was last updated. (Some Web pages automatically display the current date, and you should not confuse this date with the date when the site was last updated.) Then, check the dates of individual articles. Even if a site has been updated recently, it may include information that is out-of-date. You should also see if the links on a site are still live. If a number of links are not functioning, you should question the currency of the site.

Is the source comprehensive? A source is **comprehensive** if it covers a subject in sufficient breadth and depth. How comprehensive a source needs to be depends on your purpose and your audience as well as on your assignment. For a short essay, an op-ed from a newspaper or a short article might give you enough information to support your points. A longer paper, however, would call for sources that treat your subject in depth, such as scholarly articles or even whole books.

You can determine the comprehensiveness of a source by seeing if it devotes a great deal of coverage to your subject. Does it discuss your topic in one or two paragraphs, or does it devote much more space to it — say, a chapter in a book or a major section of an article? You should also try to determine the level of the source. Although a source may be perfectly acceptable for high school research, it may not be comprehensive enough for college research.

USING *WIKIPEDIA* AS A SOURCE

Wikipedia — the most popular encyclopedia on the Web — has no single editor who checks entries for accuracy, credibility, objectivity, currency, and comprehensiveness. In many cases, the users themselves write and edit entries. For this reason, many college instructors do not consider *Wikipedia* to be a credible source of information.

Exercise 3

Choose one source from the library and one from the Internet. Then, evaluate each source to determine if it is authoritative, accurate, objective, current, and comprehensive.

17

Integrating Sources and Avoiding Plagiarism

After you have gathered and evaluated your sources, it is time to think about how you can use this material in your essay. As you take notes, you should record relevant information in a computer file or in a note-taking application. These notes should be in the form of *paraphrase, summary*, and *quotation*. When you actually write your paper, you will **synthesize** this source material, blending it with your own ideas and interpretations — but making sure that your own ideas, not those of your sources, dominate your discussion. Finally, you should make certain that you do not inadvertently commit plagiarism.

Paraphrasing

When you **paraphrase**, you use your own words to restate a source's ideas in some detail, presenting the source's main idea, its key supporting points, and possibly an example or two. For this reason, a paraphrase may be only slightly shorter than the original.

You paraphrase when you want to present the information from a source without using its exact words. Paraphrasing is useful when you want to make a difficult discussion easier to understand while still giving readers a good sense of the original.

Keep in mind that when you paraphrase, you do not use the exact language or syntax of the original source, and you do not include your own analysis or opinions. The idea is to convey the ideas and emphasis of the source but not to mirror the order of its ideas or reproduce its exact words or sentence structure. If you decide to include a particularly memorable word or phrase from the source, be sure to put it in quotation marks. Finally, remember that because a paraphrase relies on a writer's original ideas, *you must document the source.*

GUIDELINES FOR WRITING A PARAPHRASE

- Read the source you intend to paraphrase until you understand it.
- Jot down the main points of the source.
- As you write, retain the emphasis of the original.
- Make sure that you use your own words and phrases, not the language or syntax of your source.
- Do not include your own analysis or opinions.
- Be sure to provide documentation.

Here is a passage from page 22 of the article *"Wikipedia* and Beyond: Jimmy Wales's Sprawling Vision" by Katherine Mangu-Ward, followed by a paraphrase.

ORIGINAL

An obvious question troubled, and continues to trouble, many people: how could an "encyclopedia that anyone can edit" possibly be reliable? Can truth be reached by a consensus of amateurs? Can a community of volunteers aggregate and assimilate knowledge . . . ?

PARAPHRASE

According to Katherine Mangu-Ward, there are serious questions about the reliability of *Wikipedia*'s articles because any user can add, change, or delete information. There is some doubt about whether *Wikipedia*'s unpaid and nonprofessional writers and editors can work together to create an accurate encyclopedia (22).

Exercise 1

Select one or two paragraphs from any essay in this book, and then paraphrase them. Make sure your paraphrase communicates the main ideas and key supporting points of the passage you selected.

Summarizing

Unlike a paraphrase, which restates the ideas of a source in detail, a **summary** is a brief restatement, in your own words, of a passage's main idea. Because it is so general, a summary is always much shorter than the original.

When you summarize (as when you paraphrase) you use your own words, not the words of your source. Keep in mind that a summary can be one sentence or several sentences in length, depending on the length and complexity of the original passage. Your summary expresses just the main idea of your source, not your own opinions or conclusions. Remember, because a summary expresses a writer's original idea, *you must document your source.*

GUIDELINES FOR WRITING A SUMMARY

- Read the source you intend to summarize until you understand it.
- Jot down the main idea of the source.
- Make sure that you use your own words and phrases, not the words and sentence structure of your source.
- Do not include your own analysis or opinions.
- Be sure to provide documentation.

Here is a summary of the passage from the article "*Wikipedia* and Beyond: Jimmy Wales's Sprawling Vision" by Katherine Mangu-Ward.

SUMMARY

According to Katherine Mangu-Ward, *Wikipedia*'s reliability is open to question because anyone can edit its articles (22).

Exercise 2

Write a summary of the material that you paraphrased for Exercise 1. How is your summary different from your paraphrase?

Quoting

When you **quote**, you use a writer's exact words as they appear in the source, including all punctuation, capitalization, and spelling. Enclose all words from your source in quotation marks — *followed by appropriate documentation*. Because quotations distract readers, use a quotation only when you think a writer's exact words will add something to your discussion. In addition, too many quotations will make your paper look like a collection of other people's words. As a rule, unless you have a definite reason to quote a source, you should paraphrase or summarize it instead.

WHEN TO QUOTE SOURCES

1. Quote when the original language is so memorable that paraphrasing would lessen the impact of the writer's ideas.
2. Quote when a paraphrase or summary would change the meaning of the original.

3. Quote when the original language adds authority to your discussion. The exact words of an expert on your topic can help you make your point convincingly.

GUIDELINES FOR QUOTING

- Put all words and phrases that you take from your source in quotation marks.
- Make sure that you use the *exact* words of your source.
- Do not include too many quotations.
- Be sure to provide documentation.

Exercise 3

Reread the passage you chose to paraphrase in Exercise 1, and identify one or two quotations that you could include in your paraphrase. Which words or phrases did you decide to quote? Why?

Integrating Source Material into Your Writing

When you use source material in your writing, your goal is to integrate this material smoothly into your discussion. To distinguish your own ideas from those of your sources, you should always introduce source material and follow it with appropriate documentation.

Introduce paraphrases, summaries, and quotations with a phrase that identifies the source or its author. You can place this **identifying phrase** (also called a *signal phrase*) at the beginning, in the middle, or at the end of a sentence. Instead of always using the same words to introduce your source material — *says* or *states,* for example — try using different words and phrases — *points out, observes, comments, notes, remarks,* or *concludes.*

IDENTIFYING PHRASE AT THE BEGINNING

According to Jonathan Dee, *Wikipedia* is "either one of the noblest experiments of the Internet age or a nightmare embodiment of relativism and the withering of intellectual standards" (36).

IDENTIFYING PHRASE IN THE MIDDLE

Wikipedia is "either one of the noblest experiments of the Internet age," Jonathan Dee comments, "or a nightmare embodiment of relativism and the withering of intellectual standards" (36).

IDENTIFYING PHRASE AT THE END

Wikipedia is "either one of the noblest experiments of the Internet age or a nightmare embodiment of relativism and the withering of intellectual standards," Jonathan Dee observes (36).

Synthesizing

When you write a **synthesis**, you combine paraphrases, summaries, and quotations with your own ideas. It is important to keep in mind that a synthesis is not simply a collection of your sources' ideas. On the contrary, a synthesis uses source material to support *your* ideas and to help readers see the topic *you* are writing about in a new way. For this reason, when you write a synthesis, it is important to differentiate your ideas from those of your sources and to clearly show which piece of information comes from which source.

The following synthesis is a paragraph from the model MLA paper that begins on page 742. This paragraph synthesizes several sources to present an overview of *Wikipedia*, focusing on the ease with which its text can be edited. The paragraph begins with the student's own ideas, and the rest of the paragraph includes source material that supports these ideas.

A wiki allows multiple users to collaborate in creating the content of a website. With a wiki, anyone with a browser can edit, modify, rearrange, or delete content. It is not necessary to know HTML (hypertext mark-up language). The word *wiki* comes from the word *wikiwiki*, which means "quick" or "fast" in Hawaiian. The most popular wiki is *Wikipedia*, a free, Internet-based encyclopedia that relies on the collaboration of those who post and edit entries. Anyone can write a *Wikipedia* article by using the "*Wikipedia* Article Wizard" or edit an entry by clicking on the "Edit" tab. Readers can easily view the revision history of an entry by clicking on "View History" ("Help: Page History"). For its many advocates, *Wikipedia*'s open and collaborative nature makes it a "collectively brilliant creation" (Chozick). This collaboration enables *Wikipedia* to publish a wide variety of entries on timely, unusual, and specialized topics (see fig. 1) According to Casper Grathwohl, President, Dictionaries Division, and Director, Global Business Development at Oxford University Press, it "has become increasingly clear that [*Wikipedia*] functions as a necessary layer in the Internet knowledge system, a layer that was not needed in the analog age." At this time, the site contains 30 million articles in 287 languages ("*Wikipedia*").

> **GUIDELINES FOR WRITING A SYNTHESIS**
>
> 1. Identify the key points discussed in each of your sources.
> 2. Identify the evidence that your sources use to support their views.
> 3. Clearly report what each source says, using summaries, paraphrases, and quotations. (Be sure to document your sources.)
> 4. Show how the sources are related to one another. For instance, do they agree on everything? Do they show directly opposite views, or do they agree on some points and disagree on others?
> 5. Decide on your own viewpoint, and show how the sources relate to your viewpoint.

Exercise 4

Look at the Model Student Research Paper that begins on page 742. Choose a paragraph (other than the one on page 723) that synthesizes source material. What kind of information (summary, paraphrase, or quotation) is being synthesized?

Avoiding Plagiarism

Plagiarism — whether intentional or unintentional — occurs when a writer passes off the words or ideas of others as his or her own. (Ideas can also be in the form of visuals, such as charts and graphs, or statistics.) Students plagiarize for a number of reasons. Some take the easy way out and buy a paper and submit it as if it were their own. This **intentional plagiarism** compromises a student's education as well as the educational process as a whole. Instructors assign papers for a reason, and if you do not do the work, then you miss a valuable opportunity to learn. For most students, however, plagiarism is **unintentional**.

Plagiarism can be the result of carelessness, poor time management, not knowing the conventions of documentation, laziness, or simply panic. For example, some students do not give themselves enough time to do an assignment, fail to keep track of their sources, inadvertently include the exact words of a source without using quotation marks, forget to include documentation, or cut and paste information from the Internet directly into their papers. In addition, some students have the mistaken belief that if information they find online does not have an identifiable author, it is all right to use it without documentation. Whatever the reason, whenever you present information from a source as if it were your own (either intentionally or unintentionally), you are committing plagiarism — and *plagiarism is theft*.

TIPS FOR AVOIDING PLAGIARISM

You can avoid plagiarism by keeping careful notes and by following these guidelines:

- **Give yourself enough time to do your research and to write your paper.** Do not put yourself in a position where you do not leave enough time to give your assignment the attention it requires.
- **Begin with a research plan.** Make a list of the steps you intend to follow, and estimate how much time they will take.
- **Ask for help.** If you run into trouble, don't panic. Ask your instructor or a reference librarian for help.
- **Do not cut and paste downloaded text directly into your paper.** Summarize and paraphrase this source material first. Boldface or highlight quotation marks so that you will recognize quotations when you are ready to include them in your paper.
- **Set up a system that enables you to keep track of your sources.** Create computer files where you can store downloaded source information. (If you photocopy print sources, maintain a file for this material.) Create another set of files for your notes. Make sure you clearly name and date these files so that you know what is in them and when they were created.
- **Include full source information for all paraphrases and summaries as well as for quotations.** As you write, clearly differentiate between your ideas and those of your sources. Do not forget to include documentation. If you try to fill in documentation later, you may not remember where your information came from.
- **Keep a list of all the sources you have downloaded or have taken information from.** Make sure that you always have an up-to-date list of the sources you are using.

The easiest way to avoid plagiarism is simple — give credit where credit is due. In other words, document all information you borrow from your sources (print or electronic) — not just paraphrases, summaries, and quotations but also statistics, images, and charts and graphs. It is not necessary, however, to document **common knowledge** — information that most people will probably know or factual information that is available in several different reference works. (Keep in mind that even though *information* might be common knowledge, you cannot use the exact *words* of a reference source without quoting the source and providing appropriate documentation.)

WHAT TO DOCUMENT

You Must Document

- All word-for-word quotations from a source
- All summaries and paraphrases of material from a source
- All ideas — opinions, judgments, and insights — that are not your own
- All tables, graphs, charts, statistics, and images you get from a source

You Do Not Need to Document

- Your own ideas
- Common knowledge
- Familiar quotations

Avoiding Common Errors That Lead to Plagiarism

The following paragraph is from *The Cult of the Amateur: How Today's Internet Is Killing Our Culture* by Andrew Keen. This paragraph, and the four rules listed after it, will help you understand and avoid the most common causes of plagiarism.

ORIGINAL

The simple ownership of a computer and an Internet connection doesn't transform one into a serious journalist any more than having access to a kitchen makes one into a serious cook. But millions of amateur journalists think that it does. According to a June 2006 study by the Pew Internet and American Life Project, 34 percent of the 12 million bloggers in America consider their online "work" to be a form of journalism. That adds up to millions of unskilled, untrained, unpaid, unknown "journalists" — a thousandfold growth between 1996 and 2006 — spewing their (mis)information out in the cyberworld. (Andrew Keen. *The Cult of the Amateur: How Today's Internet Is Killing Our Culture.* New York: Doubleday, 2007. 47. Print.)

1. Identify Your Source

PLAGIARISM

One-third of the people who post material on Internet blogs think of themselves as serious journalists.

The writer does not quote Keen directly, but he still must identify Keen as the source of his paraphrased material. He can do this by adding an identifying phrase and parenthetical documentation.

CORRECT

According to Andrew Keen, one-third of the people who post material on Internet blogs think of themselves as serious journalists (47).

2. Place Borrowed Words in Quotation Marks

PLAGIARISM

According to Andrew Keen, the simple ownership of a computer and an Internet connection doesn't transform one into a serious journalist any more than having access to a kitchen makes one into a serious cook (47).

Although the writer cites Keen as his source, the passage incorrectly uses Keen's exact words without putting them in quotation marks. The writer must either place the borrowed words in quotation marks or paraphrase them.

CORRECT (BORROWED WORDS IN QUOTATION MARKS)

According to Andrew Keen, "The simple ownership of a computer and an Internet connection doesn't transform one into a serious journalist any more than having access to a kitchen makes one into a serious cook" (47).

3. Use Your Own Wording

PLAGIARISM

According to Andrew Keen, having a computer that can connect to the Internet does not make someone a real reporter, just as having a kitchen does not make someone a real cook. However, millions of these people think that they are real journalists. A Pew Internet and American Life study in June 2006 showed that about 4 million bloggers think they are journalists when they write on their blogs. Thus, millions of people who have no training may be putting erroneous information on the Internet (47).

Even though the writer acknowledges Keen as his source and provides parenthetical documentation, and even though he does not use Keen's exact words, his passage closely follows the order, emphasis, and phrasing of the original. In the following passage, the writer uses his own wording, quoting one distinctive phrase from his source.

CORRECT

According to Andrew Keen, although millions of American bloggers think of themselves as journalists, they are wrong. As Keen notes, "The simple ownership of a computer and an Internet connection doesn't transform one into a serious journalist any more than having access to a kitchen makes one into a serious cook" (47).

4. Distinguish Your Own Ideas from Your Source's Ideas

PLAGIARISM

The anonymous writers of *Wikipedia* articles are, in some ways, similar to those who put material on personal blogs. Although millions of American bloggers think of themselves as journalists, they are wrong. "The simple ownership of a computer and an Internet connection doesn't transform one into a serious journalist any more than having access to a kitchen makes one into a serious cook" (Keen 47).

In the preceding passage, it appears that only the quotation in the last sentence is borrowed from Keen's book. In fact, the ideas in the second sentence are also Keen's. The writer should use an identifying phrase (such as

"According to Keen") to acknowledge the borrowed material in this sentence and to indicate where it begins.

CORRECT

The anonymous writers of *Wikipedia* articles are, in some ways, similar to those who put material on personal blogs. According to Andrew Keen, although millions of American bloggers think of themselves as journalists, they are wrong. As Keen notes, "The simple ownership of a computer and an Internet connection doesn't transform one into a serious journalist any more than having access to a kitchen makes one into a serious cook" (47).

Avoiding Plagiarism with Online Sources

Most students know that using long passages (or entire articles) from a print source without documenting the source is plagiarism. Unfortunately, many students assume that borrowing material found on a website or elsewhere online without documentation is acceptable. However, such borrowing is also plagiarism. Just as you do for print sources, you must always document words, ideas, or visuals you get from online sources.

Exercise 5

Select an essay that you have written this semester that refers to a reading selection in this book. Reread both your essay and the selection in the book, and then decide where you could add each of the following:

- A quotation
- A summary of a paragraph
- A paraphrase of a paragraph

Exercise 6

Insert a quotation, a summary, and a paraphrase into the essay you reviewed for Exercise 5. Then, check to make sure that you have not committed plagiarism. Finally, consult Chapter 18 to help you document your sources correctly.

Documenting Sources: MLA

When you **document**, you tell readers where you have found the information you have used in your essay. The Modern Language Association (MLA) recommends the following documentation style for essays that use research.* This format consists *of parenthetical references* in the body of the paper that refer to a *works-cited* list at the end of the paper.

Parenthetical References in the Text

A **parenthetical reference** should include enough information to guide readers to a specific entry in your works-cited list.

A typical parenthetical reference consists of the author's last name and the page number: (Mangu-Ward 21). If you use more than one work by the same author, include a shortened form of the title in the parenthetical reference: (Mangu-Ward, "*Wikipedia* and Beyond" 25). Notice that the parenthetical references do not include a comma after the title or "p." before the page number.

Whenever possible, introduce information with a phrase that includes the author's name. (If you do so, include only the page number in parentheses.)

> According to Andrew Keen, the absence of professional reporters and editors leads to erroneous information on *Wikipedia* (4).

Place documentation so that it does not interrupt the flow of your ideas, preferably at the end of a sentence.

---

* For further information, see the seventh edition of the *MLA Handbook for Writers of Research Papers* (New York: Mod. Lang. Assn., 2009) or the MLA website at mla.org.

The format for parenthetical references departs from these guidelines in the following special situations:

1. When you are citing a work by two authors

It is impossible to access all websites by means of a single search engine (Sherman and Price 53).

2. When you are citing a work without a listed author

The technology of wikis is important, but many users are not aware of it ("7 Things").

3. When you are citing an indirect source

If you use a statement by one author that is quoted in the work of another author, indicate this by including the abbreviation qtd. in ("quoted in").

Marshall Poe notes that information on *Wikipedia* is "not exactly expert knowledge; it's common knowledge" (qtd. in Keen 39).

4. When you are citing an electronic source

Sources from the Internet or from library databases often do not include page numbers. If the electronic source uses paragraph, section, or screen numbers, use the abbreviation par. or sec., or the full word screen, followed by the corresponding number, in your documentation. (If the citation includes an author's name, place a comma after the name.)

On its website, *Wikipedia* warns its writers and editors to inspect sources carefully when they make assertions that are not generally held in academic circles ("Verifiability," sec. 3).

If the electronic source has no page numbers or markers of any kind, include just the name(s) of the author(s). Readers can tell that the citation refers to an electronic source when they consult the works-cited list.

A *Wikipedia* entry can be very deceptive, but some users may not realize that its information may not be reliable (McHenry).

GUIDELINES FOR FORMATTING QUOTATIONS

Short Quotations

Quotations of no more than four typed lines are run in with the text. End punctuation comes after the parenthetical reference (which follows the quotation marks).

According to Andrew Keen, on *Wikipedia*, "the voice of a high school kid has equal value to that of an Ivy League scholar of a trained profession" (42).

Long Quotations

Quotations of more than four lines are set off from the text. Indent a long quotation one inch from the left-hand margin, and do not enclose the passage in quotation marks. The first line of a long quotation is not indented even if it is the beginning of a paragraph. If a quoted passage has more than one paragraph, indent the first line of each subsequent paragraph one-quarter inch. Introduce a long quotation with a colon, and place the parenthetical reference one space after the end punctuation.

> According to Katherine Mangu-Ward, *Wikipedia* has changed the world:
>> *Wikipedia* was born as an experiment in aggregating information. But the reason it works isn't that the world was clamoring for a new kind of encyclopedia. It took off because of the robust, self-policing community it created. . . . Despite its critics, it is transforming our everyday lives; as with Amazon, Google, and eBay, it is almost impossible to remember how much more circumscribed our world was before it existed. (21)

NOTE: Ellipses indicate that the writer has deleted some words from the quotation.

The Works-Cited List

The works-cited list includes all the works you **cite** (refer to) in your essay. Use the following guidelines to help you prepare your list.

GUIDELINES FOR PREPARING THE WORKS-CITED LIST

- Begin the works-cited list on a new page after the last page of text.
- Number the works-cited page as the next page.
- Center the heading Works Cited one inch from the top of the page; do not underline the heading or put it in quotation marks.
- Double-space the list.
- List entries alphabetically according to the author's last name.
- Alphabetize unsigned articles according to the first major word of the title.
- Begin each entry flush with the left-hand margin.
- Indent second and subsequent lines one-half inch.
- Separate each division of the entry — author, title, and publication information — by a period and one space.

The following sample works-cited entries cover the situations you will encounter most often. Follow the formats exactly as they appear here.

Articles

GUIDELINES FOR MLA ARTICLE CITATIONS

To cite a periodical article in MLA style, follow these guidelines:

1. List the author, last name first.
2. Put the title of the article in quotation marks and italicize the title of the periodical.
3. Include the volume and issue number (when applicable), the year and date of publication, and the pages on which the full article appears (without the abbreviation *p.* or *pp.*).
4. Finally, include the medium of publication (*Print, Web,* and so on).

Journal Articles. A **journal** is a publication aimed at readers who know a lot about a particular subject — English or history, for example.

ARTICLE IN A JOURNAL

Provide the volume number followed by a period and the issue number. Leave no space after the period between the volume and issue numbers. List the date of publication (in parentheses), the pages of the article, and the medium of publication.

> Markley, Robert. "Gulliver and the Japanese: The Limits of the
> Postcolonial Past." *Modern Language Quarterly* 65.3 (2004):
> 457-80. Print.

ARTICLE IN A JOURNAL THAT USES ONLY ISSUE NUMBERS

For a journal that uses only issue numbers, cite the issue number, publication date, page numbers, and medium.

> Adelt, Ulrich. "Black, White, and Blue: Racial Politics in B. B. King's
> Music from the 1960s." *Journal of Popular Culture* 44 (2011):
> 195-216. Print.

Magazine Articles. A **magazine** is a publication aimed at general readers. For this reason, it contains articles that are easier to understand than those in journals.

ARTICLE IN A MONTHLY OR BIMONTHLY MAGAZINE

Frequently, an article in a magazine does not appear on consecutive pages — for example, it might begin on page 43, skip to page 47, and continue on page 49. If this is the case, include only the first page, followed by a plus sign.

> Edwards, Owen. "Kilroy Was Here." *Smithsonian* Oct. 2004: 40+. Print.

ARTICLE IN A WEEKLY OR BIWEEKLY MAGAZINE (SIGNED OR UNSIGNED)

> Schley, Jim. "Laid Off, and Working Harder Than Ever." *Newsweek*
> 20 Sept. 2004: 16. Print.
>
> "Real Reform Post-Enron." *Nation* 4 Mar. 2002: 3. Print.

ARTICLE IN A NEWSPAPER

> Bykowicz, Julie. "Man Faces Identity Theft Counts; College Worker
> Accused of Taking Students' Data." *Sun* [Baltimore] 18 Sept. 2004:
> 2B. Print.

EDITORIAL OR LETTER TO THE EDITOR

> "An Un-American Way to Campaign." Editorial. *New York Times*
> 25 Sept. 2004, late ed.: A14. Print.

REVIEW IN A NEWSPAPER

> Scott, A. O. "Forever Obsessing about Obsession." Rev. of *Adaptation,*
> dir. Spike Jonze. *New York Times* 6 Dec. 2002: F1+. Print.

REVIEW IN A WEEKLY OR BIWEEKLY MAGAZINE

> Urquhart, Brian. "The Prospect of War." Rev. of *The Threatening Storm:*
> *The Case for Invading Iraq,* by Kenneth M. Pollack. *New York*
> *Review of Books* 19 Dec. 2002: 16-22. Print.

REVIEW IN A MONTHLY MAGAZINE

> Jones, Kent. "The Lay of the Land." Rev. of *Sunshine State,* dir. John
> Sayles. *Film Commentary* May/June 2002: 22-24. Print.

Books

GUIDELINES FOR MLA BOOK CITATIONS

To cite a print book in MLA style, follow these guidelines:

1. List the author with last name first.
2. Italicize the title.
3. Include the city of publication.

4. Use a shortened form of the publisher's name — for example, *Bedford* for *Bedford/St. Martin's.* Use the abbreviation *UP* for *University Press,* as in *Princeton UP* and *U of Chicago P.*
5. Include the date of publication, followed by a period.
6. Include the medium of publication (Print).

The two illustrations that follow show where to find the information you need for your book citations.

Title Page

Copyright © 2010 by Robert McCrum

All rights reserved
Printed in the United States of America
First Edition

For information about permission to reproduce selections from this book,
write to Permissions, W. W. Norton & Company, Inc.,
500 Fifth Avenue, New York, NY 10110

For information about special discounts for bulk purchases, please contact
W. W. Norton Special Sales at specialsales@wwnorton.com or 800-233-4830

Manufacturing by Courier Westford
Book design by Ellen Cipriano
Production manager: Devon Zahn

Library of Congress Cataloging-in-Publication Data

McCrum, Robert.
Globish : how the English language became the world's language /
Robert McCrum, — 1st ed.
p. cm.
Includes bibliographical references and index.
ISBN 978-0-393-06255-7
1. English language—History. 2. English language—Globalization.
I. Title.
PE1075.M57 2010
420.9—dc22

2010008157

W. W. Norton & Company, Inc.
500 Fifth Avenue, New York, NY 10110
www.wwnorton.com

W. W. Norton & Company Ltd.
Castle House, 75/76 Wells Street, London W1T3QT

1 2 3 4 5 6 7 8 9 0

Copyright Page

McCrum, Robert. *Globish: How the English Language Became the*

World's Language. New York: Norton, 2010. Print.

BOOKS BY ONE AUTHOR

McCrum, Robert. *Globish: How the English Language Became the World's*

Language. New York: Norton, 2010. Print.

BOOKS BY TWO OR THREE AUTHORS

List authors in the order in which they are listed on the book's title
page. List second and subsequent authors with first names first.

Bigelow, Fran, and Helene Siegel. *Pure Chocolate*. New York: Broadway,

2004. Print.

BOOKS BY MORE THAN THREE AUTHORS

List only the first author, followed by the abbreviation *et al.* ("and others").

> Ordeman, John L., et al. *Artists of the North American Wilderness:*
> *George and Belmore Browne.* New York: Warwick, 2004. Print.

TWO OR MORE BOOKS BY THE SAME AUTHOR

List two or more books by the same author in alphabetical order according to title. In each entry after the first, use three unspaced hyphens (followed by a period) instead of the author's name.

> Angelou, Maya. *Hallelujah! The Welcome Table: A Lifetime of Memories*
> *with Recipes.* New York: Random, 2004. Print.
>
> ---. *I Know Why the Caged Bird Sings.* New York: Bantam, 1985. Print.

EDITED BOOK

> Whitman, Walt. *The Portable Walt Whitman.* Ed. Michael Warner. New
> York: Penguin, 2004. Print.

TRANSLATION

> García Márquez, Gabriel. *Living to Tell the Tale.* Trans. Edith Grossman.
> New York: Knopf, 2004. Print.

REVISED EDITION

> Bjelajac, David. *American Art: A Cultural History.* 2nd ed. New York:
> Prentice, 2004. Print.

ANTHOLOGY

> Kirszner, Laurie G., and Stephen R. Mandell, eds. *Patterns for College*
> *Writing: A Rhetorical Reader and Guide.* 13th ed. Boston: Bedford,
> 2015. Print.

ESSAY IN AN ANTHOLOGY

> Gansberg, Martin. "Thirty-Eight Who Saw Murder Didn't Call the
> Police." *Patterns for College Writing: A Rhetorical Reader*
> *and Guide.* 13th ed. Ed. Laurie G. Kirszner and Stephen R.
> Mandell. Boston: Bedford, 2015. 128-32. Print.

MORE THAN ONE ESSAY IN THE SAME ANTHOLOGY

List each essay separately with a cross-reference to the entire anthology.

> Gansberg, Martin. "Thirty-Eight Who Saw Murder Didn't Call the
> Police." Kirszner and Mandell 128-32.

Kirszner, Laurie G., and Stephen R. Mandell, eds. *Patterns for College Writing: A Rhetorical Reader and Guide.* 13th ed. Boston: Bedford, 2015. Print.

Staples, Brent. "Just Walk On By: A Black Man Ponders His Power to Alter Public Space." Kirszner and Mandell 238-43.

SECTION OR CHAPTER OF A BOOK

Gordimer, Nadine. "Loot." *"Loot" and Other Stories.* New York: Farrar, 2004. 1-6. Print.

INTRODUCTION, PREFACE, FOREWORD, OR AFTERWORD

Ingham, Patricia. Introduction. *Martin Chuzzlewit.* By Charles Dickens. London: Penguin, 1999. x-xxxii. Print.

MULTIVOLUME WORK

Malory, Thomas. *Le Morte D'Arthur.* Ed. Janet Cowen. 2 vols. London: Penguin, 1986. Print.

ARTICLE IN A REFERENCE WORK

For familiar reference works that publish new editions regularly, include only the edition (if given) and the year of publication.

"Civil Rights." *The World Book Encyclopedia.* 2006 ed. Print.

For less familiar reference works, provide a full citation.

Wagle, Greta. "Geisel, Theodor [Seuss]." *The Encyclopedia of American Literature.* Ed. Steven R. Serafin. New York: Continuum, 1999. Print.

Internet Sources

GUIDELINES FOR MLA INTERNET CITATIONS

When citing an Internet source, include the following information:

1. The name of the author or editor of the site
2. The title of the site (italicized)
3. The site's sponsor or publisher (if no sponsor or publisher is identified, write *N.p.*)
4. The date of electronic publication (if no publication date is available, write *n.d.*)
5. The medium of publication: *Web.*
6. The date you accessed the source

ENTIRE INTERNET SITE (SCHOLARLY PROJECT, INFORMATION DATABASE, JOURNAL, OR PROFESSIONAL WEBSITE)

The Dickens Project. Ed. Jon Michael Varese. U of California, Santa Cruz, 2004. Web. 2 Dec. 2013.

International Dialects of English Archive. Dept. of Theatre and Film, U of Kansas, 2004. Web. 4 Dec. 2013.

Words of the Year. Amer. Dialect Soc., 2008. Web. 18 Feb. 2014.

DOCUMENT WITHIN A WEBSITE

"Child and Adolescent Violence Research at the NIMH." *National Institute of Mental Health,* NIMH, 2005. Web. 2 Apr. 2013.

PERSONAL WEBSITE

Lynch, Jack. Home page. Jack Lynch, n.d. Web. 2 Jan. 2014.

ENTIRE ONLINE BOOK

Austen, Jane. *Pride and Prejudice.* 1813. *The Literature Network.* Web. 30 Nov. 2013.

Fielding, Henry. *The History of Tom Jones, a Foundling.* Ed. William Allan Nielson. New York: Collier, 1917. *Bartleby.com: Great Books Online.* Web. 29 Nov. 2012.

PART OF AN ONLINE BOOK

Radford, Dollie. "At Night." *Poems.* London, 1910. *Victorian Women Writers Project.* Web. 17 Mar. 2013.

ARTICLE IN AN ONLINE SCHOLARLY JOURNAL

Condie, Kent C., and Jane Silverstone. "The Crust of the Colorado Plateau: New Views of an Old Arc." *Journal of Geology* 107.4 (1999): 387-97. Web. 9 Aug. 2013.

ARTICLE IN AN ONLINE REFERENCE BOOK OR ENCYCLOPEDIA

"Croatia." *The World Factbook 2013.* CIA, 8 Oct. 2004. Web. 30 Dec. 2013.

ARTICLE IN AN ONLINE NEWSPAPER

Krim, Jonathan. "FCC Preparing to Overhaul Telecom, Media Rules." *Washingtonpost.com.* Washington Post, 3 Jan. 2003. Web. 6 Jan. 2007.

ONLINE EDITORIAL

"Ersatz Eve." Editorial. *New York Times on the Web.* New York Times, 28 Dec. 2002. Web. 5 Jan. 2013.

ARTICLE IN AN ONLINE MAGAZINE

Press, Eyal, and Jennifer Washburn. "The At-Risk-Youth Industry."
Atlantic Online. Atlantic Monthly Group, Dec. 2002. Web. 3 Jan.
2012.

REVIEW IN AN ONLINE PERIODICAL

Chocano, Carina. "Sympathy for the Misanthrope." Rev. of *Curb Your
Enthusiasm,* dir. Robert Weide, prod. Larry David. *Salon.* Salon
Media Group, 4 Dec. 2002. Web. 17 Sept. 2010.

POSTING TO A DISCUSSION LIST

Thune, W. Scott. "Emotion and Rationality in Argument." *CCCC/97
Online.* N.p., 23 Mar. 1997. Web. 11 Nov. 2005.

BLOG POST

Singer, Judy Reene. "Why I Wrote My Elephant Books." *Romance Blog*
8 June 2013. Web. 9 Aug. 2013.

YOUTUBE VIDEO

Bruni, Frank. "Famous Interviews." Online video clip. *YouTube.*
YouTube, 26 Nov. 2012. Web. 21 Oct. 2013.

Other Internet Sources

A PAINTING ON THE INTERNET

O'Keeffe, Georgia. *Evening Star, III.* 1917. Museum of Mod. Art, New
York. *MoMA: The Museum of Modern Art.* Web. 9 Nov. 2013.

A PHOTOGRAPH ON THE INTERNET

Cartier-Bresson, Henri. *William Faulkner, 1947.* Natl. Portrait Gallery,
Washington, D.C. *Tête à tête: Portraits by Henri Cartier-Bresson.*
Web. 8 Oct. 2013.

A CARTOON ON THE INTERNET

Trudeau, Garry. "Doonesbury." Comic strip. *Washingtonpost.com.*
Washington Post, 7 Apr. 2005. Web. 5 May 2011.

A MAP OR CHART ON THE INTERNET

"Fort Worth, Texas." Map. *US Gazetteer.* US Census Bureau, n.d. Web.
26 Oct. 2012.

MATERIAL ACCESSED ON A CD-ROM, DISKETTE, OR MAGNETIC TAPE

In addition to the publication information, include the medium (CD-ROM, for example) and the distribution vendor, if relevant (UMI-Proquest, for example).

> Aristotle. "Poetics." *The Complete Works of Aristotle.* Ed. Jonathan
>   Barnes. 2 vols. Princeton: Princeton UP, 1984. CD-ROM. Clayton:
>   InteLex, 1994.
>
> "Feminism." *The Oxford English Dictionary.* 2nd ed. New York: Oxford
>   UP, 1992. CD-ROM. Vers. 3.1. 2004.

EMAIL

> Sullivan, John. "Re: Headnotes." Message to Laurie G. Kirszner. 13 Dec.
>   2013. Email.

COMPUTER SOFTWARE OR VIDEO GAME

Provide the name of the author or developer of the software, if available; the title of the software, italicized; the publisher or distributor and publication date; and the software platform (for example, Xbox 360 or PlayStation 3).

> *Sid Meier's Civilization IV: Colonization.* Take 2 Interactive, 2008.
>   Windows.

MATERIAL FROM A LIBRARY DATABASE

For material retrieved from a library database such as *InfoTrac, LexisNexis, ProQuest,* or *EBSCOhost,* list the publication information for the source and provide the name of the database (such as *LexisNexis Academic*), italicized; the publication medium; and the date you accessed the source.

> Benjamin, Roy. "The Stone of Stumbling in *Finnegans Wake.*" *Journal
>   of Modern Literature* 31.2 (2008): 66-78. *Academic OneFile.* Web.
>   7 Apr. 2011.
>
> Carter, Jeff. "The Missing Piece of Education Reform." *Washington Post*
>   18 May 2008, regional ed.: B8. *LexisNexis Academic.* Web. 31 Mar.
>   2012.
>
> Prince, Stephen. "Why Do Film Scholars Ignore Media Violence?"
>   *Chronicle of Higher Education* 10 Aug. 2001: B18. *Academic
>   Research Premier.* Web. 14 Feb. 2011.

Other Nonprint Sources

ELECTRONIC BOOK

> Moe, Richard. *Roosevelt's Second Act: The Election of 1940 and the
>   Politics of War.* New York: Oxford UP, 2013. Kindle file.

TELEVISION OR RADIO PROGRAM

"Prime Suspect 3." Writ. Lynda La Plante. *Mystery!* PBS. WNET, New
    York, 28 Apr. 1994. Television.

FILM, DVD, OR CD

Doubt. Dir. John Patrick Shanley. Perf. Meryl Streep, Philip Seymour
    Hoffman, Amy Adams, and Viola Davis. Miramax, 2008. DVD.

Man on Wire. Dir. James Marsh. Perf. Philippe Petit. Discovery Films,
    2008. Film.

PERSONAL INTERVIEW

Huffington, Arianna. Personal interview. 7 May 2013.

Model Student Research Paper in MLA Style

The following research paper, "The Limitations of *Wikipedia*," by Philip
Lau, follows MLA format as outlined in the previous pages.

Lau 1

Philip Lau

Professor Carroll

English 101

5 December 2013

The Limitations of Wikipedia

Introduction

When students get a research assignment, many immediately go to the Internet to find sources. Searching the Web, they may discover a *Wikipedia* article on their topic. But is *Wikipedia* a reliable reference source for a research paper? There is quite a controversy over the use of *Wikipedia* as a source, but

Thesis statement

the consensus seems to be that it is not. Although *Wikipedia* can be a good starting point for general information about a topic, it is not suitable for college-level research.

A wiki allows multiple users to collaborate in creating the content of a website. With a wiki, anyone with a browser can edit, modify, rearrange, or delete content. It is not necessary to know HTML (hypertext mark-up language). The word *wiki* comes from the word *wikiwiki*, which means "quick" or "fast" in Hawaiian. The most popular wiki is *Wikipedia,* a free, Internet-based encyclopedia that relies on the collaboration of those who post and edit entries. Anyone can write a *Wikipedia* article

Paragraph combines factual information found in more than one source: information and statistics from Wikipedia *articles, quotations from Chozick and Grathwohl*

by using the *"Wikipedia* Article Wizard" or edit an entry by clicking on the "Edit" tab. Readers can also view the revision history of an entry by clicking on "View History" ("Help: Page History"). For its many advocates, *Wikipedia*'s open and collaborative nature makes it a "collectively brilliant creation" (Chozick). This collaboration enables *Wikipedia* to publish a wide variety of entries on timely, unusual, and specialized topics (see fig. 1). According to Casper Grathwohl, President, Dictionaries Division, and Director, Global Business Development at Oxford University Press, it "has become increasingly clear that [*Wikipedia*] functions as a necessary layer in the Internet knowledge system, a layer that was not needed in the analog age." At this time, the site contains 30 million articles in 287 languages ("*Wikipedia*").

Lau 2

© Creative Commons/Wikipedia

Fig. 1. *Wikipedia* entry for a chemical compound. "Pentamethylcyclopentadiene."
Wikipedia, the Free Encyclopedia. Wikimedia Foundation, 3 July 2013. Web.
9 Dec. 2013.

Paragraph combines student's ideas with quotations from "No Original Research"

Wikipedia contains two kinds of content. The first kind of
content is factual — that is, information that can be verified or
proved true. Factual material from reliable sources is more
trustworthy than material from other sources. *Wikipedia*'s own
site states, "In general, the most reliable sources are peer-
reviewed journals and books published in university presses;
university-level textbooks; magazines, journals, and books
published by respected publishing houses; and mainstream
newspapers" ("No Original Research"). Most reliable publications
have staff whose job it is to check factual content. However,
because *Wikipedia* relies on a community of contributors to write
articles, no single person or group of people is responsible for
checking facts. The theory is that if enough people work on an

Lau 3

article, factual errors will be found and corrected. However, this assumption is not necessarily true.

The second kind of content consists of opinions. Because they are personal beliefs or judgments, opinions — by definition — tend to be one-sided. Because *Wikipedia* entries are supposed to be objective, *Wikipedia*'s policy statement stresses the importance of acknowledging various sides of issues and maintaining a sharp distinction between opinions and facts ("Neutral Point of View"). In addition, *Wikipedia* warns users against believing everything they read, including what they read on *Wikipedia*: "Anyone can create a website or pay to have a book published, then claim to be an expert . . ." ("Identifying Reliable Sources"). It also advises readers to examine sources carefully, especially when they make claims that are "contradicted by the prevailing view within the relevant community, or that would significantly alter mainstream assumptions, especially in science, medicine, history, politics, and biographies of living people" ("Verifiability"). However, everything is up to users; no editor at *Wikipedia* checks to make sure that these guidelines are followed.

In spite of its stated policies, *Wikipedia* remains susceptible to certain problems. One problem is the assumption that the knowledge of the community is more valuable than the knowledge of acknowledged experts in a field. In other words, *Wikipedia* values crowd-sourced information more than the knowledge of an individual specialist. In his book *You Are Not a Gadget,* computer scientist and pioneer of virtual reality Jaron Lanier argues that *Wikipedia*'s authors "implicitly celebrate the ideal of intellectual mob rule" (144). According to Lanier, "Wikipedians always act out the ideal that the collective is closer to the truth and the individual voice is dispensable" (144). Adherence to this ideal can have serious consequences for the accuracy of *Wikipedia* entries. For example, historian Timothy Messer-Kruse, an expert on American labor history,

Paragraph combines student's own ideas with quotations from multiple Wikipedia *entries*

Lau 4

attempted to edit a *Wikipedia* article to correct a factual
error in the entry on the 1886 Chicago Haymarket Riot. Although
Messer-Kruse has published extensively on the subject, his
correction was rejected. Messer-Kruse's subsequent attempts to
correct the entry — which had multiple errors — were
dismissed as well. In an article he wrote for the *Chronicle of
Higher Education,* Messer-Kruse recounted the experience,
including a telling comment from one of the site's editors, with
whom he had an online exchange:

> If all historians save one say that the sky was green
> in 1888, our policies require that we write, "Most
> historians write that the sky was green, but one says
> the sky was blue." As individual editors, we're not in
> the business of weighing claims, just reporting what
> reliable sources write.

In other words, *Wikipedia*'s policy is to present all views, even
incorrect ones, provided they are published in a reliable source
("Neutral Point of View").

Another problem with *Wikipedia* is the ease with which
entries can be edited. Because anyone can edit entries, individuals
can vandalize content by inserting incorrect information, obscene
language, or even nonsense into articles. For example, entries
for controversial people, such as President George W. Bush,
financier George Soros, or Scientology founder L. Ron Hubbard,
or for controversial subjects, such as abortion, are routinely
vandalized. Sometimes the vandalism can be extremely harmful.
One notorious case of vandalism involved John Seigenthaler, a
journalist and former administrative assistant to Attorney
General Robert Kennedy, who was falsely accused in *Wikipedia*
of being involved in the assassinations of John F. Kennedy and
Robert Kennedy. Ultimately, Seigenthaler contacted *Wikipedia*
founder Jimmy Wales, threatened legal action, and even tracked
down the writer who had inserted the libelous accusation. If a
friend had not alerted Seigenthaler to the vandalized entry, it

*Paragraph
combines
quotations from
two* Wikipedia
*entries and Lanier
as well as a long
quotation from
Messer-Kruse; it
includes student's
summary of
Messer-Kruse's
story and
student's own
ideas*

*Paragraph
contains student's
summary of
Seigenthaler's
story from
Torrenzano and
Davis's* Digital
Assassination,
*as well as
paraphrases and
quotations from
the book*

Lau 5

would have likely remained in place, with its false claim that Seigenthaler was "a suspected assassin who had defected to the Soviet Union for 13 years" (Torrenzano and Davis 60–63).

In addition to misinformation and vandalism, bias is another problem for *Wikipedia.* Some critics have accused the site of having a liberal bias. Writing for the Web publication *Human Events,* Rowan Scarborough notes that observers on the right have "long complained of *Wikipedia*'s liberal bias that infects voters with unflattering profiles of their candidates." In fact, a competitor, *Conservapedia,* lists many examples of this skewed coverage in *Wikipedia* entries ("Examples of Bias in *Wikipedia*"). Other critics have identified different kinds of biases on the site. For example, a 2010 survey of *Wikipedia* contributors suggested that "less than 15 percent of its hundreds of thousands of contributors are women" (Cohen). This imbalance indicates a significant lack of women's perspectives on the site. In response, Sue Gardner, the executive director of the Wikimedia Foundation, has "set a goal to raise the share of female contributors to 25 percent by 2015" (Cohen). Still, these accusations of bias raise questions about the credibility of *Wikipedia.*

As Gardner indicates, *Wikipedia* has tried to correct some of the problems that its critics have noted. For example, in response to criticism of its policy of allowing writers and editors to remain anonymous, Wales changed this policy. Now, writers and editors have to provide their user names and thus take responsibility for the content they contribute. In addition, *Wikipedia* has made it possible for administrators to block edits originating from certain Internet domains and to prevent certain writers and editors from posting or changing information. However, authorship is still a problem. Most readers have no idea who has written an article that they are reading or whether or not the writer can be trusted. Given *Wikipedia*'s basic philosophy, there is no way to solve this problem.

Paragraph contains paraphrase from "Examples of Bias in Wikipedia*," quotations from Scarborough and Cohen, and the student's own conclusions*

Lau 6

Of course, even traditional encyclopedias have shortcomings. For example, a 2005 study by the journal *Nature* found that although *Wikipedia* included errors, the *Encyclopædia Britannica* also did (Giles). *Britannica* — the oldest English-language encyclopedia still in print at the time — ceased print publication in 2012 after 244 years (Rousseau). However, this venerable source of information persists online because people still value its expertise and trust its credibility. As Jorge Cauz, the president of Encyclopædia Britannica, Inc., observes, "While *Wikipedia* has become ubiquitous, *Britannica* remains a consistently more reliable source. In other words, *Britannica* brings scholarly knowledge to an editorial process" (qtd. in Rousseau). Although that editorial process is not a 100 percent guarantee of accuracy, *Britannica*'s staff of dedicated experts and specialists is more reliable than anonymous *Wikipedia* posters. Moreover, conscientious and knowledgeable editors work to make sure that entries are clear, logical, coherent, and grammatically correct. The same cannot be said for *Wikipedia*, which is known for its inconsistent treatment of subjects and its ungrammatical and awkward prose.

Paragraph contains ideas found in several sources and the student's own ideas

Supporters of *Wikipedia* defend the site against charges of bias and errors, pointing out that even respected peer-reviewed journals have problems. For example, some reviewers of articles submitted for publication in peer-reviewed journals may have conflicts of interest. A reviewer might reject an article that challenges his or her own work, or editors may favor certain authors over others. Also, it may be possible for a reviewer to identify the work of a rival, especially if the number of people working in a field is relatively small, and let bias influence his or her evaluation of an article. Another problem is that it takes a long time for articles in peer-reviewed journals to get into print. Critics point out that by the time an article in a peer-reviewed journal appears, it may be outdated. In short, peer-reviewed journals may not be

Lau 7

either as objective or as up-to-date as many readers think they are.

Conclusion

Despite their problems, articles that appear in an edited encyclopedia or journal are more trustworthy than those that appear in *Wikipedia*. These articles are thoroughly reviewed by editors or go through a peer-review process (that is, they are screened by experts in a field), and for this reason, they can be considered reliable sources of information. *Wikipedia*, however, is not a reliable research source. The fact that almost anyone can contribute an article or edit one at any time raises serious questions about *Wikipedia*'s reliability. In addition, many articles contain factual errors. Although some errors are found and corrected immediately, others remain for a long time or go entirely unnoticed. Finally, articles frequently reflect the biases or political agendas of contributors and, as a result, present a one-sided or inaccurate view of a subject. All in all, *Wikipedia*'s open-source philosophy makes it more prone to errors, inconsistencies, poor writing, and even vandalism, and for this reason, it should be used with caution. Perhaps the best that can be said of *Wikipedia* is that it is a good starting point for research. Although it is a useful site for getting an overview of a subject before doing in-depth research, it should not be considered a credible or authoritative academic source.

Lau 8

Works Cited

Chozick, Amy. "Jimmy Wales Is Not an Internet Billionaire."
    New York Times. New York Times, 30 June 2013. Web.
    2 Dec. 2013.

Cohen, Noam. "Define Gender Gap? Look Up *Wikipedia*'s
    Contributor List." *New York Times* 31 Jan. 2011: A1+. Print.

"Examples of Bias in *Wikipedia*." *Conservapedia*. Conservapedia,
    18 Oct. 2013. Web. 1 Dec. 2013.

Giles, Jim. "Internet Encyclopædias Go Head to Head." *Nature*
    438 (2005): 900-901. Print.

Grathwohl, Casper. "*Wikipedia* Comes of Age." *Chronicle of
    Higher Education*. Chronicle of Higher Education, 7 Jan.
    2011. Web. 1 Dec. 2013.

"Help: Page History." *Wikipedia*. Wikimedia Foundation, 16 Oct.
    2013. Web. 1 Dec. 2013.

"Identifying Reliable Sources." *Wikipedia*. Wikimedia
    Foundation, 29 Nov. 2013. Web. 1 Dec. 2013.

Lanier, Jaron. *You Are Not a Gadget: A Manifesto*. London: Allen
    Lane, 2010. Print.

Messer-Kruse, Timothy. "The 'Undue Weight' of Truth on
    Wikipedia." *Chronicle of Higher Education*. Chronicle of
    Higher Education, 12 Feb. 2012. Web. 2 Dec. 2013.

"Neutral Point of View." *Wikipedia*. Wikimedia Foundation,
    3 Dec. 2013. Web. 3 Dec. 2013.

"No Original Research." *Wikipedia*. Wikimedia Foundation,
    15 Nov. 2013. Web. 1 Dec. 2013.

Rousseau, Caryn. "*Encyclopædia Britannica* to End Print
    Editions." *Yahoo! News*. Yahoo-ABC News Network,
    13 Mar. 2012. Web. 1 Dec. 2013.

Scarborough, Rowan. "*Wikipedia* Whacks the Right." *Human
    Events*. The Human Events Group, 27 Sep. 2010. Web.
    2 Dec. 2013.

Lau 9

Torrenzano, Richard, and Mark Davis. *Digital Assassination:*
     Protecting Your Reputation, Brand, or Business against
     Online Attacks. New York: St. Martin's, 2011. Print.
"Verifiability." *Wikipedia*. Wikimedia Foundation, 26 Nov. 2013.
     Web. 1 Dec. 2013.
"*Wikipedia*." *Wikipedia*. Wikimedia Foundation, 3 Dec. 2013.
     Web. 3 Dec. 2013.

APPENDIX

Documenting Sources: APA

APA style was developed by the American Psychological Association and is commonly used in the social sciences. Sources are cited to help readers in the social sciences understand new ideas in the context of previous research and show them how current the sources are.*

There are several reasons to cite sources. Readers expect arguments to be well supported by evidence and want to be able to locate those sources if they decide to delve deeper. Citing sources is also important to give credit to writers and to avoid plagiarism.

Using Parenthetical References

In APA style, parenthetical references refer readers to sources in the list of references at the end of the paper. In general, parenthetical references should include the author and year of publication. You may also include page numbers if you are quoting directly from a source. Here are some more specific guidelines:

- Refer to the author's name in the text, or cite it, along with the year of publication, in parentheses: Vang asserted . . . (2004) or (Vang, 2004). When quoting words from a source, include the page number: (Vang, 2004, p. 33). Once you have cited a source, you can refer to the author a second time without the publication date so long as it is clear you are referring to the same source: Vang also found . . .
- If no author is identified, use a shortened version of the title: ("Mind," 2007).
- If you are citing multiple works by the same author or authors published in the same year, add a lowercase letter with the year: (Peters, 2004a), (Peters, 2004b), and so on.

---

* American Psychological Association, *Publication Manual of the American Psychological Association*, Sixth Edition (2010).

- When a work has two authors, cite both names and the year: (Tabor & Garza, 2006). For three to five authors, cite all authors in the first reference, with the year; for subsequent references, use the first author followed by et al. When a work has six or more authors, use the first author's name followed by et al. and the year: (McCarthy et al., 2010).
- Omit page numbers or dates if the source does not include them. (Try to find a .pdf version of an online source if it is an option; it will usually include page numbers.)
- If you quote a source found in another source, indicate the original author and the source in which you found it: Psychologist Gary Wells asserted . . . (as cited in Doyle, 2005, p. 122).
- Include in-text references to personal communications and interviews by providing the person's name, the phrase "personal communication," and the date: (J. Smith, personal communication, February 12, 2014). Do not include these sources in your reference list.

Parenthetical citations must be included for all sources that are not common knowledge, whether you are paraphrasing, summarizing, or quoting directly from a source. If a direct quotation is forty words or less, include it within quotation marks without separating it from the rest of the text. When quoting a passage that is more than forty words long, indent the entire block of quoted text one-half inch from the left margin, and do not enclose it in quotation marks. It should be double-spaced, like the rest of the paper.

GUIDELINES FOR PREPARING THE REFERENCE LIST

Start your list of references on a separate page at the end of your essay. Center the title References at the top of the page.

- Begin each reference flush with the left margin, and indent subsequent lines one-half inch.
- List your references alphabetically by the author's last name (or by the first major word of the title if no author is identified).
- If the list includes references for two or more sources by the same author, list them in order by the year of publication, starting with the earliest.
- Italicize titles of books and periodicals. Do not italicize article titles or enclose them in quotation marks.
- For titles of books and articles, capitalize the first word of the title and subtitle as well as any proper nouns. Capitalize words in a periodical title as in the original.

When you have completed your reference list, go through your paper and make sure that every reference cited is included in the list in the correct order.

Examples of APA Citations

The following are examples of APA citations.

Periodicals

ARTICLE IN A JOURNAL PAGINATED BY VOLUME

Shah, N. A. (2006). Women's human rights in the Koran: An
interpretive approach. *Human Rights Quarterly, 28*, 868–902.

ARTICLE IN A JOURNAL PAGINATED BY ISSUE

Lamb, B., & Keller, H. (2007). Understanding cultural models of
parenting: The role of intracultural variation and response style.
Journal of Cross-Cultural Psychology, 38(1), 50–57.

MAGAZINE ARTICLE

Collins, L. (2009, April 20). The vertical tourist. *The New Yorker, 85*(10),
68–79.

NEWSPAPER ARTICLE

DeParle, J. (2009, April 19). Struggling to rise in suburbs where failing
means fitting in. *The New York Times,* pp. A1, A20–A21.

Books

BOOKS BY ONE AUTHOR

McCrum, R. (2010). *Globish: How the English language became the
world's language.* New York, NY: Norton.

BOOKS BY TWO TO SEVEN AUTHORS

Guerrero, L. K., & Floyd, K. (2006). *Nonverbal communication in close
relationships.* Mahwah, NJ: Erlbaum.

BOOKS BY EIGHT OR MORE AUTHORS

Mulvaney, S. A., Mudasiru, E., Schlundt, D. G., Baughman, C. L.,
Fleming, M., VanderWoude, A., . . . Rothman, R. (2008). Self-
management in Type 2 diabetes: The adolescent perspective. *The
Diabetes Educator, 34*, 118–127.

EDITED BOOK

Brummett, B. (Ed.). (2008). *Uncovering hidden rhetorics: Social issues
in disguise.* Los Angeles, CA: Sage.

ESSAY IN AN EDITED BOOK

Alberts, H. C. (2006). The multiple transformations of Miami. In
   H. Smith & O. J. Furuseth (Eds.), *Latinos in the new south:*
   Transformations of place (pp. 135–151). Burlington, VT: Ashgate.

TRANSLATION

Courville, S. (2008). *Quebec: A historical geography* (R. Howard, Trans.).
   Vancouver, Canada: UBC.

REVISED EDITION

Johnson, B., & Christensen, L. B. (2008). *Educational research:*
   Quantitative, qualitative, and mixed approaches (3rd ed.). Los
   Angeles, CA: Sage.

Internet Sources

ENTIRE WEBSITE

Secretariat of the Convention on Biodiversity, United Nations
   Biodiversity Programmes. (2005). *Convention on biological*
   diversity. Retrieved from http://www.biodiv.org/

WEB PAGE WITHIN A WEBSITE

The great divide: How Westerners and Muslims view each other.
   (2006, July 6). In *Pew global attitudes project.* Retrieved from
   http://pewglobal.org/reports/display.php?ReportID=253

UNIVERSITY PROGRAM WEBSITE

National security archive. (2009). Retrieved from George Washington
   University website: http://www.gwu.edu/~nsarchiv/

JOURNAL ARTICLE FOUND ON THE WEB WITH A DOI

Because websites change and disappear without warning, many publishers have started adding a Digital Object Identifier (DOI) to their articles. A DOI is a unique number that can be retrieved no matter where the
article ends up on the Web.

To locate an article with a known DOI, go to the DOI system website at
http://dx.doi.org/ and type in the DOI number. When citing an article that
has a DOI (usually found on the first page of the article), you do not need
to include a URL in your reference or the name of the database in which
you may have found the article.

Geers, A. L., Wellman, J. A., & Lassiter, G. D. (2009). Dispositional
   optimism and engagement: The moderating influence of goal
   prioritization. *Journal of Personality and Social Psychology, 94,*
   913–932. doi:10.1037/a0014746

JOURNAL ARTICLE FOUND ON THE WEB WITHOUT A DOI

> Bendetto, M. M. (2008). Crisis on the immigration bench: An ethical
> perspective. *Brooklyn Law Review, 73,* 467–523. Retrieved from
> http://brooklaw.edu/students/journals/blr.php/

JOURNAL ARTICLE FROM AN ELECTRONIC DATABASE

The name and URL of the database are not required for citations if a
DOI is available. If no DOI is available, provide the home page URL of the
journal or of the book or report publisher.

> Staub, E., & Pearlman, L. A. (2009). Reducing intergroup prejudice and
> conflict: A commentary. *Journal of Personality and Social
> Psychology, 11,* 3–23. Retrieved from http://www.apa.org
> /journals/psp/

ELECTRONIC BOOK

> Katz, R. N. (Ed.). (2008). *The tower and the cloud: Higher education in
> an era of cloud computing.* Retrieved from http://net.educause
> .edu/ir/library/pdf/PUB7202.pdf

VIDEO BLOG POST

> Baggs, A. (2007, January 14). In my language [Video file]. Retrieved
> from http://www.youtube.com/watch?v=Jny1M1hI2jc

PRESENTATION SLIDES

> Hall, M. E. (2009) *Who moved my job!? A psychology of job-loss
> "trauma"* [Presentation slides]. Retrieved from http://www.cew.wisc
> .edu/docs/WMMJ%20PwrPt-Summry2.ppt

Model Student Paper in APA Style

The following research paper follows APA format as outlined in the
preceding pages. Note that this paper has the same content as the MLA
paper on pages 742–49 but follows APA conventions. For this reason, it
includes an abstract, a title page, and internal headings.

Running head: THE LIMITATIONS OF *WIKIPEDIA*   1

The Limitations of *Wikipedia*

Philip Lau

English 101

Professor Carroll

December 5, 2013

Abstract

Wikipedia is an online encyclopedia with entries that are
created and updated by users rather than by editors. This
essay examines the benefits and drawbacks associated with
Wikipedia's open-forum approach. *Wikipedia* contains
information about a great number of topics and could be a good
resource for students who are trying to narrow the focus of their
essays. However, many educators believe that this information
is unreliable and therefore should not be used for scholarly
research. They are concerned that entries that can be edited by
anyone, regardless of their expertise on the subject, might not
be accurate. Although *Wikipedia* strives to be as accurate as a
traditional encyclopedia, there has been at least one case where
inflammatory and untrue information remained on the site for
months and being disseminated through other outlets as fact.
Because there is no way to determine the expertise of the
authors or the validity of the information on *Wikipedia*, it
should not be considered a reliable source.

The Limitations of *Wikipedia*

Introduction

When students get a research assignment, many immediately go to the Internet to find sources. Searching the Web, they may discover a *Wikipedia* article on their topic. But is *Wikipedia* a reliable reference source for a research paper? There is quite a controversy over the use of *Wikipedia* as a source, but

Thesis statement

the consensus seems to be that it is not. Although *Wikipedia* can be a good starting point for general information about a topic, it is not suitable for college-level research.

A wiki allows multiple users to collaborate in creating the content of a website. With a wiki, anyone with a browser can edit, modify, rearrange, or delete content. It is not necessary to know HTML (hypertext mark-up language). The word *wiki* comes from the word *wikiwiki*, which means "quick" or "fast" in Hawaiian. The most popular wiki is *Wikipedia*, a free, Internet-based encyclopedia that relies on the collaboration of those who post and edit entries. Anyone can write a *Wikipedia* article

Paragraph combines factual information found in more than one source: information and statistics from Wikipedia *articles, quotations from Chozick and Grathwohl*

by using the "*Wikipedia* Article Wizard" or edit an entry by clicking on the "Edit" tab. Readers can easily view the revision history of an entry by clicking on "View History" ("Help: page history," 2013). For its many advocates, *Wikipedia*'s open and collaborative nature makes it a "collectively brilliant creation" (Chozick, 2013). This collaboration enables *Wikipedia* to publish a wide variety of entries on timely, unusual, and specialized topics (see Figure 1). It has certainly altered the way people think about research. Moreover, *Wikipedia* has increasingly become a "necessary layer in the Internet knowledge system, a layer that was not needed in the analog age" (Grathwohl, 2011). At this time, the site contains 30 million articles in 287 languages ("*Wikipedia*," 2013).

Wikipedia's Two Kinds of Content

Wikipedia contains two kinds of content. The first kind of content is factual — that is, information that can be verified or

THE LIMITATIONS OF *WIKIPEDIA*   4

© Creative Commons/Wikipedia

Figure 1. *Wikipedia* entry for a chemical compound. Pentamethylcyclopentadiene (2013, July 5). *Wikipedia*. Retrieved from http://en.wikipedia.org/wiki
/Pentamethylcyclopentadiene.

*Paragraph
combines
student's
ideas with
quotations from
"No Original
Research"*

proved true. Factual material from reliable sources is more
trustworthy than material from other sources. *Wikipedia*'s own
site states, "In general, the most reliable sources are peer-
reviewed journals and books published in university presses;
university-level textbooks; magazines, journals, and books
published by respected publishing houses; and mainstream
newspapers" ("No Original Research," 2013). Most reliable
publications have staff whose job it is to check factual content.
However, because *Wikipedia* relies on a community of
contributors to write articles, no single person or group of
people is responsible for checking facts. The theory is that if

enough people work on an article, factual errors will be found and corrected. However, this assumption is not necessarily true.

The second kind of content consists of opinions. Because they are personal beliefs or judgments, opinions — by definition — tend to be one-sided. Because *Wikipedia* entries are supposed to be objective, *Wikipedia*'s policy statement stresses the importance of acknowledging various sides of issues and maintaining a sharp distinction between opinions and facts ("Neutral Point of View," 2013). In addition, *Wikipedia* warns users against believing everything they read, including what they read on *Wikipedia*: "Anyone can create a website or pay to have a book published, then claim to be an expert . . ." ("Identifying reliable sources," 2013). It also advises readers to examine sources carefully, especially when they make claims that are "contradicted by the prevailing view within the relevant community, or that would significantly alter mainstream assumptions, especially in science, medicine, history, politics, and biographies of living people" ("Verifiability," 2013). However, everything is up to users; no editor at *Wikipedia* checks to make sure that these guidelines are followed.

Paragraph combines student's own ideas with quotations from multiple Wikipedia entries

Errors and Other Problems with *Wikipedia*

In spite of its stated policies, *Wikipedia* remains susceptible to certain problems. One problem is the assumption that the knowledge of the community is more valuable than the knowledge of acknowledged experts in a field. In other words, *Wikipedia* values crowd-sourced information more than the knowledge of an individual specialist. In his book *You Are Not a Gadget,* Lanier (2010) argues that *Wikipedia*'s authors "implicitly celebrate the ideal of intellectual mob rule" (p. 144). According to Lanier, "Wikipedians always act out the ideal that the collective is closer to the truth and the individual voice is dispensable" (p. 144). Adherence to this ideal can have serious

THE LIMITATIONS OF *WIKIPEDIA*   6

Paragraph combines quotations from two Wikipedia entries and Lanier, as well as a long quotation from Messer-Kruse; it includes student's summary of Messer-Kruse's story and student's own ideas

consequences for the accuracy of *Wikipedia* entries. For example, historian Timothy Messer-Kruse, an expert on American labor history, attempted to edit a *Wikipedia* article to correct a factual error in the entry on the 1886 Chicago Haymarket Riot. Although Messer-Kruse has published extensively on the subject, his correction was rejected. Messer-Kruse's subsequent attempts to correct the entry — which had multiple errors — were dismissed as well. In an article he wrote for the *Chronicle of Higher Education*, Messer-Kruse recounted the experience, including a telling comment from one of the site's editors, with whom he had an online exchange:

> If all historians save one say that the sky was green in 1888, our policies require that we write, "Most historians write that the sky was green, but one says the sky was blue." As individual editors, we're not in the business of weighing claims, just reporting what reliable sources write. (Messer-Kruse, 2012)

In other words, *Wikipedia*'s policy is to present all views, even incorrect ones, provided they are published in a reliable source ("Neutral Point of view," 2013).

Another problem with *Wikipedia* is the ease with which entries can be edited. Because anyone can edit entries, individuals can vandalize content by inserting incorrect information, obscene language, or even nonsense into articles. For example, entries for controversial people, such as President George W. Bush, financier George Soros, or Scientology founder L. Ron Hubbard, or for controversial subjects, such as abortion, are routinely vandalized. Sometimes the vandalism can be extremely harmful. One notorious case of vandalism involved John Seigenthaler, a journalist and former administrative assistant to Attorney General Robert Kennedy, who was falsely accused in *Wikipedia* of being involved in the assassinations of

Paragraph contains student's summary of Seigenthaler's story from Torrenzano and Davis's Digital Assassination, as well as paraphrases and quotations from the book

John F. Kennedy and Robert Kennedy. Ultimately, Seigenthaler contacted *Wikipedia* founder Jimmy Wales, threatened legal action, and even tracked down the writer who had inserted the libelous accusation. If a friend had not alerted Seigenthaler to the vandalized entry, it would have likely remained in place, with its false claim that Seigenthaler was "a suspected assassin who had defected to the Soviet Union for 13 years" (Torrenzano & Davis, 2011, pp. 60–63).

In addition to misinformation and vandalism, bias is another problem for *Wikipedia.* Some critics have accused the site of having a liberal bias. Writing for the Web publication *Human Events,* Scarborough (2010) noted that observers on the right have "long complained of *Wikipedia*'s liberal bias that infects voters with unflattering profiles of their candidates." In fact, a competitor, *Conservapedia,* lists many examples of this skewed coverage in *Wikipedia* entries ("Examples of Bias in *Wikipedia*," 2013). Other critics have identified different kinds of biases on the site. For example, a 2010 survey of *Wikipedia* contributors suggested that "less than 15 percent of its hundreds of thousands of contributors are women" (Cohen, 2011). This imbalance indicates a significant lack of women's perspectives on the site. In response, Sue Gardner, the executive director of the Wikimedia Foundation, has "set a goal to raise the share of female contributors to 25 percent by 2015" (Cohen, 2011). Still, these accusations of bias raise questions about the credibility of *Wikipedia.*

As Gardner indicates, *Wikipedia* has tried to correct some of the problems that its critics have noted. For example, in response to criticism of its policy of allowing writers and editors to remain anonymous, Wales changed this policy. Now, writers and editors have to provide their user names and thus take responsibility for the content they contribute. In addition, *Wikipedia* has made it possible for administrators to block edits

Paragraph contains paraphrase from "Examples of Bias in Wikipedia," quotations from Scarborough and Cohen, and the student's own conclusions

originating from certain Internet domains and to prevent certain writers and editors from posting or changing information. However, authorship is still a problem. Most readers have no idea who has written an article that they are reading or whether or not the writer can be trusted. Given *Wikipedia*'s basic philosophy, there is no way to solve this problem.

Of course, even traditional encyclopedias have shortcomings. For example, a study by the journal *Nature* found that although *Wikipedia* included errors, the *Encyclopædia Britannica* also did (Giles, 2005). *Britannica* — the oldest English-language encyclopedia still in print at the time — ceased print publication in 2012 after 244 years (Rousseau, 2012). However, this venerable source of information persists online because people still value its expertise and trust its credibility. As Jorge Cauz, the president of Encyclopædia Britannica, Inc., observes, "While *Wikipedia* has become ubiquitous, *Britannica* remains a consistently more reliable source. In other words, *Britannica* brings scholarly knowledge to an editorial process" (Rousseau, 2012). Although that editorial process is not a 100 percent guarantee of accuracy, *Britannica*'s staff of dedicated experts and specialists is more reliable than anonymous *Wikipedia* posters. Moreover, conscientious and knowledgeable editors work to make sure that entries are clear, logical, coherent, and grammatically correct. The same cannot be said for *Wikipedia*, which is known for its inconsistent treatment of subjects and its ungrammatical and awkward prose.

Comparison to Traditional Sources

Supporters of *Wikipedia* defend the site against charges of bias and errors, pointing out that even respected peer-reviewed journals have problems. For example, some reviewers of articles submitted for publication in peer-reviewed journals may have conflicts of interest. A reviewer might reject an article that

Paragraph contains ideas found in several sources and the student's own ideas

challenges his or her own work, or editors may favor certain authors over others. Also, it may be possible for a reviewer to identify the work of a rival, especially if the number of people working in a field is relatively small, and let bias influence his or her evaluation of an article. Another problem is that it takes a long time for articles in peer-reviewed journals to get into print. Critics point out that by the time an article in a peer-reviewed journal appears, it may be outdated. In short, peer-reviewed journals may not be either as objective or as up-to-date as many readers think they are.

Conclusion

Conclusion

Despite their problems, articles that appear in an edited encyclopedia or journal are more trustworthy than those that appear in *Wikipedia*. These articles are thoroughly reviewed by editors or go through a peer-review process (that is, they are screened by experts in a field), and for this reason, they can be considered reliable sources of information. *Wikipedia*, however, is not a reliable research source. The fact that almost anyone can contribute an article or edit one at any time raises serious questions about *Wikipedia*'s reliability. In addition, many articles contain factual errors. Although some errors are found and corrected immediately, others remain for a long time or go entirely unnoticed. Finally, articles frequently reflect the biases or political agendas of contributors and, as a result, present a one-sided or inaccurate view of a subject. All in all, *Wikipedia*'s open-source philosophy makes it more prone to errors, inconsistencies, poor writing, and even vandalism, and for this reason, it should be used with caution. Perhaps the best that can be said of *Wikipedia* is that it is a good starting point for research. Although it is a useful site for getting an overview of a subject before doing in-depth research, it should not be considered a credible or authoritative academic source.

References

Chozick, A. (2013, June 30). Jimmy Wales is not an Internet
     billionaire. *The New York Times*. Retrieved from http://
     nytimes.com

Cohen, N. (2011, January 31). Define gender gap? Look
     up *Wikipedia*'s contributor list. *The New York Times*,
     p. A1+.

Examples of bias in *Wikipedia*. (2013, October 18).
     Conservapedia. Retrieved December 3, 2013, from http://
     www.conservapedia.com/Examples_of_Bias_in_Wikipedia

Giles, J. (2005). Internet encyclopaedias go head to head.
     Nature, 438, 900-901.

Grathwohl, C. (2011, January 11). *Wikipedia* comes of age.
     Chronicle of Higher Education. Retrieved from http://
     chronicle.com

Help: page history. (2013, October 16). *Wikipedia*. Retrieved
     December 1, 2013, from http://en.wikipedia.org/wiki
     /Help:Page_history

Identifying reliable sources. (2013, November 29). *Wikipedia*.
     Retrieved December 3, 2013, from http://en.wikipedia
     .org/wiki/Wikipedia:Identifying_reliable_sources

Lanier, J. (2010). *You are not a gadget: A manifesto*. London,
     England: Allen Lane.

Messer-Kruse, T. (2012, February 12). The "undue weight" of
     truth on *Wikipedia*. *Chronicle of Higher Education*.
     Retrieved from http://chronicle.com

Neutral point of view. (2013, December 3). *Wikipedia*. Retrieved
     December 2, 2013, from http://en.wikipedia.org/wiki
     /Wikipedia:Neutral_point_of_view

No original research. (2013, November 15). *Wikipedia*. Retrieved
     December 1, 2013, from http://en.wikipedia.org/wiki
     /Wikipedia:No_original_research

THE LIMITATIONS OF *WIKIPEDIA*   11

Rousseau, C. (2012, March 13). *Encyclopædia Britannica* to end
    print editions. *Yahoo! News.* Retrieved from http://news
    .yahoo.com/encyclopaedia-britannica-end-print-editions
    -234637805.html

Scarborough, R. (2010, September 27). *Wikipedia* whacks the
    right. *Human Events.* Retrieved from http://www
    .humanevents.com/2010/09/27/wikipedia-whacks-the
    -right

Torrenzano, R., & Davis, M. (2011). *Digital assassination:
    Protecting your reputation, brand, or business against
    online attacks.* New York, NY: St. Martin's Press.

Verifiability. (2013, November 26). *Wikipedia.* Retrieved
    December 2, 2013, from http://en.wikipedia.org/wiki
    /Wikipedia:Verifiability

Wikipedia. (2013, December 3). *Wikipedia.* Retrieved
    December 2, 2013, from http://en.wikipedia.org/wiki
    /Wikipedia

GLOSSARY

Abstract/Concrete language Abstract language names concepts or qualities that cannot be directly seen or touched: *love, emotion, evil, anguish.* Concrete language denotes objects or qualities that the senses can perceive: *fountain pen, leaky, shouting, rancid.* Abstract words are sometimes needed to express ideas, but they are very vague unless used with concrete supporting detail. The abstract phrase "The speaker was overcome with emotion" could mean almost anything, but the addition of concrete language clarifies the meaning: "He clenched his fist and shook it at the crowd" (anger).

Allusion A brief reference to literature, history, the Bible, mythology, popular culture, and so on that readers are expected to recognize. An allusion evokes a vivid impression in very few words. "The gardener opened the gate, and suddenly we found ourselves in Eden" suggests in one word (*Eden*) the stunning beauty of the garden.

Analogy A form of comparison that explains an unfamiliar element by comparing it to another that is more familiar. Analogies also enable writers to put abstract or technical information in simpler, more concrete terms: "The effect of pollution on the environment is like that of cancer on the body."

Annotating The technique of recording one's responses to a reading selection by writing notes in the margins of the text. Annotating a text might involve asking questions, suggesting possible parallels with other selections or with the reader's own experience, arguing with the writer's points, commenting on the writer's style, or defining unfamiliar terms or concepts.

Antithesis A viewpoint opposite to one expressed in a *thesis.* In an argumentative essay, the thesis must be debatable. If no antithesis exists, the writer's thesis is not debatable. (See also **Thesis**.)

Antonym A word opposite in meaning to another word. *Beautiful* is the antonym of *ugly. Synonym* is the antonym of *antonym.*

Argumentation The form of writing that takes a stand on an issue and attempts to convince readers by presenting a logical sequence of points supported by evidence. Unlike *persuasion*, which uses a number of different appeals, argumentation is primarily an appeal to reason. (See Chapter 14.)

Audience The people "listening" to a writer's words. Writers who are sensitive to their audience will carefully choose a tone, examples, and

767

allusions that their readers will understand and respond to. For instance, an effective article attempting to persuade high school students not to drink alcohol would use examples and allusions pertinent to a teenager's life. Different examples would be chosen if the writer were addressing middle-aged members of Alcoholics Anonymous.

Basis for comparison A fundamental similarity between two or more things that enables a writer to compare them. In a comparison of how two towns react to immigrants, the basis of comparison might be that both towns have a rapidly expanding immigrant population. (If one of the towns did not have any immigrants, this comparison would be illogical.)

Body paragraphs The paragraphs that develop and support an essay's thesis.

Brainstorming An invention technique that can be done individually or in a group. When writers brainstorm on their own, they jot down every fact or idea that relates to a particular topic. When they brainstorm in a group, they discuss a topic with others and write down the useful ideas that come up.

Causal chain A sequence of events when one event causes another event, which in turn causes yet another event.

Cause and effect The pattern of development that discusses either the reasons for an occurrence or the observed or predicted consequence of an occurrence. Often both causes and effects are discussed in the same essay. (See Chapter 10.)

Causes The reasons for an event, situation, or phenomenon. An *immediate cause* is an obvious one; a *remote cause* is less easily perceived. The *main cause* is the most important cause, whether it is immediate or remote. Other, less important causes that nevertheless encourage the effect in some way (for instance, by speeding it up or providing favorable circumstances for it) are called *contributory causes*.

Chronological order The time sequence of events. Chronological order is often used to organize a narrative; it is also used to structure a process essay.

Claim In Toulmin logic, the thesis or main point of an essay. Usually the claim is stated directly, but sometimes it is implied. (See also **Toulmin logic**.)

Classification and division The pattern of development that uses these two related methods of organizing information. *Classification* involves searching for common characteristics among various items and grouping them accordingly, thereby imposing order on randomly organized information. *Division* breaks up an entity into smaller groups or elements. Classification generalizes; division specifies. (See Chapter 12.)

Cliché An overused expression, such as *beauty is in the eye of the beholder, the good die young,* or *a picture is worth a thousand words.*

Clustering A method of invention whereby a writer groups ideas visually by listing the main topic in the center of a page, circling it, and surrounding it with words or phrases that identify the major points to be addressed. The writer then circles these words or phrases, creating new clusters or ideas for each of them.

Coherence The tight relationship between all the parts of an effective piece of writing. Such a relationship ensures that the writing will make sense to readers. For a piece of writing to be coherent, it must be logical and orderly, with effective *transitions* making the movement between sentences and paragraphs clear. Within and between paragraphs, coherence may also be enhanced by the repetition of key words and ideas, by the use of pronouns to refer to nouns mentioned previously, and by the use of parallel sentence structure.

Colloquialisms Expressions that are generally appropriate for conversation and informal writing but not usually acceptable for the writing you do in college, business, or professional settings. Examples of colloquial language include contractions; clipped forms (*fridge* for *refrigerator*); vague expressions such as *kind of* and *sort of*; conversation fillers such as *you know*; and other informal words and expressions, such as *get across* for *communicate* and *kids* for *children.*

Common knowledge Factual information that is widely available in reference sources, such as the dates of important historical events. Writers do not need to document common knowledge.

Comparison and contrast The pattern of development that focuses on similarities and differences between two or more subjects. In a general sense, *comparison* shows how two or more subjects are alike; *contrast* shows how they are different. (See Chapter 11; see also **Point-by-point comparison**; **Subject-by-subject comparison**.)

Conclusion The group of sentences or paragraphs that brings an essay to a close. To *conclude* means not only "to end" but also "to resolve." Although a conclusion does not review all the issues discussed in an essay, the conclusion is the place to show that those issues have been resolved. An effective conclusion indicates that the writer is committed to what has been expressed, and it is the writer's last chance to leave an impression or idea with readers.

Concrete language See **Abstract/Concrete language**.

Connotation The associations, meanings, or feelings a word suggests beyond its literal meaning. Literally, the word *home* means "one's place of residence," but *home* also connotes warmth and a sense of belonging. (See also **Denotation**.)

Contributory cause See **Causes**.

Deductive reasoning The method of reasoning that moves from a general premise to a specific conclusion. Deductive reasoning is the opposite of *inductive reasoning*. (See also **Syllogism**.)

Definition An explanation of a word's meaning; the pattern of development in which a writer explains what something or someone is. (See Chapter 13; see also **Extended definition**; **Formal definition**.)

Denotation The literal meaning of a word. The denotation of *home* is "one's place of residence." (See also **Connotation**.)

Description The pattern of development that presents a word picture of a thing, a person, a situation, or a series of events. (See Chapter 7; see also **Objective description**; **Subjective description**.)

Digression A remark or series of remarks that wanders from the main point of a discussion. In a personal narrative, a digression may be entertaining because of its irrelevance, but in other kinds of writing it is likely to distract and confuse readers.

Division See **Classification and division**.

Documentation The formal way of giving credit to the sources a writer borrows words or ideas from. Documentation allows readers to evaluate a writer's sources and to consult them if they wish. Papers written for literature and writing classes use the documentation style recommended by the Modern Language Association (MLA). (See Chapter 18.)

Dominant impression The mood or quality that is central to a piece of writing.

Essay A short work of nonfiction writing on a single topic that usually expresses the author's impressions or opinions. An essay may be organized around one of the patterns of development presented in Chapters 6 through 14 of this book, or it may combine several of these patterns.

Euphemism A polite term for an unpleasant concept. (*Passed away* is a euphemism for *died*.)

Evidence Facts and opinions used to support a statement, position, or idea. *Facts*, which may include statistics, may be drawn from research or personal experience; *opinions* may represent the conclusions of experts or the writer's own ideas.

Example A concrete illustration of a general point.

Exemplification The pattern of development that uses a single extended *example* or a series of shorter examples to support a thesis. (See Chapter 8.)

Extended definition A paragraph-, essay-, or book-length definition developed by means of one or more of the rhetorical strategies discussed in this book.

Fallacy A statement that resembles a logical argument but is actually flawed. Logical fallacies are often persuasive, but they unfairly manipulate readers to win agreement. Fallacies include begging the question; argument from analogy; personal (*ad hominem*) attacks; jumping to a conclusion (hasty or sweeping generalizations); false dilemmas (the either/or fallacy); equivocation; red herrings; you also (*tu quoque*); appeals to doubtful authority; misleading statistics; *post hoc* reasoning; and *non sequiturs*. See the section on "Recognizing Fallacies" (page 535) for explanations and examples.

Figures of speech (also known as *figurative language*) Imaginative language used to suggest a special meaning or create a special effect. Three of the most common figures of speech are *similes, metaphors,* and *personification.*

Formal definition A brief explanation of a word's meaning as it appears in the dictionary.

Formal outline A detailed construction that uses headings and subheadings to indicate the order in which key points and supporting details are presented in an essay.

Freewriting A method of invention that involves writing without stopping for a fixed period — perhaps five or ten minutes — without paying attention to spelling, grammar, or punctuation. The goal of freewriting is to let ideas flow and record them.

Grounds In Toulmin logic, the material that a writer uses to support a claim. Grounds may be evidence (facts or expert opinions) or appeals to the emotions or values of an audience. (See also **Toulmin logic.**)

Highlighting A technique used by a reader to record responses to a reading selection by marking the text with symbols. Highlighting a text might involve underlining important ideas, boxing key terms, numbering a series of related points, circling unfamiliar words (or placing question marks next to them), drawing vertical lines next to an interesting or important passage, drawing arrows to connect related points, or placing asterisks next to discussions of the selection's central issues or themes.

Hyperbole Deliberate exaggeration for emphasis or humorous effect: "I froze to death out in the storm"; "She has hundreds of boyfriends"; "Senior year passed by in a second." The opposite of hyperbole is *understatement.*

Imagery A set of verbal pictures of sensory experiences. These pictures, conveyed through concrete details, make a description vivid and immediate to the reader. Some images are literal ("The cows were so white they almost glowed in the dark"); others are more figurative ("The black-and-white cows looked like maps, with the continents in black and the seas in white"). A pattern of imagery (repeated images of, for example, shadows, forests, or fire) may run through a piece of writing.

Immediate cause See **Causes**.

Inductive reasoning The method of reasoning that moves from specific evidence to a general conclusion based on this evidence. Inductive reasoning is the opposite of *deductive reasoning*.

Informal outline A list of points to be developed in an essay.

Instructions A kind of process essay whose purpose is to enable readers to *perform* a process. Instructions use the present tense and speak directly to readers: "Walk at a moderate pace for twenty minutes."

Introduction An essay's opening. Depending on the length of an essay, the introduction may be one paragraph or several paragraphs. In an introduction, a writer tries to encourage the audience to read the essay that follows. Therefore, the writer must choose tone and diction carefully, indicate what the paper is about, and suggest to readers what direction it will take.

Invention (also known as *prewriting*) The stage of writing when a writer explores the writing assignment, focuses ideas, and ultimately decides on a thesis for an essay. A writer might begin by thinking through the requirements of the assignment — the essay's purpose, length, and audience. Then, using one or more methods of invention — such as *freewriting, questions for probing, brainstorming, clustering*, and *journal writing* — the writer can formulate a tentative thesis and begin to write the essay.

Irony Language that points to a discrepancy between two different levels of meaning. *Verbal irony* is characterized by a gap between what is stated and what is really meant, which often has the opposite meaning — for instance, "his humble abode" (referring to a millionaire's estate). *Situational irony* points to a discrepancy between what actually happens and what readers expect will happen. This kind of irony is present, for instance, when a character, trying to frighten a rival, ends up frightening himself. *Dramatic irony* occurs when the reader understands more about what is happening in a story than the character who is telling the story does. For example, a narrator might tell an anecdote that he intends to illustrate how clever he is, while it is obvious to the reader from the story's events that the narrator has made a fool of himself because of his gullibility. (See also **Sarcasm**.)

Jargon The specialized vocabulary of a profession or academic field. Although the jargon of a particular profession is an efficient means of communication within that field, it may not be clear or meaningful to readers outside that profession.

Journal writing A method of invention that involves recording ideas that emerge from reading or other experiences and then exploring them in writing.

Looping A method of invention that involves isolating one idea from a piece of freewriting and using this idea as a focus for a new piece of freewriting.

Main cause See **Causes**.

Metaphor A comparison of two dissimilar things that does not use the words *like* or *as* ("The small waves were the same, chucking the rowboat under the chin . . ." — E. B. White).

Narration The pattern of development that tells a story. (See Chapter 6.)

Objective description A detached, factual picture presented in a plain and direct manner. Although pure objectivity is impossible to achieve, writers of science papers, technical reports, and news articles, among others, strive for precise language that is free of value judgments.

Outline See **formal outline**; **informal outline**.

Paradox A statement that seems self-contradictory or absurd but is nonetheless true.

Paragraph The basic unit of an essay. A paragraph is composed of related sentences that together express a single idea. This main idea is often stated in a single *topic sentence*. Paragraphs are also graphic symbols on the page, mapping the progress of the ideas in the essay and providing visual breaks for readers.

Parallelism The use of similar grammatical elements within a sentence or sentences. "I like hiking, skiing, and to cook" is not parallel because *hiking* and *skiing* are gerund forms (*-ing*) while *to cook* is an infinitive form. Revised for parallelism, the sentence could read either "I like hiking, skiing, and cooking" or "I like to hike, to ski, and to cook." As a stylistic technique, parallelism can provide emphasis through repetition — for example, "Walk groundly, talk profoundly, drink roundly, sleep soundly" (William Hazlitt). Parallelism is also a powerful oratorical technique: "Until justice is blind to color, until education is unaware of race, until opportunity is unconcerned with the color of men's skins, emancipation will be a proclamation but not a fact" (Lyndon B. Johnson). Finally, parallelism can increase *coherence* within a paragraph or an essay.

Paraphrase The restatement of another person's words in one's own words, following the order and emphasis of the original. Paraphrase is frequently used in source-based papers, where the purpose is to use information gathered during research to support the ideas in the paper.

For example, Bruce Catton's "Grant was the modern man emerging; beyond him, ready to come on the stage, was the great age of steel and machinery, of crowded cities and a restless burgeoning vitality" (page 395) might be paraphrased as, "Grant was a man of a new era; following him, glimpsed but not fully seen, was the time of new technologies, with its crowded urban life and growing restlessness."

Personification   Describing concepts or objects as if they were human ("the chair slouched"; "the wind sighed outside the window").

Persuasion   The method a writer uses to move an audience to adopt a belief or follow a course of action. To persuade an audience, a writer relies on the various appeals — to the emotions, to reason, or to ethics. Persuasion is different from *argumentation*, which appeals primarily to reason.

Plagiarism   Presenting the words or ideas of someone else as if they were actually one's own (whether intentionally or unintentionally). Plagiarism should always be avoided.

Point-by-point comparison   A comparison in which the writer first makes a point about one subject and then follows it with a comparable point about the other subject. (See also **Subject-by-subject comparison**.)

Post hoc **reasoning**   A logical fallacy that involves looking back at two events that occurred in chronological sequence and wrongly assuming that the first event caused the second. For example, just because a car will not start after a thunderstorm, one cannot automatically assume that the storm caused the problem.

Prewriting   See **Invention**.

Principle of classification   In a classification-and-division essay, the quality the items have in common. For example, if a writer were classifying automobiles, one principle of classification might be "repair records."

Process   The pattern of development that presents a series of steps in a procedure in chronological order and shows how this sequence of steps leads to a particular result. (See Chapter 9.)

Process explanation   A kind of process essay whose purpose is to enable readers to understand a process rather than perform it.

Purpose   A writer's reason for writing. A writer's purpose may, for example, be to entertain readers with an amusing story, to inform them about a dangerous disease, to move them to action by enraging them with an example of injustice, or to change their perspective by revealing a hidden dimension of a person or situation.

Quotation   The exact words of a source, enclosed in quotation marks. A quotation should be used only to present a particularly memorable statement or to avoid a paraphrase that would change the meaning of the original.

Refutation The attempt to counter an opposing argument by revealing its weaknesses. Three of the most common weaknesses are logical flaws in the argument, inadequate evidence, and irrelevance. Refutation greatly strengthens an argument by showing that the writer is aware of the complexity of the issue and has considered opposing viewpoints.

Remote cause See **Causes**.

Rhetorical question A question asked for effect and not meant to be answered.

Rogerian argument A strategy put forth by psychologist Carl Rogers that rejects the adversarial approach that characterizes many arguments. Rather than attacking the opposition, Rogers suggests acknowledging the validity of opposing positions. By finding areas of agreement, a Rogerian argument reduces conflict and increases the chance that the final position will satisfy all parties.

Sarcasm Deliberately insincere and biting irony — for example, "That's okay — I love it when you borrow things and don't return them."

Satire Writing that uses wit, irony, and ridicule to attack foolishness, incompetence, or evil in a person or idea. Satire has a different purpose from comedy, which usually intends simply to entertain. For a classic example of satire, see Jonathan Swift's "A Modest Proposal," page 699.

Sexist language Language that stereotypes people according to gender. Writers often use plural constructions to avoid sexist language. For example, *the doctors . . . they* can be used instead of *the doctor . . . he.* Words such as *police officer* and *firefighter* can be used instead of *policeman* and *fireman.*

Simile A comparison of two dissimilar things using the words *like* or *as* ("Hills Like White Elephants" — Ernest Hemingway).

Slang Informal words whose meanings vary from locale to locale or change as time passes. Slang is frequently associated with a particular group of people — for example, bikers, musicians, or urban youth. Slang is inappropriate in college writing.

Subject-by-subject comparison A comparison that discusses one subject in full and then goes on to discuss the next subject. (See also **Point-by-point comparison**.)

Subjective description A description that contains value judgments (*a saintly person*, for example). Whereas objective language is distanced from an event or object, *subjective language* is involved. A subjective description focuses on the author's reaction to the event, conveying not just a factual record of details but also their significance. Subjective language may include poetic or colorful words that impart a judgment or an emotional response (*stride, limp, meander, hobble, stroll, plod,* or *shuffle* instead of *walk*). Subjective descriptions often include *figures of speech.*

Summary The ideas of a source as presented in one's own words. Unlike a paraphrase, a summary conveys only a general sense of a passage, without following the order and emphasis of the original.

Syllogism A basic form of deductive reasoning. Every syllogism includes three parts: a major premise that makes a general statement ("Confinement is physically and psychologically damaging"); a minor premise that makes a related but more specific statement ("Zoos confine animals"); and a conclusion drawn from these two premises ("Therefore, zoos are physically and psychologically damaging to animals").

Symbol A person, event, or object that stands for something more than its literal meaning.

Synonym A word with the same basic meaning as another word. A synonym for *loud* is *noisy*. Most words in the English language have several synonyms, but each word has unique nuances or shades of meaning. (See also **Connotation**.)

Thesis An essay's main idea; the idea that all the points in the body of the essay support. A thesis may be implied, but it is usually stated explicitly in the form of a *thesis statement*. In addition to conveying the essay's main idea, the thesis statement may indicate the writer's approach to the subject and the writer's purpose. It may also indicate the pattern of development that will structure the essay.

Topic sentence A sentence stating the main idea of a paragraph. Often, but not always, the topic sentence opens the paragraph.

Toulmin logic A method of structuring an argument according to the way arguments occur in everyday life. Developed by philosopher Stephen Toulmin, Toulmin logic divides an argument into three parts: the *claim*, the *grounds*, and the *warrant*.

Transitions Words or expressions that link ideas in a piece of writing. Long essays frequently contain *transitional paragraphs* that connect one part of the essay to another. Writers use a variety of transitional expressions, such as *afterward, because, consequently, for instance, furthermore, however,* and *likewise*. See the list of transitions on page 57.

Understatement Deliberate de-emphasis for effect: "The people who live near the Mississippi River are not exactly looking forward to more flooding"; "Emily was a little upset about failing math." The opposite of understatement is *hyperbole*.

Unity The desirable attribute of a paragraph in which every sentence relates directly to the paragraph's main idea. This main idea is often stated in a *topic sentence*.

Warrant In Toulmin logic, the inference that connects the claim to the grounds. The warrant can be a belief that is taken for granted or an assumption that underlies the argument. (See also **Toulmin logic**.)

Writing process The sequence of tasks a writer undertakes when writing an essay. During *invention*, or *prewriting*, the writer gathers information and ideas and develops a thesis. During the *arrangement* stage, the writer organizes material into a logical sequence. During *drafting and revision*, the essay is actually written and then rewritten. Finally, during *editing and proofreading*, the writer puts the finishing touches on the essay by correcting misspellings, checking punctuation, searching for grammatical inaccuracies, and so on. These stages occur in no fixed order; many effective writers move back and forth among them. (See Chapters 2–5.)

ACKNOWLEDGMENTS

Sherman Alexie. "Indian Education." From *The Lone Ranger and Tonto Fistfight in Heaven*. Copyright © 1993, 2005 by Sherman Alexie. Used by permission of Grove/Atlantic, Inc., and Nancy Stauffer Associates. Any third-party use of this material, outside of this publication, is prohibited. All rights reserved.

Nicole Allan and Derek Thompson. "The Myth of the Student Loan Crisis." © 2013 The Atlantic Media Co., as first published in the *Atlantic* magazine. All rights reserved. Distributed by Tribune Content Agency, LLC.

Don Banks. "What Price Football?" Reprinted by permission of *Sports Illustrated*.

Suzanne Berne. "Ground Zero." From the *New York Times,* November 17, 2012. © 2012 The New York Times. All rights reserved. Used by permission and protected by the Copyright Laws of the United States. The printing, copying, redistribution, or retransmission of this Content without express written permission is prohibited.

Judy Brady. "I Want a Wife." Reprinted by permission of the author.

Gwendolyn Brooks. "Sadie and Maud." Reprinted by consent of Brooks Permissions.

Max Brooks. "The Movies That Rose from the Grave." Copyright © Guardian News & Media Ltd., 2006.

Amanda Brown. "Love and Other Catastrophes: A Mix Tape." Reprinted by permission of the author.

José Antonio Burciaga. "Tortillas." Reprinted by permission of Rebeca Burciaga.

Nina Burleigh. "Would Football without Concussions Still Be Football?" Reprinted by permission of the *New York Observer*.

Bruce Catton. "Grant and Lee: A Study in Contrasts." Copyright © U.S. Capitol Historical Society. All rights reserved.

Zev Chafets. "Let Steroids into the Hall of Fame." From the *New York Times,* June 20, 2009. © 2009 The New York Times. All rights reserved. Used by permission and protected by the Copyright Laws of the United States. The printing, copying, redistribution, or retransmission of this Content without express written permission is prohibited.

Linda Chavez. "The Case for Birthright Citizenship." Reprinted by permission of the author.

Kate Chopin. "The Storm." Reprinted by permission of the Louisiana State University Press.

Amy Chua. "Why Chinese Mothers Are Superior." Reprinted with permission of the *Wall Street Journal*. Copyright © 2011 Dow Jones & Company, Inc. All rights reserved worldwide. License number 3334230128853.

Judith Ortiz Cofer. "The Myth of the Latin Woman: I Just Met a Girl Named Maria." From *The Latin Deli: Prose and Poetry*. Copyright © 1993 by Judith Ortiz Cofer. Reprinted by permission of the University of Georgia Press.

Billy Collins. "Aristotle." From *Picnic, Lightning* by Billy Collins, © 1998. Reprinted by permission of the University of Pittsburgh Press.

Norman Cousins. "Who Killed Benny Paret?" Reprinted by permission of the Norman Cousins Family Partnership.

778

Junot Díaz. "The Money." First published in the *New Yorker* and reprinted by permission of Junot Díaz and Aragi, Inc.

Lars Eighner. "On Dumpster Diving." From *Travels with Lizbeth*. Copyright © 1993 by Lars Eighner. Reprinted by permission of St. Martin's Press. All rights reserved.

Stephanie Ericsson. "The Ways We Lie." Copyright © 1992 by Stephanie Ericsson. Originally published by the *Utne Reader*. Reprinted by permission of Dunham Literary as agent for the author.

Stanley Fish. "Getting Coffee Is Hard to Do." From the *New York Times*, August 5, 2007. © 2007 The New York Times. All rights reserved. Used by permission and protected by the Copyright Laws of the United States. The printing, copying, redistribution, or retransmission of this Content without express written permission is prohibited.

Daniel J. Flynn. "Football Does a Body Good (Nannyism Doesn't)." From the *American Spectator*, May 18, 2012. Reprinted by permission of the *American Spectator*.

Alan Dean Foster. "Living with Fire." From the *New York Times*, July 2, 2013. © 2013 The New York Times. All rights reserved. Used by permission and protected by the Copyright Laws of the United States. The printing, copying, redistribution, or retransmission of this Content without express written permission is prohibited.

Martin Gansberg. "Thirty-Eight Who Saw Murder Didn't Call the Police." From the *New York Times*, March 27, 1964. © 1964 The New York Times. All rights reserved. Used by permission and protected by the Copyright Laws of the United States. The printing, copying, redistribution, or retransmission of this Content without express written permission is prohibited.

Henry Louis Gates Jr. "'What's in a Name?'" From *Dissent* 36.4 (Fall 1989), pp. 487–95. Reprinted with permission of the University of Pennsylvania Press.

Jeb Golinkin. "Why Parents Should Let Their Kids Play Dangerous Sports." Reprinted by permission of the *Week*.

Lawrence Otis Graham. "The 'Black Table' Is Still There." Pages 181–83 from *Member of the Club: Reflections on Life in a Racially Polarized World* by Lawrence Otis Graham. Copyright © 1995 by Lawrence Otis Graham. Reprinted by permission of HarperCollins Publishers.

Pamela Haag. "Your Social Life: Are You a Fox or a Hedgehog?" Reprinted by permission of the author.

Linda M. Hasselstrom. "A Peaceful Woman Explains Why She Carries a Gun." Reprinted by permission of Fulcrum Publishing.

Ann Hodgman. "No Wonder They Call Me a Bitch." Reprinted by permission of the author.

Shirley Jackson. "The Lottery." From *The Lottery* by Shirley Jackson. Copyright © 1948, 1949 by Shirley Jackson. Copyright renewed 1976, 1977 by Laurence Hyman, Barry Hyman, Mrs. Sarah Webster, and Mrs. Joanne Schnurer. Reprinted by permission of Farrar, Straus and Giroux, LLC.

Jamaica Kincaid. "'Girl.'" From *At the Bottom of the River* by Jamaica Kincaid. Copyright © 1983 by Jamaica Kincaid. Reprinted by permission of Farrar, Straus and Giroux, LLC.

Martin Luther King Jr. "Letter from Birmingham Jail." Reprinted by arrangement with the Heirs to the Estate of Martin Luther King Jr. c/o Writers House as agent for the proprietor, New York, NY. Copyright © 1963 Dr. Martin Luther King Jr. Copyright renewed 1991 by Coretta Scott King.

David Kirby. "Inked Well." Reprinted by permission of the author.

Maggie Koerth-Baker. "Why Rational People Buy into Conspiracy Theories." From the *New York Times*, May 26, 2013. © 2013 The New York Times. All rights reserved. Used by permission and protected by the Copyright Laws of the United States. The printing, copying, redistribution, or retransmission of this Content without express written permission is prohibited.

Ellen Laird. "I'm Your Teacher, Not Your Internet-Service Provider." Reprinted by permission of the author.

Chris Lewis and Layla Zaidane. "Here's Your Crisis: Student Loan Debt Isn't a Myth." Copyright © Generation Progress (genprogress.org). Reprinted by permission of the Center for American Progress.

Malcolm X. "My First Conk." From "Homeboy," in *The Autobiography of Malcolm X* by Malcolm X, as told to Alex Haley. Copyright © 1964 by Alex Haley and Malcolm X. Copyright © 1965 by Alex Haley and Betty Shabazz. Used by permission of Random House, an imprint and division of Random House, LLC. All rights reserved.

Farhad Manjoo. "No, I Do Not Want to Pet Your Dog." From *Slate,* May 20, 2006. Copyright © 2006 The Slate Group. All rights reserved. Used by permission and protected by the Copyright Laws of the United States. The printing, copying, redistribution, or retransmission of this Content without express written permission is prohibited.

Arthur Miller. "Get It Right: Privatize Executions." From *Echoes Down the Corridor: Collected Essays, 1944–2000* by Arthur Miller, edited by Stephen Centola. Copyright © 1992, 2000 by Arthur Miller. Used by permission of Viking Penguin, a division of Penguin Group (USA), LLC.

Janice Mirikitani. "Suicide Note." From *Shedding Silence* by Janice Mirikitani. Copyright © 1987 by Janice Mirikitani. Used by permission of the author and Celestial Arts, an imprint of the Crown Publishing Group, a division of Random House, LLC. All rights reserved.

Jessica Mitford. "The Embalming of Mr. Jones." Reprinted by permission of the Estate of Jessica Mitford. Copyright © 1963, 1978 by Jessica Mitford. All rights reserved.

Bich Minh Nguyen. "Goodbye to My Twinkie Days." From the *New York Times,* April 21, 2002. © 2002 The New York Times. All rights reserved. Used by permission and protected by the Copyright Laws of the United States. The printing, copying, redistribution, or retransmission of this Content without express written permission is prohibited.

George Orwell. "Shooting an Elephant." From *A Collection of Essays by George Orwell.* Copyright © 1950 by Sonia Brownell Orwell. Copyright renewed 1978 by Sonia Pitt-Rivers. Reprinted by permission of Houghton Mifflin Harcourt Publishing Company. All rights reserved.

Joshua Piven and David Borgenicht. "How to Retrieve a Candy Bar Stuck in the Lunchroom Vending Machine." From *Worst-Case Scenario Survival Handbook: Work.* Copyright © 2003 by Joshua Piven and David Borgenicht. Used with permission of Chronicle Books, LLC, San Francisco. Visit chroniclebooks.com.

Anna Quindlen. "Homeless." From *Living Out Loud* by Anna Quindlen. Copyright © 1988 by Anna Quindlen. Used by permission of Random House, an imprint and division of Random House, LLC, and International Creative Management. All rights reserved.

Deborah L. Rhode. "Why Looks Are the Last Bastion of Discrimination." Reprinted by permission of the author.

Heather Rogers. "The Hidden Life of Garbage." Excerpt from *Gone Tomorrow: The Hidden Life of Garbage.* Copyright © 2005 by Heather Rogers. Reprinted by permission of the New Press (www.thenewpress.com).

Marjane Satrapi. Excerpt from *Persepolis II: The Story of a Return* by Marjane Satrapi. Translation copyright © 2004 by Anjali Singh. Used by permission of Pantheon Books, an imprint of the Knopf Doubleday Publishing Group, a division of Random House, LLC. All rights reserved.

Carolyn Foster Segal. "The Dog Ate My Flash Drive, and Other Tales of Woe." This essay originally appeared, in a slightly different form, under the title "The Dog Ate My Disk, and Other Tales of Woe," in the *Chronicle of Higher Education,* 2000.

David Skorton and Glenn Altschuler. "Do We Really Need More Guns on Campus?" From *Forbes,* February 21, 2013. © 2013 Forbes. All rights reserved. Used by permission and protected by the Copyright Laws of the United States. The printing, copying, redistribution, or retransmission of this Content without express written permission is prohibited.

Gayle Rosenwald Smith. "The Wife-Beater." Reprinted by permission of the author.

Bonnie Smith-Yackel. "My Mother Never Worked." Reprinted by permission of the author.

Brent Staples. "Cutting and Pasting: A Senior Thesis by (Insert Name)." From the *New York Times,* July 13, 2010. © 2010 The New York Times. All rights reserved. Used by permission and protected by the Copyright Laws of the United States. The printing, copying, redistribution, or retransmission of this Content without express written permission is prohibited. "Just Walk On By: A Black Man Ponders His Power to Alter Public Space." Reprinted by permission of the author.

Dana Stevens. "Your Flip-Flops Are Grossing Me Out." From *Slate,* July 3, 2013. © 2013 The Slate Group. All rights reserved. Used by permission and protected by the Copyright Laws of the United States. The printing, copying, redistribution, or retransmission of this Content without express written permission is prohibited.

Students for Concealed Carry. "Why Our Campuses Are *Not* Safer without Concealed Handguns." Reprinted by permission of Students for Concealed Carry.

Students for Gun-Free Schools. "Why Our Campuses Are Safer without Concealed Handguns." Reprinted by permission of Students for Gun-Free Schools.

Maia Szalavitz. "Ten Ways We Get the Odds Wrong." Reprinted by permission of the author.

Amy Tan. "Mother Tongue." Copyright © 1989 by Amy Tan. First appeared in the *Threepenny Review.* Reprinted by permission of the author and the Sandra Dijkstra Literary Agency.

Deborah Tannen. "Sex, Lies, and Conversation." Author's own adaptation of text; the adaptation (about 5.5 book pages in length) appeared in the *Washington Post,* June 24, 1990, from *You Just Don't Understand* by Deborah Tannen. Copyright © 1990 by Deborah Tannen. Reprinted by permission of HarperCollins Publishers.

Timothy Wheeler. "There's a Reason They Choose Schools." Copyright © 2014 by National Review, Inc. Reprinted by permission.

E. B. White. "Once More to the Lake." From *One Man's Meat.* Text copyright © 1941 by E. B. White. Copyright renewed. Reprinted by permission of Tilbury House Publishers, Thomaston, Maine, and International Creative Management. All rights reserved.

George F. Will. "An Argument to Be Made about Immigrant Babies and Citizenship." From the *Washington Post,* March 28, 2010. © 2010 Washington Post Company. All rights reserved. Used by permission and protected by the Copyright Laws of the United States. The printing, copying, redistribution, or retransmission of this Content without express written permission is prohibited.

Juan Williams. "Songs of the Summer of 1963 . . . and 2013." From the *Wall Street Journal,* August 26, 2013. © The Wall Street Journal by News Corporation, Dow Jones & Co. Reproduced with permission of DOW JONES COMPANY in the format "Republish in a book" via Copyright Clearance Center.

William Zinsser. "College Pressures." Copyright © 1979 William K. Zinsser. Originally appeared in *Blair & Ketchum's Country Journal,* Vol. VI, No. 4, April 1979. Reprinted by permission of the author.

e-Readings on LaunchPad Solo

Arte Ideas. "Plastic Bags: How Convenience Is Killing Our Planet" (infographic). Reprinted by permission of Arte Ideas.

Born Free Foundation. "Simba Goes Home to Africa" (video). Reprinted by permission of the Born Free Foundation/Raw Cut.

Dear Motorist. "Dear Motorist: Pledge to Share the Road" (video). Reprinted by permission of My ID, product of ENDEVR.

Kerri MacDonald and Jonathan Blaustein. "Food for a Dollar" (essay with photos). From the *New York Times,* October 8, 2010. © 2010 The New York Times. All rights reserved. Used by permission and protected by the Copyright Laws of the United States. The printing, copying, redistribution, or retransmission of this Content without express written permission is prohibited. Photographs reprinted by permission of Jonathan Blaustein.

Johannes Vermeer. *Girl with a Pearl Earring* (painting). Reprinted by permission of Mauritshuis, The Hague.

Voxy. "What Are the Hardest Languages to Learn?" (infographic). Reprinted by permission of Voxy.

Wired. "What's Inside Coffee?" (video). June 28, 2013. Copyright © Wired.com/Condé Nast. "Making a Mint" (video). May 18, 2013. Copyright © Wired.com/Condé Nast.

Diane Yang. "Greek Yogurt vs. Original Yogurt" (infographic). Reprinted by permission of Diane Yang.

INDEX

Entries followed by a **e** symbol may be found online at
macmillanhighered.com/patterns.

Missing something? Instructors may assign the online materials that accompany this text. To access them, visit **macmillanhighered.com /patterns13e**.

Inside LaunchPad Solo for *Patterns for College Writing*

Tutorials

Critical Reading > Active Reading Strategies
Critical Reading > Reading Visuals: Purpose
Critical Reading > Reading Visuals: Audience
Documentation > Do I Need to Cite That?
Documentation > How to Cite an Article in MLA Style
Documentation > How to Cite a Book in MLA Style
Documentation > How to Cite a Database in MLA Style
Documentation > How to Cite a Database in APA Style
Documentation > How to Cite a Web Site in MLA Style
Documentation > How to Cite a Web Site in APA Style
Digital Writing > Photo Editing Basics with GIMP
Digital Writing > Audio Editing with Audacity
Digital Writing > Presentations
Digital Writing > Word Processing
Digital Writing > Online Research Tools
Digital Writing > Job Search/Personal Branding

LearningCurve Quizzes

Critical Reading
Topic Sentences and Supporting Details
Topics and Main Ideas
Working with Sources (MLA)
Working with Sources (APA)
Commas, Fragments, Run-Ons and Comma Splices, Active and Passive Voice, Appropriate Language, Subject-Verb Agreement

e-Readings

Born Free Foundation, *Simba Goes Home to Africa* [video]
Johannes Vermeer, *Girl with a Pearl Earring* [painting]
Kerri MacDonald and Jonathan Blaustein, *Food for a Dollar* [essay with photographs]
Wired, Making a Mint [video]
Arte Ideas, *Plastic Bags: How Convenience Is Killing Our Planet* [infographic]
Diane Yang, *Greek Yogurt vs. Original Yogurt* [infographic]
Wired, What's Inside Coffee? [video]
Voxy, *What Are the Hardest Languages to Learn?* [infographic]
NASA, *What Is a Black Hole?* [infographic]
Dear Motorist, *Dear Motorist: Pledge to Share the Road* [video]

Resources for Instructors Using

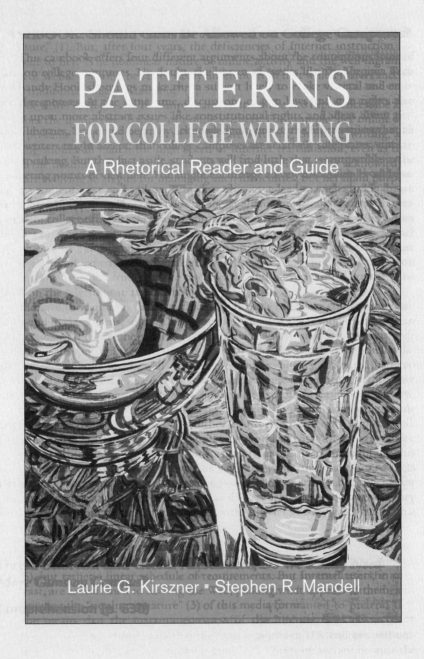

PATTERNS

FOR COLLEGE WRITING

A Rhetorical Reader and Guide

Laurie G. Kirszner ▪ Stephen R. Mandell

Resources for Instructors Using

Patterns for College Writing

A RHETORICAL READER AND GUIDE

THIRTEENTH EDITION

LAURIE G. KIRSZNER
UNIVERSITY OF THE SCIENCES, EMERITUS

STEPHEN R. MANDELL
DREXEL UNIVERSITY

with the assistance of
JEFF OUSBORNE

Bedford/St. Martin's
Boston ◆ New York

Copyright © 2015, 2012, 2010, 2007 by Bedford/St. Martin's

All rights reserved. No part of this book may be reproduced, stored in a retrieval system, or transmitted in any form or by any means, electronic, mechanical, photo-copying, recording, or otherwise, except as may be expressly permitted by the applicable copyright statutes or in writing by the Publisher.

9 8 7 6 5 4
f e d c b a

For information, write: Bedford/St. Martin's, 75 Arlington Street, Boston, MA 02116 (617-399-4000)

ISBN 978-1-4576-9942-9

Preface

Our main purpose in this manual to accompany the thirteenth edition of *Patterns for College Writing* is to save the instructor time in choosing assignments and in working with the questions that follow each selection. For each reading in *Patterns*, we include a paragraph or two on the teaching opportunities it affords, and we sometimes add a personal comment on how we like to approach a favorite selection in our own classes. We also supply the answers that we had in mind as we constructed the questions. Most of the questions are open to a range of worthwhile answers, some of them perhaps more pointed and interesting than our own; not only do we encourage and applaud interpretations that differ from ours, but we would be grateful to hear about them from anyone willing to take the time to write to us. (Wherever appropriate, paragraph numbers are included in the answers so that instructors can easily refer to the text.)

Except for the chapter on combining the patterns, the first selection in each chapter on a rhetorical pattern (Part Two, Chapters 6–14) is a visual text—a photo, an ad, or a piece of fine art—that visually reinforces the chapter's basic rhetorical concept. It is followed by *Reading Images* questions, a *Journal Entry*, and *Thematic Connections*, which help students see how the rhetorical pattern operates in a visual format. A multimodal selection for each chapter is at macmillanhighered.com/patterns.

The reading selections in *Patterns* range in subject across much of the college curriculum. They are meant to acquaint students with the rhetorical options open to them as they write for their college courses, and to show how the reading techniques presented in the introduction and Chapter 1 and the writing strategies discussed and illustrated in Chapter 2 and throughout the book become crucial to the effectiveness of a finished piece. The selections are also meant to stimulate class discussion and serve as springboards for student writing assignments.

After each essay by a professional writer we ask three types of questions: *Comprehension, Purpose and Audience,* and *Style and Structure. Comprehension* questions help students test their understanding of basic content. The questions focus attention on facts, details, and references that are necessary for comprehension; underscore the major points of each essay; and lead students through the logical progression of a writer's ideas.

Purpose and Audience questions focus on how the writer's intent and sense of his or her readers establish boundaries for the essay and govern other decisions the writer must make—for example, how much detail, or what different kinds of detail, must be supplied for one audience as opposed to another. These questions ask students to imagine themselves in the author's place and to consider, from the evidence of the essay, how the audience was perceived.

Style and Structure questions focus on the stylistic and structural options the authors have exercised. Particular attention is paid to organization, sentence structure, and word choice.

Following the questions about each essay is a *Writing Workshop* prompt, which asks students to use a particular rhetorical strategy and to write something in response (though not necessarily in reply) to the essay they have read. Some of the assignments require students to assume various roles and to address different audiences; others ask them to write in their own voices, drawing as necessary on the materials in the essay for examples, facts, or quotations.

Except for Chapter 14 on argumentation, each of the chapters on a single rhetorical pattern includes a poem or a short story that illustrates the pattern. After each of these poems or stories we ask *Reading Literature* questions that focus students on many of the same concerns that they consider for the essays—rhetorical organization, diction, imagery, and meaning. We want students to see that writers of various genres are involved in making many of the same choices.

After each selection by a professional writer, we include a *Journal Entry* prompt, a question that will stimulate students to examine and clarify their own value systems. We believe that regularly writing responses to these questions will assist students in developing good thinking, reading, and writing skills and, frequently, in generating paper topics. *Combining the Patterns* questions follow each professional essay. These encourage students to see other patterns at work within the dominant pattern of the essay.

Also included after each selection by a professional writer are *Thematic Connections*, which encourage students to perceive relationships between selections (including the student essays) they have read. The *Thematic Connections* can be used for classroom discussion or as topics for reading-based student essays.

At the end of each rhetorical chapter is a comprehensive list of *Writing Assignments*, some asking students to connect two or more selections. A suggested *Collaborative Activity* for writing follows this list.

Chapter 15, Combining the Patterns, presents one student essay and three professional essays, each of which demonstrates several different patterns within a single piece of writing. The student essay and the first professional essay have been annotated to identify these various patterns.

Part Three and the appendix include a step-by-step discussion of writing a research paper as well as guidelines for citing and documenting both print and online sources. They give advice about using quotation, paraphrase, and summary, as well as avoiding plagiarism, and include two sample student research papers. A glossary defines terms important to good writers. We have cross-referenced them, whenever useful, to discussions within the text.

Peer-editing worksheets, to be used with writing assignments for Chapters 6–15, appear in this manual.

In all cases we have tried to make the questions and writing assignments interesting, challenging, and accessible. We would be grateful for suggestions that might improve both this manual and *Patterns for College Writing*. Comments may be sent to us c/o Bedford/St. Martin's, 75 Arlington Street, Boston, MA 02116.

Laurie G. Kirszner
Department of Humanities
University of the Sciences, Emeritus
Philadelphia, PA 19104

Stephen R. Mandell
Department of Humanities–Communications
Drexel University
Philadelphia, PA 19104

Contents

ⓔ Available in LaunchPad Solo: **macmillanhighered.com/patterns**

Model Syllabi

We have included two sample syllabi that we hope will show you the flexibility you have with the thirteenth edition of *Patterns for College Writing*. The first uses the text's rhetorical approach for a 10-week term; the second uses both a thematic and a rhetorical approach for a 14-week term.*

SYLLABUS — RHETORICAL APPROACH:
10-week term, 3 meetings per week

Instructors can tailor readings to suit their own students' abilities and interests.

WEEK	ACTIVITIES
1	**Introduction**
	Chapter 1: Reading to Write: Becoming a Critical Reader
	Chapters 2–5: The Writing Process
	Diagnostic Essay
2	**Narration and Description, Chapters 6 and 7**
	Introduction
	Readings
	Narrative or Descriptive Essay
3	**Exemplification, Chapter 8**
	Introduction
	Readings
	Exemplification Essay
4	**Process, Chapter 9**
	Introduction
	Readings
	Process Essay
5	**Cause and Effect, Chapter 10**
	Introduction
	Readings
	Cause-and-Effect Essay
6	**Comparison and Contrast, Chapter 11**
	Introduction
	Readings
	Comparison-and-Contrast Essay
7	**Classification and Division, Chapter 12**
	Introduction
	Readings
	Classification-and-Division Essay

*Suggestions for modifying these syllabi are discussed in this manual's introduction to Part One of the text.

SYLLABUS — THEMATIC / RHETORICAL APPROACH:

14-week term, 3 meetings per week

This syllabus is organized primarily around a thematic approach; however, included with each theme is a rhetorical mode that the essays on the theme illustrate. Of course, instructors may modify the syllabus by deleting the rhetorical introductions and supplementing the units with additional selections (by professional or student writers) on the theme for each week. A thematic table of contents follows the regular contents in the text.

WEEK	ACTIVITIES
1	**The Writing Process**

Chapter 1: Reading to Write: Becoming a Critical Reader
Chapters 2–5: The Writing Process
Writing Activity: Diagnostic Essay

2   **Autobiography**

Using Narration: Introduction to Chapter 6
Family Relationships:
"The Money," Junot Díaz
"'Girl,'" Jamaica Kincaid
"My Field of Dreams," Forte
"Suicide Note," Janice Mirikitani
Writing Assignment: Essay on a Family Relationship

3   **Autobiography**

Using Description: Introduction to Chapter 7
Life Lessons:
"Goodbye to My Twinkie Days," Bich Minh Nguyen
"Shooting an Elephant," George Orwell
"Once More to the Lake," E. B. White
"My First Conk," Malcolm X
Writing Assignment: Essay on an Epiphany
PEER-EDITING WORKSHOP

4   **Education**

Using Exemplification: Introduction to Chapter 8
"Indian Education," Sherman Alexie
"I'm Your Teacher, Not Your Internet-Service
    Provider," Ellen Laird
"College Pressures," William Zinsser
"Cutting and Pasting: A Senior Thesis by
    (Insert Name)," Brent Staples
Writing Assignment: Essay on Education

Using the End-of-Chapter Collaborative Activities

Chapters 6–15 in this edition of *Patterns for College Writing* conclude with a *Collaborative Activity* that allows students to work together to produce a paper or class presentation based on a particular rhetorical strategy. Although we don't expect that most instructors will assign a *Collaborative Activity* with every chapter for which they assign an individual paper, we do encourage you to give students at least one or two opportunities to complete an assignment collaboratively. A collaborative writing assignment allows students to witness a variety of writing styles and writing habits; it also provides a writing situation that students generally take seriously because they recognize that others' grades depend on their performance. Moreover, collaboration is a real-world activity; students should realize that much writing in business and professional settings is produced collaboratively, either with a different person taking on each different stage of the writing process (research, drafting, editing, and so forth) or with each person contributing a section to a larger report that is then refined and edited by the group. Finally, the assignments that call for class presentations give students practice in oral rhetoric, a skill that has many academic and professional real-world applications.

Following are a few suggestions for setting up collaborative activities:

Make sure each group has a "leader." Although peer-editing groups can often be assigned randomly, collaborative groups generally work best if they are balanced in terms of individual members' abilities and the dynamics of the group. In assigning groups — particularly for the first few times — keep in mind that each should include at least one student you can depend on to motivate the others to keep the project moving forward. These "leaders" will not necessarily be the most adept writers, but rather those students who are outgoing and responsible and who consistently make positive contributions to class discussion. For writing projects it can also be a good idea to see that each group has a good editor as well — a student whose command of grammar, mechanics, and spelling is strong.

Provide an explicit schedule. Most collaborative activities can be completed in one and a half to two and a half weeks (three to five class sessions); a few may require even less time. Generally, on the day you introduce the assignment, you should give students time in class to get started and provide a written schedule so they will know from the start what activities need to be divided up. Students should come prepared to meet at least briefly with their group, bringing with them whatever materials are due for that session. It is up to you whether to require group meetings outside of class (although activities involving group drafting, such as the one at the end of Chapter 7, will almost have to involve some group work out of class, unless you're willing to devote several complete class sessions to the task).

Here's a typical schedule for the most common kind of *Collaborative Activity*, which asks each group member to contribute a paragraph or section individually. (Note that the suggested activities for any of the four days could be extended into an outside meeting.)

Day 1: Give the assignment and allow class time for the group discussion suggested by the assignment or for planning.

Day 2:	Have students bring drafts of their contributions for review and revision suggestions by other group members; have groups discuss possible strategies for the introduction and conclusion and determine who will draft each.
Day 3:	Have students bring revised drafts of their contributions and the draft introduction and conclusion; have groups work to revise the individual parts into a whole essay and then determine which member will put together the full draft.
Day 4:	Have groups meet to discuss and revise the full draft and then determine who will edit the final version.
Day 5:	Final version due; allow time for each group member to proofread quickly before collecting.

You might ask the groups to provide multiple copies of their final drafts to share in rotation with the other groups.

Allow for group self-evaluation. As groups are meeting in class, feel free to observe and even join each group for a few minutes to answer questions or make suggestions. If you observe a student behaving in a way seriously detrimental to the functioning of the group, you might want to talk to that student privately; but in general, try to give each group responsibility for "policing" lack of contribution or other inappropriate behavior. For example, if you grade a collaborative assignment, do so using points, and then require each group to determine collectively how many points each individual member will receive. Once the assignment is complete, you might also ask members to write a brief evaluation of the workings of their group to share — perhaps anonymously — with the rest of the group.

At several points during the semester, you may want to have students write briefly about their experience working with groups generally: what they've learned about group decision making and group dynamics as well as their own usual function in groups.

Introduction: How to Use This Book

The introduction discusses reading as it relates to the writing process. It is extremely important because many students have not learned to read actively by the time they reach college. Instead, they do little more than move their eyes across the lines of print — reading their textbooks as if they were reading a light novel. The introduction prepares students to read critically, so the activities you use with it can prepare students to read — and to discuss — the materials in this (and any) text. The introduction is especially important if you are using the text as the source of material for reading-based essays.

Reading the Selection and Responding to an Essay

As you discuss Henry Louis Gates's essay and the study questions that follow it, you will want to stress not only the ways the textbook can be used but also the kinds of questioning strategies that will make students better readers. You will also want to emphasize the questions that can lead to multiple answers — and consider reasons Gates might have had for leaving some details open to more than one interpretation. Explain that not every question has a single "right" answer, but explain as well that students need to be able to justify their responses from within an essay.

If your course calls for students to write reading-based (rather than personal) essays, you will want to focus very carefully on the discussions of *Thematic Connections*. Used throughout the text, these sections can be the source of subject matter for many essays. Using these in early discussions will illustrate for students the kinds of critical skills they will need in order to write effective essays based on selections from the text.

You may also want to point out the questions under *Combining the Patterns* following the Gates essay. Questions about subsidiary patterns used within a dominant pattern follow every essay in the text. These questions can help students see that most writing mixes patterns at least to some degree, an idea that is reinforced in Chapter 15, where we include four longer, more complex essays.

A final note about the questions following the readings. You may find, with the Gates essay as well as with the other essays throughout the book, that you do not want — or need — to deal with every question in class. For example, a class of fairly advanced readers might find the *Comprehension* questions a bit basic; you might want to stress style or audience rather than how patterns are combined. In fact, we have included more questions than we expect every instructor to use in order to provide the greatest degree of flexibility. You should certainly choose and assign questions for discussion according to your students' needs and the particular focus of your writing instruction.

PART ONE: The Writing Process

Part One presents an overview of the entire writing process, from deciding on a topic through revising and editing the first draft. You may want to spend two or more weeks on these five chapters, having students work their way through the entire process as they complete their first paper for the class. You might even work through the chapters in Part One in conjunction with the first pattern chapter you assign. For example, you might have your students read and discuss the essays in Chapter 6 and then have them draft and revise narrative essays of their own based on the guidelines in Part One. In any case, rather than assign students to read all of Part One at once, you will probably want to assign one chapter per class session.

Whatever your choice, you will want to link carefully the concepts discussed throughout the rest of Part One to those discussed in Chapter 1, "Reading to Write," in order to make the reading/writing connection clear for students who see these activities as only loosely related. We have structured the introductions on reading and writing to assist you in making this connection: In Part One, Laura Bobnak's essay, with its multiple drafts, explicitly connects reading and writing since it responds to an assignment derived from the Gates essay — which is printed in the introduction. As you work your way through other chapters in the text, remind students to read actively and to consider various ideas in their readings as potential paper topics. Encourage your students to read selections once for overall content and a second time to see the interplay between the writers' choices and their impact on readers. As you discuss various concepts in Part One, tell your students that throughout the term you will ask them to identify the thesis statement in a selection; to point to major transitions; and to discuss stylistic and thematic subtleties that can only be understood by rereading difficult passages, looking up unfamiliar words, and considering them in context. Encourage students to continue using their highlighting and annotating skills. Ask them to use the questions after each selection to test their understanding before coming to class. Remind them that they will have to make many of the same choices the writers of the selections did; for this reason, developing greater awareness as readers helps them become better writers.

In class, closely focus your discussions on a writer's choices. Students will have a far clearer understanding of purpose, audience, occasion, and other concepts covered in Part One if you guide them both as they read and as they respond to your questions in class. Require students to keep journals with their responses to formal *Journal Entries* throughout the text as well as any other responses they may have to the text's selections. (You may wish to give a credit/no credit grade to encourage students to stretch and explore their own thinking.) Point out to students the value Laura Bobnak's journal entry (p. 39) had in the writing of her paper. Occasionally during the term, ask students to freewrite, brainstorm, or cluster using one or more of the *Writing Workshop* prompts at the end of reading selections so they see that what they read is vitally linked to what they write.

In Part One, by necessity, we discuss writing as a linear process, but as experienced writers know, it might more accurately be described as a series of spirals. We outline the steps of the writing process in succession, but point out that they can also be performed simultaneously and recurrently. Whether or not you decide to stress this approach depends on the needs of your students. We prefer to give beginning writers a simple, concrete structure rather than overwhelm them with options they cannot fully understand or take advantage of.

Chapters 2 and 3 focus on the prewriting stage of the writing process. Most students entering college underrate prewriting. Thus the techniques we provide to narrow a topic, find something to say, develop a thesis, and arrange ideas will probably be new to them. You may find that, at first, students will resist using the techniques we present. Often a class or two devoted to illustrating prewriting can give students an understanding of how this preliminary work helps inform an entire essay. For example, you may want to tell students that using questions for probing closely parallels their normal thought processes. With these questions, students can construct a framework for the various topics they encounter. Your students should see these questions—and other techniques discussed in Chapters 2 and 3—as systematic ways both of exploring a topic's potential and of organizing the topic's presentation—whether the essay is personal or reading-based.

In Chapter 4 we focus on drafting and revision. Often students fail to understand that "finishing" a rough draft involves more than proofreading or correcting errors in grammar and spelling. They are unaware of the need to reconsider the quality of an essay's ideas and its organization into paragraphs and sentences. They do not realize that revision goes on throughout all the stages of their writing. To familiarize students with revision, we take them through three drafts of the sample essay; and, after each student essay in the chapter introductions, we include a Focus on Revision section, which suggests how an already effective essay could be made stronger. To guide your students as they revise, we include Revision and Editing Checklists for easy reference. Encourage students to use these aids.

We also include Guidelines for Peer Critiques and provide a sample peer critique following Laura Bobnak's first draft. (Model peer-editing worksheets for each chapter—like the one used to critique Bobnak's draft—appear in the introduction to each rhetorical mode.) Such critiques can be enormously useful in improving both a specific paper and students' overall sense of the connection between their writing and an audience's reading. As they critique their classmates' drafts, encourage students to be specific—to avoid simple "yes" or "no" answers, to refer to examples or passages within the draft, and to offer suggestions that might be incorporated into a subsequent draft. Also make it clear that, while they should take their peer readers' remarks seriously, writers need not follow every suggestion they receive. Ultimately, each writer must make his or her own decisions about how to go about revising a draft.

One possibility for peer critiquing in the classroom is to conduct class sessions as "writing workshops" on days when drafts are due. On these days you may require two or three students to photocopy their drafts and bring copies to class to distribute. After each of the students reads his or her paper aloud, a discussion (guided by the questions on the appropriate peer-editing worksheet found at the back of this manual) can follow. If possible, try to distribute drafts before the class in which they are to be discussed, so students can fill out peer-editing worksheets in advance. In any case, remind peer critics that their role is to make helpful suggestions, not to correct errors or impose their ideas on the draft they are critiquing. To reinforce this point, instruct them to write their comments on the worksheets, not directly on the photocopied draft.

If you want students to work in small groups, set up these groups well ahead of time so students know how many photocopies to make. (If you want to avoid the expense and possible confusion of making a number of photocopies, you can assign students to work in pairs; in this case they can simply exchange papers.)

Even if students are working in very small groups, with an "audience" of only one or two other students, it is still a good idea to require them to read their drafts aloud. Both student authors and their audiences will hear errors and inconsistencies that they may overlook when reading silently, and hearing students read aloud will sometimes alert you to reading difficulties they have.

Finally, be sure each student whose draft is the subject of a peer critique session knows to take careful notes about the other students' comments and suggestions and to ask for clarification when necessary.

As students revise their drafts—especially for your earlier assignments—you will want to make sure they recognize that an effective essay does not necessarily follow a five-paragraph formula. In fact, such a formula can impose restrictions on the development of a student's ideas. Students should see that, like Laura Bobnak's essay, their own work should proceed organically, with the structure and organization growing out of the development of their ideas. As the semester progresses, you should also eventually encourage students to depart from the confining structure of the informal outlines presented in the text. For example, they can certainly move beyond a "there are three reasons" thesis statement and a simple restatement of their thesis in the conclusion.

The final chapter in Part One focuses on editing and proofreading. It is not meant to substitute for a complete handbook of grammar and usage, but we have tried to cover the most common mechanical problems in student writing. The main point for students to glean from the chapter is that technical correctness, effective sentence construction and word choice, and proper manuscript format are crucial to their credibility as writers. You might suggest that, before they turn in their final drafts, students always use the checklists at the ends of each of the five sections of Chapter 5 as guides to editing and proofreading their essays. (Because the checklists are relatively brief, this should not be an overwhelming task for students.) If you find in reading his or her essays that a student consistently makes errors not covered in Chapter 5, you might suggest adding that problem as an item on the appropriate checklist.

Although *Patterns* does not require students to use computers, we have made suggestions in Tech Tip boxes throughout Part One for those who do. You can use a variety of techniques to facilitate computer revision. For example, you can encourage students to put topic sentences in a draft in bold print—a form of review outlining—to help them analyze their papers' structure. You can also demonstrate (or have demonstrated) the ease with which they can rearrange whole sections of a paper by cutting and pasting, and the use of spell checkers and interactive software that raises such questions as the number of *be* verbs in a draft. You can even have them critique each other's documents, and you may want to react to students' work yourself, placing your comments in the file where they will be most helpful. Make sure your students understand that they should print out a hard copy of a draft sometime before they present a finished essay. Too few of them notice their mechanical errors on the screen. Also insist that your students keep backup copies of all their work.

To reinforce the various concepts of Part One, we suggest that you have students complete the exercises included throughout Chapters 1–5. You can have students work on these exercises individually or in small groups. You may want to assign all the exercises or just some of them. Later, as you assign and discuss selections in the text, you may wish to adapt some of the exercises in Part One to help students generate and organize ideas for reading-based essays by using one or more *Thematic Connections* included with a particular selection. Of course you may wish to reproduce essays your students have written and ask your class to discuss them.

1: Reading to Write: Becoming a Critical Reader

One way to help students read and respond critically is to conduct a simple exercise with class members. As you discuss the concept that reading is "a two-way street," ask where students grew up—near your school, in distant areas of your state, in other states, or even in other countries. You can then discuss what differences such diversity can make in the reading and writing process. Similar questions can be asked about students' ages and backgrounds—ethnic, economic, and so forth.

As you discuss Chapter 1, you will want to stress differences between subjective and objective responses—and the extent to which each is appropriate in the reading/writing process. Students will need reminders of the "rules" for validating an interpretation because many have not learned to do close readings of a text. Push your students beyond the recall level, and insist that they turn to the text to support their interpretations. When students distort, overlook details, or add irrelevant details, systematically ask them to point to evidence in the text. At first, many students will expect you to signal the right answer. Not telling them that they are wrong reinforces the concept that a text may lend itself to more than one interpretation. When you ask students to turn to the text, you may also discover another valid interpretation—one you had not anticipated. Saying as much enlivens discussions throughout the term as you and your students become a community of scholars. Students will quickly learn to question and respond in appropriate ways.

Define both *highlighting* and *annotating*, and ask students to do both as they read Chapter 1. When they come to class, you might ask them what questions would have been fair for you to have asked, had you quizzed them on their first reading assignment. Students will be happy to demonstrate that they read closely—and relieved that they are to receive reinforcement for good reading skills. Peer groups can also be used to reinforce the kinds of information students should have discovered in their first reading assignment.

Exercise 1—Previewing (p. 20)

Students may be unfamiliar with marking up books and may in fact be resistant to doing so. You might encourage them by letting them know that even the best readers mark up their texts and use highlighting to identify important sections of an article.

Exercise 2—Annotating (p. 26)

You might stress that actively reading a text is both an important step in understanding the issues it raises as well as the beginning of the process of response that leads to formal writing. Summary is also an important part of that process.

Exercise 3—Working with a Visual (p. 28)

Although students may consider themselves to be visually literate, most have never actively analyzed a visual to the point of highlighting and annotating it. You might encourage students to think of this exercise as a dialogic process in which they ask themselves questions about the image and then examine it for possible answers to those questions.

2: Invention

Exercise 1—Setting Limits (p. 33)

1. A history of animal testing in medical research labs is too broad a topic for a two- to three-page paper. Without further narrowing, this topic could not be treated adequately in such a short essay.
2. This kind of topic is typical of an essay examination. Before writing an answer, a student should narrow the topic by deciding what points to discuss about the effectiveness of bilingual education programs. The number of points and the depth of the discussion are determined by the two hours allotted for the exam and the number of other questions.
3. An interpretation of Andy Warhol's soup cans is an unlikely in-class essay assignment for courses other than art history. This topic requires more knowledge about art than most students ordinarily would have, and research would be impossible under the circumstances.
4. An examination of a school's policy on plagiarism would be suitable for an email to a college paper.

Exercise 2—Setting Limits (p. 33)

The purpose of this exercise is to make students aware of the different audiences they encounter daily. An even more important realization for students is that they accommodate themselves rhetorically to each of these audiences. Levels of diction, subjects, and strategies are adjusted to suit the various audiences.

Exercise 3—Questions for Probing (p. 36)

1. Limited topic
2. General subject
3. Limited topic
4. General subject
5. Limited topic
6. Limited topic
7. General subject
8. General subject
9. Limited topic
10. Limited topic

Exercise 4—Questions for Probing (p. 36)

Students should be encouraged to use the questions for probing. This exercise lets them practice generating limited topics from general subjects. Here, you can demonstrate to them that even the most mundane general subjects can yield several interesting and workable limited topics. This is the first step in breaking down many students' preconceptions that they have nothing to say.

Exercise 5—Freewriting (p. 38)

Your students may have difficulty at first and may begin several topics before they find one they can focus on. They may also wish to repeat Exercise 4, generating topics for different general subjects.

Exercise 6—Freewriting (p. 38)

Students who have narrowed their topics sufficiently in Exercise 5 should be able to continue to freewrite from the responses they generate. However, you may have to provide assistance for some students.

Exercise 7—Brainstorming, Clustering, and Making an Informal Outline (p. 43)

This exercise not only reinforces the concepts introduced in the previous section but also enables students to progress from a general subject, to a limited topic, to a list of ideas that could be discussed in a paper, and to a rough outline of the first draft. Depending on their own learning styles, students will likely develop a preference for either clustering or informal outlining. This is a good time to tell students that some assignments, such as midterm and final examination questions, result from the narrowing of general subjects to limited topics. Knowing this can help students to prepare for such assignments and to complete them effectively by practicing the techniques described.

Exercise 8—Developing a Thesis (p. 47)

1. This is a statement of fact, rather than an opinion; therefore, it is not a thesis statement.
2. Although this statement expresses an opinion, it is still too general to be a good thesis. You will want to compare this with item (3).
3. This is a thesis statement; the paper would discuss the specific characteristics of the policy and the ways that it needs to be changed.
4. This is a thesis statement; the paper would demonstrate the reasons why community college makes a better choice for some students than a four-year college or university.
5. This is a statement of fact, rather than an opinion; therefore, it is not a thesis statement.
6. This is a topic, not a thesis statement.
7. This is a thesis statement; the paper would demonstrate how these courses would prevent violence in schools.
8. You will want to compare this to item (10). Although this statement expresses an opinion, it still lacks the clear limits of a good thesis.

9. This is a statement of fact rather than an opinion; therefore, it is not a thesis.
10. This is a thesis statement; the paper would demonstrate how prospective employers check Facebook material as well as discuss what material to avoid putting online.

Exercise 9—Developing a Thesis (p. 48)

Students' thesis statements will vary. You may want to put several of them on a transparency for evaluation in class. Push your students beyond platitudes and stress clear wording.

Exercise 10—Developing a Thesis (p. 48)

This exercise enables students to progress through the entire prewriting process. As students do this assignment, reinforce the importance of prewriting and tell them that this process should play a major part in all their writing assignments.

Exercise 11—Formulating an Effective Thesis Statement (p. 49)

Students should be reminded that effective thesis statements are often the product of revising earlier attempts to ensure that they are neither too broad nor too narrow.

3: Arrangement

Exercise 1—The Introduction (p. 55)

Examples for each kind of introduction in the text include the following:

Background information: "The Case for Birthright Citizenship" (Ch. 14)
Definition: "Getting Coffee Is Hard to Do" (Ch. 9)
Anecdote or story: "Just Walk On By" (Ch. 8)
Quotation: "Your Social Life: Are You a Fox or a Hedgehog?" (Ch. 11)
Surprising statement: "Shooting an Elephant" (Ch. 6)
Contradiction: "A Peaceful Woman Explains Why She Carries a Gun" (Ch. 10)
Fact or statistic: "Thirty-Eight Who Saw Murder Didn't Call the Police" (Ch. 6)

Exercise 2—Body Paragraphs (p. 60)

Any essay in the text could be used for this exercise, but you should probably limit students to paragraphs of five or more sentences.

Exercise 3—Thesis and Body Paragraphs (p. 60)

A good choice for this exercise is "Sex, Lies, and Conversation" (Ch. 11).

Exercise 4—The Conclusion (p. 62)

Examples for each kind of conclusion in the text include the following:

> Review of key points: "Why Chinese Mothers Are Superior" (Ch. 11)
> Recommendation: "I'm Your Teacher, Not Your Internet-Service Provider" (Ch. 11)
> Prediction: "The Movies That Rose from the Grave" (Ch. 10)
> Quotation: "The Myth of the Latin Woman: I Just Met a Girl Named Maria" (Ch. 8)

Exercise 5—Formal Outlines (p. 64)

Some students find making formal topic outlines a difficult task. If you assign this exercise, you should carefully go over the sample outline in the text and also demonstrate how to construct an outline, using either the board or an overhead projector.

4: Drafting and Revising

Exercise 1—The First Draft (p. 66)

Remind students that first drafts do not have to be perfect. Encourage them to write as fluently as possible without stopping to make minor corrections or worrying too much about spelling and punctuation—particularly if doing so interrupts the flow of their writing.

Exercise 2 and Exercise 3—Revising the Draft (p. 79)

You may wish to combine these two exercises, having students revise their drafts after they have been read and commented on by another student or students. You might also choose to comment yourself on their first drafts before having students revise.

Exercise 4—Labeling the Essay (p. 79)

Labeling their own essays, as we labeled the student essay on pages 76–78, can help students see clearly the key parts of their essays as well as how their essays are developed. Students should realize that such labeling can also be useful as they read essays by other writers, helping them to identify thesis statements and main points and where introductions end and conclusions begin.

5: Editing and Proofreading

Exercise 1 — Editing for Grammar and Punctuation (p. 88)

As students edit for grammar and punctuation, they should try to begin to identify their most likely trouble spots. You might encourage students to read their essays aloud as they edit, carefully observing their use of punctuation. This can sometimes help writers spot errors they might miss while reading silently.

Exercise 2 — Running a Grammar Check (p. 89)

Before students make additional changes based on a grammar check, you might take the time to have them share with you the specific corrections suggested by the program. You might easily identify parts of the essay that are highlighted as incorrect when, in fact, they contain no errors. Recognizing such problems may help students learn not to rely solely on grammar-check programs in editing their essays.

Exercise 3 — Checking for Sentence Style and Word Choice (p. 91)

Remind students that their choices in terms of sentence style and word choice are elements of drafting and revising as well as editing. They should be aware that they need to consider these issues throughout the writing process and not just at the end.

Exercise 4 — Proofreading (p. 92)

Many writers find that they proofread more effectively if they work on a hard copy of what they have written rather than read through it on a computer screen. If you are not bothered by a few handwritten corrections made on student essays, you might encourage students to proofread the final printout of their papers one last time before they hand them in.

Exercise 5 — Checking for Manuscript Format (p. 93)

It's a good idea to provide students with written guidelines for your preferred manuscript format when you make your first writing assignment. Students can thus follow these guidelines when they begin to draft and so not have to go back at a later stage to reformat.

PART TWO: Readings for Writers

The introduction and Chapter 1, "Reading to Write: Becoming a Critical Reader," both in the text and in this manual, discuss how the readings in this part and their apparatus can be used.

Note that the headnotes in this edition have been revised or newly drafted to provide information not only about the author but also about the cultural or historical context crucial to understanding the reading. We have come to recognize that what we consider "common knowledge"—the extent of racial segregation prior to the 1960s, prevailing attitudes in the early days of the feminist movement, and how patterns of immigration have changed over the last hundred years, to cite a few examples—is not immediately available to many students in their teens and early twenties. In addition, some readings assume familiarity with certain historical facts or events that are *not* common knowledge today. In such cases, we have included in the headnote enough background information to help students read and understand the essay.

6: Narration

Most first-year students seem to feel comfortable with narration because they have usually done a significant amount of first-person writing in high school. This does not necessarily mean, of course, that beginning students will already have mastered narrative writing. As the chapter moves through progressively more demanding narratives, you can gradually encourage your students to identify the techniques that can help them make their personal narratives more effective—dialogue, sentence variety, sharp detail. Eventually, you may ask your classes to experiment with other kinds of narrative writing, such as narrative journalism.

One way of handling the unit on narration is to assign the chapter's readings in the sequence in which they appear in the text, beginning with the paragraph by Barry Lopez on page 97. The paragraph is useful because it allows you to illustrate the pattern quickly and helps you to teach the use of narrative examples as well. You might then have students work with the panels from the graphic novel *Persepolis II* (p. 112) as a way of recognizing the visual aspects of narratives and how they can be translated into prose.

Junot Díaz's "The Money" is a wry account from the writer's childhood. In it, he narrates the story of a time that his family's apartment was broken into while they were on vacation. His tone is dryly comic, but "The Money" is a subtle and revealing sketch of his life in a Dominican-immigrant family. In "Living with Fire," Alan Dean Foster recalls his experience with a devastating fire near his home in Arizona. You can then move to "My Mother Never Worked," which focuses on the meaning of work in the domestic sphere. The essay uses a relatively informal style and simple vocabulary but employs flashbacks and effective descriptive detail. After your students read Gansberg's "Thirty-Eight Who Saw Murder Didn't Call the Police," you can discuss the differences between personal and journalistic narrative.

Next you can read Orwell's "Shooting an Elephant," which employs various narrative techniques to analyze political ideas as well as personal reactions. Finally, you can move your students from narrative essays into the realm of fiction with Sherman Alexie's "Indian Education." While clearly autobiographical, Alexie's short story is also a work of the imagination with a somewhat unconventional structure. Divided into thirteen sections—one for each of the narrator's first twelve school years and a final postscript ironically titled "Class Reunion"—it provides a perhaps startling insight into the cultural discrimination and personal difficulties faced by Native Americans living on reservations. Along with the nonfiction narratives, it also suggests the range of options available to writers of narration.

Thematic Connections at the end of each of these selections suggest other readings in the text that you may wish to assign during your narrative unit.

Marjane Satrapi, From *Persepolis II* (GRAPHIC FICTION)

Persepolis II (in which these panels appear) is the sequel to *Persepolis*, an autobiographical graphic novel by Marjane Satrapi. It depicts her childhood and adolescence in Iran after that country's Islamic revolution of 1979. The *Journal Entry* for this reading could allow some discussion of how narrative involving visuals with some dialogue and brief verbal transitions differs from narration that relies solely on words.

Reading Images (p. 113)

1. The narrator of the comic presents the classroom scene by explaining that students are now segregated by gender to keep them on a morally straight path. The anatomy professor announces to her class that in the past, the students would have done anatomical drawings from nude models, but now models must be covered. She says that they should make the best of it and draw the completely shrouded model. The students silently listen. Then, they try to view the model from all different angles and directions, but none of her body parts is visible to draw. Finally, after implying that the class never learned to draw the human body, the narrator closes by saying that the students did learn to draw drapes.

2. The main visual elements that connect the panels are the black shrouds of the students. The visual focus moves from the shrouded students receiving instructions from their professor, to an image of the shrouded students attempting to draw the shrouded model, to linked images of the covered model herself from four successive angles. The expressionless faces of the students and model in each panel are also significant, as they do not change or reveal any response. The clearest verbal transitions are indicated in the single sentence that connects the last five panels, which uses a comma, prepositional phrases, and ellipses to create a sentence of rhythm and motion.

3. Satrapi is showing the jarring social effects of the Islamic revolution on the education of women. There's an implied contrast between the procedures and rules in classrooms now and the way they were before. As the professor says, "Things have changed."

Thematic Connections

The Myth of the Latin Woman (p. 230): Judith Ortiz Cofer discusses the stereotype of Latin American women as it applies to her life—and to how she and other Latinas are perceived. She writes about both the modesty expected of her during her Catholic girlhood and the precocious, feminine sexuality often attributed to women with her ethnic and cultural background. How could these religious and cultural views be compared or contrasted with those depicted by Satrapi?

The Ways We Lie (p. 471): Is there a kind of lying going on in the selection from *Persepolis II*? Stephanie Ericsson categorizes and analyzes the different types of lies we tell others—and ourselves. Do the students in the comic participate in a kind of "delusion"? "Groupthink"? In such a society, would lying necessarily become a "survival mechanism"?

The Wife-Beater **(p. 514):** Satrapi's panels focus on the strict dress code imposed on women after the Iranian revolution of 1979. Doubtless, such rules were, in part, expressions of male dominance. Gayle Rosenwald Smith writes about a well-known style of undershirt, which people commonly refer to as a "wife-beater." For the writer, the clothing is fine, but she is disturbed by the name, which suggests male dominance and "teaches the wrong thing about men" (15).

Your Flip-Flops Are Grossing Me Out **(p. 687):** As Satrapi's work suggests, clothing restrictions can reflect deeper values or principles. In this tongue-in-cheek essay, Dana Stevens considers the growing prevalence of flip-flops in our society, and sees not only the practical and aesthetic problems with this footwear, but the social significance as well: "The crux of the flip-flop problem, for me, lies in the decoupling of footwear from foot with each step—and the attendant decoupling of the wearer's behavior from the social contract" (3).

Born Free Foundation, *Simba Goes Home to Africa* (VIDEO)

Students should find the story of Simba emotionally engaging. You might discuss the degree to which the film uses—or avoids—anthropomorphism; that is, the often sentimental attribution of human qualities to animals, especially in the context of stirring human emotions. You can also examine the strengths and weaknesses of documentary film—images of people being interviewed, voice-overs, shots with captions, footage of the film's "characters," etc.—as a vehicle for narration.

Comprehension

1. The trip takes twenty-six hours.
2. McKenna refers specifically to Land Rover and Kenya Airways for their support. Both brands are featured in the film.

Purpose and Audience

1. The ostensible purpose of this video is to present an informative and emotionally resonant account of the return of an abused and neglected lion to Africa. But it also serves to increase awareness of such animals, as well as highlight the work of the Born Free Foundation. So its purpose is also to persuade viewers to support this charity—and, less directly, highlight the support of companies such as Land Rover and Kenya Airways.
2. The intended audience would be anyone interested in animal welfare or wildlife preservation. At the same time, the film could also be seen as a more direct appeal to those inclined to support the Born Free Foundation.

Mode

1. You might use this question to discuss the quality and range of YouTube videos generally. On the one hand, the site is known for amateur—and often silly—content. On the other hand, it can be used to present sophisticated and highly

polished videos like the story of Simba. As the Born Free Foundation likely wishes to present itself as a competent, effective, and professional organization doing good work, a more amateurish video production would likely undermine its overall message.

2. The filmmakers use music deliberately. For example, the soundtrack for Simba's journey to the Belgian airport is guitar-based, nondescript Western rock music; at the 4:01 mark, the music shifts to more stylized and "exotic" percussion-heavy music that implies a narrative transition to "Africa." For the last minute and a half of the film, the narration drops out altogether, replaced by the sound and images of a local drum choir and Simba at the sanctuary. This seems to reinforce the film's story line that the lion is "home."

Junot Díaz, *The Money*

On one level, Díaz's personal narrative is a detective or crime story—what he describes as "the Case of the Stupid Morons" (12). On other levels, it is a vignette about a precocious first-generation immigrant, an account of life in a crime-ridden neighborhood, a story about the bonds between immigrants in America and the relatives they leave in their home countries. The selection should get students to think about how they can shape material from their own lives into revealing—and entertaining—narratives. You might note that Díaz the adult narrator at times finds his youthful self a mystery: "Where the hell did I get these ideas? I have not a clue" (10). Such moments highlight the fact that when we write autobiographically, we are writing about someone who is not quite our own "self." Indeed, personal writing often requires us to write about a character who, in some ways, is separate and perhaps even fictional, as we have to imagine motives or emotional states years after the events narrated.

Also, Díaz's essay provides an opportunity to discuss style and voice. The prose is sharp and distinctive: the writer uses diction shifts, fragments, understatement, sarcasm, and other stylistic techniques to transform a childhood memory into a rich, funny, sad, and ironic story about growing up in a poor immigrant family—a family that is haunted by the even poorer relatives it left behind in the Dominican Republic.

Comprehension (p. 116)

1. Díaz is explicit about his family's poverty in the first paragraph. His mother had no regular job; his father's employment was inconsistent. He refers to the way his "already broke family [had] to live even broker" (1). Later in the essay, his family's lack of money is implied by the description of the neighborhood they live in.

2. For Díaz's grandparents, the money in this "stash" was critical for their "material support" (1). Díaz and his siblings "knew that to touch it would have meant a violent punishment approaching death" (2). The money is essential for Díaz's grandparents, left behind in the Dominican Republic, but it also helps them "negotiate the absence, the distance, caused by [the family's] diaspora" (1). The money has an important meaning besides its financial value, even as its financial value was greater in Santo Domingo.

3. He realizes that his friends are guilty in "one of those moments of mental clarity . . . [w]hen the nictitating membrane obscuring the world suddenly lifts"

(8). He then tricks them during a visit to the park, breaks into his friend's apartment, and finds the stolen money and Dungeons and Dragons books.

4. He means that he expected his mother to be more grateful, to "run around with joy" (14), or become happy, but she does not. The "fifteen hundred or so miles" refers to the distance between New York City and Santo Domingo, Dominican Republic.

Purpose and Audience (p. 116)

1. Díaz's diction and range of reference is broad; it suggests a writer who is not only in control of his material and his prose, but who revels in the playful possibilities of language and style, moving from the phrase "[my mother] swore that we had run our gums to our idiot friends" (7) to "the nictitating membrane obscuring the world suddenly lifts" (8) within just a few sentences. He assumes his audience hears both his high notes and his low notes without much explanation—and that they find the incongruity amusing. His use of diction matches his range of reference, and he takes it for granted that his readers will be familiar with Dostoyevsky's *Crime and Punishment* ("Raskolnikov glances") and the Encyclopedia Brown book series. You might need to explain some of the references to students, who may not know these books.

2. As this is a personal narrative and not a sustained argument, students may answer this question in different ways. One possibility: "I once solved a crime, recovered my family's stolen money, and saved my grandparents from starving, but no one threw me a party—or even noticed." Such a sentence could open the essay, as it captures the main storyline. But in "The Money," Díaz is as interested in sketching a colorful, darkly comic vignette of his childhood and his family's relationship to money as he is in articulating a conventional thesis statement and supporting it with evidence.

3. The primary purpose of this essay—particularly given Díaz's style—is expressive: Díaz is sharing a memory. Yet the essay also informs, as it provides a representative snapshot of life in an immigrant family at the time: "All the Dominicans I knew in those days sent money home" (1). His anecdote provides a revealing—and informative—portrait of a time and a place, as well as of the lives of first-generation Americans. The essay includes implicit commentary on life in a neighborhood where, according to Díaz, people would not call the police if they saw a person breaking into an apartment. But his purpose is not persuasive.

Style and Structure (p. 116)

1. Díaz uses a one-sentence paragraph to signal a shift and narrow the essay's focus: "And that summer it was ours" (5). He uses a two-sentence paragraph to provide a sharp, comic summary: "And that was how I solved the Case of the Stupid Morons. My one and only case" (12). You might want to discuss the use of short paragraphs as a stylistic choice in personal or expressive writing, while noting that one-sentence paragraphs are usually out of place in formal academic writing.

2. The writer's use of fragments in this essay contributes to its informal, conversational tone: at times, "Money" sounds like a story that Díaz is telling the reader aloud, rather than writing on the page. This is often a matter of rhythm

and emphasis. The writer could have used complete sentences — and a fully formed paragraph — to elaborate on the guilt and shame the children felt, but the fragment captures it concisely and starkly.

3. Rhetorical questions serve different purposes in the essay. For example, "So what happened?" in paragraph 3 exemplifies Díaz's conversational style *and* sets up the next few paragraphs for Díaz to narrate the answer (and any narrative is almost always, on some level, an answer to that question). He uses rhetorical questions to connect with the experiences of his audience: "You know when you get one of those moments of mental clarity?" (8). Perhaps he also tries to anticipate his readers' questions — or frame his own about the behavior of his childhood self: "Where the hell did I get these ideas?" (10). You might point out that writers should use rhetorical questions carefully. When overused, they can lead to a sense that the writer has run out of things to say — or never had much to say to begin with.

4. He refers to the thieves repeatedly as *dopes* and *dolts*. Students should have different responses (e.g., the insults might seem childish). You might note that Díaz's word choice emphasizes the thieves' stupidity rather than, say, their moral turpitude, their dishonesty, or their *un*friendly behavior.

5. Díaz provides the details of the crime (what happened) in the third paragraph. He gives context by noting that burglaries were common in his neighborhood and that it was his family's "turn" (4–5). He then discusses the effects of the crime on his different family members (6–7). In paragraph 8, Díaz suddenly identifies the perpetrators in a moment of "mental clarity." He hatches — and implements — his plan to retrieve the stolen goods (9–11). In paragraph 12, he sums up his detective story. He then provides the tale's ironic denouement in paragraphs 13 and 14: the thief complaining about being robbed and Díaz's mother's indifferent response to Díaz solving the crime.

Combining the Patterns (p. 117)

Díaz implies the contrast between his family in America and his relatives in Santo Domingo. The contrast centers on the value of money: the financial support from Díaz's mother means that his grandparents can eat meat and have electricity. The implication seems to be that Díaz's family in America is poor and often broke, but the poverty of his relatives in the Dominican Republic is worse. The writer could elaborate on this distinction; it might add to the significance of his mother's "stash." At the same time, such a paragraph might overshadow the description of the deprivations of Díaz's family in the United States.

Thematic Connections

Indian Education (p. 142): In this short story, Alexie writes about a smart but awkward young Native American attending a reservation school. You might have students consider the stylistic similarities between "Indian Education" and "The Money": in both examples, the writers take painful or difficult childhood memories (note that both protagonists are precocious) and transform this material into powerful, darkly comic pieces of writing.

The Ways We Lie (p. 471): Stephanie Ericsson catalogs, defines, and explains ten different types of lying, from white lies to delusion. You might suggest that students analyze "The Money" using Ericsson's classifications. For example, what kinds of lies does the youthful Díaz tell as part of his scheme to recover his family's money? Are they justified?

Tortillas **(p. 506):** Díaz suggests that a strong bond connects his family in America to his grandparents in the Dominican Republic, despite the vast distance: in a way, the money represents that connection, which is why the money is so important to Díaz's mother. For José Antonio Burciaga, the bond to his ethnic and cultural heritage is the tortilla. You might encourage students to consider the stylistic differences between Díaz and Burciaga, who takes a more sentimental approach to writing about his childhood.

Alan Dean Foster, *Living with Fire*

In this personal essay, Alan Dean Foster recounts his experience facing a 2013 wildfire near his home in Prescott, Arizona. Ultimately, the fire burned over 8,500 acres and destroyed many buildings and homes. Foster's narrative is powerful but understated. You might want to discuss how he achieves this quality, as he evokes the sublimity, terror, and immediacy of a conflagration without reaching for highly emotional language. This stylistic choice supports one of the themes of his essay, the fortitude and understatement of people who choose to live in proximity to potential calamities and face those terrors with quiet dignity. "A knowing look, a regretful nod convey all that needs to be said," he writes. "People living in proximity to disaster don't shout; they just prepare in case it turns and comes for them" (15). The narrative becomes a defense of living in naturally beautiful places, regardless of their danger: "No place is safe. Not on this planet. So you choose your home for what you love about it, and not what you fear" (18). Students may question or even challenge this argument or measure it against their own ideas about where they want to live and why.

Comprehension (p. 120)

1. He is confused because he is used to seeing distant fires, which "score the blue sky with a thin haze" (4). This fire is different — "massive, a darker brown, moving too fast, and flush with orange" (4).
2. According to Foster, "technology is the first thing that flees." He is "reduced" (7) to checking the wind direction by throwing weeds into the air.
3. He writes that his mind was telling him to move and flee from danger, but he was visually drawn to the fire and could not stop staring at it (8).
4. The Granite Mountain Hotshots are a firefighting unit, "the best," according to Foster (10).
5. Foster emphasizes the quiet, dignified, and stoic quality of these people. They do not need words like "horrible" and "tragedy." Instead, they convey their emotions in a "knowing look" or "regretful nod" (15). Instead of shouting, they take care of practical necessities and preparations.
6. According to the writer, they live in these areas "[b]ecause such places are beautiful, are peaceful, and, for better or worse, are home" (18).

Purpose and Audience (p. 120)

1. One variation on the essay's thesis: "People choose to live in proximity to risk and danger for the beauty and peace of such places; they choose their homes based on their love, not their fear." Foster wants to explain the appeal of places

subject to natural disaster and to answer the question, why live with such a threat?

2. Foster assumes his audience may be skeptical or curious about why people live in places where the risk of fires is great: "Why stay there, people who live elsewhere must wonder as they watch such tragedies unfold. Why not move someplace where you don't spend every summer wondering if your house is going to burn down" (16).

3. The story adds to the tragedy, as nineteen of the firefighters died. It also contributes to Foster's overall themes of risk and courage. Readers may wonder why people like Foster live where he does; they may also wonder why people choose such dangerous jobs.

4. Students may agree that every place has its risks and that we all are at the mercy of "Mother Nature's dark side" (19) to some degree. At the same time, they may want to push back against the idea that all such choices are equal (for example, people who choose to live in places that are prone to flooding or storm damage may incur damages that require society to compensate them through federal aid or insurance).

Style and Structure (p. 121)

1. Foster's analogy about this method for starting a fire helps illustrate why the southwestern mountains of the United States are so prone to wildfires.

2. He is referring to words like "[t]errible calamity" and "horrible tragedy" (15). In this paragraph, he links an understated way of using language (or not using it at all) with the way residents of his region go about their lives: practically, quietly, soberly, determinedly, and with few overt displays of emotion.

3. The adjective denotes the apocalypse: the complete destruction of the world. It has its origins in the Greek word for *uncover*; it also carries the biblical connotations of the *end times*.

4. Students may have various responses. Although he seems transfixed by the sublimity of the fire at first, Foster accepts its tragic consequences; at the same time, he uses the occasion to explore, explain, and defend the reasons people choose to live in such high-risk areas. His prose style reflects a practical, understated approach to living. In the final paragraph, for example, he moves from considering big, unmanageable fears of the fire and "Mother Nature's dark side" (19) to everyday concerns about feeding hummingbirds and shooing away coyotes.

Combining the Patterns (p. 122)

Foster incorporates description into his narrative in the first four paragraphs, where he sets the stage for the fire, and in paragraph 6, where he describes it. Given the overall purpose of his essay, Foster limits his use of description and focuses on narrative action because he knows that his audience will want to be told the story of the fire; its actual description is less important.

Thematic Connections

Ground Zero (p. 175): Foster's essay retells his confrontation with the terrifying, apocalyptic, and sublime spectacle of a wildfire. In "Ground Zero," Suzanne

Berne describes a similar confrontation with the unsettling absence left by the attacks of September 11, 2001. Students might want to consider the style of the two writers, as both attempt to deal with powerful and emotional material in ways that are understated and almost meditative.

The Storm (p. 198): In "Living with Fire," the awesome power of "Mother Nature's dark side" (19) seems terrifying and impersonal, even as Foster tries to make sense of his personal confrontation with it. In Kate Chopin's "The Storm," a sudden storm leads two former lovers to rekindle their passionate affair spontaneously and briefly. Would students characterize the storm in this story as an example of "Mother Nature's dark side"? If nature is destructive in "Living with Fire," is it creative in "The Storm"?

A Peaceful Woman Explains Why She Carries a Gun (p. 353): Here, Linda M. Hasselstrom justifies her own choice to carry a handgun. Focusing on her vulnerability as a woman living and traveling alone, the writer draws on personal experience and observation to make her argument. Does her attitude toward risk and personal choice seem similar to Foster's?

Homeless (p. 510): In a way, Foster's essay becomes a meditation on the meaning of home — and the choice of where and how we live. In "Homeless," writer Anna Quindlen suggests that home "is everything." She claims to love her home "with a ferocity totally out of proportion to its appearance or location" (4). In what ways is her notion of home — and its significance — compatible with Foster's?

Bonnie Smith-Yackel, *My Mother Never Worked*

A discussion of the rationale behind the injustices Smith-Yackel finds in our Social Security laws is bound to produce lively debate, as is the issue of whether Mrs. Smith really "worked." This narrative can be examined in light of its original appearance in *Women: A Journal of Liberation,* a small (now defunct) feminist publication in the mid-1970s, its subsequent appearance in *Ms.,* and its continued relevance today. Students may also want to talk about the differences between "men's work" and "women's work," between the duties of farm wives and the duties of city wives who are not employed outside the home, and between the responsibilities of homemakers in Mrs. Smith's generation and in the present.

Comprehension (p. 126)

1. Martha Smith worked very hard at raising her children, doing farm chores, and maintaining a household, but she did not work outside the home for pay — the only kind of work recognized by the government.
2. According to the government, Martha Smith is not eligible for a death benefit because she was never employed.
3. The government defines *work* as an activity performed for compensation.

Purpose and Audience (p. 126)

1. The essay's thesis is that, although Martha Smith did not work outside the home, the work she did should be considered valuable enough to entitle her to Social Security benefits. The thesis is never explicitly stated because the accumulation of concrete details argues the author's point more forcefully than would a direct statement.

2. This essay might have found sympathetic audiences in other publications. For example, had it appeared in a magazine aimed at homemakers, many of these readers, regardless of their opinions about feminism, might have seen similarities between Martha Smith's story and their own (or their mothers') situations.
3. She mentions little about her father because the thesis of the essay does not concern him.
4. Students, depending on where they are from, may find the essay dated because the rural way of life described is less common now. The issue the author raises, however, remains the same. A stay-at-home wife and mother is eligible for Social Security benefits only through her wage-earning husband.

Style and Structure (p. 126)

1. Most students will find the title effective because it introduces the irony that runs through the essay and is summed up in the conclusion.
2. The frame provides the bureaucratic definition of *work,* which is contrasted in the essay with the meaning of *work* for the individual. It also establishes the contrast between the impersonal efficiency of the present and the warm memories of the past. These contrasts produce the irony that makes the essay so effective.
3. She uses transitional words and phrases that mention the season or month and year.
4. The many specific, concrete details make it clear that the writer, unlike the Social Security office, feels her mother *did* work.
5. This repetition emphasizes Martha Smith's accomplishments by indicating that she continued to work even after illness and old age had set in.
6. Students will come up with a number of different examples, probably simpler and more modern in tone. Discuss how Smith-Yackel's choice of words fits the time in which the events occurred.

Combining the Patterns (p. 127)

Passages that suggest a process explanation include paragraphs 16–18 and 21; all relate the daily chores of a farm family. If Smith-Yackel had written her essay entirely as a process explanation, she would have had to eliminate most of the specifics regarding her mother's character and personality, particularly the passages about her parents' courtship (11–12), the births of their children (13, first sentence of 17, and 19), and the details about her mother's later years. The essay would no longer be about her mother.

Thematic Connections

Midnight (p. 217): This student essay also focuses on hardworking parents, here Asian immigrants who labor in a dry-cleaning sweatshop more than twelve hours a day for substantially less than the minimum wage. Although Grace Ku does not say so specifically, it is possible that her parents were working illegally; if so, no contributions were being made by their employer to Social Security. According to the bureaucracy that Smith-Yackel dealt with, Ku's parents may also have "never worked."

"Girl" (p. 259): In Jamaica Kincaid's short story, a mother gives her daughter severe and specific advice about how to grow up to be a "lady" and "not the slut you are so bent on becoming." The monologue includes exacting instructions on the domestic role of women, whether pleasing their spouses or cooking, washing, and cleaning. You might use these two essays to discuss how the labor of women has often been central to societies and yet relegated to second-class status. You could also discuss how the expectations about women—and "women's work"—have changed over the years.

Aristotle (p. 481): Smith-Yackel frames her essay at its beginning and its ending with a phone call to the Social Security Office. In between, she recalls her hardworking mother's life, but the ironic central insight of the story only emerges at the conclusion, when the Social Security official claims that her mother "never worked" (32). Billy Collins's poem investigates beginnings, middles, and endings: how they structure and give meaning in both art and life and how they shape our understanding and expectations. You might have students place elements of the mother's life story into the structure of Collins's poem. Or they may consider the shape and meaning of their own future lives and careers in light of "Aristotle."

I Want a Wife (p. 502): Judy Brady's highly ironic examination of "women's work" can provide an especially interesting pairing with "My Mother Never Worked." Both describe in detail what has traditionally been "expected" of a wife and mother, albeit in two different worlds—one rural and working class, the other urban and professional. Students might discuss the similarities and differences between these two images and what they suggest in terms of class and generational distinctions. They might also consider whether our ideas about the roles of wife and mother have changed in the twenty or so years since these pieces were written.

Martin Gansberg, *Thirty-Eight Who Saw Murder Didn't Call the Police*

This is an essay that never fails to interest students. Some background about the 1964 incident and the public outcry it generated can open class discussion; the students will probably take it from there, volunteering information about similar incidents they have experienced or heard about. You might want to summarize for the class the psychological experiments described in the widely anthologized essay "Why People Don't Help in a Crisis" and try to examine the motives of those who watched but didn't act. You can also ask students to clip newspaper articles about similar situations—which are surprisingly easy to find. Finally, you can ask your students how they think they might react in such a situation.

Comprehension (p. 131)

1. Kitty Genovese was first stabbed shortly after 3:20; the ambulance arrived at 4:25, but the people did not come out until after it drove away. Thus, over an hour elapsed.
2. The neighbors' excuses ranged from not wanting to get involved to assuming the attack was a lovers' quarrel to being tired or afraid. One woman replied, "I don't know" (29).

Purpose and Audience (p. 131)

1. The article was intended to make its audience aware of society's general apathy and of the responsibility to correct it. It probably has very much the same impact today as it did in 1964, leading readers to wonder whether they would have come to the victim's aid.
2. The article's main point is "If someone had called the police in time, Kitty Genovese might have been saved." Gansberg has Assistant Chief Inspector Lussen (who is accustomed to crime) express his being shocked by the "good people" (4) who did not call the police. His responses are counterpointed by the weak excuses made by witnesses. An overt statement of the thesis would detract from the contrast.
3. Gansberg's description of Austin Street establishes the area as an ordinary American neighborhood. The idea that such a crime can happen anywhere, to anyone, increases the article's impact. In addition, many middle-class readers of the *New York Times,* Gansberg's original audience, could identify with the residents of such a neighborhood.
4. Gansberg prints the police department's telephone number both to inform his readers and to persuade them how simple it would have been to get help.

Style and Structure (p. 131)

1. Gansberg's precision helps to establish him as an authority on his subject, someone who has investigated these events thoroughly. This precision makes the reader more likely to accept Gansberg's thesis.
2. The words and phrases that most clearly reveal the writer's anger include the ironic *respectable, law-abiding citizens* (1), and *good people* (4).
3. Many of the briefest paragraphs (3, for instance, or the concluding paragraph) are effective because their brevity makes them stand out. Others (16, for example) include a single line of dialogue and thus would stand as separate paragraphs in any essay. In general, then, the paragraphing probably is effective. Nevertheless, students may feel that the presentation of events is choppy and that combining paragraphs could eliminate this problem.
4. The repetition of the word *assailant* matches the relentlessness of the attack. The word is also commonly used in reporting crimes. *Attacker* has the same meaning as *assailant,* although the latter is probably more commonly used in the media. *Murderer,* while it ultimately describes the crime, does not necessarily convey the sense of relentless attack since murders can seem relatively passive—in the case of a poisoning, for instance.
5. The dialogue makes the article more compelling by presenting the participants as real people with whom readers may identify.
6. The ironic comment by a police detective about the people finally coming out much too late expresses the writer's dismay.

Combining the Patterns (p. 132)

More descriptive detail about the neighborhood (6, 8–9, 18, and 25), about Kitty Genovese (7), and about her killer (22) would certainly add color and drama to the piece; the result would be something closer to a detailed magazine profile than to Gansberg's straightforward news story. The neighbors he interviewed do suggest some of their reasons for not getting involved, but if he were not reporting as a journalist, Gansberg might have concluded by offering his own analysis of causes. Students may be divided over the effectiveness of doing this because it would be difficult in such an analysis to go beyond simple moralizing about people's indifference. As it is, readers are left to struggle with their own conclusions and to consider what their own responses — and motivations — might be.

Thematic Connections

Shooting an Elephant (p. 133): The piece by Orwell offers an interesting contrast to Gansberg's account. Orwell was egged on to shoot the elephant by a crowd eager for a show, and Kitty Genovese's killer was abetted by thirty-eight neighbors who ignored her calls for help. Both stories also raise issues of morality and personal responsibility. Orwell uses recalled experience to clarify his own failings; the episode is something of a turning point in his life. Is there any suggestion that Kitty Genovese's neighbors gained any similar insight?

The Lottery (p. 308): In Shirley Jackson's celebrated short story, a group of rural townspeople stand by half-watching, half-participating in a violent tragedy. In what sense is Jackson's story a commentary on such real-life behavior? How might students explain why people in circumstances like these fail to take action?

Who Killed Benny Paret? (p. 337): Norman Cousins's indictment of prizefighting focuses on another aspect of violence in the United States. Students may well want to broaden their discussion to include movies, cartoons, video games, contact sports, and other aspects of popular culture that suggest "prevailing mores" (30) about violence in contemporary American society. Have we become so accustomed to violence that we are immune to shock when violence occurs in real life?

A Peaceful Woman Explains Why She Carries a Gun (p. 353): In this essay, Linda M. Hasselstrom makes the point that a "pistol is not the only way to avoid being raped or murdered in today's world, but, intelligently wielded, it can shift the balance of power and provide a measure of safety" (26). Clearly, if Kitty Genovese had been carrying a gun, she probably would not have been murdered. Do students agree with Hasselstrom that carrying a gun is a good way of protecting oneself?

George Orwell, *Shooting an Elephant*

Before discussing "Shooting an Elephant," you will probably need to provide students with some background about imperialism. This should include the extent of the British Empire, the purposes and methods of imperialism, and its effects on native populations or on the system's enforcers. Parallels could be drawn with American military forces stationed abroad or with the Vietnam War, with which students may be more familiar. A more helpful way of illustrating Orwell's predicament might be to ask students to put themselves in the position of a white police officer responding to an emergency in a black ghetto during times of unrest. While the situations are certainly quite different, the inner conflicts they produce may be similar.

Many students probably will have read either *Animal Farm* or *1984;* Orwell's views about political oppression in these novels can enlighten the discussion of "Shooting an Elephant."

Comprehension (p. 139)

1. Orwell is hated because he is a European police officer and therefore a symbol to the Burmese of British imperialism. Despite his position, Orwell had mixed feelings. "Theoretically . . . [he] was all for the Burmese" because he was convinced that imperialism was evil. But he also considered the Burmese "evil-spirited little beasts who tried to make [his] job impossible" (2).
2. The local officials want something done about the elephant because it has been running loose and damaging property. The crowd, on the other hand, wants to be entertained. Orwell notes that they want him to shoot just as an audience wants a magician to perform a trick; their faces were "happy and excited" (7) as they watched. Also, the crowd *expected* Orwell to shoot; they considered it his duty.
3. Orwell says he decided to kill the elephant "solely to avoid looking [like] a fool" (14). He realizes that he really has no choice; by accepting his position as an imperialist, he has destroyed his own freedom. Thus, like other imperial rulers, "in every crisis he has got to do what the 'natives' expect of him" (7). He hesitates because he feels it would be murder to shoot the elephant, which appears peaceful and harmless. He also feels that killing the elephant is "comparable to destroying a huge and costly piece of machinery" (6) and would cause a hardship for the beast's owner.
4. Orwell believed that the coolie's death justified his decision to shoot the elephant.

Purpose and Audience (p. 139)

1. The narrative reveals the true nature of imperialism by showing how it oppresses the rulers as well as the ruled.
2. Orwell's essay is strongly persuasive; he hoped to convince his audience of the evils of imperialism, not just provide them with an informative account of his experiences in Burma. Orwell probably expected his audience to be surprised by his potentially controversial views on imperialism. As a consequence, he explains his mixed feelings, the incident, and his resulting recognitions in great detail so his audience can come to understand his perspective.
3. The essay's thesis is that imperialism is an evil practice that enslaves both the rulers and the ruled.

Style and Structure (p. 139)

1. Orwell's first sentence attracts the reader's attention; the rest of the paragraph presents the story's setting and introduces the conflict between the Burmese and the Europeans. The actual narrative begins with paragraph 3, "One day something happened."
2. Orwell writes this narrative in order to show the effect the incident had on him; he is the story's dominant character. Therefore, his voice is logically the one heard above all others. Given Orwell's purpose, this narrative technique strengthens his essay.
3. Orwell devotes two paragraphs to the elephant's misery to show how much its death upset him. It is clear to the reader that the shooting is no casual event to Orwell.

4. The parenthetical comments in this essay may represent a sudden change in tone or subject, as in paragraph 4, or simply an explanatory aside to the reader, as in paragraphs 8 and 11. In both cases, the comments are isolated so they do not jar the reader with their abruptness.

5. Some equivalent expressions might be *cause trouble* for *raise a riot, called me* for *rang me up, garbage truck* for *rubbish van, damaged* for *inflicted violence, a little excitement* for *a bit of fun,* and *I think* for *I daresay.* Your students will probably think of some equally acceptable examples. Other "Britishisms" include *chucked up my job* (2) and *looking a fool* (14).

6. The speaker feels he must choose between two worlds and that he is caught in a dichotomy. Paragraphs 4 and 14 reinforce this theme by showing sharply contrasted differences at all levels in the society.

Combining the Patterns (p. 141)

The contrasts Orwell implies between himself (along with others among the British ruling class in Burma) and the Burmese are primarily differences between those who rule and those who are ruled within an imperialist system. Orwell is an intruder, and the Burmese are native to the country; he is comparatively well-off, and they are comparatively poor; he has power, and they are powerless (although he notes that, ironically, his "power" is basically a sham because, like other "tyrants," he "has got to do what the 'natives' expect of him . . . to appear resolute" even when he is uncertain [7]). However, setting these contrasts in sharp opposition in a separate paragraph would tend to undercut Orwell's central point about the ambiguity inherent in the power relationships he describes.

Thematic Connections

Thirty-Eight Who Saw Murder Didn't Call the Police **(p. 128):** The preceding piece by Martin Gansberg offers an interesting contrast to Orwell's story. Orwell was egged on to shoot the elephant by a crowd eager for a show, and Kitty Genovese's killer was abetted by thirty-eight neighbors who ignored her calls for help. Both stories also raise issues of morality and personal responsibility. Orwell uses recalled experience to clarify his own failings; the episode is something of a turning point in his life. Is there any suggestion that Kitty Genovese's neighbors gained any similar insight?

Just Walk On By **(p. 238):** In this essay Brent Staples also considers issues of power and powerlessness and, in particular, the extent to which poor young black men may find themselves in a situation similar to the one Orwell describes: adopting a powerful persona—an intimidating mask of fearsomeness—that hides an essential powerlessness. The point Staples makes is that every day he must fight against such stereotypes that lead to suspicion and fear.

The Untouchable **(p. 494):** Orwell's essay can remind students that India had an additional "caste," one not described by Ajoy Mahtab in "The Untouchable"—British "sahibs." Students can quickly infer how Orwell, who was born in India, must have reacted to India's caste system and why. You can also remind your students of Mahatma Gandhi. Ask them to consider how Gandhi's passive resistance parallels the role of the Burmese natives in Orwell's shooting of the elephant and how his use of passive resistance further illustrates Orwell's thesis.

Sherman Alexie, *Indian Education* (FICTION)

This short story is unusual in that it is told as a series of vignettes, or short anecdotes, spanning the narrator's life from first through twelfth grades, with each section relating an incident that occurred in each grade. You might focus students' attention on the cumulative effect of this series of vignettes, a question that is discussed in the second item under *Reading Literature*. Another interesting topic of discussion is whether one of these vignettes might have been expanded into a more traditional narrative exploring the one incident in detail. Could the effect have been the same? Students might also consider how well they think Alexie succeeds in bringing his narrator to life. For example, does he seem to age appropriately from one vignette to the next? (Most will probably agree that he does, beginning as a little troublemaker and growing into an increasingly serious and sensitive thinker.) Finally, if you focus on literature in any detailed way in your course, you might ask students to think about the relationship between autobiography and fiction. As the headnote preceding the selection suggests, Alexie's own youth had much in common with that of his narrator, and life as he presents it fictionally on the reservation is actually very close to the truth. What does this autobiographical aspect contribute to Alexie's themes?

Reading Literature (p. 147)

1. Alexie indicates the passage of time by using headings that refer to each school year from the first to twelfth grade. Students should recognize that in a piece of fiction, this technique is quite efficient. Adding more traditional transitional phrases (such as, "When I was in the second grade") would make this read more like an essay — although varying such transitions from grade to grade could prove challenging.
2. In general, the incidents described for each grade have in common that they suggest the difficulties the narrator faced in his childhood, scorned by his reservation friends because he was different, stereotyped by the white world, surrounded by poverty and lack of opportunity. And yet, in the face of this adversity, he learns to succeed on his own terms.
3. "There is more than one way to starve" suggests that those on the reservation become spiritually as well as economically deprived. "Sharing dark skin doesn't necessarily make two men brothers" follows from the story the narrator tells of being stereotyped as an alcoholic by a Chicano teacher. "[E]verything looks like a noose if you stare at it long enough" points to the sense of hopelessness many Native Americans face in contemplating what seems a history of failure following the arrival of Europeans.

Thematic Connections

The Money (p. 114): You might have students consider the stylistic similarities between "Indian Education" and "The Money": one is fiction and the other is nonfiction, but both writers take painful or unsettling childhood material (note that both protagonists are precocious) and transform it into powerful, darkly comic pieces of writing.

College Pressures (p. 448): Students might consider similarities and differences among the various kinds of pressure facing students from different ethnic and socioeconomic groups.

The Dog Ate My Flash Drive, and Other Tales of Woe (p. 457): Carolyn Foster Segal classifies the various excuses that students use to avoid coming to class or completing assignments. In her essay, the students are conniving and dishonest; in Alexie's story, teachers and school authorities are petty and misguided. Why do you think relationships between students and instructors can be so difficult? Both of these readings are comic, but their comic elements are fundamentally different. How would you explain this difference?

The Declaration of Independence (p. 550): This founding document of the United States, with its famous assertion that "all men are created equal," was never intended to apply to the native populations of North America. How has this fact and its subsequent interpretations affected the lives of Native Americans over the last two and a quarter centuries?

7: Description

Many college students have previously written descriptions that involve painting verbal pictures of places or things, something the introductory paragraph by James Agee does with lush concreteness. Invoking the senses of sight, hearing, and touch, the paragraph is a good place to begin your descriptive unit. A subjective description, it offers colors, shapes, and movement, as well as a variety of tactile and auditory sensations, in both literal and figurative images. Although the language is a mixture of objective and subjective words and phrases, overall the paragraph focuses on the writer's impressions.

Having discussed the paragraph, students will need you to help them expand their ideas about the use of description. The selections within this chapter were chosen to demonstrate stylistic diversity. In "Goodbye to My Twinkie Days," Bich Minh Nguyen describes not only the sight, smell, taste, and texture of Twinkies, but she also "reads" them and their pop-cultural significance — along with their connection to her childhood as a Vietnamese immigrant. Suzanne Berne describes a place, the environs of rubble of the World Trade Center six months after it was destroyed by a horrifying terrorist attack, from two perspectives: her initial sense that what she is viewing is "absence" and her dawning realization that there is a great deal to see at — and around — the site. Ann Hodgman begins her essay by announcing a long-standing curiosity: "I've always wondered about dog food." In making her investigation, Hodgman takes a comically unappetizing but richly descriptive look at nearly every aspect of her subject. Heather Rogers provides a nightmarish description of contemporary garbage disposal; her vivid evocation of an enormous Pennsylvania dump not only indicts supposedly "environmentally friendly" modern waste management methods, but also unrestrained consumerism. Perhaps the most difficult essay in this group is "Once More to the Lake" by E. B. White. White's vocabulary and intense imagery could be challenging for some students, and we recommend that you discuss several of the shorter essays before assigning his. If you include works of literature in your course, you will want to end your unit with Kate Chopin's short story "The Storm" to show the ways a fiction writer uses description of people as well as of the physical environment to heighten a story's impact and to contribute to a story's themes. Classroom discussions can focus on the uses that both essay and fiction writers make of description and the techniques they use to convey ideas and impressions to their readers.

Students should be encouraged to experiment and to open themselves up to the possibilities inherent in description.

Also, classroom discussions can concentrate on thematic threads that run through the selections, which also reflect a variety of cultures. Several of the selections deal with death as a means of understanding life.

Ansel Adams, *Jeffrey Pine—Sentinel Dome* (PHOTO)

American photographer Ansel Adams (1902–1984) is best known for his iconic black-and-white photographs of the American West. In this 1940 image, Adams captured the rugged beauty of a Jeffrey Pine tree that had grown—almost inexplicably—out of a slab of granite on top of Sentinel Dome, a mountain peak in Yosemite National Park in California. As they describe the image, students can consider the sources of its power and fascination: before it fell in 2003, the Jeffrey Pine was one of the most photographed trees in the world. Adams's photograph is haunting and evocative, but of what? Does it reveal some truth about the natural world?

Reading Images (p. 169)

1. The tree is bent severely and seems to have grown sideways, from left to right; its pine needles are in tufts and clumps. The tree is gnarled, twisted, and windswept. In the foreground, the earth looks dry, hard, and sandy; back a little farther, there is a slab of granite, from which the tree is growing. In the background, there seems to be a valley, and in the distance, mountains rise.
2. This question should give students a chance to think figuratively and perhaps even poetically about photographic images. For example, they might think of the tree as a stooped but enduring elderly person; inversely, they could even turn the tree itself into a metaphor (for endurance, persistence, or improbability).
3. Students may have different impressions of the image. That the tree is growing out of granite might strike them as surprising or wondrous. The image also evokes a strong sense of slow time, harsh nature, and persistent living things.

Thematic Connections

Once More to the Lake (p. 191): Adams's image evokes the timeliness of nature, especially as it exists independently of human limitations. In "Once More to the Lake," E. B. White considers time's effects on nature and memory from his perspective as a father, revisiting one of his favorite places: "I wondered how time would have marred this unique, this holy spot—the coves and streams, the hills that the sun set behind, the camps and the paths behind the camps."

The Kiss (p. 390): The Jeffrey Pine in the Ansel Adams photograph seems to be sculpted by nature. In Rodin's *The Kiss*, we view a sculpture made by human hands—among the most famous sculptures in the world. You might ask students how interpreting images of nature is different from reading art created by humans. But you should also remind them that Adams's photo is "staged" in its own way.

The Untouchable (p. 494): Adams's image can be seen as one of persistence in the face of powerful forces over long periods of time. In this essay, student writer Ajoy Mahtab writes about "untouchables": a taboo group of people who have traditionally lived outside of India's caste system. They have endured centuries of being shunned, despised, and oppressed. While the designation has (theoretically) been done away with in modern India, "old traditions linger on, and a deep-rooted fear passed from generation to generation does not disappear overnight" (3).

Tortillas (p. 506): For writer José Antonio Burciaga, tortillas are an enduring tie to his Mexican childhood and heritage. In fact, their significance is mythic, as he traces the origins of the "lowly corn cake" (8) to the "great god Quetzalcoatl" (3) from Mayan mythology.

Johannes Vermeer, *Girl with a Pearl Earring* (PAINTING)

This iconic painting should get students responding to visual art and sharing their responses. As you will likely be framing the discussion in terms of writing and description, students may be less intimidated by the idea of capital-A "Art" and more inclined to interpret or respond to *Girl with a Pearl Earring* in everyday language. It might be helpful to keep the focus on description and on how precise description can lead to persuasive or lively interpretations.

Comprehension

1. You might point out that the name of the painting refers to a detail: the pearl earring that draws the viewer's sight to the center of the painting. But students might discover any number of smaller elements as they consider the image: the white reflections on the woman's pupils, as well as the simulated reflection of light at the corners of her mouth and on her lower lip; the blue coloring of the turban and its relationship to other colors in the painting; the visible cracks in the paint.
2. This open-ended question should encourage students to share their own responses as they "read" the painting. Is she sad, coy, pleased, shy, resigned, frightened? Does the image objectify the woman in the manner of a modern advertisement? Ask what they see and why, and then discuss what accounts for disparate reactions.

Purpose and Audience

1. As suggested by the *Writing Projects* question below, viewers have had different responses to the painting, including Edward Snow's interpretation of it as an image of grief. You might use this question to discuss the aims of art, as well as the difference between the medium of visual art and the medium of prose. For example, would students prefer a painting that had an obvious "thesis" or "point"? Why or why not?
2. Students might want to connect this question to their own experience with other works of art that resonate with them personally, but that also seem to have some universal appeal. Do they own prints of other painters' works?

Mode

1. For this question, you might want to touch briefly on the work of a critic like Walter Benjamin, who discussed such issues in his famous essay "The Work of Art in the Age of Mechanical Reproduction": "Even the most perfect

reproduction of a work of art is lacking in one element: its presence in time and space, its unique existence at the place where it happens to be.... The presence of the original is the prerequisite to the concept of authenticity." Ask students what makes a print or reproduction less "authentic" than an original, even if it is essentially a flawless reproduction. Does a copy of *Girl with a Pearl Earring* mean something different from the original hanging in the museum?

2. For this question, you could discuss how such a title orients the viewer of the painting in a certain way. Does the phrase "Girl with a Pearl Earring" capture the meaning better than "Head of Young Girl"? These are all translations, of course, but does the sound of the phrase matter too?

Bich Minh Nguyen, *Goodbye to My Twinkie Days*

In this stylish and perceptive essay, Nguyen eulogizes the Hostess Twinkie as an American icon and comments on the way American food culture has changed since her childhood. She also writes as a child of Vietnamese immigrants: for her, the snack cakes are intimately tied to her youthful desire to assimilate and belong in America. But if "Goodbye to My Twinkie Days" is a eulogy for the Twinkie from a first-generation immigrant, it is also a lament for lost youth and the shared popular culture of her American childhood. Nguyen is almost Proustian in her approach: "I didn't think the Twinkie would thrill the way it used to, and it didn't. But it tasted like memory" (7). You might ask students to notice how she brings multiple sensory impressions to bear in her vivid and descriptive writing.

Comprehension (p. 173)

1. Nguyen buys the Twinkies out of nostalgia for the personal and cultural significance of the snack cakes. She purchases them to "pay [her] respects" (1). For the writer, Twinkies evoke her childhood—and not merely memories of her elementary school lunchroom, but the idea that, for a Vietnamese immigrant, "Twinkies were a ticket to assimilation" (5). At the end of the essay, she says she will store her Twinkies so she can "taste [her] way back to [her] childhood" if she wants to (9).

2. Nguyen associates Twinkies with the process of assimilation. They also recall a time when "junk foods seemed to represent an ideal of American indulgence" (5).

3. For the writer, eating Twinkies (as opposed to eating food associated with her immigrant parents, for example) is a rite of passage into a shared American popular culture. The snack cakes also provide an idealized image for a child longing to be more "westernized," with their "golden cake, more golden than the hair I wished I had" (5).

4. If Twinkies represent an ideal of assimilation for Nguyen, they also suggest a derogatory term for Asians *too* willing to assimilate: "To be a twinkie is to be a sellout: yellow on the outside, white on the inside" (6).

5. Generally, she claims that the loss of Twinkies will lead to the loss of a shared connection to a shared popular culture of the past. But more personally, Nguyen also ties the loss to her youth and to a time when she "dreamed of all the possibilities yet to be consumed" (9).

Purpose and Audience (p. 173)

1. Nguyen assumes her audience's relative familiarity with the snack cakes. She refers to their status as unhealthy "junk food" using the first person: "we're not supposed to eat like this anymore" (2); "[w]e know it's bad, and that's why we want it" (4). Her essay is based on the premise that Twinkies provide a communal connection to the pop culture of the past, a connection she assumes her readers will share. In short, Nguyen is not introducing her audience to an unfamiliar topic; rather, she is proposing that her readers consider the significance of a familiar food item.

2. Nguyen's purpose is to highlight the underappreciated significance of an iconic junk-food product and to note the loss of both her personal past (as she grows older) and the loss of a shared popular-culture connection among a wider group of people: "Losing the Twinkie will mean losing a connection to our shared past; it will be another part of the long goodbye to our youth. As Hostess goes under, we become older" (8).

3. The dominant impression of this essay is in its claim that the end of the Twinkie is a significant loss, both for Nguyen personally and for American popular culture generally.

Style and Structure (p. 173)

1. The introduction establishes both the broader rationale for her essay (the news that Hostess was going out of business) and her connection to the Twinkie (her desire to "pay [her] respects" to it). The practice of paying respects is usually associated with attending funerals, so in a sense, Nguyen's opening paragraph sets the tone for a eulogy. The rest of the essay also answers a question implied in these two sentences: why would the writer want to "pay respects" to a snack cake?

2. Nguyen refers to Michael Pollan because he embodies trend in the way an influential segment of educated (and often affluent) Americans think about food: that processed foods are bad and unhealthy; that snack cakes like Twinkies should not be eaten by children; that we need to "bake our own cakes now, eat whole grain bread, and try to follow those grocery store Food Rules" (8). The "Food Rules" come from a book by Pollan that offers advice on how and what to eat.

3. Stylistically, the use of the colon in the paragraph's second sentence is apt. Nguyen makes a statement ("For Asian-Americans, to be a twinkie is to be a sellout"). The colon brings the sentence to a halt; the material after the colon explains the metaphorical meaning of "twinkie" as it applies to Asian "sell-outs." The full stop emphasizes the explanation, as well as the punch of the insult, more strongly than a comma would. The semicolon is often an effective way to link closely related independent clauses—in this case, two clauses describing a cartoon cowboy and his sidekick. The semicolon highlights the connection between the two images and ideas.

4. The writer uses the term *junk food* as it is commonly applied to food with little or no nutritional value, but that appeals strongly to our cravings for excessively sweet, salty, processed, or otherwise "unhealthy" snack foods and empty calories. The designation connotes guilty or unhealthy pleasures, as well as self-indulgence.

5. Her descriptions are largely subjective. She offers interpretations of the packaging, from the name "Hostess" to the images of a cowboy and his "swarthy chocolate" (6) sidekick, which subtly imply, perhaps, kitschy and perhaps unintentional retroracism (The Lone Ranger and Tonto). Her description of the Twinkie itself is explicitly personal, as it recalls her elementary school lunchroom. Even though she does name specific chemical ingredients ("shortening," "corn syrup"), these elements lead her back to the subjective: "But it tasted like memory" (7).

Combining the Patterns (p. 174)

Nguyen refers to the practical threat to the existence of the Twinkie, which is a labor dispute between a corporation and associated unions. This is the "immediate" (2) cause of the Twinkie's demise. But she moves from this cause-and-effect relationship to another long-term trend. The real threat to the snack cake is a shift in the way Americans think about food and eating, a change that stigmatizes products like the Twinkie as unhealthy and unacceptable: "After all, we're not supposed to eat like this anymore" (2). The writer is interested almost exclusively in the latter causal relationship rather than the labor dispute.

Thematic Connections

My Field of Dreams (p. 106): Nguyen's essay is nostalgic. For her, Twinkies remind her of her childhood, when she "dreamed of all the possibilities yet to be consumed" (9). In "My Field of Dreams," Tiffany Forte writes about her childhood love of baseball and her dreams of playing in the major leagues. Forte writes nostalgically and reflects on a loss, as she came to accept the fact that she would never play professional baseball—even if the sport still evokes that youthful dream.

Songs of the Summer of 1963 . . . and 2013 (p. 403): If Williams is nostalgic for the "sweet" music of the March on Washington (and implicitly, his childhood), then Bich Minh Nguyen pines for the sweet, processed junk food of her youth. Her essay is personal, but like Williams's it also deals with the cultural changes of the last several decades.

Tortillas (p. 506): For Nguyen, Twinkies suggest assimilation to American culture and conjure memories from her childhood. For José Antonio Burciaga, tortillas conjure childhood memories as well, but this "lowly corn cake" (8) ties him to his Mexican cultural and familial heritage rather than to his American identity. Both essays speak to the power and meaning of food, personally and also in a wider social, cultural, and historical context.

Suzanne Berne, *Ground Zero*

Here, Berne describes a visit to the site of the twin towers of the World Trade Center some six months after the devastating terrorist attacks of September 11, 2001. (It is interesting to note that nowhere in the essay does she refer to the attacks themselves, only in paragraph 13 to the "terrible images" of the towers collapsing; she assumes her readers' recognition of the events that led to the collapse.) Berne's first response is that there is nothing to see at the site but the "absence" of what was once there. Then, "what is not there becomes visible" (7) as she begins to notice various signs that recall the collapse in paragraphs 8–9. Finally, she is able to find a vantage point from which she can actually see down into the pit (18), which turns into a highly sobering moment before "the day flowed back into itself" so that the "space fills up again" (20).

Berne is particularly adept at using adjectives in this piece. Dividing students into groups, you might assign each a different section of the essay and ask that they circle the adjectives Berne uses in that section; then have them share their responses to each section with the rest of the class. They should find that some sections contain many more adjectives than others. Where does Berne rely on vivid nouns and verbs rather than adjectives? An important point to make is that the overuse of adjectives in description is as problematic as their underuse.

If you have students who have visited the site described here, you might have them compare their responses to Berne's. A related topic for discussion or writing is the question posed to Berne in paragraph 14 ("You want tickets to the disaster?"). Is visiting the site for those who did not directly lose loved ones there essentially an act of respect? Or is it more related to the rubbernecking people do at the site of a traffic accident?

Comprehension (p. 178)

1. She means that one begins to realize the absence of what was at the site before: the destroyed towers of the World Trade Center and the lives they contained.
2. It takes "quite a while" to see all the details at ground zero because there are so many varied images to take in, from the nearby skyscraper "shrouded in black plastic" (8) to the myriad flags that surround the site. Thinking of something to say requires confronting the unspeakable destruction that took place there.
3. At the point in time when Berne visits ground zero, most evidence of the horrific images broadcast in the days following the attack has been removed, so it is difficult to "superimpose those terrible images" (13) when viewing the empty site.
4. Berne notes a kind of normalcy and "busyness" (5) in the area surrounding ground zero that contrasts starkly with what occurred there, a contrast Berne finds both unsettling and oddly comforting.
5. She means, as she says in her final phrase, that because of the many visitors, "that space fills up again." She seems to be less sarcastic here than ambiguous about her feelings.

Purpose and Audience (p. 178)

1. Berne comes closest to stating her thesis in her final sentence, although students will recognize that part of the central point regarding the "absence" she encounters is implied.
2. Berne's primary purpose seems to be to share with readers her own very personal responses to the site of ground zero when she visited.
3. On the surface, Berne seems to assume that her readers are curious about what it would be like to visit the site. However, writing for the *New York Times,* she must also know that more than a few of her readers would have visited the site themselves, so a further assumption may be that these readers would be interested in how another visitor to the site articulates her response.

Style and Structure (p. 178)

1. Students' answers may vary. In part, at least, she is suggesting that she never felt any interest in visiting lower Manhattan prior to the destruction of the World Trade Center.
2. Berne's essay is organized chronologically, beginning with her arrival at the site and ending with final reflections about herself and the other visitors there. This structure allows her to mirror for readers her own deepening impressions as she surveys ground zero and its environs.
3. As suggested in the answer to the previous question, Berne's vision of the site changes according to her changing vantage point over the course of her visit.
4. It is at the end of paragraph 17 that Berne is finally in a position to see directly into the chasm where the remains of those killed as the towers collapsed can be found. The fact of the disaster hits home at this point.
5. Berne's conclusion reinforces the idea that the site is more than an empty space; life must continue despite such an awful tragedy.
6. Berne uses the word *suddenly* here to suggest that her attention is drawn to many disparate images in very quick succession after a long period when she has, in a sense, been able to see nothing. The effect is that readers are almost bombarded with images.
7. Literally, *ground zero* is the point immediately over or below a nuclear bomb detonation. It connotes a place of great devastation, where life and property are destroyed in an act of military aggression.

Combining the Patterns (p. 179)

The contrast is between the first impression that there is "nothing" to see at ground zero — that what one initially thinks about is the absence of what was once there — with the gradual and then sudden realization that there is a great deal to see, both in terms of what remains and the activity that now surrounds the site.

Thematic Connections

From *Persepolis II* (p. 112): Berne confronts an absence where the towers once stood. Ultimately, "that space fills up again" (20) as she adjusts her perception and sees what has replaced the towers. In her graphic fiction recounting life in Iran after the 1979 Islamic revolution, Marjane Satrapi shows how the profound change in government and society affected sight and vision — that is, what could be seen and what could not. How does the practice of covering women make them less present — anatomically, socially, and otherwise? Why might such rules apply to women and not to men?

Living with Fire (p. 118): Foster's essay retells his confrontation with the terrifying, apocalyptic, and sublime spectacle of a wildfire. In "Ground Zero," Suzanne Berne describes a similar confrontation with the unsettling absence left by the attacks of September 11, 2001. Students might want to consider the style of the two writers, as both attempt to deal with powerful and emotional material in ways that are understated and almost meditative.

Shooting an Elephant (p. 133): In this classic essay, George Orwell recounts a different kind of incident that becomes a magnet for crowds of curious onlookers.

Students might use this and "Ground Zero" as a starting point for considering why people are drawn to such sites.

Once More to the Lake (p. 191): E. B. White's essay is a meditation on what Berne refers to in paragraph 13 as "mental revision," on how we remember what is no longer there, superimposing the past on the present.

Ann Hodgman, *No Wonder They Call Me a Bitch*

Here, Ann Hodgman indulges her long-standing fascination with dog food and gives a step-by-step description of an unusual taste test. Notice how the essay appeals to all the senses, from the "horrifying rush of cheddar taste" (8) in a Gaines-burger to the image of Cycle-2 dog food that "glistens nastily with fat" (11). But Hodgman also seems to revel in the packaging and language of the product ("Dogs love real beef!" [4]), as well as the mysterious euphemisms associated with it ("And what exactly *are* byproducts?" [1]). The comic effect of "No Wonder They Call Me a Bitch" depends, in part, on the contrast between the marketing claims of dog-food makers and the unsavory reality of the product.

Point out that Hodgman's essay is a natural extension of her curiosity, which she specifies in a series of questions: "I've always wondered about dog food: Is a Gaines-burger really like a hamburger? Can you fry it? Does Gravy Train actually make gravy in the dog's bowl . . . ?" (1). Ask students if they have their own curiosities about a product, place, or object. How might they carry out an investigation? You might even offer the first line of "No Wonder They Call Me a Bitch" as a prompt for discussion or an essay: "I've always wondered about _____."

Comprehension (p. 183)

1. Hodgman ate dog food because she had "always wondered" about its taste, composition, and "byproducts" (1). Given that she is a dachshund-owning food critic who grew up with dogs, her curiosity seems understandable.

2. According to Hodgman, the packaging makes claims such as "Dogs love real beef" (4) and "thick, rich, real beef gravy" (15). In reality, the food is a "lumpy, frightening, bloody, stringy horror" (14), or the gravy tastes "primarily like tap water" (15). This contrast runs through the entire essay.

3. The writer claims that O.N.E.-brand dog food is "pretty palatable" (19). She also notes that dog snacks taste better than dog food; among all of them, she prefers Bonz, a "hard-baked, bone-shaped snack stuffed with simulated marrow" (22). In contrast, she cannot bring herself even to try the Mighty Dog Prime Entree (29).

4. She quotes extensively from the packaging, which makes claims about good taste and quality. These messages are ultimately designed to appeal to dog owners, rather than the dogs themselves, so the language must show the appeal of the food in human terms, even when the effect is silly: "It's so good, your dog will think it's hot off the frying pan" (20). On one of the bags, for example, she finds a "long, long essay" explaining the ingredients (17). But Hodgman shows how the labels are misleading and euphemistic. For example, one boasts, "no meat by-products," even as the product ingredient list includes poultry by-products (4).

Purpose and Audience (p. 184)

1. "No Wonder They Call Me a Bitch" does not have an explicitly stated thesis. The essay does, however, highlight the contrast between the way dog food is packaged and advertised versus how it looks and tastes. Hodgman's experiment shatters a "cherished childhood illusion" about the product (9). The writer comments wryly on the tendency of dog-food makers and dog owners to anthropomorphize the pets or attribute sophistication to them: "Although our dogs do nothing but spend eighteen-hour days alone in the apartment, we still want them to be *premium* dogs. . . . We also want dog food that comes in a bag with an attractive design" (17).

2. The dominant impression of the essay is the comic contrast between the appealing claims of dog-food products and the disgusting reality of dog foods taste, texture, and composition. The essay also captures the humorous quality of attributing human tastes and preferences to dogs.

3. Hodgman seems to presume that her audience shares her curiosity about dog food — or at least that her readers can be made interested in the unusual topic by her own enthusiasm. For example, near the end of the essay, she writes, "I'm sure you have a few dog food questions of your own" (23). At the same time, she implicitly acknowledges the strangeness of her subject, as when she includes the response of a Purina representative: "When I told him I'd been eating dog food, he said, 'Oh, you're kidding! Oh, *no*!'" (5).

Style and Structure (p. 184)

1. Students may have a range of reactions to the title. Clearly, it's meant to be memorable, provocative, and darkly comic. At the same time, one could argue that the title is sensational and even misleading as applied to Hodgman's subject and style: the startling pun on a female stereotype reveals little about the essay's content.

2. Hodgman structures her essay around three different types of dog foods: boxed Gaines-burgers (3–9), canned (10–14), and dry (15–19). Near the end of her essay, she includes three paragraphs on dog snacks (20–22). She could have organized the essay in a different way — for example, by ranking the products in order of quality and flavor or by cost.

3. The writer develops her description thoroughly, providing vivid details about the texture, smell, taste, and appearance of the different dog foods. If anything, one might argue that she includes too much description for its own sake, as in the line "lumpy, frightening, bloody, stringy horror . . ." (14). As Hodgman is being deliberately gross, however, the overkill makes sense.

4. She uses figurative language effectively, as when she describes the flavor of Gaines-burgers as "like Play-Doh that's been sitting out on the rug for a couple of hours" (8). At the end of her essay, Hodgman writes that the simulated marrow inside a Bonz snack "look[s] like the sludge that collects in the treads of [her] running shoes" (22).

5. Hodgman claims she includes the questions and answers to "save us time" (23), even though they seem to reflect her own curiosity rather than that of her presumed readers. They also include information that does not fit neatly into her essay's organizing principle. By ending in this way, Hodgman forgoes the possibility of summing up or leaving her readers with a specific message or concluding thought.

6. Hodgman relies heavily on adjectives to evoke the texture, taste, and appearance of the dog food: *extruded* (6), *malleable* (7), *horrifying* (8), *oily* (11), *stringy* (14).

Combining the Patterns (p. 185)

Along with making the essay a clear sequence of events, the narrative elements allow Hodgman to include her comic responses and reflections as she recounts the taste test: "I shrieked and went instead for a plain chunk, which I was able to swallow only after taking a break to read some suddenly fascinating office equipment catalogues" (14).

Thematic Connections

The Embalming of Mr. Jones **(p. 301):** Both Hodgman and Jessica Mitford might make readers squeamish with their essays, but the style of each writer is different. Have students compare and contrast "No Wonder They Call Me a Bitch" and "The Embalming of Mr. Jones" in terms of objective versus subjective description. Hodgman's writing emphasizes her personal responses, whereas Mitford chooses a more detached, clinical point of view. Which approach is more unsettling, and why?

Tortillas **(p. 506):** In this essay, José Antonio Burciaga writes about a food that has a powerful hold on his imagination and reminds him of his childhood. Hodgman claims that she used to "beg" her mother to buy Gaines-burgers for their dogs; the product seemed to her a "miracle of beauty and packaging" (3). Ask students to think of a food or product from their childhood that holds a similar fascination for them. How have their views of it changed or remained the same?

On Dumpster Diving **(p. 672):** Lars Eighner claims that eating from dumpsters safely requires "using the senses" (8) among other things. According to him, people tend to throw things out that are still harmless and edible. How does Hodgman use her senses in her essay? Do sense impressions seem like a reliable guide to what's healthful or harmful? Does Hodgman consider the possibility that the dog food could make her ill?

Heather Rogers, *The Hidden Life of Garbage*

Here, the writer reveals and analyzes a subject that's often hidden — unsurprisingly so, perhaps. But, given that just one rubbish-handling company in Pennsylvania packs more than forty million pounds of garbage into its dumps daily, the issue of waste disposal would seem to merit investigation. Rogers argues that landfills are tucked away, not only because they're unsightly and unpleasant, but also because "[i]f people saw what happened to their waste, lived with the stench, witnessed the scale of destruction, they might start asking difficult questions" (3). For her, these questions cut to the heart of "our society's unrestrained consuming" (3). Even if students challenge the broader implications of Rogers's position, her essay should lead them to wonder where all our waste goes and how we should manage it effectively and responsibly in the long term. These questions become more complex as the writer casts a skeptical eye toward presumably high-tech or "environmentally responsible" (13) solutions — techniques that only mask the fundamental societal problems implied by the essay.

Students should also consider how Rogers uses description to make her point effectively. Her unflinching depictions of waste management—the "bizarre, thirty-acre nightmare" (4) of a landfill, the "toxic stew" (9) that threatens groundwater supplies, the "sickly and sour" (4) smell—all contribute to a provocative indictment of our attitude toward both consumption and garbage disposal.

Comprehension (p. 189)

1. According to Rogers, such sites are "tucked away" for the obvious reason that they are unpleasant. Yet, more important for her argument, they are also hidden so we never have to experience the scale and stench of our waste; if we did, we would question the fundamental "logic of our society's unrestrained consuming" (3).
2. The "working face" is where the actual dumping takes place: in this area, clusters of trucks, earthmovers, steamrollers, and other machines receive and compact the garbage into the landfill. Other parts of these complexes include underground liners and "capped" (10) cells, where garbage is sealed underground with dirt, plastic, and synthetic mesh.
3. Rogers thinks GROWS is aptly named because of the enormous amount of garbage it receives and the increasing volume of waste our society produces. The waste management company probably hopes GROWS sounds "environmentally responsible" (13) and technologically sophisticated. But the writer implies that all these "lavish resources dedicated to destroying used commodities and making that obliteration acceptable, even 'green'" (12) deserve our skepticism, not our approval.
4. New landfills leach vast quantities of "toxic stew" (9) that threaten groundwater in the area. These contemporary sites, which are potentially less dangerous than the dumps of the past, are still only "short-term solutions to the garbage problem" (11). The cell liners are designed to last thirty to fifty years, after which all the plastics, solvents, and other hazardous materials within them will have to be treated. According to Rogers, this time frame coincides with the "post-closure liability" (11) regulations of private landfill operators: thirty years after these sites are shuttered, the public becomes responsible for any contamination, not the owners.
5. The "repressed question" is: "what if we didn't have so much trash to get rid of?" (13). This follows her earlier suggestions that Americans are unreflective about their unrestrained consumption.

Purpose and Audience (p. 189)

1. Rogers puts her primary thesis in the third paragraph, where she connects the camouflaging of waste dumps to the logic of consumption. She defers this assertion until she's established her terms and set a descriptive scene in the first two paragraphs. In paragraph 11, she also makes provocative, debatable claims about the long-term tenability of waste management facilities such as WMI.
2. Rogers creates a dominant impression that she's revealing, in a blunt, uncompromising way, a hidden reality that's disgusting. The mood of the essay is almost nightmarish. At the same time, she suggests that this repulsive vision mirrors our own habits and unrestrained appetites, which we refuse to acknowledge.

3. Her attitude toward waste disposal seems to be that it's in the hands of irresponsible private owners fearful that visitors could "at any minute . . . uncover some illegal activity" (12). She also sees it, generally, as evidence of our overconsumption. Rogers's view of companies like Waste Management Inc. is cynical, particularly with regard to the "palpable tension" (12) evident when she visits them.

Style and Structure (p. 189)

1. She describes the process by which household refuse is distributed to various waste disposal sites: familiar trucks moving through neighborhoods, garbage cans being emptied, and trash being compacted. This description establishes the link between the routine, domestic waste of our lives, and the more hidden procedures whereby garbage ultimately is disposed.
2. A number of structural elements in the essay determine the arrangement of its details. For example, Rogers moves back and forth from writing generally about the state of waste disposal in the United States (paragraph 2, for example), to describing a specific site in detail (as she does in paragraphs 4, 7, and elsewhere). The more concrete descriptions — of seagulls diving into piles of garbage or workers "orchestrating the burial" (7) — are provided in these latter sections in which the writer is on-site at the GROWS landfill.
3. Rogers's descriptions are often highly technical and may appear objective, as when she gives the specialized names of landfill features such as the "capped" (10) cells, underground "liners" (9), and "litter netting" (8). But her word choice elsewhere reveals highly subjective responses and interpretations. For example, her statement that these "garbage graveyards are sequestered, guarded, veiled" (2) suggests not merely that dumps aren't publically prominent but that there's something secretively sinister in this placement — especially given the connotation of the word *veiled*. Similarly, the image of the landfill as a "bizarre, thirty-acre nightmare" (4) contains a subjective judgment, as does her perception of a "palpable tension at waste treatment facilities" (12).
4. She puts the term *environmentally responsible* in quotations to signal detachment and irony. The punctuation suggests that Rogers does not believe such landfills are actually environmentally responsible, even though their operators (or others) describe them with this catchphrase.
5. Her essay might be stronger if she offered some practical alternatives or possibilities, especially because she argues that the current landfills are "short-term solutions to the garbage problem" (11). This implies the need for long-term answers. But Rogers is more focused on waste as a symptom of a larger societal problem than as simply a permanent challenge to be addressed by practical, more efficient, "greener" waste management techniques. In fact, she casts a cynical eye on the "laboratories, universities, and corporate campuses" (12) that supposedly are improving trash disposal: they still don't deal with the provocative and "repressed" question at the heart of her essay.
6. *Environmental racism* refers generally to the intentional or unintentional practice of racial discrimination in the enforcement of environmental regulations and (especially) to the intentional or unintentional targeting of minority communities in the siting of polluting industries and waste dumps. This kind of discrimination might also include the exclusion of minority groups from

the private commissions and government regulatory agencies that determine policy or placement regarding polluting industries. Rogers does not provide demographic or socioeconomic information regarding the communities around Morrisville, Pennsylvania, where GROWS is located, so it's hard to infer from her essay whether she thinks environmental racism is at work. Students could research the history of the location to see how this location and community were chosen for the site.

Combining the Patterns (p. 190)

In paragraph 9, Rogers gives a detailed definition of a "liner" in a "state-of-the-art" landfill — an "underground bladder" designed to prevent groundwater contamination. But this definition hardly inspires confidence. In fact, it leads Rogers (and the reader) to consider the "100,000 gallons" of water "leach[ed]" by WMI's landfills daily: a "toxic stew" that would have "devastating" consequences if it seeped out. Similarly, she explains how cells are "capped" in paragraph 10 and illustrates how various layers of high-technology protection are put in place. Yet the paragraph ends with a vision of "outmoded appliances, dirty diapers, and discarded wrappers," which only reinforces her underlying point that these procedures are only short-term, superficial solutions.

Thematic Connections

What Happens to Plastic That Is Recycled by Us? **(p. 281):** According to Piranha Plastic's website, the company's recycling process ensures that no plastic sent to Piranha ends up in a landfill. Why is that important? In this essay, Heather Rogers looks at the significant, long-term effects of our (to her) shortsighted methods of waste disposal: "all those underground cells packed with plastics, solvents, paints, batteries, and other hazardous materials will someday have to be treated. . . ." Do students view waste disposal in the wider context of environmental consequences? Should they? How do they view practices such as recycling?

The Irish Famine, 1845–1849 **(p. 330):** In this student essay, writer Evelyn Pellicane writes about the causes — and consequences — of the Irish famine in the middle of the nineteenth century. The famine was caused by a disease that destroyed the Irish potato crops. But the disaster was worsened by other factors such as government policy errors and the "long-standing British prejudice against the Irish" (5).

Homeless **(p. 510):** Rogers's essay discusses the invisibility of landfills, as they are "places the public is not meant to see" (2). She wants to call attention to them. Similarly, Anna Quindlen wants homeless people to be visible as individuals, rather than as abstractions (the "homeless problem") or as anonymous figures, hidden away in shelters.

On Dumpster Diving **(p. 672):** Lars Eighner spent three years as a homeless person, traveling with his dog. He recounts his experiences scavenging for food and other necessities in "On Dumpster Diving." As it illustrates and examines the practical aspects of "scrounging," Eighner's essay also becomes an extended meditation on life at the margins of consumer society: "I live from the refuse of others . . . I think it a sound and honorable niche" (4). Given Rogers's criticism of consumerism, would she embrace the "lessons" of Eighner?

E. B. White, *Once More to the Lake*

In "Once More to the Lake" White evokes a vivid sense of a lake in Maine. The essay flows effortlessly and seems to be connected without a seam. White uses words masterfully, and students should be encouraged to see how he chooses just the right word to express his thoughts. Sense impressions abound as White attempts to convey to readers the way the lake looked and felt. At points the essay becomes a lyrical poem extolling the beauty and mystery of nature. It is important to tell students that White's essay is not intended as a model, but as a *tour de force* of descriptive writing.

Comprehension (p. 196)

1. The similarities and differences between White and his son concern their childhood experiences. The son relives some of White's experiences during his one trip to the lake, but White made regular childhood trips there and enjoyed a lake that had changed perceptibly by the time he returned as an adult. When he says, "I seemed to be living a dual existence," White means that, because he saw his son do the same things that he had done as a boy, he experienced the illusion that he was both father and son.
2. White keeps vacillating between the past and the present. In some ways the lake has remained the same as it was when he was a boy. But in other subtle ways the lake has changed and so has he.
3. White is disconcerted that he cannot sustain the impression that time has stood still at the lake. The change in the road shows that automobiles, not horses and wagons, now travel to the farmhouse. White seems to sense that, for him, life no longer holds the possibilities that it once did.
4. When White had visited the lake as a child, there were no outboard motors there. When he returned with his son, the sound of the roaring motors made the experience different than it had been years before.
5. White cannot maintain the illusion that he and his son are one. He realizes that like his father before him, he, too, will die.

Purpose and Audience (p. 196)

1. The thesis is complex and does not become apparent until the last line of the essay. Even though at the lake time seems to stand still, it really does not. White realizes that he, like his father, and even his son, is moving inevitably toward death.
2. The ending of this essay may come as no surprise to a careful reader. Throughout the essay White foreshadows his realization of the advance of time. The peacefulness of the lake, for example, is shattered by the harsh sound of an outboard motor. White says that "[t]his was the note that jarred, the one thing that would sometimes break the illusion and set the years moving" (10).
3. Although younger students will be able to grasp White's point, this essay appeals primarily to those in middle age. White's experience is not foreign to anyone who has watched his or her children growing up.

Style and Structure (p. 197)

1. White mainly emphasizes similarities between his childhood visits and his visit with his son. The main difference he notes is in paragraph 10, where he describes the jarring noise of the outboard motors that hadn't been present when he was a child; he also mentions the two-track road (three-track before) and the waitresses having washed their hair (7).
2. White says over and over that he feels as if he were experiencing his own childhood. He also says that although at first the lake seems unchanged, he realizes there are differences. Finally, images of summer, such as swimming and bass fishing, occur repeatedly. These repetitions reinforce the main point of his essay.
3. White's use of precise sense imagery enables him to transport his readers to the lake and have them see what he saw and feel what he felt. Much of the effect of this essay would be lost if White's audience read with detachment.
4. In his conclusion White realizes his identity with his father. No longer identifying with his son, White understands that he has taken his father's place and, like him, will eventually die.
5. There are many words your students might list, as most of the essay relies on sensory description. Although many of these words refer to the same sense, each is used in a unique way, depending on the context. Students will discover that synonyms are easy to think of but that they do not convey White's meaning as completely.

Combining the Patterns (p. 197)

By opening with a narration of his childhood visit to the lake, White sets the scene for his meditation on the inevitable advance of time that comes full circle in his concluding realization of his own mortality.

Thematic Connections

My Field of Dreams (p. 106): Both essays deal with nostalgic reminiscences of youthful summer days. White's essay looks back from a longer perspective, that of an older man, while Forte is writing from the perspective of a college-age person.

Goodbye to My Twinkie Days (p. 171): White's essay is a lyrical ode to a special place from his youth. He returns, "wonder[ing] how time would have marred this unique, this holy spot" (2). Bich Minh Nguyen returns not to a place but to a special food from her childhood, the Twinkie. For her, the snack cake is just as evocative of her youth as White's lake: "When I opened one, the smell of sugary, fake, buttery-ish vanilla took me back to my elementary school and the basketball lines on the floor of the gym that doubled as our lunchroom" (7).

The "Black Table" Is Still There (p. 348): As "Once More to the Lake" does, this essay provides an account of a return to a place. But where White might like to keep things as they were, Lawrence Otis Graham had hoped for change. He revisits his old high school and discovers—to his surprise—that the "all-black lunch table in the cafeteria" is still there. For Graham, the table is a "comment on the superficial inroads that integration has made in society" (17).

The Park **(p. 667):** Truong's essay, like White's, is a nostalgic reminiscence of early life. White's essay looks back from the perspective of an older man, while Forte is writing from the perspective of a college-age person.

Kate Chopin, *The Storm* (FICTION)

Coming after the essays by Rogers and White, Chopin's story provides a relatively simple example of descriptive writing. Set in Louisiana Creole country in the late nineteenth century, the brief narrative describes a passionate encounter between former lovers, now married to others, precipitated when the two are thrown together at the home of the wife by the advent of a violent thunderstorm. (The storm is, quite obviously, a symbol of the sudden, overwhelming intensity of the lovers' feelings for one another.) Their lovemaking leaves the two exhilarated, which ultimately—and, perhaps ironically—brings them both into closer happiness with their own spouses and children. Most of the descriptive elements of the story focus on the physical presence of the central character, Calixta, and on the storm that rages outside.

Students will learn from the headnote that the story remained unpublished for many years because readers of its day would have been scandalized by the unpunished act of adultery it depicted—even celebrated—in what would then have been seen as shockingly graphic terms. Do any find it equally scandalous today, or are people now simply more open to sexual expression? Another point to make is that, within Creole culture, men were expected to have affairs, but affairs were condemned for married women. Does such a double standard exist in any cultures students are familiar with?

Another topic students might discuss or write about is how this very visual story might be turned into a short film. Would anything have to be added or left out of such an adaptation? Could a film version of the story have the same effect as the written version, or would it necessarily create a different effect?

Reading Literature (p. 202)

1. The storm requires that Calixta's husband and son arrive home from the store later than expected and also leads Alcée to seek shelter at Calixta's home. Later, a bolt of lightning startles Calixta into Alcée's embrace, which leads eventually to their lovemaking.
2. Students' opinions may vary, but the events of the day do indeed seem to have left everyone happy—although Calixta's husband, Bobinôt, and Alcée's wife, Clarisse, would likely not be so happy if they knew the truth.
3. The details provided about Calixta suggest that she is attractive (12 and 22), nervous in the presence of Alcée (21), and passionate (23). She is also a devoted and loving wife and mother (33–36).

Thematic Connections

"Girl" **(p. 259):** The narrator of Jamaica Kincaid's "'Girl'" instructs her daughter in her roles as a woman and wife, imploring her to "walk like a lady and not like the slut you are so bent on becoming." The mother also establishes the girl's sexual role within marriage, saying, "this is how to love a man; and if this

doesn't work there are other ways, and if they don't work don't feel bad about giving up." How are these attitudes toward female sexuality similar to or different from those in "The Storm"? What is the relationship between the words *lady* and *slut*? How is female sexuality connected to—or detached from—domestic life in these two stories?

The Kiss/LOVE (p. 390): Rodin's *The Kiss* and Robert Indiana's *LOVE* sculpture both depict an image based on the idea of love, but *The Kiss* is about carnal love while *LOVE* is about love as a force that can unite humanity. Do students see a connection between the adulterous passion portrayed in the story and the Rodin sculpture? Or between the Robert Indiana sculpture and the marriage portrayed by Chopin?

The Ways We Lie (p. 471): What kind of lie do Calixta and Alcée carry out? What might be Stephanie Ericsson's response to this lie? What seems to be the narrator's response? How do students themselves respond?

Love and Other Catastrophes (p. 518): "Love and Other Catastrophes" is a tongue-in-cheek portrayal of a failed relationship spelled out entirely through song lyrics. Nonetheless, there are connections to be made with Chopin's story of adultery. Which parts of the narrative arcs of each piece reflect one another?

8: Exemplification

Before writing exemplification essays, students should understand that exemplification is a way of supporting assertions, not a rhetorical pattern. As the essays in this section show, examples can be organized in a number of ways. For example, Brent Staples uses narrative examples, while Deborah L. Rhode and Maia Szalavitz use examples to support an argument. Regardless of their form, however, the main use of examples is to explain or persuade.

When writing their first exemplification essays, students often worry about how many examples they need. They should understand that the position they want to support determines how many examples they need. The Alleen Pace Nilsen paragraph in the chapter introduction offers a starting point for this discussion. Although Nilsen's main idea appears as a topic sentence for a paragraph rather than as a thesis for an essay, it presents a general practice (the Marines' use of masculinity as part of their recruitment efforts) and therefore obligates Nilsen to provide a variety of examples. Of course, a general topic sentence can also be supported with one especially instructive example, and the same is true of essays. In most cases, though, essays will require more than a single example to fully support a thesis. For instance, Brent Staples is obliged to offer a variety of examples to support his statement that he can "alter public space in ugly ways" (2) because of his black skin. His indication that his experience is not unique among black men requires him to offer—at the very least—one other black man's experience.

Students also should realize that a personal statement or observation might not be sufficient to support some assertions. If they say, for instance, "Women do not have to face the problems they once did being admitted to medical school," they cannot expect to overcome audience skepticism with examples telling how easy it was for friends or fellow students to be accepted. To support this statement they would need to report the findings of a study involving hundreds or thousands of female applicants.

Four Tattoos: Charles Thatcher, *"Alisha, Loretta"*; Carrie Villines, *"Positive Outlook"*; Anthony Bradshaw, *"Bar Code"*; and Oscar Sánchez, *"Dragon"* (PHOTOS)

Questions 2 and 3 under *Reading Images* are important for students to consider here. The fact is that based on only these four tattoos—or even discussions with the four tattooed people themselves—students would probably not have enough information to form a valid general conclusion about people's reasons for getting tattoos. Most students would already have to have more familiarity with tattooed people to come to a thesis that could provide the basis for an essay.

Reading Images (p. 223)

1. The four tattoos actually have little in common other than that they are all positioned on the upper body and clearly reflect very different ways of expressing oneself with a tattoo.
2. Student answers will differ here (see the introductory paragraph above), but their statements could provide the topic sentence for a paragraph.
3. Again, student answers will differ. If you have no students with tattoos—or no students willing to share their reasons for having tattoos—you might ask students to talk about people they themselves know who have tattoos and why they chose to get them.

Thematic Connections

Medium Ash Brown (p. 277): Here student Melany Hunt recalls her impulsive decision to dye her hair—with disastrous results. Students might think about this essay and the photos of tattoos in terms of what happens when people regret changes they make to their physical appearance.

My First Conk (p. 283): In this excerpt from his autobiography, Malcolm X recalls the intensely painful process of hair straightening that many African Americans endured during the middle years of the twentieth century in order to have "good" hair (that is, hair that resembled that of white people). The tattooing process is also painful. What are people's different reasons for enduring it?

The Wife-Beater (p. 514): Many people associate tattoos—even those worn by women—with an attempt to enforce a sense of hypermasculinity, particularly when tattoos are large and prominently displayed. Does the popular name applied to the kind of T-shirt Gayle Rosenwald Smith writes about—shirts worn by both males and females and called "wife-beaters" by both—also suggest an emphasis on hypermasculine values? If so, what might this say about our culture?

Inked Well (p. 692): In this essay, David Kirby examines the contemporary prevalence of tattooing: the number of people with tattoos in the United States has increased significantly in the last decade. But he also explores the history of the practice, including the popularity of tattooing among aristocrats in the nineteenth century. The essay traces a change in Kirby's attitude as well—from believing that tattoos "were for either lowlifes or those who wanted to pretend they were" to his assertion that "tattoos are now officially OK by me" (22). Does "Four Tattoos" reinforce or challenge your views of this "body art"? What judgments do you make of people who have tattoos?

Kerri MacDonald and Jonathan Blaustein, *Food for a Dollar* (ESSAY WITH PHOTOGRAPHS)

In this series of photographs, photographer Jonathan Blaustein attempts to present food as it "really is." But along with the aesthetics of his images, the exhibit implies other questions about global commerce, American food culture, the value of money, different definitions of food, and the illusions of advertising. You might point out the different sensibilities—and even socioeconomic or cultural classes of consumption—suggested by the items in these photographs. The foods range from a fast-food cheeseburger and "potted meat food product" to saffron and escargot.

Comprehension

1. Blaustein was initially inspired by a cheeseburger in a New Mexico fast-food restaurant: "What caught his eye, though, was another menu, which featured a double cheeseburger for the same price. That additional piece of meat, and the extra slice of cheese, somehow didn't change the price." From there, he decided to see what food he could buy for a dollar—and photograph the food as it really looks.
2. He only uses food he finds in New Mexico because he wants to "let the global supply chain work its magic." The goal is to let his viewers "visualize" and think about how "interconnected global commerce can be."

Purpose and Audience

1. Students may have different responses and interpretations of these images. Clearly, Blaustein has a particular aesthetic goal. He creates some of the "same illusions as the ad industry," but does so to "represent [food] as it really is." Yet his purposes go beyond the art or representation. For example, he wants viewers to think about the "global supply chain" and international commerce.
2. Blaustein seems to assume he is producing art for a relatively affluent and educated audience that reads the *New York Times* blog. He expects them to make connections between an image of an American cheeseburger or a Chinese candy necklace and global commerce or the meaning of "food culture." The very notion of turning food into art in this way or asking questions like "What is food?" or "How should food be represented visually?" suggests a detachment from the prosaic concern of eating food to ward off hunger.

Mode

1. This question allows students to question Blaustein's artistic choices and assumptions about representation, just as he questions "images in the mass media." It also raises the issue of how to present something as it "really is." One might argue that *any* artistic choice—lighting, angle, arrangement, composition—suggests a certain level of artifice on the part of a photographer.
2. Students can use this question to explore their own reactions to the images—and what interests them most. For some, the choice might be formal or aesthetic or personal; for others, an image might touch upon the economic or commercial concerns that Blaustein discusses.

Farhad Manjoo, *No, I Do Not Want to Pet Your Dog*

Farhad Manjoo's "No, I Do Not Want to Pet Your Dog" was published as part of a regular Slate.com feature called "A Fine Whine." In this series, writers choose a peeve, an irritation, or some hidden-in-plain-sight, seemingly minor problem that nevertheless justifies a "rant." Manjoo's topic is likely to provoke strong responses in students on both sides of this issue. But you may want to begin by asking students if Manjoo is successful in his attempt at a written "whine," regardless of whether they agree with him or not. After all, the adjective *whiny* is a pejorative, so why would anyone choose to read an essay that is, as the writer admits, "curmudgeonly" and "churl[ish]" (15)? As a writer, how is it possible to fashion a long complaint that is entertaining, informative, funny, and readable, rather than off-putting or obnoxious? What do students think of this as a genre of writing? Also, you may want to keep the focus on Manjoo's overall intent. Clearly, he is not a "dog person" (8), as he admits. However, his targets here are dog owners and our culture, generally, not so much dogs themselves.

Comprehension (p. 227)

1. Manjoo seems to be serious, even though he may be using overstatement. His point is that pet dogs are now allowed to roam wherever they—and their owners—wish in "urban America," even "in places that used to belong exclusively to humans, and sometimes only to human adults" (6). Moreover, he is referring to the assumption that people must happily accept dogs in these spaces.

2. The writer includes several specific objections to dogs throughout his essay: they are dangerous and can be frightening (5, 13–14); they can cause allergic reactions (14); and they are dirty and do not respect social or physical boundaries (14). He finds them irritating in the same way that other people might find his two-and-a-half-year-old son irritating (16). One assumes that if cats were as omnipresent as Manjoo assumes dogs are, he would be irritated by them, as well.

3. Students may have a variety of responses to this question, depending (in part) on their geographical and cultural backgrounds or personal preferences (among many other factors). You might point out that Manjoo is talking primarily about pet dogs in relatively affluent urban spaces (gyms, "nice restaurants" (18), museums, etc.).

4. This information adds an element of seriousness to Manjoo's essay, which risks coming off as the "curmudgeonly" rant of a "churl" (15). His point that more Americans seek medical attention for dog bites than they do for choking and falls adds interest to his article, as well; for most people, these will be surprising facts.

5. For Manjoo, his son is like a dog because he can be loud and inconsiderate, he can violate people's personal spaces, and he can be messy and hard to restrain. Manjoo loves his son, but he does not assume other people will appreciate the child's chaotic presence in adult spaces (like "nice restaurants"). So, out of consideration for others in public places, he handles his son as if he were "handling nuclear waste" (18). Manjoo wants dog owners to extend the same consideration.

Purpose and Audience (p. 227)

1. Manjoo addresses different audiences at different moments, but this argument is primarily a call to action to his "fellow doggie skeptics": "Let's take back the peace we're owed" (21). You might point out Manjoo's subtle shifts from third person to second person in the essay. For example, he refers to "dog owners" in a section where he poses a hypothetical example about dogs in the workplace (10–12). But later in the essay, he addresses dog owners directly: "But let's leave aside the possibility that I'm scared (maybe legitimately!) of your dog, since you've assured me your dog loves people, and there's no chance you could be wrong. What if I'm allergic? Or what if I just plain hate your dog?" (14). Manjoo is not making a *Rogerian Argument* in this essay or trying to find common ground with dog owners; even his comparison with his son is more of a criticism of dog owners than an expression of empathy. He has a clear point of view and (for the most part) an uncompromising position: he does not want to pet your dog.

2. Perhaps the best expression of the writer's controlling idea is the proposal at the end of the essay: "Let's take back the peace we're owed. The next time your young, happy co-worker brings in his dog for the day, tell him the office is not a canine playpen. It's time to take that dog home" (21). He builds up to this statement by establishing several different premises throughout the essay (that dogs are omnipresent, that dogs can be irritating, that many owners are careless, etc.). As his position seems counterintuitive and cranky (as well as controversial and perhaps even offensive to dog owners), he saves the proposal for his conclusion.

3. Manjoo's essay can serve different purposes. If he cannot make dogs less pervasive or present in urban spaces, he would like dog owners to be more considerate and mindful. But he also wants to encourage other "doggie skeptics" (21) (he assumes there are many others) to stand up for themselves and resist the "cultural assumption that everyone must love dogs" (10). On another level, Manjoo is airing a grievance — and taking a deliberately provocative position — for the entertainment of his readers.

Style and Structure (p. 228)

1. Manjoo's anecdote is effective because it illustrates nearly every aspect of the problem that he is addressing: the omnipresence of dogs, the presumption of their owners, the assumption that everyone loves dogs, the potential danger of such pets in a place like a gym, the acquiescence of other people working out, and his own discomfort with the animal. It is a representative example that captures the essence of his grievance.

2. You might point out that Manjoo addresses different segments of his audience at different points in the essay: dog lovers, dog owners, those who may be ambivalent about dogs, and his fellow "doggie skeptics" (21). His tone varies. He seems to be exasperated when speaking directly to the dog owners (14); in contrast, he is encouraging to those who agree with him (21).

3. He tries makes the point that "doggie skeptics" (21) may be transformed into dog lovers by familiarity with such pets (or, perhaps, such people may be cowed by a society that requires them to love dogs). Given the pop-cultural prevalence of zombies over the last several years, some may find it timely and striking. Others might see it as an overstatement.

4. The writer is joking with this analogy between dogs and the music of Maroon 5. He asks readers to "imagine if, everywhere you went, whatever you did, Maroon 5 was always playing" (8). He concedes that this is a bad analogy because the band is enormously popular, so the comparison only reinforces the popularity of dogs. Moreover, given the band's prominence, Manjoo might also be implying that Maroon 5's music is "always playing" wherever people go.

5. These rhetorical questions highlight the ways in which the dog's presence in the gym is unnatural, "distracting," and "potentially dangerous" (8). There is an implied rhetorical question here, as well: why is no one else noticing this and asking these obvious questions?

6. At times, Manjoo is exasperated with dog owners (the rhetorical questions in paragraph 14); elsewhere, he is sarcastic: "Oh, OK then! I guess I'll just take your word for it [that your dog loves people], and forget for the moment that 1,000 Americans a day go to emergency rooms because of dog bites" (13). He tries to reason with them—perhaps condescendingly—by comparing his relationship with his son to dog lovers with their pets. He also scolds them, implying that they are rude: "But dog owners? They seem to suffer few qualms about their animals' behavior" (20).

Combining the Patterns (p. 229)

Manjoo uses these narratives to illustrate his points. His first anecdote shows the problems with dogs that he will address throughout the essay: it establishes their ubiquity, their effects on social space, and their presence in a culture where everyone is assumed to like dogs. The second narrative is more overtly explanatory: he introduces the section about his son by writing, "To give you a sense of how I feel when I'm accosted by your dog, let's replace that animal with my two-and-a-half-year-old son" (16). He uses the anecdote to communicate his frustration and discomfort with dogs to dog owners in a way that they might be able to understand.

Thematic Connections

Shooting an Elephant (p. 133): Carolyn Foster Segal classifies the various excuses that students use to avoid coming to class or completing assignments. Orwell examines the actions he took leading up to shooting the elephant and concludes that he decided to kill the elephant "solely to avoid looking like a fool" (14), which is a weak excuse for his actions.

No Wonder They Call Me a Bitch (p. 180): In this essay, writer Ann Hodgman indulges her long-standing curiosity about the composition and taste of various brands of dog food. But she also writes about the relationships owners have with their pets: "Although our dogs do nothing but spend eighteen-hour days alone in the apartment, we still want them to be *premium* dogs" (17). You might have students compare Hodgman's attitude toward dogs with Manjoo's.

Your Flip-Flops Are Grossing Me Out (p. 687): Manjoo examines the social and ethical implications of dog ownership in a light-hearted essay. In a similarly tongue-in-cheek way, Dana Stevens considers the growing prevalence of flip-flops in our society, and sees not only the practical and aesthetic problems with this footwear, but the social significance as well: "The crux of the flip-flop problem, for me, lies in the decoupling of footwear from foot with each step—and the attendant decoupling of the wearer's behavior from the social contract."

45

Judith Ortiz Cofer, *The Myth of the Latin Woman: I Just Met a Girl Named Maria*

In this widely anthologized essay, Cofer—Puerto Rican by birth—considers cultural differences between young Latina-American women and their counterparts from other backgrounds and how these differences have created certain negative stereotypes she herself has experienced. In addition to narrating several telling encounters, she relies on description and comparison and contrast to suggest some of the differences between her Latina and non-Latina classmates when she was a schoolgirl in the 1960s; cause and effect to explicate some reasons for these differences (as well as their results); and example to suggest some of the typical stereotypes Latinas endure. Implicitly, her essay is an argument to get Anglo readers to see past such stereotypes.

One way to begin discussion, especially if your class is made up primarily of students in their teens and twenties, is to pose the question of whether there may be any generational differences that color your students' responses. Cofer's essay was originally published in the late 1980s. Since then, Latino/Hispanic culture has come to permeate life in the United States more fully than it did at that time. Are the kinds of stereotypes Cofer writes about as pervasive now as they were when she was writing? Do images of Latina women in the media have the same connotations today as those she writes about? Obviously, you should encourage any Latina students to share some of their own experiences. How likely do your students think it would be for a Hispanic-looking woman today to suffer the kind of humiliating experience that Cofer writes about in paragraphs 9 and 10?

Another good subject for discussion is the persona Cofer presents. She comes off as very reasonable and very sympathetic in treating a subject that could lend itself to vehemence or victimization. How do students respond to this persona?

Comprehension (p. 235)

1. By "cultural schizophrenia," Cofer means that her family maintained its Puerto Rican customs at home while she had to learn how to behave in the Anglo world (*schizophrenia* is popularly used to mean "split personality").
2. Cofer received the conflicting message that she was to behave properly but to dress in ways that Anglo friends found provocative.
3. The first story makes the point that Cofer's appearance obviously is that of a Latina; the second that because of their culture, Puerto Rican girls of her day created a flashier image than their classmates; and the third that even when she was supposed to be the guest of honor at a function, she was taken to be a serving person.
4. Cofer says that Latin women are stereotyped as "sexual firebrand[s]" (6) or as menials and domestics.
5. In paragraph 7, Cofer attributes Latin women's "flashy" (4) attire to the environment of Puerto Rico ("a riot of primary colors") and to its climate ("where showing your skin was one way to keep cool as well as to look sexy"), as well as to the culture of Puerto Rico (women "were protected by the traditions, mores, and laws of a Spanish/Catholic system of morality and machismo"). Outsiders see their dress as sexually provocative.
6. The myth of the Latin woman is that she is a "hot tamale" (6).
7. Cofer presents herself in a way that shatters the stereotype she describes. We find her essay entirely successful.

Purpose and Audience (p. 235)

1. This is a good subject for discussion. In fact, Cofer's implied thesis would seem to be a combination of these three statements: "A woman whose appearance marks her as Latina is subject to unpleasant stereotypes that mask a much more interesting set of realities."
2. Cofer's point here is that Latin women without her education and professional associations are constantly subjected to stereotypes while she no longer is. She hopes readers will sympathize with these women and try to see beyond the stereotypes.
3. Its purpose — to get readers to look beyond Anglo stereotypes of Latin women — makes clear that it was intended primarily for an Anglo audience.

Style and Structure (p. 236)

1. We find this an effective opening because it demonstrates forcefully the way Cofer is regarded by outsiders because of her Latin appearance, the central subject of her essay. In addition, it's a good story, well told.
2. With "erotically charged" and "studied indifference," Cofer is suggesting the tone of the public mating game she is describing. Although "lost in translation" refers literally to a meaning that is difficult to express when moving from one language to another, here Cofer is using it to suggest how differently Anglo males ("mainstream culture") respond to similar stimuli, as it were.
3. We don't believe this discussion should have come earlier, as it is not the main point of Cofer's essay. And while an argument could be made for its deletion, the story about the luncheon is probably the most dramatic and telling in the essay.
4. From the first paragraph of her essay onward, Cofer provides several examples of stereotyping as well as of the disparity between the Latina stereotype and herself. All of her examples support her thesis.
5. Student interpretations may differ, but we interpret Cofer's poem to mean Anglo women hope for acceptance outside of their culture.
6. Students likely will find that, except for *senorita*, the Spanish words have no direct English equivalent (and even *senorita* makes more sense in context).

Combining the Patterns (p. 237)

Cofer uses a series of narrative examples in her piece. These personal stories bring her points vividly to life for readers and help to put readers in her situation as she describes it. The main disadvantage of using narrative examples, however, is that her evidence is anecdotal; her personal experiences may or may not accurately reflect the experiences of others in similar situations. Using other kinds of examples, such as statistics or references to studies on race and gender, might be effective, but would make for a very different essay. Cofer's narrative structure is her own personal style; it creates an emotional connection and makes for an effective essay.

Thematic Connections

"What's in a Name?" (p. 2): Cofer uses a series of narrative examples in her piece to discuss examples of racism she has encountered. These personal stories bring her points vividly to life for readers and help to put readers in her situation

as she describes it. Gates, too, uses narrative to recall incidents of racism from his boyhood.

Indian Education (p. 142): Cofer — Puerto Rican by birth — considers cultural differences between young Latina-American women and their counterparts from other backgrounds and how these differences have created certain negative stereotypes she herself has experienced. Similarly, Alexie tells of difficulties and challenges he faced due to stereotypes.

Just Walk On By (p. 238): Brent Staples considers stereotypes from his perspective as an African-American man. These two essays make an excellent pairing and would provide good subjects for an essay of comparison and contrast.

Brent Staples, *Just Walk On By: A Black Man Ponders His Power to Alter Public Space*

One way of approaching Staples's essay is to tell students about Lennel Geter, a black man in Texas who served jail time because of mistaken identity, which began when a woman saw him eating in a park each day and assumed his black skin was evidence that he was dangerous. She identified him as the man who had robbed a fast-food store. Students should also be aware of Yusuf Hawkins, a young black man who was killed in 1989 when he entered a white New York City neighborhood to inquire about a car that was for sale. You will want to ask students to consider the emotional effects of always being suspect. You will also want to stress Staples's fairness and ability to identify with his audience — a technique important for any writer of persuasion. Finally, you might ask students to identify Staples's clear topic sentences and to consider the number and kinds of examples he uses for each assertion.

Comprehension (p. 241)

1. Calling the woman a "victim" has meaning on more than one level. Staples's description of the woman makes clear that she *feels* like a victim, which, in a sense, makes her one. Staples understands that her fear is genuine: "It was clear that she thought herself the quarry of a mugger, rapist, or worse" (2). Primarily, however, the word *victim* is ironic. Since Staples was only "stalking sleep" (2), *he* is the victim of her paranoia.

2. He has the power to "alter public space" because people, fearing him because he is black, react as if any public space were a danger zone. They flee from such zones or even become a hazard to Staples himself in an attempt to protect themselves from imaginary dangers.

3. Staples walks the streets at night because he is an insomniac (2). He also refers to his walks as "constitutionals" (14).

4. As Staples describes it in paragraph 8, a "young thug" is created when he is "seduced" by the cultural idea that it is "only manly" to "frighten and intimidate." When he first robs someone who offers no resistance, he sees himself as a "tough guy," and "myth and reality merge." Poor men are more likely to become thugs because they are powerless in a culture that values power "in work and in play and even in love." Their powerlessness causes them to see chivalric, romantic nonsense as literal. Men with power are less apt to romanticize it.

5. Staples uses a variety of tactics to appear less threatening: He stays away from nervous people on subway platforms, especially when he is casually dressed; he waits before entering building lobbies when he sees nervous people; he is extremely pleasant when stopped by police; and he whistles well-known classical melodies when walking on relatively deserted streets.

Purpose and Audience (p. 242)

1. Staples states his thesis in paragraph 6. He acknowledges that some people may experience genuine fear of blacks, but he says that is "no solace against the kind of alienation that comes of being ever the suspect, against being set apart, a fearsome entity"—solely because of the color of one's skin.
2. Staples presents his appeal logically (This is what happens to me and other black men: these are the facts; these are the consequences), but students are likely to feel that it is because they sympathize with Staples emotionally that they best come to understand the point he is trying to make.
3. Staples seems to presume a white audience, in which case the preconceptions he must challenge are (1) that it is reasonable to fear all black male strangers, or (2) that white people don't really discriminate between black and white male strangers. He uses the example of himself as a way of challenging these preconceptions.
4. Staples's first sentence is intentionally misleading because the woman he describes was a "victim" only in her own mind. Staples's intention is ironic surprise, which works well in context.

Style and Structure (p. 242)

1. Podhoretz provides evidence that "New York mugging literature" exists. In addition, he illustrates a they/we approach to race relations when he says blacks "were tougher than we were, more ruthless"—as if all members of an ethnic community were identical. His remarks are, as Staples suggests, "infamous" (5); they create alienation.
2. The opening anecdote, developed with irony, is highly effective. In concrete detail, it presents a "victim" "running in earnest" from Staples's "beard and billowing hair" and "bulky military jacket" (1). An insensitive reader might make the same mistake that the "victim" did in thinking that Staples is a thug. However, in the second paragraph, Staples makes clear that his appearance did not make him dangerous—which is the point he tries to make in the essay. A sensitive reader will recognize his ironic use of "victim" from the "discreet, uninflammatory distance" (1) he maintained from the woman. Had Staples begun with an angry statement of his thesis, the unconscious bigot might have seen reason to be suspicious.
3. Staples offers many examples, but his assertion that "standard unpleasantries" occur with police and "others whose business it is to screen out troublesome individuals *before* there is any nastiness" (3) needs to be illustrated. He could also strengthen the essay with more examples of other innocent blacks who have had experiences similar to his. Although he uses an example of one other reporter, his assertion that "such episodes are not uncommon" (11) is sweeping.
4. Staples presents his examples in essentially chronological order, beginning with the first time he realized as a young adult "the lethality nighttime pedestrians

attributed to [him]" (7), moving on to the late 1970s and early 1980s when he was working in Chicago, and ending in the present—although he breaks this order in paragraphs 4–6 when he jumps forward to the present. Some students might see a strictly chronological order as preferable.

5. Synonyms for *thug* include *hoodlum, gangster, mugger,* and *gunman.* The more general meaning of *thug* suits Staples's purpose. The connotations of the others are either too weak or too strong.

Combining the Patterns (p. 243)

For the purposes of this essay, a narrative case study is probably more than is necessary—after all, Staples isn't writing about thugs, per se. You might direct students to another widely anthologized Staples essay, "A Brother's Murder," in which he does trace his brother's evolution into a thug.

Thematic Connections

The "Black Table" Is Still There **(p. 348):** Lawrence Otis Graham's essay offers a complementary perspective on black–white relationships and perceptions across racial lines.

A Peaceful Woman Explains Why She Carries a Gun **(p. 353):** Brent Staples, a black man, writes here about the fear he inspires in white pedestrians after dark, and the suspicions he raises by his very presence in places where a black man is not expected to be found. Unlike the white men Hasselstrom writes about threatening her, Staples himself does nothing threatening to justify such fear. Students might think about different approaches to protecting oneself from violence. Are they right to be wary, as Staples describes his "victims"? Given such wariness and suspicion, what might happen if more people routinely carried guns? Would the streets likely be safer or more violent?

The Ways We Lie **(p. 471):** Two of Stephanie Ericsson's categories of lying have particular pertinence to Staples's essay: facades (you might ask students the extent to which they think the actions Staples describes in his conclusion constitute a facade) and stereotypes/clichés.

The Wife-Beater **(p. 514):** Gayle Rosenwald Smith argues here that this popular nickname for a kind of sleeveless T-shirt creates "ugly stereotypes [that] are both obvious and toxic" (6). She suggests that such stereotypes can create a cultural climate in which violence against women is acceptable.

Deborah L. Rhode, *Why Looks Are the Last Bastion of Discrimination*

As Rhode writes, prejudice against "'unsightly' individuals" (1) has a long history in the United States. It has even been codified in American law. While the government no longer permits racial or gender discrimination, it does allow "businesses, schools, and other organizations to indulge their own prejudices" with respect to appearance (2). Rhode, a legal scholar, gives several contemporary and persuasive examples of appearance- or weight-based discrimination and their resulting lawsuits. She claims that "[s]uch cases are common" (6): according to one poll by the Employment Law Alliance, for example, "16 percent of workers reported being victims of appearance discrimination more generally—a figure comparable to the percentage who in other surveys say they have experienced sex or race discrimination" (7). Indeed, she argues that appearance-related bias is comparable to racial and other prejudices, and offers qualified support for laws banning such prejudices in the workforce.

Rhode carefully addresses various counterarguments—that attractiveness is a legitimate factor in making hiring decisions, for example, and that banning such discrimination will "trivialize other, more serious forms of bias" (20). Her scrupulous attention to the other side of the argument helps make her own case stronger. Students should bring a variety of opinions to this provocative topic. How do they evaluate Rhode's choice of examples? How well do the examples support her main point?

Comprehension (p. 248)

1. In a legal context, "looks are the last bastion of acceptable bigotry" because, despite expanded protections against racism, sexism, age-ism, and other prejudices, "bias based on appearance remains perfectly permissible in all but one state and six cities and counties" (2). Research suggests the deep roots of such biases, regardless of our race, sex, age, and cultural background: "Facial symmetry and unblemished skin are universally admired. Men get a bump for height, women are favored if they have hourglass figures . . ." (8). Our culture generally privileges attractive people, who are paid more, are more likely to get hired, and more likely to be viewed as "intelligent, likable and good" (9).

2. Aside from some state and local jurisdictions, the government allows appearance discrimination because such biases are not viewed in the same way as racism, sexism, and other prejudices.

3. According to Rhode, less attractive people face a variety of disadvantages: they are "less likely to be hired and promoted, and they earn lower salaries, even in fields in which looks have no obvious relationship to professional duties" (10). Similarly, "unattractive plaintiffs receive lower damage awards," while less attractive criminal defendants may get longer prison sentences (11).

4. Opponents of banning appearance-based discrimination make several arguments—that "attractiveness is job-related" and "can affect the company's image and its profitability" (16), and that legislation would "trivialize other, more serious forms of bias" (20). Rhode addresses and refutes these points specifically. She points out that so far, antidiscrimination laws "have not produced a barrage of loony litigation or an erosion of support for civil rights remedies generally" (22).

5. Rhode concedes that the laws are "unevenly enforced" (23) and that she does not want to "overstate the power of legal remedies" (24). But she argues that such bans have a "positive effect by publicizing and remedying the worst abuses" (23). They may also "play a modest role in advancing healthier and more inclusive ideals of attractiveness" (24).

Purpose and Audience (p. 248)

1. Rhode assumes that her readers are vaguely aware that appearance is important. But she suggests that most people are unaware of the depth and

widespread effects of this general bias: "We all know that appearance matters, but the price of prejudice can be steeper than we often assume" (3).

2. Rhode's broad range of studies and examples imply that her readers and the general population probably hold preconceptions and biases about appearance. According to one study, notions of attractiveness are "quite consistent, even across race, sex, age, class, and cultural background" (8).

3. The writer states her thesis in the concluding paragraph: she shows readers how to arrive at her conclusion. In the essay, Rhode establishes the reality of appearance discrimination to a potentially skeptical audience, shows how legal remedies would work, and addresses counterarguments. Essentially, she proves the reasons for her thesis before she states it outright.

4. Rhode's purpose is to inform and persuade. She tries to establish the reality and importance of appearance discrimination with her examples; then she attempts to persuade readers that legal remedies can "play a modest role in advancing healthier and more inclusive ideals of attractiveness" (24).

Style and Structure (p. 248)

1. Rhode's examples illustrate the serious and widespread effects of appearance-based discrimination. Her goal is to show that these cases are "common" (6) and that this prejudice affects society on several different levels—in education, employment, and even the justice system. The number and range of examples strengthen her point.

2. The writer asks this question because she wants it to seem obvious after all of her examples and evidence. The question implies that readers have considered the case and likely agree with Rhode that appearance discrimination is a real problem in need of a real solution. It also allows her to shift into her refutation of the counterarguments.

3. Rhode focuses on two main counterarguments: that market demands sometimes require appearance discrimination (16) and that banning appearance discrimination might "trivialize other, more serious forms of bias" (20). She addresses both directly and effectively; moreover, she makes a persuasive argument (especially after all her examples in the first part of the essay) that looks-based prejudice is analogous to racial discrimination, rather than being somehow less "serious."

4. She uses relevant statistics convincingly, and this evidence follows naturally from her argument and examples. For instance, she writes about a woman rejected for a job as a bus driver because of her weight, although the company did no testing to determine if the candidate could do the job (3). Later, Rhode cites statistics showing that physical appearance does affect hiring practices (10). So while her cases are striking, she also provides research to back up her anecdotal examples. The statistical evidence is more convincing than additional examples would be because picking several individual examples at random does not necessarily reflect a larger pattern. Statistics, if they are reliable, better show an overall trend.

5. Rhode strives to be relatively neutral in her language. For example, she uses the word *unattractive*, which is less charged than *ugly* or *unsightly*. At the same time, she highlights the insensitive language of those who practice appearance discrimination, including one description of a woman "waddling down the hall" (3).

Combining the Patterns (p. 249)

By using comparison and contrast, Rhode counts on a certain reaction from readers. The nineteenth-century Chicago ordinance seems like an offensive, slightly amusing example from a less tolerant time. Most readers will have an instinctive reaction against it: we do not have laws like that anymore. Rhode's point, however, is that such discrimination still takes place, although we no longer give the prejudice the force of law. Rather, these biases still flourish with the passive acceptance of the government.

Thematic Connections

Indian Education (p. 142): In this short story, Sherman Alexie writes about the discrimination and harassment of a Native-American student. In what ways do the protagonist's problems stem from stereotypes about his appearance? Alexie's style and tone are comic, even though the subject is sobering. Do the comic elements of the story trivialize a serious issue? Why or why not?

Four Tattoos (p. 222): You might ask your students what, if any, stigmas they attach to tattoos. They might also consider the different kinds of tattoos that are present in these photos. How, if at all, do they think differently about each of the people with the tattoo? Does it make a difference if the tattoo is of a flower or a cartoon character? Does a large amount of tattooing make a difference (as in the Oscar Sánchez photograph)? Also ask your students to consider the kinds of situations that might change the context for their views on tattooing. If they were interviewing job candidates, would they feel influenced by multiple tattoos on an applicant? Should they? What do they think Rhode would say about such a situation?

The Myth of the Latin Woman (p. 230): Judith Ortiz Cofer considers the myth and image of the Latin woman as well as how people project their preconceptions onto Latinas. As the victim of such stereotyping, Cofer often finds herself treated like a character in a "cartoon-populated universe" (10). Ask students how this problem is applicable to overweight people. Where do such stereotypical images come from? How are they misleading?

My First Conk (p. 283): In this excerpt from his autobiography, Malcolm X recalls the intensely painful process of hair straightening that many African Americans endured during the middle years of the twentieth century in order to have "good" hair—that is, hair that resembled that of white people. As with Rhode's, the piece deals with changing one's appearance—in this case choosing to suffer physically to conform to societal norms. Malcolm X sees hair-straightening conks as "self-degradation." Those who get them "violate and even mutilate their God-created bodies" (23).

Your Flip-Flops Are Grossing Me Out (p. 687): In a legal context, Rhodes writes, "looks are the last bastion of acceptable bigotry" because, despite expanded protections against racism, sexism, age-ism, and other prejudices, "bias based on appearance remains perfectly permissible in all but one state and six cities and counties" (2). Stevens finds a superficial or apparently trivial phenomenon (flip-flops) and suggests that it is the manifestation of a larger, more serious subject or problem (a breakdown of the social contract). Both writers suggest that seemingly trivial marks of appearance mask larger and more important societal issues.

Inked Well (p. 692): David Kirby provides a social history of the tattoo and its various connotations, including criminality, patriotism, decadent aristocracy, and self-expression. He writes that the practice "goes back to the dawn of human history" (20). From tattoos and piercings to conks, breast augmentation, and cosmetic surgery, what does this urge to alter ourselves physically represent? What warnings might Rhode provide on the dangers of such alterations?

Maia Szalavitz, *Ten Ways We Get the Odds Wrong*

Szalavitz enumerates ten ways in which people misunderstand the odds, from our fear of spectacular unlikely events to our tendency to downplay the risks of "natural" phenomena, such as too much sun exposure. You might have students offer their own examples to complement the writer's (or challenge them). You can also focus on some of Szalavitz's more general claims. For example, she writes, "Risk arguments cannot be divorced from values" (22). What does that mean exactly? If it is rational for us to look at empirical evidence or impersonal statistics and determine the relative safety of a behavior, how do "values" enter into an essentially mathematical calculation?

Szalavitz writes about — and complicates — the stereotype that younger people are more prone to risky behavior. You could start a discussion by asking students about their own views of risk management. How do they manage uncertainty about the outcome of their actions? Where do they see risk in their lives? Szalavitz claims that parents "worry endlessly" (16) about dangerous driving, teen pregnancy, and drug abuse; do these worries seem exaggerated? What risks and threats do students perceive that, perhaps, older people minimize or miss altogether?

Comprehension (p. 255)

1. She means that our instinctive assessment of risk is effective in the context of our evolutionary development, even if our instincts now lead us astray in the modern world: "Faced with a precipice or a predator, the brain is biased to make certain decisions. Our biases reflect the choices that kept our ancestors alive" (3).
2. We have been unable to develop effective reactions to contemporary risks because we did not evolve to respond to them. Our risk-response system developed over many thousands of years to deal with threats like animal predators, not with fast foods, chemical insecticides, car accidents, or "fear-mongering politicians" (3).
3. As she writes, the risks of "speedy motorized vehicles are newcomers on the landscape of life" (6). In contrast, our instinctive fear of snakes is an emotional response that evolved over a long, long time. That also means we instinctively react to cars coming toward us the way we react to predators (by freezing), which is the wrong response. We fear spectacular unlikely events because "fear strengthens memory"; the "drama and excitement of improbable events make them appear to be more common" than greater threats that are more likely to happen (7). Furthermore, media coverage exaggerates this phenomenon (7). We fear cancer more than heart disease, even though the latter is a greater risk, because we are "ill-prepared to deal with risks that don't produce immediate negative consequences" (9). We fear our neighbor's pesticides but not our own because if we voluntarily choose — or feel like we control — a risky action, then we worry less. If we think we will receive benefits from risk, we are more willing to downplay it (11–12). We speed while wearing seat belts because they give us

a false sense of security and because humans engage in "risk compensation": we modulate behavior to keep risk at a constant level (14–15). We fear radiation from nuclear power more than we fear radiation from sunlight because we have bias toward the familiar and natural: "We see what's 'natural' as safe — and regard the new and 'unnatural' as frightening" (26).

4. Our "risk thermostat" refers to our individual tolerances and preferences around risks; Szalavitz contrasts this to the notion of broadly "risk-taking personality" (20). People may have different settings for different kinds of risks. Thus, a person who sunbathes without sunscreen and drives dangerously may be cautious or risk averse when making investments or choosing heart-healthy foods.

5. When we overestimate the risks of the world, we subject ourselves to chronically elevated stress, which can harm us physically and psychologically (28). Understanding our innate biases can help us identify real threats to our safety and well-being; this understanding can also help us avoid "freaking out" over more dramatic or spectacular risks that are highly unlikely to occur (29).

Purpose and Audience (p. 256)

1. Szalavitz provides examples of common risks and threats, as well as our responses to them. She also explains how our risk responses evolved to deal with different threats than we face today. Without knowing the information in the first four paragraphs, readers would likely have only a vague idea what the writer is referring to in the thesis (What emotions? "[S]nap judgements" about what? Sensible when?).

2. This essay focuses on hard-wired cognitive biases and evolutionary tendencies that are common to all human beings, so implicitly, Szalavitz assumes her readers share them. Her use of the first-person "we" suggests, rhetorically, that she shares them, as well.

3. The writer's purpose is to inform readers about risks — and about the way our instinctive responses to threats may be counterproductive or even harmful. But she also has a practical and persuasive purpose: to examine our biases and show us how we can "adjust for them," manage risks more effectively, and live safer lives (29).

4. You might point out that while *Psychology Today* is aimed at readers with an interest in psychology, it is not an academic or professional journal published for experts in the field. As a journalist rather than a researcher, Szalavitz generally avoids highly specialized jargon or highly esoteric research. For example, she uses quotations from experts instead of quoting long passages from specialized publications. But general-interest readers might be more interested in more practical "how-to" advice about managing risk in their lives than the psychological or evolutionary background on the topic. So the article could be revised to include more specific suggestions about how to adjust for cognitive biases.

Style and Structure (p. 256)

1. The enumerated sections guide the reader through the different ways people misunderstand risks and threats. Indeed, while the essay uses exemplification and cause and effect, it also uses classification to sort different types of

cognitive biases and tendencies. Without the headings, readers might have a hard time distinguishing between the various categories and keeping the writer's examples straight.

2. The writer's range of examples is broad, thorough, and accessible. Her examples from everyday life (e.g., people at the wheel of four-wheel-drive vehicles are more likely to lose control during snowy conditions) help reinforce the notion of real, daily risks that are hidden in plain sight. Some students may be inclined to think that more specific instances are always better than fewer, but too many examples can be a problem in some cases: they can become distracting or take focus away from the writer's overall point.

3. Szalavitz uses scholarly authority effectively in her essay. She incorporates outside sources to answer questions and provide explanations. As she wants to highlight the relationships among evolutionary development, human responses to risk in the modern world, and various cognitive biases, the work of experts and researchers is essential. If she wrote entirely from personal observation, the examples — and any insights about them — would be limited by her own experience.

4. For the most part, the order of the examples is arbitrary. Some of them could be rearranged without changing the overall meaning of the essay (say, II and IV). Others cannot be: her final example ("We Should Fear Fear Itself") is a summation that leads to the essay's conclusion.

5. Szalavitz defines those words in their precise, technical sense, as she is writing in the context of psychology and empirical brain science. They are common words that some might use — or readers might interpret — loosely or vaguely, but she wants to keep their fundamental meaning consistent and specific. For example, the word *risk* can evoke a number of meanings or connotations in everyday conversation. However, she pares it down to its essential meaning in the context of her discussion: "uncertainty about the outcome of actions."

Combining the Patterns (p. 258)

In paragraph 6, Szalavitz discusses the evolutionary causes of our apparently irrational responses to certain risks and threats: spiders, snakes, fast driving, oncoming cars. This is one of the key insights of the essay; that is, our instinctive perception of risk did not evolve to deal with many practical threats in the modern world. In paragraph 10, Szalavitz highlights the cause-and-effect relationship between our difficulty understanding how small risks add up (the cause) and unwanted pregnancies (the effect).

Thematic Connections

Ground Zero (p. 175): Szalavitz writes that "we fear spectacular, unlikely events" (7), especially as we see images of such events repeated in the media. She refers specifically to September 11, 2001, noting that the "odds of dying [in such a terror attack] are infinitesimal" (28). In Suzanne Berne's "Ground Zero," the writer visits the site of the attack and contemplates the meaning and significance of the empty space — literally and figuratively. Ask students how Szalavitz's essay might help us manage our fear and anxieties about such attacks, as well as give us insight into why we react the way we do. Does it also give us any insight about why we might be drawn to the scenes of such events, as Berne is?

The Ways We Lie (p. 471): Stephanie Ericsson's essay classifies and catalogues various types of lying. How might we use lies — to others and ourselves — to manage our anxieties about risks and threats? For example, are those who "substitute one risk for another" (as Szalavitz writes in paragraph 13) while believing they make themselves safer behaving dishonestly? You might pay special attention to Ericsson's section on "delusion," a form of lying that she characterizes as a "survival mechanism" (33) that we use to deal with fears and risks.

Why Parents Should Let Their Kids Play Dangerous Sports (p. 616): In her essay, Szalavitz specifically cites the risks around high school sports (22–23). In contrast, Jeb Golinkin argues that parents may be becoming too risk averse about athletics: "Physical safety matters. But our collective obsession with protecting our children from harm threatens to turn out a generation of children ill-equipped spiritually or emotionally to deal with the brave new world order in which only the tough and the persistent will thrive" (10). After reading Szalavitz's essay, do students think Golinkin is getting the odds wrong here?

Jamaica Kincaid, *"Girl"* (FICTION)

At first, students may be disoriented by "'Girl'," as it does not seem like a conventional short story. It contains no real narrative, no plot, and little dialogue. Instead, Kincaid's brief fiction is a remarkable exercise in style: in a single sentence, the story conjures the domineering and often cruel voice of a mother telling her daughter how to be a woman. The mother offers a string of examples, covering a range of tasks, taboos, and behaviors — from the mandatory ("always eat your food in such a way that it won't turn someone else's stomach") to the forbidden ("don't squat down to play marbles — you are not a boy, you know"). In the process, the story evokes the limited sphere and strictly prescribed roles of women, as well as the harsh attitude the mother takes toward her daughter. For example, she repeatedly warns the girl to avoid "looking like the slut I know you are so bent on becoming," but the warning sounds more like bitter resignation.

You might begin by asking students about their own experience with parental advice. What is the mother in this story trying to achieve? What does she fear? Does she seem well-meaning, mean-spirited, or both? What view of gender roles comes across in the story? How might that view be different if the story showed a father advising a son? "'Girl'" provides a good opportunity to talk about stylistic choices as well. Why use a single sentence? We barely hear the daughter's voice in the story. Would "'Girl'" be more effective if Kincaid had included the daughter's responses to — and reflections on — the mother's advice?

Reading Literature (p. 260)

1. The speaker is a mother speaking to her daughter. The cultural setting is presumably Antigua, an island in the British West Indies.
2. The remarks suggest strict requirements for females, which include subservience to men and their needs. At the same time, "'Girl'" implies that women have some power over men ("this is how to bully a man"). "Being female," however, requires a wide range of skills and behaviors — from the domestic and sexual to the socially duplicitous ("this is how you smile to someone you don't like at all").

3. The story has obvious social and political implications. For example, the mother's advice does not suggest any educational or professional aspirations for the daughter or much of a role outside the domestic sphere.

Thematic Connections

"What's in a Name?" **(p. 2):** African-American scholar and writer Henry Louis Gates Jr. writes in this essay about his father being called "George" by a white man, though this was not his name. When the young Gates questions this, his father replies, "He calls all colored people George" (11), which is meant to diminish them and rob them of their individuality. Kincaid's short story is told from the point of view of a mother giving advice to her daughter. The mother in the story is domineering and cruel; however, unlike the white man in Gates's essay, the mother presumably means well for her daughter, and her advice is intended to help her negotiate what will likely be a difficult life.

My Mother Never Worked **(p. 123):** Bonnie Smith-Yackel's mother worked tirelessly on the family's farm for decades, tending livestock, sewing, cooking, and raising several children, among many other tasks. But "My Mother Never Worked" shows how society has often refused to acknowledge the domestic sphere as a site of "real work." Does the mother in "'Girl'" consider her own role—and the role she anticipates for her daughter—real "work"? What value does the work have in Kincaid's story?

I Want a Wife **(p. 502):** Writing in the 1970s, feminist Judy Brady takes an ironic look at stereotypical roles for women and men. Is there any overlap between Brady's characterization of a wife and the role the speaker in "'Girl'" imagines for her daughter?

9: Process

If your students have never written how-to essays, they are likely to assume that this pattern is useful only for recipes and scientific experiments. Even students who have written process essays will probably not have experimented much beyond "How to Play Monopoly." This, then, is your chance to introduce your classes to the possible uses and variations of process writing.

The paragraph in the chapter introduction from a college biology textbook allows you to review the difference between instructions and process explanations and the differences in person and tense these forms require. Your students can easily see how the writer would have altered the paragraph if he were giving instructions rather than explanations.

The first essay in the chapter, "My First Conk," draws on personal experience and uses process analysis as a vehicle for social criticism. Malcolm X uses his step-by-step account of how he got his hair conked for the first time to illustrate the degrading rituals African Americans were willing to go through to look like whites; his tone becomes increasingly angry. In "Getting Coffee Is Hard to Do," Stanley Fish deconstructs the complicated procedure of ordering coffee in a modern coffee bar. He reveals the complexities and difficulties in a familiar process that many take for granted. The dryly comic parody, "How to Retrieve a Candy Bar Stuck in the Lunchroom Vending Machine," gives a detailed set of instructions for dealing with recalcitrant candy machines. Similarly, though more biting and more ironic, is Arthur Miller's "Get It Right: Privatize Executions," which imagines executions as public events, not unlike professional sports contests, with a paying audience and a series of ritual activities. At heart, his essay is an indictment of capital punishment.

If you assign Jessica Mitford's "The Embalming of Mr. Jones," you will probably want to devote an entire class to the essay because the grisly subject matter and subtleties of tone and style will require a good deal of explanation. Shirley Jackson's "The Lottery" logically follows Mitford's essay since it also contains grisly subject matter used as a medium of social criticism.

By the end of the chapter, your students should have a dramatically altered sense of how flexible and significant process writing can be.

Piranha Plastics, *What Happens to Plastic That Is Recycled by Us?* (INFOGRAPHIC)

You may want to use this diagram to start a larger discussion about recycling, a practice that has become prevalent — even ubiquitous — over the last several years. How conscious are students of it? Do they think it is helpful? Do they understand how it works? Do they give much thought to the waste they produce?

Reading Images (p. 281)

1. Student responses may vary, depending on their learning styles and even personal preferences. One could easily imagine this explanation in prose form, particularly if it was presented in enumerated steps. A paragraph would require words such as *first, second, then, after,* and *finally.*
2. Student responses will vary. Some icons may be confusing or ambiguous — for example, the figure in the upper left of the flow chart holding money (What is being paid for? Plastic products? The services of Piranha Recycling?). The diagram also seems to elide the new plastic products created and "resold on the open market," as well as the kinds of plastic products that are discarded.
3. The ostensible purpose of this diagram is to inform about a process. But it also functions as an advertisement for Piranha Plastics. You might ask why the creators thought it was necessary to note that Piranha washes plastics with "biodegradable soap and water." This seems to suggest an environmentally conscious audience.

Thematic Connections

The Hidden Life of Garbage (p. 186): According to Piranha Plastics' website, the company's recycling process ensures that no plastic sent to Piranha ends up in a landfill. Why is that important? In this essay, Heather Rogers looks at the significant, long-term effects of our (to her) shortsighted methods of waste disposal: "all those underground cells packed with plastics, solvents, paints, batteries, and other hazardous materials will someday have to be treated" (11). Do students view waste disposal in the wider context of environmental consequences? Should they? How do they view practices such as recycling?

***Once More to the Lake* (p. 191):** Piranha Plastics is in the business of recycling. But people often see recycling as less of a commercial concern and more of a process that is supposed to help preserve the environment and the natural world. But what does it mean to "preserve" nature, which—like people—is always changing? E. B. White's "Once More to the Lake" filters a natural setting through the changing perceptions and sensibilities of a writer as he ages. In this lyrical and nostalgic essay, the lake of White's childhood vacations, a place "infinitely remote and primeval" (3) to him in his youth, becomes a medium for him to meditate on the nature of time itself.

***On Dumpster Diving* (p. 672):** People generally understand recycling as it is shown in the Piranha Plastics diagram—an impersonal process involving discarded products and packaging. Lars Eighner focuses on a more intense and personal version of recycling: he writes about a period in his life when he subsisted on what he could find in public garbage containers. His essay encourages readers to investigate their assumptions about materialism and waste.

Wired, Making a Mint (VIDEO)

This video provides a concise, illuminating account of how candy canes are made. You might want to have students consider how the medium influences the substance of process analysis or explanation. What aspects of the process is the video best at presenting? Which aspects might it downplay or have a harder time conveying?

Comprehension

1. The primary ingredients are corn syrup, sugar, and water.
2. Workers transfer the candy-cane mixture at various points in the process (e.g., in and out of the "puller"); they make the stripe patterns; they bend the canes in a mold; they taste the canes.

Purpose and Audience

1. The video is informative, primarily, but it is also supposed to be entertaining—a glimpse into a process that (perhaps) viewers have wondered about, but never have seen.
2. *Wired*'s audience is composed of people who are interested in technology and how things work. They are likely to have an innate curiosity about manufacturing processes such as this one, even though it is (in some ways) old fashioned.

Mode

1. The music is light and amusing. It gives the video a playful, semicomic quality. You might ask students how different music (industrial, classical, etc.) might change the meaning or effect of the video.
2. Students may have different reactions to this. On the one hand, the video—with its quick cuts and amusing music—makes the process seem relatively

easy. On the other hand, the process might include repetition, boredom, or physical exertion or stress that the video does not show. A labor union video presentation might present the grim or even dangerous side of the manufacturing process; an advertisement might focus on the fun or whimsical side of candy making. Likewise, the process might be presented in a different light if the workers spoke in the video.

Malcolm X, *My First Conk*

If you have a class composed largely of white eighteen-year-olds, you may have to provide some background on Malcolm X for them, although they may be familiar with Spike Lee's movie version of his life. Some explanation of the methodology of *The Autobiography of Malcolm X* is also in order. Although students may be familiar with Alex Haley's work, particularly the book and television versions of *Roots,* they will probably not know that Haley first met Malcolm X in the course of interviewing him for *Playboy* and that Malcolm X, pleased with this interview, proposed that he dictate an account of his life to Haley. For further information on the working relationship between Malcolm X and Haley, consult the epilogue of *The Autobiography of Malcolm X.*

Comprehension (p. 286)

1. A conk is a smooth, thick mane of chemically straightened hair. Malcolm X wants to get his hair conked so that he will have hair "as straight as any white man's" (21). At the time the process was performed, the conk was a status symbol; at the time he writes about it, he considers it a symbol of degradation.
2. Shorty asks Malcolm X to buy lye, eggs, potatoes, Vaseline, soap, two combs, a rubber hose and apron, and a pair of gloves. The purpose of each is explained in the context of the process.
3. The major stages of the process include preparing the congolene, applying Vaseline, combing in the congolene, lathering and spray-rinsing, drying the hair, applying Vaseline, combing the hair, and trimming the conk with a razor. All the stages are presented in chronological sequence.

Purpose and Audience (p. 286)

1. Malcolm X does not present the selection as a set of instructions because he does not intend his audience to perform the steps themselves; in fact, he advises against it. He merely explains an incident from his past.
2. The thesis is that trying to look like a white man is degrading and that blacks should concentrate on their brains, not their appearances, to get ahead.
3. Although conking is no longer a widespread practice, Malcolm X's general argument about black pride is still relevant. This thesis can be applied to many other instances of conformity (see *Writing Workshop,* p. 287, question 1) and to any race.
4. This emphasis on his discomfort supports his thesis by showing how much he was willing to endure for the dubious achievement of having straight hair.
5. Malcolm X's narrative is a personal illustration of his central point about the sacrifices people will make to conform.

Style and Structure (p. 286)

1. Some of the transitional words Malcolm X uses to move from step to step are *then, as, also, when, but, then, until,* and *finally.*
2. The process begins in paragraph 5; it ends in paragraph 19.
3. He uses the quotation marks to indicate sarcasm.
4. Suggested substitutions include *avoided* for *beat, room* for *pad, substance* for *glop, very* for *real, stylish* for *sharp, sophisticated* for *hip.* The substitutions weaken the essay because they are inconsistent with the overall tone.

Combining the Patterns (p. 287)

A definition of a conk would certainly include description, showing in words what the result was intended to look like. (The result is briefly described in paragraph 21.) It might also include cause and effect, indicating more about how the chemical nature of the process worked, and perhaps set up a contrast with a natural style. Students may have different ideas about where such additions might be inserted.

Thematic Connections

Four Tattoos **(p. 222):** Malcolm X sees hair-straightening conks as "self-degradation." Those who get them "violate and even mutilate their God-created bodies" (23). Do you think he would view these various tattoos in the same way? Do you? Why or why not? Is this form of "mutilation" different?

Just Walk On By **(p. 238):** The people in "My First Conk" treat their hair in order to "look 'pretty' by white standards" (23). Consider the impulse at that time to look more "white" as well as the significance of straight hair. In "Just Walk On By," Brent Staples writes about how he's often perceived in public as a criminal or a threat because he is a black man. As a result, he whistles Beethoven or Vivaldi sometimes as a "tension-reducing measure" (14): it signals to his potential "victims" that he is not a stereotype. But is that gesture a form of living up to "white standards"? What do Beethoven and Vivaldi signify?

Why Looks Are the Last Bastion of Discrimination **(p. 244):** Malcolm X sees getting a conk as degrading and "self-defacing" (26): a painful, pathetic attempt to live up to "white" standards of beauty. In her essay, Deborah L. Rhode considers how narrow standards of physical attractiveness still lead to discrimination and injustice.

Medium Ash Brown **(p. 277):** This student essay in the introduction to this chapter seems in many ways patterned after "My First Conk." The process described by Melany Hunt is that of dyeing her hair using a commercial product. While not painful, as the process of conking was for Malcolm X, the dye job leaves Hunt's hair "the putrid greenish-brown color of a winter lawn" (7). As she concludes, "I still have no idea what prompted me to dye my hair" (9). Students might want to consider why we want to change our appearances, and what happens when the attempt backfires.

Inked Well **(p. 692):** In Malcolm X's essay, the conk represents a self-degrading aspiration to look white, or appear "'pretty' by white standards" (23), regardless of the pain involved. Such body modifications have meanings both personal and cultural. David Kirby provides a social history of the tattoo and its various connotations, including criminality, patriotism, decadent aristocracy, and self-expression. He writes that the practice "goes back to the dawn of human history" (20). From tattoos and piercings to conks, breast augmentation, and cosmetic surgery, what does this urge to alter ourselves physically represent?

Stanley Fish, *Getting Coffee Is Hard to Do*

In "Getting Coffee Is Hard to Do," Stanley Fish takes an everyday practice — one familiar to most students — and analyzes its many components and complexities. According to Fish, ordering a cup of coffee used to be a quick, easy process. You sat down at the counter of an unpretentious diner and told a waitress or waiter what you wanted. "Twenty seconds later, tops," your order arrived as you were "settling into the sports page" (4). The sophisticated modern coffee shop, with its indie music, soft lighting, and complicated jargon, presents a new set of difficulties, which Fish sees through the lens of business management: the consumer faces a "coordination problem" (1). That is, when you order a grande café au lait, that task has "multiple and shifting components, the time for completion is limited, and your performance is affected by the order and sequence of the actions you take" (1). Fish's process explanation not only reveals how this procedure is carried out, but also suggests that its characteristics are evident in other places as well, and are representative of a "growing practice of shifting the burden of labor to the consumer" (12).

Comprehension (p. 290)

1. Fish describes the traditional process of getting coffee as a simple, brief transaction in a diner. He contrasts the details of the diner setting with that of a contemporary coffee shop, but the fundamental difference between the two experiences is in the ordering procedures: the "burden of labor" has now been shifted from the employees ("those who take your money" [12]) to the consumer.
2. Diners are nondescript, brightly lit, and full of Formica and linoleum. Today's coffee bars are "all wood or concrete floors," with self-consciously hip music playing and "photographs of urban landscapes" (5) on the walls.
3. Modern coffee-bar customers face various obstacles. They may be intimidated by the implied sophistication of the setting; coffee drinks are complicated and have strange names that are hard to remember and pronounce; there's no place to stand while waiting for your order to arrive; there's a "staggering array" of "accessories" (8) to manage once your coffee arrives.
4. Ultimately, Fish blames the difficulties in a modern coffee bar on a trend toward making the consumer do the work previously done by those paid to make and serve coffee.
5. As far as paying for the coffee, Fish does comment: "it costs a lot, $3 and up. And worst of all, what you're paying for is the privilege of doing the work that should be done by those who take your money. The coffee shop experience is just one instance of the growing practice of shifting the burden of labor to the consumer" (12). However, he does not address the sometimes awkward gap between ordering coffee and understanding when payment should be made — either before or after the delivery of the coffee. Perhaps Fish sees making the payment as a relatively stress-free part of the transaction and decided not to use column space to account for it.

Purpose and Audience (p. 290)

1. The first two paragraphs place the procedures — and difficulties — of ordering coffee into the context of business management. They give the reader a way of perceiving the general principle behind the specific problem Fish describes. Without this explanation, the third paragraph's reference to a "coordination problem" would be hard to understand.
2. The writer is describing the specific problems in getting a cup of coffee, but there are broader implications of his essay. People tend to presume that modernity and progress make for more ease and efficiency. Fish is pointing out that, even if we don't notice it, the current way of getting coffee is more difficult and less efficient than it was in the past. He sees this as part of a general shift in consumerism that requires customers to do more work (12).
3. He asserts his thesis in paragraph 2.
4. He does exaggerate the difficulty. For example, his parenthetical aside, "no bathroom breaks" (6), overstates the length of time it generally takes to order coffee. Even the initial analogy he uses with regard to coordination problems — a "general deploying troops" (2) — suggests hyperbole: there's no serious comparison to be made between a large military operation and ordering coffee. But the exaggeration is comic, and it also makes readers think about the real complexities of a procedure that they probably take for granted.
5. The "you" implied by the author seems to be Fish himself at times, as when he refers to the names of coffee drinks — labels that "never pass [his] lips" (6). But he's clearly presuming some level of identification with the reader. The second-person point of view adds to a sense of immediacy in the process explanation, which is heightened by the use of the present tense.

Style and Structure (p. 290)

1. Paragraphs 2, 3, 7, and 11 are all single sentences. Paragraph 2 could, possibly, be combined with the introduction, as it's an elaboration on the idea of the "coordination problem." The other three one-sentence examples serve as transitions (respectively) from stages in the process: from generalities about the "coordination problem" to the specific example of getting coffee; from the problems around ordering coffee to the difficulties the customer faces after the coffee arrives; from the obstacles around getting "accessories" (8) to the "problem of finding a seat" (11). Paragraph 11 could be extended, as it implies a whole new set of difficulties for the coffee bar patron.
2. The steps in the process are: entering the coffee shop and feeling intimidated; getting in line and waiting behind people making complicated drink orders; ordering your coffee; unsuccessfully trying to find a place to stand while your coffee is being made; trying to keep out of the way of others; receiving your coffee; trying to get "accessories" (milk, sugar, napkins) as others try to do the same thing; trying to find a seat. The process may be broken down into three stages: arriving and ordering coffee; waiting for it to arrive; and dealing with the "coordination problem" once you get your drink.
3. The premise of the essay, that coffee bar customers face "coordination problems," is itself a caution. Fish also reminds readers that they cannot take "bathroom breaks" (6) while waiting in line. Fish may include these notes

because his audience is so familiar with the process that they're no longer even aware that (for example) they "strive for a ballet of courtesy" (10) as they put milk or sugar in their coffee. He's not giving "how-to" instructions; rather, he's explaining how a process works, and connecting it to other processes (see paragraph 2 or paragraph 12).

4. Fish assumes his audience has a certain level of coffee-ordering knowledge, which might limit the necessity of a "how-to" article. More important, Fish wants to highlight a process that his readers are already familiar with and show its components and implications in a new light. Instructions would have been less suited to this purpose.

5. Some words pertaining to the specialized world of coffee include *arabica* (a kind of coffee grown at high altitude), *barista* (a person skilled in making coffee drinks), *espresso* (a concentrated coffee beverage), *French press* (a device for brewing coffee in which grounds and hot water are pressed through a strainer), and *latte* (a coffee beverage made with hot milk).

6. The writer seems puzzled, annoyed, and mildly amused. Implicitly, he also laments the loss of simplicity represented by the diner in paragraph 4. He's puzzled by the names of coffee drinks. His figurative language (bumper cars, ballet) suggest amusement with some parts of the process. But Fish seems genuinely annoyed at the "pain and trouble" (12) of expensive coffee — and the notion that the burden of labor has been shifted to the consumer even as prices have risen.

Combining the Patterns (p. 291)

The introduction provides a definition of *coordination problem*. Fish uses the specific procedure of getting coffee (as well as other, briefer examples) to illustrate and exemplify this general business principle. Paragraphs 4 and 5 compare and contrast ordering coffee at a diner versus a contemporary coffee bar. These two paragraphs also provide concrete descriptions of a diner and a coffee bar. In paragraphs 8–10, he narrates the complicated action of getting milk, sugar, napkins, stirrers, and so forth.

Thematic Connections

How to Retrieve a Candy Bar Stuck in the Lunchroom Vending Machine (p. 292): Stanley Fish writes about a "coordination problem" at coffee shops. Joshua Piven and David Borgenicht write about a less sophisticated (but equally frustrating) problem for those seeking ease and convenience: snacks that get stuck in vending machines. But while Fish wants to comment on a societal trend, Piven and Borgenicht dryly parody the conventions of "how-to" articles.

Tortillas (p. 506): Here, José Antonio Burciaga provides an extended meditation on the tortilla. The essay combines personal history, ethnic history, and process explanation. For Burciaga, tortillas are a food enmeshed in a specific culture. Can the same be said for the coffee that Fish describes?

The Declaration of Independence (p. 550): While Fish complains about the difficulty of getting coffee, the writers of this founding document attack the "repeated injuries and usurpations" of the king of England. You might have students consider the Declaration as a process analysis: the process in which tyranny becomes unbearable and justifies revolution.

Joshua Piven and David Borgenicht, *How to Retrieve a Candy Bar Stuck in the Lunchroom Vending Machine*

First, you might want to see if students catch the ironic quality of this selection. The humor of Piven and Borgenicht — here, and in their many other, similar instruction manuals for various quandaries and situations — is in their deadpan approach. They mimic the flat, imperative writing evident in "how-to" guides and other instructional materials. You might point out that even the most seemingly voiceless or styleless forms of writing (whether instruction manuals, warning labels, or ingredient lists) have stylistic conventions and a distinctive tone. Piven and Borgenicht focus only on candy bars. For a class activity, you might have students extend these instructions to other kinds of vended products and automated machines (soda machines or even washers at a laundromat, for example).

Comprehension (p. 294)

1. The first step — and the title — suggests what happened previously: a person has put money in a vending machine and ordered a candy bar, but the candy bar has become stuck.
2. One of the assumptions in Step 2 is that the person has enough money to risk trying to obtain the same candy bar, which may get stuck again. Step 3 might be a safer choice: you are more likely to end up with an item, even if your original choice remains stuck.
3. Students probably have their own experiences with stuck vending machine products. As vending machines are designed to promote speed, ease, and convenience, it would be ironic and comic to spend a significant amount of time (say, half an hour) trying to retrieve a stuck candy bar.

Purpose and Audience (p. 294)

1. There are different choices. One possibility: "If your candy bar gets stuck in a vending machine, there are several strategies you can use to retrieve it." While this thesis is implied by the title, students should be encouraged to see that such a thesis, as well as an introductory paragraph, would be needed to make this piece acceptable for writing in most academic contexts.
2. Any reader who has ever lost money in a vending machine — or who uses vending machines regularly — might find these instructions useful. People who own or service vending machines, as well as people in charge of the spaces where vending machines are located (e.g., a school lunchroom) might find some of the advice objectionable (e.g., Step 5, which involves rocking the machine back and forth). But students should keep in mind that Piven and Borgenicht write mostly to entertain their audience.
3. The illustration does show the process of rocking the machine back and forth ("not side-to-side"), which illustrates Step 5. But it also highlights the way in which these instructions are a parody of "how-to" articles: such instructional writing often includes illustrations of the process, with a human figure like the one in "How to Retrieve a Candy Bar Stuck in the Lunchroom Vending Machine."

Style and Structure (p. 294)

1. Other essays in the text are not composed entirely of numbered lists identifying each step in a process. This selection also includes alternative steps in the process. The most obvious absence here is that of introductory and concluding paragraphs.
2. The present tense and the imperative mood of this selection identify it as a set of instructions rather than a process explanation.
3. Readers may use these instructions the next time a vending machine item gets stuck. But "How to Retrieve a Candy Bar Stuck in the Lunchroom Vending Machine" is also written for the amusement of readers who may never follow the advice in the selection.
4. The writers include cautions and reminders in Step 1 (many machines are designed to sense when an item has not dropped and to return your money), in Steps 4 and 5 (vending machines can cause injury; do not hit or press the glass front of the machine), and in the concluding "Be Aware" note about the difficulty and danger of reaching into vending machines.
5. The writers use paragraphs and numbers to move readers from one step to the next. Students will probably understand that numbers work as substitutes for transitional words and expressions (e.g., *first, second, next, finally*).
6. They use the words *item*, *snack*, and *selection*. They might have used the generic term *product* or even a specific brand name (Snickers bar).

Combining the Patterns (p. 295)

Given the range of products available in vending machines, they might have considered the relative tendency of different items to get stuck (bags of chips vs. candy bars) or the difference between food items and vended beverages. They might have also tailored different techniques for retrieving different kinds of vending machine products.

Thematic Connections

Goodbye to My Twinkie Days (p. 171): Piven and Borgenicht offer deadpan advice about retrieving snacks stuck in malfunctioning vending machines. In "Goodbye to My Twinkie Days," Bich Minh Nguyen writes about Twinkie snack cakes in both a wider cultural context and a deeply personal context.

Getting Coffee Is Hard to Do (p. 288): As the writers do in "How to Retrieve a Candy Bar Stuck in the Lunchroom Vending Machine," Stanley Fish focuses on a process that should be quick and easy: getting coffee. But in the workings of contemporary coffee shops (like Starbucks), he finds needless complications, frustrating complexity, and an overall "coordination problem."

Rube Goldberg Machine (p. 335): Piven and Borgenicht offer complex directions on how to retrieve a candy bar from a vending machine; similarly, the Rube Goldberg contraption illustrates an overly complex way of achieving a simple goal.

Tortillas (p. 506): Vending machines have a utilitarian purpose — dispensing snacks, drinks, and "convenience foods" quickly and easily. José Antonio Burciaga considers one of the original utilitarian convenience foods: the tortilla, a "lowly corn cake" (8). In the process, he reflects on the heritage of the tortilla and its connection to his own cultural and ethnic inheritance.

Arthur Miller, *Get It Right: Privatize Executions*

Miller here shows us that the function of process in an essay can take some unusual forms. His purpose is neither to inform by setting out instructions for how to do something nor to describe the stages of an actual process. Rather, his purpose is to argue against capital punishment by describing executions with a horrifying pragmatism as public spectacles, to be attended by thousands and surrounded by the rituals of a sporting event. By outlining its hypothetical stages in vivid—if ironic—detail, he hopes to show readers that, even when not public, executions are a barbarous exaction of punishment.

One way to begin discussion is to ask students when they first realized Miller's true purpose. He doesn't begin to state it directly until the last few paragraphs of the essay, but he does provide ironic asides, as mentioned in question 5 under *Style and Structure*, that give hints of where he is going. And his description of the actual death in paragraph 13 and his reference to its reminding "those not contemplating murder . . . of how lucky they are to have been straight and honest in America" fairly directly suggest where he stands on the issue of capital punishment.

If you also plan to use Swift's "A Modest Proposal" (p. 699), you may want to refer back to Miller's essay to help students see that Swift is up to very much the same thing—laying out an outrageous plan in order to argue for the very opposite.

Comprehension (p. 298)

1. Miller describes the hypothetical process of a public execution. The steps in the process Miller describes are (1) the positioning of the electric chair on a platform in the stadium; (2) the singing of "The Star-Spangled Banner"; (3) the governor's description of the condemned's crimes; (4) the bringing of the condemned to the platform by uniformed officials; (5) a minister or priest's benediction; (6) a statement by the condemned; (7) the strapping of the condemned into the electric chair; (8) the entrance of the hooded executioner; (9) the pulling of the switch on a signal from the governor; and (10) the gruesome death of the condemned.

2. Student ideas may vary here, although the basic premise that such executions would take place in a sports arena with people paying up to $300 dollars for a ticket is itself quite outrageous.

3. Miller does not support capital punishment, as his final three paragraphs make clear.

4. Miller says that executions should be privatized rather than performed by the government because "government . . . is incapable of doing anything right" (2). Under current circumstances, "the thing is a total loss, to the convicted person, to his family, and to society" (3).

5. Proceeds from privatized executions could be used to compensate the prison where the condemned was held or contributed "to a trust fund for prisoner rehabilitation" (4). Public executions would also "provide a most powerful lesson for anyone contemplating murder" (13) and "an intense and educational experience" for the audience (14).

6. Miller's implication is that the use of alternating current to electrocute people is unwise, his point being that capital punishment is wrong.

Purpose and Audience (p. 298)

1. Miller probably chose this abrupt opening because he felt it would get his audience's immediate attention. It certainly is successful in achieving this purpose.
2. Miller likely expects various reactions: shock and even anger from those who don't recognize his real purpose and a measure of amusement from those who do (this is, after all, a very clever way to argue against capital punishment). You might want to ask students about their initial response.
3. Miller's real purpose is to suggest the barbarity of capital punishment, to make the point that "in executing prisoners we merely add to the number of untimely dead without diminishing the numbers of murders committed" (18). Miller would ultimately like to see capital punishment abolished.

Style and Structure (p. 299)

1. Paragraphs 2 and 3 could be combined, as could paragraphs 4 and 5, 14 and 15, and 18 and 19. Paragraph 5, however, has a stronger ironic effect by itself, and the point of paragraph 18 might be less obvious were it combined with paragraph 19. Short paragraphs are especially effective in the description of the stages of the process, as each focuses on only one stage or on two that are closely related.
2. The process begins in paragraph 7 and ends with paragraph 13.
3. Miller uses transitional words and phrases throughout that are related to time: *once the audience was seated*, *when she stepped down* (8); *then* (9); *next* (10); *finally* (12); and *instantly* (13). The only paragraph detailing the process that does not include some sort of transition is paragraph 11, and students may feel that a transition might be appropriate.
4. Miller also refers to the execution as an "occasion" (7), as "such proceedings" (16), and as a "spectacle" (17), the connotation of all of which is that of a major event. The word *execution* itself is essentially neutral and clinical, and thus suits Miller's tongue-in-cheek purpose. A substitute, such as "putting the condemned to death" or "electrocuting the condemned," would be more highly charged.
5. All three statements are intended to be amusing in context. The point that "no solution to any profound social problem is perfect" follows the objection that public executions might actually motivate people to commit murder. The reference to "offend[ing] good taste" comes as part of a process that itself offends good taste. And the condemned knowing "that he had not lived his life for nothing" is rather meaningless, considering that he is dead. Such phrases suggest to canny readers that Miller has another purpose in mind.
6. Miller suggests that public executions would be like sporting events in that they would take place in an arena drawing huge crowds and that they would involve rituals, such as the singing of "The Star-Spangled Banner." In the context of the essay and Miller's purpose, the analogy seems valid, but Miller doesn't really intend it to be valid literally. He doesn't believe executions should take place at all, let alone public executions.

Combining the Patterns (p. 300)

Miller's implied thesis is that capital punishment is barbaric and should be abolished. He hopes that his ironic description of a hypothetical public execution will encourage readers to agree, but not all students will likely feel that this description in itself is enough evidence to support this thesis. He doesn't actually consider or refute objections to his real argument; although in paragraph 16 he admits a possible objection to public executions that he does refute, he does not do so seriously. Like many arguments about highly controversial topics, Miller's essay probably wouldn't sway many hard-core proponents of the other side.

Thematic Connections

Shooting an Elephant (p. 133): In this famous essay, George Orwell shows readers that he felt he wrongly "executed" an elephant in order to save face as a colonial officer before a crowd of hostile Burmese subjects. Students might think about one main argument against capital punishment—that those later proved innocent have been condemned to death and even executed.

The Lottery (p. 308): Shirley Jackson's short story details another—but very different—process of public execution, though one that is no less barbaric. With Miller's essay, it would provide a good opportunity for analysis of comparison and contrast.

Who Killed Benny Paret? (p. 337): Norman Cousins's description of the killing of one boxer by another during a televised match provides an excellent pairing with Miller's essay. Here we find a popular sport that supports Miller's idea that there would be an eager audience for public executions. How might Miller respond to Cousins and Cousins to Miller?

A Modest Proposal (p. 699): Miller ironically—and absurdly—proposes privatizing executions for profit and entertainment. In "A Modest Proposal," Jonathan Swift also uses irony to suggest a barbaric solution to poverty, famine, and over-population in Ireland: "[A] young healthy child well nursed is at a year old a most delicious, nourishing, and wholesome food, whether stewed, roasted, baked, or boiled" (9). Like Miller, Swift's persona is that of a sensible, logical observer. But how does irony allow both writers to be both reasonable and absurd simultaneously? Does this satirical technique seem like a good way of addressing or solving social problems?

Jessica Mitford, *The Embalming of Mr. Jones*

You should have no trouble getting students to participate in a discussion of this essay; your problem will more likely be getting them to move beyond the essay's content to focus on style and organization. You might open the discussion by asking whether students feel embalming is a necessary process. You might also ask students whether they think Mitford is being fair in her attack, and where her bias is most obvious. An interesting footnote on the book from which this piece is excerpted is Mitford's essay "My Way of Life Since *The American Way of Death*," reprinted in her 1979 book *Poison Penmanship* (Knopf).

Comprehension (p. 306)

1. Mitford asserts that the public actually knows less about embalming than they used to because embalming is no longer done at home.
2. Mitford compares the embalmer unfavorably to the surgeon, describing the embalmer's technique as "crudely imitative of the surgeon's" (5). Later, in

paragraph 12, she likens the embalmer to a sculptor and a cosmetician, again unfavorably since the techniques described are neither artistic nor skillful.

3. The major stages of the process of embalming and restoration are laying out the body; draining out the blood and pumping in embalming fluid; removing the contents of the chest cavity and replacing them with cavity fluid; creaming the face; replacing any missing parts of the body; reducing swelling or filling out hollow areas; positioning the lips; shaving, washing, dressing, and applying makeup to the body; and, finally, casketing.

Purpose and Audience (p. 306)

1. Her thesis is that, if the public knew more about embalming, they might wonder whether they really wanted or needed to have it done.
2. Mitford seems prepared to have her audience disagree with her controversial thesis. Using such a critical, ironic tone for a sensitive topic reveals this.
3. Yes, she is muckraking in this essay. As her thesis indicates, she views her purpose as a kind of public service and expects her remarks to surprise, even shock, her readers. She suggests that undertakers are guilty of concealing information from the public that might threaten their business.
4. Mitford's judgmental tone helps to persuade readers that the process is in some ways ridiculous. Although her tone may not encourage readers to trust her entirely, they trust her enough to consider her thesis seriously. If she had presented the material more factually, she would probably diminish the interest of her readers.

Style and Structure (p. 306)

1. The essay is written in present tense, but its sentences are statements, not commands, and it employs third, not second, person.
2. Mitford's list of materials includes quasi-surgical tools, chemical preparations, and "aids to prop and stabilize" the body. The tools are described as "crudely imitative of the surgeon's," the oils and creams are labeled "bewildering," and one piece of equipment is given the negative connotation of "old-fashioned stocks." In general, then, the effect on the reader is likely to be negative.
3. To reveal her negative feelings about the industry, Mitford stresses the way embalmers distort language. She points, for example, to corruptions like *demi-surgeon* (5), understatements like *quite discouraging* (11), coinages like *casketing* (17), and euphemisms like *young female subjects* (8).
4. There are numerous examples of words that suggest surgical technique and cosmetic artistry that your students might list. It should be apparent to them that the number of surgical terms far exceeds the number of cosmetic terms, indicating that Mitford's intention is to ridicule that area of the embalming process more than the other.
5. Mitford quotes experts out of context and then echoes their words in contexts of her own. Examples of this technique include *rudimentary, not to say haphazard* (7), and *intestinal fortitude* (11, 15). She thus presents her remarks in a negative light and supports her thesis that the consumer should beware.
6. Some of the transitions Mitford uses to move from one stage of the process to another are: *To return to Mr. Jones* (8), *The next step* (10), *This done* (10), *The*

embalmer . . . returns to the attack (12), *The patching and filling completed* (16), and *Jones is now ready for casketing* (17).

7. Examples abound. See paragraphs 4, 7, 10, 11, 14, 15, 17, and 18. Mitford's many quotations from mortuary handbooks, even the brand names of the mortuary supplies, are also presented sarcastically throughout. The tone certainly serves Mitford's purpose, but it could put off some readers — particularly if they have recently lost a loved one.

Combining the Patterns (p. 307)

Paragraph 8 describes the different colors of embalming fluid, and beginning with paragraph 11, every paragraph includes some description of the corpse before and after "restoration." Each of these descriptive details suggests the artificiality and gruesomeness of the process and supports Mitford's thesis that if people knew more about it, they might be less likely to subject deceased loved ones to the procedure.

Thematic Connections

My First Conk (p. 283): The process described by Malcolm X earlier in this chapter is, like embalming, a gruesome procedure, and the restorative part of the embalming process serves a similar function: artificially creating an image that conforms to a culturally determined standard of attractiveness or acceptability. (As Mitford ironically notes, "*il faut souffrir pour être belle*" [14].) While embalming may not be a debasing act, as Malcolm X suggests conking is, students may certainly want to question its necessity.

The Movies That Rose from the Grave (p. 359): Mitford's essay provokes our reluctance to confront the uncomfortable facts of our mortality. In contrast, Max Brooks's essay reveals our enduring cultural fascination with the dead — and the undead — in the popularity of zombie movies. What aspects of death do these two essays reveal, respectively? Why might we find the images in "The Embalming of Mr. Jones" repulsive, even as we find grotesque and violent tales of the "living dead" alluring?

The Ways We Lie (p. 471): Obviously, embalming — and much of the ritual of funerals in the United States — can be seen as a certain kind of self-protective lie. Friends and family members want to see the deceased "one last time" so they can "say goodbye," but few would be willing to face a corpse *au naturel*. Stephanie Ericsson would probably classify our funeral practices in the category of *delusion*. Ask students to consider her final four paragraphs in particular. Is our avoidance of facing the reality of death a healthy aspect of our culture? If we began to treat death more honestly, would other aspects of our lives perhaps improve?

Shirley Jackson, *The Lottery* (FICTION)

Many of your students will have read Jackson's short story, but they will, in all likelihood, not have focused on it as detailing a process. Even more smoothly than Malcolm X's "My First Conk," it combines narration with process. Your discussion can help students differentiate between the two related forms of writing. Seeing the lottery that the villagers conduct each year as an inflexible process can also help students recognize that rituals are processes — although many evolve and change over time. Realizing that the villagers perform a traditional *scapegoating* will allow students to recognize other cruel traditions—traditions that continue to be observed for reasons similar to Mr. Warner's illogical justification that "[t]here's *always* been a lottery" (32). Malcolm X also participated in a painful tradition when he conked his hair for many years without thinking about its significance. He later came to feel self-contempt precisely because he was unthinking in his observance of a harmful tradition. Discussing the conditions that make observing a particular tradition a valuable process and the conditions that make it harmful can help students become more thoughtful about themselves and about the world in which they live.

Reading Literature (p. 315)

1. The first step of the process is preparation the night before the lottery is to be held. A slip of paper for each of the villagers—including the one with the black spot—is placed in the black box. The second step occurs the next day when the villagers gather in the square—first the children, with the boys piling up the stones; then the women; and finally the men. When everyone is gathered, the black box is brought to the square and placed on a three-legged stool. Mr. Summers, the lottery official, is then sworn in, and a roll call checks the attendance of the villagers. The next step is the first drawing of lots. After the family holding the paper with the black marks is identified, a "ballot" for each individual in that family is placed back in the box. When the family member who draws the black spot is identified, the final step of the process—the stoning of that person—occurs.

    Although the villagers still perform all of the steps in the process, they no longer understand the original significance of the steps. The only clue to the original meaning comes when Mr. Warner says, "Used to be a saying about 'Lottery in June, corn be heavy soon'" (32)—which suggests that the lottery must have been a fertility ritual. Now, however, a lack of logic marks the way each step is performed. The black box is used because "no one liked to upset even as much tradition as was represented by the black box" (5). Slips of paper are used instead of the original wood chips "because so much of the ritual had been forgotten or discarded"—which allows Mr. Summers to successfully argue that wood chips for a growing village take up too much space (6). The swearing-in used to involve "a recital of some sort . . . a perfunctory, tuneless chant" with the lottery official standing "just so," but "this part of the ritual had been allowed to lapse" (7). During the drawing itself, Mr. Summers merely speaks to each participant. The original "ritual salute" has been forgotten—further evidence that the lottery is not held because of its original meaning to the villagers (7). When the second drawing occurs, Mr. Summers asks the family members because "it was the business of the official of the lottery to ask such questions formally" (13). "Although the villagers had forgotten the ritual and lost the original black box, they still remembered to use stones" (74). These explanations are not particularly logical.

2. Although the village has forgotten the lottery's original significance, the fact that the villagers still perform all of the steps of the process, especially the stoning, suggests a dark, cruel side to the villagers, and perhaps to humankind in general—cruelty for its own sake and a sinister need to scapegoat.

3. As a scapegoat story, "The Lottery" has universal implications. Cruel, un-thinking traditions are maintained in many places in modern civilization. For example, novices are still forced to undergo hazing in order to be accepted into some military schools, fraternities, and sororities. Periodically someone dies from the cruelty of these traditions. Certainly, the Star of David pinned to the chests of Jews in Nazi Germany was the equivalent of the black spot — on an almost incomprehensible scale. Wherever and whenever someone is scapegoated — because of position, skin color, religious or ethnic background — the equivalent of the lottery occurs, and the individual is sacrificed to fill some dark need of the group.

Thematic Connections

Thirty-Eight Who Saw Murder Didn't Call the Police (p. 128): Martin Gans-berg's newspaper report about a woman in New York City being murdered while her neighbors listened to her screams for help, refusing to get involved, is another kind of horror story about an almost banal evil at the heart of a community. Al-though Kitty Genovese was not a scapegoat, the actions of her neighbors suggest a lack of human feeling that parallels that of the townspeople who turn on Tessie Hutchinson. Students may well say that "The Lottery" is fiction and that nothing like its story would actually happen, but they have to admit the reality of stories such as Kitty Genovese's. You might expand the discussion to include other ex-amples of members of our society "not getting involved" in the problems of others, from abused spouses or children to homeless people to functional illiterates. We would all probably say that, unlike Kitty Genovese's neighbors, we wouldn't ignore a person being attacked outside our window. Why, then, do we so easily ignore others with different kinds of troubles?

Shooting an Elephant (p. 133): Students should be able to see that Orwell be-comes a scapegoat when he feels forced by the Burmese crowd to kill the elephant. He feels he has to act as a traditional "sahib": "A sahib has got to act like a sahib" — or be laughed at. He is, therefore, "an absurd puppet pushed to and fro by the will of those yellow faces behind" (7). Tessie Hutchinson's protest at being scapegoated is more understandable than Orwell's lack of protest. She fears being stoned to death; he fears being laughed at. The Burmese natives show the same dark excite-ment that the villagers exhibit when they throw their stones at Tessie. The natives are a "sea of yellow faces . . . faces all happy and excited over this bit of fun" (7). The natives' "devilish roar of glee" (11), like the stone throwing, comes from the dark side of humanity.

Get It Right: Privatize Executions (p. 296): Miller's purpose is to argue against capital punishment by describing executions with a horrifying pragmatism as public spectacles, to be attended by thousands and surrounded by the rituals of a sporting event. By outlining its hypothetical stages in vivid — if ironic — detail, he hopes to show readers that, even when not public, executions are a barbarous exac-tion of punishment. Miller's implied thesis is that capital punishment is barbaric and should be abolished. Shirley Jackson's short story details another — but very different — process of public execution, though one that is no less barbaric. As a work of literature, it is subject to multiple interpretations, unlike Miller's straight-forward ironic essay.

10: Cause and Effect

Students are likely to find the concept of cause and effect intriguing but difficult; they may tend to oversimplify causal relationships or mistake chronology for causality. It is probably wise, then, to begin your discussion of cause and effect by illustrating terms (such as main and contributory causes and immediate and remote causes) with concrete examples drawn from current news events or from your students' own experience.

When the class has a working knowledge of terms and can apply them accurately, you can proceed to the readings. Since so many students confuse cause and effect with narration, beginning with two shorter examples will be helpful — the paragraph by Tom Wicker, which emphasizes effects, and the student essay on the Irish famine, which emphasizes causes. Then, you can move to the more complex cause-and-effect relationships examined in the chapter. Lawrence Otis Graham's "The 'Black Table' Is Still There" examines cause and effect in the context of race relations, as well as the writer's change of attitude over time. Max Brooks's "The Movies That Rose from the Grave" looks at the multiple causes and effects of our culture's enduring fascination with zombies. You might have students freewrite briefly about the causes and effects of one of the Chapter 6 selections (narration) and then discuss in class what they have written. Janice Mirikitani's "Suicide Note" may help clarify the difference between narration and cause and effect: ask students to infer the cause for the speaker's suicide from the narrative of the poem. Together, you might brainstorm for a cause-and-effect paper to show that students' causal analysis of the poem must take a form different from the original.

Jeffrey Coolidge, *Rube Goldberg Machine* (PHOTO)

Students may not know the origin of the term *Rube Goldberg machine*, even if they have heard it used. Goldberg (1883–1970) was an American cartoonist and inventor known for designing needlessly complicated devices that performed simple tasks. In addition to identifying the causal connections in this image, students might consider the ways in which *Rube Goldberg machine* has become a designation — and a metaphor — for *any* apparatus, mechanism, or system that uses needlessly complex or intricate causes and effects to achieve a particular purpose. It has been applied to everything from the workings of the human brain to the American health-care system. Ask students to come up with their own examples. What causes needless complexity? What are its effects?

Reading Images (p. 335)

1. The elaborate contraption's purpose is to turn a light on and off. The task could be accomplished by a single person pulling the chain on the light.
2. Nearly every event has a cause and effect in this image. It does not include the initial cause of the boxing glove's motion. The image does present a causal chain, where A (the boxing glove striking) causes B (the bowling ball rolling), which causes C (the pin falling), and so on.
3. The end result is a lightbulb turning on or off. In this machine, the main cause and the immediate cause appear to be the same: the movement of the

artificial hand that pulls the string that operates the lightbulb (which mimics the simple way a single person could turn the light on and off). But perhaps the causal chain is more complex: for example, the bird flying out of the cage and the hatchet falling on the string are remote causes, yet they are also essential to the final result.

Thematic Connections

Getting Coffee Is Hard to Do (p. 288): Stanley Fish analyzes the process of getting coffee at a contemporary coffee shop. In particular, he focuses on the "coordination problem" of what should be a simple procedure: the mismanagement of a "task [with] multiple and shifting components" (1). In what way is he describing a Rube Goldberg machine here? What has caused this needless complexity?

How to Retrieve a Candy Bar Stuck in the Lunchroom Vending Machine (p. 292): In both the Rube Goldberg image and in the visual essay by Piven and Borgenicht, there is an ironic quality: the reward at the end does not seem to justify the difficulty of the process. The various steps described by Piven and Borgenicht seem like overkill in a way that is similar to the complexity of the steps in the Rube Goldberg photo.

Aristotle (p. 481): In this poem, Billy Collins explores the nature of beginnings, middles, and endings. In the beginning, "Almost anything can happen" (l. 2); in the middle, "Things have had time to get complicated" (l. 28); the end is "what everything comes down to" (l. 71). Ask students how a Rube Goldberg machine might fit into Collins's poem, either literally or metaphorically.

Love and Other Catastrophes (p. 518): In this unusual piece of fiction, Amanda Brown traces the course of a romantic relationship through a chain of songs. Note, however, that the story both begins and ends with Eric Carmen's "All by Myself." Does it suggest that romance often follows the pattern of a Rube Goldberg machine: odd causal chains, needless complexity, and a simple, obvious result that might have been achieved more easily?

Arte Ideas, *Plastic Bags: How Convenience Is Killing Our Planet* (INFOGRAPHIC)

This infographic provides an overview of the harmful consequences of plastic bags; it also includes proposals for reducing their use and identifies the practical benefits of the proposals. You might point out how the writers not only identify negative effects and suggest solutions, but also show the direct cause-and-effect relationships between those solutions and the positive consequences of those solutions. You might also emphasize how the designers integrate data into the infographic, as well as provide visual representations of causal relationships to illuminate that data.

Comprehension

1. According to the infographic, it takes one thousand years for a plastic bag to degrade.
2. The writers propose a tax on the use of plastic bags, increased recycling of plastic bags, and the switch to more environmentally friendly reusable bags.

76

Purpose and Audience

1. The primary purposes of the infographic are to inform and persuade. The writers seek to inform readers of the harmfulness of plastic bags and persuade them to change their behaviors and support the writers' proposals.
2. The writers view their audience as educable and persuadable; they assume that by providing information (such as the number of marine animals killed as a result of plastic bags), they can inform their readers — and perhaps change attitudes and behaviors. The writers also seem to assume that their readers care about the environment.

Mode

1. Students should provide a range of responses to this question. You might ask them what suggestions they would make for adding more information to the infographic, removing information, or presenting information in a different way.
2. The writers present cause-and-effect relationships at several points in the infographic. The "Impact" section is probably the most obvious place, as *impact* suggests effects and consequences — as when the writers claim that plastic bags cause the death of 100,000 marine animals. But the other sections show cause and effect as well, as in the claim that taxing plastic bag consumption has reduced consumption in Ireland by 93.5 percent.

Norman Cousins, *Who Killed Benny Paret?*

Violence in sports — particularly in hockey, soccer, and boxing — remains a topic of great interest to students, who frequently have experienced it as players and as spectators. For this reason, class discussion of "Who Killed Benny Paret?" is usually lively. In this discussion you might consider whether sports have become more or less violent since this essay was written in 1962 and ask the class to try to account for the change. Has increased television coverage of sports, for instance, had any effect on violence in sports? Do the fans really want to see violent confrontations? You might also examine the *results* of this type of violence. For instance, does violence among the players lead to violence in the audience? Could frequent exposure to brutality in sports make people more tolerant of violence in other situations?

Comprehension (p. 339)

1. Jacobs believes people come to see a prizefight because they want to see a man hurt. Cousins strongly agrees, as the rest of the essay demonstrates.
2. The immediate cause of Paret's death was the blow to the head he suffered during the fight. Remote causes considered by the investigators included the referee's failure to stop the fight, the doctors' willingness to certify Paret's physical fitness, and the manager's role in encouraging Paret to fight. Cousins feels the main cause of Paret's death was the crowd that wanted to see him hurt.
3. Cousins feels it is senseless to investigate the referee's role because the referee did not have "primary responsibility" (9) for the outcome of the fight; he only acted as the crowd expected him to.
4. "The point" is that people want prizefighting to continue just as it is.

Purpose and Audience (p. 339)

1. The thesis of this essay is that Paret did not have to die; he died because the crowd wanted to see a man get hurt.
2. The case received a lot of publicity at the time of Paret's death. Even a month later, the essay would have moved readers to feel vaguely guilty about Paret's death. Because boxers continue to be killed during fights, the essay still forces readers to question their own motives as spectators.
3. This essay, which first appeared in the *Saturday Review,* is aimed at a well-educated general audience. It is probably too strongly negative to impress either of the other groups; for those readers, Cousins would have presented a subtler argument.
4. Cousins writes as if he expects his audience to be receptive to his thesis but not necessarily to agree with it. He tries to win sympathy for his position by building sympathy for Paret and other fighters.

Style and Structure (p. 339)

1. Cousins is eloquent and forceful, but the amount of detail is adequate only for an audience predisposed to accept his thesis. Many people, however, would find his argument to be slight. The fight promoter's testimony is one important piece of supporting evidence — but only one. Instead of accumulating other support, Cousins uses loaded language, saying "it is futile to investigate the referee's role and . . . [i]t is nonsense to talk about prize fighting as a test of boxing skills" (9). He asserts that "[n]o crowd was ever brought to its feet screaming and cheering" because of skill in a boxing match (9), but he fails to describe crowds at contests of skill instead of mayhem. He also neglects to interview referees and other participants.
2. Because the crowd pays to see a fighter hurt, if the referee stops the fight, the crowd boos; if the fighters dodge and weave skillfully, the crowd is quiet; if the referee does not halt the fight, thus allowing a fighter to be hit hard, the crowd comes alive.
3. In his conclusion, Cousins again refutes the two most obvious — but erroneous — explanations of Paret's death. The conclusion is effective because it firmly reiterates the cause on which the essay focuses and it forcefully sums up the essay's position.
4. a. For football, acceptable substitutions might include *general manager* for *promoter; football games* for *prize fights; on the field* for *in the ring; temperamental quarterbacks* for *boxing artists; dodging, weaving, grabbing, punching, and running* for *feinting, parrying, weaving, jabbing, and dancing; killers and hitters and maulers* for *killers and sluggers and maulers; victory* for *knockout;* and *players/play* for *fighters/fight.* (*Referee* would stay the same.)
   b. "The crowd wants the victory; it wants to see a man stretched out on the field. . . . It is nonsense to talk about football as a test of skills. No crowd was ever brought to its feet screaming and cheering at the sight of two teams beautifully running and breaking through each other's lines."

Combining the Patterns (p. 340)

The narrative introduction establishes Jacobs as an authority on boxing, someone whose negative feelings about the crowd seem justified. Because of his authority, his opinions lend strong support to the thesis Cousins presents. Cousins might have returned to his meeting with Jacobs at the conclusion to offer a final quotation to clinch his argument.

Thematic Connections

Let Steroids into the Hall of Fame **(p. 21):** In Cousins's essay, promoter Mike Jacobs says that people do not watch boxing to see a "tea party"; rather, they "come out to see a man hurt" (5). Students might consider the role of sports fans in Zev Chafets's essay, which argues that Major League Baseball and the Baseball Hall of Fame should accept the use of steroids in the game: if players "want to use anabolic steroids, or human growth hormone or bull's testosterone, it should be up to them" (12). Chafets believes that fans will accept these performance-enhancing substances. Given that baseball is ultimately an entertainment industry, should fans have the final say about such rules? Why or why not?

Thirty-Eight Who Saw Murder Didn't Call the Police **(p. 128):** Students can consider whether frequent exposure to prizefights (and to other forms of violence on television) can produce thirty-eight witnesses to murder who are not alarmed enough to call the police. (See also *Thematic Connections*, "Thirty-Eight Who Saw Murder Didn't Call the Police," p. 21 of this manual.)

Shooting an Elephant **(p. 133):** Both Cousins and Orwell discuss the power of public opinion. Looking at their essays together is one way of evaluating Cousins's use of evidence. Orwell recounts his own experience. Cousins, on the other hand, recounts no firsthand experience and fails to interview referees who, he says, continue fights because of pressure from spectators.

The Lottery **(p. 308):** Shirley Jackson's famous short story recounts, in fictional terms, a violent ritual that many have read as emblematic of human culture. As with the boxing fans who egg fighters on to greater brutality, the characters in "The Lottery" egg each other on to strike out violently themselves. Students may want to think about the roots of violence: Are humans at heart a violent species checked only by a veneer of civilization? Or is violent behavior an aberration that marks only a small number of people? Why are people drawn to violent spectacles? How, for example, do students account for the popularity of violent films and video games among so many people today?

Maggie Koerth-Baker, *Why Rational People Buy into Conspiracy Theories*

This essay should provoke a wide-ranging discussion. As the author points out, most Americans believe in at least one political conspiracy theory. Ask students about their own beliefs in conspiracies or experiences with people who hold conspiracy theories. As Koerth-Baker notes, some conspiracies are true (e.g., Watergate); she refers to one historian's observation that "conspiracy theories wouldn't exist in a world in which real conspiracies don't exist" (9). How do students separate the "real" ones from the untrue ones? She quotes a psychologist who claims that "[t]he best predictor of belief in a conspiracy theory is belief in other conspiracy theories" (3). Does this claim hold true for students?

Make sure to keep the discussion respectful, as some may take their views very seriously. But you might use conflict and disagreement over this or that conspiracy theory to discuss both "confirmation bias" (10) and the "backfire effect" (11). How do people deal with information that contradicts their opinions or with facts that do not fit their theories? These questions get at the heart of critical thinking. Indeed, you may want to use this essay to discuss logical fallacies that can creep into conspiracy theories, such as red herrings, appeals to doubtful authority, *post hoc* reasoning, and hasty generalizations.

Comprehension (p. 345)

1. You might ask students to identify the defining traits of conspiracy theories, which usually include claims that a manipulative, shadowy, or secret group of people have planned and caused some crime or event. They typically involve a cover-up: there may be an official account of the event, but conspiracy theorists dismiss such explanations as part of a wider deception or whitewashing of the "real story." Examples include the belief that the Boston Marathon bombings were perpetrated by a "mysterious Saudi with high-level connections" or even by a "rogue branch" of the U.S. government (1); fears of subversive Freemason, Catholic, or communist infiltration of the United States (4); the belief that George W. Bush helped plan the September 11 attacks (13); and the belief that the U.S. government created AIDS to harm African Americans (14).

2. They mean that a belief in conspiracies is a temperamental or psychological tendency, as well as a way of understanding reality. Such belief does not stem so much from any particular event as it is a way of interpreting all events. That is why "[t]he best predictor of belief in a conspiracy theory is belief in other conspiracy theories" (3).

3. "Confirmation bias" is our tendency to accept facts and information that reinforce or affirm what we believe, while filtering out or minimizing information that contradicts our point of view. The "backfire effect" is a phenomenon in which "efforts to debunk inaccurate political information can leave people more convinced that false information is true than they would have been otherwise" (11). In other words, stating the facts will not persuade people to change their point of view; instead, doing so will often cause people to dig in and hold on to false beliefs more firmly.

4. Belief in conspiracy theories seems more common in people with low self-worth, "especially with regard to their sense of agency in the world at large" (6). Such beliefs probably correlate with strong democratic principles because conspiracies often entail secretive, nefarious plotters "manipulating and circumventing the democratic process" (9).

5. The Internet helps to "perpetuate paranoia" because it exposes people to "alternative narratives" (11) and explanations of events. Moreover, conspiracy theorists and believers connect and identify with each other online; this "tribalism" leads them to "reinforce misguided beliefs" (12).

6. Rational people buy into conspiracy theories because (among other reasons) "[p]erfectly sane minds possess an incredible capacity for developing narratives" (5). That is, when we face threats, disasters, frightening events, and uncertainty, our brains try to analyze, interpret, reassess, and process information in a way that is coherent and meaningful. Plus, it can be comforting and emotionally satisfying to feel like we know the "truth" while others do not (8).

7. She believes that conspiratorial thinking can be "pernicious" (5). It can make people feel like they are in control of events or important issues, even when they are not. She cites a study that suggests that exposure to conspiracies can leave people disengaged and apathetic in the face of real problems (13).

Purpose and Audience (p. 345)

1. Koerth-Baker is a science journalist, writing for a general audience in the *New York Times*. Her style reflects her purpose: she is sharing information and research, particularly the work of psychologist Viren Swami. This purpose is distinctive from that of a scientist or specialist writing for other specialists in a field. Koerth-Baker needs to reach a wider audience and introduce them to ideas without being too technical or specialized.

2. All the experts and authorities she cites (across a range of disciplines) support her point about the persistence of conspiracy theories, as well as the ways in which these theories are more than merely individual responses to specific events. From Viren Swami and scientist Paul Whalen to Richard Hofstadter, her sources suggest that a tendency toward conspiratorial thinking is a temperamental trait, a psychological impulse, and a comprehensive way of making sense of the world.

3. Conspiracy theorists are often dismissed as marginal crackpots and crazy people: a clear line can be drawn between people who believe that, say, extraterrestrial aliens run the U.S. government and people who do not. Koerth-Baker's point is that conspiratorial thinking is a broadly human, psychological phenomenon that even rational people (like her implied audience) engage in at times. As she points out with the statistic in paragraph 5, most people "believe in at least one conspiracy theory."

4. As written, none of these statements makes an ideal thesis, but as prompts, they should start a conversation about what this essay is about — and encourage students to articulate a thesis in their own words. The first example could be revised into a thesis along the lines of: "Conspiracy theories and theorists may seem crazy, but most people — even the sanest among us — share a tendency toward conspiratorial thinking and even paranoid beliefs." The last two examples seem more like supporting examples or secondary aspects of the topic than prospective thesis statements.

Style and Structure (p. 346)

1. The writer focuses on effects primarily in paragraphs 13 and 14. For example, she writes about how a belief in conspiracy theories can lead to apathy, disengagement, and high-risk behaviors.

2. There are different causal chains running through the essay. For example, Koerth-Baker shows how moments of powerlessness and uncertainty stimulate part of the brain (the amygdala), which sends "the rest of the brain into analytical overdrive," which, in turn, prompts attempts at creating a "coherent and understandable narrative" (7). This causal chain, which results in the creation of explanatory stories about things that happen, can lead to conspiracy theories and paranoia. You might point out that causes and effects blend with each other in this essay. For example, do people believe in conspiracies because

they feel powerless and cynical? Or do people feel powerless and cynical because they are inclined to believe in conspiracy theories?

3. The use of the term *paranoia* is common outside clinical and medical contexts. You might want to consider the different ways a psychiatrist might apply the term and the way someone might use the word in general, everyday conversation ("I am really paranoid about something getting spilled on this dress"). Similarly, you might ask whether there are times when being "paranoid" is rational or sensible.

Combining the Patterns (p. 347)

Koerth-Baker uses several different examples of conspiracy theories in this essay. Obviously, such instances can be helpful when explaining a point. But note that her purpose is not to compile a catalogue or history of curious or prominent conspiracies; rather, her focus is on explaining the prevalence of such thinking and its relationship to certain psychological tendencies in human beings.

Thematic Connections

Ground Zero (p. 175): According to Koerth-Baker's article, people sometimes turn to conspiracy theories to make sense of anxiety, uncertainty, and upsetting events. Conspiracies can provide meaningful, explanatory narratives — even if these accounts are false. In "Ground Zero," Suzanne Berne visits the site of the September 11, 2001, attacks, and finds herself — and others — struggling to understand what she is seeing: "Again and again I heard people say, 'It's unbelievable.' And then they would turn to each other, dissatisfied. They wanted to say something more expressive, more meaningful" (12). How might such an event lead to paranoia and conspiratorial thinking? How does Berne avoid that tendency in her essay?

Just Walk On By (p. 238): In this selection, Brent Staples writes about the fear he instills in people merely by being a black man walking in public: he hears car doors lock, and he sees women cross the street to avoid him. While this is a personal essay, Staples's account suggests the problematic nature of race in America. But it is also an essay about paranoia and the toll it can take on those who are the object of irrational fear: Staples observes, "In time, I learned to smother the rage I felt at so often being taken for a criminal" (12). You might have students consider how difference — racial, cultural, national, and otherwise — can contribute to paranoia.

The Lottery (p. 308): Shirley Jackson's haunting and eerily understated story about small-town customs and scapegoating might make a provocative counterpoint to Koerth-Baker's essay. Conspiracy and paranoia are often aroused by the fear of outsiders, but Jackson's tale is about a close-knit community. What cultural or psychological need does the story's ritual serve for members of that community? What is it a response to, if anything?

The Ways We Lie (p. 471): In this essay, Stephanie Ericsson identifies and classifies various types of lying, from "white lies" to delusion. You might have students consider the ways such lies can abet — or overlap with — conspiratorial thinking. For example, how are conspiracy theories related to the practices of ignoring the plain facts, relying on stereotypes, or participating in groupthink? Likewise, how might conspiracy theorists respond to criticism by using dismissal?

Lawrence Otis Graham, *The "Black Table" Is Still There*

Graham's essay about the "self-imposed" segregation of black students in his junior high school cafeteria — something he was saddened to see was still in effect when he returned to the school almost fifteen years after he had been a student there in the 1970s — is likely to spark interesting class discussion. For one thing, Graham describes himself as having had mostly white friends in junior high and so avoided the "black table" because he feared that if he sat there he would lose them. He also describes the "blatantly racist" (13) behavior of some of his white friends — behavior he endured without protest, still blaming the black students, rather than "white bigotry" (11), for their self-segregation. Finally he notes that his junior high school cafeteria in fact included a number of tables segregated by ethnicity, gender, and personal interests. Why, he asks, does a "black table" receive so much more criticism than these other forms of self-segregation? Opinion on these issues will vary, but it is likely that students can point to concrete examples of such self-segregation in their own lives — perhaps even on campus.

Comprehension (p. 350)

1. The "black table" is the cafeteria table where the few black students in a largely white school choose to eat together, separate from other students.
2. He was surprised because he expected more integration after fourteen years.
3. See paragraph 14. Where students sat depended on race, religion, gender, ethnicity, and personal interests.
4. He was afraid he would lose all his white friends if he did.
5. As a student, he blamed the other black students for segregating themselves. Now he sees the causes as more complex: blacks wanting to associate with blacks as other groups tend to do and the lingering racism that continues to make blacks uncomfortable with whites.

Purpose and Audience (p. 350)

1. Graham states his thesis in the first sentence of his final paragraph.
2. The opinions and anecdotal evidence Graham offers seem to be enough for his purpose of drawing a personal conclusion. But students may not think he succeeds in supporting a larger argumentative thesis.
3. Black and white students may respond differently to Graham's portrait of himself as a lone African-American man breaking color barriers in a largely white world. Some students may think that a bit more information about the racial/ethnic makeup of the school might be interesting.
4. Answers here will vary. To change his audience's view of "black tables" would seem to be his conscious purpose.
5. Throughout, Graham suggests that he was closer to white culture than to black culture as a youth.

Style and Structure (p. 351)

1. Again, black and white students may have different responses. You might ask if *African-American table* has different connotations. Students may offer some

pejorative terms as they invent names for the other tables. If so, explore what this suggests about the nature of such labels.

2. Graham asks rhetorical questions in paragraphs 3, 7, and 10. These suggest his attempt to work through the issues both as a young student and as an adult.
3. These quotations suggest the dilemma he faced — scorned by blacks, yet a black "voice" for whites. Answers will vary as to the need for more quotations.
4. Graham focuses basically on finding causes.
5. Graham's personal, informal style is appropriate for the personal nature of his conclusions.

Combining the Patterns (p. 352)

Paragraph 14 classifies students according to where they sit in the lunchroom — and, by extension, according to how they identify themselves. Students will likely come up with other such categories. This strategy is appropriate because Graham's purpose is to get readers to think about the nature of such classifications.

Thematic Connections

Indian Education (p. 142): Sherman Alexie writes in this short story about a different form of segregation in education: the reservation schools attended by Native Americans. Unlike most of his peers, Alexie's protagonist chooses to attend junior high and high school at a school in town attended by mostly white students. Like those at the "black table" in Graham's essay — and like Graham himself — Alexie's protagonist finds himself part of a definite minority, though he does what he can to fit in. Reading these two selections offers an opportunity to consider how minorities find a voice for themselves within the dominant culture of an educational institution.

The Myth of the Latin Woman (p. 230): Here, Judith Ortiz Cofer examines clichés about Latina women and how they've affected her as a Puerto Rican growing up in the United States: "wanting like most children to 'belong,' I resented the stereotype that my Hispanic appearance called forth from many people I met" (2). But the stereotype persists into Cofer's adulthood. Is she an "integrating" Latin woman, just as Graham is an "integrating black person" (16)? In what ways is her relationship to her ethnic identity like Graham's relationship to his race?

Just Walk On By (p. 238): Graham describes himself as an "integrating black person" (16). Brent Staples offers another example of the dilemma facing an "integrating black person" who faces a certain level of stereotyping by whites.

College Pressures (p. 448): William Zinsser's essay focuses on education in a different sense: the burnout college students can experience, particularly at highly competitive institutions like those Graham helped to integrate.

Linda M. Hasselstrom, *A Peaceful Woman Explains Why She Carries a Gun*

This essay is a good example of a personal causal explanation — Hasselstrom is not attempting to explain the causes of some social phenomenon, but only to explain what led her, a self-described pacifist, to begin carrying a gun. At the same time, she raises larger questions about equality between women and men and about the power their greater strength gives men over women. One way to begin discussion would be to ask if any of the women in your class would carry—or would consider carrying—a gun to protect themselves specifically from sexual assault (as opposed to, say, robbery). Another is to question students about their experiences with the kinds of threatening situations in which Hasselstrom finds herself.

Comprehension (p. 357)

1. Hasselstrom carries a gun for self-protection after having too often found herself in situations in which she felt threatened by men.
2. Students should easily be able to point to the specific events that led to her decision.
3. She considered acquiring a CB radio, and she studied kung fu. The first she rejected because she realized that in calling for help she might in fact attract an assailant, and she came to see that her kung fu skills required expertise if she were to protect herself successfully from a large man. In one instance, she mentions the possibility of carrying Mace, but says that she was warned by local police that Mace is illegal; in fact, Mace remains an alternative to a gun.
4. She mentions her reluctance in paragraphs 12 and 25.
5. She again refers to the dangers of carrying a gun in her final paragraph.
6. She means that before she drew her gun, the men considered her an easy mark and felt no compunction about giving her a hard time. Once they realized she had a gun, though, they did what she requested.

Purpose and Audience (p. 357)

1. In her introduction, Hasselstrom suggests that she writes only because others might find her personal reasoning interesting. Students may recognize, however, that her larger purpose is to examine the physical balance of power between women and men.
2. Paragraph 5 serves to suggest the extent to which women are vulnerable. While Hasselstrom doesn't say whether she herself has been raped, the story about an actual rape victim graphically demonstrates the danger.
3. Students will probably see the essay as speaking more acutely to women; however, we believe it has something to say to men as well. After all, Hasselstrom's central point is that if men behaved differently, she wouldn't need to carry a gun.
4. If not necessarily to agree, Hasselstrom clearly wants readers to at least understand her decision. She most clearly responds to readers' challenges with her final story of using the gun to achieve respect from the men trespassing on her property.

Style and Structure (p. 357)

1. Students might see it as a weakness that Hasselstrom doesn't try to explain the extent to which women generally are in danger of assault. But because she is not really arguing that other women should carry guns—only explaining her personal reasons for doing so—relying only on her own experiences seems appropriate.

2. The main cause is clearly Hasselstrom's encounters with threatening men. Contributory causes include the fact that she doesn't feel she has viable alternatives and, perhaps, the fact that her husband at the time carried a gun.

3. Try to get students to see that it's not so much the fact that she is a woman that Hasselstrom uses to justify her decision; it is the fact that some men use their greater strength to intimidate women. If this didn't happen, a gun wouldn't be necessary.

4. Students might have fun coming up with possible situations that might result from Hasselstrom's virtually always carrying a gun. The larger question is whether they can imagine her actually killing someone — and when, if ever, this might be justified, especially for a pacifist. (See paragraph 13, where she describes "rehearsing . . . the precise conditions that would be required before I would shoot someone." Why isn't she more specific here?)

5. We find Hasselstrom successful at presenting herself as a peaceful woman who only reluctantly carries a gun. Students may suggest, however, that she seems to take a certain ironic delight in brandishing her weapon.

6. Examples include *changed the balance of power* (24 and, with a variation, 26) and the revised Colt slogan in paragraph 25.

Combining the Patterns (p. 358)

Narrative passages include paragraphs 4, 6, 7, 8, and 17–23. They are clearly essential to Hasselstrom's purpose in the essay. Students probably won't feel that any should be briefer or deleted.

Thematic Connections

Thirty-Eight Who Saw Murder Didn't Call the Police **(p. 128):** This essay examines a famous murder case in Queens, New York, in which many neighbors witnessed a woman's murder, but did not call the police. You might have students consider the contrasts with Hasselstrom: while she carries a gun, in part, because she lives in a remote and isolated area, Kitty Genovese was killed in a populated urban area. Which setting seems more stereotypically "dangerous"? What does each essay suggest about the vulnerability of women, in particular?

Just Walk On By **(p. 238):** Brent Staples, a black man, writes here about the fear he inspires in white pedestrians after dark, and the suspicions he raises by his very presence in places where a black man is not expected to be found. Unlike the white men Hasselstrom writes about threatening her, Staples himself does nothing threatening to justify such fear. Students might think about different approaches to protecting oneself from violence. Are they right to be wary, as Staples describes his "victims"? Given such wariness and suspicion, what might happen if more people routinely carried guns? Would the streets likely be safer or more violent?

The Wife-Beater **(p. 514):** In discussing this popular name for a kind of T-shirt, Gayle Rosenwald Smith argues that the term trivializes, if not actively encourages, violence against women. As part of her argument, she cites statistics regarding the levels of violence suffered by women at the hands of husbands and boyfriends. Do students agree that many young people take violence against women too lightly? Popular rap music lyrics, for example, have often been charged with misogyny. Should women feel as concerned about their physical well-being as Linda Hasselstrom is?

Do We Really Need More Guns on Campus? **(p. 628):** Hasselstrom makes a very personal case for her gun ownership. In "Do We Really Need More Guns on Campus?," David Skorton and Glenn Altschuler argue that colleges should be free to enact their own gun policies—particularly restrictions on weapons on campus. How do students think Hasselstrom would react to this essay? Is her argument compatible with Skorton and Altschuler's?

Max Brooks, *The Movies That Rose from the Grave*

Given the prevalence of zombies in popular culture, Max Brooks's essay should spark an informed and lively discussion of the topic. It was written in 2006, so students will be able to add newer examples; moreover, they should also be able to evaluate some of the claims and predictions that Brooks makes. Did the "dust" of 2001 to 2010 settle, bringing a "semblance of stability"—and a waning in the power of zombies? The writer briefly contrasts zombies with vampires and werewolves at the end of this essay, designating the latter as "more conventional monsters" (13). Do students agree? Do vampires, for example, speak to us about certain fears and anxieties in the same way Brooks claims zombies do?

One of the most valuable aspects of his essay is the way Brooks encourages readers to think in terms of allegory and metaphor: the popularity of zombies is itself like a zombie; fictional movies and stories about the undead allow us to work through real fears about real current events. Encourage students to consider popular culture in this way and discover its wider themes, meanings, and significance.

Comprehension (p. 362)

1. Brooks focuses more on tracing the different origins of zombies—for example, the west African legend in which wizards "transform a living human into a mobile, docile, obedient corpse" (4) or the "hostile, flesh-eating ghoul" in George A. Romero's *Night of the Living Dead* (5)—than on providing formal definition. But his point is not the singular meaning of zombies; rather, he is interested in discussing the way their meaning and form have changed and developed (across a range of media forms) to meet various social, cultural, and psychological needs.
2. He answers the first question in paragraphs 4–9; he answers the second question in paragraphs 10–12; he answers the final question in paragraph 13.
3. According to Brooks, myths concerning the reanimation of the dead go back as far as the epic of Gilgamesh, but the word *zombie* can be traced back to a west African legend (4).
4. Romero transformed the zombie from a "harmless, voodoo-created" figure into a "hostile, flesh-eating ghoul" (5). His monster's origins were scientific (radiation) rather than magical (a voodoo elixir or spell).
5. "Horocalypse" combines the words *horror* and *apocalypse*. This movie genre presents the collapse of civilization in conjunction with a "walking plague" of zombies seeking to "stamp out humanity" (6).
6. Brooks sees the current popularity of zombies as a response to contemporary events: "[t]errorism, war, viral outbreaks, and natural disasters have created a global undercurrent of anxiety" (11). Brooks also notes that "[z]ombie movies present people with an outlet for their apocalyptic anxieties" (12). You might have students explore the notion that zombies can be interpreted allegorically

or metaphorically—for fears of disease, concerns about science, or even cultural preoccupations with death or disaster.

7. Brooks sees zombies as meeting certain collective cultural needs and arising in response to particular anxieties. He believes their popularity will likely ebb at some point, but that means that zombies will "simply retreat underground again, waiting patiently for the day when they rise again" (13).

Purpose and Audience (p. 362)

1. Brooks seems to expect his readers to be at least somewhat familiar with current examples of zombies in popular culture; for example, he uses the first-person plural in his opening paragraph to refer to "our own fascination with what popular culture now refers to as the 'living dead'" (1). But he does not presume his readers know the specific origins of zombies in myth and legend (implied by his rhetorical question, "Where did these creatures come from?" [3]). Brooks also makes the point that for a long time, the living dead were a cult subgenre of horror ("largely underground" [2]), so he does not presume readers are familiar with the more obscure examples of the genre he gives in paragraph 7; at the same time, he does expect them to recognize well-known instances in popular culture, such as Michael Jackson's *Thriller* video, which "immortalized dancing zombies" (7).

2. The thesis of the essay might be stated as: "While our fascination with zombies may wax and wane, the monsters will always be with us—dominating our popular culture or waiting to rise again—because they speak to some of our deepest fears." Brooks includes general variations on this claim in both his opening paragraph and his conclusion.

Style and Structure (p. 362)

1. Student responses should vary. While you might encourage students to limit their use of exclamations in their own writing, Brooks is playfully echoing the cry of a character in a zombie movie in his opening sentence. He is also introducing the key metaphor of his essay: that our cultural preoccupation with zombies is like a zombie itself.

2. He means that the current popularity of zombies is, in part, a cultural response to "[t]errorism, war, viral outbreaks, and natural disasters" (11). Current events make people anxious; "[z]ombie movies present people with an outlet for their apocalyptic anxieties without directly confronting them" (12). You might use this insight to discuss horror and even science fiction stories and movies more broadly. That is, how do our fictional monsters and on-screen horrors serve as allegories and metaphors for real-world fears?

3. Brooks mostly focuses on causes, but he does consider some effects. For example, he claims that watching *Dawn of the Dead*—and knowing that it is a fiction that can be turned off—leads people to have "a feeling of control, a rare and valuable thing these days" (12).

4. According to Brooks, the word *zombie* can be traced back to west African folklore and legend (4). The word *zombie* connotes a reanimated but brain-dead corpse; it can also be used to describe a mindless or unthinking person. The word *ghoul* suggests a sinister, supernatural, demonic being, with more volition than a zombie.

Combining the Patterns (p. 363)

Brooks uses an extended example in paragraph 5 because he is explaining a formative and pivotal moment in the evolution of the zombie as a pop-cultural phenomenon—when George A. Romero's *Night of the Living Dead* "replaced the image of a harmless voodoo-created zombie with a hostile, flesh-eating ghoul that swelled its numbers to pandemic proportions" (5). He uses briefer examples later because they can all be traced back to Romero's fundamental reconception of the monsters.

Thematic Connections

Ground Zero (p. 175): Brooks sees the popularity of zombies as a response to current events (like terrorist attacks) and a "global undercurrent of anxiety" (11). In a sense, the monsters give us a fictional "outlet" (12) for our apocalyptic fears. Writer Suzanne Berne confronts that anxiety more directly and literally in "Ground Zero," where she recounts her visit to the empty space left by the September 11 terrorist attacks: "And by the act of our visiting—whether we are motivated by curiosity or horror or reverence or grief, or by something confusing that combines them all—that space fills up again" (20).

The Embalming of Mr. Jones (p. 301): As reanimated corpses and walking dead, zombies provide a fantastical, imaginary, and horrific vision of death—dead bodies, in particular. Jessica Mitford takes a more clinical approach in this essay, which follows the embalming process of a dead man with clinical detachment. Is there horror here, too? Does Mitford's detached style make death more familiar and understandable? Or does it make death stranger and more disturbing?

Aristotle (p. 481): In the popularity of zombies, Brooks sees an outlet for people preoccupied with "apocalyptic anxieties" (12): fears about the end of civilization or the world itself. Billy Collins's poem ponders beginnings, middles, and endings. In making connections between Brooks and Collins, you may want to emphasize the power of endings—as Collins writes, "what we have all been waiting for, / what everything comes down to" (ll. 70–71): our dread of death, our desire for closure, our fascination with doomsday fantasies (like the zombie apocalypse).

Janice Mirikitani, *Suicide Note* (POETRY)

Suicide, more than most subjects, calls for causal analysis, and teenage suicides are all too frequent in this country. In one way or another, suicide may have personally touched the lives of many of your students. Some may have heard of situations in which one teen's suicide, reported widely in the press, led to a series of others. They may also be aware of despairing college students who have killed themselves. Discussing such suicides and trying to understand them can be vital to many of your students. You may want to make your students aware of your campus's mental health resources.

You will want to focus on the raw materials Mirikitani gives in narrative form, which suggest the complex chain that causes her speaker to commit suicide. In addition to discussing the cause-and-effect relationships in "Suicide Note," you will want to discuss Mirikitani's artistry. Her use of repetition and concrete image patterns will increase your students' sense of the ways in which language can be used.

1. Being a daughter in a family that values sons more than daughters is a less immediate but fundamental cause of the student's suicide. The speaker says,

   > If only I were a son . . .
   > I would see the light in my mother's
   > eyes, or the golden pride reflected
   > in my father's dream
   > of my wide, male hands worthy of work
   > and comfort. (ll. 10, 12–16)

   A causal chain operates from the fundamental cause. As a daughter, she is not praised as she believes a son would be. This, in turn, causes a lack of self-esteem: she feels "not good enough   not pretty enough   not smart enough." Her lack of self-esteem is explicitly tied to her gender: if she were a son, she asserts, "I would swagger through life / muscled and bold and assured, / drawing praises to me" (ll. 17–19). Feeling that she has disappointed her parents by being a daughter, she cannot live with feeling that she has further let them down by not getting a perfect 4.0 grade point average.

2. She believes she would be loved and praised more and would be "virile / with confidence" (ll. 20–21). Whether she would have been happier as a son is difficult to determine. If her parents really do value sons more than daughters, a son would have very likely developed a stronger sense of self-worth — which is fundamental to happiness. However, she may also mistakenly blame her parents' cultural biases for her unhappiness.

3. Mirikitani uses repetition as a means of communicating the extent of the speaker's unhappiness and desperation. The refrain "not good enough   not pretty enough   not smart enough" makes her unhappiness and desperation all-encompassing. She is obsessed with her sense of unworthiness. Other repetitions — "I've worked very hard," "I apologize," and "sorries / sorries," — suggest her driving need to live up to her parents' expectations and her sense of shame.

   Mirikitani also effectively uses image patterns to communicate the speaker's despair. Bird imagery communicates her fragile self-image. She feels weak and inadequate — only a "sparrow / sillied and dizzied by the wind" (ll. 38–39). "[P]erched / on the ledge of [her] womanhood," she is "fragile as wings. / . . . / sillied and dizzied by the wind / on the edge" (ll. 32–40), and her wings are "crippled" (l. 45). Her suicide note, "like birdprints in snow" (l. 2), will leave no lasting imprint.

   Repeated snow and ice imagery also communicates the speaker's despair. Snow and ice are frozen potential, not water in life-giving form. "Each failure [is] a glacier / . . . / Each disappointment, / ice above my river" (ll. 25–28). Her "[c]hoices [are] thin as shaved / ice," and her "[n]otes shredded / drift like snow" (ll. 49–51). She will fly from her ledge while "[i]t is snowing," and "the snow burdens [her] crippled wings" (ll. 36, 45). Her "bird bones" will be buried beneath "this white and cold and silent / breast of earth" (ll. 58, 62–63). Ironically, her grave will be marked by an evergreen.

Thematic Connections

Midnight (p. 217): This student essay focuses on hardworking parents, here Asian immigrants who labor in a dry cleaning sweatshop more than twelve hours a day for substantially less than the minimum wage.

Why Chinese Mothers Are Superior **(p. 408):** Amy Chua compares Chinese and Western parenting styles. Many American parents would consider her methods abusive: her children were not allowed to "attend a sleepover"; "have a playdate"; "be in a school play"; "complain about never being in a school play"; or "watch TV or play computer games," among other harsh restrictions (1). No doubt these rules would lead to a certain level of stress in the children.

College Pressures **(p. 448):** The notes to Carlos at the beginning of "College Pressures" suggest the sense of desperation felt by many college students. William Zinsser also analyzes the reasons many students become desperate—no doubt, in some cases, desperate enough to commit suicide. In a "brutal economy" (20), they, their parents, and their peers feel they must major in "pre-rich" (28) and compete without respite to find "an edge" (16) over other students. Caught in "webs of love and duty and guilt" (28), like Mirikitani's speaker, they fail to understand that they have "the right to fail" (14) and to use their educations to discover who they are and enrich their lives. Zinsser is emphatic about the solution: "Ultimately it will be the students' own business to break the cycles in which they are trapped" (39). (See also *Thematic Connections*, "College Pressures," p. 22 of this manual.)

Aristotle **(p. 481):** Mirikitani's poem explores the nature and meaning of an ending, as the young speaker explains why she is killing herself. Billy Collins's "Aristotle" looks at the structures of beginnings, middles, and endings including suicide (the poem alludes to poet Sylvia Plath's suicide in line 65). How does this self-destructive act violate the form and expectations of this Aristotelian principle? You might have students compare "Suicide Note" with "Aristotle" as poems. How is their rhythm, imagery, or diction similar? How might students incorporate a line or image from Mirikitani's poem into Collins's poem—or vice versa?

11: Comparison and Contrast

Students have several problems with comparison and contrast. They often fail to appreciate the importance of prewriting when they write a comparison-and-contrast paper. The result can be a jumbled presentation that makes it difficult to understand the basis of comparison or, at times, exactly what elements are being compared. This situation occurs especially during examinations and in-class writings when time is short. In the chapter introduction we stress the necessity of planning when we discuss both point-by-point and subject-by-subject comparisons. Even so, we have found that you cannot repeat this advice enough to students.

Another problem students have is realizing that they have to compare the same or similar elements for each subject they discuss. Having your students outline one or two of the essays in this section can illustrate that writers do follow this strategy when they write. Make sure students understand that if they don't discuss the same or similar points for each subject, they are not actually comparing or contrasting anything.

Finally, students should understand that comparison-and-contrast essays need transitions to make them flow smoothly. Signals indicate movement from one point to another, highlight similarities and differences, and eliminate choppiness to help readers follow a discussion. Revision exercises concentrating on transitions can help students appreciate the importance of this concern.

We chose the two paragraphs in the chapter introduction to illustrate the difference between comparison and analogy. You will need to explain both the value of a good analogy and its logical limits. Students should understand that analogies can be vivid, suggest important relationships, and draw readers into an essay by calling on whatever they already know, but they should also understand that analogies can be trivial or even faulty when similarities are assumed that do not exist.

We chose the selections in this chapter to illustrate the variety of ways that comparison and contrast can be used. The selections begin with the images of Rodin's sculpture *The Kiss* and Indiana's sculpture *LOVE*, which offer clear visual material to compare and contrast. Next, Bruce Catton's "Grant and Lee: A Study in Contrasts" uses a point-by-point strategy to compare the two Civil War generals; it makes an excellent opening assignment. Catton's essay is followed by Pamela Haag's "Your Social Life: Are You a Fox or a Hedgehog?" Haag takes a contrast conceived by the Greek poet Archilochus and made famous by the philosopher Isaiah Berlin and applies it to contemporary social life. In "Songs of the Summer of 1963 . . . and 2013," Juan Williams compares the music and poetry of the civil rights era with contemporary hip-hop culture. Amy Chua, in "Why Chinese Mothers Are Superior," compares Chinese and Western parenting styles. Ellen Laird's "I'm Your Teacher, Not Your Internet-Service Provider" looks at the differences and similarities between teaching online classes and teaching in a traditional classroom. Deborah Tannen's "Sex, Lies, and Conversation" examines how gender affects communication styles. Finally, Gwendolyn Brooks's poem "Sadie and Maud" expands the use of comparison and contrast into the realm of literature.

Auguste Rodin, *The Kiss*, and Robert Indiana, *LOVE* (Sculptures)

Students might be interested to learn that these two sculptures were created some eighty years apart, Rodin's in the mid-1880s and Indiana's in the mid-1960s. In part, their differences can be accounted for by the prevailing artistic movements of these two eras.

Reading Images (p. 392)

1. The two sculptures share the characteristic of being larger than life. In addition, both could be titled "Love." Their shared theme provides a sufficient basis for comparison.
2. Except in terms of theme, students are likely to find few, if any, similarities between the two sculptures, but they will be able to list a number of differences: *The Kiss* depicts figures, the *LOVE* sculpture depicts a word; *The Kiss* is essentially realistic, the *LOVE* sculpture is essentially conceptual; *The Kiss* suggests passion, the *LOVE* sculpture suggests whimsy; *The Kiss* focuses on the love between men and women, the *LOVE* sculpture focuses on love in a more generalized sense.
3. Student responses will vary, but one possible statement that could be made based on the points of contrast between the two sculptures is "Rodin's *The Kiss* and Robert Indiana's *LOVE* sculpture both depict an image based on the idea of love, but *The Kiss* is about carnal love while *LOVE* is about love as a force that can unite humanity."

92

Thematic Connections

The Storm **(p. 198):** Kate Chopin's short story, like the Rodin sculpture, is a depiction of passionate lovemaking. Considering that the two were created at approximately the same time in the late 1880s, why might Chopin's story have been seen as so much more scandalous?

Sex, Lies, and Conversation **(p. 421):** Do the details of Rodin's *The Kiss* suggest any innate differences between men and women? If so, how might they be related to the kinds of differences Deborah Tannen writes about in her essay?

Love and Other Catastrophes **(p. 518):** Stringing together the titles of songs by artists like Madonna and Otis Redding, Amanda Brown illustrates the story arc of romantic love. Ask students if Brown's story shares enough characteristics with the Rodin and Indiana sculptures to establish a basis for comparison. If it does, what are the shared characteristics? If it does not, what does this suggest about the nature of love?

Diane Yang, *Greek Yogurt vs. Original Yogurt* (INFOGRAPHIC)

Over the last few years, Greek-style yogurt has become enormously popular in the United States. But even students who are not yogurt eaters should find this infographic interesting and visually striking, as it uses clever graphics and numerical data to break down the differences between Greek yogurt and regular yogurt. You might use this visual to highlight the ways in which a graphic can be too visually dense, as some of the information may be hard to process without repeated viewing.

Comprehension

1. According to the infographic, 28 percent of Americans eat yogurt on a daily basis.
2. The straining process gives yogurt its tangy flavor; Greek yogurt is strained twice, which makes it tangier than original yogurt.

Purpose and Audience

1. The purpose of this infographic is primarily informative: it illustrates and explains the differences between Greek yogurt and original yogurt. It is designed to help readers make more informed choices as consumers, based on comparative nutritional information.
2. The primary intended audience for this infographic is people choosing between Greek yogurt and original yogurt. But it would also appeal to anyone curious about yogurt, nutrition, and food choices.

Mode

1. Students should find many examples, including the use of differently colored yogurt icons, scales, and numerical data to contrast the two foods according to their calorie counts, sodium, protein, and sugar.
2. The infographic is clever and visually engaging. However, some may find it busy or even unclear in certain places. For example, the writer includes the

statistic, "7 out of 25 people would prefer Greek yogurt over regular yogurt." It is an unusual fraction; also, the infographic does not clarify whether the people polled were daily yogurt eaters or not. Likewise, the lower left-hand corner of the infographic includes two pie charts with percentages of calcium in the two foods. The percentages seem to refer to the recommended daily allowance of calcium, but that is not made clear.

Bruce Catton, *Grant and Lee: A Study in Contrasts*

This essay is a classic point-by-point comparison. First Catton discusses Lee, the aristocratic representative of tidewater Virginia. Next he presents Grant, the son of a tanner, who was everything Lee was not. He moves from generalizations about each man to the ways they differed in character and orientation. You might point out to students how, beginning with paragraph 12, Catton sums up his discussion of Lee and Grant with a point-by-point comparison. This is a good opportunity to discuss strategy and to ask students why Catton uses both types of comparisons in his essay. In this essay, topic sentences and transitions are important. The questions in *Style and Structure* ask students to consider these elements, and you might want to go further, devoting an entire class to these issues.

Comprehension (p. 396)

1. Grant and Lee met at Appomattox Court House to work out the terms for Lee's surrender, thus "bringing the Civil War to its virtual finish" (2).
2. Lee represented the aristocratic values of tidewater Virginia. He stood for a privileged class of landowners whose values and responsible leadership ideally were to repay the society that recognized their status. This regional ideal was embodied in Lee, "as if he himself was the Confederacy" (6). In contrast, Grant, who grew up on the western frontier, was independent, self-reliant, and democratic. He was committed to the nation as a whole and to its prosperity.
3. Grant and Lee contrast most strikingly in their attitudes about society. Lee saw himself in terms of his own locality: "He lived in a static society which could endure almost anything except change" (10). On the other hand, Grant believed in the nation as a whole, a "broader concept of society" defined by "growth, expansion, and a constantly widening horizon" (11).
4. Both men were "marvelous fighters" whose "fighting qualities were really very much alike" (13). Each had tenacity, fidelity, daring, and resourcefulness. And most important, each was able "to turn quickly from war to peace once the fighting was over" (16).
5. Catton suggests that "succeeding generations of Americans" are in debt to Grant and Lee because of the way they were able to "turn quickly from war to peace once the fighting was over" (16).

Purpose and Audience (p. 396)

1. The aristocratic current, represented by Lee, is based on a class structure ruled by the elite. The democratic current, represented by Grant, is based on individualism and a strong sense of national community. These differences have always defined two strong currents in America, from Jefferson and Hamilton onward, and they are still apparent in debates between conservative Republicans and liberal Democrats.

2. Catton uses Grant and Lee to represent "the strengths of two conflicting currents that, through them, had come into final collision" (3). Although their differences produced collision, their strengths made reconciliation possible. By comparing them, Catton makes a statement about the strengths of the American character and its ability to reconcile differences.
3. Catton's thesis is that Grant and Lee embodied two conflicting currents in America, the democratic and the aristocratic.

Style and Structure (p. 396)

1. Catton uses point-by-point comparison since he includes too many points for an effective subject-by-subject comparison. An audience would have difficulty remembering all the details about the first subject once the essay moved to the second.
2. These topic sentences establish the comparison and contrast; moreover, they indicate whether Grant or Lee will be the focus of the paragraph. They also unify the essay by providing transitions from one paragraph to another.
3. Examples of transitions in this essay include *These men* (2), *They were two strong men* (3), *Grant . . . was everything Lee was not* (7), *Yet along with this feeling* (9), *And that, perhaps, is where the contrast . . . becomes most striking* (10), and so forth.
4. Catton uses the meeting at Appomattox as a frame for his essay. His major concern is Lee and Grant and the currents they represent, not the events during the meeting.
5. To do this exercise correctly, students will have to be sensitive to context. For example, although *manners* is a synonym for *deportment,* it does not convey the notion of *cultivated,* which is required by the context.

Combining the Patterns (p. 397)

Paragraphs 9, 10, and 11 also use exemplification. Each suggests contrasting characteristics of the Westerner and the Virginia aristocrat.

Thematic Connections

Ground Zero (p. 175): Catton uses Grant and Lee to explore "poignant, dramatic contrasts in American history" (2). Writer Suzanne Berne visits "ground zero" of the 2001 terrorist attacks on the World Trade Center and finds its emptiness powerfully affecting and evocative. What kind of revealing contrasts can be drawn from the 2001 attacks? What do they say about America? For example, can we draw a stark distinction between the United States before September 11, 2001, and the country after the attacks? What would be the basis for such a comparison?

The Declaration of Independence (p. 550): The Declaration of Independence provides an underlying framework for discussing historical U.S. goals and values. Students might consider ways the Civil War tested the powers of this crucial document written by Thomas Jefferson.

Letter from Birmingham Jail (p. 563): Catton asserts that Robert E. Lee fought for an ideal, but criticizes it by tying it to images from the Middle Ages—to the age of chivalry, knighthood, and English squires—dated images that depend on the existence of a subordinate class. Just as feudalism required the subjugation of peasants, so Lee's "feeling that it was somehow of advantage to human society to have pronounced inequality in the social structure" (5) required the subjugation of blacks. In his "Letter from Birmingham Jail," Martin Luther King Jr. shows that such inequalities continued to exist for blacks a century after the Civil War and calls on the ministers to whom he is writing—and by extension, all Americans—to stand up "for what is best in the American dream and for the most sacred values in our Judaeo-Christian heritage, thereby bringing our nation back to those great wells of democracy which were dug deeply by the founding fathers in their formulation of the Constitution and the Declaration of Independence" (44).

Should American Citizenship Be a Birthright? **(Debate; p. 591):** In Catton's essay, Lee and Grant come to stand for different ways of being an "American." In the debate over birthright citizenship, Linda Chavez and George F. Will hold contrasting positions on birthright citizenship: the principle that anyone born in the United States is automatically an American citizen. Do the two writers also suggest contrasting views of what it means to be an American?

Pamela Haag, *Your Social Life: Are You a Fox or a Hedgehog?*

Haag compares and contrasts traditional social life with its newer, online variant—particularly Facebook. To begin, you might ask students about their own online habits, their definitions of friendship, and their view of social life, generally. For example, do they accept Haag's fundamental distinction between online and offline relationships? Or, do they see the two as complementary extensions of each other? The writer focuses almost entirely on Facebook, but how do her premises and argument apply to other applications such as Snapchat and Twitter? You can also have students respond to the quiz at the conclusion of the essay—and perhaps add some questions of their own.

Haag's use of the fox and the hedgehog parable is ingenious, but you might think critically about the analogy: What are its limitations? What problems arise when you view issues, problems, or questions using a dichotomy like this? To that end, you might point out that in her fifth paragraph Haag acknowledges a potential pitfall. Indeed, perhaps this essay's most notable stylistic quality is its circumspection: the writer is clearly open to the possibility that she is wrong in her hypothesis. Ask students how they might revise the essay into a more pointed or even polemical argument. What would they add? What would they leave out? How would the stylistic and tonal shift change the overall meaning of the essay?

Comprehension (p. 401)

1. According to the traditional formulations of Archilochus and Isaiah Berlin, "the fox knows many things about a little, but the hedgehog knows one big thing" (1).
2. The parable works well for contemporary social life because it can help frame the distinction between the past, in which people had a few close friends and knew a lot about them, and the present, in which people have many friends— particularly online—about whom they know a "million little things" (2–3).
3. According to Haag, online social networks have a bias toward making users into foxes. As she writes, "Our attention is dispersed quickly and pithily across hundreds if not thousands of people; we know a little about an awful lot of people" (8). She sees these interactions as "pure fox" (10).

4. Current research suggests that a large percentage of Americans (but not a majority) do not have a single friend in the "hedgehog" sense of the word *friendship* (17). Haag speculates that Facebook could make such isolation worse, even as the site could give the superficial illusion of expanding and deepening a lonely person's social life (19).

5. Haag means that Facebook can give the feeling and appearance of connection with others, but these online relationships are not as meaningful, lasting, or fulfilling as close, face-to-face friendships are.

Purpose and Audience (p. 401)

1. While Haag expects readers to be open to her line of thinking (as in the quiz she includes), she also seems aware that some readers might be skeptical of her point of view. Her claims are qualified and even tentative at times. For example, she writes that she is "questioning" (6) the effects of Facebook on our emotional lives: this is different from making a strong claim. Similarly, she writes that she is "not wedded to [her] hypothesis," even though Facebook "seems to be inclining us toward the fox social life" (7). Later in the essay, she anticipates a skeptical response from some readers: "My intention isn't to sound like a Luddite crank . . ." (16). Overall, her argument seems exploratory: she is making claims and building a case, but she wants to lead readers through her thinking and her examples.

2. Her thesis, in qualified phrasing, is in paragraph 7. It might be stated as: "If the parable of the fox and the hedgehog can be applied to our friendships and social lives, then online networking sites like Facebook are turning us all into foxes." You might ask students if a more forceful statement of the thesis would improve the essay.

3. This essay seeks to persuade readers to accept the analogy of the fox and the hedgehog as it applies to contemporary social life. Haag even includes a quiz so that her audience can participate. But the essay is also personal and exploratory: Haag has observed a phenomenon—in her own life and in the culture at large—and wants to understand and explain it. By doing so, the writer seeks to enlighten her readers.

Style and Structure (p. 401)

1. Haag's approach is based on questioning, as she notes in paragraph 6. The title asks readers to question their own social lives using the framework—the fox and the hedgehog—proposed by the writer. A more assertive title ("The Internet Is Killing the Hedgehog" or "We Are All Foxes Now") would misrepresent her style, tone, and approach.

2. The first paragraph explains the parable of the fox and the hedgehog. The second paragraph begins explaining how the parable is applicable to social life; it also argues that, in the past, most people were hedgehogs.

3. Haag uses point-by-point comparison early in her essay to explain the meaning of *hedgehog* and *fox* in the context of social media. The approach is effective: having established the basic contrast, she can then explore each on its own more thoroughly. Had she used a rigid, back-and-forth, point-to-point structure for the entire essay, her writing would likely become repetitive and tedious.

4. Given the nature of her essay, Haag uses relatively few transitions to cue her readers (e.g., the word *but* in her first paragraph). You might ask students to identify places where she could have included more of them to heighten a comparison or a contrast. For example, she might have started her third paragraph with the phrase *In contrast*. In paragraph 4, she might have begun the sentence with *While* or used a comma and the word *but* instead of a semicolon.

5. You might point out that it is generally not acceptable to end an academic writing assignment with a quiz rather than a conclusion. But paragraph 19 could, arguably, serve as Haag's conclusion; it proposes a paradox in the form of a question, which can be an effective way of ending an essay. The quiz does fit her larger purpose: to get readers to think about their own social lives in terms of foxes and hedgehogs.

6. Student responses will vary; you might take this as an opportunity to talk about how the level of formality of vocabulary must suit the needs of the anticipated audience, making word choice a rhetorical act.

Combining the Patterns (p. 402)

The narrative paragraph illustrates the general points Haag makes in paragraphs 8–10: that her attention is dispersed by Facebook; that she got caught up in skimming and clicking on the site over the course of two hours; that her social appetite is satisfied superficially, but she only really knew one of the several posters she was corresponding with; that her "things to do" social list remained undone. In short, her fox-like online experience crowded out her "real" social life (12–13).

Thematic Connections

No, I Do Not Want to Pet Your Dog (p. 224): As Haag does in her essay, Farhad Manjoo considers the significance and consequences of a cultural trend he has observed: the omnipresence of dogs in urban society, as well as the prevalent assumption that everyone likes dogs. You might usefully contrast the tone and style of these essays. Haag is cautious and circumspect in her "questioning" (6) of Facebook's effect on our social lives. In contrast, Manjoo takes a deliberately provocative approach to his subject and his argument.

I'm Your Teacher, Not Your Internet-Service Provider (p. 415): Ellen Laird's pointed examination of Internet distance learning makes for an excellent pairing with Haag's essay. While Haag compares and contrasts contemporary online social life with its traditional, offline counterpart, Laird compares and contrasts traditional classroom teaching with the experience of teaching online college courses. You might place special emphasis on the way the Internet changes the relationship between instructor and student, as Laird describes near the end of her essay.

Sadie and Maud (p. 428): Philosopher and critic Isaiah Berlin famously deployed the analogy of the fox and the hedgehog in an essay analyzing the fiction of Leo Tolstoy. Have students approach this poem by Gwendolyn Brooks with the parable and see if it lends any unifying insight to the characters in the text. What does Sadie seem to know? What does Maud seem to know? Does the poem suggest that one kind of knowing is superior to the other?

I Want a Wife (p. 502): Judy Brady's essay looks at conflicts between wives and husbands, in this case based on stereotypical assumptions about the roles each should fulfill within a marriage. While Haag compares online vs. traditional social life, Brady compares the gender role expectations that often came with marriage in the 1970s and that still may exist today.

Juan Williams, *Songs of the Summer of 1963 . . . and 2013*

In this alternately nostalgic and scolding essay, Juan Williams longs for the "sweet" (20) poetry and music that, for him, defined the 1963 March on Washington and the civil rights era. He cites the music of artists like Bob Dylan; Peter, Paul, and Mary; and Curtis Mayfield as an "inspiring" (18) soundtrack for the "American struggle for racial justice" (14). In contrast, he finds hip hop "degrading" (2) and "malignant" (18); he sees it as harmful to minority families and race relations; he also criticizes contemporary civil rights leaders for their failure to denounce rap for its violence and misogyny.

Students — especially those who are knowledgeable about current music — should be able to bring informed opinion and insight to the topic. Williams's treatment of older music is fine-grained and thorough, but his analysis of hip hop may seem perfunctory or shallow to some. Do students think Williams makes good points here? Is his argument too reductive in its characterizations of music from two different eras? You might also discuss the ways in which music — past and current — can capture a cultural moment or particular zeitgeist.

Comprehension (p. 406)

1. Williams is referring to the rhetoric at the march and Martin Luther King Jr.'s "I Have a Dream" speech, in particular: King began improvising and using a "musical, chanting reprise" (3). You might explore the definition of *poetry* and *poetic* here. What makes language — or even an event itself — poetry? Must it be beautiful? True? Inspiring? Transcendent? Williams claims that King's poetry "rose above . . . reality" (6). Does that mean the rhetoric was untrue?
2. According to Williams, the movement was at an impasse, especially regarding integration and civil rights legislation. *Brown v. Board of Education* had been decided almost a decade earlier, ending the separate-but-equal doctrine, but few schools were integrated. Williams notes that "[t]he Civil Rights Act was stuck in Congress" (6). It had also suffered other setbacks, like the murder of Medgar Evers, as well as violent clashes with the police in the South and across the country.
3. Williams sees the songs as reflecting a sense of "unity, promise, and purpose" (9). Students may or may not be familiar with these songs. If they are not, you might play them in class. You might also explore the idea that music can catch the mood of a cultural moment, or even provide social prophecy. Songs like "Blowin' in the Wind" (1962) and "A Change Is Gonna Come" (1963) heralded imminent political and social changes.
4. All these songs captured the spirit of the age and suggested that times were changing. They also caught the desire and hope for peaceful social and political progress, as, for example, Sam Cooke's "A Change Is Gonna Come," which Williams describes as an "anthem of yearning for a nation without racial rancor" (11).
5. According to Williams, hip hop is "malignant" and "self-aggrandizing" (18), although he is not explicit about how it reflects the cultural mood today.

However, he does believe that rap lyrics harm "poor and minority families" (20). You might ask students if Williams's comparison is fair or credible. For example, he focuses on music by Jay-Z and Lil Wayne. But can students think of other hip-hop artists or songs that are closer in sensibility to the "sweet," socially conscious music that Williams seems to long for?

Purpose and Audience (p. 406)

1. Williams assumes his audience will have a general familiarity with the 1963 March on Washington and the iconic status of Martin Luther King Jr.'s speech. But he does not assume that his readers will recall that at the time of the event, the "civil rights movement was stalled" (6). Similarly, he cites some well-known songs ("Blowin' in the Wind," "People Get Ready"), but he also quotes specific lyrics (and tells the stories behind the songs) to remind his audience of the music's topical and social relevance to its time.

2. The writer generally assumes that readers will have probably heard of songs like "Blowin' in the Wind" and artists like Bob Dylan. But he provides background information on them and cites specific lyrics; this gives insight into the connections between the artists, the songs, and the events at the time.

3. Williams's purpose seems to be to exalt the "sweet" quality of 1960s protest music and its uplifting and unifying message of promise, while criticizing contemporary hip hop for being "malignant, self-aggrandizing" (18), and harmful. He seems to be arguing that the superior music of the civil rights era is representative of a more noble or idealistic time. You might ask students whether Williams's view is too nostalgic — and whether his characterization of hip hop is accurate.

Style and Structure (p. 406)

1. The first two paragraphs present a condensed version of Williams's entire argument: the importance of music at the March on Washington (and in the culture at the time) and the contrast between the uplifting music during the civil rights era and "today's degrading rap music" (2).

2. Students should have their own variations on a similar claim: "compared with the uplifting, unifying, and idealistic music at the March on Washington, today's hip hop is confusing, depressing, and harmful."

3. Williams focuses almost entirely on music from 1963; clearly, he has much affection for it and engages in nostalgia about it. He also seems more familiar with the music from the civil rights era. Readers might question the fairness of the argument, however. For example, in contrasting early 1960s folk and protest music with Jay-Z's "current hit," is Williams comparing apples to apples? Would it make more sense to compare 1960s folk and protest music with more socially conscious and politically minded hip hop? Indeed, a representative sample of actual "hits" from 1963 ("He's So Fine," "Surf City," "Blue Velvet") shows little or none of the social consciousness referred to by Williams. Students who are contemporary music fans should be able to provide insight into these questions.

4. The writer shifts in paragraph 18, with the phrase: "Now, half a century after the lyrical promise . . ."

5. Williams emphasizes that, along with the innate degradations of hip hop, "today's civil rights leaders" (20) have contributed to the problem by failing to denounce the genre's celebration of violence and misogyny. This reinforces his overall point about the decline of minority and civil rights "culture" over the last fifty years.

6. For the music of 1963, the writer uses adjectives like *hopeful* (13), *uplifting* (16), and *inspiring* (18). For contemporary music, Williams deploys adjectives like *degrading* (2) and *malignant* (18).

Combining the Patterns (p. 407)

Williams uses exemplification frequently. For instance, in paragraphs 13 through 16, he focuses on the example of Curtis Mayfield's "People Get Ready"; by doing this, he can highlight lyrical themes, place the song in its historical and cultural context, and show its influence on later artists such as Bob Marley and Bruce Springsteen. All of these strategies help support his main point about the music of the past.

Thematic Connections

Goodbye to My Twinkie Days (p. 171): If Williams is nostalgic for the "sweet" music of the March on Washington (and implicitly, his childhood), then Bich Minh Nguyen pines for the sweet, processed junk food of her youth. Her essay is personal, but it also suggests the cultural changes of the last several decades: "We might bake our own cakes now, eat whole grain bread, and try to follow those grocery store Food Rules, but who among us can forget being sugar-shocked by processed goods?" (8).

Once More to the Lake (p. 191): While Williams nostalgically focuses on the music of the past as a manifestation of certain social and cultural trends, E. B. White's qualified and meditative nostalgia for the lake vacations of his youth is much more personal: "It seemed to me, as I kept remembering all this, that those times and those summers had been infinitely precious and worth saving" (9). But White is not naive about being able to "save" the past, as the essay ultimately suggests a deep awareness of time's passage and his own mortality.

The "Black Table" Is Still There (p. 348): In this essay, Lawrence Otis Graham considers the meaning and significance of the "black table": a cafeteria table at a predominantly white school, at which the few black students eat together, separate from other students. Students might consider this phenomenon in the wider context of civil rights history and "progress," as suggested by Williams in his essay.

Letter from Birmingham Jail (p. 563): Williams writes about the "poetry" of Martin Luther King Jr.'s August 28, 1963, "I Have a Dream" speech (3). You might have students consider King's famous "Letter from Birmingham Jail," written in April 1963, as poetry, too. Williams notes that poetry can rise above "reality" (6). How does King's language in this letter aspire, inspire, incite, sing, and soar? In what ways is it "sweet" music?

Amy Chua, *Why Chinese Mothers Are Superior*

In "Why Chinese Mothers Are Superior," Amy Chua outlines her child-rearing methods, which she attributes to her Chinese cultural heritage. Many American parents would consider her methods abusive: her children were not allowed to "attend a sleepover"; "have a playdate"; "be in a school play"; "complain about not being in a school play"; or "watch TV or play computer games," among other harsh restrictions (1). Chua considers the term "Chinese mother" to be widely inclusive (it might even exclude mothers of Chinese heritage who do not follow a strict plan for raising their children). She says, "What Chinese parents understand is that nothing is fun until you're good at it" (6), and her results seem to prove her point: her daughter Sophia, for instance, played the piano at Carnegie Hall in 2007. As you present this selection in class, keep in mind that students may not understand where Chua is being ironic or playful. You might want to point out sections where she seems to go over the top, and ask students if they think she's being entirely serious.

There are over eight thousand comments on the online version of this article, which appeared in the *Wall Street Journal* on January 8, 2011. Chua wrote it as a promotional piece for her parenting memoir, *Battle Hymn of the Tiger Mother* (2011). Clearly, the piece touched a nerve, and your students will no doubt be interested in weighing in on Chua's practices. Are her methods abusive, as some have claimed, or are the results worth the effort?

Comprehension (p. 412)

1. Chua means that working hard to master a skill is rarely "fun" and that children will "never want to work" if given the choice (6). Therefore, parents must override the preferences of their children, rather than giving in to a child's laziness, frustration, and inability to defer gratification.

2. Chua's husband disagrees with her view that children are "permanently indebted to their parents" (17). In contrast to Chinese parents, who "believe that their kids owe them everything" (16), he claims: "It's parents who foist life on their kids, so it's the parents' responsibility to provide for them. Kids don't owe their parents anything" (17).

3. Chinese parents can do things that seem "unimaginable" (9) to their Western counterparts because of three differences between the two "parental mindsets" (11): Western parents are worried about their children's "self-esteem" in a way that Chinese parents are not (12); Chinese parents "believe that their kids owe them everything" (16) while Western parents do not (17); and Chinese parents "believe that they know what is best for their children and therefore override all of their children's own desires and preferences" (18).

4. She insists that Chinese parents do care about their children and would "give up anything" for them. They just use an "entirely different parenting model" (19).

5. According to Chua, Chinese parenting practices give children skills, help them understand their own capabilities, inculcate work habits, and give children "inner confidence that no one can ever take away" (22).

Purpose and Audience (p. 412)

1. Chua refers to stereotypes of Chinese parents—for example, that they "produce children who display academic excellence, musical mastery, and professional success" (3). She also points to "all these new books . . . portraying Asian mothers as scheming, callous, overdriven people indifferent to their kids' true interests" (21).

2. The writer thinks her readers will be relatively unreceptive and even hostile to her point of view. She acknowledges that "Chinese parents can do things that would seem unimaginable—even legally actionable—to Westerners" (9). Moreover, she includes this clarification: "Don't get me wrong: It's not that Chinese parents don't care about their children" (19). Her need to establish such a basic premise implies a resistant audience.

3. The most general expression of Chua's thesis comes in her conclusion. As Chua's argument will be provocative and counterintuitive to many of her readers, this placement makes sense. The thesis comes after she has walked her reader through her arguments; it has the weight of evidence, explanation, and argumentation behind it.

4. The editors of the essay probably chose this title because it is provocative and sensational; it also plays on the anxieties of American parents, who may be worried about China's growth as an international power.

Style and Structure (p. 413)

1. The general pretext for Chua's essay is that Westerners wonder how Chinese parents produce so many high-achieving children. So she begins with a list of surprising things her daughters were "never allowed to do" (1). Because the list consists of common children's activities (sleepovers, acting in school plays, watching TV), it immediately establishes the profound and striking differences between Chinese and Western parenting.

2. Chua primarily uses a point-by-point comparison (for example, in paragraphs 9–10). This approach is effective because the essay makes a complex argument and discusses several different points regarding Chinese and Western parents. At the same time, Chua's writing never falls into a monotonous back-and-forth pattern; she varies the structure of her sentences and paragraphs and provides different kinds of evidence. For example, she contrasts Chinese and Western attitudes by using a personal anecdote in paragraph 9.

3. Chua presents a variety of evidence. When examining the cultural stereotypes of Western and Chinese parenting, she refers to an article in the *Wall Street Journal* (3) and "new books" that portray Asian mothers as "callous" and "overdriven" (21). Although she also cites polling research that reveals the "marked and quantifiable differences between Chinese and Westerners" (5), she mostly relies on anecdotal or hypothetical examples as well as personal observations to make her points: "I've noticed that Western parents are extremely anxious about their children's self-esteem" (12).

4. That the writer was born in the United States does not undercut her argument. In fact, she acknowledges that the specific nationality of parents is irrelevant: "I'm using the term 'Chinese mother' loosely. I know some Korean, Indian, Jamaican, Irish, and Ghanaian parents who would qualify too" (2). She suggests that parenting styles are a choice, not a birthright (2).

5. At the end of her essay, the writer emphasizes that both Western and Chinese parents "want to do what's best for their children" (21), but they do so in different ways. She also makes judgments about Western parents: they "seem perfectly content to let their children turn out badly" (21), and they emphasize "individuality" and "positive reinforcement" (22). But she implies that Chinese parents do a better job of preparing their children for the future (22).

She might have ended with a more specific claim, but presumes that her readers will have understood her point.

6. She means that a person does not have to be Chinese (literally) to be a "Chinese mother." The parenting styles are defined by expectations, attitudes, and behaviors, not by ethnicity or national identity. Chinese mothers do not worry about their children's self-esteem; they demand and expect perfection in academic and musical performance; they believe their children "owe them everything" (16) and that they know what is best for their children. In contrast, Western parents respect their children's individuality and personal passions; they provide "positive reinforcement and a nurturing environment" (22).

Combining the Patterns (p. 414)

Chua uses exemplification and exemplification paragraphs throughout her essay. For instance, in paragraph 5, she uses statistical examples to support her statement that "there are tons of studies out there showing marked and quantifiable differences between Chinese and Westerners when it comes to parenting." In paragraph 9, she illustrates how "Chinese parents can do things that would seem unimaginable . . . to Westerners" by using the example of Chinese mothers telling their daughters, "Hey fatty — lose some weight."

Thematic Connections

Indian Education (p. 142): Chua describes the different styles of Western parents and Chinese parents. She finds the Chinese approach superior. What role do parents seem to play in Sherman Alexie's "Indian Education"? Have students consider whether the protagonist would have benefited from having demanding parents, as opposed to a mother and a father who "sat in separate, dark places in [their] HUD house and wept savagely" (26). Do the character's main problems stem from a lack of parental discipline? Why or why not?

Suicide Note (p. 364): In this poem by Japanese-American writer Janice Mirikitani, an Asian-American teenager reflects on the extreme pressures that have led her to commit suicide: "dear mother and father. / I apologize / for disappointing you" (ll. 4–6). How might this poem function as a response to Chua's essay? Does it imply the potential dangers of "Chinese parents"? Can readers dismiss it because it is only a poem, or because depression is a mental illness rather than a result of parenting styles? How might parents find a balance between high expectations for a child (on the one hand) and the dispiriting repetition of "not good enough   not strong enough   not good enough" (on the other)?

College Pressures (p. 448): At the opening of his essay about the difficulties of college life, William Zinsser lists a series of explanations from students for why they are behind in their work. What allowances would Chua make for such explanations? We suspect not many.

Mother Tongue (p. 463): Amy Tan reflects on her Chinese immigrant mother, as well as her mother's idiosyncratic English, which shaped the writer's upbringing and "almost had an effect on limiting my possibilities in life" (15). Tan also notes how Chinese-American students excel at math and engineering. What is her explanation for this? How is it different from Chua's? Does Tan's mother sound like a "Chinese mother," as Chua defines the term? Why or why not?

Ellen Laird, *I'm Your Teacher, Not Your Internet-Service Provider*

This compare-and-contrast essay examines the differences between traditional classroom teaching and online teaching, in which instruction and pedagogy are presented over the Internet. Since the subject matter is essentially the same whether a class is on-site or online, one might think the distinctions in presentation would be superficial. Indeed, Ellen Laird initially had a "romance" with distance teaching; she even found preparing and posting new assignments a "thrilling adventure" (1). But, after four years, the deficiencies of Internet instruction are apparent to her: "The nonlinear nature of online activity and the well-ingrained habits of Web use involve behavior vastly different from that which fosters success in the traditional college classroom" (3).

The writer then goes on to compare and contrast the two experiences; she also describes the distinctive "habits" of online learners. For example, her online students presume that the processes of reading, researching, thinking, writing, and teaching should all match the high speed of Internet transmission, even as they ignore the deadlines and time-sequencing of Laird's syllabus. She acknowledges there are evolving strategies for managing such difficulties, but her main purpose is to warn prospective distance teachers that "instruction in person and online are day and night" (19). Students may consider how the Internet would change — and is changing — their own educational experience. Many professors are now building Web components into courses, even in traditional on-site classes. Laird says there are "rewards" (19) to online teaching, but does her essay actually suggest any positive aspects to this method of instruction?

Comprehension (p. 418)

1. The "honeymoon" is over because Laird had high hopes for — and early pleasures with — online teaching. But, after four years, she finds she's disappointed with the experience and struggling to make her online courses work.
2. Laird describes several general and specific contrasts between Internet teaching and classroom-based teaching. Generally, the Web encourages attitudes, habits, and behaviors "vastly different" (3) from those that usually foster success in on-site learning. She explains these general distinctions more specifically with concrete examples, such as the ways students ignore deadlines or presume egalitarianism — or even intimacy — with instructors in ways they do not in traditional courses.
3. She means that online instructors usually are trained in software use, file organization, and other technical aspects of such teaching. But this emphasis on technology and process misses the real difficulties instructors are going to face and the more problematic differences between online teaching and classroom education.
4. A classroom-based course usually has a syllabus with a clear sequence of assignments and due dates. The students do not view it as a "menu" of options (5), but rather a linear schedule of requirements. But Internet users, in contrast, are accustomed to surfing the Web, picking what appeals to them, and enjoying the "nonlinear nature" (3) of this media form.
5. She means that the instantaneousness of the Internet does not actually change the pace of human processes such as thinking, reading, and writing.

Reflection and research still require time; these activities are not fundamentally altered by the bandwidth of a cable connection or the speed of a modem, even though technology may create expectations and illusions to the contrary. Education remains a slow, deliberative process.

Purpose and Audience (p. 419)

1. The essay's thesis is that online and classroom teaching are profoundly different, because the Internet encourages habits of mind and behavior antithetical to success in traditional on-site learning; prospective teachers need to prepare themselves for these particular differences.
2. Despite the implications of her title, Laird is primarily addressing potential online instructors, as well as those who train them (4, 19). However, the "declarative sentences" (4) that structure her essay are from her syllabus.
3. Laird illuminates differences between online teaching and traditional instruction that an emphasis on technology may ignore; she is trying to identify these differences and prepare prospective instructors to deal with them. In these particular aims, she is successful.
4. Laird appears to presume that her readers are familiar with the existence and prevalence of online teaching. But she does not presume they are familiar with the specifics of it, or, for example, with the training distance educators typically receive (4).

Style and Structure (p. 419)

1. The essay is mostly a point-by-point comparison, which contrasts specific aspects of student attitudes and behaviors as they differ in class and online. Some of her points (in paragraphs 11 and 12, for example) do not suggest a comparison with traditional courses. This structure is best for longer essays that compare several points, as Laird's does. A subject-by-subject comparison would be more difficult to read, because we would have to keep track of all the contrasts throughout the paper.
2. These boldface sentences are tart, witty reminders for her students on her syllabus, but they also reveal the particular difficulties of online teaching. In this essay, they serve as topic headings for each of the problems Laird identifies and analyzes.
3. For the most part, Laird seems to take a negative view of online teaching as it exists now. She's particularly aware of the ways the Internet creates expectations, as well as habits of mind and behavior, that seem antithetical to traditional ideas about reading, writing, and learning (3, 7). Similarly, she does not give a list of advantages provided by online teaching. But Laird concludes on a qualified, hopeful note in her final paragraph, even though she offers no specific strategies for online instructors, other than patience and commitment.
4. She indicates how students respond to online teaching, as well as how they chafe and "howl electronically" (6) when she imposes traditional course requirements on them (asking that assignments be done in order, etc.). But she does not extensively explore how they feel about these courses in comparison to traditional classes. Since Laird's essay is directed mostly at prospective online instructors, her focus seems appropriate as it is.

5. Laird's conclusion implies that "strategies to manage these and similar difficulties" are evolving as the practice of online learning becomes more prevalent. She must be managing them in some way, because she persists in teaching and welcomes both "its challenges and its rewards" (19). But her main point is to warn prospective teachers that distance teaching can be problematic and to let them know that they must "brace themselves" (19) for the important, specific differences. By way of contrast, it is not really a "how-to" essay for becoming a better instructor.

6. As the analogy is used in this context, *wedding reception* implies social formality, order, structure, hierarchy, restraint, decorum, and tradition. In contrast, *rave* suggests informality, nonlinearity, disorder, egalitarianism, and intimacy.

Combining the Patterns (p. 420)

These two paragraphs of personal narrative establish that Laird was initially optimistic about online teaching; that she has experience as an in-class instructor and so can make credible comparisons; and that she has been asked, in the past, to demonstrate that her Internet composition courses are the "equivalent" (implicitly, in quality and rigor) of her traditional courses. Laird could have opened her essay in any number of ways: she could have started with a revealing, exemplifying anecdote or example of the differences she discusses in her essay.

Thematic Connections

Indian Education (p. 142): In her essay, Laird explores the nature of the relationship between instructors and their students. Ask students how they would characterize the relationship the protagonist of "Indian Education" has with his teachers. Laird implies that the "egalitarian" (17) quality of online learning may undercut the respect she receives from students. Does the main character in "Indian Education" respect his teachers? Should he?

What I Learned (and Didn't Learn) in College (p. 440): In her essay, Laird compares and contrasts two methods of instruction for college courses: Internet distance education with traditional classroom teaching. Martinez's student essay classifies college classes into the categories of ideal, worthless, disappointing, and unexpectedly valuable.

College Pressures (p. 448): Writing in the late 1970s, William Zinsser reminds students that "the road ahead is a long one and that it will have more unexpected turns than they think" (12). He worries that undergraduates face overwhelming pressures—from professors, peers, their families, and society. How does his attitude toward students differ from Laird's? How is it similar? Do you think Zinsser would approve of online courses and their "egalitarian atmosphere" (17)? Have developments like online teaching and email increased "college pressures" or lessened them?

The Dog Ate My Flash Drive, and Other Tales of Woe (p. 457): Carolyn Foster Segal classifies and analyzes the various excuses that college students use to avoid turning in their work—or showing up for class at all. What view of students comes across in this essay? Does it seem similar to the image presented by Laird? Do you think Internet communication (email, for example) enables students in their alibis?

Deborah Tannen, *Sex, Lies, and Conversation*

Tannen contrasts male and female communication styles, suggesting that many misunderstandings between heterosexual couples are due less to real personal differences than to misread conversational signals. She looks first at differences between the way girls communicate with girls and the way boys communicate with boys and the resulting "misalignments in the mechanics of conversation" among men and women (6–13). She then describes differences in the way males and females read their conversational partners' responses (14–20) and differences in men's and women's reasons for talking (21–22). Her concluding paragraphs offer hope that by recognizing these differences as "cross-cultural" (23), unhappy couples will be able to better understand one another. A good place to begin discussion is by asking students whether they think Tannen's examples are basically superficial stereotypes or whether they can see themselves in the men or the women she describes. Ask for specific exceptions to Tannen's generalizations. Do any such exceptions prove — or disprove — the rule?

Comprehension (p. 425)

1. At the beginning of her article, Tannen offers an example of a husband doing most of the talking in public and a wife doing most of the talking at home.
2. Women most often complain that their partners don't listen or talk to them.
3. Three basic behaviors give women the impression that men do not listen: men tend to face away from each other in conversation, they often switch topics instead of following up with questions, and they make less listener-noise than women.
4. Men often respond to listener-noise as overreaction or impatience. In addition, women are more likely to "finish each other's sentences, and anticipate what the other is about to say," which men interpret as "interruption, intrusion, and lack of attention" (18).
5. Understanding differences in communication style can lead couples to modify their conversational behavior in ways that the other will respond to more positively. Even without such modifications, women can recognize that a man's failure to participate in the kind of conversation they expect from their close female friends does not necessarily indicate a "failure of intimacy" (25) and simply accept the difference without taking offense.

Purpose and Audience (p. 426)

1. Tannen's thesis is stated in two parts: in paragraph 2 and at the beginning of paragraph 8.
2. Tannen's purpose is basically to inform. She doesn't directly advocate any change in male and female communication styles, suggesting that understanding the differences can help couples avoid misunderstandings.
3. Tannen clearly intends an audience of general readers, both men and women. (The essay originally appeared in the *Washington Post*.) The terms she uses and the concepts she explains are accessible to virtually any educated person, and she doesn't limit her discussion to one gender.

Style and Structure (p. 426)

1. Because she is writing to provide information most people are not aware of, it is best that she state her thesis early in order to orient readers so they can understand the specific points that follow.

2. This is a point-by-point comparison, which allows Tannen to enumerate clearly the differences in several specific conversational activities.

3. Tannen's use of scholarly studies and statistics helps her suggest that the differences she describes are not simply based on her own observations but that they are supported by the work of other experts and by objective research.

4. Tannen's tone is positive, generally hopeful that husbands and wives can reduce the frictions caused by problems of cross-cultural communication.

5. Tannen's concluding call for cross-cultural understanding in "these times of resurgent ethnic conflicts" (26) may strike some readers as a bit too far-reaching for her particular subject. Not everyone will agree that a resolution to racial and ethnic conflict might be more easily achieved if men and women in the United States learn to better understand their conversational differences.

6. Tannen doesn't use much professional jargon. Among the few examples are *organizational structures and interactive norms* (7), *physical alignment* and *topical alignment* (13), and *listener-noise* (17) and *participatory listenership* (18). Opinion will differ as to the effectiveness of such jargon in the essay. Tannen generally defines her terms directly or through example, and the professional jargon tends to make her authority more credible.

Combining the Patterns (p. 427)

The anecdote provides an example of the point Tannen makes throughout her essay—that women and men communicate in different ways but remain largely unaware of these differences, which leads to misunderstandings. The story is itself amusing and serves to establish Tannen's informal, friendly style.

Thematic Connections

I Want a Wife (p. 502): Judy Brady's essay also looks at conflicts between wives and husbands, in this case based on stereotypical assumptions about the roles each should fulfill within a marriage. How might Tannen respond to Brady's portrait of a wife? Do the differences Tannen suggests between men and women in any way justify the popularly held stereotypes of male-female roles?

The Wife-Beater (p. 514): This essay by Gayle Rosenwald Smith takes aim at the popular term for a fashionable kind of T-shirt worn by young people. To call a shirt a "wife-beater" is, for this writer, to suggest that violence against women is either something to joke about or to accept as the norm. Tannen does not consider the extent to which miscommunication between spouses may lead to angry altercations, but students might think about how differences between the way men and women communicate can lead to violence against women.

Love and Other Catastrophes (p. 518): Stringing together the titles of songs by such artists as Madonna and Otis Redding, Amanda Brown captures the story arc of a romantic relationship. You might ask your students to consider the gender perspective of the narrator. Is Brown's text the expression of a distinctively feminine point of view, or could this story apply to men and women equally?

Declaration of Sentiments and Resolutions **(p. 556):** Writing in the nineteenth century, suffragist and activist Elizabeth Cady Stanton declares that men have "usurped the prerogative of Jehovah himself" (17) and demands "equal participation" (33) in the trades and professions. She claims that married women are "civilly dead" (8); within patriarchal society, men have destroyed women's confidence in their own powers and forced them to lead "dependent and abject" (18) lives. How are Stanton's nineteenth-century demands for civil, social, and legal equality connected to Tannen's present-day calls for better communication between men and women? Does Tannen's essay suggest a power relationship between the genders? Do the prerogatives of patriarchy endure in the way men and women converse with each other?

Gwendolyn Brooks, *Sadie and Maud* (POETRY)

Brooks's poem compares two sisters, one of whom conformed to convention and the other of whom rebelled against it. While a surface reading of the poem might suggest a "good sister" / "bad sister" dichotomy, students should recognize that Brooks is after something much more subtle here. Although Sadie may have been wild by nature and even irresponsible in her behavior, she lived life large and passionately; Maud's life, as suggested by the final stanza, was far more drab and confined. Sadie at least left a "heritage" (l. 15), albeit a difficult one; it appears that Maud will leave behind none. Students should note that the poem tells readers much more about Sadie (thirteen lines are devoted to her) than about Maud (seven lines, two of which also refer to "Ma and Papa") and that, although Maud is mentioned first in the poem itself, Sadie is mentioned first in the title. Ask students specifically how they interpret the image of Sadie scraping life "[w]ith a fine-tooth comb" in lines 3 and 4 and the repetition of this image in the poem's next-to-last stanza. Another interpretive question is why Brooks uses the phrases "said her last so-long" in line 13 and "thin brown mouse" in line 18.

Reading Literature (p. 429)

1. Brooks compares two extremes for women: one plays by the rules and pursues an education but ends up sadly "all alone" (l. 19); the other breaks the rules, pursuing life's pleasures and giving birth to two illegitimate children, then dies young (note, though, that "said her last so-long" [l. 13] is a surprisingly chipper way of noting someone's death). Brooks indicates her shifts in subject as simply as possible, by introducing each sister's name.

2. The poem may tempt some readers to see stereotypes—what might in Brooks's day have been called the "loose woman" on the one hand and on the other the "old maid." In fact, though, the sympathy the poet brings to describing both sisters' lives suggests that she doesn't see them as stereotypes at all, but as women who make choices and face the consequences of those choices. (It should also be noted that neither of these stereotypes needs be confined to African-American women; they are familiar within all ethnic groups.)

3. Student responses will likely vary. Getting an education is clearly associated here with bettering oneself, and it could be said that Brooks is commenting on the limited opportunities society made available to women—and particularly black women—at the time the poem was written. Note that while "Maud . . . went to college" (l. 17), nowhere does the poem suggest that she had any sort of career.

My Mother Never Worked (p. 123): Bonnie Smith-Yackel focuses on the meaning of work in the domestic sphere as a way to explore the meaning of motherhood; Brooks is also concerned with the role of motherhood in a meaningful life.

The Myth of the Latin Woman (p. 230): Judith Ortiz Cofer examines cultural stereotypes of Latina women. Brooks is also interested in this topic as it applies to African-American women.

"Girl" (p. 259): In her poem, Brooks writes, "Sadie bore two babies / Under her maiden name. / Maud and Ma and Papa / Nearly died of shame" (ll. 9–12). The narrator of Jamaica Kincaid's "'Girl'" has similar concerns about her daughter, whom she urges to "walk like a lady and not like the slut you are so bent on becoming." Brooks's poem implies alternative choices through education, even if the process transforms Maud into a solitary, "thin brown mouse" (l. 18).

Declaration of Sentiments and Resolutions (p. 556): Elizabeth Cady Stanton's call for women's rights, written almost a century before Brooks's poem, grew out of the larger abolitionist movement and its call for human rights more generally in the United States.

12: Classification and Division

A natural way to begin studying classification and division is to look closely at Gregory Rawlins's paragraph from "Pregnant with Possibility." Note that the paragraph begins with a clear topic sentence defining three categories of people based on the effect that computer technology is having on their economic status. Rawlins then goes on to develop this central idea and to make an important point about the people in each category. Finally, he explains why he uses the word *races* in referring to his three categories in order to make a larger point about them.

Remind students that, as they write any essay, they are classifying and dividing — classifying bits of information into categories that may become paragraphs, dividing a topic into parts, and so on. You might also review the many ways we use classification and division to simplify our lives — in everything from libraries to classified ads, from biological hierarchies to technical reports. You can easily devise an exercise to illustrate how we classify and divide: items on a list of twenty-five television shows, for instance, can be classified according to format (sitcom, detective story, etc.), degree of popularity, time of broadcast, or any of several other principles. Once students have practiced arranging the titles in various groupings, you can show them how they might use these categories as support for several different thesis statements concerning television programming.

The selections in this chapter use classification and division for a wide range of purposes. The opening visual text is a somewhat shocking government document that charts how immigration authorities between 1892 and 1931 classified those not permitted entry to the United States based on the causes for which they were turned away. Then, students can readily relate to William Zinsser's essay "College Pressures," focusing on four kinds of pressures college students face. They'll also likely relate to the essay by Carolyn Foster Segal, a college English instructor who categorizes the kinds of excuses students offer for not having work ready to turn in on time. In the essay following, novelist Amy Tan focuses on language, classifying the different "Englishes" she uses when communicating with different audiences; in the subsequent essay, Stephanie Ericsson uses division to suggest the many kinds of lies we tell ourselves and others. Finally, Billy Collins's poem "Aristotle" uses classification and division to investigate the nature of beginnings, middles, and endings — in art and in life.

Ellis Island Immigration Museum/NPS, *Key to Chalk Marks Designating Medical Conditions of Immigrants, Ellis Island* (CHART)

Immigration to the United States reached an all-time high during the decade between 1900 and 1910, numbering some eight million. This increase was spurred by poverty and famine in Europe, the need for workers in the United States brought about by greater industrialization, innovations such as the telegraph that allowed for speedier communication between the United States and Europe, and improvements in ocean travel that made the journey across the Atlantic quicker. Still, many would-be immigrants were turned away at Ellis Island and other entry points because, rightly or not, they were deemed unsuitable in some way. As this image suggests, a number of perceived medical conditions were considered reason for denying entry. One issue you might have students consider is that of the authorities actually marking symbols representing these conditions on immigrants' clothing. Can this be thought of as inherently demeaning?

Reading Images (p. 446)

1. Possible principles of classification for the symbols include type of condition, severity of condition, and result of condition. Type of condition probably makes the most sense.
2. Using type of condition as the principle of classification, likely categories are general physical ailment (back, eyes, face, feet, heart, and lungs), specific physical disease or condition (conjunctivitis, trachoma, goiter, hernia, lameness, pregnancy, and favus), and mental illness (senility, suspected mental illness, and definite signs of mental illness).
3. According to the website of the U.S. Citizenship and Immigration Services, current possible disqualifications for immigrants fall into four categories: communicable disease of public health significance, lack of required vaccinations, physical or mental disorders that lead to harmful behavior, and drug abuse or addiction. Among the communicable diseases listed are severe acute respiratory syndrome (SARS), tuberculosis, leprosy, HIV/AIDS, syphilis, and other sexually transmitted diseases. Students can read about this at USCIS.gov.

Thematic Connections

Why Looks Are the Last Bastion of Discrimination (p. 244): Using several contemporary and persuasive examples, Deborah L. Rhode shows how appearance-based biases remain the "last bastion of acceptable bigotry" (2). But prejudice against the "unsightly" (1) has a long history in the United States; it has even been codified into American law at different times. Are such practices — now and in the past — similar to the methods used at Ellis Island? Did immigration officials back then have a right to discriminate against the sick, disabled, or pregnant based on their perceived conditions? Would such officials have that power today? Why, or why not?

The Untouchable (p. 494): The markings designating medical considerations were a way of deciding who was fit to enter the United States and who was not. In his essay, Ajoy Mahtab considers perhaps a more profound designation traditionally used in India: "untouchable." The name refers to a group that lived outside the country's caste structure and that was "shunned far more than lepers": untouchables, "who were not considered even human, people who defiled with their very touch" (2). Students might consider the way similar notions of purity and contamination have impinged on debates about immigration in America.

Should American Citizenship Be a Birthright? (Debate; p. 591): While immigrants to America no longer pass through Ellis Island, the discussions of immigration remain lively and contentious. In this debate, writers George F. Will and Linda Chavez offer different points of view on "birthright citizenship": the principle that anyone born in the United States is automatically an American citizen.

Wired, What's Inside Coffee? (VIDEO)

Paired with "What Are the Hardest Languages to Learn?," this video should help students understand the difference between division and classification. As an example of division, it begins with the "whole" (coffee) and breaks the drink into its individual parts. "What's Inside Coffee?" is also remarkably dense and informative, given that it breaks down coffee (and its physiological effects) in less than two minutes. You might discuss why the video makers highlight specific components or aspects of coffee, but not others. For example, they focus on its health benefits, but do not analyze any of its possible negative effects. What does this suggest about their purpose and audience?

Comprehension

1. The main ingredient in a cup of coffee is water.
2. Coffee has compounds that fight bacteria in the mouth and protect the brain from free radicals.

Purpose and Audience

1. The primary purpose of this video is to provide an informative and entertaining breakdown of the main elements of coffee; it is aimed specifically at people who drink the beverage.
2. The video makers assume a basic level of science education on the part of viewers, as they present information quickly and expect viewers to be familiar with terms such as *neurotransmitters*, *antioxidants*, and *free radicals*. Likewise, they assume viewers will not be intimidated by scientific terms such as *3,5 dicaffeoylquinic acid*.

Mode

1. Students may have different responses to this question. For example, the presentation of chemistry in this video is probably different from the kind one would find in a chemistry textbook. The video makers do a good job of

highlighting important components of coffee, as well as its effects on human physiology, but some viewers may find it difficult to recall the information after the video ends.

2. The video conveys a playful and fun tone, style, and purpose. The stylized graphics fit the video, which, after all, is designed to analyze something many viewers find appetizing and appealing. Realistic images of rotting meat or cockroaches, for example, would undercut that purpose and clash with the tone of the video.

Voxy, *What Are the Hardest Languages to Learn?* (Infographic)

Students will likely have had personal experiences trying to learn a foreign language; those insights will be a useful starting point for discussing this infographic. You might note that, among the factors that determine how difficult a language is to learn, the writers do not include the learner's innate ability. Ask students if that is also a factor — and why the makers of this infographic may have left it out.

Comprehension

1. Factors include the complexity of the language, as well as its similarity to a person's native language or other languages he or she knows; the time he or she devotes each week to learning the language; the availability of learning resources; and the learner's motivation.
2. According to the infographic, a person will need to spend around forty-four weeks to achieve proficiency.
3. Chinese is difficult because it is tonal (a change in tone changes the meaning of a word). Chinese also uses thousands of characters and a complex writing system.

Purpose and Audience

1. Voxy is a service for people who wish to learn foreign languages, so the infographic probably has an implicit marketing and advertising purpose. But it is also informative, and could help prospective learners make decisions based on its classifications and its analyses of languages. The data is from the U.S. State Department's Foreign Service Institute.
2. As Voxy is a company that provides language instruction, the target audience is people who are thinking about learning another language. But readers may include anyone who is interested in languages and their relative difficulty.

Mode

1. Among other reasons, knowing the number of people who speak a language may give some sense of the language's utility and prominence. The icons shed light on different regions of the world where a particular language is spoken; this information might be useful to travelers, as well as those interested in the geographical and cultural "reach" of various languages.

2. Students should have different responses, but you might ask them to consider what information they might add to the infographic.

William Zinsser, *College Pressures*

You will probably want to discuss this essay first in your classification unit because its subject matter is so close to students and because it so clearly demonstrates meaningful use of the pattern. From Zinsser's essay, you can raise any number of classification issues: the basis for the system, the logic behind the order in which categories are presented, questions about any overlapping categories, and the significance of the system.

As you assign the essay, you might ask students to consider causes of student suicide in this country. Of course, the causes are varied and complex, but they often include academic pressures. As you discuss the selection, you will want to emphasize Zinsser's belief that students "have the power to shape their own future" (39) and to discuss ways in which they can do so. You might also ask your students how closely Yale students parallel students elsewhere. Are the concerns of most Yale students trivial compared to pressures faced by students at state universities or community colleges, for instance? (Don't forget to remind students that Yale students, too, may have severe financial problems.)

Comprehension (p. 454)

1. Zinsser advises students that their futures are unpredictable, with turns they will not expect, and that there is time to make changes of careers, jobs, attitudes, and approaches.

2. He wishes them "some release from the clammy grip of the future" (13) so that they will have the chance to enjoy each stage of their education, to experiment, and to learn that failure is not fatal and can even be valuable. He believes his wish is naive because America worships achievement and lauds the successful in the media.

3. Zinsser identifies economic, parental, peer, and self-induced pressures.

4. Zinsser blames no one. He sees only victims, not villains, because the pressures to compete are all too real.

5. Zinsser evaluates students by the range of their learning, their curiosity, and their willingness to take risks. He cares little about their grades. In contrast, he sees employers evaluating them on the basis of their having taken a narrow spectrum of safe subjects and earned uniformly high grades.

6. Women are under even more pressure than men because society is so slow to recognize their leadership potential for jobs traditionally reserved for men.

7. The "new pauperism" causes professors to spend their time publishing to avoid "perishing" in a shrinking profession. Consequently, they do not spend as much time with students as many would like.

8. Ultimately students themselves must accept responsibility for eliminating college pressures. They are the ones who can find faith in themselves and refuse to be shaped by external pressures.

9. Because students have too many choices for the limited time they have available, sports and other extracurricular activities cause them further anxiety. Students adapt by selecting activities with a foreseeable end rather than choosing ongoing activities.

115

Purpose and Audience (p. 455)

1. Zinsser's thesis is that students who are victims of enormous economic, parental, peer, and self-induced pressures must, nonetheless, free themselves — as only they can. Without discounting the difficulties, Zinsser intends to effect change, to make students aware that they can free themselves from "the clammy grip of the future" (13).

2. Very likely students would most feel the impact from Zinsser's ideas since they generally feel pressured without realizing that they can free themselves. Other potential audiences have more experience with academic and professional life.

3. In paragraphs 42–46, Zinsser hopes to make readers aware that anxiety even drives students' extracurricular pursuits: he sees students as "largely ignoring the blithe spirit inside who keeps trying to come out and play" (46) because of faulty American values.

4. Zinsser believes that his readers, for the most part, share the values that cause student anxiety and obsession without being aware of the impact these values have. However, he also believes that they can be enlightened. His assumption about the materialism of his audience is not entirely valid; many parents are already enlightened and do not insist that their students major in "pre-rich" (28), and many employers look for qualities not shown on transcripts. Of course, Zinsser's assumptions are not without some foundation, although they need to be qualified. Certainly his assumption that Yale students are typical of students nationally could lead him to overgeneralize.

Style and Structure (p. 455)

1. Zinsser effectively uses the introductory notes to Carlos to personalize students' struggling for success.

2. Zinsser signals his classification in paragraph 15 with his explicit statement of the four types of pressure. He begins his first category in paragraph 16 when he discusses the typical question of today's students: how can they find an "edge" for getting into the professional schools that almost guarantee their earning large incomes after graduation? He indicates the completion of the final category when he asserts that the student, "as a driven creature who is largely ignoring the blithe spirit inside" (46), is the product of values that make him or her feel both driven and fearful.

3. Paragraphs 22 and 31 are transitional. Each introduces a new type of pressure by closely linking it to the one just discussed.

4. Zinsser has several options for referring to groups of mixed gender, including "he or she" and "he/she." The least obtrusive option is to make both antecedents and pronouns plural. Because it is unobtrusive, it is the preferred option. Certainly the most controversial option, at least in academic situations, is to use a plural pronoun to refer to a singular indefinite pronoun; however, this usage does sometimes appear in respected publications. Discuss your preferences and your logic with your students. The issue of gender usage creates an opportunity for you to discuss the notion of language as dynamic rather than fixed — a concept that will surprise some of your students.

5. Quotations from deans and students at Yale support Zinsser's thesis.

6. Economic pressures drive parents who, in turn, pressure students. Thus the two types of pressure overlap. Students feeling driven by economic and parental

pressures are further pressured by seeing other students outclass them, and therefore they drive themselves even further. Zinsser's acknowledgment that the categories overlap strengthens the essay, making it clear that the pressures combine to trap students.

7. Zinsser discusses economic pressure first since it generates parental pressure. Both external pressures foster pressures inside the academic environment. Zinsser ends with self-induced pressure to emphasize the individual student who suffers.

8. Students who leave notes to Carlos are *supplicants* (9), and achievement is the *national god* that is venerated and glorified as the state religion (14). Colleges, students, and their parents, like religious ascetics, belong to a *brotherhood of paupers* (20). The language suggests that Zinsser believes American materialism has replaced (or even become) religion in American society.

Combining the Patterns (p. 456)

In the opening paragraphs, Zinsser cites notes from students that exemplify the pressures they face, and he refers to specific students as examples in paragraphs 30 and 32. Other examples include the comments from deans in paragraph 16, the specifics about Yale and Harvard in paragraph 17, and the examples of the "brutal economy" in paragraphs 20–21. All the examples help make Zinsser's point more concrete. Additional examples of specific students might add to readers' understanding.

Thematic Connections

Suicide Note (p. 364): The suicide note written by Janice Mirikitani's student and the accompanying note about an actual Asian-American student who leaped to her death from her dormitory suggest how intensely parental pressures, real or assumed, can weigh on students. In her note, the girl apologizes to her parents "for disappointing you" repeatedly explaining, "I've worked very hard" (ll. 6–7). She clearly suffers from being caught in what Zinsser calls "one of the oldest webs of love and duty and guilt" (28). Zinsser does not mention suicide, but news articles appear with some frequency about student suicides that can be traced to academic pressures. Your students can benefit from discussing this link — and from your informing them about your school's resources for troubled students. Be sure they understand that Zinsser does not blame anyone for the pressures but does suggest a solution. (See also *Thematic Connections*, "Suicide Note," p. 91 of this manual.)

Why Chinese Mothers Are Superior (p. 408): Both writers deal with the cost and outcomes of high expectations. While Amy Chua believes that her parenting style is the one that produces the best results, she does not focus on the possible negative consequences it may produce. In contrast, Zinsser is concerned about the consequences that high expectations may have on college students.

I'm Your Teacher, Not Your Internet-Service Provider (p. 415): In "College Pressures," Zinsser writes, "Part of the problem is that [college students] do more than they are expected to do" (35). Compare this characterization of undergraduates with the description of them in Ellen Laird's essay. Do they seem to be over-exerting themselves? What "pressures" does distance education relieve? Which ones might it exacerbate?

The Dog Ate My Flash Drive, and Other Tales of Woe **(p. 457):** Writer and college instructor Carolyn Foster Segal considers student excuses for turning work in late — or not at all. They range from dubious family emergencies to the "totally bizarre" (1). All of these alibis, however, seem to be summed up by the cliché for this kind of excuse-making alluded to in her title. The writer even keeps a cartoon tacked to her office door, which shows a cat explaining to his feline teacher: "The dog ate my homework" (1). In her essay, the students are conniving and dishonest. In contrast, Zinsser's essay presents a more sympathetic view of students as it focuses on the stress and difficulties they can experience, particularly at highly competitive institutions.

Is the Student Loan Crisis a Myth? **(Debate; p. 578):** Zinsser includes the economic and financial pressures that students face, as well as the problem of debt. Writing in the late 1970s, he claims that America is "witnessing . . . the creation of a brotherhood of paupers" (20). Ask students to consider this claim in light of the current debate about the student loan crisis. Does Zinsser's assertion suggest that concerns about student debt are perennial and therefore perhaps subject to hype or exaggeration? Or is there something different about student debt now that makes it more of a crisis?

Carolyn Foster Segal, *The Dog Ate My Flash Drive, and Other Tales of Woe*

This essay — a catalog of student excuses for late work compiled by an English professor — may immediately appeal more to instructors than to students, some of whom may feel Segal's characterizations are unfair. What is important to get students to realize is that Segal is writing humorously for an audience of college instructors. Her intention is not to malign students but to set out in an entertaining way experiences all instructors share to some extent. The fact that the same excuses are offered over and over by different students "week after week, semester after semester, year after year" (1) obviously frustrates Segal, but here she finds it more comical than annoying. If you have excuses you've heard over and over from students (or any that are, like one of Segal's categories, "totally bizarre"), by all means share them with your class. One lesson students should come away with is the knowledge that instructors do generally see through false excuses.

At the same time, students will find this a very clear model of classification and division — and one that can probably inspire them to think of good topics for their own essays using this pattern. You might also have them experiment on their own or in groups with Segal's very clever syntax in sentences like "My best friend was up all night and I had to (a) stay up with her in the dorm, (b) drive her to the hospital, or (c) drive to her college because (1) her boyfriend broke up with her, (2) she was throwing up blood . . . , or (3) her grandfather/grandmother died." You might have them use this model to write a similar sentence about excuses one might give to a police officer for speeding, to a parent for coming in late, or to a friend for forgetting a date or a birthday.

Comprehension (p. 460)

1. Segal states her thesis in the final two sentences of her opening paragraph. She is classifying the types of excuses her students offer to explain why an assignment that is due is not complete.

118

2. Students may not feel the statement is fair, but they should recognize that Segal means it as a joke.
3. Student responses will vary. Segal's point, of course, is that in most cases such excuses are untrue.
4. Again, student responses will vary. Depending on your own policies regarding accepting late work, you might let students know why you feel the need to enforce such policies. You might also ask about the policies of their other instructors.
5. One thing Segal hopes to instill in students is a sense of personal responsibility; she expects them to hand in work on time and, if this is not possible, to accept the consequences. Student opinion will vary as to whether reading this essay would impart this lesson to her students.

Purpose and Audience (p. 461)

1. Segal has noted that the response from college instructors was sympathetic; she heard from many readers whose experiences matched hers almost exactly. They also found her essay entertaining. College students guilty of offering such excuses on a regular basis might find that the essay hits a little too close to home.
2. Segal is not writing to students particularly, so it is not likely that her purpose is to change students' habits. For a readership of college teachers, it is more likely her purpose is to entertain; she could be letting off steam, but her humorous tone suggests otherwise.
3. Segal lists specific excuses here, using what seem like students' own words, in order to show how lame they are. The final one, with its many mistakes, suggests that technological excuses are often written rather than given in person. Most students will find this an effective strategy.

Style and Structure (p. 461)

1. Listing her categories is not exactly necessary for Segal, but doing so provides a helpful forecast of what the essay will cover.
2. Students may see a slight overlap, as the final excuse under "the evils of dorm life" — the student whose roommate attacked him with a hammer — could well rank as "totally bizarre." It would not be easy to combine any of the categories, though clever students may think of categories Segal doesn't include, such as what might be called the vicissitudes of life — "my knapsack containing my paper was stolen," and so forth.
3. Segal's order seems to go from the most common ("the grandmother of all excuses" [2]) to the least ("the totally bizarre" [8]). This order makes sense logically.
4. The first three categories are comparable in that they each offer a variety of brief, related examples of excuses. The final category offers only two extended examples of excuses, so it is not strictly comparable, but it nonetheless provides a satisfying conclusion to the essay.
5. The reference to *Little Women* and *Pilgrim's Progress* in paragraph 3 is an example of Segal's sarcasm, as is her discussion of the excuse "My best friend's mother killed herself" in paragraph 5 and the "evil roommate"/"innocent victim" discussion in paragraph 6. Most college instructors would see such

sarcasm as appropriately humorous because they would consider such excuses as ripe for sarcasm. Students may respond differently.

6. College-related terms include *syllabus* and *dorm life* (1); *extensions* (2); *adjunct* and *professor* (5); *graduate school* (6); *commuter student* (8); and *absence, withdraw from the course*, and *dropped the class* (9).

7. References to the "grandfather/grandmother died" excuse appear in paragraphs 2, 4, and 6, while references to "throwing up blood" appear in paragraphs 4, 6, and 7. Segal seems to single out the first excuse because it is so common and the second because it is such a wild claim.

8. Other examples of phrases that lend Segal's essay a breezy tone are "plot development" (2); "no professor can prove otherwise!" and "off week" (5); and "her phrase" (10). This casual tone serves Segal's purpose to entertain.

9. You may have students who can add to the list in paragraph 7. Subcategories might be general computer problems (examples one and seven), printer problems (examples two through five), and Internet connection (examples six, eight, and nine).

Combining the Patterns (p. 462)

Segal's two concluding narratives are necessary to suggest the "totally bizarre" nature of the specific excuses she writes about. Such narratives are not really necessary elsewhere in the essay because the excuses in the other categories are more generic—although the story in paragraph 6 of the student whose roommate attacked him with a hammer might have been expanded on.

Thematic Connections

Cutting and Pasting: A Senior Thesis by (Insert Name) (p. 17): Segal's section entitled "The Evils of Technology" lists the "electronically enhanced" explanations students now use to justify late or missing work (7). Her essay is relatively lighthearted. In Brent Staples's "Cutting and Pasting: A Senior Thesis by (Insert Name)," the implications of new technologies (and new forms of academic dishonesty) are more serious: "The Pritchard axiom—that repetitive cheating undermines learning—has ominous implications for a world in which even junior high school students cut and paste from the Internet instead of producing their own writing" (9). The problem of "electronically enhanced" plagiarism should provoke a lively discussion among students.

I'm Your Teacher, Not Your Internet-Service Provider (p. 415): In this essay, Ellen Laird compares and contrasts Internet distance education with traditional classroom teaching. How might online learning exacerbate the student tendencies Segal identifies in "The Dog Ate My Flash Drive, and Other Tales of Woe"? How would you propose that both Segal and Laird better manage these problems?

College Pressures (p. 448): At the opening of his essay about the difficulties of college life, William Zinsser lists a series of explanations from students for why they are behind in their work. How are these explanations different from the kinds of excuses Segal writes about? What would Segal make of such explanations? Is there a difference that these students are writing to an adviser rather than to an instructor?

The Ways We Lie (p. 471): Assuming that most of the excuses Segal writes about are, indeed, untruths, into which of Stephanie Ericsson's categories of lying might they best be placed? Or would they require a category that Ericsson doesn't list? Ericsson might call them "out-and-out lies," but students might think otherwise.

Amy Tan, *Mother Tongue*

The daughter of Chinese immigrant parents, Amy Tan describes the four "Englishes [she] grew up with" (2), focusing on their relation to her mother: the "simple" English she spoke to her mother, her mother's "broken" English, her "watered-down" translations of her mother's Chinese, and her imaginatively realized "perfect" translations of her mother's "internal language." Tan does not name these categories until her next-to-last paragraph, but she provides examples throughout: paragraphs 4–9 discuss her "simple" English and her mother's "broken" English, with Tan concluding ruefully that as a child she was embarrassed by her mother's English; paragraphs 10–14 give examples of her "watered-down" translations; and her final paragraphs describe her attempts to capture her mother's "internal language." In paragraphs 15–18, Tan suggests her purpose in considering these "Englishes": to explain the difficulties Asian-American students have with English, particularly English achievement tests, and the reason they end up pursuing degrees in math and science.

At some point you may want to ask students—even those whose families are native English speakers—how different their "home language" is from the language they encounter at school. What difficulties do they have adjusting to "academic English"?

Comprehension (p. 468)

1. See the discussion of Tan's categories in the introduction above.
2. She identifies the categories in her next-to-last paragraph. Students might suggest that this identification could have come earlier to make the structure of the essay clearer from the start. You might point out that this might have made the essay seem more formal.
3. Only the final category is not clearly illustrated. Tan might have provided an example from one of her books to do so, but her conclusion might then have had less force.
4. Her mother's English was a handicap when her mother needed to communicate about important matters with native English speakers in positions of authority—her stockbroker, for example, and hospital personnel. Other examples might include dealings with the police, the courts, government agencies, and the like.
5. Tan was embarrassed by her mother's English as a child, and she also believes that the language she heard at home contributed to her lowered scores on language achievement tests. But in adulthood the same language became an inspiration to her as a novelist.
6. Tan attributes her difficulty in answering questions on achievement tests to the fact that she could not easily limit the possibilities; her mind, she suggests, didn't process language in a simple either/or pattern. It is certainly possible that Tan's imagination—which would lead to her success as a

writer—contributed as much to the problem as did the level of her family's language skills.
7. Because they score higher on math achievement tests than on language tests, Tan suggests that many Asian-American students are being steered to majors in math and science, effectively cutting them off from creative writing. Other explanations might include the possibility that such students simply feel more comfortable with more technical subjects.

Purpose and Audience (p. 468)

1. Tan uses her opening to show that she is writing from personal experience, not from extensive study. She doesn't intend her ultimate claims about Asian-American students to be definitive.
2. The level of detail she offers about immigrant culture suggests that Tan expects her audience to be composed largely of native English speakers.
3. Tan focuses fairly equally on her mother and on the subject of language, but her larger purpose is to make a point about language.

Style and Structure (p. 468)

1. Both Tan's diction and her organizational structure are relatively informal. For an audience of nonexperts, such informality seems appropriate, but achieving credibility with a more expert audience would require a more formal style.
2. She includes the example to suggest what the "family talk" she grew up with sounds like. The impression it gives is that her mother's English is indeed "broken," which is the effect Tan intended.
3. Students may have different opinions about this and, like Tan, will probably have difficulty coming up with a more neutral term. You might ask what this difficulty suggests about the way speakers like Tan's mother are viewed in American society.
4. These passages demonstrate the contrast between Tan's command of English and her mother's.
5. *Mother tongue* generally refers to one's native language. Here the phrase refers more exactly to Tan's mother's language, the language of home for the writer.
6. The "terrible line" shows Tan reaching to find an English suitable for formal expression—and in doing so, using diction that is artificial and stilted. The style she uses for the essay is more natural and fluid.

Combining the Patterns (p. 470)

The narration Tan uses adds color and vividness to the essay and is crucial to making her point concrete. No other strategy would be quite so appropriate, although the anecdotes do serve as examples.

Thematic Connections

Midnight (p. 217): This student essay focuses on hardworking parents, here Asian immigrants who labor in a dry cleaning sweatshop more than twelve hours a day for substantially less than the minimum wage. Like Tan's mother, they speak broken English, and that has limited their job opportunities. Ku writes, "Even though they did not speak, their eyes said, 'We hate our jobs, but we work so that our children will have better lives than we do.' "

Why Chinese Mothers Are Superior (p. 408): The daughter of Chinese immigrant parents, Tan focuses on language, classifying the different "Englishes" she uses when communicating with different audiences. Tan is writing primarily about the relationship she has with her immigrant mother, whose "language . . . helped shape the way [she] saw things, expressed things, made sense of the world" (7). Amy Chua focuses on parenting styles and the need to instill a sense of discipline and a strong work ethic in her children. Both writers understand that certain expectations must be met—Tan's mother will not be cheated, and Chua upholds the lessons she learned from her own parents. While Tan focuses on clear communication, Chua focuses on discipline.

The Park (p. 667): Tan writes about growing up as the daughter of an immigrant mother whose language limited Tan's perceptions of her and "almost" limited Tan's "possibilities in life" (15). But she also developed strategies for negotiating this doubleness. How does Truong's account of his experiences with his friend at the park suggest their own strategies for dealing with their lives as immigrants and outsiders? If no fence had ultimately kept them from the park, how might their own possibilities have been "limited"?

Stephanie Ericsson, *The Ways We Lie*

Stephanie Ericsson analyzes the effect of lying by dividing lies into ten different categories, moving from the most personal to those that affect our world in the most profound ways. Admitting that we can't really eliminate lies entirely from our lives, Ericsson nonetheless suggests that to create a sea change that will grant us as a public "our *right* to trust" (36) the media, politicians, and others, we must begin on the smallest level: "Maybe if I don't tell the bank the check's in the mail I'll be less tolerant of the lies told me every day" (37).

One way to begin discussion is to have students provide some examples of their own for Ericsson's categories, particularly white lies, deflecting, omission, dismissal, and delusion. Ask whether there are any times when they feel justified in telling a lie (most will say "yes"); then ask if there are any times when they feel it is justified for someone else to lie to them (a much more difficult question).

Comprehension (p. 478)

1. (1) *White lies* are generally "harmless untruth[s]" (1). (2) *Facades* are roles we play, often to impress others. (3) *Ignoring the plain facts* is a kind of lying to oneself. (4) *Deflecting* is distracting others from something negative about oneself or refusing to respond when accused of inappropriate behavior. (5) *Omission* is the leaving out of pertinent facts that don't correspond with the image one wants to present. (6) *Stereotypes and clichés* "shut down original thinking" and result in "[a]ll the 'isms' " (21–22). (7) *Groupthink* is a combination of other forms of lying in which a group's loyalty to itself outweighs any other value, including the truth. (8) *Out-and-out lies* are attempts to "refashion reality" and can be "easily confronted" (27). (9) *Dismissal* is ignoring "feelings, perceptions, or even the raw facts of a situation" (28), particularly as they relate to others. (10) *Delusion* is "the tendency to see excuses as facts," "the mind's ability . . . to support what it wants to be the truth" (32).

2. Lies are often necessary to protect the feelings of others and to help us present the most positive images of ourselves. In addition, delusion is a "survival mechanism" (33).

3. White lies can delude people into a false sense of security or hope. Facades can be used to "seduce others into an illusion" (11). Ignoring the plain facts can lead to all kinds of harm, particularly when criminal behavior is involved. Deflecting can let people hide what they don't want others to know by making it look as though they're being honest; it is also a way of resisting justified criticism. Omission on a historical level can keep people ignorant of their true past. Stereotypes "close minds and separate people" (22). Groupthink leads to poor decision making. Out-and-out lies can refute reality unless they are caught. Dismissal can result in mental illness. Delusion allows us to ignore our most serious problems.

4. Out-and-out lies are the most "honest" lies; that is, the liar knows he or she is lying and expects you to suspect the lie.

5. Dismissal often involves things that can't be "proved" unless we delve deeply. As long as we don't delve deeply, we can continue to believe that the problem doesn't exist.

Purpose and Audience (p. 478)

1. Ultimately, Ericsson attacks lying. As she says in her conclusion, "Our acceptance of lies becomes a cultural cancer that eventually shrouds and reorders reality until moral garbage becomes as invisible to us as water is to a fish" (35). She ends by encouraging readers, at least implicitly, to think carefully before telling even little lies in order to become "less tolerant" (37) of the larger lies that surround us.

2. Ericsson's is a fairly liberal slant, most evident in the examples she offers in paragraphs 5, 12, 15, 18–20, 24–25, and 33. She seems to have imagined a fairly liberal audience, but it's clear that people of all political stripes are concerned about politicians' lying and lying in the media — although they might define those lies differently.

Style and Structure (p. 478)

1. Ericsson's informal opening serves to draw readers in. She establishes common ground by telling about her own lies and noting that we all lie.

2. The quotations from a wide variety of time periods and sources serve to universalize the points she is making. Students, unfamiliar with many of these sources, may see them as interruptions.

3. Generally, each discussion includes an example or two, and Ericsson's evaluation of when that category of lie is beneficial and how it is harmful. Sometimes, however, she omits the discussion of benefits — one assumes because she sees no benefit in that category of lie. The discussions are not exactly balanced, however; some are more detailed than others. Students might feel that more balance would set up each category more clearly.

4. Ericsson basically moves from the least to the most problematic kinds of lies — although students will not necessarily agree with her ranking system. Some, for example, might see ignoring the plain facts as more harmful than deflecting or omission.

5. Rhetorical questions help emphasize the point that lying is a double-edged sword, sometimes beneficial, sometimes harmful. Ericsson wants us as a society to find alternatives to lying, yet she has no simple answer as to how this might be accomplished.

6. Colloquialisms include *Sure I lie . . .* (3); *ducked out* (6); *looks great . . . looks like hell* (8); *crawls into a hole* (16); *mouth like a truck driver* (22); and *good-ole-boy* (25). They lend a certain informality and accessibility to her prose, which most readers should view positively.

7. Ericsson cites historians and psychologists, the very sorts of experts one would expect in a research paper on lying. Student opinion will vary regarding the need for other citations.

8. Ericsson also uses the feminine indefinite pronoun in paragraph 4, but she uses the male indefinite pronoun in paragraph 8. It is unlikely that students would find these few shifts distracting.

9. In both her conclusion and her introduction, Ericsson uses personal experience, quotation, and rhetorical questions. Her conclusion echoes much of the important language in the introduction as well.

Combining the Patterns (p. 480)

The dictionary definition is probably not necessary, but it does allow Ericsson to establish common terminology before discussing behaviors that readers might not have thought of as lying before.

Thematic Connections

"What's in a Name?" **(p. 2):** Henry Louis Gates's essay offers the story of a childhood incident that revealed to him the extent to which African Americans were considered inferior by whites. Ericsson's discussion of stereotypes is pertinent here, as is her discussion of facades. Brent Staples's "Just Walk On By" (p. 238) and student Mark Cotharn's "Brains versus Brawn" (p. 377) also deal with stereotypes.

The Money **(p. 114):** In this darkly comic personal narrative, Junot Díaz recounts an incident from his childhood in which his family's house was burglarized. You might have students use Ericsson's categories to identify and analyze the types of lies in Díaz's essay.

Thirty-Eight Who Saw Murder Didn't Call the Police **(p. 128):** Have students decide, on the basis of the quotations in Martin Gansberg's newspaper article, what kind of lying the thirty-eight witnesses exhibited. The most likely categories are ignoring the plain facts and dismissal, with stereotypes playing a role in some instances.

The Hidden Life of Garbage **(p. 186):** Heather Rogers writes vividly about contemporary waste disposal; she indicts the consumer society that produces so much garbage, as well. By focusing on the veiled and euphemized ways we conceal the "stench" and the "scale of the destruction" (3), do you think the writer reveals dishonesty? When she puts quotations around the words "environmentally responsible" (13), does she suggest that the phrase is a lie?

The Lottery **(p. 308):** Students will easily see Shirley Jackson's short story as an example of groupthink. Tessie Hutchinson also uses deflection when she argues that the lottery drawing was unfair.

Billy Collins, *Aristotle* (POETRY)

Billy Collins is known for his self-consciously accessible poetry, and students should have relatively little trouble with the diction and theme of "Aristotle." Despite the clear language, however, the poem is witty, sophisticated, and allusive, drawing on a range of references from John Milton to Sylvia Plath. This selection is not a classification-and-division essay, of course, but it speaks to the way we divide art, stories, plots, plays, journeys, and lives. It also reflects and enacts our need for beginnings, middles, and ends. This is true of the writer ("It is me hitting the period" [l. 63]) and the reader ("you closing the book" [l. 64]). Once you have established your students' relative comprehension of the poem, you might ask them what images they would add to Collins's examples. Consider specific passages as well: How does a plot "congeal" (l. 35)? What does the speaker mean when he claims that the end is "what we have all been waiting for" (l. 70) and "the destination we cannot help imagining" (l. 72)? Why did Collins choose the title "Aristotle" for this poem?

Reading Literature (p. 483)

1. "Aristotle" explores beginnings, middles, and ends. The poem suggests that the categories are discrete, as indicated by three distinctive verse paragraphs that begin "This is the beginning," "This is the middle," "And this is the end."
2. The poet treats the categories in similar terms. He provides a range of examples and images for each category, from beginnings ("the creation of light" [l. 4], curtains rising, wheels beginning to turn), to middles (a letter hidden under a pillow, an aria rising in pitch, a climbing party stuck on a ledge), and endings (the last elephant in a parade, a person closing a book, the image of poet Sylvia Plath about to commit suicide). Each category is necessary and equal, as required by Aristotle.
3. Collins's poem has an openness and a free-associative quality that should encourage students to think of their own examples. They might consider images from songs, books, movies, relationships, life as a student, family life, and video games, among other sources.

Thematic Connections

Ground Zero **(p. 175):** Suzanne Berne writes about the difficulty of trying to "superimpose" media images of the 9/11 attacks onto the "industrious emptiness" (13) where the towers fell. Her goal is to "understand better" what she is "looking at" (14), as she stares at the empty site and tries to make sense of the event. Does "Ground Zero" imply that the fall of the towers entailed both an ending and, ultimately, another beginning?

Once More to the Lake **(p. 191):** E. B. White revisits a lake from his childhood and reflects on time and change. Are there lines or images in this essay that could fit into the categories of "Aristotle"? For example, how might the last sentences of "Once More to the Lake" correspond to the poem's "endings" section? Is White attempting to change or complicate beginnings, middles, and endings?

"Girl" **(p. 259):** In Jamaica Kincaid's " 'Girl,' " a mother gives severe and sometimes mean-spirited advice to her daughter on how to be a woman. How does the mother imagine the beginning, middle, and end of her daughter's life? What ending does she have in mind for her?

Suicide Note (p. 364): Janice Mirikitani's poem reveals the meaning of an ending, as the young speaker explains why she is committing suicide. How does this self-destructive act violate the structure of beginning-middle-ending? Point out the allusion in "Aristotle" to Sylvia Plath's suicide (l. 65). You might also have students compare "Suicide Note" and "Aristotle" as poems. How are their rhythm, diction, and imagery similar? How might students incorporate a line or an image from Mirikitani's poem into Collins's poem — or vice versa?

Love and Other Catastrophes (p. 518): Stringing together the titles of songs by such artists as Madonna and Otis Redding, Amanda Brown captures the story arc of a romantic relationship. How would students divide Brown's account into separate categories? Does it have a clear beginning, middle, and ending, or does it suggest more than three distinct elements? Discuss how students would divide up these stages.

13: Definition

Because definition encompasses all the patterns of arrangement, this chapter presents a good opportunity for review. A logical beginning model for your discussion is Desmond Morris's paragraph defining *altruism* because it compactly illustrates the combination of two techniques. As you read the essays in this chapter, you can show your students that these definition techniques and others can structure not only paragraphs but also sections of longer pieces and even whole essays, poems, or stories. You should also emphasize that any essay can include examples of several rhetorical patterns studied throughout the text. This might also be a good time to look back at earlier essays in which a definition is central — *work* in "My Mother Never Worked" and *lie* in "The Ways We Lie," for example.

U.S. Census Bureau, *U.S. Census 2010 Form* (QUESTIONNAIRE)

Reproduced here are the boxes on the 2010 Census Form in which people were asked to identify themselves first as "Hispanic, Latino, or Spanish" or not and then by "race." The form offers many choices, and some critics have questioned whether the many choices cause more confusion than clarity and perhaps even skew the reported results. For example, figures released by the Census Bureau in 2003 showed that Hispanics accounted for a larger percentage of the total U.S. population than did blacks, and some attributed this to the fact that people could, beginning in 2000, check off more than one box.

If questions regarding race might be a sensitive topic in your classroom, you might have students simply write about the questions posed below rather than conducting a class discussion.

Reading Images (p. 500)

1. Students' answers will vary. You might ask whether the request to define oneself in terms of "race, religion, or ethnicity" provides any students with too limited a set of options and, if so, why.

2. Again, students' answers will vary. You might note that the form uses the term *race* rather loosely; anthropologists generally define only three races: Caucasoid (roughly, white), Negroid (roughly, black), and Mongoloid (roughly, Asian). It is also becoming increasingly clear that genetically racial differences are minuscule compared to the vast number of genes shared by all human beings.
3. Again, students' answers will vary. Students who consider themselves of mixed race may have the most to contribute to the conversation.

Thematic Connections

"What's in a Name?" (p. 2): African-American scholar and writer Henry Louis Gates Jr. writes in this essay about his father being called "George" by a white man, though this was not his name. When the young Gates questions this, his father replies, "He calls all colored people George," which is meant to diminish them and rob them of their individuality. The census form, in contrast, is an objective measure of race.

Indian Education (p. 142): The census form asks people to define themselves according to their "origin" and "race." Does Sherman Alexie's "Indian Education," which focuses on a Native American (or "American Indian" according to the census form), suggest any general definition of a racial category? How does the main character's racial identity emerge through the narrative?

The Myth of the Latin Woman (p. 230): The census form presumes to be neutral and objective; it does not ostensibly ascribe different characteristics to different races or national origins. In contrast, Cofer's personal essay explores the myths about Latin women: cultural stereotypes that include the "sizzling" female "hot tamale" (6), along with "Maria the housemaid" (11).

Mother Tongue (p. 463): Amy Tan explores the meaning of her mother's—and her own—Chinese-American identities through the prism of her mother's idiosyncratic use of the English language.

On Dumpster Diving (p. 672): In this essay, Lars Eighner recounts his life as a wandering, homeless, Dumpster-diving "scavenger" or "scrounger." His account is also (among other things) a guide on how to survive on what other people throw away. You might have students consider how the Census Bureau views figures like Eighner. Are they essentially nonexistent?

NASA, *What Is a Black Hole?* (INFOGRAPHIC)

This infographic takes a complex scientific phenomenon and presents it in simple language and visuals. You might discuss the effectiveness of this form as a way of presenting difficult concepts like singularity and the notion that an "infinitely small point" can have the mass of many suns. You might even ask what questions the infographic leaves—and how students might revise it to include answers to those questions.

Comprehension

1. The point is called a "singularity."
2. The infographic identifies two different types of black holes: stellar and supermassive.

Purpose and Audience

1. The goal of this infographic is informative, as it explains the composition and development of black holes. The infographic also aims to define a complex astronomical phenomenon in a way that is accessible to general readers.
2. The audience for this infographic is a general audience, not scientists or specialists. The diction and rough measurements (for example, "a bunch of our suns") as well as the humor ("spaghettification") suggest this direct and accessible approach to explaining black holes.

Mode

1. This infographic uses process, as it shows, step by step, the development of black holes. It also uses comparison and contrast (of the two types of black holes) as well as exemplification (the hypothetical example of the spaceship and the event horizon).
2. Students should have a range of responses, depending, perhaps, on their level of preexisting knowledge of astronomy and black holes. The infographic might include other information, such as how scientists observe black holes or where the closest black hole to Earth is.

Judy Brady, *I Want a Wife*

This essay comments satirically on the demands placed on wives and mothers. You might begin by asking your students whether Brady overstates her case.

Comprehension (p. 504)

1. She means a devoted "servant." This ideal wife exists in the pages of some women's magazines and in the minds of some men and women.
2. Some specific duties include washing clothes, cleaning, cooking, babysitting, and typing. The five categories are child care, household chores, cooking, managing social life, and providing for sexual needs.
3. She feels she must do the jobs of both husband and wife.
4. She might leave if she found a more suitable wife. In that case, her first wife would take care of the children.

Purpose and Audience (p. 504)

1. It exaggerates the role of wife and mother to ridicule it. Most feminists would agree — perhaps in varying degrees — with her thesis. Students may not see this essay as likely to appear in any publication today.
2. The thesis, which is implied, is that too much is expected of wives.
3. No. She is merely using this to make her point.

Style and Structure (p. 504)

1. This repetition reinforces her thesis and introduces a list of new reasons why she wants a wife.

2. No. In fact, the length of the paragraphs draws attention to the statements being made.
3. Students can find a number of verbs that are repeated, and they should be able to determine how they affect the tone of the essay.
4. She omits the pronouns because she means to suggest that her wife—or any wife—could just as easily be male as female.
5. Students will readily see that many of these words are used sarcastically.

Combining the Patterns (p. 505)

Brady uses exemplification and description as the major patterns in her definition—and contrasts between images of wives and husbands are implied. The implied contrasts might in fact be seen as the most important for Brady's purposes.

Thematic Connections

My Mother Never Worked (p. 123): Even Brady's exhausting job description for a wife falls short of the work performed by Bonnie Smith-Yackel's mother, Martha. Students can discuss the extent to which a woman's life has improved since 1921, when Martha Smith became a wife, or make the necessary additions to turn Brady's essay into "I Want a Farm Wife."

Sex, Lies, and Conversation (p. 421): See *Thematic Connections,* "Sex, Lies, and Conversation," p. 93 of this manual. Deborah Tannen's essay provides a good opportunity to think about male-female stereotypes—and what actually governs gender roles.

Declaration of Sentiments and Resolutions (p. 556): This early feminist document, written by Elizabeth Cady Stanton in 1848, will give students a sense of how far women had—or had not—come by the time Brady wrote her essay in the early 1970s. (If you are old enough, you may remember the advertising jingle for Virginia Slims cigarettes, introduced at about this time: "You've come a long way, baby / to get where you got to today. / You've got your own cigarette now, baby. / You've come a long, long way.") A more important issue, perhaps, is what advances women have made since "I Want a Wife" was first published. See also *Thematic Connections,* "Declaration of Sentiments and Resolutions," p. 111 of this manual.

José Antonio Burciaga, *Tortillas*

This lighthearted look at a staple of Mexican cuisine is an especially good example of definition. Not only is it interesting and immediately accessible, but it also shows the combination of rhetorical techniques that can go into making an extended definition: narration (1, 3), cause and effect (2), process (4), exemplification (5, 7–8), description (6), and comparison (6). You might begin discussion by asking what students remember first when they think of tortillas as described by Burciaga; then have them decide why the technique used to make that point is particularly effective.

Comprehension (p. 508)

1. A tortilla is a flat, round corn cake that is fried or steamed.

2. Tortillas may be filled with a variety of fillings and rolled into tacos. They may be filled with cheese and grilled (*quesadillas*). They may be deep-fried (*flautas* or *gorditas*). More whimsically, they can be used as a mask or hat, as an artist's canvas, or even as the basis for a miraculous vision.

3. Burciaga is not entirely serious here, yet he does mean to suggest the fundamental role tortillas play in Mexican culture.

Purpose and Audience (p. 508)

1. The thesis might be paraphrased as "Although we take tortillas for granted, they are in fact a special part of Mexico's cultural heritage." Burciaga doesn't state his thesis sooner because he wants to lead us to this understanding in his conclusion.

2. Students may have different opinions about Burciaga's intended audience. He certainly assumes that his audience is already familiar with tortillas because he spends very little time describing them, but this doesn't necessarily mean that he expects readers to be of Mexican descent. Given the level of detail and the tone, it would seem that Burciaga is writing for a general audience that includes both Chicanos and non-Chicanos.

3. Burciaga is trying in a lighthearted, humorous way to "elevate" the tortilla in his readers' minds, to show how versatile, even meaningful, it is. If he tried to be more serious, he would probably be less convincing because he might seem to be overstating his case.

4. For Burciaga tortillas are a representation of his childhood and of his cultural heritage.

Style and Structure (p. 508)

1. The brief formal definition comes in paragraph 6. It is clear that Burciaga assumes an audience that already knows what a tortilla is and so does not feel the need to provide an introductory definition. The definition in paragraph 6 serves to highlight the versatility of tortillas.

2. Burciaga doesn't define three Spanish words in paragraph 4: *mercado* (market), *masa* (the cornmeal dough from which tortillas are made), and *deliciosas* (delicious). He clearly assumes that readers will be familiar with these words or that their meanings will be clear in context. Note that he also doesn't define the Yiddish word *yarmulke* (skullcap) in paragraph 2.

3. Burciaga doesn't use synonyms, although he uses a helpful analogy at the beginning of paragraph 3; and he doesn't discuss the word's origin, although he traces its appearance in Mayan mythology. Neither does he use negation as part of his definition, probably because little would be gained by doing so.

4. See question 2, above. *Jalapeños* are hot green peppers used in much Mexican and southwestern cooking.

Combining the Patterns (p. 509)

See the introduction to this entry for a survey of the rhetorical patterns Burciaga uses.

Thematic Connections

Goodbye to My Twinkie Days (p. 171): For Burciaga, tortillas evoke both his childhood and his ethnic heritage. Bich Minh Nguyen's meditation on the Twinkie is a variation on a similar theme, as she ties the snack cake to both childhood memories and broader issues of assimilation into American life and culture.

Once More to the Lake (p. 191): Both Burciaga and E. B. White invoke childhood memories that represent their cultural heritage and that suggest deeply satisfying and meaningful rituals. In both cases the past seems to permeate the present, creating a warm feeling of nostalgia. Students might consider the differences in tone between the two essays.

The Case for Birthright Citizenship (p. 593): Burciaga was born in America, but he values — and holds on to — the "lowly corn cake" as an important part of his Mexican heritage. Writing in the context of the immigration debate, Linda Chavez argues that an "expansive view of who is an American" is critical to the "successful assimilation of millions of newcomers" (8). Does his fascination with tortillas suggest Burciaga's resistance to assimilation? How does sharing the cuisine and eating customs of a country figure into the assimilation process? How does the United States assimilate foods — as well as people — from other cultures?

The Park (p. 667): Student Michael Huu Truong's essay is also a reminiscence of childhood that focuses on culture and assimilation. Note that except for Bruce Lee, the heroes the two boys (one Vietnamese, the other Korean) imagine themselves to be are all American icons: Abbott and Costello, Superman, Clint Eastwood, the Bionic Man. Does assimilation mean losing one's heritage, or can assimilation result in something "truly bicultural," like Burciaga's children putting peanut butter and jelly on tortillas?

Anna Quindlen, *Homeless*

"It has been customary to take people's pain and lessen our own participation in it by turning it into an issue, not a collection of human beings," writes Anna Quindlen in her meditation on the problem of homelessness (8). Yet, the idea of "homelessness" as an abstract "problem" is exactly what she wants to question in this classic essay. You might begin by asking students about their own definitions of *home*: What does it mean? What connotations does it have? How is it different from *house* or *shelter*? Do they accept Quindlen's claims about the centrality and importance of home ("That is everything" [9])?

You should also note that Quindlen consciously avoids using data, statistics, social science, or any real empirical lens to view homelessness. Instead, she prefers the personal and the anecdotal, like the story of Ann that opens the essay. This is deliberate, of course, but it may lead to the question: Is empathy enough, on its own? In concentrating on details and individuals, does Quindlen lose sight of broader, structural issues (social, economic, or otherwise) that could be useful in lessening the number of people without homes? You might even ask students how they might revise the essay to incorporate significant data or specific proposals, while retaining its focus on individual connection.

Comprehension (p. 512)

1. Quindlen tries to question and redefine these designations. For example, she sees terms like *homeless* and *homeless people* as language that turns the problems

and the pain of real human beings into issues and abstractions (8–9). She wants us to see homelessness as a quality that goes beyond not having "shelter from the elements" (3). When individuals like the ones she describes experience "homelessness," they lack a place for the deepest aspects of their selves and personal identities, as indicated by Quindlen's proverbial rhetoric: "You are where you live" (2) and "Home is where the heart is" (4). Her definition of *home* is almost ineffable, as she illustrates in paragraph 4: "[Home] is everything."

2. By *homes*, she does not mean houses or shelters. She means home as a secure, stable place, to which a person has a deep, personal connection.

3. In paragraph 4, Quindlen uses her own relationship to her home to illustrate what she means by "home" in paragraph 3. It is a place of "certainty, stability, predictability, privacy."

4. Quindlen means that these people are not an abstraction or a generalized social problem ("homelessness") or "issue." Rather, they are all real, specific individuals with specific needs and lacks. She wants her readers to perceive them as such, and truly understand their pain (8).

Purpose and Audience (p. 512)

1. This strategy introduces — and supports — Quindlen's main point: "homelessness" is not an abstract social issue that can be solved by providing more homeless shelters. Instead, Quindlen wants us to view the problem through a different lens: Ann is an individual with no home — and all that fact entails.

2. Quindlen's thesis could be stated as: "We should not view homelessness as an abstract social issue; rather, we should see it as a collection of individual human beings who lack the most basic necessity for a dignified human existence: a home, and all the that the word *home* entails." She makes similar claims throughout the essay, as in her final paragraph: "They are not the homeless. They are people who have no homes" (9).

3. The writer seemed to want to reframe the problem of homelessness for readers who may have gotten inured to it: "It has been customary to take people's pain and lessen our own participation in it by turning it into an issue, not a collection of human beings" (8). In the 1980s, the problem of homelessness was a more prominent social issue than it is now, but in the wake of the financial collapse, chronic high unemployment, and a housing crisis, her essay may strike readers as poignant and relevant.

Style and Structure (p. 513)

1. Many sentences throughout the essay reveal Quindlen's feelings, including her concluding ones: "My God. That is everything" (9). Implicitly, her entire essay is a call for empathy, a quality of feeling she demonstrates during her interaction with Ann: "There was no need for discussion. I knew what she was trying to tell me, for it was something I had often felt" (2). Students may have different views of this emotional approach to the topic. Can the problem of too many people without homes be "solved" without a big-picture view, broad strokes, and policies that address it as a social issue? Is it more important to have empathetic interactions with individuals?

2. She uses compare and contrast to show how our sense of—and relationship with—the idea of "home" has changed. In the past, it was tied to family and

rooted in a specific place where we lived and died. Now, homes are temporary; they are less tied to specific people and places, as we "move on to something else and something else again" (5). This has diminished our understanding of their centrality and importance.

3. While empirical data might help readers understand the broad contours and social implications of homelessness, Quindlen is explicitly trying to avoid viewing the issue through the lens of social science or policy making.

4. An example of definition by negation can be found in the third paragraph, where Quindlen attempts to redefine "homeless people" as individuals without homes: "I'm not simply talking about shelter from the elements, or three square meals a day, or a mailing address."

5. Quindlen begins her essay with exemplification. Ann is a specific instance of homelessness as the particular problem of one individual. Quindlen uses description in the second paragraph, when she describes the home that Ann used to own.

6. This question should get students to think about the meaning of *home*, as well as its complex connotations and implications. For Quindlen, a home is good and necessary in and of itself; its value is innate. In contrast, *real estate* implies property owned for its potential financial value. Yet, in the United States (in particular) *owning* a home suggests a rootedness and, perhaps, even virtue. Can places we rent temporarily be "homes"?

Combining the Patterns (p. 513)

Quindlen wants to persuade readers to view homeless people, and the problem of homelessness, in a specific way. She seems to want her audience to participate in the real pain of those without homes instead of "turning it into an issue" (8). While she focuses on empathy and "details" (9) here, her essay might benefit from some data on the extent of the problem of homelessness. Quindlen could also provide a more specific proposal or course of action for those who want to help the homeless.

Thematic Connections

"What's in a Name?" (p. 2): In "Homeless," Quindlen considers the definition and significance of something most of us take for granted: our homes. In fact, her essay might be retitled "What's in a Home?" In " 'What's in a Name?,' " Henry Louis Gates Jr. reflects on the significance of another thing that we take for granted: our names and the respect accorded to us by those who address us properly. While many readers are probably familiar with common racial slurs, Gates focuses on a less obviously offensive term, "George," which, nevertheless, left a deep impression on him as a child.

Midnight (p. 217): Grace Ku writes about growing up with parents who worked long hours in unpleasant jobs at a dry-cleaning plant. The result is a poignant meditation on the meaning of work and sacrifice. You might ask students to consider the connections between Quindlen's idea of "home" and the idea of "work" that emerges from Ku's essay.

On Dumpster Diving (p. 672): Lars Eighner's guide to living on the street out of garbage cans and Dumpsters considers what it means to be poor and lack economic opportunity. In this essay he describes a period in his life when he was homeless and forced to subsist on what he could scrounge from public garbage containers. Because Eighner's writing is graceful and nuanced, he is able to vividly portray his experience such that students may come to understand him as a complex, specific person, not simply a generic "homeless" person.

Gayle Rosenwald Smith, *The Wife-Beater*

Depending on your age and fashion sense, you may or may not be familiar with the term *wife-beater* to describe a tank-style T-shirt. One way to begin discussion is to ask students whether they are familiar with this meaning of the term and whether they have used it themselves. If many have used it, ask whether Smith has opened their eyes in any way in arguing that the use of the term is disturbing and leads to a climate that tolerates violence against women. (You will surely have some students who will think Smith should "lighten up" and who will argue that the term is more a joke than anything else.)

You will probably want to have students consider contemporary culture more generally in terms of what Smith refers to in paragraph 11 as a return to male dominance. Many commentators have over the past decade noted a backlash against feminism that has younger men and women embracing more traditional gender roles in their relationships. Do students see such a trend? In addition, do male rappers, sports figures, and other celebrities popular with young men create a climate in which "manliness" is equated with violence, as Smith suggests in her conclusion?

In terms of teaching this essay as a rhetorical model, you'll need to point out that, while definition is central to the points Smith is trying to make, hers is not a conventional essay of definition, using a variety of patterns to define a particular object or concept. This is at heart an argumentative essay and, thus, provides an excellent transition to the next chapter.

Comprehension (p. 516)

1. "Wife-beater" is the nickname for a white, skinny-ribbed, tank-style T-shirt originally worn by men as an undershirt and now fashionable with men and women as an outer garment or under a jacket. Smith is disturbed by the name because its casual use suggests that spousal abuse is acceptable among those who use the term.

2. When she says "The name is the issue," she seems to mean that the fact that such shirts themselves are "all the rage" (1) is not a matter of concern to her — only what they are called. When she says "It's not just the name that worries me," she means that she fears the use of the term is an example of a possible "return . . . to male dominance where physical abuse is acceptable as a means of control." There's no real contradiction here.

3. In paragraphs 13–16, Smith suggests that she fears a causal connection between the acceptance of the term *wife-beater* and high rates of family violence, particularly when she notes that most people who use the term are under 25 and that the average age of batterers is 31. Students should recognize, though, that she does not actually claim a causal connection.

4. This does not really undercut her argument because she has made the point earlier that it is not the popularity of the shirt that disturbs her, but rather the popularity of the slang term for it.

5. Smith feels that because many women find men who wear the shirt attractive and "manly," *manly* comes to equal *violent*, leading perhaps to young women tolerating violent behavior against themselves.

Purpose and Audience (p. 516)

1. There are a number of possible reactions to Smith's opening sentence. Most immediately, readers are likely to be curious about what she means by "them" and so continue reading. In the context of her essay as a whole, this opening suggests that, if her concerns are correct, then the problem may be widespread.
2. Smith is clearly encouraging readers to think twice about using the term and even abandon its use altogether. But she also wants readers to recognize that violence against women is something our culture should be concerned about and we should discourage in any way that we can.
3. She seems to have a fairly broad audience in mind including both young adults and older readers. She does not seem to be writing only to those who wear such T-shirts because she is careful to explain what they are to readers who may not have heard of them, but it is also clear that her imagined audience includes those who use the term.
4. A possible paraphrase of Smith's thesis: "Casual use of the term 'wife-beater' as the nickname for a popular style of T-shirt contributes to a cultural climate that condones and even encourages violence against women."

Style and Structure (p. 516)

1. The fact that the sleeveless shirt is so popular is part of the source of Smith's concern about what it is called. Students will probably see this as an effective opening.
2. One effect of including the dictionary definition is to show that the term has become so widely used that it has found its way into dictionaries. Another is to support her contention that the term refers openly to spousal abuse.
3. Students' answers will vary. Based on Smith's suggestion that the shirt's name should connote flattery rather than violence, one possibility is "hunkshirt."
4. At the end of her first paragraph, Smith mentions that this particular style of T-shirt has not achieved such popularity since the leading male character in the film *A Streetcar Named Desire* made it popular in the 1950s. (For readers familiar with the film, this historical fact will immediately call up the image of Marlon Brando wearing such a shirt and so help them visualize it; for others, it probably serves little rhetorical purpose.) Then, in paragraphs 6–9, she traces several possible histories of the term to link it to spousal abuse.
5. Smith quotes three statistics in paragraph 13 to suggest a link between the popularity of the term *wife-beater* among young people and the high levels of violence against women.
6. Dictionary.com offers this definition: "n. a sleeveless undershirt. (Indicating a low regard for the wearers of the garment . . .)." Merriam-Webster does not note a negative connotation; it simply says, "a man's white tank top." The website Thefreedictionary.com defines the term as "a man who hits his wife," without indicating its use as a name for a garment.

Combining the Patterns (p. 517)

Students' opinions will likely vary. Smith does not really establish a cause-and-effect relationship but rather suggests that even the possibility of one is reason enough to abandon the name. In fact, hard information is not available to establish such a relationship, although students might consider the extent to which the term reflects stereotypes of gender relations that are also seen in other aspects of contemporary culture.

Thematic Connections

Four Tattoos (p. 222): You might ask your students to consider socioeconomic connections between tattoos and "wife-beater" shirts. What signals do such fashion choices send?

My First Conk (p. 283): Malcolm X recalls undergoing the painful process of hair straightening popular among black men prior to the 1960s. Like Smith, he encourages a change in how a popular fashion statement is regarded as a way to combat pernicious stereotypes.

A Peaceful Woman Explains Why She Carries a Gun (p. 353): Linda Hasselstrom's essay describes a culture in which the possibility of violence against women is so prevalent that she has begun carrying a gun for protection. One theme students might consider is whether women have reason to fear violence in most parts of the United States and, if so, whether gender stereotypes may be responsible for such violence.

Your Flip-Flops Are Grossing Me Out (p. 687): Stevens finds a superficial or apparently trivial phenomenon (flip-flops) and suggest that it is the manifestation of a larger, more serious subject or problem (a breakdown of the social contract, for example). Similarly, Smith suggest that the name for a particular t-shirt embeds larger societal issues having to do with gender and violence.

Amanda Brown, *Love and Other Catastrophes: A Mix Tape*

Students should appreciate Amanda Brown's clever account of an archetypal romantic relationship using only the titles of popular songs. They should also connect with the story's universality, touching upon themes of loneliness, infatuation, love, betrayal, and heartbreak in remarkably few words. You might begin by discussing what is being defined here as well as the story's pattern of development. What stages of love do specific songs represent? Does the reader need to be familiar with the songs to understand the story? You can also move to the content of "Love and Other Catastrophes"—for example, Brown ultimately implies a cynical (or "catastrophic") view of love. Can students imagine another set of songs and another storyline? Is Brown's text the expression of a distinctively feminine point of view, or could this story apply to men and women equally?

Reading Literature (p. 519)

1. The story defines *love* in the context of a romantic relationship.
2. Several patterns of development are used: exemplification (each song title is an example of a specific stage in a relationship, such as infatuation for "I'll Tumble 4 Ya"), process (the author traces a romantic relationship from stage

to stage), and classification and division (the writer implicitly identifies the subclasses or distinctive elements of a relationship, such as commitment, betrayal, and reconciliation).

3. According to the story, the progress of a romantic relationship is full of turmoil and drama, leading ultimately to failure. The meaning of "other catastrophes" is open to interpretation, but it may refer to all the specific disappointments and reversals that make up a relationship.

Thematic Connections

The Storm (p. 198): Kate Chopin's story describes a passionate and unpunished adulterous encounter that, ironically, leaves two lovers happier and more connected to their respective spouses and children. Students might consider how "The Storm" complicates notions of infatuation, commitment, and betrayal. Is the tryst described in the story a "catastrophe" in any way?

The Kiss/LOVE (p. 390): As "Love and Other Catastrophes" does, these two sculptures provide an image — and suggest the meaning — of love. Which seems most compelling and "true"? What stage of love in Brown's story does Auguste Rodin's sculpture correspond to? What song title might match the concept of love proposed by Robert Indiana's *LOVE*? How might "Love and Other Catastrophes" be expressed in a visual or sculptural medium?

The Ways We Lie (p. 471): In this essay, Stephanie Ericsson divides lies into ten different categories and analyzes their effects. Students might consider the role of lying in love and romance. As Brown's story suggests, dishonesty might include the obvious "out and out lies" of betrayal. Do romantic relationships encourage (or even require) lying in subtle ways — via facades, ignoring the plain facts, a delusion?

I Want a Wife (p. 502): Judy Brady gives a satirical view of the demands placed on wives and mothers. How does Brady's view of marriage differ from the image presented in "Love and Other Catastrophes"? Does "I Want a Wife" imply that love and marriage are ultimately a "catastrophe" for women?

The Wife-Beater (p. 514): "Wife-beater" is the nickname for a white, skinny-ribbed, tank-style T-shirt originally worn by men as an undershirt and now fashionable with men and women as an outer garment or under a jacket. Gayle Rosenwald Smith is disturbed by the name because its casual use suggests that spousal abuse is acceptable among those who use the term. Smith thus characterizes the term *wife-beater* as having a negative connotation. Similarly, Brown portrays the negative side of having a relationship, though she writes in a more humorous way than Smith.

14: Argumentation

Argumentation is a difficult rhetorical form for students to understand. In the chapter introduction we take pains to describe it and relate it to the other types of writing we have discussed. Although our primary emphasis is the appeal to reason, we recognize the emotional dimension that most good arguments possess. At the risk of oversimplifying the issue, however, we do not discuss in any depth the other appeals acceptable for persuasive writing. We choose to focus on argumentation because it is the principal form of persuasion used in college and because many beginning student writers confuse appeals to emotion with the feeling that "because I feel it is right, it must be."

Our suggestion is that you spend a good deal of time emphasizing the rhetoric of argumentation. You can illustrate to students that a good argument usually relies on a number of patterns of development. In order to convince an audience, they should use all of the rhetorical tools at their disposal. Indeed, the paragraph taken from Daniel Pink's *To Sell Is Human: The Surprising Truth about Moving Others* uses cause and effect and exemplification prominently. Notice how both these patterns not only support the paragraph's thesis, but also provide important context and orient the reader.

Carefully illustrate for students how writers support their assertions. You can, for example, ask students to point out the information Thomas Jefferson uses to support his points. You can also ask students to judge the quality and effectiveness of the deductive argument he presents. Elizabeth Cady Stanton's *Declaration of Sentiments and Resolutions*, which is modeled on Jefferson's Declaration, and other essays included in the unit can also be examined for their uses of evidence. Pointing out inadequate evidence is another effective way to teach students. Some of the questions at the ends of selections will help your students make such judgments.

One of the more exciting and challenging aspects of argumentation is refutation, which requires students to develop a dynamic and subtle sense of audience. Earlier in the semester students were concerned with presenting information to an audience, but now they not only have to evaluate an audience, they also must anticipate and react to its probable responses to a subject. We suggest you begin with "Letter from Birmingham Jail." You will want to explore King's excellent uses of induction and deduction and then to consider his care in refuting his opposition. If students use a highlighter to mark each time King addresses his opponents' view, they will see that these refutations organize King's tightly logical argument.

To further sharpen students' awareness of the need to identify audience and refute arguments, we have grouped essays into five widely debated subjects. The first debate provides contrasting viewpoints on the student loan crisis; as many students have probably taken out loans for their education, the subject should generate lively discussion. The second grouping considers the contentious issue of immigration, but does so from an angle that may be unfamiliar to students: the practice and merits of birthright citizenship. Next are four essays that address the current controversy over the violence and physical consequences of football, in particular, and risky sports, more generally. This casebook suggests a variety of provocative questions: How protective should parents be of their children? Does the athletic and entertainment value of sports such as football justify the risk of permanent brain damage to players? Do dangerous activities have an inherent value for those who participate — and those who watch? The second casebook focuses on another contentious topic, particularly in the wake of the mass shootings of the past several years. Students are likely to be somewhat familiar with debates about gun rights and gun laws, but this collection of arguments places the controversy in the immediate context of college campuses.

In these debates and casebooks, students are presented with multiple sides of each issue. As a result, they can more clearly see refutations at work. Before asking students to write a full argumentative essay, have them write a short essay in which they refute a specific argument. This assignment will help them build up to more demanding argumentation assignments.

The section on deductive and inductive reasoning is intended as an introduction to logic. Our purpose is to give an overview of the basic principles of logic and to provide a list of the problems in reasoning that plague many student writers. You can use this section as the subject for a class discussion, or you can refer students to it as the need arises. For more information on reasoning and logic we suggest you consult *With Good Reason: An Introduction to Informal Fallacies* by S. Morris Engel (St. Martin's Press).

StopTextsStopWrecks.org, *You Don't Want Them Responding to Your Text* (AD)

This public service advertisement is sponsored by the National Highway Traffic Safety Administration (NHTSA). According to its website, nhtsa.gov, the "NHTSA was established by the Highway Safety Act of 1970 and is dedicated to achieving the highest standards of excellence in motor vehicle and highway safety. It works daily to help prevent crashes and their attendant costs, both human and financial."

Reading Images (p. 549)

1. The ad is directed at those who might text while driving but who might not be aware of the dangers of this practice.
2. The ad's headline says "You don't want them responding to your text"? The image of the ambulance supports this point by suggesting the danger inherent in texting while driving, that such a practice can lead to crashes and injuries. The headline suggest that such injuries would be to the driver, but of course others (pedestrians, other drivers, and passengers) could be hurt as well.
3. The ad appeals primarily to emotions, but asks viewers to consider the logical relation between texting and crashes.
4. The website StopTextsStopWrecks.org includes additional information and resources such as videos, facts about texting and driving, and tips to prevent the practice.

Thematic Connections

Ten Ways We Get the Odds Wrong (p. 250): Szalavitz enumerates 10 ways in which people misunderstand the odds, from our fear of spectacular unlikely events to tendency to downplay the risks of a "natural" phenomenon, too much sun exposure. She writes that "ancient threats like spiders and snakes cause fear out of proportion to the real danger they pose, while experiences that should frighten us — like fast driving — don't" (6).

The Embalming of Mr. Jones (p. 301): Mitford details the embalming process with detachment and precision. She also reflects on the "reticence" of morticians to provide "public information" about such a common procedure. The anti-texting ad attempts to bring to light the dangers of texting while driving.

The Lottery (p. 308): In Jackson's celebrated short story, a group of rural townspeople stand by half-watching, half-participating in a violent tragedy. It brings to the mind the possibility of a passenger passively accepting texting by a driver. You might ask your students how they handle such a situation. Are they aware of the danger? Do they typically try to stop such behavior? Why or why not?

Who Killed Benny Paret? **(p. 337):** Cousins's essay focuses on violence in the boxing ring, which contributes to serious injury and even death. What might be seen as the links between the dangers of driving and violence in sports?

Dear Motorist, *Dear Motorist: Pledge to Share the Road* (VIDEO)

This video argues that drivers must be more conscious and considerate of the safety of cyclists. You might discuss how the video makers avoid simply scolding motorists or commanding them to drive in certain ways. Instead, they take a more subtle approach, highlighting individual cyclists and their stories. They also urge cyclists to be more conscientious and self-aware. "Dear Motorist" appeals to pathos: students might have different responses to its highly emotional approach, but they should understand how the creators of the video are using it to support their purpose.

Comprehension

1. According to a figure in the video, everyone's "worst fear" is to kill or injure another person.
2. The noncyclist speaks as the husband of a biker: he talks about how his wife was almost hit by a motorist. His presence in the video shows that cyclists are not the only ones affected by safety issues.

Purpose and Audience

1. The purpose of the video, according to its producers, is to save at least "one" cyclist. But its more general aim is to make motorists more aware—and respectful—of cyclists so there are fewer accidents and deaths.
2. The video takes a conciliatory and understanding attitude toward its audience. You might note that, while the video is serious and plays on emotions, its tone is not preachy or hectoring. Its creators go out of their way to acknowledge the frustrations of motorists, as well as the need for cyclists to obey laws and be conscientious on the road.

Mode

1. In the context of the video's argument, the juxtaposition of these images over the death of a cyclist plays upon the emotions of viewers, or pathos. It highlights the profound loss that such a death entails—in this case, for the family of the biker.
2. Part of the purpose of the video is to show the various individuals who are cyclists—wives, husbands, sons, fathers, mothers, and friends. The effect is to highlight these individual stories and roles, and suggest the significance of each one of these people—or any other cyclist on the road.

Thomas Jefferson, *The Declaration of Independence*

The Declaration of Independence stands as a classic model of deductive argument. It begins with a major premise, progresses to a minor premise, and draws a logical conclusion. Often, students approach this document with a closed mind and see it as a musty, boring piece of history that has nothing to do with them. Many students have never read it and are surprised to see how clear and exciting it really is. You might point out to them how genuinely revolutionary it was and how it shocked the world when it first appeared. Once students realize this fact, they can have great fun analyzing the rhetorical strategy that Jefferson and the other writers employed. Especially interesting in this regard are the many grievances that the document lists. Not only do they make for an interesting class discussion, but they also show the lengths to which the writers felt they had to go to establish the reasonableness of their case.

Comprehension (p. 553)

1. Paragraph 2 enumerates the self-evident truths that Jefferson asserts: "that all men are created equal, that they are endowed by their Creator with certain unalienable rights, that among these are life, liberty and the pursuit of happiness. That to secure these rights, governments are instituted among men, deriving their just powers from the consent of the governed. That whenever any form of government becomes destructive to these ends, it is the right of the people to alter or to abolish it, and to institute new government, laying its foundation on such principles and organizing its powers in such form, as to them shall seem most likely to effect their safety and happiness."
2. Governments derive "their just powers from the consent of the governed" (2).
3. Paragraphs 3–31 list the reasons that justify the break with Great Britain.
4. Jefferson concludes that the British crown no longer deserves allegiance because it no longer protects the rights of the governed.

Purpose and Audience (p. 553)

1. The major premise of Jefferson's argument is that all men are created equal. He could not have done more to establish that premise in this essay and still have accomplished his purpose.
2. Jefferson structures the Declaration like a formal argument in logic. In paragraph 2, he states the general premises upon which he bases his argument. In paragraphs 3–31, he states specific justifications for the actions of the colonies. Finally, in paragraph 32, he sums up his argument and states his conclusions.
3. Jefferson realized that he would have to address several very distinct audiences. The Declaration announced to Great Britain that the colonies no longer owed allegiance to the crown; to other European countries that the colonies were free states that would trade, wage war, and make alliances independent of Great Britain; and to the colonists themselves that some of their number were ready to fight for independence. Jefferson surely knew that some people would never accept his conclusions no matter how well reasoned they were—as evidenced by the strong and continued support of the king by many of the colonists.
4. In paragraphs 2, 30, and 31, Jefferson effectively anticipates the opposition and presents convincing evidence that all reasonable approaches have been attempted.
5. Jefferson speaks of his "British brethren" to emphasize the cultural bonds that connected the colonies with England. By doing this, he hopes to gain empathy from his audience. In part, this was also an effort to defuse the violent reaction that Jefferson expected from the British.

6. Jefferson states his thesis, so to speak, in the final paragraph. Because its claim is so decisively revolutionary, it is necessary that he present all pertinent evidence before stating it directly.

Style and Structure (p. 554)

1. Jefferson primarily uses deductive reasoning. The Declaration of Independence resembles a syllogism. It begins with a major premise, progresses to a minor premise, and ends with a conclusion. Jefferson argues that his major premise is "self-evident" (2). However, when he provides evidence that his minor premise is sound (3–29), he reasons inductively.
2. In addition to the syllogistic structure discussed above, Jefferson uses the language of formal logic to create transitions between sections. He introduces his premises by saying, "We hold these truths to be self-evident." He then prefaces the list of grievances by saying, "To prove this, let facts be submitted to a candid world" (2). Finally, he begins his conclusion by saying, "We, therefore, the Representatives of the United States of America" (32).
3. Jefferson includes all twenty-eight grievances to establish the reasonableness of the colonists' position. Summarizing them or stating only a few of them would materially weaken the Declaration, since anyone not already inclined to agree with the colonists would suspect they are being unfair to the king and his government.
4. Jefferson concludes with "We, therefore" to emphasize the deductive structure of the document and the reasonableness of his argument. He has effectively built to this conclusion with the long list of evidence that precedes it.
5. Your students will find numerous examples of words with negative connotations, including *abuses, usurpations, despotism, injuries, forbidden, invasions, obstructed, plundered, ravaged,* and *burnt.* These words portray the actions of the king in a strongly negative light, justifying the Declaration of Independence. Had Jefferson used more neutral words, the case against the king would not have seemed so strong nor the action of the colonists so justified.
6. Jefferson's text includes a number of words that may be unfamiliar to students: *usurpations, evinces, prudence, sufferance, tyrant, dissolutions, quartering, perfidy,* and *magnanimity.* Whether students prefer their updated versions will depend to some extent on their sophistication as writers. Certainly, they are bound to sound less formal and incantatory.

Combining the Patterns (p. 555)

History suggests that Jefferson's examples are relevant, representative, sufficient, and effective. Implicit in the examples is a pattern of cause and effect (the effects of British policies on the colonists); students might consider whether making this pattern more explicit would add to the argument.

Thematic Connections

The "Black Table" Is Still There (p. 348): Pairing the Declaration of Independence with Lawrence Otis Graham's essay about self-segregation in a suburban junior high school provides an opportunity to consider the extent to which the values embodied in the Declaration have been achieved in contemporary U.S. life. Is it possible for groups to be separate but equal?

Grant and Lee: A Study in Contrasts **(p. 393):** Consulting both the Declaration and Bruce Catton's essay, students should determine how the Confederate cause differed from Jefferson's cause. Both involved throwing off a government that participants deemed to be unjust.

Aristotle **(p. 481):** Billy Collins's poem investigates the structure and meaning of beginnings, middles, and endings. He writes that the beginning is "where you find / the creation of light, a fish wriggling onto land, / the first word of *Paradise Lost* on an empty page" (ll. 3–5). The ending, on the other hand, is "me hitting the period / and you closing the book" (ll. 63–64). How does the Declaration of Independence conform or deviate from this Aristotelian structure? As a founding document of the United States, how does the Declaration function as *both* a beginning and an ending?

Letter from Birmingham Jail **(p. 563):** This country, founded on a belief that "all men are created equal," failed to extend that equality to blacks. Although slavery was discussed by the Founding Fathers, political differences led them to essentially ignore the problem. Students may not know that Jefferson himself was a slaveholder. Ask your students to read the Declaration of Independence a second time. As they reread the list of abuses the colonists believed justified their actions, ask them to keep in mind the injustices that Martin Luther King Jr. talks about. Many of Jefferson's complaints have parallels in slavery and, later, in segregation. Ask students to reread King's "Letter from Birmingham Jail" as well. Because of its length and complexity, they will need a second reading. As they reread, have them mark King's explicit and implicit references to Jefferson, the Declaration of Independence, and the Constitution. Doing so will help them appreciate and understand King's arguments and gain a stronger sense of their country's history.

Elizabeth Cady Stanton, *Declaration of Sentiments and Resolutions, Seneca Falls Convention, 1848*

You will want to make sure that students read the headnote before tackling this selection because it provides important background information. You will probably also want to study this essay after the class has worked on the Declaration of Independence (or after you are sure that students are reasonably familiar with the Declaration of Independence) because Stanton's 1848 Declaration very deliberately echoes Jefferson's; she expected her audience to immediately recognize the parallels. Like Jefferson's Declaration, hers is also a justification for rebelling against the shackles of a despotic government, but her target is the governmental, legal, and societal sanctions of the day that prevented women from sharing equally with men the "unalienable rights" of "life, liberty and the pursuit of happiness."

It should be clear to students that women of Stanton's day were less than even second-class citizens; they barely shared in the rights of citizenship at all. As Stanton acknowledges, most men and many women themselves simply accepted as a given that women were intellectually and emotionally inferior to men and unfit for any pursuits beyond keeping house and raising a family. The only serious profession open to women was that of novelist and even this was considered somewhat suspect. At the same time, women were generally held to a far higher moral standard than were men, and any breach of decorum on their part was grounds for censure. Moreover, it was unusual for women to inherit property, and when they married, they and everything they owned became, by law, their husband's property. In its day, Stanton's Declaration was nothing less than revolutionary.

If you have a dramatic bent, you might enjoy reading some passages here aloud to students. This selection was intended as much a document to be heard as to be read.

Comprehension (p. 560)

1. The declaration of sentiments is necessary, out of "respect to the opinions of mankind," to "declare the causes" that have led "one portion of the family of man" (that is, women) to assume a new position in the world, one "to which the laws of nature and of nature's God entitle them" (1).

2. These "self-evident" truths are that men and women are equals, that they share the basic rights of "life, liberty, and the pursuit of happiness," and that it is the government's responsibility "to secure these rights" for all citizens.

3. The injuries are detailed in paragraphs 4–18. They include women not being allowed to vote and the consequences of this disenfranchisement (4–7); the legally restricted status of wives, including their inability to hold property on their own (8–11); the taxation of single women by a government that does not represent them (12); the highly restricted opportunities for women in terms of employment and education (13–15); the enforcement of a different moral code for men and women (16); the arbitrary assignment to women of a limited "sphere of action" (17); and the resulting lack of confidence and self-respect that make women "willing to lead a dependent and abject life" (18). Students' opinions may differ as to the relative importance of these injuries; they might consider how many paragraphs are devoted to each.

4. Stanton writes that she expects a reception marked by "misconception, misrepresentation, and ridicule" (20) and that she and her fellow conventioneers "shall employ agents, circulate tracts, petition the State and National legislatures, and endeavor to enlist the pulpit and the press in our behalf" (20).

5. Women, Stanton concludes, should share the same rights enjoyed by men—to choose one's "station in society" (23), to "speak and teach . . . in all religious assemblies" (26), to speak in public more generally (28), and to vote (30). In paragraph 32, she asserts as "self-evident" that "equally with man," women should be able to "promote every righteous cause by every righteous means." It is "self-evident falsehood" that women are incapable of doing this.

Purpose and Audience (p. 560)

1. While Stanton's audience at the Seneca Falls Convention was made up primarily of women, she clearly expected her Declaration to be read by men. As the final paragraph makes clear, it is a call to action to both men and women. Given prevailing sentiments, women would, by and large, be more immediately receptive to the argument than men.

2. Perhaps Stanton's most effective strategy is couching her Declaration so that it echoes the Declaration of Independence, considered a model of reasonable argument. At the end of paragraph 3, she is also quick to offer proof to back

up her assertions. Then in paragraph 21 she cites the great legal commentator Blackstone as a way of supporting her position. While some contemporary readers may think that Stanton is overstating the case, women of her day were, in fact, denied all the rights she claims.

3. Stanton states her thesis in paragraph 19, waiting until she has detailed the "disenfranchisement" and "degradation" of women before proposing her solution.

4. Stanton's primary purpose is to stir up the convention's delegates in order to encourage them to begin lobbying for change. At the same time, she hopes to provoke a debate that will ultimately serve to change people's ideas and behavior.

Style and Structure (p. 561)

1. The main advantage of this strategy was that the Declaration of Independence was given great moral weight and was seen as a model of rational argument. A disadvantage is that her use of the Declaration as a model might have been seen as a kind of sacrilege, a trivialization of this important document.

2. In fact, these truths were no more "self-evident" in Stanton's day than were the truths Thomas Jefferson posed as "self-evident" when the Declaration of Independence was written. Because these are beliefs, however, Stanton could have done little to establish their validity.

3. Stanton's major premise is that, equally with men, women are guaranteed certain rights and that when these rights are abridged, those affected may seek change ("insist upon the institution of a new government" [2]). Her minor premise is that men have abridged the rights of women. Logically, this leads to her conclusion that women must insist upon change.

4. "To prove this" provides a transition from the statement of the minor premise to supporting evidence in paragraph 3, while the transition "now" leads from the previous list of injuries to Stanton's conclusion in paragraph 19. Then, beginning in paragraph 22, each new item is introduced with *"Resolved."* Most students will see these transitions as effective.

5. Students' opinions may vary. Note that Stanton implicitly denies that opposition to her position has any validity whatsoever. She essentially bases her argument on the assertion that because the laws of God apply equally to men and women, so should the laws of man.

6. Paragraph 13 is a good possibility here. It might be paraphrased: "Men have set aside for themselves almost all ways of earning a living, and any jobs women can take pay only low wages. Women are barred from pursuing any career, valued by men, that leads to wealth or distinction. Women cannot be religious leaders, doctors, or lawyers."

Combining the Patterns (p. 562)

Students should recognize that because they accurately summarize the way women of Stanton's time were subordinated, her examples are relevant and representative. She certainly offers sufficient examples, but the effectiveness of her examples will ultimately depend on one's beliefs regarding the equality of men and women.

My Mother Never Worked (p. 123): Bonnie Smith-Yackel's essay suggests that what has traditionally been considered women's work is still undervalued in contemporary society. Students might consider why it continues to be uncommon for married men to take on the primary role of housekeeper and stay-at-home dad.

A Peaceful Woman Explains Why She Carries a Gun (p. 353): Despite the many gains women have made in terms of human rights since Stanton wrote her Declaration in 1848, circumstances still exist where women are at the mercy of men, as Linda M. Hasselstrom writes in this essay. Living in the rural West, Hasselstrom recounts a number of menacing encounters—ranging from simple harassment to the threat of rape—with men who thought they could take advantage of her because she is a woman. To equal the playing field, she decided to purchase and learn how to use a pistol for protection against such people. Paragraphs 22–24 of Stanton's Declaration go to the heart of the issue of equality between men and women, but Hasselstrom suggests that in some situations only a weapon can help achieve that equality.

I Want a Wife (p. 502): This classic essay can be tied in neatly with the preceding "My Mother Never Worked" entry.

The Declaration of Independence (p. 550): As suggested in the introductory remarks to this chapter, you will probably want to study the Declaration of Sentiments and Resolutions in conjunction with the Declaration of Independence, which provided Stanton with her rhetorical model. Students might compare the two, looking for places where Stanton adheres closely to her model versus where she varies from it significantly. Why does she choose to follow Jefferson's words closely? Why are her variations necessary to her purpose?

Martin Luther King Jr., *Letter from Birmingham Jail*

King's letter is an excellent illustration of a complex argument. Many critics have pointed out the similarities between it and the Declaration of Independence. Both documents attack injustice and take pains to establish the reasonableness of their positions. Like Jefferson, King realizes that the specific audience he is addressing (the king and Parliament in Jefferson's case) is not the only audience to whom he must appeal. He is aware that people all over the world are watching the events in which he is involved. His carefully crafted argument aligns him with the three men to whom he feels he is spiritual heir: Jefferson, Thoreau, and Gandhi. Many students will not be familiar with these men or the fact that they all sought to influence public opinion by acts of civil disobedience. A short summary of their lives and causes will enable students to perceive some of the subtleties of King's argument. This essay offers a good opportunity to introduce the term *allusion* and to show students how King makes conscious reference to the Declaration of Independence, the Bible, and "Civil Disobedience."

Comprehension (p. 576)

1. King says that he receives so much criticism he would have to spend all his time answering it. He decided to answer this criticism because he feels that his fellow clergymen are men of good will and that their criticisms were sincerely set forth (1).

2. Since the demonstrations occurred after an election in Birmingham, the clergymen think that King and his associates have not allowed the new administration enough time to act.

3. King says that "Birmingham is probably the most thoroughly segregated city in the United States" (6) and mentions brutality, unfair courts, and bombings. Because the city fathers "consistently refused to engage in good-faith negotiation" (6) and because promises made by white merchants were broken (7), King says, "We had no alternative except to prepare for direct action" (8).

4. For African Americans, *wait* usually means *never*, as King observes in paragraph 13.

5. King defines two types of laws, *just* and *unjust:* "A just law is a man-made code that squares with the moral law or the law of God. An unjust law is a code that is out of harmony with the moral law" (16).

6. King says that condemning nonviolent protests because they precipitate violence is "like condemning a robbed man because his possession of money precipitated the evil act of robbery" (25). He goes on to say that "as the federal courts have consistently affirmed, it is wrong to urge an individual to cease his efforts to gain his basic constitutional rights because the quest may precipitate violence" (25).

7. King is disappointed that the white churches did not support him. Some, he says, have been outright opponents.

Purpose and Audience (p. 576)

1. King's purpose is to reach and inspire white clergymen in the South to support his cause. By establishing his setting as the Birmingham city jail, he hopes to make his audience sympathetic and to demonstrate his commitment to his cause. By defining his audience as "fellow clergymen," King can address them as "men of genuine good will," an assumption that is basic to his argument.

2. Throughout his letter, King scolds his fellow clergymen for being insensitive to the moral rightness of his cause. He does this in paragraphs 5, 12, 13, 15, 23, 24, 25, 26, 27, 32, 33, 34, 35, and 36. Although King says he believes his audience comprises men of good will, it is clear from his didactic tone throughout these passages that he has his doubts about their altruism.

3. King is aware that his letter will be picked up by the press and read by a wide general audience. His detailed description of the situation in Birmingham (already familiar to the clergymen) is one indication of this fact.

4. King's implied thesis is that men of good will should support the demonstrations in Birmingham by the Southern Christian Leadership Conference.

Style and Structure (p. 576)

1. In the first paragraph, King says that since his audience of clergymen are men of good will, he will try to answer their statements patiently and reasonably.

2. King addresses the possible objections of his audience in paragraphs 5, 12, 15, 25, and 27.

3. King makes the transition from one section of his argument to another with rhetorical questions and statements that directly address his audience. For instance, when moving from his introduction (4) to his definition of the prob-

lem (5), he says, "You deplore the demonstrations taking place in Birmingham." When turning from the end of his definition of the problem (9) to a discussion of direct action (10), he says, "You may well ask, 'Why direct action?' " After this section ends with paragraph 14, King introduces his discussion of just and unjust laws with the statement, "You express a great deal of anxiety over our willingness to break laws" (15).

4. King is seeking support from all of the United States' major religions; therefore, he carefully reinforces his arguments with references to Jewish, Catholic, and Protestant philosophers. Also, he wants to establish that his conclusions are basic to Western philosophical thought.

5. King uses appeals to authority to indicate that his argument is supported by the writings and teachings of famous philosophers and theologians.

6. King's explanation of why he came to Birmingham is an example of inductive reasoning. His examination of just and unjust laws is an example of deductive reasoning.

7. King tries to reestablish a harmonious relationship with his audience by first asking their forgiveness if he has overstated the truth (46). He then reasserts his common bond with the other clergymen and ends with a remark that asserts his optimism about the future (47). Students are likely to find King's strategy successful.

8. Allusions to the Bible appear in paragraphs 3, 21, 25, 26, and 31. These allusions refer to events or teachings in scripture that support King's position of justice, equality, and love.

9. King is alluding to the phrase "my cup runneth over" in Psalm 23. With this allusion, King reinforces the point that he, too, is walking "through the valley of the shadow of death" and, because of his faith, "will fear no evil." Thus King effectively uses a biblical reference to express his impatience.

Combining the Patterns (p. 577)

Passages of narration include paragraphs 7–9, 14, 32, and 35–36. Each of these narratives shows how King and his African-American followers have been disappointed by the policies of the white power elite.

Thematic Connections

Indian Education (p. 142): King writes about the "ominous clouds of inferiority" formed in the minds of black children and the way that prejudice distorts their personalities by encouraging an "unconscious bitterness toward white people" (14). He famously advocated nonviolent resistance. How does the child protagonist in Sherman Alexie's story deal with prejudice? Does his personality seem "distorted" by it? Is his violence justified?

Just Walk On By (p. 238): Brent Staples examines the vestiges of the color line in the United States. As a large black man, he is often perceived as a threat by white strangers on the street. Though no longer faced with the possibility of being lynched, in some communities African Americans still suffer the consequences of stereotyping both by citizens and the police. King writes in the midst of the civil rights era, when African Americans were seeking broad change in American laws and social institutions; Staples writes about a more subtle — and personal — aspect of race relations that is largely independent of the law. Are King's points still relevant in the context of stereotyping and misunderstandings between the races? If so, how?

The "Black Table" Is Still There (p. 348): In writing about self-segregation in a suburban junior high school, Lawrence Otis Graham suggests the extent to which racial polarities continue to exist more than forty years after the height of the civil rights movement, when King's letter was written. You might ask students to consider how King would view the current state of race relations in the United States if he were alive today. Would he feel that most of his goals have been achieved? Or would he be disappointed at how little progress has been made?

Should American Citizenship Be a Birthright? (Debate; p. 591): King writes that the "goal of America is freedom"; of his supporters and his cause, he claims, "Abused and scorned though we may be, our destiny is tied up with America's destiny" (41). How are King's claims here — and throughout his argument — applicable to debates about immigrants, generally, and the issue of birthright citizenship, specifically? How is the destiny of immigrants "tied up with America's destiny"?

DEBATE: Is the Student Loan Crisis a Myth?

Over the last several years, the student debt crisis has been a relatively prominent story in our media and our politics. Even President Barack Obama has regularly commented on the issue, as have other high-profile officials and candidates seeking office. No doubt, the lasting effects of the 2008 financial collapse, several years of chronically high unemployment, and a cultural preoccupation with debt, generally, have brought this crisis to the forefront of America's national conversation. But on a more practical level, financial questions about higher education are likely at the forefront of your students' minds, too. Is money borrowed for college "good" debt or "bad" debt? How much debt is too much? What is a college degree worth? Should its value be measured financially, or are there other important standards? For some students with loans, the question might be more basic: "How am I ever going to make enough money to pay these off?"

The writers in this debate take starkly contrasting positions. The *Atlantic*'s Allan and Thompson argue that the "crisis" is overblown, that student debt is manageable, and that a college degree remains an excellent investment. Lewis and Zaidane counter that the *Atlantic* writers "looked for crisis in the wrong places" (4). Indeed, these infographics provide an opportunity to discuss that exact point: Where do we look to make arguments? What information, data, statistics, and evidence are most important, and what data is unimportant, or even misleading? Both infographics present "facts," so how is it possible to come to entirely different, mutually exclusive conclusions, when all the writers are using factual evidence (in good faith) to support their points?

Have students identify and explain which data points seem most persuasive to them. For example, the *Atlantic* writers look at the relative unemployment rates for people with various levels of education. Their evidence suggests that a college degree is enormously helpful on the job market. But what does that correlation leave out, as it is presented by Allan and Thompson? Similarly, do students think that Lewis and Zaidane's formulation — "53% of recent grads are unemployed or not using their degree" — is a legitimate statistic? What does "not using" a degree mean, exactly, in this context?

This debate should allow students to share their opinions of an issue vitally important to their lives and careers. The debate may also cut across related topics (class, education, work, the value of money) that are tightly tied to personal convictions or experiences. But encourage students to defend their positions with evidence, as well as subjective opinion and anecdotes.

Nicole Allan and Derek Thompson, *The Myth of the Student Loan Crisis*

Comprehension (p. 583)

1. The average student who received aid owed $17,360 (infographic, point 2). The figure is important because it reveals that the average student owed less than the "full" price for college tuition. It is also slightly more than the average Harvard student owed during the same period, suggesting that student debt at highly competitive colleges may not be worse than student debt at less competitive or state schools, despite the Ivy League sticker price ($57,950 at Harvard).
2. The writers worry that these "horror stories"—which are "as rare as they are terrifying" (point 3)—might discourage young people from enrolling in college.
3. According to the study, low-income families are "likely to overestimate the cost of college"; they may also be "scared off by the complexity of financial-aid forms" (point 6).
4. They mean that the long-term financial benefits of a degree outweigh the short-term savings of not going to college. Citing the average earnings and unemployment rates for those with degrees versus those without them, the writers argue that the "economic value of college . . . is indisputable" (point 4).

Purpose and Audience (p. 584)

1. The purpose of the infographic is to both inform and persuade. The writers argue that current fears about a student debt crisis are exaggerated; they try to establish this point by demonstrating that "horror stories" (point 3) are not statistically representative. They also provide data showing the enduring financial value of a college degree as a wise investment.
2. The audience for this piece seems broad. It would include prospective college students and their parents (especially). It might also include policy makers, educators, journalists, and media figures who read the *Atlantic:* they would likely be interested in arguments that undercut conventional wisdom or dispelled popular myths. The magazine's demographic is highly educated, relatively affluent, and curious about current events, politics, culture, and policy. But its articles and graphics are also disseminated more broadly through the Internet.
3. The infographic, as a whole, presumes that readers have heard a lot about the student debt crisis and, perhaps, accept it as factually accurate. This is evident in their opening paragraph, which refers to the "national anxiety" over the issue. The writers also address secondary, commonly held preconceptions—for example, that college degrees are no longer financially valuable. They address these perceptions with empirical data and statistical evidence.
4. The thesis might be stated as: "Despite national anxiety over students drowning in college debt, the crisis is overblown, college is financially accessible even to low-income families, and an investment in higher education remains the best bet around."

Style and Structure (p. 584)

1. The charts and graphs of an infographic help present data, statistics, and empirical evidence visually. So, for example, the pie chart is persuasive in countering stories about college students "drowning in $100,000+ debt": it shows thin slivers of those in that relatively rare position. At the same time, graphics can obscure nuances. For example, the graph supporting point number 4 (the economic value of college) presents degree levels, but not majors or fields of concentration. That is, it implies that all degrees at each level (A.A., B.A., M.A., Ph.D.) are equally valuable. But median weekly earning may vary by major or field of study, and this graph elides that factor.

2. The writers show the unemployment rate and the median weekly earnings of people with different education levels, from high school dropouts to Ph.D.s. The graph presents clear evidence of the economic value of college: generally, the higher the level of education, the higher the median income and the lower the unemployment rate (those with professional degrees are slightly better off than those with Ph.D.s). However, some might ask about other variables: areas of study, majors, professional fields, or the relative value of particular colleges, universities, and professional schools.

3. In point 5, the writers compare the financial return of associate's and bachelor's degrees favorably to investments such as stocks, AAA-rated bonds, and gold. In the most basic terms, *investment* means spending time or money for future gain—especially financial gain. Students may have different opinions of the time and money spent on education. Some may be utilitarian and financially minded; others might see college as an investment in something intangible or even priceless.

Combining the Patterns (p. 585)

The writers rely on classification and division throughout their infographic: they use it to divide and classify students by their financial aid status (points 1–2); they divide indebted students by amount owed (point 3); they divide and classify people by level of education (point 4); and they classify and divide different kinds of investments (point 5).

Thematic Connections

The Money (p. 114): In this personal essay (and humorous detective story), writer Junot Díaz gives an account of the time his family was robbed during his childhood. But his narrative also provides insight into the meaning of money for a poor Dominican family in the United States that, nevertheless, managed to save and send money to poorer relatives.

Ten Ways We Get the Odds Wrong (p. 250): Allan and Thompson write primarily to dispel myths and misconceptions about the value of college and the "crisis" of student debt. They suggest that these misunderstandings can cause people to act in ways that do not advance their self-interest. The "horror stories" may discourage young people from making a wise investment in a college degree. In "Ten Ways We Get the Odds Wrong," Maia Szalavitz discusses our tendency to be persuaded by this kind of melodramatic or spectacular storyline. You might ask students how Szalavitz would view the issue of college debt. Would she see it as a real risk, or would the benefits of investing in a college degree seem like a good bet?

College Pressures (p. 448): Although William Zinsser's essay was published in 1979, he was already aware of the economic and financial pressures that faced college students. He was also mindful of the problem of student debt: "Everything is up. Deficits are up. We are witnessing in America the creation of a brotherhood of paupers—colleges, parents, and students, joined by the common bond of debt" (20). Are the problems Zinsser writes about here similar to the ones students face today? Or are they different?

Chris Lewis and Layla Zaidane, *Here's Your Crisis: Student Loan Debt Isn't a Myth*

Comprehension (p. 588)

1. According to the writers, multiple factors support the claim that the student debt crisis is real, including increases in the number of student loan delinquencies and defaults, the imminent surplus of degree holders on the job market, and the steep rise in the costs of public universities since 1988.

2. The suggestion is that students have invested time and money earning a degree in a field and preparing for a specific career, but that after graduation, they are taking jobs unrelated to their training or area of interest. This has implications for the unemployment rate of college graduates: a person with a degree may be employed as a waiter in a restaurant, for example, but may have spent four years (and acquired student loan debt) training for a career in architecture. The writers see this as a problem.

3. Debtors are *delinquent* when they fall behind in loan payments, or fail to make their required, scheduled payments on time. Debtors go into *default* when they fail to make any payments on their loans—usually after a period of 270 days.

4. The cost of public universities has doubled in that time. The writers focus on public universities because, in principle, such institutions—which receive public funding—are supposed to be affordable and accessible to Americans.

Purpose and Audience (p. 588)

1. One version of the thesis may be stated as: "Despite recent claims to the contrary, rising levels of student debt and the increasing costs of college are a national crisis."

2. The intended audience includes college students and recent graduates—particularly ones facing debt problems (Generation Progress focuses mostly on college students and student activism). But the infographic probably has other intended readers, as well. Generation Progress is a Washington, D.C.-based political policy and advocacy organization, so its messages are directed at "opinion leaders," public officials, and policy makers. As it is a response to an *Atlantic* infographic, it is also directed at the kind of educated and (likely) affluent readers who would be familiar with that magazine.

3. The purpose of the infographic is to inform and persuade. It is a response to claims, like the one in the *Atlantic* infographic, that the student debt crisis is a myth. The writers wish to demonstrate to readers that the crisis is real.

4. The writers provide background on the *Atlantic* infographic in their opening paragraphs, so they do not assume that their readers are familiar with it. Students will likely have different views of the fairness of the presentation. That diversity of opinion might give insight into the ways empirical evidence and statistics can be selected and presented. For example, the *Atlantic* infographic indicates that those with college degrees have a relatively low unemployment rate, while the Generation Progress writers claim, "The employment prospects for young grads are pretty gloomy" (4). Similarly, the issue of graduates "not using" their degrees is also open to interpretation. Is an anthropology or history major with a decent paying job in marketing or sales evidence of the "gloomy" job market for graduates?

Style and Structure (p. 589)

1. Students will have different opinions about what they find persuasive. These views may reflect on their own ideas about the use—and value of—a college education, as well as their sense of their own career prospects.
2. You might compare the visual presentation of this infographic with that of the *Atlantic*'s. For example, the graphics here are not as precise or elaborate as Allan and Thompson's. Also, Lewis and Zaidane do not integrate their accompanying text into the graphics as Allan and Thompson do, but place an explanatory list below the infographic.
3. The tone of the language is serious. While the first line of the introductory text ("The student loan crisis is a myth") is used ironically and the heading "The Student Loan Crisis Is (Not) a Myth" has a "not" inserted as if it were written by hand, the writers are straightforward in their approach. Lewis and Zaidane say, directly, that Allan and Thompson "looked for crisis in the wrong places" (4) and that "they're wrong" (graphic). They see the student debt problem as a real crisis with real-world consequences; their tone reflects that view.
4. In this context, *myth* means a misconception, false story, or commonly held belief that is untrue. Students may be more familiar with the use of the term *myth* in the context of Greek mythology or other ancient beliefs.

Combining the Patterns (p. 590)

The key word for this infographic is "crisis." As a response to the *Atlantic*'s suggestion that there is no crisis, Lewis and Zaidane argue that the problems faced by college students, recent graduates, and future graduates meet the definition of that word. As the writers say in their final sentence, after presenting their evidence: "That's what we call a crisis."

Thematic Connections

I'm Your Teacher, Not Your Internet-Service Provider (p. 415): As Lewis and Zaidane point out, the costs of higher education have increased significantly over the past two and a half decades. In response, some colleges and universities are using online courses to supplement traditional face-to-face classes; other institutions present their instruction almost entirely online. These can cut down on costs. Ellen Laird provides a sobering assessment of distance learning, even as she asserts that she will continue to teach online courses.

154

The Dog Ate My Flash Drive, and Other Tales of Woe (p. 457): In this essay, Carolyn Foster Segal considers the excuses students use — or fabricate — to avoid turning in assignments. You might have students consider this issue in the context of debates about the value of college as an investment of time and money. While discussions about how much college costs are important, they may take the focus away from another important factor in the value of higher education: the effort, engagement, and conscientiousness of students.

DEBATE: Should American Citizenship Be a Birthright?

The following essays appeared in 2010, a year in which several public officials — including House Speaker John Boehner (R-Ohio) — discussed the possibility of ending or revising the practice of birthright citizenship. While students will likely be familiar with immigration and naturalization controversies, they may be less familiar with debates about the meaning and history of the Fourteenth Amendment, which traditionally has conferred citizenship on anyone born in the United States. Make sure they read the debate overview, which will give them essential background information on the issue. You might begin discussion by pointing out the distinction between *jus soli* ("right of the soil") and *jus sanguinis* ("right of blood"); these two principles suggest notions of citizenship — and perhaps even different ideas about the meaning of America. Ask students whether the United States has a unique obligation to rely on the principle and practice of *jus soli*.

You might also ask them about their own immigrant heritage. How do they view their own citizenship status and that of their ancestors? What does their background contribute to their stances on these issues? Both Linda Chavez and George F. Will are writing in the context of the controversial debate about immigration. Do students see birthright citizenship as central to that controversy or as a distraction from more substantive aspects of the immigration issue? Chavez argues that ending birthright citizenship will "jeopardize the electoral future of the GOP by alienating Hispanics" (3). What role should such political considerations play in formulating policy? Will makes the case that the tradition of birthright citizenship is based on a misreading of the Fourteenth Amendment. He proposes an interpretation that conforms "with what the authors of its text intended, and with common sense, thereby removing an incentive for illegal immigration" (1). This debate should be an excellent way for students to join the nationwide conversation about immigration, the terms of which will have important implications for all Americans in the present and future.

Linda Chavez, *The Case for Birthright Citizenship*

Comprehension (p. 595)

1. Chavez is writing in response to Republican leaders in Congress, who are considering changing the Fourteenth Amendment to "deny citizenship to children born here to illegal immigrants" (1).
2. The writer argues that changing birthright citizenship will damage the Republican Party: "It will unquestionably jeopardize the electoral future of the GOP by alienating Hispanics" (3). As Hispanics constitute the "largest minority and fastest-growing segment of the U.S. population" (3), Chavez thinks that Republicans will have to appeal to them to win elections in the future.

3. Chavez writes that as a "class of aliens," the Chinese were "every bit as un-popular as present-day illegal immigrants" (5). In the nineteenth century, Chinese immigrants came here to work as "common laborers" (5) and aroused resentments in native workers who had to compete for jobs.

4. According to the writer, there was no category of "illegal alien" when the Four-teenth Amendment was adopted because immigration was "unrestricted and unregulated" at the time (4).

Purpose and Audience (p. 595)

1. Her thesis is stated in paragraph 3. Possible restatement: "The GOP should not repeal birthright citizenship, because doing so will hurt the Republican Party politically and ultimately undermine what it means to be an American."

2. Chavez is primarily addressing Republicans and conservative Americans, who are likely to be more open to repealing birthright citizenship and to care about the political prospects of the Republican Party. In her conclusion, she explic-itly warns conservatives not to "betray" American history (9), which "has been largely one of continuously expanding the community of people regarded as Americans" (8). This appeal would likely resonate with Republican readers.

3. Politicians can use resentments against illegal immigration for political advan-tage, especially if voters believe that immigrants are taking jobs and using ser-vices or resources that should only be the privileges or rights of legal citizens.

4. In Chavez's account, American history "has been largely one of continuously expanding the community of people regarded as Americans, from native-born whites to freed slaves to Indians to naturalized citizens of all races and eth-nicities" (8). Her convincing argument against restricting immigration appeals to this historical narrative. In contrast, those proposing repeal are working against the broad—and broadly appealing—themes and trends of the Ameri-can storyline.

Style and Structure (p. 596)

1. Chavez addresses the counterargument that the Fourteenth Amendment was "never intended to grant rights to the offspring of illegal aliens" (4). She also addresses the constitutional arguments against birthright citizenship by citing the case *U.S. v. Wong Kim Ark* (6). The court has consistently upheld that decision's analysis of birthright citizenship; therefore, those seeking to repeal the provision now are arguing against long-settled law.

2. According to Chavez, opponents of birthright citizenship claim that "the Four-teenth Amendment was passed after the Civil War to guarantee citizenship to freed slaves, and that it was never intended to grant rights to the offspring of illegal aliens" (4). Chavez writes that this argument is a *non sequitur*: the Four-teenth Amendment granted rights to slaves: it does not follow that it should not grant similar rights to "illegal aliens" because there was no such category at the time of its adoption: "immigration was unrestricted and unregulated" (4).

3. Chavez starts with a bold statement of her argument: "Repealing birthright citizenship is a terrible idea" (3). Though she takes the chance that such a bold assertion will turn off some readers, many will find her position intriguing enough to continue reading. If she had stated her case more subtly, she would have run the risk of her opening not grabbing her readers' attention.

4. Chavez's argument appeals to the authority of the Supreme Court. While such appeals are problematic when the authority is questionable, it is usually acceptable to rely on the authority of Supreme Court decisions that are consistently upheld.

5. The writer draws an analogy between illegal aliens now and Chinese immigrants in the past. She reinforces the similarity by noting that Chinese immigrants occupied a similar place in both society and the labor force.

6. You might have students investigate how the term is misleading. For example, the parents of so-called anchor babies do not receive automatic citizenship or immunity from deportation merely by having a child on U.S. soil.

Combining the Patterns (p. 597)

In this section, Chavez uses exemplification: her examples —"from native-born whites to freed slaves . . . to naturalized citizens of all races and ethnicities" (8) — support her general claim. There's a narrative implicit here, too: the "story" of America is one in which the community of Americans is always expanding.

Thematic Connections

Goodbye to My Twinkie Days (p. 171): Chavez discusses questions of citizenship and assimilation mostly in the context of law. In her essay, Bich Minh Nguyen writes about assimilation and belonging in the context of American popular culture. As she recalls, "Twinkies were a ticket to assimilation: the golden cake, more golden than the hair I wished I had, filled with sweet white cream. Back then, junk foods seemed to represent an ideal of American indulgence" (5).

Midnight (p. 217): This student essay focuses on Asian immigrants who labor in a dry cleaning sweatshop more than twelve hours a day for substantially less than the minimum wage. Ku writes, "Even though they did not speak, their eyes said, 'We hate our jobs, but we work so that our children will have better lives than we do.'" Ku is able to get the education in America her parents were not able to get in their home country.

Mother Tongue (p. 463): Amy Tan writes about the "different Englishes" she speaks as the daughter of Chinese immigrants. What role does language play in assimilation? How important is learning English to becoming (as Chavez might put it) a "good American"?

U.S. Census 2010 Form (p. 500): The census form offers several choices for ethnic and racial identification, although some critics wonder whether the variety of options causes more confusion than clarity. Do the different labels and categories imply different ways of "belonging" in America?

George F. Will, *An Argument to Be Made about Immigrant Babies and Citizenship*
Comprehension (p. 600)

1. Will claims that correcting a misinterpretation of the Fourteenth Amendment's first sentence would "drain some scalding steam from immigration arguments" (1). This rereading would bring the amendment in line with its authors' intentions and with common sense.

2. According to the writer, the principle and practice of birthright citizenship "flow[s]" from a misinterpretation of the Fourteenth Amendment (2).
3. Graglia claims that a parent from a poor country " 'can hardly do more for a child than make him or her an American citizen, entitled to all the advantages of the American welfare state' " (3). He implies that such parents have children in America to take advantage of government programs.
4. Will first argues that the amendment's authors did not intend to grant birthright citizenship because there were no illegal immigrants and no laws restricting immigration at the time. Then he argues that it is unreasonable to "presume that [the amendment's authors and ratifiers] would have wanted to provide the reward of citizenship to the children of violaters of those laws" *had such laws existed at the time* (5). His second point relies on a hypothetical as well as on assumptions about the views of those who framed the Fourteenth Amendment.
5. The citizenship provision of the Fourteenth Amendment originally excluded Native Americans; it still excludes the children of foreign diplomatic officers.

Purpose and Audience (p. 600)

1. Restatement of thesis: "Correcting a long-standing misinterpretation of the Fourteenth Amendment would bring the law into accord with its framers' intent, lead to a more reasonable understanding of birthright citizenship, and quiet some of the controversy in the immigration debate."
2. Will's purposes are to bring attention to what he sees as a long-standing misreading of the Constitution and to encourage others to accept his point of view.
3. Will's audience is the general readership of the *Washington Post*'s opinion page. These readers are likely to be interested in politics and political debates, even if they are not part of any specialized professional or political group. The audience for the *Texas Review of Law and Politics* probably includes lawyers and legal scholars. Moreover, the publication has an avowedly conservative point of view, as it seeks to provide "thoughtfully and intellectually rigorous conservative articles" (as stated on the journal's website).

Style and Structure (p. 601)

1. Essentially, Will wants to change a major premise in the immigration debate. Presently, the children of illegal immigrants are granted citizenship because the Constitution gives it to them. If the Fourteenth Amendment is reinterpreted to mean that the children of illegal immigrants are not granted citizenship, then it must follow that these children cannot be citizens by birth.
2. The essay would have benefited from a wider range of sources than only Graglia. Will's reliance on this single scholar weakens his argument.
3. To Will, readings of the Fourteenth Amendment allowing for birthright citizenship are unreasonable and at odds with common sense. Given the long history of reading the amendment in that way, however, his argument would have been made stronger had he addressed the specific assumptions, claims, and interpretations of his opponents.
4. This conclusion reinforces his claim in paragraph 5 about the "huge waves of illegal immigration" that have washed over the United States. By citing these statistics, Will ties his argument — which is relatively dry, legalistic, and

abstract — to real-world facts and the specific consequences of the law as it is practiced now.

5. According to Will, the definition of *citizen* should be altered in light of a more reasonable interpretation of the Fourteenth Amendment. As the law is interpreted now, the children of illegal aliens are (by definition) American citizens. Changing the interpretation would change the definition of *American citizen* and exclude these children.

6. Arguments over such labels have been a consistent part of the so-called "culture wars" or controversies over "political correctness." The term *Indian* is ultimately a misnomer, used by early European settlers in America who thought they had arrived in Asia. The more contemporary term *Native American* emphasizes the sense that indigenous Americans predated European settlers. But that newer label also homogenizes them into a monolithic unit (rather than Navajo or Eskimo, for example).

Combining the Patterns (p. 602)

Will relies on classification and division when he argues that the children of illegal immigrants are like the children of Native Americans and foreign diplomatic officers; therefore, they should be legally classified as the children of resident aliens and excluded from birthright citizenship.

Thematic Connections

The Money (p. 114): Will writes about the history of birthright citizenship, focusing mostly on the legal question. But he does touch upon the issue of "divided allegiance" (6). Díaz came to the United States at the age of six and is now a U.S. citizen. As they come across in this personal narrative, however, do Díaz and his family seem like "Americans"? How are their loyalties and allegiances divided across national borders?

Indian Education (p. 142): Will's column notes that Native Americans were historically excluded from full citizenship. In this short story, Sherman Alexie writes about a Native American who chooses to attend mostly white schools. How does he deal with his minority status and his sense of self as an outsider?

U.S. Census 2010 Form (p. 500): This census form encourages residents to identify themselves in terms of race and ethnicity. Are such labels important in this context? Do they suggest anything about the nature and composition of the United States?

CASEBOOK: Is Football Too Dangerous?

While at first glance, this casebook might seem a little narrow, or perhaps of interest only to sports fans, the question above cuts across a wide variety of topics, among them the centrality of sports entertainment to American life and culture; the value of sports for spectators and participants; parenting, and the prerogatives of parents over the choices of their children; the evaluation of risks; the American preoccupation with protecting children from danger and the consequences of risky behavior; and the role of group activities in encouraging physical, psychological, and emotional health.

Make sure that, along with reading the essays, students read the casebook overview and the background information in each headnote. These offer useful information on various issues related to the casebook question, from recent scientific research on head injuries to a broad summary of football's history. You could start discussion by asking students about their own experiences watching and participating in dangerous sports. While most of these essays focus on football, students can bring in other sports, as well. Indeed, you might even start with Jeb Golinkin's essay, which takes the broadest approach to the question and makes the loftiest claims in favor of playing dangerous sports. How do students weigh the benefits of such activities against the risks? Do they think that the current media focus on the issue is overblown? If they are fans of sports like football or events like the X Games, do they feel any complicity in — or responsibility for — the physical damage suffered by players?

Finally, encourage students to make connections to larger cultural and social issues, as the writers do here. For example, Golinkin ties his argument to what he sees as America's waning economic power and an increasingly unforgiving and competitive "new world order" (10). Likewise, Daniel Flynn ultimately argues that contact sports such as football help toughen children up and rescue them from their overprotected and sterile adolescent lives. Do students agree about the importance and value of these activities? Can children learn these lessons and skills elsewhere — and with less physical risk?

Don Banks, *What Price Football?*

Comprehension (p. 607)

1. The money was to be paid to over 4,500 retired NFL players and their families. The settlement was the result of consolidated lawsuits brought against the league by players and families, who sought restitution for the effects of head injuries. The claimants argued that the NFL knew about the dangers of the game and bears some responsibility.
2. He means that as more people become aware of how dangerous the game is, the less likely they will be willing to play — or, let their children play in youth leagues. By "feeder system," he means organizations like Pop Warner, high school football teams, and college football programs. The "unintended consequences" are the debilitating effects of head injuries.
3. He means that changing the game now to make it safer will help preserve football for the future. That will benefit fans of the game, as well as the players; spectators will not only enjoy the NFL in the future, but they will be able to do so without feeling guilty about the damage it does to players.
4. Banks does not focus on — or present — much "hard evidence" here, so students may have mixed opinions about his justifications for the claim. But he seems to presume his audience is familiar with the emerging evidence of football's harmful effects on the brains of players.

Purpose and Audience (p. 607)

1. Banks's rhetorical question is directed at the sports fans who read *Sports Illustrated* — and others, as well: "It's a question that needs to be asked by everyone who has a sporting interest in the game" (14). Implicitly, it must be answered by those people, too.

160

2. Banks states his thesis in the fifth paragraph. It could be stated as: "For the safety of football players and the future of the sport, we need to accept changes now that make the game safer."

3. The writer clearly has an affection for the game, but believes that its physical costs have become too high. Fans are his primary audience, given the publication where he writes. He includes himself among them, as indicated by his use of the first-person plural: "We have to let the game change, and we have to embrace that change" (5).

4. The writer's purpose is to persuade football fans to accept — and "embrace" — changes in the game to make it safer. He wants the game to change so that it can last, not so that it can be abolished.

Style and Structure (p. 607)

1. Examples of cause-and-effect relationships in the essay include Banks's claim that fears about football's dangers may cause the NFL's "feeder system" to "dry up" (12). He also argues that embracing changes to the game in the present will protect the game in the future, especially if what we know about the effects of the brain trauma brought about by the game today "wind[s] up being just the tip of [a] scary iceberg" (11).

2. He puts quotation marks around the word *settlement* because it is euphemistic legal jargon that covers over the fact that the lawsuit "didn't really settle anything" (1). He means not only that the brain-damaged players are still debilitated, but also that the legal dispute marks the beginning of a process — of accepting the dangers of the game, of asking questions, of changing the rules — not the end of one. He puts quotation marks around *ruining* because he disagrees with the idea that new rules will ruin football; rather, Banks believes that such rule changes are essential to saving the game.

3. He compares helmet-to-helmet hits to behaviors that seem self-evidently irrational and dangerous; in the driving example, Banks is implicitly comparing "common-sense" laws that require people to wear seat belts with football rules that will protect the heads of football players. In his view, if we accept one, we should accept the other.

4. Banks is distinguishing narrowly legal terms from broader issues of moral and ethical responsibility and accountability. He wants the NFL (and everyone involved with the sport) to actively and responsibly work to make football safer because it is the right thing to do, not out of fear of litigation.

5. These imperative sentences provide proposals for how fans should react to rule changes. Some might find the tone preachy, but Banks subtly stays in the first-person plural ("let's not whine" [10]), so he holds himself to the same standards he expects of his readers.

Combining the Patterns (p. 608)

He uses examples to clarify and persuade. Banks's most prominent use of exemplification is in paragraphs 9 and 10, where he gives clarifying examples of specific rule changes that might make the sport safer: banning crown-of-the-helmet hits and eliminating kickoffs. But Banks also cites these instances to argue that fans should react to such changes with acceptance rather than resistance.

Thematic Connections

Thirty-Eight Who Saw Murder Didn't Call the Police **(p. 128):** This news report about the famous 1964 case of Kitty Genovese being beaten and killed while her neighbors in Queens, New York, ignored her calls for help suggests the ways in which people may be "responsible" without being "liable" or "culpable." Students might discuss the ways in which football fans might bear some responsibility for the damage done to players by the game's violence.

Ten Ways We Get the Odds Wrong **(p. 250):** Don Banks believes football "has been played far too dangerously for too long" (4). In "Ten Ways We Get the Odds Wrong," Maia Szalavitz enumerates and classifies the common ways in which people misunderstand and miscalculate risk. You might have students evaluate Banks's argument through the prism of Szalavitz's claims about risk assessment. Does Banks "get the odds wrong"? Do football players get the odds wrong when they knowingly choose to play a dangerous sport? How should parents decide whether to let their children play football?

Who Killed Benny Paret? **(p. 337):** Before professional football became the focus of scrutiny for its violence, many argued that professional boxing was excessively violent and dangerous. In this classic essay about the death of a prizefighter, Norman Cousins asks some of the same questions about prizefighting that people are now asking about the NFL. He also notes the seemingly willful blindness of those investigating Paret's death who downplayed the significance of head trauma caused by the human fist: "In short, the investigators looked into every possible cause except the real one" (8).

Nina Burleigh, *Would Football without Concussions Still Be Football?*

Comprehension (p. 613)

1. She is referring to a rash of revelations about the dangers of football, lawsuits against the NFL, the "Penn State scandal, pro player suicides, college and high school deaths, and brain injuries at all levels" (6). They have brought much bad publicity to the sport.

2. The study found that NFL players have four times the risk of developing Alzheimer's disease as people in the general population. She includes these results because they support the claim that football is dangerous; as the study was released in 2012, it also supports her assertion that football "reached a crisis point" (7) that year.

3. She qualifies the assertion by noting that "knocking brains out of their own and other men's heads is what they signed up for" (13).

4. According to Burleigh, the median salary for NFL players is $770,000. The average career of a player lasts three and a half years.

5. The Pop Warner league phased out flag football because the players' "parents insisted on the full-contact version" of football (26).

Purpose and Audience (p. 614)

1. She means that the scene at the Southbridge "peewee" football game was darkly comic, as young children were being taken off the field with injuries

requiring emergency medical care. But the game continued, nevertheless. Her references to Monty Python and *South Park* suggest that her audience will understand the black humor of her account. She also assumes that readers will get the pop-culture references.

2. She loves football; for her, the game is ennobling and aesthetically pleasing, even its violence. She finds the "[p]rimal savagery" of it irresistible. Her tone is exalted and a little overstated (e.g., the word *troglodytes*), but the reader might suspect she is describing a guilty pleasure.

3. Burleigh seems to see her readers as open to her point of view, although she has to qualify her position in paragraph 23 so that the audience knows she is a football fan. The first ten paragraphs of her essay, with their cascade of anecdotes, statistics, and negative news about football, suggest that her audience may not be familiar with just how bad things have gotten for the sport.

4. Given the amount of information she packs into this dense essay, she clearly wants to inform her audience about the current state of football and its physical costs — "a pretty bill to pay for couch-potato thrills" (24). But she also wants to argue that "real changes have to start at the local level" (27). For that purpose, she is addressing parents and asserting that they should "demand" stiffer rules for youth-league and high school football (27).

Style and Structure (p. 614)

1. Her anecdote is a darkly funny, true story, which shows that the violence and risks of football are just as present in "peewee" leagues as they are in the NFL. It supports her main point because ultimately she argues that changes in the game (to make it safer) must begin at the local level with the parents of children who play the sport.

2. The sentence ties the absurd but resonant introductory story to the rest of the essay by self-consciously evoking sentimental football clichés ("invigorating autumn air," "the crack of a beer at the tailgate"), and then ending on a sour note: "boys with men in showers." The latter point evokes the Penn State football scandal. All of this is captured by the phrase "the glory and delirium of American football," which implies unclear thinking.

3. The term refers to a person's sound mind, memory, and understanding. To be *non compos mentis* is a legal term that means that one is not of sound mind. Burleigh is writing in the context of a legal settlement (where people are compensated for their devastating injuries with money) *and* the real-world suffering of players like Mike Webster, who suffered from dementia because of his football career. Her use of the term creates a deliberate incongruity of diction; the effect is both sad and grimly comic.

4. The comparisons suggest that football has a way of dehumanizing its players and turning them (at least partially) into property and commodities; the players are like animals in the service of a "multibillion-dollar obsession that thrives on their new blood" (25). Her point about the scouts shows that this process occurs even at the high school level.

5. Burleigh seems serious, if a little skeptical that rule changes can make the game much safer. She notes that three marquee quarterbacks were removed from games after suffering concussions; according to her, this is "unusual" and "likely related to the NFL's newfound consideration for players' brains" (22).

Combining the Patterns (p. 615)

Burleigh uses description effectively in the essay. For example, she demonstrates her affection for the game of football in paragraph 23 with a vividly descriptive, almost poetic rendering of the game's beauty and violence. That she is a fan of the game ("I love these brutes") is a key part of her argument: she is not writing to disparage the game, but rather to suggest changes to preserve something that she likes.

Thematic Connections

Indian Education (p. 142): As her opening anecdote and her prose style indicate, Nina Burleigh has a sense of the darkly comic and the absurd, an aesthetic sensibility she shares with Sherman Alexie. In this short fiction, told as a series of vignettes, Alexie offers the story of a Native-American boy at an Indian school. While Burleigh appreciates the beauty of football, Alexie's protagonist discovers aesthetic satisfaction in basketball: "it felt good, that ball in my hands, all those possibilities and angles. It was mathematics, geometry. It was beautiful" (31).

Ten Ways We Get the Odds Wrong (p. 250): While Burleigh discusses concussions in the NFL, her main proposal is that parents need to get involved in making football safer at younger levels of the game. You might have students analyze the risks of the sport through the prism of Maia Szalavitz's essay, which examines our cognitive biases and our tendencies to misunderstand risks and threats.

Who Killed Benny Paret? (p. 337): Burleigh loves football, but when she surveys the damage it does to players, she concludes that such problems are a "pretty bill to pay for couch-potato thrills" (24). Still, she acknowledges that violence is part of the game's appeal. In "Who Killed Benny Paret?," Norman Cousins examines the death of a prizefighter in the ring, as well as the amoral quality of violent sports as a spectacle. As one promoter tells Cousins, "[Fans] come out to see a man hurt. If they think anything else, they're kidding themselves" (5).

Brains versus Brawn (p. 377): In a student essay, Cotharn relates the special treatment he received as a football player in a high school where football was highly valued, and the opposite treatment when he moved to a more academically demanding school. The essay speaks to the high value some put on football, and the complex feelings it arouses.

Jeb Golinkin, *Why Parents Should Let Their Kids Play Dangerous Sports*

Comprehension (p. 618)

1. Golinkin claims that it is an "undeniable fact that the sports we love are killing the athletes we worship for playing them" (4). He cites anecdotal evidence (the cases of Caleb Moore and Junior Seau), as well as recent research on the chronic brain damage suffered by football players.
2. For Golinkin, dangerous sports include hockey, soccer, rugby, skiing, snowboarding, and baseball, as well as other "extreme" activities (like freestyle snowmobiling). They all have an element of physical risk and even violence, but for the writer, they (along with all sports) "represent something noble about the human spirit" (8).

3. The writer claims that these sports are ennobling (8). They teach participants lessons about teamwork and the need to push limits (9–10); they further people's "spiritual development," and help prepare children for a world in which "only the tough and the persistent will thrive" (10).
4. For Golinkin, Moore's death was tragic. But it also has an element of greatness and nobility because "Moore died doing what all great humans do in one way or another: Pushing the limits of the possible" (9).
5. The writer believes that children will face a harsh and competitive world "in which only the tough and the persistent will thrive" (10). He does not specify the meaning of "new world order," but he does imply that America's global advantages and privileges are diminishing. If children are overprotected, they may succumb to "complacency and fear"; they may grow up ill-equipped to deal with lives that are not "easy, or safe, even for the competent" (10).

Purpose and Audience (p. 618)

1. Golinkin states his thesis in paragraph 7. This placement allows him to acknowledge and concede several premises: that our players and participants face real costs for sports thrills, that dangerous sports are deservedly facing scrutiny, and that he understands the real risks of these activities and does not take these dangers lightly. But those premises ultimately support his point because the risks and dangers are a fundamental part of the value of dangerous sports—and part of the reason children should be allowed to play them.
2. The title is provocative: it is a claim that appears to go against conventional wisdom (that sports are becoming too dangerous to play). It also suggests a surprising, counterintuitive argument that should make readers curious.
3. Golinkin presumes his audience might be skeptical. He accepts the premise that conventional wisdom has turned against "dangerous" sports. He even quotes Barack Obama on the topic, noting that the president's opinion—that sports may be becoming too dangerous for children—"reflect[s] the views of many parents in the United States" (8). The writer also accepts that parents want to be protective of their children, but tries to use that to his rhetorical advantage: "We would do well to remember that spiritual development is every bit as important as physical safety" (10).

Style and Structure (p. 618)

1. Golinkin's introduction accepts—and reinforces—a common parallel: that risky, dangerous contemporary spectator sports like football and the X Games are appealing because of their violence and danger. Viewers derive the same entertainment from them that ancient Romans derived from blood sports like gladiator fighting. By using this comparison, Golinkin demonstrates his honesty and thus appeals to ethos: he does not try to soft-pedal the nature of these activities, or their costs. As he says later, the "sports we love are killing the athletes we worship for playing them" (4).
2. The rhetorical question sets up the answer, which is his thesis: that children should be allowed to play such sports. The question signals his shift from acknowledging the serious dangers of these sports to defending his claim that parents should let their children play them anyway.

3. By using *we* and *our*, he avoids sounding preachy or unnecessarily judgmental. For example, if he wrote, "The sports you love are killing the athletes you worship" rather than, "The sports we love . . . ," readers might feel singled out or attacked. The first-person plural puts the writer on the same level as the audience.

4. These paragraphs do not undermine his argument because he claims that the danger of these sports is an essential part of their value — and part of the reason children should be allowed to play them. At the same time, these paragraphs are more grounded and empirical than what comes later; they concede an "undeniable fact" (4). The second section is more speculative and abstract. Students may have different opinions about what part of the essay is more persuasive or effective.

5. Golinkin might have included more empirical evidence to support his claims about the value of sports. Similarly, he might have provided analysis that placed the risks of different activities in perspective. For example, are the dangers of youth-league soccer really comparable to the dangers of the X Games or college rugby?

6. In this context, the word *competent* appears to refer to the elemental qualities that usually make people effective: common sense, a work ethic, conscientiousness, prudence, foresight, the ability to defer gratification, and other basic virtues and skills. Golinkin means that even people with these capabilities will have a hard time competing in the future.

Combining the Patterns (p. 620)

Golinkin uses cause and effect at different points in the essay. The causal relationships most central to his overall argument and purpose are that letting children play dangerous sports will make them team-oriented, tough, resilient, and competitive, and that forbidding them to play may make them fearful, complacent, and spiritually stunted (10–11).

Thematic Connections

Let Steroids into the Hall of Fame (p. 21): Chafets argues that a new line needs to be drawn in Major League Baseball — a line that would accept the use of performance-enhancing drugs in the sport. Like Golinkin, Chafets accepts that there are complexities around issues of sports performance, that there are positives and negatives inherent in sport.

Ten Ways We Get the Odds Wrong (p. 250): Golinkin weighs the risks of dangerous sports against the benefits that children may derive from playing them — as well as the risks of not letting children participate. Maia Szalavitz provides a provocative analysis and discussion of the biases and blind spots that make us poor assessors of such risks.

Brains versus Brawn (p. 377): Golinkin discusses youth sports in the context of physical risk. In "Brains versus Brawn," student Mark Cotharn gives an account of his experience as a high school athlete, first at a school where he is privileged as a star quarterback, and then at a school with a "weak" football team where his athletic status makes him the target of discrimination. Is this experience valuable for Cotharn? You might ask students to consider this essay in light of Golinkin's argument that sports participation teaches important lessons.

***Why Chinese Mothers Are Superior* (p. 408):** Golinkin worries about overprotected American children becoming complacent, fearful, and unable to compete in a tough "new world order" (10). Amy Chua's controversial essay about the differences between Western and Chinese parenting gives credence to Golinkin's fears. According to Chua, Western parents focus on nurturing individuality and positive reinforcement. In contrast, Chinese parents "believe that the best way to protect their children is by preparing them for the future, letting them see what they're capable of, and arming them with skills, work habits and inner confidence that no one can ever take away" (22).

Daniel J. Flynn, *Football Does a Body Good (Nannyism Doesn't)*

Comprehension (p. 623)

1. In his opening paragraphs, Flynn refers to some of the events that have recently damaged football's reputation, including the revelation that the New Orleans Saints had a bounty program that paid bonuses to players for injuring opponents and the suicide of Junior Seau (4).

2. The writer finds the analogy misleading. Flynn claims that there is "strong evidence . . . that cigarettes cause cancer." In contrast, he argues that there is "no evidence, just speculation, that football caused Junior Seau to kill himself" (6).

3. He seems to place much of the blame on journalists, who have "parlayed a few tragic anecdotes among tens of thousands of retired professional athletes into a national anti-football frenzy" (7).

4. The study reported that former NFL players generally lived longer than men in the general population; they also had "lower rates of cancer and heart disease" (8).

5. Flynn sees these sports as healthy exercise; he believes that such "strenuous outdoor activity is a fine remedy for what ails climate-controlled, obese, antiseptic adolescence" (19).

Purpose and Audience (p. 623)

1. Flynn's essay is not explicitly political, but he does write from a libertarian/populist conservative perspective, in line with the *American Spectator*. He is contemptuous of fretful journalists and the intellectual "[e]ggheads" (17) of the "smart-set" (18); he is skeptical of rules and regulations that might inhibit certain kinds of personal choices; he is suspicious of intellectuals, for whom a "cultural tic masquerades as a public-health crusade" (17). Overall, he seems to think American children risk becoming "wuss[es]" (20) because of the well-meaning "nannyism" of wonks and do-gooders.

2. Flynn takes a deliberately provocative and iconoclastic position in the essay; his purpose is to question and criticize prevailing wisdom and an "anti-football frenzy" (7).

3. Given the readership of the *American Spectator*, he is likely writing for many people already inclined to agree with his general perspective. For example, his dismissive approach to misguided journalists and resentful "[e]ggheads" (17) seems aimed at affirming the views of those who already see such figures with skepticism or contempt.

Style and Structure (p. 624)

1. He addresses opposing points of view primarily in paragraphs 5 through 11. Flynn structures his argument as a response to those he disagrees with because he is not only making a case that playing football is good for young people; he is also making a case against conventional wisdom and the "anti-football frenzy" (7) provoked by journalists and others.

2. Essentially, he accuses journalists of jumping to conclusions and making a hasty generalization based on too little evidence ("a few tragic anecdotes") (7). You might point out that much of the discussion of football's consequences is also based on recent research into the neurocognitive problems caused by head traumas. Flynn does not address this.

3. Flynn uses one-sentence paragraphs for both emphasis and tone. So, for example, paragraph 9 is a sarcastic rhetorical question; paragraph 12 emphasizes the odd disparity between people's views of dangerous activities like swimming and skiing, and less dangerous sports like football; and paragraph 18 is an ironic comment on the apparent myopia of intellectuals.

4. *Hysteria* usually refers to exaggerated or uncontrollable emotion or excitement, particularly when the emotions are shared by a group of people. The word has its origins in the Greek word *hysterikos*, which means "of the womb." Indeed, hysteria was often considered a condition particular to women. Flynn's point is that American boys risk becoming "wuss[es]" (20) if they are not allowed to play football; the notion that anti-football sentiment is "hysterical" suggests that this belief is unmanly and effeminate.

5. Flynn closes by emphasizing that prohibitions on football may make American children into wusses or wimps. Students should have different opinions of this conclusion. But clearly, Flynn ends with a perspective on American life that goes beyond merely a defense of football.

Combining the Patterns (p. 625)

Flynn looks at several cause-and-effect relationships in this essay. In some cases, he argues against causal connections ("There's no evidence . . . that football caused Junior Seau to kill himself" [6]). He thinks the current "anti-football frenzy" has been caused by journalists (7). He argues that playing football leads to good health and toughness.

Thematic Connections

Let Steroids into the Hall of Fame (p. 21): As Flynn does, Zev Chafets takes a provocative position in this essay. He argues against the prevailing conventional wisdom that performance-enhancing drugs are hurting baseball: "Chemical enhancement won't kill the game; it is the cover-up that could be fatal" (10). He claims that the baseball purists need to replace their sentimental "mythology" with "realism" and "honesty" (11). Ask students if they think Flynn would agree with Chafets's argument.

Who Killed Benny Paret? (p. 337): In this classic essay, writer Norman Cousins explores the death of a prizefighter who was killed after a boxing match in 1962. Cousins touches on many of the same questions and issues that are now associated with debates about the dangers of football.

A Peaceful Woman Explains Why She Carries a Gun (p. 353): In this essay, Linda M. Hasselstrom reflects on her own decision to carry a gun and what her gun ownership means. Among other things, the weapon serves as an equalizer in dangerous confrontations: "A pistol is not the only way to avoid being raped or murdered in today's world, but, intelligently wielded, it can shift the balance of power and provide a measure of safety" (26).

CASEBOOK: Should Guns Be Allowed on College Campuses?

This casebook offers four different arguments about the contentious issue of guns on college campuses. No doubt, the horror of events like the Virginia Tech and Sandy Hook shootings make this a subject likely to evoke visceral and emotional responses. At the same time, discussions of gun laws and gun rights also touch upon more abstract issues like constitutional rights and ideas about personal liberties. You could begin by acknowledging one of the few premises that all these writers might accept: that college campuses are relatively safe places, statistically speaking. But that fact aside, students will find little that is compatible in the competing points of view here. You might encourage a lively discussion by addressing the contentiousness head-on: Why does this issue lead to such starkly drawn battle lines? For example, Timothy Wheeler's polemic practically drips with contempt for college officials who want to prohibit firearms on campuses. Where does the passion — and deep sense of conviction — come from on both sides of the topic? Does it originate in primal fear? Steadfast devotion to individual rights? Distrust in the ability of experts and officials to keep us safe? As an in-class activity, you might want to divide students into two groups and have them debate the issue based on the selections in the casebook.

Many of the claims in these articles speak directly to college students on campuses and in classrooms, so test these assertions against the responses of those in your class. Would they be inhibited or anxious if more students were armed? Would they feel safer? Likewise, three of these articles discuss the emotional volatility of undergraduates, as well as their presumed tendency (disputed here) to abuse alcohol and drugs. Ask if these factors are real or exaggerated. Do they have any bearing on the issue at hand? Make sure students read the casebook overview, as well as the background material in each headnote; this information will provide helpful perspective and context. The authorial information is vital here, as well. Three of these selections were written by advocates and activists for specific causes; two of these three are the products of advocacy organizations. You might use this as an opportunity to talk about the way such advocacy informs, shapes, or restricts arguments. That is true even on the level of prose style: the articles by Students for Gun-Free Schools and Students for Concealed Carry read, in some ways, as if they were written by committee. Contrast them with Wheeler's essay, which has such a distinctive, individual voice.

David Skorton and Glenn Altschuler, *Do We Really Need More Guns on Campus?*

Comprehension (p. 630)

1. Skorton and Altschuler state that the "vast majority of U.S. colleges and universities, public and private, prohibit guns" (2). This is important because the

writers suggest that colleges should be able to set their own policies, without the interference of legislators: overwhelmingly, these institutions choose to ban firearms. It is also important because, under the current policies, colleges and universities are "safer than most public spaces in the United States" (8).

2. Shootings on both school and college campuses—including the Virginia Tech massacre in 2007—have made gun policies a source of controversy and debate.

3. During an active shooter situation, campus police would have tremendous difficulty distinguishing between "good" guys and "bad" guys at a scene "where more than one person [was] firing a gun" (10). As one campus police chief asked, "When you're responding to a situation like that, and someone's in plain clothes with a gun, who's the bad guy? Who are you going to take out to save the lives of the ten thousand other students you're trying to protect?" (10).

4. Colleges are relatively safe, in terms of homicide. But the writers characterize college students as a "a cohort that includes emotionally volatile young men and women and abusers of alcohol and drugs" (12). Skorton and Altschuler think that allowing them to have guns will likely lead to more campus suicides, accidental shootings, and deadly disputes.

Purpose and Audience (p. 630)

1. The writers are trying to persuade readers that colleges and universities should be able to set their own policies; they want to encourage their audience to oppose legislation that would take this authority away from colleges and universities. They are also informing readers of these legislative efforts, as well as of other facts and viewpoints that support their thesis—for example, that college campuses are relatively safe and that guns may make them more dangerous.

2. Students may have different views on this question. But given Skorton and Altschuler's purposes and writing situation, these representative examples are sufficient to establish the writers' basic premises.

3. The purpose of paragraph 8 is to establish that colleges and universities are relatively safe places—an important point, given the horror and spectacle of high-profile shootings such as the one at Virginia Tech. Given that fact, the writers build a case that more guns might make campuses more violent and deadly—and shootings less rare.

Style and Structure (p. 631)

1. They state their thesis in the last sentence of the first paragraph. One variation on the statement could be: "As they have in the past, colleges and universities should be allowed to set their own gun policies; current legislation seeking to take that authority away from them and allow more guns on campuses will make colleges more dangerous places."

2. The writers quote and restate opposing arguments in paragraph 6, which focuses on the Second Amendment and safety; over the next several paragraphs, Skorton and Altschuler provide counterarguments. In doing so, they primarily address safety issues, although they do mention the Second Amendment

argument in passing ("By all means, let's get on with the national and state-level debate about how best to balance second-amendment rights with public safety" [14]). The writers seem more interested in practical arguments about campus safety than they are in abstract debates about constitutional rights.

3. The sentence follows Skorton and Altschuler's restatement and quotation of their opponents' arguments. Their tone implies that those who take the opposing position do not really know or understand what "actually happens on college campuses" (7). It suggests that gun rights advocates, like David Burnett, make arguments that are disconnected from practical reality. The sentence is a way for Skorton and Altschuler to implicitly claim, "We will now provide facts."

4. In the context of Skorton and Altschuler's argument, these are legitimate and credible authorities. At the same time, you might ask students how far that authority goes. For example, if a gun rights advocate found and then quoted a college provost and a campus police chief from other universities who disagreed with Skorton and Altschuler's position, would their opinions negate the point made in paragraph 10?

5. When *categorically* is used in this way, it means "without qualifications." It is a way of strengthening a statement or claim; in essence, the modifier indicates that the statement is unambiguous, objective, and indisputable. Note that when the word is deployed accurately, the person making such a claim ("categorically") cannot spin or back-pedal on the statement.

Combining the Patterns (p. 632)

In paragraphs 2 through 4, the writers use classification and division to discuss differences in state gun laws and university polices on handguns. Skorton and Altschuler want to make the point that, despite some variations, colleges and universities have come to an approximate consensus about prohibiting guns on campuses. As campuses are relatively safe places, the writers want these institutions to retain their authority to implement gun polices as administrators see fit.

Thematic Connections

Thirty-Eight Who Saw Murder Didn't Call the Police (p. 128): Martin Gansberg's newspaper report is about a woman in New York City being murdered while her neighbors listened to her screams for help, refusing to get involved. You might ask your students if getting involved in the issue of allowing guns on college campuses would prompt them to support one side of the issue or another. Do they see the issue as one of protection from a mentally unstable shooter or from a registered gun owner who attempts to step into a dangerous situation and creates even more danger?

College Pressures (p. 448): In this classic essay, William Zinsser discusses the various pressures on students: financial, social, academic, social, and self-imposed. Does his portrait of undergraduates in the 1970s match Skorton and Altschuler's description of a "cohort that includes emotionally volatile young men and women and abusers of alcohol and drugs" (20)? Do the problems Zinsser writes about remain more important today than the risk of campus shootings?

Students for Gun-Free Schools, *Why Our Campuses Are Safer without Concealed Handguns*

Comprehension (p. 639)

1. In the debate about gun laws, people lose sight of the fact that American colleges and universities are "some of the safest places in our country" (2). This is important to the writers' main point: they believe that colleges are safe because "campuses in almost all cases, have remained gun-free" (2).

2. The Brady Report claims that gun violence is likely to increase if firearms are allowed on campuses because of the following factors: "(1) [t]he prevalence of drugs and alcohol; (2) [t]he risk of suicide and mental health issues; (3) [t]he likelihood of gun thefts; and (4) [a]n increased risk of accidental shootings" (8).

3. "Shall-issue" policies mean that "officials may not arbitrarily deny an application [for concealed carry permits] to those who meet a basic set of requirements" (18).

4. The "bottom line" is that passing a background check and qualifying for a concealed carry permit does not guarantee a person is a law-abiding citizen. The writers cite various examples of shooters who passed background checks and who had concealed carry permits; they also refer to research demonstrating that "those who obtain concealed carry permits can pose a threat to public safety" (21).

Purpose and Audience (p. 640)

1. As an advocacy and activist organization, Students for Gun-Free Schools are explicitly committed to a particular cause and a particular point of view. Consequently, their writing purpose is entirely persuasive; the goal of this essay is not fundamentally analytical, exploratory, expressive, or even informative. Every argument, claim, detail, and piece of evidence included in this text must support the organization's political goal. You might ask students whether they consider this selection "propaganda." You can also discuss how the purpose affects its style and tone: it is written in the impersonal voice of an organization, institution, or party.

2. They establish that campuses are safe places for three main reasons. First, campuses have traditionally been gun-free, and the writers attribute the safety of colleges and universities to that fact. Second, establishing this point undercuts the argument that more students need to be armed to defend themselves, as campus shootings and homicides are rare. Third, it follows that more guns on campus will make what are now safe places more dangerous; the writers make this case by referring to the 2007 Brady Campaign report (8).

3. The thesis could be stated as: "Despite the claims of gun-rights advocates, allowing more guns on campuses will make colleges and universities more dangerous and detract from the academic learning environment."

4. In its least generous interpretation, the term *gun lobby* connotes a powerful, well-funded organization devoted to the proliferation of firearms. The word *lobbyist* generally has a negative connotation: people who are paid to persuade public officials to enact (or not enact) policies favorable to the interests lobbyists represent. In characterizing their opponents in this way, Students for Gun-Free Schools are not seeking to persuade adamant gun-rights activists or advocates. Rather, they are trying to persuade those who have not made up

their minds about these issues. They are also affirming the views of (and providing arguments for) those already inclined to agree with their positions.

5. These "bullet hit rates" undercut one of the main arguments of gun-rights advocates. They claim that individuals with guns will be able to stop shooters in situations like the massacre at Virginia Tech. Yet the Students for Gun-Free Schools writers argue that "even well-trained law enforcement officers rarely hit their targets when firing at other human beings" (26). It follows that untrained concealed carry permit holders with guns would be even less effective. Worse, they would add confusion to active shooter scenes: "The potential for collateral damage is enormous, even assuming that concealed carry permit holders would make sound decisions about when to discharge their handguns" (27).

Style and Structure (p. 640)

1. The quotation marks suggest an ironic or sarcastic tone; implicitly, the writers do not agree that such a "right" exists.

2. To the degree that the writers want to align their views with "common-sense" or mainstream opinion, the poll is effective rhetorically: it suggests that the writers' position is in line with an overwhelming majority of Americans. But the results of the poll do not necessarily mean that their position is correct. Arguably, this is an example of *argumentum ad populum*, or an appeal to the people: the claim that something must be right or true because most people believe it to be so.

3. According to the writers, gun-rights advocates sometimes argue that gun-free zones (like colleges and universities) invite attacks because shooters know that the unarmed are unlikely to resist or stop a shooting. In paragraph 15, the writers provide examples of two shooters who staged their attacks in places where people put up armed resistance: a police station and a courthouse. The authors conclude, "There is no evidence that suicidal shooters would be deterred from attacks on college campuses by concealed carry permit holders" (16).

4. *Collateral damage* is most often used in the context of warfare. For example, when enemy combatants are targeted in U.S. drone strikes, resulting civilian casualties are often referred to as "collateral damage." The term is euphemistic, but it can evoke images of innocent victims and unintended deaths.

Combining the Patterns (p. 641)

The writers use comparison and contrast when they consider how effective civilian conceal and carry permit holders might be at stopping shooters. They compare and contrast the effectiveness of well-trained law enforcement officers with the potential efficacy of typical gun owners (26). This pattern supports their argument because it undercuts the claim that armed students would make college campuses safer.

Thematic Connections

Shooting an Elephant (p. 133): In this famous essay, George Orwell shows readers that he felt he wrongly "executed" an elephant in order to save face as a colonial officer before a crowd of hostile Burmese subjects. Had he not had the means to kill the elephant, he would not have reacted as he did. The Students for Gun-Free Schools essay argues that possessing a gun would encourage students to similarly escalate tense situations.

Just Walk On By (p. 238): In this essay, Brent Staples also considers issues of power and powerlessness and, in particular, the extent to which young black men may find themselves in the situation of adopting a powerful persona—an intimidating mask of fearsomeness—that hides an essential powerlessness. The point Staples makes is that every day he must fight against stereotypes that lead to suspicion and fear. Staples himself does nothing threatening to justify such fear. The Students for Gun-Free Schools essay argues that possessing a gun would encourage students to use violence to solve situations that might not call for it.

Students for Concealed Carry, *Why Our Campuses Are* Not *Safer without Concealed Handguns*

Comprehension (p. 652)

1. These state legislatures allow guns to be carried into the capitol. The writers suggest that the presence of concealed firearms does not discourage debate and discussion. Their point is to address the claim in the Students for Gun-Free Schools article that concealed guns in classrooms might discourage debate and discussion.

2. According to the writers, people generally overstate the amount of drinking among college students. They support this claim with research and the authority of an expert on the subject (11–12).

3. The writers assert that "[a]ll a concealed handgun license holder needs to know is how to use his or her concealed handgun to stop an immediate threat of death or serious bodily harm" (27). They argue that this can be accomplished in one-day training courses.

4. According to Students for Concealed Carry, their opponents' arguments "rely entirely on speculation, false assumptions, and emotion" (32).

Purpose and Audience (p. 652)

1. One variation on the thesis could be stated as follows: "Despite the speculative, emotional, and poorly considered arguments of Students for Gun-Free Schools, banning guns at colleges and universities does not make campuses safer."

2. The writers accuse their opponents of engaging in *post hoc* reasoning (*post hoc, ergo propter hoc*/After this, therefore because of this). In their article, Students for Gun-Free Schools cite the safety of colleges and universities, then claim that colleges are safe because of policies that keep guns off campuses. But Students for Concealed Carry point out that no causal connection between these two facts has been established. The writers make this charge against their opponents early because it supports one of their main points: Students for Gun-Free Schools are not only wrong; they also make bad, fallacious, and misleading arguments.

3. The writers want to reach ambivalent readers who might be persuaded by the arguments of Students for Gun-Free Schools. They write, in part, to clear up what they see as misinformation and misperception about guns and gun ownership. They want to present themselves as debunkers and appeal to readers who trust empirical data over "speculation, false assumptions, and emotion" (32). Note that in their introduction, the authors confidently claim that their cause has generated "unprecedented" public support; they suggest, moreover, that their success has caused a dubious "counter-movement" that relies on tired, "well-worn" arguments (1).

4. The writers seem to combine two views of the American public. On the one hand, they begin their article with the claim that they have generated "unprecedented media attention and public support" (1), which presents the public in a positive light. On the other hand, they assume that the public is largely ignorant about gun laws, licensing requirements, and crime statistics. Consequently, the writers downplay the importance of the public in the debate: "Public opinion does not always dictate public policy on complicated issues of public safety. The FDA does not poll the public on acceptable procedures for sanitizing meatpacking plants" (7).

5. The writers do use imagery designed to evoke an emotional response, particularly when they present the horror and fear of being defenseless in a mass shooting: "Why should a professor who is allowed the means to defend himself at the local bank and at his neighborhood church be forced to hide under his desk listening to gunshots getting closer, with no recourse but to hope and pray the gunman doesn't find him?" (18). This appeal reinforces their claim that concealed carry license holders should be able to carry their handguns on campus, as they do in church, grocery stores, and other places.

Style and Structure (p. 653)

1. The writers do a thorough job of including the arguments of Students for Gun-Free Schools. It is possible to understand this article without reading the original; however, the Students for Concealed Carry authors do not frame their opponents' arguments in a flattering or credible light.

2. The writers use analogies sparingly, but effectively. For example, they compare college campuses to "large, affluent neighborhoods" (3) and imply an equivalency between people with guns in classrooms and people with guns on the floor of the Texas and Virginia state legislatures.

3. The writers use the term *moot point* in a way that is considered distinctive to colloquial American English: to be "moot" in this context is to have no practical significance. They may mean that the point is a diversionary red herring: "this is not a debate about keeping guns out of the hands of college students" (12). In its strictest sense, the word *moot* means subject to debate, dispute, or uncertainty.

4. By labeling the organization in this way, the writers encourage readers to see it — and perceive its claims — as agenda-driven, "biased," and suspect.

5. The writers incorporate expert opinion, research, and statistics at various points in the article. For example, they use both expert opinion and a study by the Task Force on College Drinking to refute Students for Gun-Free Schools and address more general misperceptions about college alcohol abuse (9–10). Similarly, the writers use data from the Texas Department of Corrections to address Students for Gun-Free Schools claims in paragraph 23.

Combining the Patterns (p. 654)

The writers use cause and effect at various points in their article. First, you might point out that their main argument is an attempt to refute a causal relationship asserted by the Students for Gun-Free Schools article: that campuses are safe because guns are prohibited. Indeed, many of their claims dispute cause-and-effect relationships (e.g., that the possible presence of guns will discourage debate in classrooms). Second, they imply that allowing concealed carry permit holders to bring their weapons to campus may make colleges and universities safer. They quote a Louisiana State representative on the subject, who states, "If we don't try it, are we going to know?" (15).

Thematic Connections

A Peaceful Woman Explains Why She Carries a Gun (p. 353): The Students for Concealed Carry writers ask a hypothetical question: "Why should a 105-pound woman who is allowed the means to defend herself against a 250-pound would-be rapist outside of campus not be afforded that same right on campus?" (18). In "A Peaceful Woman Explains Why She Carries a Gun," Linda M. Hasselstrom provides a deeply personal and revealing answer to a similar question. But Hasselstrom writes about needing a gun in circumstances where she is isolated and vulnerable. Do students think she would agree that people should be allowed to carry guns on bustling, crowded college campuses?

The Declaration of Independence (p. 550): A founding document of the United States asserts that people have the "unalienable right" to "life, liberty and the pursuit of happiness." How far do such rights go? Do students believe that the personal right to carry a gun anywhere they choose is bound up with these rights, or "unalienable"?

Timothy Wheeler, *There's a Reason They Choose Schools*

Comprehension (p. 657)

1. Wheeler sees a "depressing" similarity in the fact that recent shootings took place at "that steadfastly gun-free zone, the school campus" (2).
2. The writer is dismissive and perhaps even contemptuous of the AMA's reaction and policy proposals. He considers the special issue of the AMA journal a "rehash" of "all the tired rhetoric of bureaucrats and public-health wonks" (3).
3. According to Wheeler, the AMA writers "studiously avoid" the "repeated failures of such feel-good steps as no-gun policies, and on the other hand the demonstrated success of armed first responders" (5).
4. The writer claims that campus anti-violence policies are based on "irrational fears more than real-world analysis of what works" (9).
5. For Wheeler, the best way to deal with such a threat is a "prepared and brave defender with the proper lifesaving tool — a gun" (12).

Purpose and Audience (p. 658)

1. Students may have different views of Wheeler's background. Does he have credibility because he is a physician? But he is not an impartial medical pro-

fessional; he is the director of an advocacy organization that lobbies for gun rights. That fact might shape the way readers understand and evaluate his argument. You might want to examine these issues in the context of Wheeler's ethos.

2. The *National Review*'s audience is primarily conservative; its readers are likely to agree with Wheeler's point of view. Given his disdain for those he disagrees with, he does not seem to be trying to persuade them. His characterization of AMA physicians, university officials, legal analysts, and "public-health wonks" (3) implies a populist distrust of "experts" and "intellectuals." Readers who share this skepticism are likely to agree — and feel affirmed.

3. One possible thesis: "As long as arrogant bureaucrats and wonks insist on ineffectual antigun policies at colleges and universities, campuses and other 'gun-free zones' will make appealing targets for mass shooters."

4. Given his negative characterizations of school officials and public-health experts as timid, out-of-touch bureaucrats, they might be offended. Ask students if this argument would be likely to change their minds. If not, how might the argument be revised to be more persuasive?

5. Wheeler sees the formation of Students for Concealed Carry as an "encouraging" sign that "college students themselves have a much better grasp on reality than their politically correct elders" (8). The writer's purpose is to advocate for allowing students to carry guns, and this organization supports his point of view. At the same time, the formation of Students for Concealed Carry also reinforces his premise that "arrogant" (5) officials and administrators are out of touch, while nonexperts know better.

Style and Structure (p. 658)

1. Wheeler addresses opposing points of view at several different places in his article; indeed, it is structured, primarily, as a response to a special issue of an AMA publication. You might point out that Wheeler mocks the diction and rhetoric of these experts, as well as their arguments. This is evident in the quoted terms in paragraph 3; the "gem" he quotes in paragraph 4; and the long "nostrum" he includes in paragraph 10, which he follows with a one-sentence paragraph: "Got that?" Clearly, he thinks this language is pompous bureaucratese, which (for him) matches its authors' detachment from reality. You might compare it with his own style, which strives for directness.

2. The writer characterizes his opponents with disdain bordering on contempt. Their arguments are "tired" (3); they are "arrogant" (5); they are "timid bureaucrats" who base their policies on "irrational fears more than real-world analysis of what works" (9).

3. Wheeler places quotation marks around these phrases because he thinks they are pompous, trite, and "tired" jargon terms from "bureaucrats and public-health wonks" (3). The punctuation implies that the writers are out of touch and that their claims should not be taken seriously.

4. Strictly speaking, a *mantra* is a sound, word, or phrase that is repeated by a person who is praying or meditating, often in a mystical context. Wheeler is using it in a colloquial sense to refer to a statement ("guns are the root cause of violence") that he believes is repeated mindlessly as conventional wisdom among "bureaucrats" and "public-health wonks."

5. In paragraph 4, Wheeler cites a specific passage from the AMA journal that he finds especially egregious and incorrect. The passage condenses nearly everything that he finds objectionable: the claim that colleges should reinforce prohibitions on guns and the assertion that officials need to discourage the belief that armed students can stop active shooters. Wheeler uses the paragraph to then pivot away from the journal article, before returning to it in paragraph 10.

6. Wheeler includes this passage because he finds it pompous, pretentious, and disconnected from reality. He implies that this prose style reflects poor thinking and substantively bad arguments.

Combining the Patterns (p. 659)

Wheeler uses comparison and contrast when he discusses how an armed student and an armed vice principal stopped two school shootings in progress, respectively (4). Implicitly, he is contrasting these situations with those on campuses where students and officials were not armed. Perhaps most pointedly, Wheeler contrasts AMA journal editor James J. James's (presumed) proposal for dealing with school shootings in paragraph 10 with his own "remedy" for confronting a "gun-wielding homicidal maniac" (12).

Thematic Connections

Thirty-Eight Who Saw Murder Didn't Call the Police **(p. 128):** Wheeler writes about the prospect of armed citizens, bravely defending themselves and the innocent when confronted with "gun-wielding homicidal maniac[s]" (12). Any such discussion must take into account how people respond to such situations in real time. In this essay, Martin Gansberg tells the story of a woman who was assaulted and murdered, even as her neighbors witnessed and heard her cries but did nothing in response. Would carrying a concealed weapon bestow on the gun owner any social obligations to others—for example, the obligation to draw the weapon and attack the attacker, rather than, say, retreating to safety?

Ground Zero **(p. 175):** In this essay, Suzanne Berne confronts the emptiness at the site of the September 11 attacks in downtown New York. She also faces a sense of helplessness and, perhaps, meaningless in the face of large-scale death and catastrophe. Such events can leave people feeling powerless, both during and after. How does possessing a handgun provide a sense of control or security in an unpredictable and often dangerous world?

15: Combining the Patterns

In this chapter are two essays—one student, one professional—that we have annotated to indicate each writer's use of multiple patterns, along with three additional (unannotated) professional essays. You may not wish to wait until you have completed the chapter on argumentation to discuss these essays. In fact, a good time to have students look at the two annotated essays might be prior to Chapter 10 or Chapter 11. At that point it can be useful for students to recognize that although their papers may be structured primarily as cause-and-effect or comparison-and-contrast essays, for example, they may well include passages of narration, description, exemplification, and process.

Another approach would be to look at the student essay in conjunction with Chapter 6. Michael Huu Truong's "The Park" is primarily a narrative essay, and you might use it early in the course to point out the interplay in most writing of the various patterns to be practiced in subsequent chapters. In conjunction with Chapter 13, you could again emphasize the use of multiple patterns by having students look at Lars Eighner's "On Dumpster Diving"—an essay of definition that, like many extended definitions, uses virtually every technique in the writer's repertoire of development strategies. You might have students read David Kirby's "Inked Well" in conjunction with other cause-and-effect essays in the text, while Jonathan Swift's "A Modest Proposal" could be read as a special form of argumentation. Alternatively, you might introduce Truong's and Eighner's essays independently at the end of the course; both demonstrate how writing patterns can be used for complex purposes.

Lars Eighner, *On Dumpster Diving*

Students are bound to find much to fascinate, appall, and stimulate discussion in Eighner's guide to living on the street out of garbage cans and Dumpsters. Writing with rueful good humor, an eye for telling detail, and an engagingly personal style, Eighner does more to suggest the day-to-day reality of homelessness than would any number of documentaries or clinical studies.

He begins with his situation and his terminology, which lead him to his thesis. Then he looks at the theory, technique, and dangers (mainly dysentery) of scavenging through garbage for food. (If your campus is a residential one, students might be especially interested in Eighner's description of why college students are among his best sources.) Then he turns to the "predictable series of stages a person goes through in learning to scavenge" (31). He next considers the collection of objects and why he hates people who scrounge for cans to turn in for cash. He explains why he has reservations about going through individual garbage cans, which leads him to think about the personal lives of those whose garbage he sifts through. He also explains the animal dangers—vermin, cats, fire ants—as well as why it is best to lower oneself into a Dumpster. He concludes by noting the two "rather deep lessons" (63) he has learned from scavenging.

It will probably be easy to get students talking about Eighner and his essay, but as part of your discussion, be sure to have students think about his intended purpose and audience. Does he really expect readers to follow his directions and advice? Or does he want to affect his audience in a different way?

Comprehension (p. 684)

1. *Dumpster diving* might be defined as "a systematic method of scouring refuse containers for items useful for living on little or no money."
2. Fruits and vegetables may be discarded for minor imperfections; pizzas may end up in a pizzeria's Dumpster because they were ordered as a prank or incorrectly made: college students often throw away food when they are going on a break ("through carelessness, ignorance, or wastefulness" [22]).
3. He avoids "game, poultry, pork, and egg-based foods" (28) and "[h]ome leftovers" (29), as well as anything that looks or smells obviously bad.

4. Obvious drawbacks include the threat of dysentery, dealing with the fire ants, and the lack of medical care and storage space. Implied drawbacks include the nastiness of rooting through garbage and the hunger that could result from several days without a successful "dive."

5. The stages of learning to scavenge are (a) scavenging at first with a sense of disgust and loathing; (b) realizing that a lot of good, usable stuff is discarded and therefore taking pleasure in scavenging; (c) becoming obsessed with scavenging to the point of trying to acquire everything one finds.

6. He also scavenges for collectible items (pocket calculators and the like), personal needs (like warm bedding), and essential drugs (like antibiotics) because he has no access to health care.

7. Can scroungers, who are usually addicts and winos, "tend to tear up the Dumpsters, mixing the contents and littering the area" (44), and Eighner is contemptuous of them because they pass up many useful items.

8. He has learned "to take what you can use and let the rest go by" (63) and that material being is transient: "mental things are longer lived than other material things" (64).

Purpose and Audience (p. 685)

1. He apparently also wants to encourage some compassion in his audience for those like himself, living on the fringe. And in his final paragraphs, he suggests an even larger purpose: to let his audience see that material things are transient.

2. Students may respond in a variety of ways to the essay — feeling everything from real sympathy to outright contempt. Try to get them to explore the reasons for their different responses.

3. There may be many reasons to explain why Eighner does not provide background information about himself. For one thing, not doing so makes him essentially anonymous — like the homeless people readers actually encounter on the streets. Also, the facts of his earlier life may not be particularly interesting — or flattering. Many students, however, are likely to think he could have explained in more detail why he ended up as he did.

4. His purpose in including such detail is probably twofold: he wants to provide an in-depth view of a subject most readers know nothing about, and he wants to suggest that homelessness is fraught with peril and difficulty.

5. His telling about the stages of scavenging is a way of helping readers imagine themselves in his place (everyone can imagine being "filled with disgust and self-loathing" [32]), and his scruples about going through individual cans are something readers can share. In addition, when he describes the process of going through a Dumpster, he does so in a way that puts his readers directly on the scene.

6. The last line is calculated to suggest that even in his distressed state he has reached a level of inner understanding through Dumpster diving that makes him better off than the "rat-race millions" (67).

Style and Structure (p. 685)

1. He describes the source of the term *Dumpster* and offers alternatives to the phrase *Dumpster diving*. These opening definitions seem appropriate to establish the subject and Eighner's tone of clarity and preciseness.

2. *Scrounging* seems less purposeful than *scavenging* (hence, his use of the term when he's trying "to be obscure"), and *foraging,* as he suggests, has come to be associated with finding food in the wilderness. *Diving,* he says, is too cute and not quite accurate in his case. So he prefers *scavenging.*

3. The one-sentence paragraphs are 2, 7, 41, and the final paragraph. The first and last are for dramatic effect; the middle two each introduce a new section of discussion and might be combined with the following paragraph.

4. The present tense adds a greater sense of immediacy than the past tense would allow.

5. Other paragraphs of lists include 14–16, 24–25, 28, 38, 40, 53, and 55. As mentioned earlier, Eighner's goal seems to be to establish a very precise, even fastidious, tone; the careful listing helps accomplish this goal.

Combining the Patterns (p. 686)

Students will have different responses here, but certainly the passages of exemplification, cause and effect, and process are particularly instructive.

Thematic Connections

The Untouchable (p. 494): In this student essay, Ajoy Mahtab defines the lowest level of the Indian caste system, "human beings treated worse than dogs and shunned far more than lepers" (2). To what extent are the homeless in the United States the "untouchables" of our society? Based on Eighner's essay, how fair do students find the attitudes toward the homeless?

Homeless (p. 510): Like Eighner, Quindlen consciously avoids using data, statistics, social science, or any real empirical lens to view homelessness. Instead, she prefers the personal and the anecdotal, like the story of Ann that opens the essay. This is deliberate, of course, but it may lead to the question: Is empathy enough, on its own? In concentrating on details and individuals, does Quindlen lose sight of broader, structural issues (social, economic, or otherwise) that could be useful in lessening the number of people without homes?

The Declaration of Independence (p. 550): The United States is founded on the notion that "all men are created equal, that they are endowed by their Creator with certain unalienable rights, that among these are life, liberty and the pursuit of happiness." What does *equality* mean in this context? Using "On Dumpster Diving" as a starting point, students might consider issues of class, privilege, and power in the United States in terms of the ideals on which the country is based.

Dana Stevens, *Your Flip-Flops Are Grossing Me Out*

Dana Stevens's "Your Flip-Flops Are Grossing Me Out" was published as part of a regular Slate.com feature called "A Fine Whine." In this series, writers choose a peeve, an irritation, or some minor, hidden-in-plain-sight problem that nevertheless justifies a "rant." In this case, Stevens targets both flip-flops and those who wear this casual footwear inappropriately. As with Farhad Manjoo's "No, I Do Not Want to Pet Your Dog," which is part of the same "A Fine Whine" series, you should ask your students if Stevens is successful in writing an amusing "whine," whether they agree with her or not. The key to the form is to find some superficial or apparently trivial phenomenon (flip-flops) and suggest that it is the manifestation of a larger, more serious subject or problem (a breakdown of the social contract, for example). Do students think Stevens is making too much of a minor peeve, or can they understand how interpreting the meaning of little things can start wider conversations and reveal larger issues? Is there something problematic about being judgmental of other people's fashion choices, as Stevens implicitly concedes in her first paragraph? You might even apply her analysis—and her standards—to the classroom. Is the classroom an appropriate setting for flip-flops? Why or why not? Like all the other essays in this section of the book, "Your Flip-Flops Are Grossing Me Out" illustrates how good writers make use of all the patterns and combine them fluently.

Comprehension (p. 690)

1. Stevens had once mentioned her intention of writing a "tirade" against flip-flops to her editor. A few years later, the "increasing prevalence" of the footwear—as well as a void created by a time of year when news is slow—prompted her to write the essay (1).

2. The paragraph provides the history of the flip-flop, but it also allows her to qualify her argument. She is not criticizing people who wear flip-flops for their "situational utility." The footwear has its place, which Stevens acknowledges. The writer is also not criticizing people who wear flip-flops in parts of the world where the flip-flop is the "only shoe that's both available and affordable." Her targets are "grown adults in affluent societies" who wear flip-flops in inappropriate situations.

3. Stevens objects to the way the flip-flop "decoupl[es]" the "footwear from foot with each step" (3). Moreover, other forms of casual footwear fulfill "most of the basic functions of shoes," allowing wearers to run, step backward, or perform necessary tasks. Their "thicker soles and foot-harnessing straps" also protect feet in a messy, litter-strewn urban environment (4).

4. She finds them appropriate for activities like going to the beach or pool, "showering at the gym, taking out the garbage," or going to the laundromat (2). She also has no objections to President Obama wearing his while visiting an ice-cream shop in Hawaii while on vacation.

5. The "crux of the flip-flop problem" is in the "decoupling of footwear from foot with each step—and the attendant decoupling of the wearer's behavior from the social contract" (3).

6. Stevens cites her own observations. She refers to the growth in sales and popularity of the Havaianas brand of flip-flops. She also recalls the 2005 incident in which Northwestern University's women's lacrosse team visited the White House; several members wore flip-flops, which started a "national conversation" about the suitability of their footwear (5).

7. The writer's primary objection to flip-flops is most evident in paragraphs 3 and 9. In essence, she finds them uncivilized and unseemly: they "gross" her out, as the title suggests. She also implies that they show "laziness and lack of character," and reflect the "half-dressed slatternliness" of their wearers (9).

Purpose and Audience (p. 690)

1. The essay is part of a Slate.com series called "A Fine Whine," which provides sharp, cranky takes on the pet peeves of various authors. Stevens's primary

purpose is to amuse: flip-flops are not really a pressing issue, nor is information about their history particularly useful. No doubt, Stevens wants to persuade readers to view the footwear in an amusing new way; also, the information about flip-flops and foot problems may be valuable. But this is not primarily an informative essay about podiatric issues. Rather, it is a funny, expressive exercise in style and observation.

2. Stevens characterizes herself as "not really one for composing tirades" (1). She claims she does not usually care about other people's grooming or fashion choices. In other words, she implies that she is not a whiner or complainer, or a particularly judgmental person. Implicitly, if she has been reduced to complaining about flip-flops, then they must really be a serious problem.

3. Stevens is writing for a sophisticated audience, many of whom live in cities. Her primary objections to flip-flops involve people who wear them in urban settings. She assumes her readers will have a broad range of references, as well, from social contract theory to the television show *Cheers*. She is writing primarily for those who might have noticed the prevalence of flip-flops in inappropriate settings, but she also addresses their wearers directly at times: "Those people — you, if you're among them — need to face the reality that you are, in essence, going barefoot, and it's grossing the rest of us out" (2).

4. The last sentence of her first paragraph sets up her main point, but it may be too noncommittal to be a thesis statement. The best statement of her thesis is probably at the end of her second paragraph. After this main claim, she provides her supporting arguments.

Style and Structure (p. 691)

1. Stevens uses expert opinion (the views of a podiatrist and a pedorthist) to support her claim that flip-flops are "bad for the health of the human foot" (6–8). She uses personal opinion throughout the essay, including her visceral objections to flip-flops (they are "grossing" her out) and her interpretation of them as a violation of the social contract (3). She relies on anecdotal evidence to support her assertion about the "growing pervasiveness" of flip-flops (5).

2. Given the substance, style, and form of this essay — it is supposed to be a crotchety rant — the title is appropriate. For example, consider how titles that might emphasize other parts of the writer's argument ("Flip-Flops May Be Harmful to Feet") would miss the essay's tone.

3. The term *flip-flop* often refers to the act of changing one's opinions or positions, especially in the context of politics. As applied to footwear, the label has an onomatopoeic quality.

4. Dana Stevens's use of the term *foot underwear* or *foot robes* evokes the informal, slatternly, too casual quality of flip-flops when they are worn in inappropriate settings. This question should get students thinking metaphorically.

Combining the Patterns (p. 691)

Stevens combines all the patterns in this essay. She opens with a brief narrative (1); she compares and contrasts appropriate situations for flip-flops with inappropriate ones (2); she classifies and divides different kinds of footwear (4); she gives an example (the lacrosse players at the White House) in paragraph 5; her explanation of how flip-flops may harm feet includes both cause and effect and process (6–7); and in renaming flip-flops in her concluding paragraph, she uses definition.

Thematic Connections

From *Persepolis II* (p. 112): In Stevens's essay, the writer claims that flip-flops essentially break the "social contract," and eliminate important barriers "between public and private, inside and outside, shod and barefoot" (3). Implicitly, she ties clothing to personal character and the foundations of civilization. In this excerpt, Marjane Satrapi covers similar subject matter, but in a much more serious context: clothing restrictions on women in Iran after the Islamic Revolution of 1979. Is the etiquette that Stevens endorses related in any way to Islamic rules requiring that women be covered? Does Satrapi's comic make Stevens's essay seem frivolous?

My First Conk (p. 283): In this essay, Malcolm X writes about a hairstyle called the "conk." To achieve this fashionable look, African Americans would subject their hair to a painful chemical process so that it would be straight—and meet implicit standards of Caucasian beauty. For Malcolm X, who writes self-deprecatingly about getting his first conk, the process came to represent a shameful "self-degradation" (23) and a loss of identity. It was also a waste of time for those who engaged in the practice: "[I]f they gave the brains in their heads just half as much attention as they do their hair, they would be a thousand times better off" (27). Like Stevens, Malcolm X is writing about the connections between personal style and much more substantive issues.

The Wife-Beater (p. 514): Where Stevens objects to flip-flops, Gayle Rosenwald Smith objects to a slang term for a type of undershirt: "The name is the issue. For they are known as 'wife beaters'" (3). She worries about the acceptance and normalization of this name, as it has toxic connotations of male dominance and spousal abuse.

Inked Well (p. 692): Here, David Kirby reflects on the increasing prevalence of tattoos in society, as well as shifting standards and assumptions about the kinds of people who get tattoos. He also considers the different ways people use tattoos so that they—the individuals who choose to be "inked"—can be "read" by others. As he writes, "The point of all this is self-expression—and we seem to be living in a time where that's what nearly everybody (word carefully chosen) wants to do, in one way or another" (21).

David Kirby, *Inked Well*

In this essay David Kirby explores the current fad for tattooing; the number of people in the United States with tattoos has increased by at least 10 percent over the last five years, and more and more tattoos are sported by members of the middle class rather than just "crooks and creeps" (9). Kirby also considers some of the history of tattooing, its popularity among the aristocracy in the nineteenth century, gradual stigmatization as it became more readily available to the masses, and recent resurgence. To get a firsthand perspective on the matter, he interviews people on the street with tattoos and comes to the conclusion that people get tattoos for many, essentially benign reasons. He also classifies two types of "tattoo narratives": the "Record Book" and the "Canvas" (18). Finally, he links tattooing to other kinds of body modifications, seeing it all as means of self-expression.

One interesting aspect of the essay is Kirby's own stance, moving from disdain for people who get tattoos (his opening example is priceless) to something almost

184

like admiration. How do students respond to this change of heart? And how does the fact that he concludes by admitting he still wouldn't get a tattoo himself affect their reading? Students obviously will have varied opinions regarding getting tattoos, so the essay may produce some lively discussion.

This essay is an excellent model for students as a piece of writing they could pursue on their own. They might consider any aspect of contemporary popular culture—something physical, such as piercings or electric-colored dyed hair; something technological, such as iPods or text messaging; a particular film or music genre; the possibilities are virtually endless—and then plan and write an essay following Kirby's lead: providing examples, giving an overview and background, researching experts as well as participants, and offering their own personal commentary, their own take on the subject.

Comprehension (p. 696)

1. You may have to explain to students that the title is a play on the term *ink well*, an old-fashioned desktop container that writing pens are dipped into.
2. Kirby's opening story provides an example of why he always believed that people with tattoos are "either bottom feeders or those who want to pretend they are" (3).
3. Kirby presents information on the history of tattoos in paragraphs 5–9, in part to provide the perhaps surprising fact that they were once the province of the aristocracy. This information is necessary for his purpose, which is to give readers an overview of the subject. He returns to this historical background in paragraph 20 in order to stretch body modification back to the dawn of human history, showing his newfound respect for the tattoo.
4. The first tattoos in the West were sported by explorers from Polynesia beginning in the eighteenth century and later by sailors from the early nineteenth century. They then became fashionable with the aristocracy through the early part of the twentieth century; the fad died out because new technology made tattoos much cheaper. By the mid-twentieth century, other than sailors, they mainly marked those on the fringes of society, such as bikers and ex-convicts.
5. Kirby has just made the point that up until recently tattoos have been a way of differentiating "Them" from "Us" (meaning the lower from the middle classes and higher). Now, people from the middle class increasingly are getting tattoos.
6. The two types of tattoo narratives Kirby identifies are the Record Book and the Canvas. The former represents an event, such as a relationship or a death; the latter represents the self and provides the opportunity for personal discovery.
7. The people Kirby talks to have gotten tattoos just because it's something to do, to cement a friendship, to act as a personal symbol, to ease emotional pain. Students should have no trouble coming up with other possible reasons.
8. Kirby has come to approve of people who get tattoos rather than simply dismiss them, primarily because of his research.

Purpose and Audience (p. 696)

1. Kirby's primary purpose is to provide information about tattoos, although he also wishes to entertain readers and explore his own feelings. He does not wish to persuade readers to get tattooed.

2. This is probably as close to Kirby's thesis as any sentence in the text. But this essay really divides into two parts, beginning with the questions he asks in paragraph 11. The answer to this question in paragraph 21 is an extension of his thesis into the present.

3. Kirby's point is that there are many ways in which people seek to alter their bodies besides tattoos, so tattoos are just one part of the spectrum and should be viewed no more negatively than a weightlifter's enlarged muscles.

Style and Structure (p. 697)

1. The Polynesian word *tatao* (meaning "to tap") is the immediate basis, but researchers suggest that the Tahitian word *tatu* ("to mark something") is a distant ancestor. A good site for tattoo slang can be found at Body Art Fun: tattoo.about.com/cs/tatfaq/a/tat_slang.htm.

2. The dominant pattern of development is exemplification, with cause and effect also playing an important role.

3. We find the markedly brief opening and conclusion effective. The opening sentence could be attached to the second paragraph, but it wouldn't have as much punch. Students will be hard pressed to come up with anything to add to the conclusion.

4. Kirby cites experts in paragraphs 3, 5, and 17 as a way of indicating the sources he has used and to expand on his own discoveries about why people get tattoos. He includes statistics in paragraph 10 to show that tattoos are growing in popularity.

Combining the Patterns (p. 697)

Kirby opens with a narration that also serves as an example. Then he uses definition (3), exemplification (4), narration (5–7), cause and effect (8), definition (9), comparison and contrast (10), cause and effect and exemplification (11–17), classification and division and exemplification (18–19), exemplification (20), cause and effect (21), and comparison and contrast (22).

Thematic Connections

Four Tattoos (p. 222): This visual text includes four photos of tattoos. Students might speculate on what these tattoos signify.

Why Looks Are the Last Bastion of Discrimination (p. 244): Kirby illustrates our tendency to judge people by their appearance. Using several contemporary and persuasive examples, Deborah L. Rhode shows how looks-based biases remain the "last bastion of acceptable bigotry" (2). These prejudices have real consequences, too, as less attractive people are "less likely to be hired and promoted, and they earn lower salaries, even in fields in which looks have no obvious relationship to professional duties" (10).

Medium Ash Brown (p. 277): Student Melany Hunt writes about dying her hair, with disastrous results. While this is not, strictly speaking, body modification, the essay provides an opportunity to discuss what people do to create the image they want to present to the world.

My First Conk (p. 283): Like the previous essay, which it inspired, this process explanation by Malcolm X deals with changing one's appearance — in this case choosing to suffer physically (as those who get tattoos do) to conform to societal norms (which is not a motivation for those who get tattoos – unless, of course, the motivation is to conform to one's peer group). This essay, "Medium Ash Brown," and Kirby's essay offer a great deal for discussion about personal image.

The Wife-Beater (p. 514): Here is another example of something once considered low-class that has been incorporated into the mainstream – wearing sleeveless undershirts, but not under a shirt. Gale Rosenwald Smith's and Kirby's essays provide a chance to think about what might be considered the coarsening of American society. What other examples can students think of?

Jonathan Swift, *A Modest Proposal*

Swift's brilliant, scathingly ironic attack on the devastating policies of the British ruling class toward an impoverished Irish peasantry is one of the classics of English prose. It will also be a challenging essay for most first-year students. Not only is the complex eighteenth-century rhetoric unfamiliar, but the essay also includes many historical references that will be difficult for students, even with footnotes. In addition, students often have trouble recognizing that Swift is adopting a persona and some may take his horrifying proposal at face value. Unless you already know the essay well and have an affinity for explaining its complexities in terms of both language and tone, you probably should reserve this essay for a course for advanced students. Even then, you should provide some historical background and make students aware that they don't need to understand every reference in order to appreciate Swift's irony and ultimate compassion. You might also point out that the main thrust of Swift's argument comes in paragraphs 3–16 and 20–30; the long digression in paragraphs 17–19 often bogs students down.

Comprehension (p. 706)

1. Swift notes the problem of poverty in Ireland and satirically proposes that such poverty could be eliminated if the children of the poor were sold to be butchered and eaten.
2. The advantages of the plan are that it would lessen the number of Catholics, that poor tenants would have an income with which to pay the landlord, that poor parents wouldn't have to maintain their children after two years of age, that taverns would benefit by increased business, and that it would encourage marriage.
3. Paragraph 29 enumerates the "alternatives," which involve the wealthy giving up a squanderous lifestyle, the uniting of the Irish people, and an increased compassion for the poor. These are what Swift is actually proposing.
4. The very outrageousness of the proposal suggests that Swift is not serious. Other clues include the overattention to detail and, of course, the seriousness of his true proposals outlined in paragraphs 29–33.
5. See answer 3 above. He rejects them to suggest the callousness with which his audience has treated the poor.

Purpose and Audience (p. 706)

1. Many British readers would likely dismiss the proposal as the rantings of a madman. Irish readers, however – at least those who realized the harm British control was doing to the country of Ireland – would understand Swift's point.

2. Swift seems to have wanted to inspire change; only by shocking the sensibilities of his audience so thoroughly could he make readers stop and consider real solutions.
3. Such computations establish the "proposer" as a meticulous, even finicky, man.
4. Only those who took the proposal seriously — or who disagreed with Swift's politics — would likely be offended.
5. He expected his conclusion to be viewed as comically ironic.

Style and Structure (p. 706)

1. The term suggests livestock; Swift's proposer is dehumanizing poor women as Swift would suggest the ruling classes have already done.
2. Paragraph 8 is a transition. Paragraph 20 is another brief transitional paragraph. Paragraphs 12 and 30 are brief for emphasis.
3. The "objections" in paragraph 29 aren't really refuted because they represent Swift's real proposals. In paragraph 30 he simply writes that there is little hope they will be put into practice.
4. Other examples include *food* (9), *excellent nutritive meat* (14), and *yearling child* (27). Again, these words dehumanize the peasantry.
5. He refers to "[a] very worthy person" in paragraph 17 and to "[s]ome persons of a desponding spirit" in paragraph 19. Such references lend an air of authenticity to the proposal by suggesting the proposer has conducted research.
6. Swift's essay is sharply ironic, and he is ridiculing the callousness of the ruling classes toward the peasants by wittily attacking their attitude.
7. By enumerating each advantage he adds a level of formality to the proposal.
8. The parenthetical asides — generally amplifications or qualifications — serve to suggest a tone of fastidious regard for exactitude.
9. He has been digressing from the subject of slaughtering infants for meat — to take up the subject of substituting adolescents for deer as the prey in hunting!
10. Swift's proposal is hardly a modest one, and the use of the word *humbly* is a common rhetorical device even today. ("I humbly propose" often introduces a major proposal.)

Combining the Patterns (p. 708)

The patterns Swift uses are description (1), cause and effect (2–3), process (4), cause and effect (5), exemplification (6–7), description (9), process (10), description (11–12), cause and effect (13), description (14–16), comparison (17), exemplification (18), description (19), cause and effect (21–28), and argumentation (29–33).

Thematic Connections

The Embalming of Mr. Jones (p. 301): Jessica Mitford uses irony in a more straightforward way to describe the fairly horrifying process of embalming.

The Irish Famine, 1845–1849 (p. 330): Student Evelyn Pellicane's essay-exam response, though focusing on a period more than a hundred years after Swift wrote, provides useful historical detail for understanding conditions of Irish life and the relationship between Ireland and Britain.

I Want a Wife (p. 502): Judy Brady's ironic look at gender expectations has a goal similar to that of "A Modest Proposal": to present an exaggerated, even outrageous, view of the status quo in order to get readers to see the situation in a new light.

Part Three: Working with Sources

This part provides an overview of the research process: looking for sources, doing research, avoiding plagiarism, and documenting sources in MLA style. Each chapter offers specific advice and includes examples from the research process of a student writer. The part concludes with the final draft of the student's paper.

The appendix includes guidelines for citing sources using APA documentation style and provides sample entries for a works-cited page, including examples of citations for electronic sources. The sample research paper follows APA guidelines.

While you will want to use much of the material on working with sources in conjunction with a formal research paper if you have students write essays analyzing any of the readings in the book, you should probably cover the material on paraphrasing, summarizing, and using quotations early on. You might use the examples in the text and have students practice paraphrasing and summarizing in class—and be careful to point out any inadvertent plagiarism.

PEER-EDITING WORKSHEETS

Following are models of peer-editing worksheets—one for each of the patterns discussed in Chapters 6–15 of the text. You may retype and duplicate these to distribute to students or adapt them to create versions of your own. The worksheets are also available on the *Patterns* website, bedfordstmartins.com/patterns. Advice about using the peer-editing worksheets appears on pages xxii–xxiii of this manual.

Peer-Editing Worksheet: Narration

1. What point is the writer making about the essay's subject? Is this point explicitly stated in a thesis statement? If so, where? If not, is the essay's thesis clearly implied? Would a stated thesis be more effective?

2. Does the writer include enough detail? Where could more detail be added? What kind of detail? Be specific.

3. Does the writer vary sentence structure and avoid monotonous strings of similar sentences? Should some sentences be combined? If so, which ones? Can you suggest different openings for any sentences?

4. Is the order in which events occur clear? Should any events be relocated? Should any transitions be added to clarify relationships between events?

5. Are verb tenses consistent? Identify any verb tenses that you believe are incorrect.

6. Does the writer avoid run-on sentences?

7. What could the writer *add* to this essay?

8. What could the writer *take out* of this essay?

9. What is the essay's greatest strength? Why?

10. What is the essay's greatest weakness? What steps should the writer take to correct this problem?

Peer-Editing Worksheet: Description

1. What is the essay's dominant impression or thesis?

2. What points does the writer emphasize in the introduction? Should any other points be included? If so, which ones?

3. Would you characterize the essay as primarily an objective or subjective description? What leads you to your conclusions?

4. Point out some examples of figures of speech. Could the writer use figures of speech in other places? If so, where?

5. What specific details does the writer use to help readers visualize what is being described? Could the writer use more details anywhere? Would a visual have helped readers understand what is being described?

6. Are all the details necessary? Do any seem excessive or redundant? Are there enough details provided to support the thesis or convey the dominant impression?

7. How are the details in the essay arranged? Would another arrangement be clearer or more effective?

8. List some transitional words and phrases the writer uses to help readers follow the discussion. Do any sentences need transitional words or phrases to link them to other sentences?

9. Do any sentences contain misplaced or dangling modifiers? If so, which ones?

10. How effective is the essay's conclusion? Does the conclusion reinforce the dominant impression?

Peer-Editing Worksheet: Exemplification

1. What strategy does the writer use in the essay's introduction? Would another strategy be more effective?

2. What is the essay's thesis? Is it specific enough? Does it prepare readers for the essay that follows?

3. What specific points do the body paragraphs make? Are these points expressed in the topic sentences?

4. Does the writer use one example or several to illustrate each point? Should the writer use more examples? Fewer? Explain.

5. Does the writer use a sufficient range of examples? Are they explained in enough depth?

6. Do the examples add interest? How persuasive are they? List a few other examples that might be more persuasive.

7. What transitional words and phrases does the writer use to reinforce the connections between examples? Should any transitional words and phrases be added?

8. In what order are the examples presented? Would another order be more effective? Explain.

9. Has the writer used a series of three or more examples in a single sentence? If so, are these examples separated by commas?

10. What strategy does the writer use in the conclusion? What other strategy could be used?

Peer-Editing Worksheet: Process

1. What process does this essay describe? How familiar were you with this process before you read the essay?

2. Does the writer include all the information the audience needs? Is any vital step or piece of information missing? Is any step or piece of information irrelevant? Is any necessary definition, explanation, or caution missing or incomplete?

3. Is the essay a set of instructions or a process explanation? How can you tell? Why do you think the writer chose this strategy rather than the alternative? Do you think this was the right choice?

4. Does the writer consistently follow the stylistic conventions for the strategy—instructions or process explanation—he or she has chosen?

5. Are the steps presented in clear, logical order? Are the steps grouped logically into paragraphs? Should any steps be combined or relocated? If so, which ones?

6. Does the writer use enough transitions to move readers through the process? Should any transitions be added? If so, where? Do the transitions clearly indicate the logical and sequential relationships between steps?

7. Does the writer avoid confusing shifts in tense, person, voice, and mood?

8. Is the essay interesting? What descriptive details would add interest to the essay? Would a visual be helpful?

9. How would you characterize the writer's opening strategy? Is it appropriate for his or her purpose and audience? What alternative strategy might be more effective?

10. How would you characterize the writer's closing strategy? Would a different conclusion be more effective? Explain.

Peer-Editing Worksheet: Cause and Effect

1. Paraphrase the essay's thesis. Is it explicitly stated? Should it be?

2. Does the essay focus on causes, effects, or both? Does the thesis statement clearly identify this focus? If it doesn't, how should the thesis statement be revised?

3. Does the writer consider *all* relevant causes or effects? Are any key causes or effects omitted? Are any irrelevant causes or effects included?

4. Make an informal outline of the essay. What determines the order of the causes or effects? Is this the most effective order? If not, what revisions do you suggest?

5. List any transitional words or phrases that the writer uses to indicate causal connections in this essay. Are any additional transitions needed to make these connections clear? If so, where?

6. Does the writer avoid *post hoc* reasoning? Are all of the writer's causal connections logical?

7. Does the writer explain each cause or effect clearly and convincingly? Are more examples or details needed to help readers understand causal connections? If so, where?

8. Do you agree with the writer's interpretation of the cause-and-effect relationships examined in this essay? Do you agree with his or her conclusions? Why or why not?

9. Has the writer avoided illogical "the reason is because" constructions in this essay?

10. Are *affect* and *effect* used correctly?

Peer-Editing Worksheet: Comparison and Contrast

1. Does the essay have a clearly stated thesis? What is it?

2. What two things are being compared? What basis for comparison exists between the two?

3. Does the essay treat the same or similar points for each of its two subjects? List the points discussed.

First subject   **Second subject**

a.   a.

b.   b.

c.   c.

d.   d.

Are these points discussed in the same order for both subjects? Are the points presented in parallel terms?

4. Does the essay use a point-by-point or subject-by-subject strategy? Is this the best choice? Why?

5. Are transitional words and phrases used appropriately to identify points of comparison and contrast? List some of the transitions used.

6. Are additional transitions needed? If so, where?

7. How could the introductory paragraph be improved?

8. How could the concluding paragraph be improved?

9. What could the writer add to this essay?

10. What could the writer take out of this essay?

Peer-Editing Worksheet: Classification and Division

1. What thesis does the body of the essay support? Is this thesis explicitly stated?

2. What whole is being divided into parts in this essay? Into what general categories is the whole divided?

3. Is each category clearly identified and explained? If not, what revisions can you suggest? (For example, can you suggest a different title for a particular category?)

4. Does the writer list the categories to be discussed? Is the list introduced by a colon (preceded by a complete sentence)?

5. Are the categories arranged in a logical order, one that indicates their relationships to one another and their relative importance? If not, how could they be rearranged?

6. Does the writer treat all relevant categories and no irrelevant ones? Which categories, if any, should be added, deleted, or combined?

7. Does the writer include all necessary items, and no unnecessary ones, within each category? What additional items could be added? Should any items be located elsewhere?

8. Does the writer treat all categories similarly, discussing comparable points for each? Should any additional points be discussed? If so, where?

9. Do topic sentences clearly signal the movement from one category to the next? Should any topic sentences be strengthened to mark the boundaries between categories more clearly? If so, which ones?

10. Could the writer use another pattern of development to structure this essay? Is classification and division the best choice? Explain.

Peer-Editing Worksheet: Definition

1. What term is the writer defining? Does the essay include a formal dictionary definition? If so, where? Does the phrasing of this definition avoid *is when* and *is where*? If no formal definition is included, should one be added?

2. Why is the writer defining the term? Does the essay include a thesis statement that makes this purpose clear?

3. What patterns does the writer use to develop the definition? What other patterns could be used? Would a visual be helpful?

4. Does the essay define the term appropriately for its audience? Does the definition help you understand the meaning of the term?

5. Does the writer use **synonyms** to develop the definition? If so, where? If not, where could synonyms be used to help communicate the term's meaning?

6. Does the writer use **negation** to develop the definition? If so, where? If not, could the writer strengthen the definition by explaining what the term is not?

7. Does the writer use **enumeration** to develop the definition? If so, where? If not, where might the term's special characteristics be listed?

8. Does the writer use **analogies** to develop the definition? If so, where? Do you find these analogies helpful? What additional analogies might help readers understand the term more fully?

9. Does the writer explain the term's linguistic origin and development? If so, where? If not, do you believe this information should be added?

10. Reread the essay's introduction. If the writer uses a formal definition as an opening strategy, try to suggest an alternative opening.

Peer-Editing Worksheet: Argumentation

1. Does the essay take a stand on an issue? What is it? At what point does the writer state his or her thesis? Is the thesis debatable?

2. What evidence does the writer include to support his or her position? What additional evidence could the writer supply?

3. Does the essay summarize and refute the opposing arguments? List these arguments.

4. How effective are the writer's refutations? Should the writer address any other arguments?

5. Does the essay use inductive reasoning? Deductive reasoning? Both? Provide an example of each type of reasoning used in the essay.

   Inductive reasoning:

   Deductive reasoning:

6. Does the essay include any logical fallacies? How would you correct these fallacies?

7. Do coordinating and subordinating conjunctions convey the logical and sequential connections between ideas?

8. How could the introduction be improved?

9. How could the conclusion be improved?

10. What would you add to make this essay more convincing?

Peer-Editing Worksheet: Combining the Patterns

1. Using the annotations for "The Park" (p. 667) or "On Dumpster Diving" (p. 672) as a guide, annotate the essay to identify the patterns of development it uses.

2. What is the essay's thesis? If it is not explicitly stated, state it in your own words. What pattern or patterns of development are suggested by the wording of the thesis statement?

3. What pattern of development determines the essay's overall structure? Could the writer use a different pattern for this purpose? Which one?

4. What patterns does the writer use to develop the body paragraphs of the essay? Explain why each pattern is used in a particular paragraph or group of paragraphs.

5. What patterns are *not* used? Where, if anywhere, might one of these patterns serve the writer's purpose?

6. Review the essay's topic sentences. Is the wording of each topic sentence consistent with the particular pattern it introduces? If not, suggest possible ways some of the topic sentences might be reworded.

Missing something? Instructors may assign the online materials that accompany this text. To access them, visit **macmillanhighered.com /patterns13e**.

Inside LaunchPad Solo for *Patterns for College Writing*

Tutorials

Critical Reading > Active Reading Strategies
Critical Reading > Reading Visuals: Purpose
Critical Reading > Reading Visuals: Audience
Documentation > Do I Need to Cite That?
Documentation > How to Cite an Article in MLA Style
Documentation > How to Cite a Book in MLA Style
Documentation > How to Cite a Database in MLA Style
Documentation > How to Cite a Database in APA Style
Documentation > How to Cite a Web Site in MLA Style
Documentation > How to Cite a Web Site in APA Style
Digital Writing > Photo Editing Basics with GIMP
Digital Writing > Audio Editing with Audacity
Digital Writing > Presentations
Digital Writing > Word Processing
Digital Writing > Online Research Tools
Digital Writing > Job Search/Personal Branding

LearningCurve Quizzes

Critical Reading
Topic Sentences and Supporting Details
Topics and Main Ideas
Working with Sources (MLA)
Working with Sources (APA)
Commas, Fragments, Run-Ons and Comma Splices, Active and Passive Voice, Appropriate Language, Subject-Verb Agreement

e-Readings

Born Free Foundation, *Simba Goes Home to Africa* [video]
Johannes Vermeer, *Girl with a Pearl Earring* [painting]
Kerri MacDonald and Jonathan Blaustein, *Food for a Dollar* [essay with photographs]
Wired, Making a Mint [video]
Arte Ideas, *Plastic Bags: How Convenience Is Killing Our Planet* [infographic]
Diane Yang, *Greek Yogurt vs. Original Yogurt* [infographic]
Wired, What's Inside Coffee? [video]
Voxy, *What Are the Hardest Languages to Learn?* [infographic]
NASA, *What Is a Black Hole?* [infographic]
Dear Motorist, *Dear Motorist: Pledge to Share the Road* [video]